Meluhha

A Visible language

S. Kalyanaraman

Sarasvati Research Center 2013

ISBN: 978-0-9911048-1-9
ISBN: 0991104811
Library of Congress Control Number: 2013918957

Sarasvati Research Center Herndon, VA, USA.

Table of Contents: Meluhha – A visible language

Executive Summary	8
The argument: hieroglyphs for a catalog of a smithy/forge	10
Alchemical tradition of symbols, Philosopher's stone	13
The argument: presenting hard alloys/smithy repertoire as hieroglyphs of Meluhha	14
The argument: presenting Meluhha artisan and *milakkhu kulsānā* 'copper forge'	22
Elamite metallurgical excellence	34
The argument: fish and antelope as hieroglyphs	36
Boat load of hard alloys and lapidary products	39
Samarra: first smelting of iron ore, 5000 BCE validated by Meluhha writing	46
Six women, with wavy hair, six scorpions: Samarra bowl	49
Continuity of artisan traditions	57
The argument: hieroglyphs of Warka vase	58
Dancing girl hieroglyph	65
Composites, pictorial nature of the Meluhha writing system	72
Kanmer: tokens in bulla as seals	76
Kanmer: Stone-turner artisan's workshop	77
Kanmer: Furnace workshop	79
Kanmer: Metal workshop	79
Documentation concerning a transaction	80
Chanhudaro *paṭṭaḍi* 'anvil, smithy, forge'	83
paṭṭaḍi – Smithy/forge Workshop	88
Trough as a hieroglyph	91

Dholavira advertisement board announcing bronze-age metalwork	94
Harosheth Hagoyim, smithy of nations	98
Lapidary-Smith Standard in procession	102
Orthographic style of the writing system	105
Metals trade catalog on a Mohenjo-daro seal	113
Meluhha – pioneers in brass and makers of tin and zinc alloys	134
Advancement from tokens/bullae to incised speech	135
Corpora of inscriptions	137
Sibri cylinder seal	156
A writing system called *mlecchita vikalpa*	161
Hieroglyptic nature of the cipher	167
Mesopotamia and Harappa	169
Proto-Elamite, potters' marks and Indus script	171
Meluhha language	172
Role of Dilmun in Indus trade with contact areas	173
Co-existence of three writing systems	174
What is the etymology of the word mīmāṃsa मीमांस ?	177
Bharata's *Nāṭyaśāstra*: *mleccha* as language, *bhāṣā*	178
Toda Mund and Sumer Mudhif	184
One Meluhhan village in Akkad (3rd millennium BCE)	190
Bronze Age Linguistic Doctrine	195
Nature of doctrine	196

Meluhha may mean the lands of the Indian Ocean	203
Languages of Meluhha (Mleccha) and Marhashi are the same	209
Narmer Palette, rebus method	221
Tamilla as a synonym of Milangka, Wilangka (Milakkha, mleccha, Pali)	250
Slanted strokes as hieroglyphs	259
Sources of Prākrits	273
Validity of mleccha usage	275
Mleccha as a Bharatiya language	291
Mleccha were bharatiya (Indians) of Indian linguistic area	291
Nahali, Meluhhan, Language 'X'	292
Evidence related to proto-Indian or proto-Indic or Indus language	293
Evidence from Śatapatha Brāhmaṇa for *mleccha vācas,* Meluhha speech	297
Mleccha words in Sumerian	307
Substrate language of Sumer and Indian lexemes	309
Apaśabda, mleccha	312
Mleccha, *lingua franca* of Bhāratam, of the 'linguistic area'	313
Indo-Iranian a product of merger in historical linguistics	314
Centum -- Sadem in Sanskrit	315
Ralayor abhedah	316
Meluhha granaries, garden, temples,avifauna, fauna, timber/woods, bronzes	323
The *meluhhan* village of Guabba	326
Guabba continued with *Meluhhan* temples	327

Guabba as a *Meluhhan* seaport	328
Proto-Munda continuity and Language X	329
Further researches: historical linguistics	330
How to reconstruct mleccha of 4th millennium BCE Indian *sprachbund*?	336
Lingua franca, *deśi*	349
Mleccha, Indus language of Indian linguistic area (*sprachbund*)	350
Characteristics of mleccha noted by Patañjali	358
Evidence from Valmiki Rāmāyaṇa	360
He 'lavah	365
Meluhha: epigraphical evidences	366
Mleccha Khandas	368
Meluhha, toponym: two Meluhhas	370
Melakkha, island-dwellers, lapidaries	383
Bronze Age Meluhha, smithy/lapidary documents, takṣat vāk, incised speech	387
Tanana mleccha	412
Haifa: find-spot of the first two 'rosetta stones'	416
Mesopotamian trade with Dilmun, Magan and Meluhha	430
Erythraen Sea and Meluhha	431
Tin from 'Meluhha'	434
Euphrates the copper river or URUDU and Tin from Meluhha	441
Sea-faring merchants of Melukkha (Meluhha) and trade route of tin ingots	442
Tilmun, Telmun, Dilmun, the land of the famous red stone	457

The Tin road	462
Tin from Meluhha; Mleccha as a language	465
Tin of Melukkha	468
Diffusion of Metallurgy: Meluhha and western Afghanistan sources of tin	473
Documenting the Tin processing tradition in India	478
Papagudem boy wearing a bangle of tin	478
Tin placer prospecting: pictorial gallery	480
Elamite < proto-afroasiatic?	482
Ubaid ceramics	484
Archaeobotanical evidence	486
Avestan later than Vedic	487
takṣa, tvaṣṭṛ, ṛbhu: carpenters	488
Technical skils of the artificer mentioned in texts	489
Tvaṣṭṛ, soma	492
Maritime, riverine Ṛgvedic culture	493
Meluhha distinct from Elamite	495
Spinner hieroglyph	503
Hieroglyph of overflowing water	509
Standard device in front of the one-horned young bull	516
Buffalo as hieroglyph and association with overflowing water	521
Goat-fish as ligatured hieroglyph	533
Identifying the hieroglyphs of Sit Shamshi bronze	538

Sacred ceremony: water ablutions to the morning sun, Shamash	539
Susa: sacred fire-smithy, model of a temple	539
Three stakes on Sit-Shamshi bronze	543
Mohenjo-daro stupa, Great Bath and Sit Shamshi bronze	545
Proto-elamite tablet with seal mark	551
The emergence of a new writing system in the Fars region	551
Common motifs on seals/tablets of bronze-age Indo-Eurasia	552
Dilmun (Failaka) seals	554
Meluhha hieroglyphs on cylinder seals and kudurru	574
Lanayor abhedah	576
Kudurru and scorpion glyph	585
Glyphs on kudurru: sun-disk, scorpion, eagle, lion, snake-hood, quadruped	586
Indus writing in Ancient Near East	587
Dilmun, sea of Magan, the power of the bull	596
Seals of Saar, Bahrain	600
ḍhāla 'shield' Rebus: *ḍhālako* 'large ingot'; *huḍa* 'ram' Rebus: *uḍu* 'boat, raft'	601
Hieroglyphs to denote iron, anvil, mint	603
Hieroglyph *khaṇḍa* 'divisions' Rebus: *kāṇḍā* 'metalware'	604
Metalware products of a forge	606
Comparable hieroglyphs of antithetical antelopes	611
Ligatured Meluhha hieroglyphs	611
Indian sprachbund contacts with Sumer, Elam, Mesopotamia	625

Meluhha

A Visible language

Executive Summary

This is a tribute to the artisans of the Bronze-age Indo-Eurasia who laid the foundations for 1) an industrial revolution with the invention of tin-bronzes and brass and 2) a cultural revolution with the invention of writing systems. The glyphs of early writing systems of Bronze-age in Ancient Near East, represent a visible language of Meluhha. A synonym of 'visible language' is 'incised speech' *takṣat vāk*, (a metaphor used in what is possibly the oldest human document, the Ṛgveda.)[1] It is likely that many unique pictorial motifs on cylinder seals of contact areas of Sumer-Elam-Mesopotamia were inspied by the Meluhha cipher since some hieroglyphs used in a metallurgy-lapidary context are also used in the contact areas, together with cuneiform texts. This calls for a re-evaluation of some art-historians' interpretation of some symbols explained in astronomical or religious contexts. Homonymous glosses matching the glyphs explain the semantics of Meluhha. The writing systems were intended to document trade and workshop processes of the bronze-age merchants, smiths and lapidaries. This context is exemplified by two terms used in ancient texts naming writing systems: 1. '*mlecchita vikalpa*' (cipher of mleccha/meluhha), a term attesed ca. 6th century

BCE by Vātsyāyana; 2. *kharoṣṭī* (cognate *harosheth hagoyim*, 'smithy of nations'). The writing systems on cylinder seals of Sumer-Elam-Mesopotamia and on Indus script corpora are based on rebus method -- rendering mleccha language metallurgy-related or bronze-age workshop-related sememes. Such sememes are attested in many languages of Indian *sprachbund* providing a framework to outlinine features of mleccha (Meluhha) language of artisans/traders of Bronze-age. Meluhha were sea-faring merchants and artisans working in tin, zinc, copper and other bronze-age alloying minerals (attested in cuneiform texts). Meluhha settlements are also attested in Ancient Near East archaeology. Meluhha Smithy (*kole.l*) denotes the divine space, a temple (*kole.l*). Implements produced in a smithy and repertoire of a smithy denote attributes of the divine. This world-view of Meluhha is discerned from hundreds of cylinder seals with hundreds of hieroglyphs – as visible language or incised Meluhha speech. A list of Meluhha glosses evidenced in Indian *sprachbund* is presented. A list of languages and dialects listed in Indo-Aryan, Dravidian and Munda lexicons annexed to the list constitutes a resource base for identifying and clustering semantics of Meluhha. The intimations of semantics conveyed by Meluhha cipher should be augmented by further language explorations and studies to detail the grammatical features of Meluhha/mleccha language. Such studies could be on the lines of Jules Bloch's *La formation de la Langue Marathe* [2] and of Prakrit grammars.

The argument: hieroglyphs for a catalog of a smithy/forge

34

Provenience: Khafaje Kh. VII 256 Jemdet Nasr (ca. 3000 - 2800 BCE) Frankfort, Henri: *Stratified Cylinder Seals from the Diyala Region*. Oriental Institute Publications 72. Chicago: University of Chicago Press, no. 34. Mythological scene: tailless lion or bear standing erect behind tree; two goats feeding at other side of tree; another tree, with bird in branches, behind monster; three-lowered buildings with door at left side; watercourse along bottom of scene. Gray limestone. 4.1x3.5cm.[3]

The cylinder seal is a catalog of a smithy: copper, iron alloy smith, turner, hard alloy metal tools, pots and pans.

The two animals are: markhor, antelope. *miṇḍāl* 'markhor' (Tōrwālī) *meḍho* a ram, a sheep (Gujarati)(CDIAL 10120); rebus: *mẽṛhẽt, meḍ* 'iron' (Munda.Ho.) *mṛeka, melh* 'goat' (Telugu. Brahui) Rebus: *melukkha* '*milakkha*, copper'.

करडणें or करंडणें [karaḍaṇē or ṅkaraṇḍaṇēṃ] *v c* To gnaw or nibble; to wear away by biting (Marathi). Rebus: *karaḍa* 'hard alloy'. *karaḍa* 'duck' Rebus: *karaḍa* 'hard alloy' *karaḍa* 'wave' Rebus: *karaḍa* 'hard alloy' *karaḍa* 'panther' Rebus: *karaḍa* 'hard alloy'. *khōṇḍa* 'leafless tree' (Marathi). Rebus: *kõdār* 'turner' (Bengali) kole.l 'temple' Rebus: kole.l 'smithy'. *khōṇḍa* A tree of which the head and branches are broken off, a stock or stump: also the lower portion of the trunk—that below the branches. (Marathi) Rebus 1: *kõdā* 'to turn in a lathe' (Bengali) Rebus 2: *koḍ* 'workshop' (Gujarati) Glyh of flowing water: *kāṇḍa* 'flowing water' Rebus: *kāṇḍā* 'metalware, tools, pots and pans'.Thus, the entire hieroglyphic composition of the cylinder seal is a smithy catalog: *karaḍ* 'nibbling' *karaḍa* 'duck' *karaḍa* 'wave' *karaḍa* 'panther' all connoting reinforcing, Rebus: *karaḍa* 'hard alloy' and work of *kõdār* 'turner' in *kole.l* 'smithy, temple' producing: *kāṇḍā* 'metalware, tools, pots and pans'.

Two goats eating from a tree on a mountaintop in proto-Elamite seals from Mundigak and Susa. After Amiet, P., 1961, *La glyptique mesopotamienne archaique*, Paris: 497; Mundigak IV.3; 3.

Plate 65. Fig. 701 in: Frankfort, H., Univ. of Chicago, Oriental Institute, Vol. LXXII, Stratified cylinder seals from the Diyala Region, Illinoi, Univ. of Chicago Press.[4]

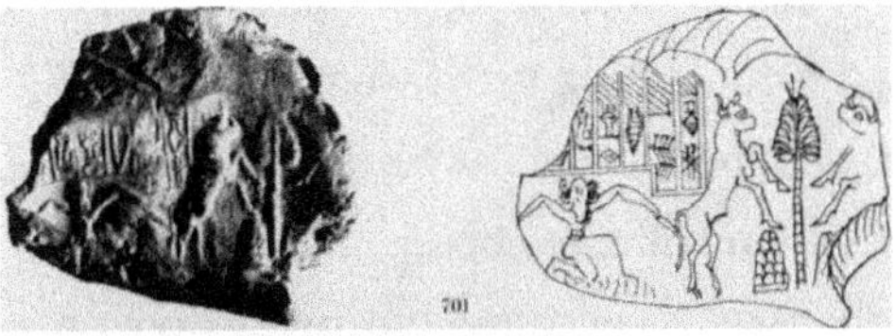

Lid of a pyxis with mistress of the animal 13th cent. BCE Minet et Beida, port of Ugarit (modern Ras Shamra), Syria The Levant Elephant ivory D. 13.7 cm. Th. 12 cm allocated to the Louvre after the Schaeffer excavation, 1929 AO 11601 Near Eastern Antiquities. The Mistress of the Animals

"This lid forms a circular scene. In the center, a female figure is holding out ears of corn to two wild goats standing on their hind legs. Many works of art from Greece and the

Levant depict female figures dominating wild or tame animals. Such scenes, which might at first glance appear to be straightforward depictions of female goatherds, are in fact generally understood as expressions of a belief in the symbolic powers of nature. A smiling young woman, her arms bent symetrically on either side of her chest, is holding out ears of corn that the two goats are nuzzling. Her profile, with the nose a continuation of the line of the forehead and her hair arranged in curls, is reminiscent of works from Crete and Santorini, as is the band with a spiral at the center of her forehead and the long wavy lock of hair at the top of her head. The costume is also pre-Hellenistic in inspiration. Her breasts are bare and she is wearing a necklace and a loose skirt made of decorated panels. She is shown sitting on a small stepped stool. Her legs are in profile, but her torso is shown face-on. The step on the right is hidden by a notched cone, on which the goat is resting its right foreleg. There is a similar object beside the goat on the left side. It is not clear what these objects represent. They may be stylized rocks like the one the young woman is sitting on, which is likewise full of holes. The entire scene was originally ringed with a decorative trim of overlapping scales. The two goats are mirror images of each other, standing on their hind legs as if in the act of stepping forward. They each have one front hoof on a cone of rock, the other close to the woman's elbow. Their bodies are powerful and slender, and the hooves are carefully detailed. Their beards are pointing forward, and their mouths are open, ready to eat the ears of corn...This disk was originally the lid of a cylindrical box made from an elephant tusk. The lid was cut out of a slice sawn vertically from the pointed end of the tusk. The box was cut from the thicker end of the tusk where there is a natural cavity containing the dental pulp tissue. The artists of Ugarit were experts in carving ivory from both elephants and hippopotamuses to produce all sorts of precious objects, such as powder boxes (round like this one or in the shape of a duck), combs, spindles, musical instruments, and parts of pieces of furniture. Elephant tusks and hippopotamus teeth were shipped in from Africa and Egypt across the Mediterranean, as proved by the cargo found in a ship wrecked off the coast of Turkey some time during the thirteenth century BCE".[5]

Alchemical tradition of symbols, Philosopher's stone

The glyptic compositions exemplified by the bronze-age artisans on hundreds of cylinder seals, sculptural friezes and a myriad metal and stone objects continue in the alchemical tradition associating mysteries and esoteric meanings to the symbols with particular reference to materials used in the alchemical experiments for transmutation of base metal into gold or electrum. Excerpts from a remarkable webpage of University of Delaware are appended to provide a backdrop to alternative explanations of symbols.

In the context of the bronze age, startin circa 5th millennium BCE in the ancient Near East, many symbols are explained as rebus renderings of Meluhha speech. There are certain intimations associating symbols to identify divinities as noted by art historians, Sumerologists and Assyriologists.

As we traverse the sacred space of hieroglyphs, transcentind the mists of time dating back to several millennia, we are left with awe and admiration for our ancestors who have attempted to convey the knowledge gained them working with minerals, creating new alloys and making tools and implements which transformed human life on the planet.

The arguments of the Philosopher's stone will continue to fascinate the way Newton was fascinated by alchemical processes. Skirting such an excursus into philosophical inquiries, arguments will be intertwined with the pictographic evidences and the memories embedded in the abiding evidence of language evolution – some select glosses of Meluhha. That such a visible language called Meluhha existed is the crux of the falsifiable theory tested with glyptic evidence.

The argument: presenting hard alloys/smithy repertoire as hieroglyphs of Meluhha

Cylinder seal. Uruk, southern Iraq About 3200-3100 BCE. Two 'safflower' hieroglyphs are shown in the field. The 'safflower' glyph adorns the Ashurbanipal reliefs of 9th century BCE. खांबोटी [*khāmbōṭī*] *f* (Dim. of खांब) A short post, a stanchion. *kampaṭṭa* 'mint, coiner'. मेंढा [*mēṇḍhā*] A crook or curved end (of a stick) Rebus: *meḍ* 'iron'. *ēraka* a reed (Pali) Rebus: *eraka* 'copper'.

karaḍa -- m. 'safflower', *°ḍā* -- f. ' a tree like the karañja ' (Prakrit); M. *karḍī*, *°ḍaī* f. ' safflower, *carthamus tinctorius* and its seed '. (CDIAL 2788). Rebus: करडा [*karaḍā*] Hard from alloy--iron, silver &c. (Marathi) *kharādī* ' turner, a person who fashions or shapes objects on a lathe' (Gujarati) *mṛeka* 'goat'. Rebus: *milakkhu* 'copper'. *kāḍ* reed Rebus: *kāṇḍa* 'tools, pots and pans, metal-ware'. *dhaṭu* m. (also *dhaṭhu*) m. 'scarf' (WPah.) Rebus: *dhatu* 'mineral (ore)'. मेंढा *mēṇḍhā* 'sheep' मेंढा 'shepherd' मेढ *mēḍha* 'stick, stake or post.' Rebus: *meḍ* 'iron'.

Hieroglyphs read rebus in Meluhha: safflower (*karaḍa* hard alloy), goat (*mṛeka, milakkhu* copper), scarf [*dhatu* minerals (ore)], reed (*eraka* copper), stake (*kāḍ kampaṭṭa* metal-ware, mint), shepherd (*mēḍ* iron).

Cylinder seal with kneeling nude heroes, ca. 2220–2159 b.c.; Akkadian Mesopotamia Red jasper H. 1 1/8 in. (2.8 cm), Diam. 5/8 in. (1.6 cm)

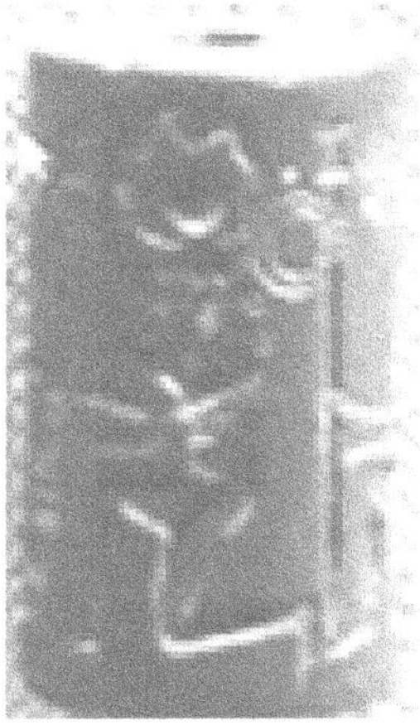

Metropolitan Museum of Art - USA

Four flag-posts(reeds) with rings on top held by the kneeling persons define the four components of the iron smithy/forge. This is an announcement of four shops, पेढी (Gujarati. Marathi). पेढें 'rings' Rebus: पेढी 'shop'. āra 'serpent' Rebus; āra 'brass'. *karaḍa* 'double-drum' *Rebus: karaḍa* 'hard alloy'.

Specific materials offered for sale/exchange in the shop are: hard alloy brass metal (*ayo,* fish); *lokhaṇḍ* (overflowing pot) 'metal tools, pots and pans, metalware'; *arka/erka* 'copper'; *kammaṭa* (a portable furnace for melting precious metals) 'coiner, mint' Thus, the four shops are: 1. brass alloys, 2. metalware, 3. copper and 4. mint (services).

erãguḍu bowing, salutation (Telugu) *iṟai* (-v-, -nt-) to bow before (as in salutation), worship (Tamil)(DEDR 516). Rebus: *eraka, eṟaka* any metal infusion (Kannada.Tulu) *eruvai* 'copper' (Tamil); *ere* dark red (Kannada)(DEDR 446).

puṭa Anything folded or doubled so as to form a cup or concavity; crucible. Alternative: *ḍhālako* = a large metal ingot (G.) *ḍhālakī* = a metal heated and poured into a mould; a solid piece of metal; an ingot (Gujarati)

Allograph: ढाल [ḍhāla] *f* (S through H) The grand flag of an army directing its march and encampments: also the standard or banner of a chieftain: also a flag flying on forts &c. ढालकाठी [ḍhālakāṭhī] *f* ढालखांब *m* A flagstaff; esp.the pole for a grand flag or standard. 2 fig. The leading and sustaining member of a household or other commonwealth. 5583 ḍhāla n. ' shield ' lex. 2. *ḍhāllā -- . 1. Tir. (Leech) "*dàl*" ' shield ', Bshk. *ḍāl*, Ku. *ḍhāl*, gng. *ḍhāw*, N. A. B. *ḍhāl*, Or. *ḍhāḷa*, Mth. H. *ḍhāl* m.2. Sh. *ḍal* (pl. *°lẹ*) f., K. *ḍāl* f., S. *ḍhāla*, L. *ḍhāl* (pl. *°lã*) f., P. *ḍhāl* f., G. M. *ḍhāl* f. WPah.kṭg. (kc.) *ḍhā`l* f. (obl. -- *a*) ' shield ' (a word used in salutation), J. *ḍhāl* f. (CDIAL 5583).

They are four Glyphs: *paṭākā* 'flag' Rebus: *pāṭaka,* four quarters of the village.

kāḍ reed Rebus: *kāṇḍa* 'tools, pots and pans, metal-ware'.

1. Pk. *kamaḍha* -- , *°aya* -- m. ' bamboo '; Bhoj. *kōro* ' bamboo poles '. 2. N. *kāmro* ' bamboo, lath, piece of wood ', OAw. *kāṁvari* ' bamboo pole with slings at each end for carrying things ', H. *kāwaṛ, °ar, kāwaṛ, °ar* f., G. *kāvaṛ* f., M. *kāvaḍ* f.; -- deriv. Pk. *kāvaḍia* -- , *kavvāḍia* -- m. ' one who carries a yoke ', H. *kāwaṛī, °ṛiyā* m., G. *kāvaṛiyɔ* m. 3. S. *kāvāṭhī* f. ' carrying pole ', *kāvāṭhyo* m. ' the man who carries it '. 4. Or. *kāmaṛā, °muṛā* ' rafters of a thatched house '; G. *kāmṛũ* n., *°ṛī* f. ' chip of bamboo ', *kāmaṛ -- koṭiyũ* n. ' bamboo hut '. 5. B. *kāmṭhā* ' bow ', G. *kāmṭhũ* n., *°ṭhī* f. ' bow '; M. *kamṭhā, °ṭā* m. ' bow of bamboo or horn '; -- deriv. G. *kāmṭhiyɔ* m. ' archer '. 6. A. *kabāri* ' flat piece of bamboo used in smoothing an earthen image '. 7. *kābīṭ, °baṭ, °bṭī, kāmīṭ, °maṭ, °mṭī, kāmṭhī, kāmāṭhī* f. ' split piece of bamboo &c., lath '.(CDIAL 2760). kambi f. '

branch or shoot of bamboo ' lex. Pk. *kaṁbi* -- , *°bī* -- , *°bā* -- f. ' stick, twig ', OG. *kāṁba*; M. *kāb* f. ' longitudinal division of a bamboo &c., bar of iron or other metal '. (CDIAL 2774). कंबडी [kambaḍī] *f* A slip or split piece (of a bamboo &c.)(Marathi)

The rings atop the reed standard: पेंढें [pēṇḍhēṃ] पेंडकें [pēṇḍakēṃ] n Weaver's term. A cord-loop or metal ring (as attached to the गुलडा of the बैली and to certain other fixtures). पेंडें [pēṇḍēṃ] n (पेड) A necklace composed of strings of pearls. 2 A loop or ring. Rebus: पेढी (Gujaráthí word.) A shop (Marathi) Alternative: *koṭiyum* [*koṭ, koṭī* neck] a wooden circle put round the neck of an animal (Gujarati) Rebus: *ācāri koṭṭya* = forge, *kammārasāle* (Tulu)

The four hieroglyphs define the four quarters of the village smithy/forge: alloy, metalware, turner's lathe-work, cruble (or, ingot).

ayo 'fish' Rebus: *ayo* 'metal, alloy'

కాండము [kāṇḍamu] *kāṇḍamu.* [Skt.] n. Water. నీళ్లు (Telugu) kaṇṭhá -- : (b) ' water -- channel ': Paš. *kaṭā´* ' irrigation channel ', Shum. *xãṭṭä.* (CDIAL 14349).

lokhãḍ 'overflowing pot' Rebus: 'tools, iron, ironware' (Gujarati)

arká1 m. ' flash, ray, sun ' RV. [√arc] Pa. Pk. *akka* -- m. ' sun ', Mth. *āk;* Si. *aka* ' lightning ', inscr. *vid -- äki* ' lightning flash '.(CDIAL 624) *அருக்கன் arukkaṉ, n. < arka. Sun; சூரி யன். அருக்க னணிநிறமுங் கண்டேன் (திவ். இயற். 3, 1).*(Tamil) agasāle 'goldsmithy' (Kannada) అగసాలి [agasāli] or అగసాలెవాడు *agasāli.* n. A goldsmith. కంసాలివాడు. (Telugu) erka = ekke (Tbh. of arka) aka (Tbh. of arka) copper (metal); crystal (Kannada) cf. eruvai = copper (Tamil) eraka, er-aka = any metal infusion (Ka.Tu.); erako molten cast (Tulu) Rebus: eraka = copper (Ka.) eruvai = copper (Ta.); ere - a dark-red colour (Ka.)(DEDR 817). eraka, era, er-a = syn. erka, copper, weapons (Ka.) erka = ekke (Tbh. of arka) aka (Tbh. of arka) copper (metal); crystal (Kannada) akka, aka (Tadbhava of arka) metal; akka metal (Te.) arka = copper (Skt.) erako molten cast (Tulu)

Alternative: *kunda* 'jasmine flower' Rebus: kunda 'a turner's lathe'. kundaṇa pure gold.

The image could denote a crucible or a portable furnace: *kammaṭa* 'coiner, mint, a portable furnace for melting precious metals (Telugu) On some cylinder seals, this image is shown held aloft on a stick, comparable to the bottom register of the 'standard device' normally shown in front of a one-horned young bull. Alternatives: *puṭa* Anything folded or doubled so as to form a cup or concavity; crucible. *Ta.* kuvai, kukai crucible. *Ma.* kuva id. *Ka.* kōve id. *Tu.* kōvè id., mould. (DEDR 1816). Alternative: Shape of ingot: దళము [daḷamu] *daḷamu.* [Skt.] n. A leaf. ఆకు. A petal. A part, భాగము. dala n. ' leaf, petal ' MBh. Pa. Pk. *dala* -- n. ' leaf, petal ', G. M. *daḷ* n.(CDIAL 6214). <DaLO>(MP) {N} ``^branch, ^twig''. *Kh.<DaoRa>(D) `dry leaves when fallen', ~<daura>, ~<dauRa> `twig', Sa.<DAr>, Mu.<Dar>, ~<Dara> `big branch of a tree', ~<DauRa> `a twig or small branch with fresh leaves on it', So.<kOn-da:ra:-n> `branch', H.<DalA>, B.<DalO>, O.<DaLO>, Pk.<DAlA>. %7811. #7741.(Munda etyma) Rebus: *ḍhālako* = a large metal ingot (G.) *ḍhālakī* = a metal heated and poured into a mould; a solid piece of metal; an ingot (Gujarati)

Stela of Ashurnasirpal II

Neo-Assyrian, about 883-859 BCE. From Nimrud (ancient Kalhu), northern Iraq. Divinities worshipped by the King are reportedly shown as symbols.

"The helmet with horns represents the supreme god Ashur; the winged disc stands for the sun god, Shamash; the crescent within a full circle is the emblem of the moon god, Sin; the fork is the thunderbolt of the storm god, Adad; and a star, the planet Venus, signifies Ishtar, goddess of love and war. The king wears a row of similar symbols on his chest, with a Maltese cross for the sun. The inscription has a prayer to the gods, a description of the rebuilding of Kalhu and ends with curses on anybody who damages the stela."[6]

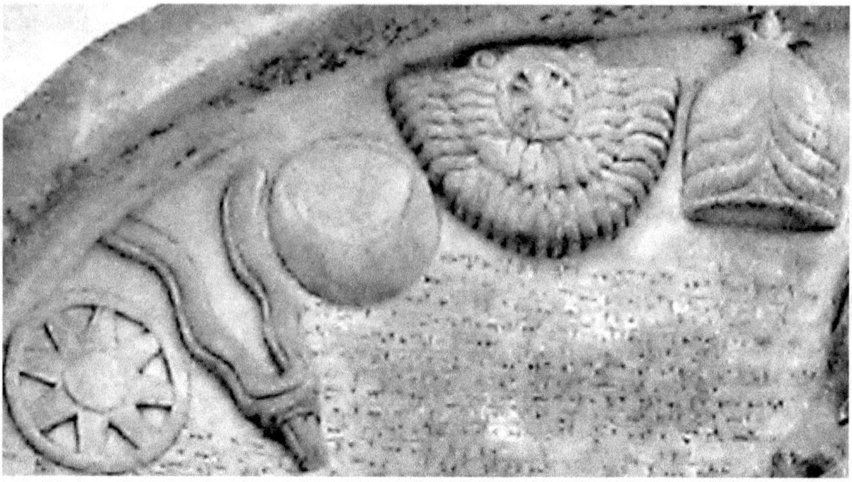

The five glyphs and suggested divine associations are (r. to l.): helmet with horns (Ashur), winged disk (Shamash), moon (Sin), fork (Adad), star (Ishtar).

“One cannot simply assume that a set of symbols, arranged in a more or less linear fashion, is writing. A good example of this can be found in the Assyrian bas relief…The pictograms arranged in a diagonal line shown in this figure are not writing – they are symbols for deities, in particular the major deities of the King Ashurnasirpal II (ninth century BCE). ” While these arguments on associations[7] are dated to the reign of the kIng 883-853 BCE, the glyphs may have originated from representation of implements and weapons of the early Bronze-age recorded on cylinder seals and other objects, predating this 9th century BCE symbolism by about two millennia. Since the smithy was viewed as a temple (*kole.l* is the word used for both meanings), the implements/metals/metalware from the smithy also had ‘divine’ associations. It is suggested that the early forms of these symbols should have denoted such implements of the bronze-age and related to the life-activities of the artisans/merchants of the times. It has been argued elsewhere that many of the glyphs are so relatable: 1. sun symbol: *arka* ‘gold, *arka/erka* ‘copper’; 2. Moon, star symbols: *uḍu* ‘star, moon’ *Rebus: uḍu* ‘boat, raft’. *meḍh* ‘Polar star’ Rebus: *meḍ* ‘iron’ [Alternative: moon sytmbol: *kammaṭa* ‘crucible’ Rebus: *kammaṭa* ‘coiner, mint, portable furnace for precious metals']; 5. *kōṇḍa* 'A circle described around a person under adjuration' (Marathi) Rebus: *kõdā* ' to turn in a lathe '; 4. fork symbol: *karaḍa* 'snarling iron' (comparable to the fork?) Rebus: *karaḍa* 'hard alloy' (used as anvil).

Such rebus readings are also suggested for symbols such as scorpion or lizard or fox or fish or serpent which are deployed on kudurru of Mesopotamia and on many cylinder seals with or without cuneiform texts, generally denoting the names of the owners of the seals.

Utu in Sumerian is the synonym of Akkadiam Shamash, sun divinity. Homonymous glosses in Meluhha point to the associations of divinity/constellation in the early Sumerian tradition, followed over centuries in Mesopotamia. Thus, even the symbols used on Kudurru and on some cylinder seals in a sacred context associating with 'divinities', there seems to be an underlying language which reinforced the deployment of the symbols. It is thus possible to explain the use of the 'moon' symbol in Mesopotamian artifacts in the context of the Meluhha word : *uḍu* which shows semantic evolution meaning references to moon, constellation, star. There are allographs which could also been used in the writing systems of Ancient Near East with symbols such as uṛu ' boatman '; uṭu Feather of an arrow; Arrow-head; *huṇḍā* ' hyena '. The 'moon' symbols shown on Ancient Near East artifacts may have connoted the rebus representation of *uḍu* 'star, moon' *Rebus: uḍu* 'boat, raft'. This argument demonstrates that one should not rush to judgement that the symbols used had no basis in language and there is no basis to conclude that the symbols were voice-less abstractions, arbitrary choices or non-linguistic representations.

uḍu f.n. ' star ' Kālid. [If isolated from uḍupa -- ' moon ', derivation from *ṛtu -- pa -- (Mayrhofer EWA i 100 with lit.) is made doubtful by the Pa. form] Pa. *uḷu* -- f. ' lunar mansion '; Pk. *uḍu* -- ; n. ' constellation '; Si. uḷu ' star '(CDIAL 1694). Allograph: uḍupa m. ' raft ' MBh. [Cf. *hōḍa* -- m. lex. prob. ← Drav., Tam. *ōṭam*] Pa. *uḷumpa* -- m.n. ' raft '; Pk. *uḍuva* -- m. ' boat '; Or. *uṛu* ' boatman '; G. *oṛvũ* n. '

small boat '; Si. mald. *oḍi* ' boat '; -- Si. *oruva* ' boat, canoe ' (CDIAL 1695). உடு; uṭu Oar, boatman's pole; ஓடம் இயக் குங் கோல். (பிங்.) hōḍa m. ' raft, boat ' lex. [← Drav., Kan. ōḍa., &c. DED 876] H. hoṛī f., holā m. ' canoe, raft '; G. hoṛī f. ' boat '; M. hoḍī f. ' canoe made of hollowed log '..hōḍa -- : Md. oḍi ' large kind of boat ' ← Drav.(CDIAL 14174).

Allographs: *huṛeāl, huṛeār* m. ' the wild hill sheep or oorial ' (Lahnda) huḍa 'ram'. உடு; uṭu Feather of an arrow; Arrow-head; *huṇḍā* ' hyena ' (Oriya)

Rebus: *huṇaï* ' offers oblation ' (Prakrit)

Rebus: Or. uṛa ' vow '; (oṭṭu ' wager ' ← Tam. oṭṭu).(CDIAL 14175)

The argument: presenting Meluhha artisan and *milakkhu kulsānā* 'copper forge'

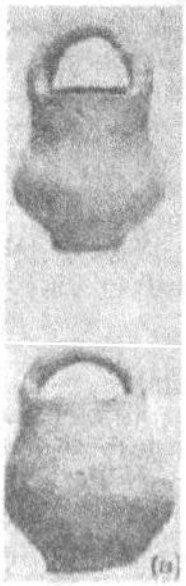

Akkadian cylinder seal bears the inscription *ṣu-i-li-ṣu/ eme-bal me-luh-ha-ki* 'Su-ilisu, Meluhha interpreter'). Musee du Louvre. Ao 22 310, Serpentine. H. 2.9 cm; Diam. 1.8 cm.[8]

kamaṇḍalu regarded as sacred possessions of ascetics were found in the Sarasvati-Sindhu civilization. The shape and handle of the vessel compare with the object shown carried by a woman accompanying the Meluhhan sea-faring merchant on an Akkadian cylinder seal. The pot carried by the woman accompanying the Meluhhan is of traditional, cultural significance in the context of water-ablution ceremonies. It is not clear if this connoted a pot containing the metalsmith's alchemical *rasa* or alchemial elixir of life or Amṛta (अमृत). In western alchemy, it was also called 'tincture' or 'powder' of alchemists. *kola* 'woman' Rebus: *kol* 'working in iron, *pañcaloha* alloy of five metals'.

Such pots related to elite people may be seen in Assyrian artifacts. Two persons flanking a stylized tree seem to be carrying implements (chisels?). Two winged persons carry *kamaṇḍalu* jars.

Assyrian Eagle Protective Spirit Also known as Apkallu griffin. Originally from 865

B.C., it can now be found at the New York Metropolitan Museum.

Assyrian Ashurnsirpal Reliefs from Nimrud, 865,

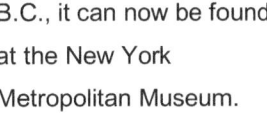

879 BCE, can now be found at the British Museum and FitzWilliam Museum. On the wrists and hanging as pendant on the necklace of an apkallu is a 'safflower' glyph (See fragment of a king's face in FitzWilliam Museum). Safflower glyphs decorate the arch around the worshipped tree in the middle on one relief. A section of wall relief was behind the king's throne. It depicts a ritual involving a stylized tree. Another panel with the same scene was opposite the center doorway of the throne room. The king is shown twice, on either side of a symbolic tree. On the left and on the right is an apkallu.

Image of apkallu, winged 'sage' in Mesopotamia carrying a pot? *eraka* 'wing' Rebus: *eraka* 'copper'. *kamaṭha* 'a water-jar' Rebus: *kammaṭa* 'mint, coiner'. The hieroglyphic depiction is that of a metalsmith working with copper alloys. Alternative: *goṭā* 'seed' (Bihari) Rebus: *khōṭ* 'alloyed ingot'.

The object carried by the king may be a pine-cone. If so, the rebus readings are: Ash. piċ -- kandə ' pine ', Kt. pṻċi, piċi, Wg. puċ, püċ (pṻċ -- kəŕ ' pine -- cone '), Pr. wyoċ, Shum. lyēwič (lyē -- ?).(CDIAL 8407). Cf. Gk. peu/kh f. ' pine ', Lith. pušìs, OPruss. peuse NTS xiii 229. The suffix –kande in the lexeme: Ash. piċ-- kandə ' pine ' may be cognate with the bulbous glyphic related to a mangrove root: Koḍ. kaṇḍe root-stock from which small roots grow; ila·ti kaṇḍe sweet potato (ila·ti England). Tu. kaṇḍe, gaḍḍè a bulbous root; Ta. kaṇṭal mangrove, Rhizophora mucronata; dichotomous mangrove, Kandelia rheedii. Ma. kaṇṭa bulbous root as of lotus, plantain; point where branches and bunches grow out of the stem of a palm; kaṇṭal what is bulb-like, half-ripe jackfruit and other green fruits; R. candel. (DEDR 1171). Rebus: *kaṇḍa* 'tools, pots and pans of metal'. Alternative: Paš. lauṛ. kayā́ ' edible pine cone '.

The Akkadian cylinder of Shu-ilishu, is is the clearest evidence for Meluhha as a language which required a translation into Akkadian, apart from evidencing Meluhha-Mesopotamia trade interactions.

The Meluhhan is accompanied by a lady carrying a kamaṇḍalu. *eme-bal,* lit: "the language turner" meant a translator of foreign languages into the local languages of Mesopotamia (Sumerian and Akkadian). The evidence of a Meluhha translator complements the evidence of Meluhha settlements in Sumer/Mesopotamia. காண்டம் kāṇṭam Ewer; கமண்டலம்.(Tamil) காண்டம் kāṇṭam , *n.* < *kāṇḍa.* 1. Water; sacred water; நீர். துருத்திவா யதுக்கிய குங்குமக் காண் டமும் (கல்லா. 49, 16). Rebus: காண்டம் kāṇṭam Weapon; ஆயுதம். (சூடா.) *khāṇḍā* 'tools, pots and pans and metal-ware'; खांडा [khāṇḍā] *m* A kind of sword, straight, broad-bladed, two-edged, and round-ended. (Marathi).

The woman accompanying the Meluhhan merchant carries a *kamaṇḍalu* on her right hand and an uncertain animal (tiger?) on her left. If it denotes a tiger, this glyph could be a phonetic determinant. kol 'tiger' (Konkani) Rebus: kol 'iron' (Ta.) kulsānā to forge (Gondi)

kola bride (Nk.); korti wife (Ko.); koḍus-, koḍc- to sprout; (P.) koṛuŋ young shoot (Pa.) (DEDR 2149) M. *kõb*, *°bā* m., *°bī* f. ' young shoot '(3249) Rebus:
Ta. kol working in iron, blacksmith; kollaṉ blacksmith. *Ma.* kollan blacksmith, artificer. *Ko.* kole·l smithy, temple in Kota village. *To.* kwala·l Kota smithy. *Ka.* kolime, kolume, kulame, kulime, kulume, kulme fire-pit, furnace; (Bell.; U.P.U.) konimi blacksmith; (Gowda) kolla id. *Koḍ.* kollë blacksmith. *Te.* kolimi furnace. *Go.* (SR.) kollusānā to mend implements; (Ph.) kolstānā, kulsānā to forge; (Tr.) kōlstānā to repair (of ploughshares); (SR.) kolmi smithy;
Kuwi (F.) kolhali to forge.(DEDR 2133).

कमठ *kamaṭha* 'a water-jar (esp. one made of a hollow gourd or cocoa-nut , and used by ascetics)' कमंडलु [kamaṇḍalu] *m n* (S) The waterpot used by the ascetic and the religious student. (Marathi)

'Based on cuneiform documents from Mesopotamia we know that there was at least one Meluhha village in Akkad at that time, with people called 'Son of Meluhha' living there. The cuneiform inscription (ca. 2020 BCE) says that the cylinder seal belonged to Shu-ilishu, who was a translator of the Meluhha language. "The presence in Akkad of a translator of the Meluhha language suggests that he may have been literate and could read the undeciphered Indus script. This in turn suggests that there may be bilingual Akkadian/Meluhha tablets somewhere in Mesopotamia. Although such documents may not exist, Shu-ilishu's cylinder seal offers a glimmer of hope for the future in unraveling the mystery of the Indus script."[9]

It is likely that the hieroglyphic narrative describes the Meluhhan as a tin (*tagara,* 'ram,goat') merchant (*damgar, tamkāru*) with competene in working with metal alloys (*kol*) -- signified by the pot (*kãwaṇḍal* Rebus: *kamaṭa* 'portable furnace'; *kammaṭa* 'coinage, mint') carried by the accompanying woman (*kola* Rebus: *kol* 'working in iron').

The Akkadian cylinder seal can be cited as a 'rosetta stone' attesting to *meluhha* as a language. A cognate term in Indic language family is: *mleccha*.

This seal together with a reference to a Meluhhan ship establishes contact between Mesopotamia and Meluhha over sea-route, in Akkadian times. Inscriptions of Gudea of Lagash (2143-2124 BCE) refer to 'the Meluhhans came up (or down) from their country' to supply wood and other raw materials for the construction of the main temple of Gudea's capital. Refernces to import of luxury items from Meluhha also occur in these inscriptions.[10] Suilisu means 'he of his god'. The logographs are read: 'bearded (su) [man protected by] the hands (su) of the god or goddess (ili).'

The antelope carried by the bearded Me-lah-ha on an Akkadian cylinder seal may be a phonetic determinant that the holder is a Meluhhan: mēlh 'goat' (Brahui); or *mṛeka* (Telugu) rebus for: melukka copper (Pali); mleccha-mukha 'copper' (Sanskrit). The antelope carried by the bearded Me-lah-ha on an Akkadian cylinder seal may be a phonetic determinant: melu-hha; also, melech, 'king'; plural form, '*melechim*'. cf. Melech Hamashiah: King Messiah; Akad: {Akkad} A city in Mesopotamia (now Iraq) which was part of Nimrod's kingdom, founded by Melech Sargon around 2350 BCE Genesis 10:10.

This glyph of holding by the throat of the animal is a phonetic determinant of the animal itself, and hence a reference to Meluhhan or *melech*, 'king' or *melukka* copper (Pali); *mlecchamukha* 'copper' (Sanskrit). *meḍh* मेढ 'merchant's helper' (Gujarati) [The suffix –*mukha* in *mlecchamukha* connotes *mũh* 'face' Rebus: *mũh* 'ingot'.]

On some glyphs, the antelope is held by its neck (*meḍa* or *melkha*). *melkhā* throat, neck (Kur.); *melque* throat (Malt.)(DEDR: 5080). *meḍa* = neck (Telugu) *meṭe* = the throat (Ka.); *men̲n̲a, men̲n̲i* (Ta.); *menne* (Ma.); *miḍaṛu* = the neck, the throat (Ta.Ma.); *meṭregaṭṭu* = a swelling of the glands of the throat (Kannada).

Ur seal (showing a person holding an antelope by its neck).

Two figures carry between them a vase, and one presents a goat-like animal (not an antelope) which he holds by the neck. Human figures wear early Sumerian garments of fleece. A man and woman jointly hold a *kamaṇḍalu* (a vase of the type shown on Shu-ili-shu cylinder seal). *kā̃waṇḍal* may be rebus *kammaṭa* 'coinage, coiner'. Thus, the glyptic message in Meluhha read rebus is: *mṛēka, mēl̲h̲* 'antelope'; *kā̃waṇḍal* 'water vessel'. Rebus: Meluhha, *meḍh* मेढ 'merchant's helper', 'copper merchant', *kammaṭa* 'coiner'. Vikalpa: *miṇḍāl* markhor (Tor.wali) *meḍho* a ram, a sheep (G.)(CDIAL 10120) Rebus: *meḍ* 'iron' (Munda). The hieroglyph of antelope carried on Meluhhan's arm is a phonetic determinant suggesting phonemic variants– *melkhā* >> *meluhha.*Mohenjo-daro Seal m0712

On a Mohenjo-daro seal (m0712), the hieroglyph (Sign 391) denoting spokes (of wheel) *ārā* Rebus *āra* 'brass' is ligatured on the neck *melkhā* of a young bull to reinforce the characteristic of the 'iron-like' hard alloy and that the merchant is *milakkha* (Pali) meaning 'Meluhha speaker, copper *–milakku, mlecchamukha* --merchant'.

Thus, the ligatured hieroglyph of young bull ligatured on neck with spoked-wheel may read rebus: *āra milakkha konda* 'spokes – throat, neck *melkhā* -- young-bull'. Meaning: brass-artisan: 'Meluhha turner, metal-work artisan' of *āra* 'spokes', Rebus: *āra* 'brass'. [Alternatives for 'neck' hieroglyph: 1. అర్రు [arru] arru. [Tel.] n. The neck. కంఠము, పశుజాతి, మెడపంపు, కుతిక, ఆపద, హాని. A sore on a bullock's neck occasioned by ploughing. ఆ యెద్దు యొక్క అర్రు కొట్టు కొనిపోయినది the bullock's neck is hurt (by the yoke.) (Telugu) A phonetic determinant of *āra* 'spokes' 2. *kand* ' throat ' (Gypsy) *khaṇṭ* f. 'word' [Gawar-Bati (Dardic)] A phonetic determinant of *kaṇḍe* 'ear of maize'?]

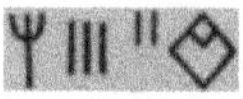1091 Text on Seal m0712:

Three linear strokes: *kolom* 'three' Rebus: *kolami* 'smithy'.

 *kōṇṭu* angle, corner (Tulu). rebus: *kõdā* 'to turn in a lathe' (Bengali) *kondā , konda* bullock, ox (Gondi) *sal* 'splinter' Rebus: *sal* 'workshop'

 *kaṇḍe* (Telugu) n. A head or ear of millet or maize. జొన్న కంకి. *kaṇḍa* -- m.n. joint of stalk (Pali) Rebus *kāṇḍa* tools, pots and pans and metal-ware. Alternative:kolmo 'sprout' Rebus kolami 'smithy'. [Glyph of Sign 347 can be viewed as a duplicated ligature of the 'sprout, stalk glyph. *dula* 'pair'; Rebus: *dul* 'cast (metal)(Santali). Thus Glyph 347 denotes metalware made from castings – *dul kāṇḍa*]

Thus, the phonetically re-inforced hieroglyphs denote brass *āra* of a Meluhha smithy where forging, work of turning on a lathe is done – *kõdā* 'lathe-turning'; *konda* 'young bull' to make tools, pots and pans and metal-ware-- *kāṇḍa*. .

Gregory Posshel notes: "Based on cuneiform documents from Mesopotamia we know that there was at least one Meluhhan village in Akkad at that time, with people called "Son of Meluhha" living there…The writing of Meluhha (the Indus script) remains undeciphered, in spite of many claims to the contrary. The inscriptions are short, and this makes the job of decipherment very difficult. To break the code, what is probably needed is a body of bilingual texts, like Jean-Francois Champollion had when he deciphered the Egyptian hieroglyphics on the Rosetta Stone. The presence in Akkad of a translator of the Meluhhan language suggests that he may have been literate and could read the undeciphered Indus script. This in turn suggests that there may be bilingual Akkadian/Meluhhan tablets somewhere in Mesopotamia. Although such documents may not exist,Shu-ilishu's cylinder seal offers a glimmer of hope for the future in unraveling the mystery of the Indus script."[11]

Antelope carried by the Meluhhan is a hieroglyph: *mlekh* 'goat' (Br.); *mr̤eka* (Te.); mēṭam (Ta.); meṣam (Skt.) Thus, the goat conveys the message that the carrier

577

is a Meluhha speaker (*milakkha* -- Pali). A phonetic determinant. *mr̤eka, mlekh* 'goat'; Rebus: melukkha Br. *mē̱ḻẖ* 'goat'. Te. *mr̤eka* (DEDR 5087)

Enthroned divinity (Ningishzida) flanked by two snakes receives two worshippers introduced by minor deity carrying staff; one worshipper carries an antelope kid, the other a bucket; scorpion and star in field Shell. 3.6x2.2cm. *meḍh* 'polar star' Rebus: *mẽṛhẽt,* 'iron' (Mu.Ho.) *meḍ, meṛed* 'iron'; *bica* 'scorpion' *bica* 'stone ore'.

आर [*āra*] A large serpent of the Boa-kind. (Marathi) Rebus: *āra* 'brass'. Alternative: Horned serpents *paṭam* , *n.* < *phaṭa*. 'cobra's hood' (CDIAL 9040). Rebus: 'sharpness of iron': *padm* (obl.*padt-*) temper of iron (Kota)(DEDR 3907); *patam* 'sharpness, as of the edge of a knife' (Tamil)

Thus, the three symbols – scorpion, star, serpent -- associated with the seated divinity on the shell cylinder seal: Rebus: *patam + meṛed-bica* = sharp

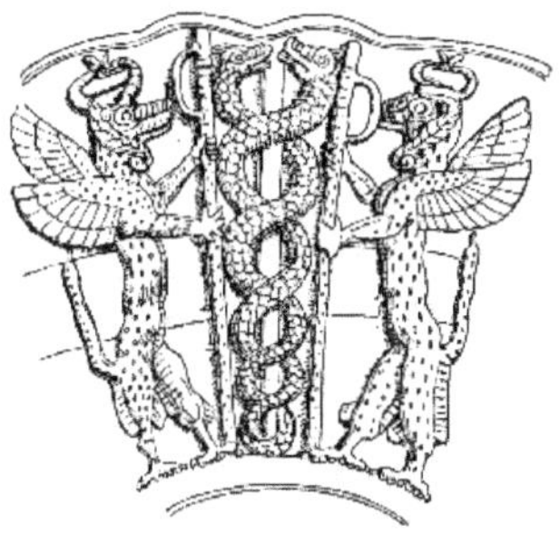

implements + iron stone ore, in contrast to *bali-bica*, iron sand ore (Munda). The Meluhhan carrying an antelope and a woman carrying a water-jar being introduced to the divinity, evoke the gyphs of Shu-ilishu cylinder seal.

The 'deity' is referred to as Ningishzida based on the tradition of two entwined serpents (mushussu) depicted s a cauduceus on Gudea's libation vase (21st century BCE), flanked by two winged foxes (cheetahsThe spotted 'foxes' may link with the following references to cheetahs:

DT Potts notes: "A well-known Old Babylonian inscription of Ibbi-Sin's from Ur (Sollberger 1965: 8, UET 8.34) records the dedication to Nanna of a statue of an ur gun-a Me-luhha-ki which the king had originally received a a gift from Marhashi and which he named 'let him catch' or 'may he catch'." (p.346) Elamites and soldiers are referred to as 'Elamites of Marhashi' (Steinkeller 1982: 262, n. 97). Ur and Marhashi had always enjoyed friendly diplomatic relationships, sometimes fortified by royal marriages. Steinkeller suggests that the ur gun-a Meluhha-ki was a spotted feline given to Ibbi-Sin,it was 'most likely a leopard (*Panthera pardus*)(Steinkeller 1982: 253

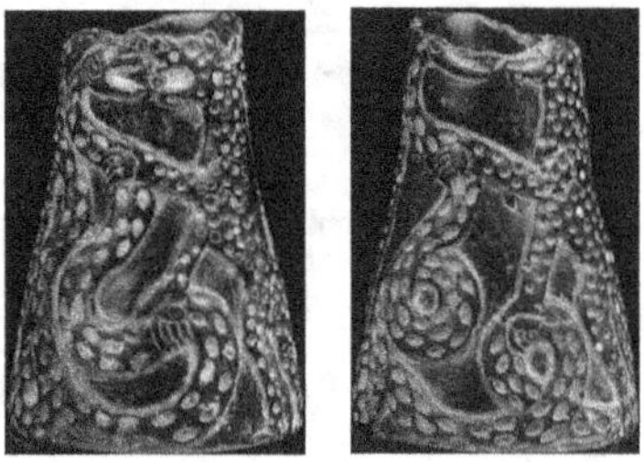

and n. 61). It could also have been a cheetah (Acinonyx jubatus vernaticus). In Hindi *chita* means 'spotted' (Yule and Burnell 1886: 187).

Gold foil feline from Tal-i Malyan, Banesh period (courtesy of WM Sumner).

It is possible that the cheetah from Meluhha was the animal given to Ibbi-Sin with the legend 'let him catch'.[12]

kindorkula, kinduakula = the panther (Munda) kolhā, kolā 'jackal'(Marathi) Rebus 1: kol 'working in iron'

Alternative: karaḍa 'tiger' Rebus: करडा [*karaḍā*] Hard from alloy--iron, silver &c. (Marathi) ?). *lōī* f., *lo* 'fox' (Western Pahari) Rebus: loh 'copper'.

The seal of Gudea of Lagash. Musee du Louvre. No. AO 22126 ca. 2120 BCE. Neo-Sumerian from the city-state of Lagash. Gudea, with shaven head, is accompanied by a minor female diety. He is led by his personal god, Ningishzida, into the presence of Enlil, the chief Sumerian god. The winged leopard (griffin or fox) is a mythological creature associated with Ningishzida, The horned helmets, worn even by the griffins, indicates divine status (the more horns the higher the rank). The writing in the background translates as: "To the god Ningiszida, his god Gudea, Ensi (governor or 'lord of the plowland') of Lagash, for the prolongation of his life, has dedicated this".

Note the winged fox at the edge of the cylinder seal and the foxes on the shoulders of the person holding the overflowing pot with Gudea.

lōī f., *lo* 'fox' (Western Pahari) Rebus: loh 'copper'. kāṇḍa 'flowing water' Rebus: kāṇḍā 'metalware, tools, pots and pans'

Figure, "nude goddess", 7000 Years of Iranian Art, no. 204.[13] On this statue, a ram is ligatured to a woman (*kola*). *meḍho* a ram, a sheep (G.)(CDIAL 10120); Rebus: *mẽṛhẽt,* 'iron' (Mu.Ho.) Rebus: meṛha, meḍhi 'merchant's clerk; (G.) Rebus: mḗdha m. ' sacrificial oblation ' RV. mēdha -- m. ' sacrifice ' (Pa.) (CDIAL 10327).

Antelope carried by the Meluhha woman accompanying the Meluhhan shown on Shu-ilishu cylinder seal is a hieroglyph: mlekh 'goat' (Br.); mṟeka (Te.); mēṭam (Ta.); meṣam (Skt.) Thus, the goat conveys the message that the carrier is a Meluhha speaker. A phonetic determinant is mṟēka 'goat' Rebus: melukkha (Meluhha).

The Meluhha is accompanied by a woman. kola 'woman' (Nahali). Rebus: *kol* 'pañcalōha, alloy of five metals' (Ta.) கொல் kol, n. 1. Iron; இரும்பு. மின் வெள்ளி பொன் கொல்லெனச் சொல்லும் (தக்கயாகப். 550). 2. Metal; உலோகம். (நாமதீப. 318.) *kola* 'blacksmith' (Ka.); Koḍ. *kollë* blacksmith (DEDR 2133). It appears that the same hieroglyphs are used: antelope, woman in the following artifact

592

produced during Jacques de Morgan's excavations at Susa (1905). He had also published the tokens. The tokens were used for categorizing property

593

items.

Ancient impression on clay; minor god introduces two worshippers, the second of whom is female and carries a bucket, to god holding cup and enthroned before fire altar; two entwined snakes behind god, another snake above hed of female worshipper; crescent in field. 2.5x2 cm. A flaming altar and a 'crucible' hieroglyph in the field.

Ancient impression on clay; minor god introducing worshipper carrying kid to god characterized by two snakes projecting from his legs; he holds cup and is attended by god with mace; crescent and dagger in field; endless-knot motif beneath inscription. 2.4x2.8 Inscription: Udurum great vizier of Tishpak. A dagger is shown on the field together with the 'crucible' hieroglyph (moon? Ingot? Mould?).

Signature tune of Elamite worshipper (Gold, Silver), Susa, Iran 12th century BCE: carrying

an antelope on his arms. Praying figure clutching a young goat Middle Elamite period, c. 1500-1200 BCE Tell of the Acropolis, Susa Gold and copper J. de Morgan excavations, 1904 Sb 2758[14]

Thus, the use of Indus glyphs on seals found in Persian Gulf including Lagash clearly relate to the Meluhhan's native language - Mleccha. An *eme-bal* might have interpreted these glyphs to Mesopotamian trade contacts. It is not necessary to assume that the Indus glyphs were adapted to represent some words or syllables of Sumerian or Akkadian language. The glyphs may simply have been read rebus in mleccha as was done for these glyphs on inscriptions of other objects inscribed found in the civilization area on such sites as Mohenjo-daro, Harappa, Chanhu-daro, Mitathal or Dholavira, Kalibangan or nearly 40 other seal discovery sites, with Indus script.

Apkallu, priest of Enki

Glyphs: giant ear of corn, eagle wings, antelope[15]

kulullu 'fish-man' (Ancient Mesopotamia)

apkallu 'sage' (Akkadian) One of seven sages. There is an Indic tradition of seven sages called saptarishi.

The word ap-kallu has parallels in indic languages (semantics, 'water', 'fish'):Aapah 'waters'.

kol ‘working in iron, blacksmith (Ta.); kollan- blacksmith (Ta.); kollan blacksmith, artificer (Ma.)(DEDR 2133) kolme = furnace (Ka.) kole.l 'temple, smithy' (Ko.); kolme smithy' (Ka.) kol = pañcalōha (five metals); kol metal (Tamil) pañcaloha = a metallic alloy containing five metals: copper, brass, tin, lead and iron (Skt.); an alternative list of five metals: gold, silver, copper, tin (lead), and iron (dhātu; Nānārtharatnākara. 82; Man:garāja’s Nighaṇṭu. 498)(Ka.) kol, kolhe, ‘the koles, an aboriginal tribe if iron smelters speaking a language akin to that of Santals’ (Santali)

xolā = tail (Kur.); qoli = id. (Malt.)(DEDR 2135).

kolli = a fish (Ma.); koleji id. (Tu.)(DEDR 2139). kōlā flying fish, exocaetus, garfish, belone (Ta.) kōlān, kōli needle-fish (Ma.)(DEDR 2241).

kōli = a stubble of jōḷa (Ka.) kōle a stub or stump of corn (Te.)(DEDR 2242). (cf. Ear of corn held in Apkallu’s right hand).

kole.l ‘smithy, temple’ (Ko.) kol ‘working in iron, blacksmith (Ta.)(DEDR 2133)

Elamite metallurgical excellence

Metallurgical excellence achieved in Elam is exemplified by this statue of Queen Napirasu.

Statue of Queen Napirasu, wife of Untash-Napirisha C. 1340-1300 BCE Tell of the Acropolis, Susa Bronze and copper J. de Morgan excavations, 1903 Sb 2731

“Queen Napirasu, Untash-Napirisha's wife, is shown standing. The figure is life-size, but the head and the left arm are damaged. She is wearing a short-sleeved gown covered in the sort of embroidery usually found on such garments. She has four bracelets on her right wrist and a ring on her left ring finger. Although her hands are crossed on her stomach, she is not in the pose usually associated with worship. The inscription on the front of the skirt is in Elamite, reflecting the kingdom's linguistic identity. This inscription gives the queen's name and titles, invokes the protection of the gods, describes the ritual offerings made to them, and calls down their curse on anyone bold enough to desecrate her likeness. The statue is placed under the protection of the god Beltiya and three deities associated with the Igihalkid Dynasty - the god Inshushinak, the god Napirisha, and his consort Kiririsha. These three deities are also depicted on the stele of Untash-Napirisha, also in the Louvre (Sb3973)..

“Elaborate metalworking techniques

“This statue of Queen Napirasu is a rare surviving likeness of a member of the royal court during the Middle Elamite period. The sheer amount of metal used - some 1,750 kg for a single work - reflects the wealth of the Elamite kingdom during Untash-Napirisha's reign. The dimensions and the finesse of the statue also reflect the skill of the Elamite metalworkers. The work must have been cast in two successive parts: a lost-wax cast for the copper and tin shell, followed by a full cast alloy of bronze and tin for the core, rather than the more usual refractory clay. The two parts are held together with pins and splints. The sides would have originally been covered with gold or silver.

“A great king and a great builder

“The reign of the Igihalkid king, Untash-Napirisha, witnessed the launch of a major construction program. The king ordered the restoration of a large number of temples and also built a new religious capital, Al-Untash-Napirisha (sometimes simply known as Al-Untash), on the site of modern-day Chogha Zanbil. The aim was to unite the different religions practiced in his kingdom in one place.

Monuments throughout the city were decorated with numerous sculptures commissioned by the king, including this statue of his wife, which was discovered in Susa but was probably moved there from Al-Untash."[16]

The argument: fish and antelope as hieroglyphs

A remarkable legacy of the use of 'fish' hieroglyph is reported from Haft Tepe excavations.[17] The site is just 10 kms. From Susa which reported a pot with 'fish' hieroglyph painted on the rim and containing metal tools and weapons.

One seal impression is reported.[18] "The seal impression is incomplete, but the remaining part contains a figure, possibly a deity, at the center, with head smeared and unclear, wearing a long garment with vertical folded skirt, seated on a simple bench with one arm bent at the elbow and the hand touching his waist while the other is extended, holding some object. In front of this figure, are two large fish above each other, with some distance between, with clearly detailed eyes, fins, and tails. Behind the seated deity, at ground level as shown by a horizontal band, is a recumbent animal, possibly a mountain goat, with straight horns sprouting from the head, which is turned backward.Behind this recumbent goat part of a tree with rounded flowers or fruit appears at the border edge of the broken side. Two more fish appear below the ground lines...Fish are rather unusual in seal designs, but they do sometimes appear. An early representation of fish appears on two seals in the Ashmolean Museum, classified by Buchanan to the Proto-historic art of the Jemdet Nasr period...there is evidence of a connection of some sort with the Proto-historic of southern Mesopotamia and southwestern Iran.

More seals with fish designs, in the British Museum, are classified by Wiseman as Jemdat Nasr-Early Dynastic I Period and other seals with fish designs are also classified to Jemdat Nasr Period by Frankfort. Some seals with fish designs are described by Legrain as Elamite, while more seals with fish designs from Susa are attributed by Pezard to the native and indigenous art of Elam. One group of seals with fish designs from Susa is attributed by Amiet to the Proto-Elamite period, and another group to the middle of the second millennium BCE and to the Medeo-Elamite period, while one example is described as a seal of the early first millennium BCE.

Two seals in the Ashmolean are described by Buchanan as Mitannean style as are many steal impressions with fish designs from Nuzi which are classified by Porada with Group XXVI of Elaborate Mitannean Stye, dated to the second half of the fifteenth century BCE…"

Painted clay head from Haft Tepe, Middle Elamite I. 28 cm. height.[19]

Haft Tepe, 'the seven mounds' in Kuzestan is 10 kms. Southeast of Susa is a large Elamite site.Several clay tablets and seal impressions found at this site containthe name 'Ka-ap-nak'. Various crafts were carried out in an artist's workshop. "Bowls with dried paint, a sawn elephant skeleton, a solidified cluster of several hundred bronze arrowheads and small bronze hooks, fragments of colored stone mosaic framed in bronze, and a butterfly pin of gold and carnelian were all found here, but the most unusual objects in the workshop are two life-size painted portrait heads of an elamite king and queen, together with a clay mask. Directly in front of this workshop is a large very large kiln composed of two long partitioned wings with a fire chamber in the center, in which both pottery and bronze apparently were baked…On one clay tablet the name of Kadashman Enlil is inscribed with an impression of the seal of King Tepti-Ahar. Apparently Tepti-Ahar, king of Elam, was a contemporary of Kadashman Enlil I, the Kassite king of

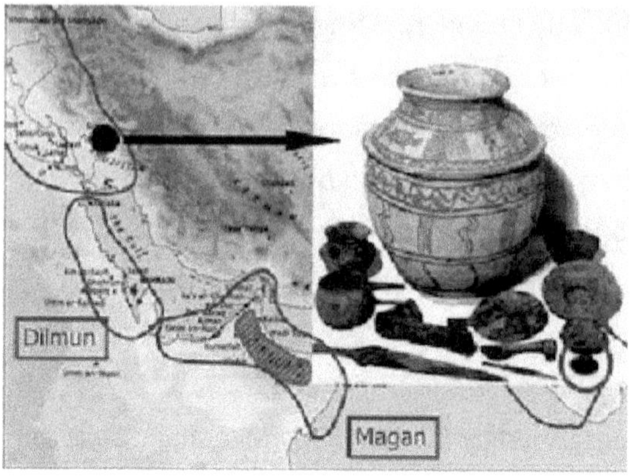

Mesopotamia, who is known to have reigned before Burnaburiash III, whose rule began around 1375 BCE."[20]

Susa pot with incised speech, from Meluhha, which contained metal artifacts. (Image thanks to Maurizio Tosi). The pot has an inscription, just below the rim, painted with 'fish' hieroglyph – the hieroglyph is determinative of the contents of the pot – ayo 'fish' Rebus: 'metal'.

On a Mohenjo-daro seal, ayo 'fish' read rebus ayas 'metal'; ḍangar 'bull' read rebus ḍhangar 'blacksmith'; koṭ 'horn; red rebus: khoṭ 'alloy'; khoṇḍ 'young bull-calf' read rebus khuṇḍ '(metal) turner'.

The ayo 'fish' hieroglyph thus adequately categorizes the metalware contents of a pot discovered in Susa.

Context for use of 'fish' glyph. This photograph of a fish and the 'fish' glyph on susa pot are comparable to the 'fish' glyph on an indus seal.

Kalibangan 37, 34

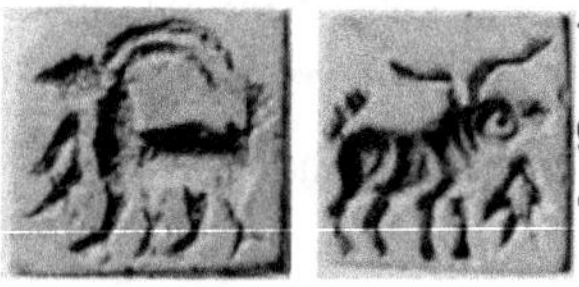

Two Kalibangan seals show an antelope and fish glyphs as the inscription. Mẽḍha 'antelope'; rebus: 'iron' (Ho.)

ayo 'fish'; rebs: ayo 'metal' (G.) [These are examples which clearly demonstrate that Indus script is a glyptic writing system and hence, all glyphs and glyptic elements have to be decoded.] *miṇḍāl* markhor (Tor.wali) *meḍho* a ram, a sheep (G.)(CDIAL 10120) iron (Ho.) *meṛed-bica* = iron stone ore, in contrast to bali-bica, iron sand ore (Munda) *meḍ* 'iron'.

m1429B. Glyphs: crocodile + fish ayakāra 'blacksmith' (Pali) kāru a wild crocodile or alligator (Telugu) aya 'fish' (Munda) The method of ligaturing enables creation of compound messages through Indus writing inscriptions.

Lothal seal. L048 ibex

Fish sign incised on copper anthropomorph, Sheorajpur, upper Ganges valley, ca. 2nd millennium BCE, 4 kg; 47.7 X 39 X 2.1 cm. State Museum, Lucknow (O.37) Typical find of Gangetic Copper Hoards. miṇḍāl markhor (Tor.wali) meḍho a ram, a sheep (G.)(CDIAL 10120) Rebus: meḍh 'helper of merchant' (Gujarati) meḍ iron (Ho.) meṛed-bica = iron stone ore, in contrast to bali-bica, iron sand ore (Munda) ayo 'fish' Rebus: ayo, ayas 'metal. Thus, together read rebus: *ayo meḍh* 'iron stone ore, metal merchant.'

Boat load of hard alloys and lapidary products

Mohenjo-daro. m1429a m1429b m1429c prism seal. Shows boat carrying metal ingots (shown by the glyphs of ox-hide ingots between two palm trees).

Sailing vessel shown on a stamp seal and on a line drawing, Mohenjodaro m1349A Mohenjo-daro seal.

"Found jammed up against the eastern wall of the tomb (at Tell Abraq) was this ivory bird figurine. The bird has a squared off tail and tufted crest, reminiscent of a tufted duck (Aythya fuligula) described in Colin Richardson's Birds of the United Arab Emirates as a 'fairly regular winter

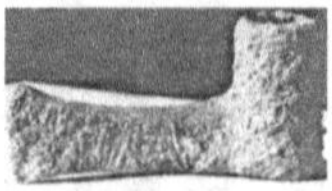

visitor...on creeks, ponds, lagoons and reservoirs in the Northern Emirates.' It is intriguing to think that Mesopotamian references to imported ivory birds from Meluhha may indeed refer to just such an object as this."[21]

A bronze axe-head from the Tell Abraq site.[22] (P. Hellyer)

Aythya faligula (Tufted duck)

dula 'pair' Rebus: dul 'cast (metal)'. *karaḍa*-- m. ' crow '(Prakrit) *karaṇḍa* 'duck' (Sanskrit) *karaṛa* 'a very large aquatic bird' (Sindhi) Rebus: करडा [karaḍā] Hard from alloy--iron, silver &c. (Marathi) *kārṇī* m. 'super cargo of a ship '(Marathi) *tamar*, 'palm tree, date palm' (Hebrew) Rebus: *tam(b)ra*, 'copper' (Prakrit) *bēṛā* m. ' large cargo boat ' (Lahnda). Alternative: bagalo = an Arabian merchant vessel (Gujarati) *bagala* = an Arab boat of a particular description (Ka.); bagalā (M.); bagarige, bagarage = a kind of vessel (Kannada) Rebus: bangala = kumpaṭi = angāra śakaṭī = a chafing dish a portable stove a goldsmith's portable furnace (Telugu) cf. bangaru bangaramu = gold (Telugu)

ayo 'fish' Rebus: ayas 'metal'. kāru 'crocodile' Rebus: kāru 'artisan'. Thus, together read rebus: ayakara 'metalsmith'

Alloys and lapidary products  Text 3246

Cast metal, alloy account

kāḍ काड् ', the stature of a man' Rebus: खडा [khaḍā] *m* A small stone, a pebble (Marathi) dula 'pair' Rebus: dul 'cast (metal)' shapes objects on a lathe' (Gujarati) *kanka, karṇaka* 'rim of jar' Rebus: *karṇaka* 'account scribe'. *kāṛṇī* m. 'super cargo of a ship '(Marathi)

Alloy ingots

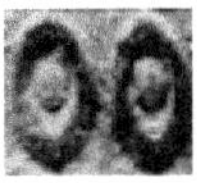

A pair of ingots with notches in-fixed as ligatures.

 *ḍhālako* 'large ingot'. खोट [*khōṭa*] 'ingot, wedge'; A mass of metal (unwrought or of old metal melted down)(Marathi) *khoṭ* f 'alloy (Lahnda) Thus the pair of ligatured oval glyphs read: *khoṭ ḍhālako* 'alloy ingots'.

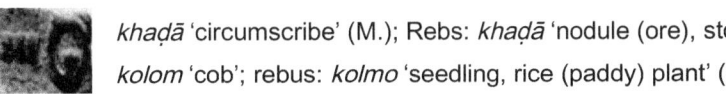

Forge: stone, minerals, gemstones

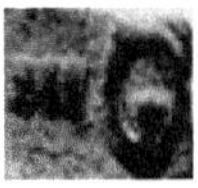

khaḍā 'circumscribe' (M.); Rebs: *khaḍā* 'nodule (ore), stone' (M.) *kolom* 'cob'; rebus: *kolmo* 'seedling, rice (paddy) plant' (Munda.) kolma hoṛo = a variety of the paddy plant (Desi)(Santali.) kolmo 'rice plant' (Mu.) Rebus: *kolami* 'furnace,smithy' (Telugu) Thus, the ligatured glyph reads: *khaḍā* 'stone-ore nodule' *kolami* 'furnace,smithy'. Alternatives: 1. *koṛuṅ* young shoot (Pa.) (DEDR 2149) Rebus: *kol* iron, working in iron, blacksmith (Tamil) kollan blacksmith, artificer (Malayalam) kolhali to forge.(DEDR 2133).2. *kaṇḍe* A head or ear of millet or maize (Telugu) Rebus: *kaṇḍa* 'stone (ore)(Gadba)' Ga. (Oll.) kanḍ, (S.) kanḍu (pl. kanḍkil) stone (DEDR 1298).

kolmo 'three' Rebus: *kolami* 'furnace,smithy'. Thus, the pair of glyphs may denote lapidary work – working with stone, mineral, gemstones.

Early Dilmun reed and sail-boat depicted on seals.[23]

1.5 A reed boat and a sailing boat depicted on seals of the Early Dilmun period.

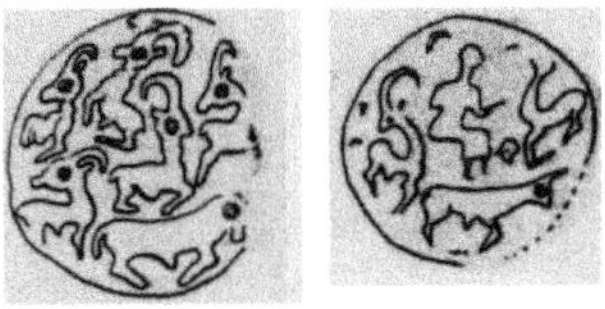

Fig.85; Susa, tablet: seal impression, Louvre Sb 11221

खांडा [*khāṇḍā*] A flock (of sheep or goats) (Marathi) Rebus: *kāṇḍā* 'metalware'.

Fig. 86; Susa, sealing:seal impression Louvre MDAI, 43, no. 240

Fig. 87; Susa, stamp seal from the Gulf, Louvre, MDAI, 43, No. 1716; depicts two goat-antelopes crouching head to tail, inside and outside an oval. Incised eyes are saucer-shaped.

Fig. 89; Susa, stamp seal from the Gulf, Teheran Museum, MDAI, 43, no. 1718; a person, naked and thin, has a stylised head shaped like a narrow arch with indentations to mark the nose and mouth. Animals have bound feet and surround a square object on which the person stands. खांडा [khāṇḍā] A division of a field. (Marathi) Rebus: *kāṇḍā* 'metalware'.

Fig.90; Susa, cylinder seal from the Gulf, Louvre, MDAI, 43, no. 2021; made of steatite; a person with a horned tiara, wearing an unevenly chequered robe; the person is attended by a naked man and alongside are two tamers grasping a pair of crossed animals.

Fig. 91; Susa, cylinder seal from the Gulf, Teheran Museum, MDAI, 43,no. 1975; steatite; three figures with stylised heads in the form of notched arches, wearing boldly chequered skirts; one is seated; the other two stand with backs turned, hold an enormous feathered arrow, and one of them extends a hand towards a stylised goat-antelope.

h503 4129 kaṇḍa 'arrow' Rebus: *kāṇḍā* 'metalware'.The arrow sign terminates 184 inscriptions (out of a total of 227 inscriptions in which the sign occurs) *karaṁḍa* 'backbone'. Rebus: *kharādī*' turner, a person who fashions or shapes objects on a lathe' (Gujarati) *karaṁḍuya* -- n. ' backbone '. (CDIAL 2670) Rebus: करडा [karaḍā] Hard from alloy--iron, silver &c. (Marathi) *kharādī*' turner, a person who fashions or shapes objects on a lathe' (Gujarati) करडा [karaḍā] Hard from alloy--iron, silver &c. (Marathi) Allograph: *kāraṇḍavamu* A kind of

antelope. కన్నెలేడి or కామిలేడిపిట్ట *kanne-lēḍi.* [Tel.] n. The bird called the Bastard Florikin: or stone-curlew. (Telugu) *karaḍa*-- m. ' crow '(Prakrit)

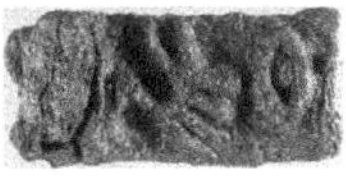

Harappa. Copper tablet (H2000-4498/9889-01) with raised script found in Trench 43. 8 identical tablets were found. The duplicates occur on steatite and faience tablets at Harappa; these may have represented a commodity or a value.[24] Yes, indeed, they are smith guild tokens like all other epigraphs of the civilization.

h1931A

h1931B
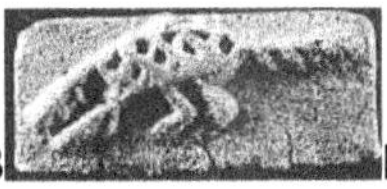
h1931C *kāru* a wild crocodile or alligator (Telugu) Rebus: *khar* 'blacksmith' (Kashmiri); *kāru* 'artisan' (Marathi).

U + || Glyph: dula pair' Rebus: dul 'cast (metal)'. Rebus: *kǒṇḍu* m. ' large cooking pot '(Kashmiri) *koṇḍa* bend (Konkani) Rebus: *kõdā* 'to turn in a lathe'(B.) कोंद *kōnda* 'engraver, lapidary setting or infixing gems' (Marathi) Alternative: *baṭhu* m. 'large pot in which grain is parched.' Rebus: *baṭi, bhaṭi* 'furnace' (Hindi) U + ||| (three linear strokes) may denote: konda 'engraver' + kolmo 'three' Rebus: kolimi 'smithy'. Thus, *kolimi konda* 'smithy engraver'.

Pair of ingots: dula 'pair' Rebus: dul 'cast (metal)'. *ḍhālako* 'a large metal ingot' (Gujarati)

Metal alloy worker, engraver/scribe, turner

1. *kaśēru* 'the backbone' (Bengali. Skt.) Rebus: Bi. H. *kaserā* m. ' worker in pewter '. (CDIAL 2989). *kāsā* 'metal alloy, bel-metal, bronze'. Alternatives: 1. riṛ 'ridge formed by the backbone' (Santali); rebus: rīti 'brass' (Skt.) 2. *karaṁḍuya* -- n. ' backbone ' L. *kaṇḍ* f., *kaṇḍā* m.

'backbone'. (CDIAL 2670).Rebus: करडा [karaḍā] Hard from alloy--iron, silver &c. (Marathi) *kāḍ* 'stone'. Ga. (Oll.) *kanḍ*, (S.) *kanḍu* (pl. kanḍkil) stone (DEDR 1298). L. *kanērā* m. ' mat -- maker '; H. *kāḍerā* m. ' a caste of bow -- and arrow -- makers '.(CDIAL 3024). H. *kanīrā* m. ' a caste (usu. of arrow -- makers) '.(CDIAL 3026).

2. *kanka, karṇaka* 'engraver, scribe'.

3. *khareḍo* 'a currycomb' Rebus: करडा [karaḍā] Hard from alloy--iron, silver &c. (Marathi) *kharādī* ' turner, a person who fashions or shapes objects on a lathe ' (Gujarati) Alternative: kāmsako, kāmsiyo = a large sized comb (G.) Rebus: kaṁsa= bronze (Te.) kaṁsá1 m. ' metal cup ' AV., m.n. ' bell -- metal N. *kasār* ' maker of brass pots ' (CDIAL 2988).

h1827A

h1827B

h1302A

h1302B

h1303A

h1303B

h1932A
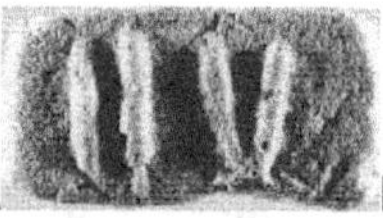
h1932B
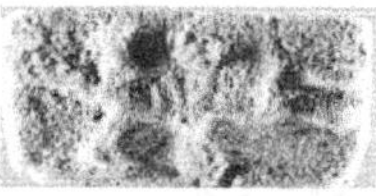
h1932C

These examples show a thre-glyph sequence including an 'E-shaped' glyph, like the teeth of a currycomb.

Identical glyphs on 8 tablets which flank the 'backbone' glyph on these tablets is an oval (variant 'rhombus') sign — like a metal ingot — and is ligatured with an infixed sloping stroke: ḍhāḷiyum = adj. sloping, inclining (G.). This example of a uniquely scripted tablet with raised Indus writing glyphs shows that copper tablets were also used in Harappa, while hundreds of copper tablets with incised script inscriptions were found in Mohenjo-daro. *dul mũh khāṇḍā* 'cast ingot tools, pots and pans and metal-ware'. The ligatured glyph (oval with infixed jag) is read rebus as: ḍhālako = a large metal ingot (G.) ḍhālakī = a metal heated and poured into a mould; a solid piece of metal; an ingot (G.) ḍhāḷiyum = adj. sloping, inclining (G.)

Indus Sign	Pottery Graffiti Symbol No.*	Plates*	Pages*
137	10-11	IXA:1-2 IXB: 1-4	10 10
139	59	XXXIII:11	20
162	3 41-42	IIIA:1-6 XXVIII:1-7 XXIXA:1-2	8 17 17
176	19	XV:1-9	12-13

* References to Lal 1960.

These eight copper tablets with raised writing were found on circular platforms. The circular platforms functioned as sorting, marketing platforms if, in the center of the circle, a storage pot containing metal artefacts, beads, ivory products etc. were kept for display, marketing, trade. [The center of the circle may also have held a drill-lathe as guild trade platforms for artisans of forge/smithy and lapidaries.] "During excavations of the circular platform area on Mound F numerous Cemetery H-type sherds and some complete vessels were recovered in association with pointed base goblets and large storage vessels that are usually associated with Harappa Period 3C." South fo the platforms was a furnace. "A large kiln was also found just below the surface of the mound to the south of the circular platforms."[25] The circular platforms are used in conjunction with the products taken out of the kiln (furnace) and large storage vessels which could have been plced in the center of any of the street platforms, constituting the main market street of early times of Harappa settlement. Circular platforms (with a dia. of 1.5 m) found within rooms (of a coppersmith) as in Padri might have served as working platforms for the brass-workers, lapidaries, artisans of the civilization or as a display counter if the room was used as a shop for sales.

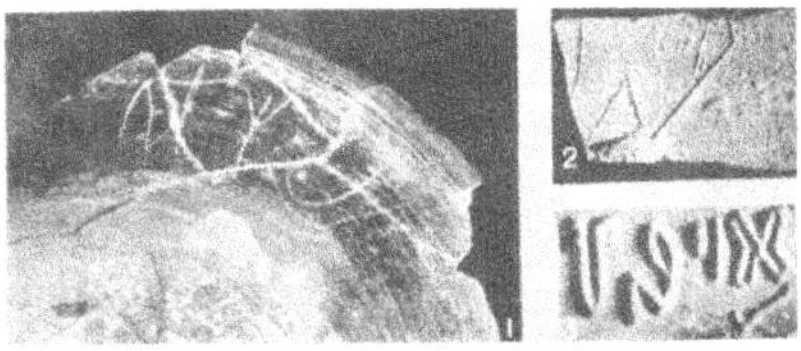

Many Indus writing glyphs continued into the chalcolithic and megalithic period as evidenced by the comparison in the table.[26]

This continuum of the writing tradition is exemplified by the use of glyphs in Chalcolithic/Megalithic sites, as for example in Sanur, Tamil Nadu.

Pottery graffiti at Sanur, a megalithic site had a glyph comparable to Sign 47/Variant Sign 48.

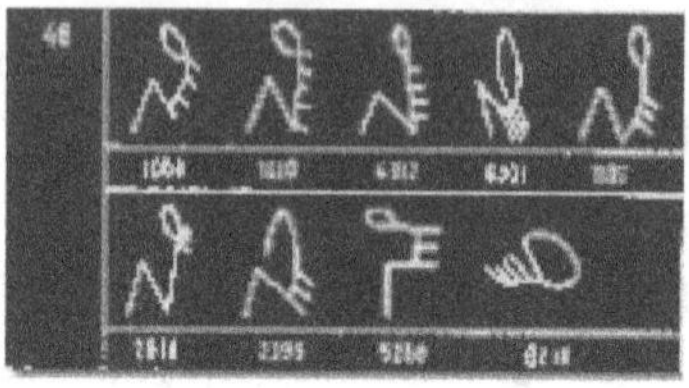

Megalithic glyph at Sanur in Tamilnadu (extreme left) and Glyphs (Signs 47 and 48) in texts at Kalibangan (right top) and Harappa (right bottom).

Kalibangan048 Mahadevan compares the Glyph (Sign 48) with a glyph on a Kalibangan seal showing a seated person occupying the entire field. This variant glyph shows backbone and ribs of a person with a large head and a massive jaw jutting forward. The complete ribcage is shown in clear detail with almost all the ribs in position, curving naturalistically on either side of the backbone.[27]

Glyph (Sign 47) is compared with the glyph in Pl. XXXI B-1 (Megalithic). The glyph also occurs in Pl. IIIA-1,3. The graffiti bearing Megalithic pottery found in Tamilnadu is assigned to ca. 2nd half of 1st millennium BCE. Lal notes: “In the case of Sanur…three symbols occur in such close proximity to one another as to give the impression of a record. It may however be added that the three symbols interchange their position on different pots producing all possible combinations.”[28]

Samarra: first smelting of iron ore, 5000 BCE validated by Meluhha writing

[quote] "The first smelting of iron [ore] may have taken place as early as 5000 BCE" at Samarra, Mesopotamia, but more commonly early iron was recovered from fallen meteors (yielding iron with a characteristic 4+% nickel content). By the middle of the fourth millennium BC, "both texts and objects reveal the presence

of iron" in Mesopotamia, from where the Jaredites departed. Just possibly they brought with them to the New World technical knowledge of that metallurgy. Sporadically throughout the Bronze Age (about 3500 BCE–1000 BCE) in the Near East, wrought (nonmeteoric) iron objects were being produced, along with continued use of the meteoric type. Yet details of the history at that time are poorly known. The find of an iron artifact from Slovakia dated to the 17th century BCE leads one researcher to lament "how little we actually know about the use of iron during the second millennium BCE." Steel is "iron that has been combined with carbon atoms through a controlled treatment of heating and cooling." Yet "the ancients possessed in the natural (meteoric) nickel-iron alloy a type of steel that was not manufactured by mankind before 1890." (It has been estimated that 50,000 tons of meteoritic material falls on the earth each day, although only a fraction of that is recoverable.) By 1400 BCE, smiths in Armenia had discovered how to carburize iron by prolonged heating in contact with carbon (derived from the charcoal in their forges). This produced martensite, which forms a thin layer of steel on the exterior of the object (commonly a sword) being manufactured. Iron/steel jewelry, weapons, and tools (including tempered steel) were definitely made as early as 1300 BC (and perhaps earlier), as attested by excavations in present-day Cyprus, Greece, Turkey, Syria, Egypt, Iran, Israel, and Jordan. "Smiths were carburizing [i.e., making steel] intentionally on a fairly large scale by at least 1000 BC in the Eastern Mediterranean area." [unquote][29]

Glyphs of Harappa and Samarra read rebus in Meluhha language: fish, peacock, eye of peacock-feather, disheveled or snarled hair, women, svastika, antelope/ram, scorpion. Rebus readings are consistent with the archaeological evidence of early iron-smelting work in Samarra.

Harappa, Pakistan. Four women with wavy hair. Glyphs showing 'eyes' of peacock-feathers, together with a glyph of ram.

kaṇ eye, aperture, orifice, star of a peacock's tail. (Tamil)(DEDR 1159a) Rebus 'brazier, bell-metal worker': கன்னான் kaṉṉāṉ , *n.* < கன்¹. [M. *kannān.*] Brazier, bell-metal worker, one of the divisions of the Kammāḷa caste; செம்புகொட்டி. (திவா.) *Ta.* kaṉ copper work, copper, workmanship (Tamil)

mora peacock; morā 'peafowl' (Hindi); rebus: morakkhaka loha, a kind of copper, grouped with pisācaloha (Pali). moraka "a kind of steel" (Sanskrit)

tagara 'ram' Rebus: tagaram 'tin'.

S. mī̃ḍhī f., °ḍho m. ' braid in a woman's hair ', L. mē̃ḍhī f.; मेढा [mēḍhā] A twist or tangle arising in thread or cord, a curl or snarl (Marathi). Rebus: mẽṛhẽt, meḍ 'iron' (Mu.Ho.) meṛed-bica = iron stone ore, in contrast to bali-bica, iron sand ore (Mu.lex.)

meṇḍa -- m. ' ram ' (Pali) Rebus: *mẽṛhẽt, meḍ* 'iron' (Mu.Ho.) *meṛed-bica* = iron stone ore, in contrast to bali-bica, iron sand ore (Mu.lex.)

Svastika, four peacocks and fish: Samarra bowl 1 Svastika in the centre. Eight fish, four peacocks holding four fish, slanting strokes surround.

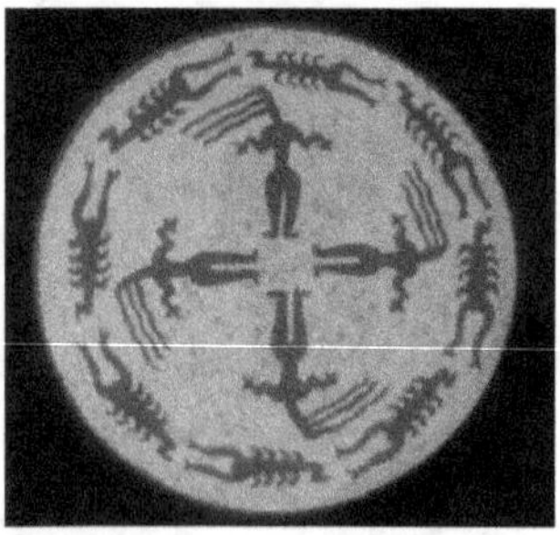

Image 1. The Samarra bowl (ca. 4000 BC) at on exhibit at the Pergamon museum, Berlin. The bowl was excavated as Samarra by Ernst Herzfeld in the 1911-1914 campaign, and described in a 1930 publication. The design consists of a rim, a circle of eight fish, and four fish swimming towards the center being caught by four birds. At the center is a swastika symbol.[30]

Glyph: ayo 'fish'; rebus: ayas 'metal'

Glyph: svastika Rebus: satthiya 'zinc', jasta 'zinc' (Kashmiri), satva, 'zinc' (Pkt.)

Samarra, Iraq, circa 5000 BCE Four women with wavy hair. Eight scorpions: Samarra bowl 2.

Image 2. Women with flowing hair and scorpions, Samarra, Iraq.[31] This image is discussed in Denise Schmandt-Besserat, When writing met art, p.19. "The design features six humans in he center of the bowl and six scorpions around the inner rim. The six identical anthropomorphic figures, shown frontally, are generally interpreted as females because of their wide hips, large thighs, and long, flowing hair…Six identical scorpions, one following after the other in a single line, circle menacingly around the women."

Six women, with wavy hair, six scorpions: Samarra bowl

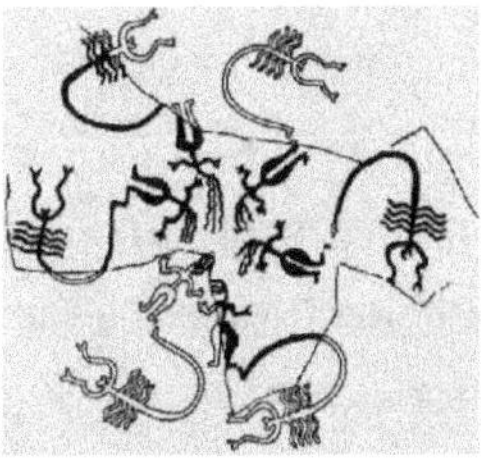

Glyphs: six (numeral) + ring of hair: आर [āra] A term in the play of इटीदांडू,--the number six. (Marathi) आर [āra] A tuft or ring of hair on the body. (Marathi) Rebus: āra 'brass'.

<raca>(D) {ADJ} ``^dishevelled" (Munda) *rabca* 'dishevelled' Rebus 1: రాచ *rāca* (adj.) Pertaining to a stone. Rebus 2: *rasāṇē* n. ' glowing embers '(Marathi). of kuṭhi 'smelter' – for, bica 'scorpion' Rebus: bica 'stone ore'. Thus, the glyphic of 'dishevelled hair' (*rāca* 'pertaining to a stone') is a semantic reinforcement of the nature of 'stone' ore represented by the 'scorpion' glyph, *bica*. *kola* 'woman' Rebus: *kol* 'working in iron'. cf. *sangatarāśi* = stone-cutting (Telugu)

bicha 'scorpion' (Assamese) Rebus: bica 'stone ore' (Munda). meṛed-bica = iron stone ore, in contrast to bali-bica, iron sand ore (Munda)

Alternative readings: *kuṭhi, kuṭi* (Or.; Sad. *koṭhi*) (1) the smelting furnace of the blacksmith; kuṭire bica duljaḍko talkena, they were feeding the furnace with ore (Santali)

gaṇḍa set of four (Santali) Rebus: *kaṇḍ* 'fire-altar, furnace' (Santali)

 Text 4304 Rendering (to) temple (guild) stone, tin smithy furnace/smelter account.

koḍi 'flag' (Ta.)(DEDR 2049). Rebus: Bshk. *kōr* ' large stone ' (CDIAL 3018).

 This glyph is comparable to the glyph on Kafajeh vase fragment possibly

depicting the Sin temple. *kole.l* 'temple' Rebus: *kole.l* 'smithy'. *kanka* 'rim of jar' Rebus: *kanka* 'scribe, account'. खांडा [*khāṇḍā*] *m* a jag, notch, or indentation (as upon the edge of a tool or weapon) Rebus: *khāṇḍā* 'metal tools, pots and pans'. *ranku* 'liquid measure' Rebus: *ranku* 'tin'. *kolom* 'sprout' Rebus: *kolami* 'smithy'. *kuṭi* 'water-carrier' Rebus: *kuṭhi* 'furnace for smelting iron ore'. The six glyphs of the inscription thus denote (catalog of): large stone for temple, metal tools, tin, smithy, smelter. The context is provided by the pictorial motifs also read rebus: Side B: Working with iron stone ore; Side A: artisan/smithy work in hard alloys, smelter and in a mint.

Pictorial motif on side b of tablet h180: a woman with legs spread out, accent on pubes: kuṭhi; rebus: kuṭhi = a furnace for smelting iron stone ore].

Harappa. h180A,B twosided bas-relief tablet Text 4304 Nude female figure upside down with thighs drawn apart and crab (?) issuing from her womb, two tigers standing face to face rearing on their hindlegs at L. Pict-92: Man armed with a sickle-shaped weapon on his right hand and a cakra (?) on his left hand, facing a seated woman with disheveled hair and upraised arms. Side A: Glyphs: Accent on pubes and copulating crocodile. *kuṭhi* 'pubes' Rrebus: *kuṭhi* 'furnace for smelting iron ore'. kāru 'crocodile' Rebus: kāru 'artisan' khar 'blacksmith'. *kamḍa, khamḍa* 'copulation' (Santali) Rebus: *kampaṭṭa* 'mint, coiner'. Glyphs: two rearing tigers: kol 'tiger' Rebus kol 'working in iron'. Alternative: *karaḍa* tiger' Rebus: *kharaḍa* 'hard alloy'. Dula 'pair' Rebus: dul 'cast metal'. Thus, the pictorial motifs depict the artisan/smithy work in hard alloys, smelter and in a mint. Side B: Glyphs: Ku. *āsī* 'scythe' Rebus: ancu 'iron' (Tocharian). raca 'dishevelled' Rebus: rāca 'pertaining to a stone'. The glphic composition thus depicts the working with iron stone ore.

Eye Idol Chalcolithic (3300-3000 BC) Northern Syria Terra-cotta H. 25 cm Gift of the Friends of the Louvre, 1991 AO 30002

Allograph: Pk. *ḍōla* -- m. ' eye ' (CDIAL 6582).Rebus: *ḍula* m. ' rolling stone ' (Kashmiri) dul 'cast (metal)'.

"A multitude of eye idols

"Eye idols are scattered over a vast region bounded by southeast Turkey (Arslantepe) to the north, Syria (Hama) to the west, and southern Mesopotamia (Telloh, Uruk, Ur) and Iranian Khuzistan (Susa) to the south. These objects are characteristic of the Proto-urban period in Uruk (3700-3100 BC) during which the first cities appeared. The many different contexts in which they were discovered (domestic, ritual, funerary, dumps) cast doubt on the strictly religious function of these objects, which vary greatly in shape, material, and style.

"In 1996, Catherine Bréniquet suggested dividing the idols into three types. Type 1, from Tell Brak, known as "eye idols," covers all the small engraved alabaster plaques evoking the upper part of a human body with the face reduced to the eyes and sometimes adorned with jewelry and headdresses. Type 2, the "large idols with spectacles," covers quite large bell- or trumpet-shaped pottery objects with a neck supporting two perforated circles. Some have been carefully shaped, smoothed and glazed, while others are quite summarily made. Our idol belongs to this type of "large idols with spectacles," present in northern Mesopotamia and Syria. Type 3, which groups "small idols with spectacles" shows strong similarities with Type 2, but these objects are much smaller and are all made of stone.

“Various interpretations

“Max Mallowan interpreted all these objects as belonging to one and the same series, evolving in shape over time. The group would have made a set of votive objects dedicated to an "eye god" venerated in the "temple" of Tell Brak. Other scholars have thought Types 2 and 3 to be lids (H. Frankfort), a set of standard weights or weights for a loom, or even firedogs to be set around a hearth. Catherine Bréniquet believes that Type 1 models - the only ones that really deserve to be called "eye idols" - should be distinguished from Types 2 and 3. The latter could well be instruments used in spinning, placed in front of the seated operator. The holes were used to separate two or three single threads, which were then twisted together. On cylinder seals from the Uruk period, such objects seem to be shown in association with spinners at work.”[32]

kaṇ eye, aperture, orifice, star of a peacock's tail. (Tamil)(DEDR 1159a) Rebus ‘brazier, bell-metal worker’: கன்னான் kaṉṉāṉ , *n.* < கன்[1]. [M. *kannān.*] Brazier, bell-metal worker, one of the divisions of the Kammāḷa caste; செம்புகொட்டி. (திவா.) *Ta.* kaṉ copper work, copper, workmanship (Tamil)

mora peacock; morā ‘peafowl’ (Hindi); rebus: morakkhaka loha, a kind of copper, grouped with pisācaloha (Pali). moraka "a kind of steel" (Sanskrit)

tagara ‘ram’ Rebus: tagaram ‘tin’.

मेढा [mēḍhā] A twist or tangle arising in thread or cord, a curl or snarl (Marathi). S. mī˜ḍhī f., °ḍho m. ‘ braid in a woman's hair ’, L. mēḍhī f.; G. mī̃ḍlɔ, miḍ° m. ‘braid of hair on a girl's forehead ’ (CDIAL 10312). Rebus: mēḍ ‘iron’ (Mu.) meṛha M. meṛhi F.’twisted, crumpled, as a horn’; meṛha deren ‘a crumpled horn’ (Santali) मेंढा [mēṇḍhā] A crook or curved end (of a stick, horn &c.) and attrib. such a stick, horn, bullock. mēṇḍha m. ‘ ram ’.

kola 'woman' Rebus: *kol* 'working in iron'
kuṛī f. ' girl' Rebus: *kuṭhi* 'smelter'

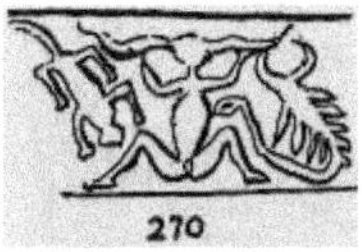

Brass-worker catalog of implements and repertoire:There are five hieroglyphs on the cylinder seal (Figure 270): 'dishevelled hair', '*pudendum muliebre'*, 'lizard', 'scorpion', 'woman'. The accent is on the sting of the scorpion: koṭṭu (koṭṭi-) to sting (as a scorpion, wasp) (Tamil) Rebus: Pk. *koṭṭaga* -- m. ' carpenter ', *koṭṭila* -- , *°illa* -- m. ' mallet '. (DEDR 3236). *koṭṭu-k-kaṉṉār* brass-workers.

In Fig. 270[33], the woman is shown with disheveled hair. A lizard is also shown in the field together with a scorpion (*bica*). <raca>(D) {ADJ} ``^dishevelled'' (Munda) *rasāṇẽ* n. 'glowing embers' (Marathi). *rabca* 'dishevelled' Rebus: రాచ *rāca* (adj.) Pertaining to a stone (ore) (*bica*).

The hieroglyphs on this seal constitute a metalware catalog set showing the attributes of a smithy/forge: smelting furnace, glowing embers, stone ore (*bica*) and anvil (airaṇ). Glyph: *araṇe* 'lizard' (Tulu) Rebus: eraṇi f. ' anvil ' (Gujarati); *aheraṇ, ahiraṇ, airaṇ, airṇī, haraṇ* f. 'anvil'(Marathi)

kuṭhi 'pudendum muliebre, vagina' Rebus: *kuṭhi* 'smelting furnace'. bichā 'scorpion' (Assamese). Rebus: bica 'stone ore'.

kola 'woman'; rebus: kol 'iron'. kola 'blacksmith' (Ka.); kollë 'blacksmith' (Koḍ) The glyphic elements shown on the tablet are: copulation, vagina, crocodile. h180 tablet.

Gyphic: 'copulation': *kamḍa, khamḍa* 'copulation' (Santali) Rebus: *kammaṭi* a coiner (Ka.); *kampaṭṭam* coinage, coin, mint (Ta.) kammaṭa = mint, gold furnace (Te.) Vikalpa: kaṇḍa 'stone (ore)'. Glyph: vagina: kuṭhi 'vagina'; rebus: kuṭhi 'smelting furnace'. The descriptive glyphics indicates that the smelting furnace is for stone (ore). This is distinquished from sand ore. Glyph: 'crocodile': karā 'crocodile'. Rebus: khar 'blacksmith'. kāru a wild crocodile or alligator (Te.) Rebus: kāruvu 'artisan'

A comparable glyphic composition is a naked woman seated with her legs spread out flanked by two scorpions. Cylinder-seal impression from Ur showing a squatting female. L. Legrain, 1936, Ur excavations, Vol. 3, Archaic Seal Impressions. This glyphic composition depicts a smelting furnace for stone ore as distinguished from a smelting furnace for sand ore. meṛed-bica = iron stone ore, in contrast to bali-bica, iron sand ore (Munda)

The squatting woman on the Ur cylinder seal impression may be showing dishevelled hair providing for rebus reading: <rabca?>(D) {ADJ} ``with ^dishevelled ^hair''. Rebus: రాచ (adj.) Pertaining to a stone. bicha, bichā 'scorpion' (Assamese) Rebus: bica 'stone ore' (Mu.) sambr.o bica = gold ore (Mundarica) Thus, the reading of the Ur cylinder seal impression may depict: *meṛed-bica* 'iron stone-ore' *kuṭhi* 'smelter, furnace'.

kuṭire bica duljad.ko talkena, 'they were feeding the furnace with ore'. (Santali) This use of *bica* in the context of feeding a smelter clearly defines *bica* as 'stone ore, mineral', in general.[34]

269

kuṭhi 'vagina'; rebus: *kuṭhi* 'smelting furnace bichā 'scorpion' (Assamese). Rebus: bica 'stone ore' as in *meṛed-bica* = iron stone ore, in contrast to *bali-bica*, iron sand ore (Mu.lex.) dul 'pair, likeness' Rebus: dul 'cast metal' (Santali) Thus the hieroglyphs connote a smelter for smelting and casting metal stone ore.

Glyphs: six (numeral) + ring of hair: आर [āra] A term in the play of इटीदांडू,--the number six. (Marathi) आर [āra] A tuft or ring of hair on the body. (Marathi) Rebus: āra 'brass'. Alternative: bhaṭa 'six '; rebus: bhaṭa 'furnace'.

satthiya 'svastika glyph'; rebus: satthiya 'zinc', jasta 'zinc' (Kashmiri), satva, 'zinc' (Pkt.)

muha -- n. 'mouth, face' (Pkt.) mũh 'face'; rebus: mũh 'ingot' (Mu.)

kul 'tiger' (Santali); kōlu id. (Te.) kōlupuli = Bengal tiger (Te.) कोल्हा [kōlhā] कोल्हें [kōlhēṃ] A jackal (Marathi) rebus: kol 'furnace, forge' (Kuwi) kol 'alloy of five metals, pañcaloha' (Tamil) kol 'working in iron, blacksmith'; kollaṉ 'blacksmith' (Tamil).

ṭagara = *tabernae montana* (Skt.) ṭagara 'antelope'; rebus: ṭagara 'tin'. Cf. cognate: tamkāru, damgar 'merchant'(Sumerian).

Other glyphic elements of the tablet:

Two tigers rearing on their hindlegs standing face to face.

Glyph: tiger: kola 'tiger'. Rebus: kol 'working in iron'
Glyph: dula 'pair'. Rebus: dul 'casting (metal).

A person carrying a sickle-shaped weapon and a wheel on his bands faces a woman with disheveled hair and upraised arm. *kundau dhiri* = a hewn stone. Rebus:) कोंद *kōnda* 'engraver, lapidary setting or infixing gems' (Marathi)

kuṭhāru 'armourer' (Skt.) The glyptic composition is decoded as kuṭhāru sal 'armourer workshop.'

Thus, the entire composition of these glyphic elements relate to an lapidary/smith's copper workshop. The hairstyle of the woman is comparable to the wavy hair shown on the Samarra bowl (Image 2. Six women, curl in hair, six scorpions). rabca 'dishevelled' Rebus: రాచ rāca (adj.) Pertaining to a stone.

Scorpion, *pudendum muliebre* as hieroglyphs to denote ore-smelting furnace
Just as the abiding continuity of tradition is evidenced by the wearing of sindhur at the hair-parting by married women in India, comparable to the sindhur shown on two terracotta figurines of Nausharo, the metaphors and puns implied by scorpion and *pudendum muliebre* are vividly representing by stone-workers who created the Khajuraho stone sculptures.

Scoprion metaphor does occur in a sexual setting on early epigraphs and on at least two sculptures from Khajuraho. It is suggested in this note that the scorpion is a hieroglyph representing a major component mineral ore used by a blacksmith/artisan working with metals and stone ores. This memory continues in a stunning recollection dated to ca. 1150 CE in Khajuraho sculptures.

The imageries shown (presented in different views from the sculptures of Kandariya Mahadev temple of Khajurato) on the sculptures are the presence of a scorpion on the thigh of a woman as she exposes her pudendum muliebtre while removing her skirt.[35]

The most emphatic rebus representation of *kuṭhi* 'the pubes of a woman' yields the homonym *kuṭhi* 'smelting furnace' (Santali)

Shown together with scorpions, the rebus reading may refer to a smelting furnace used for iron or native metal: bica 'scorpion' (Assamese); bica = stone ore containing iron (Mu.) [Sand containing iron ore has a distinct lexeme: bali (Munda).

Glyph: kuṭhi = pubes Rebus: kuṭhi, kuṭi (Or.; Sad. koṭhi) (1) the smelting furnace

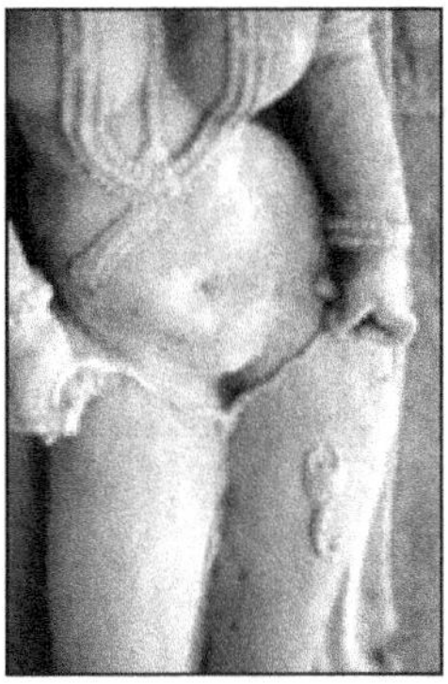

of the blacksmith; *kuṭire bica duljaḍko talkena*, they were feeding the furnace with ore; (2) the name of ēkuṭi has been given to the fire which, in shellac factories, warms the water bath for softening the lac so that it can be spread into sheets; to make a smelting furnace; kut.hi-o of a smelting furnace, to be made; the smelting furnace of the blacksmith is made of mud, cone-shaped, 2' 6" dia. At the base and 1' 6" at the top. The hole in the centre, into which the mixture of charcoal and iron ore is poured, is about 6" to 7" in dia. At the base it has two holes, a smaller one into which the nozzle of the bellow is inserted, as seen in fig. 1, and a larger one on the opposite side through which the molten iron flows out into a cavity (Mundari)

Continuity of artisan traditions

The transition from Stone Age into Bronze Age resulted in stone-workers' and lapidaries' competence being complemented by 1) invention of metallurgical technique of alloying minerals to create hard metal and metal artefacts and 2) invention of Indus writing system. Both inventions of the artisans drew upon the repertoire of mleccha (Meluhha) language of Indian linguistic area to trade with their contact areas and to create a record of their economic transactions.

Many researchers have analyzed and documented economic facets, in particular, of the Indus civilization area and their insights support the decoding of inscriptions of the civilization, in the context of economic activities by Meluhhans, who are mleccha speakers of Indus language and users of Indus script. The areas investigated by researchers and scholars also cover, in an inter-disciplinary evaluation of archaeology, literature and language of ancient times, an extensive civilization area across the Persian Gulf and in maritime trade contact with Mesopotamia. These detail the material resources used for bead-making, manufacture of grinding stones, of copper plates/utensils/tools/weapons - many with inscriptions, agricultural products used/produced, stone-work, and metallurgy including alloying, casting, forging.

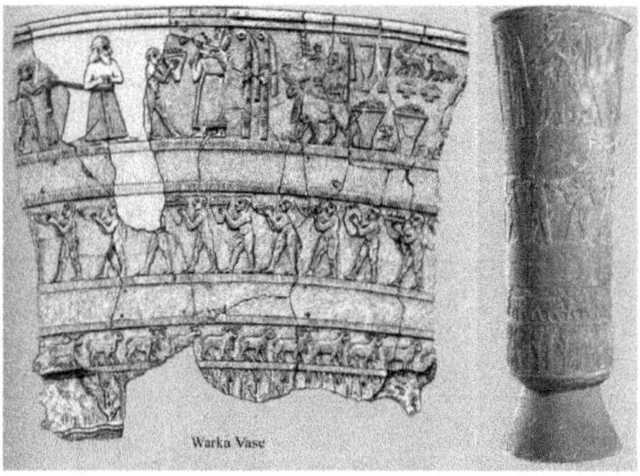

The argument: hieroglyphs of Warka vase

The reeds with ligatured scarves is a remarkable glyph which occurs on a Uruk cylinder seal and also on Warka vase. The glyph is interpreted by art historians as the symbol of a Sumerian divinity, Inanna. I suggest that this hieroglyph read rebus, connotes meluhha incised speech.

[quote]At the time this seal was made, Uruk was one of the largest settlements in the world, estimated at around 250 hectares (about 620 acres). Such a large centre, with several thousand inhabitants, required sophisticated means of administration; this seal may have belonged to one of the most important officials. They were rolled across damp clay to seal vessels or doors with a mark of authority. The figure depicted here is often referred to as a priest-king because he undertakes activities which could be described as religious and royal (although there was no clear division of these functions in the ancient world). The beard, net-like skirt and wide band around his head distinguish him from other representationsof humans. The poles with loops were probably actually made

from reeds bound together and are the symbol of Inana, a goddess of fertility and the patron of Uruk.Large seals of this period are generally unpierced and often have an animal carved as part of the seal or cast in metal and fixed on top. These contrast with contemporary smaller schematic seals which appear to show workers, perhaps connected with the production of textiles and pottery and rows of animals.[unquote].

Warka vase, Uruk: 3000 BCE, Uruk in Southern Iraq. (Height, aprox.1,20 mts)[36]

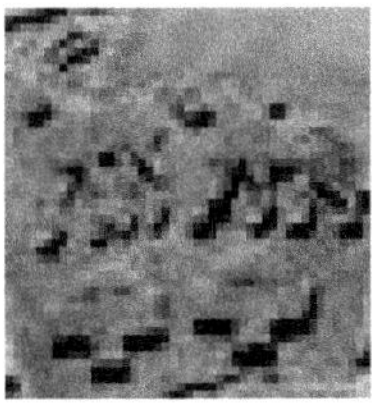

"The Warka Vase or the Uruk Vase is a carved alabaster stone vessel found in the temple complex of the Sumerian goddess Inanna in the ruins of the ancient city of Uruk, located in the modern Al Muthanna Governorate, in southern Iraq. Like the Narmer Palette from Egypt, it is one of the earliest surviving works of narrative relief sculpture, dated to c. 3,200–3000 BC. The vase was discovered as a collection of fragments by German Assyriologists in their sixth excavation season at Uruk in 1933/1934. It is named after the modern village of Warka - known as Uruk to the ancient Sumerians."

[quote] The site of Uruk, modern Warka, is located in southern Iraq about 35 kilometers east of the modern course of the Euphrates river. Settlement at the site began in the Ubaid period (5th millennium BC). In the Uruk period (4000-3000 BC) the site was the largest in Mesopotamia at 100 hectares. Uruk continued to grow in the Early Dynastic period (2900-2350 BC), reaching a size of about 400 hectares. After the end of the Early Dynastic period, the city declined in size and significance until the Ur III period (2100-2000 BC), when the ruling dynasty pursued new building projects in the Eanna precinct. It is to this period that the massive ziggurat still visible today dates. Uruk declined again after the Ur III period, and was resettled in the Neo-Assyrian (883-612 BC) and Neo-Babylonian periods (612-539 BC). [unquote] [37]

These flowers are identified as tulips, perhaps Mountain tulip or Boeotian tulip (both of which grow in Afghanistan) which have an undulate leaf. There is a possibility that the comb is an import from Bactria, perhaps transmitted through Meluhha to the Oman Peninsula site of Tell Abraq.

kand 'fire-altar' (Santali) The pair of composite glyphs together with ram and tiger glyphs may read as: tin ingot, *tagara kand mũh* and *kol kand khōṭ,* 'alloyed ingot'. An allograph for kand: kŏnḍ क्वंड् or kŏnḍa क्वंड । कुण्ड m a deep still spring (El., Gr.Gr. 145); (amongst Hindūs) a hole dug in the ground for receiving consecrated fire; cf. ạgana-kŏnḍ (p. 16*b*, l. 34) (Rām. 631). kọ̆nḍu or konḍu । कुण्डम् m. a hole dug in the ground for receiving consecrated fire kōda कोँद। कुलालादिकन्दुः f. a kiln; a potter's kiln (Rām. 1446; H. xi, 11); a brick-kiln (Śiv. 133); a lime-kiln. (Kashmiri)

A pair of *khōṭ* 'alloyed ingots' are shown atop the fire-altars. An allograph for mũh 'ingot' (Santali) : kōḍ कोड् m. a kernel (Kashmiri) खोट [khōṭa] A lump or solid bit (as of phlegm, gore, curds, inspissated milk); any concretion or clot. (Marathi) Rebus: L. *khoṭ*f. ' alloy, impurity ', *°ṭā* ' alloyed ', awāṇ. *khoṭā* ' forged '; P. *khoṭ* m. ' base, alloy ' M.*khoṭā* ' alloyed ', (CDIAL 3931)

kol 'tiger' (Kon.) Rebus: kol 'iron' (Ta.)

tagara 'ram' (Ta.) Rebus: *damgar* 'merchant' (Akk.) (Top register, ahead of the two storage jars with ingots).

pasaramu, pasalamu = quadrupeds (Telugu); pasra 'smithy, forge' (Santali) (Third register).

tagaraka *tabernae montana* (Skt.) Rebus: tagara 'tin' (Ka.) (Fourth register).

Thus, the vase describes two types of metal ingots being carried into the treasury: ingots of tin, ingots of iron.

That a metal ingot is being carried is reinforced by the head of an ox shown together with a pellet between its horns.

This depiction may be seen between the two storage jars filled with the ingots.[38]

On the top register, a scarf atop a post is shown behind two adorants standing on two 'frames of buildings' and atop a ram. The male adorant carries in his hands a glyphic comparable to the glyptic shown on the Susa ritual basin flanked by two antelope-goat composite hieroglyphs. If this glyphic denotes tamar, 'palm tree, date palm' the rebus reading would be: tam(b)ra, 'copper' (Pkt.)

The frames of buildings used in the glyphic composition are hieroglyphs:
sāgāḍā m. ' frame of a building ' (M.)(CDIAL 12859) Rebus: *jangaḍiyo* 'military guards who accompanies treasure into the treasury" (G.)
tagara 'ram' (Ta.) Rebus: *damgar* 'merchant' (Akk.) (Top register, ahead of the two storage jars with ingots).

dhatu 'scarf'; rebus: dhatu 'mineral' (Santali) dhātu 'mineral (Pali) dhātu 'mineral' (Vedic); a mineral, metal (Santali); dhāta id. (G.) H. dhāṛnā 'to send out, pour out, cast (metal)' (CDIAL 6771).

Rings on standards: pēṇḍhē पेंढें 'rings' Rebus: pēṇḍhī पेढी 'shop'. The rings atop the reed standard: पेंढें [pēṇḍhēṃ] पेंडकें [pēṇḍakēṃ] n Weaver's term. A cord-loop or metal ring (as attached to the गुलडा of the बैली and to certain other fixtures). पेंडें [pēṇḍēṃ] n (पेड) A necklace composed of strings of pearls. 2 A loop or ring. Rebus: पेढी (Gujaráthí word.) A shop (Marathi)

A pair of reeds as standard. *sangaḍa* 'pair', *kāḍ* काँड् । काण्ड: m. 'the stalk or stem of a reed, grass, or the like, straw', पेंढें 'rings' Rebus: पेढी 'shop'. *dhatu* 'scarf'. Alternative:

The rebus reading of the pair of reeds in Sumer standard is: *khāṇḍa* 'tools, pots and pans and metal-ware', dhatu 'mineral (ore)'. पेंढें 'rings' Rebus: पेढी 'shop'. Alternative: *khōṭ* 'alloyed ingots', *Ko.* goṇḍ knob on end of walking-stick, head of pin (DEDR 2081). Rebus: kǒṇḍu or konḍu । कुण्डम् m. a hole dug in the ground for receiving consecrated fire (Kashmiri) H. *gõṛā* m. 'reservoir used in irrigation '. (CDIAL 3264). अग्निकुण्डम्. A pool, well; especially one consecrated to some deity or holy purpose. (Sanskrit) *Kur.* xoṇḍxā, xōṛxā deep; a pit, abyss.
Malt. qoṇḍe deep, low lands. (DEDR 2082).

The glyphs in the composition of a pair of scarved posts are:

sangaḍa 'pair' (Marathi) Rebus: jaṅgaḍ 'entrustment articles'. The pair of pegs denote the pair of minerals dealt with: *tagara,*'tin' and *kol,* 'iron'. The pair of reed stalks read rebus: *sangaḍa kāṇḍa* 'entrustment articles' of 'tools, pots and pans, metal-ware'.
goṇḍ 'knob on end of walking-stick, head of pin' (Ko.); *khūṭ* peg, post'. Allograph: *kõdā* खोंड [khōṇḍa] m A young bull, a bullcalf. (Marathi) Rebus 1: kǒṇḍu or konḍu । कुण्डम् m. a hole dug in the ground for receiving consecrated fire (Kashmiri) Rebus 2: A. *kundār*, B. *kũdār, °ri*, Or. *kundāru*; H. *kũderā* m. ' one who works a lathe, one who scrapes ', *°rī* f., *kũdernā* ' to scrape, plane, round on a lathe '.(CDIAL 3297).

dhatu 'scarf'; rebus: 'cast mineral' (Santali); (cf. H. dhāṛnā 'to send out, pour out, cast metal)

The pegs or posts may be joints of stalk or reeds: *kaṇḍa* -- m.n. ' joint of stalk, stalk (Pali); *kāḍ* m. ' stalk of a reed, straw ' (Kashmiri); *kāḍ* n. ' trunk, stem ' (Marathi); Or.*kāṇḍa, kāṛ* ' stalk (Oriya); *kāṛā* 'stem of muñja grass (used for

thatching) (Bihari); *kānā* m. ' stalk of the reed Sara ' (Lahnda)(CDIAL 3023). Rebus: *kāṇḍa* 'tools, pots and pans, metal-ware'.

Thus the combined glyphs of *goṇḍ* knob, *kāḍ* reed, *dhatu* scarf read rebus: *kūdār* 'turner'; *konḍu* 'consecrated fire'; furnace' (Santali); *kāṇḍa* 'tools, pots and pans, metal-ware'; *dhatu* 'mineral ore'.

medhi (f.) [Vedic methī pillar, post (to bind cattle to); BSk. medhi Divy 244; Prk. meḍhi Pischel *Gr.* § 221. See for etym. Walde, *Lat. Wtb.* s. v. meta] pillar, part of a stūpa [not in the Canon?].(Pali) What are often referred to as 'temple poles' of Inanna may thus connote: the following glyphic readings: *sangaḍa* 'pair' [A word associated with the pair of storage jars, pair of 'reed' glyphs, pair of vases – glyphs shown on Warka vase.]

meḍhi 'pillar'.

dhatu 'scarf'

The rebus readings for these glyphs are:

jangaḍa 'entrustment articles' (of) *dhatu* 'iron ore'.

dhatu 'minerals' (cast in) *kaṇḍa*, furnace (fire-altar, consecrated pit). khondu id. (Kashmiri) kŏnḍ क्रंड् 'a hole dug in the ground for receiving consecrated fire' (Kashmiri) kunḍa 'consecrated fire-pit'. Allograph: koṇḍi knot of hair on the crown of the head (Telugu) Allograph: konḍu spine (Kashmiri) *kaṇḍa* 'nodule of stone ore'.

The pair of 'reed' glyphs can thus be read rebus: *sangaḍa* 'entrustment articles': *dhatu.kūdār kāṇḍa* 'iron ore turner tools, pots and pans, metal-ware'. The word *kole.l* has two meanings: smithy,

temple. Thus, the pair of 'reeds' signify sacredness associated with a temple.

kunḍa 'pot; rebus: 'consecrated fire-pit'. The 'U' glyphic is a semantic determinant to emphasize that this is a temple with a smithy furnace and a consecrated fire-pit. The structural form (*sangaḍa* 'frame of a building') within which this sign is enclosed may represent a temple: kole.l 'temple, smithy' (Ko.); kolme smithy' (Ka.) The ligatured sign may thus be read: *sangaḍa kunḍ* to mean 'entrustment articles (of) consecrated fire-altar or furnace'.

The naked person is offering a large storage jar with ingots of smithy to a person who carries on the left hand face of a bull. ḍangar 'bull' ḍāṅgar 'cattle'; rebus: *ṭhākur* ' blacksmith ' (Maithili) [The bull head carried by the person is a phonetic determinant of the identification of the person's title or profession.]

Homonym: damgar 'merchant' (Akkadian).

The person stands in front of two poles surmounted by two scarves.
Thus, the scarfed composition denotes the *damgar* 'merchant' and female (*kola*, smithy) attendant, offering *dhatu,* 'mineral', and *tam(b)ra* 'copper' from *kand,* 'furnaces (consecrated fire-altars)'. The top register of the vase records this offering on a tall storage jar containing ingots and a cob. The cob is kolmo 'seeding, rice-plant'(Munda) rebus: kolami 'smithy'; (Telugu) mũh ' ingot' (Santali).

Rebus reading from Maithili: *ṭhākur* 'blacksmith' .

sangaḍa 'pair' (Marathi) Rebus: jaṅgaḍ 'entrustment notes' indicates entrustment into the treasury by *jangaḍiyo* 'military guards who accompanies treasure into the treasury" (Gujarati)

Dancing girl hieroglyph

Bhirrana find; the potsherd with the engraving. ASI discovered by a team led by the late L.S. Rao, Superintending Archaeologist, Excavation Branch, ASI, Nagpur, belonged to the Mature Harappan period. Mr. Rao called it the "only one of its kind" because "no parallel to the Dancing Girl, in bronze or any other medium, was known" until the latest find. The "Dancing Girl" statuette made of bronze using cire perdue technique which continues to be used even today in the temple town of Eraka (copper!) Subrahmanya at Swamimalai on the banks of River Kaveri. Mr. Rao says, "... the delineation [of the lines in the potsherd] is so true to the stance, including the disposition of the hands, of the bronze that it appears that the craftsman of Bhirrana had first-hand knowledge of the former."[39] Why depict a dancing girl as a hieroglyph? Because, depiction of a dance pose is a hieroglyph to represent what was contained in the pot. The glyph encodes the mleccha word for 'iron': med. Glyph is *meḍ* 'to dance' (Munda).

Meluhha writing, *mlecchita vikalpa*, metallurgists' writing -- *takṣat vāk,* inscribed speech, is evidenced by the epigraph on a 'snarling iron'[40] of Chanhu-daro. One of the glyphs inscribed on the two snarling irons denotes the turner's anvil:

karaḍi, karaḍe an oblong drum beaten on both sides, a sort of double drum (Kannada)(DEDR 1264). Rebus: *kharādī* ' turner, a person who fashions or shapes objects on a lathe' (Gujarati) करडा [karaḍā] Hard from alloy--iron, silver &c. (Marathi) कारंडा [kāraṇḍā], करंडा karaṇḍā *m* A chump or block (Marathi). करडा [karaḍā] *m* The arrangement of bars or embossed lines (plain or fretted with little knobs) raised upon a तार of gold by pressing and driving it upon the अवटी or grooved stamp. Such तार is used for the ornament बुगडी, for the hilt of a पट्टा or other sword &c. Applied also to any similar barform or line-form arrangement (pectination) whether embossed or indented; as the edging of a rupee &c.

Allograph:

176

kharedo = a currycomb (G.) खरारा [kharārā] *m* (H) A currycomb. 2 Currying a horse. (Marathi)

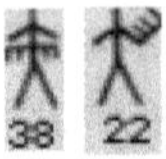
38 22

Composite 'glyphs' Mahadevan Signs 22 and 38 can be looked upon as variant ligatures, combining Signs 1 and 176 as ligaturing glyph elements, as shown on Signs 38 and 22.

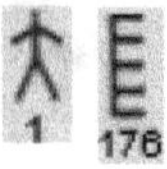
1 176

Parpola (1994) identifies 386 (+12?) signs (or graphemes) and their variant forms. Mahadevan (1977) identifies 419 graphemes; out of these 179 graphemes have variants totalling 641 forms. [See Sign List and Variants].

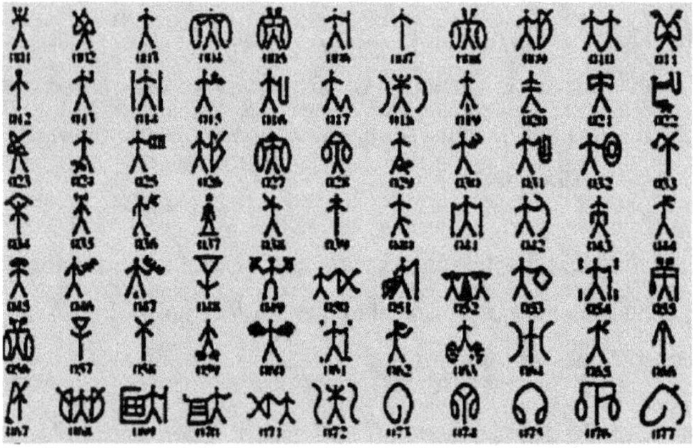

It is possible that many compilers of corpora of Indus writing use a variety of criteria to compile 'sign lists'. It may be seen from the following excert from a table of signs in one corpus[41] that a large number of ligatures appear to modify the basic sign :

What does the basic sign connote in Meluhha speech? This connotes the stature of a man: *kāḍ* काड् । पौरुषम् m. a man's length, the stature of a man (as a measure of length) (Rām. 632, zangan kaḍun kāḍ, to stretch oneself the whole length of one's body. See the suffix *-kāḍu* to denote a person: *kōḍekāḍu* a young man (Telugu) కాడు [kāḍu] or గాడు *kāḍu.* [Tel. for వాడు.] (an affix.) He, that man. సొగసుకాడు a pretty fellow. వేషగాడు a masker. Added to names, it denotes meanness or low station in life, thus: అబ్బిగాడు, సుబ్బిగాడు, as in English, a fellow name

d so and so. It is also part of the names of some animals as ఇబ్బందికాడు a leopard. బావురుగాడు a he cat. Rebus: कार [kāra] *f m* The Trap rock or

stone.(Marathi) खडा [khaḍā] *m* A small stone, a pebble (Marathi) *kāṇḍa* 'tools, pots and pans, metal-ware' Ku. *lokhaṛ* 'iron tools '; H. *lokhaṇḍ* m. ' iron tools, pots and pans '; G. *lokhãḍ* n. 'tools, iron, ironware'; M. *lokhãḍ* n. ' iron '(CDIAL 11171).

What does the sign connote in Meluhha speech? Since the ligaturing glyph connotes a currycomb, the combined ligatured glyph – Signs 22 and 38 can be read rebus as: *khareḍo + -kār lit.* 'currycomb + stretch of man's body' 'worker on a lathe, *kharaḍ* ', which compound, in spoken Meluhha morphology, gets compressed phonetically as: *kharādī* ' turner, a person who fashions or shapes objects on a lathe' (Gujarati) करडा [karaḍā] Hard from alloy--iron, silver &c. (Marathi)

कांडें [kāṇḍēṃ] 5 fig. A measure of length,-- a pole, stick, straw, thread, any thing (of definite or indefinite length) taken to measure with: also the measure so taken. *v* घे. Hence A section or defined portion (of a long wall, of an elevated platform sometimes appended to a draw-well, of a raised पाट or plantation-watercourse, of any long line of masonry). ह्याचें त्याचें कांडें पेरें मिळालें Said of two persons of mutual resemblance. कांडें पेरें घेणें to take the measurement of.

Some ligatures of Indus writing are orthographic abstractions. That one ligature set is unique is clear from the fact tht it occurs only on two glyphs [Glyphs 52 and 327 of inscription texts: One is a *loha-kāra* (metalsmith); *kāruvu* [Skt.] n. An artist, artificer. An agent (Telugu). The other is a *cunda-kāra* (ivory turner) or *kundār* 'turner']. The ligaturing glyptic elements may be read as: *kāra* or-*khar* 'smith' (Kashmiri). The lexeme *kāruvu* may explain one of Kubera's *navanidhi* (nine treasures): *kharva* which may mean 'artifice'.

Rebus: kārú -- , *°uka* -- m. ' artisan ' (Mn. Gujarati)*kāru* -- , *°uka* -- m. (Pali), *kāru* -- m. (Prakrit); A. B. *kāru* ' artist ' (Assamese. Bengali); *kāru* ' artisan, servant ' (Oriya), *kāruā* ' expert, deft ' (Oriya); *karuvā* 'artist' (Sinhala)(CDIAL 3066). *khar* 'blacksmith, artisan' (Kashmiri) - *kār* 'suffix in Marathi and Indo-Aryan languages' to denote an artisan.

Allographs:

1. *kāru* 'crocodile' (Telugu). Rebus: artisan (Marathi) *kāṛā* 'buffalo' bull (Tamil)

1

2. *kāḍ,* to stretch oneself the whole length of one's body (Marathi). See the suffix -*kāḍu* to denote a person (Telugu) –*kār, -ār* suffixes denote a person/artisan in many Indo-Aryan languages. *kāṭhā* ' measure of length '(Bengali) *kāṭhī* ' stick, measure of 5 cubits ' (Gujarati. Marathi) ' thin bamboo measuring rod ' (Assamese. Bengali)(CDIAL 3120)
3. *kāṭo* ' young buffalo bull ' (Kumaoni) *kaṭṭā*m., *°ṭī* f. ' yearling buffalo ' (Punjabi)
4. *khaṛam* wooden sandal' (Bengali)(CDIAL 3127)

1

The unligatured 'man' glyph (Sign 1) may denote an artisan, smith. A number of other glyphs which ligature with this basic glyph, may be qualifiers to designate the particular skill of the artisan. By itself, the glyph denotes *khar* 'blacksmith'.

One such ligature to designate a particular skill of the artisan (smith) may be cited:

 *khoṇḍ* 'square' is ligatured to the 'man' glyph:

 Rebus: *cundakāra* a turner J vi.339 (Pali) Cognate *kundār* 'turner'.

This is a work in cryptography and is a contribution to delineate glosses of a language called Meluhha (cognte mleccha, evidenced in ancient texts of *Manu Samhitā* and *Śathapathabrāhmaṇa*) which was the *lingua franca* of the civilization, from ca. 4th millennium BCE. The language, mleccha, is mentioned in the Great Epic Mahābhārata where an episode describes conversations Yudhishtira had with Khanaka and Vidura. Mleccha-speakers are described as *dasyu* (Iranian daha, people) in *Manu Samhitā* . Vātsyāyana's *Kāmasūtra* lists 64 arts including an art called *Mlecchita vikalpa* (lit. mleccha alternative representation) which is interpreted as a reference to cryptography.

सांगड sāṅgaḍa A body formed of two or more (fruits, animals, men) linked or joined together; सांगडणी [sāṅgaḍaṇī] *f* (Verbal of सांगडणें) Linking or joining together. सांगडणें [sāṅgaḍaṇēṃ] *v c* (सांगड) To link, join, or unite together (boats, fruits, animals). 2 Freely. To tie or bind up or unto. (Marathi) Rebus: *sā̃gaṛh* m. ' line of entrenchments, stone walls for defence ' (Lahnda).(CDIAL 12845) Allograph: saṅgaḍa 'lathe'.

Harappa. Molded tablet. (Kenoyer)[42] Plano convex molded tablet showing a female battling two tigers and standing above an elephant. A single Indus script depicting a spoked wheel is above the head of the deity. Material: terra cotta Dimensions:

3.91 length, 1.5 to 1.62 cm width Harappa, Lot 4651-01 Harappa Museum, H95-2486 Meadow and Kenoyer 1997

m308 Seal arā 'spokes'. आर [āra] A term in the play of इटीदांडू,--the number six. (Marathi) Rebus: āra 'brass'. kāṇá ' one -- eyed ' (RV.Pali.Prakrit) *kāṛa, °ṛī* f. ' blind ' (Ash.)(CDIAL 3020). kaṉ copper work, copper, workmanship (Tamil) Thus, the 'eye' glyph, 'six spokes' glyph connote: kaṉṉār 'brass-worker'.

kola 'woman' Rebus: kol 'working in iron' kola

'tiger' Rebus: kol 'working in iron'. கன்னான் kaṉṉāṉ , *n.* < கன்[1]. [M. *kannān.*] Brazier, bell-metal worker.

S. *vāraṇu* 'to shut, forbid' (CDIAL 11553) Rebus: bharat (5 copper, 4 zinc and 1 tin)(P.) bharan or toul alloy of brass or zinc and bronze. (B.)

On the reverse, an individual is spearing a water buffalo with one foot pressing the head down and one arm holding the tip of a horn. A gharial [lizard?] is depicted above the sacrifice scene and a figure seated in yogic position, wearing a horned headdress, looks on. The horned headdress has a branch with three prongs or leaves emerging from the center.

మేడెము [mēḍemu] or మేడియము *mēḍemu.* [Tel.] n. A spear or dagger. Rebus: *meḍ* 'iron'.

- kolhe (iron-smelter; kolhuyo, jackal) Rebus: kol, kollan-, kollar = blacksmith (Tamil)
- kol 'to kill' (Tamil)
- ibha 'elephant' Rebus: ibbo 'merchant'; ib 'iron'.

Pictorial motifs (ornamental figure, leafless tree): *kola* 'boat' of *kõdār* 'turner'.

- *kaṭái* ' buffalo calf '(Gaw.) *kāṭo* ' young buffalo bull ' (Kumaoni) (CDIAL 2645).Rebus: *kāḍ* 'stone ore', *bhāṭi* 'kiln', *kaṇḍa* 'fire-altar', bharat 'copper-zinc-tin-alloy'. khareḍo = a currycomb (Gujarati) Rebus: *kharādī* ' turner, a person who fashions or shapes objects on a lathe' (Gujarati)
- *kamaḍha* 'penance'; rebus: *kampaṭṭam* 'mint' (Ta.) *kūtī* = bunch of twigs (Skt.) kuṭhi 'smelting furnace' (Santali)
- *karā* 'crocodile' (Santali) Rebus: *karāvu* 'artisan, smith'.

kolsa = to kick the foot forward, the foot to come into contact with anything when walking or running; kolsa pasirkedan = I kicked it over (Santali)

mēṛsa = v.a. toss, kick with the foot, hit with the tail (Santali)

mẽṛhẽt iron; ispat m. = steel; dul m. = cast iron; kolhe m. iron manufactured by the Kolhes (Santali); meṛed (Mun.d.ari);

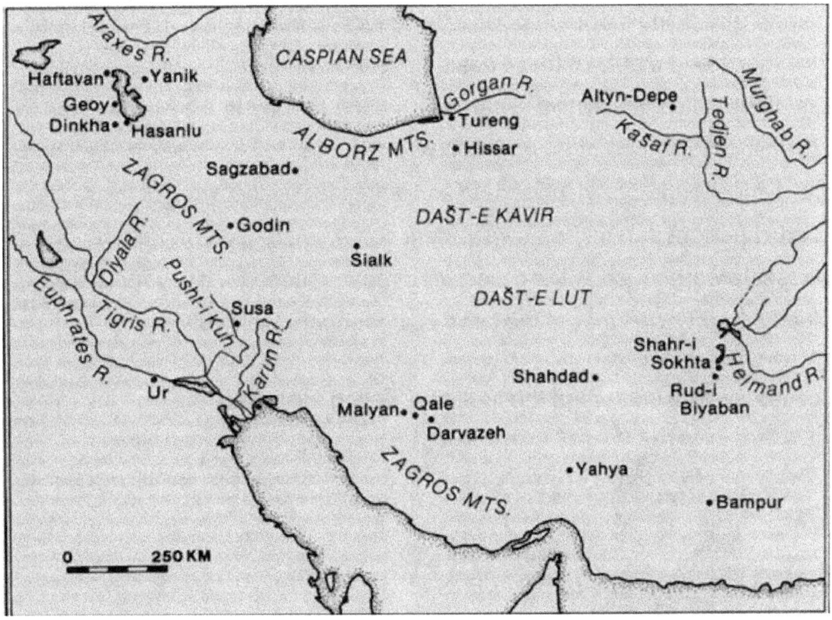

meḍ (Ho.)(Santali.Bodding)

Location of Altyn-Depe, a Meluhha language contact area

Altyn-Depe; metal (silver) seal from southern Turkmenistan with the pictograph

of a ligatured animal with three heads. Indian influence is seen in the three-headed ligature which occurs on the silver seal from Altin-Depe. "The Harappan influence observed in southern Turkmenia, however, also indicates trade routes going northwest. It was apparently largely this northenr trade of Harappa which led to the rise of Mundigak in southern Afghanistan, which was located advantageously to control the supply of copper and lapis lazui going to the towns of the Indus Valley. The close resemblance bewteen the unpainted pottery of southern Turkmenia, Seistan and southern Afghanistan is no coincidence. In Mundigak, this similarity with the Turkmenian sites extends to metal seals as well as to seals made of stone and baked clay, with their incised designs...The seals are an important pointer where social organization is concerned...Practically all the basic forms and motifs of these seals have their origin in the various magic symbols of the Late Chalcolithic. Seal impressions on clay in the Middle Bronze Age material indicate one of their functions: thus, one clay figurine of a bull had a brand, a symbol of property, incised on its flank. It is well known that livestock played an important part in the development of the institutuion of property; since only two seals were found in the collective tomb mentioned.., it is very likely that the valued property was that of the large clan, not personal property."[43]

Composites, pictorial nature of the Meluhha writing system

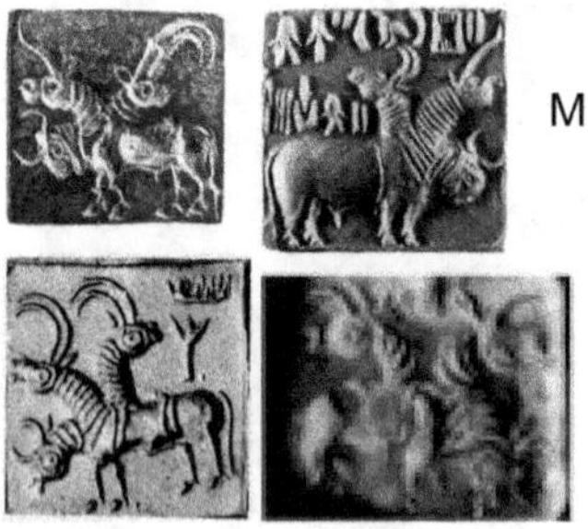

M1169a, m1170, m1171 seals. Bet Dwarka conch-shell seal.

sangaḍi = joined animals (M.) Rebus: *sãgaṛh* m. ' line of entrenchments, stone walls for defence '

(Lahnda)(CDIAL 12845) sang संग् m. a stone (Kashmiri) sanghāḍo (G.) = cutting stone, gilding; sangatarāśū = stone cutter; sangatarāśi = stone-cutting; sangsāru karan.u = to stone (S.), cankatam = to scrape (Ta.), sankaḍa (Tu.), sankaṭam = to scrape (Skt.) The three worker categories represented by the hieroglyphs are: engraver (lapidary), smith, helper of merchant: *kondh* 'young bull', kōnda bullock (Kol.)(DEDR 2216). Rebus: *kũdār* 'turner, brass-worker'.*kõdār* 'turner' (Bengali) कोंद kōnda 'engraver, lapidary setting or infixing gems' (Marathi) *ḍhangra* 'bull'. Rebus: *ḍhangar* 'blacksmith'. *mṛeka* 'goat'. Rebus: *milakkhu* 'copper' Rebus: *meṛh* 'helper of merchant'.

The standard device, sangada, is shown as relatable, rebus, to stone-workers called sangataras. संगतराश lit. 'to collect stones, stone-cutter, mason.[44]' The contribution of Randall W. Law co-authored with Prabhakar VN and Tejas Garge has been linked in the decoding of 1) a Mitathal seal[45] with Indus script and underlying language and 2) glyphs of standard device, heifer and scarf used on the Indus inscriptions.

The cumulative conclusion drawn from these contributions is that the primacy of economic activities necessitated the invention and use of a writing system to convey messages using the language – lingua franca – of the civilization. This inference is consistent with the insight provided by James Muhly: invention of alloying tin with copper to create bronze alloy heralding the Bronze Age had to be linked with another invention: the writing system used in economic activities, in trade transactions, in particular.

The objects on which the Indus script is inscribed are part of the material artefacts discovered through archaeological excavations. It is, therefore, reasonable to evaluate the writing system on these inscribed objects in the context of other economic activities of the civilization – activities such as cultivation of rice, millet or maize (glyphs related to which had been used in the script), mining of mineral resources, lapidary crafts on precious- and semi-precious stones – turning the stones into beads used on necklaces and other ornaments, bones, ivory, stone-work related to ring-stones – used as architectural supports in buildings, grinding stones – used in households for grinding cereals or pulses into edible flour, metallurgical activities of alloying minerals into metals, casting and forging them into household utensils or artisan tools or weapons.

The challenge of decoding the writing system is, in effect, the challenge of identifying the words used by the people of the civilization engaged in such economic activities – without invoking an a priori assumption of a religious or political basis for the use of glyphs of the writing system.

It has been shown that a Mohenjodaro tablet inscribed with three glyphs: standard device, heifer and scarf – decoded rebus related to the workshop of stone-workers and mineral-workers or miners.

As Randall Law has demonstrated, the stone work covered a variety of resources: grinding stone, chert, steatite, agate, vesuvianite-grossular, alabaster, and limestone. In addition to these resources, bone, ivory, copper, tin, arsenic, meteoric iron were also used to produce artefacts as archaeologically attested.

In what language and with what words did the creators of the urbanized civilization refer to these resources?

Decryption of Indus script cipher of hieroglyphs is premised on the Indian linguistic area and consistent with the principle of occam's razor, uses a simple rebus method to read all the glyphs – pictorial motifs with glyptic elements and signs with glyptic elements – as based on words of the Indus (Meluhha) language from a repertoire of artisans' work attested archaeologically. The semantic framework of the Indus language is independently delineated by a comparative *Indian Lexicon*[46] which provides the glosses for matching words with glyptic elements of Indus writing and identifying homonyms which render the message content of inscriptions. The set of glosses from the Indian linguistic area lead to a decipherment of the messages as representations of the repertoire of artisans, veritable catalogs compiled by – stone0-workers, lapidaries, miners and smiths. The underlying language – for glosses which render the glyptic elements and concordant homonyms -- is not exclusive Munda or exclusive Sanskrit or exclusive Dravidian but the lingua franca which included glosses from all three language families – with glosses borrowed from one another. Confirmation for the decipherment comes from the cultural continuum including punch-marked coins and sculptural glyphs of the historical periods which continued to use the glyphs of Indus writing. Evidence is also provided to equate the Indus language with a language category called mleccha (cognate: meluhha) attested in Mesopotamian texts, in an archaeological context and attested in ancient Indian texts which point to mleccha as a language with shared super-set of glosses, as *lingua franca* clearly distinguishable from literary language – just as Prākṛtam is distinguishable from Samskṛtam. Thus, mleccha is construed as the set of glosses shared in the Indian *sprachbund* in contact situations and the context of history of changes in phonetic forms and/or semantic expansions of glosses.

MS 2814
Royal inscription commemorating defeat of Oman and Indus Valley.
Sumer, 2100-1800 BC

A clue is provided by the inscriptions already decoded in a known language in a known writing system: Mesopotamian cuneiform inscriptions.

MS 2814, a cuneiform inscription. MS in Neo Sumerian and Old Babylonian on clay, Sumer, 2100-1800 BCE, 1 tablet, 14,8x14,0x3,3 cm (originally ca. 16x14x3 cm), 3+3 columns, 103 lines.

The royal inscription on the Sumerian clay tablet of 2100 to 1800 BCE, commemorates defeat of Magan, Melukkham, Elam (?) and Amurru – linking Oman and Indus Valley.

Commentary: The text was copied from a Sargonic royal inscription on a statue in the Ur III or early Old Babylonian period. Magan was at Oman and at the Iranian side of the Gulf. Meluhha or Melukham was the Indus Valley civilisation (ca. 2500-1800 BCE). This is one of fairly few references to the Indus civilisation on tablets. The 3 best known references are: 1. Sargon of Akkad (2334-2279 BCE) referring to ships from Meluhha, Magan and Dilmun; 2. Naram-Sin (2254-2218 BC) referring to rebels to his rule, listing the rebellious kings, including '(..)ibra, man of Melukha'; and 3. Gudea of Lagash (2144-2124 BCE) referring to Meluhhans that came from their country and sold gold dust, carnelian, etc. There are further references in literary texts. After ca. 1760 BCE Melukha is not mentioned any more. For Indus MSS in The Schøyen Collection, see MS 2645 (actually linking the Old Akkadian and Indus civilisations), MSS 4602, 4617, 4619, 5059, 5061, 5062 and 5065. Exhibited: Tigris 25th anniversary exhibition. The Kon-Tiki Museum, Oslo, 30.1. - 15.9.2003.[47]

Kanmer: tokens in bulla as seals

Three Kanmer tokens strung together as bulla to categorise turners' work

An evidence comes from Kanmer, for the use of tablets created with duplicate

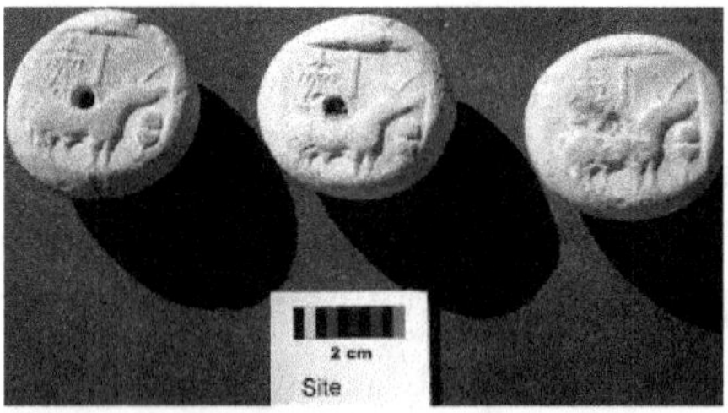

seal impressions on three clay sealings.[48] These tablets may have been used the same way tokens and bullae were used -- as category tallies of lapidary workshops – a remarkable parallel with the system of bullae and tokens in use in Sumer/Elam/Mesopotamia.

Three clay sealings from Kanmer with 'one-horned young bull' (unicorn) motif. Top view of the three Kanmer sealings with different motifs suggesting different uses/users.

The ligatured glyph used as an inscription on the three Kanmer tokens is mirrored on a Mohenjo-daro Seal m162:

m1162. Mohenjo-daro seal with the same hieroglyph which appears on Kanmer circular tablets.  Glyph 33. Text 2068

The ligatured glyph 33 denotes Rebus: करडा [karaḍā] Hard from alloy--iron, silver &c. (Marathi) *kharādī*' turner' (Gujarati) *karaḍo –kār* : an artisan-turner who works on a lathe – on hard alloys: కరటి [karaṭi] *karaṭi*. [Skt.] n. An elephant. ఏనుగు (Telugu)

kāḍ, to stretch oneself the whole length of one's body (Marathi). See the suffix -*kāḍu* to denote a person (Telugu) *–kār, -ār* suffixes denote a person/artisan in many Indo-Aryan languages. Rebus: khar 'blacksmith'; *kāru 'artisan, smith'.*

khareḍo = a currycomb (G.) खरारा [*kharārā*] *m* (H) A currycomb. 2 Currying a horse. (Marathi) Rebus: करडा [*karaḍā*] Hard from alloy--iron, silver &c. (Marathi) *kharādī*' turner' (Gujarati)

Rebus 1: *karaḍo, karāḍī* 'a goldsmith's tool' (Gujarati) Rebus 2: *karaḍu, kharaḍe, karḍu* 'rough, as an account' (Kannada); *kharaḍem* a rude sketch, foul copy' (Marathi)

koḍ 'one' (Santali); rebus: *koḍ* 'workshop' (G.) Thus, the inscription on Kanmer tokens reads: करडा [karaḍā] Hard from alloy--iron, silver &c. (Marathi) *karaḍā koḍ* 'hard alloy workshop'; *kharādī koḍ* 'turner's workshop'.

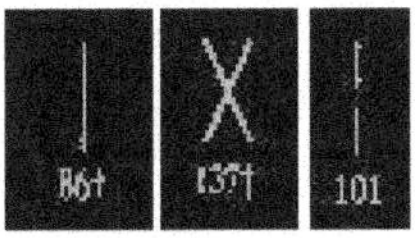

Kanmer: Stone-turner artisan's workshop

Pictorial motif is identical on the three Kanmer tokens. Glyph: koḍiyum 'young bull' (G.) Rebus: koḍ 'workshop

(Kuwi) Glyph: sangaḍa 'lathe' (Marathi) Rebus 1: : jangaḍ 'entrusted articles on approval basis'.Rebus 2: sangaḍa 'association' (guild). Rebus 2: sangatarāsu 'stone cutter' (Telugu). Rebus 3: sangar 'fortification wall' (Pushto).

It is a category mistake to call these as 'seals'. These are three duplicate tablets created with seal impressions (glyphs: one-horned young bull, standard device, PLUS two text inscription glyphs (or 'signs' as written characters): one long linear stroke, ligatured glyph of body + 'currycomb' glyph. There are perforations in the center of these duplicate seal impressions which are tablets and which contained identical inscriptions. It appears that three duplicates of seal impressions -- as tablets -- were created using the same seal.

Obverse of these tiny 2 cm. dia. tablets show some incised markings. It is unclear from the markings if they can be compared with any glyphs of the Indus script corpora. They may be 'personal' markings like 'potter's marks' – designating a particular artisan's workshop (working platform) or considering the short numerical strokes used, the glyphs may be counters (numbers or liquid or weight measures). More precise determination may be made if more evidences of such glyphs are discovered. Excavators surmise[49] that the three tablets with different motifs on the obverse of the three tablets suggest different users/uses. They may be from different workshops of the same guild but as the other side of the tablets showed, the product taken from three workshops is the same.

Kanmer. A large number of bead-making goods — 150 stone beads and roughouts, 160 drill bits, 433 faience beads and 20,000 steaite beads — were found here, indicating the site's importance as an industrial unit. Agate quarries were also located at a distance of 20 kilometres (12 mi) from the site.[50]

The compound glyph on the 3 circular tablets of Kanmer refers to stone and bronze workshop. This reading is consistent with the archaeological finds at Kanmer.

It would appear that the three tablets (seal impressions) originated in three distinct phases of the lapidary/smithy processes, based on the following rebus readings of three distinct sets of incised glyphs on the obverse of the tablets. The three phases are: mineral workshop, furnce workshop (smithy), metal workshop (forge).

The markings on the obverse of these three clay sealings may also be read rebus:

dāṭu = cross (Te.); dhatu = mineral (Santali)

sal stake, spike, splinter, thorn, difficulty (H.) Rebus: sal 'workshop' (H.)

kod. 'one' (Santali); rebus: kod. 'workshop' (G.)

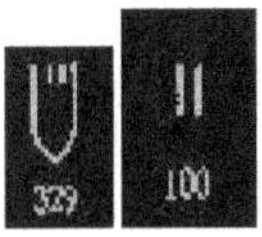

Kanmer: Furnace workshop

aṭar 'splinter' (Ma.); aḍaruni 'to crack' (Tu.) Rebus: aduru 'native metal (Kannada) sal stake, spike, splinter, thorn, difficulty (H.) Rebus: sal 'workshop' (H.)

baṭa = a kind of iron (G .) baṭa = rimless pot (Kannada)

S. baṭhu m. 'large pot in which grain is parched, large cooking fire', baṭhī f. 'distilling furnace'; L. bhaṭṭh m. 'grain—parcher's oven', bhaṭṭhī f. 'kiln, distillery', awāṇ. bhaṭh; P. bhaṭṭh m., °ṭhī f. 'furnace', bhaṭṭhā m. 'kiln'; S. bhaṭṭhī keṇī 'distil (spirits)'. (CDIAL 9656)

Kanmer: Metal workshop

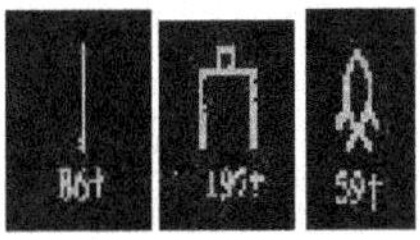

ayo, hako 'fish'; ās = scales of fish (Santali); rebus: aya = iron (G.); ayah, ayas = metal (Skt.)

Decoding of the identical inscription on the three tablets of Kanmer.

Glyph: One long linear stroke. koḍa 'one' (Santali) Rebus: koḍ 'artisan's workshop' (Kuwi)

Glyph: meḍ 'body' (Mu.) Rebus: meḍ 'iron' (Ho.) Ligatured glyph : aḍar 'harrow'

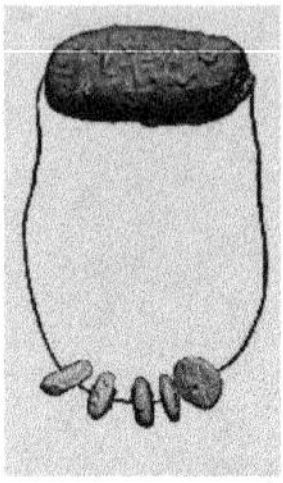

Rebus: aduru 'native metal' (Kannada). Thus the glyphs can be read rebus. Glyph: koḍiyum 'young bull' (G.) Rebus: koḍ 'workshop (Kuwi) Glyph: sangaḍa 'lathe' (Marathi) Rebus 1: Rebus 2: sangaḍa 'association' (guild). Rebus 2: sangatarāsu 'stone cutter' (Telugu). The output of the lapidaries is thus described by the three tablets: *aduru meḍ sangaḍa koḍ* 'iron, native metal guild workshop'.

'...it now appears that practically all of the raw material of the raw stone and metal that Harappans used came from highlands surrounding the Indus valley.'[51]

Documentation concerning a transaction

Bulla for holding a string of complex counting tokens concerning a transaction.

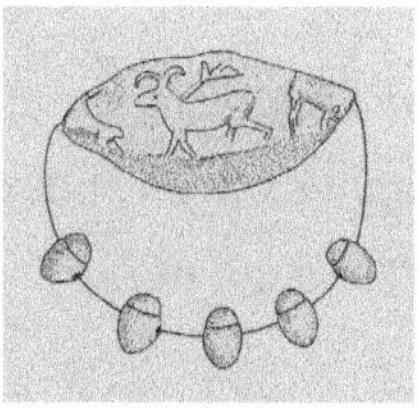

"Bulla in clay, Syria/Sumer/ Highland Iran, ca. 3500-3200 BC, 1 oblong bulla, diam. 2,5x6,5 cm, rollsealed with a line of animals walking left or 2 men standing with arms raised, pierced for holding a string of counting tokens.

Context: For another bulla of the same type, see MS 5113. Commentary: The bulla originally locked the ends of a string with a number of complex counting tokens attached to it, representing 1 transaction. The string with the tokens was hanging outside the bulla like a necklace. If the string had, say, 5 disk type tokens representing types of textiles, this number could not be tampered with without breaking the seal. The tokens could also be entirely enclosed in the centre of the bulla, see MSS 4631, 4632 and 4638. Tokens were used for accounting purposes in the Near East from the Neolithic period ca. 8000 BC until ca. 3200 BC, when they were superseded by counting tablets and pictographic tablets. Some of the earliest tablets have actual tokens impressed into the clay to form numbers and pictographs, and some of the pictographs were illustrations of tokens, see MS 4551."[52]

Proposed reconstruction of a string of complex tokens held by a solid oblong bulla. Drawing by Ellen Simmons.[53] The way the tokens were strung together to constitute the bulla is indicative of the type of use made of Kanmer tokens (or, tablets with Indus writing).

"MS 4631 Schoyen Collection. Bulla in clay, Syria/Sumer/ Highland Iran, ca. 3700-3200 BC, 1 spherical bulla-envelope (complete), diam. ca. 6,5 cm, cylinder seal impressions of a row of men walking left; and of a predator attacking a deer, inside a complete set of plain and complex tokens: 4 tetrahedrons 0,9x1,0 cm (D.S.-B.5:1), 4 triangles with 2 incised lines 2,0x0,9 (D.S.-B.(:14), 1 sphere diam. 1,7 cm (D.S.-B.2:2), 1 cylinder with 1 grove 2,0x0,3 cm (D.S.-B.4:13), 1 bent paraboloid 1,3xdiam. 0,5 cm (D.S.-B.8:14). *Context:* Total number of bulla-envelopes worldwide is ca. 165 intact and 70 fragmentary. *Commentary :* While counting for stocktaking purposes started ca. 8000 BC using plain tokens of the type also represented here, more complex accounting and recording of agreements started about 3700 BC using 2 systems: a) a string of complex tokens with the ends locked into a massive rollsealed clay bulla (see MS 4523), and b) the present system with the tokens enclosed inside a hollow bulla-shaped rollsealed envelope, sometimes with marks on the outside representing the hidden contents.

"The bulla-envelope had to be broken to check the contents hence the very few surviving intact bulla- envelopes. This complicated system was superseded around 3500-3200 BC by counting tablets giving birth to the actual recording in writing, of various number systems (see MSS 3007 and 4647), and around 3300-3200 BC the beginning of pictographic writing (see MSS 2963 and 4551).

"Exhibited: The Norwegian Intitute of Palaeography and Historical Philology (PHI), Oslo, 13.10.2003-06.2005."[54]

Distribution of Tokens in the Middle East.[55] "...the number of token shapes which was limited to about 12 around 7500 BC, increased to some 350 around 3500 BC, when urban workshops started contributing to the redistribution economy. Some of the new tokensstood for raw materials such as wool and metal while others represented finished products, among them textiles, garments, jewelry, bread, beer and honey."[56]

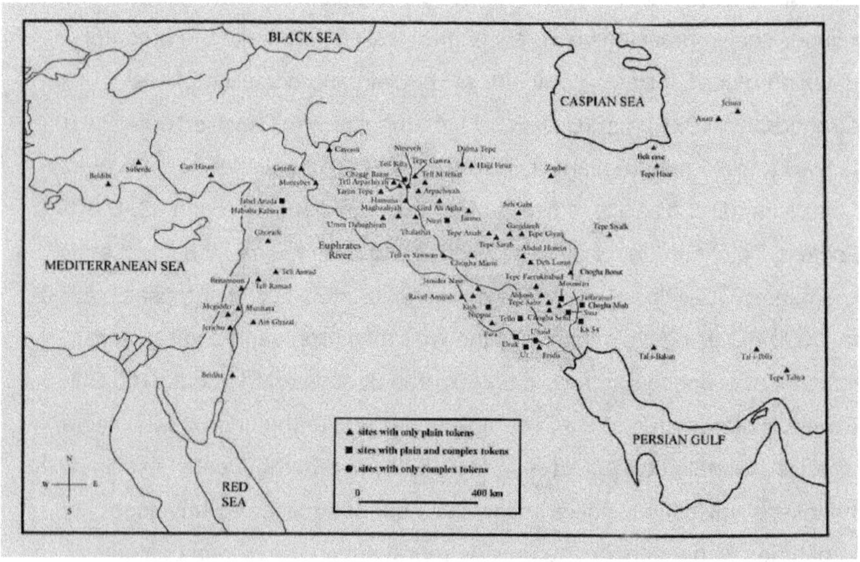

Harappa potshed dated to about 3500 BCE makes the Indus Script earliest writing system of the world.

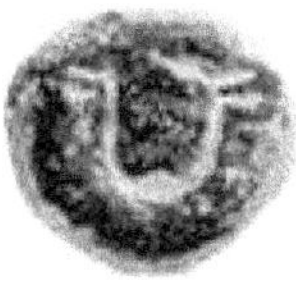

Rim-of-jar glyph. Seal. Daimabad. Ca. 1400 BCE. *kanka* 'rim-of-jar' Rebus: *kanka* 'engraver, scribe'.

There is now a consensus among linguists that India of ancient tmes, say 3rd millennium BCE, was a linguistic union called *sprachbund*. Words which can be identified as related to Indian *sprachbund* have been documented in an *Indian Lexicon*[57] organized in 8000 semantic clusters. Many words show cognates (similar sounding words with similar meanings) in Munda, Dravidian and Indo-Aryan language families and these words relate also to stoneware and metalware catalogued on Indus Script inscriptions.

This work complements the work on the hieroglyphs of the script of Meluhha (mleccha) with a focus on the use of the glyptics of the script in civilization areas of Meluhha, Magan, Dilmun, and Mesopotamia/Sumer. The writing system continued among metallurgists who created the mints for early coins; in India, these were punch-marked coins of many janapadas (republics). Kota language documents the smithy as a temple. Kole.l means, 'smithy, temple in Kota village (Kota); kwala.l Kota smithy (Toda)(DEDR 2133). Koles were iron-smelters. The scribe was karṇaka (kanka in mleccha) represented rebus by the rim of a jar. This glyph becomes the glyph used with the highest frequency on Indus script epigraphs. The scribe had arrived as an artisan with capability and skills to write on copper plates and to inscribe/punch-mark on early coins with incised Meluhha speech.

Chanhudaro *paṭṭaḍi* 'anvil, smithy, forge'

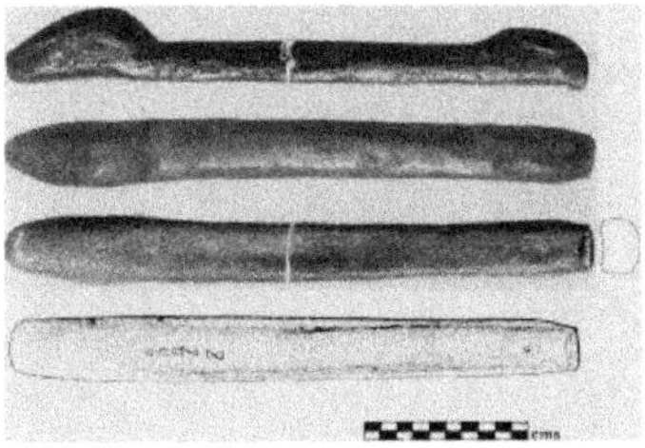

Snarling iron, anvil -- *kolimi kōnda kharādī* smithy, engraver, turner -- as read from Chanhudaro inscribed tool.

Inscribed Chanhu-daro Snarling iron, 2529H, ASI, Central Antiquities Collection. 74.1/48

Snarling irons from the first quarter of the 20th century, after Otto 1922: 45 fig.

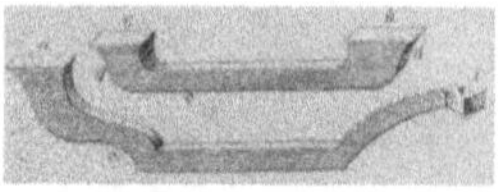

41-2. Used like special anvils for the raising of metal vessels.

The Chanhu-daro snarling alloy (ingot) has an inscription using Indus (Meluhha) writing with five glyphs and a dot glyph. The dot glyph is a notch upon the edge of the bronze snarling tool read rebus as: खांडा [khāṇḍā] *m* A jag, notch, or indentation (as upon the edge of a tool or weapon). Rebus: *kāṇḍa* 'tools, pots and pans and metal-ware'. Thus, theinscription denotes that this is a metalsmith'stool for lathe and forging work.

Chanhujodaro39A1 Chanhudaro39A2

Text of inscription

Three piled up U glyphs, two 'drum' glyphs. *koṇḍa* bend (Konkani)

Enclosure signs of the field: ( ) *kuṭila* = bent, crooked (Skt.Rasaratna samuccaya, 5.205) Humpbacked *kuḍilla* (Pkt.) Rebus: *kuṭila, katthīl* =

bronze (8 parts copper and 2 parts tin) [cf. āra-kūṭa, 'brass' (Skt.) The glyphs (Signs 312 to 315) thus connote one, two, three, seven brass implements – example, anvil as a 'snarling iron', used in the forge. The inscription deploys the hieroglyphs of 'double drum' *karaṭa-* 'a kind of drum' Rebus: *karaḍo, karāḍī* 'a goldsmith's tool' (Gujarati) The glyphs could also connote stylized pair of 'steps or sandals': *meṭṭa* the foot; meṭṭu మెట్టు a shoe, slipper. పాదరక్ష. plu. meṭlu మెట్లు. sandals Rebus: *meḍ* 'iron'. Alternative: *koṇḍa* bend (Konkani) Rebus: *kõdā* 'to turn in a lathe'(B.) कोंद *kōnda* 'engraver, lapidary setting or infixing gems' (Marathi) Allograph: *kŏnḍu* m. ' large cooking pot '(Kashmiri) *kolmo* 'three' Rebus: kolimi 'smithy/forge'. Thus, the inscription describes the snarling iron, lapidary's/smith's tool used in a forge.

Ta. karaṭi, karaṭi-ppaṟai, karaṭikai a kind of drum (said to sound like a bear, karaṭi). *Ka. karaḍi, karaḍe* an oblong drum beaten on both sides, a sort of double drum. / Cf. Skt. *karaṭa-* a kind of drum. (DEDR 1264). Rebus: करडा [*karaḍā*] Hard from alloy--iron, silver &c. (Marathi) *kharādī* ' turner, a person who fashions or shapes objects on a lathe' (Gujarati)

கரடி² *karaṭi, n.* [T. *gariḍi*, K. *garuḍi.*] 1. Fencing; சிலம்பம். 1262 *Ta. karaṭi, karuṭi, keruṭi* fencing, school or gymnasium where wrestling and fencing are taught. *Ka. garaḍi, garuḍi* fencing school. *Tu.* garaḍi, garoḍi id. *Te. gariḍi, gariḍī* id., fencing. గరిడి [gariḍi] or గరిడీ *gariḍi.* [Tel.] n.Fencing, sword play. సాము. A dancing school, a fencing school. సాముకూటము. గరడీల సాము, or గరిడీవిద్య sword play, gymnastics. A place చోటు. Nearness. సమీపము, చెంత. గరిడిముచ్చు a rogue who pretends to be a good man. మంచివానివలె దగ్గరనుండి సమయము చూచి దొంగిలించే దొంగ. (కళా. ii.)

Rebus: करडा [karaḍā] Hard from alloy--iron, silver &c. (Marathi)

Kalibangan065E Kalibangan065a Text 8024

  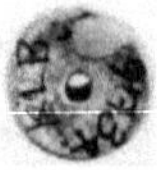

Rebus 1: करडा [karaḍā] Hard from alloy--iron, silver &c. (Marathi) karaḍo, karāḍī 'a goldsmith's tool' (Gujarati) kharādī ' turner, a person who fashions or shapes objects on a lathe' (Gujarati) Rebus 2: karaḍu, kharaḍe, karḍu 'rough, as an account' (Kannada); kharaḍem a rude sketch, foul copy' (Marathi)

khareḍo = a currycomb (G.) खरारा [kharārā] *m* (H) A currycomb. 2 Currying a horse. (Marathi)

The dot glyph is a notch upon the edge of the bronze snarling tool read rebus as: खांडा [khāṇḍā] *m* A jag, notch, or indentation (as upon the edge of a tool or weapon). Rebus: *kāṇḍa* 'tools, pots and pans and metal-ware'.

There are 3 U glyphs: *kolmo* 'three' (Munda) Rebus: *kolimi* 'forge, smithy' (Telugu). *baṭhu* m. ' large pot in which grain is parched' (Sindhi) Rebus: *bhāṭhā* ' kiln '(Awadhi). The three U glyphs together read: *kolimi bhāṭhā* 'forge, smithy (with) smelter/furnace'.

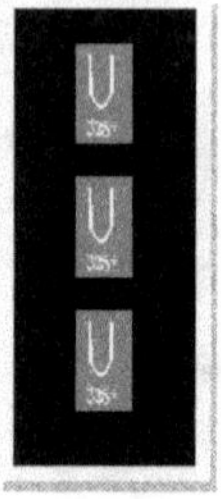

The pair of glyphs preceding the 3 U glyphs are comparable to the pair of feet shown on some seals (discussed further in this note).

aṭai அடை 'anvil' (Tamil) combined with the U glyph which is *baṭhu* yields the compound lexeme: பட்டடை[1] *paṭṭaṭai* (Tamil); cognate *paṭṭaḍi* smithy, forge (Kannada)

The inscription on the 'snarling iron' of Chanhudaro can thus be read as: *kolami paṭṭaḍi* 'anvil for smithy/forge'. The inscription accurately describes in Meluhha (Mleccha) language the function served by the anvil for raising vessels in a smithy/forge.

Reference to *aṭai, aḍi* அடை 'anvil' yields the clue to the rebus readings of 'feet, footprint' glyphs which occur on seals, discussed further in this note.

Tepe Yahya. Seal impressions of two sides of a seal. Six-legged lizard and

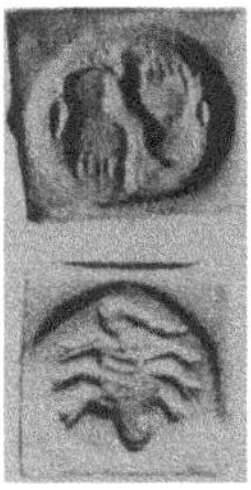

opposing footprints shown on opposing sides of a double-sided steatite stamp seal perforated along the lateral axis. Lamberg-Karlovsky 1971: fig. 2C Shahr-i-Soktha Stamp seal shaped like a foot. āra 'six' Rebus: 'brass'. *araṇe* 'lizard' Rebus: *eraṇi, airaṇ* ' anvil '. *meṭ* sole of foot, footstep, footprint (Ko.); *meṭṭu* step, stair, treading, slipper (Te.)(DEDR 1557). Rebus: मेढ *meḍh* 'merchant's helper' (Pkt.); *meḍ* 'iron' (Munda). The two-sided Tepe Yahya seal records an implement: a snarling iron (anvil: *airaṇ, eraṇi*) for brass (*āra*) and iron (*meḍ*).

Alternative: *aṭi* foot, footprint (Tamil) Rebus: *aḍe, aḍa, aḍi* the piece of wood on which the five artisans put the article which they happen to operate upon, a support (Kannada)

Glyph: araṇe 'lizard' (Tulu) Rebus: eraṇi f. ' anvil ' (Gujarati); aheraṇ, ahiraṇ, airaṇ, airṇī, haraṇ f. (Marathi)

Glyphs: six (numeral): आर [āra] A term in the play of इटीदांडू,--the number six. Rebus: āra 'brass'.

Alternative: Glyph: bhaṭa 'six' (G.) rebus: baṭa = kiln (Santali) baṭa = a kind of iron (Gujarati)

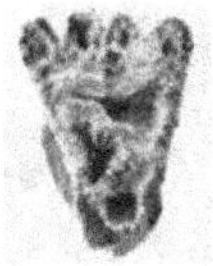

Ia. 18

[Note: six legs shown on the lizard glyph]

The rebus readings are: āra 'brass' *aṭai-kal* 'anvil', *airaṇ* 'anvil', that is, brazier's anvil.

Shahdad seal (Grave 78)

paṭṭaḍi – Smithy/forge Workshop

Circular working platform as a workshop (anvil, smithy, forge)Examples of worker's platforfms at Harappa.

The circular platforms could have served as prastara for the articles taken for display from out of the storage pots. "During excavations of the circular

platform area on Mound F numerous Cemetery H-type sherds and some complete vessels were recovered in association with pointed base goblets and large storage vessels that are usually associated with Harappa Period 3C." South fo the platforms was a furnace. "A large kiln was also found just below the surface of the mound to the south of the circular platforms."[58] The circular platforms are used in conjunction with the products taken out of the kiln (furnace) and large storage vessels which could have been plced in the center of any of the street platforms, constituting the main market street of early times of Harappa settlement. Circular platforms (with a dia. Of 1.5 m) found within rooms (of a coppersmith) as in Padri might have served as working platforms for the brass-workers, lapidaries, artisans of the civilization or as a display counter if the room was used as a shop for sales.

ಪಟ್ಟಲೆ paṭṭalĕ. A district, a community. (R.).

ಪಟ್ಟಡಿ paṭṭu 2-aḍi 4. = ಪಟ್ಟಡೆ, q. v. (My.; SS. 399). 2, = ಪಟ್ಟದಿಮನೆ (My.). — ಪಟ್ಟಡಿಮನೆ. A workshop (ಅಡಿಕ್ಕಟ್ಟ, ಶಿಲ್ಪಶಾಲೆ Sl. 108; My.).

ಪಟ್ಟಡಿ paṭṭu 2-aḍi 4. = ಪಟ್ಟಡೆ, q. v. (My.; SS. 399). 2, = ಪಟ್ಟದಿಮನೆ (My.). — ಪಟ್ಟಡಿಮನೆ. A workshop (ಅಡಿಕ್ಕಟ್ಟ, ಶಿಲ್ಪಶಾಲೆ Sl. 108; My.).

ಪಟ್ಟಡಿ paṭṭu 2-aḍi 4. = ಪಟ್ಟಡೆ, q. v. (My.; SS. 399). 2, = ಪಟ್ಟದಿಮನೆ (My.). — ಪಟ್ಟಡಿಮನೆ. A workshop (ಅಡಿಕ್ಕಟ್ಟ, ಶಿಲ್ಪಶಾಲೆ Sl. 108; My.).

paṭṭar-ai community; guild as of workmen (Ta.); pattar merchants; perh. Vartaka (Skt.) వడ్లబత్తుడు *vaḍrangi.*

[Tel.] n. A carpenter. బత్తుడు *battuḍu*. n. A worshipper. భక్తుడు. The caste title of all the five castes of artificers as వడ్లబత్తుడు a carpenter. కడుపుబత్తుడు one who makes a god of his belly. L. xvi. 230.(Telugu) The merchant, *battuḍu, pattar* is shown in a worshipful state kneeling in adoration on many inscriptions. It is reasonable to assume that the economic principles of Sarasvati-Sindhu (Indus) civilization and facets of *dharma* would have found their echoes – as continuing legacies -- in ancient India which is a major part of the civilization area. In the As noted by Nicholas Kazanas[59] In the use of vārt(t)ā in Sanskrit to connote economic activities, i.e. manufacture, trade etc., it is underscored that these activities were not divorced from ethics and religion. '...; in a Rgvedic hymn the girl Apāla speaks distinctly of her father's cultivated field. [Rgveda VIII, 33 5-6]. But such references show occupation and use, not ownership. Ownership, as we know it, would be shown indisputably only if there was mention of sale, exchange, or giving away of land. There are no such references in the Hymns. The head of a tribe or community or hamlet often gives away gifts – as in the hymn on Liberality (Dakṣiṇā, a RV X, 107) or the Vālakhilya hymns 7 & 8 (RV VIII, 55 & 56) etc. The gifts are gold and jewels, cattle, steeds, skins and the like...Thus dharma denotes religion and religious laws but also secular law and, at the same time, the duties, religious and civil, that a man has to perform towards himself, his family, the State-officials, other members of the community, the priests and holy men, strangers, the environment and gods! It is all dharma, aspects of universal Natural law. (pp.11-12). In the post-vedic literature, in Baudhāyana, we find mention of a householder who lives by the mode called "ṣannivartanī", which is a kind of tenant farming. "He cultivates six nivartanas [a nivartana=6000 sq ft] of fallow land giving a share to the owner, or soliciting his permission (to keep the whole produce)."[III, 2, 2,. SBE XIV, p 288] ... Kauṭilya's *Arthaśāstra*[60] presents both private property and royal property in land; there are also vast uninhabited tracts, wastes and jungles, which seem to belong to the State as a whole. These last are used for new settlements (śūnyaniveśa : settlement or occupation of vacant land). Such settlements (forms of colonization) are small or large villages from 100 to 500 families (grāma; II, 1,2).

… Bṛhaspatisūtra XIX, 26: "A privy, a fireplace, a pit or a receptacle for leavings of food and other (rubbish), must never be made very close to the house of another man" …Specialized craftsmen, tradesmen and other occupations, formed guilds and developed their own professional codes. Many law-givers enjoin that these should be respected by the ruler. In fact Yājñavalkya ordains (I,361) that the king should compel such guilds to comply with their own rules. (pp. 8, 18-19, p 32).[61]

One side of a two-sided tablet m0478, 0479, 0480. in bas relief. Kneeling adorant carrying a U-shaped rimless pot in front a tree. Note: The kneeling motif also occurs on Sit Shamshi bronze.

Obverse of the tablets show this narrative. Pict-111: From R.: A woman with outstretched arms flanked by two men holding uprooted trees in their hands; a person seated on a tree with a tiger below with its head turned backwards; a tall jar with a lid.

Many such circular working platforms were discovered. A lexeme of indian linguistic area which described a circular working platform of the type found at harappa: ku. Pathrauṭī f. ' pavement of slates and stones '(cdial 8858)
Ta. paṭṭaṭai, paṭṭaṟai anvil, smithy, forge. Ka. Paṭṭaḍe, paṭṭaḍi anvil, workshop.

Te. Paṭṭika, paṭṭeḍa anvil; paṭṭaḍa workshop.(dedr 3865). கடைசற்பட்டரை kaṭaicaṟ-paṭṭarai , n. < id. +. turner's shop; கடைசல்வேலைசெய்யுஞ் சாலை. pathūrū f. ' level piece of ground, plateau, small village '; s. patharu m. ' rug, mat '; or. athuripathuri ' bag and baggage '; m. pāthar f. ' flat stone '; omarw. pātharī ' precious stone '.(CDIAL 8857) allograph indus script glyph: pātra 'trough' in front of wild/domesticated/composite animals. pattar 'trough' (dedr 4079) 4080 ta. cavity, hollow, deep hole; pattar (dedr 4080) rebus: பத்தர்[2] pattar ,

n. < t. battuḍu. a caste title of goldsmiths. it was a smiths' guild at work on circular platforms of harappa using tablets as category 'tallies' for the final shipment of package with a seal impression.

On seal m1186A a kneeling adorant makes offerings. bārṇe, bāraṇe = an offering of food to a demon; a meal after fasting, a breakfast (Tu.) barada, barda, birada = a vow (Gujarati) Rebus: baran, bharat (5 copper, 4 zinc and 1 tin)(P.B.)

A similar kneeling adorant now holds a wide-mouthed, rimless pot and makes an offering to the tree.

kǒṇḍu m. ' large cooking pot '(Kashmiri) Rebus: *kõdā* 'to turn in a lathe' (B.) कोंद *kōnda* 'engraver, lapidary setting or infixing gems' (Marathi) + . bārṇe, bāraṇe = an offering of food to a demon; a meal after fasting, a breakfast (Tulu) Rebus: baran, bharat (5 copper, 4 zinc and 1 tin)(Punjabi.Bengali.) That is, turner working with copper, zinc and tin minerals.

Alternative reading: baṭhu m. 'large pot in which grain is parched (Sindhi) Rebus; bhaṭṭhā m. 'kiln' (P.) baṭa = a kind of iron (G.) bhaṭa 'furnace' (g.) baṭa = kiln (santali); baṭa = a kind of iron (g.) bhaṭṭha -- m.n. ' gridiron (pkt.) baṭhu large cooking fire' baṭhī f. 'distilling furnace'; l. bhaṭṭh m. 'grain—parcher's oven', bhaṭṭhī f. 'kiln, distillery', awāṇ. bhaṭh; p. bhaṭṭh m., ṭhī f. 'furnace', bhaṭṭhā m. 'kiln'; s. bhaṭṭhī keṇī 'distil (spirits)'. (CDIAL 9656) Thus, the reading of the composite glyph: kneeling adorant + pot is read rebus: *meḍ pattar + bhaṭa* 'iron urnace (of) merchant guild'.

Trough as a hieroglyph

Examples of 'trough' glyph are shown in front of wild, domesticated and composite animals — an evidence for the use of 'trough' glyph as a hieroglyph, together with the 'animal' glyph. The 'trough' glyph denoted the working platform and the 'animal' glyph denoted the product type (e.g. copper, gold, metal alloy, output of furnaces (of various types), minerals).

That trough is a hieroglyph is evident from the glyph shown in front of a rhinoceros which was not a domesticated animal.

pattar 'trough' (Ta.), rebus paṭṭar-ai community; guild as of workmen (Ta.); pattar merchants (Ta.); perh. vartaka (Skt.) pātharī 'precious stone' (OMarw.) (CDIAL 8857) gaṇḍá 'rhinoceros', kāṇḍā id. Rebus: *kāṇḍa* 'tools, pots and pans and metal-ware' The combination of the hieroglyphs of rhinoceros + trough thus connote a guild (*pattar, paṭṭar-ai*) of metalware artisans.

Alternative: Glyph and rebus decoding: Patharī 'stone cup' (Kumaoni) Rebus: OMarw. Pātharī 'precious stone'.

Stamp seal with a water-buffalo, Mohenjo-daro. "As is usual on Indus Valley seals that show a water buffalo,this animal is standing with upraised head and both hornsclearly visible. (Mackay, 1938b, p. 391). A feeding trough is placed in front of it, and a double row of undecipherable script fills the entire space above. The horns are incised to show the natural growth lines. During the Akkadian period, cylinder seals in Mesopotamia depict water buffaloes in a similar pose that may have been copied from Indus seals (see cat. No.135)(For a Mesopotamian seal with water buffalo, see Parpola1994, p. 252 and Collon 1987, no.529 – Fig. 11)."(JMK –Jonathan Mark Kenoyer, Professor of Anthropology, University of Wisconsin, Madison) (p.405). பத்தர்[1] pattar , n. 1. See பத்தல், 1, 4, 5. 2. Wooden trough for feeding animals; தொட்டி. பன்றிக் கூழ்ப்பத்தரில் (நாலடி, 257).

ḍhangar 'trough'; ḍhangar 'bull'; rebus: ḍhangar 'blacksmith'

Seal. Chanhudaro 22a *ḍhangar* 'bull'. Rebus: *ḍhangar* 'blacksmith' pattar 'trough'. Rebus: pattar (Ta.), battuḍu (Te.) goldsmith guild (Tamil.Telugu)

‘Pannier’ glyph: खोंडी [khōṇḍī] *f* An outspread shovelform sack (as formed temporarily out of a कांबळा, to hold or fend off grain, chaff &c.) Rebus: *kõdā* ‘to turn in a lathe’ (Bengali) कोंद *kōnda* ‘engraver, lapidary setting or infixing gems’ (Marathi) Alternative: K. kŏthul, lu m. ‘ large bag or parcel ’ (CDIAL 3511) Rebus: *kṓṣṭhaka* ‘treasury’ (Skt.); *kóṭṭhi* ‘temple treasury’ (WPah.); *koṭho* ‘warehouse’ (G.)(CDIAL 3546).

Text 6115 Glyph shown as an ingot. Rebus: खोट [*khōṭa*] ‘ingot, wedge’; A mass of metal (unwrought or of old metal melted down)(Marathi) *khoṭ* ‘alloy (Lahnda) Hence खोटसाळ [khōṭasāḷa] *a* (खोट & साळ from शाला) Alloyed--a metal. (Marathi) Bshk. *khoṭ* ‘ embers ’, Phal. *khūṭo* ‘ ashes, burning coal ’; L. *khoṭā* ‘ alloyed ’, awāṇ. *khoṭā* ‘ forged ’; P. *khoṭ* m. ‘ base, alloy ’ M.*khoṭā* ‘ alloyed ’, (CDIAL 3931)

goṭā ‘seed’ Bihari) *khōṭ* ‘alloyed ingot’; *kolmo* ‘rice plant’.

kolom ’sprout’; *kolom* = cutting, graft; to graft, engraft, prune; *kolma hoṛo* = a variety of the paddy plant (Desi)(Santali.) *kolmo* ‘rice plant’ (Mu.) Rebus: *kolami* ‘furnace,smithy’ (Te.) *koḍi* ‘flag’ (Ta.)(DEDR 2049).Rebus: *koḍ* ‘workshop’ (Kuwi) dula ‘pair’; rebus: dul ‘cast (metal)(Santali) Vikalpa: baddī = ox (Nahali); baḍhi = worker in wood and metal (Santali) ḍāngrā = a wooden trough just enough to feed one animal. cf. iḍankaṟi = a measure of capacity, 20 iḍankaṟi make a paṟṟa (Malayalam) ḍangā = small country boat, dug-out canoe (Or.);ḍõgā trough, canoe, ladle (H.)(CDIAL 5568). Rebus:ḍānro term of contempt for a blacksmith (N.) (CDIAL 5524)

Other examples of trough as a hieroglyph on Indus writing seals shown in front of animals.

m1928a m1928b h087 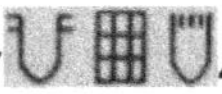 4240

m0266.  1306 m0267 Water-buffalo 2257

 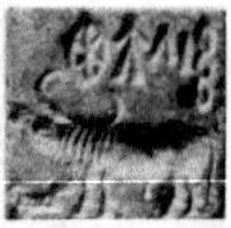  

m0268 Water-buffalo 2445 1804 Pict-39 Ox-antelope with a long tail; a trough in front.

A trough is shown in front of some domesticated animals and also wild animals like rhinoceros, tiger, elephant. The trough glyph is clearly a hieroglyph, in fact, a category classifier. Trough as a glyph occurs on about one hundred inscriptions, though not identified as a distinct pictorial motif in the corpus of inscriptions. Why is a trough shown in front of a rhinoceros which was not a domesticated animal? A reasonable deduction is that 'trough' is a hieroglyph intended to classify the animal 'rhinoceros' in a category.

Dholavira advertisement board announcing bronze-age metalwork

The signboard measuring 3 metres long, must have been placed above the north

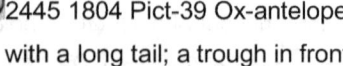

 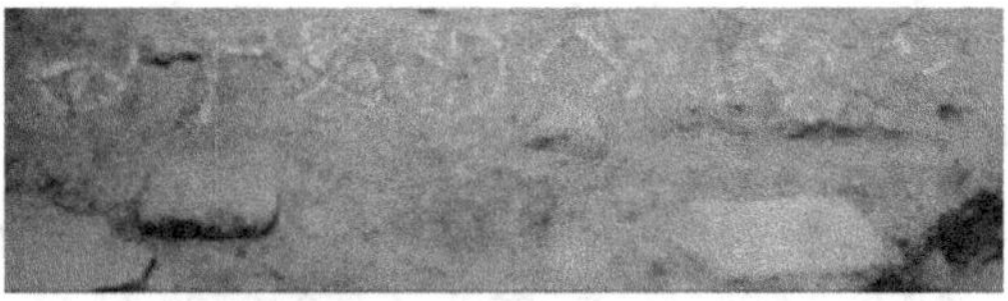

gate of the citadel that existed at the Harappan city of Dholavira. All the signs in white gypsum may have made the board visible from afar.[62] Each glyph is 35 cm to 37 cm tall and 25 cm to 27 cm wide, made of baked gypsum and inlaid on a wooden board. The 10 signs constitute an exquisite work of artisans. Each sign is made of several gypsum fragments pieced together.
Welcome message, advertisement board on the Northern Gateway which leads into citadel of Dholavira.

Surrounding and to the south, east and west of Dholavira are other industrial/ artisan sites of Rann of Kutch, of Sindhu-Sarasvati civilization -- and nearby

Sheffield of the Ancient Near East, Chanhu-daro on the right bank of River Sarasvati.

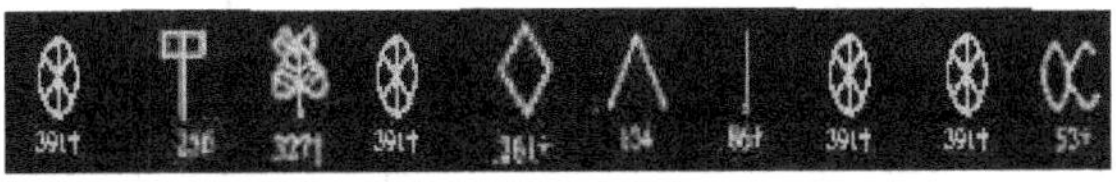

Dholavira Sign-board mounted on a gateway (a reconstruction).

The Meluhhan organization and (perhaps the world's earliest) corporate form of trade is matched by the world's first gigantic, advertisement display board in Dholavira mounted on a gateway of the fort which describes the copper-based smithy-forge work offered by artisans working inside the fort. The repetition of 'nave-of-wheel' glyph divides the announcement in three segments, each related to coppersmithy work.

eraka 'nave-of-wheel', 'moltencast, copper'; *arā* 'spokes', *āra* 'brass'. Rebus: *eraka, era, era* = syn. *erka*, 'copper, weapons' (Kannada).

1. Working in ore, molten cast copper, lathe (work), producing weapons
2. Native metal tools, pots and pans, metalware, turning/engraving (molten cast copper)
3. Copper-/brass-smith mint, furnace (smelter), workshop (molten cast copper -- is the refrain repeated three times as 'nave of wheel' hieroglyph Glyph 391.)

The entry through the port of Dholavira opens up the Meluhha Bronze Age industrial complex.

Copper-brass ingots, metalware, smelter, smithy/forge

Nave + notch glyphs on Text 1061 read:

six (numeral): आर [āra] A term in the play of इटीदांडू,--the number six. Rebus: āra 'brass'. eraka 'nave' Rebus eraka 'copper' + खांडा [*khāṇḍā*] *m* a jag, notch, or indentation (as upon the edge of a tool or weapon); rebus: *khāṇḍā* 'metal tools, pots and pans', thus denoting copper tools, pots and pans.

ḍabu 'an iron spoon' (Santali) Rebus: ḍab, ḍhimba, ḍhompo 'lump (ingot?)' (Munda) Rebus: baṭa = a kind of iron (G.) bhaṭa 'furnace' (G.) *kuṭam* 'pot' (Tamil) *koḍẽ* n. ' earthen saucer for a lamp ' (Marathi). Rebus: kuṭhi 'smelter'. *குடம்¹ kuṭam, n. < குட. cf. kuṭakuṭam K. kuṭa, M. kuṭam.] 1. Water-pot; நீர்வைக்கும் குடம். (பிங்.). See குடதாடி. Hub a wheel; வண்டிக்குடம்.*(Tamil) Rebus: *kuṭhi* 'smelter'.

kolom'sprout'; kolom = cutting, graft; to graft, engraft, prune; kolma hoṛo = a variety of the paddy plant (Desi)(Santali.) kolmo 'rice plant' (Mu.) Rebus: kolami 'furnace,smithy' (Te.)

Segment 1: The word eraka means 'nave- of-wheel'. The word also means 'copper'; *eraka* 'molten cast (metal). *eraka, era, era* = syn. *erka*, 'copper, weapons' (Kannada) arā 'spokes' Rebus: āra 'brass'. dula 'pair' Rebus: *dul* 'cast (metal)'. *ḍato* 'claws or pincers of crab' Rebus: *dhatu* 'ore'; kamaṭha 'crab' Rebus: kammaṭa 'mint, coiner'. Together, the three glyphs read rebus: dul āra eraka 'brass copper casting' kammaṭa 'mint, coiner'.

Segment 2: āra eraka 'brass, copper'; khoṇḍ square Rebus: kõdā ' to turn in a lathe'; कोंद *kōnda* 'engraver, lapidary setting or infixing gems' (Marathi) ; šen ' roof ' Rebus: seṇi, śreṇi 'guild'; koḍa 'one (numeral)' Rebus: koḍ 'artisn's workshop'. Together, the four glyphs read rebus: āra eraka 'brass, copper' koḍ seṇi 'artisan workshop guild'. An alternative reading for the 'roof' glyph: *aḍaren, ḍaren* lid, cover (Santali) Rebus: *aduru* 'native metal' (Ka.) *aduru* = gaṇiyinda tegadu karagade iruva aduru = ore taken from the mine and not subjected to melting in a furnace (Kannada) (Siddhānti *Subrahmaṇya śāstri's new interpretation of the Amarakośa*, Bangalore, Vicaradarpana Press, 1872, p. 330)

An alternative for the 'one(numeral)' glyph: खांडा [khāṇḍā] *m* A jag, notch, or indentation (as upon the edge of a tool or weapon).
(Marathi) Rebus: *khāṇḍā* 'tools, pots and pans, metal-ware'.

Segment 3: *āra eraka* 'brass, copper'; *kamaṛkom, kamaḍha* 'ficus' (Santali) Rebus: *kammaṭa* 'mint, coiner'. Alternative: *loa* 'ficus religiosa' + *kār* ligature Rebus: *lohār, lohāra* 'coppersmith, blacksmith' (Lahnda. Prakrit)

khuṇṭa, khuṭī 'peg' *khũṭi* 'pin' Rebus: *kuṭhi* 'smelter'; kūṭa 'workshop', kuṇḍamu 'a pit for receiving and preserving consecrated fire' (Te.) kundār kũdār, kũdāri 'turner'.Together, the three glyphs read rebus: *āra eraka* 'brass, copper' *lohār* 'smith' *kammaṭa* 'mint, coiner' *kuṭhi* 'smelter'.

The advertisement board thus announces the facilities of a smelter, artisan's workshop guild for brass, copper casting. There is also a pun on the word *du āra* which may also refer to Dwara(ka), the gateway to the bronze-age metallurgical facility in Dholavira (also called in village name: *koṭḍa*).

The complete message of the huge signboard, an advertisement hoarding with 15 inch high lettering could be seen by seafaring merchants entering from Persian Gulf or navigating the Rivers Sarasvati and Sindhu towards the northern gate of Dholavira.

The complete message read in three segments, inviting traders/artisans into a Meluhha copper metalworking and lapidary (engraving, bead-making) complex of Bronze Age sites not far from Dholavira (Kotda) to the seafaring merchants and artisans from Dilmun, Magan, Elam, Mesopotamia, Sumer and even beyond from places such as Altyn Depe or Haifa (Israel) where evidences for use of documents with Indus writing have been found.

Thus was conceived a monumental documentation for Meluhhan artisanal competence using the gigantic-sized hoarding on the northern gateway of Kotda, Dholavira fortification.

This verily constitutes the Bronze Age Standard of Eurasia – apart from being a Meluhha Standard. Ancient Near East Bronze Age Meluhha, smithy/lapidary documents, *takṣat vāk*, incised speech [Evidence from sites surrounding Bhuj in Kutch: Kanmer, Dholavira, Gola Dhoro (Bagasra), Shikarpur, Khirsara, Surkotada, Desalpur, Konda Bhadli, Juni Kuran, Narapa].

Harosheth Hagoyim[63], smithy of nations

Etymology of harosheth is variously elucidated, while it is linked to 'chariot-making in a smithy of nations'.

Harosheth Hebrew: חרושת הגויים; is pronounced khar-o-sheth? Most likely, (haroshet) a noun meaning a carving. Hence, *kharoṣṭī* came to represent a 'carving, engraving' art, i.e. a writing system. Harosheth-hagoyim See: Haroshet [Carving]; a forest; agriculture; workmanship;Harsha [Artifice: deviser: secret work]; workmanship; a wood.[64] Cognate with haroshet: karṣá m. ' dragging ' Pāṇ., ' agriculture ' Āp.(CDIAL 2905).karṣaṇa n. ' tugging, ploughing, hurting ' Mn., ' cultivated land ' MBh. [kárṣati, √kr̥ṣ] Pk. karisaṇa -- n. ' pulling, ploughing '; G. karsaṇ n. ' cultivation, ploughing '; OG. karasaṇī m. ' cultivator ', G. karasṇī m. -- See *kr̥ṣaṇa -- .(CDIAL 2907). *Harosheth-hagoyim* is the home of general Sisera, who was killed by Jael during the war of Naphtali and Zebulun against Jabin, king of Hazor in Canaan (Judges 4:2). The lead players of this war are the general Barak and the judge Deborah. The name Harosheth-hagoyim obviously consists of two parts. The first part is derived from the root , which HAW Theological Wordbook of the Old Testament treats as four separate roots (harash I, II, III, & IV). The verb (harash I) means to engrave or plough. HAW Theological Wordbook of the Old Testament reads, "The basic idea is cutting into some material, e.g. engraving metal or plowing soil." Derivatives of this verb are: (harash), meaning engraver; (haroshet) a noun meaning a carving. This word is equal to the first part of the name Harosheth-hagoyim; (harish), meaning plowing or plowing time; (maharesha) meaning ploughshare; (harishi), a word which is only used in Jona 4:8 to indicate a certain characteristic of the sun - vehement (King James) or scorching (NIV). The verb (harash II) most commonly denotes refraining from speech or response, either because one is deaf or mute, or because one doesn't want to respond. None of the sources indicates a relation with the previous root, and perhaps there is none, but on the other hand, perhaps deafness was regarded in Biblical as either being marked or else cut or cut off. The noun (horesh) from root (hrsh III) occurs only in Isaiah 17:9 and has to do with a wood or forest. The noun (heresh) from root (hrsh IV) occurs only in Isaiah 3:3 and probably means magical art or expert enchanter, or something along those lines. The second part of the name, hagoyim, comes from the definite article (ha plus the common word (goy) meaning nation, people, gentile. This word comes from the assumed root (gwh), which is not translated but which seems to denote things that are surpassed or left behind. Other derivatives are: (gaw a and gew), meaning back, as in "cast behind the back," i.e. put out of mind (1 Kings 14:9, Nehemiah 9:26, Isaiah 38:17); (gewiya), meaning body, either dead or alive (Genesis 47:18, Judges 14:8, Daniel 10:6). The meaning of the name Harosheth-hagoyim can be found as any combination of the above. NOBS Study Bible Name List reads Carving Of The Nations, but equally valid would be Silence Of The Gentiles or Engraving Of What's Abandoned. Jones' Dictionary of Old Testament Proper Names reads Manufactory for Harosheth and "of the Gentiles" for Hagoyim.[65]

This may suggest a fresh look at and reconsideration of the messages conveyed by thousands of cylinder seals which depict many animals, including antelopes, goats, rams, scorpions or composite animals with wings. Some of these explained in sacred contexts, may also be explained as hieroglyphs of bronze-age life activities. They are read rebus by literate-language communities, instead of merely explaining away some representations -- only as objects of art appreciation -- to be hunting or banquet scenes or metaphors in the context of assumed rituals in temples or communities.

The design known as the animal file *motif* is extremely early in Sumerian and Elamitic glyptic; in fact is among the oldest known glyptic designs.

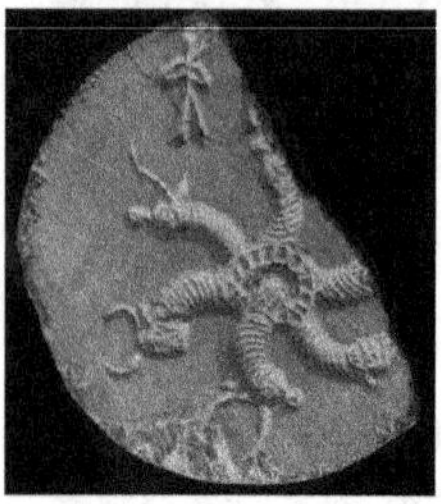

A characteristic style in narration is the use of a procession or group of animals to denote a professional group. The grouping may connote a smithy-shop of a guild -- *pasāramu.*

Mohenjo-daro seal m417 six heads from a core.*śrēṇikā* -- f. ' tent ' lex. and mngs. ' house ~ ladder ' in *śriṣṭa -- 2, *śrīḍhi -- . -- Words for ' ladder ' see śrití -- . -- √śri]H. *sainī, senī* f. ' ladder '; Si. *hiṇi, hiṇa, iṇi* ' ladder, stairs ' (GS 84 < *śrēṇi* --).(CDIAL 12685). Woṭ. šen ' roof ', Bshk. šan, Phal. Šān(AO xviii 251) Rebus: seṇi (f.) [Class. Sk. śreṇi in meaning "guild"; Vedic= row] 1. A guild Vin iv.226; J i.267, 314; iv.43; Dāvs ii.124; their number was eighteen J vi.22, 427; VbhA 466. ° -- pamukha the head of a guild J ii.12 (text seni --). — 2. A division of an army J vi.583; ratha -- ° J vi.81, 49; seṇimokkha the chief of an army J vi.371 (cp. senā and seniya). (Pali)

Glyphs: six (numeral): आर [āra] A term in the play of इटीदांडू,--the number six. Rebus: āra 'brass'.

This denotes a mason (artisan) guild -- seni -- of 1. brass-workers; 2. blacksmiths; 3. iron-workers; 4. copper-workers; 5. native metal workers; 6. workers in alloys.

The core is a glyphic 'chain' or 'ladder'. Glyph: kaḍī a chain; a hook; a link (G.); kaḍum a bracelet, a ring (G.) Rebus: kaḍiyo [Hem. Des. kaḍaio = Skt. sthapati a mason] a bricklayer; a mason; kaḍiyaṇa, kaḍiyeṇa a woman of the bricklayer caste; a wife of a bricklayer (G.)

The glyphics are:

1. Glyph: 'one-horned young bull': *kondh* 'young bull'. 'Pannier' glyph: खोंडी [khōṇḍī] *f* An outspread shovelform sack (as formed temporarily out of a कांबळा, to hold or fend off grain, chaff &c.) Rebus: *kõdā* 'to turn in a lathe' (Bengali) *kũdār* 'turner, brass-worker'. कोंद *kōnda* 'engraver, lapidary setting or infixing gems' (Marathi)
2. Glyph: 'bull': *ḍhangra* 'bull'. *Rebus: ḍhangar* 'blacksmith'.
3. Glyph: 'ram': *meḍh* 'ram'. Rebus: *meḍ* 'iron'
4. Glyph: 'antelope': *mṛeka* 'goat'. Rebus: *milakkhu* 'copper'. Vikalpa 1: *meluhha* '*mleccha*' 'copper worker'. Vikalpa 2: *meṛh* 'helper of merchant'.
5. Glyph: 'zebu': *khũṭ* 'zebu'. Rebus: *khũṭ* 'guild, community' (Semantic determinant of the 'jointed animals' glyphic composition). *kūṭa* joining, connexion, assembly, crowd, fellowship (DEDR 1882) Pa. *gotta* 'clan'; Pk. *gotta, gōya* id. (CDIAL 4279) Semantics of Pkt. lexeme *gōya* is concordant with Hebrew *'goy'* in *ha-goy-im* (lit. the-nation-s). Pa. *gotta* -- n. ' clan ', Pk. *gotta* -- , *gutta* -- , amg. *gōya* -- n.; Gau. *gū* ' house ' (in Kaf. and Dard. several other words for ' cowpen ' > ' house ': gōṣṭhá -- , Pr. *gū´ṭu* ' cow '; S. *goṭru* m. ' parentage ', L. *got* f. ' clan ', P. *gotar, got* f.; Ku. N. *got* ' family '; A. *got -- nāti* ' relatives '; B. *got* ' clan '; Or. *gota* ' family, relative '; Bhoj. H. *got* m. ' family, clan ', G. *got* n.; M. *got* ' clan, relatives '; -- Si. *gota* ' clan, family ' ← Pa. (CDIAL 4279). Alternative: adar ḍangra 'zebu or humped bull'; rebus: aduru 'native metal' (Ka.); ḍhangar 'blacksmith' (H.)
6. The sixth animal can only be guessed. Perhaps, a tiger (A reasonable inference, because the glyph 'tiger' appears in a procession on some Indus script inscriptions. Glyph: 'tiger?': *kol* 'tiger'.Rebus: *kol* 'worker in iron'. Vikalpa (alternative): perhaps, rhinoceros. gaṇḍa 'rhinoceros'; rebus: khaṇḍ 'tools, pots and pans and metal-ware'. Thus, the entire glyphic composition of six animals on the Mohenjodaro seal m417 is semantically a representation of a *śrēṇi*, 'guild', a *khũṭ* , 'community' of smiths and masons.

Stamp seal from Latifia showng a zebu bull.[66]

This guild, community of smiths and masons evolves into Harosheth Hagoyim, 'a smithy of nations'.

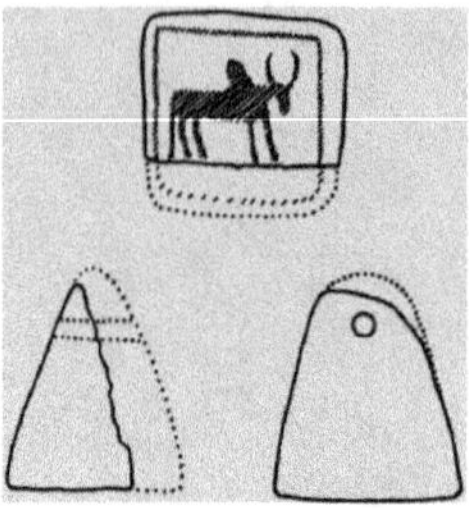

The artistic deployment of hieroglyphs on a procession is also seen on one side of Narmer palette.

A note[67] explains the hieroglyphs on the Mohenjo-Daro tablets showing a procession of standard-bearers as the standard of the civilization.

The procession is a celebration of the graduation from stone-cutting or making of stone-beads -- *sanghāḍo* -- community (or artisan guild) to a bronze-age guild of metal (mineral and alloy)-turners in smithy/forge or mint, *kammaṭa*.

Lapidary-Smith Standard in procession

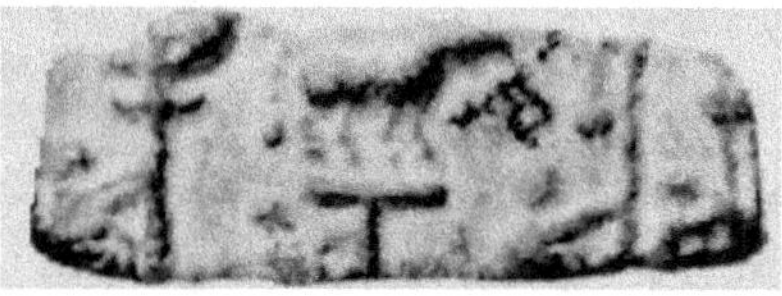

Mohenjo-daro tablets m0490, m0491 tablets.

These tablets from Mohenjo-daro show four standard-bearers in a procession advertising the products and technologies offered by them: perforated beads, mineral (ores), turner (wood-metal-shell-stone-mason), from fortified workshop, consignments offered *jangad*, approval-basis, which is a unique commercial transaction practiced even today among diamond merchants of Surat.

1. *kandi* (pl. –l) necklace, beads (Pa.) Ga. (P.) *kandi* (pl. –l) bead, (pl.) necklace; (S.2) *kandiṭ* bead (DEDR 1215). *kandil, kandīl* = a globe of glass, a lantern (Kannada) Rebus: *kaṇḍ* 'fire-altar'.

2. *dhàṭṭu* m. 'woman's headgear, kerchief'; *dhaṭu* m. (also *dhaṭhu*) m. 'scarf' (WPah.); rebus: *dhātu*'mineral' (Skt.), *dhatu* id. (Santali).

3. *kōḍu* horn (Kannada. Tulu. Tamil) खोंड [*khōṇḍa*] m A young bull, a bullcalf. (Marathi) Rebus 1: কুঁদন, কোঁদন [kuṅdana, kōṅdana] n act of turning (a thing) on a lathe; act of carving; act of bragging. কুঁদ [kuṅda] n a (turner's) lathe.কুঁদ¹ [kuṅda¹] v to turn (a thing) on a lathe, to shape by turning on a lathe; to carve (Bengali) Rebus 2: कोंड [*kōṇḍa*] A circular hamlet; a division of a मौजा or village, composed generally of the huts of one caste. खोट [*khōṭa*] Alloyed--a metal (Marathi).

4. सांगड [*sāṅgaḍa*] That member of a turner's apparatus by which the piece to be turned is confined and steadied (Marathi) *sanghāḍo* (G.) cutting stone, gilding (G.) Rebus: जांगड [*jāṅgaḍa*] f (Hindi) Goods taken from a shop, to be retained or returned as may suit: also articles of apparel taken from a tailor or clothier to sell for him. 2 or जांगड वही The account or account-book of goods so taken.(Marathi)

Late Uruk and Jemdet Nasr seal; ca. 3200-3000 (?) BC; marble; cat.3; loop bore; an antelope with two tigers, one with head turned. kola 'tiger' Rebus: kol 'working in iron'. tagara 'antelope' Rebus: tagara 'tin'. krammara 'head turned back' Rebus: kamar 'smith, artisan'.

Banner: খোঁড [*khōṇḍa*] m 'a young bull' Rebus: কোঁদন [*kōṅdana*], 'turning on a lathe'

The standard-bearer glyph bearing the one-horned young bull is replicated on a mosaic panel found in the Temple of Ishtar in Mari (Tell-Hariri), Syria.

Frieze of a mosaic panel Circa 2500-2400 BCE Temple of Ishtar, Mari (Tell Hariri), Syria Shell and shale André Parrot excavations, 1934-36 AO 19820. Figures carved in mother-of-pearl, set on a wooden panel covered with a layer of bitumen. Inlaid mosaics of lapis lazuli or pink limestone.

"Reconstruction of the original panel is based on guesswork, since shell pieces are missing. The soldiers wear helmets, carry spears or adzes, and are dressed in kaunakes (fleecy skirts or kilts) and scarves. The dignitaries wear kaunakes and low fur hats, and each carries a long-handled adze on the left shoulder. Their leader appears to be a shaven-headed figure: stripped to the waist and wearing kaunakes, he carries a standard showing a bull standing on a pedestal. The lower register, on the right, features traces of a chariot drawn by onagers, a type of wild ass."[68]

On the top register, a person is a standard bearer of a banner holding aloft the one-horned young bull which is the signature glyph of Indus writing. The banner is comparable to the banner shown on two Mohenjo-daro tablets.

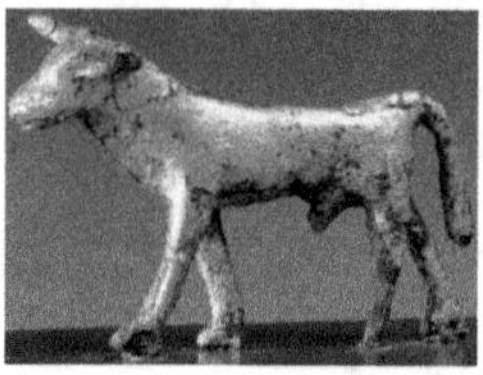

Gilded bullock known as the Golden Calf Middle Bronze Age, 1900-1800 BCE Byblos, the Levant Lost-wax bronze cast, gold leaf H. 37 cm; W. 55 cm Maurice Dunand excavation, gift of the Lebanese Republic, 1930 AO 14680

"This statuette of a young bullock represents the animal form of Reshef or Baal, god of storms. He was worshipped in Byblos, where many offerings were dedicated to him, including steles, weapons, and figurines such as this, which were placed inside vases. The covering of gold leaf is reminiscent of the episode of the Golden Calf in the Bible, when the tribes led through the desert by Moses forsook their god to worship false idols (Exodus 32)...The statuette represents a young bullock walking in a calm, non-threatening manner...The bronze was cast using the lost-wax process, found in a vase buried in the foundations of a shrine in Byblos...The site of Byblos - the Greek name for the city now known as Jbeil in Arabic and Gubla in Semitic languages - dates from the seventh millennium BCE...The young bullock of Byblos is clearly associated with a youthful god, as distinct from El, the father of the gods, who is sometimes depicted in the form of an older, more powerful bull."

Orthographic style of the writing system

The following are examples of Indus script inscriptions with only pictorial motifs and/or only one or two signs.

M838 seal. Seal impression, Ur (Upenn; U.16747); dia. 2.6, ht. 0.9 cm.; Gadd, PBA 18 (1932), pp. 11-12, pl. II, no. 12; Porada 1971: pl.9, fig.5; Parpola, 1994, p. 183; water carrier with a skin (or pot?) hung on each end of the yoke across his shoulders and another one below the crook of his left arm; the vessel on the right end of his yoke is over a receptacle for the water; a star on either side of the head (denoting supernatural?). The whole object is enclosed by 'parenthesis' marks. The parenthesis is perhaps a way of splitting of the ellipse. An unmistakable example of an 'hieroglyphic' seal.[69]

m1405At Pict-97: Person standing at the center pointing with his right hand at a bison facing a trough, and with his left hand pointing to the sign

kuṭi 'water carrier' (Telugu) kuṭhi = kiln (Santali) kuṛī f. 'fireplace' (H.); krvṛı f. 'granary (WPah.); kuṛī, kuṛo house, building'(Ku.)(CDIAL 3232) kuṭi 'hut made of boughs' (Skt.) guḍi temple (Telugu) [The bull is shown in front of the trough for drinking; hence the semantics of 'drinking'.]

Listed by Koskenniemi and Parpola and cited by Diwiyana.[70] Ligatured glyph of three sememes:
1. *meḍ* 'body' (Mu.); rebus: 'iron' (Ho.); Glyph: 'full stretch of one's arms': kāḍ 2 काड् । पौरुषम् m. a man's length, the

stature of a man (as a measure of length) (Rām. 632, zangan kaḍun kāḍ, to stretch oneself the whole length of one's body. So K. 119). Rebus: kāḍ 'stone'. Ga. (Oll.) kanḍ, (S.) kanḍu (pl. kanḍkil) stone (DEDR 1298).

2. *kuṭi* 'water carrier' (Te.) Rebus: *kuṭhi* 'smelter furnace' (Santali).

3. खांडा [*khāṇḍā*] *m* a jag, notch, or indentation (as upon the edge of a tool or weapon); rebus: *khāṇḍā* 'metal tools, pots and pans'.

Thus, together, the composite glyph reads rebus: *kāḍ kuṭhi khāṇḍā* 'stone (ore) smelter metalware'.

Fish + notch: *ayo* 'fish' + खांडा [khāṇḍā] *m* A jag, notch, or indentation (as upon the edge of a tool or weapon). Rebus: khāṇḍa 'tools, pots and pans, and metal-ware'. *ayaskāṇḍa* is a compounde word attested in Pāṇini.

Together with meḍ 'body', rebus: meḍ 'iron', the rebus reading of the 'body with spread feet' may read rebus: *meḍ pattar* 'iron (workers) guild'. This glyph if ligatured with a notch-glyph, the reading is: *meḍ pattar khāṇḍā* 'iron guild tools pots and pans'. खांडा [khāṇḍā] *m* A jag, notch, or indentation (as upon the edge of a tool or weapon). Rebus: khāṇḍa 'tools, pots

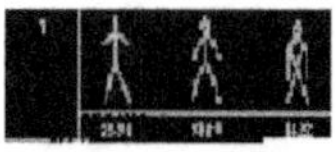

and pans, and metal-ware'.

Alternative: kāḍ 2 काड् । पौरुषम् m. a man's length, the stature of a man (as a measure of length) (Rām. 632, zangan kaḍun kāḍ, to stretch oneself the whole length of one's body. So K. 119). Rebus: kāḍ 'stone'. Ga. (Oll.) kanḍ, (S.) kanḍu (pl. kanḍkil) stone (DEDR 1298). *dhaṛu* 'body' (Sindhi) Rebus: *dhatu* 'ore'

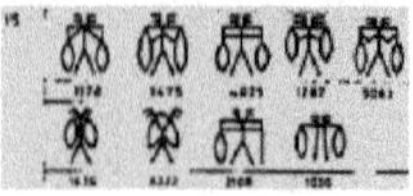

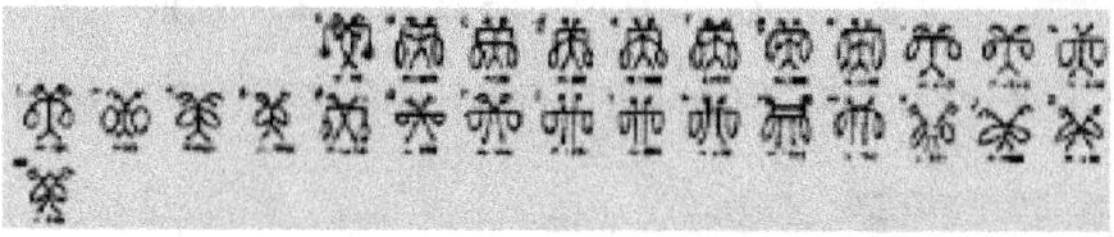

(Santali) *badhoria* 'expert in working in wood'(Santali).

The most frequently occurring glyph -- rim of jar -- ligatured to Glyph 12 becomes Glyph 15 and is thus explained as a *kanka, karṇaka:* 'furnace scribe' and is consistent with the readings of glyphs which occur together with this glyph. Kan-ka may denote an artisan working with copper, kaṉ (Ta.) kaṉṉār 'coppersmiths,

blacksmiths' (Ta.) Thus, the phrase kaṇḍ karṇaka may be decoded rebus as a brassworker, scribe. karṇaka 'scribe, accountant'.

Glyph15 variants (Parpola)

Indus inscription on a Mohenjo-daro tablet (m1405) including 'rim-of-jar' glyph as component of a ligatured glyph (Sign 15 Mahadevan) This tablet is a clear and unambiguous example of the fundamental orthographic style of Indus Script inscriptions that: both signs and pictorial motifs are integral components of the message conveyed by the inscriptions. Attempts at 'deciphering' only what is called a 'sign' in Parpola or Mahadevan corpora will result in an incomplete decoding of the complete message of the inscribed object.

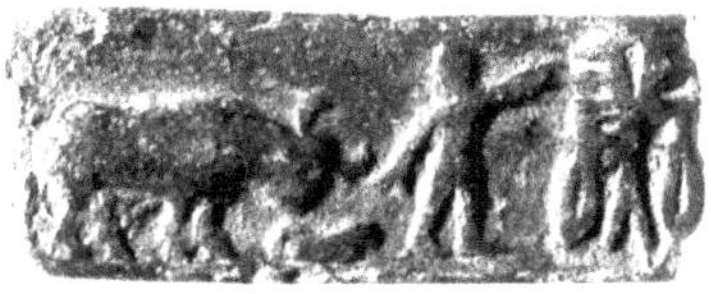

This inscribed object is decoded as a professional calling card: a blacksmith-precious-stone-merchant with the professional role of copper-miner-smelter-furnace-scribe.

m1405At Pict-97: Person standing at the center points with his right hand at a bison facing a trough, and with his left hand points to the ligatured glyph.

The inscription on the tablet juxtaposes – through the hand gestures of a person - a 'trough' gestured with the right hand; a ligatured glyph composed of 'rim-of-jar' glyph and 'water-carrier' glyph (Glyph 15) gestured with the left hand.

The inscription of this tablet m1405 is composed of four glyphs: bison, trough, shoulder (person), ligatured glyph -- Glyph 15 (rim-of-jar glyph ligatured to water-carrier glyph).

Each glyph can be read rebus in mleccha (meluhhan).

ḍangur m. 'bullock', rebus: ḍāṅro 'blacksmith' (N.) pattar 'trough' (Ta.), rebus paṭṭar-ai community; guild as of workmen (Ta.); pattar merchants (Ta.); perh. vartaka (Skt.) pātharī 'precious stone' (OMarw.) (CDIAL 8857)

meḍ 'body' (Mu.); rebus: meḍ 'iron' (Ho.); eṛaka 'upraised arm' (Ta.); rebus: eraka = copper (Ka.)

Ligature 1 in composite glyph: kan-ka 'rim of jar' (Santali), rebus karṇaka 'scribe, accountant' (Pa.); vikalpa: 1. kāraṇika -- m. 'arrow-maker' (Pa.) 2. khanaka 'miner, digger, excavator' (Skt.). Ligature 2 in composite glyph: kuṭi 'water-carrier' (Telugu), rebus: kuṭhi 'smelter furnace' (Santali)

The composite message is thus: blacksmith, merchant, copper smelter scribe.

Vikalpa: pattar 'trough'; rebus pattar, vartaka 'merchant'. பத்தல் pattal, n. பத்தர்[1] pattar 1. A wooden bucket;மரத்தாலான நீரிறைக்குங் கருவி. தீம்பிழி யெந்திரம் பத்தல் வருந்த (பதிற்றுப். 19, 23). பத்தர்[2] pattar , n. < T. battuḍu. A caste title of goldsmiths; தட்டார் பட்டப்பெயருள் ஒன்று. பட்டடை[1] paṭṭaṭai , n. prob. படு[1]- + அடை[1]-. 1. [T. paṭṭika, K. paṭṭaḍe.] Anvil; அடைகல். (பிங்.) சீரிடங்காணி னெறிதற்குப் பட்ட டை (குறள், 821). 2. [K. paṭṭaḍi.] Smithy, forge;கொல்லன் களரி பத்தல் pattal , n. 1. A wooden bucket; மரத்தாலான நீரிறைக்குங் கருவி. தீம்பிழி யெந்திரம் பத்தல் வருந்த(பதிற்றுப். 19, 23). பத்தர்[1] pattar , n. 1. See பத்தல், 1, 4, 5. 2. Wooden trough for feeding animals; தொட்டி. பன்றிக் கூழ்ப்பத்தரில் (நாலடி, 257).
paṭṭar-ai community; guild as of workmen (Ta.); pattar merchants; perh. vartaka (Skt.)

paṭṭarai 'workshop' (Ta.) pattharika [fr. patthara] a merchant Vin ii.135 (kaŋsa˚).(Pali) cf. Pattharati [pa+tharati] to spread, spread out, extend J i.62; iv.212; vi.279; DhA i.26; iii.61 (so read at J vi.549 in cpd ˚pāda with spreading feet, v. l. patthaṭa˚). -- pp. patthaṭa (q. v.). பத்தர் pattar, n. perh. vartaka.

Merchants; வியாபாரிகள். (W.) battuḍu. n. The caste title of all the five castes of artificers as vaḍla b*, carpenter.

 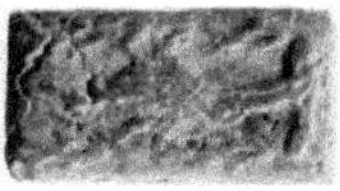  h172A h172B 5305 This is a frequently occurring terminal pair of signs:  Sign 342 (164), Sign 48 (114); the pair occurs also on 13 copper tablets).

'Crocodile' + 'fish' ligatured glyph on one side of h172 tablet. ayo 'fish' Rebus: ayas 'metal'. kāru 'crocodile' Rebus: kāru 'artisan'. Thus, together read rebus: ayakara 'metalsmith'

Ka. eṟakil, eṟake a roof, thatch. (DEDR 528) *kŏnḍu* m. ' large cooking pot '(Kashmiri) Rebus: *kõdā* 'to turn in a lathe'(B.) कोंद *kōnda* 'engraver, lapidary setting or infixing gems' (Marathi) Thus, the ligatured glyph denotes a coppersmith.

G.*karā* n. pl. 'wristlets, bangles'; S. *karāī* f. 'wrist' (CDIAL 2779). Rebus: *khār* खार् 'blacksmith' (Kashmiri)

khareḍo = a currycomb (Gujarati) Rebus: करडा [karaḍā] Hard from alloy--iron, silver &c. (Marathi) *kharādī* ' turner, a person who fashions or shapes objects on a lathe' (Gujarati)
kanka, karṇaka 'rim of jar' Rebus: *karṇaka* 'account scribe'.

ḍhanga 'crook' *Rebus: dhangar* 'blacksmith'. Alternative: अंकडा [aṅkaḍā] *m* (अंक S) Also अकडा *m* A hook or crook, a curved end gen. (M.) Rebus 1: अखाडा [akhāḍā] *m* (H) A community, or the common place of residence or of assembly, of persons engaged in study or some particular pursuit; a college, a disputation-hall, a gymnasium, circus, arena. Hence, A club or clubroom; a stand of idlers, loungers, newsmongers, gossips, scamps. 2 An order of men. Ex. गोसाव्यांचे अठरा अखाडे आहेत.(M.) Rebus 2: 'chisel': Pk. *āhōḍaï* ' strikes, beats '; S. *ahoṛaṇu, ahuṛ°* ' to roughen a millstone by pricking with a chisel ', *ahoṛo* m. ' stonecutter's chisel ';

M. *ahaḍṇī* f. ' brazier's instrument for smoothing down dints in new -- made vessels '. (CDIAL 1036).

Ras-al-Junayz. Copper  seal. kolom 'three' (Mu.) Rebus: kolami 'furnace, smithy' (Te.) Two silver seals at Mohenjodaro, two copper seals at Lotha, 8 molded copper tablets at Harappa and copper seals at Lothal and at Ras al-Juayz are rare uses of metal as a medium for conveying messages.

dāṭu = cross (Telugu) Rebus: *dhatu* = mineral (Santali) H. *dhāṭnā* 'to send out, pour out, cast (metal)' (CDIAL 6771).

Sign 130 *ḍhanga* = a crook used for pulling down the branches of trees, for goats, sheep and camels (Punjabi) Rebus: *dhangar* 'blacksmith' (Maithili) *ḍangar* 'blacksmith' (Hindi)

Thus, the pair of glyphs read rebus: *dāṭu* 'cross' Rebus: *dhāṭ* 'cast mineral'.

ḍhanga 'crook' *Rebus: dhangar* 'blacksmith'.

Hoofed platform

m1181 Seal. Mohenjo-daro. Three-faced, horned person (with a three-leaved branch on the crown), wearing bangles and armlets and seated on a hoofed platform.

Text of inscription. खुर [khura] m S A hoof. See the derivative खूर; (खुरा, not खुऱ्या) The heel (of a shoe or sandal). (Marathi) Rebus: kuraga 'an instrument of goldsmiths, etc., a sort of anvil (Kannada). khurāryā खुरा or ऱ्या [khurā or ṛyā] m An instrument of farriers, goldsmiths, and other smiths, a sort of anvil. Otherwise called वटांग & संधन.(Marathi)

Allograph: kuranga, kurangaka 'a species of antelope, an antelope, a deer' (Kannada). *Kol.* (Hislop) kori antelope. *Pa.* kuri id. *Ga.* (Oll.) kuruy deer. *Go.* (Tr. etc.) kurs (*pl.* -k) deer, antelope (*Voc.* 792). *Kui* kruhu (*pl.* kruhka), (P.) krusu (*pl.* kruska) barking deer, jungle sheep. *Kuwi* (S.) kluhu antelope; (Su.) kruhu (*pl.* kruska (P.) kurhu antelope. ? *Ma.* kūran hog-deer. / Cf. Skt. kuraṅga- a species of antelope, antelope or deer in general. (DEDR 1785).

khōṭasāḷa, forge (for alloys) shown on a Bahrain seal

Tracking the Meluhhan seafaring merchant. Indus Valley seal found in Bahrain (Roaf 1982; Crawford 1998) (After Fig. 9.5 in Harriet EW Crawford, 2004, Sumer and Sumerians, Cambridge University Press, p. 189). “There is a famous inscription in which Sargon boasts that the boats of Dilmun, Magan and Meluhha are moored at the quays of Agade (Sollberger and Kupper 1971). It is probably to this period, or perhaps a little earlier, that the site of Ras al-Junayz (now known as Ras al-Jinz), on the south-east tip of the Arabian peninsula, shold be dated. Tosi has suggested that this may have been a staging-post for the Meluhhan boats on their long journey from the Indus upto the head of the Gulf (Tosi 1984: Cleuziou and Tosi 2000). Weights and seals (Fig. 95) identical to those in use in the Indus valley were found on the island of Bahrain, enabling us to track these Harappan merchants futher along their route. It is even suggested that there may have been colonies of foreign merchants resident in some of the major Sumerian cities about this time or a little later (Parpola et al., 1977). Perhaps it was these colonies which commissioned cylinder seals like the examples recovered from Ur and from Tell Asmar which are decorated with typical Indus motifs. There is also an Agade seal which appears to show a Meluhhan interpreter translating to a local ruler for a party of foreigners (Lamberg-Karlovsky 1981)” (Harriet EW Crawford, 2004, pp. 189-190).

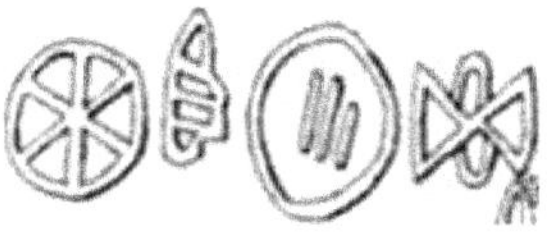

Text of inscription with four glyphs on Bahrain seal. The text seems to describe ‘a snarling iron tool to shape ingots into metalware vessels (in a) smithy/forge (using) copper and brass ore nodules.' supplied by *baḍhi* ('rhinoceros' glyph) -- 'an expert carpenter, worker in wood and metal'. Alternative reading of 'rhinoceros' glyph: *gaṇḍá* 'rhinoceros' Rebus: *khaṇḍ* 'tools, pots and pans and metal-ware' Alternative: *baḍhia* = a castrated boar, a hog (Santali) Rebus: *baḍhi* 'a caste who work both in iron and wood' (Santali) baḍhoe 'a carpenter, worker in wood'; badhoria 'expert in working in wood'(Santali)

 *karaḍi, karaḍe* an oblong drum beaten on both sides, a sort of double drum (Kannada)(DEDR 1264). *kharādī* ' turner, a person who fashions or shapes objects on a lathe' (Gujarati)

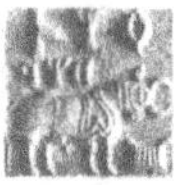

 *ḍhālako* 'large ingot'. खोट [*khōṭa*] 'ingot, wedge'; A mass of metal (unwrought or of old metal melted down)(Marathi) *khoṭ* 'alloy (Lahnda) Hence खोटसाळ [khōṭasāḷa] *a* (खोट & साळ from शाला) Alloyed--a metal. (Marathi) (Fist glyph from r. on Line 1 of Seal. Chanhudaro 22a Text 6115).

Composite glyph identified as a ligature of two component glyphs:

The ligatured glyph could read rebus: 'ingot turner': *karaḍ khōṭ or karaḍ ḍhālako.* Hence, the ligatured glyph could connote a descriptive depiction of the snarling iron used for forging; on this tool was inscribed the basic 'turner' glyph was.

 kolmo 'three' Rebus: kolimi 'smithy/forge'. *khaḍā* 'circumscribe' (M.); Rebus: *khaḍā* 'nodule (ore), stone' (Marathi)

 *ḍhālako* 'large ingot'. Two short linear strokes: sal 'splinter' Rebus: sal 'workshop'.

 arā 'spokes' Rebus: arā 'brass'.eraka 'nave of wheel' Rebus: eraka 'copper'.

Metals trade catalog on a Mohenjo-daro seal

The glyphic composition denotes a *sodagor*, trader of mineral ores, metal-ware, ingots of bronze, brass, tin and iron.

Broken seal m0304 Mohenjo-daro, reconstructed

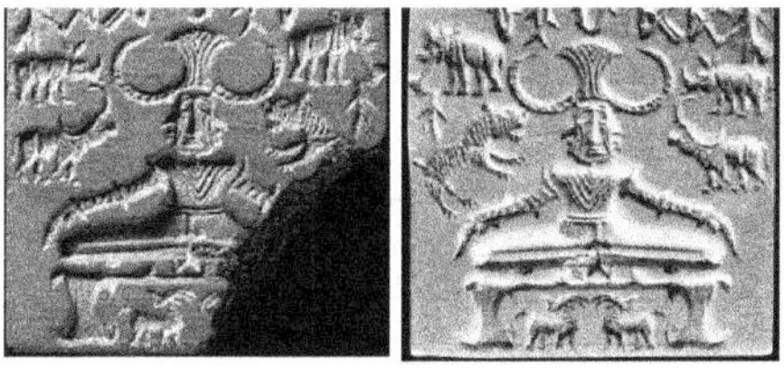

Reconstructed as a seal impression using seal m0304 creating a pair of antelopes and a pair of hayricks below the platform (stool) base (After J. Huntington).

The platform glyphs read rebus:

Decoding a pair: dula दुल । युग्मम् m. a pair, a couple, esp. of two similar things (Rām. 966) (Kashmiri); dol 'likeness, picture, form' (Santali) Rebus: dul 'to cast metal in a mould' (Santali) dul meṛeḍ cast iron (Mundari. Santali)

Kur. kaṇḍō a stool. Malt. kanḍo stool, seat. (DEDR 1179) Rebus: kaṇḍ = a furnace, altar (Santali) H. *lokhaṇḍ* m. 'iron tools, pots and pans'; G. *lokhā̃ḍ* n. 'tools, iron, ironware', the word *khaṇḍ* denotes 'tools, pots and pans and metal-ware'.

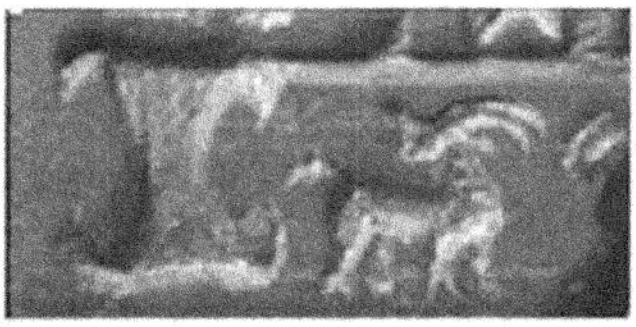

Glyphs in composition of the platform: stool of a pair of hayricks flanking a pair of antelopes: *kā̃ṛ* 'stack of stalks of large millet'(Maithili) Rebus: *khaṇḍ* 'tools, pots and pans and metal-ware' (Gujarati). Vikalpa: kuntam 'haystack' (Te.)(DEDR 1236) Rebus 1: kuṇḍamu 'a pit for receiving and preserving consecrated fire' (Te.) kunda a turner's lathe (Skt.)(CDIAL 3295) Rebus 2: kundan 'pure gold'. kuṇḍamu 'a pit for receiving and preserving consecrated fire' (Telugu)

Ta. takar sheep, ram, goat, male of certain other animals (yāḷi, elephant, shark). பொருநகர் தாக்கற்குப் பேருந் தகைத்து (குறள், 486).Ma. takaran huge, powerful as a man, bear, etc. Ka. tagar, ṭagaru, ṭagara, ṭegaru ram. Tu. tagaru, ṭagarů id.

Te. tagaramu, tagaru id. / Cf. Mar. tagar id. (DEDR 3000). Rebus 1: tagromi 'tin, metal alloy' (Kuwi) takaram tin, white lead, metal sheet, coated with tin (Ta.); tin, tinned iron plate (Ma.); tagarm tin (Ko.); tagara, tamara, tavara id. (Ka.) tamaru, tamara, tavara id. (Ta.): tagaramu, tamaramu, tavaramu id. (Te.); ṭagromi tin metal, alloy (Kuwi); tamara id. (Skt.)(DEDR 3001). trapu tin (AV.); tipu (Pali); tau, taua lead (Pkt.); *tū̃* tin (P.); ṭau zinc, pewter (Or.); tarūaum lead (OG.); *tarvū̃* (G.); tumba lead (Si.)(CDIAL 5992). Rebus 2: damgar 'merchant'.

The pair of antelopes have their heads turned backwards. క్రమ్మర *krammara*. adv. Again. క్రమ్మరిల్లు or క్రమరబడు Same as క్రమ్మరు. krəm back'(Kho.) (CDIAL 3145) Rebus: karmāra 'smith, artisan' (Skt.) kamar 'smith' (Santali) The two antithetical antelopes thus denote: *tagar kamar* 'tin artisan, tin smith, tin merchant.'

The five glyphs on either side of the seated person read rebus:

ib, 'elephant', *dhaṛu* 'body', *ib* 'iron' *dhatu* 'ore'; *kol* 'tiger', *kol* 'iron'.

gaṇḍá 'rhinoceros', kaṇḍ 'fire-altar, furnace', *khaṇḍ* 'tools, pots and pans and metal-ware'

kāṛā 'buffalo' bull (Tamil) *khaḍā* 'nodule (ore), stone' (Marathi). Alternative: கண்டி kaṇṭi buffalo. *gaḍa* 'large stone mould'

Alternaive: Elephant: కరటి [karaṭi] *karaṭi*. [Skt.] n. An elephant. ఏనుగు (Telugu) Rebus: *kharādī* ' turner' (Gujarati)Alternative: ibha (glyph). Rebus: ibbo (merchant of ib 'iron')

Tiger: kola (glyph). Rebus: kol (working in iron, kolami 'smithy/forge')

Leap of tiger: S. kuḏaṇu ' to leap '; L. kuḏaṇ ' to leap, frisk, play '; P. kuddṇā ' to leap ', Ku. kudṇo, N. kudnu, B. kūdā, kõdā; Or. kudibā ' to jump, dance '; Mth. kūdab ' to jump ', Aw. lakh. kūdab, H. kūdnā, OMarw. kūdaï, G. (CDIAL 3411, 3412) Rebus: kunda 'turner' kundār turner (A.)

Alternative: baḍhia = a castrated boar, a hog (Santali) Rebus: baḍhi 'a caste who work both in iron and wood' (Santali) baḍhoe 'a carpenter, worker in wood'; badhoria 'expert in working in wood'(Santali)

Glyphs constituting the seated person composition: Villa+ge chief brass-worker, metals turner (*kundār*).

A person is shown seated in 'penance'.

kamaḍha 'penance' (Pkt.) Rebus: kammaṭi a coiner (Ka.); kampaṭṭam coinage, coin, mint (Ta.) kammaṭa = mint, gold furnace (Te.) Thus, the over-arching message of the inscription composed of many hieroglyphs (of glyphic elements) thus is a description of the offerings of a 'mint or coiner (workshop with a gold furnace)'.

Glyph: kuṇḍī 'crooked buffalo horns' (Lahnda.) Rebus: kuṇḍī = chief of village (Prakrit). The artisan is kundakara— m. 'turner' (Skt.); H. kũderā m. 'one who works a lathe, one who scrapes' (CDIAL 3297).

ḍabe, ḍabea 'large horns, with a sweeping upward curve, applied to buffaloes' (Santali) Rebus: *ḍab*, ḍhimba, ḍhompo 'lump (ingot?)', clot, make a lump or clot, coagulate, fuse, melt together (Santali)

Glyph of a 'clump' between the horns: *kuṇḍa* n. ' clump ' e.g. *darbha-kuṇḍa* — Pāṇ.(CDIAL 3236). Rebus: *kūdar* 'brass-worker, turner'. Vikalpa (alternative): kūdī, kūṭī 'bunch of twigs' (Skt.) Rebus: kuṭhi 'smelter furnace' (Santali)

daṭṭi 'waistband' (Kannada)(DED 2465) Ku. dhaṛo 'piece of cloth', N. dharo, B. dhaṛā; Or. dhaṛā 'rag, loincloth', dhaṛi ' rag '; Mth. dhariā 'child's narrow loincloth'.(CDIAL 6707). Rebus: dhatu '(ore) mineral' (Skt.) G.*karā* n. pl. 'wristlets, bangles'; S. *karāī* f. 'wrist' (CDIAL 2779). Rebus: *khār* खार् 'blacksmith' (Kashmiri)

Rebus reading of glyphic elements of the 'bristled (tiger's mane) face'

There are two glyphic elements denoted on the face.

mũh 'face'; rebus: metal ingot (Santali) mũhã = the quantity of iron produced at one time in a native smelting furnace of the Kolhes; iron produced by the Kolhes and formed like a four-cornered piece a little pointed at each end; mūhā mẽṛhẽt = iron smelted by the Kolhes and formed into an equilateral lump a little pointed at each end; kolhe tehen me~ṛhe~t mūhā akata = the Kolhes have to-day produced pig iron (Santali)

Shoggy hair; tiger's mane. *sodo bodo, sodro bodro* adj. adv. 'rough, hairy, shoggy, hirsute, uneven';*sodo* [Persian. *sodā*, dealing] trade; traffic; merchandise; marketing; a bargain; the purchase or sale of goods; buying and selling; mercantile dealings (Gujarati) sodagor = a merchant, trader;*sodāgor* (P.B.) (Santali.) The face is depicted with bristles of hair, representing a tiger's mane.*cūḍā, cūlā, cūliyā* tiger's mane (Pkt.)(CDIAL 4883).Rebus: cūḷai 'furnace, kiln, funeral pile' (Te.)(CDIAL 4879; DEDR 2709). Thus the composite glyphic composition: 'bristled (tiger's mane) face' is read rebus as: sodagor mũh cūḷa 'furnace (of) ingot merchant'.

mũh 'face; *mũhe* 'ingot' (Santali)

Animal glyphs around the seated person, glyphics: buffalo (*sal*), boar (rhinoceros, *baḍhoe*), elephant (*ib*), tiger (jumping, *kũdā kol*).

The four animal glyphs surrounding the seated person thus connote, rebus: workshop (*sal*), worker in both iron and wood (*baḍhi*), merchant (*ibbho*), turner-smith (*kũdā kol*),

Alternative reading: sal '*bos gaurus*'; rebus: sal 'workshop' (Santali) Vikalpa 1: ran:gā 'buffalo'; ran:ga 'pewter or alloy of tin (ran:ku), lead (nāga) and antimony (añjana)'(Santali) Vikalpa 2: kaṭamā 'bison' (Ta.)(DEDR 1114)

ibha ‘elephant’ (Skt.) Rebus: ibbho 'merchant' (cf.Hemacandra, *Desinamamala*, vaṇika). ib ‘iron’ (Santali) karibha ‘elephant’ (Skt.); rebus: karb ‘iron’ (Ka.)

Decoding the text of the inscription

 Text 2420 on m0304

Line 2 (bottom): ‘body’ glyph. *dhaṛu* ‘body’ (Sindhi) Rebus: *dhatu* ‘ore’ (Santali) Alternative 1: *mēd* ‘body’ (Kur.)(DEDR 5099); *meḍ* ‘iron’ (Ho.) Alternative 2: Glyph: kāḍ 2 काड् । पौरुषम् m. a man's length, the stature of a man (as a measure of length) (Rām. 632, zangan kaḍun kāḍ, to stretch oneself the whole length of one's body. So K. 119). Rebus: kāḍ ‘stone’. Ga. (Oll.) kanḍ, (S.) kanḍu (pl. kanḍkil) stone (DEDR 1298).

Line 1 (top) The first set of three glyphs are read rebus: *dhatu kuṭi(l)* ‘mineral (ore) smelter furnace’ (Santali) *kuṭila, katthīl* = bronze (8 parts copper and 2 parts tin) [The ligature of the ‘body’ glyph reinforces the ligatured glyph ‘claws of crab’ reads rebus: *daṭo* ‘claws’ Rebus: *dhatu* ‘mineral’]

 A खांडा *khāṇḍā* ‘jag’ infixed inside *kanka* ‘rim of jar’ glyph is read as the phrase: *kaṇḍa kanka*, ‘furnace account, scribe’: cf. *kul -- karṇī* m. ‘village accountant’ (Marathi); *karṇikan* id. (Tamil) கணக்கு kaṇakku, n. cf. gaṇaka. [M. kaṇakku] 1. Number, account, reckoning, calculation, computation (Tamil) kaṇḍ ‘fire-altar’ (Santali)

ayo ‘fish’ (Mu.); rebus: ayo ‘metal’ (Gujarati); ayas ‘alloy’ (Sanskrit) *ayo kanka* ‘fish+ rim-of-jar’ rebus: metal (alloy) account (*kaṇakku*) scribe.

kuṭilikā- smith's tongs.(DEDR 2052). *kuṭila, katthīl* = bronze (8 parts copper and 2 parts tin)(CDIAL 3230).

Sign 229. Alternative: sannī, sannhī = pincers, smith's vice (P.) Rebus: seṇi 'guild'.

  'Body' glyph ligatured to 'pincers' glyph is a phonetic determinant of the nature of ore - *kanḍ* 'stone': *dhaṛu* 'body' (Sindhi), *ḍato* 'claws or pincers of crab' (Santali) rebus: dhatu 'ore' (Santali) kāḍ 2 काड् । पौरुषम् m. a man's length, the stature of a man (as a measure of length) (Rām. 632, zangan kaḍun kāḍ, to stretch oneself the whole length of one's body. So K. 119). Rebus: kāḍ 'stone'. Ga. (Oll.) kanḍ, (S.) kanḍu (pl. kanḍkil) stone (DEDR 1298).

ḍato 'claws or pincers (chelae) of crabs'; *ḍaṭom, ḍiṭom* to seize with the claws or pincers, as crabs, scorpions; *ḍaṭkop* = to pinch, nip (only of crabs) (Santali) Vikalpa: erā 'claws'; Rebus: era 'copper'.

Chanhu-daro inscriptions (Selected rebus Meluhha readings)

Inscriptionson both sides of a copper-plate:

  Chanhu-daro40A, 40B 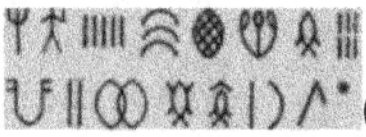 6306

 Glyphs: six (numeral) + ring of hair: आर [āra] A term in the play of इटीदांडू,-- the number six. (Marathi) आर [āra] A tuft or ring of hair on the body. (Marathi) Rebus: āra 'brass'. Alternative: *bhaṭa* 'six' (G.) Rebus: *bhaṭa* 'furnace' (Santali)

ayo 'fish' (Mu.) Rebus: aya '(alloyed) metal' (G.)

kolmo 'three' Rebus: kolami 'smithy, forge' (Telugu) *paṭṭaḍi* 'anvil'.

mõṛē 'five (count)'. Rebus 1: Md. *moḍenī* ' massages, mixes '. (CDIAL 9890) Pa. *mōdanā* -- f. ' blending (?)(CDIAL 10356). Rebus 2: *manḍua* 'booth, shed' meḍ 'body ' (Mu.) Rebus: meḍ 'iron' (Ho.) Alternative: Glyph: 'full stretch of one's arms': kāḍ 2 काड् । पौरुषम् m. a man's length, the stature of a man (as a measure of length) (Rām. 632, zangan kaḍun kāḍ, to stretch oneself the whole length of one's body. So K. 119). Rebus: kāḍ 'stone'. Ga. (Oll.) kanḍ, (S.) kanḍu (pl. kanḍkil) stone (DEDR 1298).

kolom 'sprout' Rebus: kolami 'smithy, forge' (Telugu)

) Pa. kuṭila— 'bent', n. 'bend' Rebus: kuṭila, katthīl = bronze (8 parts copper and 2 parts tin) [cf. āra-kūṭa, 'brass' (Skt.) (CDIAL 3230)

koḍa 'in arithmetic, one' (Santali); rebus: *koḍ.* 'artisan's workshop' (Kuwi)

ayo 'fish' (Mu.); rebus: aya '(alloyed) metal' (G.) Fish + corner, *aya koṇḍa*, 'metal turned, i.e., forged'.

Fish + scales aya ãs (amśu) 'metllic stalks of stone ore. *ãs*, cognate with *añc* 'iron' (Tocharian) may be a determinative of 'iron' as the 'metal'. Hence, the ligatured glyph may connote 'iron or stony metal'.

dula 'pair' (Kashmiri) Rebus: dul 'cast (metal)'.)) Pa. kuṭila— 'bent', n. 'bend' Rebus: kuṭila, katthīl = bronze (8 parts copper and 2 parts tin) [cf. āra-kūṭa, 'brass' (Skt.) (CDIAL 3230). Thus, the pair of 'oval' glyphs read: *dul kuṭila* 'bronze cast metal'.

dula 'pair' Rebus: dul 'cast (metal)'

kanka 'rim (of jar, kaṇḍ)' (Santali) kárṇa— m. 'ear, handle of a vessel' RV., Glyph: kaṇḍ kanka, kaṇḍ karṇaka 'rim of jar' (Santali. Sanskrit). Rebus: furnace account (scribe). khanaka m. one who digs , digger , excavator Rebus karṇaka 'scribe, accountant'.

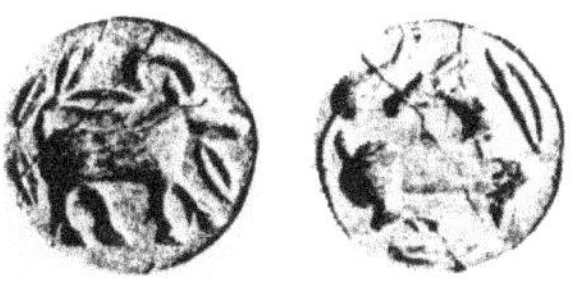

Chanhudaro Seal obverse and reverse. The oval sign of this Jhukar culture seal is comparable to other inscriptions. Fig. 1 and 1a of Plate L. After Mackay, 1943

Chanhudaro Seal obverse and reverse. The oval sign of this Jhukar culture seal is comparable to other inscriptions. Fig. 1 and 1a of Plate L. After Mackay, 1943

Glyph shown together with sting of scorpion on Urseal 1. Rebus: खोट [*khōṭa*] 'ingot, wedge'; A mass of metal (unwrought or of old metal melted down)(Marathi) *khoṭ* 'alloy (Lahnda) Hence खोटसाळ [khōṭasāḷa] *a* (खोट & साळ from शाला) Alloyed--a metal. (Marathi) Bshk. *khoṭ* ' embers ', Tor. *khōr* ' ashes '; Phal. *khūṭo* ' ashes, burning coal '; L. *khoṭā* ' alloyed ', awāṇ. *khoṭā* ' forged '; P. *khoṭ* m. ' base, alloy ' M.*khoṭā* ' alloyed ', (CDIAL 3931)

Glyph: tagaru 'ram' (Tulu) Rebus: tagarm 'tin' (Kota). damgar 'merchant' (Akkadian)

Another antelope is looking back. Hieroglyph of 'looking back' connoting an artisan. Thus the seal shows that the holder of the seal is a artisan and trader in tin ingots: krammaru 'turning back' Rebus: karmāra 'smith, artisan' (Skt.) kamar 'smith' (Santali)

Chanhudaro. Seal impression. Fig. 35 of Plate LII. After Mackay, 1943.  6235 *tagaraka tabernae montana* (Skt.) Rebus: tagara 'tin' (Ka.)

kanka 'rim (of jar, kaṇḍ)' (Santali) kárṇa— m. 'ear, handle of a vessel' RV., Glyph: kaṇḍ kanka, kaṇḍ karṇaka 'rim of jar' (Santali. Sanskrit). Rebus: furnace account (scribe). khanaka m. one who digs , digger , excavator Rebus karṇaka 'scribe, accountant'.

Chanhudaro17a  6122

koḍiyum 'young bull'(G.) koḍe 'young bull' (Telugu) खोंड [khōṇḍa] m A young bull, a bullcalf. Rebus: कोंडण [kōṇḍaṇa] f A fold or pen. (Marathi) koḍ 'workshop' (G.)

kanka 'rim (of jar, kaṇḍ)' (Santali) kárṇa— m. 'ear, handle of a vessel' RV., Glyph: kaṇḍ kanka, kaṇḍ karṇaka 'rim of jar' (Santali. Sanskrit). Rebus: furnace account (scribe). khanaka m. one who digs , digger , excavator Rebus karṇaka 'scribe, accountant'

dhaṛu 'body' (Sindhi) Rebus: *dhatu* 'ore' (Santali) bhaṭa 'warrior' Rebus: bhaṭa 'furnace'. Alternative: meḍ 'body ' (Mu.) Rebus: meḍ 'iron' (Ho.) One horned body. *meḍ* 'body ' (Mu.) Rebus: *meḍ* 'iron' (Ho.) *koḍu* 'horn' Rebus: *koḍ* 'workshop'. Thus, *koḍ meḍ* 'iron workshop'.

Glyph shown as an ingot. Rebus: खोट [*khōṭa*] 'ingot, wedge'; A mass of metal (unwrought or of old metal melted down)(Marathi) *khoṭ* f 'alloy (Lahnda) Hence खोटसाळ [khōṭasāḷa] *a* (खोट & साळ from शाला) Alloyed--a metal. (Marathi) Bshk. *khoṭ* ' embers ', Phal. *khūṭo* ' ashes, burning coal '; L. *khoṭā* ' alloyed ', awāṇ. *khoṭā* ' forged '; P. *khoṭ* m. ' base, alloy ' M.*khoṭā* ' alloyed ', (CDIAL 3931) *Kor.* (O.)

Chanhudaro2  6128

koḍiyum 'young bull'(G.) koḍe 'young bull' (Telugu) खोंड [khōṇḍa] m A young bull, a bullcalf. Rebus: कोंडण [kōṇḍaṇa] f A fold or pen. (Marathi) koḍ 'workshop' (G.)

sangaḍa 'lathe' (G.) Rebus: jaṅgaḍ 'entrusment articles'.

ranku 'liquid measure'. Rebus: ranku 'tin' (Cassiterite)

tagaraka *tabernae montana* (Skt.) Rebus: tagara 'tin' (Ka.)

kanka 'rim (of jar, kaṇḍ)' (Santali) kárṇa— m. 'ear, handle of a vessel' RV., Glyph: kaṇḍ kanka, kaṇḍ karṇaka 'rim of jar' (Santali. Sanskrit). Rebus: furnace account (scribe). khanaka m. one who digs , digger , excavator Rebus: karṇaka 'scribe, accountant'

Chanhudaro15a  6213 Temple workshop hard alloy account

koḍa 'in arithmetic, one' (Santali); rebus: *koḍ*. 'artisan's workshop'

(Kuwi)

guḍḍu, guḍḍi eyeball, egg (Kannada) guḍi 'temple' (Telugu).

khareḍo = a currycomb (Gujarati) Rebus: करडा [karaḍā] Hard from alloy--iron, silver &c. (Marathi)

kanka 'rim (of jar, kaṇḍ)' (Santali) Rebus: karṇaka 'scribe, accountant'.

 6131This is the only text on a large Chanhu-daro seal and occurs together with 'one-horned young bull' glyph.

Kur. kaṇḍō a stool. Malt. kanḍo stool, seat. (DEDR 1179) Rebus: kaṇḍ = a furnace, altar (Santali.)

Mth.*ḍagar* ' road ', H. *ḍagar* f., *ḍagrā* m., G. *ḍagar* f. (CDIAL 5523) Rebus: damgar 'merchant' (Akkadian) Thus, together the composite glyph reads: *kaṇḍ damgar* 'furnace (of) merchant'.

Chanhudaro21a  6209 Fish + scales aya ãs (amśu) 'metllic stalks of stone ore. *ãs*, cognate with *añc* 'iron' (Tocharian) may be a determinative of 'iron' as the 'metal'. Hence, the ligatured glyph may connote 'iron or stony metal'.

kanka 'rim (of jar, kaṇḍ)' (Santali) kárṇa— m. 'ear, handle of a vessel' RV., Glyph: kaṇḍ kanka, kaṇḍ karṇaka 'rim of jar' (Santali. Sanskrit). Rebus: furnace account (scribe). khanaka m. one who digs , digger , excavator Rebus karṇaka 'scribe, accountant'

kuṭi 'water-carrier (woman)' (Telugu); rebus: *kuṭhi* 'furnace, smelter' (Santali)

Thus, together, the composite glyph reads: *kuṭi kanka* 'furnace scribe'.

Pict-40 Ox-antelope with a long tail; a trough in front.  6121

miṇḍāl markhor (Tor.wali) *meḍho* a ram, a sheep (G.)(CDIAL

10120)

Rebus: *meṛh* 'helper of merchant'. *loa* 'ficus religiosa' Rebus: *loh* 'copper'. Rim-of-jar glyph: kanka 'scribe, accountant'. The device in front: *sangaḍa* 'lathe' Rebus: jaṅgaḍ 'entrusment articles' (Gujarati).

Seal Bull ID 73. *ḍabu* 'an iron spoon' (Santali) Rebus: *ḍab, ḍhimba, ḍhompo* 'lump (ingot?)' (Munda) The pairing (duplicating) glyph may denote a pair of bangles: *sangaḍa* 'pair'. *karā* n. pl. 'wristlets, bangles' (Gujarati) *karāī* f. 'wrist' (Sindhi)(CDIAL 2779). Rebus: khār खार् 'blacksmith' (Kashmiri) Alternative: *dula* 'pair' Rebus: *dul* 'cast (metal)'. खोट [*khōṭa*] 'ingot'. kolmo 'three' Rebus: kolami 'smithy/forge'. Rim-of-jar glyph: *kanka* 'scribe, accountant'. Thus, blacksmith ingot account (rendered to) workshop.

Regular and upside-down views of dagger chape 539-333 BCE Iran Bone H. 30 cm; W. 45 cm; D. 10 cm. The bone is carved in slight relief. Antoine-Barthélémy Clot Bey collection N 8336 (MN 1376). A lion devours an ibex. *aryeh* 'lion' Rebus: *arā* 'brass'.

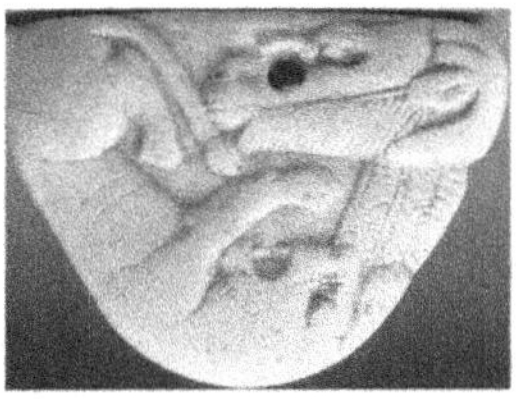

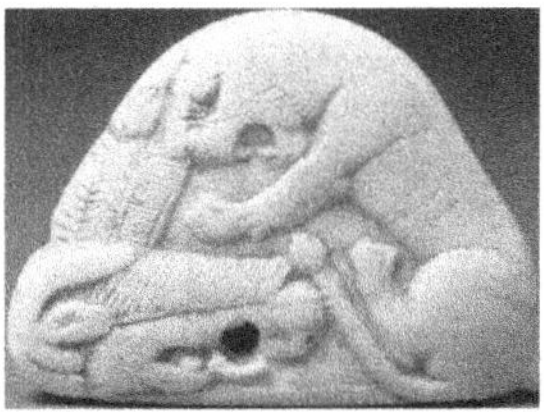

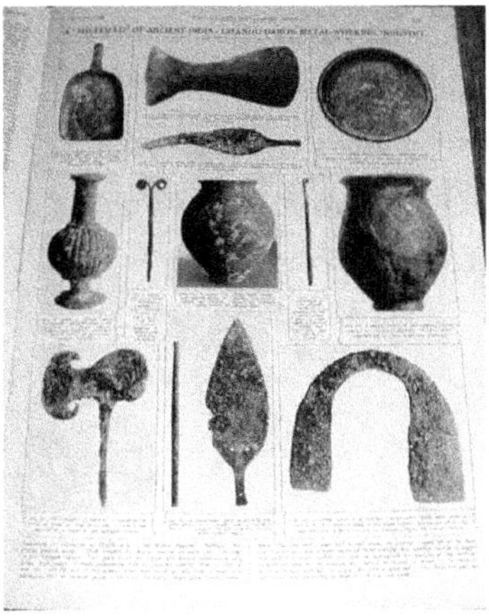

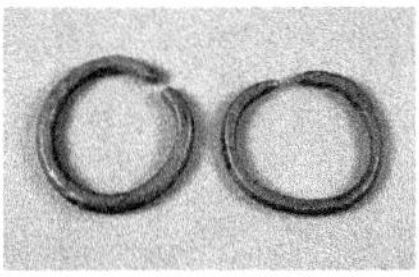

miṇḍāl markhor (Tor.wali) *meḍho* a ram, a sheep (G.)(CDIAL 10120) Rebus: *meḍh* 'helper of merchant' (Gujarati) *meḍ* iron (Ho.) *meṛed-bica* = iron stone ore, in contrast to bali-bica, iron sand ore (Munda) The hieroglyphs on the dagger chape thus connote: merchant in brass and iron.

A 'Sheffield of Ancient India': Chanhu-Daro's Metal working Industry. Illustrated London News 1936 – November 21st, p.909. 10 x photos of copper knives, spears , razors, axes and dishes.

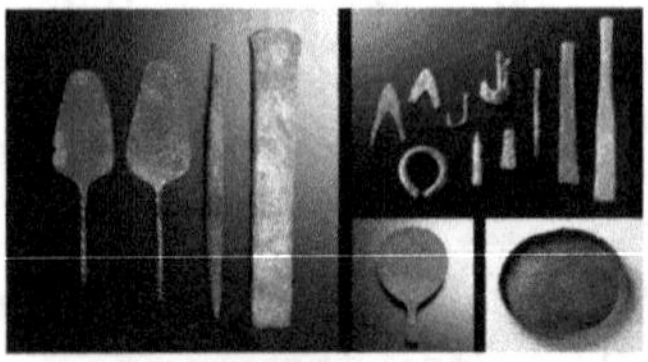

Harappans made knives, weapons, bowls and figures from bronze.

Two copper/bronze bangles, one from Harappa and the other from Mohenjo-daro. The bangles were made from a round hammered rod bent in a full circle. The space between the ends of the bangle would be pried apart to slip it over the wrist. Dimensions of left bangle: 6 cm diameter, 0.73 cm thickness.[71]

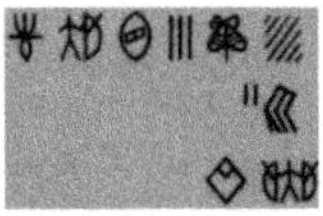

That a scribe of a smithy was involved in making the seals is evidenced by a Chanhudaro seal.

Chanhudaro Seal 023 Text 6402. The text reading provided by Mahadevan can be used as a reference to the corpus concordance of variant glyphs. A broad-axe is shown as a hieroglyph. *tagara* 'ram' Rebus: *damgar* 'merchant'. The sel thus shows a merchant of copper (alloy) axe. kāmaṭhum = a bow; kāmaḍī, kāmaḍum = a chip of bamboo (G.) kāmaṭhiyo a bowman; an archer (Sanskrit) Rebus: kammaṭa = portable furnace (Te.) kampaṭṭam coiner, mint (Tamil) Glyph of two bows in two hands of the archer: dula 'two' Rebus: dul 'cast (metal)'. *kāḍ* 2 काड् a man's length, the stature of a man (as a measure of length); rebus*: kāḍ* 'stone'; Ga. (Oll.) *kanḍ* , (S.) *kanḍu (pl. kanḍkil)* id.

The glyphic composition is a combination of an 'ingot' ligatured to 'ingot smithy'

'seedling: *kolmo* 'seeding, rice-plant' (Munda) rebus: *kolami* 'smithy'; (Telugu) goṭa 'numerative particle' (Maithili) Rebus: *khoṭ* f 'alloy (Lahnda) Hence खोटसाळ [khōṭasāḷa] *a* (खोट & साळ from शाला) Alloyed--a metal. (Marathi) खोट [*khōṭa*] 'ingot, wedge'; A mass of metal (unwrought or of old metal melted down). (Marathi)Alternative: *mũh* ' ingot' (Santali).

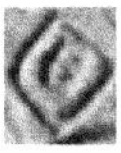

khoṇḍ square (Santali) Rebus: *kõdā* ' to turn in a lathe ' (Bengali) **कोंद** *kōnda* 'engraver, lapidary setting or infixing gems' (Marathi) **कोंड** [*kōṇḍa*] A circular hamlet; a division of a **मौजा** or village, composed generally of the huts of one caste (possibly, a turner's hamlet). Ku. koṭho 'large square house' Rebus: Md. koṛāru 'storehouse'. Infixed is sal 'splinter' Rebus: sal 'workshop'.

pasaramu, pasalamu 'an animal, a beast, a brute, quadruped' (Telugu) Rebus: *pasra* 'smithy' (Santali);

Glyph: 'splinter' sal 'splinter'. Rebus: sal 'artisan's workshop'. खांडा [khāṇḍā] *m* A jag, notch, or indentation (as upon the edge of a tool or weapon. Rebus: *kāṇḍa* 'tools, pots and pans and metal-ware'.

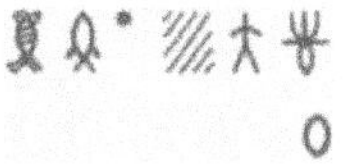

urseal159845 Ur [The first sign looks like an animal with a long tail – as seen from the back and may have been the model for the orthography of Sign 51 as noted in Mahadevan corpus].

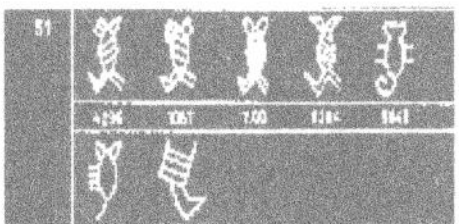

Variants of Glyph 51. Many allographs of glyph 51 seek to emhasise the 'sting' of the scorpion. Seal impression; UPenn; steatite; bull below a scorpion; dia. 2.4cm.; Gadd, PBA 18 (1932), p. 13, Pl. III, no. 15; Legrain, MJ (1929), p. 306, pl. XLI, no. 119; found at Ur in the cemetery area, in a ruined grave .9 metres from the surface, together with a pair of gold ear-rings of the double-crescent type and long beads of steatite and carnelian, two of gilt copper, and others of lapis-lazuli, carnelian, and banded sard. The first sign to the left has the form of a flower or perhaps an animal's skin with curly tail; there is a round spot upon the bull's back.

Glyph of musk-rat. Or, is it glyph of scorpion? If it denotes a scorpion, some rebus readings are: *koṇḍi* 'sting of scorpion'; rebus: kundār turner (Assamese)

Glyph *Ka. koṇḍi* the sting of a scorpion. *Tu. koṇḍi* a sting. *Te. koṇḍi* the sting of a scorpion.(DEDR 2080).

Rebus: kuṇḍī = chief of village. kuṇḍi-a = village headman; leader of a village (Prakrit) i.e. śreṇi jeṭṭha chief of metal-worker guild. khŏḍ m. 'pit', khōḍü f. 'small pit' (Kashmiri. CDIAL 3947), kuṭhi 'smelter furnace' (Mu.) kuṇḍamu 'a pit for receiving and preserving consecrated fire' (Te.) kundār turner (A.); kũdār, kũdāri (B.); kundāru (Or.); kundau to turn on a lathe, to carve, to chase; kundau dhiri = a hewn stone; kundau murhut = a graven image (Santali)

If the orthography denotes a mouse, the rebus readings are: suṇḍa 'musk-rat' (Kannada) Rebus: *cundakāra* a turner J vi.339 (Pali)

loha-kāra (metalsmith).

Glyph 'leaf, petal': A 'leaf' glyph has to be distinguished from a 'petals' glyph because the leaf orthography is clearly representative of the *ficus* genus which attains sacredness in later historical periods in the Indian linguistic area. Allograph: *kamaḍha* 'ficus religiosa' (Skt.) *kamaṛkom* 'ficus' (Santali) Rebus: *kampaṭṭam* coiner, mint (Tamil) *kammaṭa* =

portable furnace for melting precious metals (Telugu) Glyph: *loa* = a species of fig tree, ficus glomerata, the fruit of ficus glomerata (Santali) Rebus: *lo* 'iron' (Assamese, Bengali); *loa* 'iron' (Gypsy) *lauha* = made of copper or iron (Gr.S'r.); metal, iron (Skt.) *loha-kāra* a metal worker, coppersmith, blacksmith Miln 331 (Pali) Glyph 'fig, ficus glomerata': మేడి [mēḍi] *mēḍi.* [Tel.] అత్తి, ఉదుంబరము. మేడిపండు the fruit of this tree. *Ka.* mēḍi glomerous fig tree, *Ficus racemosa*; opposite-leaved fig tree, *F. oppositifolia. Te.* mēḍi *F. glomerata. Kol.* (Kin.) mēṛi id. [*F. glomerata* Roxb. = *F. racemosa* Wall.](DEDR 5090). Rebus: *meḍ* 'iron' (Ho.)

Moulded tablets from Trench 11 Harappa (Kenoyer); m1186; m488C adorant with 'scarf'; markhor in front, with rings (or neck-bands, scarves) on neck. Ficus leaves flanking the horned person.

kolmo 'three' Rebus: kolami 'smithy, forge'.

kundau, kundhi corner (Santali) *kuṇḍa* corner (S.); *kūṭ* corner, side (P.)(CDIAL 3898). *khoṇḍ* square (Santali) Rebus 1: *kund* lathe (A.); *kundiba* to turn and smooth in a lathe (A.); *kũd* lathe (B.); *kũdā, kõdā* to turn in a lathe (B.); *kūnda* lathe (Or.); *kũdibā, kūdibā* to turn (Or. > *kũd* lathe (Kur.); *kund* brassfounder's lathe (Bi.); *kunnā* to shape on a lathe (H.); *kuniyā* turner (H.); *kunwā* turner (H.)(CDIAL 3295). kundār turner (A.) kũdār, kũdāri (B.); kundāru (Or.); kundau to turn on a lathe, to carve, to chase; *kundau dhiri* = a hewn stone; kundau murhut = a graven image (Santali) Rebus 2: *khũṭ* 'community, guild' (Mundari) कोंद *kōnda* 'engraver, lapidary setting or infixing gems' (Marathi)

Pict-40 Ox-antelope with a long tail; a trough in front. Chanhudaro  6121

koḍiyum 'heifer'(G.) koḍe 'heifer' (Telugu) खोंड [khōṇḍa] m A young bull, a bullcalf. Rebus: कोंडण [kōṇḍaṇa] f A fold or pen. (Marathi) koḍ 'workshop' (G.) কুঁদন, কোঁদন [kuṅdana, kōṅdana] n act of turning (a thing) on a lathe; act of carving (Bengali)

sangaḍa 'lathe' (G.) Rebus: jaṅgaḍ 'entrusment articles'.

kanka 'rim (of jar, kaṇḍ)' (Santali) kárṇa— m. 'ear, handle of a vessel' RV., Glyph: kaṇḍ kanka, kaṇḍ karṇaka 'rim of jar' (Santali. Sanskrit). Rebus: furnace account (scribe). khanaka m. one who digs , digger , excavator Rebus karṇaka 'scribe, accountant'

Kalibangan 067 Antelope with long tail + two glyphs of ficus religiosa. *mẽḍha* 'antelope'; rebus: *meḍ* 'iron' (Mu.) Alternative: *tagara* 'antelope' Rebus: *tagara* 'tin'; *damgar* 'merchant'. *loa* 'fig leaf' (Santali): Rebus: *lo* 'iron' (Assamese, Bengali); *loa* 'iron' (Gypsy) Allograph: *lo* = nine (Santali); *no* = nine (B.) *on-patu* = nine (Ta.)

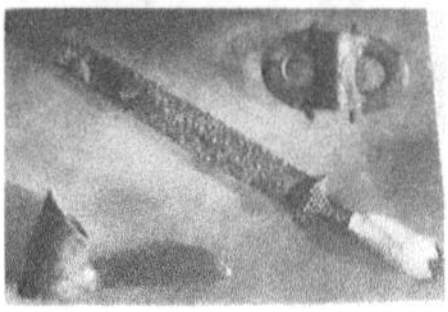

M0592 copper plate. Double-axe hieroglyph. Compare with double-axe (together with axe and dagger) of finds in a Ur grave.[72]

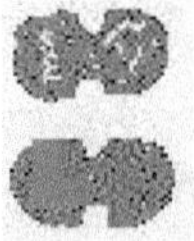

4407 Field Symbol 129

h818At

h818Bt

4376

h817At

h817Bt

h971Ait

h971Bit

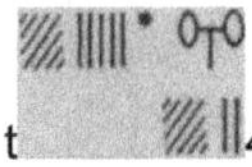
4557

h232A

h232B tablet in bas relief

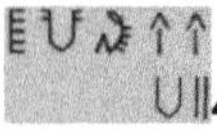
4368 Harappa tablets in the shape of double-axe

tabar 'a broad axe' (Punjabi). Rebus: *tam(b)ra* 'copper'.

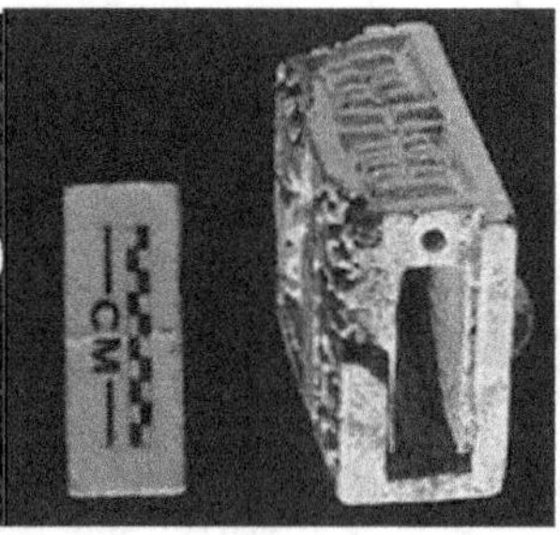

Gola Dhoro. Socketed seal with a sliding lid. Inscribed on three sides. This socketed seal (GD1) was discovered in the gateway of the city wall at Gola Dhoro (Bagasra).[73] The socket might have held a lid to enclose a tablet containing some other message(s) to complete the metalware catalog created by the inscriptions on three sides of the uniquely fashioned seal. *sangaḍa* 'lathe, furnace'. Rebus: *jangad* 'entrustment note' (Gujarati)

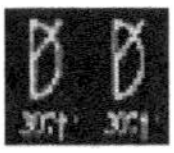

Two glyphs of bow+arrow are inscribed on the seal. These compare with the bow+arrow held by archer on Chanhudaro seal 023. kāmaṭhum = a bow; kāmaḍī, kāmaḍum = a chip of bamboo (G.) kāmaṭhiyo a bowman; an archer (Sanskrit) Rebus: kammaṭa = portable furnace (Te.) kampaṭṭam coiner, mint (Tamil) Glyph of two bows in two hands of the archer: Glyph: *dol* 'likeness, picture, form' dula दुल । युग्मम् m. a pair, a couple, esp. of two similar things (Kashmiri Rām. 966). ḍol 'the shaft of an arrow, an arrow' (Santali) Rebus: dul meṛeḍ cast iron (Mundari. Santali) *dul* 'to cast metal in a mould' (Santali) pasra meṛed, pasāra meṛed = syn. of koṭe meṛed = forged iron, in contrast to dul meṛed, cast iron (Mundari)

kundau, kundhi corner (Santali) *kuṇḍa* corner (S.); *kūṭ* corner, side (P.)(CDIAL 3898). *khoṇḍ* square (Santali) Rebus *kund* lathe (A.) sal "stake, spike, splinter, thorn, difficulty" (H.) Rebus: sal 'workshop' (Santali) kundau, *kundhi* corner (Santali) *kuṇḍa* corner (S.)*: khoṇḍ* square (Santali) Rebus: *kũd* ' lathe '.

Allograph: *Ka.* kunda a pillar of bricks, etc. *Tu.* kunda pillar, post. *Te.* kunda id. *Malt.* kunda block, log. ? Cf. Ta. kantu pillar, post.(DEDR 1723). *கற்கந்து kaṟ-kantu* , *n.* < கல் +. Stone pillar; கற்றூண். கற்கந்தும் எய்ப்போத்தும் . . . அனை யார் (இறை. 2, உரை, 27).

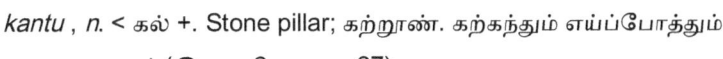

bhaṭa 'warrior' Rebus: baṭa = kiln (Santali); baṭa = a kind of iron (G.)

khaḍā 'circumscribe' (M.); Rebs: khaḍā 'nodule (ore), stone' (M.) ayo 'fish'; rebus: ayas 'metal, iron' (Pan.Skt.) aḍaren, ḍaren lid, cover (Santali) Rebus: aduru 'native metal' (Ka.)

Alternative: Woṭ. šen ' roof ', Bshk. šan, Phal. šān(AO xviii 251) Rebus: seṇi (f.) [Class. Sk. śreṇi in meaning "guild"; Vedic= row] Thus, the glyphic composition reads: stone-metal-guild khaḍā ayas seṇi (glyphic: circumscribe+fish+roof).

GD3?

??

Gola-Dhoro seal. kolom 'sprout' Rebus: kolami 'smithy, forge'. kolmo 'three' Rebus: kolami 'smithy, forge'. An alternative reading could be: tagaraka 'tabernae montana' Rebus: tagaram 'tin'. Thus, the inscription may read: tagaram kolami 'tin smithy/forge'.

Gola Dhoro (Bagasra) GD5 seal. Rebus readings of inscription:

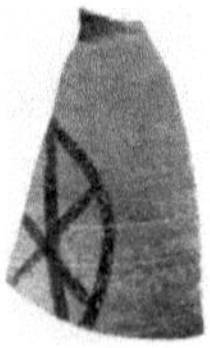 

Surkotada 4  9094

Glhyph 391 Glyph: nave of wheel; Rebus: Molten cast copper

GD5

era, er-a = eraka = ?nave; erakōlu = the iron axle of a carriage (Ka.M.); cf. irasu (Kannada) [Note Sign 391 and its ligatures Signs 392 and 393 may

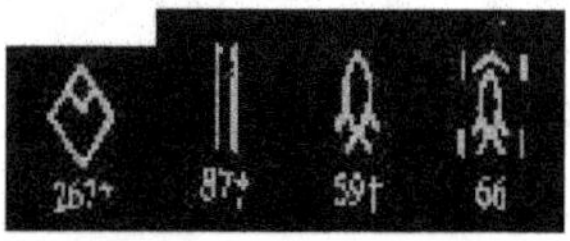

connote a spoked-wheel, nave of the wheel through which the axle passes; cf. arā, spoke] eraka, era, er-a = syn. erka, copper, weapons. Rebus: er-r-a = red; eraka = copper (Ka.) erka = ekke (Tbh. of arka) aka (Tbh. of arka) copper (metal); crystal (Kannada) eraka, er-aka = any metal infusion (Ka.Tu.); erako molten cast (Tulu) agasāle, agasāli, agasālavāḍu = a goldsmith (Telugu) cf. eruvai = copper (Tamil)

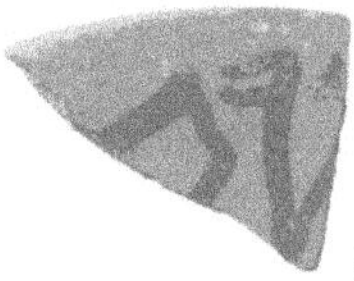 Surkotada3c  9093  Glyph:

rhombus. *khoṇḍ* square (Santali) Rebus: *kõdā* 'to turn in a lathe' (Bengali) कोंद *kōnda* 'engraver, lapidary setting or infixing gems' (Marathi)

Glyph composition: rim of jar + notch, jag खांडा [khāṇḍā] *m* A jag, notch, or indentation (as upon the edge of a tool or weapon).

(Marathi) Rebus: *khāṇḍā* 'tools, pots and pans, metal-ware'. *kaṇḍa kanka* 'rim of jar' (Santali)*kaṇḍa* 'furnace, fire-altar' (Santali);

khanaka 'miner' karNaka 'scribe' (Skt.) Thus the composite glyph reads: *kanka khāṇḍā* 'scribe metal tool, pots and pans, metalware'.

kundau, *kundhi* corner (Santali) *kuṇḍa* corner (S.)*: khoṇḍ* square (Santali) *khuṇṭa2 ' corner '. 2. *kuṇṭa -- 2. [Cf. *khōñca --] 1. Phal. *khun* ' corner '; H. *khũṭ* m. ' corner, direction ' (→ P. *khũṭ* f. ' corner, side '); G. *khũṭrī* f. ' angle '. <-> X kōṇa -- : G. *khuṇ* f., *khū̃ṇɔ* m. ' corner '. 2. S. *kuṇḍa* f. ' corner '; P. *kũṭ* f. ' corner, side ' (← H.).(CDIAL 3898).

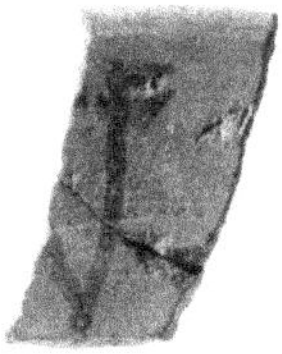 Surkotada 6  9095

Glyph composition: rim of jar + notch, jag खांडा [khāṇḍā] *m* A jag, notch, or indentation (as upon the edge of a tool or weapon).

 (Marathi) Rebus: *khāṇḍā* 'tools, pots and pans, metal-ware'.

khaḍā 'circumscribe' (M.); Rebs: *khaḍā* 'nodule (ore), stone'

 (M.) *kolmo* 'paddy plant' (Santali); Rebus:*kolimi* 'smithy, forge' (Te.) *kolom* = cutting, graft; to graft, engraft, prune; kolma hoṛo = a variety

of the paddy plant (Desi)(Santali.) Thus the glyph comosition reads: *khaḍā kolimi* 'ore (mineral) smithy/forge'.

Metal blade/ploughshare smithy/forge

kolmo 'paddy plant' Rebus: kolimi 'smithy, forge'.

phāla 'board' Rebus: 'ploughshare'.

Thus the pair of glyphs read: *phāl kolimi* 'metal blade/ploughshare smithy/forge'.

kaṇḍa kanka 'rim of jar' (Santali) *kaṇḍa* 'furnace, fire-altar' (Santali); *khanaka* 'miner' karNaka 'scribe' (Skt.)
Surkotada 2 9092 *dhātu* 'mineral' + *dul ḍhālako* 'cast mineral ingot'+ *kanka khāṇḍā* scribe -- 'tools, pots and pans, metal-ware'+ *khaḍā kolimi* 'ore (mineral) smithy/forge'+ *phāl kolimi* 'metal blade/ploughshare smithy/forge'+ *kaṇḍa kanka* 'furnace, fire-altar' ; khanaka 'miner' *karṇaka* 'scribe'.

ḍato = claws of crab (Santali) ḍato 'claws or pincers (chelae) of crabs'; ḍaṭom,

ḍiṭom to seize with the claws or pincers, as crabs, scorpions; ḍaṭkop = to pinch, nip (only of crabs) (Santali) Rebus: dhātu = mineral (Skt.)

ḍhālako = a large metal ingot (G.) *ḍhālakī* = a metal heated and poured into a mould; a solid piece of metal; an ingot (G.) dula 'pair' Rebus: dul 'cast (metal)' Thus the composite glyph of claws of crab + pair of ingots read: *dul ḍhālako* 'cast mineral ingot'.

Surkotada1  9091

eraka 'nave' Rebus: erka 'copper, weapons'

Glyph: 'archer': kamāṭhiyo = archer; kāmaṭhum = a bow; kāmaḍ, kāmaḍum = a chip of bamboo (G.) kāmaṭhiyo a bowman; an archer (Sanskrit) Rebus: kammaṭi a coiner (Ka.); kampaṭṭam coinage, coin, mint (Ta.) kammaṭa = mint, gold furnace (Te.)

kolmo 'paddy plant' (Santali); Rebus: *kolimi* 'smithy, forge' (Te.) *kolom* = cutting, graft; to graft, engraft, prune; kolma hoṛo = a variety of the paddy plant (Desi)(Santali.) + 'splinter' glyph: sal 'splinter' Rebus: sal 'workshop'. Thus, the pair of glyphs read: *kolimi sal* 'smithy/forge workshop'.

gaṇḍa 'four' (Santali); rebus: *kaṇḍ* fire-altar, furnace' (Santali) + *kolmo* 'paddy plant' (Santali); Rebus: *kolimi* 'smithy, forge' (Te.). Together, the pair of glyphs read: *kaṇḍ kolimi* smithy/forge (with) fire-altar.

The entire inscription Text 9091 on Surkotada1 Seal thus reads: *eraka* 'copper molten cast' + *kammaṭa* 'mint' + *kolimi sal* 'smithy/forge workshop' + *kaṇḍ kolimi* smithy/forge (with) fire-altar.

The invention of writing corresponded to the economical needs of a society at a time when the development of cities increased number of exchanges and transactions. This form of writing was inscribed on a soft material, clay and incised into steatite and other stones. The first tablets date from the Late Uruk period, in Mesopotamia, and the Proto-Elamite period in Iran. They often bear the mark of one or two cylinder seals, proof that an administrative check or an agreement between two parties had taken place.

A dominant feature which characterizes hieroglyphic compositions of Ancient Near East is the action of animals rushing forward to attack or beat or frisking animals. There is a Meluhha hieroglyph read rebus which explains this feature as the work of a metal turner working in a forge/smithy:

kuṅdana, kōṅdana 'attack, leap' Rebus: *kuṅdana, kōṅdana* n act of turning (a thing) on a lathe; act of carving (Bengali)

Meluhha – pioneers in brass and makers of tin and zinc alloys

[quote] "...the earliest brass in the world was in the Harappan site of Lothal and then in the early PGW site of Atranjikhera. The primacy of zinc metallurgy in India is established by three kinds of evidences: (a) second millennium BCE radiocarbon dating of zinc ore mine in Southern Rajasthan, (b) fourth century BCE brass vase in Taxila assaying 34% zinc, and (c) second century AD literature of Nagarjuna describing distillation of zinc…(paper) details…large scale zinc manufacture in medieval Zawar and the unique phenomenon of a technology transfer from India to the western world…The earliest method of making brass was possibly the cementation process in which finely divided copper fragments were intimately mixed with roasted zinc ore (oxide) and reducing agent, such as charcoal, and heated to 1000 degrees C in a sealed crucible. Zinc vapour formed dissolved into the copper fragments yielding a poor quality brazz, zinc percentage of which could not be easily controlled. Fusion of zinc with copper increases the strength, hardness and toughness of the latter. When the alloy is composed of 10-18% zinc, it has a pleasing golden yellow colour. It can also take very high polish and literally glitter like gold. For this property, brass has been widely used for casting statuary, covering temple roofs, fabricating vessels, etc…Lothal (2200-1500 BCE) showed one highly oxidized antiquity (No. 4189), which assayed 70.7# copper, 6.04# zinc, 0.9% Fe and 6.04% acid-soluble component (probably carbonate, a product of atmospheric corrosion)…Most of the brass samples in ancient India contained variable proportions of Zn, Sn and Pb…During the Harappan era, copper used to be alloyed with tin and arsenic; since these were scarce commodities, alternative alloying elements had to be looked for. Artisans in the Rajasthan-Gujarat region might have stumbled on to zinc ore deposit as a new source of alloying element…(Taxila vase BM 215-284)…dated to the 4th century BCE. This brass sample contains 34.34% zinc, 4.25% Sn, 3.0% Pb, 1.77% and 0.4% nickel. This is very strong evidence for the availability of metallic sinc in the 4th century BCE. Possibly India was the first to make this metal zinc (rasaka) by the distillation

process, as practiced for other metal mercury (rasa)...The pseudo-Aristotelian work, 'On marvelous things heard' mentioned: "They also say that amongst the Indians the bronze is so bright, clean and free from corrosion that it is indistinguishable from gold, but that amongst the cups of Darius there is a considerable number that could not be distinguished from gold or bronze except by color."...The Indian emphasis was on the 'gold-like' brass and not on the zinc metal...The discovery of three important hoards of metallic art objects at Mahudi of north Gujarat, Lilvadeva (north-east) and Akota of central Gujarat, dated between 6th and 11th centuries AD, proved that the artisans there had developed four varieties of alloys: (a) bronze, (b) zinc-bronze, (c) lead brass, and (d) conventional brass...The technical term ārakūṭa for brass persisted through centuries and we find this mentioned in the 4th century AD Jaina text Angavijja (as hārakūḍa) and also in Amarakośa (450 AD)...Pliny mentioned the Latin term aurichalcum (golden copper), made in India from cadmia, identified as calamine or the zinc ore. Samuel Beal suggested that the name cadmia came from Calamina, a port at the mouth of the Indus, which negotiated the export of the ore or the alloy of zinc. Ball, however, suggested that the port was Calliana or Kalyan near Bombay. The sixth century AD traveler Sopater had mentioned Calliana exporting brass...The earliest reference to zinc as a metl is found in Nagarjuna's Rasa-Ratnākara. In one passage (RR 3) it was mentioned: "What wonder is that rasaka (zinc or zinc ore) roasted with three parts of śulva (copper) converts the latter into gold". Actually, this was gold-coloured 25% zinc-brass, also known as pīta-tāla (pitala) or yellow alloy."...jast (derived from Sanskrit jaśada or zinc)...On brass and zinc metallurgy, the primacy of India in the ancient and medieval world is now beyond any dispute." [unquote][74]

Advancement from tokens/bullae to incised speech

The continued use of hieroglyphs of Indus writing together with cuneiform texts is a characteristic feature of the evolution of writing in ancient Near East as it progressed from the use of tokens and bullae to the use of glyphs to denote many metallurgical categories. A method of rebus readings evidenced for Narmer palette in Egypt applied to the Indus writing glyphs reveals Meluhha (mleccha) substrate lexemes from Indian *sprachbund*.

Tokens of Susa evolve into hieroglyphic Indus writing in ancient Near East

Shape of a token representing one ingot of metal, Susa, Iran, ca. 3300 BCE.

Complex tokens representing (from r. to l.) – (Top row) one sheep, one jar of oil, one ingot of metal, one garment; (Bottom row) one garment, ?, one honeycomb. Musee du Louvre.

The development of the power of abstraction as illustrated by the evolution of counting in the ancient Near East. Tokens indicates that counting was first done concretely in one-to-one correspondence. The claytokens, that appeared in the Near East about 7500 BC, abstracted the goods they represented. For example a cone abstracted a measure of grain. About 3300 BC, when tokens were kept in envelopes, markings on envelopes abstracted the tokens held inside. Abstract numbers are the culmination of the process, following the invention of writing. 'For example, the number of token shapes which was limited to about 12 around 7500 BC, increased to some 350 around 3500 BC, when urban workshops started contributing to the redistribution economy. Some of the new tokens stood for raw materials such as wool and metal while others represented finished products, among them textiles, garments, jewelry, bread, beer and honey.[75]

The token shape used for 'metal' continues to be used as a hieroglyph on Indus writing.

Source: "Catalogue de l'exposition: LUT/xabis 'Shahdad'- Premier Symposium Annuel de la recherche Archéologique en Iran, Festival de la Culture et des arts, 1972," and published in Tehran. The text on p. 20 (French portion of the publication) identifies the bulla (No. 54 in the catalogue) as "Boule en terre cuite rouge creuse qui contient des cailloux. Décor estampé. Diam: 6 cm, Xabis "Shahdad" Kerman. 2ème moité du IV mill. av. J.-C. No. F.258/48."

Corpora of inscriptions

Indus writing heralds a major advance in bronze-age, expanding the accounting documentation for metalware and metallurgical processing categories.

Indus Writing hieroglyphs compiled in corpora (of about 7000 inscriptions[76]), comprise over 100 'pictorial motifs' and over 400 'signs'[77] in vogue in ancient Near East bronze-age.

The evidence of the corpora, together with the lexemes of Indian *sprachbund* provide a method for validating the rebus readings of hundreds of hieroglyphs to categorise and account for work-in-process transactions from furnace or smelter to the forge (on workers' platforms) and for compiling metalware/stoneware catalogs of minerals/stones used, metals and alloys smelted or forged, to document on seals with one-horned young bull + standard device (*sangaḍa*), for example as *jangad* transactions (consignments couriered on approval basis) from workshops to merchants/intermediary agents in Meluhha settlements along the Persian Gulf, Elam and Sumer/Mesopotamia.

Hundreds of hieroglyphs are read rebus using the substrate lexemes of Indian *sprachbund* to decipher the inscriptions in Indus writing.

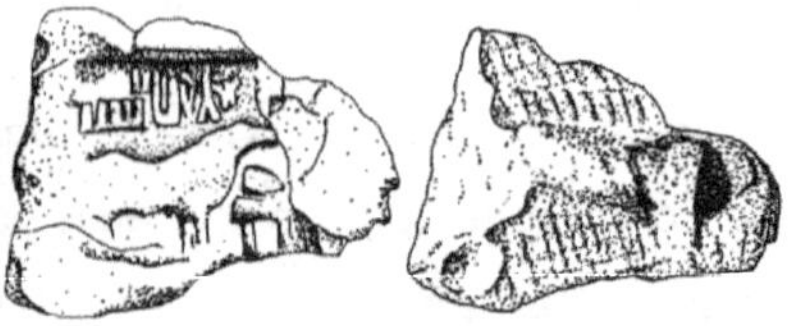

"…an imprint of (Indus (Sarasvati-Sindhu)) seal upon the fragment of a clay label from a bale of cloth had also been published by Father Scheil[78] and this was said to come from the site of Umma, the neighbor city of Lagash…(Gadd, 1932, pp.3-32.)Sealing. Umma. Text 9811  Impression of a seal from Umma. One-hornd young bull. Scheil 1925. Indicative of the receipt of goods from the Sarasvati-Sindhu and of the possible presence of Indus traders in Mesopotamia. Tell Asmar seals, together with ceramics, knobbed ware, etched beads and kidney shaped inlay of bone provide supporting evidence for this possibility.

Mohenjo-daro seal. m0301 baradh 'bull' (Gujarati); baddi (Nahali)

Sign 48: baraḍo = spine, the backbone, back (Gujarati)

Glyph: baraḍo = spine; backbone; the back; baraḍo thābaḍavo = lit. to strike on the backbone or back; hence, to encourage; baraḍo bhāre thato = lit. to have a painful backbone, i.e. to do something which will call for a severe beating (Gujarat) man.uk.o a single vertebra of the back (G.)

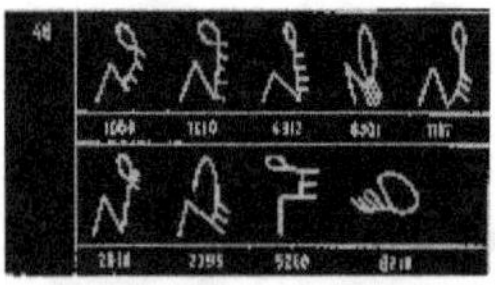

Rebus: baraḍo (vardhaki). Rebus: baraḍo, vardhaka 'carpenter, mason' (Santali. Sanskrit) *baḍhi* 'a caste who work both in iron and wood' (Santali) barduga = a man of acquirements, a proficient man (Ka.) Rebus: bharatiyo = a caster of metals, a brazier; bharatar, bharatal, bharatal. = moulded; an article made in a mould (G.) bharata = casting metals in moulds; bharavum =

to fill in; to put in; to pour into (Gujarat) bhart = a mixed metal of copper and lead; bhartīyā = a barzier, worker in metal; bhaṭ, bhrāṣṭra = oven, furnace (Skt.)

maruḍiyo = one who makes and sells wristlets, and puts wristlets on the wrists of women (Gujarat) maraḍa = twisting; a twist; a turn; marad.avum = to twist, to turn; maraḍāvum = to bend; maroḍa = a twist, a turn; writhing, a bend; maroḍavum = to writhe, to twist, to contort; to bend (Gujarati)

bhāraṇ = to bring out from a kiln (G.) bāraṇiyo = one whose profession it is to sift ashes or dust in a goldsmith's workshop (Gujarat) baran, bharat (5 copper, 4 zinc and 1 tin)(P.B.) In the Punjab, bharata = a factitious metal compounded of copper, pewter, tin (M.) In Bengal, an alloy called bharan or toul was created by adding some brass or zinc into pure bronze. bharata = casting metals in moulds; bharavum = to fill in; to put in; to pour into (Gujarat) Bengali. ভরন [bharana] n an inferior metal obtained from an alloy of coper, zinc and tin.

kuṭam 'pot' (Tamil) *koḍẽ* n. ' earthen saucer for a lamp ' (Marathi). Rebus: kuṭhi 'smelter'. *குடம்¹ kuṭam, n. < குட. cf. kuṭakuṭam K. kuṭa, M. kuṭam.] 1. Water-pot; நீர்வைக்கும் குடம். (பிங்.). See குடதாடி. Hub a wheel; வண்டிக்குடம்.*(Tamil) Rebus: *kuṭhi 'smelter'.*

bharaḍo a devotee of Śiva; a man of the bharaḍā caste in the brāhman.as (G.) baraṛ = name of a caste of jat- around Bhaṭiṇḍa; baraṛaṇḍā melā = a special fair held in spring (Punjabi) bharāḍ = a religious service or entertainment performed by a bharāḍī; consisting of singing the praises of some idol or god with playing on the ḍaur (drum) and dancing; an order of aṭharā akhāḍe = 18 gosāyī group; bharāḍ and bhāratī are two of the 18 orders of gosāyī

(Marathi) bārṇe, bāraṇe = an offering of food to a demon; a meal after fasting, a breakfast (Tulu) barada, barda, birada = a vow (Gujarati) vrata id. (Sanskrit)

Ganweiwala. Surface find tablet on a mound (2007). Hieroglyphs on both sides of the tablet.

Side 1: Glyph of 'canopy' over the seated person: *koṇḍa* bend (Konkani) Allograph: *kǫ̃nḍu* m. ' large cooking pot '(Kashmiri) Rebus: *kõdā* 'to turn in a lathe'(B.) कोंद *kōnda* 'engraver, lapidary setting or infixing gems' (Marathi) Alternative: Woṭ. šen ' roof ', Bshk. Šan, Phal. šān(AO xviii 251) Rebus: seṇi (f.) [Class. Sk. śreṇi in meaning "guild"; Vedic= row] A guild Vin iv.226; J i.267, 314; iv.43; Dāvs ii.124; their number was eighteen J vi.22, 427; VbhA 466. ° -- pamukha the head of a guild J ii.12 (text seni --).

The person is seated in penance: *kamaḍha* 'penance'; rebus: *kampaṭṭam* 'mint, coiner' (Tamil.Malayalam) Hence, the top register glyphic composition connotes: turner-engraver-coiner-guild.

மேடை mēṭai , *n.* [T. *mēḍa.*] 1. Platform, raised floor (Tamil) Rebus: *meḍ* 'iron' (Ho.)

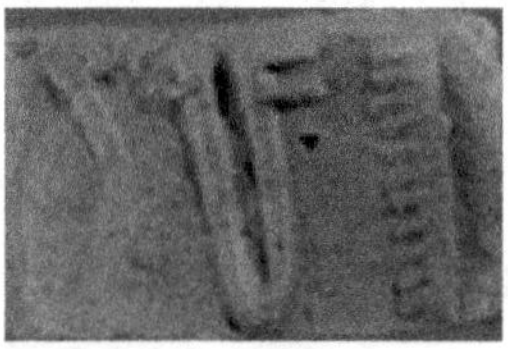

Glyph of adorant: *Ka.* eṟagu to bow, be bent, crouch, come down, alight, fall upon, attack, enter, join, accrue to; *n.* a bow, obeisance; eṟagisu to cause to bow, etc.; eṟaka coming down, etc. *Tu.* eraguni to bow *Te.* eṟãgu, erãgu to descend, bow or make obeisance, prostrate oneself; erãguḍu bowing, salutation Ta. iṟai (-v-, -nt-) to bow before (as in salutation), worship (DEDR 516). Rebus: eraka, er-aka any metal infusion (Ka.Tu.) eruvai 'copper' (Ta.); ere dark red (Ka.)(DEDR 446).

Side 2: Text of inscription on Ganweriwala tablet; 3 glyphs.

kharedo = a currycomb (Gujarati) Rebus: *kharādī* ' turner, a person who fashions or shapes objects on a lathe' (Gujarati)
kanka 'rim-of-jar' Rebus: *kanka* 'engraver, scribe'.

koṇḍa bend (Konkani) Rebus: *kõdā* 'to turn in a lathe'(B.) कोंद *kōnda* 'engraver, lapidary setting or infixing gems' (Marathi)

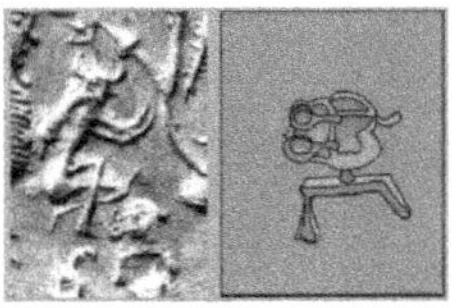

bahulā = Pleiades (Skt.) bagaḷā = name of a certain godess (Te.lex .) Rebus: bagalo = an Arabian merchant vessel (Gujarati)

WPah. dhaṭu m. (also dhaṭhu) m. 'scarf' (CDIAL 6707); Rebus: Pa. dhātu 'mineral'. (See scarf covering pigtail of kneeling person, in prayer)

Ka. eṟagu to bow, be bent, crouch, come down, alight, fall upon, attack, enter, join, accrue to; *n.* a bow, obeisance; eṟagisu to cause to bow, etc.; eṟaka coming down, etc. *Tu.* eraguni to bow *Te.* eṟãgu, erãgu to descend, bow or make obeisance, prostrate oneself; erãguḍu bowing, salutation Ta. iṟai (-v-, -nt-) to bow before (as in salutation), worship (DEDR 516). Rebus: eraka, er-aka any metal infusion (Ka.Tu.) eruvai 'copper' (Ta.); ere dark red (Ka.)(DEDR 446).

Te. garĩṭe, gaṇṭe, geṇṭe spoon, ladle. *Kol.* (SR.) gāṭe spoon; (Kamaleswaran). *Kuwi* (S.) garti (brass) spoon. *Ta.* karaṇṭi spoon or ladle. *Ma.* karaṇṭi spoon. (DEDR 1267). Rebus: *kharādī* ' turner, a person who fashions or shapes objects on a lathe' (Gujarati) Rebus: *kharādī* ' turner, a person who fashions or shapes objects on a lathe' (Gujarati)

m0516Atm0516Bt 3398 [Copper tablet; side B perhaps is a graphemic representation of an antelope; note the ligatured tail comparable to the tail on m273, b012 and k037]

rīṛ high mountain (WPah.)(CDIAL 10749a) Rebus: *rīti* 'yellow brass, bell metal': rīti2 f. ' yellow brass, bell metal ' Kathās., *rītika* -- n. ' calx of brass ', *°kā* -- f. ' brass ' lex. 2. rīrī -- , *rirī* -- f. ' yellow brass ' lex. [Ac. to AO xviii 248 Dard. forms < *raktikā -- 2] 1. Dm. *rit* ' copper ', Gaw. *rīt* (→ Sv. *rīda* NoPhal 49); Bshk. *rīd* ' brass ', Tor. *žit* f. 2. Pk. *rīrī* -- f. ' brass '; Sh. *rīl* m. ' brass, bronze, copper '.(CDIAL 10752). Alternative: *ḍāngā* = hill, dry upland (B.); *ḍāg* mountain-ridge (H.)(CDIAL 5476). Rebus: *dhangar* 'blacksmith' (Maithili) *ḍangar* 'blacksmith' (Hindi)

கண்டம்[3] kaṇṭam , *n.* < *khaṇḍa*. Piece, cut or broken off; fragment, slice, cutting, chop, parcel, portion, slip; துண்டம். செந்தயிர்க் கண்டம் (கம்பரா. நாட்டுப். 19).Rebus: *khaṇḍa* 'tools, pots and pans and metal-ware'.

kanka, karṇaka 'rim of jar' Rebus: *karṇaka* 'account scribe'.

The pictograph on m516 B (antelope) appears on a tin ingot found in Haifa, Israel. The antelope may be connoted by *ranku*, deer. Rebus: *ranga* = tin. Kur. *xolā* tail. Malt. *qoli* id. (DEDR 2135). Rebus: *kol* 'working in iron' (Tamil)

B009 markhor (*capra falconeri heptneri*).

Banawali10  9204 xolā = tail (Kur.); qoli id. (Malt.)(DEDR 2135). Rebus: kol 'pañcalōha' (Ta.) கொல் kol, n. Iron. (Tamil) Dm. *mraṅ* m. 'markhor' *Wkh. merg f. 'ibex'* (CDIAL 9885) Tor. *miṇḍ* 'ram', *miṇḍāl* 'markhor' (CDIAL 10310) Rebus: meḍ 'iron' (Ho.) kolom 'sprout' Rebus: kolami 'smithy/forge'. eae 'seven' (Santali); rebus: eh-ku 'steel' (Ta.) gaṇḍa 'four' (Santali) Rebus: kaṇḍ fire-altar, furnace' (Santali) tagaraka 'tabernae montana' Rebus: tagaram 'tin'.

Courtyard with turners' workshops

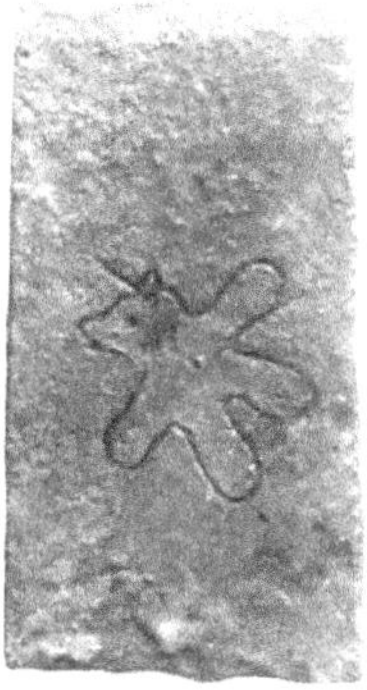

h1018 copper plate. Star-fish? Gangetic octopus?

m297a. seal. 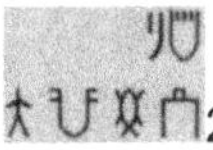2641

veṛhā octopus, said to be found in the Indus (Jaṭki lexicon of A. Jukes, 1900) Rebus: L. *veṛh*, *vehṛ* m. fencing; Mth. *beṛhī* granary; L. *veṛhā*, *vehṛā* enclosure containing many houses; *beṛā* building with a courtyard (WPah.) (CDIAL 12130)

koḍ 'horn' Rebus: koḍ = artisan's workshop (Kuwi)

खोंड [khōṇḍa] m A young bull, a bullcalf (Marathi) Rebus: *kõdār* 'turner' (Bengali)

मेड [mēḍa] *f* (Usually मेढ q. v.) मेडका *m* A stake (Marathi) meḍa 'pillar' (Go.) Rebus: meḍ 'iron' (Ho.)

kāṭhī = body, person; *kāṭhī* the make of the body; the stature of a man (Gujarati) Rebus: *khātī* 'wheelwright' (H.)

Epigraphs in the corpora are related to stone-, mineral-, metal-ware catalogs, continuing the bullae-tokens tradition of account-keeping in bronze-age. Almost all glyphs are remarkably unambiguous and vivid with specific orthographic features, including those glyphs which are referred to as geometric designs or dotted circles or svastika or ligatured composite animals (with glyptic elements

such as 'human face', 'trunk of elephant', 'forelegs of a bovine', 'hindlegs of a feline') or ligatured signs (such as a a 'rim-of-jar' glyph ligatured to a 'water-carrier' glyph).

Shahdad cylinder seal: copper turner, smith- artisan, merchant.

khōṇḍa 'leafless tree' (Marathi). Rebus: *kõdār* 'turner' (Bengali)

Nine flower stems: *lo, no* 'nine' (B.); Rebus: *loh* 'copper'

(Santali) kola 'woman' (Nahali)

Rebus: kol 'working in iron' (Tamil)

Shahdad. Drawing of cylinder seal impression. (p.661).

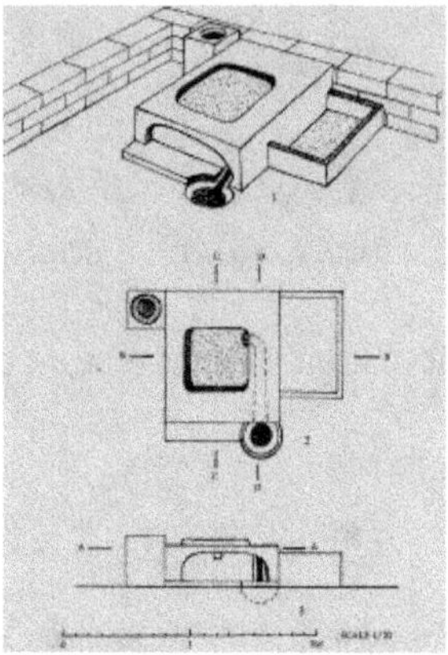

Shahdad. Metal foundry kiln, Site D "Shahdad (Islamis Khabis) is to be remembered as one of the East Iranian Centres for making metal artefacts in the 3rd millennium BCE. During the years 1971-77 an archaeological mission working in the Lut area under my supervision discovered a wide variety of metal objects in the three main burial grounds A,B and C. Over a period of seven years about 700 broke or unbroken metal objects were discovered...From the study of the metal workshops in 1977, we learned that the base metal copper had been extracted and used in three stages: a) ore smelting, b) purification and c) moulding...The upper side of the plates have embossed moulded figures of living creatures, such as crabs, fish, snakes and gazelles...The abundance of rich copper mines and skillfully mad artefacts in the vicinity of Shahdad supports the view that the prehistoric people of Shahdad were peaceful artisans engaged in the art of producing earthenware, stonework and domestic metal artefacts...The large decorated metal plates discovered in the main cemeteries, especially, confirm that the Shahdad workshop did not just make a few modest articles, but was producing work of great historical significance in the 3rd millennium BCE. It can also be concluded that similar plates, mainly that found at Tepe Hissar, and perhaps some of the others presented in this work, could likely come from the southeastern region of Iran."[79]

Glyph: tagaru 'ram' (Tulu) Rebus: tagarm 'tin' (Kota). damgar 'merchant' (Akk.) క్రమ్మరు [krammaru] v. n. To turn, return, go back (Telugu) Rebus: kamar 'smith, artisan' (Santali). Mth. *kamarsārī* 'smithy' (CDIAL 2899). Thus, the seal depicts two roles, designated by two antelope styles: one walking in profile and another antelope with its head turned back to denote roles of merchant and of artisan working with tin (mineral).

Ur cylinder seal with *taberna montana* plant, BM 122947 (U. 16220), enstatite; Legrain, 1951, No. 632; Collon, 1987, Fig. 611; A soft-stone flask, 6 cm. tall, from Bactria (northern Afghanistan) showing a winged female deity (?) flanked by two flowers similar to those shown on the comb from Tell Abraq.[80] Humped bull stands before a plant, feeding from a round manger or a bundle of fodder (or, probably, a cactus); behind the bull is a scorpion and two snakes; above the whole a human figure, placed horizontally, with fantastically long arms and legs.

ḍhanga = tall, long shanked; *maran: ḍhangi aimai kanae* = she is a big tall woman (Santali.) Rebus: *ḍhangar* 'blacksmith'. Vikalpa: tampur 'long-legged' (Santali) Rebus: tāmrá ' dark red, copper -- coloured '

tagara 'tabernae Montana tulip'. Rebus: *tagaram* 'tin'.

kāṛe ' thorny ' (Nepali) *kāṭī, kāṭī* f. ' thorn bush ' (Marathi). (CDIAL 2679). Rebus: *khāṇḍā* 'tools, pots and pans, metal-ware' (Marathi).

khũṭ m. ' Brahmani or zebu bull ' (G.) Rebus: *khũṭ* 'community, guild' (Santali) *kunda* 'turner' kundār turner (A.)

Glyph: *bicha* 'scorpion' (Assamese) Rebus: *bica* 'stone ore' (Munda) *paṭam* , *n.* < *phaṭa.* 'cobra's hood' (CDIAL 9040). Rebus: 'sharpness of iron': *padm* (obl.*padt-*) temper of iron (Kota)(DEDR 3907); *patam* 'sharpness, as of the edge of a knife' (Ta.mil)

This is a glyph showing five petals on a Harappa potsherd dated to ca. 3500 BCE, a glyph which is variant of the depiction on Shahdad cylinder seal. Characteristic of *tabernae montana* tulip flower which is a fragrant flower used as hair-dressing is that it has five petals. So, the word *tagaraka* has two meanings: 1. 'hair fragrance'; 2. *tabernae montana* 'tulip' (Sanskrit). Rebus: A homonym *tagara* means 'tin' (Kannada); tagromi 'tin, metal alloy' (Kuwi); takaram tin, white lead, metal sheet, coated with tin (Ta.); tin, tinned iron plate (Malayalam); tagarm tin (Kota); tagara, tamara, tavara id.(Kannada) tamaru, tamara, tavara id. (Tamil): tagaramu, tamaramu, tavaramu id. (Telugu); ṭagromi tin metal, alloy (Kuwi); tamara id. (Sanskrit.)(DEDR 3001). trapu tin (AV.); tipu (Pali); tau, taua lead (Pkt.); tũ_ tin (P.); ṭau zinc, pewter (Or.); tarũaum lead (OG.); tarvu~ (G.); tumba lead (Si.)(CDIAL 5992).

"The origins of Indus writing can now be traced to the Ravi Phase (c. 3300-2800 BC) at Harappa. Some inscriptions were made on the bottom of the pottery before firing. Other inscriptions such as this one were made after firing. This inscription (c. 3300 BC) appears to be three plant symbols arranged to appear almost anthropomorphic. The trident looking projections on these symbols seem to set the foundation for later symbols such as those seen in 131."

Slide 131. Inscribed sherd, Kot Dijian Phase. This sign was carved onto the pottery vessel after it was fired and may indicate the type of goods being stored in the vessel or the owner of the vessel itself. Another possible explanation is that this symbol represents a deity or spirit to which the contents of the vessel were sacrificed. This symbol becomes very common in the later Indus script.

The sign on this potsherd (with five petals as in *tabernae montana, tagaraka*) is stylized as Sign 162 (with three prongs) and Sign 165 (with five petals). Sign 167 shows five petals (and variants show many more branches).

The 'tulip' glyph is seen on a cylinder seal of Ur (cf. Gadd) and also on an axe from Tabraq, on Warka vase:

Tell Abraq axe[81] with epigraph ('tulip' glyph + a person raising his arm above his shoulder and wielding a tool + dotted circles on body).

gōṭī 'round pebble Rebus: *koṭe meṛed* = forged iron (Munda). Thus, it is a forged axe.

Glyph: *eṛaka* 'upraised arm' (Tamil) Rebus: *eraka* 'copper' (Kannada)

Glyph: *tagara* '*tabernae montana*', 'tulip'. Rebus: *tagara* 'tin'. Thus, the two glyphs, tulip and upraised arm denote tin + copper as the minerals alloyed to create the axe.

Some examples of use of comparable hieroglyphs from, Indus writing corpora may be cited:

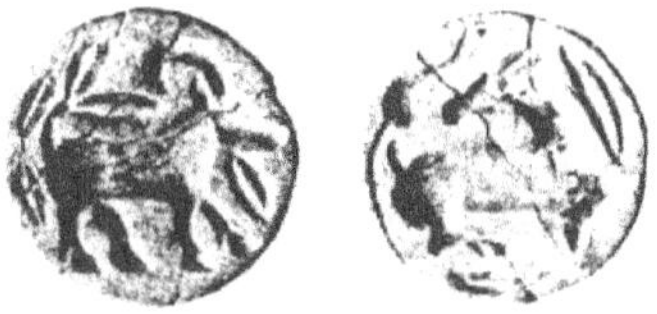

Chanhu-daro Seal obverse and reverse. The oval sign of this Jhukar culture seal is comparable to other inscriptions. Fig. 1 and 1a of Plate L. After Mackay, 1943. The hieroglyphs of the seal relate representations of bun ingots to two orthographic representations of 'antelopes': one is shown walking, the other is shown with head turned backwards. A flower is shown, perhaps, a representation of petals of tulip, *tabernae Montana* or petals of lotus

Stamp seal from Susa , at Louvre Museum. "Susa is one of the oldest known settlements of the world, possibly founded about 4200 BC, although the first traces of an inhabited village have been dated to ca. 7000 BCE. The seal depicts

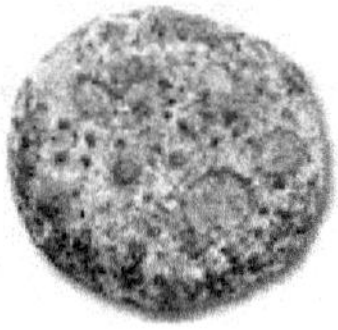

two goat-antelopes head to tail, outside an oval."

Tin bun ingot. Late Bronze Age, 10th-9th century B.C.E. Salcombe shipwreck, 300 yards off the South Devon coast, England, 2009.

urseal8Seal; BM 118704; U. 6020; Gadd PBA 18 (1932), pp. 9-10, pl. II, no.8; two figures carry between them a vase, and one presents a goat-like animal (not an antelope) which he holds by the neck.

meḍa 'neck' (Te.) *mēṭam* = goat (Ta) Rebus: *meḍ* 'iron' (Ho.) *mẽṛhẽt* = iron

(Ore)(Munda) [Allograph: *mẽt* = the eye (Santali) , orthography: dotted circle.] The kamandalu is held jointly by two persons.

meṭ sole of foot, footstep, footprint (Ko.); meṭṭu step, stair, treading, slipper (Te.)(DEDR 1557). Rebus: मेढ 'merchant's helper' (Pkt.); *meḍ* 'iron' (Munda). Alternative reading: Glyph: 'foot, hoof': Ku. *khuṭo* ' leg, foot ', *°ṭī* ' goat's leg '; N. *khuṭo* ' leg, foot '(CDIAL 3894). S. *khuṛī* f. ' heel '; WPah. paṅ. *khūṛ* ' foot '. khura m. ' hoof ' KātyŚr̥. 2. *khuḍa -- 1 (*khuḍaka* -- , *khula°* ' ankle -- bone ' Suśr.). [← Drav. T. Burrow BSOAS xii 376: it belongs to the word -- group ' heel <-> ankle -- knee -- wrist ', see *kuṭṭha --](CDIAL 3906). *Ta.* kuracu, kuraccai horse's hoof. *Ka.* gorasu, gorase, gorise, gorusu hoof. *Te.* gorija, gorise, (B. also) gorije, korije id. / Cf. Skt.khura- id.

(DEDR 1770). Allograph: (Kathiawar) *khũṭ* m. ' Brahmani or zebu bull ' (G.) Rebus: *khũṭ* 'community, guild' (Santali)

ḍhanga = tall, long shanked; *maran: dhangi aimai kanae* = she is a big tall woman (Santali.) Rebus: ḍhangar 'blacksmith

kāṭhī = body, person; *kāṭhī* the make of the body; the stature of a man (G.) *khātī* 'wheelwright' (H.) Vikalpa: *meḍ* 'body'. Rebus: meḍ 'iron' (Ho.)

Margiana, stamp seal: obverse, attacking lion; reverse: a bull copulating with a woman.

kamḍa, khamḍa 'copulation' (Santali) Rebus: kammaṭi a coiner (Ka.); kampaṭṭam coinage, coin, mint (Ta.) kammaṭa = mint, gold furnace (Te.) *ḍangar* 'bull' Rebus: *ḍhangar* 'blacksmith.

Pict-98

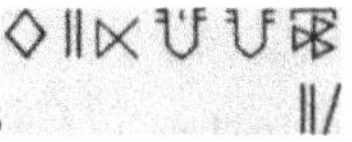

6113 Pict-98 kamḍa, khamḍa 'copulation' (Santali) Rebus: kammaṭa 'mint, coiner'.

Slanted strokes

dolio 'spotted antelope' (deśi. Hemachandra[82]); *dolo* 'the eye' (deśi. Hemachandra). Rebus: dul 'to cast metal in a mould' (Santali) It is possible that 'fish-eyes' or 'eye stones' referred to in ancient Mesopotamian texts as imports from Dilmun (Akkadian IGI-HA, IGI-KU6) mentioned in Mesopotamian texts., refer to the hieroglyph of dotted circle (hieroglyph: fish-eye or antelope-eye) connotes *dol* 'eye'; rebus: *dul* 'cast metal'.

M1909. Pict-49 Uncertain animal (antelope? quadruped) with dotted circles on its body.

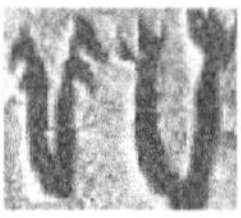

This seal has Glyph 347, 342 sequence, which is a terminal pair with 110 occurrences. An additional glyph shown in front of the animal is: a sloped/slanted stroke.

dula 'pair' *Rebus: dul* 'cast metal'. *kolom* 'sprout' Rebus: *kolami* 'forge/smithy'. *kaṇḍ kanka* 'furnace account scribe'.

ṭagara 'antelope'; தகர் takar, *n.* [T. *tagaru*, K. *tagar.*] 1. sheep; ஆட்டின்பொது. (திவா.) 2. ram; செம் மறியாட்டுக்கடா. (திவா.) பொருநகர் தாக்கற்குப் பேருந் தகைத்து (குறள், 486). Rebus: tagara 'tin'.

kōṭu (in cmpds. *kōṭṭu-*) horn (Tamil);(DEDR 2200). Rebus: *khōṭ* 'alloyed' (Punjabi) koṭe 'forged (metal) (Santali) koṭe meṛed = forged iron (Mu.)

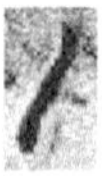

The hieroglyph of a slanted stroke in front of the animal on m1909 is: *dhāḷ* 'a slope'; 'inclination of a plane' (G.); ḍhāḷiyum = adj. sloping, inclining (G.) Rebus: ḍhālako = a large metal ingot (G.) ḍhālakī = a metal heated and poured into a mould; a solid piece of metal; an ingot (Gujarati) Antelope: miṇḍāl 'markhor' (Tōrwālī) meḍho a ram, a sheep (G.)(CDIAL 10120); rebus: mẽṛhẽt, meḍ 'iron' (Mu.Ho.) meṛed-bica = iron stone ore, in contrast to bali-bica, iron sand ore (Munda)

The ligatured animal can be read as a set of allographs:

Phonetic determinant of kandi 'beads' and kaṇḍ 'furnace' is the tusk glyph, which is read khaṇḍ 'ivory'; rebus: kaṇḍ = altar, furnace (Santali) kaṇḍ = altar, furnace (Santali) लोहकारकन्दुः f. a blacksmith's smelting furnace (Kashmiri) payĕn-kōda पयन्-कौंद । परिपाककन्दुः f. a kiln (a potter's, a lime-kiln, and brick-kiln, or the like); a furnace (for smelting)]. Kāndavika = a baker; kandu = an iron plate or pan for baking cakes etc. (Kannada) jaṇḍ khaṇḍ = ivory (Jatkī) khaṇḍī = ivory in rough (Jatkī); gaṭī = piece of elephant's tusk (S.) Alternative: kāg 'boar's tusk'; rebus: kāgar 'portable brazier'.

kandi 'hole, opening' (Ka.); kan 'eye' (Ka.); rebus: kandi (pl. –l) necklace, beads (Pa.) Thus, the entire ligatured animal is decoded rebus: meḍ pasra kāgar kandil 'iron smithy, forge, portable furnace, beads'. Pa.kandi (pl. –l) necklace, beads. Ga. (P.) kandi (pl. –l) bead, (pl.) necklace; (S.2) kandiṭ bead (DEDR 1215).

kandil, kandīl = a globe of glass, a lantern (Kannada)

Ka. kaṇḍi, kiṇḍi, gaṇḍi chink, hole, opening. Tu. kaṇḍi, khaṇḍi, gaṇḍi hole, opening, window; kaṇḍeriyuni to make a cut. Te. gaṇḍi, gaṇḍika hole, orifice, breach, gap, lane (DEDR 1176). kandhi = a lump, a piece (Santali.) Rebus: *kaṇḍ* 'stone (ore)'.

Ta. kaṇ 'star of a peacock's tail'.

Glyph: dotted circles. Rebus: *khāṇḍa* 'tools, pots and pans and metal-ware'.

Glyph: One long linear stroke. koḍa 'one' (Santali) Rebus: koḍ 'artisan's workshop' (Kuwi)

Glyph: Two long linear strokes. dol 'likeness, picture, form' [e.g., two tigers, two bulls, sign-pair.] Kashmiri. dula दुल । युग्मम् m. a pair, a couple, esp. of two similar things (Rām. 966) Rebus: dul 'cast metal' (Munda)

Thus, the composite glyph ||/ frequently occurring on Chanhu-daro inscriptions[83] can be read as slanted stroke followed by a pair of straight linear strokes: *dhāḷ*, 'slanted (stroke)' + dula 'pair or two'; read rebus: *ḍhālako* 'a large metal ingot' (Gujarati) + *dul* 'cast (metal)'. Thus, the composite glyph is read as a large cast metal ingot.

Glyph91 is a variant showing two slanted strokes followed by a straight linear stroke.

koḍa 'one' (Santali) Rebus: *koḍ* 'artisan's workshop' (Kuwi).

The composite glyph is read rebus: *ḍhālako dul* , 'large cast metal ingot" + *koḍ* 'artisan's workshop'. That is, a workshop (making) large cast metal ingots.

The three strokes together may read: kolmo 'three' (Mu.); rebus: kolimi 'smithy' (Telugu).

The following are Chanhu-daro inscriptions using the slanted strokes which signify large ingots of cast metal:

Chanhu-daro14a

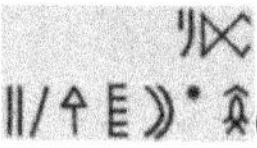

6108

Chanhu-daro29

6403

Pict-108 [*Chanhu-daro Excavations*, Pl. LI, 18] 6118

Chanhu-daro. Seal impression. Fig. 35 of Plate LII. After Mackay, 1943.

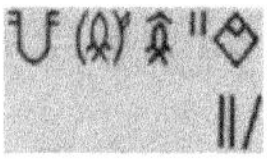

6124

6133

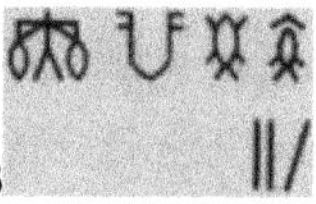

6202

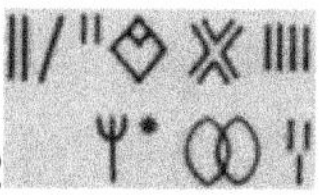

6203

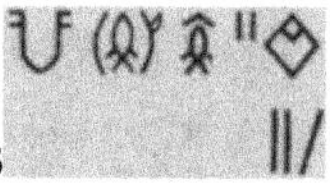

6204

6218

6233 Gharial

Allographs [kamḍa, khamḍa 'copulation' (Santali)]

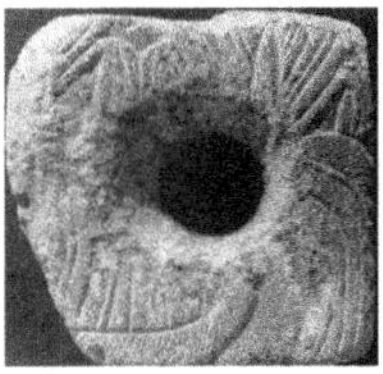 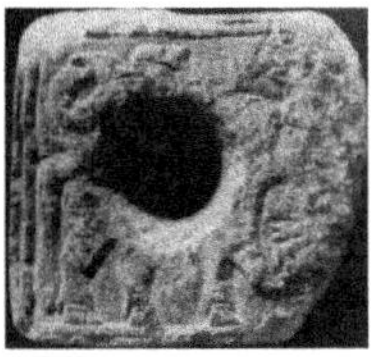

kamaṭha crab (Skt.)

kamaṛkom = fig leaf (Santali.)

kamarmaṛā (Has.), kamaṛkom (Nag.); the petiole or stalk of a leaf (Mundari)

kamat.ha = fig leaf, religiosa (Skt.)

Glyph: 'archer': kamāṭhiyo = archer; kāmaṭhum = a bow; kāmaḍ, kāmaḍum = a chip of bamboo (G.) kāmaṭhiyo a bowman; an archer (Sanskrit)

Tepe Yahya. Two sides of Tepe Yahya ('weight'?) fragment apparently reused as door socket during IVB times. One side depicts palms, and the other has a representation of a humped bull with a scorpion set above its back. *tamar*, 'palm tree, date palm' (Hebrew) Rebus reading would be: *tam(b)ra*, 'copper' (Prakrit)

m1540 copper tablet kamaṛkom = fig leaf (Santali.) kamarmaṛā(Has.), kamaṛkom (Nag.); the petiole or stalk of a leaf (Mundari)

kamāṭhiyo = archer; kāmaṭhum = a bow; kāmaḍī, kāmaḍum = a chip of bamboo (G.) kāmaṭhiyo a bowman; an archer (Sanskrit)

Provenance: 1. Bronze age site, Kalenao near the Turkmeni frontier, North West Afghanistan.

Commentary: While numerous Indus Valley stamp seals are known (cf. MS 2394), this is the only known cylinder seal (MS 2645) with the hitherto undeciphered Indus Valley script. Furthermore, this is one document linking together over land two of the great civilisations of the Old Akkadian period in Mesopotamia and the Indus Valley. Sea-borne trade has been known for a long time, and documented in practical terms

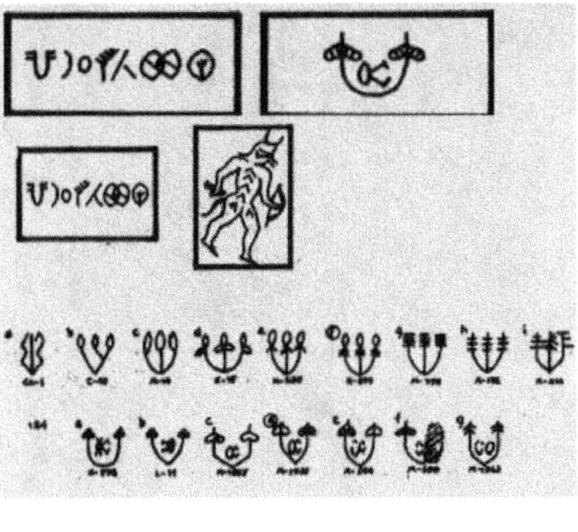

by the Norwegian explorer and scientist, Thor Heyerdahl, in his expedition with the reed boat, Tigris, in 1977.

Allographs of a duplicated ‘leaf’ glyph, ligatured with ‘crab-claws’ glyph and U (‘rimless pot’) glyph – shown on one copper tablet [After Parpola, 1994, fig. 13.15] seems to be a comparable rebus reading of the archer shown on another

copper tablet. The archer shown on one copper tablet seems to be a synonym of a ligatured complex glyph -- the ‘leave’s ligatured with crab and ‘U’ glyph on another copper tablet since the inscription on the obverse of each of the tablets is identical. [cf. Parpola, 1994, fig. 13.13] This ligatured complex glyph appears on two seals- one from Harappa and another from Lothal. Leaves ligatured with crab is a sign which occurs on these seals and with similar sign sequences.[84]
Seal Chanhujodaro (Mackay 1943: pl. 51: 13). Bison (gaur) trampling a prostrate person (?) underneath. Impression of a seal from Chanhujodaro (Mackay 1943: pl. 51: 13). The prostrate ‘person’ is seen to have a very long neck, possibly with neck-rings, reminiscent of the rings depicted on the neck of the one-horned bull normally depicted in front of a standard device.

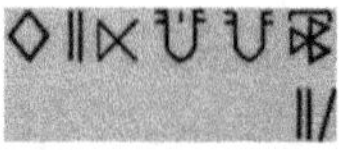
6113 Pict-98

Ta. meṭṭu (meṭṭi-) to spurn or push with the

foot. *Ko.* meṭ- (mec-) to trample on, tread on; meṭ sole of foot, footstep, footprint. *Malt.* maḍye to trample, tread. (DEDR 5057) Rebus: meḍ ‘iron’ (Ho.)

Seal impression/line-drawing. Tepe Yahya. Stone stamp seal (glyptique catalogue no 57). Persian Gulf-type circular steatite stamp seal with hemispherical knob pierced through for suspension with horned caprid, moon crescent, two small drillings, and bovid head arrayed around the edge. Dia.15mm.h.9mm.

Crescent is a stylized bun-ingot.

The use of pictorial motifs to convey information is vividly seen on Dilmun seals which use glyphs comparable to the Indus script glyphs.

A field symbol in Mahadevan corpus. Pict-49 Uncertain animal with dotted circles on its body. *ḍhāḷ* = a slope; the inclination of a plane (G.) Rebus: : *ḍhāḷako* = a large metal ingot (Gujarati)

piserā = a small deer brown above and black below (H.)(CDIAL 8365). Rebus: pasra = a smithy (Santali) blacksmith's forge (Sad.)

Obverse of steatite Dilmun stamp seal from Failaka Island (c. 2000 BCE). A

human figure and a variety of animals – two antelopes one with its head looking backward; possibly a scorpion at the feet of the human figure. A dotted circle is seen above one antelope and a vase in between the antelope and the human figure. *ḍhanga* = tall, long shanked; *maran: ḍhangi aimai kanae* = she is a big tall woman (Santali.) Rebus: *ḍhangar* 'blacksmith'. tagara 'ram' Rebus: damgar 'merchant' (Akkadian).[85]

eṛaka 'upraised arm' (Tamil) Rebus: eraka = copper (Kannada) kaṇḍa 'pot' Rebus: kaṇḍ 'fire-altar, furnace'. bica 'scorpion' Rebus: bica 'stone ore'. *gōṭī* 'round pebble Rebus *khoṭ* f 'alloy (Lahnda) *tagara* 'ram' Rebus: *damgar* 'merchant'. *meḍh* 'antelope' *meḍho* 'iron'; meḍho 'merchant'

Bhirrana. Allograph: Kur. xolā tail. Malt. qoli id. (DEDR 2135). [The 'short-tail' is a hieroglyph which is ligatured to an 'antelope' – as a hieroglyph read rebus. Such a ligatured-tail evolved into a 'sign' of the Indus script which appears on inscribed copper-tablets.] Rebus: kol 'working in iron (metal), blacksmith (in this case, tin-smith)'. *kolom* 'sprout' Rebus: *kolami* 'smithy'.

baṭa 'six' (hence six short strokes)(G.); rebus: bhaṭa 'furnace, smelter' (Santali). Glyphs: six (numeral) + ring of hair: आर [āra] A term in the play of इटीदांडू,--the number six. (Marathi) आर [*āra*] A tuft or ring of hair on the body. (Marathi) Rebus: *āra* 'brass'.

The stalk in front of the antelope is explained rebus: kolmo 'rice-plant' (Santali); rebus: kolami 'smithy/forge' (Te.) The antelope orthography shows a 'ram': tagara 'ram'; if the plant is tabernae montana, tagaraka 'tabernae montana'; rebus: tagara 'tin'. The seal shows an artisan-merchant who has a smelter to produce tin ingots.Antelope: meḷh 'goat' (Br.) Rebus: meṛha, meḍhi 'merchant's clerk; (G.) meḍho 'one who helps a merchant' vi.138 'vaṇiksahāyah' (deśi. Hemachandra). Cf. meluhha-mũh > mleccha-mukha 'copper (ingot)'.

Sibri cylinder seal

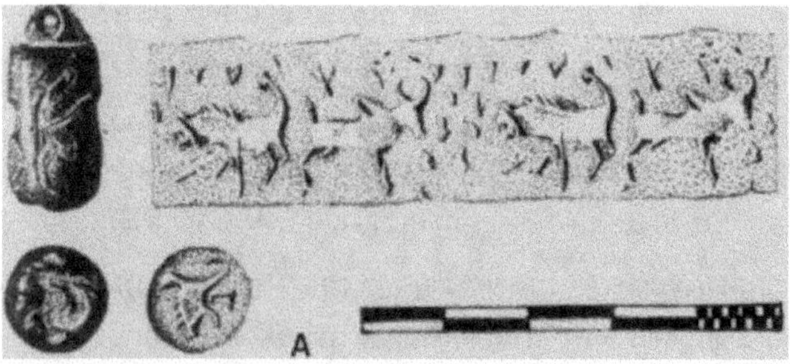

The hieroglyphs of 'zebu' and 'tiger' on Shahdad standard is also shown on a Sibri cylinder seal.

Sibri cylinder seal with Indus writing hieroglyphs: notches, zebu, tiger, scorpion?

Rebus readings of zebu and 'tiger'? on the cylinder seal shown on 7.31d: *khũṭ* m. ' Brahmani or zebu bull ' (G.) Rebus:*khũṭ* 'community, guild' (Santali) kola 'tiger' Rebus: kol 'working in iron'; pañcaloha, alloy of five metals (Tamil).

Each dot on the corner of the + glyph and the short numeral strokes on a

cylinder seal of Sibri, may denote a notch: खांडा [khāṇḍā] *m* A jag, notch, or indentation (as upon the edge of a tool or weapon). (Marathi) Rebus: *khāṇḍā* 'tools, pots and pans, metal-ware'. The numerical strokes on the seal may denote the number of 'ingots?' of iron made for the guild by the artisan who owned the cylinder seal. It may also denote that he was a worker in 'iron' for the smithy guild. An allograph to denote a guild is: footprint shown on some seals.

The + glyph of Sibri evidence is comparable to the large-sized 'dot', dotted circles and + glyph shown on this Mohenjo-daro seal m0352 with dotted circles repeated on 5 sides A to F.

Rebus readings of m0352 glyphs:

1. Round dot like a blob -- . Glyph: raised large-sized dot -- (*gōṭī* 'round pebble);

2. Dotted circle *khaṇḍa* 'A piece, bit, fragment, portion'; kandi 'bead';

3. A + shaped structure where the glyphs 1 and 2 are infixed. The + shaped structure is *kaṇḍ* 'a fire-altar' (which is associated with glyphs 1 and 2)..

Rebus readings are: 1. *khoṭ* m. 'alloy'; 2. *khaṇḍā* 'tools, pots and pans and metal-ware'; 3. *kaṇḍ* 'furnace, fire-altar, consecrated fire'.

Glyphs around the 'dotted circle' in the center of the composition: gōṭī 'round pebble; Rebus 1:L. *khoṭ* f 'alloy, impurity', *°ṭā* 'alloyed', awāṇ. *khoṭā* 'forged'; P. *khoṭ* m. 'base, alloy' M.*khoṭā* 'alloyed' (CDIAL 3931) koṭe meṛed = forged iron (Mu.) Rebus 2: kōṭhī] f (कोष्ट S) A granary, garner, storehouse, warehouse, treasury, factory, bank. *khoṭā* 'alloyed' metal is produced from *kaṇḍ* 'furnace, fire-altar' yielding *khaṇḍā* 'tools, pots and pans and metal-ware'. This word *khaṇḍā* is denoted by the dotted circles.

Damb Sadat burial vessel: pair of zebu or *bos indicus*

adar ḍangra 'zebu, *bos indicus*'.

- native metal (aduru)

- smith (ḍhangar)

- dol = likeness, picture, form (Santali) Rebus: dul m. = cast iron (Santali)

karā̃ n. pl. 'wristlets, bangles' (Gujarati); *karāī* f. 'wrist' (Sindhi)(CDIAL 2779). Rebus: *khār* खार् 'blacksmith' (Kashmiri) Thus, the Damb Sadat burial vessel indicates that the person was a blacksmith *khār*, working with native metal *aduru.*

Allograph: *aṭar* 'a splinter' (Ma.) *aṭaruka* 'to burst, crack, sli off,fly open; *aṭarcca* ' splitting, a crack'; *aṭarttuka* 'to split, tear off, open (an oyster) (Ma.); *aḍaruni* 'to crack' (Tu.) (DEDR 66) Rebus: *aduru* 'native, unsmelted metal' (Kannada) *aduru ganiyinda tegadu karagade iruva aduru'*, that is, ore taken from the mine and not subjected to melting in a furnace (Kannada).

Use of image field -- for art, for writing

The choice of a glyph by a scribe is NOT arbitrary. The scribe is attempting to communicate specific information about his core life-activity through writing. Orthographic styles used are so vivid that the glyphs are unambiguously recognizable as objects familiar to the creator/sender/receiver of the glyphs.

The choice of glyphs and unambiguous nature of the glyphs point to underlying phonetization of the glyphs. That is, the word used to phonetically refer to the objects chosen to be represented as glyphs. Many glyphs chosen in Indus writing are unambiguous references to animals and stoneware objects.

See, for example, the repeated choice of glyphs of a rhinoceros, a crocodile, a tiger, a one-horned young bull, a zebu bull, a trough in front of wild or domesticated animal, rim of a jar or a wide-mouthed rimless pot. Many Indus script epigraphs contain a prime line represented by the pictorial motif (animal or groups of animals or composite animal or animal -- tiger/antelope -- looking back, person seated on a tree branch, persons vaulting over an animal). This prime line is followed on the remaining space of the inscribed object with a sequence of an average of about 5 or 6 signs. The signs and the pictorial motif have to be read together, as integral components of the message transmitted. If the pictorial motif is ignored and decoding focusses only on the signs/sign sequences (say, in search of syntax or grammatical indicators), some categorical information sought to be conveyed may be lost in the arbitrary, selective process chosen for decoding.

Since the glyphs are unambiguous, the glyphs could be recognized as incised speech, related to glosses of Meluhha.

A remarkable clue comes from an alabaster vase from Uruk, Iraq c. 3500 to 3000 BCE (36 cms., Iraq

Museum, Baghdad). "...records the festival of the New Year. On the top band of carving a man presents a basket to a woman, either the mother goddess Inanna or her priestess, behind whom other gifts are piled up: more baskets, vases and a ram supporting clothed statuettes or figures of a man and a woman. Beneath this there is a procession of men carrying more gifts; they are naked, as men were usually represented when approaching the gods. Alternating ewes and rams fill the lowest register above a frieze of date palms and ears of barley. This is the earliest instance of an artist exploiting the possibilities of the defined 'image field', in which figures stan on a firm ground line in an area that could be understood as representing space. It is significant that it accompanied the invention of writing. The regularity of direction, spacing and grouping so evident in the Uruk vase corresponds to that of writing, as may also the use of parallel bands to create a tiered composition, with one row of scenes above another -- a system that was to be used for the next 5000 years, especially for narrative illustration. On the Uruk vase the sequence is hierarchical rather than chronological. Each frieze is a continuous procession without beginning or end..." (Hugh Honor and John Fleming, 1982, *A world history of art*, London, Laurence King Publishing Ltd.) Inanna is signified by two bundles of reeds behind her.

Indus script seal impressions point to the use of the glyphs on packages transmitted from one place to another. It is a reasonable hypothesis that the glyphs are phonetized to represent professions (as identifiers of the producer of the product or place of production of the commodity) or commodities (as identifiers of the contents of the packages).

Thus, function determines the form (orthography) of a glyph which is, generally, a representation of a noun, a substantive created by the bronze-age artisan.

As sea-faring merchants, the artisan/smith guilds of Sarasvati-Sindhu civilization areas, had continued the practice of preparing mleccha smith guild tokens, with incised speech, in contemporaneous interaction areas west of Sindhu and with civilizations across and beyond the Persian Gulf. This monograph presents a view that the Indus script was a writing system invented to communicate information – in the language of the inventors -- on the technologies, resources, and processes involved in the production and distribution of select commodities surplus to the requirements of the inventors. Such a writing system also involved communicating information about administrative structures (such as guilds of artisans) which supported/authenticated the production process. The Indus script decoded speech of artisans who had experimented with and developed skills in mining and metallurgy.

Thus, the writing system was a complementary technology, used to enhance or to substitute oral communication (or speech) related to metallurgical technologies. Almost all the epigraphs of the script (including epigraphs incised on metallic weapons/tools/ copper tablets, painted on bangles and a gold pendant, incised on a gold fillet headband and a steatite pectoral ornament) are professional guild tokens, authenticating the traded alloy/metal/mineral products, decoding the underlying mleccha speech. The guild tokens were, thus, professional calling cards of the guilds which could also be used to create sealed impressions on packages traded in an impressive long-distance trade.

In one instance, the token of a smithy/forge guild was exhibited on a monolithic sign-board on a gate of the fortification in Dholavira. (Dholavira. Northern gateway of the citadel with a sign-board.)[86]

So can the cognate glyphs on Proto-elamite, Magan, Mesopotamian and Dilmun seals – exemplified by the Gadd seals or seals from Saar (Magan) – and on two tin ingots, be decoded as metallurgical repertoire of mleccha smith guilds.

A writing system called *mlecchita vikalpa*

Almost the entire Indus writing corpora are veritable metalware and stoneware catalogs.

The underlying sounds of *daḷ* 'petal' and rebus reading: *ḍhālako* 'large ingot' explain the hieroglyphs, accompanying the two antelope hieroglyphs, on the following Two sides of Chanhudaro seal:

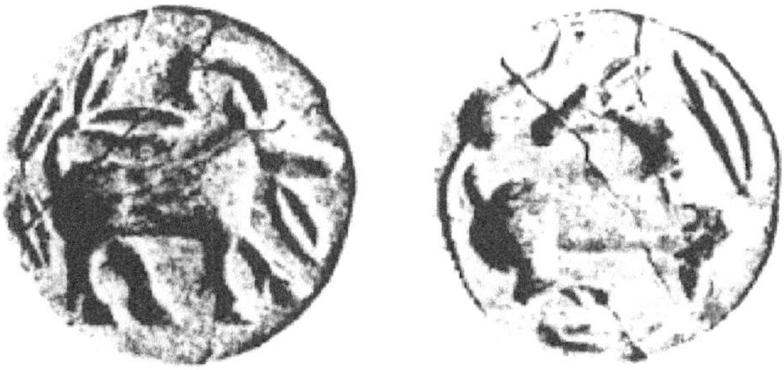

Chanhu-daro Seal obverse and reverse. The oval sign of this Jhukar culture seal is comparable to other inscriptions. Fig. 1 and 1a of Plate L. After Mackay, 1943.

The hieroglyphs of the seal relate representations of bun ingots to two orthographic representations of 'antelopes': one is shown walking, the other is shown with head turned backwards. A flower is shown, perhaps, a representation of petals of tulip, tagaraka '*tabernae montana' Rebus: 'tin' Rebus: damgar 'merchant' Rebus: kammara 'artisan'*.

Rebus: *meḍ* 'iron' (Ho.Mu.) mḗdha m. ' sacrificial oblation ' RV. Pa. *mēdha* -- m. ' sacrifice '; Si. *mehe*, *mē* sb. ' eating ' ES 69.(CDIAL 10327).

Allograph: *meṭ* knee-joint (Marathi) मेट [mēṭa] *n* (मिटणें) The knee-joint or the bend of the knee. मेटें खुंटीस बसणें To kneel down. *Go.* (L.) meṇḍā, (G. Mu. Ma.) minḍa knee (*Voc.* 2827). *Konḍa* (BB) meḍa, meṇḍa id. *Pe.* menḍa id. *Manḍ.* menḍe id. *Kui* menḍa id. *Kuwi* (F.) menda, (S. Su. P.) menḍa, (Isr.) meṇḍa id. (DEDR 4677)

Allograph: मेड [mēḍa] *f* (Usually मेढ q. v.) मेडका *m* A stake, esp. as bifurcated. Go<meDa>(Z) [meRa] {N} ``^pillar, ^fence^post". *Des.<meRa>(M) `poles in a fence'.(Munda).

Allograph: The six curls on the kneeling person's head denote an copper-brass smelter:

erugu = to bow, to salute or make obeisance (Telugu) Rebus: eraka 'copper'.

Glyphs: six (numeral) + ring of hair: आर [āra] A term in the play of इटीदांडू,--the number six. (Marathi) आर [āra] A tuft or ring of hair on the body. (Marathi) Rebus: arā 'brass'.

मेढा mēḍhā A twist or tangle arising in thread or cord, a curl or snarl. (Marathi) Rebus: meḍ 'iron' (Ho.) *bhaṭa* 'six (hair-curls)' Rebus: *bhaṭa* 'furnace'.

saman = to offer an offering, to place in front of; front, to front or face (Santali) Rebus: *samṛobica*, stones containing gold (Mundari) samanom = an obsolete name for gold (Santali) [*bica* 'stone ore' (Munda): *meṛed-bica* = iron stone ore, in contrast to *bali-bica*, iron sand ore (Munda]

TABLE 1 [Possehl, Gregory L. and Gullapalli, Praveena, 1999] RADIOMETRIC DATES FOR MEGALITHIC IRON IN PENNINSULAR INDIA		
SITE AND PERIOD	**LAB NO.**	**CALIBRATED DATE BC/AD (1δ CAL) (CALIB-3 PROGRAM)**
RADIOCARBON DATES		
Hallur, Period IB, Late Neolithic	TF-586	1415 (1310) 1134 BC
	TF-576	1679 (1522) 1426 BC
Hallur, Period II, Neolithic/Iron Age Overlap	TF-575	1255 (1039) 918 BC
	TF-573	1116 (976, 965, 935) 837 BC
	TF-570	1378 (1196, 1181, 1165, 1141, 1139) 1007 BC
Kakoria, Megalithic	TF-179	AD 1646 (1673, 1779, 1797, 1945, 1953) 1954
	TF-183	AD 1643 (1672, 1781, 1795, 1946, 1953) 1954
Korkai, Megalithic	TF-987	906 (818) 795 BC
Naikund, Megalithic	BS-94	797 (759, 676, 658, 641, 550) 405 BC
	BS-92	782 (522) 398 BC
Paiyampalli, Megalithic	TF-828	333 (102) BC AD 9
	TF-824	AD 1183 (1271) 1294
	TF-823	800 (764, 614, 606) 410 BC
	TF-825	AD 1262 (1294) 1396
Paiyampalli, Neolithic/Megalithic Transition	**TF-827**	**2033 (1892) 1747 BC**
Paiyampalli, Late Southern Neolithic	TF-833	1735 (1499, 1481, 1456) 1223 BC
	TF-829	AD 978 (1027) 1176
	TF-832	AD 1193 (1278) 1300
	TF-829 (BS)	AD 787 (897, 910, 958) 1015
Palavoy, Neolithic/Megalithic Transition	TF-700	1855 (1680) 1526 BC
Satanikota, Megalithic	BS-202	AD 544 (635) 672
	BS-201	AD 340 (427) 554
	BS-204	8081 (8018) 7927 BC
	BS-203	6458 (6372) 6182 BC
Takalghat, Pre-Iron Megalithic	TF-783	796 (759, 676, 658, 641, 550) 406 BC
	TF-784	768 (487, 442, 424) 395 BC
	TF-784 (BS)	758 (401) 264 BC
THERMOLUMINESCENCE DATES		
Kumaranhalli	PRL-TL-47	1290±90 BC
	PRL-TL-50	1270±170 BC
Gufkral (RADIOCARBON DATES, PERIOD II , MEGALITHIC IRON AGE)	**BS 434**	**2195 (2035) 1900** CALIBRATED DATE BC
	BS 431	**1885 (1747) 1677**
	BS 433	**2131 (1945) 1779**
	BS 371	**1888 (1747) 1674**

Cylinder seal and impression: cattle herd at the cowshed. White limestone, Mesopotamia, Uruk Period (4100 BC–3000 BC). Louvre Museum.

Cylinder seal and impression: cattle herd in a wheat field. Limestone, Mesopotamia, Uruk Period (4100 BC–3000 BC).

kuṇḍa n. 'clump' (Sanskrit) A phonetic determinant of the young bull *kõdā* खोंड [khōṇḍa] m 'A young bull, a bullcalf'. (Marathi) read rebus: *kũderā* m. 'one who works a lathe'. Alternative: The cob is kolmo 'seeding, rice-plant'(Munda) rebus: kolami 'smithy'; (Telugu)

The mleccha-speaking artisans invented alloying of metals and a writing system. Like the postman in *Father Brown*, the linguistic area (*sprachbund*) of India circa 5500 years ago has gone unnoticed simply because it is all around us, as a dialectical continuum stretching from Kanyakumari to Kashmir, from Dholavira to Dacca. The prehistory of the civilization is also all around us emphasizing the cultural continuity for over 5500 years to the present day. Our ancestors have delivered the messages in emphatic glyphs constituting over 7,000 epigraphs anchored on lexemes of the linguistic area of the civilization. The sounds represented by the glyphs relate to the sounds of a language called mleccha -- *Milakkha bhāsā* ! We had somehow not noticed the postman for the last 150 years, ever since the first seal was discovered close to the Sarasvati river basin. It is possible to identify both the mleccha messenger and the mleccha messages. To quote, Tolkāppiyam, "ellāc collum poruḷ kuṛittanavē" (Tol. Col. Peya. 1), i.e. all words are semantic indicators. Hence, the use of rebus to denote *res* 'things'.

Many glosses of mleccha (meluhha) are retained in many languages of Indian *sprachbund*. This evidence facilitates rebus reading of hieroglyphs on Indus writing.

Evidence has accumulated over the years since 1872 when Alexander Cunningham published the first reproduction of a seal from Harappa. Cunningham was Director of the Archaeological Survey of India from 1871 to 1885.

Illustrated London News 1936 - November 21st. A 'Sheffield of Ancient India: Chanhu-Daro's metal working industry 10 X photos of copper knives, spears, razors, axes and dishes.

American explorer of Boston Museum of Fine Arts, EJH Mackay, was so deeply impressed by the technological excellence of metal vessels, tools and weapons, excavated from Chanhu-daro that he was thrilled to call the revolutionary industrial site as the Sheffield of the Ancient Near East in *Illustrated London News* of November 21, 1936 with an accompanying photograph. This proved to be as dazzling as the gold of Egypt or wealth of Sumer. Chanhu-daro is on the right-bank of Vedic River Sarasvati. Megalithic iron in India, a chronology[87]

Bronze statue of a woman holding a small bowl, Mohenjo-daro; copper alloy made using cire perdue method (DK 12728; Mackay 1938: 274, Pl. LXXIII, 9-11)

The polemics of Aryan Invasion/Migration or Out of India Theories need not detain us here, in this enquiry related to identification of glosses of mleccha (meluhha), the most likely Indus language, and the underlying sounds used on Indus writing of metalware catalogs.

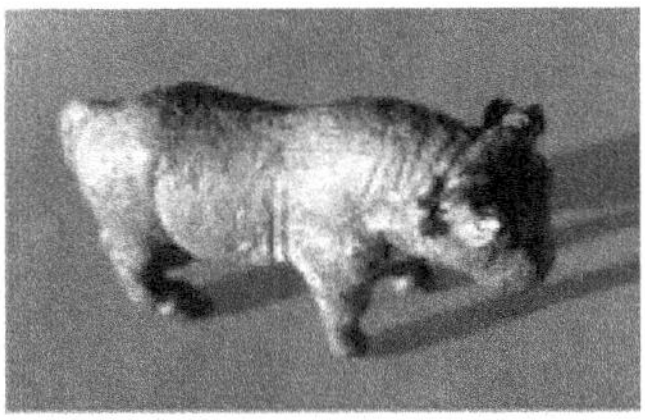

“The ‘Dancing Girl’ (Mohenjo-daro), made by the lost-wax process; a bronze foot and anklet from Mohenjo-daro; and a bronze figurine of a bull (Kalibangan). (Courtesy: ASI) "Archaeological excavations have shown that Harappan metal smiths obtained copper ore (either directly or through local communities) from the

Aravalli hills, Baluchistan or beyond. They soon discovered that adding tin to copper produced bronze, a metal harder than copper yet easier to cast, and also more resistant to corrosion. Whether deliberately added or already present in the ore, various 'impurities' (such as nickel, arsenic or lead) enabled the Harappans to harden bronze further, to the point where bronze chisels could be used to dress stones! The alloying ranges have been found to be 1%–12% in tin, 1%–7% in arsenic, 1%–9% in nickel and 1%–32% in lead. Shaping copper or bronze involved techniques of fabrication such as forging, sinking, raising, cold work, annealing, riveting, lapping and joining. Among the metal artefacts produced by the Harappans, let us mention spearheads, arrowheads, axes, chisels, sickles, blades (for knives as well as razors), needles, hooks, and vessels such as jars, pots and pans, besides objects of toiletry such as bronze mirrors; those were slightly oval, with their face raised, and one side was highly polished.

The Harappan craftsmen also invented the true saw, with teeth and the adjoining part of the blade set alternatively from side to side, a type of saw unknown elsewhere until Roman times. Besides, many bronze figurines or humans (the well-known 'Dancing Girl', for instance) and animals (rams, deer, bulls...) have been unearthed from Harappan sites. Those figurines were cast by the lost-wax process: the initial model was made of wax, then thickly coated with clay; once fired (which caused the wax to melt away or be 'lost'), the clay hardened into a mould, into which molten bronze was later poured. Harappans also used gold and silver (as well as their joint alloy, electrum) to produce a wide variety of ornaments such as pendants, bangles, beads, rings or necklace parts, which were usually found hidden away in hoards such as ceramic or bronze pots. While gold was probably panned from the Indus waters, silver was perhaps extracted from galena, or native lead sulphide...While the Indus civilization belonged to the Bronze Age, its successor, the Ganges civilization, which emerged in the first millennium BCE, belonged to the Iron Age. But recent excavations in central parts of the Ganges valley and in the eastern Vindhya hills have shown that iron was produced there possibly as early as in 1800 BCE. Its use appears to have become widespread from about 1000 BCE, and we find in late Vedic texts mentions of a ‘dark metal’ (krṣṇāyas), while earliest texts (such as the Rig-Veda) only spoke of ayas, which, it is now accepted, referred to copper or bronze.”

The direction of 'borrowings' is a secondary component of the philological excursus; there is no universal linguistic rule to firmly aver such a direction of borrowing. Certainly, more work is called for in delineating the structure and forms of meluhha (mleccha) language beyond a mere list of metalware glosses.

Hieroglyphic nature of the cipher

A word is defined as a linguistic unit which links tightly together one or more morphemes and is a unit of language which carries meaning.

The following two categories of lexemes are collated in the process of analyzing the Indus writing cipher:

(1) words which are adaptable for hieroglyphic representation ('image' words);

(2) words related to the artefacts of the bronze-age civilization ('tool or product' words).

Using the rebus principle, homonyms with substantive meanings are identified: such as the tools of jeweller-smithy, turner, miner, smith, metals-trader, mint. (A homonym is one of a group of words that share the same spelling and the same pronunciation but have different meanings.)

The following examples demonstrate the method of ligaturing glyptic elements to create ‘incised speech’.

Ligatured Sign 15 combines glyptic element of ‘rim-of’-jar’ superscripted on ‘water-carrier’ glyptic element. Sign 342 

   Ur. Gadd PBA 18 Seal impression. Harappa seal h073. Daimabad seal 01 seal.

Each glyptic element incised is a word, a unit of speech of Meluhha language.

Rim of jar = *kanka, karṇaka* Rebus: *karṇaka* 'account scribe'.

Water-carrier = *kuṭi* (Telugu). [The jar is *kaṇḍa* Rebus: *ke~ṛe~ ko~ṛe~* an aboriginal tribe who work in brass and bell-metal (Santali)]

Rebus reading of Ligatured Sign 15 is: *kuṭi kanka*, 'furnace scribe' (Santali).

Sign 15 has many variants in the texts.

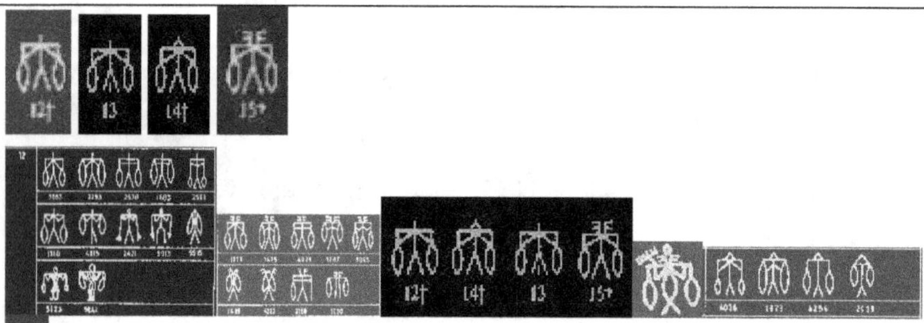

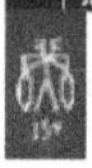 Signs 12, 13, 14, 15 and 342

"...More recent archaeological researches in East Arabia have brought to light many finds which are related to the presence of Indus valley people. In the settlements of Hili 8 and Maysar-1, both of which have been investigated, Indus valley pottery is frequently found. Seals with Indus valley script and typical iconography indicate influences in Makkan down to the level of business organization. Marks identifying pottery in Makkan were taken from those used in the Indus valley, including the use of the signs on pottery used in the Indus valley. The discovery of a sea-port-- which may be ascribed to the Harappans-- at Ra's al-Junayz on Oman's east coast by an Italian expedition would seem to indicate that trade routes should be viewed in a more differentiated fashion than has been done upto now."[88]

Written sources indicate existence of foreigners in Mesopotamia: 'interpreters from Meluhha', 'Meluhhan village'. For example, texts refer to an Assyrian trading outpost at Kultepe. Proof came with an archaeological find. 'If the tablets and their sealed envelopes had not been found, in fact, we might never have suspected the existence of a merchant colony.'[89]

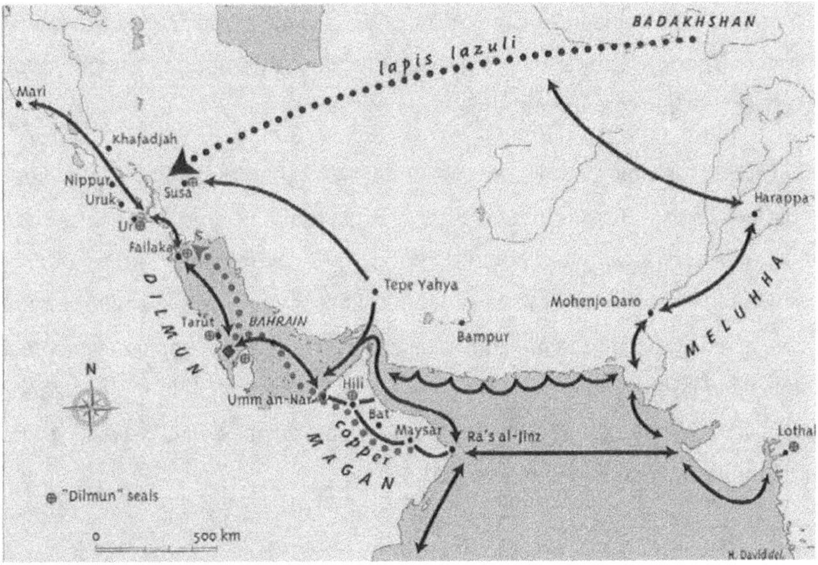

Mesopotamia and Harappa

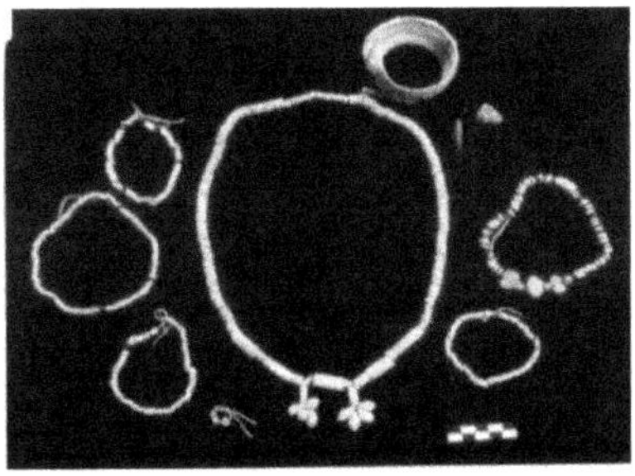

By early third millennium BCE, the Sindhu-Sarasvati doab was teeming with settlements which had known metallurgy, a system of weights, town-planning and also the use ofinscriptions to conduct trade in an extensive contact area. Many glyphic elements deployed on Indus writing by Meluhha speakers also gets deployed on many cylinder seals and artifacts, many with accompanying cuneiform texts in Sumerian/ Akkadian/Elamite.[90] This monograph explores the continuity of this hieroglyph tradition into the historical periods in India consistent with other cultural markers which continue in Hindu civilization traditions (markers such as worship of shivalinga, wearing of shankha bangles, wearing of sindhur in the parting of the hair, continued use of cire perdue technique for casting bronze murti-s, wearing of uttariyam comparable to the garment worn by the 'priest', yogic postures, postures of sitting in penance). The hieroglyph tradition continues most pronouncedly in the tradition of punch-marked and cast coins from circa 1000 BCE[91]. Some glyptic styles are also evident in Begram ivories and on the sculptures of Bharhut and Sanchi stupas and other architectural monuments.

6500 BCE is the date of the woman's burial with ornaments including a wide bangle of *śankha*. Nausharo. Burial ornaments made of shell and stone disc beads, and *turbinella pyrum* (sacred conch, *śankha*) bangle.[92] The nearest source for this shell is Makran coast of 500 km. near Karachi. *śankha, turbinella pyrum*, is a signature tune of Hindu civilization, since it is a species which occurs principally in Indian Ocean coastline. The date of the bangle found at Nasharo is instructive. It is dated to 6500 BCE, the date coterminous with the early proto-Elamite potters' marks identified by DT Potts.

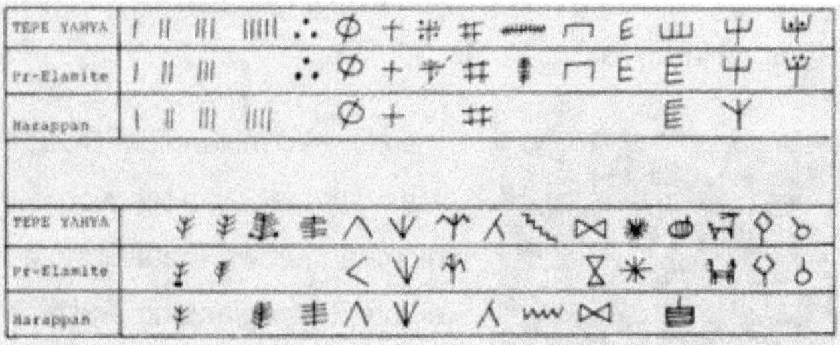

FIG. 4. - Comparison of signs in the Tepe Yahya potter's mark corpus, the Proto-Elamite script, and the Harappan script.

Proto-Elamite, potters' marks and Indus script

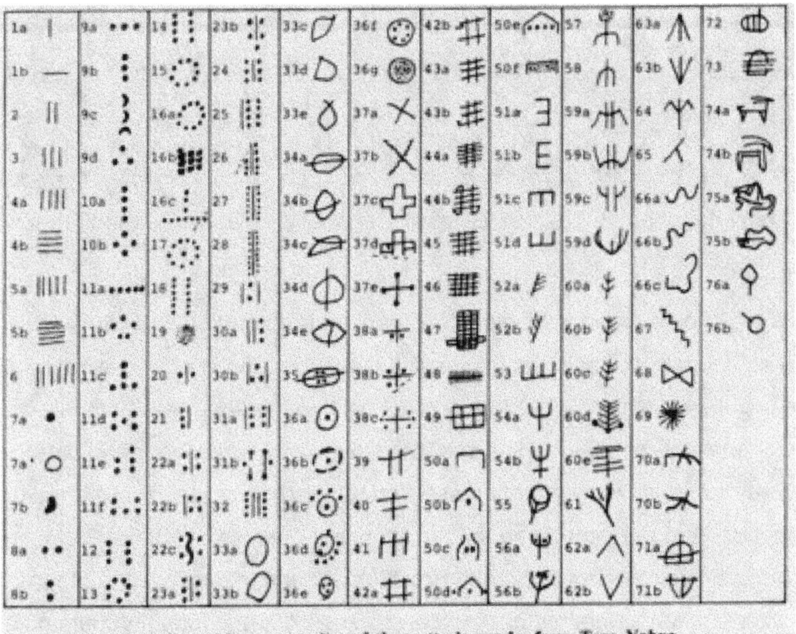

FIG. 5. – Master sign list of the potter's marks from Tepe Yahya.

Reviewing about 400 potter's marks from Tepe Yahya in Kerman province,

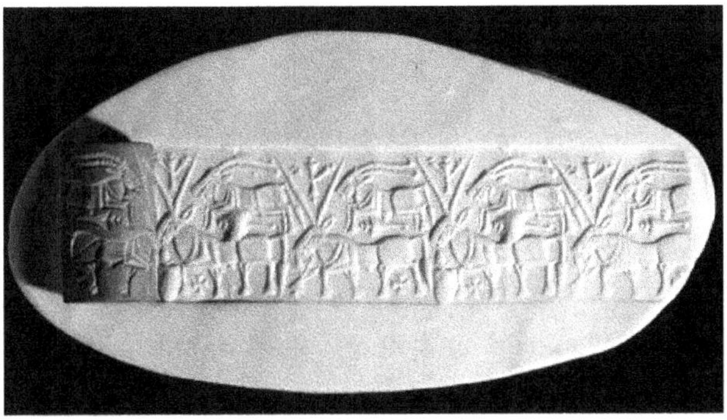

southern Iran, Potts proposes hypotheses concerning the possibility of a relationship between Proto-Elamite and Harappan scripts and in particular, that the Proto-Elamite writing system is ancestral to the Mature Harappan script. Proto-Elamite script was used between c. 3400 to 2800 BCE.[93]

Proto-Elamite, about 3000-2700 BC Cylinder seal. British Museum ME 116720. H. 4.9 cm Dia 2.9 cm

"This seal, of pale green volcanic tuff, is derived from earlier Uruk-style seals depicting animals, but belongs to a stylistic tradition found not in Mesopotamia but in south-western Iran. The heavy emphasis on the shoulders and haunches of the animals divides the bodies into three segments which are often patterned. Some seals of this type were impressed on tablets bearing the Proto-Elamite script which died out later in the third millennium. On many of these Proto-Elamite seals animals adopt human postures and these may have led to the appearance in Mesopotamia of such creatures as the bull-man and human-headed bulls."[94]

Meluhha language

The monograph identifies Meluhha language of Bronze-age, following 1) analyses of stages in the evolution of counting, using tokens and bullae, and epigraphical evidences of writing systems of Ancient Near East and 2) relating the language to *parole* of artisans and traders in a region identified by toponyms, Dilmun-Magan-Meluhha-baluhhu which extends from Failaka to Lothal. In the toponym Meluhha-baluhhu, Neo-Assyr. *baluh.h.u* 'galbanum' is suffixed, just as Inde was recognized by the Egyptian word, *sindh* denoting 'cotton' or Assyrian *sinda* denoting, from as erly as 7th century BCE, 'wood from Sindh'.

The work identifies a language called Mleccha or Meluhha which was the *parole* among stone and metal artisans of the civilization. This language is mentioned in the Great Epic Mahabharata where an episode describes conversation between

Yudhishtira and Vidura. Mleccha-speakers are described as dasyu (Iranian daha, people) in Manusamhita. Vatsyayana's Kamasutra lists 64 arts including an art called Mlecchita vikalpa (lit. mleccha alternative representation) which is Indus Script Cryptography. The work portrays lives of ancient people called Meluhha or Mleccha trading in stoneware, metalware and artisans engaged in building fortifications and multi-storied structures and organised into artisan-trade guilds, as janapada-s, without centralized rulers or kings.

Role of Dilmun in Indus trade with contact areas

Dilmun (present-day Bahrain) and Magan (or Makan, present-day Oman) of Arabian Peninsula had trade connections with the Indus. Maysar, Ra's al-Hadd and R'as al-Junayz -- sites in Oman; Tell Abrak (United Arab Emirates) -- sites in Bahrain and Failaka; Ur, Nippur, Kish and Susa -- sites in Mesopotamia between Tigris-Euphrates and in Elam, have provided evidence of Indus trade presence. Sutkagen-dor and Sokta-koh were ports near today's Iran border and indicate the role of sea-faring in Indus trade. A remote Indus trade outpost was perhaps Shortughai, on the Oxus in Afghanistan, beyond the Hindu Kush range of mountains.
Dilmun has produced seals with Indus inscription, Linear Elamite inscribed atop an Indus-stylized bull and a tablet with cuneiform -- all simultaneously being used ca. 2000 BCE:

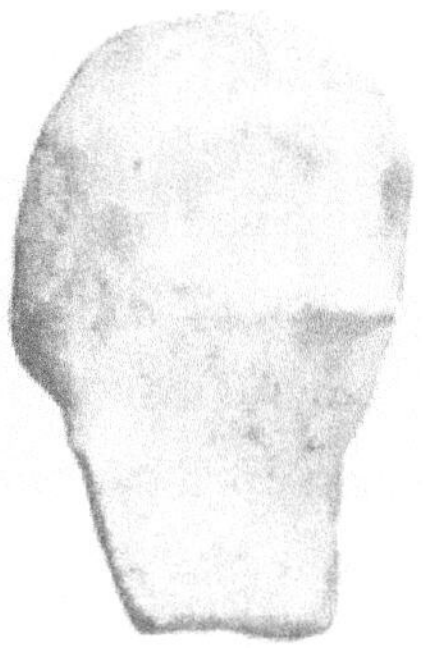

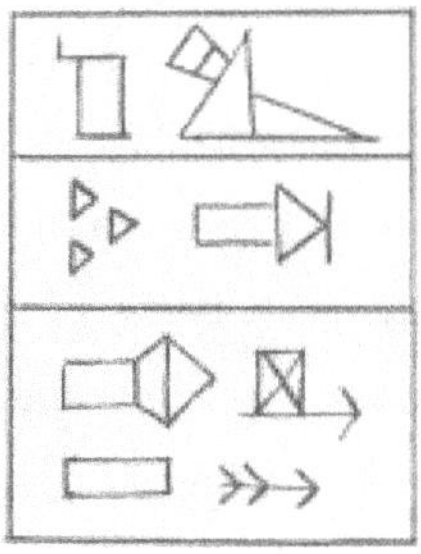

Mesopotamian-ike bearded terracotta head excavated at Lothal.[95]
The ships of Dilmun, from the foreign lands, brought him (Ur-Nanshe) wood as a tribute (?). Copy of cuneiform text with translation: From an inscription of Ur-Nanshe that speaks of timber-carrying Dilmun boats. (Kramer, ibid., p.49.)

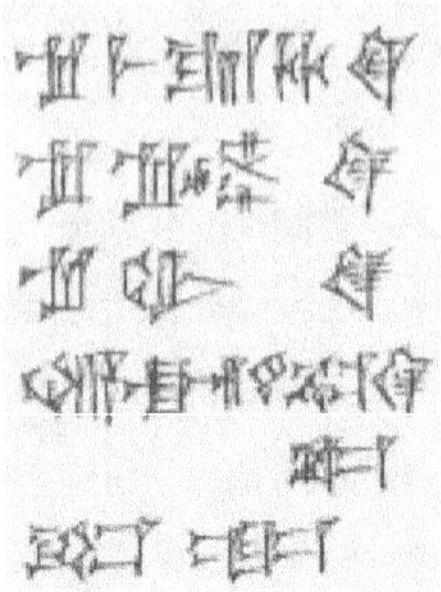

The ships from Meluhha, the ships from Magan, the ships from Dilmun, he made tie up alongside the quay of Agade. From a inscription of Sargon the Great boasting that the boats of Dilmun lay anchored at the docks of Agade. (Kramer, ibid., p.49).

"…such culturally significant words as engar (farmer), udul (herdsman), shupeshdak (fisherman), apin (plow), apsin (furrow), nimbar (palm), sulumb (date), tibira (metal worker), simug (smith), nangar (carpenter), addub (basket maker), ishbar (weaver), ashgab (leather worker), pahar (potter), shidim (mason), and perhaps even damgar (merchant), are probably all Ubaidian rather than Sumerian, as has been usually assumed. And should th inscriptions on the Indus seals contain not only the name of the consignor or consignee of the goods to which their clay impressions were attached, but also his occupation, it is not impossible that one or another of the above listed words will be found among them. Another crucial word which may turn out to be Ubaidian, is Ea, one of the two names by which Mesopotamian water god is known in the cuneiform texts, the other being Enki…For while the latter is a typical Sumerian compound with the meaning 'Lord of the Earth,' Ea is a word whose linguistic affiliations are still uncertain; it might well be his original Ubaidian name which the Sumerians changed to Enki when they incorporated him into their pantheon." (Kramer, ibid., pp.51-2).

Co-existence of three writing systems

"The presence in Dilmun of these three different writing systems –de fabrication locale, meaning the co-existence of Linear Elamite, the Indus script, and lastly the Mesopotamian cuneiform, all simultaneously being used ca. 2000 BCE, does demonstrably argue in favour of what archaeology has already proven: that Dilmun's role as a leading commercial center in the Mesopotamian world-system also places it at the crossroads of civilizations as far as languages and cultureis concerned. (As Glassner notes, the fact that archaeological discoveries reveal these three writing systems to be coexisting and simultaneously used in Dilmun at this time (ca. 2000 BC) is not at all inconceivable. He writes: “Trois écritures seraient doncsimultanément en usage, à Dilmun, autour de 2000, deux d'entre elles sont notées sur des cachets *le linéaire élamite etl'harrapéen+, la troisième *le cunéiforme mésopotamien+ l'est sur des tablettes. Le fait est parfaitement concevable: ne serait l'origine étrangère des trois écritures, la situation est tout à fait comparable à celle de la Crète où, dans la première moitié du 2 e millénaire, trois écritures coexistent dont l'une, notamment, de caractère linéaire (linéaire A), est notée sur des tablettes d'argile. On sait, d'autres part, que les Vay de Côte d'Ivoire utilisent également trois écritures.”[96] Trans. “Three scripts are simultaneously in use in Dilmun around 2000 BCE, two of them are noted on the Elamite tablets -- Linear A + Harappan + third, Mesopotamian cuneiform -- on the shelves. The foreign origin of three scripts is conceivable. The situation is quite similar to that of Crete where, in the first half of the 2nd millennium BCE, three scripts coexisted, in particular, linear A is noted on clay tablets. We know, on the other hand, that Ivory Coast also used three scripts.” As far as the reason for their usage, Glassner suspects that it had something to do with the commercial trading activities occurring at this time. In relation to discoveries made in Magan, they are also quite significantly comparable to the Dilmunite finds, and there has even been unearthed in Magan a locally fabricated seal which contains the same Indus signs as one discovered in Lothal, the ancient Indus port city, It can therefore be observed that in many ways these archaeological findings do establish some legitimate grounds for discussing the shared linguistic and/or cultural hybridity (or plurality) of the societies of Magan (Oman), Dilmun (Bahrain), and Meluhha (Indus).

The fact that these same three lands are often mentioned together in the Mesopotamian (cuneiform) records and even –often in the same sentence, as Bibby[97] remarks does lend further support to the archaeological finds in making valid cross-cultural links between these ancient peoples. Not unlike the ancient Dilmunites, it would not then be entirely inconceivable to think of the Indus business people as similarly being exposed to these other contemporary writing systems, most notably such as those of neighbouring Elam (either the proto-Elamite or later Linear Elamite script) or the Mesopotamian cuneiform that dominated the Gulf trade in which they were actively engaged".[98]

Stone cone, 2 in. high. Originally part of the foundation of a temple, ca. 1800 BCE. Palace of Rimum, servant of the god Inzak, man of (the tribe of) Agarum.

"The toponym Meluhha is found in cuneiform texts of the mid- to late third millennium BCE. An inscription of King Sargon of Akkad states that the boats of Dilmun, Magan, and Meluhha docked at the quays of Akkad. The names always occur in this sequence, and Meluhha is therefore thought to have been the farthest away. It is usually identified with the Indus valley, Gujarat, and the Harappan culture. The identification is strengthened by the nature of the commodities brought from Meluhha. These included special woods such as ebony, gold, ivory, carnelian, and lapis. Most arrived in Mesopotamia in an unworked state, but etched carnelian beads and long tubular beads of the same material were undoubtedly made in the Indus. Many of the materials originated in the Indus, but others such as lapis were traded on from further afield. It is not clear what was received in return, as few goods of Mesopotamian origin have been found in the Indus. Some Meluhhan merchants apparently lived in a special settlement near Lagash, suggesting that the trade was not exclusively in the hands of Mesopotamian merchants. A seal of the Agade period identifies its owner, who bears the Akkadian name Šu-ilišu, as a Meluhhan interpreter. The name Meluhha disappears from the texts after the third millennium, when the Indus civilization declined and direct contact apparently ceased. However, in the Neo-Assyrian period the name reappears, now used to denote Nubia and Ethiopia, which supplied some of the same goods previously obtained from the Indus."[99]

This is a contribution to hermeneutics, the science of discovering new meanings and interpretations in 'all those situations in which we encounter meanings that are not immediately understandable but require interpretive effort'.[100]

The disputation or interpretive effort is comparable to the hermeneutics of mīmāṃsa in the Indian tradition:

What is the etymology of the word mīmāṃsa मीमांस ?

mīm f. ' brain ' (Torwali) + अंस *m. du.* the two shoulders or angles of an altar. आस् Brahman. Speech. Thus, it is an intellectual inquiry, deep reflection delivered in parts on the mantra texts. मीमांसकः [मान् विचारे स्वार्थे सन् ण्वुल्] 1 One who investigates or inquires into, an investigator, examiner. -2 A follower of the system of philosophy called मीमांसा [मान्-विचारे स्वार्थे सन् अ] 1 Deep reflection, inquiry, examination, investigation; अथातो व्रतमीमांसा Bṛi. Up.1.5.21; रसगङ्गाधरनाम्नीं करोति कुतुकेन काव्य- मीमांसाम् R. G.; सैषा आनन्दस्य मीमांसा भवति Tait. Up.; so दत्तक°, अलंकार° &c. -2 N. of one of the six chief *darśanas* or systems of Indian philsophy. (It was originally divided into two systems :-- the पूर्वमीमांसा or कर्ममीमांसा founded by Jaimini, and the उत्तरमीमांसा or ब्रह्ममीमांसा ascribed to Bādarāyaṇa; but the two systems have very little in common between them, the first concerning itself chiefly with the correct interpretation of the ritual of the Veda and the settlement of dubious points in regard to Vedic texts; and the latter dealing chiefly with the nature of Brahman or the Supreme Spirit. The पूर्वमीमांसा is, therefore, usually, styled only मीमांसा or *the* Mīmāṁsā, and the उत्तर- मीमांसा, वेदान्त which, being hardly a sequel of Jaimini's system, is now considered and ranked separately.) मीमांसाकृतमुन्ममाथ सहसा हस्ती मुनिं जैमिनिम् Pt.2.34. -Comp. -कारः, -कृत् *m.* N. of Jaimini. మీమాంస *mīmāmsa.* [Skt.] n. A discussion or disputation held to find out the truth regarding anything. ప్రమాణైరర్థ విచారణ, ప్రమాణములచేత నిజముగ్రహించడము. Polemical divinity. Theological criticism. The name of one of the six great Indian philosophical systems, పూర్వ మీమాంస is a system of ritualism.ఉత్తరమీమాంస is a system practically the same as the వేదాంతము, జ్ఞానకాండ.(Telugu).

Bharata's *Nāṭyaśāstra*: *mleccha* as language, *bhāṣā*

Realising that this is but a beginning and that we have miles to go in delineating the diffusion of language communities and movement of mleccha (*bhāratīya*) language-speakers in space and time, *mlecchaśabda* (mleccha glosses) will be identified following the evidence of *Nāṭyaśāstra* XVII.29-30)[101]: *dvividhā jātibhāṣā ca prayoge samudāhṛtā mlecchaśabdopacārā ca bhāratam varṣam āśritā* 'The jātibhāṣā (common language), prescribed for use (on the stage) has various forms. It contains words of *mleccha* origin and is spoken in Bhāratavarṣa only...'

The speech of the commoners is distinguished from that of priests also containing words of mleccha origin. This may be a reference to vocables of Dravidian and Austro-asiatic languages.[102]

In Tamil, the word மொழி² moḻi, *n.* < மொழி-, 'word' occurs in Tolkāppiyam: மறைமொழி தானே மந்திர மென்ப (தொல். பொ. 481). Cognate etyma are: muṟaṅku (muṟaṅki-) to roar, thunder, make loud noise, be noised abroad, be made public (Tamil); miṟaku, miṟāvu drum (Malayalam); miṛi- to speak, utter (*Konḍa*); ? *To.* mïḷ good points in argument (in assembly), directions given in building. (DEDR 4989); மழலை maḻalai , *n.* < மழ. 1. Prattling, babbling, lisping of children; குழந்தைகளின் திருந்தாச் சொல். தம்மக்கண் மழலைச்சொற் கேளாத வர் (குறள், 66).

Shafer[103] has a Tib-Burm. etymology **mlt´se*; Southworth 1990: 223 reconstructs PDrav. 2 **muzi/mizi* 'say, speak, utter'.

Evidence for *mleccha* spoken in India, prior to 8th century BCE

Since *mlecchita*[104] *vikalpa* (cipher-writing) is a term used Vātsyāyana's *Kāmasūtra*, the underlying language, *mleccha*, was *lingua franca* or parole, prior to 8th century BCE, when Nandi transcribed the work. An early version of

Kāmasūtra, pre-dates eighth century BCE. Alain Danielou discusses the predecessors of Vātsyāyana: "The first formulation of the *Kamaśāstra,* or rules of love, is attributed to Nandi, Shiva's companion. During the eighth century BCE, Śvetaketu, son of Uddālaka, undertook the summary of Nandi's work.The date is known, since Uddālaki and Śvetaketu are the protagonists of the Brihat Aranyaka Upanishad and Chandogya Upanishad, which are usually dated to this period and contain important passages connected with erotic science. A man of letters called Babhru, together with his sons or disciples, known as the Babhravya, made an important written work, summarizing the too-vast work of Śvetaketu. The Babhravya came originally from Panchala, a region located between the Ganges and the Yamuna, to the south of present-day Delhi, but most probably lived in the city of Pataliputra, the great center of the kingdom of Chandragupta, which resisted Alexander's invasion in the fourth century and became the seat of the Ashoka empire a century later...The text of Suvarnanabha must date from the first century BCE, since it mentions a king of Kuntala (to the south of Pataliputra), named Shatakarni Shatavahana who reigned at this time and who killed his wife accidentally in the course of sadistic practices. On the other hand, Yashodhara, at the beginning of his commentary, attributes the origin of erotic science to Mallanaga, the 'prophet of the Asuras' (the ancient gods), meaning to prehistoric times. Nandi, Śiva's companion, is then said to have transcribed it for manking today. The attribution of the first name Mallanaga to Vatsyayana is due to the confusion of his role as editor of the *Kāmasūtra* with that of the mythical creator of erotic science."[105]

Shrinivas Tilak notes that King Salivahana demarcated Sindhu rastra as the nation of the Aryas that lay east of the Sindhu river (*sthāpita tena maryāda mlecchāryānām pṛthak pṛthak. Sindhu sthānam iti jñeyam rāṣṭram āryasya ca uttamam. Mleccha sthānam param sindhoh kritam tena mahātmanā*: Pratisarga Adhyāya 2). Commenting on Jaiminisutra (1:3.10), Śabara discusses whether meaning of some Vedic words like *pica, nema* (not common among the Aryas but well preserved by mlecchas) should be derived from Sanskrit roots or from their actual usage by mlecchas. Śabara advocates the use of such words as used and understood by mlecchas and recommends their incorporation at the Prakrit (lokavani) level. In Tantravārttika (#150, 153 on Jaiminisutra 1:3.10), Kumarila discusses mlecchas in detail and recommends learning from their professions and skills in agriculture, building houses, producing silk products, making harnesses, astrology and drama – and related terminology and words used by mlecchas. Prabhakara also rejects parochial efforts to derive all mleccha words from Sanskrit roots and notes the need for recognizing the actual usage by mlecchas.[106] In Baudhayana, there is an intimation of deviant behavior in the beef-eating habits of mlecchas: gomāmsa khādako yastu, viruddham bahu bhāṣate, sarvācāra vihīnasya mleccha iti abhidhīyate).[107]

Early references to mleccha (meluhha) do indicate it as a dialect and NOT as a toponym or as an ethnonym (a term referring to speakers or groups of people). The distinction between *ārya vācas* and *mleccha vācas* is only in reference to, respectively, the grammatical or non-grammatical forms of the lingua franca.

That a term should have been coined to represent the writing system of mleccha language is also significant. That it was called mlecchita vikalpa and that a study of this cryptography was a prescribed art by Vātsyāyana should make us pause and rethink the early 'meaning' of mleccha. The famous Mesopotamian cylinder seal (showing the meluhhan merchant carrying the also refers to cognate meluhha as a language (requiring an interpreter).

Parpola A. and S. suggest that the Sumerian Meluhha and Sanskrit mleccha refer to the same people or land, indicating that the term Meluhha originally referred to Baluchistan/Indus-Sarasvati valley.[108] C. J. Gadd proposed that Sanskrit mleccha '(non-Vedic- Aryan)' may be a survival of the original Indian name from which Sumerian Meluhha was derived. Corresponding Pali word is noted: *milakkha.*

That the parole of mleccha impacted by influences from languages in contact, is exemplified by the following glosses --including homonyms read rebus-- related to the most frequently-occuring glyphtic elements of Indus writing: one-horned young bull. *kōnda* bullock (Kol.) *kōḍiya, kōḍe* young bull (Telugu) Rebus: *kun̆da* 'a (turner's) lathe'

koṭiyum [*koṭ, koṭī* neck] a wooden circle put round the neck of an animal (Gujarati) [cf. the orthography of rings on the neck of one-horned young bull].

Te. kōḍiya, kōḍe young bull; *adj.* male (e.g. kōḍe dūḍa bull calf), young, youthful; kōḍekāḍu a young man. *Kol.* (Haig) kōḍē bull. *Nk.* khoṛe male calf. *Konḍa* kōḍi cow; kōṛe young bullock. *Pe.* kōḍi cow. *Manḍ.* kūḍi id. *Kui* kōḍi id., ox. *Kuwi* (F.) kōdi cow; (S.) kajja kōḍi bull; (Su. P.) kōḍi cow.(DEDR 2199). *Ka.* gōnde bull, ox. *Te.* gōda ox. *Kol.* (SR.) kondā bull; (Kin.) kōnda bullock. *Nk. (Ch.)* kōnda id. *Pa.* kōnda bison. *Ga.* (Oll.) kōnde cow; (S.) kōndē bullock. *Go.* (Tr.) kōnḍā, (other dialects) kōnda bullock, ox (*Voc.* 972). (DEDR 2216). खोंड [khōṇḍa] *m* A young bull, a bullcalf. 2 A variety of जोंधळा. कोंडण [kōṇḍaṇa] गोठा [gōṭhā] A fold or pen. (Marathi).

Ta. kōṭu (in cpds. kōṭṭu-) horn, tusk, branch of tree, cluster, bunch, coil of hair, line, diagram, bank of stream or pool; kuvaṭu branch of a tree;kōṭṭāṉ, kōṭṭuvāṉ rock horned-owl (cf. 1657 Ta. kuṭiñai). Ko. ko·ṛ (obl. ko·ṭ-) horns (one horn is kob), half of hair on each side of parting, side in game, log, section of bamboo used as fuel, line marked out. To. kw ṛ (obl. kw ṭ-) horn, branch, path across stream in thicket. Ka. kōḍu horn, tusk, branch of a tree; kōṟ horn. Tu. kōḍů, kōḍu horn. Te. kōḍu rivulet, branch of a river. Pa. kōḍ (pl. kōḍul) horn. Ga. (Oll.) kōr (pl. kōrgul) id. Go. (Tr.) kōr (obl. kōt-, pl. kōhk) horn of cattle or wild animals, branch of a tree; (W. Ph. A. Ch.) kōr (pl. kōhk), (S.) kōr (pl.kōhku), (Ma.) kōṛu (pl. kōẖku) horn; (M.) kohk branch (Voc. 980); (LuS.) kogoo a horn. Kui kōju (pl. kōska) horn, antler. (DEDR 2200). korā 'horns' (Marathi)

గోతము [gōtamu] or గోతాము *gōtamu* n. A sack, a bag (Telugu) Pa. *kotthalī* -- f. ' sack (?) '; Pk. *kotthala* -- m. ' bag, grainstore ' (*kōha* -- m. ' bag ' < **kōtha*?); K. *kŏthul, °lu* m. ' large bag or parcel ', *kothüjü* f. ' small do. '; S. *kothirī* f. ' bag '; Ku. *kuthlo* ' large bag, sack '; B. *kūthlī* ' satchel, wallet '; Or. *kuthaḷi, °thuḷi, kothaḷi, °thiḷi* ' wallet, pouch '; H. *kothlā* m. ' bag, sack, stomach (see *kōttha --) ', *°lī* f. ' purse '; G. *kothḷɔ* m. ' large bag ', *°ḷī* f. ' purse, scrotum '; M. *kothḷā* m. ' large sack, chamber of stomach (= *peṭā ċā k°*) ', *°ḷẽ* n. ' sack ', *°ḷī* f. ' small sack '; -- X gōṇī´ -- : S. *gothirī* f. ' bag ', L. *gutthlā* m. (CDIAL 3511) 3545 kṓṣṭha1 m. ' any one of the large viscera ' MBh. [Same as kṓṣṭha -- 2? Cf. *kōttha --] Pa. *koṭṭha* -- m. ' stomach ', Pk. *koṭṭha* -- , *kuṭ°* m.; L. (Shahpur) *koṭhī* f. ' heart, breast '; P. *koṭṭhā, koṭhā* m. ' belly ', G. *koṭhɔ* m., M. *koṭhā* m. (CDIAL 3545). Rebus: S. *koṭāru* m. ' district officer who watches crops, police officer ' (CDIAL 3501). Cf. *kṓṣṭhaka* 'treasury' (Skt.); *kóṭṭhi* 'temple treasury' (WPah.); *koṭho* 'warehouse' (Gujarati) (CDIAL 3546).

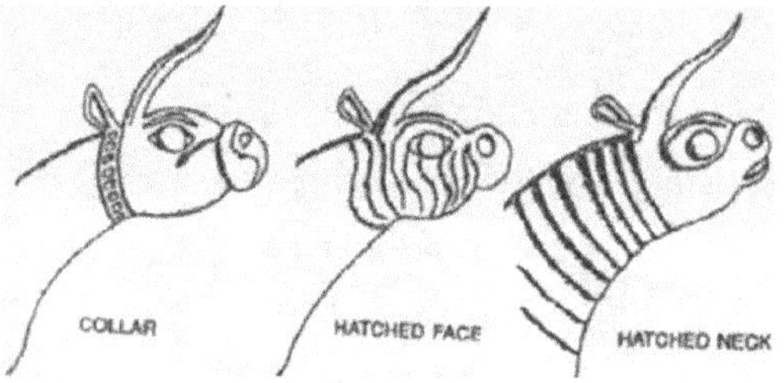

खोट [*khōṭa*] *f* A mass of metal (unwrought or of old metal melted down); an ingot or wedge. (Marathi)

ācāri koṭṭya = forge, *kammārasāle* (Tulu) *koṭḍī* a room (Gujarati) *koḍ* = artisan's workshop (Kuwi); place where artisans work (Gujarati) *koḍ* = a cow-pen; a cattlepen; a byre (Gujarati) *goṛa* = a cow-shed; a cattleshed; *goṛa orak* = byre (Santali.) *goṭho* [Skt. *koṣṭha* the inner part] a warehouse.

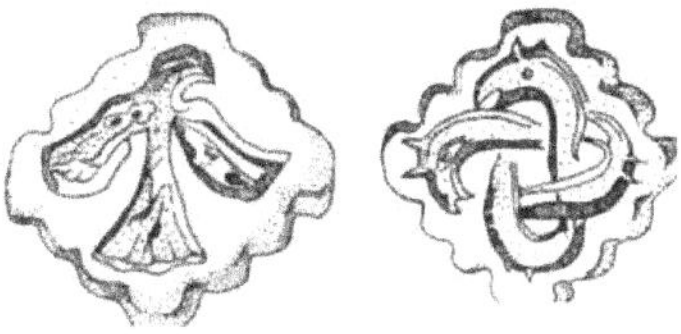

M1390, Text 2868; m0451, Text 3235; h166 Harappa Seal; Vats 1940, II: Pl. XCI.255 . Two seals from Gonur 1 in the Murghab delta; dark brown stone (Sarianidi 1981 b: 232-233, Fig. 7, 8); eagle engraved on one face.

Eagle incised on the lid of perhaps a compartmented box made of chlorite. Tepe Yahya. (After Fig. 9.7 in Philip H. Kohl, 2001, opcit.)

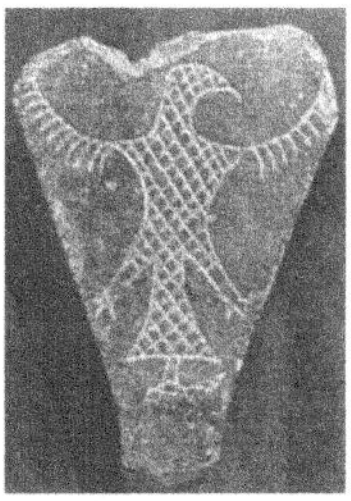

Eagle incised on a ceremonial axe made of chlorite. Tepe Yahya. (After Fig. 9.6 in Philip H. Kohl, 2001, opcit.)

The association of pajhar 'eagle' with a + glyph on h166 points to the association of the + with pasra 'smithy' (Santali) pasra = a smithy, place where a black-smith works, to work as a blacksmith; kamar pasra = a smithy; pasrao lagao akata se ban:? Has the blacksmith begun to work? pasraedae = the blacksmith is at his work (Santali.)

 Unprovenanced Harappan-style cylinder seal impression; Musee du Louvre; cf. Corbiau, 1936, An Indo-Sumerian cylinder, *Iraq* 3, 100-3, p. 101, Fig.1; De Clercq Coll.; burnt white agate; De Clercq and Menant, 1888,

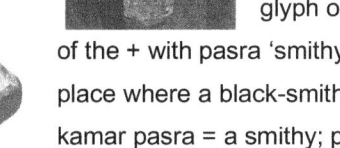

No. 26; Collon, 1987, Fig. 614. A hero grasping two tigers and a buffalo-and-leaf-horned person, seated on a stool with hoofed legs, surrounded by a snake and a fish on either side, a pair of water buffaloes. Another person stands and fights two tigers and is surrounded by trees, a markhor goat and a vulture above a rhinoceros. 9905 Prob. West Asian find Pict-117: two bisons facing each other.

Toda Mund and Sumer Mudhif

A Toda temple in Muthunadu Mund near Ooty, India. *Kur.* xolā tail. *Malt.* qoli id.(DEDR 2135) The 'tail' atop the reed-structure banner glyph is a phonetic determinant for kole.l 'temple, smithy'.

Alternative: *pajhaṛ* = to sprout from a root (Santali) Rebus: *pasra*'smithy, forge' (Santali)

m0702 Text 2206 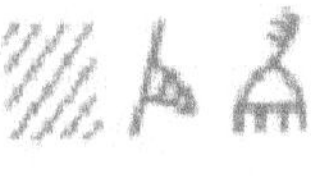 Glyph 39, a glyph which compares with the Sumerian mudhif or Toda munda structure.

[Kannada. *kōḍu*] tusk; யானை பன்றிகளின் தந்தம். மத்த யானையின் கோடும் (தேவா. 39, 1). Rebus: खोट [khōṭa] A lump or solid bit (as of phlegm, gore, curds, inspissated milk); any concretion or clot. (Marathi) Rebus: L. *khoṭ*f. ' alloy, impurity ', *°ṭā* ' alloyed ', awāṇ. *khoṭā* ' forged '; P. *khoṭ* m. ' base, alloy ' M.*khoṭā* ' alloyed ', (CDIAL 3931) kole.l = smithy (Ko.) Rebus: *Kuwi* (F.) kolhali to forge. *Koḍ.* kollë blacksmith. (DEDR 2133).

Reading 1: kole.l = smithy, temple in Kota village (Ko.) Rebus 1: *Ta.* kol working in iron, blacksmith; kollaṉ blacksmith. *Ma.* kollan blacksmith, artificer. *Ka.* kolime, kolume, kulame, kulime, kulume, kulme fire-pit, furnace; (Bell.; U.P.U.) konimi blacksmith (Gowda) kolla id. *Koḍ.* kollë blacksmith. *Te.* kolimi furnace.
Go. (SR.) kollusānā to mend implements; (Ph.) kolstānā, kulsānā to forge; (Tr.) kōlstānā to repair (of ploughshares); (SR.) kolmi smithy (*Voc.* 948).
Kuwi (F.) kolhali to forge. (DEDR 2133). Rebus 2: *Ko.* kole·l smithy, temple in Kota village. *To.* kwala·l Kota smithy (DEDR 2133).

Reading 2: goṭ = the place where cattle are collected at mid-day (Santali); goṭh (Brj.)(CDIAL 4336). Goṣṭha (Skt.); cattle-shed (Or.) koḍ = a cow-pen; a cattlepen; a byre (G.) कोठी cattle-shed (Marathi) कोंडी[kōṇḍī] A pen or fold for cattle. गोठी [gōṭhī] f C (Dim. Of गोठा) A pen or fold for calves. (Marathi)
On a cylinder seal from Uruk, a professional group of workers in a smithy are shown as a procession of young bull calves and other quadrupeds emerging out of the smithy.

Cylinder seal and impression: cattle herd at the cowshed. White limestone, Mesopotamia, Uruk Period (4100 BC–3000 BC). Louvre Museum.

33

Herd near building surmounted by emblems consisting of poles flanked by two or three pair of rings, calves emerging from building near what seem to be troughs. Gray limestone with shell rings set in top and base; silver axle and loop. 6x3.6cm.

Cylinder seal with humans and animals (left) and impression (right), ca. 3300–2900 B.C.; Late Uruk–Jamdat Nasr. Mesopotamia. Magnetite and copper; H. 8.5 cm (3 3/8 in.); Diam. 4.8 cm (1 7/8 in.). Magnesite. Visitors of the Ashmolean Museum, Oxford AN 1964 744. Is the identity of the god responsible for the mudhif conveyed through the use of a symbol emerging from the top of the hut?[109]

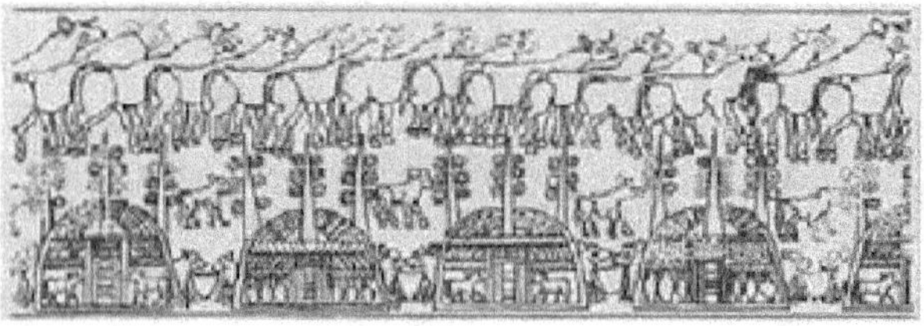

Drawing of an impression from a Uruk period cylinder seal. Glyptic representation of cattle and calves in byres.(After Sherratt 1981: Fig. 10.12)[110]

In the lower field of this seal appear three reed cattle byres. Each byre is surmounted by three reed pillars topped by rings, a motif that has been suggested as symbolizing a male god, perhaps Dumuzi. Within the huts calves or vessels appear alternately; from the sides come calves that drink out of a vessel between them. Above each pair of animals another small calf appears. A herd of enormous cattle moves in the upper field. There are three reed decorations atop the mudhif (or, Toda mund). kāḍ 1 काँड् । काण्डः m. the stalk or stem of a reed, grass, or the like, straw. In the compound with dan 5 (p. 221*a,* l. 13) the word is spelt kāḍ. Rebus: khāṇḍa 'tools, pots and pans, and metal-ware'.

Sumerian mudhif facade, with uncut reed fonds and sheep entering, carved into a gypsum trough from Uruk, c. 3200 BCE. This trough was found at Uruk, the largest city so far known in southern Mesopotamia in the late prehistoric period (3300-3000 BC). The carving on the side shows a procession of sheep (a goat and a ram)

Carved gypsum trough from Uruk. Two lambs exit a reed structure. A bundle of reeds (Inanna's symbol) can be seen projecting from the hut and at the edges of the scene. The British Museum. WA 120000, neg. 252077 Part of the right-hand scene is cast from the original fragment now in the Vorderasiatisches Museum, Berlin.

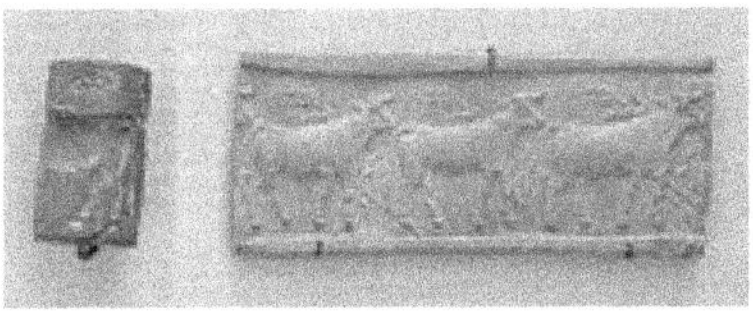

Cylinder seal and impression: cattle herd in a wheat field. Limestone, Mesopotamia, Uruk Period (4100 BC–3000 BC).

kuṇḍa n. 'clump' (Sanskrit) A phonetic determinant of the young bull *kōḍā* खोंड [khōṇḍa] m 'A young bull, a bullcalf'. (Marathi) read rebus: *kūderā* m. 'one who works a lathe'. Alternative: The cob is kolmo 'seeding, rice-plant'(Munda) rebus: kolami 'smithy'; (Telugu).

Mudhif and three reed banners. A cow and a stable of reeds with sculpted columns in the background. Fragment of another vase of alabaster (era of Djemet-Nasr) from Uruk, Mesopotamia. Limestone 16 X 22.5 cm. AO 8842, Louvre, Departement des Antiquites Orientales, Paris, France. Six circles decorated on the reed post are semantic determinants of Glyph:

Glyphs: six (numeral) + ring of hair: आर [āra] A term in the play of इटीदांडू,--the number six. (Marathi) आर [āra] A tuft or ring of hair on the body. (Marathi) Rebus: āra 'brass'. Alternative: *bhaṭa* 'six'. Rebus: *bhaṭa* 'furnace'.

काँड् । काण्डः m. the stalk or stem of a reed, grass, or the like, straw. In the compound with dan 5 (p. 221*a*, l. 13) the word is spelt kāḍ. The rebus reading of the pair of reeds in Sumer standard is: *khāṇḍa* 'tools, pots and pans and metal-ware'. Thus, together, the rebus reading is: *khāṇḍ āra* 'maker of metalware'.

Quadrupeds exiting the mund (or mudhif) are *pasaramu, pasalamu* 'an animal, a beast, a brute, quadruped' (Telugu) పసరము [pasaramu] or పసలము *pasaramu.* [Tel.] n. A beast, an animal. గోమహిషహోతి.

Rebus: pasra = a smithy, place where a black-smith works, to work as a blacksmith; kamar pasra = a smithy; pasrao lagao akata se ban:? Has the blacksmith begun to work? pasraedae = the blacksmith is at his work (Santali.) pasra meṛed, pasāra meṛed = syn. of koṭe meṛed = forged iron, in contrast to dul meṛed, cast iron (Mundari) పసారము [pasāramu]

or పసారు *pasārdmu.* [Tel.] n. A shop. అంగడి. Allograph: pacar = a wedge driven ino a wooden pin, wedge etc. to tighten it (Santali.) Allograph: pajhar 'eagle'.

Text 1330 (appears with zebu glyph). Shown as exiting the kole.l 'smithy' are *kol* 'blacksmiths' and *kũderā 'lathe-workers'.*

The young bulls emerging from the smithy. *kõdā* खोंड [khōṇḍa] m A young bull, a bullcalf. (Marathi) Rebus 1: kŏṇḍu or konḍu । कुण्डम् m. a hole dug in the ground for receiving consecrated fire (Kashmiri)Rebus 2: A. *kundār*, B. *kũdār*, *°ri*, Or. *kundāru*; H. *kũderā* m. ' one who works a lathe, one who scrapes ', *°rī* f., *kũdernā* ' to scrape, plane, round on a lathe '.(CDIAL 3297).
खांडा [khāṇḍā] *m* A jag, notch, or indentation (as upon the edge of a tool or weapon). Rebus: khāṇḍa 'tools, pots and pans, and metal-ware'. kole.l = smithy (Ko.) Rebus: *Kuwi* (F.) kolhali to forge. *Koḍ.* kollë blacksmith. (DEDR 2133).

ayo 'fish' Rebus: ayas 'metal'.

kuṭila 'bent'; rebus: kuṭila, katthīl = bronze (8 parts copper and 2 parts tin) कथली [kathalī] *f* (कथील) A certain vessel made of tin. कथली [kathalī] *a* (कथील) Composed of tin; relating to tin. (Marathi)

[cf. āra-kūṭa, 'brass' (Skt.) (CDIAL 3230) kuṭi— in cmpd. 'curve' (Skt.)(CDIAL 3231).

kanka 'rim of jar' Rebus: *karṇika 'accountant'. kul -- karṇī* m. 'village accountant' (Marathi); *karṇikan* id. (Tamil) கணக்கு kaṇakku, n. cf. gaṇaka. [M. kaṇakku] 1. Number, account, reckoning, calculation, computation (Tamil) Rebus: 'to engrave, write; lapidary': <kana-lekhe>(P) {??} ``??". |. Cf. <kana->. %16123. #16013. <lekhe->(P),,<leke->(KM) {VTC} ``to ^write". Cf. <kana-lekhe>. *Kh.<likhae>, H.<lIkhAna>, O.<lekhIba>, B.<lekha>; Kh.<likha>(P), Mu.<lika>. %20701. #20541. (Munda etyma) Kashmiri: khanun खनुन् । खननम् conj. 1 (1 p.p. khonu for 1, see s.v.; f. khüñü to dig (K.Pr. 155, 247; L. 459; Śiv. 59, 746, 994, 143, 1197, 1214, 1373, 1754; Rām. 343, 958, 1147, 1724; H. xii, 6); to engrave (Śiv. 414, 671, 176; Rām. 1583). khonu-motu खनुमतु; । खातः perf. part. (f. khüñümütsü) dug (e.g. a field, or a well); engraved. mŏhara-khonu म्वहर-खनु; or (Gr.M.) mŏhar-kan । मुद्राखननकारुः m. a seal-engraver, a lapidary (El. *mohar-kand*). -wöjü । *अङ्गुलिमुद्रा f. a signet-ring. DEDR 1170
Ta. kaṇṭam iron style for writing on palmyra leaves. *Te.* gaṇṭamu id.

DEDR 1179 *Kur.* kaṇḍō a stool. *Malt.* kanḍo stool, seat. **గడమంచె** *gaḍa-manche*. n. A wooden frame like a bench to keep things on. గంపలు మొదలగువాటిని ఉంచు మంచె.

Kuiper cites from Southworth the following examples of glosses, testifying to a 'strong foreign impact' on proto-Indo-Aryan or mleccha: *kūṭa*, 'house'; *kuṇḍa*, 'pot, vessel'; ū*rdara*, 'a measure for holding grain'; *apūpa*, 'cake'; *odana*, 'rice dish'; *karambha*, 'a kind of gruel'; *piṇḍa*, 'a lump of flesh';*ulūkhala*, 'mortar'; *kārotara*, 'sieve, drainer'; *camriṣ,* 'ladle'; *kośa*, 'cask, bucket'; *kṛśana*, 'pearl'; *kīnāśa, kīnāra*, 'ploughman'; *khilya*, 'waste piece of land'; *lāngala*, 'plough'; *sīra*, 'plough'; *phāla,* 'ploughshare'; *tilvila*, 'fertile, rich'; *bīja*, 'seed'; *pippala*, 'berry of the *ficus religiosa*'; *mūla,* 'root'; *khala*, 'threshing floor'; *ṛbīsa*, 'volcanic cleft'; *kevaṭa*, 'cave, pit'; *kṛpīṭa*, 'thick or firewood'; *śakaṭī,* 'cart'; āṇi, 'linch-pin'; *vāṇi,* 'swingle tree'; *kuliśa*, 'axe'; *kūṭa*, 'mallet'.[111]

One Meluhhan village in Akkad (3rd millennium BCE)

Though cylinder seals are normally associated with Metopotamian civilization, Sibri and Kalibangan have yielded cylinder seals, but with unique glyphs of the script. SR Rao found a Gulf seal at Lothal. Claiming that an area of 1.3 million sq.km. was covered, Joshi, Bala and Ram call it 'Sarasvati civilization' or 'Sarasvati culture'.[112]

In Sargon I's reign (ca. 2370 BCE), a reference is made to 'holder of a Meluhha ship' . A seal in British Museum (ca. 2250 BCE) lists enemies of King Naram-Sin, among them is a 'man of Meluhha' by the name of _ibra."

Meluhha was used as a personal name for some people. Urkal, Ur-dlam were called the 'son of meluhha'. A person called nin-ana is identified with the village of meluhha. Meluhha was also identified with specific products: giS-ab-ba-me-luhha (abba wood); giS-ha-lu-ub (Haluppu wood).

[quote] Numerous Mesopotamian documents, spanning several centuries, refer to the lands of Meluhha, Makkan, and Dilmun. Modern scholars identify Meluhha with the Indus Valley, Makkan with the Makran and Omani coasts, and Dilmun with Bahrain, Failaka, and the adjacent Arabian coastline. These three far-flung lands were important partners in the immense trade network in which Mesopotamia participated. A brief overview of the major literary references includes:

- Sargon's inscription referring to Meluhhan ships docked at Akkad.
- References to a Meluhhan ship-holder and a Meluhhan interpreter.
- Gudea of Lagash inscriptions (ca. 22nd cent. BCE): 'the Meluhhans came up (or down) from their country to supply wood and other raw materials for the construction of the main temple of Gudea's capital.'
- References to luxury items being imported from Meluhha.
- References to a Meluhhan workers village.[unquote][113]

It is fascinating to note that by the Ur III Period, the Meluhhan (Harappan) workers residing in Sumeria had Sumerian names, leading Parpola, Parpola, and Brunswig to comment that 'three hundred years after the earliest textually documented contact between Meluhha and Mesopotamia, the references to a distinctly foreign commercial people have been replaced by an ethnic component of Ur III society' (Parpola et al. 1977:152). Here we have an undeniable economically-based presence of Indus traders maintaining their own distinct village in a distant peripheral location over a considerable span of time.][114]

Meluhha lay to the east of Magan and linked with carnelian and ivory. Carnelian! Gujarat was a carnelian source in the ancient world. Possehl locates meluhha in the mountains of Baluchistan and meluhhan use magilum-boat.[115] sinda refers to date-palm.[116]

Many scholars have noted the contacts between the Mesopotamian and Sarasvati Sindhu (Indus) Civilizations, in terms of cultural history, chronology, artefacts (beads, jewellery), pottery and seals found from archaeological sites in the two areas.

"...the four examples of round seals found in Mohenjodaro show well-supported sequences, whereas the three from Mesopotamia show sequences of signs not paralleled elsewhere in the Indus Script. But the ordinary square seals found in Mesopotamia show the normal Mohenjodaro sequences. In other words, the square seals are in the Indian language, and were probably imported in the course of trade; while the circular seals, although in the Indus script, are in a different language, and were probably manufactured in Mesopotamia for a Sumerian- or Semitic-speaking person of Indian descent..." [G.R. Hunter,1932. Mohenjodaro--Indus Epigraphy, JRAS: 466-503] On the contrary, it is possible that Meluhhans in settlements used the Indus writing on circular seals in mleccha (meluhha), if the sequences of glyphs are properly decoded.

The acculturation of Meluhhans (probably, Indus people) residing in Mesopotamia in the late third and early second millennium BC, is noted by their adoption of Sumerian names.[117] "The adaptation of Harappan motifs and script to the Dilmun seal form may be a further indication of the acculturative phenomenon, one indicated in Mesopotamia by the adaptation of Harappan traits to the cylinder seal." (Brunswig et al, 1983, p. 110).

"Indian-style" seals have been found in Sumeria. In 1932, CJ Gadd published such seals from Mesopotamia (some of these are identified as Dilmun seals coming from Failaka and Bahrein – gulf islands). Massimo Vidale notes: "As the identification of the land of Meluhha with the coastal areas controlled by the Indus Civilization is almost universally accepted, the textual evidence dealing with individuals qualified as "men" or "sons" of Meluhha or called with the ethnonym Meluhha, living in Mesopotamia and of a "Meluhha village" established at Lagash (and presumably at other major cities as well) unexcapably points to the existence of enclaves settled by Indian migrants …Meluhhan ships exported to Mesopotamia precious goods among which exotic animals, such as dogs, perhaps peacocks, cocks, bovids, elephants (? Collon 1977) precious woods and royal furniture, precious stones such as carnelian, agate and lapislazuli, and metals like gold, silver and tin...Akkadian text records that Lu-sunzida 'a man of Meluhha' paid to the servant Urur, son of Amar-lu-KU 10 shekels of silver as payment for a tooth broken in a clash. The name Lu-sunzida literally means 'Man of the just buffalo cow', a name that, although rendered in Sumerian, according to the authors does not make sense in the Mesopotamian cultural sphere, and must be a translation of an Indian name..."[118]

Head of an Indian from the Persepolis stairway reliefs.

A remarkable link between the invention of alloying and the birth of writing has been noted: "The Early Bronze Age of the 3rd millennium BCE saw the first development of a truly international age of metallurgy... The question is, of course, why all this took place in the 3rd millennium BCE... It seems to me that any attempt to explain why things suddenly took off about 3000 BCE has to explain the most important development, the birth of the art of writing... As for the concept of a Bronze Age one of the most significant events in the 3rd millennium was the development of true tin-bronze alongside an arsenical alloy of copper..."[119] Arsenical bronze occurs in the archaeological record across the globe, the earliest artifacts so far known have been found on the Iranian plateau in the 5th millennium BCE.[120]

A revolution comparable to organized farming during the Neolithic occurred in the Bronze Age. The revolution was the result of the invention of alloying tin with copper to produce tin-bronze. One ton of tin when alloyed with 10 tons of copper could produce 11 tons of bronze. Tin bronzes replaced naturally occurring arsenical copper bronzes because tin was prospected and distributed in a widespread area of anient Near East – an area which extended from Rakhigarhi (near Delhi) to Haifa (Israel). In this area, either copper was smelted and alloyed with tin to produce tin-bronze, or alloyed bronze was directly obtained by trade from a nearby production area called Meluhha. This trade was destined for Sumer or Mesopotamia through the transit areas called Dilmun, Magan and Elam. Evidence exists for Meluhhan settlements to authenticate this trade.[121]

Damaged cicular clay furnace, comprising iron slag and tuyeres and other waste materials stuck with its body, exposed at Lohsanwa mound, Period II, Malhar, Dist. Chandauli. Bronze Age is characterized by the widespread use of copper and its alloy bronze. In some parts of the globe, Iron Age intruded directly on the Neolithic, as in the evidence of iron smelting in Lohardiva, Malhar and Raja Nal ki Tila of Ganga basin, dated to ca 18th century BCE.[122]

Some metalware terms which spread across a wide contact area of the Bronze Age may be cited merely as a reference list to explore further the spread of specific sememes as in the case of *ayas* 'metal, bronze'. Given that the Celtic derivations appear unsatisfactory Vennemann (1998: 464-465) offers the meaning 'copper island' for *Ériu* deriving from Paleosemitic Etyma from Hebrew *'-y-* 'island' and Akkadian *werûm, erû,* Assyrian often *eriu(m)* 'copper, bronze'. From paleosemitic *'y-wr'(m) 'copper island' constructed and vocalised as **'iy+weri'um, *iyweri'im*, it would be possible for such a construct to pass easily as a loanword into Greek, Latin and Celtic.[123]

Some names fo metals[124]

midnycia "copper bowl" in Ukrainian (*mid'* "copper").

Munda

med 'iron'

— Slavic

Мед [Med] *Bulgarian*

Медзь [medz'] *Belarusian*

Měď *Czech*

Miedź *Polish*

Медь [Med'] *Russian*

Meď *Slovak*

Мідь [mid'] *Ukrainian*

Bronze Age Linguistic Doctrine

How did the Meluhh (Mleccha) language, Munda, Dravidian and Indo-Aryan language families constitute themselves into an Indian *sprachbund*? Bronze Age imperative!

Bronze Age intensified the prospecting for key alloying minerals to create metal tools, pots and pans. This led to movements of lapidaries, miners and metalsmiths to move, in search of mineral resources, to places far-off from their homes.

The new revolutionary products created from precious stones, minerals of tin and zinc alloyed with copper to create bronze and brass ingots, metal tools, sharp and heavy, non-brittle metal weapons, metal pots and metal pans, by lapidaries, miners and metalsmiths resulted in a demand for the stoneware and metalware across a wide area extending from Rakhigarhi (Delhi, India) to Haifa (Israel). This demand necessitated long-distance trade by sea-faring artisans and merchants. This trade also necessitated the invention of writing systems to document the nature of products traded and identify the parties involved in the trade contracts. One such writing system was Indus Writing which provided rebuses using Meluhha (Mleccha) words to describe and incise (*takṣat vāk*, incised speech) words as Indus inscription texts and pictorial motifs which are verily stoneware and metalware catalogs. These catalogs were complemented by cuneiform texts to specify contracting parties and contract terms for the trade.

Thus, the Bronze Age imperative led to increased exchange of technical terms, particularly those related to metalwork, which were absorbed into various languages of the contact areas involved with the production and trade of stoneware and metalware. This Bronze Age absorption of technical terms is comparable to the terms generated by the communications revolution of recent decades involving computers and cell-phones which have been incorporated into lexicons of languages all over the globe.

The Meluhha prospectors, artisans and traders established settlements in Sumer and Mesopotamia and had trade agents along the Persian Gulf in Dilmun and Magan, as evidenced by cuneiform texts and seals/tablets with incised Indus writing, categorized as Dilmun or Failaka or Persian Gulf seals.

The Bronze Age imperative which impacted languages is briefly delineated by the phrase, Bronze Age Linguistic Doctrine. An outline of this doctrine need not be detained by polemics of Aryan Invasion or Migration Theories or Out of India Theories since direction of borrowings is not required to be specified to delineate the Indian *sprachbund*, a linguistic area which included many cognate semantic clusters with terms necessitated by the inventions of the Bronze Age.

Nature of doctrine

A doctrine is postulated as an informative proposition or truth claim of objective reality. A doctrine gains the attributes of an authoritative dogma. Doctrines are common in theological domain but it is surprising to find a doctrine in the domain of language studies.

One such doctrine postulated by linguists to explain cognate glosses among Indo-European languages was the Aryan Invasion Theory (with variants such as

Aryan Migration or Trickle-in Theories). This doctrine sought to explain many glosses in a category called Indo-Aryan languages. The doctrine was, simply that Aryan-speakers invaded India and forced their Indo-European language on the natives' and forced modifications in the natives' tongue or speech, creating Indo-Aryan. Counter-arguments have been advanced that an Out of India Theory is also consistent with the evidence of glosses in Indo-Aryan languages cognate with Indo-European and polemical views point to many areas as possible *urheimat*, original homeland of IE speakers.

An alternative to the Aryan Invasion Linguistic Doctrine is proposed to explain the essential semantic unity of many ancient Indian languages of the Bronze Age. Many cognate metallurgical terms invented during the Bronze Age were adopted within the speech area — cutting across Munda, Dravidian and Indo-Aryan language families. Bronze Age Linguistic Doctrine explains the *raison d'etre* for the formation of Indian *sprachbund*, a language union because tin-bronzes resulted in a revolution in ways of living of the people living and identified with the *sprachbund*. Earlier arsenical bronzes from the Anatolian peninsula of Turkey produced brittle weapons that shattered on impact. Widespread and large-scale use of bronze for tools such as ploughshare, hammer, sickle changed the nature and scale of daily activities and use of bronze for sharp swords, spear or arrow tips and other weapons changed the nature of warfare and areal contacts and relationships. With bronze and later iron tools, stone cutting, dressing, and sculpting were possible. The revolutionary nature of cultural change brought about by the use of bronze is comparable to the revolution witnessed in the use of modern computers and mobile phones or in the wake of industrial revolution, the use of railway trains for long-distance or commuter travel. Such technological inventions profoundly alter the speech forms in vogue all over the world with the common use of lexical terms such as train, ticket, cell-phone, call – in almost all languages of the globe.

The ruling IE linguistic doctrine is now on its last legs of decay: the fate of doctrines is that If once true, is always true and if once false, is always false.

The situation calls for a new doctrine to replace the terms of the decayed linguistic doctrine of Aryan Invasion because mere trickle-in by tourists cannot explain displacement of entire sets of languages or speech of 'natives' and there is no archaeological evidence for any Aryan invasion.

Doctrinal reconciliation, without calling for capitulation, is possible by postulating a replacement doctrine which explains the realities in three dimensions to reconstruct the living of life over millennia: anthropology/archaeology, culture (value systems) and language.[125]

The presentation occurs in the context of his effort to seek unity in the church, reconciling varying church doctrines. Lindbeck notes that religion refers to "a kind of cultural and/or linguistic framework or medium that shapes the entirety of life and thought ... it is similar to an idiom that makes possible the description of realities, the formulation of beliefs, and the experiencing of inner attitudes, feelings, and sentiments." [Lindbeck, *The Nature of Doctrine*, 33] Lindbeck mentions that Wittgenstein conceives of private languages as "logically impossible." [Lindbeck, *The Nature of Doctrine*, 38] However, on a closer reading, one finds that 'logical impossibility' is not a category in which Wittgenstein is working as much as the category of 'sense' [*Sinn*] and 'non-sense' [*Unsinn*].[126]

Even in physics or chemistry, a theory alters the facts to be observed and use of observation terms. This is demonstrated by shifts from Aristotlean to Newtonian to Einsteinian physics and from Darwinian biology to Genetic chemistry. Similarly, in the IE linguistic doctrine of Aryan Invasion Theory, the term 'invasion' was modified by using terms such as 'migration' or 'trickle-in' to explain the reality of features of Indo-Aryan languages which were found to be in common with other Indo-European languages. This theory soon ran into rough weather by questions raised by archaeological realities and by the presence of a large number of agricultural terms in many Indo-Aryan languages which had no cognates in other Indo-European languages. This led to the amendment of the doctrine of Aryan Invasion Theory to posit an Indian *sprachbund*, a linguistic area where different language families absorbed core language features from one another to create a linguistic union called the *sprachbund*. This doctrinal capitulation is merely an attempt to still retain the framework of a linguistic theory positing an essential unity of Indo-European (IE) languages including the Indo-Aryan languages. This capitulation runs into further rough weather when linguists began to see the presence of Munda words in Sanskrit and affinities between Munda and Dravidian languages.

An event more profound than the Aryan invasion or trickle-in was the advent of the Bronze Age which had a decisive impact on the realities of material life, culture and language. The Bronze Age created an adventure of ideas and experiments in metallurgy in relating man to the material world which travelled far and wide without requiring large scale movements or migrations of people. The Bronze Age in reality solidified the Indian *sprachbund*. Hundreds of etyma of Munda, Dravidian and Indo-Aryan languages have provided cognates for the semantics of a particular metalware term, clearly pointing to the emergence of the *sprachbund* with the incorporation of such terms. Vidura conversing with Yudhishtira in Mleccha (Meluhha) language is attested in the Great Epic. The specific reference to the language and rebus readings of Indus writing hieroglyphs incorporate meluhha (mleccha) within the *sprachbund*. And, this incorporation occurred in the Bronze Age.

From an anthropological or archaeological perspective, the march of time is viewed in linear sequence with Stone Age, Bronze Age and Iron Age, a classification proposed by a Danish antiquarian, Christian Jürgensen Thomsen. A refinement of the period of transition to Bronze Age is a Neolithic Age. Isaac Taylor in *The Origin of the Aryans*, 1889, mentions the Mesolithic as "a transition between the Palaeolithic and Neolithic Periods." Neolithic (New Stone) Age begins about 10,200 BCE in some parts of ancient Near East and ending between 4,500 to 2,000 BCE. This Age is commonly seen as related to the beginning of a revolution called farming. The Age ended when copper age or bronze age or iron age tools became widespread. The Age is characterized by the cultural advances in domestication of animals.

In the context of documentation for languages, writing systems occur during the

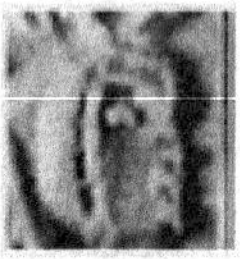

Bronze Age. Viable writing systems arose in Indus (hieroglyphs *mũh* 'face'. *mũhe* 'ingot'.), China (oracle bone script), Near East (cuneiform – related to Sumerian, Akkadian or Elamite or Hittite

or Ugaritic), Egypt

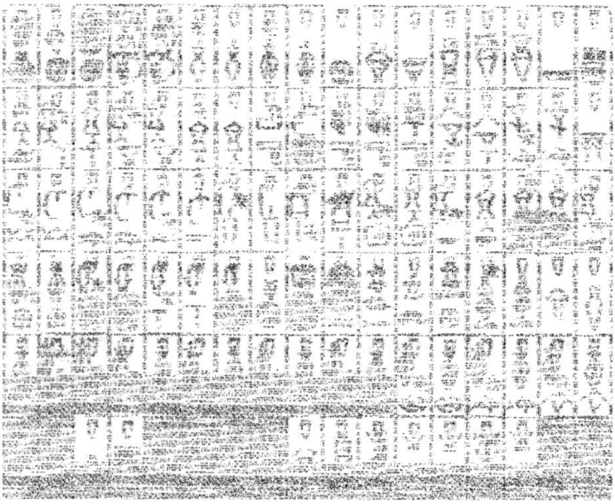

(hieroglyphs Determinative hieroglyph for copper/bronze), and the Mediterranean (Linear B 'bronze').

Musée du Louvre. A complex token shaped like a bun-ingot denoted metal ingot, Susa, ca. 3300 BCE. Bronze inscriptions (金文, i.e. "text on metal") preceded by a century the oracle bone script.

Proto-cuneiform metals list. Composite text of "Archaic Metals".[127]

Mleccha speech is mentioned in an ancient Vedic text, *Śatapathabrāhmaṇa* (3.2.1.18-24) which speaks of *asuryā vāk*. The text is dated to 8th century BCE. After the Asura were deprived of speech (vāk) which was offered to fire for purification while reciting *anuṣṭubh*, the asura shouting *he'layo he'layo* got defeated. No Vedic adherent should speak such mleccha (speech). Ṛgveda also attest to a writing system by the phrase, *takṣat vāk,* 'incised speech'.[128]

A remarkable evidence relates to the presence of Meluhhan traders in the Persian Gulf region (which links Meluhha – Indus valley – with Mesopotamia): "Several tablets refer to a colony of acculturated Meluhhan traders in Lagash."[129]

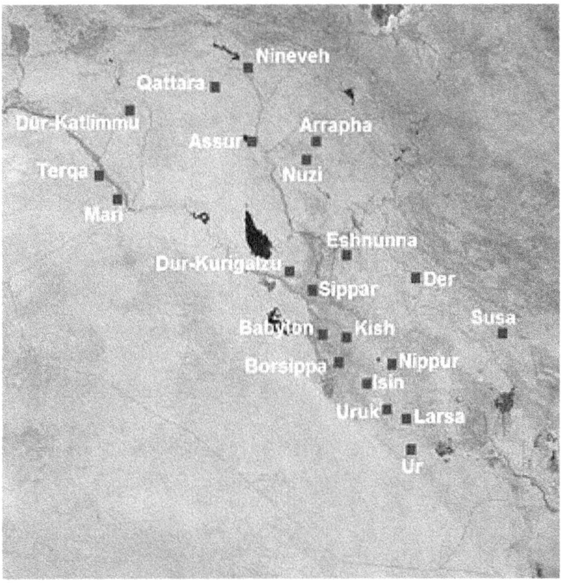

This is matched by genetic evidence from Terqa (Tell Ashara) in Mesopotamia linking Sumerians and Meluhhans: "Ancient DNA methodology was applied to analyse sequences extracted from freshly unearthed remains (teeth) of 4 individuals deeply deposited in slightly alkaline soil of the Tell Ashara (ancient Terqa) and Tell Masaikh (ancient Kar-Assurnasirpal) Syrian archaeological sites, both in the middle Euphrates valley. Dated to the period between 2.5 Kyrs BC and 0.5 Kyrs AD the studied individuals carried mtDNA haplotypes corresponding to the M4b1, M49 and/or M61 haplogroups, which are believed to have arisen in the area of the Indian subcontinent during the Upper Paleolithic and are absent in people living today in Syria. However, they are present in people inhabiting today's Tibet, Himalayas, India and Pakistan. We anticipate that the analysed remains from Mesopotamia belonged to people with genetic affinity to the Indian subcontinent since the distribution of identified ancient haplotypes indicates solid link with populations from the region of South Asia-Tibet (Trans-Himalaya). They may have been descendants of migrants from much earlier times, spreading the clades of the macrohaplogroup M throughout Eurasia and founding regional Mesopotamian groups like that of Terqa or just merchants moving along trade routes passing near or through the region."[130]

"Research was also carried out by another team (Sołtysiak et al 2013) examining fifty-nine dental non-metric traits on a sample of teeth from 350 human skeletons excavated at three sites in the lower middle Euphrates valley. This showed a stable population until after the Mongolian invasion which resulted in a large depopulation of northern Mesopotamia in the 13th century CE. The final major change occurred during the 17th century with Bedouin tribes arriving from the Arabian Peninsula... In the case of one of the studied specimens the researchers analysed both mtDNA and nuDNA sequences… Origins in the Indian subcontinent.The studied individuals carried mtDNA haplotypes corresponding to the M4b1, M49 and/or M61 haplogroups, which are believed to have arisen in the area of the Indian subcontinent during the Upper Palaeolithic and are absent in people living today in Syria. However, these same haplogroups are present in people inhabiting today's Tibet, Himalayas, India and Pakistan.

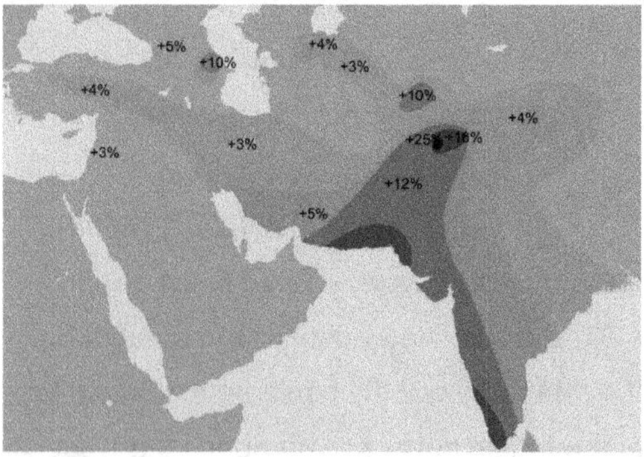

Distribution of haplogroup L of Y-Chromosome – Possible time of origin 25,000-30,000 years BP. Image. Wikimedia

The suggestion is that these analysed remains from Mesopotamia belonged to people with a genetic affinity to the Indian subcontinent as the distribution of identified ancient haplotypes indicates a solid link with populations from the region of South Asia-Tibet (Trans-Himalaya)."[131]

Meluhha may mean the lands of the Indian Ocean[132]

“The text may date back to 2300 BCE and has come to us in a bilingual version, in Sumerian and Akkadian, probably compiled six hundred years later in Old Babylonian times. Here is the Akkadian version according to H. Hirsch: MA me-lukh-kha MA ma qan-ki MA dilmun-ki in gar-ri-im si a-ga-de-ki ir-ku-us ‘...made the Meluhha ships, the Makkan ships, the Dilmun ships tie up alongside the quay of Agade.’ The names of the countries Meluhha, Makkan and Dilmun designate coastal regions which for the Sumerians were aligned as a single roué in the Lower Sea. Sargon’s text mentions them all together for the first time as parts of a single compartment in the geography of his time. Perhaps the most appropriate image is that of an upsidedown funnel which narrows from the Erythraean Sea until it flows into lower Mesopotamia, conveying goods and products from a much broader area towards the major centres of production and consumption.”[133]

"Meluhha was certainly the most distant of the countries beyond the sea the list of its products which were embarked there is among the richest and most varied and comprises precious stones, (chalcedony, cornelian and lapis luzuli) copper, gold and other prized metals, ebony, the wood of sissoo, the gis-ab-be 'sea

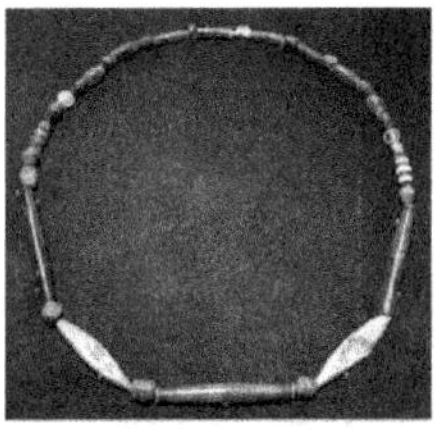

wood' (maybe mangrove) cane, peacocks and roosters. The texts also speak of ships, skilled sailors and sophisticated inlaid furniture...seafaring merchants from the distant lands of Dilmun, Meluhha and Maakan tied up at Akkads quay during Sargon's reign 2334-2279 BC. Copper was shipped directly from Maakan. During the reign of Gudea of Lagas, copper diorite and wood were delivered from Maakan and Meluhha delivered rare woods, gold *Tin* lapis Lazuli and carnelian to Lagas.There are no records indicating that ships from Meluhha docked in Sumeror that Sumerian seamen were themselves in Meluhha.""Tukulti-Ninurta refers to himself as 'King of the Upper and Lower Seas and ruler over Dilmun and Meluhha."

Mesopotamian carnelian, lapis lazuli, and gold beads, restored as a necklace, l. 14.3 cm, mid-third millennium BCE from Iraq, Kish, Mound A, Burial A51. Chicago, the Field Museum of Natural History, inv. no. 228533. Examples of long-barrel carnelian cylinder beads from Chanhu-daro (after Mackay 1943: Pl. LXXXI) were discovered in Tello in contexts datable to the time of Gudea or the Ur III period. Amongst the earliest evidence of Harappan carnelian in

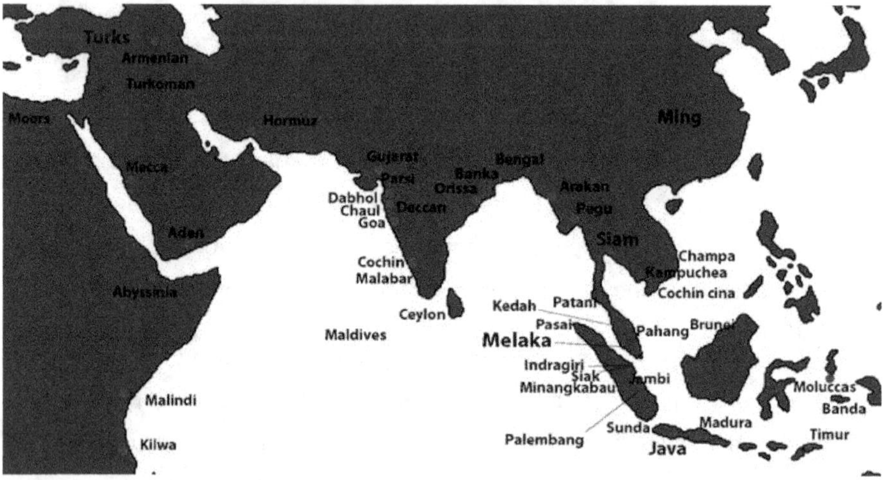

Mesopotamia15 are four 14-15-cm-long barrel-cylinder beads (Fig. XII. 7) from the Royal Cemetery at Ur (Tosi 1980:450).

Could the tin of Meluhha have come from Indonesia? "The Indonesians were sailors, crossing the Indian Ocean to settle Madagascar in the Bronze Age. The Persian Gulf, Gulf of Aden, Bay of Bengal, and Red Sea, along with the Indian Ocean were all together called the Erythrian Sea and people from the Erythrian Sea settled Sideon and Tyre; eventually becoming Phoenicans. Meanwhile, people from Indonesia moved through Melanesia to the Pacific and became Polynesians, so the two cultures Phoenicians and Polynesians are related."[134]

Map showing the locations of the Melaka (Molucca) islands, a traditional center of clove cultivation, and Terqa, where cloves have been discovered in an Old Babylonian context, ca. 1700 BCE.

Terqa structures on a mound.

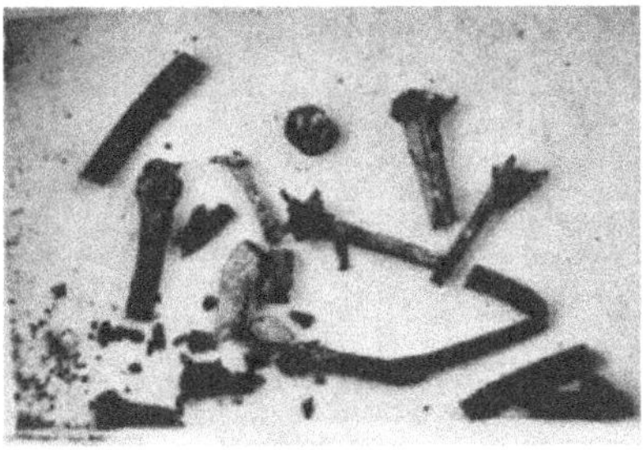

Carbonized spices found in a jar in the pantry room. These second millennium sices included cloves which were possibly traded from the Moluccas.[135]

"In the pantry of a house belonging to an individual named Puzurum, dated by tablets to c. 1700 BCE or slightly thereafter, were found 'a handful of cloves...well preserved in a partly overturned jar of a medium size' (Buccellati 1983:19; cf. Buccellati and Kelly-Buccellati 1983:54)...cloves are native to Molucca islands off the coast of Indonesia and whether or not it was via India that they arrives in Mesopotamia, from which they were transhipped up the Euphrates to Syria, they are almost certainly of Moluccan origin (Reade 1986: 331)...no consensus exist on whether the word is of Sumerian (Hempel 1993: 53) or non-Sumerian (Parpola and Parpola 1975: 205-38) origin...Terqa cloves bear witness to the extroardinary range of Mesopotamia's contacts in the second millennium, even if they reached Syria via Harappan, Dilmunite, and/or Babylonian middle men."[136]

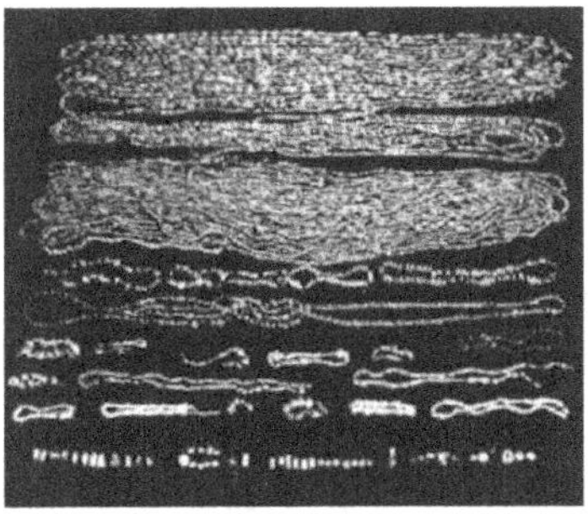

There are 550 cuneiform tablets from Terqa held at the Deir ez-Zor Museum.

The entire bead cache of the altar room. Here, the thousands of carved, semi-precious stones are strung for recording ease. They were, most likely, strung and buried in a cloth bag beneath the cella floor as a hiding place.

A small but very important find reflecting the scope of Terqa's international trade connections was indicated by the contents of a jar in the pantry of Puzurum-a few kernels of cloves. This spice was not known in the west before Romah times, and more significantly, is known to have been grown only in the distant Far East on the Molucca Islands. Long distance trade routes to the Indian sub-continent probably followed the coastline to the East. That a middleclass private individual like Puzurum not only possessed this spice but used it for cooking indicates a high degree of trans-cultural absorption. "[137]

"From Indonesia's Moluccas (Maluku) Islands to the rest of the world come the tiny but powerful flowerbuds we know as cloves. More accurately, cloves are flowerbuds from the *Syzygium aromaticum* tree that are picked before opening and dried in the sun until they resemble the little reddish-brown batons. Called *kutakaphalah* in Sanskrit, *qaranful* in Arabic or *karyphyllon* in ancient Greek (as well as *cengkeh* in North Moluccan Malay) and mentioned in the Rāmāyaṇa and later Sanskrit medical texts (*Caraka Samhita*) from the 1st Century BCE wherein the cloves were recommended along with nutmeg to freshen the breath."[138]

The discovery of cloves in Terqa is matched by the discovery of cinnamon in Tel Dor, located about 19 miles to the south of Haifa, Israel. "Phoenician flasks from this site, dating back around 3000 years, were among those that contained

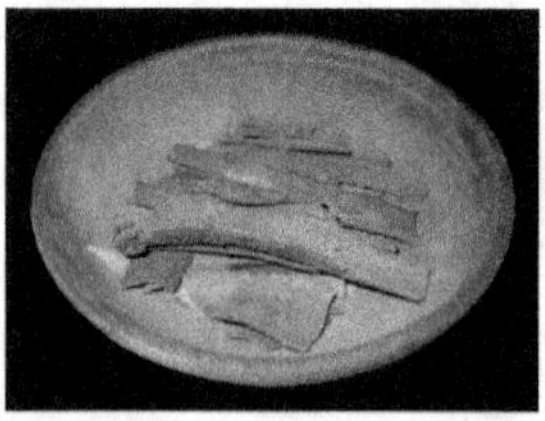

cinnamaldehyde, the compound that gives cinnamon its flavor. These finds indicate the existence of trade that brought cinnamon from the Far East to the area of modern day Israel...Researchers analyzing the contents of 27 flasks from five archaeological sites in Israel...have found that...the spice was stored in these flaks"[139]

Barks from cinnamomum verum, found naturally in southern India, Sri Lanka and Myanmar.

The cuneiform characters *meluh-ha* should be read with an alternative phonetic value: *me-lah-ha.*[140] me-lāh-ha are a clan from a Sindhi tribe known as Mohāna. *Mallah* also known as mohāna of Sindh, are traditional boatmen of ancient India, Nepal and East India who trace their roots to *niṣāda* people of *Mahābhārata*. In Baluchistan, mohana are referred to as Medes of Makran. In Arabic it means 'moving like bird's wing'. In Bengali and Bihari, the words majhi, mahishya, mandalji, machua and *mallah* refer to communities affiliated with the river and the sea. [The cuneiform characters meluh-ha should be read with an alternative phonetic value: me-lah-ha.[141] me-lāh-ha are a clan from a Sindhi tribe known as Mohāna.]

An etymology for the word Mohenjo-daro can be suggested: The word, *dāṛo* in Sindhi means 'feast given to the relatives in honour of the dead'. Mohenjo-, the prefix may be explained by Mohana, 'boatment of Sindh'.

The Louvre has also excavated a cemetery near the structures that have been dated as far back as 7,500 years. [142] Was the ziggurat a mound of the dead (like Mohenjo-daro stupa), making it a shrine to venerate the ancestors?

A reference to Meluhha, as 'the black land', occurs in the myth 'Enki and the world order' which reads:

The lands Magan and Dilmun

Looked up at me, Enki,

Moored (?) the Dilmun-boat to the ground (?),

Loaded the Magan-boat sky high;

The Magilum-boat of Meluhha,

Transports and silver and gold,

Brings them to Nippur for Enlil, the king of all the lands.

The Sumerian literary composition dealing with Ninurta and the turtle has been published by CJ Gadd in UET 6/1 2. This text shows Anzu bird carrying the tablets of fate away from Enki (not Enlil). After Ninurta (divinity of storm, wind and rain, comparable to Rgveda Indra) successfully defeated the Anzu bird, he, the hero, is caught by a turtle.[143] This myth is a memory recollected about the *kūrma avatāra* in the ten Hindu *Daśāvatārā* incarnations of Viṣṇu.

Magilum boat is 'the Boat of the West': the Epic of Gilgamesh mentions: "All living creatures born of the flesh shall sit at last in the boat of the West, and when it sinks, when the boat of Magilum sinks, they are gone."

"...the language of Marhasi [Bampur area, just west of Iranian Baluchistan] is different from that of the Simaskians [Tepe Yahya in southern Central Iran], and only very partially Elamite-related."[144] This Marhasi language could have been Meluhha. Many 'Indian' words of Mesopotamia[145] -- gisabba-meluhha (abba wood, thorn tree) and mesu, wood of the plains of Magan; si-in-da-a, si-in-du, Sindh wood, zaza cattle (zebu?), gis'immar (s'imbala, s'almali, 'salmalia malabarica'), ili 'sesame' (Akkad. ellu 'sesame oil' [cf. el̤l̤u 'sesamum indicum' (DravidianO] -- might have been transmitted by Dilmun (Bahrain) traders.

Languages of Meluhha (Mleccha) and Marhashi are the same

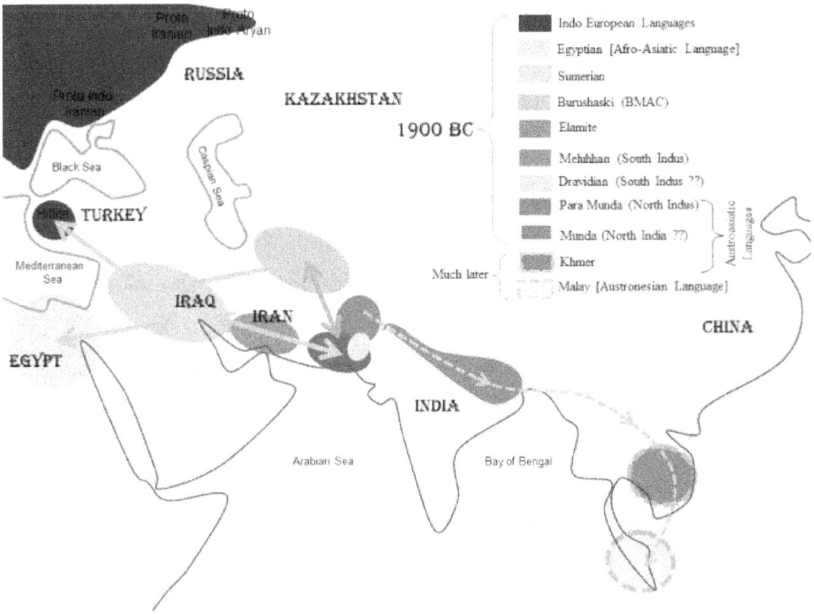

I suggest that Shahdad and Tepe Yahya were important sites (which included Meluhhan settlements) of Marhashi. The inscriptional evidence of Indus writing in these settlements attest to the trade contacts between Meluhha and ancient Elam (south-eastern Iran), close to Baluchistan.

Researchers have suggested various locations for Marhashi. It refers to the lands situated to the east of Ur, during the period of Ur III state. It has also been called Old Akkadian Barahshum. Some place it in 'the perimeter of Kerman and eastern Fars' (Stein Keller 1982: 255) or in Iranian Baluchistan (Vallat 1993: CXIII). Carl Lamberg-Karlovsky suggests that the size of Shahdad (over 100 ha.)in Kerman makes Shahdad a possible capital of Marhashi; Tepe Yahya, a site in Kerman might have been one of the smaller towns of Marhashi (Lamberg-Karlovsky 2001: 278-279). As DT Potts notes, Sharkalisharri or his son went to Marhashi and married a Marhashian (Westenholz 1987: nos. 133 and 154). In the 18th year of Shulgi's reign, Shulgi's daughter became queen of Marhashi. 'The water buffaloes so beloved by the Sargonic seal cutters must have come to Babylonia as diplomatic gifts from Meluhha.' (Westenholz 199: 102; Boehmer 1975:4).

Ancient Near East: Shahdad bronze-age inscriptional evidence, a tribute to Ali Hakemi[146]

This is a tribute to the splendid archaeological work done by Ali Hakemi in Shahdad. Hakemi, Ali, 1997, *Shahdad, archaeological excavations of a bronze age center in Iran*, Reports and Memoirs, Vol. XXVII, IsMEO, Rome. 766 pp. Vase depicting a leopard fighting a snake. Late 3rd-early 2nd millennium BCE.

Black steatite. H. 14.5 cm; Diam. 8.5 cm. AO 31595. The inscription engraved on the truncated conical vase reads: "Innana and the Snake."[147]

This vase in the shape of a truncated cone is decorated with a motif often found on steatite recipients from the 3rd millennium BC: a leopard fighting a snake. The fight certainly refers to an episode in trans-Elamite mythology. Chlorite vases were luxury objects produced for export.

Nippur vessel with combatant snake and eagle motif. Istanbul Museum. The design is raised above the base; the vessel of chlorite was found in a mixed Ur III context at Nippur in southern Mesopotamia.

खरडा [kharaḍā] A leopard. खरड्या [kharaḍyā] *m* or खरड्यावाघ *m* A leopard (Marathi). Kol. keḍiak tiger. Nk. khaṛeyak panther. Go. (A.) khaṛyal tiger; (Haig) kariyāl panther Kui kṛāḍi, krānḍi tiger, leopard, hyena. Kuwi (F.) kṛani tiger; (S.) klā'ni tiger, leopard; (Su. P. Isr.) kṛaʔni (pl. -ŋa) tiger. / Cf. Pkt. (DNM) karaḍa-id. (CDIAL 1132+). Rebus 1: *kharādī* ' turner, a person who fashions or shapes objects on a lathe' (Gujarati) Rebus 2: करड्याची अवटी [karaḍyācī avaṭī] *f* An implement of the goldsmith.

Alternative: Go. *kula* ~ *kul* ~ *ku:* `tiger, panther'. (Munda etyma)

paṭam , *n.* < *phaṭa.* 'cobra's hood' (CDIAL 9040). Rebus: 'sharpness of iron': *padm* (obl.*padt-*) temper of iron (Kota)(DEDR 3907); *patam* 'sharpness, as of the edge of a knife' (Tamil)

The combat glyphs depicting panther/leopard and snake-hoods may thus denote 1. that the metalware is fashioned or shaped on a lathe by *kharādī* (glyph: kharaḍā ' A leopard.') and 2. that the metalware is tempered, sharp *padm* metal (glyph: *paṭam* 'sharpness, temper of iron').

I am thankful to Prof. Mehdi Mortazavi Assoc. Professor, University of Sistan and Baluchestan for the links and references provided. His insights and encouragement are gratefully acknowledged and have led me to this monograph. For the opinions expressed herein, I am responsible.

Pierre Amiet summarises Hakemi's report with a brilliant exposition: "The discovery, long after that of the great Mesopotamian civilization, just after World War I, of an urban civilization which emulated that of Sumer in the Indus Valley, followed even more recently by the equally impressive civilization of Turkmenia, immediately raised the question of what presumably happened in the immense territory between th two, represented by the Iranian plateau...(Aurel Stein) had crossed Baluchistan and Kerman, ultimately reaching, on the westward side, the only historical entity of Iran predating the Persians – the ancient country of Elam – to all intents and purposes part of Mesopotamia, although essentially a country of mountaineers. In its geographic duality in which the mountain valleys of Fars were associated with the lowlying plains of Susiana, Elam, which was also an ethnic duality, was presumably linked with a hinterland that had remained in the wings of history and comprised the Kerman mountains dominating the salt pans of the Lut Desert. The province which was traditionally rich in stones and metals, and scantly explored by the pioneers, must have been a home to the major witnesses of what Gordon Childe as early as 1934 called the 'mechanism of the spread' of the conquests of civilization...in eastern Bactria, bounded the wide loop of Amu Darya, the site of Shortughai corresponds to a settlement of ‘colonists’ from Harappan India, with their characteristic pottery, who saw to the transit of copper and doubtless also of lapis lazuli. These observations seem to be indicative of what probably happened in western Bactria where fortresses housing stores, as at Dashly Tepe, may have been built by a merchant-colonist elite to guarantee trade with the workshops set up either at Shah-I Sokhta or at Shahda and Tepe Yahya and, through them, with Elam, as well as by sea, with Mesopotamia. Unlike Anatolia, where the intense metalworking activity does not seem to have produced any art specific to a given civilization or else highly customized before the 2nd millennium, Iran thus appears to hav been a huge community enlivened by a network of very long routes spreading out from the towns and villages of craftsmen who were creating a different art and using a wide range of techniques, perhaps simulated by Elam. These craftsmen worked copper and soft, colored stones, such as chlorite and alabaster, found locally, together with imported hard stones such as carnelian and lapis lazuli. They must have come into close contact with the transporters, presumably nomadic, according to the tradition of the bearers of the intercultural style. Shahdad lay at the crossroads of these routes, the one running north-south from Gorgan and Tepe Hissar and passing through Tepe Yahya on its way to the Persian Gulf, and those crossing the Lut desert or skirting it through Bampur, towards the north and south of the Hindu Kush and from there into India.” (Introduction, pp.8 - 10)

Inter-Iranian trade community from Harappa settled on the crossroads at Shahdad?

Plate 1. The upper section of the Shahdad Standard, grave No. 114, Object No. 1049 (p.24)

Steppe eagle *Aquila nipalensis*

Shahdad standard.

Two possible rebus readings: *1. pajhaṛ* 'kite'. *Rebus: pasra* 'smithy, forge' (Santali) 2. śyēná m. 'hawk, falcon, eagle' RV.Pa. sēna -- , °aka -- m. 'hawk ', Pk. sēṇa -- m.; WPah.bhad. śeṇ 'kite'; A. xen ' falcon, hawk ', Or. seṇā, H. sen, sẽ m., M. śen m., śenī f. (< MIA. *senna --); Si. sen 'falcon, eagle, kite'. (CDIAL 12674) Rebus 1: senaka a carter ThA 271 (=sākaṭika of Th 2, 443) (Pali) sēnāpati m. ' leader of an army ' AitBr. [sḗnā -- , páti --] Pa. *sēnāpati* -- , *°ika* -- m. 'general', Pk. *sēṇāvaï* -- m.; M. *śeṇvaī, °vī, śeṇai* m. 'a class of Brahmans', Ko. *śeṇvi*; Si. *senevi* 'general' (CDIAL 13589). Rebus 2: seṇi (f.) [Class. Sk. Śreṇi in meaning "guild"; Vedic= row] 1. A guild Vin iv.226; J i.267, 314; iv.43; Dāvs ii.124; their number was eighteen J vi.22, 427;

Abb.3: Die Standarte von Shahdad (a: Aufnahme des Verfassers, b: nach Hakemi, A. [1997])

VbhA 466. ° -- pamukha the head of a guild J ii.12 (text seni --).

Kur. kaṇḍō a stool. Malt. kanḍo stool, seat. (DEDR 1179) Rebus: kaṇḍ = a furnace, altar (Santali.)
kola 'woman' (Nahali). Rebus: kol 'working in iron'; pañcaloha, alloy of five metals (Tamil).

"The shaft is set on a 135 mm high pyramidal base. The thin metal plate is a square with curved sides set in a 21 mm wide frame. On the plate there is a figure of a goddess sitting on a chair and facing forward. The goddess has a long face, long hair and round eyes. Her left hand is extended as if to take a gift...a square garden divided into ten squares. In the center of each square there is a small circle. Beside this garden there is a row of two date palm trees...Under this scene the figure of a bull flanked by two lions is shown...The sun appears between the heads of the goddess and, one of the women and it is surrounded by a row of chain decorative motives." (p.271, p.649). The inscriptional evidence discovered at this site which is on the crossroads of ancient bronze-age civilizations attests to the possibility of Meluhha settlements in Shahdad, Tepe Yahya and other Elam/Susa region sites. The evolution of bronze-age necessitated a writing system -- the answer was provided by Indus writing using hieroglyphs and rebus method of rendering Meluhha (mleccha) words of Indian *sprachbund.*

Shown are the glyphs of 1. zebu and 2. tigers which are also glyphs on Indus writing which I decode as related respectively to 1. blacksmithy on unsmelted metal (Adar Dhangar, zebu) 2. working with alloys (kol, tiger) !!! The tree is a smelter furnace (kuTi). The endless-knot motif is iron (*meḍ*, 'knot, iron').

The accounting system had advanced beyond bullae-tokens to a writing system to prepare stone-, metal-ware catalogs on thousands of inscriptions using mleccha language for Indus writing.

Other glyphs used at Shahdad as evidenced by the drawings and artefacts unearthed by Ali Hakemi:

aya 'fish' (Munda) Rebus: aya 'metal (alloy)' (Sanskrit) (cf. Motif shown on copper/bronze plates).

On Shahdad standard there is an endless knot motif like a chain. This motif also appears on Indus writing.

If the date palm denotes tamar (Hebrew language), 'palm tree, date palm' the rebus reading would be: tam(b)ra, 'copper' (Pkt.) Alternative: *kuṭi* 'tree' Rebus: *kuṭhi* 'smelter furnace' (Santali)

But in one Indian language -- Kannada -- tamara means 'tin': tagarm tin (Ko.); tagara, tamara, tavara id. (Kannada)

The endless knot motif on Indus writing is as shown on the copper plate of Mohenjo-daro. This is a lot different from the continuous endless chain shown on Shahdad standard.

Another comparable motif on Indus writing is a 'chain' like a beaded chain as shown on some seals.

If there is a word to describe the Shahdad glyph of endless knot motif, there are two possibilities: *meḍhā* 'tangle in cord' rebus: *meḍ* 'iron'.

Another set of words from Indian *sprachbund*:

Glyph: kaḍī a chain; a hook; a link (G.); kaḍum a bracelet, a ring (G.) Rebus: kaḍiyo [Hem. Des. kaḍaio = Skt. sthapati a mason] a bricklayer; a mason; kaḍiyaṇa, kaḍiyeṇa a woman of the bricklayer caste; a wife of a bricklayer (G.)

m1406 A and B

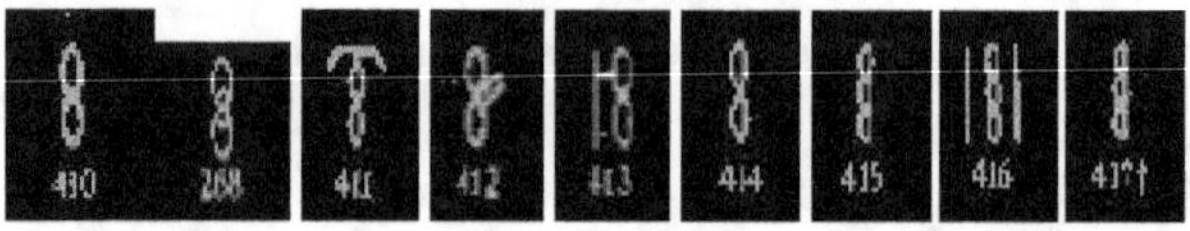

Mohenjo-daro m1406 Seal Drummer vaulting over. Endless knot  (chain like beads) motif. Rebus message: alloying (mixing) zinc (sattiya).  Casting (metal, iron, bronze, bell-metal); big stone mason. kaḍī a chain; a hook; a link (G.); kaḍum a bracelet, a ring (G.) Rebus: kaḍiyo [Hem. Des. kaḍaio = Skt. sthapati a mason] a bricklayer; a mason; kaḍiyaṇa, kaḍiyeṇa a woman of the bricklayer caste; a wife of a bricklayer (G.) A pair of chain-links may be read rebus: *dul kaḍī* 'cast stone (ore)'.

Kalibangan seal. k020 Glyphs: threaded beads + water-carrier. goṭā 'seed' (Bi.); goṭa 'numerative particle' (Mth.Hindi)(CDIAL 4271) Rebus: koṭe 'forging (metal)(Mu.) kuṭi 'water-carrier' (Telugu); Rebus: kuṭhi 'smelter furnace' (Santali)

m1457A,B copper plate Mohenjo-daro Endless knot motif 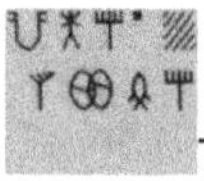 Text 2904

मेढा *mēḍhā* A twist or tangle arising in thread or cord, a curl or snarl. (Marathi) Rebus: *meḍ* 'iron' (Ho.) meṛhao = to entwine itself, wind round, wrap around, roll up (Santali.) [Note the endless knot motif].Rebus: mẽṛhẽt, meḍ 'iron' (Mu.Ho.)

Alternative: *ḍhompo* = knot on a string (Santali) ḍhompo = ingot (Santali)

Further samples of glyphs on artifacts may be cited.

Grooved lid (exterior and interior). Tepe Yahya. Possibly a lid to a compartmented box, common at Shahdad. The exterior has an incised depiction of an eagle on the top and bands of incised triangles running along the sides. 10.5 cm. wide.

Animals in procession: Two gazelles (antelopes?), stalks, two tigers

Two eagles, sprout between, lion, antelope, stalks between

tagara 'ram' Rebus: tagaram 'tin'

aryeh 'lion' Rebus: āra 'brass'

kuṇḍa n. ' clump ' e.g. *darbha -- kuṇḍa* -- Pāṇ. (CDIAL 3236). Rebus: Skt. kuṇḍa- round hole in ground (for water or sacred fire), pit, well, spring (DEDR 1669).

kolom'sprout'; kolom = cutting, graft; to graft, engraft, prune; kolma hoṛo = a variety of the paddy plant (Desi)(Santali.) kolmo 'rice plant' (Mu.) Rebus: kolami 'furnace,smithy' (Te.)

eṟaka 'wing' (Telugu) Rebus: eraka 'copper'.

pajhar 'eagle'; rebus: pasra 'smithy'.

"This object in the form of a truncated cone is a base for a ritual offering, carved with animals. Elamite period, mid-3rd millennium BC Tell of the Acropolis, Susa, Iran Bituminous rock H. 19 cm; Diam. 11 cm Jacques de Morgan excavations, 1908 Lions and gazelles passant; eagles protecting their young Sb 2725 The lower register shows two highly stylized eagles, upright, as if resting on their tail feathers. Their wings and talons are spread to protect the chicks beneath them."[148]

Stone vase from Mesopotamia Late Uruk period, about 3400-3200 BCE. Ht. 1.2 cm. It shows a bull, goat and ram.

adar ḍangra 'zebu or humped bull'; rebus: aduru 'native metal' (Ka.); ḍhangar 'blacksmith' (H.) aduru = *gaṇiyinda tegadu karagade iruva aduru* = ore taken from the mine and not subjected to melting in a furnace (Ka. Siddhānti Subrahmaṇya' Śastri's new interpretation of the Amarakośa, Bangalore, Vicaradarpana Press, 1872, p.330); adar = fine sand (Ta.); ayir – iron dust, any ore (Ma.) Kur. adar the waste of pounded rice, broken grains, etc. Malt. adru broken grain (DEDR 134). *Ta.* ayil iron. *Ma.* ayir, ayiram any ore. *Ka.* aduru native metal. *Tu.* ajirda karba very hard iron. (DEDR 192).

ranku 'antelope'Rebus: ranku = tin (santali)

tagara 'ram' Rebus: tagaram 'tin'.

A neo-Babylonian cylinder seal shows the Sumerian hero Gilgamesh circa 900-700 BCE. Glyphs of bull-men with horns and eagle in the field. aryeh 'lion' Rebus: arā 'brass'. *kõdā* खोंड [khōṇḍa] m A young bull, a bullcalf. (Marathi) Rebus 1: kŏṇḍu or konḍu । कुण्डम् m. a hole dug in the ground for receiving consecrated fire (Kashmiri) Rebus 2: A. *kundār*, B. *kũdār*, *°ri*, Or. *kundāru*; H. *kũderā* m. 'one who works a lathe, one who scrapes ', *°rī* f., *kũdernā* ' to scrape, plane, round on a lathe '.(CDIAL 3297). The crossed animals thus denote: brass-turner.

Copper alloy vase decorated with animal friezes, Susa, Iran, (1200-1000 BCE)- 11.5 cm high (Louvre)

Cylinder seal impression. Iraq museum.[149]

Sumerian white marbe cylinder seal. Early Dynastic, Circa 3200-3000 B.C. Engraved with a temple facade with a gateway, a gatepost to the left, together with a standing nude hero with a sword in one hand, holding a small quadruped in the other, to their left a stag.

Hieroglyphs from a vase in Tell Asmar (29-27th cent. BCE). Pair of tigers, pair of zebu; a person holding two hooded-snakes; eagle and lion attacking a zebu. *paṭam* , *n.* < *phaṭa.* 'cobra's hood'

phaṭa n. ' expanded hood of snake ' MBh. 2. *phēṭṭa -- 2. [Cf. *phuṭa* -- m., *°ṭā* -- f., *sphuṭa* -- m. lex., *°ṭā* -- f. Pañcat. (Pk. *phuḍā* -- f.), *sphaṭa* -- m., *°ṭā*-- f., *sphōṭā* -- f. lex. and phaṇa -- 1. Conn. words in Drav. T. Burrow BSOAS xii 386]1. Pk. *phaḍa* -- m.n. ' snake's hood ', *°ḍā* -- f., M. *phaḍā* m., *°ḍī* f.2. A. *pheṭ*, *phēṭ.* (CDIAL 9040). Rebus: 'sharpness of iron': *padm* (obl.*padt-*) temper of iron (Kota)(DEDR 3907); *patam* 'sharpness, as of the edge of a knife' (Tamil)

pajhaṛ 'eagle'; allograph: pajhaṛ = to sprout from a root. Rebus: pasra 'smithy' (Santali)

One motif that is remarkably unique in Mesopotamian seals is the LION. Only a tiger motif appears on the seals of the Sarasvati Sindhu civilization. The closest

to a lion motif is the bristled-hair (like a lion's mane) on the face of the three-faced, fully adorned, horned, seated person surrounded by animals and an inscription.

aryeh 'lion'. Rebus: *āra* 'brass, alloy of zinc and copper' as in *ārakūṭa* (Skt.) *ayir* 'iron dust, any ore' (Malayalam). The semantics of ayir as a reference to 'any ore (perhaps an alloying mineral to harden copper)' is significant and may explain the dominance of the lion hieroglyph on hundreds of Mesopotamian inscriptions, cylinder seals and artifacts and often in juxtaposition to the bull hieroglyph.

Cylinder seal: lion and sphinx over an antelope[150] Period: Late Cypriot II Date: ca. 14th century B.C.E. Geography: Cyprus Culture: Cypriot Medium: Black-grey steatite Dimensions: 0.83 in. (2.11 cm) Classification: Stone-Cylinder Seal Credit Line: The Cesnola Collection, Purchased by subscription, 1874-76 Accession Number: 74.51.4313

ṭagara 'antelope'; ḍāgar 'horned cattle' (K.) rebus: ḍāṅgar 'blacksmith' (H.) damgar, tamkāru 'merchant, trader'(Sumerian).

At the back of the lion are depicted: three dots and face of ox. *aryeh* 'lion'. Rebus: *āra* 'brass' as in ārakūṭa (Skt.) ayir = iron dust, any ore (Ma.) The 'dot' glyph is an allograph for mũhe 'face'; rebus: mũh 'ingot' (Santali) : kōḍ कोड् m. a kernel (Kashmiri) खोट [khōṭa] alloyed ingot (Marathi). kōḍ कोड् m. a kernel (Kashmiri) खोट [khōṭa] alloyed ingot (Marathi). Thus, the lion ligatured with three dots behind its head on a Cypriot seal denotes: *āra* 'brass *khoṭ* 'alloyed ingots'. The depiction of a bull's head together with an antelope is significant and recalls the association of bull's head with oxhide ingots. The antelope looking backwards is flanked by a lion (with three dots at the back of the head) and a winged animal woman's face with talons on feet of tiger?) kola 'woman'; kol 'tiger'; rebus: kol 'smithy'. eṟaka 'wing' (Telugu) Rebus: eraka 'copper'.

Th eagle is ligatured to a feline. pajhaṛ 'eagle'; allograph: pajhaṛ = to sprout from a root. Rebus: *pasra* 'smithy' (Santali). The ligature is a reinforcement of the semantics of *pasra* 'smithy' working with copper, zinc alloys to produce brass.

Thus, the ligatured glyph together with a 'human face' on the Cypriot seal denotes: copper smithy. The information transferred by the hieroglyphs on the cylinder seal impression: tagar 'antelope'; rebus: damgar 'merchant' Rebus: ḍāṅgar 'blacksmith' (H.) is thus flanked by an alloyed ingot (from) copper smithy. muha -- n. 'mouth,face ' (Pkt.) mũh 'face'; rebus: mũh 'ingot' (Munda)

Narmer Palette, rebus method

Connections between glyphs and intended meanings are provided by the rebus method. If two similar sounding words have different meanings -- one, pictorial meaning and the other metallurgical meaning -- and if this happens consistently for hundreds of word-pairs, the application of the rebus method for writing is a reasonable deduction. Similar was the method used on Narmer palette in Egypt.

N'r meant 'cuttle fish'; M'r meant 'awl'. Together, they gave the Emperor's name and so, N'r + M'r pictorials are shown in front of this person.

The Narmer Palette (Great Hierakonpolis Palette) Cairo J.E. 14716, C.G. 32169 Hierakonpolis (Horus Temple 'Main Deposit') h. 63,5 cm dated from ca. 31st century BCE.[151] The Egyptologist Bob Brier has referred to the Narmer Palette as "the first historical document in the world". (Brier, Bob. *Daily Life of the Ancient Egyptians*, A. Hoyt Hobbs 1999, p.202). At the top of both sides of the Palette are the central serekhs bearing the rebus symbols n'r (catfish) and m'r (chisel) inside, being the phonetic representation of Narmer's name. The Narmer Palette is a 63-centimetre tall (2.07 ft), shield-shaped, ceremonial palette, carved from a single piece of flat, soft dark gray-green siltstone.[152]

It appears that the entwined snakes has a Sumerian connection.

The glyph of entwined snake-hoods together with an eagle appear on a Uruk cylinder seal.

Jasper cylinder seal and clay impression: monstrous lions and lion-headed eagles, Mesopotamia, Uruk Period (4100 BC–3000 BC). Department of Oriental Antiquities, Richelieu wing, ground floor, room 1a, case 2 MNB 1167 Louvre.

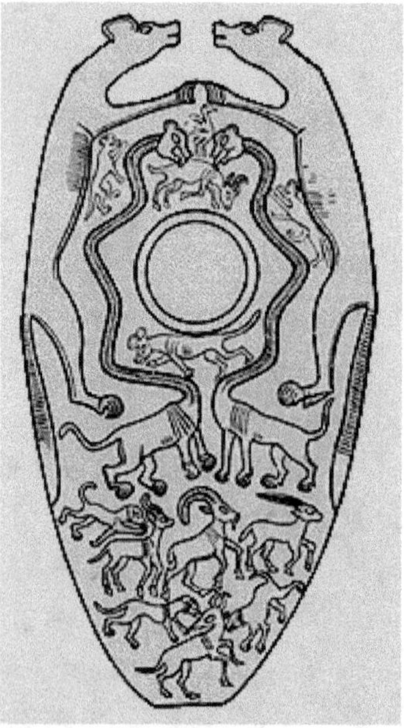

The glyphs include two entwined snake-hoods with faces of a feline and a winged feline shown between the entwined tails of the animals.

This is a scene from a ceremonial make-up palette c. 3300 BCE. Two jackals face standing up face each other. Two snakes flanking a circle have tiger-heads in place of the snake-hoods, licking a ram. Some suggest that this may be an import from Sumer to the Nile Valley. Source: The depiction of rams in the context of faces of tigers is a metallurgical determinative that the sharpness, tempered metal sought to be achieved by the process of alloying is related to copper. Hence, the tiger glyphs could connot bronze or arsenic alloys of copper. A pair of tiger glyphs then indicate cast bronze or arsenic alloys – cast perhaps into bun ingots or cast into weapon or tool shapes hardened enough to be made with sharpened edges.[153]

By the Early Dynasty III period, the Mesopotamian craftsmen had mastered the techniques for working copper, lead, silver, gold and tin. The Royal Cemetery at Ur has yielded a corpus of metal work where true tin bronze is found, apart from the common arsenical bronze and precious metals: gold, silver and electrum. Metal blades were produced in many sizes to serve as arrows, spears, daggers. Also found are sickles and hoes. Axes come in many shapes and sizes, some cast and some hammered with the tang beaten round a haft. Muhly (1983) quotes a passage from the late third millennium Laws of Eshnunna that a workman issued with tools for the harvest must return the same weight of metal at the end of the season, even if some of it is scrap. This is an indication that temples had metalsmithies where metal could be melted down and recast. Sumerian Simug was the metalsmith. In the Ur III period, the royal mausoleum of Shulgi at Ur yielded scraps of gold leaf which seem to have been part of architectural decoration, as was the case in the Jemdat Nasr period where the altar of the Eye temple at Tell Brak was decorated with gold leaf. The texts state that large numbers of metal-workers were employed by both the temple and the palace to produce a whole range of goods from tools to jewellery. These workers at Ur worked in groups under a foreman who reported to a general overseer. An assay office issued the metals to the foreman and weighed the finished article before counter-signing the receipts issued by the general overseer. In provincial towns, the governor himself issued metal from the treasury. Private metal merchants handled the supply of raw materials.[154]

The motif snake-hoods ligatured with tiger faces, is similar to the entwined snake hoods shown on Narmer Palette c. 31st century BCE.

Below the procession shown on Narmer Palette, two men are holding ropes tied to the outstretched, intertwining necks of two serpopards confronting each other, mythical felines with bodies of leopards (or more likely lionesses or tigers, given that there are no spots indicated) and snakelike necks. The circle formed by their exaggeratedly curving necks is the central part of the Palette, which is the area where the cosmetics would be ground.

These animals have been considered an additional symbol for the unification of Egypt, but it is a unique image in Egyptian art and there is nothing to suggest that either animal represents an identifiable part of Egypt, although each had lioness war goddesses as protectors and the intertwined necks may represent the unification of the state. Similar images of such mythical animals are known from other contemporaneous cultures, and there are other examples of late-predynastic objects (including other palettes and knife handles) which borrow similar elements from Mesopotamian iconography.[155]

The Narmer Palette (Great Hierakonpolis Palette) Cairo J.E. 14716, C.G. 32169 Hierakonpolis (Horus Temple 'Main Deposit') h. 63,5 cm dated from ca. 31st century BCE.[156] The Egyptologist Bob Brier has referred to the Narmer Palette as "the first historical document in the world".[157] At the top of both sides of the Palette are the central serekhs bearing the rebus symbols n'r (catfish) and m'r (chisel)

inside, being the phonetic representation of Narmer's name. The Narmer Palette is a 63-centimetre tall (2.07 ft), shield-shaped, ceremonial palette, carved from a single piece of flat, soft dark gray-green siltstone.[158]

Obverse side

The obverse side of the Narmer Palette shows some images which parallel

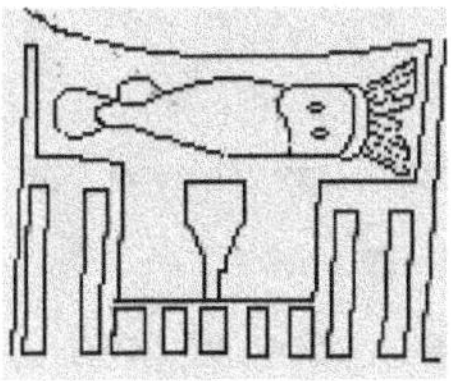

images used in Uruk. The bottom registers shows a bull and two entwined snake-hoods. At the top of both sides of the Palette are the central serekhs bearing the rebus symbols *n'r* (catfish) and *m'r* (chisel) inside, being the phonetic representation of Narmer's name.[159] The serekh on each side are flanked by a pair of bovine heads with highly curved horns, thought to represent the cow goddess Bat.

Below the bovine heads is what appears to be a procession, with Narmer

depicted at almost the full height of the register (a traditional artistic representation emphasizing his importance) shown wearing the Red Crown of Lower Egypt, whose symbol was the papyrus. The first two standard-bearers on the procession carry poles superfixed with hieroglyphs of 'bird + scarves'. baṭa = quail (Santali) Rebus: baṭa = furnace (Santali) bhrāṣṭra = furnace (Skt.) baṭa = a kind of iron (G.) bhaṭa 'furnace' (G.) baṭa = kiln (Santali). WPah.kṭg. dhàṭṭu m. ' woman's headgear, kerchief ', kc. dhaṭu m. (also dhaṭhu m. ' scarf ', J. dhāṭ(h)u m. Him.I 105). dhaṭu m. (also dhaṭhu) m. 'scarf' (WPah.) (CDIAL 6707) Rebus: dhatu = mineral (Santali) dhātu 'mineral (Pali) dhātu 'mineral' (Vedic); a mineral, metal (Santali); dhāta id. (G.) H. dhāṛnā 'to send out, pour out, cast (metal)' (CDIAL 6771).

He holds a mace and a flail, two traditional symbols of kingship. To his right are the hieroglyphic symbols for his name.

Behind him is his sandal bearer, whose name may be represented by the rosette appearing adjacent to his head, and a second rectangular symbol that has no clear interpretation but which has been suggested may represent a town or citadel.[160] Immediately in front of the pharaoh is a long-haired man, accompanied by a pair of hieroglyphs that have been interpreted as his name: *Tshet* (this assumes that these symbols had the same phonetic value used in later hieroglyphic writing). Before this man are four standard bearers, holding aloft an animal skin, a dog, and two falcons. At the far right of this scene are ten decapitated corpses, with heads at their feet, possibly symbolizing the victims of Narmer's conquest. Above them are the symbols for a ship, a falcon, and a harpoon, which has been interpreted as representing the names of the towns that were conquered.

At the bottom of the Palette, a bovine image is seen knocking down the walls of a city while trampling on a fallen foe. Because of the lowered head in the image,

this is interpreted as a presentation of the king vanquishing his foes, "Bull of his Mother" being a common epithet given to Egyptian kings as the son of the patron cow goddess.[161] This posture

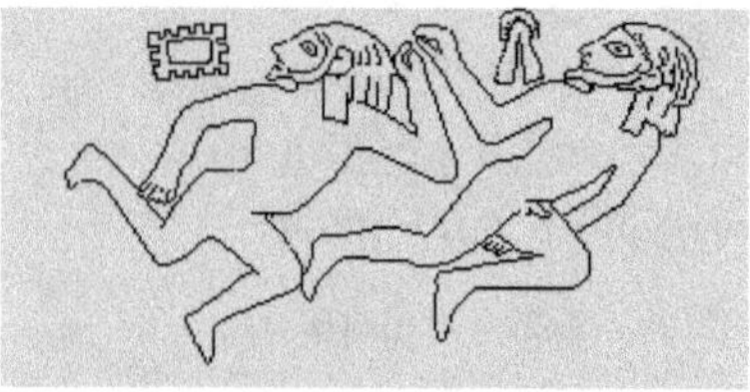

of a bovine has the meaning of "force" in later hieroglyphics.

Reverse side

Repeating the format from the other side,

two human-faced bovine heads, thought to represent the patron cow goddess Bat, flank the serekhs. Some authors suggest that the images represent the vigor of the king as a pair of bulls.

A large picture in the center of the Palette depicts Narmer wearing the White Crown of Upper Egypt, whose symbol was the flowering lotus, and wielding a mace. To his left is a man bearing the king's sandals, again flanked by a rosette symbol. To the right of the king is a kneeling prisoner, who is about to be struck by the king. A pair of symbols appear next to his head, perhaps indicating his name or indicating the region where he was from.

Above the prisoner is a falcon, representing Horus, perched above a set of papyrus flowers, the symbol of Lower Egypt. In his talons, he holds a rope-like object which appears to be attached to the nose of a man's head that also emerges from the papyrus flowers, perhaps indicating that he is drawing life from the head. The papyrus has often been interpreted as referring to the marshes of the Nile Delta region in Lower Egypt, or that the battle happened in a marshy area, or even that each papyrus flower represents the number 1,000, indicating that 6,000 enemies were subdued in the battle.

Below the king's feet is a third section, depicting two naked, bearded men. They are either running or are meant to be seen as sprawling dead upon the ground. Appearing to the left of the head of each man is a hieroglyphic sign, the first a walled town, the second a type of knot, likely indicating the name of a defeated town.[162]

Kafajeh vase fragment. The vase was found in level IX of the Sin temple. It carries a contest scene typical of Mesopotamian prototypes.[163] The top register shows two tigers standing on their hindlegs held back by a person, with bovine-hoofs, in the middle. The bottom register shows a pair of 'buildings'.

These tiger motifs and two tigers standing on their hindlegs and facing each other on the Sumerian or Narmer palettes are comparable to *kola*, the jackals or tigers shown on the Harappa tablet h1971.

h1971B Harappa. Three tablets with identical glyphic compositions on both sides: h1970, h1971 and h1972. Seated figure or deity with reed house or shrine at one side. Left: H95-2524; Right: H95-2487.

On this Harappa tablet, the two animals look like jackals *(hyena?cheetah?)* *huṇḍā* ' hyena ' (Oriya) Rebus: *huṇaï* ' offers oblation ' (Prakrit) Rebus: *uḍu* 'boat, raft'. Eraka 'wing' Rebus: eraka 'copper'. See cauaceus on Gudea's libation vase.Rings on standards: pēṇḍhē पेंढें 'rings' Rebus: pēṇḍhī पेंढी 'shop'.

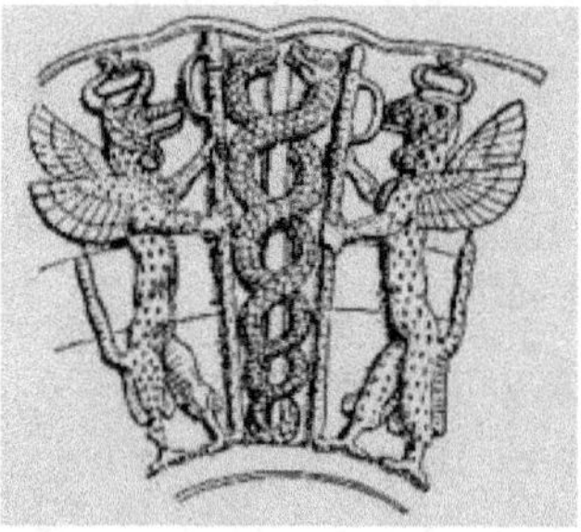

[quote]"Gudea's libation vase", 21st cent BCE[164]

The vase carries an inscription across the figures which establishes it as a gift to the god Ningishzida by Gudea, lord of Lagash. Ningishzida was a minor deity, a special patron of Gudea. Ningishzida is depicted in several works as presenting Gudea to Nin-girsu, the patron deity of Lagash. The scene is a large caduceus, two snakes twining around a central staff, flanked by two genii. The caduceus is interpreted as the god Ningishzida himself. [unquote]

Rebus readings: Glyph: *kola* 'tiger'. Rebus: *kol* 'pañcaloha, alloy of five metals, working in iron'. Glyph: when the head of the tiger is elongaged to appear like a snake's hood: Glyph: 'snake's hood': *paṭam*. Rebus: *padm* 'temper, sharpness (of metal)'. If the ram glyph denotes *melakku* 'copper'. or meḍ 'metal', the tiger glyph denotes an alloy of minerals: kol. When elongated like a snake's hood, the tiger represents a sharpened, tempered alloy – *padm kol* -- which can produce sharp tools, sharp as the edge of a knife and weapons. Pair of snake-hoods is relatable to the glyph: dula 'pair'. Rebus: dul 'cast (metal). Thus a pair of tigers with elongated necks made to look like snake-hoods cnnote 'cast alloy tempered metal.' Such a snake-hood is shown on Indus script inscriptions by the tail of a composite animal to look like a snake's hood.

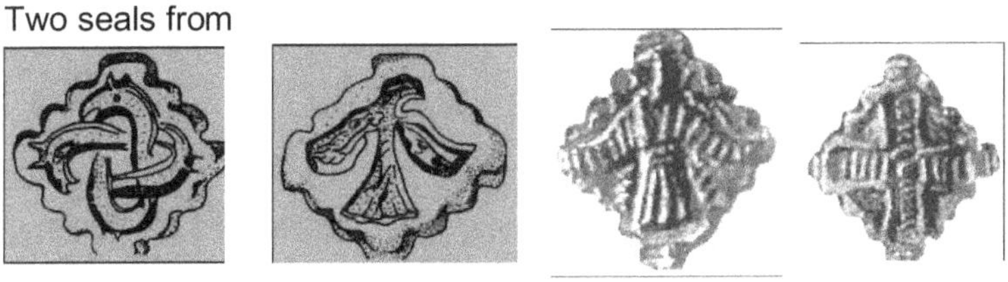

Two seals from Gonur 1 in the Murghab delta; dark brown stone (Sarianidi 1981 b: 232-233, Fig. 7,8).

Abru 'wing' (Akkadian/Assyrian) Rebus: abāru 'lead', 'antimony' abaru 'be strong, powerful; strength, power' (annaku is most unlikely to be lead rather than tin. Cf. CAD A(II): 126: AHw 49)(Akkadian/Assyrian).

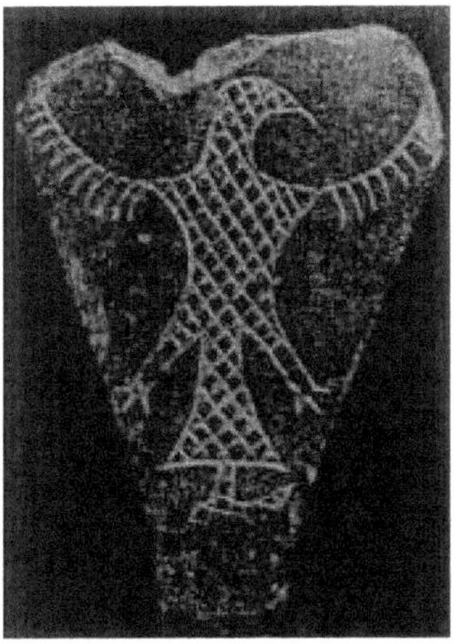

Eagle incisedon a ceremonial axe made of chlorite. Tepe Yahya. (After Fig. 9.6 in Philip H. Kohl, 2001).

The ligature of winged feline is paralleled on a painted terracotta vessel from Baluchistan. (Provenance unknown) Nal pot ca 2800 BCE; ficus leaves, tiger, with a wing, ligatured to an eagle. The eagle's wing is ligatured to a tiger shown on a register, together with ficus leaves and fish on other three registers. eṟaka 'wing' (Telugu) Rebus: erako 'molten cast' (Tulu) ayo 'fish' Rebus: ayo 'metal (alloy). kol 'tiger' + eraka 'wing' Rebus: kola 'forge' eraka 'copper'. kul 'tiger' (Santali); kōlu id. (Telugu) kōlupuli = Bengal tiger (Te.) कोल्हा [kōlhā] कोल्हें [kōlhēṃ] A jackal (Marathi) rebus: kol 'furnace, forge' (Kuwi) kol 'alloy of five metals, pañcaloha' (Tamil) kol 'working in iron, blacksmith'; kollan̠ 'blacksmith' (Tamil). *loa* 'ficus religiosa' Rebus: *loh* 'copper' (Santali) . pajhaṛ 'eagle'; allograph: pajhaṛ = to sprout from a root. Rebus: *pasra* 'smithy' (Santali). The ligature is a reinforcement of the semantics of *pasra* 'smithy' working with copper, zinc alloys to produce brass.

Cylinder seal and modern impression: 2250–2150 BCE late Akkadian period Mesopotamia Chert; H. 1 1/16 in. (2.8 cm). Pro-elamite glyptics.The owner of the seal was Balu-ili, a high court official whose title was Cupbearer[165].

Harappa tablet.  h188A

 h188B  4325

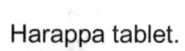

h1973B h1974B Two tablets. One side shows a

person seated on a tree branch, a tiger looking up, a crocodile on the top register and other animals in procession in the bottom register. kāru 'crocodile' (Telugu). Rebus: artisan (Marathi) Rebus: khar 'blacksmith' (Kashmiri) kola 'tiger' Rebus: kol 'working in iron'. Heraka 'spy' Rebus: eraka 'copper'. *khōṇḍa* 'leafless tree' (Marathi). Rebus: *kõdār* 'turner' (Bengali)

Looking back: krammara 'look back' Rebus: kamar 'smith, artisan'.

Glyph: seven: eae 'seven' (Santali); rebus: eh-ku 'steel' (Ta.)

खांडा [khāṇḍā] *m* A jag, notch, or indentation (as upon the edge of a tool or weapon). Rebus: khāṇḍa 'tools, pots and pans, and metal-ware'. Alternative: *aṭar* 'a splinter' (Ma.) *aṭaruka* 'to burst, crack, sli off,fly open; *aṭarcca* ' splitting, a crack'; *aṭarttuka* 'to split, tear off, open (an oyster) (Ma.); *aḍaruni* 'to crack' (Tu.) (DEDR 66) Rebus: *aduru* 'native, unsmelted metal' (Kannada) Alternative: *sal* 'splinter' Rebus: *sal* 'artisan's workshop'.

G. khuṇ f., khū̆ṇɔ m. ' corner '.2. S. kuṇḍa f. ' corner '; P. kūṭ f. ' corner, side ' (← H.). (CDIAL 3898) Phal. Khun ' corner '; H. khūṭ m. ' corner, direction ' (→ P. khūṭ f. ' corner, side '); G. khūṭṛī f. ' angle '. Rebus: khūṭ 'guild, community'.

Kolhes; iron produced by the Kolhes and formed like a four-cornered piece a little pointed at each end; mūhā me~r.he~t = iron smelted by the Kolhes and formed into an equilateral lump a little pointed at each end; kolhe tehen me~r.he~tko

mūhā akata = the Kolhes have to-day produced pig iron (Santali.)

Thus the message conveyed by the text is that the metalware -- a*yaskāṇḍa* -- is of guild, community workshop -- *khūṭ sal.*

Details of the tiger + spy + leafless tree glyphics are clearly seen on a Mohenjodaro seal m0309.

There are two glyphic elements on this composition: 1. Person sitting on a tree-branch (Spy) -- eraka 2. Leafless tree -- *khōṇḍa.* Rebus: eraka *kõdār* 'copper turner'

Mohenjo-daro seal m03092522

Ko. er uk- (uky-) to play 'peeping tom'. *Kui* ēra (ēri-) to spy, scout; *n.* spying, scouting; *pl action* ērka (ērki). ? *Kuwi* (S.) hēnai to scout; hēri kiyali to see; (Su. P.) hēnḍ- (hēṭ-) id. *Kur.* ērnā (īryas) to see, look, look at, look after, look for, wait for, examine, try; ērta'ānā to let see, show; ērānakhrnā to look at one another. *Malt.*ére to see, behold, observe; érye to peep, spy. Kur. ēthrnā. / Cf. Skt. heraka- spy, Pkt. her- to look at or for, and many NIA verbs (DEDR 903). *hērati 'looks for or at'. 2. hēraka -- , *°rika* -- m. 'spy' lex., *hairika* -- m. 'spy' Hcar., 'thief' lex. [J. Bloch FestschrWackernagel 149 ← Drav., Kui *ēra* 'to spy', Malt. *ére* 'to see']1. Pk. *hērai*'looks for or at' (*vihīraï*'watches for'); K.ḍoḍ. *hērūō* 'was seen'; WPah.bhad. bhal. *he_rnū* 'to look at' (bhal. *hirāṇū* 'to show'), pāḍ. *hēraṇ*, paṅ.*hēṇā*, cur. *hērnā*, Ku. *herṇo*, N. *hernu*, A. *heriba*, B. *herā*, Or. *heribā* (caus. *herāibā*), Mth. *herab*, OAw. *heraï*, H. *hernā*; G. *hervũ* 'to spy', M. *herṇẽ*.2. Pk. *hēria* -- m. 'spy'; Kal. (Leitner) "*hériu*" 'spy'; G. *herɔ* m. 'spy', *herũ* n. 'spying'. WPah.kṭg. (Wkc.) *hèrnõ*, kc. *erno* 'observe'; Garh. *hernu* 'to look'.(CDIAL 14165).

Glyphics read rebus: *kol kammara* 'iron smith' [*kola* 'tiger' (Telugu); *krammaru* 'head turned back' (Telugu)]; *eraka* 'copper' [*heraka* 'spy']; *khōṇḍa* 'leafless tree' (Marathi) Rebus: *kõdār* 'turner' (Bengali)

Glyphs on text 2522 inscription

V284 Glyph: *kōṇṭa* 'corner' (Nk.); Tu. *kōṇṭu* 'angle, corner' (Tu.). G. khuṇ f., khūˇṇɔ m. '

corner '.2. S. kuṇḍa f. ' corner '; P. kūṭ f. ' corner, side ' (← H.). (CDIAL 3898) Phal. khun ' corner '; H. khū̃ṭ m. ' corner, direction ' (→ P. khū̃ṭ f. ' corner, side '); G. khū̃ṭṛī f. ' angle '. Rebus: *kõdā* 'to turn in a lathe' (B.) कोंद *kōnda* 'engraver, lapidary setting or infixing gems' (Marathi) কুঁদন, কোঁদন [kuňdana, kōňdana] n act of turning (a thing) on a lathe; act of carving; act of rushing forward to attack or beat; act of skip ping or frisking; act of bragging.কুঁদ [kuňda] n a (turner's) lathe.কুঁদ1 [kuňda1] v to turn (a thing) on a lathe, to shape by turning on a lathe; to carve (Bengali) kunda1 m. ' a turner's lathe ' lex. N. *kū̃dnu* ' to shape smoothly, smoothe, carve, hew ', *kū̃duwā* ' smoothly shaped '; A. *kund* ' lathe ', *kundiba* ' to turn and smooth in a lathe ', *kundowā* ' smoothed and rounded '; B. *kū̃d* ' lathe ', *kū̃dā*, *kõdā* ' to turn in a lathe '; Or. *kū̆nda* ' lathe ', *kū̃dibā*, *kū̃d°* ' to turn ' (→ Drav. Kur. *kū̃d* ' lathe '); Bi. *kund* ' brassfounder's lathe '; H.*kunnā* ' to shape on a lathe ', *kuniyā* m. ' turner ', *kunwā* m. (CDIAL 3295). कोंद *kōnda* 'engraver, lapidary setting or infixing gems' (Marathi) kundakara m. ' turner ' W. A. *kundār*, B. *kū̃dār*, *°ri*, Or. *kundāru*; H. *kū̃derā* m. ' one who works a lathe, one who scrapes ', *°rī* f., *kū̃dernā* ' to scrape, plane, round on a lathe '.(CDIAL 3297). Four corners marked may denote a worker guild working with 4 types of pure metal and alloyed ingots (copper + arsenic/tin/zinc).

Glyph: 'splinter' sal 'splinter'. Rebus: sal 'artisan's workshop'. खांडा [khāṇḍā] *m* A jag, notch, or indentation (as upon the edge of a tool or weapon. Rebus: *kāṇḍa* 'tools, pots and pans and metal-ware'.

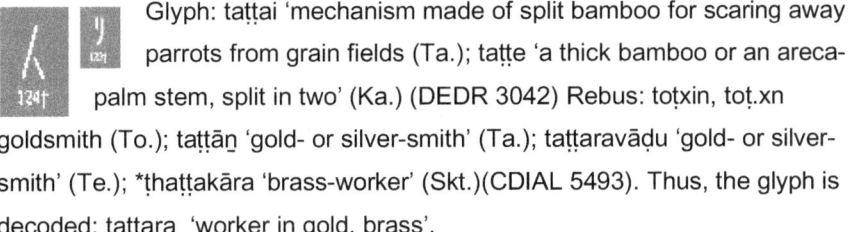

Glyph: taṭṭai 'mechanism made of split bamboo for scaring away parrots from grain fields (Ta.); taṭṭe 'a thick bamboo or an areca-palm stem, split in two' (Ka.) (DEDR 3042) Rebus: toṭxin, toṭ.xn goldsmith (To.); taṭṭāṉ 'gold- or silver-smith' (Ta.); taṭṭaravāḍu 'gold- or silver-smith' (Te.); *ṭhaṭṭakāra 'brass-worker' (Skt.)(CDIAL 5493). Thus, the glyph is decoded: taṭṭara 'worker in gold, brass'.

Glyph: *kaṇḍa kanka* 'rim of jar'. Rebus: furnace (stone ore) account (scribe).

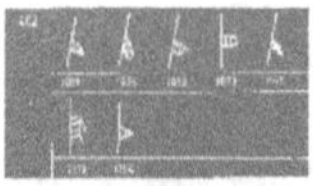  Allographs of Glyph 402 Glyph: *koḍi* 'flag' (Ta.)(DEDR 2049). Rebus: *koḍ* 'workshop' (Kuwi)

Glyph: *ayo, hako* 'fish'; a~s = scales of fish (Santali). Rebus: aya = iron (G.); ayah, ayas = metal (Skt.)

 Glyph: one long linear stroke. koḍa, koṛa = in arithmetic one; 4 koṛa or koḍa

 = 1 gaṇḍa = 4 (Santali) Rebus: koḍ, 'artisan's workshop' (Kuwi.)

The text inscription reads rebus: Lathe-turner metal-ware workshop; brass-worker, furnace (stone ore) account (scribe); metal artisan's workshop.

kõdā 'lathe-turner'; *kāṇḍa* 'tools, pots and pans and metal-ware'. *sal* 'artisan's workshop'. taṭṭara 'worker in gold, brass'; *kaṇḍa kanka* furnace (stone ore) account (scribe); *koḍ* 'workshop'; *aya* 'metal'; *koḍ* 'artisan's workshop'

Thus set 2 is distinctively a different set of trade loads compared to set 1.

Set 2 has copper ingots of ironsmith, worker in wood and iron, smith working in iron with smithy/forge.

Set 1 has the trade loads of ironsmith with smithy/forge workshop, smith working as coiner in mint, with a smelter and artisan's workshop.

Thus, two specialist guilds of workers' bronze age products are being collected together to further compile the bills of lading for the two trade loads.

Kramer notes: "Although the meaning of several words and phrases is uncertain, the sense of the passage as a whole is quite clear: the people of Magan and Meluhhha are depicted as bringing their products by bote – note that the Magilum-boat is here clearly identified with Meluhha – to Enlil's temple in Nippur, that is, of course to Sumer…it must have been common knowledge that these countries supplied Sumer with many of its economic necessities either through forced tribute or commercial exchange or both…A second relevant passage from the same myth, consisting of sixteen lines, contains Enki's blessing of Meluhha…it is obvious that the poet knew Meluhha (designated here, too, as 'the black land') as a prosperous and populous country rich in trees, reeds, bulls, *dar*-birds – note that the *dar*-birds of Meluhha are also known from the economic documents, which provides additional proof that the poet did not invent his description of the country – *haia*-birds, and sundry metals."[166] Kramer goes on to identify Meluhha with Dilmun.

The exclamation in the Sumerian myth: 'Let the magilum-boats of Melukkha transport gold and silver for exchange!' Enki and Ninkhursag (lines 1-9, Tr. by B. Alster) has references to the products of Melukkha: 'The land Tukrish shall transport gold from Kharali, lapis lazuli, and bright...to you. The land Melukkha shall bring carnelian, desirable and precious, sissoo-wood from Magan, excellent mangroves, on big-ships! The land Markhashi will (bring) precious stones, *duṣia*-stones, (to hand) on the breast, mighty, diorite-stones, u-stones, *ṣumin*-stones to you!'. 'Melukkha' is cognate with Pali 'milakkha'.

See: Ancient Near east Anzu, falcon-shaped fire-altar Uttarakhand, turning *aṁśú* (Rigveda), *ancu* (Tocharian) in smithy.[167] From Purulia, Uttarakhand, a brick altar identified as Syenachiti. The structure is in the shape of a flying eagle Garuda, head facing east with outstretched wings. In the center of the structure is the chiti is a square chamber yielded remains of pottery assignable to circa first century B.C. to second century AD. In addition copper coin of Kuninda and other material i.e. ash, bone pieces etc and a thin gold leaf impressed with a human figure tentatively identified as Agni have also been recovered from the central chamber.

A parallel in Pahlavi is senmurw, Sina-Mru (Pazand), a fabulous, mythical bird (also called simorgh). The name derives from Avestan merayo saeno 'the bird Saena', originally a raptor, either eagle or falcon, etymologically identical Sanskrit syena.

Senth century BCE cylinder seal found in Israel depicting the battle of Ninurta and Anzu. Nili Wazana, in a brilliant exposition on Anzu and Ziz asks and tentatively answers the question: "Were the Israelites acquainted with the Epic of Anzu?" She cites this rendering of a seventh century BCE cylinder seal portraying the battle of Ninurta and Anzu, discovered in Israel.[168]

Zu or Anzu (from An 'heaven' and Zu 'to know' in Sumerian language), as a lion-headed eagle, ca. 2550–2500 BCE, Louvre. Votive relief of Ur-Nanshe, king of Lagash, representing the bird-god Anzu (or Im-dugud) as a lion-headed eagle. Alabaster, Early Dynastic III (2550–2500 BCE). Found in Telloh, ancient city of Girsu. H. 21.6 cm (8 ½ in.), W. 15.1 cm (5 ¾ in.), D. 3.5 cm (1 ¼ in.)

The seventh century BCE cylinder seal found in Israel, is paralleled in an Akkadian cylinder seal.

ḍāngā = hill, dry upland (B.); *ḍā̃g* mountain-ridge (H.)(CDIAL 5476). Rebus: *dhangar* 'blacksmith' (Maithili) *ḍangar* 'blacksmith' (Hindi) *kāṇḍa* 'flowing water' Rebus: *kāṇḍā* 'metalware, tools, pots and pans'.

"On the mountainside Anzu and Ninurta met … Clouds of death rained down, an arrow flashed lightning. Whizzed the battle force roared between them." Anzu

Epic, tablet 2,in S. Dalley, Myths from Mesopotamia (Oxford - New York, 1989), p. 21.

Anzu or Zu, as a lion-headed eagle, ca. 2550–2500 BCE. Anzu(d) bird is the divine storm-bird which stole the 'Tablets of Destiny' from Enlil,inventor of the mattock (a key agricultural pick, hoe, ax or digging tool of the Sumerians) and hid the tablets on a mountain-top.

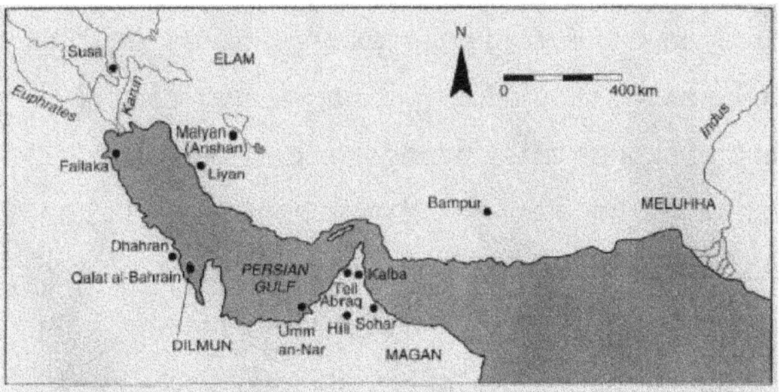

Map by D.T. Potts 2003 "Anshan, Liyan, and Magan circa 2000 BCE." N.F. Miller, K. Abdi and W.M. Summer (eds.) *Yeki Bud, Yeki Nabud: Essays on the Archaeology of Iran in Honor of William M. Sumner (Monographs Series (Cotsen Institute of Archaeology at Ucla), 48,)*, pp.156-160.

Magilum Boat (Magilum: from Sumerian ma-gi-lum, a ship of the netherworld) in Sumerian mythology was one of the valuable items seized by Ninurta, patron divinity of Lagash. This spoil was hung on an unknown part of his chariot according to the ancient source, cf. lines 40-63:

"(Ninurta) brought forth the Magilum boat from ...... his *abzu*. ...The warrior Ninurta, with his heroic strength, wreaked his vengeance (?). 52-54. On his shining chariot, which inspires terrible awe, he hung his captured wild bulls on the axle and hung his captured cows on the cross-piece of the yoke. 55-63. He hung the Six-headed wild ram on the dust-guard. He hung the Warrior dragon on the seat. He hung the Magilum boat on the .... He hung the Bison on the beam. He hung the Mermaid on the foot-board. He hung the Gypsum on the forward part of the yoke. He hung the Strong copper on the inside pole pin (?). He hung the Anzud bird on the front guard. He hung the Seven-headed serpent on the shining cross-beam."

Shamash, the sun god, rising in the morning from the eastern mountains between (left) Ishtar (Sumerian: Inanna), the goddess of the morning star, and (far left) Ninurta, the god of thunderstorms, with his bow and lion, and (right) Ea

(Sumerian: Enki), the god of fresh water, with (far right) his vizier, the two-faced Usmu. *Courtesy of the trustees of the British Museum*

Jules Bloch's work on formation of the Marathi language[169] has to be expanded further to provide for a study of evolution and formation of Indian languages in the Indian language union (sprachbund). Providing an example from the Indian Hieroglyphs used in Indus Script as a writing system, a stage anterior to the stage of syllabic representation of sounds of a language, is identified. Unique geometric shapes required for tokens to categorize objects became too large to handle to abstract hundreds of categories of goods and metallurgical processes during the production of bronze-age goods. In such a situation, it became necessary to use glyphs which could distinctly identify, orthographically, specific descriptions of or cataloging of ores, alloys, and metallurgical processes. About 3500 BCE, Indus script as a writing system was developed to use hieroglyphs to represent the 'spoken words' identifying each of the goods and processes. A rebus method of representing similar sounding words of the lingua franca of the artisans was used in Indus script. This method is recognized and consistently applied for the lingua franca of the Indian *sprachbund.* That the ancient languages of India, constituted a *sprachbund* (or language union) is now recognized by many linguists. The *sprachbund* area is proximate to the area where most of the Indus script inscriptions were discovered, as documented in the corpora. That hundreds of Indian hieroglyphs continued to be used in metallurgy is evidenced by their use on early punch-marked coins. This explains the combined use of syllabic scripts such as Brahmi and Kharoshti together with the hieroglyphs on Rampurva copper bolt, and Sohgaura copper plate from about 6th century BCE. Indian hieroglyphs constitute a writing system for meluhha language and are rebus representations of archaeo-metallurgy lexemes. The rebus principle was employed by the early scripts and can legitimately be used to decipher the Indus script, after secure pictorial identification.

"In his commentary on the *Kāma-sūtra*, Yaśodhara describes two kinds of *mlecchita-vikalpa* (cryptography). One is called *kauṭilyam* in which the letter substitutions are based upon phonetic relations -- the vowels become consonants, for example. A simplification of this form is called *durbodha.* Another kind of secret writing is *mūladeviyā.* Its cipher alphabet consists merely of the reciprocal one with all other letters remaining unchanged. *mūladeviyā* existed in both a spoken form -- as such it figures in Indian literature and is used by traders, with geographical variations -- and a written form, in which case it is called *gūḍhalekhya."*[170] Richard Burton translates 'mlecchita vikalpa' as one of the 64 arts mentioned in Vātsyāyana's *Kāma-sūtra* as follows: "the art of understanding writing in cypher, and the writing of words in a peculiar way." Writing in cypher. Vikalpa is an alternative representation of language, in this case, spoken words expressed in writing (cypher). In vidyāsamuddeśa śloka (verse detailing the objective of learning the arts) two other language-related arts listed by Vātsyāyana, in addition to *mlecchita vikalpa,* are: *deśabhāṣā jñānam* and *akṣara muṣṭika kathanam* (that is: knowledge of dialects of the land and story-telling using fingers and wrists, that is, hand-gestures and finger-gestures forming mudra-s). In this triad, it is logical to interpret mlecchita vikalpa as cypher writing made by mleccha.

Goddess Vāk belonged to the mleccha, says *Śatapathabrāhmaṇa* (3,2,I, 18ff.) Rigveda has a sūkta 10.125 addressed to Vāk. Mleccha in Pali is *milakkha or milakkhu* to describe those who dwell on the outskirts of a village.[171] Mleccha speech is not Vedic; mleccha speech is corrupt pronunciation of Prākrits: *na āryā mlecchanti bhāṣābhir māyayā na caranty uta* 'aryas do not speak with crude dialects like mlecchas, nor do they behave with duplicity'. (MBh. 2.53.8).

Post-Vedic, a milakkhu is disconnected from vāc [refined speech, for e.g. samskṛtam, as distinguished from the natural (spoken dialect or parole or *lingua franca*) Prakrit] and does not speak Vedic; he spoke Prakrit. Pali lexicon: milakkha [cp. Ved. Sk. mleccha barbarian, root mlecch, onomat. after the strange sounds of a foreign tongue, cp. babbhara & mammana] a barbarian, foreigner, outcaste, hillman S v.466; J vi.207; DA i.176; SnA 236 (°mahātissa -- thera Np.), 397 (°bhāsā foreign dialect). The word occurs also in form *milakkhu* (q. v.)

The term, mleccha, should be differentiated from another term, pāṣaṇḍa, who were opposed to the doctrines of the times. There is no indication whatsoever in any text that mleccha were pāṣaṇḍa; the mleccha were in fact an integral and a dominant part of the community called in the Rigveda bhāratam janam – the people of the nation of Bhārata (RV 3.53.12). Similarly, there is no indication whatsoever that mleccha were a distinct linguistic entity. The only differentiation indicated in the early texts that mleccha is 'unrefined' speech, that is, the *lingua franca* (as distinct from the dialects used in mantra-s or Samskṛtam). According to Geiger and Kern, the Pali term, milāca meaning 'forest dweller' was the original variant of milakkhu and was used in Jatakas and Digha Nikaya (Wilhelm 1956: 524). [Pali lexicon: Milāca [by -- form to milakkha, viâ *milaccha>*milacca> milāca: Geiger, *P.Gr.* 622; Kern, *Toev.* s. v.] a wild man of the woods, non -- Aryan, barbarian J iv.291 (not with C.=janapadā), cp. luddā m. ibid., and milāca -- puttā J v.165 (where C. also expls by bhojaputta, i. e. son of a villager).]

Thus mleccha is a reference to a common dialect, the spoken tongue in the Indic language family. Mleccha in Sanskrit is milakkhu in Pali, and the term describes those who dwell on the outskirts of a village. [Shendge 1977, pp.389-390: "Mleccha first occurs in ŚB III.2.1.24…The point made towards the end of the passage is that those who speak like Asuras are the mlecchas…But from the usage of the word milakkhu (as in Dīghanikāya III.264, Samyuttanikāya V.466, Vinaya III.28 etc.), it seems to be more a generic term used to describe all those who lived in the outskirts of the village (*paccantimesu janapadesu paccājāyanti aviññātāresu milakkhesu,* i.e., born on the outskirts of the janapada amongst the unknown milakkhus)."]. [Pali lexicon: Milakkhu [the Prk. form (A -- Māgadhī, cp. Pischel, *Prk. Gr.* 105, 233) for P. milakkha] a non -- Aryan D iii.264; Th 1, 965 (°rajana "of foreign dye" trsl.; Kern, *Toev.* s. v. translates "vermiljoen kleurig"). As milakkhuka at Vin iii.28, where Bdhgh expls by "Andha -- Damil' ādi."]

What distinguished mleccha and arya, when used in reference to language-speakers or dialect-speakers, were only places of habitation, norms of behavior and dialectical variations in parole (ordinary spoken language) juxtaposed to grammatically 'correct' Samskṛtam or inscriptional Prakrits or Pali.

On the meaning of *Ardhasamskṛtam* and semantic clusters from Indian *sprachbund*

While discussing the rules for the use of solid instruments, Bharata in *Nāṭyaśāstra* defines the term, *saindhavaka* as a regional dialect. *Saindhavaka* is dependent on the Prākrit language current in the region of Sindhu. It should have musical accompaniments and songs. The *vādya* should be of the varieties of *vitasta* and *ālipta mārgas*. Here there should not be any text (for representation). Abhinavagupta notes that it consists of harsh and coarse language. It is in this that poets compose regional plays like ḍombika, Bijaka etc. which are the pastimes of the folk. (31.359-360)

Abhinavagupta notes that *rāsaka* called *rādhāvipralambha* composed by Bhejjala uses mainly *saindhava* language. (R.S. Nagar III, p. 70).

In the context of the use of language for Dhruvā songs, Abhinavagupta explains the use of the term *ardhasamskṛtam* by Bharata in 32.397. In 32.396 to 397, Bharata notes: "Generally the language for the Dhruvā is *śaurasenī*. For Narkuṭa the language is Māgadhi. For celestials the Dhruvā song is prescribed in Sanskrit and for men the language should be half Sanskrit (meaning the mixture of Sanskrit and Prākrit or any regional language)." Abhinavagupta explains that *ardhasamskṛtam* refers to the mixed language used in Kashmir by the name *śāṭakula* and the language used in *dakṣiṇāpatha* by the name of *maṇipravāla*. NP Unni notes that a 14th century text of Kerala titled *Līātilakam* in Malayalam is also known as *maṇipravāla lakṣaṇa*. This work is said to defined maṇipravāla language as *'bhāṣāsamskṛtayogo maṇipravālam'*. Thus, *śāṭakula* and *maṇipravāla* may be cited as examples of *ardhasamskṛtam*.

In 27.48 in the chapter related to siddhi-vyañjakam (indication of success), Bharata notes one of the characteristics of arbitrators who will assess the virtues and blemishes of dramatic performance is that they should be knowledgeable in matters of dress, pious by nature and proficient in regional languages, apart from expertise in arts and artifacts. The technical term used by Bharata is: *deśabhāṣā vidhānajñāh.*

Tarlekar notes: "The use of the Prākrit dialects in Sanskrit plays of the classical period points to the fact that these, together with Sanskrit were intelligble to the spectators. The hero speaks in Sanskrit and the heroine responds in Prākrit and the hero further goes on in Sanskrit. All this would not have been possible if both were not intelligible to the characters concerned and the spectators. In the popular plays like Prahasana, the people's language, that is, Prākrit was dominant."[172]

Massimo Vidale[173] notes: "Should we be surprised by this announced 'collapse'? From the first noun in the title of their paper, Farmer, Sproat and Witzel are eager to communicate to us that previous and current views on the Indus script are naïve and completely wrong, and that after 130 years of illusion, through their paper, we may finally see the truth behind the dark curtains of a dangerous scientific myth."

An excellent introduction to the introduction of writing system by Meluhha traders is provided by Massimo Vidale:

[quote] In Mesopotamia and in the Gulf, the immigrant Indus families maintained and trasmitted their language, the writing system and system of weights of the motherland (known in Mesopotamia as the "Dilmunite" standard) as strategic tools of trade. Their official symbol of the gaur might have stressed, together with the condition of living in a foreign world, an ideal connection with the motherland. Nonetheless, they gradually adopted the use of foreign languages and introduced minor changes in the writing system for tackling with new, rapidy evolving linguistic needs. [unquote][174]

Indus language was proto-Prākrit (or proto-Indo-Aryan); प्राकृत *n.* any provincial or vernacular dialect cognate with Sanskrit (esp. the language spoken by women and inferior characters in the plays , but also occurring in other kinds of literature and usually divided into 4 dialects, viz. *Śaurasenī, Māhārāṣṭrī, Apabhramśa, Paiśācī* शौरसेनी, माहाराष्ट्री, अपभ्रंश and पैशाची) (Monier-Williams, p.703). Providing an example from the Indian Hieroglyphs used in Indus Script as a writing system, a stage anterior to the stage of syllabic representation of sounds of a language, is identified. Unique geometric shapes required for tokens to categorize objects became too large to handle to abstract hundreds of categories of goods and metallurgical processes during the production of bronze-age goods. In such a situation, it became necessary to use glyphs which could distinctly identify, orthographically, specific descriptions of or cataloging of ores, alloys, and metallurgical processes. About 3500 BCE, Indus script as a writing system was developed to use hieroglyphs to represent the 'spoken words' identifying each of the goods and processes. A rebus method of representing similar sounding words of the lingua franca of the artisans was used in Indus script. This method is recognized and consistently applied for thelingua franca of the Indian *sprachbund*. That the ancient languages of India, constituted a*sprachbund* (or language union) is now recognized by many linguists. The *sprachbund* area is proximate to the area where most of the Indus script inscriptions were discovered, as documented in the corpora.

These Meluhhans were the speakers of mleccha vācas who used mlecchita vikalpa, the Indus script with hieroglyphs as devices – devices which continue into the historical periods on punch-marked coins produced in mints from Gandhara to Karur in Sarasvati civilization area.That hundreds of Indian hieroglyphs continued to be used in metallurgy is evidenced by their use on early punch-marked coins. This explains the combined use of syllabic scripts such as Brahmi and Kharoshti together with the hieroglyphs on Rampurva copper bolt, and Sohgaura copper plate from about 6th century BCE.Indian hieroglyphs constitute a writing system for meluhha language and are rebus representations of archaeo-metallurgy lexemes.

"Indo-Aryan languages have a long history of transmission, not only in the form of literary works and treatises dealing with logical, philosophical, and ritual matters but also in phonetic, phonological, and grammatical descriptions. The languages are divisible into three major stages: Old-, Middle- and New- (or Modern-) Indo-Aryan. The first is represented by an enormously rich literature stretching over millennia, including Vedic texts and later literary works of various genres. In addition, we are privileged to have knowledge of the details of Old Indo-Aryan of different eras and areas through extraordinarily perceptive descriptions of phonetics and phonology relative to traditions of Vedic recitation in prātiśākhya works and Pāṇini's Aṣṭādhyāyī, the brilliant set of rules describing the language current at around the fifth century BCE, with important dialectical observations and contrasts drawn between the then current speech and earlier Vedic usage. Moreover, observations by Yāska (possibly antedating Pāṇini) and Patañjali (second century BCE) inform us about some dialect features of Old Indo-Aryan in early times...Speakers of Sanskrit were aware from early on not only of differences between their current language and Vedic but also of areal differences at a given time. Well known examples stem from Yāska and Patañjali, who speak of usages proper to the Kamboja, Saurāṣṭra, the east and midlands, as well as of Arya speakers. It is noteworthy that śav is said to occur in Kamboja, a northwestern people whom in his commentary on Nirukta 2.2 Durga refers to as Mleccha (Bhadkamkar 1918: 166.5-6: gatyartho dhātuh kambojeṣv eva bhāṣyate mleccheṣu prakṛtyā prayujyata ākhyAtapadabhāvena): śyav, śav, śiyav 'go' are used in Avestan and Old Persian... Patañjali refers to the use of hamm 'go' in Saurāṣṭra. Another feature of the speech of this area is noted in the metrical version of the Pāṇinīyaśikṣā, which says that nasalized vowels as in arām 'spokes' of RV 8.77.3b (khe arām iva khedayā'(...pushed...down) like spokes in the wheel navel with an instrument for pressing together') are pronounced in the manner that a woman from Saurāṣṭra pronounces takram 'buttermilk': takraM, with a fully nasalized final vowel (PS 26: yathā Saurāṣṭrikā nārī takrām ity abhibhāṣate evam rangāh prayoktavyā khe arām iva khedayā'). Patañjali is well aware of the r/l alternation in particular lexical terms...Old Indo-Aryan was of course dialectically differentiated (See Emeneau 1966). The earliest distribution of dialect areas would have to stem from Vedic times, and the texts, right back to the Rgveda, show evidence of dialect differences, reflected, for example, in the use of forms of the type dakṣi and dhakṣi 'burn' (Cardona 1991)...There is a large variety of Prākrits, traditionally named after regions and their inhabitants: Māhārāṣṭrī, *Śaurasenī* and so on. Thus, Bharata mentions (NZ 17.48: māgadhy avantijā prācyā *Śaurasenī* ardhamāgadhl bāhlikā dākṣiṇātyā ca sapta bhāṣāh prakīrtitā) seven languages as being well known: Māgadhl, the language of Avanti, the language of the east, *Śaurasenī*, Ardhamāgadhl, Bāhllkā, and the language of the south. Theoreticians of poetics and grammarians of Prākrits also enumerate and characterize different Prākrits, among wich Māhārāṣṭrī is given the highest status...The closest thing we have comparable to a dialect map of Middle Indo-Aryan is represented by Aśoka's inscriptions of the third century BCE. As has been recognized (See Bloch 1950: 43-5, Aśokan/Pāli section 1.2), the major rock edicts show that east, nortwest and west constitute three major dialect areas...Arya has various meanings centering about the notion of noble, venerable, honorable, but this term was explicitly used with reference to a particular group of people, characterized by the way they spoke...Patanjali uses the phrases āryā bhāṣante 'Aryas say' and āṣryāṣh prayunjate 'Aryas use'. In the comparable passage of his Nirukta, Yāṣska (Nir. 2.2 [161.11-13]) says śavatir gatikarmā kambojeṣv eva bhāṣyate...vikāram asyāryeṣu bhāṣante śava it 'śav meaning 'go' is used only in Kamboja...in the Arya community one uses a derivate (vikāram 'modification) śava 'corpse' '. Here, Yāska uses the locative plural āryeṣu parallel to kambojeṣu, both terms referring to communities in which particular usages prevail...The Indian subcontinent has long been home to speakers of languages belonging to different language failies, principally Indo-European (Indo-Aryan), Dravidian, and Austro-Asiatic (Munda). It is to be expected that speakers of these languages who were in contact with each other should have been subject to possible influence of other languages on their own. Scholars have long been aware of and remarked on the changes which the language reflected in the earliest Vedic underwent over time, gradually becoming more and more 'Indianized', so that one can speak of an Indian linguistic area (Emeneau 1956, 1971, 1974, 1980, Kuiper 1967). Scholars have also differed concerning the degree of influence exerted by Munda or Dravidian languages on Indo-Aryan at different stages and the manner in which such influence was made felt. It is proper to emphasize from the outset that Old Indo-Aryan should be viewed as encompassing a variety of regional and social dialects spoken natively, developing historically in the way any living language does, and whose speakers interacted in a society where diglossia and polyglossia were the norm. Sanskrit speakers show an awareness of these facts. Thus, it is not only historically true that early Vedic root aorists of the type akar, agan were gradually replaced by forms of the types akārṣū, āgamat but also that Yāska and Patañjali were aware of such changes and brought the fact out in their paraphrases; see Mehendale 1968: 15-33. Pāṇini accounted for major features of Vedic which differed from his current language. In addition, such early native speakers of Sanskrit give us evidence of attitudes towards different varieties of speech which should be taken into consideration... Patañjali recounts the dialogue: A certain grammarian (kaścid vaiyākaraṇah) says to a chariot driver, ko 'sya rathasya pravetā 'Who is the driver of this car?' The driver answers, āyuṣmann aham prājitā 'Sir, I am the driver', upon which the grammarian accuses him of using an incorrect speech form (apaśabda). The driver retorts that the grammarian knows what should obtain by rule (prāptijnah) but not what is desired (iṣṭijnah): this term is desirable (iṣyata etad rūpam), Patañjali doubtless reflects a historical change in the language between Pāṇini 's time and area and his. At the same time, he is clearly willing to countenance that usage could include terms which a strict grammarian might consider improper. And he puts this in terms of a contrast between a grammarian and a charioteer. Another famous Mahābhāṣya passage concerns sages (Ṛṣi-) who were characterized by the way they pronounced the phrases yad vā nah and tad vā nah: yar vā nah, tar vā nah. Although these sages spoke with such vernacular features, they did not do so during ritual acts...On the contrary, both accepted forms and those considered incorrect served equally to convey meanings, and what distinguished corrrect speech was that one gaind merit from such usage accompanied by a knowledge of its grammatical formation. One must recognize also that the standard speech could include elements which originally were not part of the Sanskrit norm. Moreover, Śabara remarks (on JS 1.3.5.10 [II.151]) that although authoity (pramāṇam) is granted to a learned elite (śiṣṭāh whose behaviour is authoritative with respect to what cannot be known directly (yat tu śiṣṭācārah pramāṇam iti tat pratyakṣānavagate 'rthe) and who are experts (abhiyuktāh) as concerns the meanings of terms, nevertheless Mlecchas are more expert as concerns the care and binding of birds (yat tv abhiyuktāh śabdārtheṣu śiṣṭā iti tatrocyate: abhiyuktatarāh pakṣiṇAm poṣaṇe bandhan ca mlecchāh). Consequently, when it comes to terms like pika- 'cuckcoo', which Aryas do not use in any meaning but which Mlecchas do (ZBh. 1.3.5.10 [II.149]: atha yāṇ chamdān āryā na kasmimścid artha ācaranti mlecchās tu kasmimścit prayunjate yathā pika...), authority is granted to Mleccha usage...There is thus evidence to show that before the second century BCE and possibly before Pāṇini 's time Mlecchas who inhabited areas outside the bounds of āryāvartta could be absorbed into the prevalent social system and that terms from speech areas such as that of the Kambojas could be treated as Indo-Aryan...Arya brāmaṇas normally were not supposed to engage in discourse with Mlecchas, but they had to do so on occasion. In brief, the picture is that of a society in which an Arya group considered itself the carrier of a higher culture and strived to keep this culture and the language associated with it but at the same time had necessarily to interact with groups like Mlecchas, whose language and customs were considered lesser. The result of such interaction, both with other Indo-Aryans who spoke dalects with Middle Indo-Aryan features and with non-Indo-Aryans, was that Sanskrit was effected through adoption of lexical terms and grammatical features...There is no cogent reason to consider that such changes due to contact had not been carried out gradually over generations for a long time before. Modern views. Although scholars generally agree that Old Indo-Aryan was indeed affected by 'autochthonous' languages and that there is indeed a South Asia linguistic area (see, e.g., Emeneau 1956, 1980, Kuiper 1967, Masica 1976), there are disagreements concerning the possible degree to which such effects should be seen in early Vedic and whether the features at issue could reflect also developments from Indo-European sources. In addition to the extent and sources of lexical borrowings, the main points of contention concern four features commonly considered characteristic of a South Asian linguistic area: (1) a contrast between retroflex and dental consonants, (2) the use of quotative particle (Skt. iti), (3) the use of absolutives (Skt. -tvā, ya), (4) the general unmarked word subject-object-verb...As to what non-Indo-Aryan languages are concerned, obvious candidates are Dravidian and Munda languages. The number of such borrowings into early Indo-Aryan has been the topic of ongoing debate...It has also to be admitted that the archaeological evidence available does not serve to confirm Indo-Aryan migrations into the subcontinent. Moreover, there is no textual evidence in the early literary traditions unambiguously showing a trace of such migration...In an email message kindly conveyed to me by S. Kalyanaraman (11 April 1999)...Baudhāyanaśrautasūtra passage...this text cannot serve to document an Indo-Aryan migration into the main part of the subcontinent..."[175]

Apaśabda, mleccha

Lingua franca, deśi

Mleccha, Indus language of Indian linguistic area (*sprachbund*)

Characteristics of mleccha noted by Patañjali

Hanuman chooses *parole* (mānuṣīm vāk)

Meluhha: epigraphical evidences

The earliest reference to *mleccha* as a language occurs in *Śatapathabrāhmaṇa* in 3.2.1.24. This *mleccha* speech (of a person speaking indistinctly or corruptly and who may or may not be an adherent of Vedic thought) is connected with Sumerian *Meluhha.*

Pali, a dialect in the region of Mathura, Gujarat and Vindhya has a different form: *milakkha, milakkhu* closer to Meluhha. *Milakkha, Milakkhu* [Ved. Sk. *mleccha* barbarian, root mlecch onomat. after the strange sounds of a foreign tongue] a barbarian, foreigner, outcaste, hillman S v.466; J vi.207; DA i.176; SnA 236 ; (˚*bhāsā* foreign dialect); Milakkhu [the Prk. form (A -- Māgadhī, cp. Pischel, *Prk. Gr.* 105, 233) for P. milakkha] a non -- Aryan D iii.264; Th 1, 965 (˚rajana "of foreign dye" trsl.; Kern, *Toev.* s. v. translates "vermiljoen kleurig").
As milakkhuka at Vin iii.28, where Bdhgh expls by "Andha -- Damil' ādi." Milāca [by -- form to milakkha, viâ *milaccha>*milacca> milāca: Geiger, *P.Gr.* 622; Kern, *Toev.* s. v.] a wild man of the woods, non -- Aryan, barbarian J iv.291 (not with C.=janapadā), cp. luddā m. ibid., and milāca -- puttā J v.165 (where C. also expls by bhojaputta, i. e. son of a villager). (Pāli).

Geiger and Kern thus view milāca meaning 'forest dweller' as the original variant of milakkha. The word milāca was used in Jātakas and Dīgha Nkāya.[176]

The term mleccha should also be differentiated from another term, pāṣaṇḍa, who were opposed to the doctrines of the times. There is no indication, whatsoever, in any text that mlecha were pāṣaṇḍa. On the contrary, mleccha were, in fact, an integral and a dominant part of the community denoted by the usage Bhāratam Janam in Ṛgveda (RV 3.53.12).

Similarly, there is no indication in the texts that mleccha were a distinct linguistic entity. The only differentiation indicated in the early texts is that mleccha deployed 'unrefined' speech, that is, the *lingua franca* or *parole* (as distinct from the dialects used in mantra-s or literary Samskṛtam).

What distinquished mleccha and ārya, when used in reference to language-speakers or dialect-speakers, were only places of habitation, norms of behaviour and dialectical variations in parole (ordinary spoken language) juxtaposed to grammatically 'correct' literary Samskṛtam or inscriptional Prakrits or Pali.Thus mleccha is a reference to a common dialect, the spoken tongue in the Indic language family.

Forms closer to mleccha are found in Kashmiri *britshun*, 'to weep and lament, wail, as when a child cries for some coveted object, or when it is left motherless while still a child.'Sindhi *milis*, Punjabi *milech, malech* 'weep, lament'; W. Pahari *melc.h.* 'dirty'. Other cognates are: *bAxdhl* 'Bactria' (E. Iranian); *balhi-ka* (Av.) The sound-shift from hh, kh to ch may parallel the forms: *ákṣi* n. ' eye ' RV; Pa. Pk. *akkhi -- , acchi --*; K. *ȧchi, acch, acchī*, S. *akhi* f., L. *akkh* (CDIAL 43).

In *Abhidhāna Cintāmaṇi* of Hemacandra, twelve synonyms are given for tāmram, 'copper' including the words: *mleccha, mlecchaśāvarabhedā, mlecchamukha.* The full list is: *tāmram mlecchamukham śulvam raktam dvaṣṭamudumbaram mlecchaśāvarabhedākhyam markatāsyam kanīyasam brahmavarddhanam variṣṭham sīsantu sīsapatrakam.*

Theragāthā in Pali refers to a banner dyed the colour of copper: milakkhurajanam (The Thera and Theragāthā, PTS, Verse 965: *milakkhurajanam rattam garahantā sakam dhajam; tithiyānam dhajam keci dhāressanty avadātakam*; K.R. Norman tr., Theragāthā: Finding fault with their own banner which is dyed the colour of copper, some will wear the white banner of sectarians.

Tamilla as a synonym of Milangka, Wilangka (Milakkha, mleccha, Pali)

Mizalai, 'child's soft speech' is a toponym referring to Chola region in Tamil. An earlier variant of Meluhha is me-lah-ha cognate with Pali milakkha. *Milakkha bhāsā* is clearly used as a reference to a language in *Digha Nikāya and Vinayaka* texts.

"This is something about Pali on the northern Thai fringe, or about Sri Lanka in the Chiangmai valley: The term Lawa was used in reference to highland outsiders in Lanna and Shan States. Its longer form is Damilawa , and is said to derive from the Sanskrit Damila, the same term as informed the Buddhist Sri Lankan ethnic term Tamil for their non-Buddhist Others. The root of the term lay in Sinhalese chronicle accounts of the state and its dark-skinned enemies. Thus, along with the localization of Buddhism in mainland Southeast Asia came certain aspects of ethnic ranking and prejudice that contributed to rulers' ability to contextualize in universalistic terms their rule and the peoples that it excluded. Many Chiangmai chronicles used the term Tamilla for Lawa. Some used the term Milangka. Wilangka, a variant on that term, was used among Lawa in reference to their chief who lost out to the lowland forces. Milangka is derived from Milakkha, the Pali language equivalent to the Sankrit Mleccha ("savages")."[177]

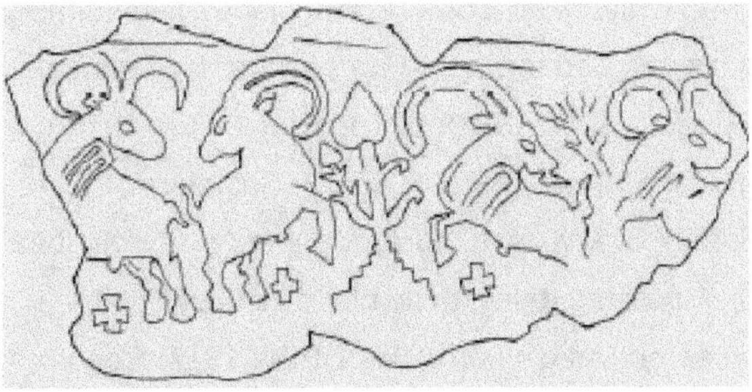

Cylinder seal reconstructed. Drawing extrapolates from fragments. Two rampant caprids against a stepped platform surmounted by tree with the third caprid and four-sided crosses (Potts 1980: figs. 13,15, pls. 17-19, 25).

Three caprids. Tepe Yahya. Cylinder seal reconstructed from seven fragments. To the left of this pair is a third caprid rampant with head turned back whose horns are viewed frontally rather than in profile. Beneath the belly of each animal is a four-sided cross. There are 9 fragments of clay slab wall sealings. Wall plaster is preserved on the reverse of most fragments. Seal is carefully rolled along horizontal axis of sealing. Lamberg-Karlovsky 1971: pls. 4, 5; cf. Fig. 10.27 in Pittman, 2001, opcit. Two caprids with heads turned back rampant against a stepped platform (mountain) surmounted by a tree. *pasaramu, pasalamu* 'an animal, a beast, a brute, quadruped' (Telugu) Rebus: *pasra* = a smithy (Santali).

Antelopes Type 1: miṇḍāl 'markhor' (Tōrwālī) meḍho a ram, a sheep (G.)(CDIAL 10120); rebus: mẽṛhẽt, meḍ 'iron' (Mu.Ho.) Antelope has head turned backwards. క్రమ్మర *krammara.* adv. Type 2: melh 'goat' (Br.); milakkhu 'copper' (Pali) Type 3: tagara 'ram' Rebus: tagara 'tin' damgar 'merchant' (Akkadian)

Again. క్రమ్మరిల్లు or క్రమరబడు Same as క్రమ్మరు. krəm back'(Kho.) karmāra 'smith, artisan' (Skt.) kamar 'smith' (Santali). *kaṇḍ,* 'a furnace, fire-altar' (Santali)

meḷh 'goat' (Br.) Rebus: meḍho 'one who helps a merchant' vi.138 'vaṇiksahāyah' (deśi. Hemachandra). Allograph: meṛgo = with horns twisted back; meṛha, m., miṛhi f.= twisted, crumpled, as a horn (Santali)

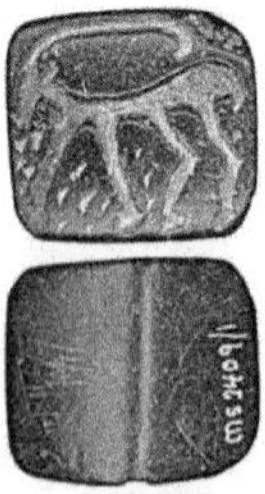

loa 'ficus religiosa' Rebus: *loh* 'copper' (Santali)

Stamp seal, large ibex walking left. Black steatite or chlorite, North Syria or Anatolia, 4th millennium BC, 1 rectangular gabled stamp seal, 4,7x5,1x1,3 cm, pierced through. *Provenance:* 1. Erlenmeyer Collection, Basel (before 1958-1981); 2. The Erlenmeyer Foundation, Basel (1981-1997); 3. Sotheby's 12.6.1997:8. *kala* stag, buck (Ma.); *kal a.r.* Nilgiri ibex (Ko.); *kalai* stag, buck, male black monkey (Ta.); *kalan:kompu* stag's horn (Ta.)(DEDR 1312) Rebus: kallan mason (Ma.); *kalla* glass beads (Ma.); *kalu* stone (Kond.a); *xal* id., boulder (Br.)(DEDR 1298).

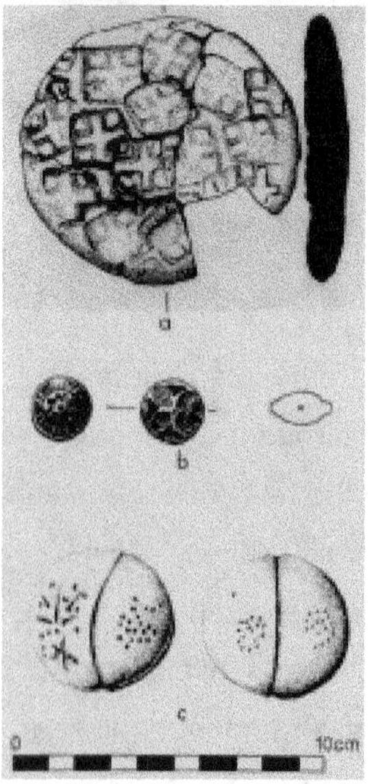

Sibri. a. Impressed Terracotta plaque. b. Block steatite bead seal c. inscribed terracotta ball (possibly a bulla holding tokens). (After Fig. 7.31 in Jarrige, C., et al., 1995/6, Mehrgarh Field Reports 1974-1985: from Neolithic times to the Indus civilization. Sind, Pakistan: the Dept. of culture and tourism, Govt. of Sindh, Pakistan. Glyphs: Four-sided crosses: Rebus reading of + glyph or four-sided cross glyph is also shown with dots on four corners of the

+ glyph, on the bulla shown on terracotta plaque of Sibri. The + glyph may denote a fire-altar (of temple). *kaṇḍ* 'furnace, fire-altar' (Santali) khondu id. (Kashmiri) kŏnḍ क्ंड् 'a hole dug in the ground for receiving consecrated fire' (Kashmiri) kunḍa 'consecrated fire-pit'. *ayaskāṇḍa* is explained in Panini as 'excellent quantity of iron' or 'tools, pots and pans and metal-ware'. [It is possible that there were allographs to depict the word: *kāṇḍa.* The allographs are: arrow-glyph; large dot; notch as a short numeral stroke (for example, ligatured on a fish-glyph or a 'rim-of-jar' glyph; dotted circle.]

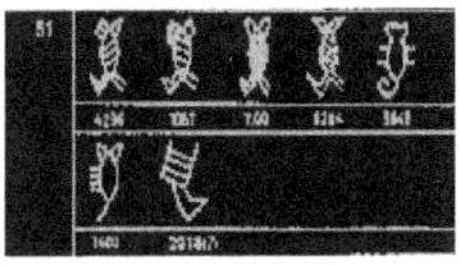

Variants of Sign 51.

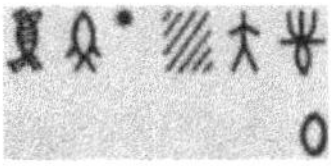

urseal11Seal; UPenn; a scorpion and an elipse [an eye (?)]; U. 16397; Gadd, PBA 18 (1932), pp. 10-11, pl. II, no. 11 [Note: Is the 'eye' an oval representation of a bun ingot made from *bicā,* sand ore?]

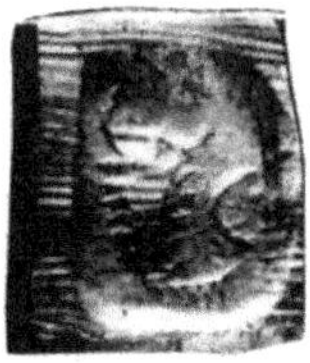

Rectangular stamp seal of dark steatite; U. 11181; B.IM. 7854; ht. 1.4, width 1.1 cm.; Woolley, Ur Excavations, IV (1956), p. 50, n.3. 16397; Gadd, PBA 18 (1932), pp. 10-11, pl. II, no. 11, urseal15 Ur Seal impression; UPenn; steatite; bull below a scorpion; dia. 2.4cm.; Gadd, PBA 18 (1932), p. 13, Pl. III, no. 15; Legrain, MJ (1929), p. 306, pl. XLI, no. 119; found at Ur in the cemetery area, in a ruined grave .9 metres from the surface, together with a pair of gold ear-rings of the double-crescent type and long beads of steatite and carnelian, two of gilt copper, and others of lapis-lazuli, carnelian, and banded sard. *koṇḍi* the sting of a scorpion.).Rebus: *kõdā* 'to turn in a lathe' (Bengali) कोंद *kõnda* 'engraver, lapidary setting or infixing gems' (Marathi) *mũh* metal ingot (Santali) *mũhã* = the quantity of iron produced at one time in a native smelting furnace of the Kolhes; iron produced by the Kolhes and formed like a four-cornered piece a little pointed at each end; mūhā mẽṛhẽt = iron smelted by the Kolhes and formed into an equilateral lump a little pointed at each end; kolhe tehen *mẽṛhẽt mūhā akata* = the Kolhes have to-day produced pig iron (Santali.) *bica* 'scorpion' Rebus *bica* 'stone ore'. *kammaṭa* 'coiner, mint, a portable furnace for melting precious metals (Telugu)

M0308 Mohenjo-dari Seal. Significance of six in the six side-locks: Glyphs: six (numeral): आर [āra] A term in the play of इटीदांडू,--the number six. Rebus: āra 'brass'. Thus, the eye + six (numeral) glyphs read rebus: kannār 'brass-smiths'. taṭu 'to hinder, stop' Rebus: dhatu 'mineral ore'. kola 'tiger' Rebus: kol 'working in iron'

Aragonite (shell) cylinder seal with a contest scene.Mesopotamia.Early Dynastic Period, about 2400-2350 BCE. "Two hero figures wrestle with a stag while two gods (distinguished by their horned head-dress) grapple with a human-headed bull and a bull. These gods wear an early

style of head-dress with multiple horns either side of a small cone; for later versions of this head-dress, see the seal of Adda, also in the British Museum."[178]

White calcite (marble) cylinder seal with a combat scene. Probably from southern Iraq Early Dynastic period, about 2700 BCE. "Although similar figures are depicted earlier in Iran, the 'bull-man', with human head and torso, and the horns, lower body and legs of a bull, first appears in Iraq around 2750 BCE. Bull-men are often seen on cylinder seals, where they appear either singly, in pairs or even in triplicate, fighting animals standing on their hind legs (generally, as here, lions). The meaning of the bull-man is unclear..."[179]

Tell Suleimeh Cylinder seal. A fish over a short-horned bull and a bird over a one-horned bull; cylinder seal impression, (Akkadian to early Old Babylonian). Gypsum. 2.6 cm. Long 1.6 cm. Dia. Tell Suleimeh (level IV), Iraq; IM 87798; (al-Gailani Werr,1983, p. 49 No. 7). [Drawing by Larnia Al-GailaniWerr. Cf. Dominique Collon 1987, First impressions: cylinder seals in the ancient Near East, London: 143, no. 609] *kondh* 'young bull'; खोंड [*khōṇḍa*] m A young bull, a bullcalf. (Marathi) Rebus: *kūdār* 'turner' (Bengali) *karaḍa* 'aquatic bird, duck' Rebus: *karaḍa* 'hard alloy' Alternative: baṭa = quail (Santali) Rebus: baṭa = furnace (Santali) bhrāṣṭra = furnace (Skt.) baṭa = a kind of iron (G.) bhaṭa 'furnace' (G.) baṭa = kiln (Santali). *ḍangar* 'bull' Rebus: *ḍangar* 'blacksmith' (Hindi) *ayo* 'fish' Rebus: *ayo, ayas* 'metal'.

Seal. Marshall, 1931, *Mohenjo-Daro and the Indus Civilization*, Vol. 3, Plate CVI #93

kanka 'rim-of-jar' (Santali) *karṇaka id. (Skt.)* Rebus 1: *kaṇakku* 'account' *karṇaka* scribe (Skt.) Rebus 2: kánaka n. ' gold ' MBh. Pa. *kanaka* -- n., Pk. *kaṇaya* -- n., MB. *kanayā* ODBL 659, Si. *kanā* EGS 36.(CDIAL 2717). *கனகம் kaṉakam, n. < kanaka. 1. Gold; பொன். காரார்வண்ணன் கனகமனையானும் (தேவா. 502,*

9)(Tamil) aya 'fish' (Mu.); rebus: aya 'metal' (G.) ayo kanka 'fish rim-of-jar' rebus: metal (alloy) account (*kaṇakku*) scribe. *kolom* 'cob'; rebus: *kolmo* 'seedling, rice (paddy) plant' (Munda.) Rebus: kolami 'furnace,smithy' (Te.) Since a pair of 'sprout.rice-plant' glyphs are used in ligature, the pair connotes : dula 'pair'; Rebus: dul 'cast (metal)(Santali) Thus, the ligatured glyph denotes dul kolami 'cast smithy'.

Glyph: *vartakara ' making turns (of the quail) '. [Pop. etym. for vártikā -- (*vartīra* -- m. Suśr., *°tira* -- m. lex.)? -- varta -- 1, kará -- 1] Ku. B. *baṭer* ' quail '; Or. *baṭara, batara* ' the grey quail '; Mth. H. *baṭer* f. ' quail '; -- →
P. *baṭer, °rā* m., *°rī* f., L. *baṭērā* m., S. *baṭero* m.; K. *bāṭuru* m. ' a kind of quail ', *baṭēra* m. ' quail '.(CDIAL 11350).

Rebus: vartaka -- 2 n. ' bell -- metal, brass ' lex. vartalōha n. ' a kind of brass (i.e. *cup metal?) ' lex. [*varta -- 2 associated with lōhá -- by pop. etym.?] Pa. *vaṭṭalōha* -- n. ' a partic. kind of metal '; L.awāṇ. *valṭōā* ' metal pitcher ', *valṭoh, ba°* f., *vaṭlohā, ba°* m.; N. *baṭlohi* ' round metal vessel '; A. *baṭlahi* ' water vessel '; B. *bāṭlahi, bāṭulāi* ' round brass cooking vessel '; Bi. *baṭlohī* ' small metal vessel '; H. *baṭlohī, °loī* f. ' brass drinking and cooking vessel ', G. *vaṭloi* f. WPah.kṭg. *bəlṭóɔ* m. ' large brass vessel '.(CDIAL 11357). *pattar* merchants (Tamil); perh. Vartaka (Skt.)

Cylinder seal. Iraq.[180] Glyphs: crossed-bullmen, crossed-lions, bull, bison(?), naked person with upraised arm, plunging a dagger into a lion's back.

erka = ekke (Tbh. of arka) aka (Tbh. of arka) copper (metal); crystal (Kannada) ḍangar 'bull' (Hindi) Rebus: ḍhangar 'blacksmith' (Hindi).

Arye 'lion' Rebus: arā 'brass'.

கண்டி kaṇṭi buffalo bull (Tamil) Pk. *gaḍa* -- n. 'large stone'? (CDIAL 3969) K. *garun*, vill. *gaḍun* ' to hammer into shape, forge, put together '. (CDIAL 3966). kaḍiyo [Hem. Des. kaḍa-i-o = (Skt. Sthapati, a mason) a bricklayer, mason (G.)]

eṛaka 'upraised arm' (Tamil) Rebus: eraka = copper (Kannada)

Glyph 'spear': మేడెము [mēḍemu] or మేడియము *mēḍemu*. [Tel.] n. A spear or dagger. ఈటె, బాకు. Rebus: meḍ 'iron' (Ho.)

Tell Abraq. Bronze dagger. Contained 12 % tin. Charred wood at the base of the tang had fragments of Dalbergia Sissoo, commonly known as Pakistani rosewood. Sissoo was rare in the ancient Near East.[181]

Akkadian Cylinder Seal (c. 2200 BCE).[182]

Glyph: six curls on hair. Glyphs: six (numeral) + ring of hair: आर [āra] A term in the play of इटीदांडू,--the number six. (Marathi) आर [āra] A tuft or ring of hair on the body. (Marathi) Rebus: āra 'brass'. Alternative: baṭa 'six' Rebus: baṭa 'furnace'. kaṇḍi 'buffalo' Rebus: kāṇḍ 'metalware'. Thus, *kāṇḍ āra* 'maker of metalware.'

aryeh 'lion' Rebus: āra 'brass'. arka 'sun' Rebus: agasāle 'goldsmithy'. meḍha 'ram' Rebus: meḍ 'iron'. meḍh 'helper of merchant'. ḍhangar 'bull' Rebus: ḍhangar 'blacksmith'. Thus, *āra ḍhangar* 'brass-smith'.

Cylinder seal with contest scene, 2350–2150 B.C. Mesopotamia Albite H. 15/16 in. (3.4

cm), Diam. 7/8 in. (2.3 cm) Gift of Nanette B. Kelekian, 1999 (1999.325.4).
"...Contests between heroes and animals first appeared in cylinder seals in the

late fourth millennium B.C., and by the middle of the third millennium B.C., the combatants, which might include mythological opponents, had assumed heroic status...A standing nude bearded hero with five visible sidelocks of hair (the traditional sixth curl is hidden by his raised right arm) grasps a water buffalo that is rearing on its hind legs. The head of the water buffalo is pushed back by the hero's right hand... Such imagery demonstrates cultural interaction resulting from trade and possibly diplomatic connections between the Akkadian empire and the Indus Valley (Harappan) civilization. Between the hero and the water buffalo is a small female in a long robe, perhaps holding a vessel. The hero's ally in the contest scene is a bull-man, shown full-face with the horns, ears, and lower body of a bull. In Akkadian-period contest scenes, the bull-man is almost invariably, as here, in conflict with a lion. A horned animal lies between the two combatants. A two-column cuneiform inscription names the seal owner as Ishri-ilum."[183]

Sumerian seal (carved cylinder), early dynastic period (third millenium B.C.). British Museum.

Glyph: six curls on hair. Glyphs: six (numeral) + ring of hair: आर [āra] A term in the play of इटीदांडू,--the number six. (Marathi) आर [āra] A tuft or ring of hair on the body. (Marathi) Rebus: āra 'brass'.

Alternative: baṭa 'six' Rebus: baṭa 'furnace'. aryeh 'lion' Rebus: *āra* 'brass'. *kondh* 'one-horned young bull' Rebus: kunda a turner's lathe (Skt.)(CDIAL 3295). Thus, *āra kund āra* 'brass-turner'.

Slanted strokes as hieroglyphs

M1909. Pict-49 Uncertain animal (antelope? quadruped) with dotted circles on its body.

dolio 'spotted antelope' (deśi. Hemachandra); *dolo* 'the eye' (deśi. Hemachandra). Rebus: dul 'to cast metal in a mould' (Santali) It is possible that 'fish-eyes' or 'eye stones' referred to in ancient Mesopotamian texts as imports from Dilmun (Akkadian IGI-HA, IGI-KU6) mentioned in Mesopotamian texts., refer to the hieroglyph of dotted circle (hieroglyph: fish-eye or antelope-eye) connotes *dol* 'eye'; rebus: *dul* 'cast metal'.

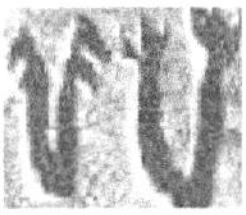

This seal has Glyph 347, 342 sequence, which is a terminal pair has 110 occurrences in Indus writing corpora.

An additional glyph shown in front of the animal is: a sloped/slanted stroke.

dula 'pair' *Rebus: dul* 'cast metal'. *kolom* 'sprout' Rebus: *kolami* 'forge/smithy'. *kaṇḍ kanka* 'furnace account scribe'.

m̤ṟeka 'goat'(Telugu) *mlekh* 'goat' (Brahui); mēṭam (Ta.); meṣam (Skt.) Rebus: *milakkha* 'copper' (Pali) Alternative: t*agara* 'antelope'; தகர் takar, *n.* [T. *tagaru,* K. *tagar.*] 1. sheep; ஆட்டின்பொது. (திவா.) 2. ram; செம் மறியாட்டுக்கடா. (திவா.) பொருநகர் தாக்கற்குப் பேருந் தகைத்து (குறள், 486). Rebus: tagara 'tin'.

*Glyph: tusk on nose of goat: *khaṇḍ* 'ivory' Rebus: *khāṇḍa* 'tools, pots and pans and metal-ware'. Alternative: *kōṭu* (in cmpds. *kōṭṭu-*) horn (Tamil);(DEDR 2200). Rebus: *khōṭ* 'alloyed' (Punjabi) koṭe 'forged (metal) (Santali)

The hieroglyph of a slanted stroke in front of the animal on m1909 is: *dhāḷ* 'a slope'; 'inclination of a plane' (G.); *ḍhāḷiyum* = adj. sloping, inclining (G.) Rebus: *ḍhālako* = a large metal ingot (G.) *ḍhālakī* = a metal heated and poured into a mould; a solid piece of metal; an ingot (Gujarati) Antelope: miṇḍāl 'markhor' (Tōrwālī) meḍho a ram, a sheep (G.)(CDIAL 10120); rebus: mẽṛhẽt, meḍ 'iron' (Mu.Ho.)

The ligatured animal can be read as a set of allographs:

Phonetic determinant of kandi 'beads' and kaṇḍ 'furnace' is the tusk glyph, which is read khaṇḍ 'ivory'; rebus: kaṇḍ = altar, furnace (Santali) kaṇḍ = altar, furnace (Santali) लोहकारकन्दुः f. a blacksmith's smelting furnace (Kashmiri) payĕn-kōda पयन्-कोँद । परिपाककन्दुः f. a kiln (a potter's, a lime-kiln, and brick-kiln, or the like); a furnace (for smelting)]. Kāndavika = a baker; kandu = an iron plate or pan for baking cakes etc. (Kannada) jaṇḍ khaṇḍ = ivory (Jatkī) khaṇḍī = ivory in rough (Jatkī); gaṭī = piece of elephant's tusk (S.) Alternative: kāg 'boar's tusk'; rebus: kāgar 'portable brazier'.

kandi 'hole, opening' (Ka.); kan 'eye' (Ka.); rebus: kandi (pl. –l) necklace, beads (Pa.) Thus, the entire ligatured animal is decoded rebus: meḍ pasra kāgar kandil 'iron smithy, forge, portable furnace, beads'. Pa.kandi (pl. –l) necklace, beads. Ga. (P.) kandi (pl. –l) bead, (pl.) necklace; (S.2) kandiṭ bead (DEDR 1215). kandil, kandīl = a globe of glass, a lantern (Kannada)

Ka. kaṇḍi, kiṇḍi, gaṇḍi chink, hole, opening. Tu. kaṇḍi, khaṇḍi, gaṇḍi hole, opening, window; kaṇḍeriyuni to make a cut. Te. gaṇḍi, gaṇḍika hole, orifice, breach, gap, lane (DEDR 1176). kandhi = a lump, a piece (Santali.) Rebus: *kaṇḍ* 'stone (ore)'.

Ta. kaṇ eye, aperture, orifice, star of a peacock's tail. Ma. kaṇ, kaṇṇu eye, nipple, star in peacock's tail, bud. Ko. Kaṇ eye. To. Koṇ eye, loop in string. Ka. Kaṇ eye, small hole, orifice. Koḍ. Kaṇṇï id. Te. Kanu, kannu eye, small hole, orifice, mesh of net, eye in peacock's feather. Kol. Kan (pl. kanḍl) eye, small hole in ground, cave. Ga. (Oll.) kaṇa (pl. Kaṇul) hole; (S.) kanu (pl. Kankul)eye. Go. (Tr.) kan (pl. Kank) id.; (A.) kaṛ (pl. Kaṛk) id. Konḍa kaṇ id. Pe. Kaṇga (pl. –ŋ, kaṇku) id. Manḍ. Kan (pl. –ke) id. Kui kanu (pl. Kan-ga), (K.) kanu (pl. Kaṛka) id. Kuwi (F.) kannū (S.) kannu (pl. Kanka), (Su. P. Isr.) kanu (pl. Kaṇka) id. (DEDR 1159a). Pa. kanḍp- (kanḍt-) to look for, seek. Ga. (Oll.) kanḍp- (kanḍt-) to search. Ta. Kāṇ (kāṇp-, kaṇṭ-) to see, consider, investigate, appear, become visible; n. sight, beauty Te. Kanu (allomorph kān-), kāncu to see (DEDR 1443)

B. kan ' eye of corn, particle ', kanā ' piece of dust, kanī ' atom, particle '; Or. kaṇa, ṇā ' particle of dust, eye of seed, atom ', kaṇi ' particle of grain '; Oaw. Kana ' drop (of dew) ' M. kaṇ m. ' grain, atom, corn ', kaṇī f. ' hard core of grain, pupil of eye, broken bit ', kaṇẽ n. ' very small particle ' (CDIAL 2661)

Glyph: dotted circles. Rebus: *khāṇḍa* 'tools, pots and pans and metal-ware'.

Glyph: One long linear stroke. koḍa 'one' (Santali) Rebus: koḍ 'artisan's workshop' (Kuwi)

Glyph: Two long linear strokes. dol 'likeness, picture, form' [e.g., two tigers, two bulls, sign-pair.] Kashmiri. dula दुल । युग्मम् m. a pair, a couple, esp. of two similar things (Rām. 966) Rebus: dul 'cast metal' (Munda)

Thus, the composite glyph ||/ frequently occurring on Chanhu-daro inscriptions[184] can be read as slanted stroke followed by a pair of straight linear strokes: *dhāḷ*, 'slanted (stroke)' + dula 'pair or two'; read rebus: *ḍhālako* 'a large metal ingot' (Gujarati) + *dul* 'cast (metal)'. Thus, the composite glyph is read as a large cast metal ingot.

Glyph 91 is a variant showing two slanted strokes followed by a straight linear stroke.

koḍa 'one' (Santali) Rebus: *koḍ* 'artisan's workshop' (Kuwi).

The composite glyph is read rebus: *ḍhālako dul*, large cast metal ingot" + *koḍ* 'artisan's workshop'. That is, a workshop (making) large cast metal ingots.

The three strokes together may read: kolmo 'three' (Mu.); rebus: kolimi 'smithy' (Telugu).

The following are Chanhu-daro inscriptions using the slanted strokes which signify large ingots of cast metal:

 Chanhu-daro14a 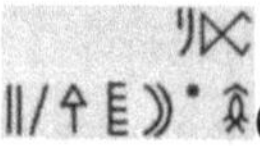 6108  Chanhu-daro29

 6403

 Pict-108 [*Chanhu-daro Excavations*, Pl. LI, 18]  6118

Chanhu-daro. Seal impression. Fig. 35 of Plate LII. After Mackay, 1943.  6124

 6133 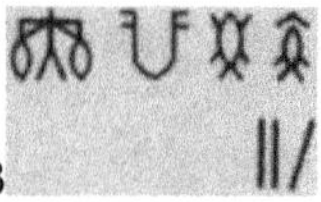 6202 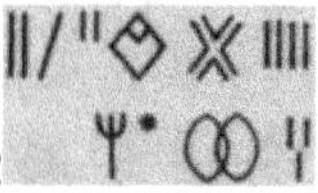

6203 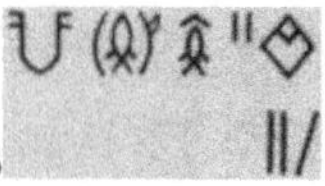 6204  6218

 6233 Gharial

Proto-Elamite, Susa ca. 4000 BCE. Stone. *adar ḍangra* 'zebu or humped bull'; rebus: *aduru* 'native metal' (Kannada) ḍhangar 'blacksmith' (Hindi) *aryeh* 'lion' Rebus: *arā* 'brass'. Brass-smith, native-metal-smith. Royal Ontario Museum[185]

Sumerian dynastic seal ca. 2500 BCE.British Museum. Cylinder seal.

Mesopotamia.[186] *tamar* "palm tree, date palm." (Hebrew) Rebus: *tam(b)ra* = copper (Pkt.) tagara 'ram' Rebus: tagaram 'tin' damgar 'merchant'. aryeh 'lion' Rebus: āra 'brass'. kamaṭha 'bow' Rebus: kampaṭṭa 'mint, coiner'

Ancient near Eastern cylinder seal, Marcopoli Collection (Beatrice Teissier, 1985, Univ. of California Press).

Ka. koṇḍi the sting of a scorpion. *Tu.* koṇḍi a sting. *Te.* koṇḍi the sting of a scorpion. (DEDR 2080). bica 'scorpion' Rebus: bica 'stone ore'. మేడెము [mēḍemu] or మేడియము *mēḍemu.* [Tel.] n. A spear or dagger. (Telugu) Rebus: meḍ 'iron' (Ho.) Antelope has head turned backwards. క్రమ్మర *krammara.* adv. Again. క్రమ్మరిల్లు or క్రమరబడు Same as క్రమ్మరు. krəm back'(Kho.) karmāra 'smith, artisan' (Skt.) kamar 'smith' (Santali) tagara 'ram' Rebus: tagaram 'tin'. aryeh 'lion' Rebus: āra 'brass'.

Ta. kōṭaram monkey. *Ir.* kōḍa (small) monkey; kūḍag monkey. *Ko.* ko·ṛṇ small monkey. *To.* kwṛṇ monkey. *Ka.* kōḍaga monkey, ape. *Koḍ.* ko·ḍë monkey. *Tu.* koḍañji, koḍañja, koḍaṅgů baboon. (DEDR 2196). Rebus: koḍ = the place where artisans work (Gujarati)

Allograph: khonḍu 'divided into parts' (Kashmiri)

Sumerian cylinder seal impression.[187]

Ta. meṭṭu mound, heap of earth Rebus: meḍ 'iron' (Ho.)

arka 'sun' Rebus: agasāle 'goldsmithy'.

Warka vase . Antelope, ingot tiger, ingot, face of bull, procession of bovidae, tabernae Montana stalks

Ka. koṇḍi the sting of a scorpion. *Tu.* koṇḍi a sting. *Te.* koṇḍi the sting of a scorpion. (DEDR 2080). Rebus: *kund* ' brassfounder's lathe ' (Bihari)(CDIA 3295). *kõdā* 'to turn in a lathe' (Bengali) कोंद *kōnda* 'engraver, lapidary setting or infixing gems' (Marathi)

kamaṭha 'frog' (Skt.); kampaṭṭa 'mint' (Ma.) kampaṭṭam coinage, coin (Ta.); kammaṭṭam, kammiṭṭam coinage, mint (Ma.); kammatia coiner (Ka.)(DEDR 1236) kammaṭa = coinage, mint (Ka.M.) kampaṭṭa-k-kūṭam mint; kampaṭṭa-k-kāran- coiner; kampaṭṭa- muḷai die, coining stamp (Tamil)

miṇḍāl markhor (Toṛwali) *meḍho* a ram, a sheep (G.)(CDIAL 10120)

Rebus: meḍ (Ho.); mẽṛhet 'iron' (Mu.Ho.)mẽṛh t iron; ispat m. = steel; dul m. = cast iron (Munda)

Cylinder-seal impression; a griffin and a tiger attack an antelope with its head turned back. The upper register shows two scorpions and a frog; the lower register shows a scorpion and two fishes.Syro-Mitannian, fifteenth to fourteenth centuries BCE, Pierpont Morgan Library, New York.[188]

There is evidence for the presence of meluhhan (Indus valley people) along the Persian Gulf region, along the sea/river route to Mari, on the right bank of Euphrates river, Mesopotamia.

"...More recent arcaheological researches in East Arabia have brought to light many finds which are related to the presence of Indus valley people. In the settlements of Hili 8 and Maysar-1, both of which have been investigated, Indus valley pottery is frequently found. Seals with Indus valley script and typical iconography indicate influences in Makkan down to the level of business organization. Marks identifying pottery in Makkan were taken from those used in the Indus valley, including the use of the signs on pottery used in the Indus valley. The discovery of a sea-port-- which may be ascribed to the Harappans-- at Ra's al-Junayz on Oman's east coast by an Italian expedition would seem to indicate that trade routes should be viewed in a more differentiated fashion than has been done upto now."[189] 'If the tablets and their sealed envelopes had not been found, in fact, we might never have suspected the existence of a merchant colony.'[190]

The city-state of Lagash (ca. 2060: king Shulgi) records a toponym about the presence of a 'Melukkhan village'.[191] The word 'Melukkha' also appears, occasionally, as a personal name in cuneiform texts of the Old Akkadian and Ur III periods.

Seals of the Indian civilization have been found in Mesopotamia and Iran at Kish (modern Tell Ingharra), Ur, Tell Asmar, Nippur (modern Nuffar), and Susa; a shard with an inscription has been found at Ras al-Junayz, the southeastern extremity of the Oman Peninsula; seal impressions of the civilization have been found at Umma (Tell Jokha) and Tepe Yahya; pottery of the civilization has been found at Ras al-Junayz, Asimah, Maysar, Hili 8, Tell Abraq -- in Oman and United Arab Emirates. Susa, Qalat al-Bahrain, Shimal (Ras al-Khaimah) and Tell Abraq (Umm al-Qaiwain) -- sites around the Arabian Gulf -- have yielded cubical weights of banded chert (unit weight: 13.63 grams) which are the hall-mark of the civilization.

In Ras al-Janyz, in the southeast coast of Oman, a large quantity of bitumen was found in a mud-brick storeroom; the surmise is that the bitumen was used to caulk reed or wooden boats. This find also points to a significant presence of traders from the Indian civilization, during the late third and early second millennium, in Magan (Oman). A copper seal with a Sarasvati hieroglyph was discovered at Ras-al-Junayz. (The port has a green-back turtle reserve). Turtle or tortoise shells were an item of trade from Meluhha, according to Mesopotamian records. “Mats, sarcophagi, coffins and jars, used for funeral practices, were often covered and sealed with bitumen. Reed and wood boats were also caulked with bitumen. Abundant lumps of bituminous mixtures used for that particular purpose have been found in storage rooms of houses at Ra's al-Junayz in Oman. Bitumen was also a widespread adhesive in antiquity and served to repair broken ceramics, fix eyes and horns on statues (e.g. at Tell al-Ubaid around 2500 BC). Beautiful decorations with stones, shells, mother of pearl, on palm trees, cups, ostrich eggs, musical instruments (e.g. the Queen's lyre) and other items, such as rings, jewellery and games, have been excavated from the Royal tombs in Ur.”[192]

“While Prof. Thomson maintained that a Munda influence has probably been at play in fixing the principle regulating the inflexion of nouns in Indo-Aryan vernaculars, such influence appeared to be unimportant to Prof. Sten Konow... Prof. Przyluski in his papers, translated here, have tried to explain a certain number of words of the Sanskrit vocabulary as fairly ancient loans from the Austro-Asiatic family of languages. He has in this opened up a new line of enquiry. Prof. Jules Bloch in his article on Sanskrit and Dravidian, also translated in this volume, has the position of those who stand exclusively for Dravidian influence and has proved that the question of the Munda substratum in Indo-Aryan cannot be overlooked...In 1923, Prof. Levi, in a fundamental article on *Pre-Aryen et Pre-Dravidian dans Vinde* tried to show that some geographical names of ancient India like Kosala-Tosala, Anga-Vanga, Kalinga-Trilinga, Utkala-Mekala and Pulinda-Kulinda, ethnic names which go by pairs, can be explained by the morphological system of the Austro-Asiatic languages. Names like Accha-Vaccha, Takkola-Kakkola belong to the same category. He concluded his long study with the following observation, “ We must know whether the legends, the religion and the philosophical thought of India do not owe anything to this past. India has been too exclusively examined from the Indo-European standpoint. It ought to be remembered that India is a great maritime country... the movement which carried the Indian colonization towards the Far East... was far from inaugurating a new route...Adventurers, traffickers and missionaries profited by the technical progress of navigation and followed under better conditions of comfort and efficiency, the way traced from time immemorial, by the mariners of another race, whom Aryan or Aryanised India despised as savages." In 1926, Przyluski tried to explain the name of an ancient people of the Punjab, the Udumbara, in a similar way and affiliate it to the Austro-Asiatic group. (cf. *Journal Asiatique*, 1926, 1, pp. 1-25, Un ancien peuple du Pendjab — les Udumbaras: only a portion of this article containing linguistic discussions has been translated in the Appendix of this book.) In another article, the same scholar discussed some names of Indian towns in the geography of Ptolemy and tried to explain them by Austro-Asiatic forms...Dr. J. H. Hutton, in an interesting lecture on the Stone Age Cult of Assam delivered in the Indian Museum at Calcutta in 1928, while dealing with some prehistoric monoliths of Dimapur, near Manipur, says that " the method of erection of these monoliths is very important, as it throws some light on the erection of prehistoric monoliths in other parts of the world. Assam and Madagascar are the only remaining parts of the world where the practice of erecting rough stones still continues....The origin of this stone cult is uncertain, but it appears that it is to be mainly imputed to the Mon-Khmer intrusion from the east In his opinion the erection of these monoliths takes the form of the lingam and yoni. He thinks that the Tantrik form of worship, so prevalent in Assam, is probably due to " the incorporation into Hinduism of a fertility cult which preceded it as .the religion of the country. The dolmens possibly suggest distribution from South India, but if so, the probable course was across the Bay of Bengal and then back again westward from further Asia. Possibly the origin was from Indonesia whence apparently the use of supari (areca nut) spread to India as well as the Pacific." (From the Introduction by PC Bagchi and SK Chatterjee, 1 May 1929).

Kuiper notes: " ...a very considerable amount (say some 40%) of the New Indo-Aryan vocabulary is borrowed from Munda, either via Sanskrit (and Prākṛt), or via

Prākṛt alone, or directly from Munda; wide-branched and seemingly native, word-families of South Dravidian are of Proto-Munda origin; in Vedic and later Sanskrit, the words adopted have often been Aryanized, resp. Sanskritized. "In view of the intensive interrelations between Dravidian, Munda and Aryan dating from pre-Vedic times even individual etymological questions will often have to be approached from a Pan-Indic point of view if their study is to be fruitful. It is hoped that this work may be helpful to arrive at this all-embracing view of the Indian languages, which is the final goal of these studies." F.B.J. Kuiper, 1948, Proto-Munda Words in Sanskrit, Amsterdam, Verhandeling der Koninklijke Nederlandsche Akademie Van Wetenschappen, Afd.Letterkunde, Nieuwe Reeks Deel Li, No. 3, 1948, p.9.[193] Emeneau notes: "In fact, promising as it has seemed to assume Dravidian membership for the Harappa language, it is not the only possibility. Professor W. Norman Brown has pointed out (The United States and India and Pakistan, 131-132, Cambridge, Harvard University Press, 1953) that Northwest India, i.e. the Indus Valley and adjoining parts of India, has during most of its history had Near Eastern elements in its political and cultural make-up at least as prominently as it had true Indian elements of the Gangetic and Southern types.[194] The passage is so important that it is quoted in full: 'More ominous yet was another consideration. Partition now would reproduce an ancient, recurring, and sinister incompatibility between Northwest and the rest of the subcontinent, which, but for a few brief periods of uneasy cohabitation, had kept them politically apart or hostile and had rendered the subcontinent defensively weak. When an intrusive people came through the passes and established itself there, it was at first spiritually closer to the relatives it had left behind than to any group already in India. Not until it had been separated from those relatives for a fairly long period and had succeeded in pushing eastward would I loosen the external ties. In period after period this seems to have been true. In the third millennium B.C. the Harappa culture in the Indus Valley was partly similar to contemporary western Asian civilizations and partly to later historic Indian culture of the Ganges Valley. In the latter part of the next millennium the earliest Aryans, living in the Punjab and composing the hymns of the Rig Veda, were apparently more like their linguistic and religious kinsmen, the Iranians, than like their eastern Indian contemporaries. In the middle of the next millennium the Persian Achaemenians for two centuries held the Northwest as satrapies. After Alexander had invaded India (327/6-325 B.C.) and Hellenism had arise, the Northwest too was Hellenized, and once more was partly Indian and partly western. And after Islam entered India, the Northwest again was associated with Persia, Bokhara, Central Asia, rather than with India, and considered itself Islamic first and Indian second. The periods during which the Punjab has been culturally assimilated to the rest of northern India are ew if any at all. Periods of political assimilation are almost as few; perhaps a part of the fourth and third centuries B.C. under the Mauryas; possibly a brief period under the Indo-Greek king menander in the second century BC; another brief period under the Muslim kingdom of Delhi in the last quarter of the twelfth century A.D.; a long one under the great Mughals in the sixteenth and seventeenth centuries A.D.; a century under the British, 1849-1947.'

"Though this refers to cultural and political factors, it is a warning that we must not leap to linguistic conclusions hastily. The early, but probably centuries-long condition in which Sanskrit, a close ally of languages of Iran, was restricted to the northwest (though it was not the only language there) and the rest of India was not Sanskritic in speech, may well have been mirrored earlier by a period when some other language invader from the Near East-a relative of Sumerian or of Elamitic or what not-was spoken and written in the Indus Valley-perhaps that of invaders and conquerors-while the indigenous population spoke another language-perhaps one of the Dravidian stock, or perhaps one of the Munda stock, which is now represented only by a handful of languages in the backwoods of Central India.

"On leaving this highly speculative question, we can move on to an examination of the Sanskrit records, and we find in them linguistic evidence of contacts between the Sanskrit-speaking invaders and the other linguistic groups within India...the early days of Indo-European scholarship were without benefit of the spectacular archaeological discoveries that were later to be made in the Mediterranean area, Mesopotamia and the Indus Valley... This assumption (that IE languages were urbanized bearers of a high civilization) led in the long run to another block-the methodological tendency of the end of the nineteenth and the beginning of the twentieth century to attempt to find Indo-European etymologies for the greatest possible portion of the vocabularies of the Indo-European languages, even though the object could only be achieved by flights of phonological and semantic fancy... very few scholars attempted to identify borrowings from Dravidian into Sanskrit...The Sanskrit etymological dictionary of Uhlenbrck (1898-1899) and the Indo-European etymological dictionary of Walde and Pokorny (1930-1932) completely ignore the work of Gundert (1869), Kittel (1872, 1894), and Caldwell (1856,1875)... It is clear that not all of Burrow's suggested borrowings will stand the test even of his own principles...'India' and 'Indian' will be used in what follows for the subcontinent, ignoring the political division into the Republic of India and Pakistan, and, when necessary, including Ceylong also... the northern boundary of Dravidian is and has been for a long time retreating south before the expansion of Indo-Aryan... We know in fact from the study of the non-Indo-European element in the Sanskrit lexicon that at the time of the earliest Sanskrit records, the R.gveda, when Sanskrit speakers were localized no further east than the Panjab, there were already a few Dravidian words current in Sanskrit. This involves a localization of Dravidian speech in this area no lather than three millennia ago. It also of course means much bilingualism and gradual abandonment of Dravidian speech in favor of IndoAryan over a long period and a great area-a process for which we have only the most llsd of evidence in detail. Similar relationships must have existed between Indo-Aryan and Munda and between Dravidian and Munda, but it is still almost impossible to be sure of either of these in detail... The Dravidian languages all have many Indo-Aryan items, borrowed at all periods from Sanskrit, Middle Indo-Aryan and Modern Indo-Aryan. The Munda languages likewise have much Indo-Aryan material, chiefly, so far as we know now, borrowed rom Modern Indo-Aryan, thogh this of course llsdes items that are Sanskrit in form, since Modern

Indo-Aryan borrows from Sanskrit very considerably. That Indo-Aryan has borrowed from Dravidian has also become clear. T. Burrow, The Sanskrit Language, 379-88 (1955), gives a sampling and a statement of the chronology involved. It is noteworthy that this influence was spent by the end of the pre-Christian era, a precious indication for the linguistic history of North India: Dravidian speech must have practically ceased to exist in the Ganges valley by this period... Most of the languages of India, of no matter which major family, have a set of retroflex, cerebral, or domal consonants in contrast with dentals. The retroflexes include stops and nasal certainly, also in some languages sibilants, lateral, tremulant, and even others. Indo-Aryan, Dravidian, Munda and even the far northern Burushaski, form a practically solid bloc characterized by this phonological feature... Even our earliest Sanskrit records already show phonemes of this class, which are, on the whole, unknown elsewhere in the Indo-European field, and which are certainly not Proto-Indo-European. In Sanskrit many of the occurrences of retroflexes are conditioned; others are explained historically as reflexes of certain Indo-European consonants and consonant clusters. But, in fact, in Dravidian it is a matter of the utmost certainty that retroflexes in contrast with dentals are Proto-Dravidian in origin, not the result of conditioning circumstances... it is clear already that echo-words are a pan-Indic trait and that Indo-Aryan probably received it from non-Indo-Aryan (for it is not Indo-European)... The use of classifiers can be added to those other linguistic traits previously discussed, which establish India as one linguistic area ('an area which includes languages belonging to more than one family but showing traits in common which are found not to belong to the other members of (at least) one of the families') for historical study. The evidence is at least as clear-cut as in any part of the world... Some of the features presented here are, it seems to me, as 'profound' as we could wish to find... Certainly the end result of the borrowings is that the languages of the two families, Indo-Aryan and Dravidian, seem in many respects more akin to one another than Indo-Aryan does to the other Indo-European languages. (We must not, however, neglect Bloch's final remark and his reasons therefor: *'Ainsi donc, si profondes qu'aient ete les influences locales,*

Ils n'ont pas conduit l'aryen de l;inde... a se differencier fortement des autres langues indo-europeennes.)"[195]

The profundity of these observations by Emeneau and Bloch will be tested through clusters of lexemes of an *Indian Lexicon*[196], which relate to the archaeological finds of the civilization.

Tamil and all other Dravidian languages have been influenced by Sanskrit language and literature. Swaminatha Iyer [Swaminatha Iyer, 1975, Dravidian Theories, Madras, Madras Law Journal Office] posits a genetic relationship between Tamil and Sanskrit. He cites GU Pope to aver that several Indo-European languages are linguistically farther away from Sanskrit than Dravidian. He cites examples of Tamil and Sanskrit forms of some glosses: hair: mayir, s'mas'ru; mouth: vāya, vā c; ear: s śevi, śrava; hear: kēḷkeṇ (Tulu), karṇa; walk: śel, car; mother: āyi, yāy (Paiśāci). Evaluating this work, Edwin Bryant and Laurie Patton note: "It is still more simple and sound to assume that the words which need a date of contact of the fourth millennium BCE on linguistic grounds as loan words in Dravidian might be words originally inherited in Dravidian from the Proto-speech which was the common ancestor of both Dravidian and Indo-Aryan...It will be simpler to explain the situation if both Indo-Aryan and Dravidian are traced to a common language family. In vocables they show significant agreement. In phonology and morphology the linguistic structures agree significantly. It requires a thorough comparative study of the two language families to conduct a fuller study. "[197] The influence of Vedic culture is profoundly evidenced in early sangam texts.[198]

It is unlikely that Akkadian was a possible underlying language because a cuneiform cylinder seal with an Akkadian inscription, showing a seafaring Meluhhan merchant (carrying an antelope) required an interpreter, Shu-ilishu, confirming that the Meluhhan's language was not Akkadian. There is substantial agreement among scholars pointing to the Indian civilization area as a linguistic area.

Sources of Prākrits

As Pischel notes: "Sanskrit is not the only source of Prākrit."[199] Pischel elaborates further: "The Prākrit language. By the term Prākrit, the Indian grammarians and rhetoricians comprehend a multitude of literary languages as the common characteristic whereof they consider Sanskrit their origin. Therefore, they generally derive the word prākṛta from prakṛiti, 'elements', 'basis', and according to them this basis is Sanskrit. So says Hemacandrs, 1,1, prakṛitih samskṛtam: tatra bhavam tata āgatam vā prākṛtam, 'Sanskrit is the basis, what originated from it or what is derived from it, is called Prākrit. Likewise Mārkaṇḍeya fol.1: prakṛitih samskṛtam tatrabhavam prākṛtamucyate...With regard to what we are to understand broadly by the term Prākrit, the Indian grammarians differ from one another. Vararuci considers Māharāṣṭrī, Paiśācī, Māgadhī and Śaurasenī as Prākrit. He would include in it also Ārṣa, Cūlikā paiśācī, and Apabhramśa. Mārkaṇḍeya...divides Prākrit into four classes: *bhāṣā, vibhāṣā, apabhramśa, paiśāca*...Under the *vibhāṣā* he includes the following five dialects: Śakarī, Cāṇḍāḷī, Śābarī, Ābhīrakī, Śākkī, and denies the status of being considered as a *vibhāṣā* to Oḍrī and Dr*āviḍ*ī... Mārkaṇḍeya (on dialects of Apabhramśa, of which) name 26; such as Pāñcāla, Mālava, Gauḍa, Oḍra, Kālingya, Kārṇāṭaka, Drāviḍa, Gurjara, and so on... Ravikara... distinguishes between two kinds of Apabhramśa. The one is based on Prākrit and differs slightly from it in flexion, composition and word-formation, and the other is a popular dialect (deśabhāṣā)...we have to consider as Apabhramśa the popular languages of India...For the drama the Bhāratīyanāṭyaśāstra accepts this, whilst it permits the actors to use, beside Śaurasenī, the language of the drama, a provincial language optionally; *Śaurasenam samāsritya bhāṣā kāryā tu nāṭake athavā chandatah kāryā deśabhāṣā prayoktṛbhih.* ..All the Prākrit languages have a series of common grammatical and lexical characteristics with the Vedic language, and such are significantly missing from Sanskrit. Such correspondences are: the comparatively greater freedom in Samdhi-rules, the change of the intervocalic ḍ, ḍh, to ḷ, ḷh; the suffix –ttana = Ved. –tvana, the svarabhakti, the gen. sing of the fem. Bases in -āe = Ved. –āyai...These alone make the hypothesis that Sanskrit was the source of the different Prākrits impossible...The inscriptions (of Aśoka), dating between the 2nd and 3rd centuries CE, that are found in caves, stūpas, plates, etc. prove that there was a popular dialect that was equally intelligible in a considerably greater part of India...The Indians include under the *Deśya* or *Deśī* class very heterogeneous elements. They consider all such words to belong to this class as they cannot trace back to Sanskrit either in form or in meaning..." (ibid., pp. 1-5).

"Candanaka says: vaam dakkhiṇattā avvaṭṭabhāsiṇo...mlecchajātinām anekadeśa bhāṣābhijñā yatheṣṭam mantrayāmah 'we southerners speak unintelligibly, because we are expert in languages of many barbarian countries, we speak just as we like." Candanaka, therefore, describes himself as a Southerner (dakṣinātya)... (ibid., p. 32).

The adjective ārya is used to differentiate the language from mleccha. Both ārya speech and mleccha speech constitute the prākṛta, the ancient form of the *lingua franca* of India. A term for speech was bhāratī (vāk) which is also related to the language of the Bharatas, giving the name bhāratavarṣa for India. "The vocabulary (of Sanskrit) was further enriched from outside Indo-Aryan itself. The pre-existing vernaculars made a sizeable contribution to the Sanskrit vocabulary...Even when all these new words have been accounted for there remains a considerable number of words in classical Sanskrit whose origin is unknown. Most were no doubt originally deśī words in the Indian terminology, and since the linguistic complexity of pre-Aryan India must have been greater than anything that now appears, we should not be surprised to find so many words whose origin remains unexplained. Such in brief are the main changes which took place in Sanskrit between the early Vedic and the classical period...The Sanskrit of the Jains is influenced by the language of the earlier Prakrit literature in the same way as the Sanskrit of the Buddhists. In vocabulary it draws more extensively than contemporary classical Sanskrit on vernacular sources, and words familiar later in Modern Indo-Aryan are often first recorded here...(Dravidian languages) were earliest influenced by Prakrit, which was the administrative language of the Sātavāhanas and their immediate successors

...The Prakrit influence in these languages, dating from the earlier period, is rapidly overlaid by extensive borrowings from the Sanskrit vocabulary. In their early classical form these languages draw on Sanskrit wholesale, and the process was continued in the succeeding periods."[200]

Validity of mleccha usage

The continuity established in the arrays of evidence adduced in this monograph lead to one hint – that the words associated with the glyphs (and meanings assigned to homonyms in the context of metalsmiths' and miners' repertoire) in *deśabhāṣā* are a continuum of the mleccha (meluhha) – the spoken, ungrammatical vernaculars as distinct from *ārya bhāṣā* which was a literary tongue with strict adherence to grammatical rules.

The continuity of the Sarasvati civilization into the historical periods has profound implications with particular reference to language evolution. The mleccha words are likely to have been borrowed into the languages and dialects spoken in the interaction areas of the civilization which extended fully along the Vedic River Sarasvati basin. There are indications that Munda-speakers moved towards the Ganga river basin as the smelting of iron ore begain circa 18th century BCE. The area of Munda-speakers is virtually coterminus with the bronze age civilization sites.

Indian linguistic and philosophical traditions recognize and acknowledge the validity of mleccha usage:

[quote]Significative Power (Śakti)

(E1-13). Sphoṭa can be classified into eight varieties: varṇasphoṭa, padasphoṭa, vākyasphoṭa (each divided into the universal or the particular), akhaṇḍa padasphoṭa, and akhaṇḍa vākyasphoṭa Of these types the vākyasphoṭa is the most important, for the sentence is the unit of speech in worldly usage. The division of the sentence into words, and further into the stems and suffixes, is only a grammatical device for analysis and has no reality…

(E37). Meaning (vṛtti) is of three kinds, primary significative power (śakti), secondary meaning (lakṣaṇā, and suggestion (vyanjanā)…

(E43). The identity and the superimposition of word and meaning are in the mind. Strictly speaking, the existence of the meaning, as well as that of the word, is only in the mind. The word is the integral sphot.a. The meaning is a vikalpa, a mental construct that comes along with the knowledge of the word and has nothing to do with the actual existence…

One cannot say that meaning is got from corrupt words through an erroneous notion of the meaningfulness. Meaning is known without any doubt (from corrupt words), hence no confusion is to be assumed. That is why women, uneducated people, and children have to be told the corrupt words, when they have doubts on hearing the correct words. The Māhābhāṣya passage, 'although meaning is known from correct as well as corrupt words, grammar gives the rules about meritorious usage', and Bhartṛhari's line 'Although there is no difference in meaningfulness, the grammatical rules are for merit and demerit in usage,' are in favor of this view. The discussion regarding the āryan and Mleccha usages in Mīmāmsā also shows this view. This discussion itself shows that both the āryan and the Mleccha usages are valid; the āryan usage is preferred as far as the Vedic terms are concerned. [unquote][201]

देश्री is first used in Bharata's Natya Shastra which refers to the regional varieties of folk dance and music elements as "Desi", and states that these are meant as pure entertainment for common people, while the pan-Indian "margi" elements are to spiritually enlighten the audience. The medieval developments of the classical Indian dance and music led to the introduction of Desi gharanas, in addition to the classical gharanas codified in Natya Shastra. The Desi gharanas further developed into the present-day adavus." In Hindustani music, a *gharānā* is a system of social organization linking musicians or dancers by lineage or apprenticeship, and by adherence to a particular musical style. A gharana also indicates a comprehensive musicological ideology. This ideology sometimes changes substantially from one gharana to another. It directly affects the thinking, teaching, performance and appreciation of music."[202]

dḗśya -- ' indigenous ' R. देशभाषा the dialect of a country; आलोच्य लक्ष्यमधिगम्य च देशभाषाः Kāvyāl.4.35 the vulgar dialect of a country (opp. to संस्कृत) , provincialism (Monier-Williams, p.496). देशी 1 The dialect of a country, one of the varieties of the Prākṛita dialect; see Kāv.1.33. -2 N. of a Rāgiṇī. -Comp. -कट्टरिः a kind of dance. -नाममाला N. of a dictionary of provincialism by Hemachandra. dēśī́ya ' peculiar to or inhabiting a country ' ŚrS. N. *desi* ' native, of the plains of India '; B. Or. *desi* ' countrymade or -- born '; OAw. *desī* m. ' inhabitant '; Mth. H. Marw. *desī* ' native ', G. M. *deśī.* (CDIAL 6555).

Meluhha (IE) presence in Sumer (3rd millennium BCE)

Sumerian *kapazum*, 'cotton' may have a cognate in *kapas* (Austro-asiatic) and *karpasa* (Sanskrit).

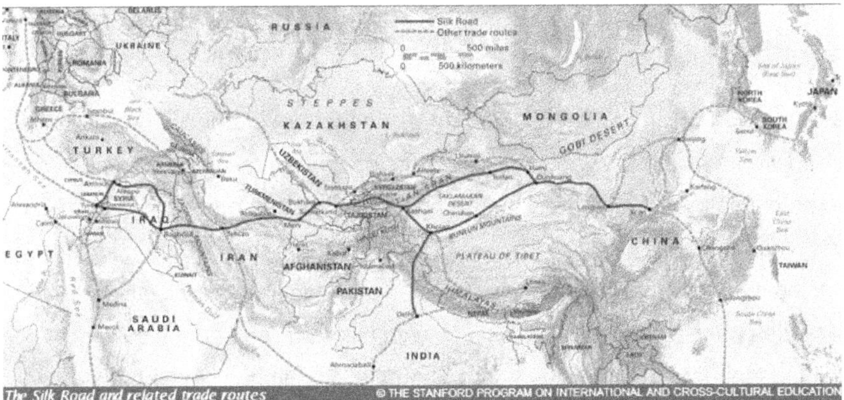

The Silk Road and related trade routes

Harmatta notes the names *Arisena* and *Somasena* in a tablet of Akkad (ca. 2200 BCE). This evidence attests to trade links between Sumeria and Meluhha.[203]

Saka dialects (kingdom of Khotan), which share features with modern Wakhi and Pashto evidence many borrowings from the Middle Indo-Aryan Prakrit. Many Prakrit terms were borrowed from Khotanese into the Tocharian languages.[204]

Map of languages along the Silk Road.

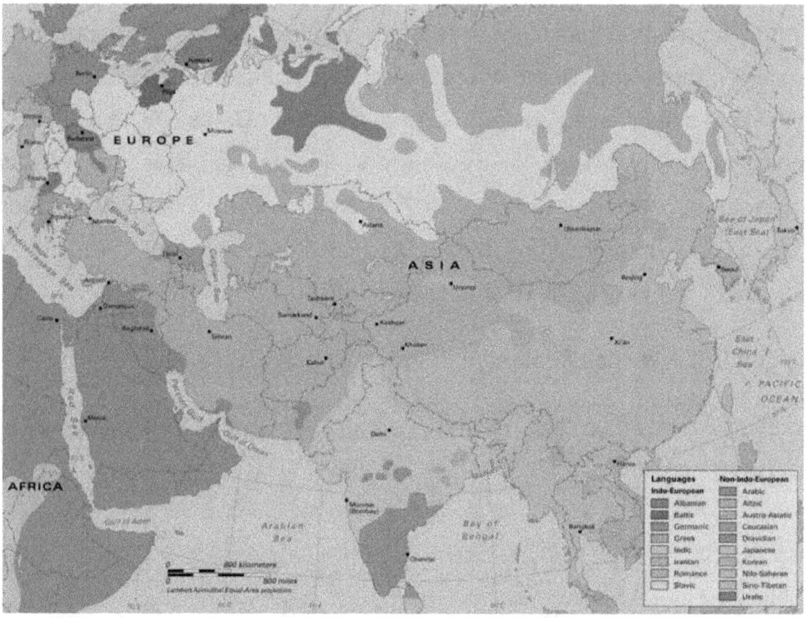

“This discussion of languages begins with those that are liturgical, the languages for which we find sacred texts or the accounts of specific religious communities. For example, followers of the Iranian prophet Zarathustra entered the Tarim Basin in the 7th century CE to establish their fire temples in Khotan; they conducted their services in the ancient Iranian language of Avestan. Buddhist missionaries possessed liturgical texts in what is known as Buddhist Hybrid Sanskrit, a language originating in northern India. Sogdian, whose homeland is west Central Asia, was employed not only by merchants but also for the religious documents of Buddhists, Manicheans, and Nestorian Christians. Whether from India or greater Iran, all of these languages were carried into the Tarim Basin by religious communities or merchants from outside the region during the 1st millennium CE".

Gostana-deśa is Prakrit name of Khotan.

Presence of Mitanni kings in northern Mesopotamia in 15th century BCE also attests to Indo-Aryan language traits. The examples cited are: assimilation of dissimilar plosives (*sapta > satta*) and interpolation of vosels to break up consonant clusters (*Indra > Indara*, example of anaptyxis). (Misra, Satya Swarup, 1992: *The Aryan Problem. A Linguistic Approach*, Munshiram Manoharlal, Delhi, p.10.) "This would imply that Middle-Indo-Aryan had developed a full millennium earlier than hitherto assumed, which in turn has implications for the chronology of the extant literature written in Middle-Indo-Aryan. In the centuries before the Mitanni texts, there was a Kassite dynasty in Mesopotamia, from the 18th to the 16th century BCE. Linguistically assimilated, they preserved some purely Vedic names: *Shunash, Maruttash, Inda-Bugash,* i.e. Surya, Marut, Indra-Bhaga (Bhaga meaning effectively 'god', cfr. Bhag-wAn, Slavic Bog.)...unlike the Iranians, who migrated from India through Afghanistan, the Kassites must have come by sea from Sindh to southern Mesopotamia...the Kassites seem to have been a warrior group moving directly from India to Mesopotamia to carry out a planned invasion which immediately gave them control of the delta area, a bridgehead for further conquests of the Babylonian heartland...At the material high tide of the Harappan culture, Mesopotamia had trade contacts with Magan, the Makran coast west of the Indus delta, with *Bad Imin*, 'the seven cities,' and with *Meluhha*, the Indus valley...*Meluhha* is the origin of Sanskrit Mleccha, Pali *Milakkhu*, 'barbarians' because of the unrefined sounds of their Prakrit and because of their cultural impurity (whether by borrowing foreign elements or simply by an indigenous decay of existing cultural standards), the people of Sindh/Meluhha were considered barbarian by the elites of Madhyadesh (the Ganga-Yamuna doab), during the Sutra period, which non-invasionists date to the late 3rd millennium BCE, precisely when Mesopotamia had a flourishing trade with *Meluhha*...according to the account given by the Babylonian priest Berosus, the Sumerians believed their civilization (writing and astronomy) had been brought to the Mesopotamian coast by sages, the first of whom was one Uana-Adapa, better known through his Greek name, *Oannes.* He was a messenger of Enki, god of the Abyss, who was worshipped at the oldest Mesopotamian city of Eridu. Like the Vedic 'seven sages', meaning both the seven clans of Vedic seers as well as the seven major stars of Ursa Major, these seven sages are associated with the starry sky; like the Matsya incarnation of Vishnu, Oannes's body is that of a fish. The myth of the Flood, wherein divine guidance helps the leader of manking (Sumerian *Ziusudra*, Sanskrit *Manu*, Akkadian *Utnapishtim*, Hebrew *Noah*) to survive, is another well-known common cultural motif…Through the Hittites, Philistines (i.e. the 'Sea Peoples' originating on the Aegean coasts and settling on the Egyptian and Gaza coasts in ca. 1200 BCE), Mitannians and Kassites, elements of IE culture were known throughout West Asia. Even ancient Israelite culture was culturally much more Indo-European than certain race theorists would like to believe."[205]

"The Ninevite Gigamesh Epic, composed probably at the end of the second millennium BC, has Utnapishtim settled "at the mouth of the rivers", taken by all commentators to be identical with Dilmun."[206]

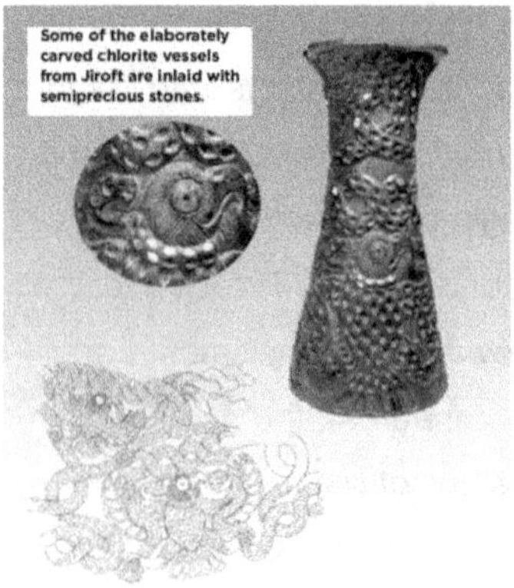

Some of the elaborately carved chlorite vessels from Jiroft are inlaid with semiprecious stones.

Lines 123-129; and interpolation UET VI/1: "Let me admire its green cedars. The (peole of the) lands Magan and Dilmun, Let them come to see me, Enki! Let the mooring posts beplaced for the Dilmun boats! Let the magilum-boats of Meluhha transport of gold and silver for exchange...The land Tukris' shall transport gold from Harali, lapis lazuli and bright... to you. The land Meluhha shall bring cornelian, desirable and precious sissoo-wood from Magan, excellent mangroves, on big ships The land Marhashi[207] will (bring) precious stones, dushia-stones, (to hang) on the breast.

The land Magan will bring copper, strong, mighty, diorite-stone, na-buru-stones, shumin-stones to you. The land of the Sea shall bring ebony, the embellishment of (the throne) of kingship to you. The land of the tents shall bring wool... The city, its dwelling gplaces shall be pleasant dwelling places, Dilmun, its dwelling place shall be a pleasant dwelling place. Its barley shall be fine barley, Its dates shall be very big dates! Its harvest shall be threefold. Its trees shall be ...-trees."[208]

Snake iconography such as that on this chlorite plaque is some of the best evidence for Jiroft's homegrown religion MORE TK.

Finds at Jiroft have challenged our understanding of how the bronze-age created crossroads of contact between Meluhha and Mesopotamia.

The chrloite vessel has eagle and 'chain' motifs as hieroglyphs *meḍhā* 'tangle in cord' Rebus: *meḍ* 'iron'. *pajhaṛ* 'eagle' Rebus: *pasra* 'smithy'.

On an artifact, the cord tangle gets depicted as snake iconography ending with the faces of felines. kol 'tiger' Rebus: kola 'working in iron'.

This impressive cup shows a man with clawed feet and one with half a bull's body holding panthers. These half-men half-beast figures are common in Jiroft's iconography.

This half-man half-scorpion chlorite figure from Jiroft's native mythology and may represent evil forces.

The tiger or panther or cheetah motifs get linked with that of a scorpion. bicha 'scorpion' (Assamese) Rebus: bica 'stone ore' (Munda). *Ka.* koṇḍi the sting of a scorpion. *Tu.* koṇḍi a sting. *Te.* koṇḍi the sting of a scorpion. (DEDR 2080). *kund* ' brassfounder's lathe ' (Bihari)(CDIA 3295). *kõdā* 'to turn in a lathe' (Bengali) कोंद *kōnda* 'engraver, lapidary setting or infixing gems' (Marathi)

In the following seals of Mohenjo-daro 'scorpion' hieroglyph is the center-piece surrounded by glyphs of a pair of bullocks, elephant, rhinoceros, tiger looking back and a monkey-like creature. On seals m1395 and m0441, the obverse shows a multi-headed tiger.

m1393t

m1394t

m440A

m0439t

m1395At

m1395Bt

m0441At

m0441Bt

Ta. kōṭaram monkey. *Ir.* kōḍa (small) monkey; kūḍag monkey. *Ko.* ko·ṛṇ small monkey. *To.* kwṛṇ monkey. *Ka.* kōḍaga monkey, ape. *Koḍ.* ko·ḍë monkey. *Tu.* koḍañji, koḍañja, koḍaṅgů baboon. (DEDR 2196). kuṭhāru = a monkey (Sanskrit) Rebus: kuṭhāru 'armourer or weapons maker'(metal-worker), also an inscriber or writer.

sangaḍa 'jointed animals' (Marathi); Rebus: *jangaḍa* 'entrustment articles'. *jangaḍiyo* 'military guard who accompanies treasure into the treasury'.

kola 'tiger' Rebus: kol 'working in iron'. *kollan* blacksmith, artificer (Ma.)(DEDR 2133)

ibha 'elephant' Rebus: ib 'iron'; ibbo 'merchant' (Gujarati)

ḍangar 'bull' Rebus ḍhangar 'blacksmith'.

Scorpion sting: koṭṭu (koṭṭi-) to sting (as a scorpion, wasp) (Tamil) Rebus: Pk. *koṭṭaga* -- m. ' carpenter ', *koṭṭila* -- , *°illa* -- m. ' mallet '. (DEDR 3236).koṭṭu-k-kaṉṉār Braziers who work by beating plates into shape and not by casting (Tamil)

A square bronze seal was discovered at Konar Sandal (Jiroft) depicting a gharial and caprid.

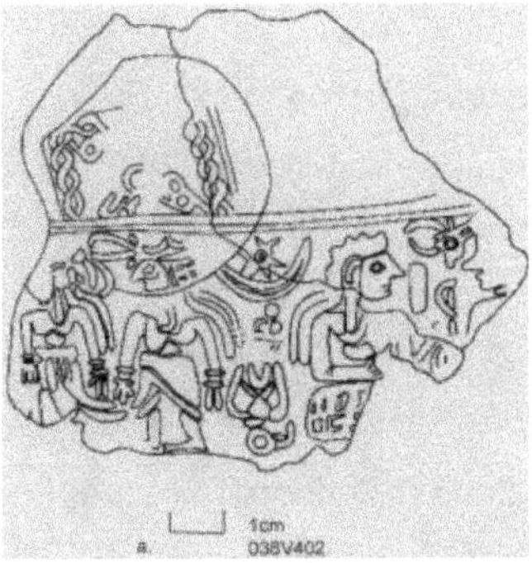

"At KSS about a dozen stamp seals were found in various operations and on the surface of the mound. They are of various types showing long distance connections especially to the east. One is a square stamp of bronze with very close parallels from the site of Lothal in the Indus Valley (Fig 28 a,b). Others are broken fragments of compartmented stamps (Fig. 28 c,d,e) similar to ones known from Bampur, Shahdad, Shahri Sokhta and as well as from sites in Central. . "There is quite a bit of robust evidence for long distance relations," says Pittman. (Pittman, H., 2008, Contribution on glyptic art. In Y. Madjidzadeh, ed., Excavations at Konar Sandal in the region of Jiroft in the Halil Basin: First Preliminary report (2002-2008). *Iran* 46: 95-103.) Source: Pittman, Holly, IX. Glyptic Art in: Excavations at Konar Sandal in th region of Jiroft in the Halil Basin: First Preliminary report (2002–2008) Youssef Madjidzadeh and Holly Pittman *Iran* Vol. 46, (2008), pp. 69-103 British Institute of Persian Studies, p. 95 ff.

a. Drawing of he carved bezel of a bronze stamp seal. KSS001surface; b. Photo of bronze stamp and a modern impression of bezel. KSS001 surface. (After Fig.

28 a,b, Pittman, H.,2011, p. 96). kakra. 'lizard'; kangra 'portable furnace'. tagaru 'ram' (Tulu) Rebus: tagarm 'tin' (Kota). damgar 'merchant'; *tamkāru, id. (Akkadian)thākur* 'smith, merchant' (Prakrit) खांडा [khāṇḍā] *m* A jag, notch, or indentation (as upon the edge of a tool or weapon). (Marathi) Rebus: *khāṇḍā* 'tools, pots and pans, metal-ware'.

After Fig. 30a.Drawing of a large sealing impressed with a cylinder and counter sealed with a stamp seal. KSS038V402. Note the head of ox on the top right corner. *mũh* 'face' (Lahnda) Rebus: *mũhe* 'ingot' (Santali).

Lothal048  7025 Lothal seal showing an antelope.

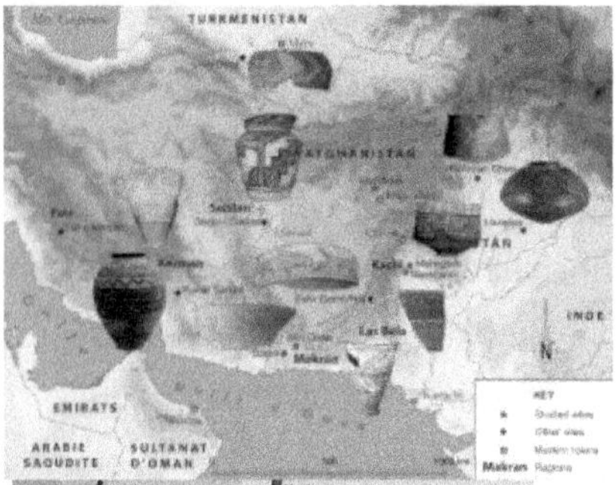

Polychrome wares in the Indo-Iranian borderlands during the 4th and 3rd millennia BCE.[209]

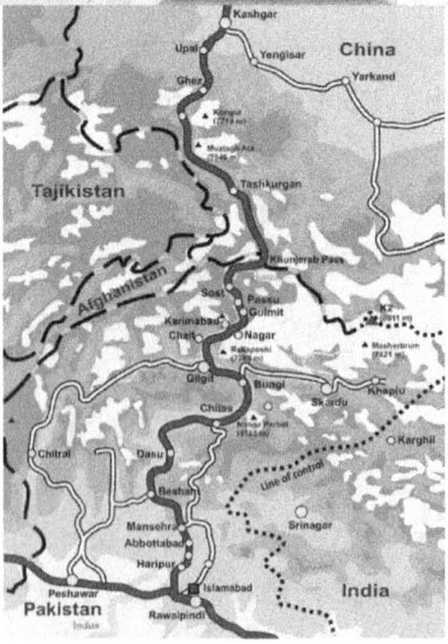

The reference to *Bad imin* is paralleled by the land *Sapta Saindhava*, 'the land of seven high places'. A cognate name, *hapta hendu*, 'seven rivers' exists in Avestan language. *Vendidad* 1.18 lists it as the fifteenth of the sixteen lands created by Mazda. [Gherardo Gnoli, *De Zoroastre à Mani. Quatre leçons au Collège de France* (Travaux de l'Institut d'Études Iraniennes de l'Université de la Sorbonne Nouvelle 11), Paris (1985)]. Vendidad also lists Airyanam Vaejah as one of the sixteen lands; the land with two months of summer and ten months of winter and which suffers from flooding at the end of winter.

Muztagh Ata, as viewed from the Karakoram Highway, which passes close to the peak and which links Gilgit–Baltistan and Khyber Pakhtunkhwa of ancient India and and the ancient Silk Road in China.

Vaejo is related to old Indic *vej/vij* (in Vedic) referring to a region of a fast-flowing river. Airyanam Vaejah may denote a region in snow-clad Himalayan ranges which could be Afghanistan highlands or Kashmir or Muztagh Ata on the norther edge of Tibetan Plateau (Xinjiang region) from which came Soma or synonym, añcu, 'iron' (Tocharian) (Vedic cognage: *amśu).*

aryānām xšaθra is a term which refers to the name of Iran with variants of MiddlePersian of *Ērān-shahr* and later, *Ērān* during Sassanian empire.

In Jaina geography, karmabhumi has six parts: one khanda was peopled by noble, meritorious good people; the other five were mleccha khandas, peopled by the rest of the inhabitants of the karmabhumi.

I suggest that Meluhha mentioned in Mesopotamian texts of 3rd-2nd millennium BCE is a language of this linguistic area. That meluhha and mleccha are cognate and that mleccha is attested as a mleccha vācas (mleccha speech) distinguished from arya vācas (arya speech) indicates that the linguistic area had a colloquial, ungrammatical mleccha speech – *lingua franca* and a grammatically correct arya speech – literary language. The substrate glosses of the *Indian lexicon*[210] are thus reasonably assumed to be the glosses of mleccha vācas, the speech of the artisans who produced the artifacts and the inscribed objects with the writing system. This assumption is further reinforced by the fact that about 80% of archaeological sites of the civilization are found on the banks of Vedic River

Sarasvati leading some scholars to rename the Indus Valley civilization as Sarasvati-Sindhu civilization.

In this context, the following monumental work by Sylvan Levi, Jules Bloch and Jean Przyluski published in the 1920's continues to be relevant, even today, despite some advances in studies related to formation of Indian languages and the archaeological perspectives of and evidences from the civilization.

Przyluski notes the principal forms of the words signifying 'man' and 'woman' in the Munda languages:

Man: hor, hōrol, harr, hǒ̃r, haṛa, hoṛ, koro

Woman: kūṛī, ērā, koṛi, kol

Comparing 'son' and 'daughter' in Santali:

Son = kora hapan; daughter = kuri hapan

"...a root kur, kor is differentiated in the Munda languages for signifying: man, woman, girl and boy. That in some cases this root has taken a relatively abstract sense is proved by Santali koḍa, koṛa, which signify 'one' as in the expression 'koḍa ke koḍa' 'each single one'. Thus one can easily understand that the same root has served the purpose of designating the individual not as an indivisible unity but as a numerical whole...Thus we can explain the analogy between the root kur, kor 'man' the number 20 in Munda kūṛī kūṛī , koḍī and the number 10 in Austro-Asiatic family ko, se-kūr, skall, gal." (ibid., pp. 28-30).

Homonym: कोल [kōla] *n* An income, or goods and chattels, or produce of fields &c. seized and sequestered (in payment of a debt). *V* धरून ठेव, सोड. 2 *f* The hole dug at the game of विटीदांडू, at marbles &c. कोलणें [kōlaṇēṃ] *v c* To strike the विटी in the hole कोली with the bat or दांडू. (In the game of विटीदांडू) 2 To cast off from one's self upon another (a work).

Ex. पैका मागावयास लागलों म्हणजे बाप लेंकावर कोल- तो लेंकबापावर कोलतो. 3 To cast aside, reject, disallow, flout, scout. कोलून मारणें To kick up the heels of; to trip up:

also to turn over (from one side to the other). किरकोळी [kirakōḷī] *f* (किरकोळ) A heap of miscellaneous articles.

An old Munda word, kol means 'man'. S. K. Chatterjee called the Munda family of languages as Kol, as the word, according to him, is (in the Sanskrit-Prākṛt form Kolia) an early Aryan modification of an old Munda word meaning 'man'. [Chatterjee, SK, The study of kol, *Calcutta Review*, 1923, p. 455.] Przyluski accepts this explanation.[211]

This area can be called speakers of 'mleccha, meluhha' or mleccha vācas according to Manusmṛti (lingua franca of the artisans). Manusmṛti distinguishes two spoken language-groups: mleccha vācas and arya vaacas (that is, spoken dialect distinguished from grammatically correct glosses).

"A *Sprachbund*...in German, plural "Sprachbünde" IPA, from the German word for "language union", also known as a linguistic area, convergence area, or diffusion area, is a group of languages that have become similar in some way because of geographical proximity and language contact. They may be genetically unrelated, or only distantly related. Where genetic affiliations are unclear, the*sprachbund* characteristics might give a false appearance of relatedness...In a classic 1956 paper titled "India as a Linguistic Area", Murray Emeneau[212] laid the groundwork for the general acceptance of the concept of a *sprachbund*. In the paper, Emeneau observed that the subcontinent's Dravidian and Indo-Aryan languages shared a number of features that were not inherited from a common source, but were areal features, the result of diffusion during sustained contact." _Common features of a group of languages in a *Sprachbund* are called 'areal features'. In linguistics, an areal feature is any typological feature shared by languages within the same geographical area. An example refers to retroflex consonants in the Burushaski,[213] Nuristani.[214]

Indian linguistic area: pre-aryan, pre-Munda and pre-dravidian in India

It will be a hasty claim to make that Old Tamil or Proto-Munda or Santali or Prakṛt or Pali or any other specific language of the Indian linguistic area, by itself (to the exclusion of other languages in contact), explains the language of the Indus civilization. In this context, the work by Sylvan Levi, Jules Bloch and Jean Przyluski published in the 1920's (loc.cit.) continues to be relevant, even today, despite some advances in studies related to formation of Indian languages and the archaeological perspectives of and evidences from the civilization.

Some glyphs of the script are yet to be decoded. Tentative readings of such glyphs yet to be validated by the cipher code key of Indus script are detailed (including decipherment of inscriptions from scores of small sites).[215] If the glyphs are unambiguously identified and read in archaeological context and the context of other glyphs of the inscription itself, it will be possible to decipher them. For this purpose, some graphemes (which have homonyms and can be read rebus) are provided from the *Indian Lexicon*[216] of the Indian linguistic area.

Graphemes:

Sign 257  Sign 197  Glyph: Peg 'khuṇṭa'; Rebus: Rebus: khũṭ 'community, guild' (Munda); kuṇḍa 'consecrated fire-pit'. round hole in ground (for water or sacred fire) (Skt.) Rebus: kūṭa 'workshop' khũṭi = pin (M.) kuṭi= smelter furnace (Santali) konḍu मूलिकादिघर्षणवस्तु m. a washerman's dressing iron (El. kunḍh); a scraper or grater for grating radishes, or the like; usually ˚ -- , the second member being the article to be grated, as in the following: -- kȧnḍi-mujü घर्षिता मूलिका f. grated radish, but mujĕ-konḍu, a radish-grater (cf. mujü). (Kashmiri) *khuṭṭa1 ' peg, post '. 2. *khuṇṭa -- 1. [Same as *khuṭṭa -- 2? -- See also kṣōḍa -- .]1. Ku. khuṭī ' peg '; N. khuṭnu ' to stitch ' (der. *khuṭ ' pin ' as khilnu from khil s.v. khī́la --); Mth. khuṭā ' peg, post '; H. khũṭā m. ' peg, stump '; Marw. khuṭī f. ' peg '; M. khuṭā m. ' post '.2. Pk. khuṁṭa -- , khoṁṭaya -- m. ' peg, post '; Dm. kuṇḍa ' peg for fastening yoke to plough -- pole '; L. khũḍī f. ' drum -- stick '; P. khuṇḍ, ḍā m. ' peg, stump '; WPah. rudh. khuṇḍ ' tethering peg or post '; A. khũṭā ' post ', ṭi ' peg '; B. khũṭā, ṭi ' wooden post, stake, pin, wedge '; Or. khuṇṭa, ṭā' pillar, post ';

Bi. (with -- ḍa --) khũṭrā, rī ' posts about one foot high rising from body of cart '; H. khũṭā m. ' stump, log ', ṭī f. ' small peg ' (→ P.khũṭā m., ṭī f. ' stake, peg '); G. khũṭ f. ' landmark ', khũṭɔ m., ṭī f. ' peg ', ṭũ n. ' stump ', ṭiyũ n. ' upright support in frame of wagon ', khũṭṛũn. ' half -- burnt piece of fuel '; M. khũṭ m. ' stump of tree, pile in river, grume on teat ' (semant. cf. kīla -- 1 s.v. *khila -- 2), khũṭā m. ' stake ', ṭī f. ' wooden pin ', khũṭaḷṇẽ ' to dibble '.Addenda: *khuṭṭa -- 1. 2. *khuṇṭa -- 1: WPah.kṭg. khv́ndɔ ' pole for fencing or piling grass round ' (Him.I 35 nd poss. wrong for ṇḍ); J. khuṇḍā m. ' peg to fasten cattle to '. (CDIAL 3893)
kola 'tiger' (Telugu); 'jackal' (Konkani); kul id. (Santali)

kol 'the name of a bird, the Indian cuckoo' (Santali)

kolo 'a large jungle climber, *dioscorea doemonum* (Santali)

Glyph: *kulai* 'a hare' (Santali)

Allograph: *kul* 'tiger' (Santali) Rebus: *kolhe* 'smelter'.

Object in front of the hare.

Glyph: 'bush, thorn': Pk. *kaṁṭiya* -- ' thorny '; S. *kaṇḍī* f. ' thorn bush '; N. *kāṛe* ' thorny '; A. *kāṭi* ' point of an oxgoad ', *kāiṭīyā* ' thorny '; H. *kāṭī* f. ' thorn bush '; G.*kāṭī* f. ' a kind of fish '; M. *kāṭī, kāṭī* f. ' thorn bush '. -- Ext. with -- *la* -- : S. *kaṇḍiru* ' thorny, bony '; -- with -- *lla* -- : Gy. pal. *ķăndī́la* ' prickly pear '; H. *kāṭīlā, kaṭ°* ' thorny '.(CDIAL 2679). kāṇṭaka -- ĀpŚr.1. Paš. *kāṛ* ' porcupine ' (cf. *kaṇṭakaśrēṇi* -- , *kaṇṭakāgāra* --). 2. S. *kāḍo* ' thorny ', Si. *kaṭu*. -- Deriv.: S. *kāḍero* m. ' camel -- thorn ', *°rī* f. ' a kind of thistle '(CDIAL 3022). Rebus: *Tu.* kandůka, kandaka ditch, trench. *Te.* kandakamu id. *Koṇḍa* kanda trench made as a fireplace during weddings. *Pe.* Kanda fire trench. *Kui* kanda small trench for fireplace. *Malt.* kandri a pit.(DEDR 1214). Rebus: *kaṇḍ* 'tools, pots and pans and metal-ware'.

Grapheme: Ta. kōl stick, staff, branch, arrow. Ma. kōl staff, rod, stick, arrow. Ko. kl stick, story of funeral car. To. kwṣ̱ stick.Ka. kōl, kōlu stick, staff, arrow. Koḍ. Klï stick. Tu. kōlů, kōlustick, staff. Te. kōla id., arrow; long, oblong; kōlana elongatedness, elongation; kōlani elongated. Kol. (SR.) kolā, (Kin.) kōla stick.Nk. (Ch.) kōl pestle. Pa. kōl shaft of arrow. Go. (A.) kōla id.; kōlā (Tr.) a thin twig or stick, esp. for kindling a fire, (W. Ph.) stick, rod, a blade of grass, straw; (G. Mu. Ma. Ko.) kōla handle of plough, sickle, knife, etc. (Voc.988); (ASu.) kōlā stick, arrow, slate-pencil; (LuS.) kola the handle of an implement. Konḍa kōlbig wooden pestle. Pe. kōlpestle. Manḍ. kūl id. Kui kōḍu (pl. kōṭka) id. Kuwi (F.)kōlū (pl. kōlka), (S. Su.)kōlu (pl. kōlka) id. Cf. 2240 Ta.kōlam (Tu. Te. Go.). / Cf. OMar. (Master) kōla stick. (DEDR 2237). कोलदंडाor कोलदांडा [kōladaṇḍā or kōladāṇḍā] m A stick or bar fastened to the neck of a surly dog. (Marathi) *Ta.* kōlam beauty, colour, form, shape, costume, attire as worn by actors, ornament. *Ma.* kōlam form, figure (chiefly of masks, dresses); idol, body, beauty. *Ka.* Kōla ornament, decoration, form, figure (chiefly of masks, dresses, etc.). *Tu.* kōla a devil-dance. *Te.* (B.) kōlamu a dance, dancing. *Go.* (Mu.) kōla the ḍanḍar dance [i.e. stick dance]; kōla pāṭa kind of song associated with the ḍanḍar dance (*Voc.* 986).(DEDR 2240).

kola [kōla] f. The bandicoot rat, *mus malibaricos* (Rajasthani)

Skanda Purana refers to kol as a mleccha community. (Hindu *śabdasagara*).

kolhe, 'the koles, are an aboriginal tribe of iron smelters speaking a language akin to that of Santals' (Santali) kōla m. name of a degraded tribe Hariv. Pk. Kōla — m.; B. kol name of a Muṇḍā tribe (CDIAL 3532). A Bengali lexeme confirms this: ক•োল[1] [kōla[1]] an aboriginal tribe of India; a member of this tribe. (Bengali) That in an early form of Indian linguistic area, kol means 'man' gets substantiated by a Nahali and Assamese glosses: kola 'woman'. See also: Wpah. Khaś.kuṛi, cur. kuḷī, cam. kŏḷā ' boy ', Sant. Muṇḍari koṛa ' boy ', kuṛi ' girl ', Ho koa, kui, Kūrkū kōn, kōnjē). Prob. separate from RV. kŕtā -- ' girl ' H. W. Bailey TPS 1955, 65; K. kūrü f. ' young girl ', kash. kōṛī, ram. kuṛhī; L. kuṛā m. ' bridegroom ', kuṛī f. ' girl, virgin, bride ', awāṇ. kuṛī f. ' woman '; P. kuṛī f. ' girl, daughter ', (CDIAL 3295). कारकोळी or ळया [kārakōḷī or ḷyā] a Relating to the country कार- कोळ--a tribe of Bráhmans (Marathi).

Mleccha as a Bharatiya language

Mleccha was substratum language of bharatiyo (casters of metal) many of whom lived in dvīpa (land between two rivers –Sindhu and Sarasvati -- or islands on Gulf of Kutch, Gulf of Khambat, Makran coast and along the Persian Gulf region of Meluhha).

Mleccha were bharatiya (Indians) of Indian linguistic area

According to Matsya Purāṇa (10.7), King Veṇa was the ancestor of the mleccha; according to Mahābhārata (MB. 12.59, 101-3), King Veṇa was a progenitor of the Niṣāda dwelling in the Vindhya mountains. Nirukta 3.8 includes Niṣāda among the five peoples mentioned in the *Ṛgveda* 10.53.4, citing Aupamanyava; the five peoples are: brāhmaṇa, kṣatriya, vaiśya, śūdra and Niṣāda. Niṣāda gotra is mentioned in the gaṇapāṭha of Pāṇini (Aṣṭādhyāyī 4.1.100). Niṣāda were mleccha. It should be noted that Pāṇini associated yavana with the Kāmboja (Pāṇini, *Gaṇapāṭha*, 178 on 2.1.72).

Mullaippāṭṭu (59-66) (composed by kāvirippūmpāṭṭinattuppon vāṇigaṇār mahā nārṇappūḍanār) are part of Pattuppāṭṭu, ten Tamil verses of Sangam literature; these refer to a chief of Tamil warriors whose battle-field tent was built by Yavana and guarded by mleccha who spoke only through gestures.[217]

Mahābhārata notes that the Pāṇḍava army was protected by mleccha, among other people (Kāmboja ,śaka, Khasa, Salwa, Matsya, Kuru, Mleccha, Pulinda, Draviḍa, Andhra and Kāñci) (MBh. V.158.20). Sūta laments the misfortune of the Kaurava-s: 'When the Nārāyaṇa-s have been killed, as also the Gopāla-s, those troops that were invincible in battle, and many thousands of mleccha-s, what can it be but Destiny?' (MBh. IX.2.36: *Nārāyaṇā hatāyatra Gopālā yuddhadurmahāh mlecchāśca bahusāhasrāh kim anyad bhāgadheyatah*?) *Mahābhārata* repeats allusion to 'thousands of mlecchas', a numerical superiority equaled by their valour and courage in battle which enhances the invincibility of Pāṇḍava (MBh. 7.69.30; 95.36).

Nahali, Meluhhan, Language 'X'

On the banks of River Narmada are found speakers of Nahali, the so-called language isolate with words from Indo-Aryan, Dravidian and Munda – which together constitute the indic language substratum of a linguistic area, ca. 3300 BCE on the banks of Rivers Sarasvati and Sindhu – a region referred to as Meluhha in Mesopotamian cuneiform records; hence the language of the inscribed objects can rightly be called Meluhhan or Mleccha, a language which Vidura and Yudhiṣṭhira knew (as stated in the Great Epic, Mahābhārata).

Elsewhere in the Great Epic we read how Sahadeva, the youngest of the Pāṇḍava brothers, continued his march of conquest till he reached several islands in the sea (no doubt with the help of ships) and subjugated the Mleccha inhabitants thereof. Brahmāṇḍa 2.74.11, Brahma 13.152, Harivaṁśa 1841, Matsya 48.9, Vāyu 99.11, cf. also Viṣṇu 4.17.5, Bhāgavata 9.23.15, see Kirfel 1927: 522: *pracetasah putraśatam rājānah sarva eva te // mleccharāṣṭrādhipāh sarve udīcīm diśam āśritāh* which means, of course, not that these '100' kings conquered the 'northern countries' way beyond the Hindukuṣ or Himalayas, but that all these 100 kings, sons of pracetās (a descendant of a 'druhyu'), kings of mleccha kingdoms, are 'adjacent' (āśrita) to the 'northern direction,' — which since the Vedas and Pāṇini has signified Greater gandhāra.[218] This can be construed as a reference to a migration of the sons of Pracetas towards the northern direction to become kings of the mleccha states. The son of Yayati's third son, Druhyu, was Babhru, whose son and grandsons were Setu, Arabdha, Gandhara, Dharma, Dhṛta, Durmada and Praceta. It is notable that Pracetas is related to Dharma and Dhṛta, who are the principal characters of the Great Epic, the *Mahābhārata*. It should be noted that a group of people frequently mentioned in the Great Epic are the mleccha, an apparent designation of a group within the country, with Bhāratam janam (Bhārata people). This is substantiated by the fact that Bhagadatta, the king of Pragjyotiṣa is referred to as mleccha and he is also said to have ruled over two yavana kings (2.13).

Evidence related to proto-Indian or proto-Indic or Indus language

A proto-Indic language is attested in ancient Indian texts. For example, Manusmṛti refers to two languages, both of dasyu (daha): ārya vācas, mleccha vācas. *mukhabāhū rupajjānām yā loke jātayo bahih mlecchavācas'cāryav ācas te sarve dasyuvah smṛtāh* Trans. 'All those people in this world who are excluded from those born from the mouth, the arms, the thighs and the feet (of Brahma) are called Dasyus, whether they speak the language of the mleccha-s or that of the ārya-s.' (Manu 10.45)] This distinction between *lingua franca* and literary version of the language, is elaborated by Patañjali as a reference to 1) grammatically correct literary language and 2) ungrammatical, colloquial speech (*deśī*).

Pāṇini explains *mleccha* as *avyaktam vāci* 'unintelligible speech'(X, 1663) and *mleccha avyakte śabde* 'mleccha unintelligible words' (1,205). This is the same as Patañjali's description of mleccha as *apaśabda* (I.1.1).

Ancient text of Panini also refers to two languages in *śikṣā*: Sanskrit and Prākṛt. Prof Avinash Sathayeprovides a textual reference on the earliest occurrence of the word, 'Sanskrit' :

triṣaṣṭiścatuh ṣaṣṭirvā varṇāh ṣambhumate matāh |

prākṛite samskṛte cāpi svayam proktā svayambhuvā || (pāṇini's śikṣā)

Trans. There are considered to be 63 or 64 varṇā-s in the school (mata) of shambhu. In Prakrit and Sanskrit by swayambhu (manu, Brahma), himself, these varṇā-s were stated.

This demonstrates that pāṇini knew both samskṛta and prākṛita as established languages. (Personal communication, 27 June 2010 with Prof. Shrinivas Tilak.)

Chapter 17 of Bharatamuni's *Nāṭyaśāstra* is a beautiful discourse about Sanskrit and Prakrit and the usage of *lingua franca* by actors/narrators in dramatic performances. Besides, Raja Shekhara, Kalidasa, Shudraka have also used the word Sanskrit for the literary language. (Personal communication from Prof. TP Verma, 7 May 2010). *Nāṭyaśāstra* XVII.29-30: *dvividhā jātibhāṣāca prayoge samudāhṛtā mlecchaśabdopacārā ca bhāratam varṣam aśritā* 'The jātibhāṣā (common language), prescribed for use (on the stage) has various forms. It contains words of mleccha origin and is spoken in Bhāratavarṣa only…' Vātstyāyana refers to mlecchita vikalpa (cipher writing of mleccha) Vātstyāyana's Kamasutra lists (out of 64 arts) three arts related to language:

- *deśa bhāṣā jñānam* (knowledge of dialects)
- *mlecchita vikalpa* (cryptography used by mleccha) [cf. mleccha-mukha 'copper' (Skt.); the suffix –mukha is a reflex of mũh 'ingot' (Mu.)
- *akṣara muṣṭika kathanam* (messaging through wrist-finger gestures)

Thus, semantically, mlecchita vikalpa as a writing system relates to cryptography (perhaps, hieroglyphic writing) and to the work of artisans (smiths). I suggest that this is a reference to Indian hieroglyphs.

It is not a mere coincidence that early writing attested during historical periods was on metal punch-marked coins, copper plates, two-feet long copper bolt used on an Aśokan pillar at Rampurva, Sohoura copper plate, two pure tingots found in a shipwreck in Haifa, and even on the Delhi iron pillar clearly pointing to the smiths as those artisans who had the competence to use a writing system. In reference to Rampurva copper-bolt: "Here then these signs occur upon an object which must have been made by craftsmen working for Asoka or one of his predessors."[219] The Indus script inscriptions using hieroglyphs on two pure tin-ingots found in Haifa were reviewed.[220]

Mahābhārata also attests to mleccha used in a conversation with Vidura. *Śatapatha Brāhmaṇa* refers to mleccha as language (with pronunciation variants) and also provides an example of such mleccha pronunciation by asuras. A Pali text, *Uttarādhyayana Sūtra* 10.16 notes: *ladhdhaṇa vimānusattaṇṇamāriattam puṇrāvi dullaham bahave dasyū milakkhuyā*; trans. ‘though one be born as a man, it is rare chance to be an ārya, for many are the dasyu and milakkhu’. Milakkhu and dasyu constitute the majority, they are the many. Dasyu are milakkhu (mleccha speakers). Dasyu are also ārya vācas (Manu 10.45), that is, speakers of Sanskrit. Both ārya vācas and mleccha vācas are dasyu [cognate *dahyu, daŋ́ha, daha* (Khotanese)], people, in general. दाशः 1 A fisherman; इयं च सज्जा नौश्चेति दाशाः प्राञ्ज- लयो$ब्रुवन् Rām.7.46.32; Ms.8.48,49;1.34. दासः ‘a fisherman’ (Apte. Lexicon) Such people are referred to in *Ṛgveda* by Viśvāmitra as ‘Bhāratam janam.’ Mahābhārata alludes to ‘thousands of mlecchas’, a numerical superiority equaled by their valour and courage in battle which enhances the invincibility of Pandava (MBh. 7.69.30; 95.36).

Excerpt from *Encyclopaedia Iranica* article[221] on cognate *dahyu* country (often with reference to the people inhabiting it): DAHYU (OIr. *dahyu-*), attested in Avestan *daxiiu-*, *daŋ́hu-* “country” (often with reference to the people inhabiting it; cf. *AirWb.*, cot. 706; Hoffmann, pp. 599-600 n. 14; idem and Narten, pp. 54-55) and in Old Persian *dahyu-* “country, province” (pl. “nations”; Gershevitch, p. 160). The term is likely to be connected with Old Indian *dásyu* “enemy” (of the Aryans), which acquired the meaning of “demon, enemy of the gods”.[222] Because of the Indo-Iranian parallel, the word may be traced back to the root *das-*, from which a term denoting a large collectivity of men and women could have been derived. Such traces can be found in Iranian languages: for instance, in the ethnonym Dahae (q.v., i) “men” (cf. Av. ethnic name [fem. adj.] *dāhī*, from *dåŋ́ha-*; *AirWb.*, col. 744; Gk. Dáai, etc.), in Old Persian *dahā* “the Daha people” (Brandenstein and Mayrhofer, pp. 113-14), and in Khotanese *daha* “man, male”.[223]

In Avestan the term did not have the same technical meaning as in Old Persian. Avestan *daxiiu-*, *dańhu-* refers to the largest unit in the vertical social organization. See, for example, Avestan *x^vaētu-* (in the Gathas) “next of kin group” and *nmāna-*“house,” corresponding to Old Persian *taumā-* “family”; Avestan *vīs-* -

"village," corresponding to Avestan *vərəzə̄na-* "clan"; Avestan *zantu-* "district"; and Avestan*daxiiu-*, *daŋhu-*.[224] The connection *daxiiu*, *daŋhu-* and *arya-* "Aryans" is very common to indicate the Aryan lands and peoples, in some instances in the plural: *airiiå daŋhāuuō,airiianąm daxiiunąm*, *airiiābiiō daŋhubiiō*.
In *Yašt* 13.125 and 13.127 five countries (*daxiiu-*) are mentioned, though their identification is unknown or uncertain; in the same *Yašt* (13.143-44) the countries of other peoples are added to those of the Aryans: *tūiriia*, *sairima*, *sāinu*, *dāha*.

In Achaemenid inscriptions Old Persian *dahyu-* means "satrapy" (on the problems relative to the different lists of *dahyāva* [pl.][225], and "district"[226]. The technical connotation of Old Persian *dahyu* is certain and is confirmed—despite some doubts expressed by George Cameron but refuted by Ilya Gershevitch—by the loanword *da-a-yau-iš* in Elamite. On the basis of the hypothetical reconstruction of twelve "districts" and twenty-nine "satrapies," it has been suggested that the formal identification of the Old Persian numeral 41 with the ideogram *DH*, sometimes used for *dahyu*[227], can be explained by the fact that there were exactly forty-one *dahyāva* when the sign *DH* was created (Mancini).

From the meaning of Old Persian *dahyu* as "limited territory" come Middle Persian and Pahlavi *deh* "country, land, village," written with the ideogram *MTA*[228] and Manichean Middle Persian *dyh*[229] At times the Avestan use is reflected in Pahlavi *deh*, but already in Middle Persian the meaning "village" is well documented; it appears again in Persian *deh*.

That Pali uses the term 'milakkhu' is significant (cf. *Uttarādhyayana Sūtra* 10.16) and reinforces the concordance between 'mleccha' and 'milakkhu' (a pronunciation variant) and links the language with 'meluhha' as a reference to a language in Mesopotamian texts and in the cylinder seal of Shu-ilishu.[230] This seal shows a sea-faring Meluhha merchant who needed a translator to translate meluhha speech into Akkadian. The translator's name was Shu-ilishu as recorded in cuneiform script on the seal. This evidence rules out Akkadian as the Indus or Meluhha language and justifies the search for the proto-Indian speech from the region of the Sarasvati river basin which accounts for 80% (about 2000) archaeological sites of the civilization, including sites which have yielded inscribed objects such as Lothal, Dwaraka, Kanmer, Dholavira, Surkotada, Kalibangan, Farmana, Bhirrana, Kunal, Banawali, Chandigarh, Rupar, Rakhigarhi. The language-speakers in this basin are likely to have retained cultural memories of Indus language which can be gleaned from the semantic clusters of glosses of the ancient versions of their current *lingua franca* available in comparative lexicons and *nighanṭu*-s (many of which are ayurvedic pharmacopeia).

Evidence from Śatapatha Brāhmaṇa for *mleccha vācas*, Meluhha speech

An extraordinary narrative account from Śatapatha Brāhmaṇa is cited in full to provide the context of the yagna in which vaak (speech personified as woman) is referred to the importance of grammatical speech in yagna performance and this grammatical, intelligible speech is distinguished from mlecccha, unintelligible speech. The example of the usage of phrase 'he 'lavo is explained by Sayana as a pronunciation variant of: 'he 'rayo. i.e. 'ho, the spiteful (enemies)!' This grammatically correct phrase, the Asuras were unable to pronounce correctly, notes Sayana. The ŚB text and translation are cited in full because of the early evidence provided of the mleccha speech (exemplifying what is referred to Indian language studies as 'ralayo rabhedhah'; the transformed use of 'la' where the syllable 'ra' was intended. This is the clearest evidence of a proto-Indian language which had dialectical variants in the usage by asuras and devas (i.e. those who do not perform yagna and those who perform yagna using vaak, speech.) This is comparable to mleccha vācas and ārya vācas differentiation by Manu. The text of ŚB 3.2.1.22-28 and translation are as follows:

yoṣā vā iyaṃ vāgyadenaṃ na yuvitehaiva mā tiṣṭhantamabhyehīti brūhi tām tu na āgatām pratiprabrūtāditi sā hainaṃ tadeva tiṣṭhantamabhyeyāya tasmādu strī pumāṃsaṃ saṃskṛte tiṣṭhantamabhyaiti tāṃ haibhya āgatām pratiprovāceyaṃ vā āgāditi tāṃ devāḥ |

asurebhyo 'ntarāyaṃstāṃ svīkṛtyāgnāveva parigṛhya sarvahutamajuhavurāhutirhi devānāṃ sa yāmevāmūmanuṣṭubhājuhavustadevaināṃ taddevāḥ svyakurvata te 'surā āttavacaso he 'lavo he 'lava iti vadantaḥ parābabhūvuḥ atraitāmapi vācamūduḥ |

upajijñāsyāṃ sa mlecastasmānna brāhmaṇo mlecedasuryā haiṣā vā natevaiṣa dviṣatāṃ sapatnānāmādatte vācaṃ te 'syāttavacasaḥ parābhavanti ya evametadveda o 'yaṃ yajño vācamabhidadhyau |

mithunyenayā syāmiti tāṃ saṃbabhūva indro ha vā īkṣāṃ cakre |

mahadvā ito 'bhvaṃ janiṣyate yajñasya ca mithunādvācaśca yanmā tannābhibhavediti sa indra eva garbho bhūtvaitanmithunam praviveśa sa ha saṃvatsare jāyamāna īkṣāṃ cakre |

mahāvīryā vā iyaṃ yoniryā māmadīdharata yadvai meto mahadevābhvaṃ nānuprajāyeta yanmā tannābhibhavediti tām pratiparāmṛśyaveṣṭyācinat |

tāṃ yajñasya śīrṣanpratyadadhādyajño hi kṛṣṇaḥ sa yaḥ sa yajñastatkṛṣṇājinaṃ yo sā yoniḥ sā kṛṣṇaviṣāṇātha yadenāmindra āveṣṭyācinattasmādāveṣṭiteva sa yathaivāta indro 'jāyata garbhobhūtvaitasmānmithunādevamevaiṣo 'to jāyate garbho bhūtvaitasmānmithunāt tāṃ vā uttānāmiva badhnāti |

Translation: 22.The gods reflected, 'That Vaak being a woman, we must take care lest she should allure him. – Say to her, "Come hither to make me where I stand!" and report to us her having come.' She then went up to where he was standing. Hence a woman goes to a man who stays in a well-trimmed (house). He reported to them her having come, saying, 'She has indeed come.' 23. The gods then cut her off from the Asuras; and having gained possession of her and enveloped her completely in fire, they offered her up as a holocaust, it being an offering of the gods. (78) And in that they offered her with an anushtubh verse, thereby they made her their own; and the Asuras being deprived of speech, were undone, crying, 'He 'lavah! He 'lavah!' (79) 24. Such was the unintelligible speech which they then uttered, -- and he (who speaks thus) is a Mlekkha (barbarian). Hence let no Brahman speak barbarous language, since such is the speech of the Asuras. Thus alone he deprives his spiteful enemies of speech; and whosoever knows this, his enemies, being deprived of speech, are undone. 25. That Yajna (sacrifice) lusted after Vaak (speech [80]), thinking, 'May I pair with her!' He united with her. 26. Indra then thought within himself, 'Surely a great monster will spring from this union of Yagna and Vaak: [I must take care] lest it should get the better of me.' Indra himself then became an embryo and entered into that union. 27. Now when he was born after a year's time, he thought within himself, 'Verily of great vigour is this womb which has contained me: [I must take care] that no great monster shall be born from it after me, lest it should get the better of me!' 28. Having seized and pressed it tightly, he tore it off and put it on the head of Yagna (sacrifice [81]); for the black (antelope) is the sacrifice: the black deer skin is the same as that sacrifice, and the black deer's horn is the same as that womb. And because it was by pressing it tightly together that Indra tore out (the womb), therefore it (the horn) is bound tightly (to the end of the garment); and as Indra, having become an embryo, sprang from that union, so is he (the sacrifice), after becoming an embryo, born from that union (of the skin and the horn). (ŚB 3.2.1.23-25). (fn 78) According to Sayana, 'he 'lavo' stands for 'he 'rayo' (i.e. ho, the spiteful (enemies)!' which the Asuras were unable to pronounce correctly. The Kaanva text, however, reads te hātavāko 'su hailo haila ity etām ha vācam vadantah parābabhūvuh (? i.e. he p. 32 ilaa, 'ho, speech'.) A third version of this passage seems to be referred to in the Mahā bhāṣya (Kielh.), p.2. (p.38). (fn 79) Compare the corresponding legend about Yagna and Dakṣiṇā (priests' fee), (Taitt. S. VI.1.3.6. (p.38) (fn 79) 'Yagnasya sīrṣan'; one would expect 'kṛṣṇa(sāra)sya sīrṣan.' The Taitt.S. reads 'tām mṛgeṣu ny adadhāt.' (p.38) (fn81) In the Kanva text 'atah (therewith)' refers to the head of the sacrifice, -- sa yak khirasta upasprisaty ato vā enām etad agre pravisan pravisaty ato vā agre gāyamāno gāyate tasmāk khirasta upasprisati. (p.39)(cf.śatapatha Brāhmaṇa vol. 2 of 5, tr. By Julius Eggeling, 1885, in SBE Part 12; fn 78-81).

Mesopotamian texts refer to a language called meluhha (which required an Akkadian translator); this meluhha is cognate with mleccha. Seafaring meluhhan merchants used the script in trade transactions; artisans created metal artifacts, lapidary artificats of terracotta, ivory for trade. Glosses of the proto-Indic or Indus language are used to read rebus the Indus script inscriptions. The glyphs of the script include both pictorial motifs and signs and both categories of glyphs are read rebus. As a first step in delineating the Indus language, an *Indian lexicon* [231] provides a resource, compiled semantically cluster over 1240 groups of glosses from ancient Indian languages as a proto-Indic substrate dictionary.[232]

Note: Coining a term, "Para-Munda", denoting a hypothetical language related but not ancestral to modern Munda languages, Witzel goes on to identify it as "Harappan", the language of the Harappan civilization. He later retracts this and posits that Harappan were illiterate and takes the glyphs of the script to be symbols without any basis in any underlying language.[233]

Ṛgveda (ṛca 3.53.12) uses the term, *'bhāratam janam'*, which can be interpreted as 'bhārata folk'. The ṛṣi of the sūkta is viśvāmitra gāthina. India was called Bhāratavarṣa after the king Bhārata. (Vāyu 33, 51-2; Bd. 2,14,60-2; lin:ga 1,47,20,24; Viṣṇu 2,1,28,32).

Ya ime rodasī ubhe aham indram atuṣṭavam

viśvāmitrasya rakṣati brahmedam bhāratam janam

3.053.12 I have made Indra glorified by these two, heaven and earth, and this prayer of viśvāmitra protects the people of Bhārata. [Made Indra glorified: indram atuṣṭavam — the verb is the third preterite of the casual, I have caused to be praised; it may mean: I praise Indra, abiding between heaven and earth, i.e. in the firmament].

The evidence is remarkable that almost every single glyph or glyptic element of the Indus script can be read rebus using the repertoire of artisans (lapidaries working with precious shell, ivory, stones and terracotta, mine-workers, metal-smiths working with a variety of minerals, furnaces and other tools) who created the inscribed objects and used many of them to authenticate their trade transactions. Many of the inscribed objects are seen to be calling cards of the professional artisans, listing their professional skills and repertoire.

The identification of glosses from the present-day languages of India on Sarasvati river basin is justified by the continuation of culture evidenced by many artifacts evidencing civilization continuum from the Vedic Sarasvati River basin, since language and culture are intertwined, continuing legacies:

Huntington notes: "There is a continuity of composite creatures demonstrable in Indic culture since Kot Diji ca. 4000 BCE."[234]

Mriga (pair of deer or antelope) in Buddha sculptures compare with Harappan period prototype of a pair of ibexes on the platform below a seated yogin.[235]

Continued use of śankha (turbinella pyrum) bangles which tradition began 6500 BCE at Nausharo;

Continued wearing of sindhur at the parting of the hair by married ladies as evidenced by two terracotta toys painted black on the hair, painted golden on the jewelry and painted red to show sindhur at the parting of the hair;

Finds of shivalinga in situ in a worshipful state in Harappa (a metaphor of Mt. Kailas summit where Maheśvara is in tapas, according to Hindu tradition);

Terracotta toys of Harappa and Mohenjo-daro showing Namaste postures and yogasana postures;

Three-ring ear-cleaning device

Legacy of architectural forms

Legacy of puṣkariṇi in front of mandirams; as in front of Mohenjo-daro stupa

Legacy of metallurgy and the writing system on punch-marked coins

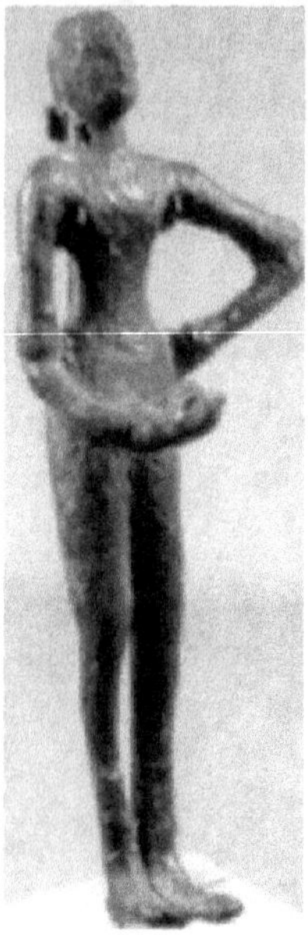

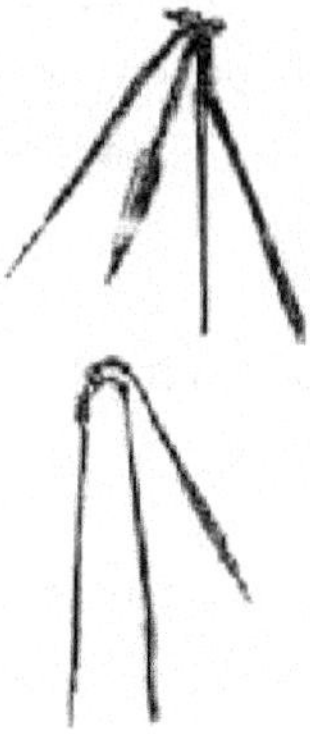

Legacy of continued use of cire perdue technique for making utsava bera (bronze murti)

Legacy: Engraved celt tool of Sembiyan-kandiyur with Sarasvati hieroglyphs: calling-card of an artisan

Legacy of acharya wearing uttariyam (shawl) leaving right-shoulder bare

Form of addressing a person respectfully as: arya, ayya (Ravana is also referred to as arya in the Great Epic Rāmāyaṇa)

Plate X [c] Lingam in situ in Trench Ai (MS Vats, 1940, Excavations at Harappa, Vol. II, Calcutta) Lingam, grey sandstone in situ, Harappa, Trench Ai, Mound F, Pl. X (c) (After Vats). "In an earthenware jar, No. 12414, recovered from Mound F, Trench IV, Square I… in this jar, six lingams were found along with some tiny pieces of shell, a unicorn seal, an oblong grey sandstone block with polished surface, five stone pestles, a stone palette, and a block of chalcedony…" (Vats, MS, 1940, Excavations at Harappa, Delhi, p. 370).

Continued use of cire perdue technique of bronze-casting. Bronze murti: cire perdue technique used today in Swamimalai to make bronze utsavabera (idols carried in procession). Eraka Subrahmanya is the presiding divinity in Swamimalai. Eraka! Copper.Devices on punch-marked coins comparable to Sarasvati hieroglyphs.

Toilet gadgets: Ur and Harappa After Woolley 1934, Vats 1941

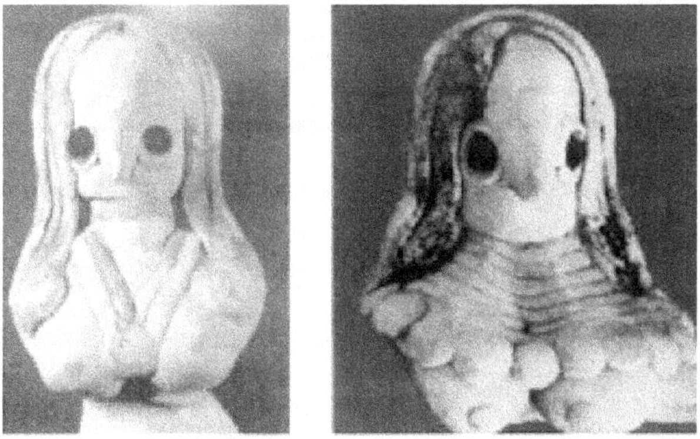

Nausharo: female figurines. Wearing sindhur at the parting of the hair. Hair painted black, ornaments golden and sindhur red. Period 1B, 2800 – 2600 BCE. 11.6 x 30.9 cm.[After Fig. 2.19, Kenoyer, 1998].

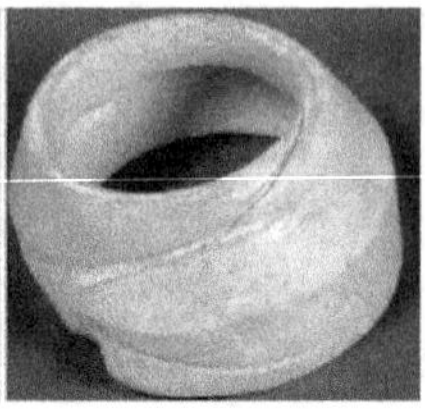
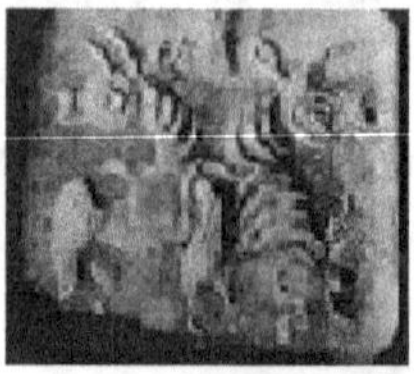
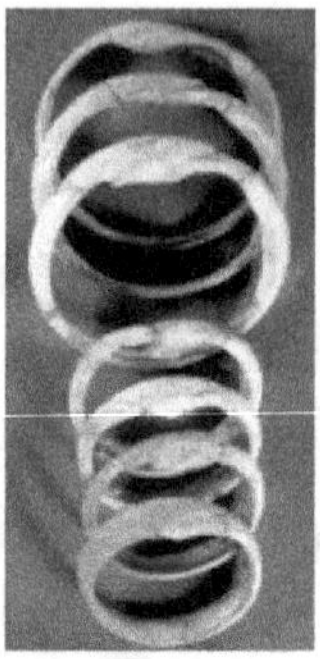
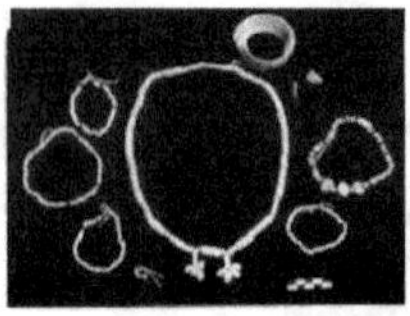

S'ankha artifacts: Wide bangle made from a single conch shell and carved with a chevron motif, Harappa; marine shell, Turbinella pyrum (After Fig. 7.44, Kenoyer, 1998) National Museum, Karachi. 54.3554. HM 13828. Seal, Bet Dwaraka 20 x 18 mm of conch shell. Seven shell bangles from burial ofan elderly woman, Harappa; worn on the left arm; three on the upper arm and four on the forearm; 6.3 X 5.7 cm to 8x9 cm marine shell, Turbinella pyrum (After Fig. 7.43, Kenoyer, 1998) Harappa museum. H87-635 to 637; 676 to 679. Modern lady from Kutch, wearing shell-bangles.

6500 BCE. Date of the woman's burial with ornaments including a wide bangle of shankha. Mehergarh. Burial ornaments made of shell and stone disc beads, and turbinella pyrum (sacred conch, s'an:kha) bangle, Tomb MR3T.21, Mehrgarh, Period 1A, ca. 6500 BCE. The nearest source for this shell is Makran coast near Karachi, 500 km. South. [After Fig. 2.10 in Kenoyer, 1998]. S'ankha wide bangle and other ornaments, c. 6500 BCE (burial of a woman at Nausharo). Glyph: 'shell-cutter's saw', *āra*

Invention of bronze-age technologies necessitated the invention and development of a writing system called Indus Script which is evidenced in corpora of about 6000 inscriptions.[236] Around 7500 BCE[237], tokens appeared and represented perhaps the early deployment of a writing system to count objects. Many geometric shapes were used for the tokens.[238] Tracing the evolution of a writing system[239], Schmandt-Besserat evalutes the next stage of keeping tokens in envelopes with markings abstracting the tokens inside and calls these abstract numbers are 'the culmination of the process…'[240] This evaluation is the starting point for identifying another stage before 'the culmination' represented by the use of syllabic representation in glyphs of sounds of a language.

That penultimate stage, before syllabic writing evolved, was the use of hieroglyphs represented on hundreds of Indian hieroglyphs.[241]

The arrival of the bronze age was maked by the invention of alloying copper with arsenic, zinc or tin to produce arsenic-alloys, and other alloys such as brass, bronze, pewter. These archaeo-metallurgial inventions enabled the production of goods surplus to the requirements of the artisan guilds. These inventions also created the imperative of and necessity for a writing system which could represent about over 500 specific categories of activities related to the artisanal repertoire of a smith. Such a large number of categories could not be handled by the limited number of geometric shapes used in the token system of accounting and documenting – goods, standard measures of grains, liquids and surface areas.[242]

The existence of Indian *sprachbund* is evidenced by the concordant lexemes used for bronze-age repertoire of bronze-age artisans. These lexemes are compiled in an *Indian Lexicon.*[243] This is a resource base for further studies in the formation and evolution of most of the Indian languages. Identifiable substrata glosses include over 4000 etyma of Dravidian Etymological Dictionary and over 1000 words of Munda with concordant semantic clusters of Indo-Aryan. That the substrata glosses cover three major language families –Dravidian, Munda and

Indo-Aryan -- is a surprising discovery. There are over 1240 semantic clusters included in the *Indian Lexicon*[244] from over 25 languages which makes the work very large, including cognate entries of CDIAL (Indo-Aryan etyma), together with thousands of lexemes of Santali, Mundarica and other languages of the Austro-Asiatic linguistic group, and, maybe, Language X. . Most glosses of the lexical archive relate to the bronze-age cultural context and possible entries are relatable rebus to Indian hieroglyphs. Many are found to be attested as substratum lexemes only in a few languages such as Nahali, Kashmiri, Kannada or Telugu or lexical entries of Hemacandra's *deśī nāmamālā (Prākṛt)*; thus, many present-day Indian languages are rendered as dialects of an Indus language or proto-Indic *lingua franca* or gloss. The identification of a particular Indian language as the Indus language has presented some problems because of the received wisdom about grouping of language families in Indo-European linguistic analyses. Some claims of decipherment have assumed the language to be Tamil, of Dravidian language family; some have assumed the language to be Sanskrit, of Indo-Aryan language family. A resolution to these problems comes from a surprising source: Manu.

The identification of mleccha as the language of the Indus script writing system is consistent with the following theses which postulate an Indian linguistic area, that is an area of ancient times when various language-speakers interacted and absorbed language features from one another and made them their own: Emeneau, 1956; Kuiper, 1948; Masica, 1971; Przyludski, 1929; Southworth, 2005.

Mleccha words in Sumerian[245]

Cuneiform writing was most probably invented in Uruk in southern Mesopotamia (modern Iraq) about 3400 - 3300 BCE.[246] It was invented to keep records of goods and services, and the language that was recorded was, as far as we can tell, Sumerian. The cuneiform script was later adopted by other people speaking languages as different as Akkadian, a Semitic language, and Hittite, an Indo-

European language. Sumerian itself is, as far as we know, not related to any other living language. It is a language isolate.

ab-ba-me-luh-ha '*abba* wood of Meluhha' (a thorn tree), *mêsu* wood 'of the plains'.

šimmar ~ RV *śalmali* at 7.50.3, 10.85.20, and *śimbala* at 3.53.22.

magilum boats of Meluhhan style (Possehl 1996).

sinda (*si-in-da-a, si-in-du*) Sindh wood, date palm, the 'red dog of Meluhha'.

The word *me-la-hha* may also be cognate with: *meṛh, meḍh,* 'copper merchant'. Another example of a substrate term: Sumerian *tibira, tabira* (Akkadian. LU2 URUDU-NAGAR =. "[person] copper-carpenter"); a word indicating borrowing from a substrate. In Pkt. tambira = copper. According to Gernot Wilhelm, the Hurrian version of *tabira* is: *tab-li* 'copper founder'; *tab-iri* 'the one who has cast (copper)'.

Sumerian shows signs of a substrate language in the use of professional names such as tibira 'copper smith', 'metal-manufacturer'; sanga 'priest', simug 'blacksmith'. The words tibira "merchant" and sanga "priest" are cognate with tam(b)ra "copper" (Santali) and sanghvi "priest who accompanies the pilgrims" (Gujarati).

Smiths (Sum. simug, Akk. nappāhum), responsible for (s)melting and casting, were distinguished from metalworkers (Sum. tibira, Akk. gurgurrum) who worked metal and created objects. These, on the other hand, were distinctly different from jewellers (Sum. zadim) and goldsmiths (Sum. ku-dim/dim, Akk. kutimmum)... Given the large number of metal tools, weapons and vessels recovered from sites in southern Mesopotamia, there is, as with ceramics, a frustrating lack of excavated workshop facilities.[247]

Substrate language of Sumer and Indian lexemes

'One of the most significant and impressive archaeological achievements of the twentieth century centers around the discovery of the ancient Indus civilization which probably flourished from about 2500 to 1500 B.C., and extended over a vast territory from the present Pakistan-Iran border to the foot of the Himalayas and to the Gulf of Cambay... That there was considerable commercial trade between Sumer and Indus land is proved beyond reasonable doubt by some thirty Indus seals which have actually been excavated in Sumer-- and no doubt hundreds more are still lying buried in the Sumerian ruins-- and which must have been brought there in one way or another from their land of origin. There is, therefore, good reason to conclude that the Sumerians had known the name of the Indus land as well as some of its more imortant featues and characteristics, and that some of the innumerable Sumerian texts might turn out to be highly informative in this respect... According to a long-known Sumerian 'Flood'-story, Dilmun, the land to which Ziusudra, the Sumerian Noah, was transported to live as an immortal among the gods, is 'the place where the sun rises', and was therefore located somewhere to the east of Sumer. In another Sumerian text, Dilmun is described as a blessed, prosperous land dotted with 'great dwellings', to which the countries of the entire civilized world known to the Sumerians, brought their goods and wares... The only rich, important land east of Sumer which could be the source of ivory, was that of the ancient Indus civilization, hence it seems not unreasonable to infer that the latter must be identical with Dilmun... there are two faces of the Indus civilization which are especially significant for its identification with Dilmun: the cult of a water deity and sea-plowing ships... the god most intimately related to Dilmun is Enki, the Sumerian Poseidon, the great Sumerian water god in charge of seas and rivers. Thus we find a Sumerian Dilmun-myth which tells the following story: Dilmun, a land described as 'pure', 'clean', and 'bright', a land which knows neither sickness nor death, had been lacking originally in fresh, life-giving water. The tutelary goddess of Dilmun, Ninsikilla by name, therefore pleaded with Enki, who is both her husband and father, and the latter orders the sun-god Utu to fill Dilmun with sweet water brought up from the earth's water-sources; Dilmun is thus turned into a divine garden green with grain-yielding fields and acres. In this paradise of the gods eight plants are made to sprout by Ninhursag, the great mother goddess of the Sumerians, perhaps more originally Mother Earth... because Enki wanted to taste them, his messenger, the two-faced god Isimud, plucks these plants one by one and gives them to his master who proceeds to eat them each in turn. Whereupon the angered Ninhursag pronounces the curse of death against Enki and vanishes from among the gods. Enki's health at once begins to fail and eight of his organs become sick. As Enki sinks fast, the great gods sit in the dust, seemingly unable to cope with the situation. Whereupon the fox comes to the rescue and after being promised a reward, he succeeds by some ruse in having the mother goddess return to the gods and heal the dying water god. She seats him by her vulva and after inquiring which eight organs of his body ache, she brings into existence eight corresponding deities-- one of these is Enshag, the Lord of Dilmun-- and Enki is brought back to life and health...

'The land Dilmun is holy, Holy Sumer--present it to him, The land Dilmun is holy, The land Dilmun is holy, the land Dilmun is pure, The land Dilmun is clean, the land Dilmun is holy... In Dilmun the raven utters no cry, The wild hen utters not the cry of the wild hen, The lion kills not... He (the god Enki) cleaned and purified the land Dilmun, Placed the goddess Ninsikilla in charge of it. '

“In fact the very name of the goddess whom Enki placed in charge of Dilmun is a Sumerian compound word whose literal meaning is 'the pure queen'... the Indus civilization depended largely on water-borne trade, coastal and riverine... one of the Sumerian rulers by the name of Ur-Nanshe, who lived as early as about 2400 B.C., speaks of timber-carrying Dilmun boats arriving at his city, Lagash... In the myth 'Enki and the World Order' mentioned earlier, Enki boasts of the moored Dilmun boats. Ivory-bearing boats from Dilmun to Ur have already been mentioned; according to the texts these also carried timber, gold, copper, and lapis lazuli. No wonder that in the 'Paradise' myth cited above, Dilmun is described as 'dockyard-house of the (inhabited) land.'...the pre-Indus settlements excavated at Harappa, Kot Diji, or Amri, which could be regarded as the forerunner of the Indus cities and towns with their carefully planned buildings and streets, their water cult and purification rites, their well-developed pictographic script, and their bustling water-borne trade...

"The names of the two great Mesopotamian rivers, the Tigris and Euphrates, or idiglat and buranun as they read in the cuneiform texts, are Ubaidian-- not Sumerian-- words. So, too, are the names of the most important centers of 'Sumer':Eridu, Ur, Larsa, Isin, Adab, Kullab, Lagash, Nippur, and Kish. In fact the word Dilmun itself may, like the word buranun for the Euphrates, be Ubaidian. More important still, such culturally significant words as engar (farmer), udul(herdsman), shupeshdak (fisherman), apīn (plow), apsin (furrow), nimbar (palm), sulumb (date), tibira (metal worker), simug (smith), nangar (carpenter), addub (basket maker), ishbar (weaver), ashgab (leather worker), pahar (potter),shidim (mason), and perhaps even damgar (merchant), are probably all Ubaidian rathern than Sumerian, as has been usually assumed... Another crucial word which may turn out to be Ubaidian, is Ea, one of the two names by which the Mesopotamian water god is known in the cuneiform texts, the other being Enki... while the latter is a typical Sumerian compound with the meaning 'Lord of the Earth', Ea is a word whose linguistic affiliations are still uncertain... The Assyrian king Tukulti-Ninurta uses in his titles the expression 'king of Dilmun and Meluhha' ... There is another king by the name of Hundaru in whose days booty taken from Dilmun consisted of objects made of copper and bronze, sticks of precious wood, and large quantities of kohl, used as an eye-paint. A crew of soldiers is sent from Dilmun to Babylon to help King Sennacherib raze that city to the ground, and they bring with them bronze spades and spikes which are described as characteristic products of Dilmun...from the myth 'Enki and the World Order', the god Enki boasts of the moored Dilmun boats.

"The lands of Magan and Dilmun
Looked up at me, Enki,

Moored (?) the Dilmun-boat to the ground (?),

Loaded the Magan-boat sky high."[248]

Lipshur litanies state: 'Melukkha...is the land of carnelian' (Sumerian NA4.GUG, Akkadian *sāmtu*). In the 17th century BC, the Neo-Assyrian king Esarhaddon called himself, 'king of the kings of Dilmun, Magan, and Melukkha'.

The Akkadian texts referring to Meluhhans also refers to mill staff (scribes, gate-keepers, reed-weavers, carpenters, maltsters, grinding-slab cutters, 'chair-bearers', boat towers, etc.) and mention of grain delivery. Meluhhans in Lagash are clearly part of domestic Ur III society.

Consistent with the focus of Akkadian texts on mill staff, it is also possible that the Indus script glyphs found on Persian Gulf sites may also refer to the professions of Meluhhans (scribes, carpenters, stone or grinding-slab cutters, etc.)

Mleccha as a Sanskrit word should also have referred to Meluhhan traders in Lagash.

Apaśabda, mleccha

For Sanskrit grammarians, Prakrits were *apaśabda* and hence labeled as *mleccha*. Lexical meaning of 'mleccha' also includes 'foreigner or outsider'. It should, however, be noted that all outsiders need not represent a common linguistic affiliation.

***Mleccha, lingua franca* of Bhāratam, of the 'linguistic area'**

> A hypothesis has been posited: Language X (cf. Masica 1991) + Proto-Munda (Proto-Prākrits) = Mleccha (vernacular of Sarasvati hieroglyphs). The hypothesis has been tested by identifying the borrowings into the Indian languages which can explain, rebus, the Sarasvati hieroglyphs in a Proto-Vedic continuum of Indian linguistic area.

Since 1956 when Emeneau referred to an ancient linguistic area in India, there has been a paradigm shift in IE linguistics as applied to the area called 'India' using terms such as areal linguistics, *sprachbund*, linguistic area.

The credit for using the term 'linguistic area' goes to MB Emeneau, even though he used the term as a translation of '*sprachbund*' invented by HV Velton in 1943. Linguistic areas are areas in which 'languages belonging to more than one family show traits in common which do not belong to the other members of (at least) one of the families'.The methodology used to recognize a linguistic area is a bifurcate one. First, a typological feature is established as pan-Indic and at the same time not extra-Indic. Second, the historical diffusion of features throughout the languages of the linguistic area are investigated through questions of lexical lists, phonology, syntactic, morphological and semantic development and sociolinguistic questions. Emeneau recognizes (1956: 1,2) that '...it is rarely possible to demonstrate this (Indo-Aryan to Dravidian) direction (except for diffusion of lexical items).

The term *sprachbund* was used in 1931 by Nikol Trubetzkoy and Roman Jakobson when they discussed the long-recognized linguistic areas such as the languages of the Caucasus or of the Balkans. The following works have been reviewed: *Language and Linguistic Area, Essays by Murray B. Emeneau,* (selected and introduced by Anwar S. Dil), 1980, Stanford University Press, California (which includes: Emeneau, MB, 1956, India as a linguistic area, in: Language, 32.3-16 Kuiper, FBJ, 1967, The genesis of a linguistic area, *Indo-Iranian Journal* 10: 81-102 Masica, Colin P., 1976, *Defining a linguistic area, South Asia*, Chicago, University of Chicago Press (Based on the author's thesis, 1971).

Indo-Iranian a product of merger in historical linguistics

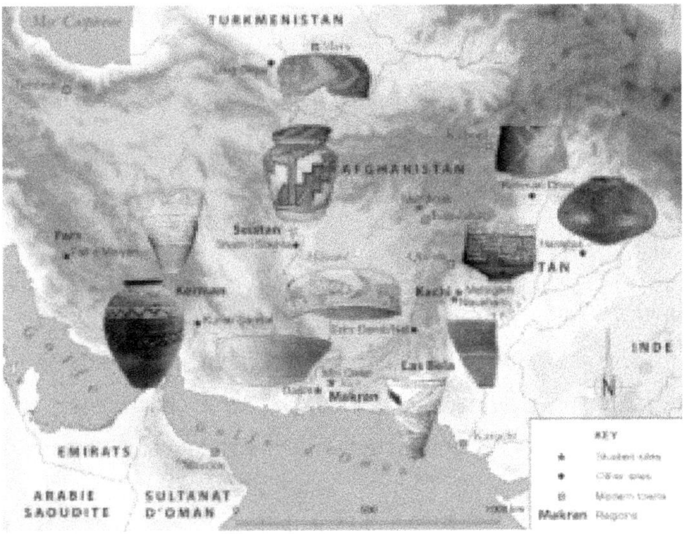

Polychrome wares in the Indo-Iranian borderlands during the 4th and 3rd millennia BCE.[249]

Indo-Iranian is the product of merger, say some IE linguists. SS Misra narrates the finds from Gypsy languages researches which indicate that Indo-Aryan a remains a in Asiatic Gypsy but it becomes a,e,o in European Gypsy.

"This confirms that original IE a was same as Skt a and remained a in the Indo-Iranian languages, but changed to a,e,o in their sister languages…Gypsy languages present evidence with the linguistic changes by repetition of what had happened several thousand years back.

Centum -- Sadem in Sanskrit

"That IE palatal *k^* has become *s'* in Sanskrit is also questionable, because in Sanskrit itself *s'* becomes *k* before *s.*. Thus the *k* which was allophonic to *s* in Sanskrit might have been generalized in the Centum languages.
Some Sadem languages also sporadically present k instead of a sibilant e.g.

Lithuanian *klausau~* < IE *k^leu-,* Skt *s'ru-,* Av *sru-,* Gk *klu-*

Lith *akmu~* < IE *ak^mon* cp Skt *as'man* Gk *a'kmo_n*, Old Church Slavic *svekry* < IE *svek^ru_,* cp Skt *s'vas'ru_,* Lat *socrus* etc.

"This shows that the allophonic nature *s': k* as shown by Sanskrit was partly disturbed in some Satdm languages and was fully lost in the highly innovating Centum languages and the allophone k has become a phoneme, replacing *s'* completely...

"...the evidence of IE *k^h* is almost nil in Sanskrit. The developments of IE *k^h, g^, g^h* as *ch, j, h* in Sanskrit can be proved otherwise mostly, as *ch, j, h* came from velar by palatalization. If we do not accept palatalization by *e* etc., there are other explanations. If origin of *s'* < *k^* is not accepted, the palatal series is eighty percent doomed.

"If the Centum velars, from IE palatal series are accepted as innovation by changing the allophonic k (<s') to a phoneme in the Centum languages, the three series system of IE guttural series almost vanishes, because the labio-velars are conjectured simply to explain certain innovations in the Centum languages.Brugmann in his 1st edition did not reconstruct a labio-velar series, but explained this as a special development in Centum.[250]

"Thus, apart from these two reconstructions viz. I IE *a, e, o* for Skt. *a* and II IE *k^* etc. for Skt *s'* etc., which are, as shown above, controversial reconstructions, Skt shows archaic features in almost all other cases. In another reconstruction, according to which IE *r* and *l* have become Indo-Iranian *r*, which further become *r* and *l* in Skt, it seems that Skt has some innovations.

Ralayor abhedah

"The theory is that in earlier portions of the Rigveda Samhitā *r* prevails and gradually *l* prevails more and more in later languages, i.e. in later Samhitās, āraṇyaka, Upaniṣad, Classical Sanskrit and finally in MIA. But in fact distribution of r and l is universally dialectical. Some languages show a preference of r as the Old Iranian languages and some show a preference of l as Chinese. If historically l replaced r in Indo-Aryan then in New Indo-Aryan languages all should show preference of r and others show preference of l, which is not the fact. Some show preference of r and others show preference of l. If we take one IE standard for distribution of r and l, we find confusion of distribution of r and l to some extent even in the languages, where it is considered to present the original distribution. Therefore, the Sanskrit Grammarians have accepted 'ralayor abhedah'.

"In all other aspects Sanskrit shows archaism and therefore, IE reconstruction is based on Sanskrit mainly. The linguistic changes found in India in the Middle Indo-Aryan stage are found amply, in Greek, Iranian and Hittite which are stamped as very old historical languages of IE."[251]

The excursus on the relationship between Indo-Iranian and Indo-Aryan presents many views on possible historical changes in PIE vowel system.

Piotr Gasiorowski notes: "The ante-PIE state of things (I mean the "origin" of the PIE vowel system) is a a matter of speculation and debate. Not so the Indo-European quality of *e. The vowel is normally reflected as mid-low to mid-high front /e/ in Old Hittite, Greek, Italic, Celtic, Germanic (with a partial shift to /i/), Slavic, Baltic and Armenian. It causes the palatalisation of various consonants in several branches and individual languages. Tocharian and Albanian show complicated developments, but these are strictly local affairs, and the reflexes in question point to a mid front vowel as well (consonants are palatalised before it in both branches) *e. In Indo-Iranian the reflex is /a/, but again velars are palatalised before it. Being a former schwa-like vowel is not enough to cause palatalisation in IIr at least, where velars are _not_ palatalised before any /i/ that reflects syllabic laryngeals or epenthetic vowels. To sum up, the comparative evidence for *e = /e/ is absolutely overwhelming. Only someone with an urgent non-linguistic agenda could have a reason to ignore it. The lapse of time between the disintegration of PIE and the Indo-Iranian merger can only be guessed at, but must have been pretty long. My private estimate is ca. 2500 years or slightly more. There is no reason to suppose that during that period the vowel was anything else but /e/-like (middish front)."[252]

The three-way vowel inventory (*a, *i, *u) was an Indo-Iranian innovation. "Consider a form like <ca-ka:r-a>, which is derived from the root <k(a)r->. The theory that it derives from the pattern *kWe-kWor-e accounts for the structure of the reduplicated perfect outside Indo-Iranian and — crucially — accounts for the peculiarities of the Sanskrit form itself. We normally expect reduplication to copy the initial consonant. In Sanskrit, however, velars are palatalised in the reduplication syllable (cf. <ja-ga:m-a> etc.). Why this should have happened before /a/ (or, worse still, only before some occurrences of /a/) is a mystery. Why <caka:ra> rather than "kaka:ra" or "caca:ra" (or "kaca:ra", for that matter)? The curious incident of Sanskrit palatalisation taking place in those cases where all the non-Indo-Iranian branches point to *e can only be a miraculous coincidence, if one accepts Misra's position. Note also that Sanskrit palatalises velars before any /i/ that corresponds to *i outside Indo-Iranian (which strengthens the argument that the "palatalising /a/" reflects an original front vowel), but there is no palatalisation before those /i/'s that do _not_ correspond to extra-Indo-Iranian *i. Why's that? And the fact that open-syllable lengthening as in the second syllable of <caka:ra> (Brugmann's Law) correlates with the occurrence of apophonic *o outside Indo-Iranian is another miraculous coincidence — needless to say, only from a strictly Misraic point of view."[253]

“The phenomenon of PIE qualitative ablaut **e* ~ **o*. In an earlier phase of the proto-language it must have been a quantitative opposition between short ***a* and long ***â*. The long vowel was backed to [*å:*], while the short vowel became fronted to [*æ*]. Under certain circumstances, long ***â* gave **ê* instead, which contrasted with short **e* < ***a*. However, long [*o(:)*] lacked a short counterpart, and could develop into a short vowel **o* in most of the PIE-speaking area [SL #12: *â* > *o*] (although in Indo-Iranian the old quantity was maintained in most open syllables — Brugmann’s Law).” Cf. Pali, where Sanskrit *e* and *o* are shortened in closed syllables.[254]

Harmatta’s dating of IIr loans in Uralic languages, is somewhat controversial because of exaggerated dating of Proto-Uralic and Proto-Finno-Ugric).

Pre-Indo-Ayan migrating out of Bharat and then coming back home is one possibility.

There could have been successive migrations out of Bharat. After each migration, a new substrate could have been absorbed by Proto-Indo-Aryan languages of Bharat.

How are the layers of borrowings in Finno-Ugric to be explained, borrowings from pre-Proto-Indo-Iranian and Proto-Indo-Iranian.[255]

Munda as the language of first contact. “One possibility would be to assume a pre-Dravidian, pre-Indo-Aryan substratum from which both language groups could have acquired the features in which they agree. Thus, Mayrhofer, Manfred (1953, *Die Substrattheorien und das Indische*, Germanisch-Romanische Monatsschrift 34, pp. 233-6) attributed the use of absolutives and quotative iti to such a substratum. One might even toy with the idea of attributing all of the features to such a substratum. However, in the absence of any evidence for contact with such a substratum, any such theory has to remain mere speculation…”[256]

"Even more important is Hock's article which discusses the possibility of Old Indo-Aryan being the PIE language and the possibility of IEs emigrating out of India (1999). Hock rightly rejects the notion that PIE was Vedic, but he is wrong in ascribing this view to Misra, who makes no such claim as far as I know...he is careful throughout his study (1992) to keep Sanskrit quite distinct from PIE...Then Hock, unaware of J. Nichols's evidence which requires a locus of dispersal at Bactria-Sogdiana (unlike his own vague "vast area from East central Europe to Eastern Russia", p. 17), nonetheless indicates that there are no substantial linguistic arguments against the proposition that IE branches moved out of India. He states that apart from the gypsy emigration, there are "three more IA languages moving out of India: Gandhari Prakrit (in medieval Khotan and farther east), and Parya (in modern Uzbekistan)...and Dumaki (close to present-day Shina)...to the outer northwestern edge of south Asia" (also in Hock 1996: 82). He states also that the PIE could 'a priori' have been 'originally spoken in India' (p. 11) and rejects the idea not on linguistic but archaeological (!) grounds (p. 13) of the kind usually employed by invasionists (horse and chariot). This, as we saw (sect. VII) is no real difficulty...He then invokes the 'principle of simplicity' as an additional difficulty (p. 16): one migration into India as against many out of it. But he ignores the fundamental fact that there is plenty of evidence of IE branches invading the areas they occupy but there is none for India: this makes considerable difference, surely. What is more, this 'simplicity' applies equally to all proposed homelands...Bactria is not far from Saptasindhu and could be a first concentration point for out-of-India travelers and subsequent dispersals...palatalization began after the various branches moved to their historical habitats (allow for some variation in the order): Hittite leaving first westward, then Tocharian to the east, then Germanic and Balto-Slavonic to the west and north-west, Celtic and Italic to the west and south-west, and finally Thraco-Phrygian and Greek (with the distinctive isoglosses they shared with the Indo-Iranians). Here too we have the difficulty of the positions of the Balto-Slavs, but, as was said, perhaps in the early period (in the 5th millennium?) they were close enough to the Indo-Iranians. Thus palatalizatin spread from the Indo-

Iranian 'core regions' to the adjacent Slavo-Balts but not the extreme limits of the 'periphery' (particularly as many non-IE cultures intervened between the Indo-Iranians and the Hittites, Phrygians and Greeks). Bryant discusses other possible OIT scenarios (146-149). The scenario with Saptasindhu as the urheimat seems much more reasonable. Or so it would be, if I accepted the theories about protolanguages and isoglosses. I don't – and this has little to do with C. Melcher's arguing (1987) that Anatolian Luvian is neither centum nor satem (where palatals have become affricates z and sibilants s; see also Hock 1991: 13-15), or with the Himalayan proto-Bangani (perhaps) being centum (Elst 1999: 122-123; Bryant, 142). We know, or rather surmise, that there was a PIE language but we don't know what it was, nor when, where and how it changed: we merely conjecture and theorize about these phenomena – and writing pseudoscientific texts just perpetuates the illusory knowledge, which becomes deception...Nobody should dismiss or ignore linguistic realities but everybody should avoid fantasies."[257]

The conclusions of Southworth about 'Indus' language, Proto-Munda and Language X are consistent and acceptable since the assumption made about the arrival of Indo-Aryan languages is not relevant for and do NOT upset his hypotheses. The *mleccha* Southworth refers to is more extensive in areal usage than suggested by his analyses. Mleccha-speaker areas according to Mahabharata and Patanjali are extensive areas covering the *lingua franca* of many regions outside of Kurukshetra – ranging from Gandhara in the west to Kosala in the East, from Kashmir in the north to Coda in the South.

What Hemachandra calls deśi seems to aptly describe this linguistic area as a continuum from the days of Sarasvati hieroglyphs.

The word *mlecchati* of Vedic, means 'speaks indistinctly'. *mliṣṭa* is referred to by Panini meaning 'spoken indistinctly or barbarously' [Monier-Williams 1899; Pali milakkha, Pkt. Milicchа; <PD *mur̤i/mir̤i 'say, speak, utter'; *muzankk 'make noise, speak' (DEDR 4989); probably connected with tamir̤ (Tamil)]. म्लेच्छनम् mlecchanam 1 Speaking indistinctly or confusedly. -2 Speaking in a barbarous

tongue.म्लेच्छित mlecchita *p. p.* Spoken indistinctly or barbarously. -तम् 1 A foreign tongue. -2 An ungrammatical word or speech. म्लेच्छितकम् Foreign or barbarous speech. म्लिष्ट mliṣṭa spoken indistinctly or barbarously Pa1n2. 7-2 , 18; indistinct speech , a foreign language. மிழலை[1] miḻalai , *n.* < மிழற்று-. cf. *mlīṣṭa.* Prattle, lisp; மழலைச்சொல். (சூடா.) மிழலை[2] miḻalai , *n.* See மிழலைக்கூற்றம். புனலம் புதவின் மிழலையொடு (புறநா. 24). miḻalai-k-kūṟṟam, *n.* < மிழலை[2] + கூற்றம். A division of *Cōḻa-nāṭu*, சோணாட்டின் ஒரு பகுதி. (புறநா. 24, உரை.)மிழற்றல் miḻaṟṟal, *n.* < மிழற்று-. 1. Speaking; சொல்லுகை. (சூடா.) 2. See மிழலை[1]. (யாழ். அக.) 3. Noise of speaking; பேசலானெழு மொலி. (யாழ். அக.)

Patanjali's Mahābhāṣya refers to asura (OIr ahura) who substitute *l* for *r* an apparent reference to poor speakers of Indo-Aryan. Parpola refers to Dasa as pre-Vedic Indo-Aryan speaking people. Deshpande (1979:1) notes that the dāsavarṇa was a reference to all the indigenous peoples. Hock notes that Balbūtha Tarukṣa, presubaly ba Dasa, is referred to as a patron of a Vedic seer. Hock also notes that the combatants of 'Battle of Ten Kings' include those with Aryan-sounding names (such as Vasiṣṭha and Bharata) and those with non-Aryan-sounding names (such as the Sṛnjayas and śimyu) on both sides.[258]

Manu 10.43-45 considered Coda, Dravida, Persian etc. as former kshatriya who sank to the level of śūdra, whether they speak the language of the mleccha or the language of arya. Kane *History of Dharmaśāstra* Vol. II, p. 383 gives the impression that these groups were bilingual, speaking both 'mleccha' language and 'ārya' language.

A more reasonable interpretation is that mleccha is the ungrammatical *lingua franca* as distinct from grammatically correct, literary bhāṣā as proto-Sanskrit. Samskṛta (refined speech) is distinguished from asura, pisaca, mleccha as dialects with incorrect pronunciation of Samskṛta. For instance, *Satapatha brāhmaṇa* notes that the mleccha-speakers failed to articulate arava(h) correctly; they uttered 'helava helava'. (te asura attavacasa he'alave he'alava 3.2.1.23). One notes that the madhyandina-branch of the śatapathi Brahmins were occasionally indifferent to correct articulation; so that they got corrupt recitation as the mleccha did.[259] "Mleccha were those who could not pronounce Samskṛta (vak) appropriately as prescribed in Svaravidhāna of the grammatical treatises. Mostly the mleccha were the Kirata, the Savara, the Pulinda (*Amarakośa*, Sundaravarga)." Akkadian maliku(m) means god, king, lord. This anecdote clearly notes mleccha as a grammatical entity, a language.

Asko and Simo Parpola (1975: 205-238) claim that *Meluhha* is the origin of the Sanskrit *mleccha*. Sargon of Akkad (c. 2200 BCE) had 'dismantled the cities, as far as the shore of the sea. At the wharf of Agade, he docked ships from Meluhha, ships from Magan.'

Copper-head from Sargonic period. Sargon?

Guabba, the Meluhhan village in Mesopotamia

"Although a Meluhhan village (e-duru me-luh-ha) integrated under the jurisdiction of Girsu/Lagash in southern Mesopotamia has been known since Sargonic times, it has never previously been identified with a specific place name. In this article the Meluhhan village has now, for the first time, been connected in a Ur III text with the well-known village/town of Guabba (Gu-ab-ba-ki) based on the (twice) published text MVN 7 420 = ITT 4 8024 from Ur III Girsu."[260]

Since Sargonic times (ca. second part of the third millennium BCE) and until the time of Gudea of Lagash, Meluhhan village (e-duru me-lu-hha) in Girsu/Lagash jurisdiction of Mesopotamia has been known to be integrated with Sumerian society and even paid taxes (known as the gun-mada-taxes[261]) to the local government. Vermaak, cites a cuneiform Ur III Girsu text specifically connecting Guabba (Gu-ab-baki) and the role played by Meluhhans in the economy, the textile industry of Girsu, in particular.[262] While Parpola et al review ten Ur III texts of Girsu/Lagash to outline activities of the neo-Sumerian Meluhhan village, Vermaak reviews 44 texts (which include 48 references to Meluhha) which describe Meluhha village with foreign descendants and "…to show that one text (MVN 7 420 = ITT 4 8024) from the Istanbul Archaeological Museum in Turkey first published by Delaporte in 1912 (ITT 4 8024) and later collated and republished by Pettinato et al. in 1978 (MVN 7 420), has never been really noticed by scholars and never received any scholarly translation or discussion regarding the *Meluhhans* in Sumer. It connects the *Meluhhan* village with the place name of Guabba."

Meluhha granaries, garden, temples,avifauna, fauna, timber/woods, bronzes
[quote] The *Meluhhan* granaries

The *Meluhhan* village was known for its granaries (ì-dub é-duru me-luh-ha) and the large amounts of royal barley that were delivered to the town of Girsu. When one calculates the amounts delivered by the *Meluhhan* granaries in comparison to other regions, towns or villages it was surprisingly high.

There are, however, two texts dating from the sixth year of Amar-Sin and the eighth year of Shu-Sin (SS 8) respectively (from Girsu) where the *Meluhhan* granary was the only deliverer of the royal barley and it seems that the various granaries had separate monthly instalments to pay.

The *Meluhhan* garden

Some references can be found to the *Meluhhan* garden (giškiri me-lu h-ha) in the Neo-Sumerian period, but no more specific details can be derived from these texts except to note that they were connected to the temple of Ninmarki. However, several types of *Meluhhan* artefacts have been identified which probably made up the *Meluhhan* garden, especially the gišab-ba me-luh-ha which is a sort of *Meluhhan* wood, or the gišab-ba could refer to some kind of water feature in a garden (see "The *Meluhhan* timber/woods" below: giškiri *me-luh-ha* dNin-marki) .

The *Meluhhan* temples

Two temples have been connected to the *Meluhhan* village in Ur III Girsu, namely those of the gods' dNanshe and dNin-marki. In a text where a number of scribes (dub-sar-me) are listed it has been summarized in three interesting lines, namely šu-nígin 6 guruš, arád dNanše-me, ugula` me-luh-ha ("A total of 6 men, servants of the god dNanshe, while the overseer is a *Meluhhan*")which definitely seems to connect the *Meluhhan* village with the temple of dNanše. This text relates to the temple of dNanshe and the *Meluhhan* official, which is a good illustration of the *Meluhhans* being incorporated into the society of southern Mesopotamia. Another text suggests that the *Meluhhans* worked in the temple of dNanše: dumu me-luh-ha erín é dNanše("the *Meluhhan* worker in the house of dNanše").

In a balanced account (níg-kas7-ak) regarding the different types of barley delivered to the temple of dNinmarki (níg-kas ak Lú-dŠul-gi šabra še é dNin-´MAR.KI`)the seal of the well-known *Meluhhan* appears twice in the text (Kišib Ur-dLamma dumu *me-luh-ha).*17 The royal barley deliveries sent to the different gardens (giškiri6 en-ne) in the region of Girsu (year 48 of Šulgi) and the *Meluhhan* garden was again connected to the temple of dNin-Marki (giškiri me-luh-ha dNin-MAR.KI-ka), but in the following line there is another temple of dNin-marki (giškiri6 dNin-MAR.KI) which was not connected to the

Meluhhan temple. This means there had to be two gardens in the same temple of dNinmarki, one as a *Meluhhan* garden and another one not.

The *Meluhhan* avifauna

The *Meluhhan* bird (dar me-luh-ha) appears five times in the Ur III texts, only once with the determinative of a bird (mušen). In most of the cases the dar has been listed together with images (alan) which indicates that in these instances the dar probably does not refer to a real bird, but to an image of a bird, maybe as a carved bird (as curio) from wood or ivory. In all instances these texts came from Ur and date from the fifteenth year of Ibbi-Sin. It has been speculated that the dar might a "multi-coloured" *Meluhhan* bird...

The *Meluhhan* fauna

Although in earlier and later texts references are made to the *Meluhhan* fauna species from other periods such as the multicoloured *Meluhhan* dog which was given as a gift to Ibbi-Sin and a *Meluhhan* cat (Akkadian *šuranu*) in a Babylonian proverb. The only *Meluhhan* fauna in the Ur III texts is a reference to the goat: máš ga mel-luh-ha, "the *Meluhhan* milk goat".

The *Meluhhan* timber/woods

Special kinds of timber/woods came into southern Mesopotamia from various places such as *Magan* and *Meluhha* from the Early Dynastic III to the Gudea period. Lexical texts confirm the import of *Meluhhan* timber which entered via the ports in the Gulf. Various kinds of *Meluhhan* wood have been identified during the Ur III and other periods and they were mostly used for different kinds of furniture. The mes me-luh-ha-wood only occurs in the Ur III texts, but also continued to be used for furniture and household utensils during the Old

Babylonian period. The gišab-ba me-luh-ha-wood had a special purpose to make *inter alia* special chairs or thrones with ivory inlays.

The *Meluhhan* bronzes

Since the Uruk III period up to the Gudea period the acquiring of bronzes from the three places Dilmun, Magan en Meluhha was well documented, however during the Ur III period only one reference was found which connects the bronze (uruda) with the *Meluhhan* village: 6 ma-na uruda *me-luh-ha.*

The *meluhhan* village of Guabba

According to the electronic UR III databases there are more than four hundred references in texts mentioning the place name Gú-ab-baki and the texts mostly originate from Girsu/Lagash.

The only reference in the Ur III texts referring to the place of Guabba as a real *Meluhhan* village comes from MVN 7 420 = ITT 4 8024 at the Istanbul Archaeological Museum in Turkey.

MVN 7 420 = ITT 4 8024

1. 490.0.0 še gur lugal 1 sìla-ta
2. še-ba gáb-ús udu gukkal
3. Gú-ab-baki-ka é-duru5 me-luh-ha-ta
4. ki Ur-gišgigir ka-gur7-ta
5. mu Ur-dLamma dumu Ka5-a ka-gur7 Gú-ab-baki-ka-šè
6. Ur-dIg-alim dumu Ur-dBa-ba6 šu ba-ti
7. gìr Ur-dun šeš-na
8. iti mu-šu-du7
9. mu An-ša-anki ba-hul

The importance of this text is that the *Meluhhan* village often referred to is now connected to the well-known place/village of Gú-ab-baki which is also mentioned twice in this text. It is also linked with a person called Ur-dLamma who has often been mentioned in several other Ur III texts (cf. Ur III databases) and seals as a *Meluhhan* (dumu me-luh-ha). If this text has been interpreted correctly, in this instance, several other texts regarding the prosopography of Ur-dLamma and the toponomy/onomastics and major activities of the place of Guabba within the region of Girsu/Lagash can now be pursued in order to form a more comprehensive insight of the foreigners living in Sumer and more specifically the *Meluhhan* population/s living together with the Sumerians and Akkadians in southern Mesopotamia. Currently, all 44 texts have been published and are available electronically referring to *Meluhha* as a place or as a qualifier (a so-called "adjective"). On the other hand the place Gú-ab-baki is to be found several hundred times in the Sargonic and Ur III texts. The challenge now would be to find as many as possible cuneiform tablets which could be related (via prosopography and onomastics) to this village which will enhance our understanding of the hybrid population of the Sumerians...

Guabba continued with *Meluhhan* temples

In the above discussion it has been concluded that the two temples which have often been associated with the *Meluhhan* village in Ur III Girsu, are namely those of the gods dNanše and dNin-mari...In a Sumerian temple hymn (TH 23)31 Guabba is twice mentioned in connected with the temple of Ninmar:

Line 291: [é-gú-ab-baki] kù-dnin-marki-ke4 "[O house of Guabba], the holy/pure Ninmar"

Line 293: é-dnin-mar-ki gú-ab-baki

"The house of Ninmar in Guabba"

In the Lamentation over Sumer and Ur the temple of Ninmar was again mentioned in connection with Guabba

Line 168: dnin-mar-ki-ra èš gú-ab-ba-ka izi im-ma-da-an-tej3(?)

"Fire approached Ninmarki in the shrine Guabba" (and)

Line 169: kù na4 za-gìn-bi má-gal-gal-la bala-šè ì-ak-e

"Large boats were transported precious metals and gem stones"

Line 170: nin-níg gur11-ra-ni hul-lu tì-la-àm kù dnin-mar-ki-ke4

"The sacred lady Ninmar was desponded of her perished goods"...

Guabba as a *Meluhhan* textile hub

...During the UR III period Guabba provides the largest group of people from Girsu working in the weaving sector, mainly women and children. In one text 4272 women and 1800 children from Guabba are listed as being in the weaving industry...

There are currently over fifty Ur III texts associating Guabba with the weaving industry of a large involvement of women. Cf. also é uš-bar dŠu-dSuen šà Gú-ab-baki-ka (BPOA 1 0061); še-ba gemé uš-bar Gú-ab-baki-ka (BPOA 1 0308)(SS 9-iii); uš-bar Gúab-baki-me (HLC 074,plate 26 = ASJ 2, 201); gemé uš-bar Gú-ab-baki-ka-ke4 (HSS 04 146)...

Guabba as a *Meluhhan* seaport

Guabba has been interpreted as a harbour town under the jurisdiction of Girsu/Lagash due to the literal meaning of the reading gú-ab-ba which did not include the determinative KI for the place name in text SRT 49 II 4, thus gú-abba ("sea-shore") in stead of the normal gú-ab-baki.39 It was supported by texts such as UET III 292 (šu-ha gú-ab-ba "fishermen of the seashore") and UET III 1294, 1297, 1302 and 1314 referring to saltwater fisherman and marine fish (cf. Zarins 1992:66).

Since pre-Sargonic and Sargonic times, references to "large boats" hint at a

trading colony which initially had direct contact with their distant ancestors…
In a Sumerian temple hymn (TH 23)40 Guabba is twice mentioned in connection with the seas:

Line 283: é ab-šà-ga lá-a ki-kù-ga dù-a

“House which extends over the midst of the sea, built on a holy place”

Line 284:

gú-ab-baki šà-zu nì-ù-tu erìn gar-gar-a

“Guabba, your interior brings forth everything, (a firmly) founded storehouse”…

[unquote]

Proto-Munda continuity and Language X

Sources of OIA agricultural vocabulary based on Masica (1979)

		Percentage
•	IE/Iir	40%
•	Drav	13%
•	Munda	11%
•	Other	2%
•	Unknown	34%
•	Total	100%

Hence, a Language X is postulated; Language ‘X’ to explain a large number of agriculture-related words with no IE cognates.[263] Since there is cultural continuity in India from the days of Sarasvati civilization, it is possible to reconstruct Language X by identifying isoglosses in the linguistic area.

Contributions of the following language/archaeology scholars have followed up on these insights of Sylvan Levi, Jules Bloch and Jean Przyluski published over 90 years ago: Emeneau, MB, Kuiper, FBJ, Masica, CP, Southworth F.[264]

Resemblances between two or more languages (whether typological or in vocabulary) can be due to genetic relation (descent from a common ancestor language), or due to borrowing at some time in the past between languages that were not necessarily genetically related. When little or no direct documentation of ancestor languages is available, determining whether a similarity is genetic or areal can be difficult.

Further researches: historical linguistics

In addition to studies in the evolution of and historical contacts among Indian languages, further researches are also needed in an archaeological context. Karl Menninger cites a remarkable instance. In the Indian tradition, finger signals were used to settle the price for a trade transaction. Finger gestures were a numeric cipher!

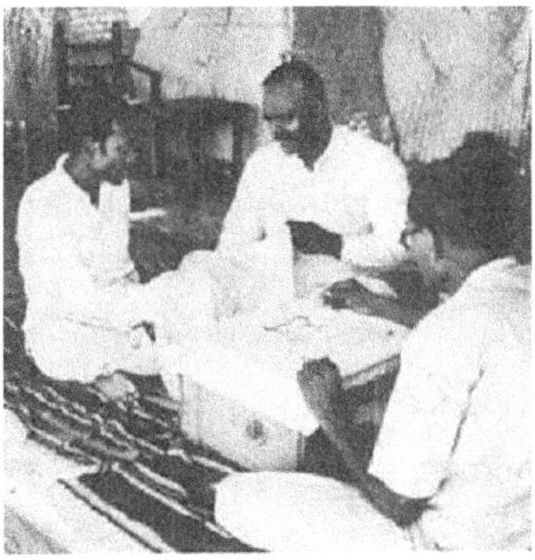

A pearl merchant of South India settling price for a pearl using finger gestures under a handkerchief.[265]

Further work on the nature of the contacts between Indian artisans and their trade associates, say, in Meluhhan settlements in the Persian Gulf region, may unravel the the nature of long-distance contacts. Could it be that the Indus language and writing were Indus Artisans' cryptographic messaging system for specifications of artifacts made in and exported from Meluhha?

Linguistics and archaeo-metallurgy: Identifying meluhha words and matching hieroglyphs with lexemes of archaeo-metallurgy

Indian Hieroglyphs are identified. This announcement in Archaeometallurgy may be taken as Kitty Hawk flight demo or Jean-Francois Champollion demonstration of Egyptian hieroglyphs. Announcing that Indus script, an unsolved puzzle for over 150 years since the first discovery of a seal by the archaeologist of British India, Alexander Cunningham, are composed of Indian hieroglyphs, the book is said to detail in about 800 pages what could possibly be the earliest invention of writing.

Hundreds of Indian hieroglyphs have been identified in the context of the bronze age and the rebus readings are comparable to the rebus method employed for Egyptian hieroglyphs. The book has related the invention of writing to the invention of bronze-age technologies of mixing copper with other ores such as arsenic, zinc, tin to create alloys like bronze, brass, pewter. The book relates the hieroglyphs to the lexemes of Indian *sprachbund*.

Use of iron was also attested during the bronze age.[266] A surprising find in matching meluhha lexemes with hieroglyphs is that, as noted by the late Gregory Possehl, an Indus archaeologist, iron was also used, though archaeo-metallurgy evidence for iron-smelters have not so far been discovered in th civilization area.

Archaeo-metallurgy studies of Sarasvati (Indus) Civilization have made some progress.[267] These studies have to be elaborated further to identify the processes of continuity evidenced by the iron smelters identified in the Ganga valley. D.K. Chakraborti and James Muhly argue that metallurgy of tin was well developed in Indus (Sarasvati) Civilization. The use of zinc as evidenced by the svastika glyphs is surprising and has to be explained further in archaeo-metallurgy context. One possibility is that zinc-bearing ores were used to create bronze alloy ingots and tools/vessels.

"A copper blade (Marshall 1931: pl. 136, f.3) found in one of the upper levels, though termed a spear-blade, may conceivably have been a knife (Plate IX, no.1). An exactly similar blade, but with a slightly longer tang, was found in the A mound at Kish (Mackay 1929a: pl. 39, gp. 3, f.4)... attention should be called to a steatite seal from Kish, now in Baghdad Museum, which bears the svastika symbol. This seal, both in shape and design upon it, exactly resembles the little square seals of steatite and glazed paste that are so frequently found at Mohenjodaro (Marshall 1931: pl. 144, f. 507-15). I do not think that I err in regarding the Kish example, which was found by Watelin, as either of Indian workmanship or made locally for an Indian resident in Sumer... The curious perforated vessels shown (Marshall 1931: pl. 84, f. 3-18) are very closely allied to perforated vessels found at Kish (Mackay 1929a: pl. 54, f. 36), especially in the fact that besides the numerous holes in the sides there is also a large hole in the base, which suggests that by this means they were supported on a rod or something similar... I have suggested, from evidence obtained by Sir Aurel Stein in southern Baluchistan, that these perforated vessels were used as heaters..."[268]

Mainstream linguistics has no way to determine a range of dates for this *sprachbund* (language union). I submit that the language union relates to the bronze age inventions and trade which is complemented by and necessitated the invention of writing. In my view, the script records the archaeometallurgy transactions using lexes of Indian *sprachbund.* The tradition continues in ancient Indian mints which produced the early punch-marked coins. The tradition is also evidenced on the Rampurva copper bolt hieroglyphs, Sohgaura copper plate inscription and Sanchi s'rivatsa hieroglyph.

Indian hieroglyphs typical of the 3rd millennium BCE: Elephant:ibh rebus:ib 'iron'; koD 'one-horned young bull' rebus: koD 'smithy'; sathiya 'svastika glyph' rebus: satiya,jasta 'zinc'; adar 'zebu' rebus: aduru 'unsmelted metal or ore'; pattar 'trough' rebus: 'smiths' guild'; kaND karNaka 'rim of jar' rebus: kaND karNaka 'furnace account scribe', ayakara 'fish+crocodile' rebus: 'metal-smith' etc.

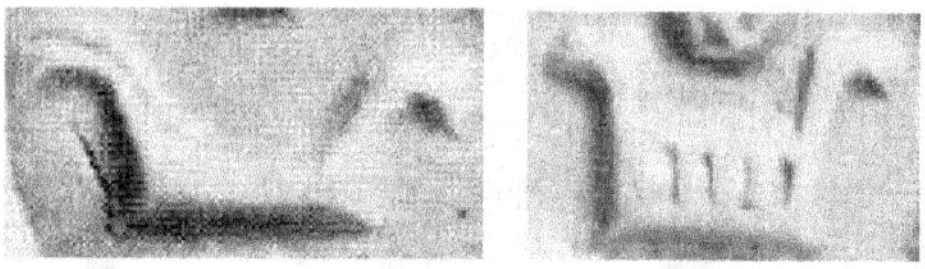

Types of trough shown in front of some animals on seals/tablets

Hundreds of such examples are discussed in *Indian hieroglyphs*[269] demonstrating that Indian hieroglyphs constitute a writing system for meluhha language and are rebus representations of archaeo-metallurgy lexemes.

After scholars review this work which covers hieroglyphs used in about 5000 indus script inscriptions of the corpora and validate the rebus readings, a mile-stone would have been recorded in the study of ancient civilizations. The identification of Indian hieroglyphs may, then, turn out to be as historic as the decoding of Egyptian hieroglyphs by Jean-Francois Champollion and be the foundation for further studies in (a) the evolution of languages of the Indian *sprachbund* (language union) and (b) archaeo-metallurgical traditions.

Tokens designed to count goods evolved over millennia into hieroglyphs to represent words denoting the bronze-age goods and processes. This stage of rebus representation of sounds of words of meluhha (mleccha language) was the stage penultimate to the culminating stage which used representation of syllables graphically in Brahmi and Kharoshti scripts. This culmination of the process for literacy and civilization was the contribution made by artisans of the bronze-age of Sarasvati civilization (also called Indus civilization).

For the specimen of mleccha speech, an alternative explanation is provided in Mahābhāṣya with a variation, helayo helayo; Sāyaṇācārya notes that the specimen of asura/mleccha speech is a variant of he'rayo, he'raya meaning, 'O the (spiteful) enemies', explained by the asuras' inability to pronounce the sounds, - r- and –y-. (Chatterjee 1957: 10-11). Is *helayo* comparable to Akkadian *ilum, elum*, 'god' or Phoenian *elyun elyun* 'high is the father of all gods?

Buddhaghosa specifies *milakkha bhāsas* or mleccha languages as those of: Andhra, Dami*ḷa,* kirāta, yoaka (yavana) (*Manorathapuraṇī* on *Ang. N* II: 289) and lauds the superiority of Māgadhabāsa over these dialects. (*Sammohavinodanī*. 388).

Adding Dravida (*andha damilādi*), the mleccha was apparently the *lingua franca,* the spoken tongue which enabled the use of Prakrits to convey Ashoka's messages through the edicts. Devala noted that anyone who had visited the Sindhus or Sauvīras should be initiated afresh.

"Buddhaghosha explains mleccha as referring to 'andha damilādi' (Andhra, Tamil, etc.) The Jaimini Dharmashastra lists some (sanskritized) Dravidian words as characteristic of mleccha speech, and Panini makes reference to the onomastic suffix –an (a Dravidian form) in the names of members of the Andhaka, Vṛṣṇi and Kuru tribes." (Southworth, opcit., fn. 30, p. 61) *śatapatha brāhmaṇa* includes in mleccha territories: Saurashtra, Gujarat and Maharashtra, but also the eastern areas (Bihar and Bengal). Mahabharata regards Anga, Vanga, Kalinga as mleccha kingdoms and that the sons of Turvasu are the Yavanas and that the sons of Anu were the Mlecchas. (*Cr. Ed.* I.80.26; Roy I.85). cf. Dharmasūtra I.1.32-33: ca. 4th cent. BCE, according to Bhandarkar.

Deshpande (1979: 48) observes: "The Baudhayana Dharmasūtra (1.1.32-33) gives us a clear idea of how the 'Vedic Aryans' viewed the 'mixed Aryans' of the outer regions: The inhabitants of ānartta, of Anga, of Magadha, of Saurāṣṭra, of the Deccan, of Upavṛt, of Sind, and the Sauvīras are of mixed origin. He who has visited the countries of the ārattas, Kāraskaras, Puṇḍras, Sauvīras, Vangas, Kalingas [or] Pranūnas shall offer a Punastoma...sacrifice [for purification]." Deshpande (1979: 48) underscores the fact that speakers of Indo-Aryan who belonged to regions other than Aryavarta considered themselves as āryas, not mlecchas. This indicates that use of the same language, but with corrupted speech, was the criterion for distinguishing Aryan-speakers – ārya vācas-- and mleccha-speakers – mleccha vācas.

A Pali text, Uttarādhyayana Sutra 10.16 notes: *ladhdhaṇa vi mānusattaṇam āriattam puṇrāvi dullaham bahave dasyū milakkhuyā*; trans. 'though one be born as a man, it is rare chance to be an ārya, for many are the dasyu and milakkhu'. Milakkhu and dasyu constitute the majority, they are the many. Dasyu are milakkhu (mleccha speakers).

Dasyu are also ārya vācas (Manu 10.45), that is, speakers of Sanskrit. Both ārya vācas and mleccha vācas are bharatiya, dasyu, people.

mlech 'to utter indistinctly' (Skt.S'Br.) *mlecchayati* id. (Dhātup. xxxii , 120); mleccha employ Prakrit form of speech. Manu notes (10.45):

mukhabāhūrupajjānām yā loke jātayo bahih mlecchavācas' cāryavācas te sarve dasyuvah smṛtāh 'All those people in this world who are excluded from those born from the mouth, the arms, the thighs and the feet (of Brahma) are called Dasyus, whether they speak the language of the *mleccha*-s or that of the ārya-s.' Caṇḍāḷa are dasyu and the meat of an animal procured by them was non-polluting (Manu VIII.66).

How to reconstruct mleccha of 4th millennium BCE Indian *sprachbund*?

Mleccha as a language category and mleccha in relation to bronze-age metal/mineral resources are correlated by the use of two maps: 1) Map of austro-asiatic speakers; and 2) Map of bronze-age sites in Southeast Asia. The trans-continental journey of mleccha-speakers and bronze-age mine-workers/smiths of Sarasvati civilization during the historical periods has to be narrated. An indication is provided by Bnei Menashe, descendants of one of the ten lost tribes of Israel. Also known as the Shinlung, the Bnei Menashe have a memory of their history of movement from the Northern Kingdom of Israel in 721 BCE. across the silk route finally ending up in Mizoram, India.

Pinnow's map of Austro-AsiaticLanguage speakers correlates with bronze age sites.[270] Map of Bronze Age sites of eastern India and neighbouring areas: 1. Koldihwa; 2.Khairdih; 3. Chirand; 4. Mahisadal; 5. Pandu Rajar Dhibi; 6.Mehrgarh; 7. Harappa;8. Mohenjo-daro; 9.Ahar; 10. Kayatha; 11.Navdatoli; 12.Inamgaon; 13. Non PaWai; 14. Nong Nor;15. Ban Na Di andBan Chiang; 16. NonNok Tha; 17. Thanh Den; 18. Shizhaishan; 19. Ban Don Ta Phet [After Fig. 8.1 in: Charles Higham, 1996, The Bronze Age of Southeast Asia, Cambridge

Übersichtskarte über die austroasiatischen Sprachen

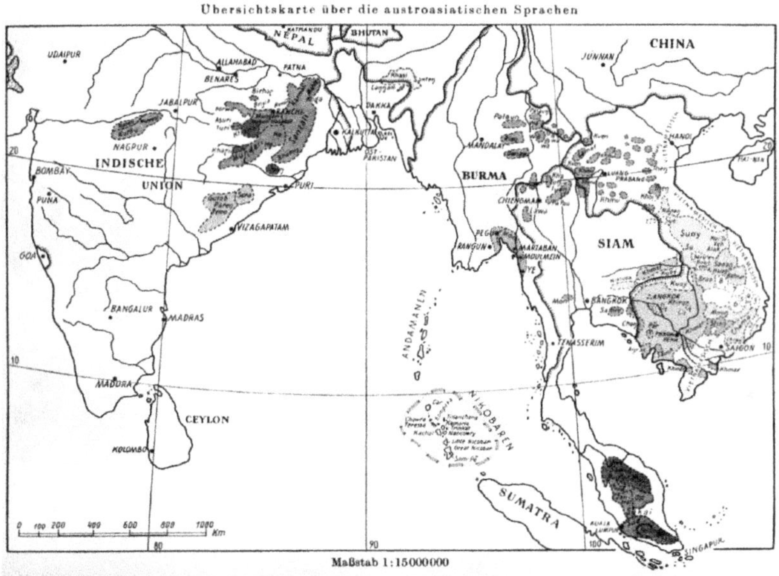

University Press].

The areal map of Austric (Austro-Asiatic languages) showing regions marked by Pinnow correlates with the bronze age settlements in Bharatam or what came to be known during the British colonial regime as 'Greater India'. The bronze age sites extend from Mehrgarh-Harappa (Meluhha) on the west to Kayatha-Navdatoli (Nahali) close to River Narmada to Koldihwa- Khairdih-Chirand on Ganga river basin to Mahisadal – Pandu Rajar Dhibi in Jharia mines close to Mundari area and into the east extending into Burma, Indonesia, Malaysia, Laos, Cambodia, Vietnam, Nicobar islands. A settlement of Inamgaon is shown on the banks of River Godavari.

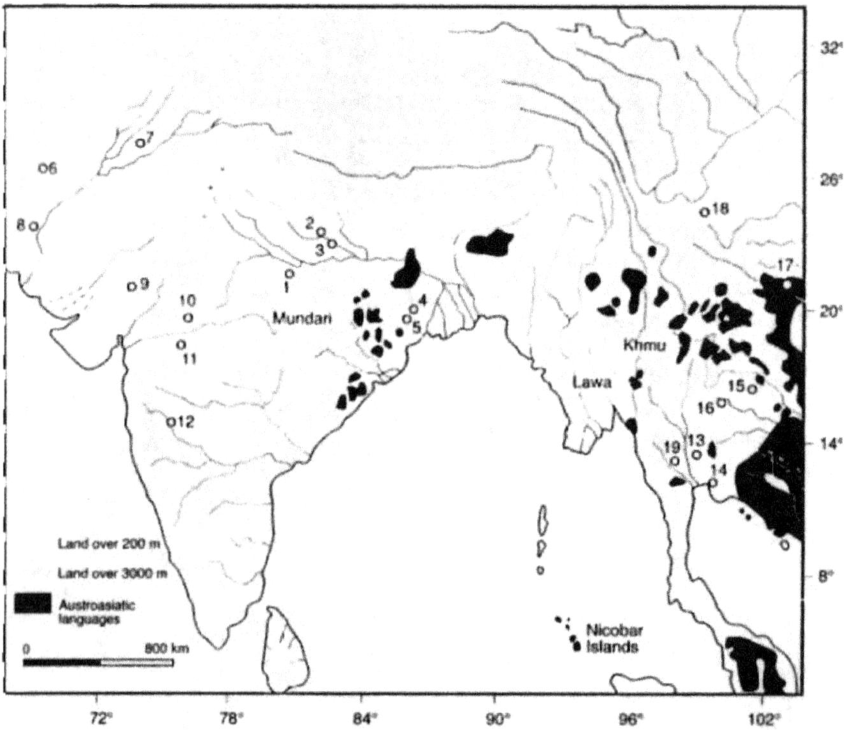

One resource for recontruction of mleccha is a work which dealt with *Prākṛit* forms.[271] *Prākṛitarūpāvatāra* literally means 'the descent of *Prākṛit* forms'. Pischel noted: "...the *Prākṛitarūpāvatāra* is not unimportant for the knowledge of the declension and conjugation, chiefly because *Simharāja* frequently quotes more forms than Hēmachandra and Trivikrama. No doubt many of these forms are theoretically inferred; but they are formed strictly according to the rules and are not without interest." (Pischel, 1900, *Grammatik der Prākṛit-Sprachen*, Strassburg, p.43). Pischel also had written a book titled, *Hēmachandra's Prākṛit grammar*, Halle, 1877. The full text of the *Vālmīkisūtra*, with *gaṇas, dēśīyas, and iṣṭis*, has been printed in Telugu characters at Mysore in 1886 as an appendix to the *ṣaḍbhāṣachandrikā*.

A format to determine the structure of *Prākṛit* is to identify words which are identical with Sanskrit words or can be derived from Sanskrit. In this process, *dēśīyas* or *dēśyas,* 'provincialisms' are excluded. One part of the work of Simharja is *samjñāvibhāga* 'technical terms'. Another is *pari bhāṣāvibhāga* 'explanatory rules'. Dialects are identified in a part called *śaurasēnyādivibhāga*; the dialects include: *śaurasēni, māgadhī, paiśācī, chūḷikā paiśācī, apabhramśa.*

Additional rules are identified beyond those employed by Pāṇini:

sus, nominative; *as*, accusative; *ṭās*, instrumental; *nēs*, dative; *nam*, genitive; *nip*, locative.

Other resources available for delineation of mleccha are: *The Prākṛita-prakāśa; or the Prakrit grammar of Vararuchi.* With the commentary Manorama of Bhamaha. The first complete ed. of the original text... With notes, an English translation and index of Prākṛit words; to which is prefixed a short introd. to Prākṛit grammar (Ed. Cowell, Edward Byles,1868, London, Trubner)

On these lines, and using the methods used for delineating *Ardhamāgadhi* language, by *Prākṛita* grammarians, and in a process of extrapolation of such possible morphemic changes into the past, an attempt may be made to hypothesize morphemic or phonetic variants of mleccha words as they might have been, in various periods from ca. 4th millennium BCE. There are also grammars of languages such as Marathi.[272]

Colin P. Masica's *Indo-Aryan Languages*, Cambridge University Press, 1993,"... has provided a fundamental, comparative introduction that will interest not only general and theoretical linguists but also students of one or more languages (Hindi, Urdu, Bengali, Punjabi, Gujurati, Marathi, Sinhalese, etc.) who want to acquaint themselves with the broader linguistic context. Generally synchronic in approach, concentrating on the phonology, morphology and syntax of the modern representatives of the group, the volume also covers their historical development, writing systems, and aspects of sociolinguistics." Thomas Oberlies' Pali grammar (Walter de Gruyter, 2001) presents a full description of Pali, the language used in the Theravada Buddhist canon, which is still alive in Ceylon and South-East Asia. The development of its phonological and morphological systems is traced in detail from Old Indic (including mleccha?). Comprehensive references to comparable features and phenomena from other Middle Indic languages mean that this grammar can also be used to study the literature of Jainism. Madhukar Anant Mehendale's *Historical Grammar of Inscriptional Prakrits* is a useful aid to delineate changes in morphemes over time. A good introduction is: Alfred C. Woolner's *Introduction to Prakrit*, 1928 (Motilal Banarsidass). "*Introduction to Prakrit* provides the reader with a guide for the more attentive and scholarly study of Prakrit occurring in Sanskrit plays, poetry and prose--both literary and inscriptional. It presents a general view of the subject with special stress on Śauraseni and Māhārāṣṭrī Praākrit system. The book is divided into two parts. Part I consists of I-XI Chapters which deal with the three periods of Indo-Aryan speech, the three stages of the Middle Period, the literary and spoken Prakrits, their classification and characteristics, their system of Single and Compound Consonants, Vowels, Sandhi, Declension, Conjugation and their history of literature. Part II consists of a number of extracts from Sanskrit and Prakrit literature which illustrate different types of Prakrit--Sauraseni, Maharastri, Magadhi, Ardhamagadhi, Avanti, Apabhramsa, etc., most of which are translated into English. The book contains valuable information on the Phonetics and Grammar of the Dramatic Prakrits--Sauraseni and Maharastri. It is documented with an Index as well as a Students'. "

It may be noted that Hemacandra is a resource which has provided the sememe *ibbo* 'merchant' which reads rebus with *ibha* 'elephant' hieroglyph.

Sir George A. Grierson's article on The Prakrit Vibhasas cites: "Pischel, in §§3, 4, and 5 of his Prakrit Grammar, refers very briefly to the Vibhāṣās of the Prakrit grammarians. In § 3 he quotes Mārkaṇḍēya's (Intr., 4) division of the Prakrits into *Bhāṣā, Vibhāṣā, Apabhraṁśa*, and *Paiśāca*, his division of the Vibhāṣās into *Śākārī, Cāṇḍālī, Śābarī, Ābhīrikā*, and *Ṭākkī* (not *Śākkī*, as written by Pischel), and his rejection of *Auḍhrī* (Pischel, *Oḍrī*) and *Drāviḍī*. In § 4 he says, "Rāmatarkavāgīśa observes that the *vibhāṣāḥ* cannot be called Apabhraṁśa, if they are used in dramatic works and the like." He repeats the latter statement in § 5, and this is all that he says on the subject. Nowhere does he say what the term *vibhāṣā* means.[273]
In *Mahābhārata,* Pahlava, śabara, śaka, Yavana, Pundra, Kirāṭa, Dramiḷa, Simbhala, Barbara, Darada and Mleccha are collectively summed up as mleccha (1.165.35-37). Name of Himalayas is given as *dāruṇa mleccha* (*Mārkandēya Purāṇa*). Bhagadatta the ruler of Prāgjyotiṣa was a mleccha heading a large number of yavanas. In Mahabharata (XVI.7.63) ābhīras are called mleccha; kings regarded as vrātya. Garuda Purana refers to madraka (Capital śākala, modern Siālkot) as mleccha.
"...Ganga, on the lower reaches of which were the kingdoms of Anga, Variga, and Kalinga, regarded in the Mahabharata as Mleccha. Now the non- Aryan people that today live closest to the territory formerly occupied by these ancient kingdoms are Tibeto-Burmans of the Baric branch. One of the languages of that branch is called Mech, a term given to them by their Hindu neighbors. The Mech

live partly in Bengal and partly in Assam. B(runo) Lieblich remarked the resemblance between Mleccha and Mech and that Skr. Mleccha normally became Prakrit Meccha or Mecha and that the last form is actually found in Sauraseni. Sten Konow[274] thought Mech probably a corruption of Mleccha. I do not believe that the people of the ancient kingdoms of Anga, Vanga, and Kalinga were precisely of the same stock as the modern Mech, but rather that they and the modern Mech spoke languages of the Baric division of Sino-Tibetan. **mlts̈e* 'tongue', Old Bodish ltśe, Kukish generally **mlei*, the combination of initial consonants *(*mlts̈-)* being simplified in various ways in different Tibeto-Burmic languages. Aspiration cannot occur after *l* in Old Bodish, and the proto-Bodish form may have been **mlts'e* for all we know, so the *cch* of Skr. *Mleccha* may come nearer the primitive affricate than anything preserved in the Tibeto-Burmic languages."[275]

At the 2004 annual meeting of the Southeast Asian Linguistic Society held in Bangkok, David Stampe reiterated the view that "India may be the homeland of Austroasiatic, and Mon-Khmer reflects an offshoot that migrated eastward". And, more recently on Monday, 16th July 2007, Gerard Diffloth has in a lecture presented some fresh arguments suggesting that "the origins of the Austroasiatic family are more likely to be found somewhere on the shores of the Bay of Bengal.

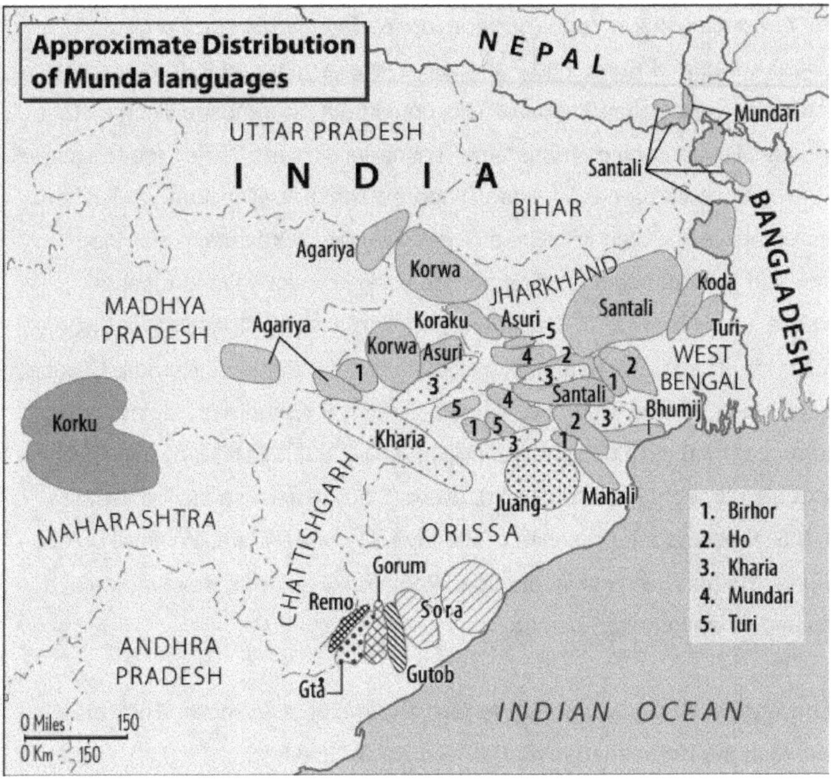

Mlecchadeśa is an area where the four varṇas were not known (VS LXXXIV.4) It is 'that land where the black antelope naturally roams, one must know to be fit for performance of sacrifice; (the tract) different from that (is) the country of the Mlecchas.'[276]

Mleccha refers to people who lived in certain parts of India. Mleccha also refers to the language spoken by these people. Mleccha was defined largely in terms of language, with particular reference to the inability to use and to use correctly, the Sanskrit language. Malayaketu of Mudrārākṣasa depends on mleccha mercenaries, in contrast to Chandragupta.[277]

Tushara (tukhara, tocharoi) were mleccha located in northwest India. MBh (1:85) refers to mleccha as descendants of Anu (Anavas), one of the sons of King

Yayati. Yayati eldest son Yadu (of Yadavas) and youngest son Puru (of Pauravas) are part of Kurus and Panchalas. Anava migrated to Iran and settled in Bactria and were called Tushara. This could be a reference to Tocharistan/ Tokharistan/Tukharistan of Tocharians/ Tokharians/Yuezhi. They are the same people who used surnames Thakurs/ Tagores/Thakkars/Thackerays. Tushara (Tocharoi) are associated with Saka (Indo-Scythians), Yavana/Yona (Indo-Greeks) and Bahlika (Bactria). The phrase used is: saka yavana tushara bahlikaśca. (*AV-Par* 57.2.5). These are people of Uttarapatha, Dasyu. (MBh. 12.65.13-15). Tushara, together with Bahlika, Kirata, Pahlava, Parada, Darada, Kamboja, Saka, Kanka, Romaka, Yavana, Trigarta, Kshudraka, Malava, Anga, Vanga brought gifts to Yudhishthira. (MBh. 2.51-2.53; 3.51). Many including Tukhara also brought millions of gold. (MBh. 2:50). Rajasuya of Yudhishthira (MBh. 3:51) records the presence of Pahlava, Darada, Kirata, Yavana, Sakra, Harahuna, Tukhara, Sindhava, Jaguda, Ramatha, Tangana, Kekaya, Malava, Munda and inhabitants of Kasmira.

Mleccha were skilled in weapons, warfare and material sciences. They also participate in the Kurukshetra war (MBh. 6:75; 8:73; 8:88).

Tocharian languages known from the manuscripts of 6th to 8th centurie were a branch of the Indo-European family. Many Tocharians migrated to Bactria in the second century BCE and later to northwest India as Yuezhi to found the Kushan empire. The term Tocharian is derived from Old Persian tuxāri-, Khotanese ttahvāra and Sanskrit tukhāra. It also refers to Takhar province of Afghanistan. There is evidence for the presence of Indo-European speakers during the Chalcolithic period (4300-3200 BCE) or perhaps, even earlier during the Neolithic period in the Ganga basin and in Sarasvati-Sindhu river valley. Sites like Girawad and Farmana have Early Harappan basal layers which contain copper and gold artifacts, as well as painted and incised pottery related to that of the Hakra Phase in the civilization. Further, the Ochre Colored and Black and Red Ware complexes have Early and/or Mature Harappan antecedents. "The implications of this are a bidirectional agricultural settlement of the Ganges Basin, with wheat, barley, sheep and goats moving in from the Middle East via Iran and the Indus region, and rice coming either from eastern Asia or representing a loal Gangetic *indica* domestication (at present, *japonica* pre-domestication cultivation in Central China pre-dates any parallel evidence in India by over 4,000 years). South Asia itself doubtless witnessed some internal domestications of humped cattle, millets, and legumes, but these do not negate the significance of the external flows. I detect in this a gradual movement downstream, between 3500 and 2000 BCE, of westerly Chalcolithic populations of Indus/Early Harappan cultural inspiration, mingling with easterly Neolithic populations, perhaps of separate lower Gangetic or Southeast Asian origin and probably rice-growing. The latter should have been at their highest densities in the strongly monsoonal regions of Orissa, Jharkhand, Bihar and Bengal, rather than in the drier upper Ganges basin, and it is precisely in these areas that Munda-speaking populations still exist in greatest numbers today. All of this implies that the Harappan urban civilization housed large populations of IE (Indo-Aryan) speakers, and probably Dravidians too, since north-western South Asia is a likely homeland region for the latter in terms of Dravidian subgrouping and place name substrata (although Southworth 2006 prefers a homeland more to the east). This is not the place to ask whether the Harappan symbol system (mnemonic notation or script?) was thereby the oldest attested Indo-European potential writing system, pre-dating Hittite and Linear B Greek by almost 1,000 years. But, interestingly Kenoyer (2006) traces the origins of some of the Harappan symbols into Hakra Phase sites in Pakistan, early in the fourth millennium BCE. Where did the Hakra Phase people come from? The 5,000 years of cultural continuity from this period onwards into early historical and modern times in the upper and middle Ganges Basin surely renders these people speakers of IE (Indo-Aryan?) languages, at least in Haryana and by association in the Indus region as well, given the theoretical position taken in this presentation that major language spreads were associated with movements of their speakers. Related IE (Indo-Iranian?)-speaking populations must have existed in Iran at the same time, even though the oldest *philological* evidence for their presence in Iran and Syria (Mitanni) does not pre-date 2000 BCE, and is mostly very much later. One observation that can be drawn from this is that historical and philological docuentation need have nothing to to diwh ethnolinguistic origin – a lesson that I believe the Hittites also teach us…If theHittites wer not natives of Anatolia, then neither comparative IE linguistics nor archaeology throw any light at all on their origins. Any discussion of Indo-Iranian/Indo-Aryan origins within the IE family inevitably brings up the whole issue of the overall origin of ancient Indo-European-speaking populations. I have given my basic opinion in *First Farmers*. In terms of modern comparative linguistic studies that include extinct subgroups such as Anatolian and Tocharian, the linguistic origin region can be placed in Anatolia, as suggested by Colin Renfrew in 1987 and supported more recently by the computational and genealogical IE subgroupings of Warnow, Ringe et al, and Gray and Atkinson. I remain unconvinced that any subgrouping argument within IE supports a Pontic steppes origin noth of the Black Sea, and regard the arguments for this from linguistic palaeontology – especially from horse, cart, and wheel vocabularies – as tangential to the real question of origins owing to the potential for early borrowing rather than absolute inherited cognacy in early phases of language family differentiation. Most of this vocabulary is anyway absent in Hittite, although I have no disagreement with Parpola's view that wheeled vehicles and their associated vocabulary items were innovated amongst IE-speaking communities. For both Tocharian and Indo-Iranian languages, there are many who also argue for a central Asian steppes homeland subsequent to that for the Ies as a whole, based on borrowings into early Uralic languages and isoglosses with Baltic and Slavic languages…"[278]

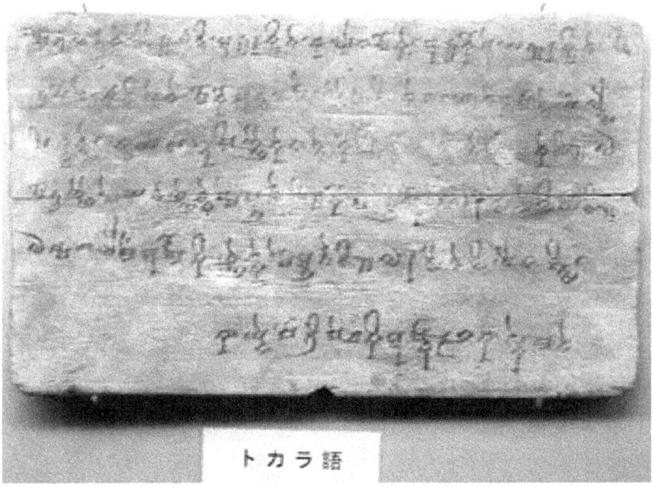

Wooden plate with inscriptions in the Tocharian language. Kucha, China, 5th–8th century. Tokyo National Museum.

A gloss identifiable as part of mleccha repertoire occurs in *Ṛgveda* and in Tocharian. The word is ancu. *Ṛgveda* refers to cognate amśu as a synonym of Soma. Tocharian attests ancu as meaning, 'iron'. (cf. Dictionary and Thesaurus of Tocharian A. Volume 1: a-j. Compiled by Gerd Carling in collaboration with Georges-Jean Pinault and Werner Winter, Wiesbaden, Harrassowitz Verlag, 2009).

Lubotsky, Alexander (2001, The Indo-Iranian substratum in: Carpelan et al., eds., Early contacts between Uralic and Indo-European: linguistic and archaeological considerations (Papers presented at the international symposium, Tvarminne, 8-10 January, 1999), Helsinki, Suomalais-Ugrilainen Seura: 304, 310) opines that ancu, 'soma plant' is the substratum source of Vedic amśu; Late Av. Asu 'Soma/Haoma plant'. Vedic amśu, 'twigs, sprigs, stalks' are units of Soma. TS I.2.11a cited in ŚB III.4.3.19): amśur-- amśuṣ ṭe deva somāpyāyatām indrāyaikadhanavide, 'let stalk after stalk of thine swell strong, O divine Soma, for Indra, the winner of one part of the booty!' In metonymy, the word amśu refers to the entire holy soma material. In Tocharian A we have *añcu, 'iron'; derived añcwāṣi, 'made of iron'. This corresponds with Toch. B eñcuwo, adjective eñcuwaññe, 'made of iron'. These words and related semantics occur in Sanskrit *ayas* 'iron, metal.' In Tocharian B *yasa* (A *was*) 'gold'. Pinault notes that Vālakhilya hymn (RV VIII.53.4c: *śīṣṭeṣu cit te madirāso amśavah*) indicates that

Soma processing also extended to non-Aryans with the use of śīṣṭa- with variants śīṣṭra-, śīrṣṭra-, with intrusive –r- (Kuiper, FBJ, 1991, Aryans in the *Ṛgveda*, Leiden Studies in Indo-European, I, Amsterdam/Atlanta: Rodopi.: 7, 70).

A hypothesis is postulated that the donor language for these forms of amśu is mleccha (meluhha).

The forms go back to CTocharian *oeñuwō which has no convincing IE etymology. Cognates are Chorasmian hncw, 'iron', 'iron tip' < Iranian *anśuwan. The reasoned conjecture is that the Tocharian words may be traceable to a common substratum language. The CTocharian word can be explained if the semantics of soma, amśu are related to electrum processing in incessant fire of about 1500 degrees centigrade continuously for 5 days and nights in ati-rātra of soma yajña.

Mleccha, *lingua franca* (deśī -- vernacular) " a very considerable amount (say some 40%) of the New Indo-Aryan vocabulary is borrowed from Munda, either via Sanskrit (and Prakrit), or via Prakrit alone, or directly from Munda; wide-branched and seemingly native, word-families of South Dravidian are of Proto-Munda origin; in Vedic and later Sanskrit, the words adopted have often been Aryanized, resp. Sanskritized. "In view of the intensive interrelations between Dravidian, Munda and Aryan dating from pre-Vedic times even individual etymological questions will often have to be approached from a Pan-Indic point of view if their study is to be fruitful. It is hoped that this work may be helpful to arrive at this all-embracing view of the Indian languages, which is the final goal of these studies."[279]

Southworth (1979) also notes that the flora terms did not come from either Dravidian or Munda. Southworth found only five terms which are shared with Munda, leading to his suggestion that "the presence of other ethnic groups, speaking other languages, must be assumed for the period in question" (205), with hardly the 'slightest hints' as to what the languages were. Out of 121 terms for plants, Southworth finds only a little over a third have Indo-European etymologies. (Southworth, 1993: 81-85) "Chapter 3. This chapter is a discussion of linguistic evidence found in old Indo-Aryan texts which indicate contact between speakers of OIA and other languages. The chapter's conclusions are summarized graphically in the map (Figure 27). Note that this map covers a period of several millennia, since it includes the probable earliest locations of Munda/AA and Dravidian languages in the subcontinent, as well as the inferred locations of earlier languages such as the 'Indus' language(s), along with the modern locations of Dravidian, Munda, and Tibeto-Burman languages, and isolated languages such as Nahali, which are not necessarily the same as their ancient locations. Section 3.2 takes up the lexical evidence, looking first of all at loanwords in OIA which seem to be fom Munda or Austro-Asiatic (AA) languages. These are the earliest identifiable foreign words in OIA, appearing in the oldest books of the *Ṛgveda*...Though many of these words do not have specific Munda/AA etymologies, the hypothesis of AA origin is supported by the presence of prefixes of types found in Munda and AA languages, which are not found in the other language families of the area. These words appear in OIA texts belonging to the entire Vedic period, indicating the presence of Munda/AA speakers in all the regions associated with Vedic texts, from Panjab to eastern Uttar Pradesh – as well as further to the east, given the connection of Munda with the rest of Austro-Asiatic. Dravidian loanwords in OIA appear at a somewhat later date...in contexts which suggest a more southerly location, possibly Sindh. These words also continue to appear in OIA throughout the Vedic period and into the Epic and Classical Sanskrit periods. A small group of controversial words suggest the possibility of an even earlier contact between Dravidian and OIA, in the period of Proto-Indo-Iranian, which if it occurred must have been separate from that reflected in the *Ṛgveda*. Apart from words attributable to languages of limited extent such as Burushaski and various (named or unnamed) Tibeto-Burman languages, an additional body of foreign words found in all periods of OIA are of unidentified origin, probably pre-Indo-Aryan and pre-Dravidian, and in some cases perhaps pre-Munda/AA. An examination of agricultural vocabulary in modern Hindi indicates that, even among words which existed in OIA, approximately 30% cannot be traced to known languages. Thus it is likely that a number of languages existed in South Asia before the arrival of the Indo-Aryan and Dravidian speakers. Only a few of these languages, such as Burushaski and Nahali, can be identified by name. The name 'Indus' is used here to designate this group of languages...Overall, the lexical and structural evidence of OIA and Dravidian languages suggests that a linguistic interaction zone or 'linguistic area' existed in South Asia before the arrival of Indo-Aryan languages in South Asia. Within the subcontinent, it involved speakers of Munda, Dravidian and 'Indus' languages, as well as the ancestors of Burushaski and other linguistic isolates...and, was probably linked to speech communities of Central Asia...

Lingua franca, deśi

Southworth notes: "Chapter 3 presents an ancient linguistic area, with different languages in contact with each other in various parts of the subcontinent, particularly in the Indus Valley. Because of certain linguistic changes, particularly the adoption of the dental-retroflex contrast in consonants, it is inferred that the contact between the 'Indus' language and the Munda/Para-Munda languages was somewhat intense, implying a fairly high degree of socio-economic integration. The same was true later of the contact between OIA (presumably both the inner and outer varieties) and the local languages, which presumably included both 'Indus' and Para-Munda. Thus we infer some sort of economic interdependence in both of these cases. If 'Indus' and Para-Munda were languages of the Indus Valley culture (respectively a local language and an inter-regional *lingua franca*), then it would not be surprising if such contact occurred; nor would it be surprising if early speakers of Indo-Aryan interacted with the local people in similar ways, given the need of pastoralists for agricultural produce. Interactions between Dravidian and Indo-Aryan speakers appear to be somewhat later, and perhaps first occurred in Sindh. Whether there are any specific archaeological assemblages which can be linked with any of these contact situations would require a separate study."[280]

Mleccha, Indus language of Indian linguistic area (*sprachbund*)

The evidences presented of continued use of Indus script glyphs during the historical periods in India and in particular, on punch-marked coin symbols relate to a historical cultural continuum in India. This leads to a reasonable inference that the language of the writing system should be a language of the people, artisans, in particular, which continues to be used even today in India since language and culture are closely intertwined phenomena in a *sprachbund* (language union).

The identification of a particular Indian language as the Indus language has presented some problems because of the received wisdom about grouping of language families in Indo-European linguistic analyses. Some claims of decipherment have assumed the language to be Tamil, of Dravidian language family; some have assumed the language to be Sanskrit, of Indo-Aryan language family. A resolution to these problems comes from a surprising source: Manu.

The evidence which comes from Manu, dated to ca. 500 BCE. Manu underscores the linguistic area: *mleccha vācas* distinguished from ā*rya vācas* (*lingua franca* or deśi distinguished from literary Sanskrit) (Manu 10.45):

mukhabāhurūpajjānām yā loke jātayo bahih

mlecchavācaś cāryavācas te sarve dasyuvah smṛtāh

"All those people of the world which are excluded from the (community of) those born from the mouth, the arms, the thighs and the feet (of Brahman) are called Dasyu, whether they speak the language of the mleccha or that of the ārya." (Buhler). Alt. Mleccha dialect speakers and ārya dialect speakers are all remembered as dasyu. Thus, it is clear that there were two dialects in the linguistic area: *mleccha vācas* and *ārya vācas.*

Dasyu is a general reference to people. Dasyu is cognate with dasa, which in Khotanese language means 'man'. It is also cognate with daha, a word which occurs in Persepolis inscription of Xerxes, a possible reference to people of Dahistan, a region east of Caspian sea. Strabo wrote :"Most of the scythians, beginning from the Caspian sea, are called Dahae Scythae, and those situated more towards the east Massagetae and Sacae." (Strabo, 11.8.1). Close to Caspian Sea is the site of Altyn-depe which was an interaction area with Meluhha and where three Indus seals with inscriptions were found, including a silver seal showing a composite animal which can be called a signature glyph of Indus writing.

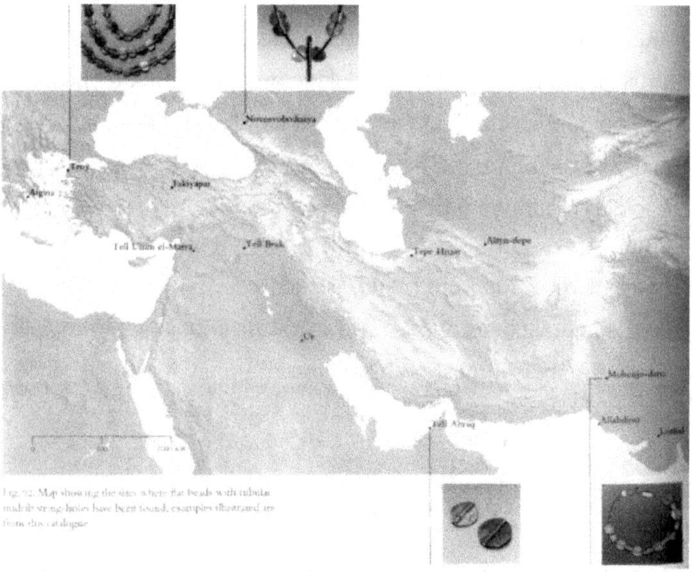

Findspots of mid-ribbed disc beads: Troy, Novosvobodosya, Tell Abraq, Mohenjo-daro.

"Jonathan Mark Kenoyer makes the suggestion (see cat. No. 278b), based on the similarity between gold and silver floral head-dresses at Ur and diadem sshown on Harappan terracottas, that some of the servants buried in the tombs of Ur may have come to Mesopotamia from the Indus valle. The facts that a gold floral ornament was also worn by queen Puabi and that in both her grave and another there were belts made of biconical carnelian beads (cat. Nos. 62,80) may further reflect the predilection of the Ur elie for Indian jewelry and fashion, including Harappan belts (see cat. No. 279)...One particular bead type made of gold and silver, a flat disk with a tubular midrib string-hole, appears to have been distributed, and probably manufactured as well, at sites along the same routes as the etched carnelian beads (see Fig.72). Such beads were found at many Indus sites, including the port of Lothal, at Altyn-depe in Turkmenistan, at Tepe Hissar in Iran, in the Royal Cemetery at Ur, at Eskiyapar and Troy in Anatolia, and on Aigina in the Aegean. (Possehl, 1996, pp. 161-162)." (Aruz, pp. 239-244)

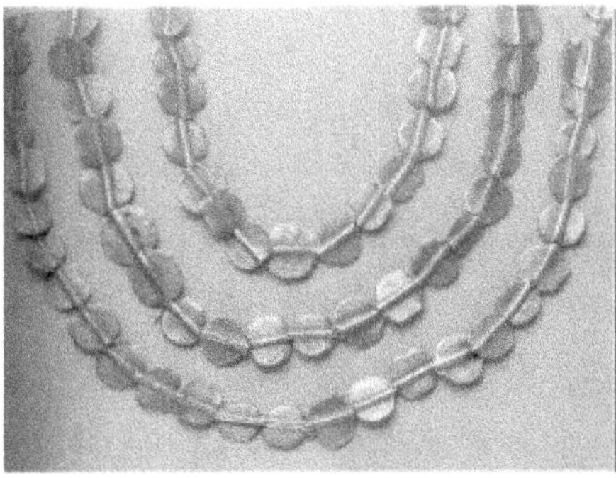
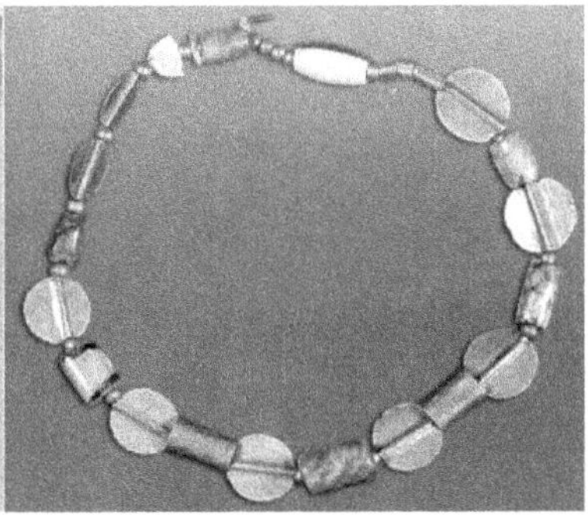

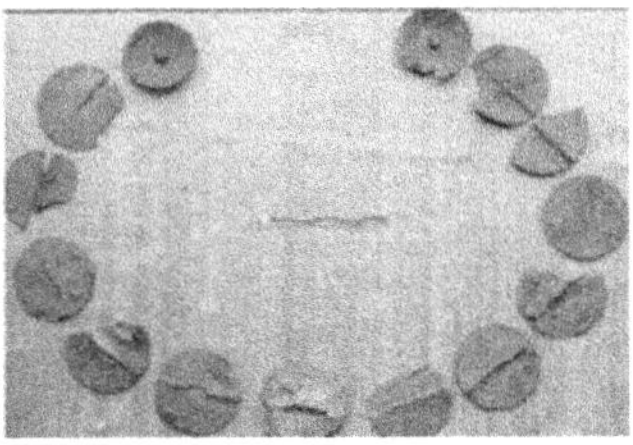
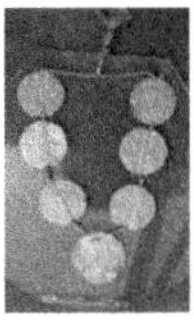

Strings of gold disc beads. Mohenjodaro. (See Kenoyer 1998, p. 140, fig 7.14, p. 201, no.16) 3rd millennium BCE.

Gold discs with midribs on a necklace found at Lothal.

Silver discs with midribs on a necklace found at Kunal.

Map of Pre-Indo-Aryan substratum languages. Indian linguistic area map, including mleccha and vedic (After F. Southworth, 2005, *Linguistic Archaeology*

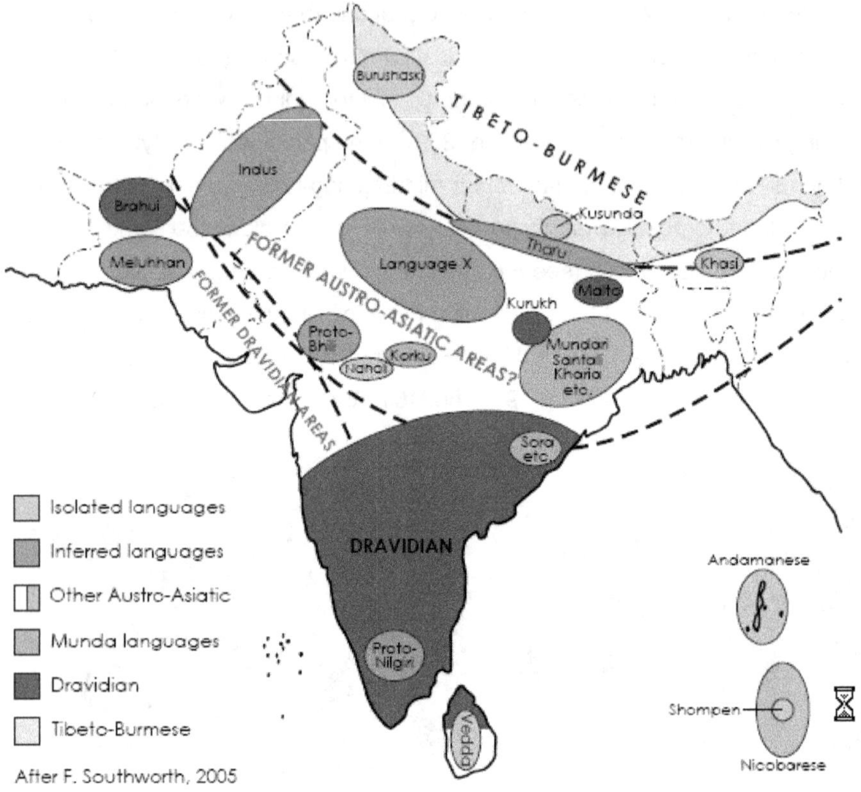

of South Asia, New York, RoutledgeCurzon, p. 65; mleccha and vedic added.)

A language family, mleccha (?Language X, Proto-Prākrit, Proto-Indo-Aryan), is attested in or derived from the ancient literature of India.

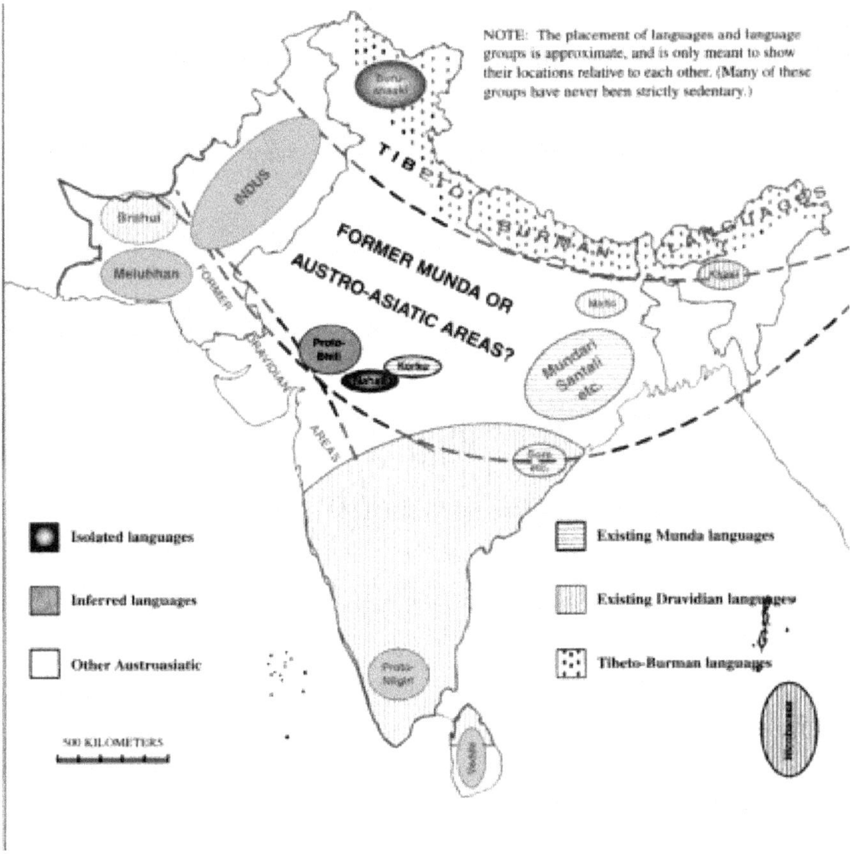

Pre-Indo-Aryan substratum languages (After Fig. 3.1 Southworth, 2005, p. 65)

This is the *lingua franca*, the spoken version of the language of the civilization of about 5000 years ago, distinct from the grammatically correct version called Samskṛtam represented in the vedic texts and other ancient literature.

Ancient texts of India are replete with insights into formation and evolution of languages. Some examples are: Bharata's *Nāṭyaśāstra*, Patanjali's *Mahābhāṣya,* Hemacandra's *Deśī nāmamālā*, Nighanṭus, Panini's *Aṣṭādhyayi*, Tolkappiyam–Tamil grammar.

The identification of meluhha (cognate: *mleccha*) as the language of the Indus writing system is consistent with the following theses which postulate an Indian linguistic area, that is an area of ancient times when various language-speakers interacted and absorbed language features from one another and made them their own:

Emeneau, MB, 1956, India as a linguistic area, *Language* 32, 1956, 3-16.

Kuiper, FBJ, 1948, Proto-Munda words in Sanskrit, Amsterdam, 1948

1967, The genesis of a linguistic area, *IIJ* 10, 1967, 81-102

Masica, CP, 1971, *Defining a Linguistic area. South Asia.* Chicago: The University of Chicago Press.

Przyludski, J., 1929, Further notes on non-aryan loans in Indo-Aryan in: Bagchi, P. C. (ed.), *Pre-Aryan and Pre-Dravidian in Sanskrit.* Calcutta : University of Calcutta: 145-149

Southworth, F., 2005, *Linguistic archaeology of South Asia*, London, Routledge-Curzon.

The divinity Vāk is said to have originally belonged to the *mlecchas*. A possible interpretation of this remarkable claim is that a clear pronouncement has been made in *Śatapathabrāhmaṇa 3.2.1.18 ff.*, that *mleccha* was the proto-language of Sarasvati-Sindhu civilization. Was this a reference to the speech of people in ancient Magadha recognized in later-day texts as Prākrit language?

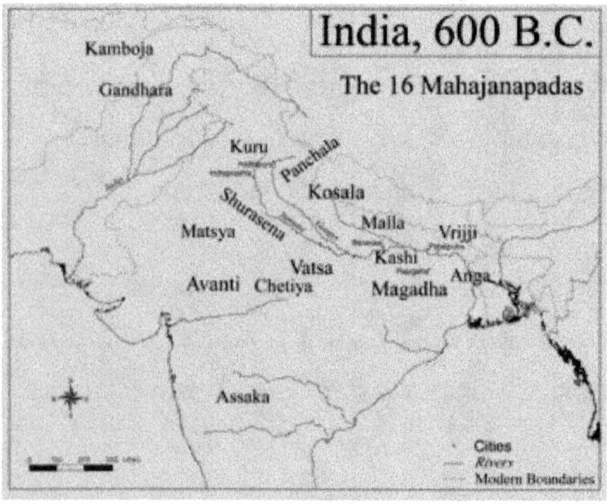

Mahābhārata lists people and their characteristics of comprehension -- linguistic in particular:

ingitajnāś ca magadhāh
prekṣitajnāś ca kosalāh

ardhoktāh kuru-pāncālāh śālvāh kṛtnānuśāsanāh

*pārvatāyāśca viṣamaāyathaiva girayas (sibayas) tatha_*

sarvajnāyavanārājan śūrās caiva viśeṣatah

mlecchāh svasamjnāniyataānānukta itaro janāh

"The magadhas comprehend gestures, the kośalas understand at a glance; the kuru-Pāncālas a speech half-uttered, the śālvas only when the whole sentence is spoken; mountaineers, like the śibi, understand with difficulty. The yavanas, O king, are omniscient, the śūras especially so. The mleccha rely on their own knowledge; 'other people cannot understand.'" (*Cr. Ed.* VIII.30.79-80; Roy VIII.45.34-35)

Southworth notes: "The term mleccha occurs often in collocation with bhāṣā 'speech' and deśa 'country, region'. It is probable that in the OIA Brahminical sources, the lands designated as mleccha-deśa included not only areas in which non-Aryan languages were spoken, but also those Indo-Aryan-speaking areas which were regarded as religiously unorthodox.)." This may explain why Magadha was known as mleccha-deśa (whether the language of that area was a form of Indo-Aryan or not), 'whereas to the Buddhists the term meant primarily those lands in which non-Aryan languages were spoken.'..It seems probable, on the basis of this evidence, that there was a good deal of bilingualism and diglossia in ancient India, with those of non-Aryan groups who dealt with the Aryan Brahmans being obliged to learn some form of Indo-Aryan (Sanskrit or Prakrit) for day-to-day communication. On the other hand, the presence of many words of foreign origin in Vedic from the earliest times indicates that this was not a one-sided process."[281]

Ṛgveda sūkta 10.125 is a monologue by Vak, the almightly feminine divinity *par excellence*, who punished the impious and who claims she is *rāṣṭrī samgamanī*, that is, the carrier of wealth along the lighted, united path of the people, the *rāṣṭram*.

Śatapathabrāhmaṇa 3,2,1,18 to 25 elaborates on this extraordinary *Ṛgveda rāṣṭra* sūkta, juxtaposing *yajña* and *Vāk* (speech):

> "Thereupon he ties a black deer's horn to the end (of his garment). Now the gods and the Asuras, both of them sprung from Prajapati, entered upon their father Prajapati's inheritance: the gods came in for the Mind and the Asuras for Speech. Thereby the gods came in for the sacrifice and Asuras for speech; the gods for yonder (heaven) and the Asuras for this (earth)." It is clear that the asura whose speech is commented upon are the children of Prajapati, they are NOT foreigners.
>
> 19. The gods said to *Yajña* (the sacrifice). 'That *Vāk* (speech) is a woman: beckon her, and she will certinly call thee to her.' Or it may be, he himself thought, 'That Vak is a woman: I will beckon her and she will certainly call me to her.' He accordingly beckoned her. She, however, at first disdained him from the distance: and hence a woman, when beckoned by a man, at first disdains him from the distance. he said, 'She has disdained me from the distance.'
>
> 23. The gods then cut her off from the Asuras; and having gained possession of her and enveloped her completely in fire, they offered her up as a holocaust, it being an offering of the gods. And in that they offered her with *anushtubh* verse, thereby they made her their own; and the Asuras, being deprived of speech, were undone, crying, *'He 'lavah! he 'lavah!'* [According to Sayana, 'He 'lavo' stands for 'he 'rayo' (i.e. ho, the spiteful enemies)!' which the Asuras were unable to pronounce correctly. The Kanva text, however reads, *te hattavako 'sura hailo haila ity etam ha vakam vadantah parababhuvuh* (? i.e. He ila 'ho, speech.']
>
> It is perhaps a third version of this passage that is referred to in the *Mahābhāṣya* (Kielh.), p.2.] For the specimen of mleccha speech, an alternative explanation is provided in Mahābhāṣya with a variation, *helayo helayo*; Sāyaṇācārya notes that the specimen of Asura/mleccha

speech is a variant of *he 'rayo, he 'raya* meaning, 'O the (spiteful) enemies', explained by the asuras' inability to pronounce the sounds, - r- and –y-. (*Mahābhāṣya* 1.1.1; KC Chatterjee, 1957, Patanjali's *Mahābhāṣya*, Calcutta, pp. 10-11; Sāyaṇa on *Śatapathabrāhmaṇa*, 3.2.1.23).

Characteristics of mleccha noted by Patañjali

Patanjali elaborates on mleccha as a dialect.

Mleccha speech did not conform to the rules of grammar (*mlecchāḥ mā bhūma iti adhyeyam vyākaraṇam*) and had dialectical variants or unrefined sounds in words (*mlecchitavai na apabhāṣitavai*) (Chatterjee, K.C., 1957, *Patañjali's Mahābhāṣya*, Calcutta. A. Mukherjee & Co.) The speech also deployed imprecise pronunciations and corrupted (ungrammatical) words : mlecchitam vispaṣṭena iti eva anyatra . tasmāt brāhmaṇena na and mlecchaḥ ha vai eṣaḥ yat apaśabdaḥ

Sets of etyma may be cited:

aduru native metal (Ka.); ayil iron (Ta.) ayir, ayiram any ore (Ma.); ajirda karba very hard iron (Tu.)(DEDR 192). I do not know how aduru evolved or is phonetically cognate vis-a-vis ayo 'iron' (Gujarati). There is a very specific explanation for the Kannada word: aduru = *gaṇiyinda tegadu karagade iruva aduru* = ore taken from the mine and not subjected to melting in a furnace.[282]

ibha 'elephant' (Samskrtam)

ibbo 'merchant' (Hemacandra Desināmamāla -Gujarati)

ib 'iron' (Santali).

కరటి [karaṭi] *karaṭi.* [Skt.] n. An elephant. ఏనుగు (Telugu) Rebus: *kharādī*' turner' (Gujarati)

There are two compounds: *milakkhu rajanam* 'copper-coloured' (Pali), *mleccha mukha* 'copper' (Samskrtam).

Why *mleccha mukha*? I think the lexeme *mukha* is a substrate lexeme.

mūh 'face, ingot' (Munda. Santali etc.); it is possible that mleccha mukha may refer to 'copper ingot'. *mũhã* = the quantity of iron produced at one time in a native smelting furnace (Santali) Mleccha, language. Mleccha, copper.

The lexical entry *mūh* 'face' (CDIAL 10158) explains why a face glyph gets ligatured in Indus writing to clear composite hieroglyphs to create *mlecchitavikalpa* (cipher mentioned by Vātsyāyana).

m1179 tagara 'ram, antelope' Rebus: tagara 'tin'; damgar 'merchant' *mūh 'face'* Rebus: *mūh* 'ingot' (Santali) m1186Am0302

The ancient text *Śatapathabrāhmaṇa* records the nature of *mleccha* speech of at least some of the speakers in the following terms: *te 'surā āttavacaso he lavo he lava iti vadantah parābabhūvuh tatraināmapi vācamūduh upajijñāsyā sa mlecchastasmānna brāhmaṇo mlecchedasuryā haiṣā vāg.*

24. The Asuras, deprived of (correct) speech, saying *he lavo, he lavah*, were defeated. This is the unintelligible speech which they uttered at that time. He who speaks thus is a mleccha. Therefore a brāhmaṇa should not speak like a *mleccha*, for that is the speech of the Asuras. Thus alone he deprives his spiteful enemies of speech; and whosoever knows this, his enemies, being deprived of speech, are undone. (*Śatapathabrāhmaṇa* 3.2.1.24).

25. The Yajna (sacrifice) lusted after Vak (speech), thinking, 'May I pair with her!' He united with her.

It appears that the use of the term *mleccha* is a reference to Prakrit as parole.

A Prakrit dialect could have been referred to by Manu as *mleccha vācas*.

As Weber comments: 'asuya' speech relates to 'Prakriic dialectic differences, assimilation of groups of consonants and similar changes peculiar to Prakrit vernaculars.' (Weber, Albrecht, *History of Indian Literature*, Fourth Edition, 1904, Popular Re-issue, 1914. London, Kegan Paul, Trench, Trubner & Co. Ltd., pp. 67-68). Bauddham and Jaina works contrast *milakkhabhāṣā* with *māgadhabhāṣā.*

Sāyaṇa comments on *ŚBr.* VI.3.1.34: *'daivam' devasambandhi vākyam samskṛtam 'mānuṣa sambandhi bhāṣāmayan ca vākyam.* Thus, bhāṣā (parole) was sought to be distinguished from 'mantra'. Were *Māhārāṣṭrī, Śurasenī, Māgadhī, Prācyā* and *Avanti* five-fold bhāṣā -- dialects of parole? (Monier-Williams, Sanskrit-English Dictionary, 1899, p. 755). [Saussure makes a distinction between two linguistic terms: *langue* ('language) and *parole* ('speech'). In this *langue* refers to the abstract, systematic rules and conventions of a signifying system and involves principles of language. *Parole* refers to concrete examples of the use of *langue*. Thus, parole is a phenomenon of language recognized as a series of speech acts made by a linguistic subject.[283]

Evidence from Valmiki Rāmāyaṇa

Slokas 5.30.16 to 21 in the 29th sarga of Sundara Kandam, provide an episode of Hanuman introspecting on the language in which he should speak to Sita. This evidence refers to two dialects: Sanskrit and mānuṣam vākyam (lit. jāti bhāṣā). In this narrative mānuṣam vākyam (spoken dialect) is distinguished from Sanskrit of a Brahmin (or, grammatically correct and well-prouncedd Sanskrit used in yajña-s).

1. "antaramtvaha māsādya rākṣasīnam iha sthitah"

2. "śanairāśvāsaiṣyāmi santāpa bahulām imām"

(Staying here itself and getting hold of an opportunity even in the midst of the female-demons (when they are in attentive), I shall slowly console Sita who is very much in distress.)

3. "aham hi atitanuścaiva vānara śca viśeṣata"

4. "vācam ca udāhariṣyāmi mānuṣīm iha samskṛtām"

(However, I am very small in stature, particularly as a monkey and can speak now Sanskrit, the human language too.)

5. "yadi vācam pradāsyami dwijātiriva samskṛtām"

6. "rāvaṇam manyamānā mām sītā bhītā bhavi ṣyati"

7. vānarasya viśeṣena kathamsyādabibhāṣaṇam

(If I use Sanskrit language like a llsde, Sita will get frightened, thinking that Rāva ṇ a has come disguised as a monkey. Especially, how can a monkey speak it?)

8. "avaśyameva vaktavyam mānuṣam vākyam arthavat"

9. "mayā śāntvayitum śakyā"

10. "nānyathā iyam aninditā"

(Certainly, meaningful words of a human being are to be spoken by me. Otherwise, the virtuous Sita cannot be consoled.)

11. "sā iyam ālokya me rūpam jānakī bhāṣitam tathā ||

rakṣobhih trāsitaa pūrvam bhuūah trūsam gamiṣyati |"

(Looking at my figure and the language, *Sita* who was already frightened previously by the demons, will get frightened again.)[284]

Hanuman chooses *parole* (mānuṣīm vāk)

The distinction between *langue* and *parole* is brought out vividly in a reference in Vālmīki *Rāmāyaṇa* to Hanuman's dilemma in choosing between *langue* and *parole* – *Samskṛtam* or *Mānuṣīm vāk* -- to converse with Devi *Sita*:

अहम् हि अतितनुः चैव वानरः च विशेषतः ।
वाचम् च उदाहरिष्यामि मानुषीम् इह संस्कृताम् ॥

यदि वाचम् प्रदास्यामि द्विजातिः इव संस्कृताम् ।
रावणम् मन्यमाना माम् सीता भीता भविष्यति ॥
वानरस्य विशेषेण कथं स्यादभिभाषणम्म् ।

अवश्यम् एव वक्तव्यम् मानुषम् वाक्यम् अर्थवत् ॥

मया सान्त्वयितुम् शक्या न अन्यथा इयम् अनिन्दिता ।

सा इयम् आलोक्य मे रूपम् जानकी भाषितम् तथा ॥
रक्षोभिः त्रासिता पूर्वम् भूयः त्रासम् गमिष्यति ।

Trans. "However, I am very small in stature, particularly as a monkey and can speak now Sanskrit, the human language too. If I use Sanskrit language like a brahmin, *Sita* will get frightened, thinking me as Ravana. Especially, how can a monkey speak it? Certainly, meaningful words of a human being are to be spoken by me. Otherwise, the virtuous *Sita* cannot be consoled. Looking at my figure and the language, *Sita* who was already frightened previously by the demons, will get frightened again." (5.30.17-21)

Hanuman concludes:

कथम् नु खलु वाक्यम् मे शृणुयान् न उद्विजेत च ||
इति संचिन्त्य हनुमान् चकार मतिमान् मतिम् |

रामम् अक्लिष्ट कर्माणम् स्व बन्धुम् अनुकीर्तयन् ||
न एनाम् उद्वेजयिष्यामि तत् बन्धु गत मानसाम् |

इक्ष्वाकूणाम् वरिष्ठस्य रामस्य विदित आत्मनः ||

शुभानि धर्म युक्तानि वचनानि समर्पयन् |
श्रावयिष्यामि सर्वाणि मधुराम् प्रब्रुवन् गिरम् ||

श्रद्धास्यति यथा हि इयम् तथा सर्वम् समादधे |

इति स बहु विधम् महाअनुभावो |
जगति पतेः प्रमदाम् अवेक्षमाणः |
मधुरम् अवितथम् जगाद वाक्यम् |
द्रुम विटप अन्तरम् आस्थितो ||

Trans. How can *Sita* hear my words without fear? Thinking in this way, the wise Hanuma made up his mind (as follows): If I eulogize Rama, who is unwearied in action and a good relation, I shall not frighten her, whose mind is directed towards that relation. Offering auspicious and righteous words about Rama the most excellent prince Ikshvaku dynasty who possesses a learned soul and myself speaking in a sweet voice, I shall make everything intelligible so that *Sita* rightly believes everything The noble-minded Hanuman, abiding in the midst of the twigs of the trees and seeing *Sita*, spoke the following words of many kinds which were not futile. (5.30.40-44)

एवम् बहु विधाम् चिन्ताम् चिन्तयित्व महाकपिः |
संश्रवे मधुरम् वाक्यम् वैदेह्या व्याजहार ह ||

राजा दशरथो नाम रथ कुन्जर वाजिनाम् |
पुण्य शीलो मह्ाकीर्तिः ऋजुः आसीन् मह्ायशाः ||

Trans. Thus reflecting on many kinds of thought, Hanuma spoke the following sweet words within the hearing range of *Sita*. There was a king named Dasaratha who was very glorious among the kings of Ikshvaku dynasty and had a virtuous disposition. He owned chariots, elephants and horses, becoming very famous. (5.31.1-2)

Śatapathabrāhmaṇa for the first time refers to Mleccha NOT in terms of referring to a group of people but to their linguistic distinctiveness. The allusion is to asura who had lost speech or vāc, since they utter incomprehensible words similar to those deployed by Mleccha-speakers. It is noted that there is a linguistic variation in the utterance by Asura of: he 'lavo he'lavah. One linguistic explanation is that these are mispronunciation of words, rather than some examples of hostile speech, noting that the correct pronunciation of the intended meaning should be: *he 'ari h'ari* (O! spiteful enemies), interchanging l with r sound which is a common feature in Prakrit dialects.

Thus, the Mleccha speakers are simply speakers of Indo-Aryan but with tendency to deploy dialectical phonetic variations. In *Aṣṭādhyāyi* (VII.2.18), *mleccha* gets semantically associated with indistinct speech. Patañjali (*Mahābhāṣya* I.14) uses the same *Śatapathabrāhmaṇa* example to cite indistinct speech forms of Mleccha dialects, calling them apaśabda (corrupt pronunciation). *Brāhmaṇa* learning grammar and language were asked to be cautious about corrupt pronunciations so as not to lead to the type of downfall which has befallen asura. It should be noted that the semantics of asura in early texts refer to their being possessed of wonderful power. Even Sarasvati is referred to *āsurī* sarasvatī linked to the root *asu* , lit. 'spiritual, divine'.

He 'lavah

He 'lavah is the only term available as an asura dialect and relatable to a maritime sailor's boat song. The *he 'lavo he'lavah* is a refrain of boatman's song. The cognate words in Dravidian etyma: kol. *elava* 'a wave'; Go. *helva* id., flood (DEDR 830). *Ka.* elā, *ele, elē, elo, elō* excl. of a familiar and friendly character, used in calling or directly addressing any person; elage ho! used in calling to females. *Tu. elā* interj. of surprise. *Kui* ēla companionship (DEDR 831).

Te. elũgu voice; *elĩgincu, elũgincu, elũgiccu* to make a noise, cry, roar, sound, resound. Pa. *iluŋg* voice. *Ga.* (S.3) lēng a tune (DEDR 835). எலுவ eluva , *n.* Man-friend, always in the voc; தோழன் முன்னிலைப்பெயர். (தொல். பொ. 220, உரை.)(Tamil) ఏలపదము [ēlapadamu] or ఏలపాట *ēla-padamu.* [Tel.] n. A carol or balled. ఏల [ēla] *ēla.* [Tel.] n. A hurrah, or hoop. A carol or catch used by rowers of boats శృంగారపు పాట."ఏటికట్ట గుడిసె వేతాం ఏరువస్తే కూడాపోదాం ఓ, ఓ, గొల్లభామా!"(The books named గరుడాచలము, ఆటభాగవతము, పారిజాతము, &c. contain many specimens of these carols.) Also, a chorus of applause. ఏలపాటలు a kind of play, a game played by children బాలక్రీడావిశేషము. See P. ii. 132. ఏలు [ēlu] *ēlu.* [Tel.] v. i. & t. To rule, govern. manage. To enjoy, to master. To possess or take. పరిగ్రహించు, పాలించు. ఏలించు *ēlintsu.* v. t. To cause one to rule. నిన్నుమాచెర్ల యేలింతును I will make you ruler of Mācherla. ఏలినవాడు *ēlina-vāḍu.* n. A ruler, lord, your honor. ఏలిక, రాజు, స్వామి. ఏలుకోటి *ēlu-kōti.* n. The people, subjects. Host assembly. ప్రజాకోటి. సకలమైనవారు. ఏలుబడి *ēlu-baḍi.* n. Government, reign. ఏలేవారు or ఏలువారు *ēlē-vāru.* n. The rulers. ఏలుకొను = ఏలు. (Telugu).

cf. Melech Hamashiah: King Messiah; Akad: {Akkad} A city in Mesopotamia (now Iraq) which was part of Nimrod's kingdom, founded by Melech Sargon around 2350 BCE Genesis 10:10; KP Jayaswal notes that *mleccha* was the Samskṛtam representation of Hebrew (Semitic) *melekh* meaning, 'king' and that the utterance: *he lavah! he lavah!* in the Śatapatha Brāhmaṇa was a specimen of *mleccha* speech; that this spech is cognate with Hebrew *ēloāh* (plural ēlōhim) meaning, 'God'.[285]

Dhavalikar traces the derivation of Meluhha terms as: *meluhha > melukha > melakkhu > milakkho mleccha.*[286]

An interpretation offered by Sengupta[287] is that *mleccha* were Phoenician, deriving the word *mleccha* from Moloch or Molech, relating them to Melek or Melqart, the god of the Phoenicians. It is unclear if this reference linking Phoenicians who were active during the latter half of the 2nd millennium BCE is a memory of the earlier millennium.

The etyma mleccha, milakkhu are research challenges. Paton[288] discusses the term *milcom* which was the name of an Ammonite god, notes that Phoenician equivalent *milk* means 'king' and that *melek* as the divine name is found in all branches of the Semitic language. Rejecting all theories about *melek*, Paton notes that *melakim* of the Semitic groups probably bore a family resemblance to each other as the Baalim did. Is the term *mleccha* derived from Akkadian *malik* (Hebrew *molech*; Phoenician *milk*) given the resemblance of the Pali terms *milakkhu* and *milakka* ? Childer's *Pali Dictionary* has the forms malikkho or malik'khako, possibly Prakrit forms of the Sanskrit word *mleccha,* 'stranger'. "The most conspicuous of the Phoenician Milkim was Melkart = Milk-kart, 'king of the city', the chief god of Tyre."

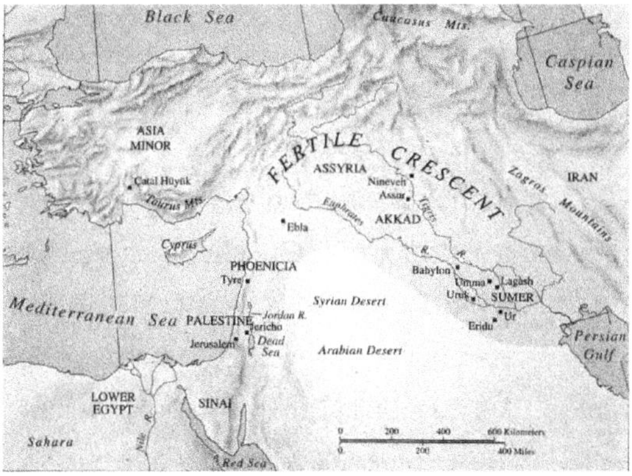

Meluhha: epigraphical evidences

Decrypting glyphs of Indus Writing is achieved by decoding of *apaśabda*. For example, on

the Seals m1118 and Kalibangan032, glyphs used are: Zebu (*bos taurus indicus*), fish, four-strokes (allograph: arrow).

काण्ड an arrow MBh._xiii , 265 Hit. (Monier-Williams, p. 269) Rebus: काण्ड abundance; a multitude , heap , quantity (ifc.) Pa1n2._4-2 , 51 Ka1s3.

ayo 'fish' (Mu.) + *kaṇḍa* 'arrow' (Skt.) *ayaskāṇḍa* 'a quantity of iron, excellent iron' (Pāṇ.gaṇ) aya = iron (G.); ayah, ayas = metal (Skt.) *gaṇḍa*, 'four' (Santali); Rebus: *kaṇḍ* 'fire-altar', 'furnace'), arrow read rebus in mleccha (Meluhhan) as a reference to a guild of artisans working with *ayas kāṇḍa* 'excellent quantity of iron' (Pāṇini) is consistent with the primacy of economic activities which resulted in the invention of a writing system, now referred to as Indus Writing.

Allograph: काण्डः kāṇḍḥ ण्डम् ṇḍam The portion of a plant from one knot to another. काण्डात्काण्ड- त्प्ररोहन्ती Mahānār.4.3. A stem, stock, branch; लीलोत्खातमृणालकाण्डकवलच्छेदे U.3.16; Amaru.95; Ms. 1.46,48, Māl.3.34.

The pictorial motif of zebu or *bos taurus indicus* has been decoded: *aḍar ḍhangar khũṭ* 'native-metal-blacksmith community (guild)(making) excellent metal'.

aḍar ḍangra 'zebu'(Santali); *ḍhangar* 'bull' Rebus: *dhangar* 'blacksmith' (Maithili) ḍangar 'blacksmith' (Hindi) *khũṭ* Brahmani bull (Kathiawar G.); khũṭro entire bull used for agriculture, not for breeding (G.)(CDIAL 3899). *khũṭro* = entire bull; *khũṭ* = brāhmaṇi bull (G.) *khuṇṭiyo* = an uncastrated bull (Kathiawad. Gujarat) *khũṭaḍum* a bullock (used in Jhālwāḍ)(G.) *kuṇṭai* = bull (Tamil) cf. *khũdhi* hump on the back; khuī̃dhũ hump-backed (G.)(CDIAL 3902). Rebus: *kūṭa* a house, dwelling (Sanskrit) *khũṭ* = a community, sect, society, division, clique, schism, stock; *khūṭren peṛa kanako* = they belong to the same stock (Santali) *khūṭ* Nag. *khūṭ, kūṭ* Has. (Or. *khūṭ*) either of the two branches of the village family. Rebus: *kuṭi*, 'smelting furnace' (Mundari).*kuṭhi, kuṭi* (Or.; Sad. *koṭhi*) (1) the smelting furnace of the blacksmith; kuṭire bica duljaḍko talkena, they were feeding the furnace with ore; (2) the name of ēkuṭi has been given to the fire which, in lac factories, warms the water bath for softening the lac so that it can be spread into sheets; to make a smelting furnace; kut.hi-o of a smelting furnace, to be made; the smelting furnace of the blacksmith is made of mud, cone-shaped, 2' 6" dia. At the base and 1' 6" at the top. The hole in the center, into which the mixture of charcoal and iron ore is poured, is about 6" to 7" in dia. At the base it has two holes, a smaller one into which the nozzle of the bellow is inserted, as seen in fig. 1, and a larger one on the opposite side through which the molten iron flows out into a cavity (Mundari)

There are over 50 epigraphs of the civilization showing *bos taurus indicus* which is decoded as a hieroglyph denoting in mleccha a metal-smithy-guild (community, *khūṭ* This reference to a community through a glyph is indicative of the early guild working in the civilization. This is a surmise that the early semantics of the word *khūṭ* may have related to such a group formation of metalsmiths and artisans.

Mleccha Khandas

There are 5 mleccha khandas in each of the 32 Videhas and Bharata and Airāvata ksetras each. Thus there are 170 (= 5 X32.+ 5 x 2) mleccha khandas in Jambūdvipa. In mleccha Khandas and 110 towns of Vidyādharas at both the srenis of 32 Videhas there exists a situation alike to that at the begining of fourth period of avasarpini and in mleccha khandas and 50 and 60 towns of Vidyadharas at southern and northern Srenīs of Vijayārdhas of Bharata and Āirivata ksetras alike to what appears from the beginning to the end of fourth period of avasarpanī.

"The Iranian homelands *Airyanam Vaejo*, described as too cold in its 10-months-long winter, and *Hapta-Hendu*, described as rendered too hot for men (i.e. the Iranians) by the wicked Angra-Mainyu, are Kashmir and Sapta-Saindhavah (Panjab-Haryana) respectively.They are considered as the first two of sixteen countries successively allotted to the Iranians, the rest being the areas where the Iranians have effectively been living in proto-historical times. This scenario tallies quite exactly with the Vedic and Puranic data about the history of the *Anavas*, one of the five branches of the *Aila/Saudyumna* people: from Kashmir, they invaded Sapta-Saindhavah, but were defeated by the *Paurava* branch (which composed the Rg-Veda) and driven northwestward."[289]

Aila outflow of the Druhyus through the northwest into the countries beyond where they founded various kingdoms. (*Bhishma's Study of Indian History and Culture* by S.D. Kulkarni, Shri Bhagwan Vedavyasa Itihasa Samshodhana Mandira, (BHISHMA) Thane, Mumbai, Vol. I, p. 298.)

Pargiter[290] in speaking of the different tribal groups, tells us that the Ailas (the Yadus, TurvaSas, Anus, Druhyus and Pūrus) were Aryans, the Ikṣvākus were Dravidians, and the eastern Saudyumna groups (named in the Purāṇas) were Austrics.

The Jain Prajñāpanā records two divisions of the people of India Milikkha and Arya, and enumerates 53 people in the former group, some of which are the Saga, Javana, Sabara, Vavvara, Hona, Romaya, Pārasa and Khasa.

Mlecchas dwelt in the Yavana, China and Kamboja countries. (MBh. VI. 9.65.) They were ignorant of Dharma. [(Gita Press) Karna Parva, 40/42-43. मद्रका सिन्धुसौवीरा धर्मं विद्दु: कथंत्विह । पापदेशोद्भवा मलेच्छा धर्मानामाविचाक्षणा: ।] Yavana were mleccha and were (unlike Madra ad Vahika) skillful people. (ibid., 45/36-37. सर्वज्ञा यवना राजञ्शूराश्चैव विशेषत: । मलेच्छा स्वयंसंज्ञानियता नानुक्त मितरे जना: ।। प्रतिरब्धास्तु वाहिका न च केचन मद्रका: ।).

In the *Mahābhārata* the Abhiras are called Mleccha We also find a reference to the oppression of the earth by the Mlecchas in the epilogue of the play Mudra-

Raksasa written by Visakhadatta where it is prayed that 'The earth may now be protected by "His Highness" along with relatives and retinue by king Candragupta'. It is probable that the play was written after the Ramagupta episode and probably the word Mleccha in this context alludes to the Sakas who were suppressed by Chandragupta II in the guise of the Gupta queen Dhruvasvamini. The word Mleccha was used to refer to both the eastern and western Anavas.

Anu (अनु) was son of Yayati and Sharmishtha. [1]Yayati had three sons from Sharmishtha –

1. Druhyu
2. Anu and
3. Puru.

The mother of Anu and Puru, (whom the Jats claim as their progenitors), was Sarmishtha, the princess of King Vrshaparvan.[291]

Meluhha, toponym: two Meluhhas

One was the region of Meluhha-Baluhhu (India), the other was the region of Meluhha-Kush (Nubia/Egypt). Could the later date texts locating Meluhha in portions of Africa relate to Meluhha-speakers who were earlier located in Baluchistan and later in Africa?

Grayson's account[292] of Sargon geography refers to a text detailing the limits of Sargon's empire: [ultu…]x ti-tur-ri Ba-zaki sha pAT (ZAG) harrAn (KASKAL) mAt Me-luh-h[aki][From…]the bridge of Baza on the edge of the road to the land Meluhha. The second line of the text refers to 'mountain of cedar'denoting western limit of the empire. The text indicates that Meluhha was situated to the east of Sargon's empire. Potts has reviewed the evidence related to Baza and discusses the two locations, mentioned at different periods, of two Meluhhas –

one in the vicinity of Baluchistn and the other in Africa (possibly a location in Nubia or Ethiopia).[293]

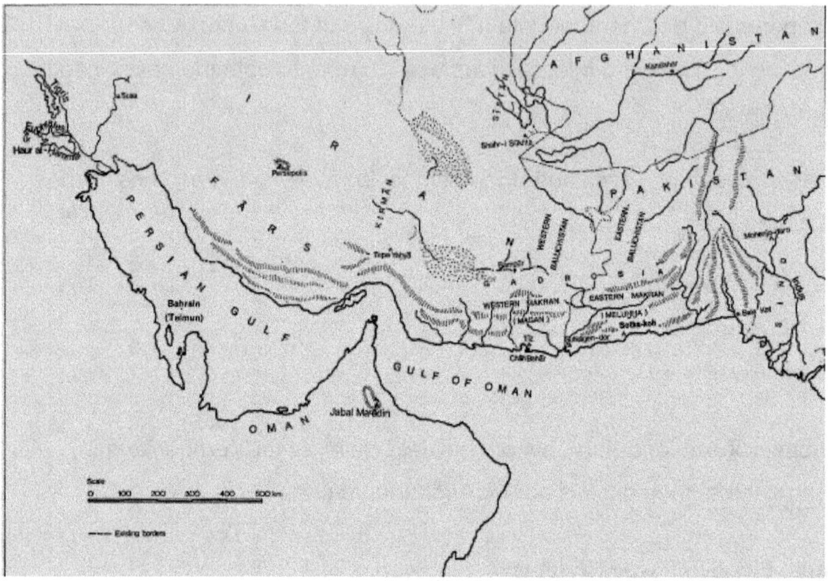

Weidner showed that there was an ‘eastern’ and a ‘western’ Meluhha in Mesopotamian evidences. Weidner proposed that texts of late third and early second millennium date locate Meluhha in southeastern Oman.[294]

Meluhha (After Fig. 1 in: Hansman, J., "A Periplus of Magan and Melukha", in *BSOAS*. London, 1973, p. 554-87. Hansman proposes that linguistically Magan always been linked with the toponym Makran (southern Baluchistan) and that Meluhha is identified with the former Khanat of Kalat which includes most of Baluchistan in Pakistan and in the south Makran in Pakistan.

"Almost from the beginning of the excavations in the ruins of the old city of Uruk in Lower Mesopotamia in 1928, work has concentrated on uncovering large parts of the temple area of that city, the holy district of Eanna... It was in these various layers and accumulations of debris covering large parts of the Eanna district that over the years more than four thousand clay tablets and fragments were found... In the Archaic Metals List we again find DILMUN in a line which due to a common denominator proves to be part of an internally cohesive group of entries. The entire list starts out with a sequence of metal vessels and continues with metal tools and weapons. This group opens with a sequence of various daggers, continues with various groups of unidentified objects and from line 23 on shows five entries with the common denominator tun2, 'axe'. The lines read in tentative translation: 'big axe', 'two-handed axe', 'one-handed axe', 'x-axe', and 'Dilmun axe'. Here most likely the differentiation bears on differences in shape, size or function; the 'two-handed axe' may mean a double-edged axe, for instance. Again, if seen as a coherent context DILMUN may be used here as equivalent to 'Dilmun-type axe'. I do not think it could just refer to the provenance of an axe but rather to specific qualities... three texts clearly are dealing with textiles but only one of them has a context which might be interpreted; tentatively it reads' 1 bale of DILMUN garment'... as the title following the one containing the sign for DILMUN we find the comosite sign for namesda, the title of the opening line of the Archaic Professions list. It is supposed that this title represents the highest official. Probably without all connotations of the terms 'ruler' or 'king' it nevertheless should be fairly close. The preceding line contains a number of signs which if translated literally could mean 'the prince of the good Dilmun-house (or temple)'. The exact meaning is elusive. To sum up, from our texts we do not get an adequate picture of the relations of Babylonia, or the city of Uruk, with Dilmun. On a general level, however, we can conclude that not only did such relations exist already by the end of the fourth millennium BC, but that these contacts apparently were not restricted to trade. To be sure, the exchange of metal and ttextiles may represent the main ties, but the existence of titles containing Dilmun in their name in normal Babylonia contexts like the Professions List point to much closer mutual contacts that would be sustained by occasional trade. The same is suggested by the existence of DILMUN in generic designations for kinds of textiles or metal tools. We certainly are entitled to assume that these relations had existed long before the emergence of writing."[295]

In the Old *Babylonian* period, some Mesopotamian seals depict a deity holding a crook. (cf. Seal 124 in Macropoli Collection). The deity also appears with his foot on a gazelle, but sometimes on a small pedestal; he wears a long robe or a kilt and on his head a horned headdress or a tall cylindrical hat. He has been identified as the god AMURRU. In texts and cylinder seal impressions his name is written d/AN.MAR.TU or d/MAR.TU, i.e., AMURRU(M), 'GOD OF THE WEST' in Akkadian. He is often loosely called the god of the Amorites because of his association in texts with the desert and steppe. He became the son of Anu the sky god and was often associated with Sin the moon god. He was referred to as the warrior god. The association with the desert is remarkable. In the Sarasvati Sindhu valley area, the arid zone on the banks of the Sarasvati river is called MARUSTHALI (now called Thar/Cholistan or Great Indian Desert). And, MARUTS are celebrated in the Rigveda as wind-gods, echoing the phenomenon of the *āndhī* or sandstorms common in the region of Thar/Cholistan desert.

"From the Ur III (2112-2004 BC) and Isin-Larsa (2025-1763) periods, we have a number of textual sources which suggest that an ethnic group of people called MAR-TU were associated with the land of Dilmun-- the first of three entities found to be trade partners with Mesopotamia from at least 2500 BC (the others being Makkan and Meluhha). From Drehem, a city near Nippur, we note the occurrence in two texts (dated to AS 2-2044 BC)(CST 254 and TRU 305) of a colophon which reads 'MAR-TU (and) Diviners coming from Dilmun' (or MAR-TU Diviners coming from Dilmun)(BUccellati 1966: 249)... In addition, other evidence suggests that the MAR-TU were associated with (sea) fishing (Civil 1961: Buccellati 1966: 90). Thus Buccellati and later Gelb concluded that the MAR-TU existed in the south in the area of the Gulf as far as Bahrain (Gelb 1968: 43; 1980: 2). Finally, this linkage is suggested by a text from Eshnunna, a Mesopotamian city on the Diyala river. In this text most likely dated to Is'aramas'u (c. 1970 BC) MAR-TU are arranged by segmented lineage affiliation (babtum).

The total states that twenty-six MAR-TU are e-lu-tum-me, a term perhaps best translated as meaning' trustworthy' or 'reliable' vis-a-vis the local Eshnunna officials. One MAR-TU from the lineage of Bas'anum is said to be a-ab-ba-ta or 'from the sea (lands)' or the land across the sea[296] the newely discovered Ibla texts mention the MAR-TU principally in connection with metal daggers (Pettinato 180: 9 and commentary) and prisoners of war (Pettinato 1981b: 120, see text TM 75G.309). (Note also the MAR-TU name Iblanum as meaning man from Ibla, Buccellati 1966: 155, 246)... From the early second millennium BC, we have a much wider body of evidence dealing with the MAR-TU. This is due to the greatly increased numbers of MAR-TU escaping the hamad and entering the settled zones. As early as S'u-Sin year (2034 BC) we see that a large defensive wall was being built in central Mesopotamia for the express purpose of keeping out the MAR-TU (the MAR-TU wall (called) the one which keeps Didanum away, Buccellati 1966: 92). Unfortunately, by the early reign of the succeeding king, Ibbi-Si, things had changed:

Reports that hostiel MAR-TU had entered the plains having been received, 144,000 gur grain (representing) the grain in its entirety was brought into Isin. Now the MAR-TU in their entirety have entered the interior of the country taking one by one all the great fortresses. Because of the MAR-TU I am not able to provide... for that grain... (Jacobsen 1953: 40)

According to the year date of Ibbi-Sin 17, some of these MAR-TU apparently came from the Gulf region: 'The year the MAR-TU, the powerful south wind who, from the remote past, have not known cities, submitted to Ibbi-Sin, the king of Ur.' (cf. also Gelb's views, 1961: 36)... Oppenheim's review of UET V suggests that Ur apparently served as a focal point and port for foreign trade, specifically with Dilmun (Oppenheim 1954: 8, n.8). A number of texts describe this activity as traders called alik Dilmun sailed to Dilmun and exchanged goods. A number of texts (e.g. UET V 286, 297, 549 and 796) clearly demonstrate that individuals with MAR-TU names were involved in the trade (e.g. in UET V 297 a certain Zuabbaum; in UET V 549 a person named Milkudanum; and in UET V 796

Alazum). This then is a clear link between Dilmun and the MAR-TU-- a hypothesis already formulated from a number of literary texts and Ur III economic records... It seems clear in summary that the MAR-TU were linked to Dilmun in a political sense (rulers in southern Mesopotamian towns), commercial agents in Mesopotamia (alik Dilmun), and inhabitants of Dilmun itself (Susa Tablet, UET V 716).[Juris Zarins, MAR-TU and the land of Dilmun, 232-249 in: Shaikha Haya Ali Al Khalifa and Michael Rice (eds.) Bahrain through the ages: the archaeology, London, KPI, 1986.]

Sir Henry Rawlinson in 1880 suggested that Dilmun of the Sumerian and Akkadian texts might be identified with Bahrain island. This was on the basis of a stone cone found by Captain Durand during an archaeological survey of Bahrain in 1879, but later lost. The text related to the temple of Inzak, elsewhere known as the god of Dilmun.[297] Since then various identifications have been suggested such as: encompassing Saudi Arabian mainland in the area called Dilmun, Iranian side of the Persian Gulf as constituting Dilmun, Al-Qurna in southern Iraq and the Indus Valley (S.N.Kramer). All these identifications suggest that not all of them are valid for all periods of Mesopotamian history. Throughout Mesopotamian history, however, Dilmun has been an important trade centre, and 'one of the remote areas which was at times within the reach of Mesopotamian political influence. Noticeable among the early texts mentioning Dilmun is that of Urnanshe who had wood transported to Mesopotamia from Dilmun (ca. 2500 BC). In the same early period copper is known to hae been exported from Dilmun to Sumer. About 2100 BC Urnammu of the 3rd dynasty of Ur reopened the Arabian Gulf trade, this time with direct contact with Magan, from which copper was exported to Mesopotamia. The Dilmun trade flourished in the Larsa period (ca. 2000-1763 BC), but then died out. After an interim of 400 years Kassite influence appears in Dilmun (early 14th century BC). It seems that at this time the only export article was dates. Under Sargon of Assyria (end of 8th century BC) Upe_ri, king of Dilmun, is recorded to have sent tribute to the Assyrian empire. In 544 BC, Dilmun disappears from Mesopotamian history when, according to an administrative document, Nabonidus, king of Babylon, had a governor there. Dilmun is also mentioned in Sumerian literary texts as a famous place of prosperity and happiness, and even of eternal life, with the result that comparisons with the Biblical paradise have been made.'[298]

On the northern coast of Bahrain, at Barbar, a Sumerian temple, which had been rebuilt three times was found. The dates for the contruction events are estimated to be: beginning of third millennium B.C., middle of the third millennium BC and for the third event, ca. 2200-2000 BC. In the first temple there were two staircases descending to a square well. This was retained in all the three phases. Peder Mortensen suggested, based on the similarity with the Khafajah and al-'Uaid temples, that the temple was for goddess Ninhursag. The mother-goddess plays an important role in the Sumerian Dilmun myth, Enki and Ninhursag. (Peder Mortensen, *Kuml 1956*: 189-198, *1970*: 385-398).

Indus valley type seals and cubical chert weights were found.[299] A bronze mirror handle was also found in the Barbar temple suggesting a link with the Kulli culture in South Baluchistan (N.Rao, *Kuml 1969*: 218-220). "....as far as the third millennium BC is concerned, the cultural relations with the early civilizations in the Indus valley and southern Iran seem to have been much more outspoken than those with Mesopotamia. (M.Tosi, Dilmun, *Antiquity*, 45 (1971): 21-25). Yet, as far as the early second millennium BC is concerned, a cultural setting has certainly been found within which the identification of Dilmun with Bahrain makes good sense... There is now wide agreement among most, but not all scholars, that from the middle of the third millennium BC, Magan and Meluhha are to be found east of Mesopotamia along the coast of the Arabian Gulf or the Arabian Sea, whereas later, from the middle of the secon dmillennium BC, Egypt, Nubia or Ethiopia must be considered.[300] The cuneiform texts certainly give the impression that at least originally they (Makan and Meluhha) were located in the same direction as Dilmun, but farther away-- and later, remembrance of this direction was demonstrably kept alive, which makes the matter rather complicated. Archaeologically it makes sense to speak of Bahrain as a station on the way to Magan and Meluhha if these two were located east of Bahrain, as the most important cultural relations of Bahrain were Indus and Iran rather than Egypt. The use of Indus measuring standards in Bahrain clearly testifies to this, and was taken for granted by the Mesopotamian traders... The most important suggestins that have been made for Magan are Makran on the Iranian coast, and the Oman peninsula. As copper has been found in the Oman, the latter possibility seems highly likely. This, however, has been questioned by W. Heimpel, according ot whom diorite statues of Naramsin and Gudea said to be made of stones from Magan cannot have come from Oman, because diorite stones big enough for these statues are reported not to exist in Oman. As a possible source he suggests a position 50 miles NNE of Bandar Abbas on the northern side of the Arabian Gulf. Meluhha is to be found along the coast of Baluchistan and the Indus valley.

A cuneiform text [Ur III (ca. 2100-2000 BC)] refers to Meluhha as a region; the list is of the Sargonic king Rimus, who conquered Parahsum, Zahar, Elam, [Balsin(?), and Meluhha.[301]

An account of the insurrection of Naram-Sin (text from the end of the third millennium BCE) mentions the rulers allied against Akkade: 'the man of Meluhha, the man of Aratta, the king of Marhasi...[another country: gap in tablet], the king of all Elam'[302]

"...there was a temple of Enzak, the god of Dilmun, on Failaka... it was Failaka that was Dilmun?...the so-called a_lik Dilmun, the sea-faring merchants of Ur... The returning merchants used to offer a share of their goods or a silver model of their boat to the temple of the goddess Ningal, and he texts tell about partnerships and the sharing of profit and losses in a way which would not fit such an easy travel as thaf from Ur to Failaka. The distance from Aba_da_n to Failaka is no more than 60 nautical miles (111 km.) and could hardly be considered a great enterprise... Another possibility would be to suggest that Dilmun was a designation not only of Bahrain, but also of other parts of the

Arabian Gulf area, among which Failaka would be counted... Dilmun is likely to the name of a rather large geographical area, including Bahrain, Failaka, Tarut, and certain parts of the Arabian littoral (During Caspers and Govindakutty, *JESHO* 21 (1978): 130; cf. the map in D.O.Edzard and G.Farber, *Repertoire Geographique des Textes Cuneiformes* 2, Wiesbaden, 1974)..."[303]

Meluhha as toponym has been the subject of scholarly inquiry and debate locating Meluhha – using Sumerian references -- as a region in the lower end of Persian Gulf to the east of Tigris-Euphrates rivers and – using late Assyrian texts (that is, from about 1500 BCE) – as a region in Egypt/Nubia/Ethiopia. Landsberger tried to resolve the contentious issue by suggesting that Magan could be located near the lower end of the Persian Gulf and earlier Meluhha located as an unspecified region east of this Magan. He added that these two regions, Meluhha and Magan were names applied in later Assyrian period to Egypt/Ethiopia because gold and ivory were imported into Mesopotamia from this 'southern Meluhha' while materials were imported into Sumer from the 'eastern Meluhha'. Herzfeld locates Magan on both sides of the Gulf of Oman and see the name Magan surviving as Makran, the coastal region of south-eastern Iran and southwestern Pakistan. Gelb locates Meluhha as the north shore of the Persian Gulf including Iran past Elam and Anshan and also the region east of there upto and including the Indus valley.[304]

"The following types of commodities are attested in connection with Makkan and Meluhha : metals and métal objects, precious metals, stone and stone objects, semi-precious stones, trees and wooden objects, boats, reeds, plants and plant deri vatives, and animais...We know of stone vases which Naram-Sin received as booty from Makkan, of a stone statuette of a Meluhha dog which Ibbi-Sin received as booty, and of an oil perfume said to have come from Makkan...Makkan is the southern shore of the Persian Gulf and of the Arabian Sea; it denotes Arabia, extending east of ancient Sumer upto and including Oman. Meluhha is the northern shore of the Persian Gulf and of the Arabian Sea;

it denotes Iran and India, extending east of ancient Elam and Anshan upto and including the Indus Valley...The evidence concerning the lapis lazuli, the sissoo-tree, and the black people of Meluhha, corresponding to the *Aithiopes* of classical times, place Meluhha between Iran and Afghanistan. The farthest extent of Meluhha in India is indicated by the imports. "[305]

Hansman cites texts of Old Akkadian and Sumerian periods attest Telmun, Meluhha and Magan:[quote] Dynasty of Akkad. *Sargon* (2370-2316 BCE) caused the ships of Telmun, Meluhha and Magan to be moored at the wharf before Agade. *Manishtusu* (2306-2292 BCE) crossed the lower sea (the Persian Gulf) in ships. He defeated 32 kings and their cities on the other side of the sea and overthrew the whole country as far as the silver mines. He took stones from the mountains below the lower sea and had statues to be made from these.

Naram-Sin (2291-2255 BCE) subjugated Magan and killed Manui, Lord of Magan. In their mountains he quarried stone which was transported to Agade to make statues.

Dynasty of Lagash

Gudea (c. 2200 BCE) brought na-ESI (probably diorite) from the mountains of Magan to Lagash, where it was used to make his statue. He brought *uṣu* wood (ebony?) and gold dust from Meluhha to Lagash. Brought also from Meluhha was Gug.Gi.RIN.E, a kind of stone, probably carnelian.

Third Dynasty of Ur

Ibbi-Sin (2029-2006 BCE), garments and wool were brought from store to trade for copper from Magan. Other imports to Ur at this period were Magan onions and Magan reeds. From Meluhha came copper, A.AB.BA wood used for making chairs and dagger sheaths, *mesu* wood, and multi-coloured birds of ivory.

Assyria

Iluṣuma (2004-1977 BCE), in a year-formula text a throne is stated to have been made from AB.BA Meluhha wood.

Dynasty of Larsa

Gungunum (1932-1906 BCE), expeditions to Telmun brought back with other cargo gold, ivory, copper, carnelian, and silver.

Babylon

Sumu-ilum (1880-1845 BCE), imports from Telmun included *mesu* wood, gold, objects inlaid with ivory, copper, and lapis lazuli.

Dynasty of Larsa

Rim-Sin (1822-1763 BCE), silver, sesame oil, and garments were sent from Larsa to Telmun for copper. This text is from the middle period of Rim-Sin's reign.

Dynasty of Mari

Yasmah-Adad (1796-1780 BCE) writes to Hammurabi of Babylon about the delay of a caravan sent by the former to Telmun.

Lexical series

Mainly HAR-ra: *hubullu* recovered in copies of the later Assyrian period but which cuneiformists generally agree are derived from lists of the Larsa period or of the end of the Third Dynasty of Ur.

IV, 98 Magan chair; IV, 99 Meluhha chair; IV, 194, Magan table; IV, 195 Meluhha table; III, 204 MES wood of Magan; III, 205 MES wood of Meluhha; III,286 date-palm of Magan; III, 287 date-palm of Meluhha; III, 155 A.AB.BA wood of Meluhha; XI, Magan copper; XI, Meluhha copper...

"Dr. Ilya Gershevitch has demonstrated convincingly that MES or MIS wood of Sumerian and Old Babylonian texts is to be identified with the Old Persian *yakā-* in an Achaemenian trilingual inscription, and that the MES *yakā-* is in fact the sissoo tree. The sissoo is found along the watercourses in both Iranian and Pakistan Makran...Legrain suggests that Magan reed may be bamboo...used for the long shafts of daggers and also as fittings for containers...The toponym Meluhha attested in Sumerian and Old Akkadian texts was apparently intended by its Mesopotamian users to identify a country located beyond Magan...In treating the location of Meluhha, therefore, Baluchistan in Pakista which lies immediately to the east of Makran/Baluchistan in Iran, perhaps merits our attention...In Sanskrit texts groups of lawless barbarians who live beyond the Sindhu, i.e. to the west of the Indus, and who do not conform to Hindu customs, are identified as Mleccha. (Bailey, pp. 584-6)...it has been noted by Gadd and Leemans that the older toponym Meluhha and this word Mleccha show certain similarities of form...these Mleccha occupied at least a part of the country where we have placed Meluhha. By what name then was the country called Meluhha in the third millennium known during the later periods in Mesopotamian history?...an essence RIQ *baluhhu*, and its gum HIL RIQ *baluhhi* are listed in Assyrian medical texts as medications used both externally and internally. Thompson has identified RIQ *baluhhu* as galbanum, an extract of the plant *Ferula galbaniflua* which is native to Eastern Iran and Afghanistan...*Meluhha > Baluhhu > Baluch* can be postulated, with *m* and *b* interchanging and with the Iranian ending *ch* replacing the non-Iranian ending of Baluhhu. In this event, it is possible that the Iranian people now called Baluch could have adapted a form of the most ancient name of the country in which they settled, even though the name is now sometimes used in a non-ethnic sense." [unquote][306]

"Mleccha-, Balōc, and Gadrōsia... Epic usage, *Mahābhārata* contrasts the *mleccha-* with *ārya-,* and has he mleccha- bhāṣā 'Mleccha language', and mleccha-vāk 'using Mleccha speech'. The Dharmasūtra text, the Manu-smṛiti, 2.23, has the mleccha-deśa- 'Mleccha country' as unfit for Brahmanical sacrifices. Localization. 1. The *Mahābhārata* places Mleccha loosely in east, north, and west. The *Rāmāyaṇa* has Mleccha for the Matsya people of Rajputana. (see S. Levi, *Journal Asiatique*, XIe Ser., XI, 1, 1918, 123). 2. Varāhamihira, c. CE 550, placed the Mleccha in the *upara-* region, the western. His *upara-* region refers to the peoples beyond the Sindhu, Indus, for whom the *Mahābhārata* had the epithet pāre-sindhavah 'beyond the Sindhu'. Varāhamihira has peoples reaching the Vokkāṇa- 'Wakhān', through Pancanada- 'Panjāb', the Pārata-, Pārada-, which is the Greek Paradhnh 'Parada-' placed by Ptolemy in Gedrosia. These Pārada- are named in the Paikuli inscription of the Sasanians and in the inscription of Shāhpur I, Parthian text, line 2, in the list *krmn skstn twgrn mkwrn p'rtn hndstn* 'Kirmān, Sakastān, Tugrān, Pārtan, Hindastān'. This position excludes Levi's proposal of the Panjāb for the Pārata-. These Indian localizations give only 'beyond the Indus'. III. Linguistic evidence. 1. (a) Later Veda, *mleccha-* and verbal *mlecchati*, with participle in the Scholiast to Pāṇini *mliṣṭa; mlecchita-* is also cited. Patanjali has the infinitive *mlecchitavai*. (b) Pali, in the oldest texts *Dīgha-nikāya* and *Vinaya, milakkhu-, milakkhuka-, milakkha-, milakkha-bhāsā,* and later *milāca-.* (c) Jaina older Ardhamāgadhī, *milikkha-* (with *vokkāṇa* and *yavana-* (Wakhān' and 'Greek'), *milakkhu-, milikkhu-, mileccha-,* and Māhārāṣṭrī *miliṭṭha-* 'speaking indistinctly'. (d) Buddhist Sanskrit mleccha-, whence Saka Khotan *mīlaicha-.* (e) New Indo-Aryan in R.L. Turner, *Comparative dictionary*, no. 10398, Kāśmīrī *mīch* (with *–ch* from older *–cch-,* not *-kṣ-*); Bengali *mech* of a Tibeto-Burmese tribe, Sinhalese *milidu, milindu* 'savage', *milis, maladu*, Panjābī *milech, malech*. The Pali *–kkh-* was explained as secondary to *–cch-* by J. Wackernagel, *Altindische Grammatik*, I, 154; but was unexplained according to Turner, loc.cit. 2. Th starting-point of the interpretation should be a form **mlekṣ-, mlikṣ-.* Within the Veda there is a variation between *–cch-* (*-ch-*) and *-kṣ-* as in Atharvaveda *ṛccharā-* beside Śukla-yajur-veda, Vājasneyi-samhitā *ṛkṣalā* – 'fetter', and within the Atharva-veda in *parikṣit-* and variant *paricchit-* 'surrounding'. Hence *Śatapathabrāhmaṇa mleccha-* may be traced to older **mlekṣa-. The kṣ* was replaced by *–kkh-* or by retroflex *–ch-* or by palatalized *–cch-* in different dialects.Within the Veda there was also variation in *kśā-, kṣa-,* and *khya-* from *kaś-*, corresponding to Avestan *xsā-* from *kas-* 'to look at'. If the oldest form had then **mlekṣa-*, this *-kṣ-* could be accepted as a substitute for the foreign velar fricative (the sound expressed in Arabic script by خ *kh*). If the word **mlekṣ-* was a foreign name, it was adapted to the usual Vedic verbal system, giving particile mliṣṭa- in the grammarians, supported by the Jaina Māhārāṣṭrī *miliṭṭha-*. The vowel *-e-* of *mleccha-* was thus adapted into the ablaut system *–e-*: *-i-*.[307]

mliṣṭa म्लिष्ट *a.* 1 Spoken indistinctly (as by barbarians), indistinct; P.VII.2.18; म्लिष्टमस्फुटम् Abh. Chin.266. -2 Barbarous. -3 Withered, faded. -ष्टम् 1 An indis- tinct or barbarous speech. -2 A foreign language.

mlēcch म्लेच्छ् or म्लेछ् 1 P., 1 U. (म्लेच्छति, म्लेच्छयति-ते, म्लिष्ट, म्लेच्छित) 1 To speak confusedly, indistinctly, or barbarously. -2 To speak distinctly (व्यक्तायां वाचि); L. D. B. म्लेच्छः [म्लेच्छ्-घञ्] 1 A barbarian, a non-Āryan (one not speaking the Sanskṛit language, or not con- forming to Hindu or Āryan institutions), a foreigner in general; ग्राह्या म्लेच्छप्रसिद्धिस्तु विरोधादर्शने सति J. N. V.; म्लेच्छान् मूर्छयते; or म्लेच्छनिवहनिधने कलयसि करवालम् Gīt.1. -2 An outcast, a very low man; (Baudhāyana thus defines the word:-- गोमांसखादको यस्तु विरुद्धं बहु भाषते । सर्वा- चारविहीनश्च म्लेच्छ इत्यभिधीयते ॥). -3 A sinner, wicked person. -4 Foreign or barbarous speech. -च्छम् 1 Copper. -2 Vermilion. -Comp. -आख्यम् copper. -आशः wheat. -आस्यम्, -मुखम् copper. -कन्दः garlic. -जातिः *f.* a savage or barbarian race, a mountaineer; पुलिन्दा नाहला निष्ट्याः शबरा वरुटा भटाः । माला भिल्लाः किराताश्च सर्वे$पि म्लेच्छजातयः ॥ Abh. Chin.934. -देशः, -मण्डलम् a country inhabited by non-Āryans or barbarians, a foreign or barbarous country; कृष्णसारस्तु चरति मृगो यत्र स्वभावतः । स ज्ञेयो यज्ञियो देशो म्लेच्छदेशस्त्वतः परः ॥ Ms.2.23. -द्विष्टः bdellium. -भाषा a foreign language. -भोजनः wheat. (-नम्) barley. -वाच् *a.* speaking a barbarous or foreign language; म्लेच्छवाचश्चार्यवाचः सर्वे ते दस्यवः स्मृताः Ms.1.45.[308]

Melakkha, island-dwellers, lapidaries

Amarakośa defines mleccha as a reference to forest people while categories of people such as niṣāda (of Vindhya mountains), ābhīra (reed-workers), kirāta, śabara, pulinda, āndhra, puṇḍra, drāviḍa, lāṭa, oḍra, darada, kāmboja, khasa, kalinda, uṣinara, mahiska, mekala, barbara, pahlava, śaka, yavana, sinhala also get designated as mleccha, milakkha or milakkhu in early texts.

Amarakośa also denotes a foreigner as *tāmra-mukha* 'copper-faced' (*Amara*, II,9,97). This term is explaind by Kṣīrasvāmin as *mleccha-deśe mukham utpattih yasya*, 'on whose origin is Mlecchadeśa, A similar explanation also fits the term *mleccha mukha*, 'copper, *tāmraṁ*' (as a mineral whose origin is Mlecchadeśa). *Abhidhāna Cintāmaṇi* (IV, 105) explains *mleccha* as 'copper' and *mleccha śavara* as 'dark copper'. Dhavalikar[309] explains why Meluhha could be identified as Gujarat: "...copper figures in various lists of different periods as coming from Meluhha. It is rather enigmatic because it is well known that India is deficient in copper. If Meluhha is to be identified with India, then it is intriguing that India should have exported copper in the third millennium. In fact one of the functions of the settlements of northern Kutch was the supply of copper to Sind...A copper ingot, plano-convex in shape, was found at Lothal...contains 99.81% pure copper...In shape...identical with those from Susa...since Gujarat or the Harappan province of western India was known to the Mesopotamians as Meluhha, copper was given the same name (Meluhha)...it is no without significance that the Dharmaśāstras referred to Gujarat as mleccha country, and hence, except on pilgrimage, visits to Gujarat were forbidden (*Vishnu Purāṇa*, IV, 24)."

Brihatsamhita places them in the West and describes them as unrighteous. (XIV, 21: निर्मार्यादा मलेच्छा ये पश्चिमदिक्स्थतास्ते च ।।) In the 'life' of Hiuen Tsang, all places to the north of Lamgham district have been described as Mi-li-ku, i.e. frontier or Mleccha lands. (S. Beal, Beal, S. 1973, *The Life of Hiuen Tsiang*, New Delhi, p.57). Rājataranginī मलेच्छा हैमवतास्थता । mentions the Mlecchas as issuing forth from the valleys adjoining the Himalayas.

The collective phrase used is: *nānāmlecchagaṇa* (MBh I.165.35-37).

The narratives accout for mlecchas with haihaya and tālanangha vanquished the regime of Bāhu of Ikṣvāku dynasty. Bauddham piṭaka texts place mleccha in paccantima (pratyanta) janapada (i.e. border territories). Samantapāsādikā on VinP I:255 refers to '*milakkhakam nāma yo koci anāriyako andhadamḷādi.*' A good indication of the mleccha-speaker community is also provided by the locations of Ashoka's edicts which included territories crossing the Vindhya mountains.

Vidura speaks to Yudhishthira in mleccha language (*mleccha vācā,* MBh. 1.135.6b). Khanaka, a dear friend of Vidura, well-skilled in ming, is sent to help the Pāṇḍava in confinement to report on how Purocana would put fire in the door of Pāṇḍava's house. *kṛṣṇa pakṣe caturdasyām rātrāv asya purocanah, bhavanasya tava dvāri pradàsyati hutāsanam, mātrā saha pradagdhavyàh pāṇḍavāh puruṣarṣabhā, iti vyavasitam pārtha dhārtarāṣṭrāsya me śrutam, kiñcic ca vidurenokto mleccha-vācāsi pāṇḍava, tyayā ca tat tathety uktam etad viśvāsa kāraṇam*: on the fourteenth evening of the dark fortnight, Purocana will put fire in the door of your house. 'The Pandavas are leaders of the people, and they are to be burned to death with their mother.' This, Pārtha (Yudhiṣṭira), is the determined plan of Dhṛtarāṣṭra's son, as I have heard it. When you were leaving the city, Vidura spoke a few words to you in the dialect of the mlecchas, and you replied to him, 'So be it'. I say this to gain your trust.(*MBh.* 1.135.4-6). This passage shows that there were two categories of Aryans distinguished by language and ethnicity, Yudhiṣṭira and Vidura. Both are aryas, who could speak mlecchas' language; Dhṛtarāṣṭra and his people are NOT aryas only because of their behaviour.

According to the Great Epic, Mlecchas lived on islands: "*sa sarvān mleccha nṛpatin sāgara dvīpa vāsinah, aram āhāryàm àsa ratnāni vividhāni ca, andana aguru vastrāṇi maṇi muktam anuttamam, kāñcanam rajatam vajram vidrumam ca mahādhanam*: (Bhima) arranged for all the mleccha kings, who dwell on the ocean islands, to bring varieties of gems, sandalwood, aloe, garments, and incomparable jewels and pearls, gold, silver, diamonds, and extremely valuable coral… great wealth." (MBh. 2.27.25-27).

A series of articles and counters had appeared in the *Journal of the Economic and social history of the Orient*, Vol.XXI, Pt.II, Elizabeth C.L. During Caspers and A. Govindankutty countering R.Thapar's dravidian hypothesis for the locations of Meluhha, Dilmun and Makan; Thapar's A Possible identification of Meluhha, Dilmun, and Makan appeared in the journal Vol. XVIII, Part I locating these on India's west coast. Bh. Krishnamurthy defended Thapar on linguistic grounds in Vol. XXVI, Pt. II: *mel-u-kku = highland, west; *teLmaN (=pure earth) ~ dilmun; *makant = male child (Skt. vīra =male offspring.[310]

The reference to gems, pearls and corals evokes the semi-precious and precious stones, such as carnelian and agate, of Gujarat traded with Mesopotamian civilization. According to Sumerian records from the Agade Period (Sargon, 2373-2247 BC), Sumerian merchants traded with people from (at least) three named foreign places: Dilmun (now identified as the island of Bahrain in the Persian Gulf); Magan (a port on the coastline between the head of the Persian Gulf and the mouth of the Sindhu river); and Meluhha. Mentions of trade with

Meluhha become frequent in Ur III period (2168-2062 BCE) and Larsa dynasty (2062- 1770 BCE). To the end of the Sarasvati Civilization period, the trade declines dramatically attesting to Meluhha being the Sarasvati Civilization. By Ur III Period, Meluhhan workers residing in Sumeria had Sumerian names, leading to a comment: '…three hundred years after the earliest textually documented contact between Meluhha and Mesopotamia, the references to a distinctly foreign commercial people have been replaced by an ethnic component of Ur III society' This is an economic presence of Meluhhan traders maintaining their own village for a considerable span of time.[311]

The epic also refers to the pāṇḍava Sahadeva's conquest of several islands in the sea with mleccha inhabitants.

Bronze Age Meluhha, smithy/lapidary documents, takṣat vāk, incised speech

Seals and tablets of the sites of Rann of Kutch and even a huge hoarding at Dholavira are smithy/lapidary documents which are catalogs of stone- and metal-ware made by Meluhha-speaking artisans of Bronze Age. Indus Writing deployed on these catalogs encodes Meluhha (Mleccha) speech sounds.

A reference also to the salty marshes of Rann of Kutch in Gujarat (and also, perhaps, the Makran coast, south of Karachi), may also be surmised, where settlements and fortifications such as Amri Nal, Allahdino, Dholavira (Kotda) Sur-kota-da, and Kanmer have been excavated – close to the Sarasvati River Basin as the River traversed towards the Arabian ocean.

At Shikarpur were found, in addition to an inscribed square terracotta tablet, two terracotta sealings with possible textile (?) marks or impressions of threat and knot, on the obverse. Thumb-nail impressions, like crescent marks are found all around one seealing which also shows a one-horned young bull joined with the heads of a bull and an antelope looking backwards (See d in Figure). A second sealing has impressions from three different inscribed seals.

The legible glyphs on seal (a) in the Figure are:

A warrior glyph.

Three linear strokes, followed by a horn glyph

Read rebus:

bhaṭa 'warrior'. Rebus: *bhaṭa* 'furnace'

kolom 'three. Rebus: *kolami* 'smithy, forge'.

kōṭ 'horn' Rebus: *khoṭa* 'ingot forged, alloy' Vikalpa: *koḍ* 'horn' Rebus: *koḍ* 'workshop'.

The thumb-nail U shaped impressions on the Shikarpur sealings may denote:

U Glyph: *baṭhu* m. 'large pot in which grain is parched.'

Rebus: *baṭi, bhaṭi* 'furnace' (H.) Rebus: *baṭa* = a kind of iron (G.) bhaṭa 'furnace' (G.) baṭa = kiln (Santali). bhaṭa = an oven, kiln, furnace (Santali) baṭhi furnace for smelting ore (the same as kuṭhi) (Santali) bhaṭa = an oven, kiln, furnace; make an oven, a furnace; iṭa bhaṭa = a brick kiln; kun:kal bhaṭa a potter's kiln; cun bhaṭa = a lime kiln; cun tehen dobon bhaṭaea = we shall prepare the lime kiln today (Santali); bhaṭa 'furnace' (G.) baṭa = kiln (Santali); bhaṭṭha -- m.n. ' gridiron (Pkt.) baṭhu large cooking fire' baṭhī f. 'distilling furnace'; L. bhaṭṭh m. 'grain— parcher's oven', bhaṭṭhī f. 'kiln, distillery', awāṇ. bhaṭh; P. bhaṭṭh m., ṭhī f. 'furnace', bhaṭṭhā m. 'kiln'; S. bhaṭṭhī keṇī 'distil (spirits)'. (CDIAL 9656)

Shikarpur 2009. Terracotta inscribed square tablet and terracott sealings with inscribed seal impressions.

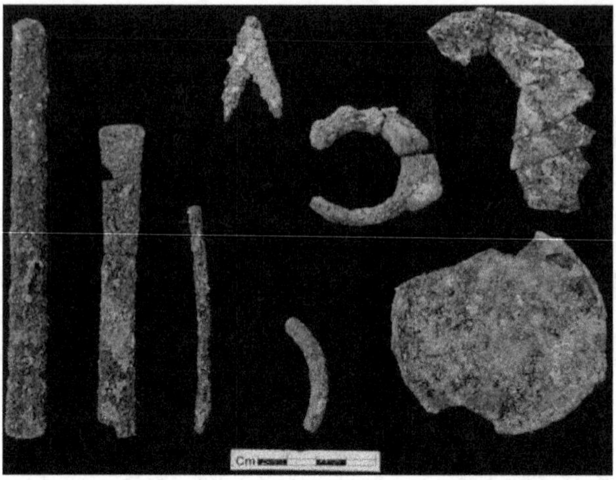

Shikarpur 2009: Copper implements.

Khirsara. During 1976-77 exploration, an Archaeological Survey of India official discovered a big cubical weight, chunks of pottery, sprinklers and spouts of red polished ware from the site. In December 2009, a team from the Vadodara division of the Archaeological Survey of India started excavation at this site after the discovery of a 300 m² fortification wall.[312]

A bar seal with writing in Harappan script. Only one other bar seal figures in the total of 11 seals found so far in Khirsara. The entire metalware catalog of the inscription on the tablet reads:

meḍ 'iron'+ tagaram'tin'+ *dul aduru* 'cast native metal'.+ *ayah, ayas* 'metal' + *aduru* = ore taken from the mine and not subjected to melting in a furnace+ *dhātu* 'mineral'+ *kolimi kanka* 'smithy/forge account (scribe)'.

Thus, the smithy forge account is for iron, tin, cast native metal, unsmelted native metal, metal (alloy), mineral.

A bar seal with writing in Harappan script. Only one other bar seal figures in the total of 11 seals found so far in Khirsara.

Rebus readings of Indus writing (from r.): मेंढरी [mēṇḍharī] *f* A piece in architecture. मेंधला [mēndhalā] *m* In architecture. A common term for the two upper arms of a double चौकठ (door-frame) connecting the two. Called also मेंढरी & घोडा. It answers to खिली the name of the two lower arms or connections. (Marathi) meḍhi 'pillar'. Rebus: *meḍ* iron'.

tagaraka 'tabernae montana' Rebus: *tagaram* 'tin' (Malayalam)

sangaḍa 'bangles' (Pali). Rebus: *sangaḍa* 'lathe, furnace'. saghaḍī = furnace (G.) Rebus: jaṅgaḍ 'entrustment articles' *sangaḍa* 'association, guild'. dula 'pair' Rebus: dul 'casting'.

aḍar 'harrow' Rebus: aduru = gaṇiyinda tegadu karagade iruva aduru = ore taken from the mine and not subjected to melting in a furnace (Kannada) dula 'pair' Rebus: dul 'casting'. Thus the composite glyph reds *dul aduru* 'cast native metal'.

ayo 'fish' (Mu.) Rebus: *aya* = iron (G.); *ayah, ayas* = metal (Skt.)

aḍar 'harrow' Rebus: aduru = gan.iyinda tegadu karagade iruva aduru = ore taken from the mine and not subjected to melting in a furnace (Kannada)

ḍato = claws of crab (Santali); dhātu = mineral (Skt.), dhatu id. (Santali)

kanka 'rim-of-jar' Rebus: furnace account (scribe); khanaka 'miner' (Skt.). kolom 'three' Rebus: kolami 'smithy, forge' (Telugu) The ligature of three strokes with rim-of-jar hieroglyph thus reads: *kolimi kanka* 'smithy/forge account (scribe)'.

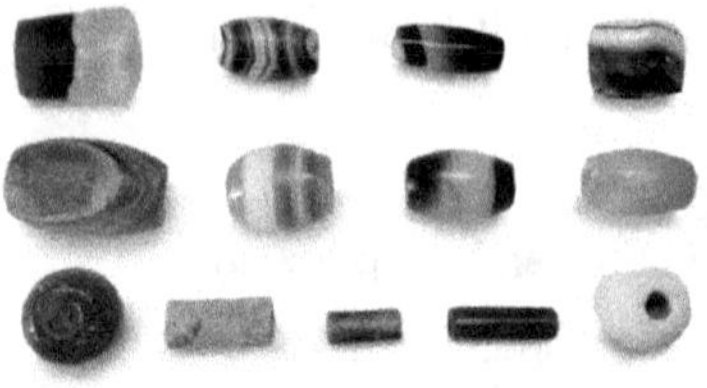

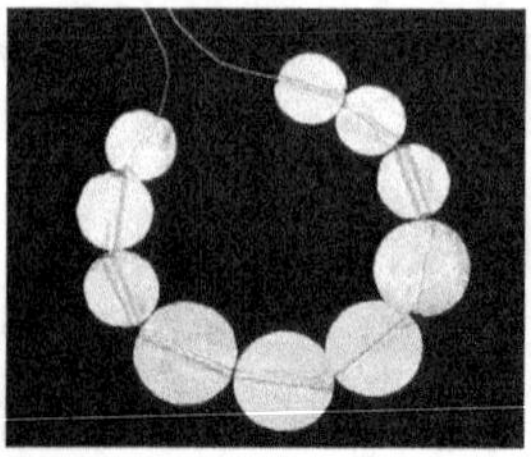

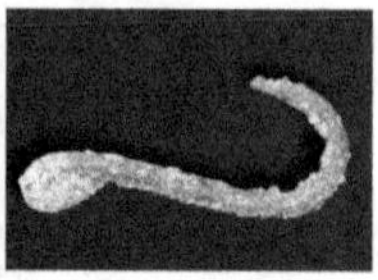

Khirsara. Beads.

Khirasra. Disc-shaped gold beads found in a pot.

Khirasra. A copper fish-hook found in a trench.Dholavira. A chessboard (on the stone slab at right) and an architectural member that resembles a Sivalinga.

Dholavira. A grinding stone at the site museum.

Kurd. *bard* ' stone '. 1. Gy. eur. *bar*, SEeur. *bạị* ' stone ', pal. *wăṭ*, *wŭṭ* ' stone, cliff '; Ḍ. *boṭ* m. ' stone ', Ash. Wg. *wāṭ*, Kt. *woṭ*, Dm. *bɔ̄ṭ*, Tir. *baṭ*, Niṅg. *bōt*, Woṭ. *baṭ* m., Gmb. *wāṭ*; Gaw. *wāṭ* ' stone, millstone '; Kal.rumb. *bat* ' stone ' (*bad -- váṣ* ' hail '), Kho. *bort*, Bshk. *baṭ*, Tor. *bāṭ*, Mai. (Barth) "*bhāt*" NTS xviii 125, Sv. *bāṭ*, Phal. *bāṭ*; Sh.gil. *băṭ* m. ' stone ', koh.*băṭṭ* m., jij. *baṭ*, pales. *baṭ* ' millstone '; K. *waṭh*, dat. *°ṭas* m. ' round stone ', *vüṭü* f. ' small do. '; L. *vaṭṭā* m. ' stone ', khet. *vaṭ* ' rock '; P. *baṭṭ* m. ' a partic. weight ', *vaṭṭā,ba°* m. ' stone ', *vaṭṭī* f. ' pebble '; WPah.bhal. *baṭṭ* m. ' small round stone '; Or. *bāṭi* ' stone '; Bi. *baṭṭā* ' stone roller for spices, grindstone '. -- With unexpl. -- *ṭṭh* -- : Sh.gur.*baṭṭh* m. ' stone ', gil. *baṭhā´* m. ' avalanche of stones ', *baṭhúi* f. ' pebble ' (suggesting also an orig. **vartuka* -- which Morgenstierne sees in Kho. place -- name *bortuili*, 2. Paš.lauṛ. *wāṛ*, kuṛ. *wō* ' stone ', Shum. *wāṛ*.(CDIAL 11348).

Elephant glyph: ibha 'elephant' (Skt.) Rebus: ib 'iron' (Santali) ibbo 'merchant'

Seal. Kanmer.

Epigraph

(Gujarati) కరటి [karaṭi] *karaṭi.* [Skt.] n. An elephant. ఏనుగు (Telugu) Rebus: *kharādī* ' turner' (Gujarati)

ayo 'fish' (Mu.); *kaṇḍa* 'arrow'; *kaṇḍa, kāṇḍa, kāḍe* = an arrow (Ka.) *kāṇḍ kāṇ kōṇ, ko~_, ka~_ṛ* arrow (Pas'.);*ka~_ḍī* arrow (G.) Cf. *kaṇṭam* 'arrow' (Ta.) Rebus: *ayaskāṇḍa* "a quantity of iron, excellent iron" (Pāṇ gaṇ)

sal "stake, spike, splinter, thorn, difficulty" (H.);

Rebus: *sal* 'workshop' (Santali); *śāla* id. (Skt.)

kundau, *kundhi* corner (Santali) *kuṇḍa* corner (S.)*:* *khoṇḍ* square (Santali) *khuṇṭa2 ' corner '. 2. *kuṇṭa -- 2. [Cf. *khōñca --] 1. Phal. *khun* ' corner '; H. *khũṭ* m. ' corner, direction ' (→ P. *khũṭ* f. ' corner, side '); G. *khũṭṛī* f. ' angle '. <-> X kōṇa -- : G. *khuṇ* f., *khū̃ṇɔ* m. ' corner '. 2. S. *kuṇḍa* f. ' corner '; P. *kũṭ* f. ' corner, side ' (← H.).(CDIAL 3898).

ಕುಂಡ kuṇḍa. = ... A hole in the ground, a pit. 2, a pot (..., ..., etc. Mr. 209; see B. 3, 80). 3, a pool,

ಕೊಂಡ kŏṇḍa. Tbh. of ಕುಂಡ (Śmd. 355; Abh. P. 10, after 183; My.). — ... N. among Brâhmaṇas (S. Mhr.). — ... A cart used at the kŏṇḍa feast (My.). — ... A feast in honor of Vîrabhadra at which Liṅgavantas carry an idol of Vîrabhadra and dance with it on live coals in a pit (My.).

Allograph: kunta 'lance, spear' (Kannada)

Rebus: kunda1 m. ' a turner's lathe ' lex. [Cf. *cunda -- 1] N. *kũdnu* ' to shape smoothly, smoothe, carve, hew ', *kũduwā* ' smoothly shaped '; A. *kund* ' lathe ', *kundiba* ' to turn and smooth in a lathe ', *kundowā* ' smoothed and rounded '; B. *kũd* ' lathe ', *kũdā, kõdā* ' to turn in a lathe '; Or. *kū̆nda* ' lathe ', *kũdibā, kũd°* ' to turn ' (→ Drav. Kur. *kũd* ' lathe '); Bi.*kund* ' brassfounder's lathe '; H. *kunnā* ' to shape on a lathe ', *kuniyā* m. ' turner ', *kunwā* m. (CDIAL 3295). kundakara m. ' turner ' W. [Cf. *cundakāra -- : kunda -- 1, kará -- 1] A. *kundār*, B. *kũdār, °ri,* Or. *kundāru*; H. *kũderā* m. ' one who works a lathe, one who scrapes

', °rī f., *kūdernā* ' to scrape, plane, round on a lathe '.(CDIAL 3297). *Ta.* kuntaṉam interspace for setting gems in a jewel; fine gold (< Te.). *Ka.* kundaṇa setting a precious stone in fine gold; fine gold; kundana fine gold. *Tu.* kundaṇa pure gold. *Te.* kundanamu fine gold used in very thin foils in setting precious stones; setting precious stones with fine gold. (DEDR 1725). **कोंद** *kōnda* 'engraver, lapidary setting or infixing gems' (Marathi)

Allograph: *Ka.* kunda a pillar of bricks, etc. *Tu.* kunda pillar, post. *Te.* Kunda id. *Malt.* kunda block, log. ? Cf. Ta. kantu pillar, post.(DEDR 1723). *கற்கந்து kaṟ-kantu* , *n.* < கல் +. Stone pillar; கற்றூண். கற்கந்தும் எய்ப்போத்தும் . . . அனையார் (இறை. 2, உரை, 27). Rebus: kunda 'lahe', 'turner'.

Ring-stones around a pillar with coping stones carved in high-relief, in a building-structure as at Dholavira

Ka. kunda a pillar of bricks, etc. *Tu.* kunda pillar, post. *Te.* kunda id. *Malt.* kunda block, log. ? Cf. Ta. kantu pillar, post.(DEDR 1723). Rebus: *kundār, kōdār* 'turner'.

kōlam 'Ornamental figures drawn on floor' Rebus: kolmi 'smithy'

 *koṭho* 'warehouse' (Gujarati)(CDIAL 3546). kanka 'account, scribe'.

Allograph: kōl 'stick' (Tamil) Rebus: kol 'working in iron'. Hence, kollan 'blacksmith, artificer' (Tamil)

m0457At 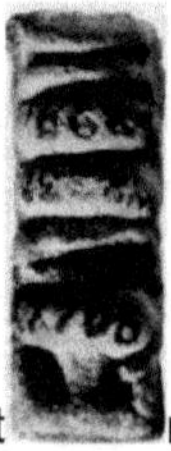m0457Bt m0457Et

m0458At m0458Bt 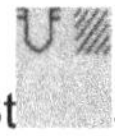3227

m0459At m0459Bt 3225

m0460At m0460Bt 3228

m0461At m0461Bt 2806 Pict-73

m0462At m0462Bt 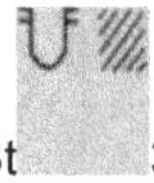3215

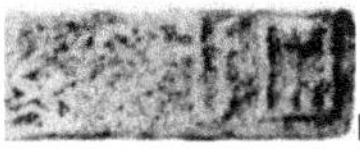m0463At m0463Bt 2813

The reconstruction of the Indus and Ghaggar-Hakra-Nara beddings[313] is

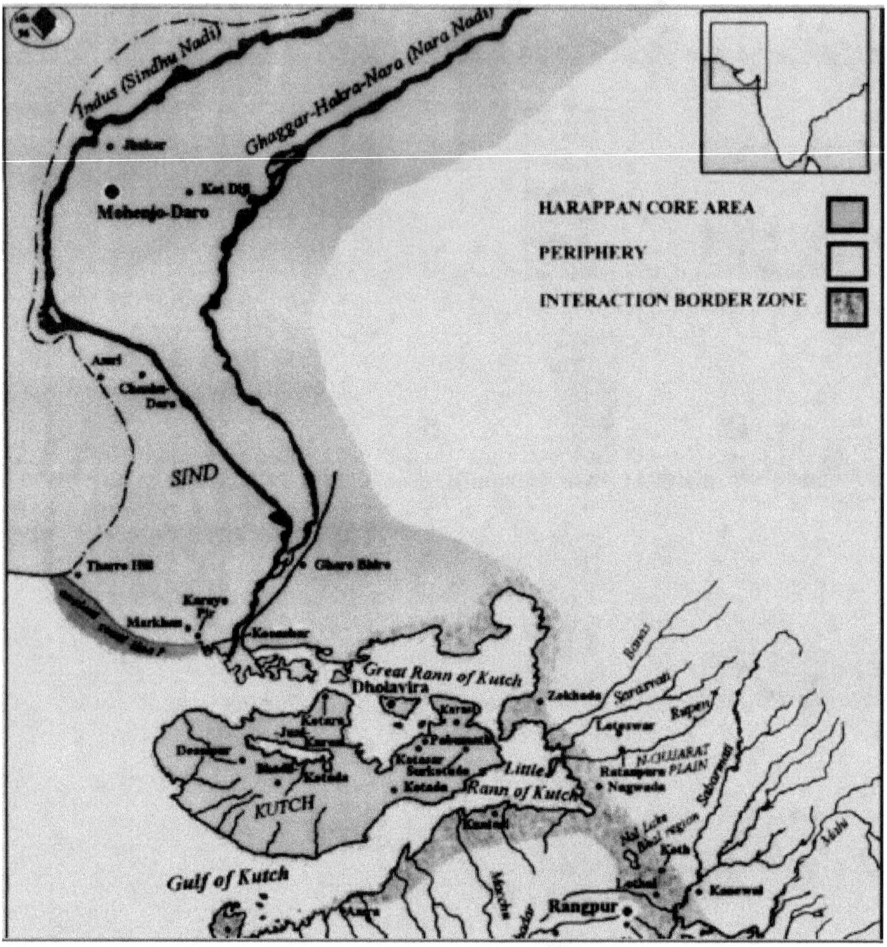

according to Flam, 1981, 1993. "According to L. Flam, not one but two rivers were flowing into the Arabian Sea during the Bronze Age: a Sindhu branch (Indus) and the Nara Nadi (Ghaggar-Hakra-Nara), the latter presently dried up. Both rivers were discharging in the east part of the delta, north of the Great Rann of Kutch. The ancient coast line of the delta is still in debate... Kutch... was an island surrounded by tidal sea in late Holocene times." (p.89)

"The Citadel fortification walls on east, north and west had entry gates. Just near the door, chambers were built at a height with roofs supported on pillars, parts of which can be seen even today. The main through-way in the citadel was segregated in three sections, marked by means of 2 polished pillars. In one of the two north gate chambers, archaeologists found a huge name board written with 10 Indus script glyphs or symbols. Each of this was made from Gypsum and was 15 inches high. Total length of this board was about 3 meters and the gypsum symbols were embedded in wood, which had rotted away later, leaving only the symbols intact. "[314]

[quote] Kachchh peninsula and the Great Rann

“The description of the Rann by A.B.Wynne in GSI Memoir Vol.9 on Geology of Kutch (1872) reads, “Its flat unbroken surface of dark silt, baked by the sun and blistered by saline encrustations, is varied only by the mirage, and great tracts of dazzlingly white salt or extensive but shallow flashes of concentrated brine; its intense silent desolation is oppressive, and save by chance a slowly passing caravan of camels or some herd of wild asses even less likely to be seen there is nothing beyond a few bleached skeletons of cattle, salt dried fish, or remains of insects brought down by floods, to maintain a distant and dismal connection between it and life which it is utterly unfitted to support”. Nothing seems to have changed in this great desolate patch of land since this passage was written in 1872 except that it is now much more difficult to wander around with abandon for security reasons.

“The Kachchh region presents an interesting case of very recent tectonic adjustments and consequential environmental changes of far reaching anthropo-geographic significance. The great Rann of today was an old inlet of the sea. A river named Puran, a distributory of Indus, formerly flowed across the western Rann to the sea along the Kori Creek, which was navigable from Lakhpat to Ali Bandar in 1808. The records mention of a fertile tract known as Saira bordering Puran river, which, according to Burnes (1835), included the country between

Lakhpat and Mundhan. The river in its upstream reaches passed into eastern Nara and this into the bed of Hakra, the lost river of the Indian desert. Fed by Sutlej and some other tributaries, it carried a powerful discharge to the sea. This system of drainage continued to flow between 8th and 16th centuries AD. Later, Sutlej gradually became a part of the Indus system, and by 1798; Hakra was merely a dry channel. The highly diminished flow in Puran was from an effluent of the Indus, over which embankments at Mora and Ali Bandar were constructed. In 1826, by some breach in the banks of Indus, a heavy discharge into the course of Puran swept away all the man-made embankments.

"The Kachchh Earthquake of 16 June 1819 had a profound effect in the entire peninsula and brought in some spectacular terrain deformation in the Great Rann. Burnes (1835), in his account of the catastrophe writes, "By the severe shock, hundreds of people perished and every fortified stronghold was shaken to its foundation. Innumerable wells and rivulets were changed from fresh water to salt water. The Brick Fort of Sindhri was overwhelmed at once with a tremendous inundation of water from the Ocean, converting the area into a 25 km long lake". A remnant of Sindhri lake still exists. [unquote] [315]

"Historical accounts suggest that the rann was occupied by a shallow navigable sea, which is confirmed by the presence of several archaeological sites belonging to the Harappan civilization, including the port town of Dholavira located on the Khadir Island. Presently also, a large part of the Rann surface gets inundated by storm tides from the west and the rest by annual monsoon precipitation." Maurya, DM, et al, Subsurface sediment characteristics of the Great Rann of Kachchh, western India based on preliminary evaluation of textural analysis of two continuous sediment cores, in: *Current Science*, Vol. 104, No. 8, 25 April 2013, p. 1071.

"Malik and others also highlighted the evolution of the delta complex of the Sarasvati and other extinct rivers of northwest India and the role of tectonic movements and aridity. In their recent investigations of the Rann of Kachtchh, they proposed that the formation of the delta complex system was a result of contribution of three rivers -- Proto Shatadru (Hakra),

Saraswati and Drishadvati Rivers. They also recorded evidence of a fragmentary delta near the western flank of the Nagar Parker Hill joining the relict channel of the Sukri, a branch of the Luni River. This is identified with the ancient Drishadvati. A sequence of neo-tectonics around 3500 to 3000 years ago caused a significant decrease in the flow of water in the Sarasvati and Drishadvati, while the Shatadru was diverted towards Indus.[316]

Dholavira. Ring-stone used tohold a pillar. Inside castle-wall.

Dholavira. Polished stone pillars

Dholavira (Kotda).The two 'sthambs', or polished pillars, which are claimed to resemble Sivalingas, in the citadel.

[quote] Bisht was non-committal when asked if the two "sthambs" found at the Dholavira site and the phallus-like stone artefacts excavated there but kept in

Purana Qila, New Delhi, looked like Sivalingas. Nauriyal said, separately: "They definitely resemble male organs. What the concept was, it is difficult to comment. Whether they were used for worship, magic, ritual or as a good omen, we do not know." On what led to the collapse of Dholavira, Nauriyal said: "The snap in the trade relationship with foreign countries, possibly." It was largely maritime trade. Goods could not be traded any more. "There must have been a host of factors and the economic factor must have been one of them," he said. [unquote][317]

These pillars evoke the imageries of a festival which is celebrated even today by Lingavantas, particularly in Karnataka.

These pillars at Dholavira could be a depiction of pillars of flame as Sivalinga.

Kalibangan: Terracotta. S'ivalinga (ASI)[318]

Plate X [c] Lingam in situ in Trench Ai[319] Lingam, grey sandstone in situ, Harappa, Trench Ai, Mound F, Pl. X (c) (After Vats). "In an earthenware jar, No. 12414, recovered from Mound F, Trench IV, Square I... in this jar, six lingams were found along with some tiny pieces of shell, a unicorn seal, an oblong grey sandstone block with polished surface, five stone pestles, a stone palette, and a block of chalcedony..."

The worship of the Shiva-Linga originated from the famous hymn in the Atharva-Veda Samhitâ sung in praise of the Yupa-Stambha, the sacrificial post. In that hymn a description is found of the beginningless and endless Stambha or Skambha, and it is shown that the said Skambha is put in place of the eternal Brahman. As afterwards the Yajna (sacrificial) fire, its smoke, ashes, and flames, the Soma plant, and the ox that used to carry on its back the wood for the Vedic sacrifice gave place to the conceptions of the brightness of Shiva's body, his tawny matted-hair, his blue throat, and the riding on the bull of the Shiva, and so on — just so, the Yupa-Skambha gave place in time to the Shiva-Linga, and was deified to the high Divinity of Shri Shankara.

The sukta begins:

Skambha Sukta (Atharva Veda X-7)

kásminn áṅge tápo asyādhi tiṣṭhati kásminn áṅga ṛtám asyādhy āhitam

kvà vratáṃ kvà śraddhāsya tiṣṭhati kásminn áṅge satyám asya prátiṣṭhitam

Trans. Which of his members is the seat of Fervour: Which is the base of Ceremonial Order? Where in him standeth Faith? Where Holy Duty? Where, in what part of him is truth implanted?

Etyma from Meluhha (Mleccha) point to *khoṇḍ* as a square (Santali) , the type of square on which two pillars are found in Dholavira. Rebus: *kõdā* 'to turn in a lathe' (Bengali). कोंद *kōnda* 'engraver, lapidary setting or infixing gems' (Marathi) *kũdar* 'brass-worker, turner'. Thus, *koṇḍ habba* is a celebration of the life-activity of the lapidaries/smiths of the civilization: *kõdā* meaning 'lathe-turning' for making perforated beads or for turning/forging metalware..This may explain why in the tablets showing procession as a festival ceremony, two hieroglyphs are carried as standards: both hieroglyphs relate to the one-horned young bull and the standard device (lathe). The related words reading hieroglyphs rebus from Meluhha (Mleccha) speech are: *kõdā sãgāḍī* Rebus words denote: 'metals turner-joiner (forge); worker on a lathe' – associates (guild)'.

This *khoṇḍ* 'square' could have been used to celebrate a festival which is called *koṇḍahabba.* The adorants walk on a bed of burning embers in fulfilment of their vows. Sucha bed of burning embers might have been laid on the square linking these two pillars of Dholavira shaped like sivalingas, symbolising pillars of fire. The significance attached to th word *khoṇḍ* may explain the local name for Dholavira: *Kotḍa.*

It is notable that a smithy was a temple for Meluhhans (Mlecchas). This is evidenced by the lexeme kole.l of Kota language which means 'smithy' and also 'temple'. Thus, a smithy is a temple -- kole.l Such a gestalt relatable to the lapidaries and smiths -- miners/metalworkers may explain why the *agamas* prescribe the procedures for invoking divinities in sculptures in a *sanctum* of a temple, adorned with metallic weapons on their multiple hands.

It is, thus, possible to hypothesise that the religious practices of the people of the civilization at Mohenjodaro, Harappa, Kalibangan (where a terracotta Sivalinga has been found) and Dholavira are represented by the continuum of *koṇḍahabba* festivals celebrated by Lingavantas.

Turner

kundau, *kundhi* corner (Santali) *kuṇḍa* corner (S.)*: khoṇḍ* square (Santali) *khuṇṭa2 ' corner '. 2. *kuṇṭa -- 2. [Cf. *khōñca --] 1. Phal. *khun* ' corner '; H. *khũṭ* m. ' corner, direction ' (→ P. *khũṭ* f. ' corner, side '); G. *khũṭṛī* f. ' angle '. <-> X kōṇa -- : G. *khuṇ* f., *khũ˘ṇɔ* m. ' corner '. 2. S. *kuṇḍa* f. ' corner '; P. *kũṭ* f. ' corner, side ' (← H.).(CDIAL 3898).

ಕುಂಡ kuṇḍa. = ಕೊಂಡ. A hole in the ground, a pit. 2, a pot (ಮಡಕೆ, ಕುಡಿಕೆ, etc. Mr. 209; see B. 3, 80). 3, a pool,

ಕೊಂಡ kŏṇḍa. Tbh. of ಕುಂಡ (Śmd. 355; Abh. P. 10, after 183; My.). — ಕೊಂಡಸ್ಥ. -ಅಸ್ಥ. N. among Brâhmaṇas (S. Mhr.). — ಕೊಂಡಬಂಡಿ. A cart used at the kŏṇḍa feast (My.). — ಕೊಂಡಹಬ್ಬ. A feast in honor of Vîrabhadra at which Liṅgavantas carry an idol of Vîrabhadra and dance with it on live coals in a pit (My.).

Evidence for Sivalinga is provided in other sites (Mohenjodaro and Harappa) of the civilization:

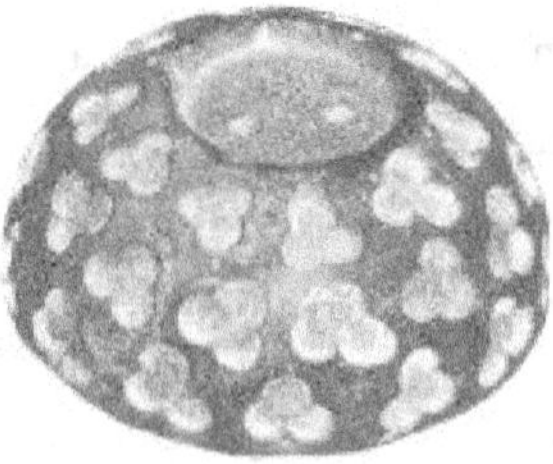

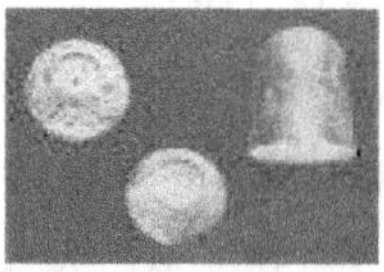

Tre-foil inlay decorated base (for linga icon?); smoothed, polished pedestal of dark red stone; National Museum of Pakistan, Karachi; After Mackay 1938: I, 411; II, pl. 107:35; Parpola, 1994, p. 218.

Two decorated bases and a lingam, Mohenjodaro.

Lingam, grey sandstone *in situ*, Harappa, Trench Ai, Mound F, Pl. X (c) (After

Vats). "In an earthenware jar, No. 12414, recovered from Mound F, Trench IV, Square I... in this jar, six lingams were found along with some tiny pieces of shell, a unicorn seal, an oblong grey sandstone block with polished surface, five stone pestles, a stone palette, and a block of chalcedony..." (Vats,MS, *Excavations at Harappa*, p. 370)

"Excavations conducted at the site for two field seasons (2003-04 and 2004-05) have revealed cultural remains of Harappan culture. The excavation has brought to light three-fold division of town planning i.e. Citadel, Middle Town and Lower Town each being fortified. Important structural findings include mud platform of 03 m height, two stadiums (one for commoners and the other for aristocrats), pillared hall and chamber on fortification wall and gateways. Besides, a good number of antiquities were discovered including a seal with unicorn and 8 letters." (Not illustrated) http://asi.nic.in/asi_exca_2005_gujarat.asp

Desalpur (Gunthli)

Desalpur seal. Desalpur sealing.
kaṇḍa kanka 'rim of jar' (Santali) kan.d.a 'furnace, fire-altar' (Santali); khanaka 'miner' karNaka 'scribe' (Skt.)

sal stake, spike, splinter, thorn, difficulty (H.); Rebus: sal 'workshop' (Santali)

aḍar 'harrow'; rebus: aduru 'native metal, unsmelted' (Ka.) kolom = cutting, graft; to graft, engraft, prune; kolma hoṛo = a variety of the paddy plant (Desi)(Santali.) kolom 'three' (Mu.) Rebus: kolami 'furnace, smithy' (Te.)

Text of Desalpur seal1. 9071.

sal stake, spike, splinter, thorn, difficulty (H.); Rebus: sal 'workshop' (Santali)

kuṭi = a slice, a bit, a small piece (Santali.Bodding) Rebus: kuṭhi 'iron smelter furnace' (Santali)

ayo 'fish'; rebus: ayas 'metal, iron' (Pan.Skt.) dol 'likeness'; rebus: dul 'cast (metal)' (Santali)

ranku 'antelope'; rebus: ranku 'tin' (Santali)

koṇḍa-miṇdi eyelid (Go.)(DEDR 4864). Rebus: meḍ 'iron' (Santali. Mundari) koṇḍa 'turned in lathe'.

kaṇḍa kanka 'rim of jar' (Santali) kaṇḍa 'furnace, fire-altar' (Santali); khanaka 'miner' karNaka 'scribe' (Skt.)

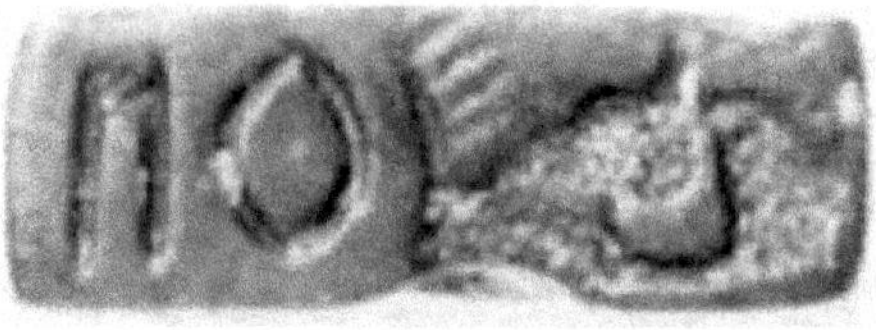

Desalpur. Seal2.

ranku 'liquid measure'; rebus: ranku 'tin' (Santali)

khaḍā 'circumscribe' (M.); Rebs: khaḍā 'nodule (ore), stone' (M.)

pajhaṛ = to sprout from a root (Santali) Rebus: pasra 'smithy' (Santali) Vikalpa: tagaraka 'tabernae montana' Rebus: tagarak 'tin' (Malayalam)

Apart from basic Harappan pottery, two script bearing seals, one of steatite and other of copper were also found; script bearing terrecotta sealings was also found.[320]

Kathāsaritsāgara[321] associates mleccha with Sind. Mleccha kings paid tributes of sandalwood, aloe, cloth, gems, pearls, blankets, gold, silver and valuable corals.

The pictorial motifs and the epigraphs of the Kanmer seal and Gola Dhoro (Bagasra) seals and sealing have been decoded as metalsmith guild tokens. Both sites are in Rann of Kutch, Gujarat.

For a small-sized settlement of less than 2 hectares, stunning arrays of copper artefacts were found: A copper vessel containing eight bangles, an axe probably used for recycling precious metal, copper knives with bone handles have been found. A unique copper battle-axe (parashu) is also an interesting find from this area and the small size of the battle-axe suggests it as presumably used for ritualistic purpose. Heavily tampered clay crucibles with copper adhering in them have been found, suggesting that they might have been used for copper smelting.

The pictorial glyphs and the sign glyphs together constitute the listing of smithy/forge/metalguild workshop repertoire.[322]

Nakula conquered western parts of Bhāratavarṣa teeming with mleccha (MBh.V.49.26 : *yah pratīcīm diśam cakre vaśe mlecchagaṇāyutām sa tatra nakulo yoddhā citrayodhī vyavasthitah*). Bṛhatsamhitā XIV.21 refers to lawless mleccha who inhabited the west: *nirmaryādā mlecchā ye paścimadiksthit āsteca.* A Buddhist chronicle, *ārya Manjuśrī Mūlakalpa*[323] associates pratyanta (contiguous)with mlecchadeśa in western Bhāratavarṣa: *paścimām diśīm āsṛtya rājāno mriyate tadā ye 'pi pratyantavāsinyo mlecchataskarajīvinah.* (trans. 'Then (under a certain astrological combination) the kings who go to the west die; also inhabitants of pratyanta live like the mlecchas and taskara.')

This metaphor defines the region fit for yajna. This metaphor also explains the movements of mleccha, such as kamboja-yavana, pārada-pallava along the Indian Ocean Rim as sea-faring merchants from Meluhha. This parallels the hindu-bauddha continuum exemplified by the Mathura lion capital withśrivatsa and Angkor Wat (Nagara vātika) as the largest Viṣṇu mandiram in the world, together with celebration of Bauddham in many parts of central, eastern and southeastern Asian continent. Mleccha were at no stage described in any text as people belonging to one ethnic, religious or linguistic group. This self-imposed restriction evidenced by all writers of the early Indian cultural tradition – Veda, Bauddha, Jaina alike – is of fundamental significance in understanding that mleccha constituted the core of the people on the banks of Rivers Sarasvati and Sindhu and were the principal architects, artisans, workers, and people, in general, of the Sarasvati-Sindhu Civilization throughout its stages of evolution through phases in modes of production – pastoral, agricultural, industrial – and interactions with neighbors, trading in surplus food products and artefacts generated and sharing cultural attributes/characteristics.

Various terms are used to describe mleccha social groups and communities: *pratyantadeś'a* (*Arthaśāstra* VII.10.16), *paccantimā janapada* (*Vinaya Piṭaka* V.13.12, vol. I, p. 197), *aṭavi, aṭavika.*[324] Some mleccha lived in border areas and forests, e.g.*pratyanta nṛpatibhir* (frontier kings: JF Fleet, CII, vol. II, 'Allahabad Posthumous Pillar Inscription of Samudragupta, text line 22, p. 116) cf. Arthaśāstra– a 4th century BCE text — I.12.21; VII.14.27; XIV.1.2; *mleccha jāti* are: *bheda,kirāta, śabara, pulinda*: *Amarakośa* II.10.20, a fifth century CE text).

In many Persian inscriptions Yauna, Gandhāra and Saka occur together. [For e.g., DC Sircar, *Selected Inscriptions*, no.2 'Persepolis Inscription on Dārayavahuṣ (Darius c. 522-486 BCE),' lines 12-13, 18, p.7; no. 5, 'Perseplis Inscription of Khshayārshā (Xerxes c. 486-465)', lines 23, 25-6, p. 12]. Thus, *yavana*may be a reference to people settled in the northwest Bhāratavarṣa (India).

There are references to Mleccha (that is, *śaka, Yavana, Kamboja, Pahlava*) in Bāla Kāṇḍa of the *Valmiki Rāmāyaṇa* (1.54.21-23; 1.55.2-3). *Taih asit samvrita bhūmih śakaih-Yavana miśritaih || 1.54-21 || taih taih Yavana-Kamboja barbarah ca akulii kritaah || 1-54-23 || tasya humkaarato jātah Kamboja ravi sannibhah | udhasah tu atha sanjatah Pahlavah śastra panayah || 1-55-2|| yoni deśāt ca Yavanah śakri deśāt śakah tathā | roma kupeṣ u Mlecchah ca Haritah sa*

Kiratakah || 1-55-3 ||.Kāmboja Yavanān caivaśakān paṭṭaṇāni ca | Anvīkṣya Varadān caiva Himavantam vicinvatha || 12 || — (*Rāmāyaṇa* 4.43.12)

The Yavanas here refer to the Bactrian Yavanas (in western Oxus country), and the Sakas here refer to the Sakas of Sogdiana/Jaxartes and beyond. The Vardas are the same as Paradas (*Hindu Polity*, 1978, p 124, Dr K. P. Jayswal; *Goegraphical Data in Early Purana*, 1972, p 165, 55 fn, Dr M. R.Singh). The Paradas were located on river Sailoda in Sinkiang (MBh II.51.12; II.52.13; VI.87.7 etc) and probably as far as upper reaches of river Oxus and Jaxartes (Op cit, p 159-60, Dr M. R.Singh).

Vanaparva of Mahābhārata notes: "......Mlechha (barbaric) kings of the śaka-s, Yavanas, Kambojas, Bahlikas etc shall rule the earth (i.e India) un-rightously in Kaliyuga..." *viparīte tadā loke purvarūpān kṣayasya tat || 34 || bahavo mechchha r\ājānah pṛthivyām manujādhipa | mithyanuśāsinah pāpa mṛṣavadaparāṇah || 35 || āndrah śakah Pulindaśca Yavanaśca narādhipāh | Kamboja Bahlikah śudrastathābhīra narottama* || 36|| MBH 3/188/34-36). Anushasanaparava of Mahābhārata affirms that Mathura, was under the joint military control of the Yavanas and the Kambojas (12/102/5). *Tathā Yavana Kambojā Mathurām abhitaś ca ye ete niyuddhakuśalā dākshiinātyāsicarminah.* Mahābhārata speaks of the Yavanas, Kambojas, Darunas etc as the fierce mleccha from Uttarapatha : *uttaraścāpare mlechchha jana bharatasattama. || 63 || Yavanashcha sa Kamboja Daruna mlechchha jatayah. | — (MBH 6.11.63-64) They are referred to as papakritah (sinful): uttara pathajanmanah kirtayishyami tanapi. | Yauna Kamboja Gandharah Kirata barbaraih saha. || 43 || ete pāpakṛtāstatra caranti prṛthivīmimām. | śvakakabalagridhraṇān sadharmaṇo narādhipa. || 44 ||* — (MBh 12/207/43-44).[325]

Yavana are descendants of Turvaśu, one of the four sons of Yayāti. The sons were to rule over people such as Yavana, Bhoja and Yādava (MBh. 1.80.23-4; Matsya Purāṇa 34.29-30). Yavana, descendants of Turvaśu are noted as meat-eaters, sinful and hence, anārya.[326] These people were brought over the sea safely by Indra (RV 6.20.12). In the Mahābhārata, sons of Anu are noted as mleccha.

Milakkhu means *anārya* (Prākrit). Jaina texts describe two groups of people: *ārya* and *milakkhu* (*Pannavana*, 1.37).

Ṛgveda notes that Yadu and Turvaśa are dāsa (RV 10.62.10):

> *sanema te vasā navya indra pra pūrava stavanta enā yajnaih*
>
> *sapta yat purah śarma śāradīr dadruiśa dhan dāsīh purukutsāya śikṣan*
>
> *tvam vrdha indraprvyarja bhūr varivasyann uśane kāvyāya*
>
> *parā navavāstvam anudeyam mahe pitre dadātha svam napātam*
>
> *tvam dhunir indra dhunimtrṇor āpah sīrā na sravantīh*
>
> *pra yat samudram ati śūra parśi pāraya turvaśam yadum svasti*

RV 6.020.10 (Favoured) by your proection, Indra, we solicit new (wealth); by this adoration men glorify you at sacrifices, for that you have shattered with your bolt the seven cities of śarat, killing the opponents (of sacred rites), killing the opponents (of sacred rites), and giving (their spoils) to Purukutsa. [Men: puravah = manuṣyah; śarat = name of an asura].

RV 6.020.11 Desirous of opulence, you, Indra, have been an ancient benefactor of Us'anas, the son of Kavi; having slain Navavāstva, you have given back his own grandson, who was (fit) to be restored o the grandfather.

RV 6.020.12 You, Indra, who make (your enemies) tremble, have caused the waters, detained by Dhuni, to flow like rushing rivers; so, hero, when, having crossed the ocean, you have reached the shore, you have brought over in safety Turvas'a and Yadu. [*samudram atipraparṣi* = samudram atikramya pratirṇo bhavasi = when you are crossed, having traversed the ocean, you have brought across Turvaśa and Yadu, both standing on the future shore, *samudrapāretiṣṭhantau apārayah*].

Nandana, another commentator of *Mānava Dharma śāstra*. X.45, defines *āryavāc as samskṛtavāc*. Thus, according to Medhātithi, neither habitation nor mleccha speech is the ground for regarding groups as Dasyus, but it is because of their particular names Barbara etc., that they are so regarded. These people were brought over the sea safely by Indra, as noted by this ṛca. This ṛca also notes that Yadu and Turvaśa (are) dāsa; and that Turvaśu is a son of Yayāti. The sons of Yayāti were to rule over people such as Yavana, Bhoja and Yādava. Turvaśu and Yadu crossed the oceans to come into Bhāratavarṣa. In this ṛca., 'samudra' can be interpreted only as an ocean. The ocean crossed by Indra, may be not too far from Sindhu. Sindhu is a 'natural ocean frontier' in *Ṛgveda*. Given the activities of the Meluhha along the Makran Coast (300 km. south of Mehergarh, in the neighbourhood of Karachi), Gulf of Kutch and Gulf of Khambat, (evidence? *Turbinella pyrum* —śankha-bangle found in a woman's grave in Mehergarh, dated to c. 6500 BCE, yes 7th millennium BCE; the type of shell found nowhere else in the world excepting the coastline of Sindhu sāgara upto to the Gulf of Mannar).

The ocean referred to may be the ocean in the Gulf of Kutch and was situated with a number of dvīpas. In places north of Lamgham district, i.e. north bank of river Kabul, near Peshawar were regions known as Mi-li-ku, the frontier of the mleccha lands.[327] *Harivamśa* 85.18-19 locates the mleccha in the Himalayan region and mleccha are listed with yavana, *śaka, darada, pārada, tuṣāra, khaśa* and *pahlava* in north and north-west Bhāratavarṣa: *sa viv ṛddho yad ā rāj ā yavan ānām mah ābalāh tata enam nṛpā mlecch āh sams'rity ānuyayaus tad ā śakās tuṣār ā daradāh pāradās tan:gaṇāh khasśāh pahlavāh śataśaścānye mlecch ā haimavat ās tathā. Matsya Purāṇa* 144.51-58 provides a list. Pracetā had a hundred sons all of whom ruled in mleccha regions in the north. [Matsya Purāṇa 148.8-9; Bhāgavata Purāṇa IX.23.16.] Bhīṣma Parvan of Mahābhārata notes that mleccha jāti people lived in Yavana, Kāmboa, Dāruṇā

regions and are listed together with several other peoples of the northern and north-western parts of Bhāratavarṣa (MBh. VI.10.63-66: *uttarāścāpare mlecchā janā bharatasattama yavanāśca śaka, kāmbojā dārun.ā mlecchajātayah*).
In *Rāmāyaṇa* IV.42.10, Sugrīva is asked to search for Sītā in the northern lands of mleccha, pulinda, sūrasena, praṣalā, bhārata, kuru, madraka, kamboja and yavana before proceeding to Himavat: *tatra mlecchān pulindāmśūrasen āmś tathaiva ca prasthalān bharatāmścaiva kurūmsśca saha madraih.* Mlecchas came from the valley adjoining the Himalaya.[328]

When Sagara, son of Bāhu, was prevented from destroying śaka, Yavana, Kāmboa, Pārada and Pāhlava after he recovered his kingdom, Vasiṣṭha, the family priest of Sagara, absolved these people of their duties but Sagara commanded the Yavana to shave the upper half of their heads, the Pārada to wear long hair and Pahlava to let their beards grow. Sagara also absolved them of their duty to offer yajna to agni and to study the Veda. [Vāyu Purāṇa 88.122. 136- 43; Brahmāṇḍa Purāṇa 3.48.43-49; 63.119-34.] This is how these Yavana, Pārada and Pahlava also became mleccha. [Viṣṇu Purāṇa 4.3.38-41.] The implication is that prior to Sagara's command, these kṣatriya communities did respect Vasiṣṭha as their priest, studied the Veda and performed yajna. [Harivamśa 10.41-45.] Śaka who were designated as kings of mleccha jāti by Bhaṭṭa Utpala (10th century) in his commentary on Bṛhatsamhitā, were defeated by Candragupta II. That the mleccha were also adored as ṛṣi is clear from the verse of *Bṛhatsamhitā* 2.15:*mlecchā hi yavanās teṣu samyak śāstram kadam sthitam ṛṣivat te 'pi pūjyante kim punar daivavid dvijāh* (The yavana are mleccha, among them this science is duly established; therefore, even they (although mleccha) are honoured as ṛṣi; how much more (praise is due to an) astrologer who is a brāhmaṇa'). *Bṛhatsamhitā* 14.21 confirms that the yavana, śaka and pahlava lived on the west. Similarly, Konow notes that Sai-wang (Saka King) mentioned in Chinese accounts should be interpreted as Saka Muruṇḍa and the territory he occupied as Kāpiśa. [Sten Konow, *CII*, vol. II, pp. xx ff; Sten Konow, EI, no. 20 'Taxila Inscription of the Year 136', vol. XIV, pp. 291-2.] Śaka migrated to Bhāratavarṣa through Arachosia via the Bolan Pass into the lower Sindhu, a region called Indo_Scythia by Greek geographers and called śaka-dvīpa in Bhāratiya texts.[329] Another view expressed by Thomas is that the migration was through Sindh and the valley of the Sindhu River. [FW Thomas, 'Sakastana', JRAS, 1906, p. 216.] Kalhaṇa notes that Jalauka, a son of Aśoka took possession of Kāśmīra, advanced as far as Kanauj, after crushing a horse of mleccha. [Rājatarangiṇī, 1.107-8.] Greek invasions occurred later, during the reign of Puṣyamitraśunga (c. 185-150 BCE). The regions inhabited by the 'milakkha' could be the Vindhyan region. The term, 'mleccha' of which 'milakkha' is a variant, could as well have denoted the indigenous people (Nahali?) or of Bhāratavarṣa who had lived on the Sarasvati River basin and who moved towards other parts of Bhāratavarṣa after the gradual desiccation of the river, over a millennium, between c. 2500 and 1500 BCE. Medhātithi, commenting on the verse of Manu, defines a language as mleccha : *asad avidyam ān|ārthās ādhu śabdatayā vāk mleccha ucyate yathā śabarāṇām kirātānām anyeyām va antyānām*: Medhātithi on*Mānava Dharmaśāstra* X.45 – 'Language is called mleccha because it consists of words that have no meaning or have the wrong meaning or are wrong in form. To this class belong the languages of such low-born tribes as the śabara-s, Kirāta and so forth…'… He further proceeds to explain that āryavāc is refined speech and the language of the inhabitants of āryāvarta, but only of those who belong to the four varṇa-s. The others are called Dasyus.: ibid. – *āryavāca āryāvartam vāsinas te cāturvarṇy ādanyajātīyatvena prasiddhas tadā dasyava ucyante* 'Arya (refined) language is the language of the inhabitants of āryāvarta. Those persons being other than the four varṇa-s are called Dasyus.'

In *Dhammapada*'s commentary on Petuvathu, Dwaraka is associated with Kamboja as its Capital or its important city.[330] See evidence below:

"*Yasa asthaya gachham Kambojam dhanharika/ ayam kamdado yakkho iyam yakham nayamasai// iyam yakkham gahetvan sadhuken pasham ya/ yanam aaropyatvaan khippam gaccham Davarkān iti*" [Buddhist Text *Khudak Nikaya* (P.T.S)]

Mleccha who came to the Rājasūya also included those from forest and frontier areas (MBh. III. 48.19:*sāgarān ūpagāmścaiva ye ca paṭṭaṇavāsinah simhal ān barbarān mlecchān ye ca jān:galavāsinah*). Bhīmasena proceeded east towards Lohitya (Brahmaputra) and had conquered several mleccha people who bestowed on him wealth of various kinds (MBh. II.27.23-24: *suhmānāmādhipam caiva ye ca sāgaravāsinah sarvān mlecchagaṇāmścaiva vijigye bharatarṣabhah evam bahu vidhān deśān vijitya pavanātmajah vasu tebhya upādya lauhityam agad balī.*[331]

Celebrations at the Kalinga capital of Duryodhana were attended by preceptors and mleccha kings from the south and east of Bhārata (MBh. XII.4.8: *ete cānye ca bahavo dakṣinām diśām āśritah mlecchā āryāśca rāj ānah prācyodicyāśca bhārata*).

Bhāgadatta, the great warrior of Prāgjyotiṣa accompanied by mleccha people inhabiting marshy regions of the sea- coast (*sāgarānūpavāsibhih*), attends the Rājasūya of Yudhiṣṭhira (MBh. II.31.9-10:*prāgjyotiṣaśca nṛpatir bhagadatto mahāyaśāh saha sarvais tathā mlecchaih sāgarānūpavāsibhih*). This is perhaps a reference ot the marshy coastline of Bengal. *Amarakośa* II, Bhūmivarga – 6: pratyanto mlecchade śah syāt; Sarvānanda in his commentary, ṭīkāsarvasva, elaborates that mleccha deśa denotes regions without proper conduct such as Kāmarūpa: *bhāratavarṣasyāntadeśah śiṣṭācārā rahitah kāmarūpādih mlecchadeśāh* [Nāmalingānuśāsana, with commentary ṭīkāsarvasva, of Sarvānanda (ed. Ganapati śāstri)]; he also cites Manu that where four varṇa-s are not established that region is mlecchadeśa. A contemporary of Harṣavardhana was Bhāskaravarman of Kāmarūpa; this king was supplanted by another dynasty founded by śālastambha who was known as a mleccha overlord.[332]

Meluhha, Mleccha areas: Sarasvati River Basin and Coastal Regions of Gujarat, Baluchistan

Meluhha referred to in Sumerian and old Akkadian texts refers to an area in Sarasvati Civilization; Asko and Simo Parpola add: '...probably, including NW India with Gujarat as well as eastern Baluchistan'.[333]

Imports from Meluhha into Mesopotamia included the following commodities which were found in north-western and western Bhāratavarṣa: copper, silver, gold, carnelian, ivory, uśu wood (ebony), and another wood which is translated as 'sea wood' – perhaps mangrove wood on the coasts of Sind ad Baluchistan.[334]

The Ur texts specifically refer to 'seafaring country of Meluhha'' and hence, Leemans' thesis that Meluhha was the west coast (modern state of Gujarat) of Bhārata. The Lothal dockyard had fallen into disuse by c.1800 BCE, a date when the trade between Mesopotamia and Meluhha also ended.[335]

In Leemans' view, Gujarat was the last bulwark of the (Indus or Sarasvati) Civilization. Records refer to Meluhhan ships docking at Sumer. There were Meluhhans in various Sumerian cities; there was also a Meluhhan town or district at one city. The Sumerian records indicate a large volume of trade; according to a Sumerian tablet, one shipment from Meluhha contained 5,900 kg of copper (13,000 lbs, or 6 ½ tons)! The bulk of this trade was done through Dilmun, not directly with Meluhha. In our view, the formative stages of the Civilization also had their locus in the coastal areas – in particular, the Gulf of Khambat, Gulf of Kutch and Makran coast, as evidenced by the wide shell-bangle, dated to c. 6500 BCE, made of turbinella pyrum or śankha, found in Mehergarh, 300 miles north of the Makran coast.

Tanana mleccha

A Jaina text, Avasyaka Churani notes that ivory trade was managed by mleccha, who also traveled from Uttaravaha to Dakshinapatha.[336] Guttila Jataka (ca.4th cent.) makes reference to itinerant ivory workers/traders journeying from Varanasi to Ujjain.[337] The phrase, *tanana mleccha* may be related to: (i) tah'nai, 'engraver' mleccha; or (ii) tana, 'of (mleccha) lineage'. 1. See Kuwi. *tah'nai* 'to engrave' in DEDR and Bsh. *then, thon*, 'small axe' in CDIAL: DEDR 3146 *Go.* (Tr.) *tarcana* (Mu.) *tarc-* to scrape; (Ma.) *tarsk-* id., plane; (D.) *task-,* (Mu.) *tarsk-/tarisk-* to level, scrape (*Voc.*1670).

Bronze age trade and cryptography: mlecchita vikalpa

This monograph presents four 'rosetta stones' to decipher the Indus script. 1. First and second are pure tin ingots with Sarasvati hieroglyphs discovered in the Haifa shipwreck; 2. Third is an Akkadian cylinder seal attesting to Meluhha as a language of bronze-age traders (sea-faring merchants); 3. Fourth is a cylinder seal from Ur showing *tabaernae montana* flower (used as hair-fragrance) which is read in Meluhha as tagaraka, rebus: tagara 'tin'. The cryptography of the writing system is mlecchita vikalpa (which is recognized by Vatsyayana as one of 64 arts).

"The fabrication of bronze represented man's first industrial revolution centering in the use of fire...Stannite on smelting yields a natural bronze. This generally steel-gray to grayish-black ore frequently has the appearance of bronze and indeed is called 'bell metal' ore. Stannite fits with the hypothesis that metallurgy was born in a polymetallic setting, where interfluxing and interalloying of ores could occur. This would most generally be a gossan cap on a copper deposit, also containing arsenopyrites and lead-silver...In Egypt in 1976, we relived the experience of predynastic prospectors for gold: of finding cassiterite in the decayed quartzes or greisens, extensions of the gold ones. It was especially rewarding to follow the trail of the bright black placer crystals up the riffles in the wadis. There can now be little question in our minds that cassiterite (SnO_2) was the ore that led toward the identification of tin and the ultimate naming of the metal as *anāku* in Akkadian. Stannite could not have performed this function... The several hundred translated tablets from Kultepe and Mari containing references to trade in *anāku* from the east, suggesting an origin for tin in Elam or Iran. After a long debate over the logogram *anāku*, it seemed that the trade item must concern tin rather than lead or exotic glazes. The reference of the geographer Strabo to tin in Drangiana, or Seistan, which tin had been exhausted."[338]

The mineral Cassiterite (SnO_2) or tinstone is usually deep brown to black in colour, but is sometimes red (ruby tin), yellow (rosin tin), and may even be colourless. Heating the tin oxide in charcoal fire or furnace yields metallic tin. The metal melts at the low temperature of 232 C, but the ore requires a smelting temperature of about 100 C. Tinstone is found in the same alluvial gravel deposits as gold; it is probable that when was being sought, the tinstone would have been noticed and the alluvial ore discovered thus.

"In the Late Bronze Age the alloy normally contained 10% Sn, but lead was introduced into castings...tin is found mainly as the mineral cassiterite (SnO_2) which is white in the pure state, but is more often contaminated with greater or lesser amounts of iron which render it brown or black...(Bronzes at Mohenjodaro--2500-2000 BC) cover a range of 3 to 26.9% Sn and it would seem that tin was sometimes available in the 500 years of occupation on this site. At Mundigak, in Afghanistan, only one out of a total of five shaft-hole axes analysed contained as much as 5% Sn...The Early Bronze Age seems to have lasted to about 300 BC in the Ganges Basin and the Deccan. In the former, Harappa-type cultures have produced a few bronzes containing 3.8 to 13.3%Sn. A site at Jorwe in the Deccan, dated to before 300 BC, produced six very simple flat axes or rectangular form and one copper bangle...Considering that India is near the well known tin deposits of Burma and Malaya, one would not be surprised to see a difference in the use of tin there, and particularly in the quantity used in the Early Bronze Age, compared with the use made of it in places not so close to known tin deposits... iron using people have occupied the area from about 2000 BC. During the Bronze Age copper ores would have been smelted with the aid of iron fluxes, and there would be a distinct possibility of iron being reduced in the bottom of the furnace."[339] The pin at Tepe Hissar 1 (ca. 3900-2900 BC) had 1.74% Sn; dagge at Geoy Tepe (ca. 2000 BC) had 0.5% Sn; dagger at Tepe Yahya (ca. 3000 BC) had 3.0% Sn; the blade and pin at Ur (ca. 2800-2500BC) had 2.4 and 1.0% Sn respectively; the fragment at Mohenjodaro (ca. 2100-1700 BC) had 1.2% Sn; dagger at Tel Asmar (ca. 2500 BC) had 2.63%Sn. There are indications that bronze was being made by 'cementing' copper with tin oxide in the Late Bronze Age. At Tepe Hissar (ca. 2100-1800 BC), only alloys containing 0.78% to 2.24%Sn were found. At Susa, alloys did not exceed 1.63% tin content even as late as 1800 BC. However, the 'Luristan Bronzes' (1500-700 BC) show the true flowering of the Bronze Age in Iran. In Crete, dilute bronzes (3.14, 3.16% Sn) appear only during the Middle Minoan I (2000 BC). Cretan Minoan double axes are mostly tin bronze (3 to 18%Sn). Moulds for these objects were found at Malli and on Melos.Evidence for trade in tin or cassiterite comes from the wreck found off the coast of Cape Gelidonia in southern Turkey; this find is dated to the Late Bronze Age (1200 BC). About 16 kg of white material containing 14% SnO_2 and 71% $CaCO_3$ were recovered from the sea bed. This may represent corroded material from a tin ingot having a cross-section of about 6 cm sq. The cargo included copper and bronze ingots and scrap metal. The ship was travelling in a westerly direction and the suggestion is that it was a Syrian ship taking copper from Cyprus to the Mycenaen civilizations in Crete or Greece. This tin was certainly not obtained in Cyprus and should have been traded from more distant places and picked up at one of the ports of call.[340]

Shipwrecked cargo exhibit in National Maritime Museum (Hebrew: המוזיאון הימי הלאומי, *HaMuze'on HaYami HaLe'umi*), a maritime and Archaeological museum in Haifa, Israel. Uruluburn shipwreck dated to the late 14th century BCE or the late Bronze Age also resulted in the discovery of copper and tin ingots being traded.

The following picture of these two ingots incised with epigraphs was published by J.D. Muhly.[341]

In the old Akkadian period, the ingots of tin are called śuqlu and weigh about 25 kg. The two ingots found at Haifa weigh about 5 kg. each.(details of the find and archaeological, archaeo-metallurgical contexts are elaborated.[342]

Some conjectures are that they could have come from Ugarit.The glyphs incised on the ingots DO NOT resemble Cypro-Minoan symbols used in Cyprus or Hittite hieroglyphs used in Ugarit or Cretan hieroglyphs ca. 1500 to 1100 BCE.

One possibility is that they were weighed at Ugarit and stamped as they travelled through the long overland caravan route...[343]

There were Meluhhans in various Sumerian cities; there was also a Meluhhan town or district at one city. The Sumerian records indicate a large volume of trade; according to a Sumerian tablet, one shipment from Meluhha contained 5,900 kg of copper (13,000 lbs, or 6 ½ tons)!

Haifa: find-spot of the first two 'rosetta stones'

At the port of Dor, south of Haifa, fisherfolk had raised about 7 tonnes of copper and tin ingots in the 1970's. In 1976 two ingots of tin were found in a shipwreck in the sea near this Phoenician port. Ingot 1 and Ingot 2; Museum of Ancient Art, Municipal Corporation of Haifa.

The epigraphs on the tin ingots have been decoded as related to ranku "antelope", ranku "liquid measure"; dhātu 'ore'; the two epigraphs on the two ingots are read rebus: ranku dhātu "tin unalloyed (i.e. pure metal)".

The modifying element | ligatured (subscripted) to X on the tin ingot inscriptions, may be read rebus: खांडा [khāṇḍā] 'notch':Marathi: खांडा [khāṇḍā] *m* A jag, notch, or indentation (as upon the edge of a tool or weapon). Rebus: *kāṇḍa* 'tools, pots and pans and metal-ware'.

kuṭilikā- smith's tongs.(DEDR 2052). Rebus: kuṭila, katthīl = bronze (8 parts copper and 2 parts tin)(CDIAL 3230). If Sign 229 'pincers' glyph is rotated right 90-degrees, the glyph will be comparable to the variant X glyph shown on the tin ingots. This X glyph is also ligatured (subscripted) with a short numeral stroke. *dāṭu* 'cross'(Telugu) Rebus: *dhatu* 'mineral' (Santali).

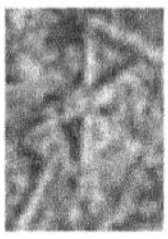

Thus, the composite glyphic composition on the tin-ingots may be read rebus as: *dhatu kuṭila khāṇḍā* 'mineral (for) bronze tools'.

ranku 'liquid measure, antelope' Rebus: *ranku* 'tin'. This glyph is annotated by the variang X glyph that the tin mineral is for (alloying to) bronze tools.

The epigraphs incised on the ingots read as hieroglyphs, depict the nature of the property items: metallic tin (ranku dhātu) read rebus in mleccha (meluhha, milakkhu), the *lingua franca* of the bronze-age civilization linguistic area.

-     [Copper tablet; side B perhaps is a graphemic representation of an antelope; note the ligatured tail comparable to the tail on m273, b012 and k037]
- ran:ku = tin (Santali)
- *ran:ku* = liquid measure (Santali)
- *ran:ku* a species of deer; *ran:kuka* (Skt.)(CDIAL 10559). See middle glyph on copper plates m0522 & m0516
- *dāṭu* = cross (Te.); dhatu = mineral (Santali)
- H. *dhāṭnā* to send out, pour out, cast (metal)' (CDIAL 6771).

 These two hieroglyphs were inscribed on two tin ingots discovered in port of Dor south of Haifa from an ancient shipwreck. They are allographs. Both are read in Meluhha (Mleccha) of Indian *sprachbund*: *ranku* 'liquid measure'; *ranku* 'antelope'.Rebus: *ranku* 'tin'. An allograph to denote tin is: tagara 'ram' Rebus: tagara 'tin'. Rebus: damgar 'merchant' (Akkadian)

dāṭu X rebus: dhatu 'mineral'. The notch subscripted to X is a hieroglyph: खांडा khāṇḍā *m* A jag, notch, or indentation (as upon the edge of a tool or weapon). Rebus: *khāṇḍā* 'tools, pots and pans, metal-ware'. खुंट [khuṇṭa] The square or area formed by the meeting of four roads; An end or a point of a street or road. Commbined with *āra* 'brass' as in ārakūṭa 'brass' (Skt.) Rebus: khũṭ 'community, guild' (Mu.); kuṇḍa 'consecrated fire-pit'. Rebus: खोट [khōṭa] an ingot or wedge or old metal melted down (Marathi) The X khuṇṭa may indicate that the tin ingot is for 'alloying' *kūṭa*. Thus, the message is 'rub -- alloying mineral' for tools, pots and pans, metalware, *khāṇḍā*

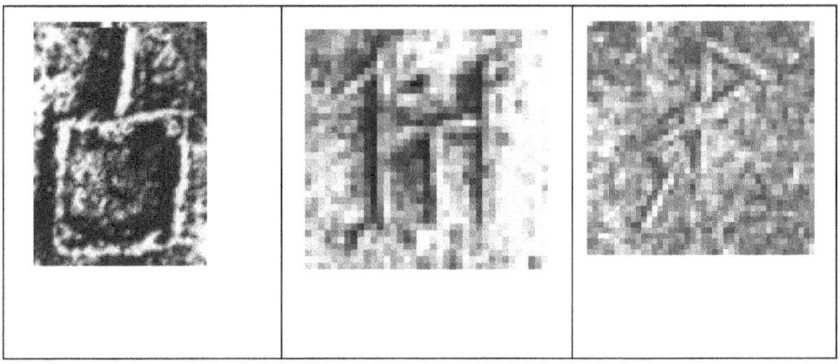

Figure 4. Three incised hieroglyphs on the tin ingots

[The first sign from the left in Figure 4 compares with Sign 278 of Harappan (also called Indus script or Sarasvati hieroglyphs) in Daniels and Bright (1996: 167). The second sign (stylized antelope) is a Harappan sign, shown in Figure 17. This second pictograph illustrated on Figure 4 incised on tin ingot 1, clearly is a stylized representation of an antelope as depicted on the Mohenjodaro copper plate inscription: (m0516b shown). The third sign, the X, seems to be more than merely an X; it is comparable to a variant of Sign 142 shown in Harappan, as may be seen from Figure 18.]

At this stage, a note on the orientation of the symbols is apposite. The two tin ingots have two signs written top to bottom, while normally Harappan writing is usually written from right to left. However, there are instances in the corpus of Harappan (Indus Script) epigraphs where the orientation of writing is top to bottom (See Figure 25 Bronze dagger with hieroglyphs) or even from left to right as on the Dholavira sign-board.

The three pictographs of Figure 4 have parallels in the inscriptions of the civilization; in m1336 the 'antelope' pictograph appears together with the 'liquid-measure' pictograph; X sign occurs on many inscriptions with many variants elaborating it as a junction or intersection of two roads:

Figure 5.Seal m1336a (All references to the text of epigraphs and Signs refer to Mahadevan 1977 and seal/tablet pictures refer to Parpola 'Corpus of Indus inscriptions', 1987 Vol. 1, 1991 Vol. 2)

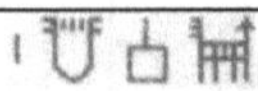
Figure 6 m1336a Text 2515 (Mahadevan)

Figure 7 Seal m1341

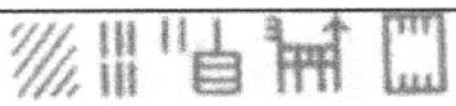
Figure 8 m1341 Text 2092

Figure 9 Two sides of tablet: m0516 (copper plate)

3398 Figure 10 Text of tablet m0516

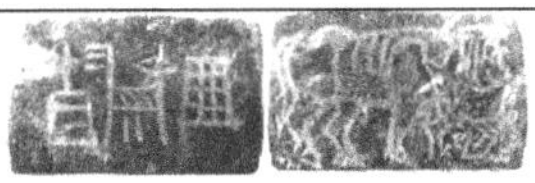
Figure 11 Two sides of tablet m0522 (copper plate)

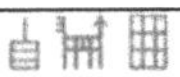
Figure 12 m0522 Text 3378

(Note: Figures 9 and 10, m0516 and m0522 are copper plates; on Figure 9, m0516 side A of the copper plate shows the antelope glyph; on Figure 10, m0522 side B the antelope glyph becomes a middle segment of a three-glyph epigraph. This is a clear demonstration of the continuum of the so-called field symbols or pictorial motifs and the so-called signs of the Indus script. Both the 'pictorial motifs or field symbols' and 'signs', a bi-partite categorization used in the corpuses of Parpola and Mahadevan, are hieroglyphs).

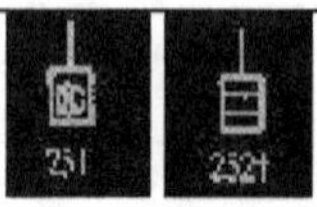

Figure 13. Signs 251, 252. ran:ku 'liquid measure (Mundari)

Figure 14. Sign 249

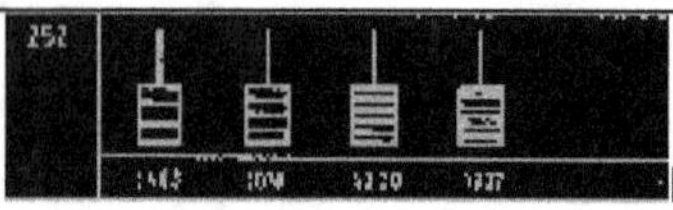

Figure 15 Sign 252 and variants

The 'liquid measure' glyph may be seen to be a liquid measure by the orthographic styles shown on Sign Variants of Sign 252 with part filling of the liquid measuring container (with a handle).

The hieroglyphs may be read:

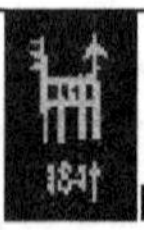

Figure 16. Sign 184 ran:ku 'antelope'.

Read rebus, the hieroglyphs connote ran:ku 'tin'.

That the 'antelope' sign is a derivative from the 'antelope' glyph is seen from the Sign Variants of Signs 182 to 184 (See Figure 17)

 V182  V184 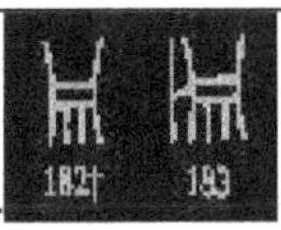

 Figure 17. Sign 182, 183, 184 and variants

Chanhudaro23 The short-tail of the antelope shown on this Chanhudaro seal (which also includes a double-axe as a pictograph) is distinctly identified on Signs 182, 183, 184 and variants. The tail is clearly the signature-tune, an orthographic characteristic, used by the artisan who is depicting an 'antelope' hieroglyph.

The sign 182 is repeatedly used on copper plate epigraphs and substitutes for an 'antelope' glyph.

Liquid measure: ran:ku; rebus: ran:ku = tin; rebus: ran:ku = antelope. Thus both liquid measure glyph and antelope glyphs are graphonyms (graphically denoting the same rebus substantive: ran:ku, 'tin'). Both the glyphs may be decoded as denoting 'tin' to describe the nature of the ingots being moved on the ships to Haifa and to Cape Gelidonya.

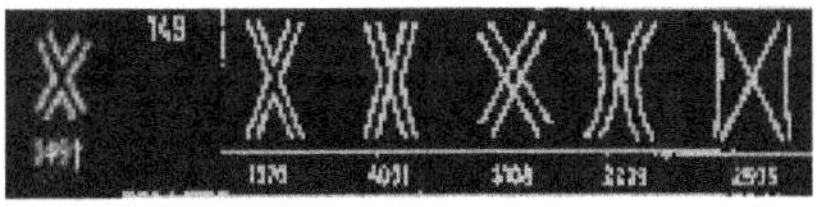 Figure 18 Sign 137, 142, 149 and variants

This glyph could connote the junction of two roads: baṭa means 'road'; rebus: baṭa means 'furnace, smelter'. An alternative interpretation for the X glyph and its variants, is possible, again in Indic family of languages. X may refer, rebus, to dhātu 'mineral' (Skt.). tātu = powder, dust, pollen (Ta.); to.0 = powdery, soft (of flour or powdered chillies)(To.). There is a possibility that the early meaning of the word, 'dhātu' was cassiterite, powdery tin mineral.

If X glyph connotes a cross over: dāṭu = cross over; daṭ - (da.ṭ-t-) to cross (Kol.);dāṭisu – to cause to pass over (Ka.); da.ṭ- (da.ṭy-) to cross (mark, stream, mountain, road)(Ko.); tāṭṭuka to get over or through (Ma.); tāṇṭu = to cross, surpass (Ta.)(DEDR 3158). In RV 6.044.23 the term used is: tridhātu divi rocaneṣu = 'three-fold amṛtam hidden in heaven' is the metaphor; and in RV 8.044.12 the term is: tridhātunā śarmanā.

Geologists have found sources for ancient tin from the work of Assur or Munda people gathering cassiterite stones from placer deposits in water-bodies.

Two minerals of great importance found their early use, during the bronze-age, in India: tin and zinc which when alloyed with the abundant copper mineral yielded the metal alloys of tin-bronze and brass products such as vessels, pots and pans, tools and weapons. The hardened metal alloys could be used to create sharp weapons like spears, arrow-heads, daggers, farm tools like ploughshares or sickles and ornaments and jewellery combined with gold, silver and perforated beads of semi-precious stones of lapis lazuli, carnelian, agate or even ivory. The availability of metal tools also resulted in techniques for sculpting polished stone pillars and ring-stones and even for creating water reservoirs cutting through sheer-rock as evidenced in Dholavira. Even Shivalingas were found in Harappa. These together with the suggestion by some researchers that the stupa mound of Mohenjo-daro may have been a ziggurat-temple provide new avenues for archaeological exploration of the cultural foundations of the ancient people of the region. Comparable cultural sequences were located in delta areas of Rann of Kutch, Gujarat (Dholavira, Kanmer, Khirsara, Surkotada), Lothal , Gujarat(Gulf of Khambat) and in areas west of River Indus in sites such as Mehergarh, Shahdad, Shortugai, Shahr-i-sokta, Tepe Yahya in Afghanistan-Baluchistan-Iran and across the Persian Gulf. These were centres of trade and commerce between India, present-day Pakistan, Afghanistan, Iran, Iraq (in areas called Elam,

Bactria-Margiana, Dilmun, Magan). The trading area evidenced by the seals usin characteristic glyphs of the writing system.

The emerging picture was that of a maritime, riverine culture with sea-faring merchants, artisans and explorers for minerals reaching far and wide upto Caucasus mountains in Europe (Altyn Depe) and Haifa, an ancient port in Israel (shipwreck yielding two pure tin ingots with Indus Script inscriptions).

Muhly notes:"A long-distance tin trade is not only feasible and possible, it was an absolute necessity. Sources of tin stone or cassiterite were few and far between, and a common source must have served many widely scattered matallurgical centers. This means that the tin would have been brought to a metallurgical center utilizing a nearby source of copper. That is, copper is likely to be a local product; the tin was almost always an import...The circumstances surrounding the discovery of these ingots are still rather confused, and our dating is based entirely upon the presence of engraves signs which seem to be in the Cypro-Minoan script, used on Cyprus and at Ugarit over the period 1500-1100 BCE. The ingots are made of a very pure tin, but what could they have to do with Cyprus? There is certainly no tin on Cyprus, so at best the ingots could have been transhipped from that island. How did they then find their way to Haifa? Are we dealing with a ship en route from Cyprus, perhaps to Egypt, which ran into trouble and sank off the coast of Haifa? If so, that certainly rules out Egypt as a source of tin. Ingots of tin are rare before Roman times and, in the eastern Mediterranean, unknown from any period. What the ingots do demonstrate is that metallic tin was in use during the Late Bronze Age...rather extensive use of metallic tin in the ancient eastern Mediterranean, which will probably come as a surprise to many people."[344] [Tin ingots were traded through the Levant in the 2nd millennium BC; in the autumn of 1976 two ingots were found 'in the sea near the Phoenecian port of Dor, south of Haifa. Ingot 1 and Ingot 2; Museum of Ancient Art, Municipal Corporation of Haifa; local fishermen had raised about 7 tonnes of copper and tin ingots in Haifa. The date of the two ingots is uncertain. The symbols incised on the ingots also resemble Cypro-Minoan symbols used in

Cyprus and Ugarit ca. 1500 to 1100 BC. May be, they were weighed at Ugarit and stamped as they travelled through the long overland caravan route right upto the western end. It is notable that Cyprus had no tin. Sources: Anon., Ingots from wrecked ship may help to solve ancient mystery.[345]

"Mari and the Tin Trade...the texts from Mari (Tell Hariri), dating mainly to the first half ot the eighteenth century BCE...(tin) came to Mari through Elam, from Susa and Anshan (now identified with the Central Iranian site of Tepe Malyan), and Elamites played a major role in the trade, especially a man named Kuyaya. Certain merchants from Mari were also heavily involved in the tin trade with Elam, among them a merchant named Ishkhi-Dagan (the two appear together in ARM 23 555). The tin came to Mari in the form of ingots (Akkadian le_'u) that weighed about ten pounds each. It is possible to obtain some idea of the relative value of this tin, for a number of the Mari texts provide a tin:silver ratio of 10:1 (the most common ratio; a few texts give ratios from 8:1 to 15:1). This is to be compared with isolated referenced to a tin:gold ratio (48:1), a confusing silver:gold ratio of 4:1 as well as 2:1, and a lead:silver ratio (1200:1). The usual copper:silver ratio at Mari was 180:1 for unrefined 'mountain' copper, with refined (litarally 'washed') copper being valued at 150:1. This means that tin was usually from fifteen to eighteen times more valuable than copper...In later texts from Nuzi (fifteenth century BCE) goods were priced in amounts of tin. An ox cost thirty-six minas of tin; an ass, twenty-four minas. During the Middle Assyrian period tin seems to have functioned as the monetary standard (temporarily replacing the customary silver). Plots of land were purchased with tin...The cuneiform archives contain a number of 'recipe' texts, giving the amounts of coper and tin used to make specified amounts of bronze. One of the earlist such texts, from Palace G at Ebla, records that 3 minas, 20 shekels of tin were alloyed with 30 minas of copper to produce 200 objects of bronze, each weighing 10 shekels. In other words, 200 shekels of tin were mixed with 1,800 shekels of copper to produce 2,000 shekels of a 10 percent tin-bronze. In one Mari text 20 shekels of tin were added to 170 shekels of refined copper from Teima at the rate of 1:8, to produce

190 shekels of bronze for a key (to the lock of a city gate)...This means that smiths at Mari were working with the metals themselves--with copper and tin--not with ores or minerals. That is no smelting was being carried out in the vicinity of the Mari palace... At the other end of the Mari trade network, the texts record that tin stored at Mari was transhipped to various cities in the Levant, from Karkamish in the north to Hazor in the south. This we learn from a remarkable tin itinerary that concludes with the recording of '1 (+) minas of tin to the Cretan; 1/3 mina of tin to the translator, chief (merch)ant among the Cretans; (dispensed) at Ugarit...' (ARM 23 556). This striking passage indicates that there were Minoan merchants (the text uses the name Kaptaru, generally taken to designate the island of Crete) doing business (perhaps also residing) at Ugarit (modern Ras Shamra) toward the beginning of the Old Palace period in Crete. Furthermore, the Minoan merchants seem to have had a translator (Akkadian, targamannum; the origin of the common European 'dragoman') who was also the leader of the Minoans doing business at Ugarit. Such translators are known from other periods of Mesopotamian history. We have the cylinder seal of a Sargonic official who served as translator for the Melukkha merchants who came to Agade from the Indus Valley, perhaps bringing with them the tin of Melukkha, a commodity mentioned in one of the statue inscriptions of Gudea, ruler of Lagash. A Mari text, dated to the ninth year of the reign of Zimri-Lim, refers to the construction of a 'small Kaptaru boat', perhaps to be taken as a model ship for ritual purposes or as the designation of a ship built for sailing to Crete. A possible parallel for this would be the Egyptian references to Byblos ships (for sailing to the ancien Syrian port of Byblos (modern Jubayl) and Keftiu ships (built for sailing to Crete)...

"Bronze certainly was being produced in Middle Minoan Crete, with production undergoing a great expansion during the Late Bronze Age, as it did on the Greek mainland...The problem is that, at present, no satisfactory analytical method for studying the provenance of tin has been discovered."[346]

"Tin and the Development of Bronze Metallurgy. Early Use of Bronze. The most important metallurgical development during the Early Bronze Age was the discovery that adding tin to copper produced a far superior metal, eventually known as bronze. In its classic form, bronze has 10 percent tin and 90 percent copper. The addition of even 2 percent tin has noticeable effects upon the hardness and working properties of copper, but anything over 16 percent tin is undesirable, for a very high tin content makes copper brittle and difficult to work. Objects such as the ax head from the A cemetery at Kish (modern Tell al-Uhaimir; Early Dynastic, or ED, IIIB), with 15.5 percent tin, are probably to be assessed as being of early, experimental alloys.

"The historical development of bronze metallurgy has been difficult to document, and locating ancient sources of tin has proved to be an even more intractable problem...the cache of human figurines from Tell Judeidah (northern Syria), the excavators' date of about 3000 (transition Amuq G-H) still seems the most probable...A pin from Tepe Gawra VIII (early third millennium) siad to have 5.6 percent tin unfortunately can no longer be located, but four artifacts from the Y cemetary at Kish, of ED I date, proved to have more than 2 percent tin. These are the earliest examples of bronze from Mesopotamia. One of these objects, a spouted jar, has 6.24 percent tin...

"Sources of Tin and the Tin Trade...The tin was brought to Asshur from some point further east, most likely Afghanistan. The Assyrian merchants purchased the tin for reshipment, by donkey caravan, and sale (at a 100 percent markup) in Anatloia...The Old Assyrian tin trade was on a large scale and enriched three generations of Old Assyrian merchant families...

"Tin exists in nature in the form of cassiterite, an oxide of tin. The cassiterite most likely utilized by Bronze Age metal workers was alluvial or placer cassiterite, popularly known as tin-stone and present as nuggets or pebbles in the beds of streams...Alluvial cassiterite was collected by panning the bed of a stream, much like the recovery of alluvial gold...Gold and tin often occur within the same general area as, for example, in the Eastern (Arabian) Desert of Egypt. Ancient Sardis, the region of the Tmolus (modern Boz Dag) mountain range and the

Pactolus River, was famous as an ancient source of alluvial gold, the source of wealth for Croesus, king of Lydia, but no placer cassiterite has been documented from Anatolia...

"The similarity in geological history suggests a possible historical connection between tin and gold, with the two metals first being used at about the same time. This seems to be exactly what happened (except for the extensive use of gold in a few of the burials from the site of Varna, on the Black Sea coast of Bulgaria, dating to the second half of the fifth millennium, and the presence of eight massive, circular objects of gold and electrum in a Chalcolithic cave deposit of the fourth millennium at Nahal Qanah in Israel).

"Bronze tools, implements, and weapons and gold jewelry appear together in the Royal Cemetery of Ur, the royal shaft graves of Alaca Huyuk, and the various treasures (really hoards) of Troy II...The same is true for the bronze metallurgy and gold jewelry of Poliochni V (yellow). All this begins in the twenty-sixth century BCE, the date of the Royal Cemetery, and continues over the next few centuries down to about 2200 BCE. As indicated above, the possibility of tin, gold, and lapis lazuli coming into Mesopotamia from Afghanistan is certainly an attractive one. Of these three raw materials, however, we can be sure of the provenance of only one. Most, if not all, of the lapis lazuli used by the Sumerians came from northeast Afghanistan, from the Sar-i Sang mines in the region of Badakhshan...As for tin and gold, it can only be said that both metals are present in significant quantities in Afghanistan and in alluvial form. The recovery of fine gold particles from streams, making use of the woolly fleece of sheep (the famous Golden Fleece of Greek legend), was still practiced in Afghanistan well into the twentieth century.

Muhly adds:"... copper is likely to be a local product; the tin was almost always an import... There is certainly no tin on Cyprus, so at best the ingots could have been transhipped from that island. How did they then find their way to Haifa? Are we dealing with a ship en route from Cyprus, perhaps to Egypt, which ran into trouble and sank off the coast of Haifa? If so, that certainly rules out Egypt as a source of tin. Ingots of tin are rare before Roman times and, in the eastern Mediterranean, unknown from any period. What the ingots do demonstrate is that metallic tin was in use during the Late Bronze Age...rather extensive use of metallic tin in the ancient eastern Mediterranean, which will probably come as a surprise to many people."[347] We do not know where the tin ingots were moulded, and where the epigraphs were incised, but it is possible to read the epigraphs using references to cryptography in Mahabharata and mlecchita vikalpa 'cryptography' mentioned by *Vātsyāyana* in *vidyā samuddeśah* (objective of education in 64 arts).

Two remarkable insights provided by Muhy and Potts have made this possible. Muhly noted, the emergence of bronze age trade and writing system may be two related initiatives which started circa 3rd millennium Before Common Era (BCE).

Potts identified a glyph in what is clearly an Indus script epigraph as *tulip montana* flower which in Indic family of languages and in many ancient ayurveda texts is called *tagaraka*, read rebus *tagara* 'tin', also tagara 'hair fragrance'. This monograph reads the epigraphs inscised on the tin ingots as Sarasvati hieroglyphs of mleccha (meluhha) language which is part of the Indic language family. (These are called 'Sarasvati hieroglyphs' because, about 80% of the archaeological sites of the so-called Indus Valley civilization are on the banks of this Vedic river). The epigraphs 'certify' the metal as *ranku*, 'tin' (moulded out of) *dhatu* 'mineral'; ranku is represented by two allographs and two related homonyms: antelope, liquid-measure both phonetically read as *ranku* dāṭu 'cross'(Telugu) is represented by X glyph, *dāṭu* 'cross'(Telugu) is a homonym meaning 'road'. Thus, bot the epigraphs together connote 'tin mineral'. The two tin ingots become the two 'rosetta stones' validating the decipherment of sarasvati hieroglyphs (so-called Indus script) as the repertoire of a smithy/ metalsmith-merchant engaged in the bronze-age trade of minerals, metals and alloys and using types of furnaces/smelters.

Mesopotamian trade with Dilmun, Magan and Meluhha[348]

Products imported into Ur from Dilmun Late third and early second millennium BC	Products imported into Ur from Magan Late third millennium BC	Products imported into Ur from Meluhha Mid-third to mid-second millennium BC
lapis lazuli	timber and wooden objects	Timber and wooden furniture
carnelian	a type of onion (?)	Copper
semi-precious stones	copper	Gold dust
ivory and ivory objects	ivory	Lapis lazuli
copper	gold dust	Cornelian
silver	cornelian	Birds (including peacock)
'fish-eyes'	semi-precious stones	Multi-coloured ivory birds
red gold	diorite	Cornelian monkey
white corals	red ochre	Red dog
various woods	goats	
dates		
[Except for the dates and 'fish-eyes', all the commodities came to Dilmun from elsewhere for onward shipment; cf. Tilmun: Edzard et al., 1977, p. 157-8; Groneberg, 1980: 237).	[Cornelian and ivory were being shipped from further east; copper and diorite were local]. Akkadian kings claimed to have campaigned in Magan and taken boody. (Potts, D., 1986).	(Ratnagar, 1981: 66ff.) Texts refer to it as the land of seafarers.

Trade interactions of bronze age[349]

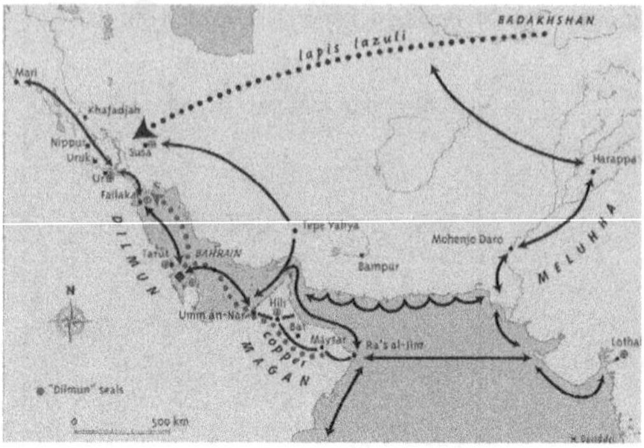

Erythraen Sea and Meluhha

Fifth century BCE Greek historian, Herodotus referred to the body of water which linked Africa, the Arabian Peninsula, Iran and the Indian subcontinent as the Erythraen sea. This sea includes the Red sea, the Gulf of Aden, Indian Ocean, Arabian Sea, Gulf of Oman and the Persian or Arabian Gulf.

"The land of Melukkha shall bring carnelian, desirable and precious, sissoo-wood from Magan, excellent mangroves, on big-ships!" said a statement in the Sumerian myth, Enki and Ninkhursag (cf. lines 1-9, trans. B. Alster). "In the late Early Dynastic period (about 2500), Ur-Nanshe, king of the Sumerian city-state Lagash, "had ships of Dilmun transport timber from foreign lands" to his capital (modern Tell al-Hiba), just as a later governor of Lagash, named Gudea, did in the mid-twenty-first century. In the early twenty-fourth century, Lugalbanda and Urukagina, two kings of Lagash, imported copper from Dilmun and paid for it with wool, silver, fat, and various milk and cereal products... That these (round stamp) seals were used in economic transactions is proven by the discovery of two important tablets bearing their impressions. One of these tablets was found at Susa, and dates to the first half of the second millennium. It is a receipt for goods, including ten minas of copper (about eleven pounds or five kilograms). The second tablet, in the Yale Babylonian Collection, is dated to the tenth year of Gungunum of Larsa (modern Tell Senkereh), that is, around 1925, and records a consignment of goods (wool, wheat, and sesame) prior to a trading voyage that almost certainly had Dilmun as its goal. Dilmun seals characteristically depict two men drinking what could be beer through straws, or two or three prancing gazelles...a merchant named Ea-nasir, who is identified as one of the ālik Tilmun, or "Dilmun traders"... Ea-nasir paid for Dilmun copper with the textiles and silver that he received from the great Nanna-Ningal temple complex at Ur...The Mari texts contain several references to Dilmunite caravans...Melukkha was a source of wood (including a black wood thought to have been ebony), gold, ivory, and carnelian...Melukkha was accessible by sea...Sargon of Akkad...boasts that ships from Dilmun, Magan and Melukkha docked at the quay of his capital Akkad...While points of contact with other regions are attested, they can hardly have accounted for the strength and individuality of civilization in the subcontinent... Unmistakably Harappan cubical weights of banded chert (based on a unit of 13.63 grams) are known from a number of sites located around the perimeter of the Arabian GUlf, including Susa, Qalat al-Bahrain, Shimal (Ras al-Khaimah), and Tell Abraq (Umm al-Qaiwain)...an inscribed Harappan shard has been found at Ras al Junayz... Harappan pottery has been found at several sites throughout Oman and the United Arab Emirates...A "Melukkhan village" in the territory of the ancient city-state of Lagash, attested in the thirty-fourth year of the reign of Shulgi (2060), may have been a settlement of Harappans, if the identification with the civilization of the Indus Valley is correct...But...there is little evidence of a Sumerian, Akkadian, or Babylonian presence in the Indus Valley... That the language of Melukkha was unintelligble to an Akkadian or Sumerian speaker is clearly shown by the fact that, on his cylinder seal, the Akkadian functionary Shu-ilishu is identified as a "Melukkhan translator"...the word "Melukkha" appears occasionally as a personal name in cuneiform texts of the Old Akkadian and Ur III periods."[350]

"Gordon Childe refers to the 'relatively large amount of social labour' expended in the extraction and distribution of copper and tin', the possession of which, in the form of bronze weaponry, 'consolidated the positions of war-chiefs and conquering aristocracies' (Childe 1941: 133)... With the publication of J.D. Muhly's monumental *Copper and Tin* in 1973,[351] an enormous amount of data on copper previously scattered throughout the scholarly literature became easily accessible... cuneiform texts consistently distinguish refined (urudu-luh-ha) [cf. loha = red, later metal (Skt.)] from unrefined copper (urudu) strongly suggests that it was matte (impure mixture of copper and copper sulphide) and not refined copper that was often imported into the country. Old Assyrian texts concerned with the import of copper from Anatolia distinguish urudu from urudu-sig, the latter term appearing when written phonetically as dammuqum, 'fine, good' (CAD D: 180, s.v. dummuqu), and this suggests that it is not just 'fine quality' but actually 'refined' copper that is in question... TIN. In antiquity tin (Sum. nagga/[AN.NA], Akk. annaku) was important, not in its own right, but as an additive to copper in the production of the alloy bronze (Sum. sabar, Akk. siparru) (Joannes 1993: 97-8)... In some cases, ancient recipes call for a ratio of tin to copper as high as 1: 6 or 16.6 per cent, while other texts speak of a 1:8 ratio or 12.5 per cent (Joannes 1993: 104)... 'there is little or no tin bronze' in Western Asia before c. 3000 B.C. (Muhly 1977: 76; cf. Muhly 1983:9). The presence of at least four tin-bronzes in the Early Dynastic I period... Y-Cemetery at Kish signals the first appearance of tin-bronze in southern Mesopotamia... arsenical copper continued in use at sites like Tepe Gawra, Fara, Kheit Qasim and Ur (Muhly 1993: 129). By the time of the Royal Cemetery at Ur (Early Dynastic IIIa), according to M.Muller-Karpe, 'tin-bronze had become the dominant alloy' (Muller-Karpe 1991: 111) in Southern Mesopotamia... Gudea of Lagash says he received tin from Meluhha... and in the Old Babylonian period it was imported to Mari from Elam...

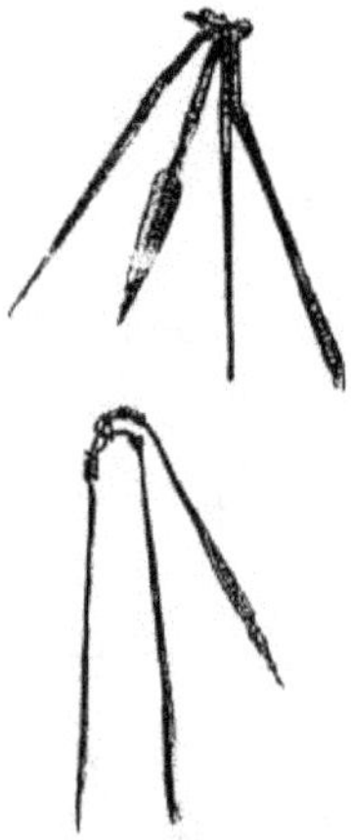

Harappan control over the Oman Sea

"Oman peninsula/Makkan lies half way between the two main civilization centres of the third millennium Middle East: Mesopotamia and the Indus valley... an increasing influence of Harappan civilization on Eastern Arabia during the last two centuries of the third millennium. This influence seems to strengthen during the early second millennium where proper Harappan objects are found all over the Oman peninsula: a cubic stone weight at Shimal, sherds of Harappan storage jars on several sites including Hili 8 (period III). Maysar and Ra's

Al-Junayz bears a Harappan inscription and Tosi (forth.) has emphasized the importance of this discovery for knowledge of Harappan control over the Oman Sea."[352]

Toilet implements from Ur and Harappa.[353]

Tin from 'Meluhha'

Aurel Stein collected a few bronzes from Shahi Tump, Mehi, Siah Damb and Segak Mound, all of which have a high tin percentage... tin was a precious commodity as is evident from the findings of bronze scraps, stored along with other valuables in copper vessels at both Harappa and Mohenjodaro.[354]

DK Chakrabarti opines[355] that during the pre-Harappan and Harappan periods, the main supply of tin was from the western regions: Khorasan and the area between Bukhara and Samarkand, through sites like Shortugai. The ancient tin mines in the Kara Dagh District in NW Iran and in the modern Afghan-Iranian Seistan could have been possible sources. Harappan metal-smiths used to conserve tin by storing and re-using scrap pieces of bronze, making low-tin alloys and substituting tin by arsenic. It is possible that some of the imported tin (like lapis lazuli) was exported to Mesopotamia.

"...According to the Larsa texts, merchants were there (in Mari and Larsa) to purchase copper and tin: the copper came from Magan in Oman, via Tilmun (Bahrain), but the origin of the tin is left in question. Tin mines in north-west Iran or the Transcaucasus are highly unlikely. Fortunately, there is evidence for another tin source in texts from Lagash. Lagash, about 50 km east of Larsa, was of minor importance except under the governorship of Gudea (ca. 2143-2124 BC). His inscriptions indicate extensive trade: gold from Cilicia in Anatolia, marble from Amurra in Syria, and cedar wood from the Amanus Mountains between these two countries, while up through the Persian Gulf or 'Southern Sea' came more timber, porphyry (strictly a purplish rock), lapis lazuli and tin.[356] There is evidence from a cylinder seal of Gudea, the king of Lagash (2143 – 2124 BCE) that tin came from Melukkha.[357]

One inscription has been translated:

> Copper and tin, blocks of lapis lazuli and ku ne (meaning unknown), bright carnelian from Meluhha.

"This is the only reference to tin from Meluhha...either Meluhha was a name vague enough to embrace Badakhshan (the northernmost province of Afghanistan) as well as some portion of the Indian subcontinent including the Indus valley, or 'tin from Meluhha' means that the metal came from some port in Meluhha -- just as 'copper from Tilmun' means copper from elsewhere shipped through the island of Bahrain. Whichever interpretation is correct, the result is the same. Tin must have come from somewhere in India, or from elsewhere along a trade route down the Indus valley. India is not without its tin locations, rare though they are...The largest deposits in India proper are in the Hazaribagh district of Bihar. 'Old workings' are said to exist... (Wheeler, R.E.M., 1953, The Indus Civilization, CUP, 58)...Tin bronzes from Gujarat are at the southernmost limit of Indus influence. The copper could have come from Rajasthan, though copper ingots at the port of Lothal, at the head of the Gulf of Cambay, suggest imports from Oman or some other Near Eastern copper mining district. Tin supplying Harappa and Mohenjo-daro, most famous of the Indus cities, may have been sent overland to Lothal for export, though the scarcity of tin in the Indus cities makes this idea unconvincing.

Homeric times refer to tin along with ivory coming from India (V. Ball, 1880, A geologist's contribution to the History of Ancient India, in: *Journal of Royal*

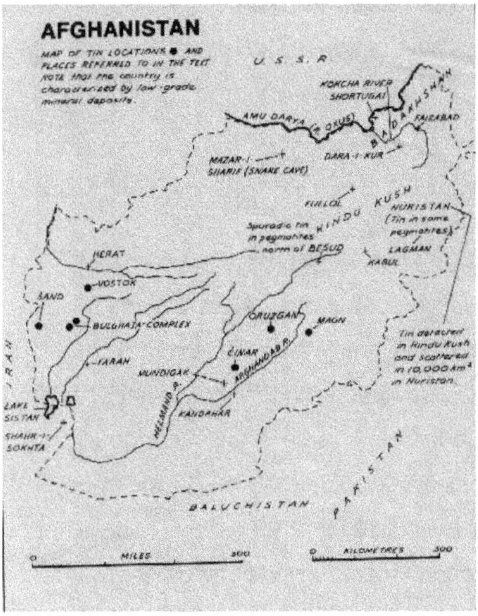

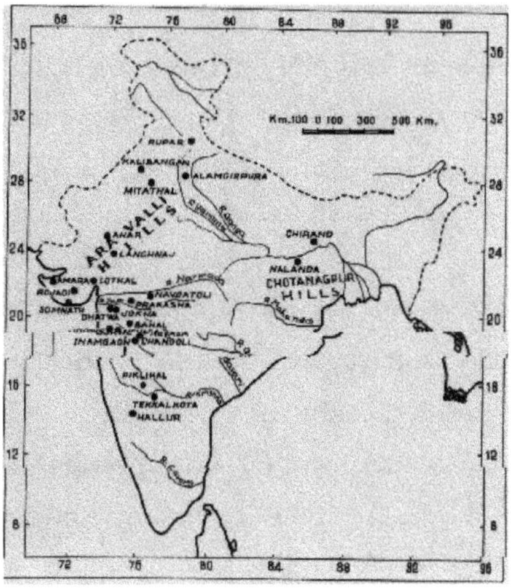

Geological Society of Ireland, Vol. 5, Part 3, 1879-89, Edinburgh, pp. 215-63). Ball reiterates Lassen's comment that the Greek word *kassiteros* was derived from *kastira* whereas Bevan feels (E.J. Rapson ed., 1921, *The Cambridge History of India*, Vol. I, Delhi, Indian Edn., S. Chand and Co., p. 351)

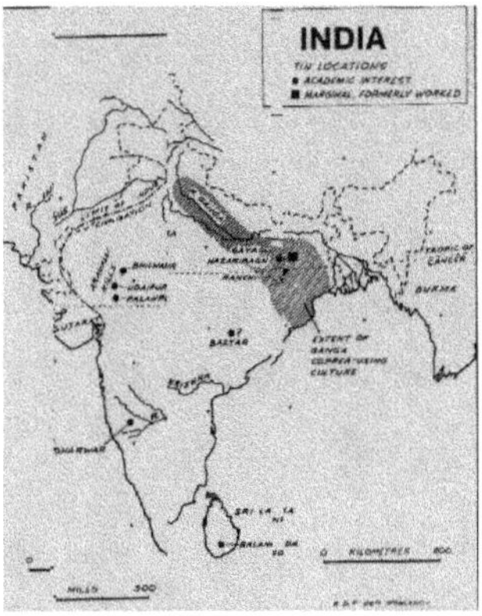

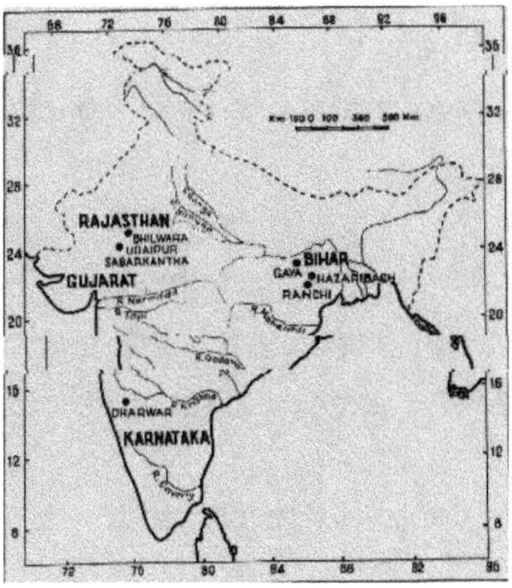

that *kastira* was derived from *kassiteros*. Such a controversy also existed about ā*rakūṭa* in Sanskrit and *oreichalkos* in Greek ('mountain copper') which refer to brass. Pliny called this *aurichalcum* or golden copper (since brass is yellow).[358]

Sources of tin in India and Afghanistan (After Pennhallurick, 1986, maps 3 and 5).

Sources of Tin for the Bronze Age in the areas close to Aravalli and Chota Nagpur Hills, India

Sites of ancient Indian excavated and copper and bronze objects (Hegde, opcit.)

"I have analyzed 38 representative metal objects, selected from among 76 objects, excavated from six post-Harappan sites: Mitathal, Ahar, Somnath, Navdatoli, Jokha, and Chandoli; distributed in Central and western India and in the Deccan plateau. These objects were recovered from the strata that are dated to ca. 1500-1000 BC. The objects included axes, chisels, knives, daggers, bracelets, and bangles. Among the 38 objects analyzed, 7 were found to be made of bronze. Their tin content varied from 3.12 to 12.82 percent. The other objects were made of copper...At Nalanda in Bihar, excavations have brought to light over five hundred metal images. These images are dated AD 800 to 1200. From among them, BB Lal selected 18 images for chemical analysis. The study revealed that 9 of the images were made of bronze. In their composition, the percentage of tin varied from 7.88 to 23.68 (Lal, 1956, p. 56)...from the foregoing, it is possible to observe that tin was used in India to produce bronze tools and ornaments during the protohistoric Bronze Age and again during historic times to produce statuary...

Out of 13 artefacts analysed from Mohenjo-daro, 6 were found to contain between 4.51% to 13.21% tin; the artefacts were: bronze rod, bronze button, bronze chisel, bronze slab, bronze chisel and bronze lump.[359]

Sites of Indian tin ore deposits (Hegde, opcit.)

Kumbharia (2 kms. east of Ambaji) is a pilgrimage centre for the Jains, which has a temple with metal images of Tīrthānkara, dated ca. 11th cent. AD. Kumbharia is located near a mountain known as Arasur which has many mines of non-ferrous metals. (cf. ancient texts: *Purātan Prabhanda San:graha*, 1030 AD and *Upades'a Saptati*, 1477 AD; the texts also refer to Ambāji in Banaskantha district of North Gujarat as sources of copper and other metals). (Swarna Kamal Bhowmik and Mudrika Jani, Literary references on metals, metallic objects of art and metal technology, in: Vibha Tripathi (ed.), 1998, *Archaeometallurgy* in India, Delhi, Sharada Publishing House).

"Tin ore deposits are known to occur in India at a number of places in Rajasthan, Gujarat, Bihar, and Karnataka. In Rajasthan, they are found in the Aravalli Hills, about 27 km north of Shahapura, near Paroli in Bhilwara district and at Soniana in Udaipur district. In Gujarat, the deposits occur within the Aravalli Hills, near Hussainpur and Palanpur, in Banaskantha district.In Bihar, tin ore deposits are reported from the Chota Nagpur Hills, in Hazaribagh, Ranchi, and Gaya districts. In Hazaribagh district, they are found at Simritari, Pihra, Chappatand, and at Nurungo. In Ranchi district, the deposits are foundat Jonha Silli and Paharsingh. In Gaya district, they are found at Dhakanahwa and Dhanras. In Karnataka, small cassiterite deposits are reported to be present in the alluvia of the streams flowing from the northern part of the Kapatgod Hills, near Dambal in Dharwar district....Cassiterite is often found in the form of water-concentrated deposits, referred to as 'stream tin'. R.F. Tylecote (1962, *Metallurgy in Archaeology*, London, Edward Arnold, p. 63), observes more likely that it was stream tin that the ancient metallurgists exploited rather than vein deposits. Vein deposits are hard to mine. Proper prospecting of the alluvial deposits of the streams that flow from the cassiterite-bearing hills in the Aravalli and Chota Nagpur ranges, is yet to be done...tin ore deposits within the proximity of the Aravalli and Chota Nagpur Hills and whether they did not form a source of ancient tin India. Our study on the source of ancient Indian copper seems to indicate this possibility. Through a spectrometric analysis and comparison of impurity patterns, we have been able to demonstrate the possibility of linking the copper in the post-Harappan copper and bronze objects with the chalcopyrite deposits in the Aravalli Hills. The chalcopyrite deposits in the Aravalli Hills form a discontinuous belt, extending over 150 km. And within the belt, there are a number of 7 to 8 m deep shafts and large slag heaps -- possible marks of ancient mining and metal-smelting activities. Among the excavated material remains, dated to ca. 1500 BC from Ahar, a site within the Aravalli Hills, there were a number of chunks of semi-fused glass-like material. This we have chemically analyzed and identified as copper metallurgical slag, a waste product of the copper smelting industry. We have therefore observed that Ahar was an ancient Indian copper smelting center. The metalworkers there appear to have exploited the locally available ores. Similarly, in Bihar chalcopyrite deposits occur at a number of places, in Hazaribagh and Singhbhum districts in the Chota Nagpur Hills. These deposits are also marked with ancient metalworking activities. In the Aravalli and Chota Nagpur Hills copper and tin ore deposits occur in proximity. There are clear indications to show that the ancient Indian metallurgists exploited the copper ore deposits occurring in the Aravalli Hills. It is likely that they took advantage of the copper ore deposits in the Chota Nagpur Hills, as well...The geographic distribution of sites, where ancient Indian bronze objects were found, supports this observation. However, this does not rule out the possibility of import of tin into India. India has had long cultural and trade contacts with Burma, Malaya and other Southeast Asian countries known for their rich deposits of tin ore. These contacts increased during the historic period...C.J.Brown and A.K. Dey (1955, *India's Mineral Wealth*, Bombay, Oxford University Press, p. 167) refer to the fact that in 1849 tin ore was being smelted in village iron furnaces at Purgo, near Parasnath in Bihar. It is therefore likely that the locally smelted tin and imported tin were both used in the production of ancient Indian bronze objects."[360]

"At Harappa, three copper alloys were used in the period 2500-2000 BC: copper and up to 2% nickel; copper and up to 5% nickel; copper with ca. 10% tin and a trace of arsenic. Ingots of tin as well as of copper were found at Harappa. (Lamberg-Karlovsky, C.C., 1967, Archaeology and metallurgy in prehistoric Afghanistan, India and Pakistan, American Anthropologist, 1967, 69, 145-62).

The rarity of the metal is seen at Mohenjo-daro where, of 64 artifacts examined, only nine were of tin bronze.[361] Ingots of tin bronze have also been found at Chanhu-daro. Yet in spite of its scarcity, tin bronze was widely used. Its occasional abundance and, in the case of the bronzes from Luristan in southern Iran, the high quality of the tin bronzes produced, equally underline the fact that rich source of tin existed somewhere...

"The archaeological evidence from Afghanistan is not unequivocal...What is surprising is the discovery in 1962 of corroded pieces of sheet metal bearing traces of an embossed design and made of a low tin content bronze (5.15%)...The uncorroded metal is thought to have contained nearer 7% tin. (Caley, E.R., 1972, Results of an examination of fragments of corroded metal from the 1962 excavation at Snake Cave, Afghanistan, Trans. American Phil. Soc., New Ser. , 62, 43-84). These fragments came from the deepest level in the Snake Cave, contemporary with the earliest occupation dated by 14C to around 5487 and 5291 BC. (Shaffer, J.G., in Allchin F.R. and N. Hammond (eds.), 1979, The Archaeology of Afghanistan, Academic Press, 91, 141-4)...If this dating is acceptable, not only is this metal the earliest tin bronze known from anywhere, but it is also an isolated occurrence of far older than its nearest rival and quite unrelated to the main development of bronze age metallurgy...

"Even more exciting is the evidence from Shortugai... In 1975, French archaeologists discovered on the surface at Shortugai, sherds of Indus pottery extending over more than a millennium - the whole span of the Indus civilization. (Lyonnet, B., 1977, Decouverte des sites de l'age du bronze dans le N.E. de l'Afghanistan: leurs rapports avec la civilisation de l'Indus, Annali Instituto Orientali di Napoli, 37, 19-35)... Particularly important is a Harappan seal bearing an engraved rhinoceros and an inscription which reinforces the belief that the site was a trading post. Shortugai is only 800 km from Harappa, as the crow flies, though the journey involves hundreds of kilometres of mountainous terrain through the Hindu Kush...Lyonnet's conclusion was that the most likely explanation for their existence was an interest in 'the mineral resources of the

Iranian Plateau and of Central Asia', to which can now be added those of Afghanistan itself. Indus contacts extended well into Turkmenia where the principal bronze age settlements, such as Altin-depe and Namasga-depe, lie close to the Iranian border…

"A fine copper axe-adze from Harappa, and similar bronze examples from Chanhu-daro and, in Baluchistan, at Shahi-tump, are rare imports of the superior shaft-hole implements developed initially in Mesopotamia before 3000 BC. In northern Iran examples have been found at Shah Tepe, Tureng Tepe, and Tepe Hissar in level IIIc (2000-1500 BC)...Tin was more commonly used in eastern Iran, an area only now emerging from obscurity through the excavation of key sites such as Tepe Yahya and Shahdad. In level IVb (ca. 3000 BCE)at Tepe yahya was found a dagger of 3% tin bronze. (Lamberg-Karlovsky, C.C. and M., 1971, An early city in Iran, Scientific American, 1971, 224, No. 6, 102-11; Muhly, 1973, Appendix 11, 347); perhaps the result of using a tin-rich copper ore. However, in later levels tin bronze became a 'significant element in its material culture' comparatble with other evidence from south-east Iran where at Shadad bronze shaft-hole axes and bronze vessels were found in graves dated to ca. 2500 BC. (Burney, C., 1975, From village to empire: an introduction to Near Eastern Archaeology, 1977, Phaidon). The richness of Tepe Yahha, Shahr-i-Sokhta, and Shadad, are all indicative of trade and 'an accumulation of wealth unsuspected from the area'. (Lamberg-Karlovsky, 1973, reviewing Masson and Sarianidi (1972) in Antiquity, 43-6)....Namazga-depe and neighbouring sites are a long way from the important tin reserves of Fergana...The origin of Near Eastern tin remains unproven; the geological evidence would favour the deposits of Fergana and the Tien Shan range..."[362]

Euphrates the copper river or URUDU and Tin from Meluhha

"A copper trade down the Euphrates is extremely ancient; the river's original name was Urudu or 'copper river'. (Hawkes, J. (ed.), 1977, *The First Civilizations*, London, Pelican: 159, 167-8)...The whole purpose of sending Assyrian merchants to Anatolia was to ensure a steady supply of Anatolian silver and some gold. In exchange they gave cloth and tin, 'transported by caravans of black donkeys bred in Assyria'. They made a profit on the cloth of 100% and on the tin of 75-100%. The quantities traded could be considerable; a cargo of 410 talents of tin (more than 12 t) is once mentioned, though for some curious reason tin prices are never recorded. Trade with Kanesh continued until ca. 1757 BC when Hammurabi of Babylon destroyed Mari (900 km. up the Euphrates) and a period of wars followed which reduced 'central Anatolia, once rich, to a land of ruins'. The Kanesh tablets give no indicatin of where Assyrian tin came from...The texts from Mari show a way out of the difficulty by also recording tin being shipped up the Euphrates, presumably from the Persian Gulf, pointing to a distant origin involving maritime trade...The Arab geographer Muqadasi stated that tin occurred at Hamadan, 560 km south-west of Tehran. As Muhly wrote, 'a mineral zone running roughly from Hamadan to Tabriz seems to fit all the evidence for the Near Eastern tin trade'.[363]

Sea-faring merchants of Melukkha (Meluhha) and trade route of tin ingots

Mleccha trade was first mentioned by Sargon of Akkad (Mesopotamia 2370 B.C.) who stated that boats from Dilmun, Magan and Meluhha came to the quay of Akkad.[364] The Mesopotamian imports from Meluhha were: woods, copper (ayas), gold, silver, carnelina, cotton. Gudea sent expeditions in 2200 B.C. to Makkan and Meluhha in search of hard wood. Seal impression with the cotton cloth from Umma (Scheil, V., 1925, Un Nouvea Sceau Hindou Pseudo-Sumerian, RA, 22/3, pp. 55-56) and cotton cloth piece stuck to the base of a silver vase from Mohenjodaro (Wheeler, R.E.M., 1965, Indus Civilization) are indicative evidence. Babylonian and Greek names for cotton were: sind, sindon. This is an apparent reference to the cotton produced in the black cotton soils of Sind and Gujarat. Ca. 2150-2000 BC, ivory from Meluhha is mentioned in connection with ivory bird figurines.[365] About 2000 BCE at Ur, ivory is attributed to Dilmun (Bahrein), perhaps shipped up the Gulf from the Indus where tusks and ivory objects were plentiful. Isin-Larsa period (ca. 2000-1800 BCE) texts refer to rods, combs, inlays, boxes, spoons, and 'breastplates' of ivory donated to temples by merchants returning from Dilmun.[366]

Gudea notes that from Magan comes bronze and from the land Meluhha are derived ushu-wood, gold, precious stones and copper. "In the power of Nina and in the power of Ningirsu for Gudea, to whom a scepter was given by Ningirsu, have Magan, Meluhha, Gubin, and the land Tilmun, each of which possesses every kind o tree, brought to Shirpurla ships (laden) with wood for his buildings" (Statue D, iv.2-12). Copper of Dilmun, Magan and Meluhha is mentioned in a text.[367]

'Melukkha' is cognate with Pali 'milakkha' or Sanskrit 'mleccha'. In Pali, 'milakkha' also means, 'copper'. In Sanskrit, 'mleccha-mukha' means 'copper'.

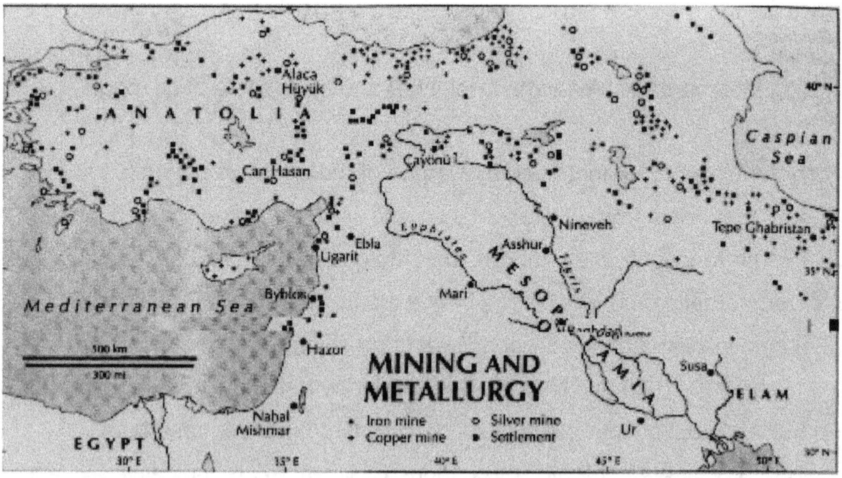

The trading route through Mari on the Euphrates to Ugarit (Mediterranean Sea) and on to Minoan Crete. This routing may explain the presence of Harappan script inscription on tin ingots found at Haifa, Israel!

[After Potts, 1995] The body of water called the Red Sea, Gulf of Aden, Arabian Gulf, Gulf of Oman and the Arabian Sea were referred to by Herodotus as the Erythraean Sea. Dilmun is identified with Bahrain, Magan with Oman and Melukkha with the Indian Civilization. Sargon of Akkad boasts that ships from Dilmun, Magan and Melukkha docked at the quay of his capital Akkad. This inscription affirms that Melukkha was accessible by the sea-route, through the Arabian gulf.There is significant evidence for the presence of people and goods from and frequent interaction with the Indian Civilization in the Mesopotamian and Gulf areas. There is, however, little evidence of a Sumerian, Akkadian or Babylonian presence in India.

"Latin *stagnum-stannum* only comes to mean 'tin' in Late Latin. The word originally designates 'a mixture of lead and silver'. Again, it si not clear why the word came to mean 'tin'. The original Latin designation for tin is not a distinct word at all, but the expression *plumbum album,* sometimes *plumbum candidum,* literally 'white lead'...Pliny refers to a practice of plating objects with tin to give them the appearance of silver:

A method discovered in the Gallic provinces is to plate bronze articles with white lead as to make them almost indistinguishable from silver; articles thus treated are called 'inoctilia'.

Recent archaeological discoveries indicate that such deceptions were practiced not only on metal objects, but also in clay. Excavations at several Mycenaean sites have produced clay vessels with surviving incrustations representing an original tinfoil covering applied with beeswax...

The Greek word for tin, Κασσίτερος/Kassiteros, is again of unknown origin...Some feel that the word is to be analyzed as *kassi-ti-ra,* 'from the land of the Kassites'. This derivation is of considerable interest in the light of the suggested connection of the Kassites with the Zagros mountains and the indications...that this area might have been an important source of tin. Yet this etymology is quite improbable and cannot be substantiated...there is no indication that the Greeks played any role in (Celtic) trade before the founding of the Massalia (modern Marseilles) around 600 BC. Since the Greeks did not come into contact with the Celtic peoples of Gaul much before the end of the seventh century BC, it would be strange to find a Celtic word already in Homer...this factor...rules out a Celtic origin for *kassiteros*...there is no common Indo-European word for tin. Of course the various Romance languages have a common word borrowed from Latin, and the various Germanic languages (with the exception of Gothic) seem to have a common word which may ultimately derive from the same source. This is all the result of a late development. The fact that Latin uses an expression like *plumbum album* to mean 'tin', indicates that the language lacked a real word for the metal...In fact, the earliest Indo-European texts, such as the Mycenaean Linear B tablets and the earliest Sanskrit texts, seem to lack a word for tin. What of Hittite? Unfortunately, here the situation is once again problematic. A word has been suggested, namely **dankui-*. However, even if correct, it says nothing significant about the source of tin in the Hittite empire. The word is clearly a manufactured one, derived from the adjective *dankui*, 'dark', very common in Hittite texts, especially in reference to the dark earth...a lexical text from Ras Shamra seems to equate the Hittite **dankui-* with Sumerian An.NA, Akkadian *ana_ku,* both words now translated 'tin.' Also, if the reference is to the black tinstone of alluvial deposits, the name is quite appropriate.

"The basic Hebrew word for tin is *bedi_l.* The principal reference is from the book of Ezekiel:

Tarshish traded with you because of your abundant wealth of every kind; she bartered with you silver, iron, tin, and lead.

This passage suggests that tin came to Israel from Tarshish, sometimes identified with the south coast of Iberia. The tin trade with Tarshish is thought to have been in the hands of the Phoenicians...this Hebrew word for tin has been compared with Sanskrit *pa_t.i_rah,* 'tin'...a late lexical word in Sanskrit, and seems to belong to that group of words which includes French *peautre,* Italian *peltro* and English *pewter.* These words all go back to an original **peltirum* or **peltrum,* often said to be of Ligurian origin...these words may all be based on the stem **pel-,* meaning 'gray, blackish'...the Old Testament has another word which may represent tin. *Ana_k* is traditionally translated 'plumb line' or 'plummet'. The most important reference is in the book of Amos:

Thus he showed me, and lo, the Lord was standing upon a wall, with a plumb line in his hand.

"...if Hebrew *anāk* is to be compared with Akkadian *anāku*, then the *Homat. anāk* should be 'a wall made of tin'. ..The Sumerian An.NA is sometimes transcribed *nagga*, but there are objections to this reading and it is best to retain the reading AN.NA, in capitals. The meaning 'tin' is established by the fact that the cuneiform texts contain recipes involving the mixture of copper [Sum. *urudu*, Akk. *eru*) with AN.NA in order to produce what can only be bronze (Sum. *zabar*, Akk. *siparru*). The first of these texts dates from the pre-Sargonic period: *1 ma.na 1/3 urudu luh ha AN.NA bi gin 13 igi 3 gal* (That is, 80 shekels of pure copper and 13 1/3 shekels of tin are mixed together, producing a bronze with a copper-tin ratio of 6:1. The Sumerian texts from the Third Dynasty of Ur uses the expression *zabar-7-la*, indicating a bronze with a copper-tin ratio of 6:1. A ratio of 7:1 is also known from this period as the following text indicates: *5 gin AN.NA 1/2 ma.na 5 gin urudu luh-ha* (Here 5 shekels of tin are mixed with 35 shekels of copper giving a copper-tin ratio of 7:1). In the Old Babylonian period, the ratio is again 6:1: *3 ma.na zabar s'a 6 ba-al.lu* (three minas of bronze mixed (in the ratio) of six (to one)

"...Such a ratio means a bronze with about 17% tin...This connection between the texts mentioning the mixture of URUDU and AN.NA and the copper-tin ratio established through the analysis of ancient Mesopotamian bronzes is one of the most convincing arguments for the translation of AN.NA as 'tin'...A bilingual literary text refers to the fire-god: urudu AN>NA III.III bi za e-me-en *s'a e-ri i u a-na-ki mu-bal-lil-s'u-nu at-ta·* (you (fire) are the one who makes an alloy of copper and tin.)...The Akkadian word seems to have cognates in Hebrew *ana_k*, Arabic *a_nuk*, Syriac *a_neka_*, Ethiopic *na_'ek,* and perhaps even Armenian *anag*...already in the Old Akkadian period, there are references to ingots of tin called *s'uqlu* and weighing about 25 kg. The Old Babylonian letters from Mari refer to tin in a form designated by the word *le_'um.* This word, usually translated 'tablet,' is also used to designate the Neo-Assyrian hinged wax-covered ivory writing board foundat Nimrud in 1953. The Mari references must be to an ingot of tin shaped something like a tablet. The Cape Gelidonya ship-wreck has now produced a Late Bronze Age example of a tin ingot. The excavator of the wreck, G.F. Bass, says of this find:

At Gelidonya, therefore, we may have the shape of the end of a tin ingot which was six centimeters on a side; the length of the bar is unknown. Such a shape would correspond to the larger ingot which we have identified in the tomb of Nebamu_n and Ipuky...

"...In addition to these ingots there also tin, as well as copper, ingots from the site of Harappa. (C.C. Lamberg Karlovsky, *American Anthropologist*, 69 (1967) 145-162, p. 149).The existence of tin ingots is well atteste for all periods and all areas of the ancient world, from ca. 2000 BC. to 400 AD. Such an ingot the Egyptians called a *nms'.t dh* and *dh* must then be the Egyptian word for tin...

"The myth of Inanna and Mount Ebih also mentions 'the high mountain land, the mountain land of carnelian and of lapis lazuli' (kur.BAD-na kur-na gug-na za-gin-na) which is of interest as there seems to be, as will be shown below, some connection between the source of tin and the sources of carnelian and lapis lazuli...since one of the exemplars of this myth mentions Enheduanna, the daughter of Sargon of Akkad, it would seem that the work may go back to the Agade period.

"...The mountains of Lūristan are also the location of the land of Barahs'e, known from the Neo-Sumerian period as Marhaśi...One of the texts from al-Rimah does refer to fifty minas of tin from the Nairi-lands. The Nairi-lands are now fairly well known, especially as they appear in the inscriptions of Tukulti-Ninurta I and Tiglath-Pileser I. They occupy the area northwest of Assyria, the region of Diyarbakir and the lands to the east of it, with a population said to be related to the later Urartaeans. The 'sea of the Nairi-lands' (*tamdi śa māt na-i-ri*) would then be identified with Lake Van...

"The reference to 'the Caphtorite' and the clear implication that tin was sent from Mari to Crete are bound to arouse heated controversy. It should come as no surprise here, as this study has repeatedly emphasized the eastern connections of Minoan metallurgy. Strange as it may seem to those rooted in the insularity of the Aegean world, we must now seriously consider the possibility that the tin used by Minoan metal-workers came to Crete from Mari. The 'itinerary' (published by G. Dossin) also implies that the representatives of Crete and Caria, together with a translator (Akkadian targamannum), received their tin at Ugarit...

"J. Bottero and M. Birot have assumed that the tin came from Iran and was brought to Mari by Elamites...The text TLC X 125 refers to 1 1/3 minas, 9 2/3 shekels of pure silver...This text may indicate that silver was brought to Larsa in order to purchase tin and that this tin was purchased in Susa. That is, Larsa did not purchase tin in the north. On the contrary, it supplied tin to the north...Old Assyrian and Old Babylonian period ca. 2000 BC to 1600 BC...The tin was sent from Sippar to Mari, and from there was re-exported to Syria and Palestine. The tin came to Sippar from Susa, either by way of Dēr and Eśnunna or by way of Larsa, coming up from the south. The beginnign of the trade, the determination of the ultimate origin of the tin, still remains to be established...A text from the reign of Gudea of Lagash (ca. 2143-2124 BC) provides a possible clue in this direction. In his elaborate cylinder and statue inscriptions Gudea provides considerable information concerning the origin of the various materials used in his extensive building program. Gudea says that the tin he used came from the land of Meluhha:

(urud)u AN>NA lagab-za-gin na(k)u NE gug-gi rin me luh ha da (copper and tin, blocks of lapis lazuli...bright carnelian from (the land of) Meluhha)

"The land of Meluhha is well known as a source of lapis lazui and carnelian. This is the only direct reference to tin from Meluhha, but the Gudea passage suggests that tin may be associated with the Meluhha trade, a trade also involving copper, lapis lazuli and carnelian. Of all the items involved here, the one which is most securely localized is lapis lazulip. The lapis lazuli used in Mesopotamia came from northern Afghanistan, from the Sar-i-Sang mine in Badahshan. No one has ever proposed that Meluhha be identified with Afthanistan. The current tendency is to identify Meluhha with Sind and the coastal region of western Pakistan. This would mean that the expression 'lapis lazuli from Meluhha' refers not to the actual source of the material, but rather to the entrepot from which it was sent to Mesopotamia. Lapis lazuli from Meluhha would then be an expression parallel to copper from Tilmun.

"It is now assumed that the references to the land of Meluhha in texts relating to the latter part of the third and early part of the second millennium BC are to be associated with the now established relations between Mesopotamia and the Harappn civilization of the Indus Valley during the Sargonic and Isin-Larsa periods. This was a sea-borne trade going down the Persian Gulf and across the Arabian Sea, such as existed in the Hellenistic, Roman, and Byzantine periods. The best known example of such a voyage is that undertaken by Nearchus, the admiral of Alexander the Great, in the year 325 BC. Nearchus set out from the newly built harbor at Pattala, near the mouth of the Indus river, with 1800 transports and galleys and 5000 sailors and marines, in September 325 BC. The entire voyage to the mouth of the Euphrates, with many wanderings and delays, took 130 days. As Nearchus first sailed down the Indus river to pattala, his voyage represents a rpecise example of how the lapis lazuli of Afghanistan could have reached Mesopotamia.

"The voyage of Nearchus was not the first recorded example of a voyage from India. According to Herodotus, the Persian king Darius (522-486 BC) ordered the Ionian admiral Scylax of Caryanda to make a voyage from India to Egypt, a journey said to have lasted three months. Scylax set sail from 'the city of Caspatyrus in the Paktyan country,' a site which cannot be securely identified but which, according to another passage in Herodotus, is to be placed in northern India near Bactria. According to R. Carpenter, the description in Herodotus '...best suits the borderland between modern Pakistan and Afghanistan.' Here, then, is another voyage down the Indus river and then west across the Arabian Sea. Such voyages, from Egypt to India, became very common by the early years of the Roman Empire. Strabo says that, in the reign of Augustus, as many as 120 ships a year sailed from the Red Sea ports of Myos Hormos and Berenice for northeast Africa and India. By the time of the emperor Tiberius, when the Greek explorer Hippalos discovered the monsoons and direct voyages to Bombay became possible, the traffic to India became so extensive that Tiberius began to worry about Rome's balance of payments. Roman hard currency was leaving the country to pay for the gems and silks of India. The so-called *Periplus of the Erythraean Sea* describes this trade in detail. At the time this text was written (late first century AD) India was importing copper, tin, and lead. Her exports included such items as ivory, agate, carnelian, pearls and tortoise shell, many of which are familiar as items associated with the Meluhha trade...

"The archaeological evidence...suggests that such contacts (between Mesopotamia and the Indus Valley) began already in the Early Dynastic period and came to an end with the close of the Isin-Larsa period. In general terms, the dates 2500-1900 BC give the approximate time range for the contacts between the two areas. The period of Mesopotamian contact seems to coincide with the period of Harappan civilization itself. That such contacts were by sea is suggested not only by the geographical setting and the known historical background, but also by references in the Mesopotamian texts to ships from Meluhha. The first such reference comes from *Sammeltafel* text, in abilingual passage relating to the reign of Sargon of Akkad. It refers to the ships of Meluhha, Magan and Tilmun which are docked at the quay of harbor of the city of Agade. The ships of Meluhha are mentioned in other Mesopotamian texts, including one which actually comes from the Old Akkadian period and is not a later copy. Another Old Akkadian text seems to refer to a sailor of a Meluhhan ship. The Sumerian myth known as *Enki and the World Order*, refers to the *magilum*-ship from Meluhha which brings gold, silver, and lapis lazuli to Nippur. The myth of *Enki and Ninhursanga* refers to the big ships brought from Meluhha. These references suggest that a Meluhha ship was a ship which came from Meluhha and that the trade with Meluhha was in the hands of the inhabitants of the Indus Valley. The presence of 'an official interpreter of the Meluhhan language' in Mesopotamia helps to confirm this impression. The most extensive description of Meluhha in cuneiform literature comes in the Sumerian myth of *Enki and the World Order*. In the translation by S.N. Kramer, the relevant passage reads:

He proceeded to the land of Meluhha,

Enki, the king of Abzu, decrees (its) fate:

'Black land, may your trees be large trees, may they be 'highland' trees,

May their thrones fill the royal palace,

May your reeds be large reeds, may the be 'highland' reeds,

May the heroes in the place of battle wield their weapons,

May yourbulls be large bulls, may they be 'highland' bulls,

May their cry be the cry of highland wild bulls,

May the great *me's* of the gods be perfected for you,

May all the *dar* birds of the highland wear carnelian beards,

May your bird be the *Haia* bird

May its call fill the royal palace,

May your silve be gold,

May your copper be tin (and) bronze,

Land, may everything; you have increase,

May your people multiply...

"This passage mentions a number of objects associated with Meluhha and listed elsewhere as coming from Meluhha. All of these items can be found in either Afghanistan or India and sometimes in both. Lapis lazuli has already been mentioned. It is found in Badahshan in northeastern Afghanistan. Carnelian is found in India. Gold, silver, and copper are all found in Afghanistan. They are also found in India. Gold has a particular association with India and there is extensive evidence for gold mining, both ancient and modern, in India, especially in the Kolar gold field, Mysore state. Gold also had a special connection with Meluhha, and the cuneiform texts refer to 'gold in its dust' from Meluhha. They also refer to silver from Meluhha. The copper from Meluhha has already been discussed.

"Besides the various stones and metals already mentioned, other natural products, said to be from Meluhha, are to be found in either India or Afthanistan. Ebony, the wood of Meluhha, is to be found in India. Ivory, said to be from Meluhha, is also from India, as is tortoise shell, which may also be another export from Meluhha. Among the birds mentioned in these texts the *dar-me-luh-ha mushen*, a variegated bird, is now thought to be some sort of chicken. The Meluhha species was known in Mesopotamia only from representations carved in ivory. The *dha-ja mushen* can now be identified as the peacock, the Indian bird par excellence. Both the dog and the cat are said to be from Meluhha, and there is evidence that both animals were domesticated by the inhabitants of the Indus Valley in Harappan times. Even the monkey may be associated with Meluhha, and there may also be an etymological connection as shown by the various words for 'monkey'.

"These are the principal products associated with the Meluhha trade. They represent exports from Meluhha, brought to Mesopotamia by traders from Meluhha in Meluhha ships...The same articles mentioned in the literary and historical texts appear as imports in the mundane economic texts of the Third Dynasty of Ur. All of the products said to be from Meluhha can be localized in Afghanistan or in the Indus Valley. This is in agreement with the generally accepted identification of Meluhha with the area of Sind and western Pakistan...The termination of this trade now seems to coincide with the collapse of Harappan civilization itself. This collapse may even be in some way responsible for the general economic decline in Mesopotamia and the absence of international trade after the Isin-Larsa period, i.e. after ca. 1900-1850 BC...The lapis lazuli of Badahshan and the other stones and metals of Afghanistan must have been brought down the Indus river to some port on the mouth of the Indus. From Afghanistan the trade route must have gone south, over the Hindu Kush by means of the Khyber Pass to Peshawar. The Peshawar plain was known to the Persians as the satrapy of Gan-dh-a_ra and, from at least the sixth century BCE, on, there existed a major trade route across Peshawar down to southern India. The cities of Chārsaddā and Taxila testify to the importance of this route. Somewhere near the mouth of the Indus there must have been a port similar to that which Alexander the Great had built at Pattala, and from here the goods were shipped west eventually to reach southern Mesopotamia.

"It is generally assumed that such a port has been found and that it is located not on the Indus but at Lothal in the Gulf of Cambay...The radiocarbon determinations from Lothal suggest that the site was in use aproximatey in the period during which the trade with Meluhha was in existence.

"Although no actual remains of boats were found, the excavations at Lothal did uncover terracotta boat models and a number of +so-called anchors of stone. It seems that industry was located right at the harbor site, for at Lothal were excavated not only factories for making agate and carnelian beads, but also the workshops of coppersmiths together with ingots of almost pure copper...

"The quay (Sumerian kar, Akkadian kārum) is mentioned frequently in cuneiform literature and was a major factor in the economic organization of ancient Mesopotamia...The quest for metals was the factor which stimulated the trowth of an organized foreign trade. The trade with Tilmun, Magan and Meluhha must, then, be seen as part of the international age of metallurgy which developed in the second half of the third millennium BC.

"The tin of Meluhha may even have something to do with the Harappan settlement at Lothal. The use of tin-bronze in the Harappan period has been outlined above. Of particular interest is the extensive use of tin-bronze at Rangpur in Gujarat. The bronzes here have a tin content of four to eleven percent. The absence of arsenic in the Rangpur bronzes and its presence in the bronzes from Harappa and Mohenjodaro indicates taht different sources of copper were used in each area. That used at Rangpur must have come from Rajasthan and this is the ore also worked at Lothal, because arsenic is also absent from the copper ingots found there. This indicates that the Harappans did not come to Lothal to obtain copper. They might have come in order to obtain tin...it should be pointed out that Gujarat has even been proposed as possible location for Meluhha."[368]

D.K. Chakrabari[369] opines that during the pre-Harappan and Harappan periods, the main supply of tin was from the western regions: Khorasan and the area between Bukhara and Samarkand. The ancient tin mines in the Kara Dagh District in NW Iran and in the modern Afghan-Iranian Seistan could have been possible sources. Harappan metal-smiths used to conserve tin by storing and re-using scrap pieces of bronze, making low-tin alloys and substituting tin by arsenic. It is possible that some of the imported tin (like lapis lazuli) was exported to Mesopotamia. A cylinder seal of Gudea of Lagash (2143-2124 B.C.) read: "copper, tin, blocks of lapis lazuli-- bright carnelian from the land of Meluhha." (Muhly, J.D., 1976, Copper and Tin, Hamden, Archon Books, pp. 306-7). Trapu is tin in the Atharva Veda (11, 8.7-8: *śyāmamayah asya māmsāni lohitamasya lohitam; trapu bhasma haritam varn.ah puṣkaramasya gandhah*) and vanga is also tin with the possible association of chalcolithic cultures in Bengal (2nd millennium B.C.) with possible links with the culture of Thailand of the same period (Solheim, W.C., Sciene, Vol. 157, p. 896). Hegde suggests the possibility that water-concentrated placer deposits referred to as 'stream tin' (alluvial cassiterite or mineral tin) in the proximity of Aravalli and Chota Nagpur Hills might have also been the sources of tin. A survey[370] covered six ancient copper ore mining and smelting sites in the Aravalli (Arbuda) hills extending over a thousand kms.: Khetri and Kho Dariba in NE, Kankaria and Piplawas in the Central part and Ambaji in SW.. A large majority of mine-pits measure 7-8 metres in dia. and 3-4 metres deep showing evidence of fire-treating of the host rocks on the mine walls to widen rock joints. The evidene indicated probable mining in the chalcolithic period. Timber supports recovered from a gallery at a depth of 120 metres at Rajpura-Dariba mines in Udaipur District were radio-carbon dated to 3120+_ 160 years before the present (1987). This correlates with the zinc-containing copper artefacts of Atran~jikhera. Finely crushed ore was concentrated by gravity separation at the smelting sites which were invariably close to the banks of hill streams. This helped separate gangue from the ore. Smelting charge was by crushed quartz equal to the weight of the ore, crushed charcoal twice the weight of the ore. Furnace walls showed evidence of residues of small, hand-made, fistfuls of spherical lumps. The smelter furnace was a small, crucible-shaped, clay-walled, slag-tapping device worked on forced draught from bellows; 'this simple furnace appears to have been continuously used in India over the millennia without little innovation.' It would appear that the facilities in the metropolis of the civilization on the banks of Sarasvati and Sindhu were only purification and fabrication facilities with limited or no smelting operations. Bun-shaped copper ingots from Ganeshwar taken through the riverine routes were perhaps carried by itinerant metal-smiths of the copper-hoard culture and fabricated in cities like Mohenjodaro and Harappa to meet the specifications of the consumers of this doab or the Tigris-Euphrates doab.[371]

Harappa. kiln.

Harappa 1999, Mound F, Trench 43: Period 5 kiln, plan and section views[372]

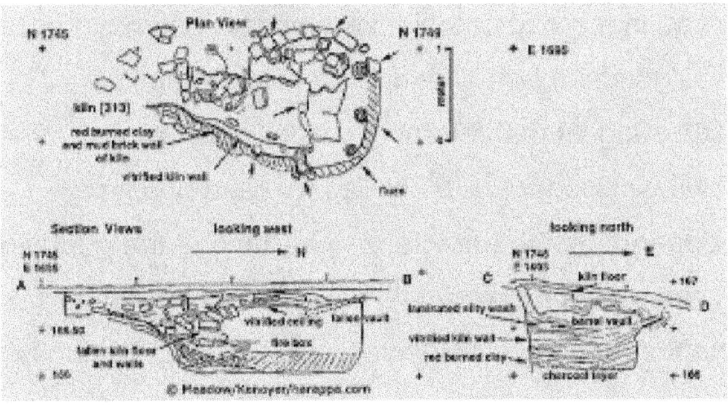

"A lengthy prehistoric sequence has been established at the important site of Mehrgarh in Pakistani Baluchistan, where an aceramic occupation beginning around 7000 BCE that formed the foundation for the later ceramic Neolithis and Chalcolithic cultures in the region has recently been documented. Despite innovations and changes in the prehistoric sequence of the greater Indus Valley, there is an essential thread of unity and a strong stamp of cultural identity throughout that underscores the essentially indigenous, deeply rooted nature of Indian civilization. While points of contact with other regions are attested, they can hardly have accounted for the strength and individuality of civilization in the subcontinent." (Potts, 1995, p. 1457).

Damaged circular clay furnace, comprising iron slag and tuyeres and other waste materials stuck with its body, exposed at lohsanwa mound, Period II, Malhar, Dist. Chandauli.[373]

Tilmun, Telmun, Dilmun, the land of the famous red stone

Documents of the Larsa period in Ur were on tablets. Volume UET V includes texts which deal with Ur as the port of entry for copper into Mesopotamia during the time of the Dynasty of Larsa. The copper was imported by boat from Telmun. (Tilmun is associated with the famous red stone, of which Gudea speaks repeatedly as being imported from Meluhha.) [quote]This 'Telmun-trade' was in the hands of seafaring merchants--called alik Telmun-- who worked hand in hand with enterprising capitalists in Ur to take garments to the island in order to buy large quantities of copper there... In our period-- that of the fifth to seventh king of the Dynasty of Larsa-- the island exported not only copper in ingots but also copper objects, beads of precious stones, and-- most of all-- ivory... Travels to Telmun are repeatedly mentioned in a group of tablets whih come patently from the archives of the temple of the goddess Ningal and list votive offerngs, incoming tithe, etc. The contexts suggest that returning sailors were wont to offer the deity in gratitude a share of their goods. In UET V 526 we read of a small amount of gold, copper and copper utensils characterized as 'tithe of the goddess Ningal from an expedition to Telmun and (from) single persons having gone (there) on their own', during the first 3 months of the year. UET V 292... listing of merchandise is more extensie; besides' red' gold, copper, lapiz lazuli in lumps, various stone beads, ivory-inlaid tables, et., we find also 'fish-eyes'--perhaps pearls. (The meaing 'pearl' for IGI.HA has been proposed by R.C. Thompson (1936y: 53, n2) on the basis of UET V... The appearance of rather numerous references to IGI.HA in Ur and especialy in connection with imports from Tilmun must be considered an argument in favor of an interpretation which is not based on philological evidence. The lack of archaeological proof for the use of pearls is of course an important arguent against the identification but its value is somewhat diminished when one considers that no ivory object has been found in Ur although the texts report on ivory as raw material as well as on ivory objects.) ... UET 78, recording ivory combs, eye-paint and certain kinds of wood, not to mention designations which we fail to understand... UET V 367: '2 mina of silver (the value of): 5 gur of oil (and of) 30 garments for an expedition to Telmun to buy (there) copper, (as the) capital for a partnership, L. and N. have borrowed from U. After safe termination of the voyage, he (the creditor) will not recognize commercial losses (incurred by the debtor); they (the debtors) hae agree to satisfy U (the creditor) with 4 mina of copper for each shel of silver as a just (price(?)].'.. babtum must denote some kind of customs or dues imposed on the merchants by the city administration... all extant Old and Neo-Babylonian contracts on partnership reserve for the tamkarum not only the invested capital (plus interest) but also an equal share of the profit yielded by the business venture... The complex legal relationship between the investing and the travelling merchant has created a number of loan types of which at least two are mentioned in the Code of Hammurabi. One of them uses the characteric term tadmiqtu. We encounter this word in the paragraphs 102-103 of the Code and in a few documents of that period... UET V 428: '5 shekels of silver as a tadmiqtu-loan PN1 has borrowed from PN2. He will return the silver at a moment (yet) to be determined (?) (This) he has sworn by the life of the king.' The specific designation of the loans as tadmiqtu 'favor, kindness' (in Sumerian: KA.sa 'friendly word') should not, in spite of the obvious etymology of these terms in both languages, induce us to presume that this business transaction was not as completely under the sway of the laws of economic life as any other loan... As to the main object of the Telmun trade, the copper (termed URUDU), we obtain most of the evidence from the letters (UET V 22,29, 71 and 81) addressed to a certain Ea-na_s.ir, a travelling merchant and importer of Telmun copper. The metal came in large quantities (UET V 796 mentions more than 13,000 minaz of copper according to the weight standard of Telmun) and often in ingots termed gubarum which weighed up to 4 talents each (UET V 678). The ingots are sometimes qualified as damqu (UET V 22,81) as is also the copper itself (UET V 20 wariam la damqam, but wariam dummuqam in UET V 5 and 6). The quoted passages do not entitle us to speak of refining of copper, because Ea-na_s.ir was not a coppersmith but a merchant and because the meaning of damqum as well asdummuqum as 'good (in quality)' is borned out by such letter passages as UET V 5:28 or 22: 10-13 ('show him 15 ingots so that he may select 6 damqu ingots' ... UET V 81, lines 33-39: 'I myself gave on account of you 19 talents of copper to the palace and S'umi-abum gave (likewise) 18 talents of copper, apart from the sealed document which we both handed over to the temple of Shamash.'... Ea-na_s.ir is supposed to have imported a large copper kettle (UET V 5:25)... UET V 428: '1 mina of...silver, 1/2 mina of... silver to buy (precious stones), 'fish-eyes' and other merchandise on an expedition to Telmun, PN2 has borrowed from PN1...'... ivory as raw material (UET V 546) as well as finished ivory objects have been imported from Telmun. Among the latter we find exactly the same objects which we know so well from the dowry inventories, etc. of the Amarna letters: ivory combs (UET V 292, 678), breast plates (UET V 279), boxes (UET V 795), inlaid pieces of furniture (UET 292) and spoons (UET V 795)... Southern Mesopotamia had to rely exclusively upon ivory imported from the East, to be exact: via Telmun... we have from Mohenjodaro actual ivory combs... UET V 82 refers to the karum as a locality in which business accounts have been settled, which in Old-Babylonian practice is normally done in the temple of Shamash... A certain Lu-En-li_l-la_ is said in UET III 1689 (Ibbi-Sin, 4th year) to have received large amounts of garments and wool from the storehouse of the temple of Nanna in order to buy copper in Makkan (nig.s'am.marudu Ma.gan ki, literally: equivalent for buying copper in M.)... When Sargon of Agade proudly proclaims (Legrain 1923: 208f., col. v-vi) that ships from or destined for Meluhha, Makkan and Telmun were moored in the harbor which was situated outside of his capital, this obviously proves the existence of flourishing commercial relations with the East... We even know the name of a person, a native of 'Great-Makkan' i.e. Ur-Nammu (UET III 1193). In the period, Makkan-- 'the country of mines' seems to have been the only importer of copper... After the collapse of the Dynasty of Ur, Telmun replaces Makkan in the Eastern trade of the city... Telmun, as against Makkan, seems never to have completely lost contact with Mesopotamia... Telmun had lost contact with the mining centers of Makkan and with those regions which supplied it with stone and timber, etc. some time between the fall of the Dynasty of Larsa and the decline of power of the Hammurabi Dynasty... It turned again into an island famous only for its agricultural products, its sweet water, etc. Copper, precious stones, and rare woods have now to come to Southern Mesopotamia either over the mountain ranges and from the West along the river routes... Sometime in the second half of the 2nd millennium B.C., Telmun seems to have come in closer contact with the rulers of Southern Babylonia (Goetze 1952)... We are fortunate indeed to have three letters at our disposal, two written by Assurbanipal's general Bel-ibni mentioning Hundaru, king of Telmun, and one written by Assurbanipal and addressed to Hundaru. The details of the dealings of the king of Telmun in his fight for survival are of little interest in the present context, far more revealing is the mention of metal (bronze), precious woods and 'kohl' i.e. eye-paint in these letters. We read of great amounts of kohl, 26 talent of bronze, numerous copper and bronze objects, of sticks of precious wood as part of the booty taken from Telmun, while another speaks of the tribute of Telmun mentioning, at the same time, bronze, perfumes and likewise 'sticks' of precious wood offered by merchants from Bit-Naialu... a passage of the inscription KAH 122 of Sennacherib which describes the tools of the crew of corvee-workers sent from Telmun to Babylon to assist the Assyrian king to tear down the city. Their tools are characterized as follows: 'bronze spades and bronze pikes, tools which are the (characteristic) product of their (native) country.' Thus, it becomes evident that Telmun has again access to the copper mines of Makkan, to the spices, perfumes and rare woods of the East... Assurbanipal's inscription in the temple of Ishtar in Niniveh mentions another island-- beyond Telmun--: '[x-y]-i-lum, king of the [ ]-people who resides in Hazmani which is an island alongside Telmun'

whose messengers had to travel a long way across the sea and overland to Assyria. [unquote][374]

"Indian metallurgists were familiar several other metals, of which zinc deserves a special mention because, having a low boiling point (907°C), it tends to vaporize while its ore is smelted. Zinc, a silvery-white metal, is precious in combination with copper, resulting in brass of superior quality. Sometimes part of copper ore, pure zinc could be produced only after a sophisticated 'downward' distillation technique in which the vapour was captured and condensed in a lower container. This technique, which was also applied to mercury, is described in Sanskrit texts such as the 14th-century Rasaratnasamuccaya. There is archaeological evidence of zinc production at Rajasthan's mines at Zawar from the 6th or 5th century BCE. The technique must have been refined further over the centuries. India was, in any case, the first country to master zinc distillation, and it is estimated that between 50,000 and 100,000 tons of zinc was smelted at Zawar from the 13th to the 18th century

CE! British chroniclers record continuing production there as late as in 1760; indeed, there is documentary evidence to show that an Englishman learned the technique of downward distillation there in the 17th century and took it to England —a case of technology transfer which parallels that of wootz steel."

An underground furnace at Ghatgaon (Madhya Pradesh), with a tribal smelting iron ore. (Courtesy: A.V. Balasubramaniam). "We should finally note that most of India's metal production was controlled by specific social groups, including so-called tribes, most of them from the lower rungs of Indian society.For instance, the Agarias of Uttar Pradesh and Madhya Pradesh are reputed iron smiths, and there are still such communities scattered across Jharkhand, Bihar, WestBengal, Kerala and Tamil Nadu. Together, they contributed substantially to India's wealth, since India was for a long time a major exporter of iron. In the late 1600s, shipments of tens of thousands of wootz ingots would leave the Coromandel Coast for Persia every year. India's iron and steel industry was intensive till the 18th century and declined only when the British started selling their own products in India while imposing high duties on Indian products. Industrially produced iron and steel unavoidably put a final stop to most of India's traditional production."[375]

Map showing locations of Mari and Ugarit. The trading route through Mari on the Euphrates to Ugarit (Mediterranean Sea) and on to Haifa. This may explain the presence of Harappan script inscription on tin ingots found at Haifa, Israel ! [Map after Markus Wafler, 'Zu Status und Lage von Taba_l', Orientalia]. Meluhha and interaction areas.

The Tin road

Muhly notes:"A long-distance tin trade is not only feasible and possible, it was an absolute necessity. Sources of tin stone or cassiterite were few and far between, and a common source must have served many widely scattered matallurgical centers. This means that the tin would have been brought to a metallurgical center utilizing a nearby source of copper. That is, copper is likely to be a local product; the tin was almost always an import...The ingots are made of a very pure tin, but what could they have to do with Cyprus? There is certainly no tin on Cyprus, so at best the ingots could have been transhipped from that island... What the ingots do demonstrate is that metallic tin was in use during the Late

Bronze Age...rather extensive use of metallic tin in the ancient eastern Mediterranean, which will probably come as a surprise to many people." (p.47)

Tin used in Indus Valley civilization is well attested. (Hegde 1978; Chakrabarti 1979; Muhly 1985: 283; Stech and Pigott 1986: 43-4). Gudea c. 2100 BC, identified Meluhha as the source of his tin (Falkenstein 1966: i.48: Cylinder B: XIV). "...tin may well often have travelled by sea up the Gulf from distribution centres in the Indus Valley. In the Old Babylonian period tin was shipped through Dilmun (Leemans 1960: 35)... It is now known that Afghanistan has two zones of tin mineralization. One embraces much of eastern Afghanistan from south of Kandahar to Badakshan in the north-east corner of the country (Shareq et al. 1977); the other lies to the west and extends from Seistan north towards Herat (Cleuziou and Berthoud 1982), the valley of the Sarkar river, where the hills are granitic. Here tin appears commonly as cassiterite, frequently associated with copper, gold, and lead, and in quantities sufficient to attract attention in antiquity. Bronzes at Mundigak, and the controversial Snake Cave artefacts, indicate local use of bronze by at least the third millennium BCE (Shaffer 1978: 89, 115, 144). A number of scholars have pointed out the possibility that tin arrived with gold and lapis lazuli in Sumer through the same trade network, linking Afghanistan with the head of the Gulf, both by land and sea (Stech and Pigott 1986: 41-4)."[376] van:ga is also tin with the possible association of chalcolithic cultures in Bengal (2nd millennium B.C.) with possible links with the culture of Thailand of the same period (Solheim, W.C., Sciene, Vol. 157, p. 896). Hegde suggests the possibility that water-concentrated placer deposits referred to as 'stream tin' (alluvial cassiterite or mineral tin) in the proximity of Aravalli and Chota Nagpur Hills might have also been the sources of tin.

Melakkha [ancient Sindhu (Indus)-Sarasvati valley] could have been the early source of ancient tin. "There is an extensive belt of placer deposits in the Malay peninsula which stretches over a distance of 1000 miles. The location of the early tin mines is lost to history, but the first documented use of tin seems to be in

Mesopotamia, followed soon by Egypt. The tin probably came in through the Persian Gulf, or down what would later be the Silk Route. Some tin has been found in central Africa, and could have supplied a small amount to Egypt. However, the earliest needs for the mineral must have been met by Indian sources, the material being carried westward by migrations from southern and eastern Asia toward the Mediterranean area or from nearby sources."[377]

A cylinder seal of Gudea of Lagash (2143-2124 B.C.) read: "copper, tin, blocks of lapis lazuli-- bright carnelian from the land of Meluhha."[378] This is evidence that tin came from Melukkha.

"Archaeologists now present evidence that dates the earliest international trade convoys to 2700 B.C. This trade of 5,000 years ago involved cargos of tin, brought from the mountains of Afghanistan overland across Iran to the city of Eshnunna (Tel Asmar in current-day Iraq) on the Tigris river in Mesopotamia. From there the cargos were transported overland, via the city of Mari on the Euphrates, to the port of Ugarit (current-day Ras Shamra) in northern Syria, and finally from there shipped to various destinations in the Middle East. Tin was an important commodity, as it was vital ingredient in the production of bronze. The bronze alloy formulated in the eastern Mediterranean in the 3rd Millennium BC brought about a revolution in economics, civilization and warfare. At that time, there were only two known sources of tin in the world: Afghanistan and Anatolia. Anatolian tin was used locally and the surplus was exported. The increased demand for tin for bronze production opened up trade with Afghanistan, and thus the first known trade route, the Tin Road, was born. This route was the predecessor of the much later, and more famous Silk Road, over which merchants traveled to and from China."[379]

Tin from Meluhha; Mleccha as a language

Tin used in Indus Valley civilization is well attested. (Hegde 1978; Chakrabarti 1979; Muhly 1985: 283; Stech and Pigott 1986: 43-4). Gudea c. 2100 BC, identified Meluhha as the source of his tin (Falkenstein 1966: i.48: Cylinder B: XIV). "...tin may well often have travelled by sea up the Gulf from distribution centres in the Indus Valley. In the Old Babylonian period tin was shipped through Dilmun (Leemans 1960: 35)... It is now known that Afghanistan has two zones of tin mineralization. One embraces much of eastern Afghanistan from south of Kandahar to Badakshan in the north-east corner of the country (Shareq et al. 1977); the other lies to the west and extends from Seistan north towards Herat (Cleuziou and Berthoud 1982), the valley of the Sarkar river, where the hills are granitic. Here tin appears commonly as cassiterite, frequently associated with copper, gold, and lead, and in quantities sufficient to attract attention in antiquity. Bronzes at Mundigak, and the controversial Snake Cave artefacts, indicate local use of bronze by at least the third millennium BCE(Shaffer 1978: 89, 115, 144). A number of scholars have pointed out the possibility that tin arrived with gold and lapis lazuli in Sumer through the same trade network, linking Afghanistan with the head of the Gulf, both by land and sea (Stech and Pigott 1986: 41-4)." (P.R.S. Moorey, 1994, Ancient Mesopotamian Materials and Industries, Oxford, Clarendon Press p. 298-299).

van:ga is also tin with the possible association of chalcolithic cultures in Bengal (2nd millennium B.C.) with possible links with the culture of Thailand of the same period (Solheim, W.C., Sciene, Vol. 157, p. 896). Hegde suggests the possibility that water-concentrated placer deposits referred to as 'stream tin' (alluvial cassiterite or mineral tin) in the proximity of Aravalli and Chota Nagpur Hills might have also been the sources of tin.

Meluhha (ancient Sindhu (Indus)-Sarasvati valley) could have been the early source of ancient tin. “There is an extensive belt of placer deposits in the Malay peninsula which stretches over a distance of 1000 miles. The location of the early tin mines is lost to history, but the first documented use of tin seems to be in Mesopotamia, followed soon by Egypt. The tin probably came in through the Persian Gulf, or down what would later be the Silk Route. Some tin has been found in central Africa, and could have supplied a small amount to Egypt.

However, the earliest needs for the mineral must have been met by Indian sources, the material being carried westward by migrations from southern and eastern Asia toward the Mediterranean area or from nearby sources."[380]

It will be an erroneous assumption to make that a writing system emerged only to write long texts. The system could have emerged to convey messages about valued artifacts in bronze age trade. "Obviously no script could have survived indefinitely as a simple mixture of pictures and puns; its scope would have been far too restricted and it would have had in course of time to evolve into a syllabic script," notes Chadwick.[381]

Yes, indeed. The Sarasvati hieroglyphs continued to be used on products manufactured in mints, such as early punch-marked coins of Asia Minor and India. The writing system of Sarasvati hieroglyphs continued on three media and not for writing long texts: 1. Line 1 of Sohgaura copper plate followed by text in Brahmi script to represent the facilities provided to itinerant smiths/merchants for metalwork; 2. About 5 devices on punch-marked coins to represent the repertoire of a mint; and 3. On sculptures of Barhut stupa and many representations in Angkor Wat, representing extraordinary ligatured glyptics such as those of makara. Two Sarasvati hieroglyphs became abiding metaphors: 1. narrow-necked jar which is shown on a Yajurveda manuscript discovered in Gujarat; 2. svastika which adorns many temple walls in India. It is possible that the glyphs and the underlying rebus or pun words, provided the basis for the choice of graphs used in the syllabic-phonetic scripts of Brahmi or Kharoshthi. "A lengthy prehistoric sequence has been established at the important site of Mehrgarh in Pakistani Baluchistan, where an aceramic occupation beginning around 7000 BCE that formed the foundation for the later ceramic Neolithis and Chalcolithic cultures in the region has recently been documented. Despite innovations and changes in the prehistoric sequence of the greater Indus Valley, there is an essential thread of unity and a strong stamp of cultural identity throughout that underscores the essentially indigenous, deeply rooted nature of Indian civilization. While points of contact with other regions are attested, they can hardly have accounted for the strength and individuality of civilization in the subcontinent."[382]

Attesting Indus trade in Mesopotamia are the following artifacts: From an Akkadian house in Tell Asmar, a cylinder seal was found depicting elephant, rhinoceros, crocodile (Frankfort, H., 1923, Tell Asmar, Khafaje, Khorsabad Seals, Oriental Instit Communications No. 16, Chicago:51; 1938:305). In Kish, a square steatite seal with 'one-horned young bull' and the Indus signs. (Found nine meters below the surface, Langdon, S., 1931, A new factor in the problem of Sumerian origins, JRAS, : 593-96). A square Indus seal was found in Kish showing 'one-horned young bull' and Indus inscription. (Langdon 1931: 593). In Umma (Tell Jokha), an impressed square clay sealing with at least ten Indus signs was found.[383] At Tell Asmar are also found Harappan-type knobbed ware, etched beads and kidney shaped inlay of bone. 'An unpublished bronze or copper knife of distinctly Harappan type was found in Hissar IIIB, while a copper axe-adze is noted from Mohenjo-daro and said to be paralleled at Hissar III.' (Lamberg-Karlovsky, 1972, Trade mechanisms in Indus-Mesopotamian interrelations, Journal of American Oriental Society, Vol. 92, No. 2, p.225).

'...the presence of a proto-literate site at Tepe Yahya, some 600-800 miles from the Indus Valley and 200-400 years prior to the formation of the Harappan culture has clear implications in generating the processes which led toward not only the development of later Indus-Elamite-Mesopotamian relations, but for the very formation of the Harappan Civilization!...'[384]

Gelb's hypothesis was that proto-Elamite, like proto-Indic (Indus script), represented a 'fully developed system' with regard to phonetization.[385] [grammatology: study of writing systems.] Gelb is right about proto-indic (Indus script). Proto-Elamite uses more abstract graphics than Indus script. Indus script is dominated by pictographs as field-symbols and many 'signs' are also pictographic, not unlike Egyptian hieroglyphs using the orthography of a pictographic style. Indus script has also evolved beyond the pictorial glyphs by evolving signs from pictographs. (E.g., water-carrier glyph as a sign; antelope as a sign).

m0516At m0516Bt 3398 [Copper tablet; side B perhaps is a graphemic representation of an antelope.

Tin of Melukkha

Some excerpts from Muhly, Forbes, Serge Cleuziou and Thierry Berthoud on sources of tin; tin of Melukkha !

Cuneiform texts from Mari on the Euphrates record the storage of 500 kilograms of tin, and shipment to cities such as Ugarit on the Syrian coast, to Dan and Hazor in Palestine, and even to Captara, i.e. Crete.[386]

"The Bronze Age exploitation of the Omani copper deposits seems to have coincided with what are most likely two related phenomena: (1) references in Mesopotamian texts to copper from Magan and to obtaining that copper either directly from Magan or through the intermediate agency of Dilmun (the island of Bahrain)-- the copper did not come FROM Dilmun but THROUGH Dilmun; and (2) the period of the Mature Harappan phase of the Indus Valley Civilization.

"This second correlation suggests that contact and trade with Mesopotamia were factors contributing to the development of the Indus Valley civilization, established in an area known to the Sumerians as the land of Melukkha. So close was the relationship that the traders of Dilmun used the same system of weights and measures as that found in the Indus Valley. From the figures given in Sumerian texts it would appear that the Dilmun shekel was about three times heavier than the standard Sumerian one. It has been thought by some scholars that transactions at Ebla (modern Tell Mardikh) were also conducted on the basis of the Dilmun shekel, but this reading of the sign in question in the Ebla texts cannot be substantiated, and all theories regarding references to Dilmun at Ebla remain conjectural.

"The amount of copper involved in this trade was quite considerable. One text from Ur (UET 5 796), dated to the reign of Rim-Sin of Larsa (1822-1763 BCE), records the receipt in Dilmun of 611 talents, 6 2/3 minas of copper (presumably from Magan). This shipment, according to the text, was weighed according to the standard of Ur, giving a modern equivalent of 18,333 kilograms (40,330 pounds) of copper. One-third of this copper was earmarked for delivery to Ea-na_s.ir of Ur, a merchant who had close connections with Magan and the Dilmun copper trade...This contact beween Metopotamia and the Indus Valley, the land of Melukkha, was clearly by sea and must have brought products across the Arabian Sea and the Persian Gulf. These products included the copper of Magan. Did they also include the tin of Afghanistan and Central Asia, perhaps the tin designated by Gudea, king of Lagash (now known to be a contemporary of Ur-Nammu, king of Ur, circa 2100 BCE), as the tin of Melukkha?

"Tin and the Development of Bronze Metallurgy. Early Use of Bronze. The most important metallurgical development during the Early Bronze Age was the discovery that adding tin to copper produced a far superior metal, eventually known as bronze. In its classic form, bronze has 10 percent tin and 90 percent copper. The addition of even 2 percent tin has noticeable effects upon the hardness and working properties of copper, but anything over 16 percent tin is undesirable, for a very high tin content makes copper brittle and difficult to work. Objects such as the ax head from the A cemetery at Kish (modern Tell al-Uhaimir; Early Dynastic, or ED, IIIB), with 15.5 percent tin, are probably to be assessed as being of early, experimental alloys.

"The historical development of bronze metallurgy has been difficult to document, and locating ancient sources of tin has proved to be an even more intractable problem...the cache of human figurines from Tell Judeidah (northern Syria), the excavators' date of about 3000 (transition Amuq G-H) still seems the most probable...A pin from Tepe Gawra VIII (early third millennium) siad to have 5.6 percent tin unfortunately can no longer be located, but four artifacts from the Y cemetary at Kish, of ED I date, proved to have more than 2 percent tin. These are the earliest examples of bronze from Mesopotamia. One of these objects, a spouted jar, has 6.24 percent tin...

"Sources of Tin and the Tin Trade...The tin was brought to Asshur from some point further east, most likely Afghanistan. The Assyrian merchants purchased the tin for reshipment, by donkey caravan, and sale (at a 100 percent markup) in Anatloia...The Old Assyrian tin trade was on a large scale and enriched three generations of Old Assyrian merchant families...

"Tin exists in nature in the form of cassiterite, an oxide of tin. The cassiterite most likely utilized by Bronze Age metal workers was alluvial or placer cassiterite, popularly known as tin-stone and present as nuggets or pebbles in the beds of streams...Alluvial cassiterite was collected by panning the bed of a stream, much like the recovery of alluvial gold...Gold and tin often occur within the same general area as, for example, in the Eastern (Arabian) Desert of Egypt. Ancient Sardis, the region of the Tmolus (modern Boz Dag) mountain range and the Pactolus River, was famous as an ancient source of alluvial gold, the source of wealth for Croesus, king of Lydia, but no placer cassiterite has been documented from Anatolia...

"Mari and the Tin Trade...the texts from Mari (Tell Hariri), dating mainly to the first half ot the eighteenth century BCE...(tin) came to Mari through Elam, from Susa and Anshan (now identified with the Central Iranian site of Tepe Malyan), and Elamites played a major role in the trade, especially a man named Kuyaya. Certain merchants from Mari were also heavily involved in the tin trade with Elam, among them a merchant named Ishkhi-Dagan (the two appear together in ARM 23 555). The tin came to Mari in the form of ingots (Akkadian le_'u) that weighed about ten pounds each. It is possible to obtain some idea of the relative value of this tin, for a number of the Mari texts provide a tin:silver ratio of 10:1 (the most common ratio; a few texts give ratios from 8:1 to 15:1). This is to be compared with isolated referenced to a tin:gold ratio (48:1), a confusing silver:gold ratio of 4:1 as well as 2:1, and a lead:silver ratio (1200:1). The usual copper:silver ratio at Mari was 180:1 for unrefined 'mountain' copper, with refined (litarally 'washed') copper being valued at 150:1. This means that tin was usually from fifteen to eighteen times more valuable than copper...In later texts from Nuzi (fifteenth century BCE) goods were priced in amounts of tin. An ox cost thirty-six minas of tin; an ass, twenty-four minas. During the Middle Assyrian period tin seems to have functioned as the monetary standard (temporarily replacing the customary silver). Plots of land were purchased with tin...

"The cuneiform archives contain a number of 'recipe' texts, giving the amounts of coper and tin used to make specified amounts of bronze. One of the earlist such texts, from Palace G at Ebla, records that 3 minas, 20 shekels of tin were alloyed with 30 minas of copper to produce 200 objects of bronze, each weighing 10 shekels. In other words, 200 shekels of tin were mixed with 1,800 shekels of copper to produce 2,000 shekels of a 10 percent tin-bronze. In one Mari text 20 shekels of tin were added to 170 shekels of refined copper from Teima at the rate of 1:8, to produce 190 shekels of bronze for a key (to the lock of a city gate)...This means that smiths at Mari were working with the metals themselves--with copper and tin--not with ores or minerals. That is no smelting was being carried out in the vicinity of the Mari palace...

"At the other end of the Mari trade network, the texts record that tin stored at Mari was transhipped to various cities in the Levant, from Karkamish in the north to Hazor in the south. This we learn from a remarkable tin itinerary that concludes with the recording of '1 (+) minas of tin to the Cretan; 1/3 mina of tin to the translator, chief (merch)ant among the Cretans; (dispensed) at Ugarit...' (ARM 23 556). This striking passage indicates that there were Minoan merchants (the text uses the name Kaptaru, generally taken to designate the island of Crete) doing business (perhaps also residing) at Ugarit (modern Ras Shamra) toward the beginning of the Old Palace period in Crete. Furthermore, the Minoan merchants seem to have had a translator (Akkadian, targamannum; the origin of the common European 'dragoman') who was also the leader of the Minoans doing business at Ugarit. Such translators are known from other periods of Mesopotamian history. We have the cylinder seal of a Sargonic official who served as translator for the Melukkha merchants who came to Agade from the Indus Valley, perhaps bringing with them the tin of Melukkha, a commodity mentioned in one of the statue inscriptions of Gudea, ruler of Lagash. A Mari text, dated to the ninth year of the reign of Zimri-Lim, refers to the construction of a 'small Kaptaru boat', perhaps to be taken as a model ship for ritual purposes or as the designation of a ship built for sailing to Crete. A possible parallel for this would be the Egyptian references to Byblos ships (for sailing to the ancien Syrian port of Byblos (modern Jubayl) and Keftiu ships (built for sailing to Crete)... "Bronze certainly was being produced in Middle Minoan Crete, with production undergoing a great expansion during the Late Bronze Age, as it did on the Greek mainland...The problem is that, at present, no satisfactory analytical method for studying the provenance of tin has been discovered." (James D. Muhly, 1995, Mining and Metalwork in Ancient Western Asia, in: Jack M. Sasson, ed. 1995, Civilizations of the Ancient Near East, Vol. III, New York, Charles Scribner's Sons, pp. 1501-1521).

"In the ancient Near East... when working gold by streaming, nodules of cassiterite (or tin-stone SnO2) were found. This cassiterite was reduced by workers already proficient in the production of gold, silver and lead. The metal obtained was held to be a kind of lead. [In Sanskrit, the term for lead is: na_ga. In Akkadian, the term for tin is: anakku). Lead and antimony were already used to increase the ease with which copper could be cast, but neither of them improved in its other qualities, notably the tensile strength. From trials with the new kind of 'lead', it would be learnt that this mixture was now improved in tensile strength as well as in ease of casting. Nor was it necessary to produce this new metal first;

unrefined copper had only to be smelted with charcoal and stream-tin to produce a new kind of 'copper' (ayas in Rigveda), namely bronze, with superior qualities for tools and weapons. At the same time, certain naturally mixed ores were also worked, and were found to give the better kind of 'copper' directly. We have no proof that the tin compound of these mixed ores was ever isolated or recognized. Furthermore, at this early stage the tin content of the bronze could not be adequately controlled, and therefore varied between fairly wide limits."[387]

Diffusion of Metallurgy: Meluhha and western Afghanistan sources of tin

"Investigators in all periods have been faced with one major fact. Because southern Mesopotamia is virtually lacking in mineral resources, the materials used to make the metal artifacts found there must have come from another locale. Thus, our research led to the metallogenic zones in Iran, Afghanistan and Oman, where ores of copper, amont others, are known to occur in substantial quantities...we have also uncovered significant new information on tin deposits which could have been exploited in antiquity...Other metals were also used for this purpose (alloying) by ancient metal workers, most notably arsenic, antimony and lead. Arsenic, in particular, played an important role in the early metallurgy of the Near East...The earliest occurrence of tin-bronze date to the 4th millennium.Though the total number of artifacts analyzed from this period is not large, those of tin-bronze are even fewer: three pins from Necropolis A at Susa (with tin contents of 4%, 8% and 2.3% respectively), and an awl from Sialk III (0.95%). In the later 4th and early 3rd millennia, greater tin values occur--5.3% in a pin from Susa B; and 5% in an axe from Mundigak III in Afghanistan; but these are still exceptional in a period characterized by the use of arsenical copper ...arond 270 BC, during Early Dynastic III in Mesopotamia...eight metal artifacts of forty-eight in the celebrated 'vase a la cachette' of Susa D are bronzes; four of them -- three vases and one axe -- have over 7% tin. The analyses of objects from the Royal Cemetery at UR present an even clearer picture: of twenty-four artifacts in the Iraq Museum subjected to analysis, eight containing significant quantities of tin and five with over 8% tin can be considered true bronzes in the traditional sense...In addition, a contemporary shaft-hole axe from Kish contains 4% tin, and significant amounts were detected in a few artifacts from Tepe Giyan and Tepe Yahya IVB in Iran, and Hili in Oman. Thus, we see an increasing pattern of tin usage...We explored the area south of Herat, where several deposits of tin were said to exist. At Misgaran, tin appears 500 meters north of a copper mine which was worked in ancient times, although the precise dates of exploitation are not known. The copper ores here contain over 600 ppm (0.06) of tin. Tin-bearing sands, which can be easily beneficiated by panning, were worked in the nearby Sarkar Valley. There too the tin was found in association with copper, green traces of which are visible throughout the landscape...Gudea of Lagash (2150-2111BCE)speaks of the tin of Meluhha...the geographer Strabo (XV.2.10) who, in referring to the inhabitants of Drangiana (modern Sistan), says that they have 'only scanty supplies of wine, but they have tin in their country'...this passage..does accord well with the discoveris in the area of Herat...There are two possible routes from Afghanistan to Mesopotamia. One crosses the northern part of the Iranian plateau, along the Elburz mountains, then through the passes in the Zagros descends to Babylonia and Assyria. In the 1st millennium it was one of the principal supply routes of eastern goods to Assyria. In the 2nd millennium the tin that Assur exported to Anatolia might have followed this route. Along it are found such sites as Tepe Sialk (where the use of tin is attested in the 4th millennium), Tepe Giyan and Tepe Hissar, wehre other finds (such as lapis lazuli at Hissar) implicate them in long-distance commerce in the 3rd millennium.

Storage jar 4th millennium BCE found at Tepe Sialk. Teheran's National Museum of Iran. The antelope depicted on the jar is also used as a glyph on proto-Elamite script. miṇḍhāl 'markhor' (Tōrwālī) Rebus: meḍ 'iron' (Munda)

Kotdiji burial shard showing leaf. Sign 326. kamaṛkom = fig leaf (Santali.) kamarmaṛā (Has.), kamaṛkom (Nag.); the petiole or stalk of a leaf (Mundari) Rebus: kampaṭṭa 'mint, coiner'. kammaṭa = mint, gold furnace (Telugu) *daṭhi, daṭi* the petioles and mid-ribs of a compound leaf after the leaflets have been plucked off, stalks of certain plants, as Indian corn, after the grain has been taken off (Santali) Rebus: dhatu 'mineral.

Cylinder seal impression, Mesopotamia. The bulls flank a mountain topped by a leaf. British Museum No. 89308 *ḍāngā* = hill, dry upland (B.); *ḍãg* mountain-ridge (H.)(CDIAL 5476). Rebus: *dhangar* 'blacksmith' (Maithili) *ḍangar* 'blacksmith' (Hindi) loa 'ficus religiosa' Rebus: lo 'copper'. dula 'pair' Rebus: dul 'cast (metal)'. Thus, a cast (metal) coppersmith.

Image parallels:

Leaf on Mountain summit Kalibangan053Sign 232

ṭākuro = hill top (N.); ṭāngī = hill, stony country (Or.); ṭāngara = rocky hilly land (Or.); ḍāngā = hill, dry upland (B.); ḍāg mountain-ridge (H.)(CDIAL 5476). Rebus: ḍānro = a term of contempt for a blacksmith (N.)(CDIAL 5524). ṭhākur = blacksmith (Mth.) (CDIAL 5488). loa 'ficus religiosa' Rebus: lo 'copper'.

kūṭamu = summit of a mountain (Telugu) Rebus: kūṭakamu = mixture (Telugu) kūṭam = workshop (Ta.) The Sign 230 which is used as a ligature element on Sign 232, thus connotes an alloyed metal, kūṭa [e.g.

copper + dhātu 'mineral (ore)' as in: ārakūṭa = brass (Skt.)]

Mcmohan cylinder seal with six signs,found in 'Swat and Seistan', unrolled photographically and the unbroken stamp-end of the seal; positive impression of the cylinder showing Harappan inscriptions.[388] A glyph on the stam-pend of the cylinder seal compares with the glyph of Sign 230, a range of three mountain summits, may be read rebus as *ḍāg* mountain-ridge Rebus: *ḍangar* 'blacksmith'. "The Seistan findspot of this seal is of great interest. Evidence exists for the movement of Indus commodities, and, therefore, Indus commercial activities in the direction of western Asia and, in return, from there to the Indus world.. Evidence for the Harappan penetration of Seistan and farther to southeastern Iran is scanty but includes at least one other Indus inscription from an impression of a sherd discovered at Tepe Yahya, period IV A (c. 2200 BCE).[389]

"The second route is by sea, along the Arabian coast of the Gulf, perhaps also going by land through souther n Iran. It was at the time of Gudea of Lagash and earlier in the Early Dynastic III period, the great supply route of eastern commodities to southern Mesopotamia. It is by this route that the copper of Makkan came, copper which analysis has shown to have originated in the peninsula of Oman. It also brought the products of Meluhha, including lapis lazuli, carnelian, copper, ivory and various woods. Nothing, however, suggests the passage of tin through this area. For example, there is little tin in the artifacts recovered at Qala'at al Bahrain, dating between 2300 and 1800 BC. Furthermore, we know from the work of Limet, who studied texts concerned with metalworking in Sumer, that Mesopotamian metalworkers did their own alloying. We suspect, therefore, that the tin moved through this area in an unalloyed state.

"Recently Oman has yielded the first signs of the use of tin in the region. The analysis of a sword from Hili, dated to the mid-3rd millennium, shows a tin content of 6.5%, and a mold of a tap hole (?) associated with the remains of a furnace held metal with a tin content of 5%. The furnace is dated after the tree-ring calibration of a radiocarbon analysis (MC 2261) to circa 2225 BC...it is clear that the tin was added to the copper and it is also clear that it did not come from Oman itself. At Umm an-Nar artifacts with tin contents on the order of 2% were recovered; the tin must have been mixed with the local copper...Meluhha...the use of tin is attested already in the late 4th or early 3rd millennium at Mundigak III in southern Afghanistan. Tin appears only in small quantities in artifacts from Sahr-i-Sokhta in eastern Iran and at Tepe Yahya in southern Iran...In the Indus Valley, the copper-tin alloy is known at Mohenjodaro.

"...Oman's trade with southeastern Iran and Baluchistan is well attested...Among the products attributed to Meluhha, lapis lazuli and carnelian are found in sites and tombs of the 3rd millennium. We can suggest with reasonable certainty that the tin used in Oman was in transit through Meluhha and that the most likely source was western Afghanistan. The discoveries of tin in artifacts at Hili, though singular, are important because the site lies in an area clearly involved in long-distance trade. However, there is no clear evidence that the site was a way-station on the route which brought tin from Afghanistan to Mesopotamia. Therefore the presence of tin at Hili indicates only that it was transported in the Gulf area, where it was also used to fill local needs.

"The collective indications are that western Afghanistan ws the zone able to provide the tin used in Southwest Asia in the 4th and 3rd millennia...In order to elucidate the questions raised by our findings, a project aimed specifically at tin-- its sources and metallurgy-- should be organized." (Serge Cleuziou and Thierry

Berthoud, Early Tin in the Near East, in: Expedition, Vol. 25, No. 1, 1982, pp. 14-19).

Documenting the Tin processing tradition in India

As the pictorial gallery demonstrates, the entire tin processing industry is a family-based or extended-family-based industry. The historical traditions point to the formation of artisan guilds to exchange surplus cassiterite in trade transactions of the type evidenced by the seals and tablets, tokens and bullae found in the civilization-interaction area of the Bronze Age.

Papagudem boy wearing a bangle of tin

"Bronze articles such as ornamental mirrors, arrowheads, pins, bangles and chisels, of both low tin and high tin content, have been recovered from Lothal, the Harappn port on the Gujarat coast, which has been dated earlier than 2200 BCE. The tin content in these articles range from 2.27% to 11.82%; however, some of the articles contain no tin. Tin is said to have been brought as tablets from Babylon and mixed with copper to make an alloy of more pleasing colour and luster, a bright golden yellow. The utilization of bronze is essential only for certain articles and tools, requiring sharp cutting edges, such as axes, arrowheads or chisels. The selection of bronze for these items indicates the presence of tin was intentional...Recent discoveries of tin occurrences in India are shown in...Fig. 11.2. However, none of these occurrences shows evidences of ancient mining activity. This is because, unlike copper ores, the mining and metallurgy of the tin ore cassiterite is simple, and leaves little permanent trace...tin ore is usually recovered by simple panning of surface deposits, often contained in gravel, which soon collapse, leaving little evidence of having once been worked. Cassiterite is highly resistant to weathering, and with its high specific gravity, it can be easily separated from the waste minerals. The simple mining and metallurgical methods followed even now by Bastar and Koraput tribals in Chattisgarh and Orissa, central India, could be an indication of the methods used in the past. These tribal people produce considerable quantities of tin without any external help, electric power or chemical agents, enough to make a modern metallurgist, used to high technology, wonder almost in disbelief. Clearly though, the technology practiced has a considerable importance for those studying early smelting practices. The history of this process is poorly known. Back in the 1880s Ball (1881) related the story of a Bastar tribal from the village of Papagudem, who was observed to be wearing a bangle of tin. When questioned as to where the metal had come from, he replied that black sands, resembling gunpowder were dug in his village and smelted there. Thus it is very likely that the present industry is indigenous, and may have a long history. That being said, neither the industry or its products appear in any historical document of any period, and thus is unlikey to have been a significant supplier of metal...The tin content of cassiterite ranges from 74.94% (mean 64.2%), showing that pebbles contain about 70% to 90% of the tin oxide, cassiterite...The ore is localized in gravel beds of the black pebbles of cassiterite which outcrop in stream beds etc. and there are other indicators, in the vegetation. The leaves of the Sarai tree (Shoria robusta) growing on tin-rich ground are often covered in yellow spots, as if suffering from a disease. (The leaves were found to contain 700 ppm of tin on analysis!) Wherever the tribals find concentrations of ore in the top soil, the ground all around the area is dug up and transported to nearby streams, rivers or ponts...The loose gravelly soil containing the tin ore is dug with pick and shovel, and carried to the washing sites in large, shoulder-strung bamboo baskets. The panning or washing of the ore is carrie out using round shallow pans of bamboo. The soil is washed out, leaving the dense casiterite ore at the bottom of the pan...The ore is smelted in small clay shaft furnaces, heating and reducing the ore using charcoal as the fuel...The shft furnaces are square at the base and of brick surmounted by a clay cylindrical shaft...The charcoal acts as both the heating and reducing agent, reducing the black cassiterite mineral into bright, white tin metal...a crude refining is carried out by remelting the metal in an iron pan at about 250 degrees C. The molten tin is then poured into the stone-carved moulds to make square- or rectangular-shaped tin ingots for easy transportation."[390]

Tin placer prospecting: pictorial gallery

Here is a pictorial gallery which encapsulates frozen time continuum in practices which are followed even today in India. From an anthropological perspective, there can be several arguments that these attest to an ancient tradition dating back to the 4th millennium BCE to validate the observations of scientists like Muhly who have documented from cuneiform texts that tin for Mesopotamia came from Meluhha:

Panning for cassiterite using bamboo pans in a pond in Orissa. The ore is carried to the water pond or stream for washing in bamboo baskets.

People panning for cassiterite mineral in the remote jungles of central India.

The ore is washed to concentrate the cassiterite mineral using bamboo pans. Base of small brick and mud furnace for smelting tin.

The tin is refined by remelting the pieces recovered from the furnace in an iron pan. The molten tin is poured into stone-carved moulds to make square- or rectangular-ingots.

Elamite < proto-afroasiatic?

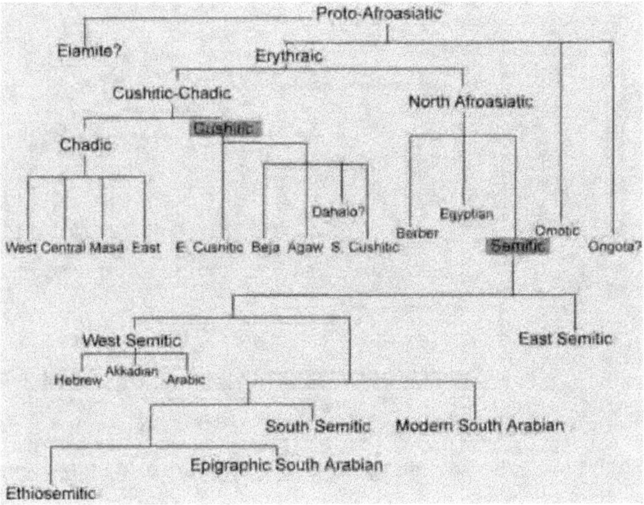

Afroasiatic classification. *Highlighted branches* are those that occur on either side of the Red Sea. (After Blench, R., Archaeology, language and the African past. Lanham: Alta Mira Press, 2006).

Semitic branch of the Afroasiatic phylum yields languages of present-day Arabian peninsula. Prior to the expansion of Islam and Arabic in the seventh century, possibly Sabaean and languages of South Semitic branch were widespread in the peninsula. Sabaean, Minaean and Qatabanian inscriptions (ca. 8th century BCE to sixth century CE) are attested. (Versteegh, 2000). It is likely that non-Semitic languages were spoken in earlier millennia. If Elamite was a Proto-Afroasiatic language, there is a possibility that Elamite might have some substrate glosses from Meluhha, given the archaeological evidence of contacts within the Middle Asia interaction sphere depicted in the map:Middle Asian interaction sphere.

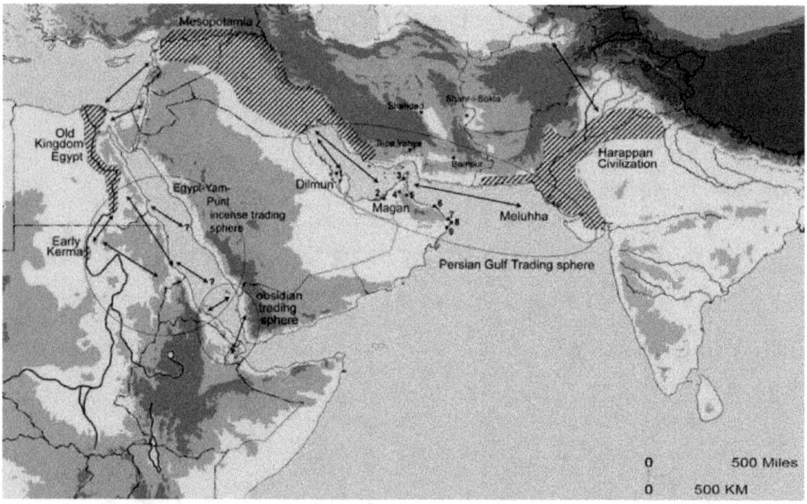

Third millennium trading spheres map: 1. Barbar; 2. Umm-an-Nar; 3. Tell Abraq; 4. Hili; 5. Wadi Suq; 6. ras al-Hamra; 7. Ras al-Hadd; 8. Ras al-Jinz; 9. as-Suwayh (After Fig. 7 in Boivin, Nicole, Roger Blench and Dorian Q. Fuller, 2009, Archaeological, Linguistic and Historical sources of ancient seafaring: A multidisciplinary approach to the study of early Maritime contact and exchange in the Arabian peninsula, Chapter 18, Petraglia, MD & J.I. Rose, eds., The evolution of human populations in Arabia, Vertebrate Paleobiology and Paleoanthropology, Spinger Science).

Arabian settlement of Hili engaged in the production and exchange of copper. Ras al-Jins, Ras al-Hadd and Ras Shiyah imported and used copper. Trade between Oman and Mesopotamia was mediated via Dilmun. (Cleuziou, S., 1996, The emeergence of oases and towns in eastern and southern Arabia. In: Afanas 'ev GE, Cleuziou S., Lukacs JR, Tosi M, eds., The prehistory of Asia and Oceania, Colloquia 16. Forli: UISPP, p. 159-65). Subsequently, Sargon of Akkad (2334-2270 BCE) boats of mooring ships destined for Meluhha, Makkan and Dilmun (Oppenheim, AL, 1954, Seafaring merchants of Ur. Journal of the American Oriental Society, ur: 6-17). A Sargonic tablet (ca. 2200 BCE) refers to a man with an Akkadian name entitled 'the holder of a *Meluhha* ship'. An Akkadian cylindr seals of Shu-ilishu, Meluhha interpreter is recorded, as seals with Indus writing appear in Mesopotamian sites. Oman records carnelian (some etched), combs, shells, shell objects, metal objects, seals and weights of Harappan provenience (Vogt, B., 1996, Bronze age maritime trade in the Indian Ocean: Harappan traits on the Oman peninsula. In: Reade J., ed., The Indian Ocean in Antiquity. London, Kegan-Paul). Indus black-slipped wareused as storage jars of large-volume, is widely distributed. (Cleuziou S. and Mery . 2002, In-between the great powers: the Bronze Age Oman peninsula. In: Cleuziou S., Tosi, M. Zarins J., eds., Essays on the Late prehistory of the Arabian Peninsula. Rome: Istituto Italiano per l'Africa l'Oriente, p. 273-316).

Ubaid ceramics

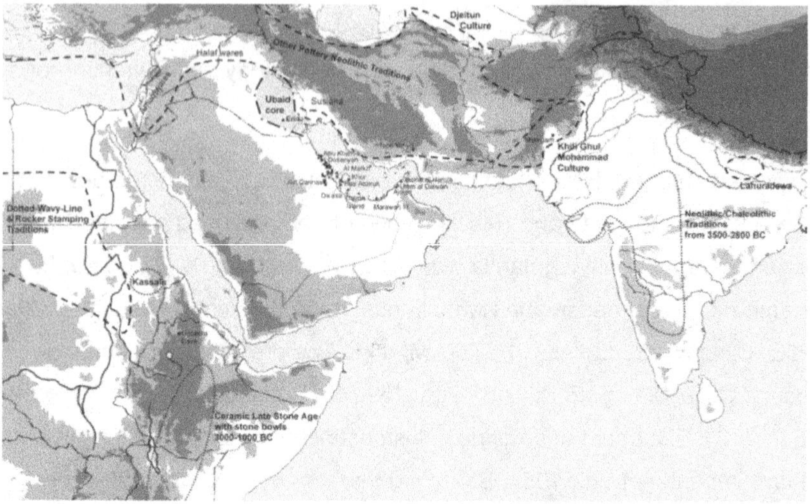

Finds of Ubaid ceramics in the Gulf (after Crawford, 1998; Carter, 2006), in relation to the core range of Ubaid pottery in Mesopotamia and other early ceramic traditions. The *dashed line* indicates the extent of early ceramic traditions of ca. 6000 BCE prior to the development of Ubaid. *Dotted areas* indicate important regional developments where ceramics were later, beginning between 3500 and 2500 BCE (East African stone bowl traditions: Barnett, 1999; South Asian traditions: Fuller, 2006; Sahara-Sudan traditions: Jesse, 2003; Kasalla: Sadr, 1991.(After Fig. 6 ibid.)[391]

Peter Bellwoods's pioneering archaeology of island cultures points to small-scale societies as major forces of cultural history. Such forces should also have influenced the spread of glosses related to the Bronze Age innovations. Boivin & Fuller point to small-scale coastal societies as pioneers who created cross-cultural contacts resulting in translocation of plants and animals in the early Indian Ocean. Such translocation might also explain the presence of Meluhha merchants and colonies of Meluhhans in Mesopotamia, in Sumer, in Elam and along the Persian Gulf as also Arabian peninsula. (Boivin, Nicole, Roger Blench and Dorian Q. Fuller, 2009, Archaeological, Linguistic and Historical sources of ancient seafaring: A multidisciplinary approach to the study of early Maritime contact and exchange in the Arabian peninsula, Chapter 18, Petraglia, MD & J.I. Rose, eds., The evolution of human populations in Arabia, Vertebrate Paleobiology and Paleoanthropology, Spinger Science).

Archaeobotanical evidence

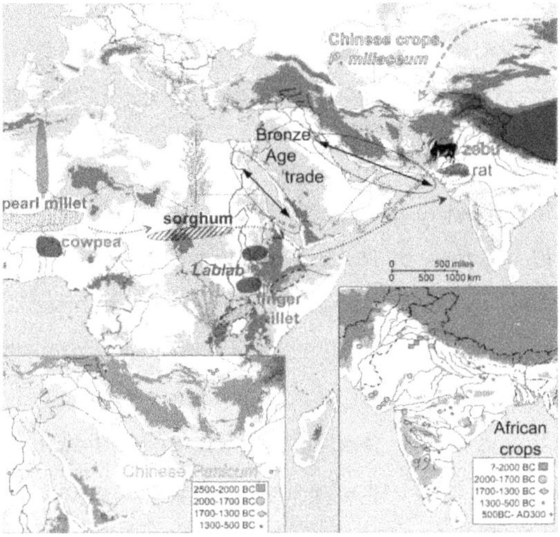

Shematic map of major Bronze Age translocations between South Asia, Arabia and Africa. Inset lower left: map of the distribution of archaeobotanical evidence of broomcorn millet (Panicum miliaceum) of Chinese origin, suggesting dispersal from South Asia to Arabia and Nubia via the sea. Inset lower right: map of the distribution of sites in South Asia with archaeobotanical evidence for one or more crops of African origin. (After Fig. 1 in Fuller et al. 2011)

Fuller et al note that some crops such as sorghum (sorhum bicolor), pearl millet (pennisetum glaucum) and finger millet (eleusine coracana) originated in Africa and arrived in India at some point in prehistory. One conjecture is that this happened perhaps ca. 2600-2000 BCE brought by Harappan seafarers. Movement of zebu cattle from India to Yemen and East Africa might also have occurred in the Harappan era. A corollary pointer is the presence of cloves from Malacca in Terqa (Tell Asmar).

Avestan later than Vedic

Vocabulary of Brahui is substantially of non-Dravidian origin and has cognates in Balochi and Sindhi languages, derived from Iranian and Indo-Aryan languages. It is likely that the present-day languages of India evidence a *dialect continuum* from the days of Indus-Sarasvati civilization. Indian Lexicon[392] documents glosses of a linguistic area pointing to common glosses in Dravidian, Austro-asiatic or Indo-Aryan or unknown sources, examples of non-Indo-European influence in Meluhha (Mleccha).[393]

Nicholas Kazanas has demonstrated that Avestan (OldIranian) is much later than Vedic. " 'Vedic and Avestan' by N. Kazanas In this essay the author examines independent linguistic evidence, often provided by Iranianists like R. Beekes, and arrives at the conclusion that the Avesta, even its older parts (the gaθas), is much later than the Rigveda. Also, of course, that Vedic is more archaic than Avestan and that it was not the Indo-aryans who moved away from the common Indo-Iranian habitat into the Region of the Seven Rivers, but the Iranians broke off and eventually settled and spread in ancient Iran."[394]

"The Avesta kows the beginning or source of the Aryans as Airyana Vaejo (Pahlavi Iran-Vej). The Avestan Vaejo corresponds to the Sanskrit bīj meaning 'beginning or source'. The Avesta describes it as a place of extreme cold that became over-crowded (Vend. I. 3-4; II. 8-18). ... Whether the Mitannian kings (1475-1280 B.C.) on the upper Euphrates were a direct offshoot of the Aryans or not their names are certainly Aryan, for example Saussatar, Artatama, Sutarna, Tusratta and Mattiuaza (H. Oldenburg: in Journal of the Royal Asiatic Society, 1909, p. 1094-1109)... Mattiuaza, in his treaty with the Hittite king Aubbiluliuma signed in 1380 B.C. at Boghazkoy, invokes not only Babylonian gods to witness the treaties, but Mitra, Varun.a, Indra, and Nāsatya in the form in which they appear in the Rigveda (S. Konow: Aryan gods of the Mitani people, 1921, pp. 4-5). They occur in the treaty as ilāni Mi-it-ra-as-si-il ilāni A-ru-na-as-si-il In-da-ra ilāni Na-sa-at-ti-ya-an-na. Since the form for Nāsatya is quite different in the

Avestan language (Naonhaithya) it is argued that the Mitannian did not speak Iranian but Indo-Aryan (E.Meyer: Sitzungsberichte der K. Preuss. Akad. der Wissen, 1908, I, p. 14f.)... The name for 'fire' in the Persian Avesta is quite different, being atar, and this does not occur in the Indian Veda except in the Vedic proper name Atharvan, which corresponds to the Avestan name of the fire priest. Agni, as a messenger between gods and man, was known to the Vedas as Narā-śamsa. This corresponds with the Avestan messenger of Ahura, Nairyō-sangha."[395]

takṣa, tvaṣṭṛ, ṛbhu: carpenters

In the Rigveda, the lexeme takṣam is used to define composition or fashioning.

apūrvyā purustamanyasmai mahe vīrāya tavase turāya; viripśane vajriṇe śantamāni vacāmsyāsā sthavīrāya takṣam (RV. VI.32.1)

Trans.: a seer has composed unprecedented, comprehensive and gratifying praises for the mighty Indra.

agnaye brahma ṛbhavasta takṣuh (RV. X.80.7):the fashioning of hymns for agni is done by the ṛbhus.

In Avestan tradition, Ahur Mazdā is conceived as a carpenter who fashions the earth from wood and who fashions bodies and souls: *gāuś-taśā: dāidi mōi yā gam taśō apas ca urvaraśca*: 'grant me thou -- who has created Mother Earth and the waters and the plants' (Yasna 51.7); *hyat nā mazdā, paourvīm g ā eoasca tas'ō daēnascā*: 'since for us, O Mazda, from the beginning Thou didst create Bodies and also Souls' (Yasna 31.11)[396] *gaus = gāv* (Skt. gau). The phrase mahigauh in RV refers to the earth. *Taśa* is from the root *taś* (Skt. *takṣ*) = to create, to fashion; to hew, to cut. The cognate lexemes are: technos (Greco-Roman), *taśyati* (Lith.)

The gavam-ayanam is a sattra related to the turning of the earth which is related to the solstice or the apparent shift of sun's motion. Mahāvrata day is the last day but one of the year; it was, as Tilak observed, a link between the dying and the coming year.[397]

gavam-ayanam is a sattra similar to ādityānām-ayanam and angi_rasām-ayanam. *Aitareya Brāhmaṇa* (iv,17) notes: "They hold the gavām-ayanam, that is, the sacrificial session called the 'cows' walk'. The cows are the ādityas (Gods of the months). By holding the session called 'the cows' walk', they also hold the ādityānām-ayanam (the walk of the ādityas)." The origin of the sattra is described as follows "The cows being desirous of obtaining hoofs and horns held (once) a sacrificial session. In the tenth month (of their sacrifice) they obtained hoofs and horns. They said, we have obtained fulfillment of that wish, for which we underwent the initiation into the sacrificial rites. Let us rise (the sacrifice being finished). Those that rose are those who have horns. Of those who, however, sat (continued the session), saying 'Let us finish the year', the horns went off on account of their distrust. It is they who are hornless (*tūparāh*). They (continuing their sacrificial session) produced vigour (u_rjam). Thence after (having been sacrificing for twelve months and) having secured all the seasons, they rose (again) at the end, for they had produced vigour (to reproduce horns, hoofs when decaying. Thus the cows made themselves beloved by all (the whole world), and are beautified (decorated) by all."[398]

Technical skils of the artificer mentioned in texts

తక్షకుడు [takṣakuḍu] *takshakuḍu.* [Skt.] n. The name of mythological serpent ఒక సర్పరాజు. The name of a race of men called Takshakas. A carpenter వడ్లవాడు.(Telugu) A memory associating an artisan with serpent glyph, a memory retained in Telugu of *āra* 'serpent' Rebus: *āra* 'brass'.

The sememe *takṣ* refers to the technical skill of fashioning metallic objects. ṛbhus do great deeds and have dexterous hands (*svapasah suhastāh*) and frame a chariot for the aśvins (RV.1.111.1; X.39.4), fashion the vigorous horses for Indra (RV. 1.20.2; 1.111.1; III.60.2) and divide the single camasa into four (RV. I.161.2). The ṛbhus fabricate the ratha (chariot)(RV. 1.111.1; IV.33.8), fashion agni for manu's sacrifice: *dyātvā yamagnim pṛthivē janiṣṭ āmāpastvaṣṭā mṛgavo yam sahobhih, īḍenyam prathamam mātariśvā devāstatakṣurmanave yajatram* (RV. X.46.) *ye aśvinā ye piratā ya ūtī dhenum tatakṣur ṛbhavo ye aśvā; ye amsatrā ya ṛdhagrodasī ye vibhvo narah svapatyāni cakruh* (RV. IV.34.9): ṛbhus fashioned the chariots for aśvins, renovated their parents, restored the cow, fabricated the horses, made armor (*amsatra*) for the gods, separated earth and heaven and accomplished the acts of good results. Sāyaṇa explains the equivalence of *tvakṣ* and *takṣ* in re: RV. I.100.15: *takṣū tvakṣū tanūkaraṇe* (to accomplish by reducing, scraping, cutting) in the context of the skills of carpentry, using *tools. Takṣa is a professional like the bhiṣak (physician) and priest (Brahman): takṣāriṣṭam rutam bhis.agabrahmā sunvantam icchat īndrāyendo pari srava* (RV. IX.112.1) The major wood-work included cutting of the sacrificial stake (yūpa), fastening of the wooden ring (cas. āla) on its top and fashioning of the wooden vessels: *yūpa vraskā uta ye yūpavāhāścas ālam ye aśvayūpāya takṣati; ye cārvate pacanam sambharantyuto teṣāmabhigūrtirna invatu* (RV. I.62.6) Tvaṣṭṛ carved the vajra, the weapon wielded by Indra to sever the limbs of vṛttra (RV. 1.32.2; 52.7; 61.6; 121.3; X.48.3; 99.1); it is *āyasam* (metallic)(RV. X.48.3) *atha tvaṣṭāte maha ugra vajram sahasrabhṛṣṭim vavṛtacchatāśrim nikāmamaramaṇasam yena navantamahi sam piṇagṛjīṣin* (RV. VI.17.10): fierce Indra, Tvaṣṭṛ constructed for thee, the mighty one, the thousand-edged, the hundred-angled thunderbolt, wherewith thou hast crushed the ambitious audacious loud-shouting *ahi= vṛttra.* RV. I.85.9: *tvaṣṭā yadvajram sukṛtam hiraṇyayam sahasrabhṛṣṭam svapā avartayat:* refers to the shaping of the thunderbolt, vajra, by skilful (*svapā= śobhanakarmā*); Sāyaṇa explains *sukṛtam* as *samyak niṣpāditam* or well made; *hiraṇyayam* as *suvarnamayam* or golden; *sahasrabhṛṣṭim* as *anekābhir dhārābhir yuktam* or 'of numerous edges'. Tvaṣṭṛ augments the strength of Indra by fashioning a vajra of overpowering vigour: *tvaṣṭā citte yujyam vāvṛdhe śavastatakṣa vajramabhibhātyojasam* (RV. I.52.7)

The transition from the lithic age to the bronze age is apparent from the description of adze or vāśi as either metallic or made of stone and used for shaping wooden vessels: *vāśībhih aśmanmayībhih* (RV. X.101.10) Rigveda refers to smelter of metals (*dhmātā*: RV. V.9.5) and the smith (*karmāra*: RV.X.72.2)[Schrader notes that the names of smiths in IE languages are often derived from the old Indo-Germanic names for stone of which the smiths' tools were originally made; e.g. hamarr (OHG); akmōn (= anvil)(Gk.); aśman (=hammer, anvil, oven)(Skt.)

Tvaṣṭṛ is shown sharpening his metallic axe while fabricating the camasa bowl used for soma (apparently, the axe is used to fashion the bowl): *śisīte nūnam paraśum svāyasam* (RV. X.53.9) The camasa created by Tvaṣṭṛ is later divided into four parts by his disciples, the ṛbhus: *uta tyam camasam navam tvaṣṭurdevasya niṣkṛtam* (RV. I.20.6); akarta caturah punah (RV. IV.33.5-6)[Commenting on RV. I.20.6, Sāyaṇa says that ṛbhus are the disciples of Tvaṣṭṛ: *tvaṣṭuh śiṣyā ṛbhavah*. Elsewhere, Sāyaṇa refers to Tvaṣṭṛ as the preceptor of the ṛbhus: *ṛbhavah tvaṣṭā yuṣmadguruh* (RV. IV. 33.5)]

The reference to ratha is: ratham suvṛtam (RV. 1.111.1). Sāyaṇa interprets this as well-built or good-wheeled: *śobhanavartanam sucakram vā* The carpenters' tools are: *svadhiti* which is used to cut and trim the wooden post: *yānvo naro devayanto nimimyurvanaspate svādhitirvā tatakṣa* (RV. III.8.6) *vāśī* and *paraśu* are also creations of divine artificers: *tvaṣṭṛ*. and *ṛbhus* (RV. I.110.5; X.53.9-10) Viṣṇu prepares the womb and Tvaṣṭṛ adorns the forms: *Viṣṇuryonim kalpayatu tvaṣṭā rūpāṇi pimśatu* (RV. X.184.1) *svadhiti* is used to create a well-made form (tvas.t.reva ru_pam sukr.tam svadhityainā:AV. XII.3.33) Atharva Veda refers to the use of *vāśī* by takṣan: *yat tvā śikvah parāvadīt takṣā hastena vāsyā* (AV.X.6.3) RV I.32.5 alludes that Indra strikes Vṛttra with vajra, as the *kuliśa* (=axe) fells a tree-trunk: *ahanvṛtramk vṛtrataram vyamsamindro vajreṇa mahatā vadhena; skandhāmsīva kulis'enā vivṛkṇā hih śyata upapṛkpṛthivyāh.* A cognate Indian lexeme is: *kulhāḍī* (a metallic blade with a cutting edge and a handle). *ṛbhu, vibhu, vāja* constitute a trinity; the ṛbhus are *saudhanvanāh* (sons of Sudhanvan). The ṛbhus are mortals who attained immortality by dint of their workmanship: *martāsah santo amṛtatvamānaśuh* (RV. I.110.4) Commenting on RV. I. 20.1, Sāyaṇa observes that ṛbhus were pious men who through penance obtained deification: manus.yah santastapasā devatvam prāptah. Aitareya Brāhmaṇa describes them as men who by austerity (tapas) obtained a right to partake of soma among gods (AB. III.30.2) *yābhih śacībhiścamasā apiśata yayā dhiyā gāmariṇīta carmaṇah; yena harī manasā niratakṣata tena devatvam ṛbhavah* samānaśa (RV. III.60.2): With those faculties by which you have fashioned the drinking bowl; with what intelligence wherewith you have covered the (dead) cow with skin, -- with what will by which you have fabricated two horses (of Indra); with those (means) ṛbhus, you have attained divinity. Macdonell derives the term ṛbhu from the root *rabh*, to grasp and explains it as handy or dexterous and identifies it with German elbe and English elf. (opcit., p. 133)

Tvaṣṭṛ, soma

Tvaṣṭṛ is the master of all forms and shaper of all animals (*tvaṣṭā rūpāṇi hi prabhuh paśūnviśvāntsamānaje*)(RV I.188.9) He is the fashioner of the quick-moving horse: *tvaṣṭurvājāyata āśuraśvah* (TS. V.I.11.3; KS. XLVI.2) The lexeme also means a fashioner or artificer.[399] Indra drinks soma in the house of Tvaṣṭṛ: *tvaṣṭugṛhi apibat somamindrah* (RV. IV.18.3) Tvaṣṭṛ is referred to as supāṇim, beautiful-handed; sugabhastim beautiful armed and ṛbhvam shining or glorious (RV. VI.49.9) *sukṛtsupāṇih svavau ṛtāvā devastvaṣṭāvase tāni no dhāt* (RV. III.54.12): May the divine Tvaṣṭṛ the able artificer, the dexterous handed, the possessor of wealth, the observer of truth,bestow upon us those things (which are necessary) for our preservation. *ugrasturāvālamibhūtyojāyathāvaśam tanvamcakra evah; tvaṣṭāramindro januṣābhibhūyāmanuṣyā somamapibaccamūṣu* (RV. III.48.4): fierce, rapid in assault, of overpowering strength, he made his form obedient to his will; having overcome Tvaṣṭṛ by his innate (vigour), and carried off the soma, he drank it (or deposited) in the ladles. These and other references lead Macdonell to surmise that Indra's father whom he slays in order to obtain the soma, is Tvaṣṭṛ.[400]

Maritime, riverine Ṛgvedic culture

The maritime/riverine nature of the Sarasvati Sindhu civilization is borne out by the archaeological finds of contacts with Sumeria, particularly in the trade of copper/bronze weapons exported from ancient India.

Rigveda has a number of allusions to the use of boats.

The vedic people had used ships to cross oceans: anarambhaṇe... agrabhaṇe samudre... śatāritram nāvam... (RV. I.116.5; cf. VS. 21.7) referring to aśvins who rescued bhujyu, sinking in mid-ocean using a ship with a hundred oars (nāvam-aritraparanīm). There is overwhelming evidence of maritime trade by the archaeological discoveries of the so-called Harappan civilization, which can now be re-christened: Sarasvati-Sindhu civilization. Some beads were reported to have been exported to Egypt from this valley (Early Indus Civilization, p. 149); Sumerians had acted as intermediaries for this trade[401] which extended to Anatolia and the Mediterranean.

Boats drown in the river Sarasvati when the river was in spate (RV. 6,61,3); Devi Aditi comes in a boat for the reciters to board (RV. 10,63,10); Soma, the king of the waterways, who covers the universe as a cloth, has boarded the boat of sacrifice; the sūrya descends the heavens on a boat (RV. 1,50,4; 5,45,10; 7,63,4; 10,88,16,17). Sudasa built an easily pliable boat to cross the Purus.n.i river (RV. 7,18,5); Agni is a boat which carries the sacrificers over the difficult path of sacrifice (RV. 1,9,7, 7-8: 5,4,9); Agni is the boat of the reciters in troubled times (RV. 3,29,1), to ford enemy lines (RV. 3,24,1); Agni is the carrier-boat of oblations to the gods (RV. 1,128,6); Agni is the boat of all wishes (RV. 3,11,3);

Indra was like a ferry-boat (RV. 8,16,11); Indra protected the boats (RV. 1,80,8); Indra is invoked to carry the reciters over the ocean of misfortune (RV. 3,32,14); Indra takes the reciters in his boat across the ocean (RV. 8,16,11); Indra saved the ship-wrecked Naryam, Turvasu, Yadu, Turviti and Vayya (RV. 1,54,6); Indra-Varuṇa sail on the boat on the celestial ocean (RV. 7,88,3); Puṣan's golden boat moves on the sky (RV. 6,58,3) Varuṇa's boat will carry the reciter on to the mid-ocean of the sky (RV. 7,88,3); Maruta helped the reciters to cross the ocean of war in a boat (RV. 5,54,4); Maruta was compared to a tempestuous ocean in which had sunk a laden ship (RV. 5,59,2); there are references to: house boat (RV. 1,40,12); long boat (RV. 1,122,15); well-furnished boat with oars (RV. 10,101,2); boats carrying foodgrains for overseas markets (RV. 1,47,6; 7,32,20; 7,63,4); boats fit to cross the ocean with oars (RV. 1,40,7); ocean-trading boats (RV. 1,50,2).[402]

Riches are obtained from the samudra (i.e. by maritime trade) (RV. 1,47,6); there were two winds on the ocean, one to put the boat to the seas and the other to bring it to shore (RV. 10,137,2).

[quote]The Elamites called their country *Haltamti.* [403] Sumerian *ELAM*, Akkadian *Elamû*, female *Elamītu* "resident of Susiana, Elamite".[404] Additionally, it is known as *Elam* in the Hebrew Bible, where they are called the offspring of Elam, eldest son of Shem (see Elam in the Bible; Genesis 10:22, Ezra4:9). The high country of Elam was increasingly identified by its low-lying later capital, Susa. Geographers after Ptolemy called it *Susiana*. The Elamite civilization was primarily centered in the province of what is modern-day Khuzestān and Ilam in prehistoric times. The modern provincial name Khuzestān is derived from the Persian name for Susa: Old Persian *Hūjiya* "Elam," in Middle Persian *Huź* "Susiana", which gave modern Persian *Xuz*, compounded with *-stån* "place". [unquote][405]

McAlpin proposes that 20% of Dravidian and Elamite vocabulary are cognates and 12% are probable cognates.[406]

Meluhha distinct from Elamite

Nine texts dated to Ur III times and references to Sargonic texts indicate activities of Meluhha and Meluhhans in Mesopotamia. Sargon refers to Meluhhan ships docked at his capital. One tablet refers to a person with an Akkadian name as 'the holder of a Meluhha ship'. Gudea, (second half of 22nd century BCE) notes that Meluhhans came with wood and other raw materials to construct the main temple in Lagash. Imports include marine shell (for containers and lamps), inlay works, agate, carnelian and perhaps ivory. To this period is assigned the cylinder seal of Shu-ilishu, 'Meluhha interpreter'. One Akkadian text notes that Lu-sunzida (lit. man of the just buffalo cow), 'a man of Meluhha' paid to the servant Urur, son of Amar-lu-KU 10 shekels of silver as a payment for a tooth broken in a clash.[407] This law seems to be an earlier version of the code of Hammurabi (1792 – 1750 B.C.E), which states that "if one knocks out the tooth of a freeman, he shall pay one-third mana of silver."[408]

"The texts indicate that Meluhhans were perceived as distinct ethnic group, living in a separate settlement but largely integrated in the contemporary Sumerian society, owning or renting land and accumulating and variously distributing their agricultural products."

(Vidale, Massimo, 2001, Growing in a foreign world. For a history of the Meluhha villages' in Mesopotamia in the 3rd millennium BCE, in: A. Panaino and A. Piras, eds., Proceedings of the fourth annual symposium of the Assyrian and Babylonian intellectual heritage project, held in Ravenna, Italy, Oct. 13-17, 2001, Milan, Universita di Bologna & Islao, 2004, p. 263).

Plaque Showing Banqueters Gypsum Early Dynastic IIIa, ca. 2600-2500 B.C. Khafajah, Sin Temple IX.
Excavated by the Oriental Institute, 1933-34 OIM A12417

Lyre-player, from one of the steles of king Gudea of Lagash. The lyre has eleven strings. Circa 2150 BCE. Tello (ancient Girsu) Limestone H. 1.20 m; W. 0.63 m; D. 0.25 m E. de Sarzec excavations, 1881 AO 52 Louvre, Departement des Antiquites Orientales, Paris, France On the stele of music, Gudea, carrying a peg and cord and followed by figures probably representing his princely heir and two priests, prepares to lay out the plan of Ningirsu's sanctuary... Behind the cantor, a musician plays on a lyre whose sound box is decorated with a bull... The making of the god's lyre gave its name to the third year of Gudea's reign, called "the year in which was made the lyre [called] Ushumgalkalamma [the dragon of the land of Sumer]."...The spirit embodied by the lyre played a part in the events leading to the building of the temple, for it appears in the dream in which the god reveals to Gudea the task he is to accomplish (Gudea Cylinders, Louvre, MNB 1512 and MNB 1511): "When, together with Ushumgalkalamma, his well-beloved lyre, that renowned instrument, his counselor, you bring him gifts [...] the heart of Ningirsu will be appeased, he will reveal the plans of his temple."...Among the divine servants of Ningirsu, it is the lyre's duty to charm his master, a god of changeable mood. It is assisted by the spirit of another lyre that brings consolation in times of darkness: "So that the sweet-toned tigi-drum should play, so that the instruments algar and miritum should resound for Ningirsu, [...] his beloved musician Ushumgalkalamma accomplished his duties to the lord Ningirsu. To soothe the heart and calm the liver [the seat of thought], to dry the tears of weeping eyes, to banish grief from the grieving heart, to cast away the sadness in the heart of the god that rises like the waves of the sea, spreads wide like the Euphrates, and drowns like the flood of the storm, his lyre Lugaligihush accomplished his duties to his lord Ningirsu."[409]

Glyph: *tambura* 'harp'; Rebus: *tambra* 'copper' (Pkt. Santali) Another example of a substrate term: Sumerian tibira, tabira (Akkadian. LU2 URUDU-NAGAR =.

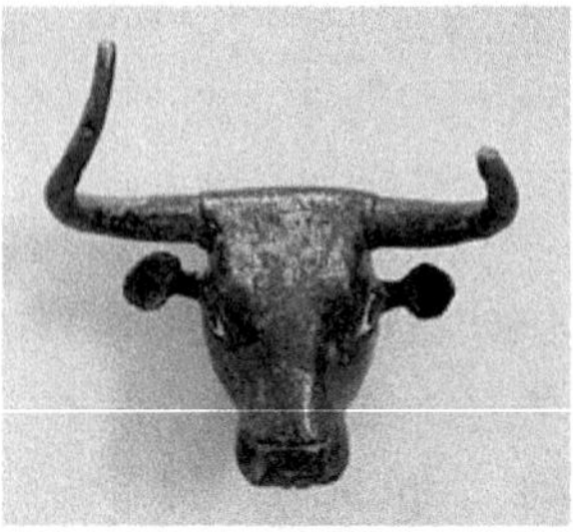

"[person] copper-carpenter"); a word indicating borrowing from a substrate. In Pkt. tambira = copper. According to Gernot Wilhelm, the Hurrian version of tabira is: tab-li 'copper founder'; tab-iri 'the one who has cast (copper)'. *ḍangar* 'bull' (Hindi) Rebus: *ḍhangar* 'blacksmith' (Hindi).

Bull head, probably affixed to the sound-chest of a lyre. Copper, mother-of-pearl and lapis lazuli, found in Telloh, ancient Girsu. Louvre Museum, Accession number AO 2676, Excavated by Ernest de Sarzec; gift of Sultan Abdul Hamid, 1896

Second dynasty of Lagash, reign of Gudea, c. 2120 BCE Tello (ancient Girsu) Limestone H. 1.20 m; W. 0.63 m; D. 0.25 m E. de Sarzec excavations, 1881 AO 52

The stele of music shows the foundation rites - performed to the sound of the lyre - of the temple built by Prince Gudea (c. 2100 BC) at his capital of Telloh (ancient Girsu), for Ningirsu, god of the state of Lagash in the Land of Sumer. The stele thus accords with the tradition of Neo-Sumerian art, which unlike that of the preceding period that focused on the warlike exploits of the rulers of Akkad, tends to show the king engaged in pious activities.[410]

"The addresses on fragments of clay at Tello prove that sealings were employed on bundles despatched from city to city."[411]

The word me-la-hha may also be cognate with: *meṛh, meḍh*, 'copper merchant' (Gujarati).

Steatite seals with the image of the short-horned bulls with lowered head from Failaka

(1), Bahrein (2-3), Bactria (4), the Iranian Plateau (5). Nr. 6 comes from the surface of the site of Diqdiqqah, near Ur. Not in scale.

2. Distribution of inscribed finds with Indus signs in Mesopotamia, in the Iranian Plateau and in the Gulf (from Parpola 1994).

3. Etched Carnelian Beads found in Mesopotamia and the Iranian Plateau. F1y, second row from below, right, bears the symbol of the Akkadian sun-god Shamash: it was evidenty manufactured by a Meluhhan beadmaker for a local Mesopotamian market or demand (from Reade 1979).

4. Distribution of etched carnelian beads from the Indus valley to the Mediterranean coast (from Reade 1979).

5. Long barrel-shaped carnelian beads from Chanhu-Daro and Mohenjo-Daro (Sindh, Pakistan) (upper row, left) and reconstruction of the drilling technique, with lithic drill-heads (upper row, right: from Mackay 1938, 1943 and Kenoyer 1997). Similar beads were manufactured and traded in late ED III Mesopotamia. The longest examples of these highly refined beads reach 13 cm. Lower row: examples of etched carnelian beads found in the Indus valley, to be compared with those found in Mesopotamia, common in early and middle Akkadian times.

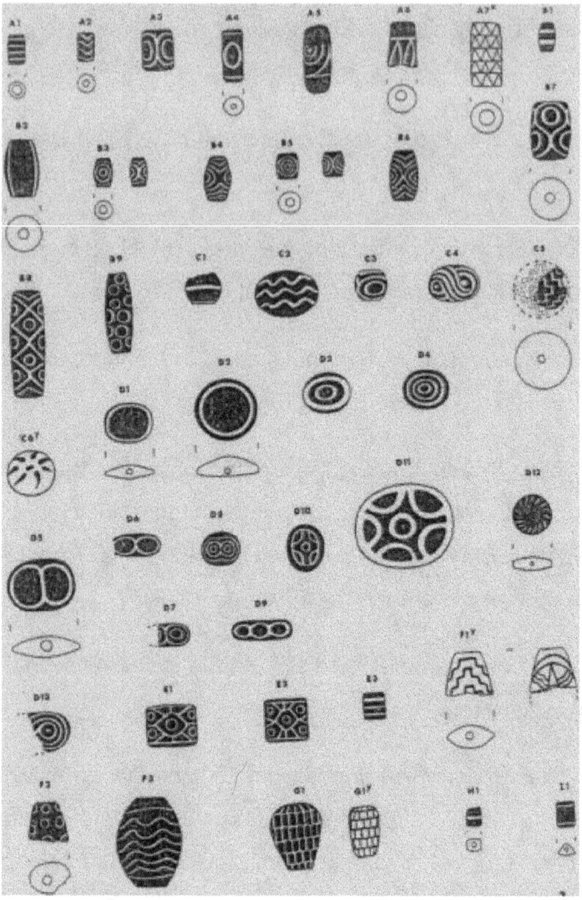

"...these beads are reliable indicators of the activities of the Meluhhan traders in Mesopotamia in the last centuries of the 3rd millennium BCE (Figs. 2,4)...It was the beads and shell trade that, in Mesopotamia, in the Gulf, most probably at Susa and possibly even in Bactria, gradually promoted the local settlement of families of specialized merchants and craftspersons from the Indus valley, who channeled along their tracks the supply of raw materials and, in general, the complex know-how of the Indus crafts. Archaeological evidence pushes back the beginning of this process toat east to the end of the 4th millennium BCE, when Late Uruk Sumerian engravers frequently employed the colummella of the Indian *shank* shell (*turbinella pyrum*) for their cylinder seals...If we have to believe to the cuneiform texts that insistently ascribe to Meluhha the lapis lazuli trade, Meluhhan traders would also have promotd the flowing, in a relatively short time, of incredible amounts of the blue stone at the courts of Ur…"(Vidale, M., pp.271-2)

Parpola et al remark that 'textual references to Meluhha and Meluhhans prior to the Ur III dynasty (relegated) that country and its inhabitants to a non-Mesopotamian, foreign status. Goods and materials were exotic to Mesopotamia and came from a distant Meluhha…' (Parpola S., A. Parpola & R.H. Brunswig, Jr. (1977) "The Meluhha Village. Evidence of acculturation of Harappan traders in the late Third Millennium Mesopotamia." Journal of Economic and Social History of the Orient, 20, 129-165. p.150).

"At the end of the 3rd millennium BC, the Ur III record from Lagash shows a community maintaining its original ethnic affiliation but successfully integrated with the Sumerian society, particularly in contexts suggesting economic and ideological interaction with temples and local cults. Meluhhans bear Sumerian names or are identified by their ethnical or professional identity. They live in a separate rural settlement identified as a "Meluhha village" somewhere in the province of Lagash; the community owns or nd and manages a central granary, that delivers rations or payments in barley to craft specialists. They appear variously involved with the management of temples and other religious institutions: one is perhaps an "inspector" of a temple, another a skipper trasporting grain for a temple's mill, another one receives a substantial payment in barley for the temple of Ninmar. To the same goddess is sacred a "Meluhha garden," possibly a precinct where fruits and flowers imported from India are cultivated. Aswe have seen, there is the possibility that "Dogs" of Meluhhan affiliation were employed by the Lagash lords as organized guards for controlling the state dockyards.[412]Plates XXI, XXII (Vidale, M.)

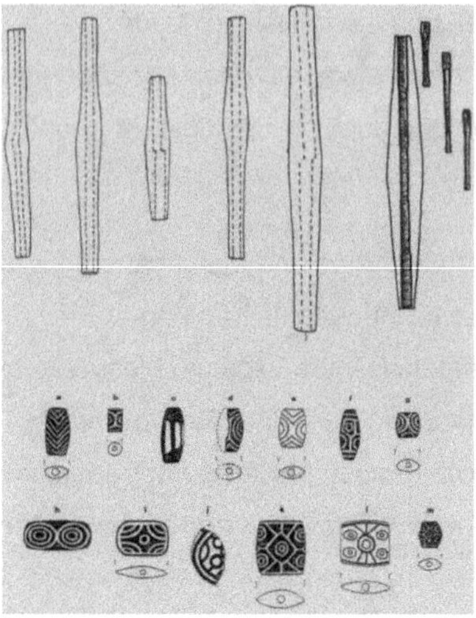

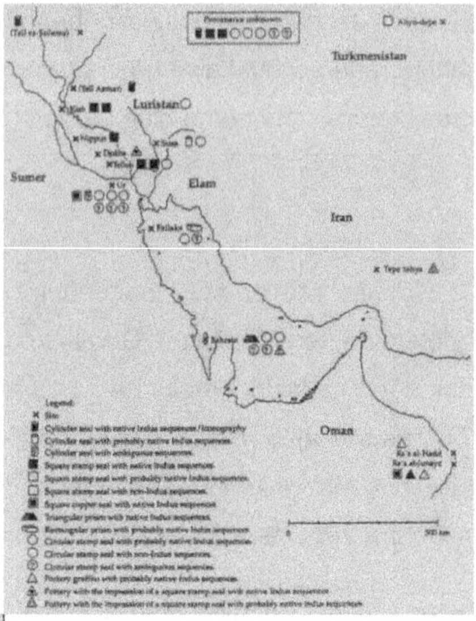

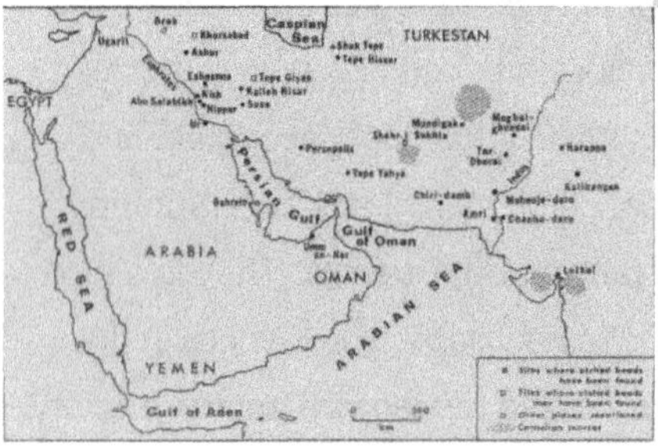

Figure 3 has the Mesopotamian symbol of Shamash, the sun-god. "As excavations at Susa brought to light examples of cylinder-like steatite seals with Indus features (Fig. 1.15), long-barreled cylinder seals and etched carnelian beads, these indicators strongly point to the presence of a Meluhhan 'craft village' in one of the capitals of ancient Elam." (Vidale, M. p.266)

Animal figures in Indus style and round seals with Indus inscriptions are reported from Mesopotamia, Failaka and Bahrain, dated to ca. latter 2 centuries of 3rd millennium BCE and to immediately later times. All round seals (Mesopotamia, the Gulf, Bactria, Iran: Fig. 2) show one animal icone, a short-horned bull with lowered head

Kish and Umma evidenced standard square Indus seals and their sealings.

Two seals with Indus bulls have cuneiform inscriptions: one (Fig. 1.6) from Mesopotamia has a pre-Akkadian inscription (hard to read).

Another seal with an Indus bull and cuneiform inscription (in the Cabinet des Medailles of Paris) is still unpublished. This has an Indus bull with lowered head. J.J. Glassner reads this as Ur.d-Ninildum dumu Ur.gi, an expression which may mean: 'dog' or 'slave' of Ninildum, son of 'Big dog' or 'Mastiff' or, alternatively, 'in charge of the mastiffs'. Ninildum is a goddess of carpentry and timber, referred to in later Babylonian texts as 'great heavenly carpenter' and 'bearer of the shiny hatchet.'

A round seal (Fig. 1.5) has a proto-Elamite inscription. A round chlorite seal coated with a gold foil, with Indus bull on one side and a mythological Bactrian creature on the opposite face (Fig. 1.4) is from a looted grave in Bactria. A lapis lazuli cylinder seal from Bactria in Schoyen collection has a boar-hunting scene together with a well-carved Indus inscription.

"As well remarked by M. Tosi "...the lack of Mesopotamian imports in the Indus Valley reveals the lesser significanceof these connections for the eastern pole.Very much like the Roman trade with India and Arabia, as described in the Erythrean Sea in the 1st century AD, the flow of goods towards the head of the Gulf in the later 3rd millennium BC was determined more by the Mesopotamian demand than by economic integration with the distant lands that supplied these goods from the shores of the Indian Ocean." (1991: 119). Sumerians and Akkadian interacted more with Dilmun sailors and traders, Indian immigrants and largely acculturated social groups than with the remote "Black Country" of Meluhha. In Mesopotamiaand in the Gulf, the immigrant Indus families maintained and trasmitted their language, the writing system and system of weights of the motherland (known in Mesopotamia as the "Dilmunite" standard) as strategic tools of trade. Their official symbol of the gaur might have stressed, together with the condition of living in a foreign world, an ideal connection with the motherland. Nonetheless, they gradually adopted the use of foreign languages and introduced minor changes in the writing system for tackling with new, rapidy evolving linguistic needs. The Indus communities in Mesopotamia developed thanks to an intimate understanding of Mesopotamian culture and markets, and to a very opportunistic behaviour. They promptly adapted their products and trade to the fast-changing political and ideological environments of the local social and cultural evolution. Their success in Mesopotamia is easily measured by their efficient adaptation, inorder of time, to the frantic politics and fights of the ED III city-states, to the Akkadian centralized bureaucracy and to the even more centralized empire established by Ur-nammu. By 2000 BC, their integration with Mesopotamian social and economic reality seems to be total. Theacculturation process involved collaboration with local religious institutions, worship of foreign divinities, production of ornaments with foreign religious symbols, adoption of "impure" foreign rituals in life and death and (it would be easy to imagine) at the eyes of their compatriots at home "eating impure food." The price of the success might have been their apparent "contamination" with Mesopotamian habits, creeds and ritual practices, a circumstance that – we may be sure – did not escape the attention of the traditional élites in the Indus valley."[413]

Spinner hieroglyph

Bas-relief fragment, called "The Spinner" Bitumen J. de Morgan excavations Sb 2834. Made of a bituminous stone, a matte, black sedimentary rock. Relief of a woman being fanned by an attendant while she is seated on a stool, holds what may be a spinning device before a table with a bowl containing a whole fish. Her hair is pulled back in a bun and held in place with a headscarf crossed around her head. Young woman spinning and servant holding a fan. Fragment of a relief known as "The spinner".[414] Susa, Iran, Neo-elamite period. An elegantly coiffed, exquisitely-dressed and well fanned Elamite woman sits on a lion footed stool winding thread on a spindle. This five-inch fragment is dated 8th century BCE. It was molded and carved from a mix of bitumen, ground calcite, and quartz. The

Elamites used bitumen, a naturally occurring mineral pitch, or asphalt, for vessels, sculpture, glue, caulking, and waterproofing.

The glyph elements connote: metal alloy smelter/furnace/workshop, making war chariots.

camara 'flywhisk' (Pkt.); cammar id. (S.) (CDIAL 4677). Rebus: *samara* 'hostile encounter, conflict, struggle, war, battle' (SankhBr.MBh.)(Monier-Williams, p. 1170).

meḍhi, miḍhī, meṇḍhī = a plait in a woman's hair; a plaited or twisted strand of hair (P.) मेढा [mēḍhā] meṇḍa A twist or tangle arising in thread or cord, a curl or snarl. (Marathi) (CDIAL 10312). [dial., cp. Prk. mĕṇṭha & miṇṭha: Pischel, Prk. Gr. § 293. The Dhtm (156) gives a root meṇḍ (meḍ) in meaning of "koṭilla," i. e. crookedness.(Pali)[415] Vikalpa: ḍhompo = knot on a string (Santali) ḍhompo = ingot (Santali) Vikalpa: cūḍa 'diadem, hairdress' (Skt.) Rebus: cūḷa 'furnace' (H.) Rebus: meḍ 'iron' (Ho.) [cf. coiffure hairstyle] Thus, the glyptic elements of woman, plaited hair can be decoded as: meḍ kolami 'iron smelter smithy'.

khattar 'attendant' (Pali) Rebus: *khāḍ* 'trench, fire-pit' (G.) kātī 'woman who spins the thread' Rebus: *khātī* 'wheelwright' (H.)

kaṇḍō 'a stool' (Kur.); Malt. kanḍo stool, seat.(DEDR 1179). Rebus: *kaṇḍ* 'furnace, fire-altar' (Santali) *khaṇḍa* 'tools, pots and pans and metal-ware'. Rebus: kāḍ 'stone'. Ga. (Oll.) kanḍ, (S.) kanḍu (pl. kanḍkil) stone (DEDR 1298).

The glyphics represent *kol khūṭ khātī,'* working in iron, a guild of wheelwrights '.

Significance of six knobs on the fish on the stool: *khoṭ* 'alloyed ingots'. Glyphs: six (numeral) + ring of hair: आर [āra] A term in the play of इटीदांडू,--the number six. (Marathi) आर [āra] A tuft or ring of hair on the body. (Marathi) Rebus: āra 'brass'.

Alternative: bhaṭa 'six' (G.) bhaṭa 'furnace' (G.)

ayo = fish (Mu.); ayas = metal (Skt.) Thus, *aya (k)āra* 'metalsmith'.

[cf.tiger's legs of the bedstead] *kōlupuli* = Bengal tiger (Te.); *kol* = tiger (Santali) *kōla* = woman (Nahali) kolo 'jackal')(Kon.) Rebus: *kol* 'metal of five alloys, *pan~caloha*, working in iron' (Tamil) Rebus: *kolami* 'smithy' (Te.) [Vikalpa: goti 'woman'; rebus; goṭ 'cow-pen'; rebus: koḍ 'place where artisans work' (Kuwi)]

kuṭhe 'leg of bedstead or chair' (Santali) Rebus: *kuṭhi* 'a furnace for smelting iron ore, to smelt iron'; *koṭe* 'forged (metal)(Santali)

kolheko kuṭhieda koles smelt iron (Santali)

The legs of the two stools shows glyphic of tiger's foot. Glyph: 'foot, hoof': Glyph: 'hoof': Ku. *khuṭo* ' leg, foot ', *°ṭī* ' goat's leg '; N. *khuṭo* ' leg, foot '(CDIAL 3894). S. *khuṛī* f. ' heel '; WPah. paṅ. *khūṛ* ' foot '. khura m. ' hoof ' KātyŚr̥. 2. *khuḍa -- 1 (*khuḍaka* -- , *khula°* ' ankle -- bone ' Suśr.). [← Drav. T. Burrow BSOAS xii 376: it belongs to the word -- group ' heel <-> ankle -- knee -- wrist ', see *kuṭṭha --](CDIAL 3906). Allograph: (Kathiawar) *khūṭ* m. ' Brahmani bull ' (G.) Rebus: *khūṭ* 'community, guild' (Santali)

kāṭi = fireplace in the form of a long ditch (Ta.Skt.Vedic) kāṭya = being in a hole (VS. XVI.37); kāṭ a hole, depth (RV. i. 106.6) khāḍ a ditch, a trench; khāḍ o khaiyo several pits and ditches (G.) khaṇḍrun: 'pit (furnace)' (Santali)

baṭa = kiln (Santali); baṭa = a kind of iron (G.) bhaṭṭhī f. 'kiln, distillery', awāṇ. bhaṭh; P. bhaṭṭh m., °ṭhī f. 'furnace', bhaṭṭhā m. 'kiln'; S. bhaṭṭhī keṇī 'distil (spirits)

Glyph: 'animals': *pasaramu, pasalamu* 'an animal, a beast, a brute, quadruped' (Telugu) Rebus: *pasra* = a smithy, place where a black-smith works, to work as a blacksmith; *kamar pasra* 'artisan smithy'; *pasrao lagao akata se ban:?* 'Has the blacksmith begun to work?' *pasraedae* 'the blacksmith is at his work' (Santali) *pasra meṛed, pasāra meṛed* = syn. of koṭe meṛed = forged iron, in contrast to dul meṛed, cast iron (Mundari.)

Figure 22 Seal impression showing female water-carrier

Water carrier with a skin (or pot?) hung on each end of the yoke across her shoulders and another one below the crook of her left arm; the vessel on the right end of her yoke is over a receptacle for the water; a star on either side of the head (denoting supernatural?). The two celestial objects depicted on either side of the water-carrier's head can be interpreted as a phonetic determinant: koḷ 'planet'. The whole object is enclosed by 'parenthesis' marks. The parenthesis is perhaps a way of splitting the ellipse. Hunter calls the use of ( ) as enclosure of the pictograph an unmistakable example of an 'hieroglyphic' seal.[416]

Some glosses which explain the 'meaning' of the pictograph:

kuṭi = a woman water-carrier (Telugu) *kuṭi* = to drink; drinking, beverage (Ta.)(DEDR 1654). Rebus: *kuṭhi* 'a furnace for smelting iron ore, to smelt iron'; *kolheko kuṭ.hieda* koles smelt iron (Santali)

An Early Dynastic II votive plaque from the Inanna temple at Nippur VIII (after Pritchard, 1969: 356, no. 646). "It has something very Harappan about it also in the lower part depicting two 'unicorn' bulls around a tree. The six dots around the head of the Harappan hero, clearly visible in one seal (Mohenjodaro, DK 11794; cf. Mackay, 1937: II, pl. 84:75) may be compared to the six locks of hair characteristic of the Mesopotamian hero from Jemdet Nasr to Akkadian times (cf. Calmeyer, 1957-71: 373). From the Early Dynastic period onwards the scene usually comprises a man fighting with one or two bulls, and a bull-man fighting with one or two lions....North-west India of the third millennium BC can be considered as an integral, if marginal, part of the West Asian cultural area."[417]

Uruk-Jamdat Nasr has also yielded some tablets with semi-pictographic writing:

Tablets with Semi-Pictographic Writing Clay Uruk-Jamdat Nasr Period (ca. 3200-2900 B.C.E.) Left: Tell Asmar Excavated by the Oriental Institute, 1933. OIM A12259. Right: Purchased in Paris, 1920. OIM A2514[418]

The hieroglyphs identifiable are: 1. Sprout; 2. Star. On Indus writing, these glyphs have specific connotations: e.g. *kaṇḍe* 'sprout' *meḍha* 'star' with rebus readings of bronze-age metalware:

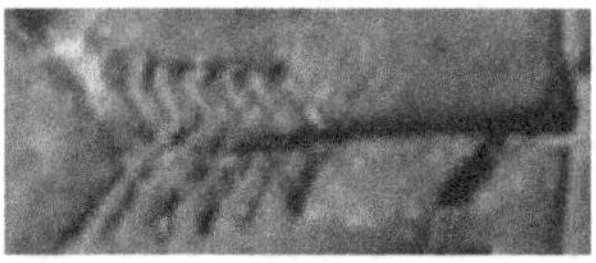

kaṇḍe. [Tel.] n. A head or ear of millet or maize. కందళము [Skt.] n. A germ or shoot, a sprout. కొత్తమొలక. కందళించు *kandaḷinṭsu*. v. n. To sprout, germinate, shoot. (Telugu) Rebus: rebus: *kaṇḍa* '(mineral)stone, meal tools, pots and pans'.

meḍha 'polar star' (Marathi). Rebus: meḍ (Ho.); mẽṛhet 'iron' (Mu.Ho.)

mẽṛhẽt iron; ispat m. = steel; dul m. = cast iron (Munda)

Cylinder seal of the priest-king. Uruk period, circa 3200 BCE. Iraq, findspot unknown. White limestone H. 6.2 cm; Diam. 4.3 cm. AO 6620

కండె [kaṇḍe] *kaṇḍe*. [Tel.] n. A head or ear of millet or maize. జొన్నకంకి.(Telugu)

“The appearance of the cylinder seal “Seals of cylindrical form appeared in Mesopotamia in the second half of the 4th millennium BC, rapidly replacing the stamp seals employed since the 5th millennium to authenticate the sealings that guaranteed the integrity of goods in storage or in transport. These small stone cylinders, carved all over, could easily be rolled in fresh clay to produce complex motifs, arranged in symbolic compositions. Reproducible at will, these impressions could thus serve as marks of ownership.

The appearance of such cylinder seals was not, however, an isolated phenomenon, but rather an integral part of a decisive transformation of society as a whole. The most important expression of this was the birth of the first cities, accompanied by the discovery of writing. The iconography of these cylinder seals thus reflects the new form of social organization prevailing in the cities, in which the dominant figure was the 'priest-king.'

“The cult of the goddess Inanna

“The 'priest-king' appears on this fragmentary cylinder seal in his cultic function, presiding at a ceremony in honor of Inanna, the Sumerian goddess of fertility, whose most important sanctuary was in the city of Uruk. Dressed in a long skirt and wearing a cap or headband denoting his status, the priest-king seems to be making an offering, probably of a wheat-sheaf, in front of the sanctuary of the goddess, symbolized by the bundle of reeds tied with a streamer. He is followed by an assistant also bearing a sheaf of wheat: their offering being symbolically intended to feed the sacred herd of Inanna. The truncated cone at the top of the cylinder is also decorated in relief with a group of sheep, the property of the goddess and of her temple.

"The offering of wheat testifies to the emblematic significance still attached to cereals, the first plants to be selected and grown. It is to be presented to Inanna, the great goddess of fertility, who governs the annual cycle of nature's regeneration. Her performance of this fundamental role depends in particular on the intensity of the worship addressed to her, and it is the responsibility of the priest-king - first among the humans who depend on her - to ensure the regularity of this worship and so guarantee the prosperity of the country."[419]

Hieroglyph of overflowing water

lo 'pot to overflow'[420] *kāṇḍa* 'water'.

Rebus: लोखंड *lokhaṇḍ* Iron tools, vessels, or articles in general.

Gudea's link with Meluhha is clear from the elaborate texts on the two cylinders describing the construction of the Ninĝirsu temple in Lagash. An excerpt: 1143-1154. Along with copper, tin, slabs of lapis lazuli, refined silver and pure Meluḫa cornelian, he set up (?) huge copper cauldrons, huge ...... of copper, shining copper goblets and shining copper jars worthy of An, for laying

(?) a holy table in the open air ...... at the place of regular offerings (?). Ninĝirsu gave his city, Lagaš

Chlorite vessel found at Khafajeh: Ht 11.5 cm. 2,600 BCE, Khafajeh, north-east of Baghdad (Photo from pg. 69 of D. Collon's 1995 *Ancient Near Eastern Art*).

The vessel was found at Khafajeh. Zebus stand back to back. A person is holding streams of water showering down onto a palm tree. A crescent and a rosette are in front of his face. The second person has a rosette at his shoulder. He has a snake in each hand and is standing between two felines. At the right of the panel, a bull is being attacked by a large bird (eagle) and a lion while another small animal (tiger?) faces the other way. This composite image was created by rotating the vessel.

Two views of the bow. which dates from c. 2700-2500 B.C. and the motif shown on it resembles that on a fragment of a green stone vase from one of the Sin Temples at Tell Asmar of almost the same date.

Zebu is shown with its characteristic hump; a male figure with long hair and wearing a kilt grasps two sinuous objects, representing running water, which flows in a continuous stream. Around the bowl, another similar male figure stands between two lionesses with their head turned back towards him; he grasps a serpent in each hand. A further scene (not shown) represents a prostrate bull which is being attacked by a vulture and a lion.

Stele of Untash-Napirisha, king of Anshan and Susa

Stele representing King Untash Napirisha, "King of Anzan and Susa"

C. 1340-1300 BCE Sandstone J. de Morgan excavations

Sb 12 Near Eastern Antiquities Sully wing Ground floor Iran, Susiana (Middle Elamite period) Louvre Museum

This stele with four registers was commissioned by the Elamite king Untash-Napirisha for the city of Chogha Zanbil. It was later moved to Susa by one of his successors, probably Shutruk-Nahhunte I. The four registers depict the god Inshushinak acknowledging the monarch's power, two priestesses accompanying the king to the temple, minor deities - half-women, half-fish - holding streams of water, and two creatures - half-men, half-mouflons - who are guardians of the sacred tree.

Cylinder seal showing running goats turning their heads, appearing in perpetual motion; ca. 2800 B.C. (Uruk IV) (M.E.L.Mallowan, 1965, *Early Metopotamia and Iran*, London, Thames and Hudson); the antelope with its head turned backward is a typical motif on the seals of the Sarasvati Sindhu civilization.

."The stele is decorated with four registers separated by a guilloche frieze framed by two serpents whose heads confront each other at the top of the stele…In the upper register, the deity Inshushinak welcomes Untash-Napirisha. Between the two figures is carved a dedication in Elamite, naming Inshushinak god of the Susa plain. ..The second register depicts Untash-Napirisha, flanked by his wife Napir-Asu and probably his mother, the priestess U-tik. The two women are accompanying the king to the temple for the ceremony. The names of the two women are carved on their forearms, which are crossed over their stomachs in the usual pose of sculpted figures of the Middle Elamite period. The third register depicts a minor goddess with a fish's tail instead of legs. She is holding streams of water flowing from several vessels. By perpetuating the water cycle, she underlines its importance in nature, particularly for plants, represented by a stylized tree in the lower register. It was believed that supernatural beings like this deity lived in Apsu. Here, the streams rather resemble ropes, mirroring the sinuous lines of the serpents. It is clear that these are Elamite deities because of the cow's ears sticking up from their hair, in addition to their human ears. In the bottom register, two creatures - half-men, half-mouflons - flank a stylized tree that represents plant life. These figures are the equivalents of the Mesopotamian half-man, half-bull figures. Their role here may be to replace the acolytes of the god Enki as nude heroes guarding his realm. By guarding the underground water, they protect the sacred tree, which represents the way that plants flourish when they are watered. These two lower registers have been carved to form a symmetrical composition."[421]

Table decorated with serpents and deities bearing vessels spouting streams of water 14th century BCE Tell of the Acropolis, Susa, Iran Bronze H. 19.5 cm; W. 15.7 cm; L. 69.5 cm Jacques de Morgan excavations, 1898 Sb 185

"This table, edged with serpents and resting on deities carrying vessels spouting streams of water, was doubtless originally a sacrificial altar. The holes meant the blood would drain away as water flowed from the vessels. Water was an important theme in Mesopotamian mythology, represented particularly by the god Enki and his acolytes. This table also displays the remarkable skills of Elamite metalworkers.

“A sacrificial table

“The table, edged with two serpents, rested on three sides on five figures that were probably female deities. Only the busts and arms of the figures survive. The fourth side of the table had an extension, which must have been used to slot the table into a wall. The five busts are realistic in style. Each of the deities was holding an object, since lost, which was probably a water vessel, cast separately and attached by a tenon joint. Water played a major role in such ceremonies and probably gushed forth from the vessels. Along the sides of the table are sloping surfaces leading down to holes, allowing liquid to drain away. This suggests that the table was used for ritual sacrifices to appease a god. It was believed that men were created by the gods and were responsible for keeping their temples stocked and providing them with food. The sinuous lines of the two serpents along the edge of the table mark off holes where the blood of the animals, sacrificed to assuage the hunger of the gods, would have drained away.

“The importance of water in Mesopotamian mythology

“In Mesopotamia, spirits bearing vessels spouting streams of water were the acolytes of Enki/Ea, the god of the Abyss and of fresh water. The fact that they figure in this work reflects the extent of the influence of Mesopotamian mythology in Susa. Here, they are associated with another Chtonian symbol, the snake, often found in Iranian iconography. The sinuous lines of the serpents resemble the winding course of a stream. It is thought that temples imitated the way streams well up from underground springs by the clever use of underground channels. Water - the precious liquid - was at the heart of Mesopotamian religious practice, being poured out in libations or used in purification rites…”[422]

According to the inscription this statue was made by Gudea, ruler of Lagash (c.

2100 BCE) for the temple of the goddess Geshtinanna. Gudea refurbished the temples of Girsu and 11 statues of him have been found in excavations at the site. Nine others including this one were sold on the art market. It has been suggested that this statue is a forgery. Unlike the hard diorite of the excavated statues, it is made of soft calcite, and shows a ruler with a flowing vase which elsewhere in Mesopotamian art is only held by gods. It also differs stylistically from the excavated statues. On the other hand, the Sumerian inscription appears to be genuine and would be very difficult to fake. Statues of Gudea show him standing or sitting. Ine one, he rests on his knee a plan of the temple he is building. On some statues Gudea has a shaven head, while on others like this one he wears a headdress covered with spirals, probably indicating that it was made out of fur. Height 61 cm.

The overflowing water from the vase is a hieroglyph comparable to the pectoral of Mohenjo-daro showing an overflowing pot together with a one-horned young bull and standard device in front.

m1656 Mohenjodro Pectoral. kāṇṭam காண்டம் kāṇṭam, *n.* < *kāṇḍa*. 1. Water; sacred water; நீர். துருத்திவா யதுக்கிய குங்குமக் காண் டமும் (கல்லா. 49, 16). <kanda> {N} ``large earthen water ^pot kept and filled at the house". @1507. #14261.(Munda) Rebus: *khāṇḍā* 'metal tools, pots and pans' (Marathi)

<lo->(B) {V} ``(pot, etc.) to ^overflow". See <lo-> `to be left over'. @B24310. #20851. Re<lo->(B) {V} ``(pot, etc.) to ^overflow". See <lo-> `to be left over'. (Munda) Rebus: loh 'copper' (Hindi) The hieroglyph clearly refers to the metal

tools, pots and pans of copper. Thus, the two words read together Rebus: lōkhaṇḍa लोखंड Iron tools, vessels, or articles in general (Marathi).

khaṇṭi 'buffalo bull' (Tamil) Rebus: *khāḍ* '(metal) tools, pots and pans' (Gujarati) கண்டி kaṇṭi buffalo bull (Tamil) kaṇḍ 'buffalo'; rebus: kaṇḍ 'stone (ore)'. *kiḍāvu.* He-buffalo; எருமைக்கடா (Malayalam) *Colloq.*கடவு³ kaṭavu , *n.* < கடா. 1. Male buffalo; எருமைக்கடா. முதுகடவு கடவி (அழகர்கல. 33). *kaḍawan hoṛ* 'a man who has buffaloes'.[423] Rebus: khāḍ 'trench, firepit' (G.) khāṛo 'pit, bog' (Nepali) "In Santali, any word may (in theory at least) be used as a verb simply by adding *a*, which is the verbal sign, and other signs to signify tense, mood etc. The *a* alone signifies the general or future tense in the active voice — used to make general statements, or statements referring to the future... The verb generally comes at the end of a sentence or phrase... (Santali language) consists of root-words and various infixes, suffixes and particles, joined together or agglutinated in such a way as to form phrases and sentences... dalgot' kedeae... dal the root word, meaning to strike or striking; got' an adverbial particle giving the sense of quickly or suddenly; ked the sign ket', denoting the past tense of the active voice, modified to ked... e ... signifying an animate object — him, or her... a the verbal sign, showing that the idea of striking is used verbally; e the short form of the 3rd personal pronoun, singular... denoting the subject — he, or she."[424]

Rebus: kāḍ 'stone'. Ga. (Oll.) kanḍ, (S.) kanḍu (pl. kanḍkil) stone (DEDR 1298). maypon̤ḍi kanḍ whetstone; (Ga.)(DEDR 4628).(खडा) Pebbles or small stones: also stones broken up (as for a road), metal. खडा [khaḍā] *m* A small stone, a pebble. 2 A nodule (of lime &c.): a lump or bit (as of gum, assafœtida, catechu, sugar-candy): the gem or stone of a ring or trinket: a lump of hardened fæces or scybala: a nodule or lump gen. CDIAL 3018 kāṭha m. ' rock ' lex. [Cf. *kānta* -- 2 m. ' stone ' lex.]

Standard device in front of the one-horned young bull

Variants of standard device shown in front of the one-horned young bull on many seals/tablets.

The diorite from Magan (Oman), and timber from Dilmun (Bahrain) obtained by Gudea could have come from Meluhha. "The goddess Geshtinanna was known as “chief scribe” (Lambert 1990, 298–299) and probably was a patron of scribes,

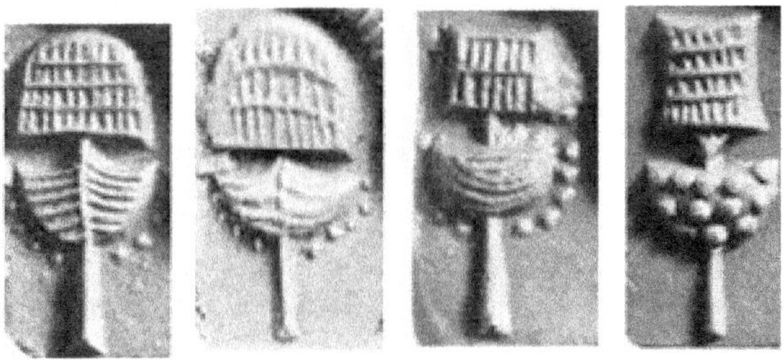

as was Nidaba/Nisaba (Michalowski 2002)."[425] That the hieroglyph of pot/vase overflowing with water is a recurring theme can be seen from other cylinder seals, including Ibni-Sharrum cylinder seal. Such an imagery also occurs on a fragment of a stele, showing part of a lion and vases. Inscription on base of skirt- God commands him to build house. Gudea is holding plans. Gudea depicted as strong, peaceful ruler. Vessel flowing with life-giving water w/ fish. Text on garment dedicates himself, the statue, and its temple to the goddess Geshtinanna. "The goddess Geshtinanna was known as “chief scribe”."[426]

Gudea Statue D Colum IV refers to Magan, Gubi and reads[427]:

1. he has constructed.
2. By the power of the goddess NINÂ,
3. by the power of the god NIN-GIRSU,
4. to Gudea
5. who has endowed with the sceptre
6. the god NIN-GIRSU,
7. the country of MÂGAN,

8. the country of MELUGHGHA,
9. the country of GUBI,
10. and the country of NITUK,
11. which possess every kind of tree,
12. vessels laden with trees of all sorts
13. into SHIRPURLA
14. have sent.
15. From the mountains of the land of MÂGAN
16. a rare stone he has caused to come;
17. for his statue

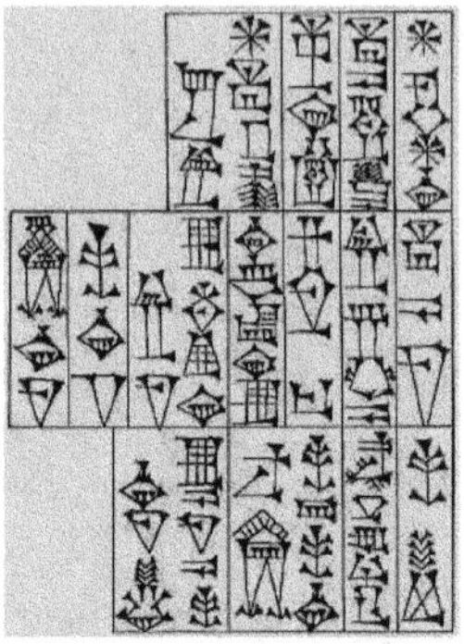

'Gudea of Lagash': The Inscription

The inscription extends over part of the right shoulder and onto the left side of the robe. The upper part, the cartouche, gives the name of the ruler, while the lower, main text speaks of the reasons for the creation of this particular statue. The cartouche translates as follows: Gudea, city ruler of Lagash, the man who built the temple of Ningishzida and the temple of Geshtinanna.The text reads:

Gudea, city ruler of Lagash, built to Geshtinanna, the queen *a-azi-mu-a*, the beloved wife of Ningishzida, his queen, her temple in Girsu. He created for her [this] statue. "She granted the prayer," he gave it a name for her and brought it into her temple.[428]

The inscriptions on the many (22) statues of Gudea and on two large cylinders, are a remarkable source of information on commodities exchanged across the interaction area. Here are some examples related to transactions with Meluhha involving gold, diorite (obtained also from Magan), Magan, Meluhha, Gubin and the Land Tilmun – supplying him with wood, describing himself as a sea-farer dealing with materials of the bronze-age including, gold, silver, bronze, copper, tin and stones such as diorite (carnelian from Meluhha) and varieties of wood. It is thus, not unreasonable to read rebus the hieroglyph of the overflowing vase and fishes on Statue N. As related to ayo 'metal (alloy), lo 'copper' and tools, pots and pans made of metal (kāṇḍā): He (Gudea) brought alabaster blocks from Tidanum, the mountain range of the Martu, using them to make... (for Ningirsu), and he mounted them in the Houseas 'skull-crashers.' In Abulāt, on the mountain range of Kimaṣ, he mined copper, and he (used it to) make for him the 'Mace-unbearable-for-the-regions.' From the land of Meluhha he brought down diorite, used it to build <...> (for Ningirsu), he brought down blocks of hulālu stone, and he (used them to) make for him the 'Mace-with-a-three-headed-lion.' He brought down gold in its fore from the land of Meluhha, ad he (used it to) make a quiver for (Ningirsu). He brought down...; be brought down halub wood from Gubin, the halub mountain, and he (used it to) make for him the bird(?) 'Mow-down-a-myriad'. He brought down a myriad(?) of talents of bitumen from Madga, the mountain range of the Ordeal river(?), and he (used it for) building the retaining wall of the Eninnu...He defeated the cities of Anṣ an and Elam and brought the booty therefrom to Ningirsu in his Eninnu...For this statue nobody was supposed to use silver or lapis lazuli, neither should copper or tin or bronze be a working (material). It is (exclusively) of diorite; let it stand at the libation place. Nobody will forcibly damage (the stone). O statue, your eye is that of Ningirsu; He who removes from the Eninnu the statue of Gudea, the ruler of Lagaṣ, who had build Ningirsu's Eninnu; who rubs off the inscription thereon; who destroys (the statue); who disregards my judgment after – at the beginning of a prosperous New Year – his god Ningirsu, my master, had (directly) addressed him within the crowd, as my god (addressed me);...He brought down diorite from the mountain of Magan and fashioned it into a statue of himself...He constructed for (Ningirsu) his beloved boat (named) 'Having set sail from the Lofty Quay', and he moored it for him at the 'Lapis Lazuli Quay' of Kasurra. He enrolled for (Ningirsu) the sailors and their captain, donating them for the House of his master...Magan, Meluhha, Gubin and the Land Tilmun – supplying him with wood---let their imber cargoes (sail) to Lagaṣ. He brought down diorite from the mountain range of Magan, and he fashioned it into a statue of his...The fierce halo (of the House) reaches upto heaven, great fear of my House hovers over all the lands, and all (these) lands will gather on its behalf from as far as where heaven ends – (even) Magan and Meluhha will descend from their mountains…The Elamites came to him from Elam, the Susians from Susa. Magan and Meluhha, (coming down) from their mountain, loaded wood on their shoulders for him, and in order to build Ningirsu's House they all joined Gudea (on their way) to his city Girsu. (Ningirsu) ordered Nin-zaga, and he brought to Gudea, the builder of the House, his copper as (much as) if it were huge quantities of grain. (Ningirsu) ordered Ninsikila, and she brought to the ruler who build the Eninnu great halub logs, ebony wood along with 'wood of the sea'. The lord Ningirsu cleared the way for Gudea to the impenetrable cedar mountain…Silver from its mountain is being brought down to Gudea, light carnelian from Meluhha spreads before him, alabaster from the alabaster mountain they are bringing down to him. When building the House with silver, the shepherd sat with the silversmith, when building the Eninnu with precious stones, he sat with the jeweler, and when building it with copper and tin, then Nintu-kalama directed before him the chief of the smiths.[429]

Fig. 8: Gudea Basin SV.7.

Baked clay H. 73.5 cm; W. 31.5 cm; Thickness 12.0 cm Ur (Iraq). IX Expedition, 1930-31. AH. Paternoster Row No. 8-10, a little above floor level Isin-Larsa and Old Babylonian 31-43-577 (U. 16959) "Large baked clay plaque featuring a goddess holding a vase overflowing with water…The goddess wears a long pleated garment with short sleeves and a horned crown with four pairs of horns. Her hair passes behind her ears and turns up at her shoulders. She holds what was probably a round-bodied jar with short narrow neck and flaring rim. Her left hand cradles the body of the vessel; her right hand grasps its neck. Streams of water gush from the vessel, flowing over her breasts and shoulders and onto the ground. A wavy line at the base of the goddess' garment likely represents the water flowing under her feet. The vase overflowing with water, Sumerian hé-gál or Akkadian hegallu, is a symbol of abundance and prosperity..."[430]

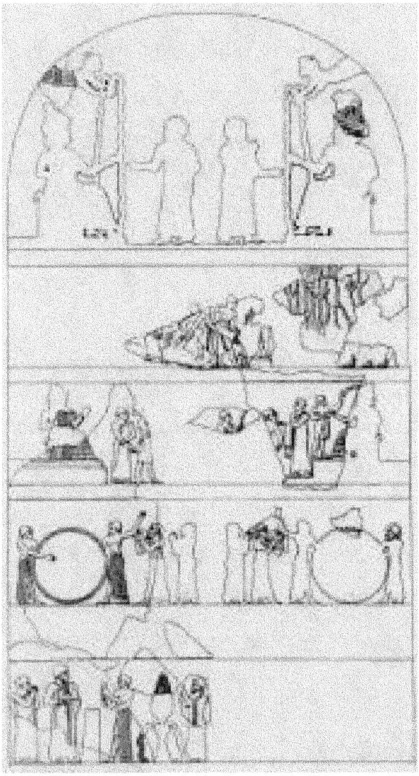

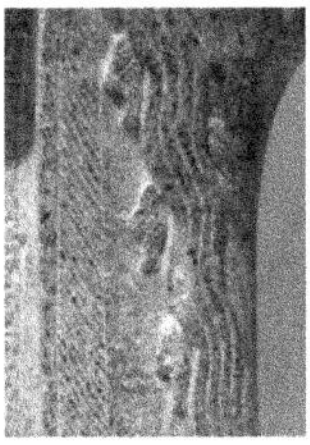

Timber and exotic stones to decorate the temples were brought from the distant lands of Magan and Meluhha (possibly to be identified as Oman and the Indus Valley).

Gudea Basin. Water overflowing from vases. : The Representation of an Early Mesopotamian Ruler ... By Claudia E. Suter "The standing statue N (Fig. 5) holds a vase from which four streams of water flow down on each side of the dress into identical vases depicted on the pedestal, which are equally overflowing with water. Little fish swim up the streams to the vase held by Gudea. This statue evidently shows the ruler in possession of prosperity symbolized by the overflowing vase."[431] (p.58)*ayo* 'fish' (Munda) Rebus: *ayo* 'iron' (Gujarati); *ayas*'metal' (Skt.) Together with *lo*, 'overflow', the compound word can be read as loh+ayas. The compound *lohāyas* is attested in ancient Indian texts, contrasted with*kṛṣṇāyas,* distinguishing red alloy metal (bronze) from black alloy metal (iron alloy). *ayaskāṇḍa* is a compound attested in Pāṇini; the word may be semantically explained as 'metal tools, pots and pans' or as alloyed metal.

Fish in water on statue, on viewer's right.

Fig. 33 Urnamma stela.

Borker-Klahn's reconstruction.

On the Urmamma Stela, she is hovering over the offering of flowing water to the ruler by the enthroned deity. In this scene the goddess underlines the gift bestowed on the ruler, and figures as a personification of it, while on the seal she may have implied and guaranteed that the petitioner who offers an antelope (?) is pleading for and will receive blessings of abundance in return. The basin of Gudea is dedicated to Ningirsu, and may be understood as a plea for prosperity as well as a boast of its successful outcome."[432]

Buffalo as hieroglyph and association with overflowing water

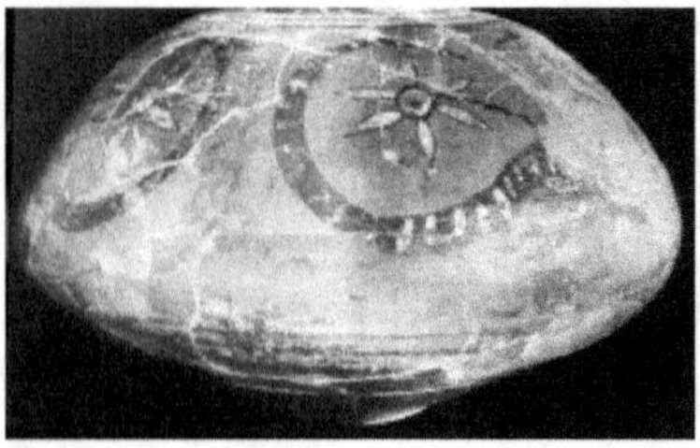

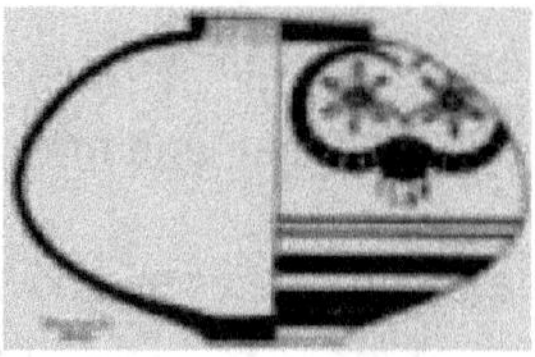

Kot Diji. Buffalo's long horns ligatured to a human (woman) face. A pair of stars are shown between the horns.

Buffalo-horned face. Painting on a jar. Kot Diji. C. 2800-2600 BCE.[433] sal *'bos gaurus,* bison'*;* sal 'workshop' (Santali) Vikalpa: rangā 'buffalo'; ranga 'pewter or alloy of tin (ranku), lead (nāga) and antimony (*añjana*)'(Santali)

meḍha 'polar star' (Marathi).

Allograph: miṇḍāl markhor (Tor.wali) meḍho a ram, a sheep (G.)(CDIAL 10120)

Rebus: meḍ (Ho.); mẽṛhet 'iron' (Mu.Ho.)mẽṛh t iron; ispat m. = steel; dul m. = cast iron (Munda)

miṇḍāl markhor (Tor.wali) meḍho a ram, a sheep (G.)(CDIAL 10120)Rebus: meḍ (Ho.); mẽṛhet 'iron' (Mu.Ho.)mẽṛh t iron; ispat m. = steel; dul m. = cast iron (Munda)

Cylinder seal and modern impression: two horned animals, rosettes Period:

Proto-Elamite Date: ca. 3100–2900 B.C. Geography: Southwestern Iran Culture: Proto-Elamite Medium: Clinoenstatite (sometimes referred to as "glazed steatite") Dimensions: H. 1 3/8 in. (3.5 cm); D. 11/16 in. (1.8 cm) Classification: Stone.[434]

The 'rosette' could be a safflower, *karaḍa* Rebus: hard alloy. The 'dotted circle' ligatured with a sprout at the back of the antelope, could be a representation of kaN 'eye' rebus: kaṇḍa 'stone, meal tools, pots and pans'.

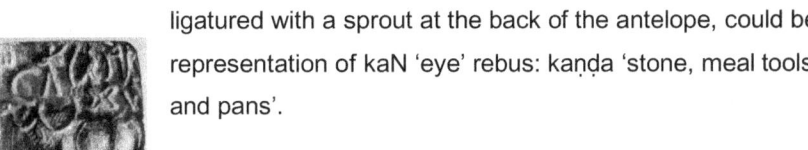

Indus seal. Water-buffalo; a trough in front. *pattar* 'trough' Rebus: *pattar* 'guild'. *khaṇṭi* 'buffalo bull' (Tamil) Rebus: kāḍ 'stone'. Ga. (Oll.) kanḍ, (S.) kanḍu (pl. kanḍkil) stone (DEDR 1298).

Buffaloes sitting with legs bent in yogic āsana. Susa Cc-Da, ca. 3000-2750 BC, proto-Elamite seals: (a-c) After Amiet 1972: pl. 25, no. 1017 (=a); and Amiet 1980a: pl. 38, nos. 581-2 (b-c)

ḍāngā = hill, dry upland (B.); *ḍā̃g* mountain-ridge (H.)(CDIAL 5476). Rebus: *dhangar* 'blacksmith' (Maithili) *ḍangar* 'blacksmith' (Hindi) Alternative: Glyph: hill: <-> Bshk. *khan* m. ' hill ', Tor. Mai. *khān*, Chil. Gau. *kān* (→ Par. *khándi* IIFL i 265) poss. all < *skandhá* -- , but prob. like Tor. (Grierson) *khaṇḍ* ' hill ', Phal. *khāṇ*, *khaṇ*, Sh.koh. *khŭ̃ṇ* m., gur. *khonn*, pales. *khōṇə*, jij. *khɔ̃ṇ* rather < khaṇḍá -- AO xviii 240. -- X maṇi – (CDAIL 13627)

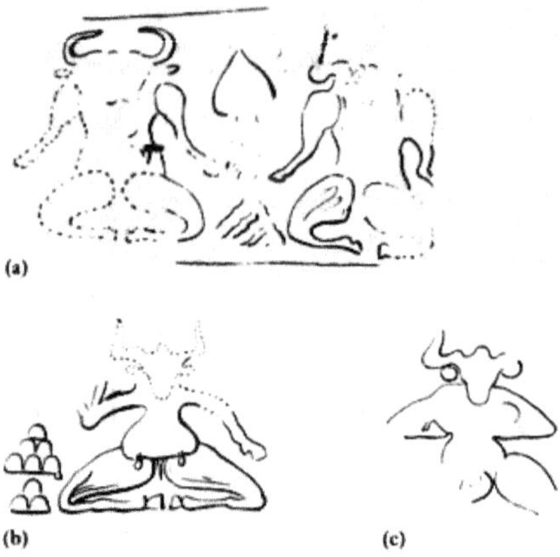

Example of use of allograph on a seal from Banawali showing women acrobats leaping over a water-buffalo:

Impression and line-drawing of a steatite stamp seal with a water-buffalo and leapers. Buffalo attack or bull-leaping scene, Banawali (after UMESAO 2000:88, cat. no. 335). A figure is impaled on the horns of the buffalo; a woman acrobat wearing bangles on both arms and a long braid flowing from the head, leaps over the buffalo bull. Two Indus script glyphs in front of the buffalo. Allograph: *kaṇḍa 'arrow'*. खांडा [khāṇḍā] *m* A jag, notch, or indentation (as upon the edge of a tool or weapon). (Marathi) Rebus: *khāṇḍā* 'tools, pots and pans, metal-ware'.

m0312 Persons vaulting over a water-buffalo. *ḍolu* 'to tumble over' Rebus: *ḍhō̃ḷ* m. 'stone'; *kaṇḍ* 'buffalo'; rebus:*kaṇḍ* 'stone (ore)'.

khanṭi 'buffalo bull' (Tamil) Rebus: kāḍ 'stone'. Ga. (Oll.) kanḍ, (S.) kanḍu (pl. kanḍkil) stone (DEDR 1298).

Glyphs: '1. arrow, 2. jag/notch':

1. kaṇḍa 'arrow' (Skt.) H. kā̃ḍerā m. ' a caste of bow -- and arrow -- makers (CDIAL 3024). Or. kāṇḍa, kāṛ 'stalk, arrow '(CDIAL 3023). *ayaskāṇḍa* 'a quantity of iron, excellent iron' (Pāṇ.gaṇ)

2. खांडा [khāṇḍā] *m* A jag, notch, or indentation (as upon the edge of a tool or weapon). (Marathi) Rebus: *khāṇḍā* 'tools, pots and pans, metal-ware'.

The message of stone ore is reinforced by the glyphics of buffalo and overthrow of an acrobat woman (*kola* 'woman'; rebus: *kol* 'smithy'):

baṭi trs. To overturn, to overset or ovethrow; to turn or throw from a foundation or foothold (Santali) baṭi to turn on the ground to any extent, or roll; uaurbaṭi, to upset or overthrow by shoving or pushing; mabaṭi to overturn by cutting, to fell trees; baṭi-n rflx. v., to lay oneself down; ba-p-aṭi repr. V., to throw each other; baṭi-o to be overturned, overthrown; ba-n-at.i vrb.n., the extent of the overturning, falling down or rolling; baṭi-n rlfx.v., to lie down; baṭi-aṛagu to bring or send down a slope by rolling; baṭi bar.a to roll again and again or here and there; baṭi-bur to turn over by rolling (Mundari) Rebus: baṭi, bhaṭi 'furnace' (H.) Rebus: baṭa = a kind of iron (G.) bhaṭa 'furnace' (G.) baṭa = kiln (Santali). bhaṭa = an oven, kiln, furnace (Santali) baṭhi furnace for smelting ore (the same as kuṭhi) (Santali)

Pict-102: Drummer and people vaulting over? An adorant?

Glyph: kaḍī a chain; a hook; a link (G.); kaḍum a bracelet, a ring (G.) Rebus: kaḍiyo [Hem. Des. kaḍaio = Skt. sthapati a mason] a bricklayer; a mason; kaḍiyaṇa, kaḍiyeṇa a woman of the bricklayer caste; a wife of a bricklayer (Gujarati) *karaḍa 'double-drum' Rebus: karaḍa* 'hard alloy'

Alternative: ḍhol 'drum' (Gujarati.Marathi)(CDIAL 5608) Rebus 1: large stone; Rebus 2: brass pot; Rebus 3: dul 'to cast in a mould'. Alt

The imagery of vaulting over is repeated. This hieroglyphic representation of 'vaulting or rolling over' is an allograph: Allographs: ḍollu. [Tel.] v. n. To fall, to roll over. పడు, పొరలు. డొలుచు [ḍolucu] or ḍoluṭsu. [Tel.] v. n. To tumble head over heels as dancing girls do (Telugu) Mth. Bhoj. Aw. lakh. Marw. G. M. *ḍhol* m. *ḍhōlayati 'makes fall'(CDIAL 5608). Glyph: *ḍhol* 'a drum beaten on one end by a stick and on the other by the hand' (Santali); *ḍhol* 'drum' (Nahali); *dhol* (Kurku); *ḍhol* (Hi.) *dhol* a drum (G.)(CDIAL 5608) డోలు [ḍōlu] [Tel.] n. A drum. Rebus 1: dul 'to cast in a mould'; dul *mẽṛhẽt, dul meṛeḍ, dul; koṭe meṛeḍ* 'forged iron' (Santali) WPah.kṭg. (kc.) Rebus 2: *ḍhō`ḷ* m. 'stone', kṭg. *ḍhòḷṭɔ* m. 'big stone or boulder', *ḍhòḷṭu* 'small id.' Him.I 87.(CDIAL 5536).

Rebus 3: K. *ḍula* m. ' rolling stone '(CDIAL 6582)

Rebus 4: Bshk. *ḍōl* ' brass pot '; K. *ḍol* m. ' bucket ', S. *ḍolu* m., P. *ḍol* m., WPah.bhal. *ḍol* n., Ku. N. B. Mth. *ḍol*, Aw. lakh. *ḍōlu*, H. *dol*, *ḍol* m., G. *ḍol* f., M. *ḍol* m. WPah.poet. *ḍōr* m. ' small pot ', kṭg. *ḍōl* m. ' bucket ', J. *ḍō̃l* m. ← H. or < **dōlla* --).(CDIAL 6583).

h182A, h182B

The drummer hieroglyph is associated with svastika glyph on this tablet (har609) and also on h182A tablet of Harappa with an identical text. kola 'tiger' Rebus: kol 'alloy of five metals, pañcaloha' (Tamil). *karaḍa 'double-drum' Rebus: karaḍa* 'hard alloy'. Alternative: ḍhol 'drum' (Gujarati.Marathi)(CDIAL 5608) Rebus: large stone; dul 'to cast in a mould'. G.*karā̃* n. pl. 'wristlets, bangles'; S. *karāī* f. 'wrist' (CDIAL 2779). Rebus 1: *gaṛā* ' to hammer into shape, form (Bengali) (CDIAL 3966). Rebus 2: Bshk. *kōr* ' large stone ' (CDIAL 3018).Rebus 3: khār खार्

'blacksmith' (Kashmiri) dula 'pair' Rebus: dul 'cast metal'. *kanka* 'Rim of jar' (Santali); *karṇaka* rim of jar'(Skt.) Rebus: *karṇaka* 'scribe' (Telugu); *gaṇaka* id. (Skt.) (Santali) Thus, the tablets denote blacksmith's alloy cast metal accounting including the use of alloying mineral *satthiya*, *jasta* 'zinc' –*satthiya* 'svastika' glyph. Alternative: *karaḍa* 'double-drum', phonetic determinant: 'panther, leopard' Rebus: करडा [*karaḍā*] Hard from alloy--iron, silver &c. (Marathi) The message may relate to hard alloy, cast metal (which can be) hammered into shape in a forge. The alloy is described as zinc alloy.

 Alternative reading: (Kashmiri)(CDIAL  Glyph: *ḍula* m. ' rolling stone ' 6582) Rebus: dul 'cast (metal)'. The glyph of two linear strokes may be phonetic determinant: dula 'pair' Rebus: dul 'cast metal'. Thus, the inscription text may render a scribe's account of the cast metal of five alloyed hard metals -- *karaḍā* --with zinc.

In a remarkable continuity of associating svastika glyph -- satthiya 'zinc', jasta 'zinc'-- with fish – ayo 'fish' Rebus: ayas 'metal' --, an altar dated to ca. 1st century BCE produces the following further links of svastika glyph with the 'nave of wheel or spokes' glyph:

Svastika glyph is associated with the glyphs of wheel and fish in the following artifact, attesting to the metallurgical documentation of the bronze-age:

Altar in the Toulouse Museum[435]

A stone altar erected in the south of France among the Pyrenees about the time of the advent of the Romans. It has a Swastika engraved on its pedestal.[436] Altar, Pyrenees (South of France). I Century BC (The altar shows a svastika and a fish – both are Sarasvati hieroglyphs of Indus writing.) In the context of metallurgists' or stone work, the glyphs read rebus: ayo 'fish' Rebus: ayo 'metal' (Gujarati) satthiya 'svastika glyph' Rebus satthiya, jasta 'zinc' (Kashmiri. Kannada); sattva 'zinc' (Prakrit) eraka 'nave of wheel' Rebus: eraka 'copper'.

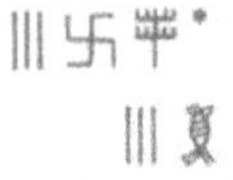

"The discovery in Altyn-Depe of a proto-Indian seal with two signs deserves special mention. V.M. Masson pointed out, that what the seal depicted was a pictogram and not just a representation of animals. In his opinion this means that some of the ancient residents of Altyn-Depe were able to read this text."[437] Altyn-tepe seals compare with an inscription on a miniature tablet, Text 4500 (Harappa. Incised miniature tablet; not illustrated). Line 2 of inscription: A pair of 'harrows' glyph: dula 'pair'; rebus dul 'cast (metal)'; aḍar 'harrow'; rebus: aduru 'native metal'. Thus, the duplicated 'harrow' glyph read rebus: cast native metal. Glyph: svastika; rebus: jasta 'zinc' (Kashmiri). Glyph 'three liner strokes': kolmo 'three'; rebus: kolami 'smithy'. Line 1 of inscription: Ligatured glyph: cunda 'musk-rat'; rebus: cundakāra 'ivory turner'; kolmo 'three'; rebus: kolami 'smithy'. Thus the Text 4500 on an incised miniature tablet read rebus: ivory turner smithy'; cast native metal, tin, smithy.

Finds at Atlyn-depe: ivory sticks and gaming pieces (?) obtained from Sarasvati Sindhu civilization; similar objects with dotted circles found in Mohenjodaro and Harappa.

Two seals found at Altyn-depe (Excavation 9 and 7) found in the shrine and in the 'elite quarter'.[438] aḍar 'harrow'; aduru 'native metal' (Ka.) kolmo 'paddy plant' (Santali); rebus: kolami 'furnace, smithy' (Te.) *sathiyā* (H.), sāthiyo (G.); satthia, sotthia (Pkt.) Svastikā sign Rebus: Kashmiri: zasath ज़स्ऺथ् or zasuth ज़सुथ् । त्रपु m. (sg. dat. zastas ज़स्तस्), zinc, spelter, pewter (cf. Hindī *jast*). jasti jasti; त्रपुधातुविशेषनिर्मितम् adj. c.g. made of zinc or pewter. jasth जस्थ । त्रपु m. (sg. dat. jastas जस्तस्), zinc, spelter; pewter. jastuvu जस्तुवु त्रपूद्भवः adj. (f. jastüvü), made of zinc or pewter.

satavu, satuvu, sattu = pewter, zinc (Ka.) dosta = zinc (Santali) jasada, yasada, yasadyaka, yasatva = zinc (Jaina Pali) ruhi-tutiya (Urdu) tuttha (Arthas'a_stra)

totamu, tutenag (Te.) oriechalkos (Gk.)

h1966A h1966B 1. Glyph: 'bull': *ḍhangra* 'bull'. *Rebus: ḍhangar* 'blacksmith'.pattar 'trough' Rebus: pattar 'guild'. dula 'pair, likenes' Rebus: dul 'cast metal. Thus the hieroglyphs denote pattar 'guild' of blacksmiths, casters of metal.

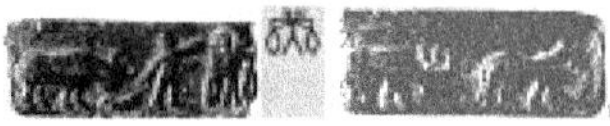

m1405At Bt

Pict-97: Person standing at the center pointing with his right hand at a bison facing a trough, and with his left hand pointing to the sign

2841 Obverse: A tiger and a rhinoceros in file. Pict-48 A tiger and a rhinoceros in file

2805 (m1431)  m1431A  m1431C

m1431D One side (m1431B) of a four-sided tablet shows a procession of a tiger, an elephant and a rhinoceros (with fishes on top?).

koḍe 'young bull' (Telugu) खोंड [khōṇḍa] m A young bull, a bullcalf. Rebus: kõdā 'to turn in a lathe' (B.) कोंद *kōnda* 'engraver, lapidary setting or infixing gems' (Marathi) कोंडण [kōṇḍaṇa] f A fold or pen. (Marathi) ayakāra 'ironsmith' (Pali)[fish = aya (G.); crocodile = kāru (Te.)] baṭṭai quail (N.Santali) Rebus: bhaṭa = an oven, kiln, furnace (Santali)

ayo 'fish' Rebus: ayas 'metal'. *kaṇḍa* 'arrow' Rebus: *khāṇḍa* 'tools, pots and pans, and metal-ware'. *ayaskāṇḍa* is a compounde word attested in Panini. The compound or glyphs of fish + arrow may denote metalware tools, pots and pans.kola 'tiger' Rebus: kol 'working in iron, alloy of 5 metals - pancaloha'. ibha 'elephant' Rebus ibbo 'merchant'; ib 'iron'. Alternative: కరటి [karaṭi] *karaṭi.* [Skt.] n. An elephant. ఏనుగు (Telugu) Rebus: *kharādī* ' turner' (Gujarati) *kāṇḍa* 'rhimpceros' Rebus: *khāṇḍa* 'tools, pots and pans, and metal-ware'. The text on m0489 tablet: loa 'ficus religiosa' Rebus: loh 'copper'. kolmo 'rice plant' Rebus: kolami 'smithy, forge'. dula 'pair' Rebus: dul 'cast metal'. Thus the display of the metalware catalog includes the technological competence to work with minerals, metals and alloys and produce tools, pots and pans. The persons involved are krammara 'turn back' Rebus: kamar 'smiths, artisans'. kola 'tiger' Rebus: kol 'working in iron, working in pancaloha alloys'. పంచలోహము *pancha-lōnamu.* n. A mixed metal, composed of five ingredients, viz., copper, zinc, tin, lead, and iron (Telugu). Thus, when five svastika hieroglyphs are depicted, the depiction is of satthiya 'svastika' Rebus: satthiya 'zinc' and the totality of 5 alloying metals of copper, zinc, tin, lead and iron.

Seal of Ibni-Sharrum, the scribe of King Sharkali-Sharri son of Naram-Sin - 2,250 B.C.

Cylinder seal. Chlorite. AO 22303 H. 3.9 cm. Dia. 2.6 cm. Musée du Louvre, Département des Antiquités Orientales, Paris AO 22303 "At the end of the Uruk period (c.3500-3100 BCE). On the Sharkalisharri cylinder, fifth king of the Akkad dynasty, two naked heroes, acolytes of Eas, water two buffaloes which carry the inscription " Cylinder seal impression of Ibni-sharrum, a scribe of Shar-kali-sharri ca. 2183–2159 BCE. The inscription reads "O divine Shar-kali-sharri, Ibni-sharrum the scribe is your servant."

కరడము or కరడు or కరుడు *karaḍamu.* [Tel.] n. A wave. అల . (Telugu) Rebus: *karaḍa* 'hard alloy' (Marathi) *kāṇḍa* 'flowing water' Rebus: *kāṇḍā* 'metalware, tools, pots and pans'.

erugu = to bow, to salute or make obeisance (Telugu) Rebus: *eraka* 'copper'. Six curls: Glyphs: six (numeral) + ring of hair: आर [āra] A term in the play of इटीदांडू,-- the number six. (Marathi) आर [āra] A tuft or ring of hair on the body. (Marathi) Rebus: āra 'brass'. Rebus: *lohār, lohāra* 'coppersmith, blacksmith' (Lahnda.Prakrit)

Thus, the kneeling adorant with six hair-curls is a smith working with copper and brass. This is consistent with the overflowing pot he offers: *lōkhaṇḍa* 'metalware': *lokhãḍ* n. 'iron'(Marthi) yields the clue to the early semantics of khāṇḍā which should have referred to tools, pots and pans (of metal). Kumaoni has semantics: *lokhaṛ* 'iron tools'. लोहोलोखंड [lōhōlōkhaṇḍa] *n* (लोह & लोखंड) Iron tools, vessels, or articles in general (Marathi). lōhakāra m. ' iron -- worker ', *°rī* -- f., *°raka* -- m. lex., *lauhakāra* -- m. Hit. Pa. *lōhakāra* -- m. ' coppersmith, ironsmith '; Pk. *lōhāra* -- m. ' blacksmith ', S. *luhāru* m., L. *lohār* m., *°rī* f., awāṇ. *luhār*, P. WPah.khaś. bhal. *luhār* m., Ku. *lwār*, N. B. *lohār*, Or. *lohaḷa*, Bi.Bhoj. Aw.lakh. *lohār*, H. *lohār*, *luh°* m., G. *lavār* m., M. *lohār* m.; Si. *lōvaru* ' coppersmith '.WPah.kṭg. (kc.) *lhwā̀r* m. 'blacksmith', *lhwàri* f. ' his wife ', Garh. *lwār* m.(CDIAL 11159).

[quote]A masterpiece of glyptic art

This seal, which belonged to Ibni-Sharrum, the scribe of King Sharkali-Sharri, who succeeded his father Naram-Sin, is one of the most striking examples of the perfection attained by carvers in the Agade period. The two naked, curly-headed heroes are arranged symmetrically, half-kneeling. They are both holding vases from which water is gushing as a symbol of fertility and abundance; it is also the attribute of the god of the river, Enki-Ea, of whom these spirits of running water are indeed the acolytes. Two arni, or water buffaloes, have just drunk from them. Below the scene, a river winds between the mountains represented conventionally by a pattern of two lines of scales. The central cartouche bearing an inscription is held between the buffaloes' horns. A scene testifying to relations with distant lands. Buffaloes are emblematic animals in glyptic art in the Agade period. They first appear in the reign of Sargon, indicating sustained relations between the Akkadian Empire and the distant country of Meluhha, that is, the present Indus Valley, where these animals come from. These exotic creatures were probably kept in zoos and do not seem to have been acclimatized in Iraq at the end of the 3rd millennium BC. Indeed, it was not until the Sassanid Empire that they reappeared. The engraver has carefully accentuated the animals' powerful muscles and spectacular horns, which are shown as if seen from above, as they appear on the seals of the Indus. The production of a royal workshop. The calm balance of the composition, based on horizontal and vertical lines, gives this tiny low relief a classical monumental character, typical of the style of the late Akkadian period. Seals of this quality were the preserve of the entourage of the royal family or high dignitaries and were probably made in a workshop whose production was reserved for this elite...Two nude heroes with long curls are represented kneeling on one knee in a strictly symmetrical composition. Each

of them holds a vase with water gushing forth, a symbol of fertility and abundance; two water buffalo are drinking from them. Underneath, a river winds its way between the mountains, represented in a conventional manner by a motif composed of two lines of scales. In the center of the composition, the text panel containing the inscription is supported on the backs of the buffalo. These animals are evidence of the relations existing between the Akkadian Empire and the region of Meluhha, identified with the Indus Valley, where they originated...[unquote] [439]

Greenstone seal

Akkadian, about 2250 BCE. Mesopotamia. “Belonging to the servant of a

prince...The inscription records the name of the owner but it is not clear; it possibly reads Amushu or Idushu. He is described as the servant of Bin-kali-sharri, a prince. The seals of two of his other servants are also known. Bin-kali-sharri was one of the sons of Naram-Sin, king of Agade (Akkad) (reigned 2254-2218 BC).”[440]

The struggle between wild animals and heroes was a popular design on seals of

this period. It is a standard Mesopotamian theme, representing the symbolic struggle between divine order and chaotic savagery. The inscription records the name of the owner but it is not clear; it possibly reads Amushu or Idushu. He is described as the servant of Bin-kali-sharri, a prince. The seals of two of his other servants are also known. Bin-kali-sharri was one of the sons of Naram-Sin, king of Agade (Akkad) (reigned 2254-2218 BC). Naram-Sin was the grandson of Sargon (reigned 2334-2279 BC), the founder of the Akkadian dynasty. The kings of the dynasty expanded their control beyond their city state of Agade through military conquest. A major building at Tell Brak in north-eastern Syria has been found with bricks stamped with the name of Naram-Sin, testifying to the extent of Akkadian control. Naram-Sin was succeeded by another son, Shar-kali-sharri (2217-2193 BC). After Shar-kali-sharri's reign a period of instability helped to bring the empire to an end."[441]

Overflowing water from a pot is a recurrent motif in Sumer-Elam-Mesopotamian contact areas – a motif demonstrated to be of semantic significance in the context of lapidary-metallurgy life activity of the artisans.

The pot carried by the woman accompanying the Meluhha sea-faring merchant could also be a hieroglyphic rebus reading of *kāṇṭa* signifying metal pots and pans and tools-- *kāṇḍa*.

The following semantic cluster indicates that the early compound: *loha* + *kāṇḍa* referred to copper articles, tools, pot and pans. The early semantics of 'copper' got expanded to cover 'iron and other metals'. It is suggested that the hieroglyph of an overflowing vase refers to this compound: *lohakāṇḍā.*

खांडा [khāṇḍā] *m* A kind of sword, straight, broad-bladed, two-edged, and round-ended (Marathi) M. *lokhāḍ* n. 'iron'(Marthi) yields the clue to the early semantics of khāṇḍā which should have referred to tools, pots and pans (of metal).

Kumaoni has semantics: *lokhaṛ* 'iron tools'. लोहोलोखंड [lōhōlōkhaṇḍa] *n* (लोह & लोखंड) Iron tools, vessels, or articles in general (Marathi).

Thus *lohakāṇḍā* would have referred to copper tools. The overflowing vase on the hands of Gudea would have referred to this compound, represented by the hieroglyphs and rendered rebus.

Goat-fish as ligatured hieroglyph

Ritual basin decorated with goatfish figures. Middle Elamite period Susa,

Iran Limestone H. 62.8 cm; W. 92

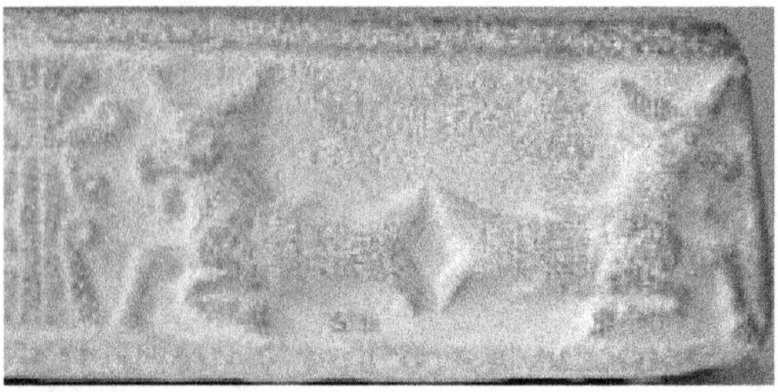

cm Jacques de

Morgan excavations, 1904-05 Sb 19). "Ce bas-relief ne porte aucune inscription et par suite nous ne pouvons dire à quelle époque il appartient; toutefois, par beaucoup de détails, je crois qu'il est permis de le considérer comme contemporain des Sargonides, c'est-à-dire du temps où l'Élam, continuellement en rapports avec Ninive et se trouvant dans son déclin, subissait l'influence de ses puissants voisins du Nord."[442]

Susa ritual basin decorated with goatfish figures, molluscs, reeds – all these are interpretable as hieroglyphs. N" 16. Tête de bé-lier à'Ea surmontant une maison posée sur une antilope munie d'un corps de poisson (fig.459 Figurations emblematiques du koudourrou N" XX); antelope fitted with a fish body.

Ea, l'antilope à corps de poisson, surmonté d'un carré dont je ne puis expliquer la Signification. Fiti. 453. — Emblèmes du koudouukou n" xv .[443] The inside of the basin consists of a series of squared steps leading down to the bottom of the dish. Traces of an inscription, too worn to be read, indicate that there was originally a text along the edges of the basin.

लोहकारनालिका f. the trough into which the blacksmith allows melted iron to flow after smelting. (Kashmiri) pattar 'trough' Rebus: pattar 'guild'. ayo 'fish' Rebus: ayas 'metal' tagara 'antelope' Rebus: tagara 'tin'. *kāṇḍa* काण्ड: m. the stalk or stem of a reed, grass, or the like, straw. In the compound with dan 5 (p. 221*a,* l. 13) the word is spelt kāḍ. Rebus: *kāṇḍa* 'tools, pots and pans and metal-ware'. The composite glyph of goat-fish thus reads: *ayaskāṇḍa* 'metalware'.

The pictographs on the ritual basin show: molluscs as center-piece flanked by a

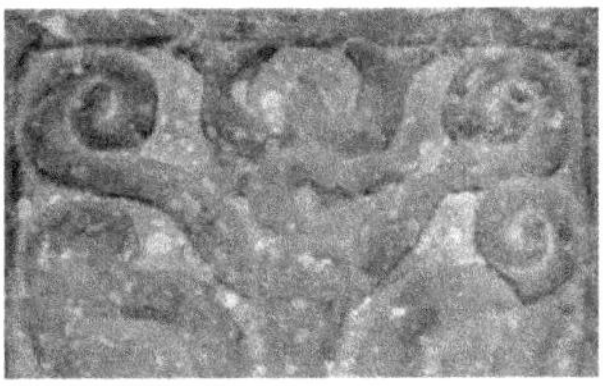

ligatured goat-fish. Molluscs as hieroglyphs occur in Indian artefacts of historical periods. Goat and fish are hieroglyphs used in Indus writing, though a ligatured goat-fish does not appear in the Indus script corpora,

there are many other examples of ligatured animals (e.g. ligatured heads of 3 or more animals; ligatured crocodile-fish).
The mollusc design compares with śrivatsa (entwined pair of fishes) and molluscs depicted on Mathura Lion Capital.

A combination of a markhor's horns + fish occurs on a copper anthropomorph of Sheorajpur, Uttar Pradesh, India.

A copper anthropomorph had a 'fish' glyph incised. Anthropomorph with 'fish' sign incised on the chest and with curved arms like the horns of a markhor. Sheorajpur (Kanpur Dist., UP, India). State Museum, Lucknow (O.37) Typical find of Gangetic Copper Hoards. 47.7 X 39 X 2.1 cm. C. 4 kg. Early 2nd millennium BCE. Tagara 'ram' + ayo 'fish'; rebus: tagara 'tin', ayo 'metal' (perhaps bronze formed by alloying copper mineral with tin mineral).

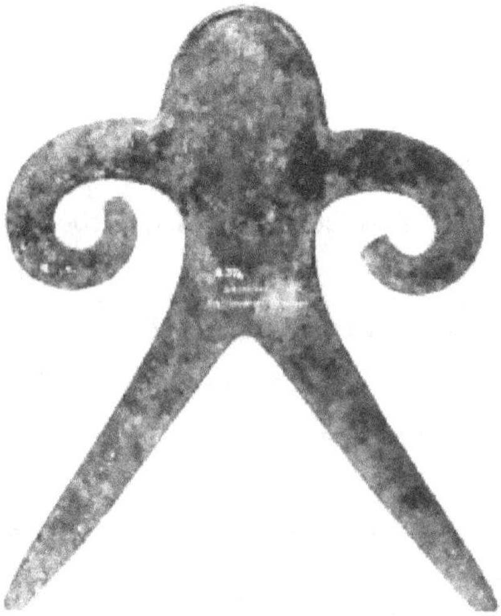

If the molluscs are stylized composition of a palm tree, the rebus reading may be: *tamar* "palm tree, date palm" (Heb.) Rebus: *tam(b)ira* 'copper' (Pkt.) The glyphic composition on Susa ritual vat thus reads: tagara, 'tin'; ayo 'alloyed bronze'; tam(b)ra 'copper'.

If the composition represents a pair of reeds, the rebus reading of the pair of reeds in Sumer standard is: *khāṇḍa* 'tools, pots and pans and metal-ware', *khōṭ* 'alloyed ingots', dhatu 'mineral (ore)'.

The reed hieroglyph may be comparable to the reed + scarf hieroglyph shown on the top register of Warka vase. dula 'pair' Rebus: dul 'cast metal'.

kāṇḍa काण्ड: m. the stalk or stem of a reed. Rebus: *kāṇḍa* 'tools, pots and pans and metal-ware'. Scarf [read rebus as dhaṭu m. (also dhaṭhu) m. 'scarf' (WPah.) (CDIAL 6707) Rebus: dhatu 'minerals' (Santali); dhātu 'mineral' (Pali) Thus reed + scarf denotes metallic minerals + metalware tools, pots and pans.

[pattara 'trough' is a glyph used in front of many types of animals including wild animals and composite animal glyphs. pātra 'trough'; pattar 'merchant'. The lexeme also connotes a 'guild'.]

Thus, the entire ritual trough may connote pattar 'guild' [pattharika [fr. Patthara] a merchant Vin ii.135 (kaŋsa˚). (Pali)] of mineral- and metal-workers and traders dealing with alloys (*ayaskāṇḍa*).

The 'reed' glyph and the 'humanface' glyph are the key hieroglyphic links to Uruk trough and Indian hieroglyphs of Indus script. The Meluhhan settlers of Uruk who created the hieroglyphs of Uruk trough, of Indus script and of the Nar Mer Palette are of the same scribe guild whose language was Indus language, mleccha (meluhha) and who had learnt the literate art of writing to represent (vikalpa) human speech sounds.

"This limestone basin dates from the 13th or 12th century BC. It was used for ritual libations. The decoration depicts goatfish figures around a sacred tree in reference to the Mesopotamian god Enki/Ea.

"A basin symbolizing the water cycle
"This basin was broken into several pieces when it was found and has been reconstituted. Used by priests in their ritual libations, liquid was poured out over the basin and was then collected for re-use. There were two types of ritual libations. The first reflected the water cycle, with water rising up from underground, filling rivers and wells. The other was an offering of beer, wine or honey, poured out for the deity in anticipation of his meal. The decoration of this basin suggests it was used for the first type of ritual libation. It is made in the

shape of the realm of Enki/Ea, Apsu, the body of fresh water lying beneath the earth and feeding all the rivers and streams. Apsu is likewise represented in the bronze model called Sit-Shamshi (Louvre, Sb2743). The fact that it was found in Susa indicates that the Elamites adopted certain aspects of Mesopotamian mythology.

"Goatfish figures around a sacred palm
"The rim of the limestone basin is decorated with a single repeated motif: two goatfish figures, or Nou, on either side of a stylized tree. These creatures were the attributes of Enki/Ea, the Mesopotamian god of underground water, symbolizing his power to replenish vegetation, represented by the sacred palm tree. A similar stylized tree can be seen on the stele of King Untash-Napirisha (Sb12). The tree consists of a central trunk with a number of offshoots curved at the tip and with three palmettes on the upper part. The image is completely stylized, bearing only a very distant resemblance to actual date palm trees. This symbol of plant life reflects the importance of date palms in the region. Dates were a staple foodstuff for the local population. This type of sacred palm was the predecessor of the sacred trees of Assyria. A relief from the palace of Assurnazirpal II in Nimrud depicts a winged spirit with a bird's head in front of just such a sacred tree (AO19849). The upper part of the basin is decorated with an intertwining pattern resembling flowing water. The inside of the basin consists of a series of squared steps leading down to the bottom of the dish. Traces of an inscription, too worn to be read, indicate that there was originally a text along the edges of the basin." Louvre Museum write-up.[444]

Identifying the hieroglyphs of Sit Shamshi bronze

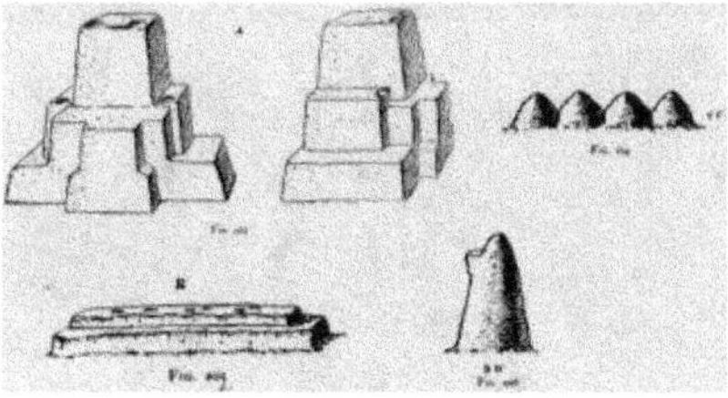

Glyph: 'stump of tree': M. khũṭ m. 'stump of tree'; P. khuṇḍ, °ḍā m. 'peg, stump'; G. *khũṭ* f. 'landmark', *khũṭɔ* m., *°ṭī* f. ' peg ', *°ṭũ* n. 'stump' (CDIAL 3893). Allograph: (Kathiawar) khũṭ m. 'Brahmani bull'(G.) Rebus: khũṭ 'community, guild' (Munda)

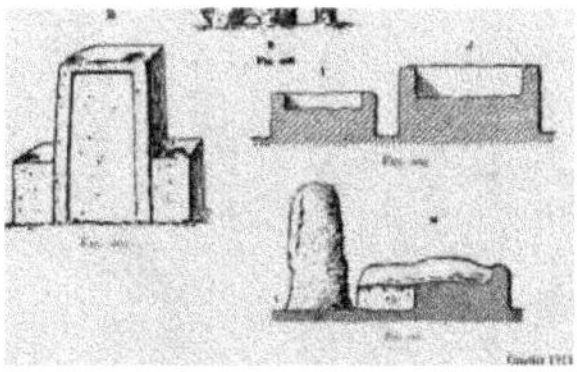

The ziggurat shown on the Sit-Shamshi bronze compares with a ziggurat which might have existed in the Stupa mound of Mohenjodaro (lit. mound of the dead), indicating the veneration of ancestors in Susa and Meluhha in contemporaneous times.Some glyphics of the bronze model have parallels in Indian hieroglyphs.

Sacred ceremony: water ablutions to the morning sun, Shamash

Susa: sacred fire-smithy, model of a temple[445]

It is suggested that there was a Meluhha settlement of traders in Susa who could read the messages conveyed by Indus script inscriptions.

	item		fastening	bronze alloy
F and G	human figures	solid	locked into the base	2% tin
A	big stepped structure	hollow	fixed by rivets	3.5% tin
B	small stepped structure	hollow	fixed by rivets	3.5% tin
H	jar	hollow	fixed by rivets	3.5% tin
M	right-angle-shaped platform	hollow, being attached by rivets, but it might be solid according to X-ray analysis	fixed by rivets	3.5% tin
E	table with depressions (made of 2 superimposed plates)	solid	bottom plate: fixed by rivets top plate: pierced with holes	3.5% tin
C	8 piles	solid	cast with the base	2% tin
I and J	2 basins	solid	cast with the base	2% tin
D and D'	2 pillars	solid	cast with the base	2% tin
L	stela	solid	not elucidated by X rays analysis	
K	3 trunks of tree	solid	not elucidated by X rays analysis	similar to the one used for the parts attached by rivets
•	(at least) 9 rivets used to hold the separate pieces to the base			
■	15 or 16 small rivets			2-3% tin, copper

Based on the evidence in Tallon & Hurtel 1992.

Tallon 1992

Sculptural segments of Sit Shamshi bronze. 1. Water ablutions. 2. Ziggurat, as temple.

The ceremony involved *lo* 'pouring (water) oblation' (Munda) for the setting sun. Rebus: *loa* 'copper' (Santali) The glyphic representations connote a guild of coppersmiths in front of a ziggurat, temple and is a veneration of ancestors. It is not unlikely that the authors of the bronze Sit Shamshi model had interacted with the groups of artisans of Mohenjo-daro who had a ziggurat in front of the 'Great bath'.

Alternative: Ta. ayam water, spring, tank, pond. Ma. ayam pool, tank. (DEDR 188). Ta. toṛi (-v-, -nt-) to be spilt. Tu. doriyuni to flow, etc. (or with 2883 Ta. cōr). Go. (Tr.) tōṛā blood which precedes the birth of a child (Voc. 1825); (ASu.) tōṛg- (water) to be spilt. Kui tōṛa (tōṛi-) to be liquid, flow, trickle. (DEDR 3523) Gu<Dalei> {V} ``to ^pour out, to ^spill (liquid), to ^scald''. *Des.<Dal->(M) `to spill, pour out'. E.g. <maj Da? Dalei-o?> `he poured water'.

Allograph: Ta. toṛu cattle-stall, manger, pound, stocks, married life, cage for wild animals; toṛuti multitude, crowd, herd, flock of birds; toṛuvam, toṛuku cattle-stall, manger; tōṛ, tōṛam cattle-stall; toṇṭu cattle pound. Ma. toṛu stable; toṛuttu stable, sheepfold, pen for goats. Ko. to·y buffalo pen. To. tu· fo·s̱ entrance of pen. Pa. -tol in: cakur-tol cattle-shed (DEDR 3526).

Ta. toṛu (-v-, -t-) to worship, adore, pay homage to; toṛukai worshipping, adoration, prayer; toṛuvu worshipping, adoration.Ma. toṛuka to salute by joining the hands, acknowledge superiority. Ka. tuṛil salutation, obeisance, bow. Koḍ. to- (topp-, tott-) to salute. Tu. turli obeisance; solma, solmè salutation. Go. (Mu.) doṛī- to bow (Voc. 1902). Pe. ṭoḍ- (ṭoṭṭ-) id. Manḍ. ṭuḍ- to bow head. ? Konḍa tuRpa- to invoke gods, fulfil a religious vow, adore, worship (DEDR 3525).

తెలుచు [telucu] or తెలుచ్చు teluṭsu. [Tel.] v. t. To bow to, to worship. మ్రొక్కు. To clear up, as a doubt తీర్చు. To make clear తెల్లముచేయు. To pray, to request ప్రార్థించు. (Telugu) தெளி[1]-தல் teḷi- To pierce, perforate; துளைத்தல். தெளிவு teḷivu , *n.* < தெளி[1]-. 1. [K. *tiḷi*, M. *teḷivu.*] Clarity, transparency, limpidness; துலக்கம். 2. [K. *tiḷi*, M. *teḷivu.*] Brightness, brilliance, as of a gem, pearl, etc. தெளி[2]-த்தல் teḷi-To take an oath, swear; சூளுறுதல். தீதிலேமென்று தெளிப்பவும் (கலித். 81, 33).(Tamil)

Tallon 1992

[quote] Akkadian name for an Elamite object in an Elamite inscription!

Sit Shamshi an Akkadian loan-word in Elamite?

"Do you know this object? I hope so. It is perhaps the most stimulating object found in the entire Ancient Near East, even if handbooks on Mesopotamian art do not talk much about it. It is a three-dimensional bronze model whose base measures 60 X 40 cm, excavated in the 1904-05 campaign by the French Mission at Susa. The scene is focused on two squatted human figures: one stretches its hands out, the other seems to be pouring water over them from a jug. Around them, there are possibly some kinds of altars, a large vessel, two basins, a stela and three trunks of trees. This act, perhaps a cultic scene which took place in the second half of the 12th century BCE, was fixed for eternity by will of Shilhak-Inshushinak (1140-1120 BCE), king of Anshan and Susa, according to the short inscription in a corner of the base. If you are so lucky as to run into a picture of it (unless you are directly visiting the Louvre Museum), looking at the caption you would learn that the name commonly given to this object is sit shamshi. Actually , this name, meaning 'the rising of the sun, sunrise' in Akkadian, appears in lines 5-6 of the inscription. But only in the unlikely event that you are both in front of the Louvre showcase with the sit shamshi in and an 'Elamist', i.e. a specialist in Elamite studies, you could go further in reading the inscription, though even an Elamist, having been ready to interpret the most stereotyped Akkadian inscription -- you know, Akkadian was very spread in Susiana --, so even an Elamist will jolt becoming aware of the language of the text. Apart from brushing up the revered edition by Scheil (1909) or Konig (1965), this is the only way to learn that the inscription is compiled in Elamite language. So, an Akkadian name for an Elamite object in an Elamite inscription!"

"Sit shamshi is the name used in an inscription of the Middle Elamite king Shilhak-Inshushinak (ca. 1150-1120 BC) to refer to its textual support, a bronze model (base 60 × 40 cm) representing in three dimensions two squatted individuals, one pouring a liquid over the hands of the other, in an open space with buildings, trees and other installations. The common interpretation of this name (meaning 'sunrise' in Akkadian) has become also the key for the understanding of the whole scene, supposedly a ritual ceremony to be performed at the sunrise in a sacred precint.

"From one hand, I would like to discuss the interpretation of Sit Shamshi as an Akkadian syntagm, considering that the inscription is written in Elamite and that sit e sham - are also known as Elamite terms. On the other hand, I would like to have feedback from scholars skilled in ritual texts from Mesopotamia, trying also to understand if there is some further element in support of the sunrise ritual interpretation. [unquote][446] "This large piece of bronze shows a religious ceremony. In the center are two men in ritual nudity surrounded by religious furnishings - vases for libations, perhaps bread for offerings, steles - in a stylized urban landscape: a multi-tiered tower, a temple on a terrace, a sacred wood. In the Middle-Elamite period (15th-12th century BC), Elamite craftsmen acquired new metallurgical techniques for the execution of large monuments, statues and reliefs. The eight bun-like ingots lining either side of the ziggurat may denote: खांडा [*khāṇḍā m* A jag, notch, or indentation (as upon the edge of a tool or weapon). *kāṇī* ' ornamental swelling out in a vessel ' (Bengali)(CDIAL 2849). Rebus: *karṇī* 'super cargo of a ship' (Marathi). Rebus: *khāṇḍa* 'tools, pots and pans, and metal-ware'. <tamja-n+m>(L) {N} ``eight years". #48162. <tamji>(L)

{N} ``^eight". *^V008 Kh.<tham>. #64641.Rebus: tam(b)ra 'copper'. If this surmise is valid, the ziggurat might have been stupa called *dhatu-garbha* or *dagoba* or *dagaba*.

Sit Shamshi. Model of a place of worship, known as the Sit Shamshi, or "Sunrise (ceremony)". Middle-Elamite period, toward the 12th century BCE. Acropolis mound, Susa, Iran. BronzeH. 60 cm; W. 40 cm Excavations led by Jacques de Morgan, 1904-5. Sb 2743 Near Eastern Antiquities, Musée du Louvre.[447] The base measures 60 X 40 cm. Sit Shamshi 'sunrise ceremony'. Discovery location: Ninhursag Temple, Acropole, Shūsh (Khuzestan, Iran).

Three jagged sticks on the Sit Shamshi bronze, in front of the water tank (Great Bath replica?) If the sticks are orthographic representations of 'forked sticks' and if the underlying language is Meluhha (mleccha), the borrowed or substratum lexemes which may provide a rebus reading are:

Three stakes on Sit-Shamshi bronze

kolmo 'three'; rebus; *kolami* 'smithy' (Telugu)

Glyph: khuṇṭ 'stump'. Rebus: khũṭ 'community, guild' (Mu.) P. *khuṇḍ, °ḍā* m. ' peg, stump 'Rebus: 1. khũṭ 'community, guild' (Mu.) 2. Skt. kuṇḍa- round hole in ground (for water or sacred fire). Vikalpa: मेंढा [mēṇḍhā] A crook or curved end (of a stick, horn &c.) and attrib. such a stick, horn, bullock. मेढा [mēḍhā] m A stake, esp. as forked. meḍ(h), meḍhī f., meḍhā m. ' post, forked stake '.(Marathi)(CDIAL 10317) Rebus: mẽṛhẽt, meḍ 'iron' (Mu.Ho.) Vikalpa 1: Thus, three jagged sticks on the Sit Shamshi bronze may be decoded as *khũṭ kolami* 'smithy guild' or, *meḍ kolami* 'iron (metal) smithy'. 'Iron' in such lexical entries may refer to 'metal'. Vikalpa 2: मेढ [mēḍha] *f* A forked stake. Used as a post. Hence a short post generally whether forked or not. मेड [mēḍa] *f* (Usually मेढ q. v.) मेडका *m* A stake, esp. as bifurcated. मेंढा [

mēṇḍhā] *m* (मेष S through H) A male sheep, a ram or tup. 2 A crook or curved end (of a stick, horn &c.) and *attrib.* such a stick, horn, bullock. मेढा [mēḍhā] *m* A stake, esp. as forked. 2 A dense arrangement of stakes, a palisade, a paling.(Marathi) Rebus1. Rebus: *meḍ* 'iron' (Mundari. Remo.) Rebus 2: मेंडका or क्या [mēṇḍakā or kyā] *a* (Preferably मेंढका or क्या) A shepherd.

Thus, three jagged sticks on the Sit Shamshi bronze may be decoded as *khũṭ kolami* 'smithy guild' or, kuṇḍa kollami 'sacred fire smithy' or, *meḍ kolami* 'iron (metal) smithy'. 'Iron' in such lexical entries may refer to 'metal'.

Sit Shamshi bronze illustrates the complex technique of casting separate elements joined together with rivets, the excavations at Susa have produced one of the largest bronze statues of Antiquity: dating from the 14th century BC, the effigy of "Napirasu, wife of Untash-Napirisha," the head of which is missing, is 1.29 m high and weighs 1,750 kg. It was made using the solid-core casting method.

"Two nude figures squat on the bronze slab, one knee bent to the ground. One of the figures holds out open hands to his companion who prepares to pour the contents of a lipped vase onto them.The scene takes place in a stylized urban landscape, with reduced-scale architectural features: a tiered tower or ziggurat flanked with pillars, a temple on a high terrace. There is also a large jar resembling the ceramic pithoi decorated with rope motifs that were used to store water and liquid foodstuffs. An arched stele stands by some rectangular basins. Rows of 8 dots in relief flank the ziggurat; jagged sticks represent trees. An inscription tells us the name of the piece's royal dedicator and its meaning in part: "I Shilhak-Inshushinak, son of Shutruk-Nahhunte, beloved servant of Inshushinak, king of Anshan and Susa [...], I made a bronze sunrise.

"Chogha Zambil: a religious capital

"The context of this work found on the Susa acropolis is unclear. It may have been reused in the masonry of a tomb, or associated with a funerary sanctuary. It appears to be related to Elamite practices that were brought to light by excavations at Chogha Zambil. This site houses the remains of a secondary capital founded by the Untash-Napirisha dynasty in the 14th century BC, some ten kilometers east of Susa (toward the rising sun). The sacred complex, including a ziggurat and temples enclosed within a precinct, featured elements on the esplanade, rows of pillars and altars. A "funerary palace," with vaulted tombs, has also been found there.

“The royal art of the Middle-Elamite period

“Shilhak-Inshushinak was one of the most brilliant sovereigns of the dynasty founded by Shutruk-Nahhunte in the early 12th century BC. Numerous foundation bricks attest to his policy of construction. He built many monuments in honor of the great god of Susa, Inshushinak. The artists of Susa in the Middle-Elamite period were particularly skilled in making large bronze pieces. Other than the Sit Shamshi, which illustrates the complex technique of casting separate elements joined together with rivets, the excavations at Susa have produced one of the largest bronze statues of Antiquity: dating from the 14th century BC, the effigy of "Napirasu, wife of Untash-Napirisha," the head of which is missing, is 1.29 m high and weighs 1,750 kg. It was made using the solid-core casting method. Other bronze monuments underscore the mastery of the Susa metallurgists: for example, an altar table surrounded by snakes borne by divinities holding vases with gushing waters, and a relief depicting a procession of warriors set above a anel decorated with engravings of birds pecking under trees. These works, today mutilated, are technical feats. They prove, in their use of large quantities of metal, that the Susians had access to the principal copper mines situated in Oman and eastern Anatolia. This shows that Susa was located at the heart of a network of circulating goods and long-distance exchange.”[448]

Mohenjo-daro stupa, Great Bath and Sit Shamshi bronze

Artisans of Susa and artisans of Mohenjo-daro were worshippers of the ancestors, offering morning prayers with water ablutions. The stupa of Mohenjo-daro should have been built over a ziggurat (memorial for ancestors) used for such water ablutions in the Great Bath situated which is located in front of the ziggurat.

A hypothesis will be formulated and tested that Sit Shamshi bronze is a replica of the sacred ceremonies by artisans -- lapidaries and metallurgists, in front of the stupa at Mohenjo-daro.

That what is referred to as the stupa of Mohenjo-daro was an early ziggurat is a plausible argument. Such an argument that the stupa structure should be related to the Indus period was first mooted by the explorer, RD Banerji whose hypotheses and arguments were countered by John Marshall.

The Great Ziggurat Ur - View
Source: Great Architecture of the World (2000)

There could have a ziggurat-type structure below the stupa for celebration by artisans. A comparable argument can be cited from the Anu ziggurat: "...lumps of metal ore were said to have been found in approximately contemporary levels of the adjacent Anu ziggurat so that metal-working in the vicinity of one or other of the temples remains a possibility." (Harriet EW Crawford, 2004, Sumer and the Sumerians, Cambridge Univ. Press, p. 168).

Ziggurat at Ur of Ur-Nammu, the first ruler of Ur III dynasty. Reconstruction by the excavator, Woolley. The south-west side of the ziggurat towards the end of the excavations from Woolley's photo album.

An artist's impression of how the Anu Ziggurat might have looked.

The reconstruction by Woolley of the Anu Ziggurat shows its similary with the Laurid Nandagarh Stupa[449] or Guldara Stupa (near Kabul) or the large stepped stupa shown Sit Shamshi bronze.

Ziggurat of Chogha Zanbil in Elam. This ziggurat is also a rectangular structure like the stepped rectangular structure shown on Sit Shamshi bronze.

Stupa area on the right; Great Bath area on the left.

The Great Bath was located to the west of the Stupa and water ablutions could have been offered at the Great Bath facing east towards the stupa of Mohenjo-daro.

"The stupa area...The loftiest of all the mounds at Mohenjo-daro is the one near the north-west corner of the site, crowned by the Buddhist stupa and monastery. Including the stupa itself, this mound rises some 72 feet above the surrounding country and 227 feet above mean sea level. On the east it breaks abruptly away to the plain; on the other three sides, where there are many solid ruins of the Indus period to resist denudation, the slope is more gradual. The Buddhist monuments on the summit of this mound were mainly excavated by Mr. RD Banerji in 1922-3; the deeper diggings in the prehistoric strata between them was started by Mr. Banerji, but chiefly done by Mr. BL Dhama under my own direction in 1925-6...The Buddhist monuments brought to light by Mr. Banerji comprise a spacious quadrangle open to the sky, with a lofty stupa in its middle and rows of monastic building enclosing it on the four sides (Pl. XVI). The whole complex of these monuments, including stupa, courtyard, and surrounding monastery, was many times repaired or rebuilt -- on each occasion at a successively higher level. Thus, the original pavement of the courtyard was 20 feet below the bottom of the stupa drum...How came it then to contain the same type of small pointed vessels (which he calls 'burial urns', but which in the Indus period were almost certainly drinking goblets) that are so characteristic of the Indus Period?...In the stupa area the most interesting feature is the large bath on the west, separated from the stupa by a distance of roughly 190 feet." (Marshall, John , ed., 1931, Mohenjo-Daro and the Indus civilization..., Repr. Delhi, Asian Educational Services, 1966, pp.113-131.) Marshall proceeds to detail an evaluation of the reconstructed stratification data and some objects found on various strata to attempt a chronological reconstruction of the stupa from the Indus period to the Kushana period which is considered to be the date for the stupa with relics, assuming 'that the Buddhists occupied Mohenjo-daro about the beginning of the third century AD and held it till the fifth century AD.'

Sit Shamshi bronze. Water ablutions on sunrise in front of the two Ziggurats.

View of the Mohenjo-daro stupa -- layout, in relation to the Great Bath. This compares with the Sit Shamshi bronze layout showing location of a water-tank in relation to two stepped ziggurats. In the Indian tradition, water ablutions are offered as sacred duty. This may explain one of the functions of the great water tank, called the Great Bath. The menhir stone shown in front of the water-tank of Sit Shamshi bronze is comparable to the Indian tradition of menhir stones venerating ancestors.

Mohenjo-daro stupa location in relation to th Great bath. Looking south at the stupa and main Citadel excavations. The people on the right side of the picture are near the Bath.

Great bath, SD Area, looking north. Brick colonnades were discovered on the eastern, northern and southern edges. It is possible that the brick colonnades

were he areas from where the water ablutions were offered in front of the stupa (Ziggurat?) – in case the layout is comparable to the layout of the water ablution ceremony for the Sun detailed on the Sit Shamshi bronze.

Corbelled drain exiting the Great Bath.

Stupa, pillared hall with paved walk-ways, L Area, Mohenjo-daro. Could this represent a structure comparable to the 'second' ziggurat shown on Sit Shamshi bronze?

Gateway with stupa in background. 'A massive block of brick architecture at the southeast corner of the 'citadel' mound was thought to represent a gateway with larg brick bastions.'[450] The stupa is perched on top of the 'citadel' mound.

A massive mud-brick platform or wall

encircles the citadel mound, Mohenjodaro. (Photo taken in 2011). The mound itself rose about 12 metres from the ground.

Views of the Mohenjo-daro stupa (Ziggurat?)

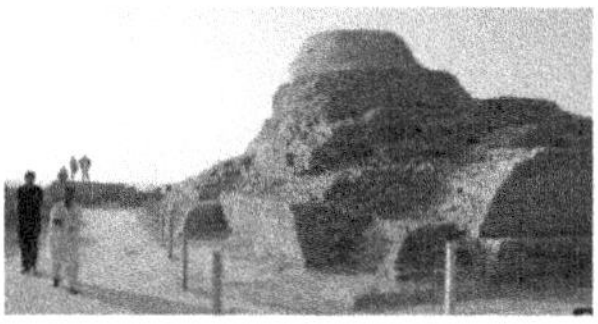

Close-up of the stupa, Mohenjo-daro.

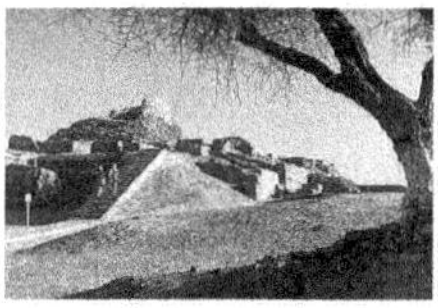

Lower town: HR Area and the stupa, Mohenjo-daro. "This general view of houses in HR area shows the color of the brick walls prior to use of mud brick and clay slurry for conservation. The lower parts of the walls have the natural reddish color of fired brick."[451]

The shape of the dome of Mohenjo-Daro stupa, in its original form, might have looked like the top

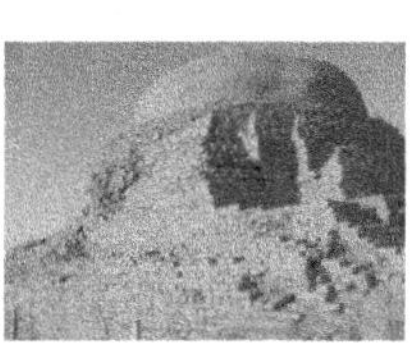

segment of the stepped ziggurat depicted on Sit Shamshi bronze.

Proto-elamite tablet with seal mark

An accounting document sealed with images of animals in human poses [quote]A large tablet

Technical information. Proto-Elamite tablet with seal mark Proto-Elamite period, circa 3100-2800 BCE Acropolis mound, Susa, Iran Clay H. 21 cm; L. 26 cm; H. of seal mark: 4.2 cm Excavations led by Jacques de Morgan, 1901 Sb 2801 Near Eastern Antiquities

This tablet is the largest from the Proto-Elamite period, corresponding to the earliest urban development in the late 4th millennium BC, in the Fars region (southwestern Iran), the present regional capital of which is Shiraz. It bears traces of three different types of administrative tools: writing, accounting and glyptics, a major art form of the period, corresponding to the use of seals. There are inscriptions of both writing and numeral signs on both sides of the tablet.

The emergence of a new writing system in the Fars region

Writing emerged in Iran nearly three centuries after being invented in southern Mesopotamia. This writing system, developed in the Fars region and called Proto-Elamite for this reason, is totally independent from the writing in use at Uruk. As no bilingual text exists that would enable us to establish an equivalence between the two systems, Proto-Elamite writing remains undecipherable.

However, the reading direction (right to left) and its horizontality have been detected.

These Proto-Elamite tablets are accounting documents. Three different numerical systems are used on the tablet: a decimal system, a sexagesimal system and a mixed system known as SE. The various operations are listed on the front side of the tablet, recapitulated, with totals, on the back at the top. New figures appear: crescent-shaped notches and dots circled with a constellation of tiny points, some of which represent fractions. A pictographical sign resembling a fringed triangle, known as the "hairy triangle," often appears, but its meaning remains unclear. A single seal was used on the document, a cylinder-seal that was rolled twice across the width of the tablet, covering most of the back of the tablet. The scene shows a bull symmetrically restraining two seated felines, alternating with a lion dominating two rearing bulls, each topped with a "hairy triangle." The animals stand on their hindlegs as if they were bipeds, a technique characteristic of the Proto-Elamite period in which animals were often depicted in a human pose. The choice of bulls and lions was deliberate, for these animals appear to personify cosmic forces, decisive in the balance of power in the world. In the scene, there is no durable winner or loser, but alternating, opposing forces that appear equal. [unquote]

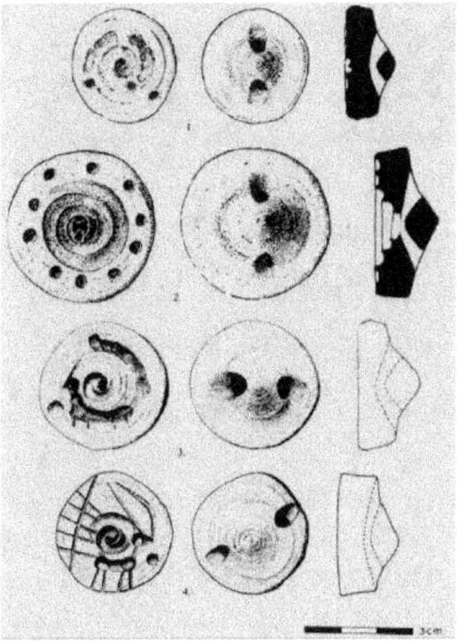

Common motifs on seals/tablets of bronze-age Indo-Eurasia

The following seals of Mesopotamia contain features reminiscent of themes depicted on the seals of the Sarasvati Sindhu civilization. Typical motifs are: rows of animals, combat, antelope or tiger with head turned, woman with thighs spread out, circle-and-dot, one-horned bull, hare, plant, snake, bird, fish. All these motifs have been explained as related to metallic weapons, in the context of the decipherment of Indus script pictorials and signs. In the Mesopotamian motifs, there are clear images related to weapons and implements.

One motif that is remarkably unique in Mesopotamian seals is the LION. Only a tiger motif appears on the seals of the Sarasvati Sindhu civilization. The closest to a lion motif is the bristled-hair (like a lion's mane) on the face of the three-faced, fully adorned, horned, seated person surrounded by animals and an inscription.[452]

Late Uruk and Jemdet Nasr seal; ca. 3200-3000 BC; serpentine; cat.1; boar and bull in procession; terminal: plant; heavily pitted surface beyond plant. *ḍangar* 'bull' Rebus: *dhangar* 'blacksmith' (Maithili) *ḍangar* 'blacksmith' (Hindi) காண்டாமிருகம் kāṇṭā-mirukam , *n.* [M. *kāṇṭāmṛgam.*] Rhinoceros; கல்யானை. Rebus: *kāṇḍā* 'metalware, tools, pots and pans'.

ca. 750-600 BC; chalcedony; cat. 285; a hero in a short kilt stands between two ibexes and graps their horns. In the field: plant in vase. In the sky: star, crescent. *miṇḍāl* 'markhor' (Tōrwālī) *meḍho* a ram, a sheep (G.)(CDIAL 10120); rebus: *mẽṛhẽt, meḍ* 'iron' (Mu.Ho.)

ca. 900-700 BC; chert;cat. 188; a rosette and a bull.

Terminal: plant (the linear striations on the bull's body are reminiscent of certain seals of the late Kassite style). The bull is pictured like the Indus one-horned bull, but in motion with 3 legs seen in profile. *karaḍa* 'safflower' Rebus: *karaḍa* 'hard alloy'. *ḍangar* 'bull' Rebus: *dhangar* 'blacksmith' (Maithili) *ḍangar* 'blacksmith' (Hindi)

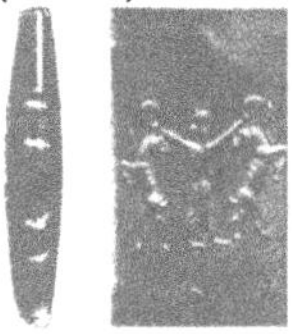

Achaemenian seal; ca. 521-400 BC; lentoid; agate. A royal figure holds two bearded ibexes at bay.

Dilmun (Failaka) seals[453]

Tell Abraq comb (TA 1649; Ivory comb with Mountain Tulip motif and dotted circles. TA 1649 Tell Abraq. [D.T. Potts, South and Central Asian elements at Tell Abraq (Emirate of Umm al-Qaiwain, United Arab Emirates), c. 2200 BC—AD 400, in Asko Parpola and Petteri Koskikallio, *South Asian Archaeology 1993*, pp. 615-666] 11x8.2x0.4cm).[454] "Both sides of the body of the comb are decorated identically with a set of three double-dotted circles arranged in a triangle. On either side of the dotted circles is a stylized flower with tw upward-curving, dentate or cronate leaves, a long stem and three lotus- or tulip-like petals...We find a strikingly similar pair of long-stemmed flowers on a series of soft-stone flasks (Fig. 3)...in southern Bactria (northern Afghanistan)..."

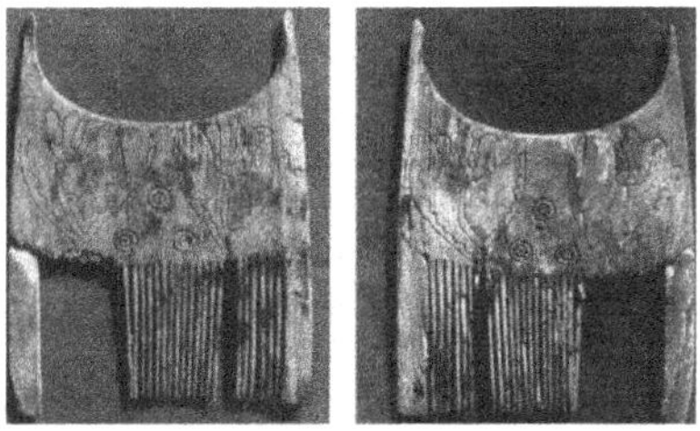

The glyph is *tabernae montana*, 'mountain tulip' – a variant of *tulip montana*. A soft-stone flask, 6 cm. tall, from Bactria (northern Afghanistan) showing a winged female deity (?) flanked by two flowers similar to those shown on the comb from Tell Abraq. Ivory comb with Mountain Tulip motif and dotted circles. TA 1649 Tell Abraq.

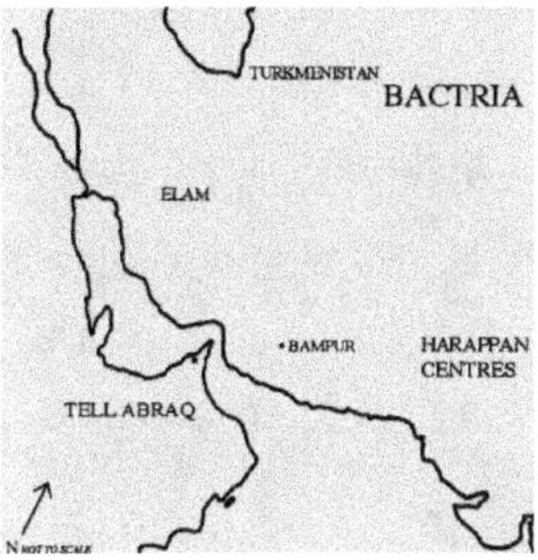

(After Fig. 3 in Potts, DT, opcit, A soft-stone flask from Bactria showing a winged female deity(?)

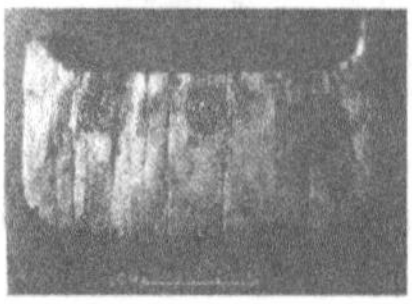

flanked by two flowers similar those shown on the comb from Tell Abraq. 6 cm. tall. (After Pottier, M.H., 1984, *Materiel funeraire e la Bactriane meridionale de l'Age du Bronze*, Paris, Editions Recherche sur les Civilisations: plate 20.150) "Indeed the mountain tulip (*Tulipa Montana* Lindl.), which occurs in Asia Minor and Afghanistan, bears a remarkable likeness to the flower on the Tell Abraq comb."(Potts, DT, opcit., p.594).

Kalibangan, Ivory comb with three dotted circles; Kalibangan, Period II.[455]

Tabernae Montana tulip is also shown on the Ur cylinder seal.

koṇḍ i the sting of a scorpion.).Rebus: *kõdā* 'to turn in a lathe' (Bengali) कोंद *kōnda* 'engraver, lapidary setting or infixing gems' (Marathi) *mũh* metal ingot

(Santali) *āra* 'serpent' Rebus: *āra* 'brass'. *tampur* 'long-legged' (Santali) Rebus: *trāmo, tām(b)o* m. 'copper' (Sindhi)

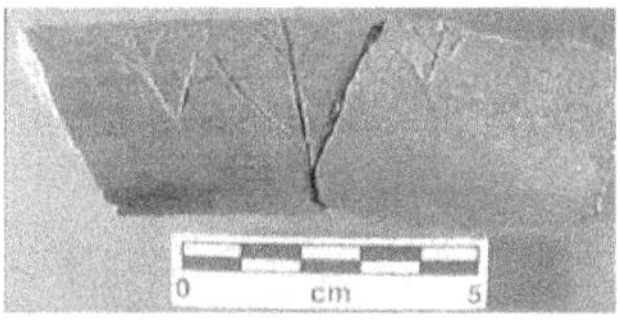

tagar = a flowering shrub; a plant in bloom (Gujarat) tagara = the shrub tabernaemontana coronaria, and a fragrant powder or perfume obtained from it, incense (Vin 1.203); *tagara-mallikā* two kinds of *gandhā* (Punjabi) *ṭagara (tagara)* a spec. plant; fragrant wood (Prakrit) *tagara* = a kind of flowering tree (Telugu) Rebus: *tagromi* 'tin metal alloy' (Kuwi)

Sign 169 takaram tin, white lead, metal sheet, coated with tin (Ta.); tin, tinned iron plate (Ma.); tagarm tin (Ko.); tagara, tamara, tavara id. (Ka.) tamaru, tamara, tavara id. (Ta.): tagaramu, tamaramu, tavaramu id. (Te.); ṭagromi tin metal, alloy (Kuwi); tamara id. (Skt.)(DEDR 3001). trapu tin (AV.); tipu (Pali); tau, taua lead

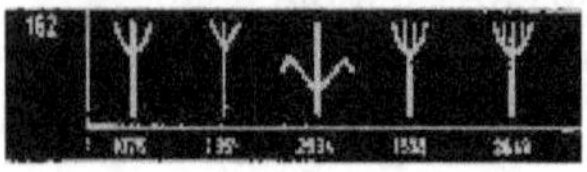

(Pkt.); *tū* tin (P.); ṭau zinc, pewter (Or.); tarūaum lead (OG.); tarvu~ (G.); tumba lead (Si.)(CDIAL 5992).

•*ran:ga ron:ga, ran:ga con:ga* = thorny, spikey, armed with thorns; edel dare ran:ga con:ga dareka = this cotton tree grows with spikes on it (Santali) ran:ga, ran: pewter is an alloy of tin lead and antimony (añjana) (Santali).

Adar ḍangra 'zebu'; rebus: aduru 'native metal' (Ka.); ḍhangar 'blacksmith' (H.)

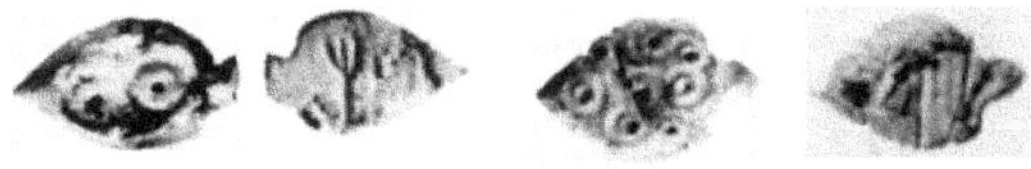

h337, h338 Texts 4417, 4426 (Dotted circles on leaf-shaped tablets) Tell Abraq comb and axe with epigraph After Fig. 7Holly Pittman, 1984, *Art of the Bronze Age: Southeastern Iran, Western Central Asia, and the Indus Valley*, New York, The Metropolitan Museum of Art, pp. 29-30].

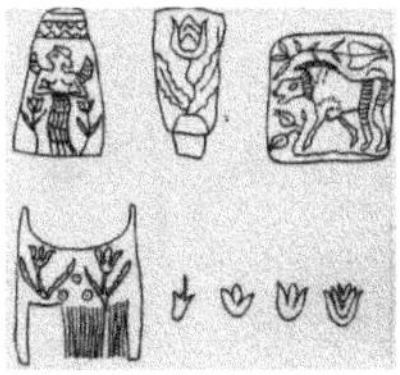

Wild tulip motif. A motif that occurs on southeast Iranian cylinder seals and on Persian Gulf seals. 1st row: Bactrian artifacts; 2nd row: a comb from the Gulf area and late trans-Elamite seals.[456]

The ivory comb found at Tell Abraq measures 11 X 8.2 X .4 cm. Both sides of the comb bear identical, incised decoration in the form of two long-stemmed flowers with crenate or dentate leaves, flanking three dotted circles arranged in a triangular pattern. Bone and ivory combs with dotted-circle decoration are well-known in the Harappan area (e.g. at Chanhu-daro and Mohenjo-daro), but none of the Harappan combs bear the distinctive floral motif of the Tell Abraq comb. These flowers are identified as tulips, perhaps Mountain tulip or Boeotian tulip (both of which grow in Afghanistan) which have an undulate leaf. There is a possibility that the comb is an import from Bactria, perhaps transmitted through Meluhha to the Oman Peninsula site of Tell Abraq.

Harappan weight TA 1356 from Tell Abraq. C. 22nd cent. BCE. Banded chert or flint weight 54.06 g. This is approx. 4 times the unit Harappan weight of 13.63 g.

Seal impression from Harappa (Kenoyer, 1998); a woman is carrying a three-petalled flower.

Crete. Inscribed Cretan copper ox-hide ingot (After Fig.82 in: Sinclair Hood, 1971, *The Minoans: Crete in the Bronze Age*, Thames and Hudson) kolmo 'paddy plant' (Santali); rebus: kolami 'furnace, smithy' (Te.)

One of the 81 fig shells (*Ficus subintermedia*) discovered at Tell Abraq, UAE. It was found adjacent to human bones within the Umm an-Nar tomb. These "feeding shells" were traditionally used by mothers to feed liquids to babies.[457]

In 1977 the Arab Archaeological Mission and the Directorate of Archaeology and Museums of the State of Bahrain excavated the mounds of Sar, near the causeway between the Kingdom of Saudi Arabia and the State of Bahrain. Shell seals were found. [Haya Al Khalifa, The shell seals of Bahrain, pp. 255-259]

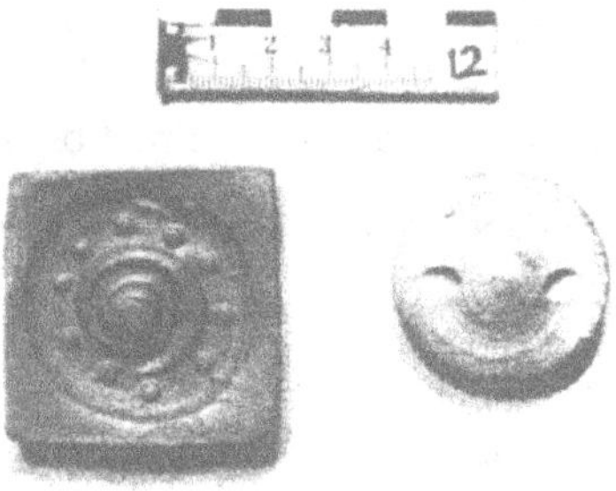

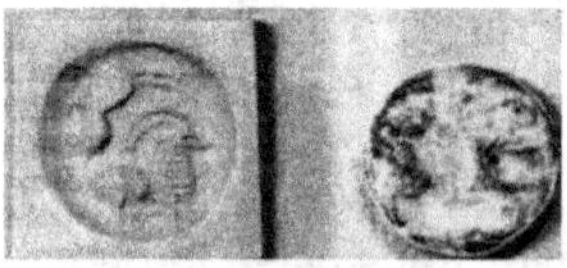

Barhain seal: ten circular depressions surround the spiral

Bahrain seal: Two antelopes

Bahrain seal: four antelope heads emanating from a star.[458]

Seals from the Near East and contacts with Sarasvati Sindhu Valley

Early Dynastic II/III seal in the 'Fara' style (after Mallowan, 1961: 75, no.34).

396

Girdled nude hero attacking water buffalo; bull-man attacking lion, inscription. Green stone. 2.5x1.5cm.

Bird-man holding gatepost emblem is brought captive by god to Ea (characterized by streams of water and five fishes) and announced by two-faced attendant Usmu. Graystone. 3.2 cm. high.

580

52

Tell Suleimeh Cylinder seal. A fish over a short-horned bull and a bird over a one-horned bull; cylinder seal impression, (Akkadian to early Old Babylonian). Gypsum. 2.6 cm. Long 1.6 cm. Dia. Tell Suleimeh (level IV), Iraq; IM 87798; (al-Gailani Werr,1983, p. 49 No. 7). [Drawing by Larnia Al-GailaniWerr. Cf. Dominique Collon 1987, First impressions: cylinder seals in the ancient Near East, London: 143, no. 609] *karaḍa* 'duck' Rebus: *karaḍa* 'hard alloy'. Alternative: *vartaka* 'quail' Rebus: *vartaka* 'bell-metal, brass'. ayo 'fish' Rebus: ayo 'metal'. *kõda* 'young bull-calf'. Rebus: *kũdār* 'turner'. कोंद kōnda 'engraver, lapidary setting or infixing gems' (Marathi) *ḍangar* 'bull' Rebus: *ḍhangar* 'blacksmith'.

Seal. Marshall, 1931, *Mohenjo-Daro and the Indus Civilization*, Vol. 3, Plate CVI #93

kanka 'rim-of-jar' (Santali) *karṇaka id. (Skt.)* Rebus 1: *kaṇakku* 'account' *karṇaka* scribe (Skt.) Rebus 2: kánaka n. ' gold ' MBh. Pa. *kanaka* -- n., Pk. *kaṇaya* -- n., MB. *kanayā* ODBL 659, Si. *kanā* EGS 36.(CDIAL 2717). *கனகம் kaṉakam, n. < kanaka. 1. Gold; பொன். காரார்வண்ணன் கனகமனையானும் (தேவா. 502, 9)*(Tamil) aya 'fish' (Mu.); rebus: aya 'metal' (G.) ayo kanka 'fish rim-of-jar' rebus: metal (alloy) account (*kaṇakku*) scribe. *kolom* 'cob'; rebus: *kolmo* 'seedling, rice (paddy) plant' (Munda.) Rebus: kolami 'furnace,smithy' (Te.) Since a pair of 'sprout.rice-plant' glyphs are used in ligature, the pair connotes : dula 'pair'; Rebus: dul 'cast (metal)(Santali) Thus, the ligatured glyph denotes dul kolami 'cast smithy'.

Stone Bowl with Farmer and Cattle. Early Dynastic Period (ca. 2900-2400 B.C.) Tell Agrab, Shara Temple. Excavated by the Oriental Institute, 1935 OIM A18144 "The fragment of an ancient stone bowl…a herdsman, carrying an implement that may be a fly wisk or goad stands between the two cows that are facing away from him. Above the central cow's back are two birds, standing back-to-back. The head of one of the calves coming out to greet its mother is visible at the right edge of the fragment."[459] What the herdsman is carrying is comparable to the reed flag shown on Warka vase.

karaṇḍa duck (CDIAL 2787). కారండవము [kāraṇḍavamu] [Skt.] n. A sort of duck. Rebus: करडा [karaḍā] Hard from alloy--iron, silver &c. (Marathi) Rebus: खरड [

kharaḍa] *f* (खरडणें) A hurriedly written or drawn piece; a scrawl; a mere tracing or rude sketch. Rebus: *kharādī* ' turner' (Gujarati) Alternative: *vartaka* 'duck' Rebus: *vartaka* 'merchant'. *vartaka* 'bell-metal, brass'.

baṭa 'quail' Rebus: baṭa 'furnace'. కర్మారము [karmāramu] *karmāramu*. [Skt.] n. A bamboo. వెదురు. కర్మారుడు *karmāruḍu*. n. An artisan. కమ్మరవాడు. (Telugu) పసరము [pasaramu] or పసలము *pasaramu*. [Tel.] n. A beast, an animal. గోమహిషహాతి. (Telugu) Rebus: పసారము [pasāramu] or పసారు *pasārdmu*. [Tel.] n. A shop. అంగడి.(Telugu)

Hammer decorated with heads of two birds and feathers 3rd Ur Dynasty, reign of Shulgi (2094-2047 BCE) Iran, Royal City of Susa, acropolis mound Bronze H. 12. 3 cm; L. 11 cm Excavations led by Roland de Mecquenem Sb 5634 *karaḍa* 'duck' Rebus: *karaḍa* 'hard alloy' (Marathi)

"This votive bronze weapon is characteristic of Iranian metalwork, of which many examples have been found at the Susa site. Decorated with birds' heads and feathers, this hammer carries an inscription in Sumerian referring to King Shulgi: "Powerful hero, king of Ur, king of Sumer and Akkad."

"A work inscribed with the name of a Mesopotamian king Shulgi, second king of the 3rd Ur Dynasty, is one of the sovereigns who marked the Neo-Sumerian period, half of which was covered by his long forty-eight-year reign.

"During this period, Susa and Elam were returned to Mesopotamia. Shulgi took control of Mesopotamia and conquered Susa, thus putting an end to the attempts of the Elamite sovereign Puzur-Inshushinak to achieve autonomy.

“Epigraphic figurines and foundation tablets in the name of Shulgi (Louvre Museum, Sb 2879 and Sb 2880) record the king's building of the temples of Ninhursag and Inshushinak on the acropolis at Susa.

“The inscription on this bronze hammer dedicated to him is in Sumerian, once more the official language in the Neo-Sumerian period, and uses the official title adopted by Shulgi's predecessor: "King of Sumer and Akkad."

“A ceremonial weapon in the Iranian tradition

“This ceremonial bronze hammer is decorated with the heads of two birds on either side of the hammer collar and curled plumage on the heel. This model has not been found in Mesopotamia, but is well documented in Luristan. A similar example (Louvre Museum, AO 24794) from this region dates from the early years of the 2nd millennium BC. Though animal motifs are a very ancient form of decoration in Iran, it was in the late 3rd and the 2nd millenniums BC that Iranian metalworkers excelled in this type of weapon, often decorated with animals.

“These bronze hammers and axes featuring animal motifs were often ceremonial weapons presented by Elamite sovereigns to their dignitaries. An illustration of this custom can be seen on the seal of Kuk-Simut, an official under Idadu II, an Elamite prince in the early years of the 2nd millennium BC (Louvre Museum, Sb 2294). This votive weapon was thus preserved for eternity in its owner's grave.”[460]

Glyph: kāru ‘crocodile’ (Telugu). Rebus: कारु [kāru] m (S) An artificer or artisan (Marathi).

The depiction of the udder of the cow and the calf together with the cowherd carrying the standard (Stone Bowl with Farmer and Cattle. Early Dynastic Period (ca. 2900-2400 B.C.) is significant as may be seen from the following semantic exposisition on the term kās ‘udder’: karuvu n. Melting: what is melted (Te.) kruciji ‘smith’ (Old Church Slavic). कारु [kāru] m (S) An artificer or artisan. 2 A common term for the twelve बलुतेदार q. v. Also कारुनारु m pl q. v. in नारुकारु. (Marathi)

Cylinder seal. Iraq.[461] Glyphs: crossed-bullmen, crossed-lions, bull, bison(?), naked person with upraised arm, plunging a dagger into a lion's back.

erka = ekke (Tbh. of arka) aka (Tbh. of arka) copper (metal); crystal (Kannada)

ḍangar 'bull' (Hindi) Rebus: ḍhangar 'blacksmith' (Hindi).

arye 'lion' Rebus: āra 'brass'.

kharāru 'a currycomb' (Kannada) khakharārā id. (Marathi) ఖరారము [kharāramu] *kharāramu*. [Skt.] n. A curry comb. గుర్రపుగొరపము. కరఫలము [karaphalamu] *kara-phalamu*. [Skt.] n. A curry comb. కరారా, గుర్రమునుతోమే గొరపము.

கண்டி kaṇṭi buffalo bull (Tamil) Pk. *gaḍa* -- n. 'large stone'? (CDIAL 3969) K. *garun*, vill. *gaḍun* ' to hammer into shape, forge, put together '. (CDIAL 3966). kaḍiyo [Hem. Des. kaḍa-i-o = (Skt. Sthapati, a mason) a bricklayer, mason (G.)]

eṛaka 'upraised arm' (Ta.); rebus: eraka = copper (Ka.)

Glyph 'spear': మేడెము [mēḍemu] or మేడియము *mēḍemu*. [Tel.] n. A spear or dagger. ఈటె, బాకు. Rebus: meḍ 'iron' (Ho.)

Cylinder seal impression; bullls and lions in conflict (British Museum No. 89538).

खोंड [khōṇḍa] m A young bull, a bullcalf. (Marathi) koḍiyum ‘young bull’ (Gujarati)

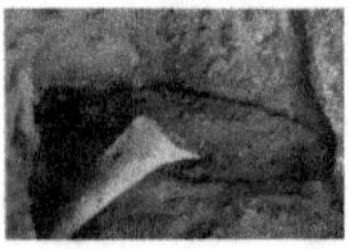

कोंद *kōnda* ‘engraver, lapidary setting or infixing gems’ (Marathi) *kõdā* ‘to turn in a lathe’(B.) aryeh ‘lion’ Rebus: *arā* ‘brass’.

Tell Abraq. Bronze dagger. Contained 12 % tin. Charred wood at the base of the tang had fragments of Dalbergia Sissoo, commonly known as Pakistani rosewood. Sissoo was rare in the ancient Near East.[462]

642

Glazed steatite . Cylinder seal. 3.4cm high; imported from Indus valley. Rhinoceros, elephant, crocodile (lizard?).Tell Asmar (Eshnunna), Iraq. IM 14674; Frankfort, 1955, No. 642; Collon, 1987, Fig. 610. *ibha* ‘elephant’ Rebus: *ibbo* ‘merchant’, *ib* ‘iron’காண்டாமிருகம் kāṇṭā-mirukam , *n*. [M. *kāṇṭāmṛgam*.] Rhinoceros; கல்யானை. Rebus: *kāṇḍā* ‘metalware, tools, pots and pans’. *araṇe* ‘lizard’ Rebus: *airaṇ* ‘anvil’. Alternative: . *kāru ‘crocodile’* Rebus: *kāru* ‘artisan’.

619

Captive bird-man brought to Ea and announced by two-faced attendant Usmu, another god following; eight-pointed star, five fishes, and standard-like motif in field. Blackstone 3.4x2cm. *lo* ‘overflowing water’ Rebus: *lo* ‘copper’. *kūdī* ‘twig’ Rebus: *kuṭhi* ‘smelter’. *kaṇḍo* ‘stool’ Rebus: *kāṇḍā* ‘metalware, tools, pots and pans’. *baṭa ‘quail’* Rebus: *baṭa* ’iron’.

622

Long-haired girdled bull-man subduing ibex; flat-capped bearded man subduing human-headed bull; lion struggling with another human-headed bull; plant and eight-pointed star I field. Shell 3.6x2cm. *kūdī* 'twig' Rebus: *kuṭhi* 'smelter'. *meḍ* 'star' Rebus: *mẽṛhẽt, meḍ* 'iron' (Mu.Ho.) *dhangar* 'bull' Rebus: *dhangar* 'blacksmith' (Maithili) *arye* 'lion' *āra* 'brass'. *miṇḍāl* 'markhor' (Tōrwālī) *meḍho* a ram, a sheep (G.)(CDIAL 10120) Rebus: *mẽṛhẽt, meḍ* 'iron' (Mu.Ho.)

623

Bearded girdled figure subduing bull attacked by lion; similar figure subduing human-headed bull; small kilted figure beneath blank inscription panel. Shell 3.5x1.9cm

Sun-god in his boat holds steering oar; anthropomorphous prow, with long-haired

120

crowned figure using punting pole, and snake-head stern; human-headed lion in boat, tied to prow; above lion, prow, vase with spout and handle, and two unrecognizable objects, one of which is perhaps a bag of seed; outside boat, goddess of vegetation, characterized by ears of grain growing from shoulder and robe, holds flowering branch, fishes and zigzags meaning water below. Shell 3.7x2.1cm. *uṛu* ' boatman' (Oriya) Rebus: *Utu* in Sumerian is the synonym of Akkadiam Shamash, sun divinity. uḍu f.n. ' star'. *arye* 'lion' *āra* 'brass'. *mũh* 'face' Rebus: *mũhe 'ingot'. paṭa* 'hood of snake'. *Rebus: padm* 'tempered, sharpness (metal)'. *ayo* 'fish' Rebus: *ayo, ayas* 'metal'. *kaṇḍe 'maize-cob'* Rebus: *kāṇḍā* 'metalware, tools, pots and pans'. *kamaṭa* 'spouted pot' Rebus: *kammaṭa* 'mint, coiner, portable gold furnace'.

611

Long-haired bearded god of fertility holding stalks of grain in each hand, while other staks spring from left shoulder; on his robe and in the field at either side are pairs of stalks; goddess of fertility (unfinished), holding plants in each hand, in front of him; two indistinct figures and personage (unfinished) with trailing robe (or lion skin) behind him. Shell 4x2.4 cm. *kūdī* 'twig' Rebus: *kuṭhi* 'smelter'. *kola* 'woman' *kol* 'working in iron'.

589

Two worshippers approach snake-god, who is holding his tail; fire altar between them and him; plant and eight-pointed star in field. Blackstone 2.2x1.2cm. *kūdī* 'twig' Rebus: *kuṭhi* 'smelter'. *meḍ* 'star' Rebus: *mẽṛhẽt, meḍ* 'iron' (Mu.Ho.) *kammaṭa* 'portable gold furnace' Rebus: *kammaṭa* 'mint, coiner'. Alternative: *kaṇḍ* 'furnace, fire-altar' (Santali) Rebus: *kāṇḍā* 'metalware, tools, pots and pans'.

613

Two flat-capped figures drinking through tubes from jar. Crescent in field Shell 3.2x1.5cm. *kuṭi* 'drink' Rebus: *kuṭhi* 'smelter'. *kūdī* 'twig' Rebus: *kuṭhi* 'smelter'. *kaṇḍo* 'stool' Rebus: *kāṇḍā* 'metalware, tools, pots and pans'.

624

Eagle in center of antithetic group of two bulls attacked by lion and man respectively; trees and lizard in field. Shell 3.5x2cm. *ḍangar* 'bull' Rebus: *ḍangar* 'blacksmith' (Hindi) *arye* 'lion' Rebus: *āra* 'brass'. *khōṇḍa* 'leafless tree' Rebus: *kõdā* ' to turn in a lathe.' *araṇe* 'lizard' Rebus: *airaṇ* 'anvil'. *pajhaṛ* 'kite' Rebus: pasra 'smithy'.

883

Fragmentary clay sealing: two antithetical bulls resting forelegs on mountain from which springs tree; nude girdled man kneeling under inscription naming Shudurul. About 3x5.5 cm. Inscription: Shudurul, mighty king of Agade, ...mah [son of...is his servant?] *ḍangar* 'bull', *ḍāg* mountain-ridge (H.)(CDIAL 5476). Rebus: *dhangar* 'blacksmith' (Maithili) *khōṇḍa* 'leafless tree' Rebus: *kõdā* ' to turn in a lathe.'

No. 883. Two lions attacking goat, each restrained by bull-man; bird of prey between bull-men, White stone; 2.7x2.1 cm. Early dynastic cylinder seal impression from Farah. Reproduced from Heinrich, Fara, Pl. 46f.

Wg. *koṇḍāl, kondāl* ' mattock, hoe '. (CDIAL 3286) *Ta.* kuntāli, kuntāḷi pickaxe. Rebus: *kõdā* ' to turn in a lathe.' *arye* 'lion' *āra* 'brass'. *meḍh* 'star', *miṇḍāl* 'markhor' (Tōrwālī) *meḍho* a ram, a sheep (G.)(CDIAL 10120) Rebus: *mẽṛhẽt, meḍ* 'iron' (Mu.Ho.) *ḍangar* 'bull' Rebus: *ḍangar* 'blacksmith' (Hindi)

801

Two girdled bull-men assailing with swords a lion which attacks bull; calf's head, plant, and indistinct motif in field. Yellow translucent stone; 3x2.5 cm. *mũh* 'face' Rebus: *mũhe* 'ingot'. *kūdī* 'twig' Rebus: *kuṭhi* 'smelter'. *ḍangar* 'bull' Rebus: *ḍangar* 'blacksmith' (Hindi) *arye* 'lion' Rebus: *āra* 'brass'

669

Adoration of seated goddess; fertility god carrying plant introduces nude worshipper followed by female worshipper carrying bucket; crescent, star, and mace in field. Shell. 3.1x1.9 cm. *kamaṭa* 'spouted pot' Rebus: *kammaṭa* 'mint, coiner, portable gold furnace'. *kūdī* 'twig' Rebus: *kuṭhi* 'smelter'. *meḍh* 'star' Rebus: *mẽṛhẽt, meḍ* 'iron' (Mu.Ho.)

671

Long-haired bull-man subduing lion; kilted hero subduing water buffalo. Gray mottled stone 2.9x1.6cm.

Two kilted men with turbans subduing two water-buffaloes, one rampant and one inverted. Shell 3x1.6cm.

663

659

Snake-god between two trees holds mace or battle-axe and receives worshipper carrying bucket. Blackstone 2.8x1.6cm. *āra* 'serpent' Rebus: *āra* 'brass'. *kuṭi* tree' Rebus: *kuṭhi* 'smelter'. *kamaṭa* 'spouted pot' Rebus: *kammaṭa* 'mint, coiner, portable gold furnace'.

662

Enthroned god holding mace receives two deities, male and female, introducing worshipper carrying sacrificial kid; male deity has stick or mace, female holds worshipper by hand; crescent, start, standard-like motif, and enigmatic object in field. Blackstone 3x1.7cm. *mṛeka, melh* 'goat' Rebus: *milakkhu* 'copper'. *meḍh* 'star' Rebus: *mẽṛhẽt, meḍ* 'iron' (Mu.Ho.) *kaṇḍ* 'furnace, fire-altar' (Santali) Rebus: *kāṇḍā* 'metalware, tools, pots and pans'. *eruvai* 'reed' Rebus: *eraka* 'copper'.

675

Ancient impression on clay; lion and ass seated, drinking through tubes from jar; nude figure in field. 4x7cm. *arye* 'lion' Rebus: *āra* 'brass' *khar m., khürü* f., 'donkey' (Kashmiri); Bshk. Kt. *kur* ' donkey' (CDIAL 3818). *khur* ' razor ' (Assamese. Bengali) (CDIAL 3727). *kuṭi* 'drink' Rebus: *kuṭhi* 'smelter'. *kaṇḍo* 'stool' Rebus: *kāṇḍā* 'metalware, tools, pots and pans'. Catalog: Brass, metalware, razor, smelter.

670

Bull-man attacking lion; nude girdled hero subduing water buffalo; battle-axe, eight-pointed star, and antelope in field; blank inscription panel. Hematite. 3.5x2.5cm.

684

Antithetic group of two bulls with two trees. Black stone 1.8x.8 cm.

Two goats flanking palm tree with bunches of dates; naked girdled figure

753

with long hair holding vase from which two streams of water flow, fishes swimming beside each stream;

761

indistinct object in field. Brown stone 1.8x1cm.

Worshipper bringing sacrificial kid to Shamash, who stands with one foot on mountain holding his saw in one hand, his beard in the other; Ishta, holding mace with two panther heads and scimitar, stands with one foot on lion, minor goddess before her; cow suckling calf above two rampant goats flanking mountain from which springs a tree; eight-pointed star and goat-fish (horns probably worn away) in field. Brown stone 3x1.7 cm.

770

Antithetic group of bison and water buffalo flanking mountain from which plants grow, both animals attacked by naked girdled figures. Gray-green stone; 3.3x1.9 cm.

Two lions, each clawing a bull, one from in front (with hindleg on bull's neck), one from behind; ram's head and hindquarters of hoofed animal in field. Calcite; 4.3x5.2 cm.

800

799

Two bull-men restraining lion which is attacking goat; antithetic group of twin goats on mountain with plant (?) between them, Calcite; 3.2x2.2 cm.

The motif is found on a Harapan tablet.. The leaf on a mountain motif is found on a seal from

Kalibangan. *ḍāngā* = hill, dry upland (B.); *ḍā̃g* mountain-ridge (H.)(CDIAL 5476). *ḍangar* 'bull' Rebus: *dhangar* 'blacksmith' (Maithili) *ḍangar* 'blacksmith' (Hindi) *miṇḍāl* 'markhor' (Tōrwālī) *meḍho* a ram, a sheep (G.)(CDIAL 10120) Rebus: *mẽṛhẽt, meḍ* 'iron' (Mu.Ho.) tagara 'antelope' Rebus: damgar 'merchant'.

Sumerian cylinder seal showing flanking goats with hooves on tree and/or mountain. Uruk period. (After Joyce Burstein in: Katherine Anne Harper, Robert L. Brown, 2002, The roots of tantra, SUNY Press, p.100)

loa = a species of fig tree, ficus glomerata, the fruit of ficus glomerata (Santali) Rebus: lo 'iron' (Assamese, Bengali); loa 'iron' (Gypsy). rebus: loh 'metal' (Skt.) Rebus: lo 'copper'. meḍha 'polar star' (Marathi). Rebus: meḍ 'iron' (Ho.)

Ur. Shell plaque. Shell plaque From Ur, Southern Iraq (c. 2,600-2,400 B.C.) Entwined in the branches of a flowering tree, two goats appear to be nibbling on its leaves. This decorative plaque, which was carved from shell and highlighted with bitumen, was also excavated from the Royal Tombs of Ur. The glyphics on this plaque are comparable to the glyphics on Tablet 1431E showing two goat glyphs flanking a tree glyph. करडणें or करंडणें [*karaḍaṇē* or *ṅkaranḍaṇēṃ*] *v c* To gnaw or nibble; to wear away by biting (Marathi). Rebus: *karaḍa* 'hard alloy'. *loa* 'ficus religiosa' Rebus: *lo* 'iron' (Assamese, Bengali); *loa* 'iron' (Gypsy) *lo* 'copper'. *ḍāngā* = hill, dry upland (B.); *ḍā̃g* mountain-ridge (H.)(CDIAL 5476). Rebus: *dhangar* 'blacksmith' (Maithili) *ḍangar* 'blacksmith' (Hindi) *miṇḍāl* 'markhor' (Tōrwālī) *meḍho* a ram, a sheep (G.)(CDIAL 10120); rebus: *mẽṛhẽt, meḍ* 'iron' (Mu.Ho.) The 'cross' glyphs flanking the ficus religiosa leaf may denote: *kaṇḍ* 'furnace, fire-altar' (Santali) . dula 'pair' Rebus: dul 'cast (metal)'. Thus, the entire glyptic composition denotes catalog of a smithy: *ḍangar* 'blacksmith' *lo* 'copper', *meḍ* 'iron', *karaḍa* 'hard alloy', *dul* 'cast (metal)'

m1430C, body of bison, three heads: bison, antelope, bull; a pair of goat(s), tree branch

Vikalpa 1: Leaf on mountain: kamaṛkom 'petiole of leaf'; rebus: kampaṭṭam 'mint'. Glyph: Vikalpa reading 2: kamaṛkom = fig leaf (Santali.) kamarmaṛā (Has.), kamaṛkom (Nag.); the petiole or stalk of a leaf (Mundari)Rebus: kampaṭṭam coinage, coin (Ta.)(DEDR 1236) kampaṭṭa- muḷai die, coining stamp (Ta.)

Orthography of the two goats on the prism tablet is comparable to the glyph on a shell plaque from Ur. Mlekh, mṛeka 'goat' (Br.Telugu); rebus: milakkhu 'copper'. डगर [ḍagara] A slope or ascent (as of a river's bank, of a small hill). A pair is dula; rebus: dul 'cast (metal)'(Santali)Rebus: ḍāṅgar 'blacksmith' (H.) Thus, the glyptic composition is read rebus: dul mlekh ḍāṅgar 'cast copper-smith'.

Alternative: Glyph: *Ta.* kōṭu summit of a hill, peak,
mountain; kōṭai mountain; kōṭar peak, summit of a tower; kuvaṭu mountain, hill, peak; kuṭumi summit of a mountain, top of a building, crown of the head, bird's crest, tuft of hair (esp. of men), crown, projecting corners on which a door swings. (DEDR 2049).

Rebus: खोट [khōṭa] *f* A mass of metal (unwrought or of old metal melted down); an ingot or wedge. Hence खोटसाळ [khōṭasāḷa] *a* (खोट & साळ from शाला) Alloyed--a metal. (Marathi) Bshk. *khoṭ* 'embers', Phal. *khūṭo* 'ashes, burning coal'; L. *khoṭ* f. 'alloy, impurity', *°ṭā* 'alloyed', awāṇ. *khoṭā* 'forged'; P. *khoṭ* m. 'base, alloy' M.*khoṭā* 'alloyed' (CDIAL 3931)

Glyph: 'broken tree branch': khōṇḍa A tree of which the head and branches are broken off, a stock or stump: also the lower portion of the trunk—that below the branches. (Marathi) Rebus 1: kõdā 'to turn in a lathe' (Bengali) Rebus 2: koḍ 'workshop' (G.)

Allograph glyph: खोंड [khōṇḍa] m A young bull, a bullcalf. (Marathi) గోద [gōda] gōda. [Tel.] n. An ox. A beast. kine, cattle.(Telugu) koḍiyum 'young bull' (G.) [kōḍiya] kōḍe, kōḍiya. [Tel.] n. A bullcalf. . k* దూడA young bull. Plumpness, prime. తరుణము. జోడుకోడయులు a pair of bullocks. kōḍe adj. Young. kōḍe-kāḍu. n. A young man.పడుచువాడు. [kārukōḍe] kāru-kōḍe. [Tel.] n. A bull in its prime. koḍiyum (G.) Rebus : B. kõdā 'to turn in a lathe'; Or. kũnda 'lathe', kũdibā, kũd 'to turn' (→ Drav. Kur. kũd 'lathe') (CDIAL 3295). कोंद *kōnda* 'engraver, lapidary setting or infixing gems' (Marathi)

M1431E shows a turner at work, assisted by a person bending on all fours. kunda 'turner' kundār turner (A.); kũdār, kũdāri (B.); kundāru (Or.); kundau to turn on a lathe, to carve, to chase; kundau dhiri = a hewn stone; kundau murhut = a graven image (Santali) kunda a turner's lathe (Skt.)(CDIAL 3295) Glyph: Br. Kōṇḍō on all fours, bent double. (DEDR 204a) The seated person is shown wearing knot of hair at back. Sūnd gaṭ (Go.) cundī the hairtail as worn by men (Kur.)(DEDR 2670). Rebus: cundakāra a turner J vi.339 (Pali) cundakāra cognate kundār.

Chanhudaro17a 6122

Glyph: 'full stretch of one's arms': kāḍ 2 काड् । पौरुषम् m. a man's length, the stature of a man (as a measure of length) (Rām. 632, zangan kaḍun kāḍ, to stretch oneself the whole length of one's body. So K. 119). Rebus: kāḍ 'stone'. Ga. (Oll.) kanḍ, (S.) kanḍu (pl. kanḍkil) stone (DEDR 1298).

m1431E. From R.—a person holding a vessel; a woman with a platter (?); a kneeling person with a staff in his hands facing the woman; a goat with its forelegs on a platform under a tree. [Or, two antelopes flanking a tree on a platform, with one antelope looking backwards?]

The turner on a lathe is depicted on this glyphic narrative. kōdā 'to turn in a lathe' (Bengali) कोंद *kōnda* 'engraver, lapidary setting or infixing gems' (Marathi)

h380 4902 A bronze dagger showing the hieroglyphs oriented from handle to edge of dagger.

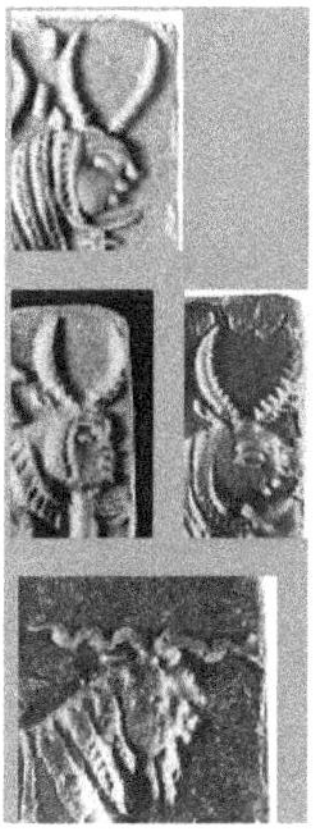

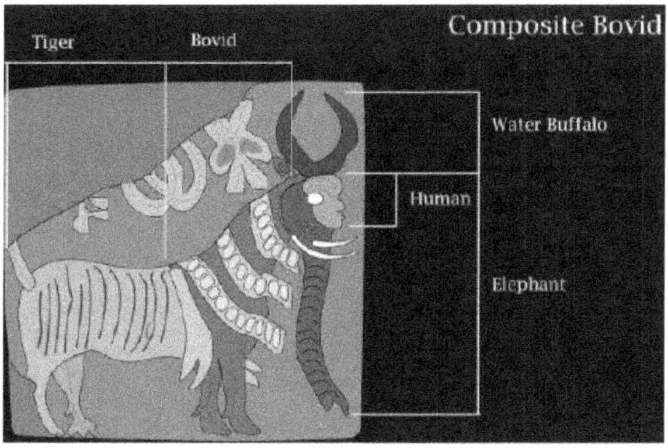

Composite bovid, ligatured components (the elements in the face shown on Seal m0304 is evidenced by zoomed in pictorial motifs from other seals).

Elements in m0304 face (Huntington 2007): two profile faces, bovine ears. Probable bristles like the bristles on a tiger's mane. The face profiles do not match with other faces profiled on other inscribed objects. The profiles of two faces however, can be compared with the profile of human face shown on this seal of a composite animal (elements: human, tiger, tiger's mane, markhor horns).

ṛanku, ranku = fornication, adultery (Telugu) This semantics explains the extraordinary glyptics employed on many epigraphs, showing the sexual act. Alternative: *kamḍa, khamḍa* 'copulation' (Santali) Rebus: *kampaṭṭa* 'mint, coiner'.

urseal18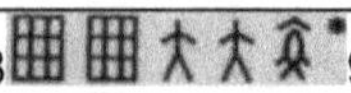9902 BM 123059. And, seal impression.

A bull mating with a cow. Seal impression . Twins, two men stand side-by-side. *dula* 'pair' Rebus: *dul* 'cast (metal) *meḍ* 'body' Rebus: *meḍ* 'iron'. Thus, the twin hieroglyph denotes cast iron. खांडा [*khāṇḍā*] A division of a field. (Marathi) Rebus: *khāṇḍā* tool, pots and pans, metalware (Marathi) The pair of glyphs of 'square with divisions' connotes: cast metalware. *ayo* 'fish' Rebus: *ayo, ayas* 'metal'. *aḍaren* 'lid' Rebus: *aduru* 'native, unsmelted metal' (Kannada)

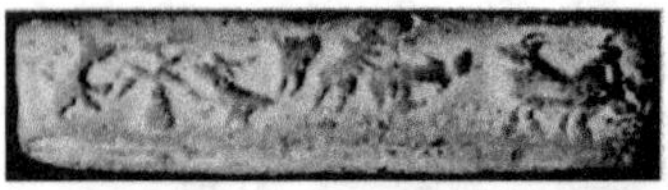
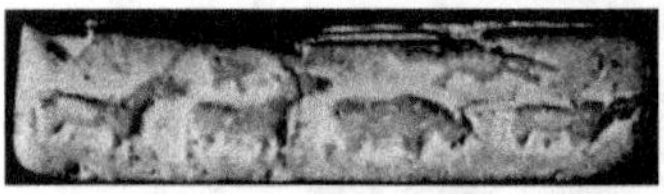
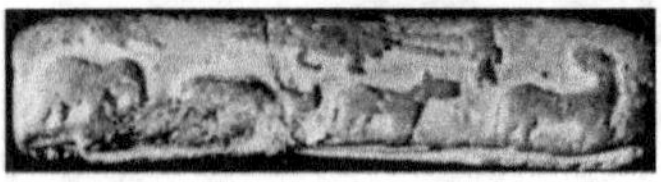

m0489a,b,c A standing human couple mating (*a tergo*); one side of a prism tablet from Mohenjo-daro (m489b). Other motifs on the inscribed object are: two goats eating leaves on a platform; a cock or hen (?) and a three-headed animal (perhaps antelope, one-horned bull and a short-horned bull). The leaf pictorial connotes on the goat composition connotes loa; hence, the reading is of this pictorial component is: lohar kamar = a blacksmith, worker in iron, superior to the ordinary kamar (Santali.)]

kāruvu 'crocodile' Rebus: 'artisan, blacksmith'. *pasaramu, pasalamu* = an animal, a beast, a brute, quadruped (Telugu) Thus, the depiction of animals in epigraphs is related to, rebus: *pasra* = smithy (Santali)

*pisera_* a small deer brown above and black below (H.)(CDIAL 8365).
ḍān:gra = wooden trough or manger sufficient to feed one animal (Mundari).
iṭan:kāṟṟi = a capacity measure (Ma.) Rebus: ḍhan:gar 'blacksmith' (Bi.)

pattar 'goldsmiths' (Ta.) patra 'leaf' (Skt.) melh 'goat' (Br.); milakkhu 'copper' (Pali)

r-an:ku, ran:ku = fornication, adultery (Telugu); rebus: ranku 'tin' (Santali)

kaulo-mengro, s. A blacksmith; kaulo ratti. Black blood, Gypsy blood (Gypsy).
mangar `crocodile' (Bal.); kula 'house'. Rebus: kolli 'fish' (DEDR 2139)

Hieroglyphs:

elephant, boar/rhinoceros, tiger, tiger face turned

heifer, antelope, bullock, brahmani bull

Rebus mleccha glosses:

Ibha, badhia, kol, krammara kol

damṛa, melh, bail, adar ḍangra

Iron (ib), carpenter(badhi), smithy (kol 'pancaloha'), alloy-smith (kol kamar)

tam(b)ra copper, milakkhu copper, bali (iron sand ore), native metal (aduru), ḍhangar 'smith'

Meluhha hieroglyphs on cylinder seals and kudurru

Implements are shown on cylinder seals as glyphs. These glyphs occur together with cuneiform inscription and also symbols such as stars and dots associated as divinity representations, according to Assyriologists and Sumerologists who have expertise in analyzing cylinder seals of Sumer, Elam, Mesopotamia A typical example is provided by VA243 cylinder seal which shows implements of dagger together with a plough.

The seal is transliterated (the Sumero-Akkadian signs in English letters) and translated into German, in the principal publication of the Berlin Vorderasiatische Museum's publication of its seal collection, Vorderasiatische Rollsiegel ("West Asian Cylinder Seals"; 1940) by Mesopotamian scholar Anton Moortgat on page 101. The seal is also called VA243 because it is number 243 in the VA Museum collection.[463]

More than 22 socketed spearheads found in a tomb at Tell Abraq.[464]

The cylinder seal also uses the Meluhha hieroglyphs of 1. Antelope carried by a Meluhhan -- Mlekh 'goat' Rebus: melukkha 'copper'; 2. A ram with long curved-back horns – tagara 'ram' Rebus: tagara 'tin (mineral)'; 3. Mountain-range. -- mēḍu 'height, rising ground, hillock' (Kannada) Rebus: meḍ 'iron' (Ho.) *ḍāngā* = hill, dry upland (B.); *ḍāg* mountain-ridge (H.)(CDIAL 5476). Rebus 1: *damgar, tamkāru* 'merchant' (Akkadian). Rebus 2: *dhangar* 'blacksmith' (Maithili) *ḍangar* 'blacksmith' (Hindi) *miṇḍāl* 'markhor' (Tōrwālī) *meḍho* a ram, a sheep (G.)(CDIAL 10120); rebus: *mẽṛhẽt, meḍ* 'iron' (Mu.Ho.)

The Dubsiga cylinder seal or VA243 clearly evidences a plough held in the hands of the seated person. One explanation is that the person represents the divinity Dagan (Hebrew Dogon), the inventor of the plough.

An alternative interpretation is provided in the context of the 'person being introduced' who could be a Meluhhan since he carries an antelope on his arms.

The word for the plough in Meluhha is: *lāṅal, nāṅal.* It is hypothesized that the plough held in the hands of the seated person on the Dubsiga cylinder seal was presented by the Meluhhan artisan/smith as a product made in his smithy/forge *kole.l*, which is his temple, *kole.l* నాగటిజోడు *nāgail+jōdu* an epithet of Balarama. How to explain the suffix - *jōdu*? మేజోడు [mējōḍu] *mējōḍu.* [H.] n. Stockings. సంగడి బావులు two wells side by side, జోడుబావులు. Thus, jōḍu connotes a 'pair'. जोड [jōḍa] *m f* (जुड S) 'A pair, a couple (of things of a sort and of which two usually go together)'. 'Friendship or close connection' (Marathi). The plough is paired with Balarama, the elder brother of Krishna in the Great Epic, *Mahābhārata.* The association of Balarama with the plough is an abiding tradition of the cultural contact area of Sarasvati-Sindhu civilization. There is a gloss for this feature: जोडगिरी [jōḍagirī] *f* Joining in with and aiding (as of a singer or Hardás). 2 Doubleness, state of consisting or of being composed of two. 3 Piecedness, composition through pieces or a piece joined. (Marathi)

Lanayor abhedah

Just as distribution of *r* and *l* is dialectical explained by *ralayor abhedah*, a remarkable interchange of *l* and *n* occurs in Indian *sprachbund.* Bengali glosses show evidence of both *lāṅal, nāṅal*, to denote the pough. One gloss which such interchange of *l* and *n* relates to the semantics of the numeral 'nine'.

Dubsiga cylinder seal (VA 243)

Line 1 = dub-si-ga “Dubsiga” [a personal name of an apparently powerful person[1]]

Line 2 = ili-il-la-at “Ili-illat” [another personal name, this time of the seal’s owner]

Line 3 = ir3-su “dein Knecht” [German for “your servant”[2]]

So the full (rather boring) inscription of VA243 reads: “Dubsiga, Ili-illat, your/his servant.”

The implement shown on the seal: Mr' hand-plough, Protodynastic Period of Egypt (from the Scorpion Macehead)

koṇḍi the sting of a scorpion (Kannada). Rebus: *kōnda* ‘engraver (Marathi)

Michael Heiser notes that the study of cylinder seals is actually a very specialized sub-discipline within Sumerology and Assyriology. An excellent general introduction is Dominique Collon's work.[465]

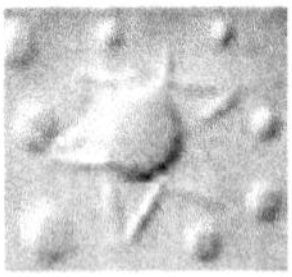

The star symbol on VA243 may stand for a deity and is surrounded by eight dots, also stars; the entire glyph complex may denote a divine council.

Sun divinity, Shamash Akkadian, is known a Utu in Sumerian.

The inscription describes an offering made by a worshipper (who is named) to a seated divinity who is associated in the seal with fertile harvest. "Since there are two other figures in the seal in addition to the seated god, and one is the offerer, the remaining figure is likely a deity also associated with the offering. In favor of this possibility are the 'implements' shown on the seal with respect to these two figures facing the seated god and the figure's headdress. Also in its favor is the fact that there are literally hundreds of such 'offering seals,' and many have a star in upper proximity to the figures' heads, signifying the figure is a deity. Since the star is surrounded by eleven other stars (dots), the artistic depiction could stand for the lead god of the Mesopotamian divine council and its other eleven (upper tier) members...The symbol of the sun god in Sumero-Mesopotamian religion was a central ciecle with extended 'arms' with wavy lines in between each 'arm', or a circle with only wavy lines. The entire symbol was...inside a circle, as below:"

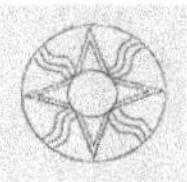

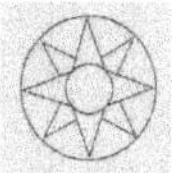

Distinct from the 'sun' symbol is the 'star' symbol:

The symbols used on Kudurru reliefs are analysed in zodiac context:

The sun symbol (Left) and star symbol (Right) are next to each other under the snake (Draco).[466]

The sun symbol (center) and star symbol (R of center) are next to each other under the snake's tail.[467]

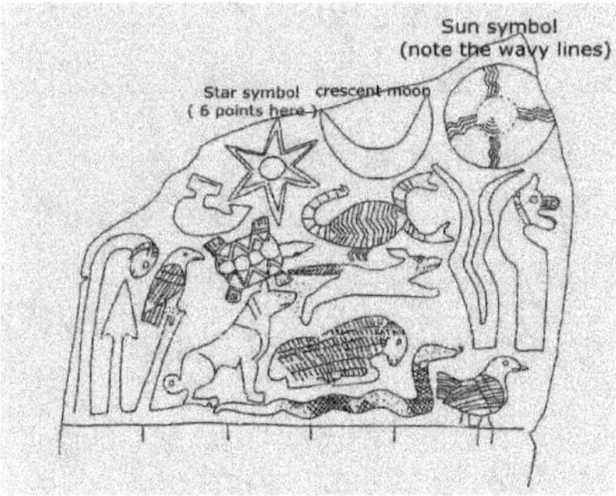

Some symbols on Kudurru reliefs and associations with smithy repertoire/implements.[468]

It is hypothesised that some symbols used on Kudurru reliefs are Meluhha hieroglyphs which have been elaborated as metalware catalogs of bronze-age. Such hieroglyphs which could have attained the attributes of divinity in Sumeria-Elam-Mesopotamia, exemplified by the temple traditions are:

1. arrowhead
2. scorpion
3. turtle or tortoise
4. snake and snake-hood
5. duck
6. fox
7. ram
8. frog
9. footstep
10. lizard

The Meluhha rebus readings are:

1. *uṭu* 'Feather of an arrow; Arrow-head' Rebus: *uḍu* 'boat, raft'.
2. scorpion *bica* 'scorpion' (Assamese) Rebus: *bica* 'stone ore'. meṛed-bica 'iron stone ore'. *koṇḍi* the sting of a scorpion.).Rebus: *kõdā* 'to turn in a lathe' (Bengali) कोंद *kōnda* 'engraver, lapidary setting or infixing gems' (Marathi)
3. turtle or tortoise *kamaṭhamu.* [Skt.] n. A tortoise. Rebus: kammaṭa (Kannada)కమటము *kamaṭamu.* [Telugu] n. A portable furnace for melting the precious metals. అగసాలెవాని కుంపటి. (Telugu)
4. snake and snake-hood *paṭam* , *n.* < *phaṭa.* 'cobra's hood' (CDIAL 9040). Rebus: 'sharpness of iron': *padm* (obl.*padt-*) temper of iron (Kota)(DEDR 3907); *patam* 'sharpness, as of the edge of a knife' (Tamil)
5. duck *karaṇḍa* 'duck' (Sanskrit) *karaṛa* 'a very large aquatic bird' (Sindhi) Rebus: करडा [karaḍā] Hard from alloy--iron, silver &c. (Marathi)
6. fox *lōī* f., *lo* m.2. Pr. *ẓūwī* 'fox' (Western Pahari)(CDIAL 11140-2). Rebus: *loh* 'copper' (Hindi).
7. ram मेंढा [mēṇḍhā] *m* (मेष S through H) A male sheep, a ram or tup.(Marathi) *meḍ* 'iron' (Mundari. Remo.)

8. Frog hieroglyph: *meḍak* 'small frog' (Gujarati) Rebus: *meḍ* 'iron' (Ho.)
9. Footstep hieroglyph: Rebus 1: Ta. aṭi foot, footprint, base, bottom, source, origin; Ma. aṭi sole of foot, footstep, measure of foot, Ko. aṛy foot (measure);To. oṛy foot. Ka. aḍi foot, measure of foot, step, pace,Te. aḍugu foot, footstep, footprint, step, pace, measure of a foot,aḍi-gar̲r̲a sandal, wooden shoe. Ga. (S.2) aḍugu footstep (< Te.). Go. (G.) aḍi beneath; (Mu.)(DEDR 72) Rebus 2: Glyph: *Ko.* meṭ- (mec-) to trample on, tread on; meṭ sole of foot, footstep, footprint. Rebus: *meḍ* 'iron' (Mundari. Remo.)
10. Lizard hieroglyph: Glyph: araṇe 'lizard' (Tulu) Rebus: eraṇi f. ' anvil ' (Gujarati); aheraṇ, ahiraṇ, airaṇ, airṇī, haraṇ f. (Marathi)

Ishtar shown on a cylinder seal[469], carrying a sickle on her left hand and associated with an eight-pointed star, stepping one foot on top of an unidentified motif. मेढ [mēḍha] The polar star (Marathi). [cf.The eight-pointed star

associated with the feminine divinity in Mesopotamian tradition.] Glyph of the implement she carries on her left hand: *koṭṭi katti* billhook (Koḍagu)

Clay impression of Akkadian cylinder seal, ca. 2334-2154 BCE. Blackstone. The Oriental Institute, The University of Chicago. *ṭaṅkam* mace (Malayalam). *ṭaṅga* 'sword, spade'.*arye* 'lion' Rebus: *āra* 'brass'.

Goddess depicted is Ishtar associated with a 'star' symbol.[470] In this example, the obvious star symbol has eight points, and is very similar in design to the star symbol of VA 243. We know it's a star and not the sun because the goddess depicted is Ishtar.

Glyph 'leaf, petal': A 'leaf' glyph has to be distinguished from a 'petals' glyph because the leaf orthography is clearly representative of the *ficus* genus which attains sacredness in later historical periods in the Indian linguistic area.

The following demonstration of the cipher indicates that the Meluhha word for 'nine' – the count of nine ficus leaves shown on Mohenjodaro Seal m0296 – was most likely *lo* 'nine'. This is reinforced by the phonetic determinant – the gloss for the ficus religiosa, *loa.*

Glyptic elements of m0296 seal impression: 1. Two heads of one-horned young bulls; 2. ligatured to a pair of rings and a standard device; 3. ligatured to a precise count of nine leaves. Read rebus: koḍiyum 'heifer, rings on neck'; खोंड [khōṇḍa] m A young bull, a bullcalf. (Marathi) గోడ [gōda] gōda. [Tel.] n. An ox. A beast. kine, cattle.(Telugu) koḍiyum (G.) Rebus : B. kõdā 'to turn in a lathe'; Or. kũnda 'lathe', kũdibā, kũd 'to turn' (→ Drav. Kur. kũd 'lathe') (CDIAL 3295). Rebus: koḍ 'workshop' (Kuwi.G.); dula 'pair' (Kashmiri); rebus: dul 'cast metal' (Mu.) *lo, no* 'nine' (B.); loa 'ficus religiosa' (Santali); rebus: loh 'metal' (Skt.); loa 'copper' (Santali) sangaḍa 'jointed animals' (Marathi); sangaḍa 'lathe' (G.) Rebus: jaṅgaḍ 'entrusment articles'. Part of the pictorial motif is thus decoded rebus: loh dul koḍ 'metal cast(ing) smithy turner (lathe) workshop'. Part of the inscription is read rebus: *ayaskāṇḍa kole.l* 'smithy, excellent quantity of iron'.

The stem in the orthographic composition relates to *sangaḍa* 'lathe/furnace' (yielding crucible stone ore nodules), the standard device which is depicted frequently in front of 'one-horned heifer'. Rebus: *sangāta* 'association, guild' or, *sangatarāsu* 'stone-cutter' (Telugu). The 'globules' glyphic joining the two ringed necks of a pair of one-horned heifers may connote: goṭi. It may connote a forge.

Glyph: 'piece'; the two rings emanating from the top of the portable furnace denote *khoṭā* 'forged'; *khoṭa* 'alloy': guḍá—1. — In sense 'fruit,  kernel' cert. ← Drav., cf. Tam. koṭṭai 'nut, kernel'; A. goṭ 'a fruit, whole piece', °ṭā 'globular, solid', guṭi 'small ball, seed, kernel'; B. goṭā 'seed, bean, whole'; Or. goṭā 'whole, undivided', goṭi 'small ball, cocoon', goṭāli 'small round piece of chalk'; Bi. goṭā 'seed'; Mth. goṭa 'numerative particle' (CDIAL 4271) Rebus: *khoṭ* m. 'base, alloy' (Punjabi) Rebus: koṭe 'forging (metal)(Mu.) Rebus: goṭī f. 'lump of silver' (G.) goṭi = silver (G.) koḍ 'workshop' (G.). Glyph: 'two links in a chain': kaḍī a chain; a hook; a link (G.); kaḍum a bracelet, a ring (G.) Rebus: kaḍiyo [Hem. Des. kaḍaio = Skt. sthapati a mason] a bricklayer; a mason; kaḍiyaṇa, kaḍiyeṇa a woman of the bricklayer caste; a wife of a bricklayer (G.) The stone-cutter is also a mason.

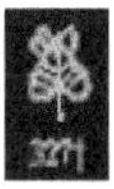

kamaḍha = *ficus religiosa* (Skt.); kamar.kom 'ficus' (Santali) rebus: kamaṭa = portable furnace for melting precious metals (Te.); kampaṭṭam = mint (Ta.) Vikalpa: Fig leaf 'loa'; rebus: loh '(copper) metal'. loha-kāra 'metalsmith' (Skt.).

Text on m296 seal.

Glyphs: ayas 'fish'. Rebus: aya 'metal'. Glyph: *kaṇḍa* 'arrow' Rebus: 'stone (ore)metal'; kaṇḍa 'fire-altar'. *ayaskāṇḍa* is explained in Panini as 'excellent quantity of iron' or 'tools, pots and pans and metal-ware'.

The last sign on epigraph 5477 and 1554 (m296 seal) is read as: kole.l = smithy, temple in Kota village (Ko.) *sāgāḍā* m. ' frame of a building ' (M.)(CDIAL 12859) Rebus: जांगड jāṅgaḍa *f* (H) Goods taken from a shop, to be retained or returned as may suit: also articles of apparel taken from a tailor or clothier to sell for him or जांगड वही The account or account-book of goods so taken.

Thus, the three text sign sequence can be explained rebus as smithy for metal of stone (ore) iron.

There are two glyphs preceding the 'fish' glyph on Text of m296 seal: *ḍhāḷako* 'a large metal ingot' and *khāṇḍā* 'tools, pots and pans, metal-ware'.खांडा khāṇḍā *m* A jag, notch, or indentation (as upon the edge of a tool or weapon). A gap in the teeth. Rebus: *khāṇḍā* 'tools, pots and pans, metal-ware'. ḍhāḷ = a slope; the inclination of a plane; m ḍhāḷiyum = adj. sloping, inclining (G.) Rebus: *ḍhāḷako* 'a large metal ingot' (Gujarati)

This is a complex, ligatured glyph with a number of glyphic elements. May denote a cast metal (copper) worker guild working with 4 types of pure metal and alloyed ingots (copper + arsenic/tin/zinc). *kūṭ* f. 'corner, side' (Punjabi) Rebus: *khoṭa* 'alloy'. Allograph: *khūṭ* 'zebu'.

Glyphic element: erako nave; era = knave of wheel. Glyphic element: āra 'spokes'. Rebus: āra 'brass' as in ārakūṭa (Skt.) Rebus: Tu. eraka molten, cast (as metal); eraguni to melt (DEDR 866) erka = ekke (Tbh. of arka) aka (Tbh. of arka) copper (metal); crystal (Ka.lex.) cf. eruvai = copper (Ta.lex.) eraka, er-aka = any metal infusion (Ka.Tu.); erako molten cast (Tu.lex.) Glyphic element: kund opening in the nave or hub of a wheel to admit the axle (Santali) Rebus: kunda 'turner' kundār turner (A.); kūdār, kūdāri (B.); kundāru (Or.); kundau to turn on a lathe, to carve, to chase; kundau dhiri = a hewn stone; kundau murhut = a graven image (Santali) kunda a turner's lathe (Skt.)(CDIAL 3295). kundan 'pure gold'. Allograph: wing: *Ta.* ciṟai, ciṟaku, ciṟakar wing; iṟai, iṟaku, iṟakar, iṟakkai wing, feather. *Ma.* iṟaku, ciṟaku wing. *Ko.* rek wing, feather. *Ka.* eṟake, eṟaṅke, ṟakke, ṟekke wing; ṟaṭṭe, ṟeṭṭe wing, upper arm. *Koḍ.* rekke wing; raṭṭe upper arm. *Tu.* ediṅke, reṅkè ing. *Te.* eṟaka, ṟekka, rekka, neṟaka, neṟi id. *Kol.* reḍapa, (SR.) reppā id.; (P.) reṛapa id., feather. *Nk.* rekka, reppa wing. *Pa.* (S.) rekka id. *Go.* (S.) rekka wing-feather; reka (M.) feather, (Ko.) wing (*Voc.* 3045). *Konḍa* ṟeka wing, upper arm. *Kuwi* (Su.) rekka wing. (DEDR 2591). *Ko.* kerŋgl, kergl feather, wing. (DEDR 1983).

Glyphic element: 'corner': khuṇṭa 'corner'. Phal. khun ' corner '; H. khūṭ m. ' corner, direction ' (→ P. khūṭ f. ' corner, side '); G. khūṭṛī f. ' angle '. <-> X kōṇa -- : G. khuṇ f., khūˇṇɔ m. ' corner '.2. S. kuṇḍa f. ' corner '; P. kūṭ f. 'corner, side' (← H.). (CDIAL 3898). Rebus: khūṭ 'community, guild' (Mu.); kuṇḍa 'consecrated fire-pit'.

The 'U' glyphic on this variant of Sign 243 could be to denote the sounds of words: 1. baṭi and 2. kuṇḍa: 1. baṭi 'broad-mouthed, rimless metal vessel'; rebus: baṭi 'smelting furnace'; 2. kuṇḍa 'pot; rebus: 'consecrated fire-pit'. The 'U' glyphic is a semantic determinant to emphasise that this is a temple with a smithy furnace and a consecrated fire-pit. The structural form within which this 'U' glyphic is enclosed may represent a temple: kole.l 'temple, smithy' (Ko.); kolme smithy' (Ka.) The structural form (*sangaḍa* 'frame of a building') within which this sign is enclosed may represent a temple: kole.l 'temple, smithy' (Ko.); kolme smithy' (Ka.) The ligatured sign may thus be read: *sangaḍa kunḍ* to mean 'entrustment articles (of) consecrated fire-altar or furnace (of) temple'.

Copper/iron

Pk. *lōha* -- m. ' iron ', Gy. pal. *li°*, *lihi*, obl. *elhás*, as. *loa* JGLS new ser. ii 258; Wg. (Lumsden) "*loa*" ' steel '; Kho. *loh* ' copper '; S. *lohu* m. ' iron ', L. *lohā* m., awāṇ. *lō`ā*, P. *lohā* m. (→ K.rām. ḍoḍ. *lohā*), CDIAL 11171-3).

Meluhha glosses may also explain the use of selected hieroglyphs in the Sumerian-Elamite- Mesopotamian writing tradition in the context of adoration of 'deities' or offerings to temples/ziggurat. Such deployment of implements and mineral/metal repertoire of a smithy/forge is consistent with the use in Kota and Toda languages, the same sememe to connote both a smithy and a temple:
kole·l smithy, temple in Kota village (Kota); kwala·l Kota smithy (Toda);
Ta. kol working in iron, blacksmith; kollaṉ blacksmith (Tamil); kollan blacksmith, artificer (Malayalam). (DEDR 2133). kuṛḷ hut; guṛy temple (Kota)
kuṛy Hindu temple (Toda); guḍi temple (Telugu); guṛi temple (Gondi)(DEDR 1655).

Rahman-dheri01A and B Rhd1: Two scorpions flanking a 'frog?' and a sign T with two holes on the top, possibly to be tied on a string.

The glyphs are: mouflon, scorpion, frog, pedestal (on which idols are carried as shown on Mohenjo-daro 'procession' tablet).

> Glyph of 'pedestal': पेढी [*pēḍhī*] f (पीठ S) A raised place upon a floor &c. as a seat or to place an idol or dishes upon. 2 The seat or stand of a shroff. Rebus: पेढी (Gujaráthí word.) *pēḍhī* 'A shop'.
>
> 'Slanted stroke' glyph: *ḍhāḷ* 'slanted' Rebus: *ḍhāḷako* 'large ingot'.
> dula 'pair' Rebus: dul 'cast metal'.
> *bica* 'scorpion' Rebus *bica* 'stone ore'.
> *meḍho* a ram, a sheep (G.)(CDIAL 10120) Rebus: *mẽṛhẽt, meḍ* 'iron' (Mu.Ho.)

The glyph like a flat T sign is comparable to the bun-ingots kept atop such a glyphic composition of Warka vase. One is a tin ingot: tagara 'ram' Rebus: tagaram 'tin'. The other is a brass ingot: *aryeh* 'lion'. Rebus: *āra* 'brass, alloy of zinc and copper' as in *ārakūṭa* (Skt.) *āram* 'brass' (Tamil) *dul* 'to cast metal in a mould' (Santali) *ḍhālako* = a large metal ingot (G.) *ḍhālakī* = a metal heated and poured into a mould; a solid piece of metal; an ingot (Gujarati).

Kudurru and scorpion glyph

Kudurru recopied under Marduk-apla-iddina I, from Susa, 12th cent. BCE. A godess wearing a tunic with pleats in the back and elbow-length sleeves, a cone-shaped headdress, and quilted slippers. Top register: sun, moon, star, scorpion: In Babylonia, a replica of boundary stone placed in a temple, recording a land grant, usually involving the crown. Land grants were made to crown prince, princess, temple officials and priests, officers and

generals, and courtiers. Personal names are accompanied by the phrase, 'his (i.e. the king's) servant'.

bicha 'scorpion' (Assamese) Rebus: bica 'stone ore' (Munda). The symbolism of the scorpion in the context of the land grants has to be investigated further.

Kudurru of Meli-Shipak commemorating a gift of land to his son Marduk-apla-iddina Kassite period, reign of Melishipak (1186-1172 BCE) Susa (where it had been taken as war booty in the 12th century BCE) Limestone J. de Morgan excavations Sb 22 This example records a gift of land made by King Melishipak to his son Marduk-Apal-Iddina. The text, which covers one whole side of the stone, records a major gift of land from the Kassite king, Melishipak, to his son, Marduk-Apal-Iddina, the future "shepherd of his country." The ownership of the land came with a number of franchises. Kudurru inscriptions are usually in two parts. The first describes the nature of the gift and the clauses attached to it. This is followed by an imprecation calling down a divine curse on anyone who opposed the gift. The gift was thus not only recorded and displayed for all to see, but also placed under divine protection.[471]

Glyphs on kudurru: sun-disk, scorpion, eagle, lion, snake-hood, quadruped

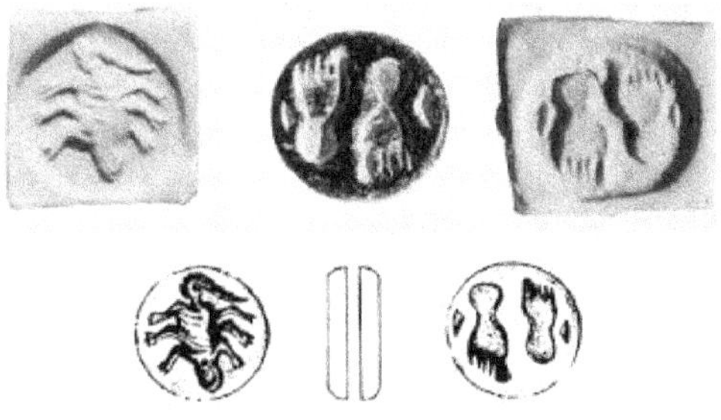

Catalogue no. 58, Double-sided steatite stamp seal, perforated along the lateral axis with opposing footprints on one side, a fantastic creature with long tail, six legs, and a head as seen from above on the other. Dia. 15mm h. 8mm.Disk seal (glyptic catalogue no. 58; 15 mm in dia. X 8 mm) Excavations at Tepe Yahya, 3rd millennium, p. 154 Tepe Yahya. Seal impressions of two sides of a seal. Six-legged lizard and opposing footprints shown on opposing sides of a double-sided steatite stamp seal perforated along the lateral axis.

Ia. 18

rebus word

Lamberg- Karlovsky 1971: fig. 2C Shahr-i-Soktha Stamp seal shaped like a foot.

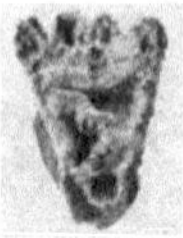

Shahdad seal (Grave 78). It is significant that a footprint is used as a seal at Shahdad. The glyph is read rebus as for 'iron':

Rebus readings:

Glyph: *meṭṭu* 'foot'. Rebus: *meḍ* 'iron' (Ho.Mu.) dula 'pair' (Kashmiri); dul 'cast (metal)(Santali). Six legs of a lizard is an enumeration of six 'portable furnaces' ; araṇe 'lizard' (Tulu) Rebus: airaṇ 'anvil' (Marathi) Alternative: kakra. 'lizard'; Rebus: kangra 'portable furnace'.

Glyphs: six (numeral) + ring of hair: आर [āra] A term in the play of इटीदांडू,--the number six. (Marathi) आर [āra] A tuft or ring of hair on the body. (Marathi) Rebus: āra 'brass'.

bhaṭa 'six' (G.) rebus: baṭa = kiln (Santali); baṭa = a kind of iron (G.) bhaṭṭhī f. 'kiln, distillery', awāṇ. bhaṭh; P. bhaṭṭh m., °ṭhī f. 'furnace', bhaṭṭhā m. 'kiln'; S. bhaṭṭhī keṇī 'distil (spirits)'. Read rebus as : *dul (pair) meḍ* 'cast iron'; *kan:gra bhaṭa* 'portable furnace' or kangra āra 'portable furnace (for) brass'.

Indus writing in Ancient Near East

After: Robert H. Brunswig, Jr., Asko Parpola, and Daniel Potts[472]

Seal and seal impression. 9908. Iraq museum; glazed steatite; perhaps from an Iraqi site; the one-horned bull, the standard are below a six-sign inscription.

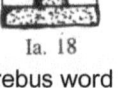

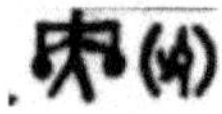

9351; Nippur; ca. 13th cent. BC; white stone; zebu bull and two pictograms.

Kassite (c. 14th century BCE). Gibson 1977.

9851; Louvre Museum; Luristan; unglazed, gray steatite; short-honed bull and 4 pictograms.

Foroughi collection; Luristan; medium gray steatite; bull, crescent, star and net square; of the Dilmun seal type.

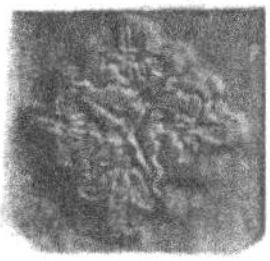

3255; Louvre Museum; Luristan; light yellow stone; seal impression; one side shows four eagles; the eagles hold snakes in their beaks; at the center is a human figure with outstretched limbs; obverse of the seal shows an animal, perhaps a hyena or boar striding across the field, with a smaller animal of the same type depicted above it; comparable to the seal found in Harappa, Vats 1940, II: Pl. XCI.255.

9701; Failaka; unglazed steatite; an arc of four pictograms above the hindquarter of a bull.

9602; seal, impression; Qala'at al-Bahrain; green steatite; short-horned bull and five pictograms. Found in association with an Isin-Larsa type tablet bearing three Amorite names.

9601; Qala'at al-Bahrain; light-grey steatite; hindquarters of a bull and two pictograms.

Seal impression; Dept. of Antiquities, Bahrain; three Harapan-style bulls;

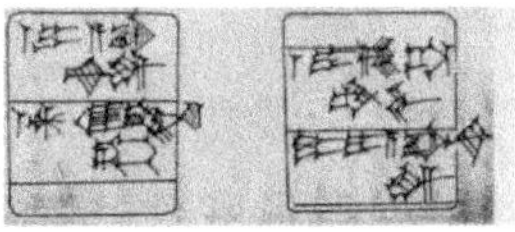

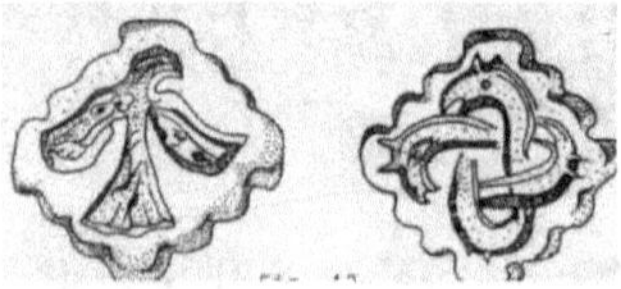

Qala'at al-Bahrain; ca. 2050-1900 BC; tablet, found in the same level where 8 Dilmun seals and six Harappan type weights were found. Three Amorite names are: Janbi-naim; Ila-milkum; Jis.i-tambu (son of Janbi-naim)

Two seals from Gonur 1 in the Murghab delta; dark brown stone (Sarianidi 1981 b: 232-233, Fig. 7, 8); eagle engraved on one face.

9702; seal, impression, inscription; Failaka; brownish-grey unglazed steatite; Indus pictograms above a short-horned bull. (Fig.3)

Steatite seals with the image of the short-horned bulls with lowered head from Failaka (1), Bahrein (2-3), Bactria (4), the Iranian Plateau (5). Nr. 6 comes from the surface of the site of Diqdiqqah, near Ur.

MS 2645, Afghanistan, 23rd-21st c. BCE

1.1

1.2

1.3

1.5

1.6

1.9

1.7

1.8

Sigilli a stampo quadrangolari di tipo indiano e pseudo-indiano

1.7 Ur Ratae. 1.8 Ur Serpentine or Steatite. 1.9 Mesootamia Pietra verde (steatite?)

2.1

2.2

2.3

Sigilli a stampo circolari con iscrizione indiana (2.1-2.10) e di tipo Arabian Gulf (3.1)

2.1 Susa Porfido verde (steatite?) 2.2 Tello (Girsu). Pietra tenera di coloro grigio-verde. 2.3 Ur Steatite invetriata. 2.4 Ur Steatite. 2.5 Ur Steatite. 2.6 Ur Steatite. 2.7 Ur Steatite invetriata. 2.8 Mesopotamia Steatite. 2.9 Mesopotamia Steatite.2.10 Mesopotamia Steatite. 3.1 Ur Steatite.

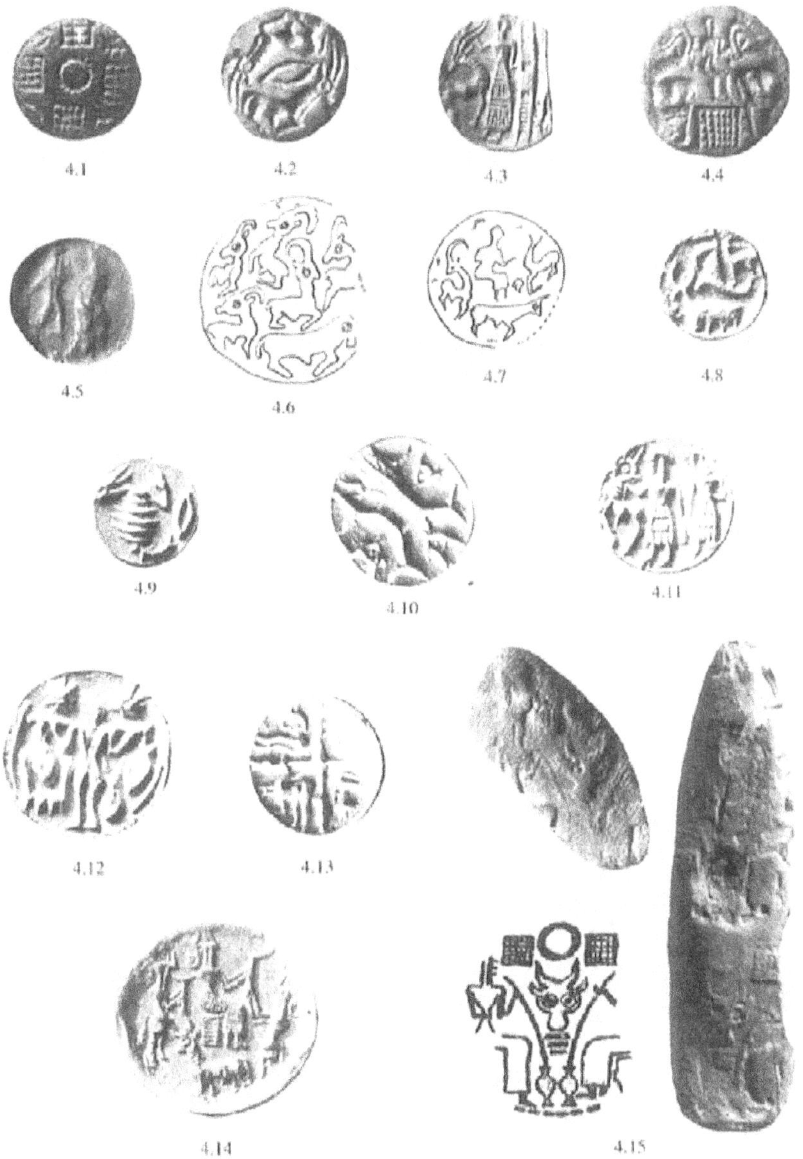

Sigilli a stampo circolari di tipo dilmunita

4.1 Ishchali Calcite. 4.2 Susa Steatite invetriata. 4.3 Susa Steatite invetriata. 4.4 Susa Statite invetriata. 4.5 Susa Steatite invetriata. 4.6 Susa Argilla. 4.7 Susa

Argilla. 4.8 Ur Steatite invetriata. 4.9 Ur Steatite. 4.10 Ur Steatite invetriata. 4.11 Ur Steatite invetriata. 4.12 Ur Steatite. 4.13 Ur Steatite invetriata. 4.14 Ur Steatite invetriata. 4.15 Ur. Argilla.

5.1

Tell Asmar Cylinder seal modern impression [elephant, rhinoceros and gharial (alligator) on the upper register][473] ibha 'elephant' Rebus: ib 'iron'. Ibbo 'merchant' (Gujarati). Alternative: కరటి [karaṭi] *karaṭi.* [Skt.] n. An elephant. ఏనుగు (Telugu) Rebus: *kharādī* ' turner' (Gujarati)

kāṇḍā 'rhinoceros' Rebus: *khāṇḍa* 'tools, pots and pans, and metal-ware'. *kāruvu* 'crocodile' (Telugu) Rebus: *kāruvu* 'artisan' (Marathi) *khar* 'blacksmith' (Kashmiri)

One side of a triangular terracotta tablet (Md 013); surface find at Mohenjo-daro in 1936. Dept. of Eastern Art, Ashmolean Museum, Oxford. *kamaḍha, kamaṭha, kamaḍhaka, kamaḍhaga, kamaḍhaya* = a type of penance (Prakrit)

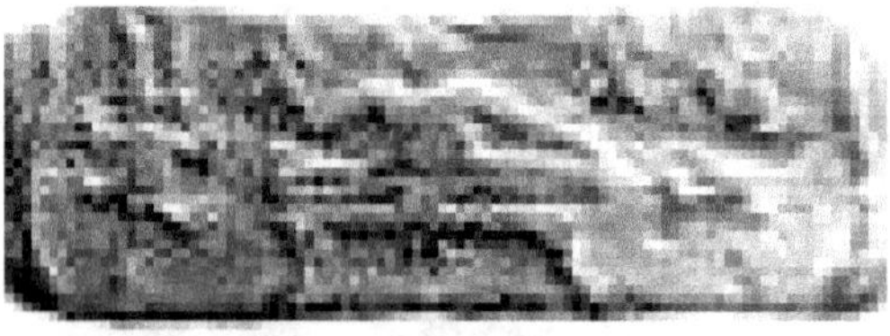

kamaṭamu, kammaṭamu = a portable furnace for melting precious metals; kammaṭīḍu = a goldsmith, a silversmith (Telugu) kãpṛauṭ jeweller's crucible made of rags and clay (Bi.); kampaṭṭam coinage, coin, mint (Tamil)

kamaṭhāyo = a learned carpenter or mason, working on scientific principles; kamaṭhāṇa [cf. karma, kām, business + sthāna, thāṇam, a place fr. Skt. sthā to stand] arrangement of one's business; putting into order or managing one's business (Gujarati)

5.3 Susa Steatite invetriata.

Cylinder seal carved with an elongated buffalo and a Harappan inscription circa 2600-1700 BCE Susa, Iran Fired steatite H. 2.3 cm; Diam. 1.6 cm Jacques de Morgan excavations, Susa Sb 2425.

"This cylinder seal, carved with a Harappan inscription, originated in the Indus Valley. It is made of fired steatite, a material widely used by craftsmen in Harappa. The animal - a bull with no hump on its shoulders - is also widely attested in the region. The seal was found in Susa, reflecting the extent of commercial links between Mesopotamia, Iran, and the Indus."[474]

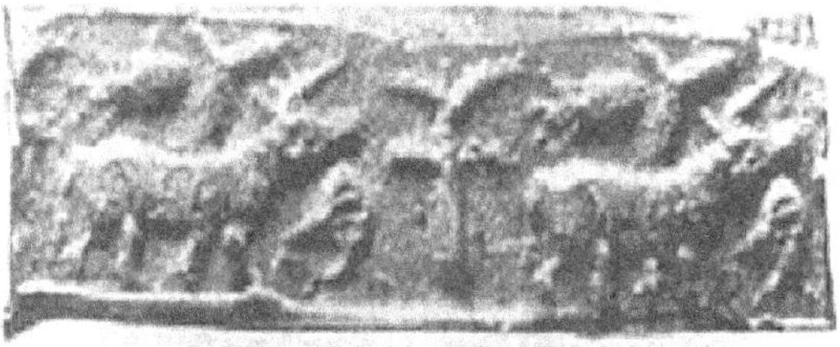

5.4

5.5

Sigilli a cilindro di tipo pseudo-indiano

5.1 Tell Asmar Steatite invetriata 5.4 Ur Conchiglia. 5.5 Mesopotamia. Apparentemente Integro

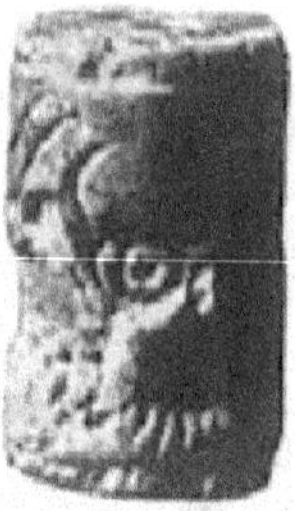

6.1

6.2

6.3

Sigilli a cilindro di tipo dilmunita

6.1 Susa Steatite inveiriata. 6.2 Susa Steatite.[475]

Seal  from Hamma. C. 2000-1750 BCE. Ingholt 1940: 62, pl. XIX.

Seal from Tello. Late 3rd millennium. During Caspers (Varint reading)

9851 Telloh

[Pierre de talc. Louvre, AO 9036. P. Amiet, Bas-relliefs imaginaries de l'Orient ancien, Paris, 1973, p. 94, no. 274...ils proviendrait de Tello, l'ancienne Girsu, une des cites de l'Etat sumerien de Lagash. Musee National De Arts Asiatiques Guimet, 1988-1989, *Les cites oubliees de l'Indus Archeologie du Pakistan*.]

Dilmun, sea of Magan, the power of the bull

Bahrain. Seal impression.Two bull-men standing before a podium. They raised a horned altar or table, which is surmounted by a crescent and sun-disc. Alsendi 1994, No. 115.

If the crescent is a stylized glyph comparable to the bottom part of the standard device, the rebus reading could be *sangaḍa* 'portable furnace'. Rebus: *jangaḍa* 'entrustment articles'. *jangaḍiyo* 'military guard who accompanies treasure into the treasury'.

arka 'sun' Rebus: erka = ekke (Tbh. of arka) aka (Tbh. of arka) copper (metal); crystal (Kannada) eraka, er-aka = any metal infusion (Ka.Tu.); erako molten cast (Tulu) *agasāle, agasāli, agasālavāḍu* = a goldsmith (Telugu)

ḍhangar 'bull' Rebus: *dhangar* 'blacksmith' (Maithili) *ḍangar* 'blacksmith' (Hindi)

खांडा [*khāṇḍā*] A division of a field. (Marathi) Rebus: *kāṇḍā* 'metalware' (Marathi)

karaṇḍa 'duck', 'water-pot' (Sanskrit) *karaṛa* 'a very large aquatic bird' (Sindhi) Rebus: करडा [*karaḍā*] Hard from alloy--iron, silver &c. (Marathi)

The pair of hieroglyphs flanking the 'partitioned square' glyph may

compare with the Kafajeh vase fragment showing Sin temple? The Meluhha word for the temple is *kole.l* Rebus: *kolami* 'smithy'; *kol* 'working in iron.' Alternative: करडा [karaḍā] *m* The arrangement of bars or embossed lines (plain or fretted with little knobs) raised upon a तार of gold by pressing and driving it upon the अवटी or grooved stamp. Rebus: करडा [karaḍā] Hard from alloy--iron, silver &c. (Marathi)

In the following two seals (Kjaerum 249 and 267), the glyphs may have the same rebus readings as on the Bahrain seal for the glyphs: crescent, sun, duck,

square. The additional glyphs on Kjaerum 267 are: 1. a harp-player: Glyph: *tambura* 'harp'; Rebus: *tambra* 'copper' (Pkt. Santali) 2. Sprout. *kolmo* 'sprout' Rebus: *kolami* 'smithy/forge'. The group of quadrupeds on Kjaerum 249 read rebus *pasaramu, pasalamu* 'an animal, a beast, a brute, quadruped' (Telugu) Rebus: *pasra* = a smithy (Santali).

Three bulls stand ranged one behind the other. A bull-man with a high head-

dress grasps one of them. Two small personages crouch before two of the bulls, one holding the horn of one of the animals (Kjaerum 249).

Kuwait-Failaka island. Many of the domed, circular stamp seals from Failaka (as from Bahrain) include references to bulls and to bull-men. A seated man plays a lyre, with three strings, in the shape of a small bull, standing on the back of a larger one, before whom stands a man wit a hammer or axe raised above its head. A fowl, podium, a branch and a crescent with a sun-disc can be seen (Kjaerum 267).

The island of Failaka (Kuwait bay) was part of Dilmun ca. 2nd millennium BCE.

The following 7 seals (Kjaerum 93, 228, 274, 143, 43, 242, 232) deploy unambiguous hieroglyphs which can be read rebus in Meluhha:

The hieroglyphs are:

- Dotted circles flanking a tree 1. Bead: kandi (pl. –l) necklace, beads (Parji). Ga. (P.) kandi (pl. –l) bead, (pl.) necklace; (S.2) kandiṭ bead (DEDR 1215). Rebus: *kāṇḍā* 'metalware' (Marathi) 2. Tree: kuṭhāru Rebus: kuṭhāru ‘armourer or weapons maker’(metal-worker), also an inscriber or writer. kuṭi ‘tree’ kuṭhi ‘smelter’.

- Monkey *Ta.* kōṭaram monkey. *Ir.* kōḍa (small) monkey; kūḍag monkey. *Ko.* ko·ṛṇ small monkey. *To.* kwṛṇ monkey. *Ka.* kōḍaga monkey, ape. *Koḍ.* ko·ḍë monkey. *Tu.* koḍañji, koḍañja, koḍaṅgů baboon. (DEDR 2196). kuṭhāru = a monkey (Sanskrit) Rebus: kuṭhāru ‘armourer or weapons maker’(metal-worker), also an inscriber or writer.

- Antelopes Type 1: *miṇḍāl* ‘markhor’ (Tōrwālī) *meḍho* a ram, a sheep (G.)(CDIAL 10120); rebus: *mẽṛhẽt, meḍ* ‘iron’ (Mu.Ho.) Antelope has head turned backwards. క్రమ్మర *krammara.* adv. Type 2: melh ‘goat’ (Br.); milakkhu ‘copper’ (Pali) Type 3: tagara ‘ram’ Rebus: tagara ‘tin’ damgar ‘merchant’ (Akkadian) Again. క్రమ్మరిల్లు or క్రమరబడు Same as క్రమ్మరు. krəm back’(Kho.) karmāra ‘smith, artisan’ (Skt.) kamar ‘smith’ (Santali)
- Flag on podium (hatched) *kōḍu* A leg of a bed, table, or chair. కాలు. (Telugu) koṭi banner, flag, streamer (Tamil) Rebus: *koḍ* ‘artisan’s workplace’. Alterntive: *Kur. kaṇḍō* a stool. *Malt.* kanḍo stool, seat. (DEDR 1179). Rebus 1: *kāṇḍā* ‘metalware’ (Marathi) Rebus 2: *kaṇḍ*, ‘a furnace, fire-altar’ (Santali)

- Duck/fowl *karaṇḍa* ‘duck’, ‘water-pot’ (Sanskrit) *karaṛa* ‘a very large aquatic bird’ (Sindhi) Rebus: करडा [*karaḍā*] Hard from alloy--iron, silver &c. (Marathi)

- Bucranium (Head of a bull) *mũh* ‘face’ Rebus: *mũh* metal ingot (Santali)

- Bull *ḍhangar* ‘bull’ Rebus: *dhangar* ‘blacksmith’ (Maithili) *ḍangar* ‘blacksmith’ (Hindi)

- Horned serpents *paṭam* , *n.* < *phaṭa.* ‘cobra's hood’ (CDIAL 9040). Rebus: ‘sharpness of iron’: *padm* (obl.*padt-*) temper of iron (Kota)(DEDR 3907); *patam* ‘sharpness, as of the edge of a knife’ (Tamil)

- Acrobats (leaping person) baṭi trs. To overturn, to overset or ovethrow; to turn or throw from a foundation or foothold (Santali) Rebus: baṭa = a kind of iron (G.) bhaṭa 'furnace' (G.) baṭa = kiln (Santali). bhaṭa = an oven, kiln, furnace (Santali) baṭhi furnace for smelting ore (the same as kuṭhi) (Santali)

- Rosette *karaḍa* -- m. ' safflower ' (Prakrit) Rebus: करडा [*karaḍā*] Hard from alloy--iron, silver &c. (Marathi)

- Sun arka 'sun' Rebus: eraka 'molten cast (copper)'

- Crescent-topped staff *sangaḍa* 'portable furnace'. Rebus: *jangaḍa* 'entrustment articles'. *jangaḍiyo* 'military guard who accompanies treasure into the treasury'.

A bull-man standing on a square podium grasps a bucranium in his hands; two antelopes, with their heads turned back, stand on either side (Kjaerum 93).

A nude man, flanked by two fowls, above the back of a bull, grasping one of its horns. A crescent-topped staff before the bull; a horizontal branch with two circles above and below the stem (Kjaerum 228).

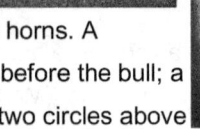

A bull stands at the lower register; a 'monster' with claws and three-fingered hands above it. A divinity sits on a square stool, reaching out towards a nude man. Behind the bull, an antelope; beneath it a hatched podium (Kjaerum 274).

Two bull-men facing each other, reaching out towards a crescent, standing raised on a hatched podium. Two horned beasts stand below the bull-men, horned serpents behind them (Kjaerum 143).

At the base, two bull-men on a hatched podium hold a standard; behind each of

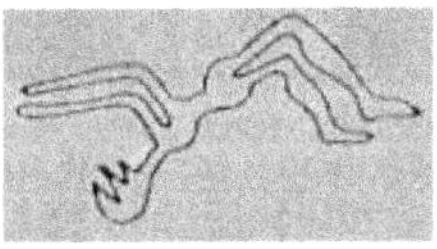

them is a rosette, like the rosette in the centre of the seal. To the right and left of the central rosette are two bulls, each with a monkey standing on its back, both granspinq a horn. Above the central rosette is an offering table from which two acrobats hang, turned on their backs. Is this analogous to a bull-leaping sequence over the bull's back? (Kjaerum 43).

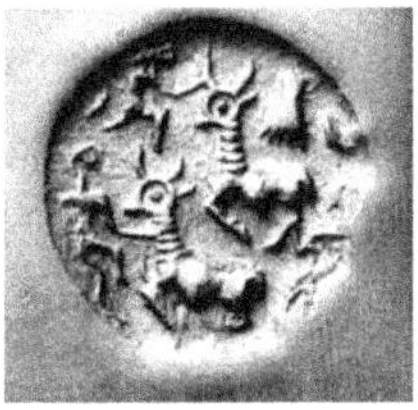

Two bulls stand with a man facing one of them and a smaller figure (a monkey?) grasping the horn of the other (Kjaerum 242).

A bull stands in the base of the seal, flanked by a rearing caprid and a snake. Above the bull a male figure is shown leaping (Kjaerum 232).

Seals of Saar, Bahrain

Many seals of Sumer, Elam and Mesopotamia and selected glyphs used on Kudurru reliefs, contain features reminiscent of themes depicted on the seals of the Sarasvati Sindhu civilization. Typical motifs are: rows of animals, combat, antelope or tiger with head turned, woman with thighs spread out, circle-and-dot, one-horned bull, hare, plant, snake, bird, fish. All these motifs have been explained as related to metallic weapons, in the context of the decipherment of Indus script pictorials and signs. In the Sumer, Elam and Mesopotamia motifs, there are clear images related to weapons and implements.

Many seals and seal impressions of Saar deploy Indus writing hieroglyphs.

Saar is a single-period Early Dilmun settlement, located on the northwest part of the island of Bahrain, founded ca. 2300 BCE. Artifacts found include copper fishhooks, bitumen nodules, and numerous shells from shellfish, including pearl oyster. The copper was produced in Bahrain; the bitumen imported from Mesopotamia. About 100 seals, used to seal packages, bales and jars, have been found at the Saar settlement, and 48 seals from the associated burial ground.[476]

***ḍhāla* 'shield' Rebus: *ḍhālako* 'large ingot'; *huḍa* 'ram' Rebus: *uḍu* 'boat, raft'**

Fig. 88; Susa, stamp seal from the Gulf, Teheran museum, MDAI, 43, no. 1717; an animal tamer wearing a skirt and grasping with one hand a goat-antelope with its head turned back and with its feet bound; with the other hand, the person holds a large object which looks like an architectural feature or shield. *ḍhāla* n. ' shield ' M. *ḍhāl* f. WPah.kṭg. (kc.) *ḍhā`l* f. (obl. -- *a*) ' shield ' (a word used in salutation), J. *ḍhāl* f. (CDIAL 5583).

Rebus: *ḍhālakī* = a metal heated and poured into a mould; a solid piece of metal; an ingot (Gujarati) Rebus: *ḍhālako* 'large ingot'

huḍa 'ram' *huṛeāl, huṛeār* m. ' the wild hill sheep or oorial ' Rebus: *uḍu* 'boat, raft'. Allograph: *uḍu* 'star, moon'.

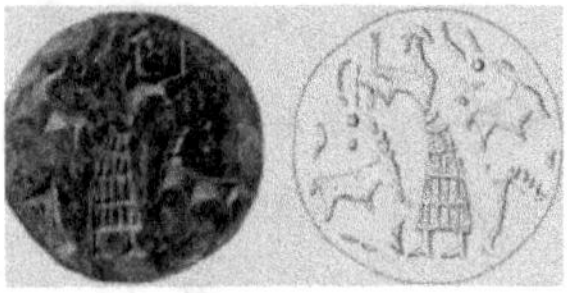

Saar. 3302:01. Mottled grey stone. Dia.2.9, height 1.1. Human figure with long legs. Oval shield? Horned animal looking back.

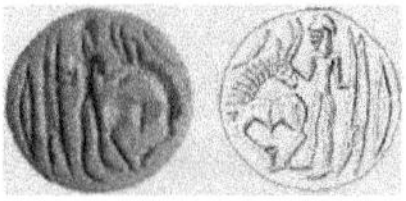

Saar. 1612:01 A man holds a shield. Antelope looks back. An oblong symbol in left field and a crescent in the right field behind the head of the animal.

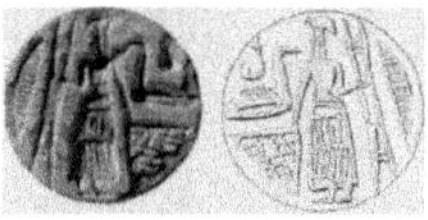

Saar. 4346:01. Dia 2.5 Ht 1.0 Standing male figure, holds a shield beyond which is a hatched, oblong motif (Large ingot?) His hand touches a triangular, hatched motif in bottom right field, below a long-necked, swimming bird with a sub-circular motif above its back, perhaps a pot or a plant.

Saar. G17:07:01 dia 1.11 ht 0.96. A bearded figure on a boat with an animal-head prow, holds an oval object (large ingot?). In the right field a plant motif with a hatched triangle above. In the left field, an antelope looking back.

Saar. 5510:15. Dia 2.2 ht 1.1. Male figure holding a long shield. Hatched rectangle linked to heads of two long-horned animals with ruffed necks. A palm-frond at the extreme edge of the seal.

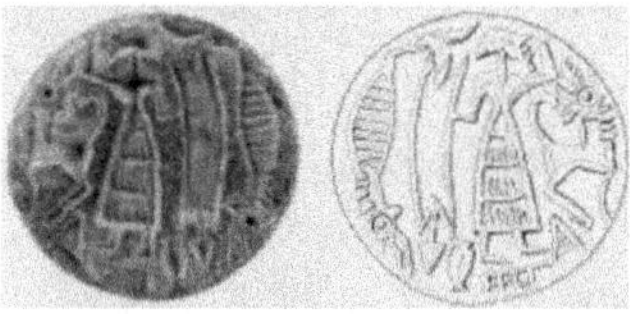

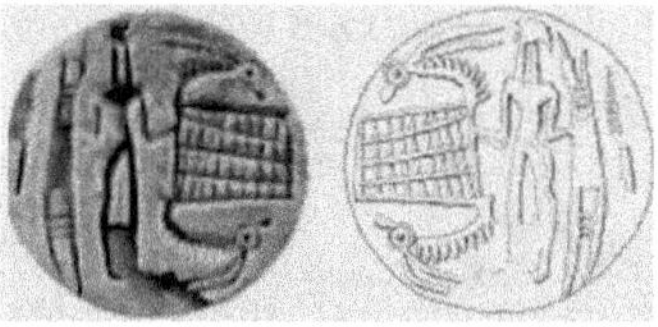

Saar. 5099:33. Dia 2.4 ht 1.2. Unusual red mottled stone. Man stands on a hatched platform with raised front, perhaps a boat with raised prow. One arm is raised above short-horned animal, with curly tail and claws on his hind-leg. Man holds large rectangular shield with a triangular spike, possibly a spear, protruding from the center of its lower edge. Three triangular motifs project from the top of it. A crescent lies above it, and below is a jar, between the shield and the man. In extreme right field is another composite animal with hatched body, possibly a scorpion, and gazelle's head.

Saar. 1853-99. Saar. 1853:97. Dark-grey clay. Reverse: string-impressions. Obverse: schematic human head on left, ladder-like motif on right (gate

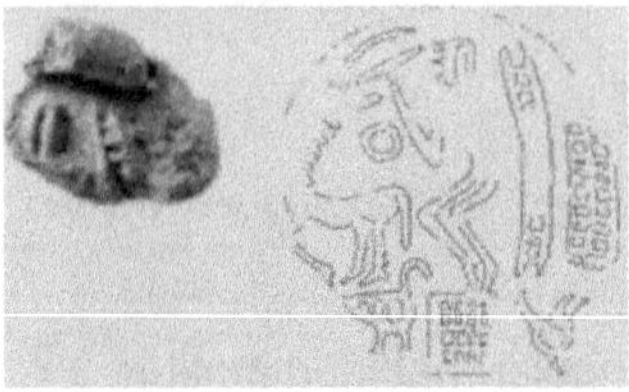

symbol?). The same impression appears on

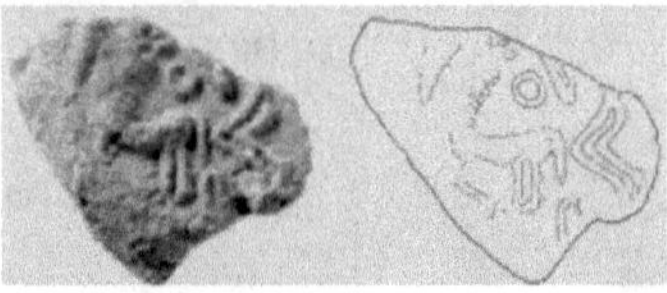

sealings 1853-96, 99, 100-106 and 109. "The drawing is a reconstruction based on all related fragments. The design can be reconstructed as follows: On the left, a standing horned animal with ruffed neck, facing left, with head turned back to center of seal, and a seated or squatting, nude, human figure who faces left, with one arm raised to the left. His feet rest on a hatched rectangle below him. To its left is a long-legged bird (duck?) with striped body, facing right, to its right is an animal head, above which are a shield symbol, and a ladder-like motif."

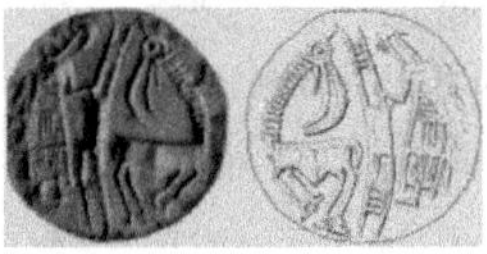

Saar. 4350:01. Dia 2.2 Ht. 1.22.Greystone. A figure holds a shield with two prongs at each end. Horned animal with ruffed neck, head stretched up and back.

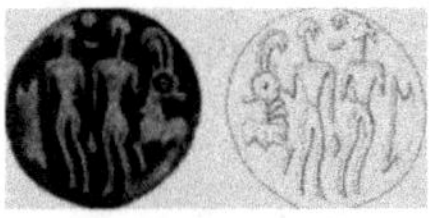

Saar. F18:33:15. Dia 2.2 ht. 0.9 Two men. Between their heads is a crescent with a possible sun above it. Animal with backswept horns. Shield-like object.

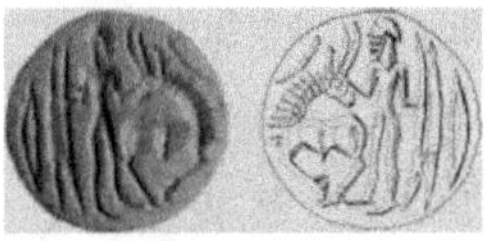

Saar. 1612:01. A person holds a shield. Antelope looks back.

Hieroglyphs to denote iron, anvil, mint

Saar seals with the glyphs: copulation, lizard and hatched triangle are explained in the context of repertoire of a smithy/forge:

kamḍa, khamḍa 'copulation' (Santali) Rebus: kammaṭa = mint, gold furnace (Telugu) *araṇe* 'lizard' Rebus: *airaṇ* 'anvil'.

meṭṭu 'hill' Rebus: *meḍ* 'iron' Alternative: *ḍāg* mountain-ridge Rebus: *dhangar* 'blacksmith'

Saar. Pale stone. G16:01:01 dia 2.0 ht 1.0. Standing male Erect penis. At right angles to him is a stylized female figure,legs wide apart, holding her feet in her arms, apparently engage in sexual intercourse with the male. On either side of her is a hatched triangle.

Saar. K16:29:08. Dia 2.47 ht. 0.75. A naked female figure, legs wide apart. To the left of her head is a lizard; to the right is an identified motif. (ingot?). Below her, at right angles to her legs is a male figure, head missing, holding his erect penis in his right hand, apparently about to enter her. In his left hand he holds a straw coming from a jar at his feet.

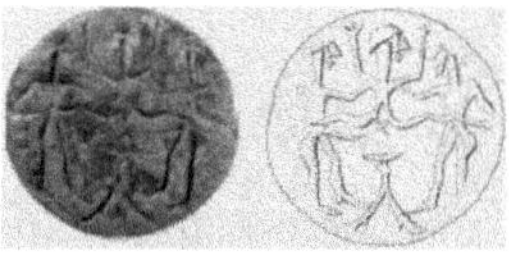

Saar. 4025:06. Dia. 2.45. Ht. 0.95. Central figure with upraised arms, legs splayed and a prominent vulva. Below her is a flat-topped stand with two hoofed legs. Standing males flank her. One has a large erect penis. *eraka* 'upraised arm' Rebus: *eraka* 'copper'.

Hieroglyph *khaṇḍa* 'divisions' Rebus: *kāṇḍā* 'metalware'

Saar. I14:20:10. Gable-backed rectangular seal. Very dark stone. 0.8x1.2x1.5. A couchant ruffed neck animal with upright horns. Above its back is a hatched square (4X7 squares). *huḍa* 'ram' Rebus: *uḍu* 'boat, raft'. *khaṇḍa* 'divisions' Rebus: *kāṇḍā* 'metalware'.

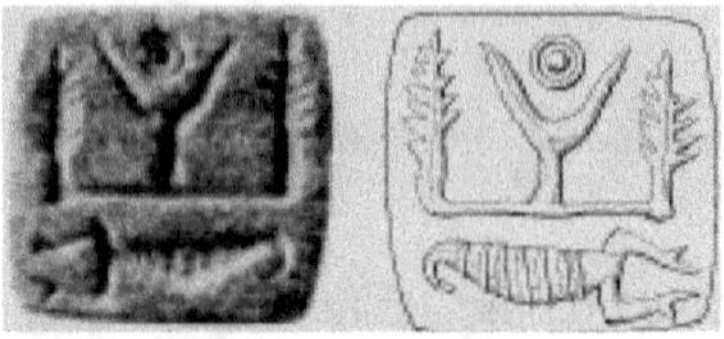

Hieroglyphs of a smithy catalog or repertoire: boat, smelter, mint, cast metal, metalware.

Saar. 6535:01. Square stamp seal.Greystone with crystalline inclusions. 1.56x1.56x0.6. Scorpion.Two palm-fronds flank a standard topped with a crescent, with a circle with central dot. *bica* 'scorpion' Rebus *bica* 'stone ore'. *kuṭi* 'tree' Rebus: *kuṭhi* 'smelter' dula 'pair' Rebus: dul 'cast metal'. *kammaṭa* 'coiner, mint, a portable furnace for melting precious metals (Telugu) *kandi* 'bead' Rebus: *khaṇḍā* 'tools, pots and pans and metal-ware'. *uḍu* 'boat, raft'.

Saar. 6580:01 Scorpion tail, three claws on foreleg of a rampant horned monster. Crescent on edge of seal. Male figure. meḍa 'neck' Rebus: meḍ 'iron' *mṛeka, melh* 'goat' Rebus: *milakkhu* 'copper'.Alternative: *meḍho* a ram, a sheep (G.)(CDIAL 10120) Rebus: *mẽṛhẽt, meḍ* 'iron' (Mu.Ho.)

Saar. 6581:01 dia 2.4 ht 0.95. Male figure holds back animal with ruffed neck and another animal with turned back. Below the man is another animal with ruffed neck.

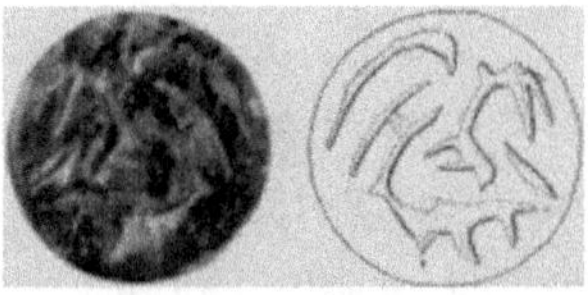

Saar. L18:27:07. Dia 1.8 ht 0.7. Persian gulf style. Difficult to interpret. Long-horned animal and possibly a second horned animal. Above the horns of the second animal, is a curved line with left end thickened. At right angles is an irregular line. (Ingots?)Two curved lines in upper right field, and a triangular mark in left field.

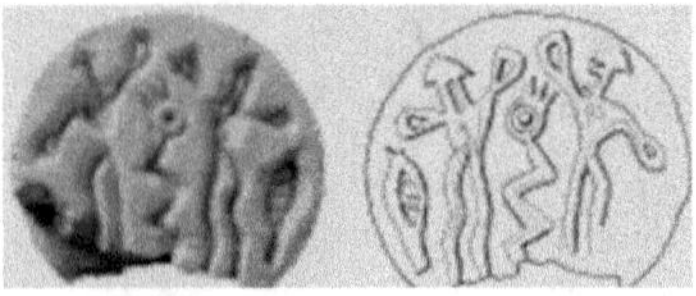

Saar. K16:29:13. Dia 0.9 ht 1.75. Schematic

design. Snake as a vertical zigzag with a beak-like antelope head. To either side is a stylized human figure with upraised arms. In the right field, a hatched motif, perhaps a fish.

Saar. 6583:01. Pale-grey steatite. Dia 3.01 ht.1.21. Antithetical bull with ruffed neck. Two antelopes flank a palm-frond. Each animal has a crescent above its back and a rosette/sun motif between its feet.

Metalware products of a forge

Hieroglyphs used on Saar and Failaka artifacts and their rebus Meluhha readings:

Saar. 1098:03. Ivory seal. Hatched square flanked by double-ended standard with crescent and sun (rosette, one with a drilled hole) at each end.

Saar. 5510:52 Seal impression. Goose-like bird looking right towards a palm-frond. Below the bird is a horizontal, hatched motif, perhaps the horizontal arm of a cross dividing up the surface of the seal.

khaṇḍa 'divisions', Rebus: *kāṇḍā* 'metalware'
kammaṭa 'crucible' Rebus: 'mint'
karaḍa 'safflower', *karaḍa* 'duck' Rebus: *karaḍa* 'hard alloy'
dula 'pair' Rebus: *dul* 'cast metal'

āra 'serpent' Rebus: *āra* 'brass'
meḍ 'step' Rebus: meḍ 'iron'
Alternative: *aḍi* 'foot' Rebus: *aṭai, aḍi* அடை 'anvil'
uṭu 'arrowhead', Rebus: *uḍu* 'boat
kuṭi 'drink' Rebus: *kuṭhi* 'smelter'.
tagara 'antelope, ram' Rebus: *damgar* 'merchant'
meḍho a ram, a sheep Rebus: *mẽṛhẽt, meḍ* 'iron'
ḍangar 'bull' Rebus: *ḍangar* 'blacksmith' (Hindi)
pattar 'trough' Rebus: *pattar* 'smiths' guild'

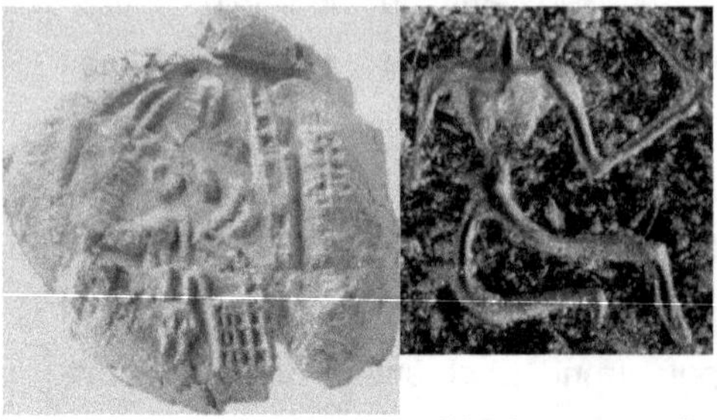

Saar. Seven separate impressions of the same seal are combined here to show the overall design (1853:97 et al. After Fig. 37, Crawford, 2000, p. 34). Saar. Pair of crossed animals (P18:33:16).

Glyph: tampur 'long-legged' (Santali) Rebus: Pa. Pkt. *tamba* -- ' red ', n. 'copper', Pk. *taṁbira* -- 'coppercoloured, red'; S.kcch. *trāmo, tām(b)o* m. 'copper'; G.*tābaṛ* n., *trābṛī, tābṛī* f. ' copper pot '; Pa. Pkt. *tamba* -- 'red ', n. 'copper' (CDIAL 5779). Hieroglyph *khaṇḍa* 'divisions' Rebus: *kāṇḍā* 'metalware'

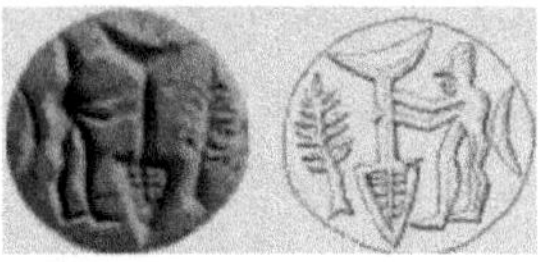

Saar. 2500:01 A standing figure holds a standard. This is a pole with a crescent at the top and a hatched triangle, apex down, at the base. Behind the figure is a crescent. At the far right edge is a tree or palm-frond.

uṭu Feather of an arrow; Arrow-head; Rebus: *uḍu* 'boat, raft'. *khōṇḍa* 'leafless tree' Rebus: *kõdā* ' to turn in a lathe.' *kammaṭa* 'portable gold furnace' Rebus: *kammaṭa* = mint, coiner'(Telugu)
ḍhālako = a large metal ingot (G.) *ḍhālakī* = a metal heated and poured into a mould; a solid piece of metal; an ingot (Gujarati)

Saar. P19:01:10. Dia 2.6 ht 1.32. Central divine figure, on stool, with headdress, holds in one hand a long straw drinking out of a pot at his feet. Below him is a scorpion. In front of him is a kneeling gazelle above damaged bird (duck?) motif. An identified symbol lies above the gazelle's head. A smaller figure stands at the back of the seated figure; he holds a crescentic object with a hatched triangle at one end. Below this is an offering stand, above which is a rosette or sun.

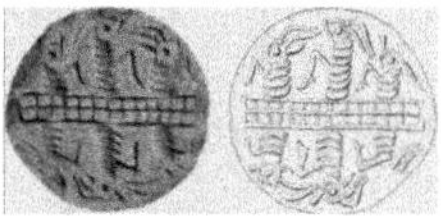

Saar. 1024:06 Hatched square. 6 antelope heads.

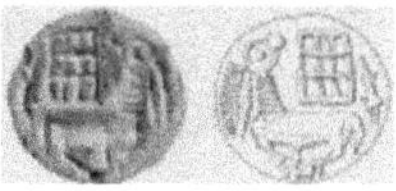

Saar. 228:02. Crouchant quadruped. Hatched square.

Fig. 99; Failaka; no. 174 impression; two bull heads emanating from a chequered square; two persons drinking; altar and sun; bull in the lower register

Fig. 100; Failaka no. 83 impression; a person flanked by two bulls, each standing atop a chequered square

Fig. 104; Failaka; no. 89 impression; bulls; antelopes; person; chequered square; trough?

Fig. 101; Failaka no. 82; entwined serpent in the middle; two antelopes standing atop a chequered rectangle; two bulls in lower register.

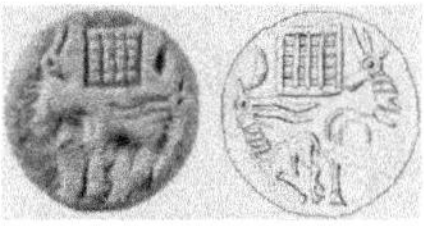

Saar. 1853:30. Two quadrupeds back-to-back. Hatchd rectagle and crescent (bun-shaped ingot?)

Saar. 1159:05. Seal impression. Possibly part of a token with hemispherical back, originally pierced for suspension. Hatched square (4X6 squares), with necks of two short-horned animals protruding from top, one looking left and one right. A three-toed rampant monster is at the left. Below is the head of animal with long back-swept horns facing left. The motif of two necks of two short-horned animals protruding from top of a hatched square is part of the images on K16:53:02 and 6539:01.

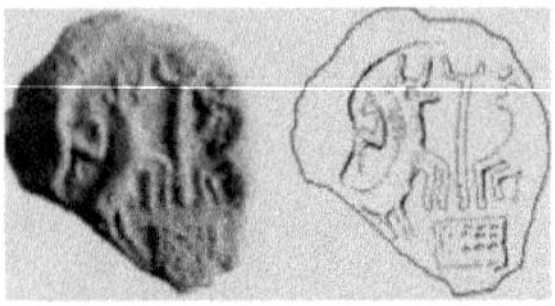

Saar. 5065:01. Standard with crescent on top, above a hatched square. To left is a rampant, horned, male animal. Second, rampant animal to right. Goose or duck in left field, looking over shoulder to the left.

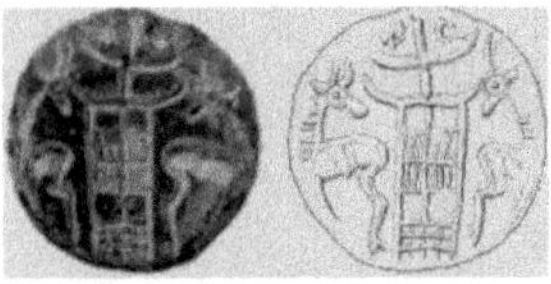

Saar. K16:08:05. Dia 2.4 ht. 1.20. Two short-horned animals. Between them is a rectangular structure, partly hatched, possibly a door or altar. The top of the rectangle is decorated with a double-crescent standard. Drilled motifs in each of the two upper crescents.

Saar. 4306:07. Dia 2.2 Ht. 0.9. Hatched rectangle in center (7X6 squares) flanked by two figures; with second, smaller one above it (4x10 squares). Behind one person is a jar with a straw in it. Part of fringed motif below the rectangle, probably a crab.

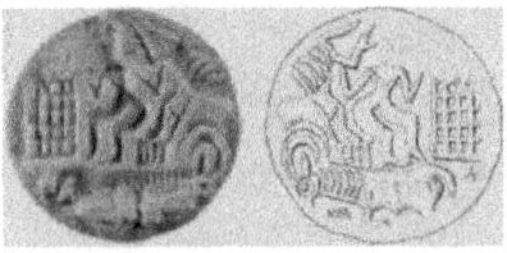

Saar. 5168:01. Dia 2.54 ht 1.1. Person with horned headdress on a vertically-hatched seat. A standing person touches the waist of the seated person with a stick/sword. Another figure behind. In the lower field is a standing bull.

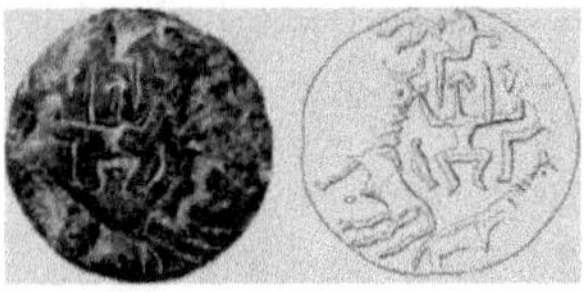

Saar. 2667:03. A figure seated on a vertically-hatched seat and a high back. A hatched rectangle to left and a scorpion claws to the right. An animal stands below with long, back-swept, notched horns. Four vertical lines below the neck.

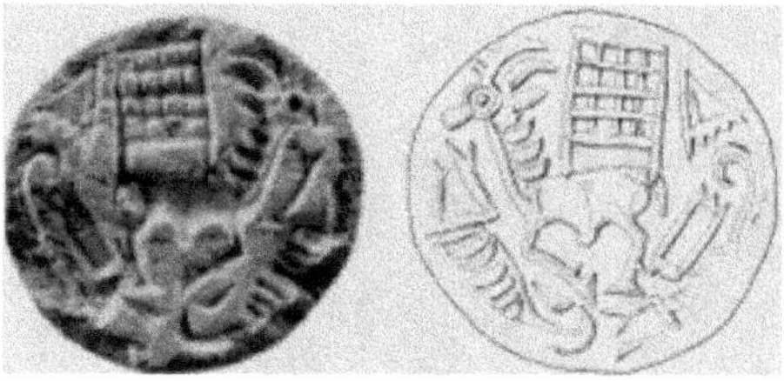

Saar. 5104:07 dia 2.4 ht 1.2 A horned animal with ruffed neck. A hatched square (4X4 squares) on its back. Possible human foot to the right of this. Rectangular motif on eft fielw with inverted scorpion below it. A second scorpion in right field. A crescent in the curve of the tail of the right scorpion.

Saar. 2109:01. Shiny whitestone. Central circle with dot in the middle. Encircled

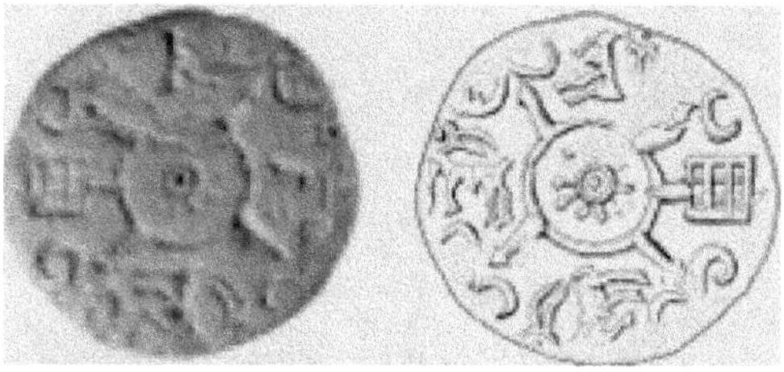

in turn by a rosette of lines and dots. Another circle surrounds the first. Radiating from this are four lines, each with a spike and a double volute at the end, on the outer edge of the seal. Each quadrant so defined contains a motif. One shows a hatched square attached to the central circle by a line; the others each contain a standing, horned, male

animal.

Comparable hieroglyphs of antithetical antelopes

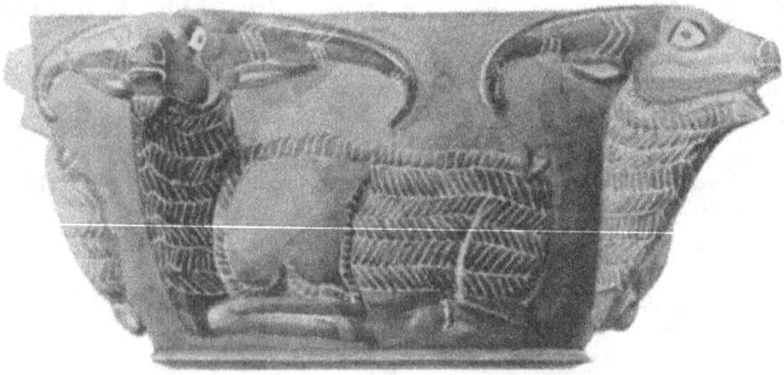

Ishchali -- Reconstruction of Mouflon Bowl (Ovis orientalis) fragment (Ish.34:117). (From water-color painting by G. Rachel Levy). Plate 32.

Ishchali -- Bronze statue of a four-faced goddess from the 'Serai' (a private house). Plate 28.

Ishchali. Side view of the bronze statue. Plate 29.

Ishchali. Side view of the bronze statue of a four-faced god from the 'Serai'. Plate 27.

"The largest of the statues is 17.30 centimeters high and shows a god in standing position, his right foot placed on the back of a reclining ram, his right hand holding a curved weapon...The statue of goddess measures 16.20 centimeters in height..."[477]

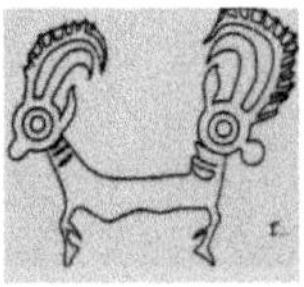

Fig. 96f: Failaka no. 260 Double (Antithetical) antelopes joined at the belly; in the Levant, similar doubling occurs for a lion.

Tell Abraq. Gold objects recovered.

pṛṣṭhá n. ‘ back, hinder part ’ Rigveda; *puṭṭhā* m. ‘ buttock of an animal ’ (Punjabi) Rebus: *puṭhā*, *puṭṭhā* m. ‘buttock of an animal, leather cover of account book’ (Marathi) tagara 'antelope' Rebus: damgar 'merchant'. This may be an artistic rendering of a 'descendant' of a ancient (metals) merchant. Hieroglyph: Joined back-to-back: pusht ‘back’; rebus: pusht ‘ancestor’. pus̱ẖt bah pus̱ẖt ‘generation to generation.’

Wadi Suq-period gold and/or electrum animal plaques from Bidiyah (a) and Qattrah (b-d).[478]

Failaka no. 267; harp with taurine sound-box

The ram could also be denoted by *ṭagara* ‘antelope’; takar, *n.* [தகர் T. *tagaru*, K. *tagar.*] 1. Sheep; ஆட்டின்பொது. (திவா.) 2. Ram; செம் மறியாட்டுக்கடா. (திவா.) பொருநகர் தாக்கற்குப் பேருந் தகைத்து (குறள், 486). Rebus: *ṭagara* ‘tin’.

Ligatured Meluhha hieroglyphs

A parallel tradition is noticed in ligatured sculpture and ligatured hieroglyphs

which are signature-tunes of Indus writing by Meluhha artisans: three-faced: tiger, bovine, elephant, 6.76 cm (h); three-headed: elephant, buffalo, bottom jaw of a feline.[479] These glyphs of elephant, buffalo and tiger occur on Mohenjo-daro Seal m0304.

Two-faced sculpture. Indus tradition.[480] The Hindu continuum in temple sculptures and iconographic tradition exemplifies[481] the representations of divinities with multiple arms and carrying

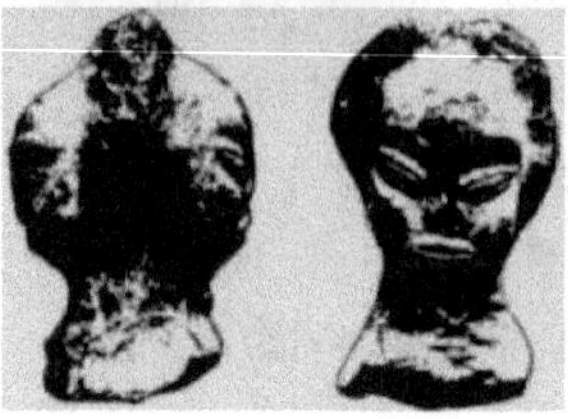

weapons and implements – a parallel with the Sumerian-Elamite-Mesopotamian tradition of depicting weapons-carrying divinities on cylinder seals. *Śvetāśvatara Upaniṣad* III.5 refers to corporeal representation of *Śiva:*

yā te rudra Śivā tanūraghorā 'pāpakāśinī/tayā nastnuvā santamayā giriśantābhicākaśthi:

Trans. That body (*tanū*) of yours O Rudra which is auspicious (*Śivā*), Not terrifying (*aghorā*), looking not evil (*apāpakāśinī*), With that most beneficent body Appear (before) us O Dweller in the mountains.

The ideas expressed in this text can be traced to *Taittirīya Samhitā* (4.5.1c) and *Vājasneyi Samhitā* (16.2).

Parel (Bombay-Maharashtra). Siva Sadasivamurti, fifth century. Deccan trap (Plaster of Paris copy), Bombay, Prince of Wales Museum, 90. Courtesy of the American Institute of Indian Studies.

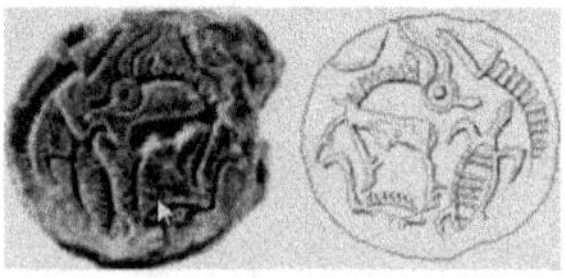

Saar. 6538:01. Upper left, a scorpion. Below it a turtle. A horned ruffed neck animal looks back. At bottom right, a bird with feathered back (duck?). In the upper right field, a crescent.

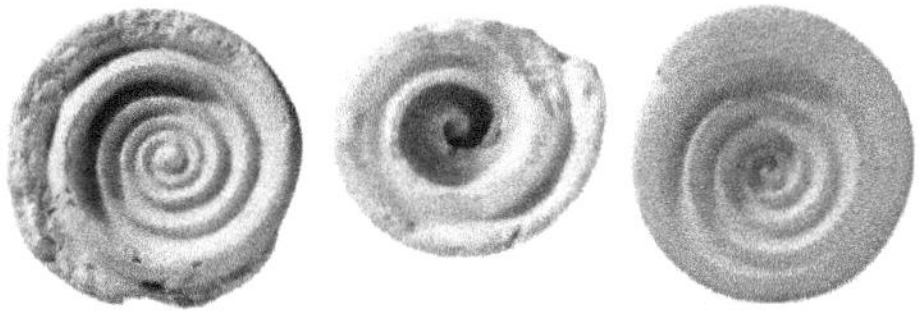

Saar. Q20:22:07 Shell-seal Saar.7001:29.Saar. 6672:04 Apex of conch shell (lambis truncate). Dia. 2.9 ht 1.3

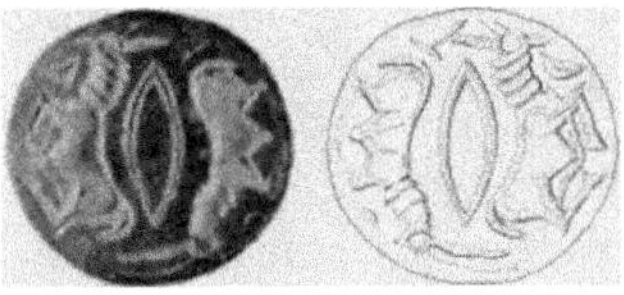

Saar. 5059:04 dia 2.21 ht 0.53. Central lozenge motif (Large ingot?). Horned animals with ruffed necks on either side. Identical example from Susa Harper et al 1992, p. 119, fig. 78.

Saar. 6580:05. Dia 2.4 ht 1.0. Male figure. A horned animal with ruffed neck looks back. To the left the man holds a seated monkey-like creature, jar motif between their heads.

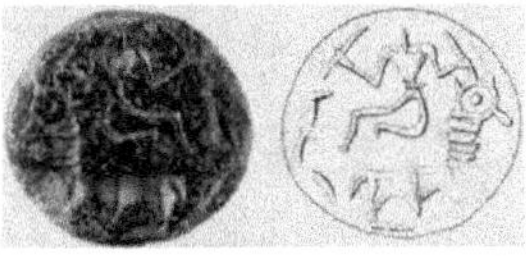

Saar. 2070:05. Man holds a straw coming out of a jar below. Animal below.

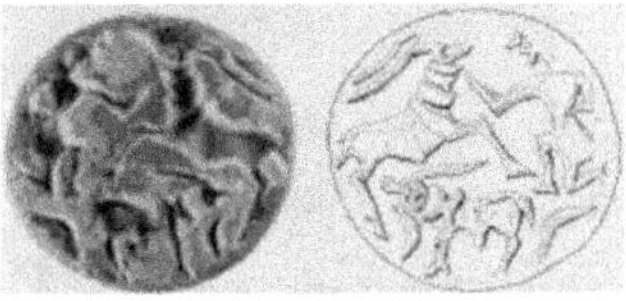

Saar. 5147:01. Dia 2.0 ht 0.88 Kneeling man. Leaping animal with a ruffed neck. Below and between them is another, smaller, long-horned animal. Crescent in lower left field and another in lower right.

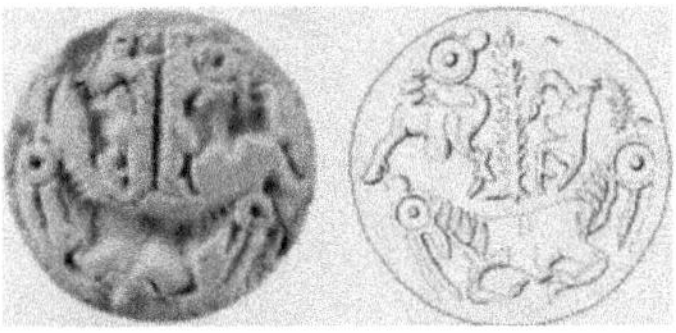

Saar. 5099:32 Dia 2.5 ht 1.3. Two antithetical antelopes joined back-to-back, look up at to animals on either side of a palm-frond.

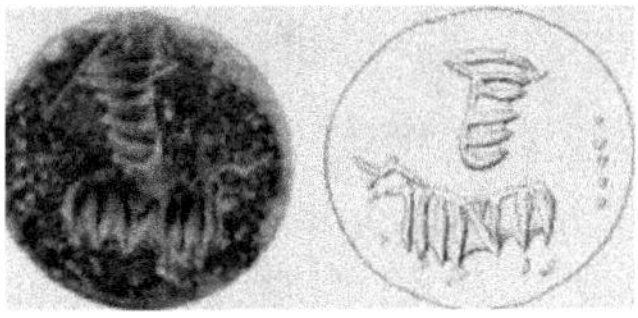

Saar. 5506:05. Dia 2.3 ht 1.05. Bull with vertically striated body. Second striated motif above its back at right angles to it, possibly another animal. String of five small triangular holes in left field.

Saar. 5510: 21. Dia 2.7 ht 0.9.Twins carrying a jar between them. A long-horned

ruffed neck animal, looking back. The right-hand figure drinks through a straw from another jar. A crescent lies on the edge of the seal between the heads of the twins. The motif of twins is comparable to the twins which appear on many Dilmun seals.

Saar. 5774: 01. Dark-grey steatite. Dia 2.2 ht 1.08. Two seated men drink through straws from a jar. Foot motif below the jar. Between their faces is another jar with down-curving straws in it.

Saar. 6087:10. Pale-grey steatite. Dia 1.9 ht 0.85. Horned animal with ruffed neck faces palm-frond. On left, a monkey-like creature.

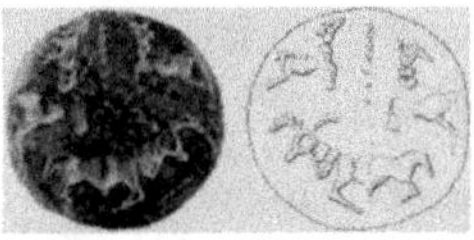

Saar. 5546:02. Dia 2.29 ht 0.65. Animal with downward curving horns. Above his back are two more horned animals flanking the remains of a palm-frond.

Saar. 2088:01. Two horned animals facing each other, flanking a fringed stalk, stylized palm tree. At the base, a scorpion facing right. *tamar*, 'palm tree, date palm' the rebus reading would be: *tam(b)ra*, 'copper' (Prakrit) tagara 'antelope' Rebus: damgar 'merchant'.

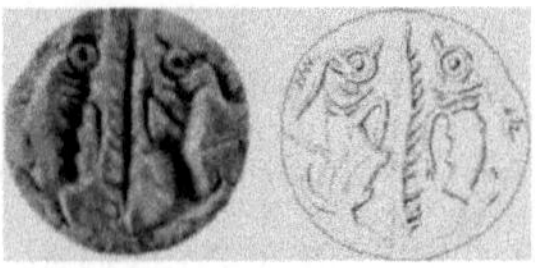

Saar. 5040:01 Dia 2.34 Ht 1.24. A central palm-frond or stylized tree, with a rampant horned animal on either side with back-swept fringed horns and flicked-up tails.

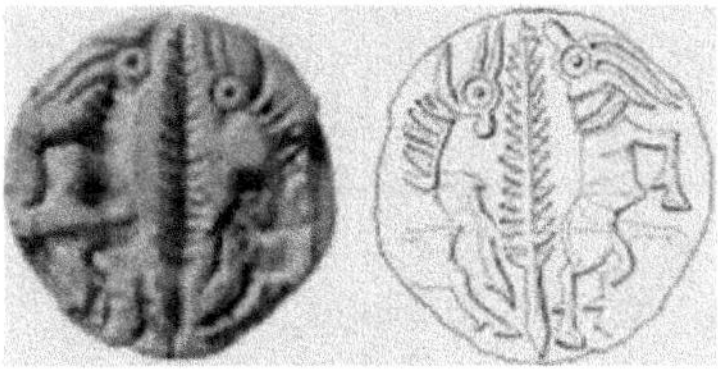

Saar. F18:33:01. Creamy stone. Dia 2.1, Ht. 1.86. Two horned animals rampant on either side of a tree or branch.

Saar. 2535:02. A seated figure. Holds a straw which comes from a jar on a stand at his feet. On the left, a standing figure with a tiered robe holding an object (fan?) above the pot.

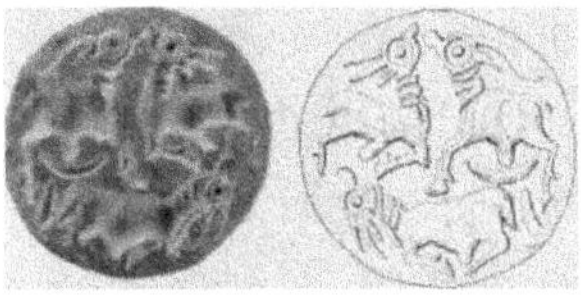

Saar. 2535:03. Horned animals with ruffed necks. Two are facing each other, the third is couchant below them.

Saar. 2171:01.Animal with ruffed neck. A broken standing figure in a short skirt. A tree/branch motif in the right field behind the neck of the animal.

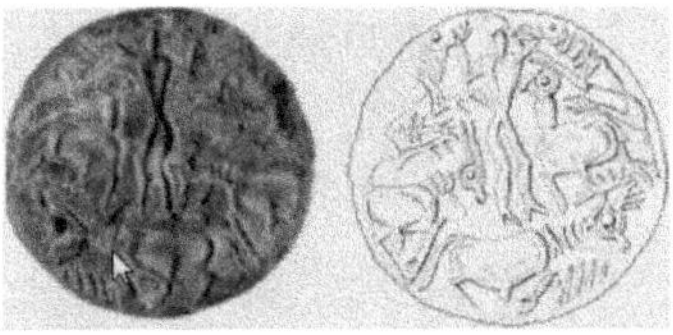

Saar. 2570:01. A figure grasps the neck of a monstrous creature with claws and possibly a lion's mane. Two other horned animals on either side of his legs. A third stands beneath his feet.

Saar. 2535:01. An incised cross divides the seal into four quadrants. Each contained head of ruffnecked animal.

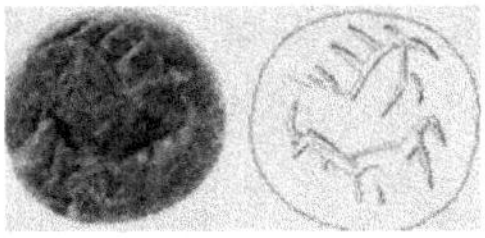

Saar. 2622:05. Two stylized horned quadrupeds, one inverted above the other.

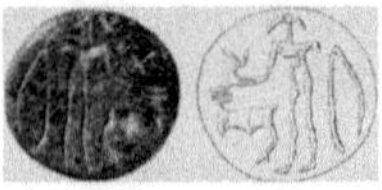

Saar. 3041:01. Unusual, bow-legged human figure with raised arms. Bull. Above its back is a bulbous motif. Below the feet of the central figure is a second horned animal. Above this, and to the left of the main figure, is a second seated human figure. A third figure, above and at right angles to the bow-legged man, has one leg raised and one arm extended.

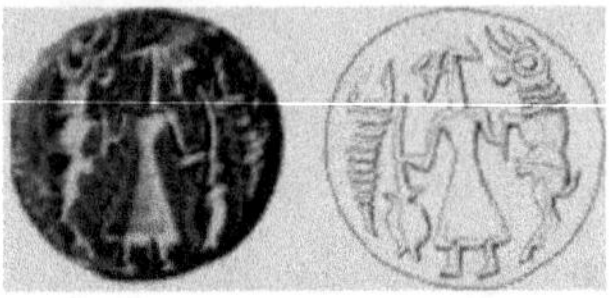

Saar. 3515:09. Dark Greystone. Human figure holds a straw in a jar. Vertical scorpion. Foreleg of a rampant bull is held by the man.

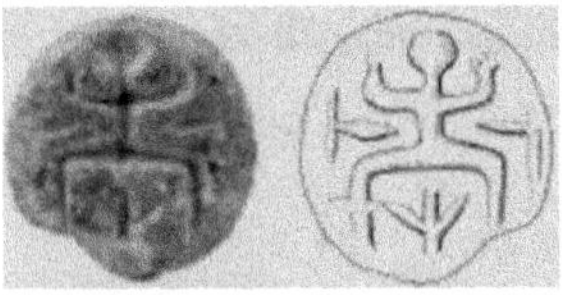

Saar. 4139:01. Schematic human figure with arms raised, legs apart. Plant motif between the legs. Unidentified motifs on either side. kolmo 'sprout' Rebus: kolami 'smithy, forge'.

Saar. 4025:14. Two registers. Top register shows a kneeling figure. Ruffed neck animals on either side. Lower register shows a second kneeling figure flanked by ruffed neck animals. The wavy, long horns divide the two registers.

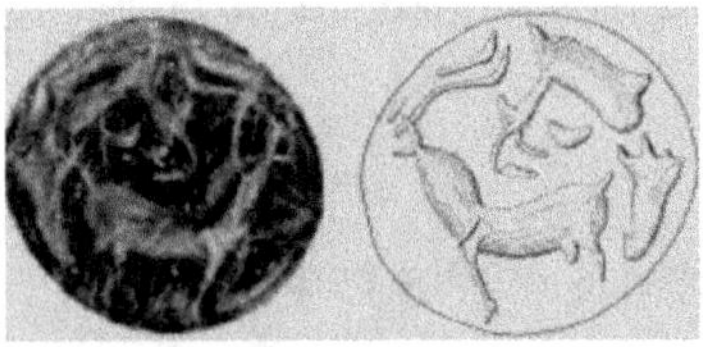

Saar. 4300:01. Greyish mottled stone. Long-horned animal. A second, smaller animal, with curved horns lies inverted over the back of the first, its head to the center. A crescent in field between the animals. A foot motif.

Saar. K16:53:10 Male flanked by two antelopes. One antelope looks back towards a crescent in the right field. Below this is a damaged foot motif.

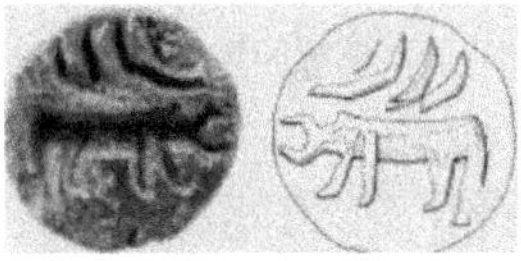

Saar. 4197:03. Mottled greystone. Dia 1.9 Ht 1.5. Stylized, horned quadruped (bull?) with three crescent-shaped symbols above its back (ingots?)

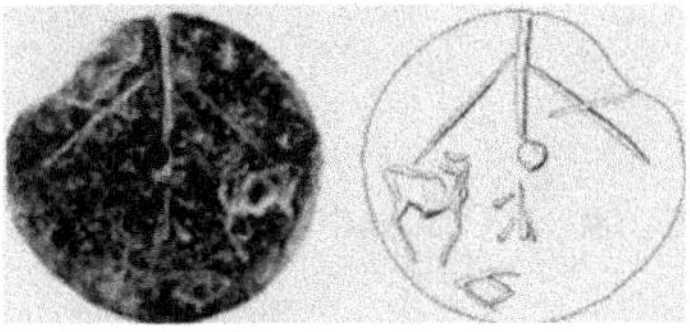

Saar. 4306:01. Dia 2.35 Ht. 0.68. Animal with ruffed neck, to right of roots of tree. Lozenge shape (fish?) below and to left of fore-legs of animal. Above are one vertical and two diagonal lines, one on either side of the vertical.

Saar. 4306:04. Dia 2.26 Ht. 0.4. Denticulated line around circumference, area

within it divided into four by deeply incised cross. Two incised rectangles, on inside the other in the center. A crab in each quadrant, with thin fringe-like legs, two have three legs on each side, two have five. Each has long pincers pointing towards center of the seal.

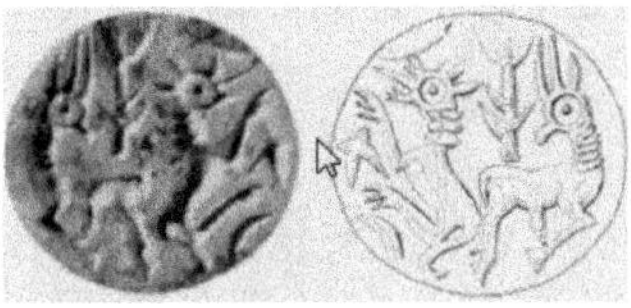

Saar. 4361:01 dia 2.43 ht 1.05. Two animals flanking a tree with crescent-shaped top. One animal has feet with large claws. Below its back legs and above its head are crescents; a four-pointed motif lies between its front and back legs.

Saar 4741:11 Cylinder seal. Creamy steatite. Length 3.05 dia 1.75 (top). Horizontal crescent with a spike in the center divides two registers. 1. Two men in tiered skirts, seated on either side of a jar, drinking through straws; a crescent in the field between the straws. 2. Two men hold another standard between them, also topped with a rather angular crescent.

kammaṭa 'portable gold furnace' Rebus: *kammaṭa* = mint, coiner'(Telugu) *kuṭi* 'drink' Rebus: *kuṭhi* 'smelter'. *ḍhāḷako* = a large metal ingot.

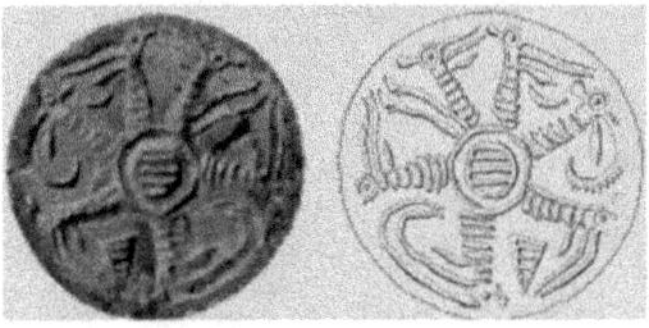

Saar. 2144:01. A naked figure with raised arms astride on an equid-like quadruped with long, ruffed neck (one horn?). Star, a vertical line topped by an open crescent containing a circle.

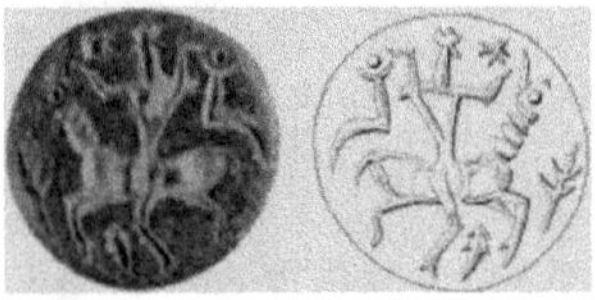

By the figure's knee is a fish, and in front of the animal a plant motif. *āra* 'six' Rebus: *āra* 'brass'. *meḍho* a ram, a sheep (G.)(CDIAL 10120) Rebus: *mẽṛhẽt, meḍ* 'iron' (Mu.Ho.)

Saar. G17:18:02 dia 2.7 ht 1.25. A wheel of six animal heads joined at the base of their necks to a hatched central circle. Filler motifs between the heads are: a hatched triangle, two wavy lines and a crescent.

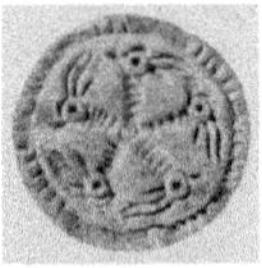

Saar. 7008:5. Creamy steatite. Dia 2.64 ht 1.24. A rotating design of five long-horned animal heads, with long, ruffed necks, joined at the center by a circle.

Saar. K16:29:03. Dia 2.03 ht 0.96. Five standing bearded figures and holding hands. Above the figures are: a crescent, six-pointed star on either side of it. Possibly a guild of artisans/merchants.

Saar. 2126:01. Seal impression. Hemispherical piece of grey clay. Reverse: Convex, with finger-prints and textile impression. Obverse: Four stylized, deeply incised, horned heads, possibly of bulls. In rotation, horns facing towards the outer rim.

Saar. K16:29:16. Four horned animals with ruffed necks.

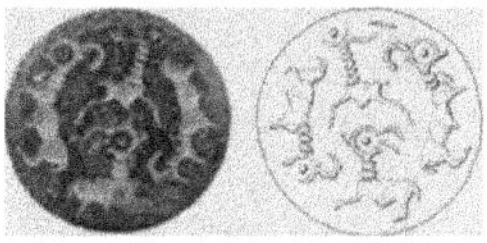

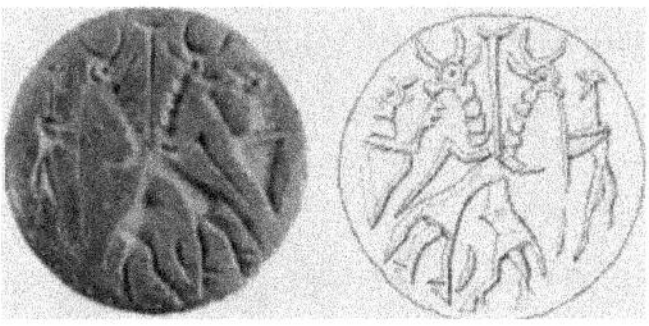

Saar. F18:33:16. Two rampant crossed horned animals. Between the animals' feet is an illegible motif, possibly a fish or an ingot. Between their heads is a standard topped with a crescent. In the left field is a person holding a spear. In the right field is a wedge-shaped motif with an animal head and raised fore-limb protruding from the top.

Sea impressions from Saar

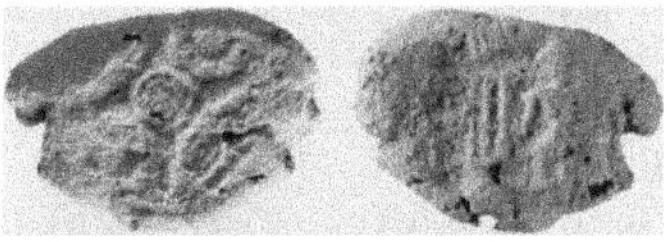

Saar. Tag impressed with two different seals (2570:11; 2.2x3.2cm)

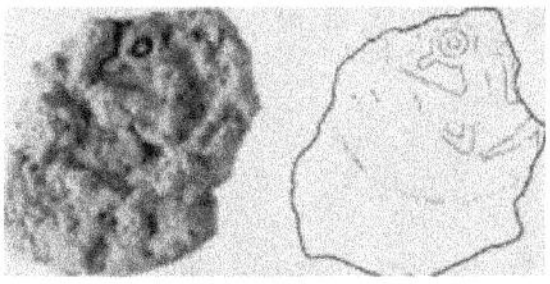

Saar. 1042:17. 2.6x1.8x0.8 Reverse: faint string-impression. Two fragments of yellow/green clay. Obverse: a horned animal looks backwards. Below is a possible second animal. To its right is a possible human figure.

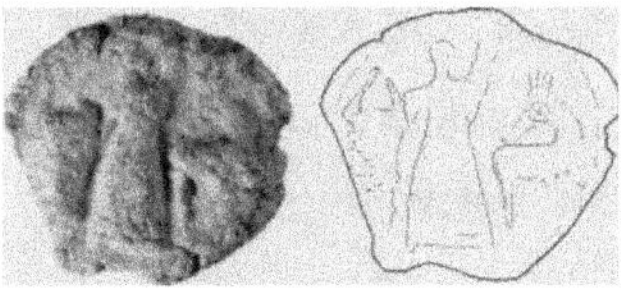

Saar. 1029: 02. 2.6x2.8x1.2 Hemispherical piece of hard, baked, red/organge clay. A standing figure. To the left of the figure is a scorpion. To the right is a horned animal, looking back.

Saar. 1042:01. 1.8x1.4x0.9. Fragment of yellow/green hardened clay. Upper torso and head of a man. In his raised hand, he appears to beholding the nose of a short-horned animal.

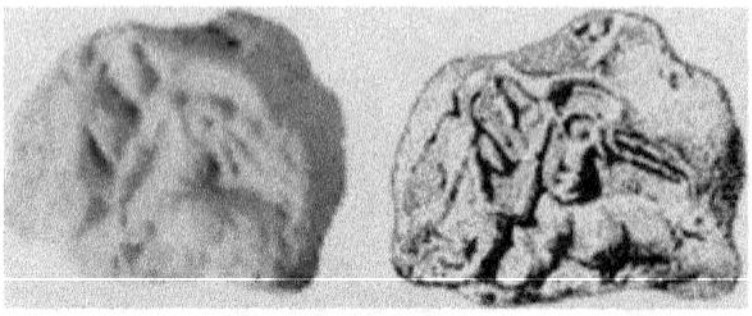

Saar 1042:18 1.8x2.1x0.75. Light-grey hardened clay. Reverse: knot impression. Obverse: two horned animals, rampant, on either side of a turtle or tortoise. A rosette or star is in the field above the head of the tortoise. Found in association with a cooking-pot.

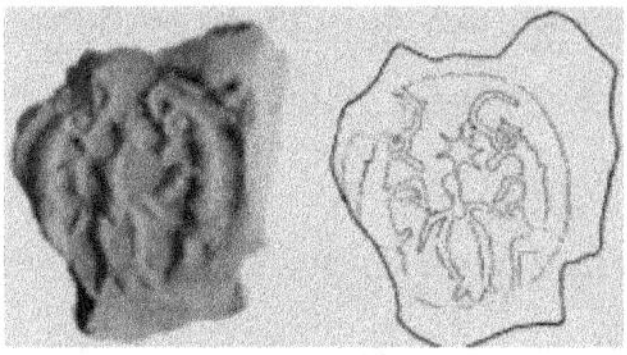

Saar. 1042:19. 2.2x2.4x0.75. Light-grey, hardened clay. Reverse: Parallel string-impressions. The very well-defined design is identical to that on 1042:18, 20, 21 and 22. Found in association with cooking pot 1042:14.

Saar. 1042:20. 1.2x1.9x0.7 Yellow/green clay. Reverse: Knot-impression. Obverse: A turtle or tortoise between the lower limbs of two rampant animals with horns. This is the same design that appears on fragments 1042:18, 19, 21, and 22. Found in association with cooking pot 1042:14.

uṭu Feather of an arrow; Arrow-head *uṭu* 'raft, boat'. Saar. 6539:01. Seal impression. "Oval disk, hard pinkish clay. Impressed on either side with different seals, each design virtually a mirror-image of the other. Side 1: An arrow-head, pointing up, inside a square. To the left of the square, a palm-frond. Above and below the square, curved lines, possibly crescents (ingots), the lower one upside-down (ingot). From the right edge of the square protrude the curved necks of two animals, heads missing. Side 2: The impression is at a diagonal to that on the first side and is a mirror image of it. An arrow-head, pointing down, inside a square. To the left, traces of a palm-frond, this time upside down. Above and below the square, the same crescents as o the first side. From the right side of

the square protrude the curved necks of two animals. The left-hand head is missing. From the same pair of seals as K16:53:02. A unifacial token with the same design was found at Qala'at al-Bahrain (Beyer 1989, p. 154, No. 284), and there is a seal from Failaka with the same design again (Kjaerum 1983, No. 52)."

Saar. K16:53:02. Both sides have a seal impression. See details above in reference to Saar. 6539:01. Seal impression.

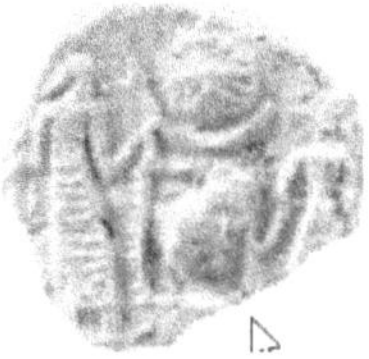

Saar. 5143:03. Two standing figures one with arms raised. Both touch a rectangular, fringed square with concave top, perhaps a podium. Above the square is a crescent, the horns of which enclose a star. Five other sealings from same seal: see 5143:02.

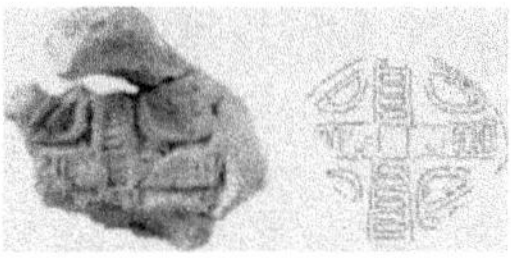

kaṇḍ 'furnace, fire-altar' (Santali) Rebus: *kāṇḍā* 'metalware, tools, pots and pans'. Saar. 5143:15. The design is divided into four fields by a cross. Arms of cross formed by rectangle filled by striations. A triangle is visible in each of the upper fields.

Comparable motif on Sibri seal, though the four streated arms are shown in X-shape:

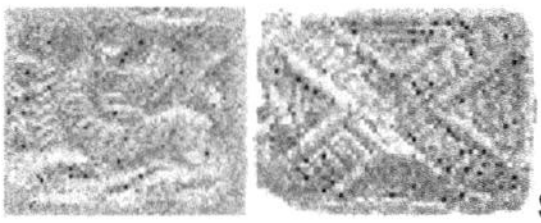
sb1 Seal Sibri.

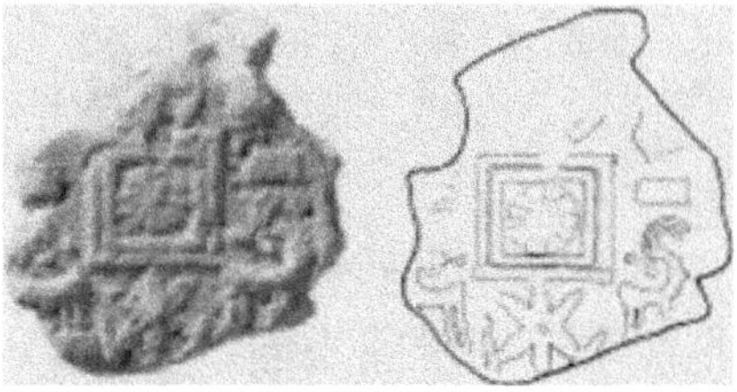

Saar. 2141:01. In the center a rosette framed by a square, a six-pointed star below the square, and a standing horned animal on either side of it. Above the horns is an unidentified motif.

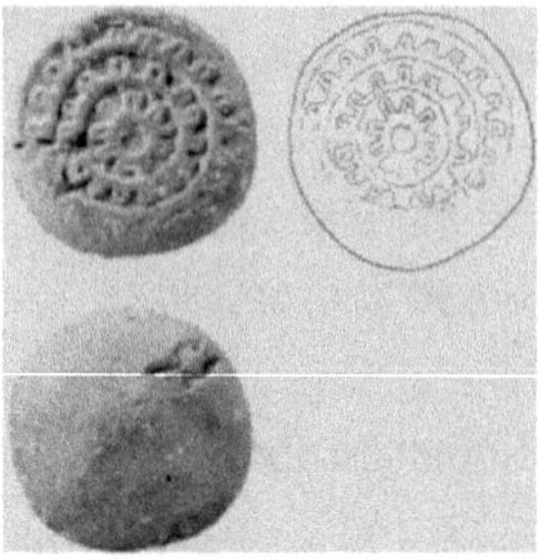

Saar. 2665:06 Seal impression. Three concentric circles, each with loops on outer edge; nine on central circle, fourteen or fifteen on the middle one, and on the outer the impression is too shallow to say. From the same seal as 5500:27. Also identical in design to a bifacial example from the Barbar temple (Beyer 1989, p.154, no. 284).

Seal 5500:27. Seal impression.

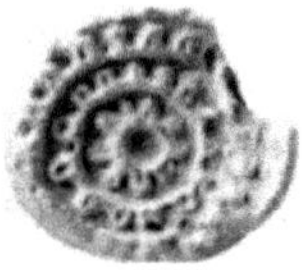

From the same seal as 2665:06

Saar. 2171:02. A tree or fond, a standing male holding a standard topped by a crescent on its back with a rosette or sun above. Another figure to the other side of the standard.

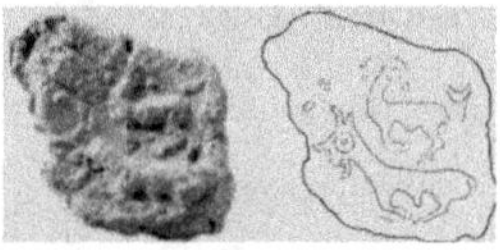

Saar 4197:01 3.3x2.4x1.05. Kneeling, male, horned quadrupet, possibly a bull, facing left. Above him a smaller, standing quadruped, facing left, looking back. To the upper right is the raised arm of a standinghuman figure, the left, unidentified motifs.

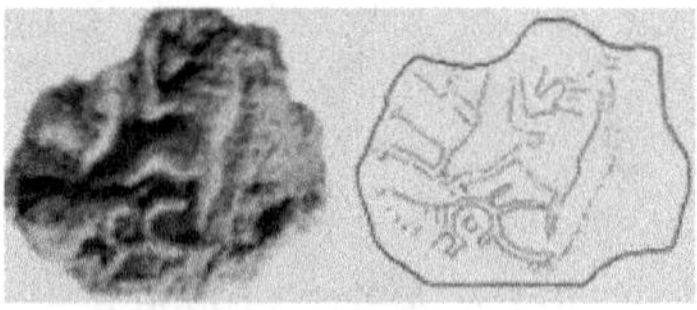

Saar. 1042:23. Upper right quadrant of a circular seal impression, a seated monkey-like creature on the right, facing left towards a short-horned animal. Below them is the head and neck of a possible bull.

Saar. 1045:01. Reverse: Deep string-impression. Obverse: A standing male figure in a skirt, facing right, arms held out

to either side. To the right, he touches the nack of a horned animal, which looks back over its shoulder at the man. A palm-frond or branch appears in the field between the man and the animal.

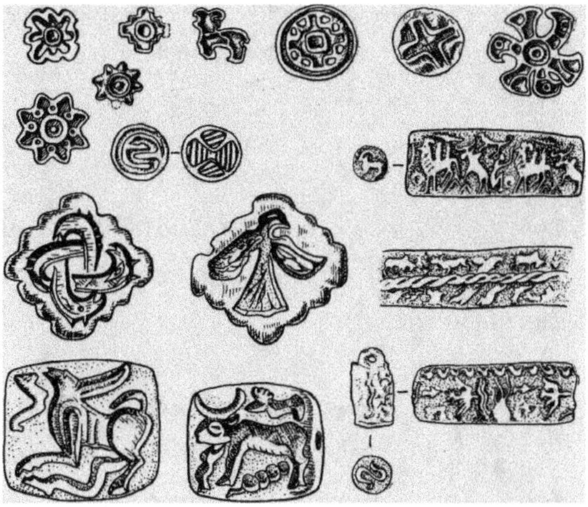

Bactria: tablet depicting an animal with its head looking back; similar pictorials are seen in seals at Chanhudaro (Mackay 1943: pl. L1). క్రమ్మరు *krammaru.* [Telugu] v. n. To turn, return, go back. Rebus: karmāra 'smith, artisan' (Skt.) kamar 'smith' (Santali) kol 'tiger' Rebus: kol 'working in iron'.

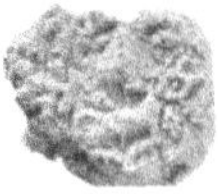

Saar. 1133:15.Reverse: knot-impression. Obverse: Seated figure on left. Short-horned animal, perhaps bull.

Saar. 1040:01 Pair of antelopes. Palm-tree, rising above the body of a scorpion.

Saar. 1853:18. Palm-tree. Seated person. Antelopes looks back. Crab.

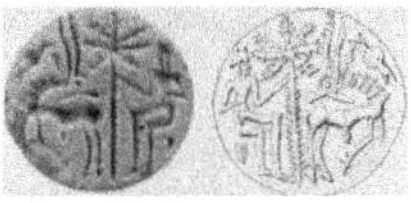

Saar. 2051:06 Two antelopes with backs turned, flanking a palm tree.

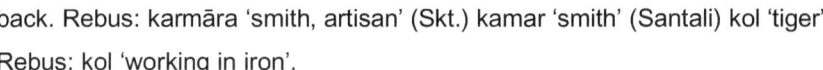

Saar. 1870:18 A man holds the horns of a

bull (?) and of a horned animal. In the field are a monkey-like creature, a jar, crescent and possibly a second jar. Below his left arm is another crescent.

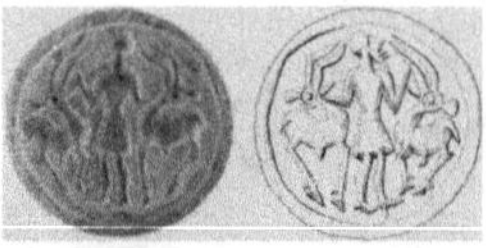

Saar. 1580:01. A person flanked by two antelopes looking back.

Saar 1841:01

Saar. 2051:06. Two quadrupeds looking back, flanking a palm-tree. Two ingots also flank the tree, above the backs of the animals.

Saar. 1870:18. A man. Bull (?) below him back-to-back with a quadruped. In upper left field is monkey-like creature, below man's right arm is a jar. In upper right field is cresent and possible second jar. Below his left arm is another crescent (ingot?)

Fig. 102; Failaka no. 126; antelopes flanking a line (standard?)

Fig. 103; Failaka no. 206; serpents held in the hands. *āra* 'serpent' Rebus: *āra* 'brass'. *mũh* 'face' Rebus: *mũhe* 'ingot'. *kūdī* 'twig' Rebus: *kuṭhi* 'smelter'.

Fig. 105; Failaka no. 204; is the person seated on a bull?

Stamp seal. Saar necropolis, Bahrain excavations 1988, Tumulus 122. Early Dilmun, c. 2000 BCE Chlorite or steatite 1.2x2.6 cm. Manama, Bahrain National Museum, Acc. No.

2626-2-90. Alsendi, 1994, no. 134; Stamp seal. Madinat Hamad necropolis. Bahrain excavations 1987-88, Tumulus 3. Early Dilmun, c. 2000 BCE. Chlorite or steatite .8x2.1 cm. Manama, Bahrain National Museum, acc. No. 2720-2-90; Stamp seal. Dar Kulayb necropolis, seson and grave unspecified. Early Dilmun, c. 2000 BCE. Chlorite or steatite 1/3x2/2 cm. Manama, Bahrain National Museum, main store. (Source: Harriet EW Crawford, Michael Rice, 2000, Traces of paradise: the archaeology of Bahrain 2500 BCE to 300 AD – an exhibition at the Brunei Gallery, Bahrain national museum, p. 101)

Stamp seal. Qal'at al-Bahrain, Danish excavations 1965 (520.ALX), Northern city wall. Early Dilmun c. 2000 BCE. Chlorite or steatite 1.3x2.1 cm. Manama, Bahrain National Museum, acc. No. 52-2-90; Bibby 1967, fig. 4d. (p.102)

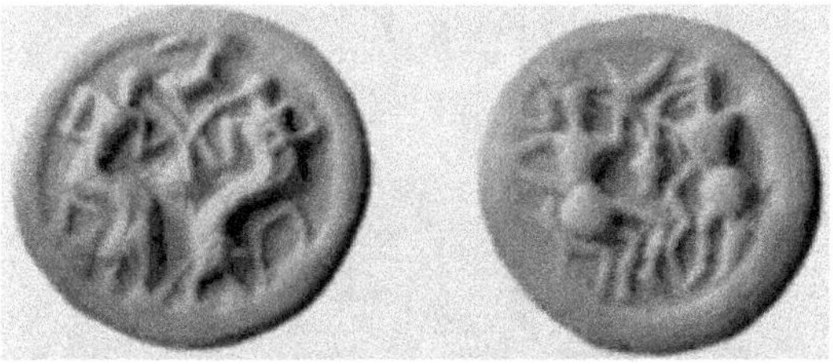

Stamp seal. Ali necropolis. Bahraini excavations 1981-82. Manama, Bahrain National Museum, acc. No. 3892-2-91.10. (p.102)

"The adaptation of Harappan motifs and script to the Dilmun seal form may be a further indication of the acculturative phenomenon, one indicated in Mesopotamia by the adaptation of Harappan traits to the cylinder seal." (Brunswig et al)[482]

Indian *sprachbund* contacts with Sumer, Elam, Mesopotamia

In terms of cultural history, chronology, artefacts (beads, jewellery), pottery and seals found from archaeological sites in the two areas are well-attested.

"...the four examples of round seals found in Mohenjodaro show well-supported sequences, whereas the three from Mesopotamia show sequences of signs not paralleled elsewhere in the Indus Script. But the ordinary square seals found in Mesopotamia show the normal Mohenjodaro sequences. In other words, the square seals are in the Indian language, and were probably imported in the course of trade; while the circular seals, although in the Indus script, are in a different language, and were probably manufactured in Mesopotamia for a Sumerian- or Semitic-speaking person of Indian descent..." (Hunter)[483]

The acculturation of Meluhhans (probably, Indus people) residing in Mesopotamia in the late third and early second millennium BC, is noted by their adoption of Sumerian names (Parpola, Parpola and Brunswig 1977: 155-159). "The adaptation of Harappan motifs and script to the Dilmun seal form may be a further indication of the acculturative phenomenon, one indicated in Mesopotamia by the adaptation of Harappan traits to the cylinder seal." (Brunswig et al, 1983, p. 110)

Stamp seal with a seated figure, animals, and landscape (left) and impression (right), mid-to-late 3rd millennium B.C. Eastern Iran. Lapis lazuli; W. 4 cm (1 5/8 in.); L. 3.1 cm (1 1/4 in.); Thickness 2.5 cm (1 in.). Trustees of The British Museum, London BM 1992-10-7, 1. "This stamp seal, with a wide perforated handle at the back, was originally almost square but, because of damage, the bottom corners are missing. Formerly two figures faced each other. Only the face, one shoulder, and one arm survive of the figure on the left (of the impression). The arm is raised and holds a tall cup. On the right is a man shown frontally with head in profile, a prominent nose and long hair hanging down his back with one lock falling beside the face. His legs are folded beneath him and covered with a skirt while his forearms lie parallel to his legs with his hands held palm to palm beneath his chest. Between the figures is a large drill hole. Above this is a horizontal line with short vertical strokes extending from it and four rows of semicircular notches. This may represent a fenced enclosure or clouds and rain. To the right is a tadpole-like creature. On the right side of the seal a goat faces left with long horns, a triple zigzag beard, and a short tail. Below and facing right is a zebu with horns shown frontally and a tail raised over its back. The scene can be related to imagery found on a copper "standard" from Shahdad in southeastern Iran, "Intercultural Style" vessels, as well as seals from the Harappan civilization. Comparisons with this material suggest that the seal originates from within the culture of southeastern Iran. During most of the third millennium B.C. western Iran was largely under Mesopotamian domination. The majority of seals are often hard to differentiate from the Early Dynastic, Akkadian, and Ur III glyptic of Mesopotamia. Occasionally, seals are marked by stylistic and iconographic peculiarities that lead us to recognize them as having been made in Elam (southwestern Iran). A different phenomenon is illustrated by the presence at Susa of a few seals from Bactria and the Gulf Region. These seals had very little influence on Elamite glyptic and appear as a result of commercial exchange. The compartmented seals are widely distributed throughout Iran although the overwhelming majority comes from western Central Asia."[484]

"Dilmun is a trading post on the 'Lower Sea'. In Mesopotamian mythology, Dilmun is the land of immortality, a favourite meeting place of the gods, which was visited by the hero Gilgamesh in his search for everlasting life. Inscriptions indicate that the ancestors of the Sumerians came from Dilmun, and it was here that they learnt the art of writing. We agree with S.N.Kramer's observations identifying Dilmun with the Sarasvati-Sindhu (Indus) valley. The God Enki is said to have given his son Inzak dominion over Dilmun. On the Lagash tablet (ca. 2520 BC) is recorded: "The ships of Dilmun from the foreign lands brought me woods". A document of ca. 1800 BC refers to an expedition "to Dilmun to buy copper there'. Sargon of Assyria (710 BC) notes that "he had received presents from the King of Dilmun, a land which lies like a fish, 60 hours away in the midst of the sea of the rising sun".[485]

An Assurbanipal clay cylinder states: Dilmun ki śa qabal tāmtim śaplīt (Dilmun is in the midst of the lower sea) (D.D. Luckenbill, Ancient Records of Assyria, *ARAB*, II 970. A Ungnad, *ZA* 31 (1917): 34, 1.9. That Dilmun was a continental coastland may be surmised from Sargon II's great Display inscription: bīt-ia-kin śa kiśād nār marrati adi pāt Dilmun (Bīt-Iakin which (extends) from the bank of the brackish river to the border of Dilmun)(Luckenbill, *ARAB*, 54 = 82 =99). Sargon II's inscription states: Upēri śar Dilmun śa mālāk 30 bēru ina qabal tāmtim śa nipih śamśi kīma nūni śitkunu narbasu (Upēri, king of Dilmun, whose resting place is 30 double hours away like a fish in the midst of the ocean of the rising sun) (Luckenbill, *ARAB*, 41,70). During the reign of Sargon of Assyria, Dilmun and Magan are stated to be "on the farther side of the lower sea" and there is also a reference to the "sea of Magan" (J.Muhly, *Copper and Tin*, p. 226; W.F. Leeman, *Foreign Trade*, p. 81, n.11; M. Weitemeyer, *Acta Orientalia*, 27 (1964): 207; E. Weidner, *AfO*, 16 (1953): 5, 1.42). The timber for the boats in Bahrain always came from India. The name of the Meluhha-boat is magilum (*Enki and the World Order* 128).[Boats which plied on the Sindhu river are called mohanna.]

"The Ninevite Gigamesh Epic, composed probably at the end of the second millennium BC, has Utnapishtim settled "at the mouth of the rivers", taken by all commentators to be identical with Dilmun." (W.F.Albright, The Mouth of the Rivers, *AJSL*, 35 (1919): 161-195).

The mouth of the rivers may relate to the Rann of Kutch/Saurashtra lying at the mouth of the Sindhu and Sarasvati rivers. In the Sumerian myth *Enki and*

Ninhursag, which recounts a Golden Age, paradise is described: "The crow screams not, the *dar*-bird cries not *dar,* the lion kills not... the ferry-man says not 'it's midnight', the herald circles not round himself, the singer says not elulam, at the outside of the city no shout resounds." The cry of the sea-faring boatmen in Indian languages on the west-coast is: ēlēlo !

Lines 123-129; and interpolation UET VI/1:

"Let me admire its green cedars. The (peole of the) lands Magan and Dilmun, Let them come to see me, Enki! Let the mooring posts beplaced for the Dilmun boats! Let the magilum-boats of Meluhha transport of gold and silver for exchange...The land Tukris' shall transport gold from Harali, lapis lazuli and bright... to you. The land Meluhha shall bring cornelian, desirable and precious sissoo-wood from Magan, excellent mangroves, on big ships The land Marhashi will (bring) precious stones, dushia-stones, (to hang) on the breast. The land

Magan will bring copper, strong, mighty, diorite-stone, na-buru-stones, shumin-stones to you. The land of the Sea shall bring ebony, the embellishment of (the throne) of kingship to you. The land of the tents shall bring wool... The city, its dwellin gplaces shall be pleasant dwelling places, Dilmun, its dwelling place shall be a pleasant dwelling place. Its barley shall be fine barley, Its dates shall be very big dates! Its harvest shall be threefold. Its trees shall be ...-trees."

Meluhha carried out bead production on a phenomenal scale resulting in the finds of millions of paste beads, thousands of agate, carnelian beads. The tomb at Tell Abraq had 600 beads including those made of lapis lauli, etched carnelian and agate, shell, paste and serpentine, almost all from Meluhha.

Ivory seal. Tell Abraq. Ibex and antelope flank a twig, scorpion, hooded-snake. *bica* 'scorpion' Rebus *bica* 'stone ore'. *kūdī* 'twig' Rebus: *kuṭhi* 'smelter'. *meḍho* a ram, a sheep (G.)(CDIAL 10120) Rebus: *mẽṛhẽt, meḍ* 'iron' (Mu.Ho.) *āra* 'serpent' Rebus: *āra* 'brass'

Steatite Dilmun seal from around 2350 BC, New National Museum, Manama, Bahrain, Middle East.[486]

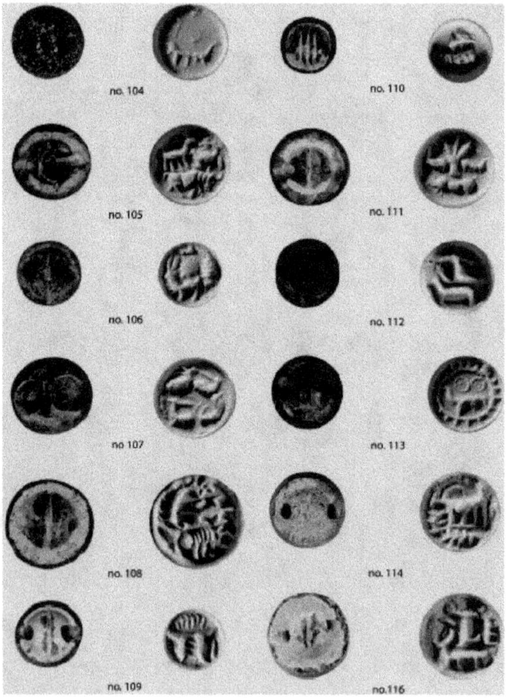

Modern Impression of a stamped seal: hunters and goats, rectangular pen (?), early 2nd millennium BCE.Gulf region (ancient Dilmun)Steatite or chlorite.H. 1/2 in. (1.27 cm). Gift of Martin and Sarah Cherkasky, 1987 (1987.96.22)

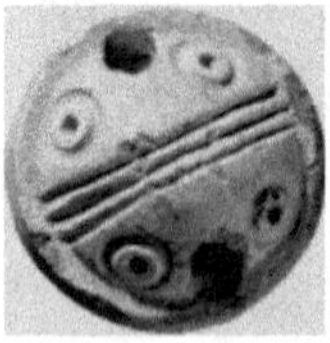

Back of proto-Dilmu seal from Saar. Dia

1.9 cm. (After Fig.10 Saar Report.[487])

khāṇḍā 'dotted circles' Rebus 1: *khāṇḍā* 'tools, pots and pans and metal-ware'. Rebus 2: kāḍ 'stone'. Ga. (Oll.) kanḍ, (S.) kanḍu (pl. kanḍkil) stone (DEDR 1298). *kolom* 'three' Rebus: *kolami* 'smithy/forge'.

"The earliest stone seals of the Gulf region were made of steatite hardened by firing and often glazed after they were carved. The impression of the hemispherical stamp seal depicted here shows a male figure in the upper field who grasps a caprid by the neck. To the left, a male figure holds a staff. Below, a recumbent caprid reclines beneath a gridded rectangle. A snake and perhaps a monkey(?) are also depicted in the field. The hemispherical form and round sealing face are typical of seals of the Gulf region, as are the incised lines and concentric circles that decorate the back of this seal."

Steffen Terp Laurssen[488] has reviewed 121 seals and seal impressions of 'Gulf type' dated to the end of 3rd millennium BCE, which 'come from a vast geographical area encompassing Bahrain, the Indus Valley (Mohenjo-daro and Chanhu-daro), Iran (Kerman, Luristan, Susa and the western Iranian plateau), Kuwait (Failaka), Mesopotamia (Ur, Girsu, Babylon and others unspecified) and the United Arab Emirates (Tell Abraq).'[489]

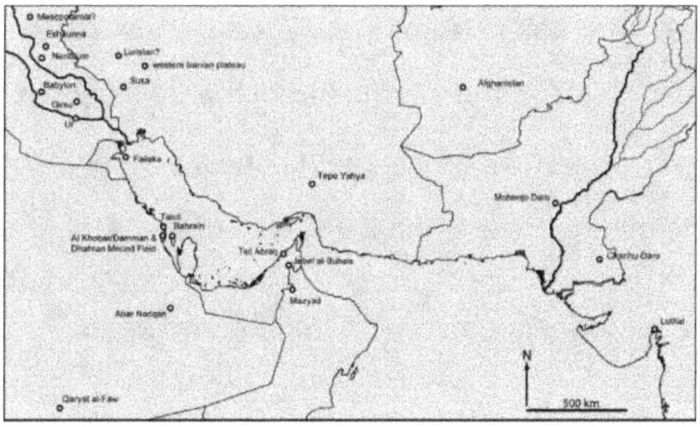

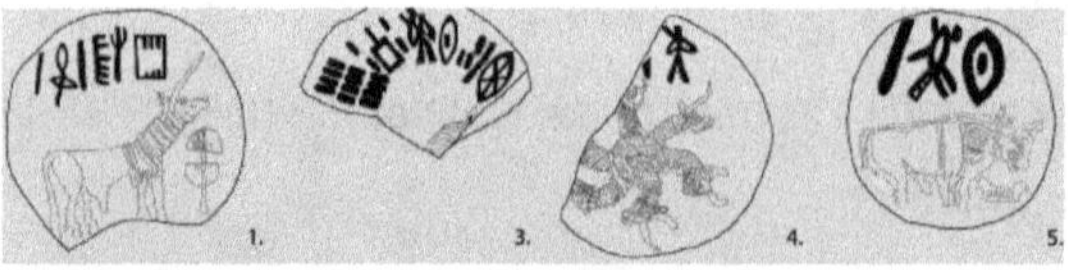

Indus Valley, and areas with which Gulf merchants traded and with whom they shared a common visual vocabulary. Distribution of Gulf and Dilmun type seals and geographical vastness of the underlying networks (After Fig. 13, Laurssen, 2010).

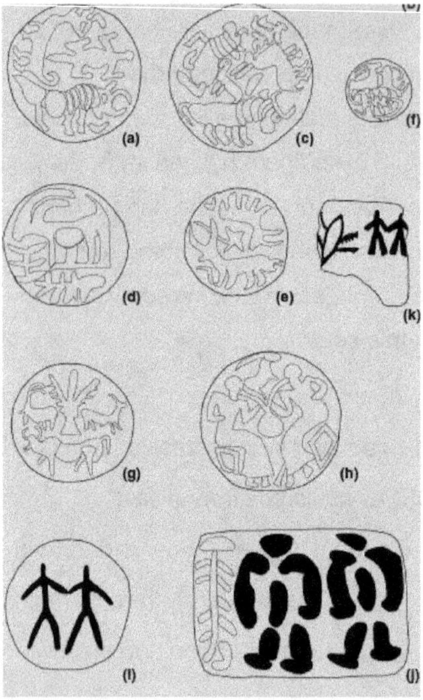

Inscribed circular seals show bison or short-horned bulls. Dominant iconographic motifs are: caprids, ibexes, scorpions, human footprints, crescents and anthropomorphic figures.[490]

Twelve Gulf type seals with pictorial motifs. (After Fig. 17, Laurssen, 2010). "The transformation of the Indus script into 'western' grammar as testified by the prefix 'twins' on the seals suggests that the process occurred in relative isolation from the Indus valley centres."[491]

The seal impressions drawings from Mohenjo-daro and Chanhu-daro seals. (After Fig. 8, Laurssen, 2010).

(a. impression drawing of a cylinder seal from Ur with a humped bull and a

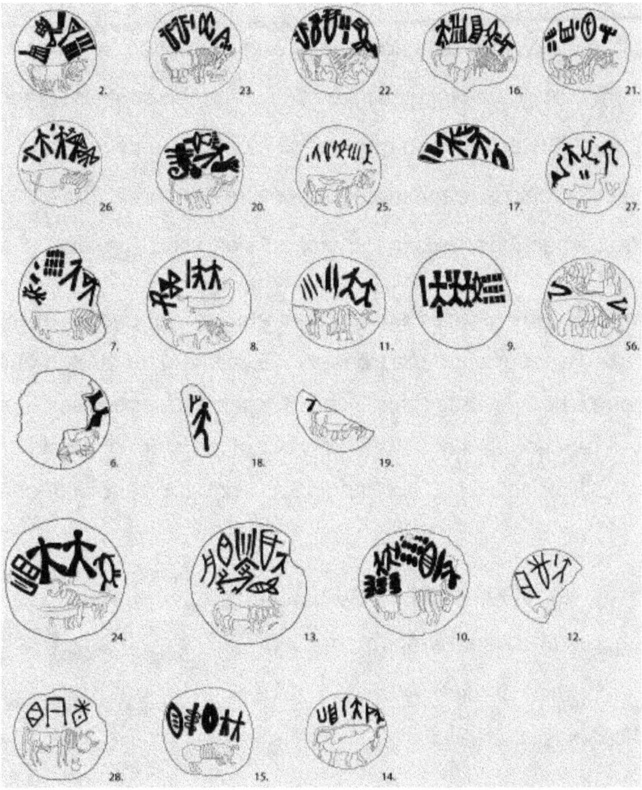

'blade of fodder' (Gadd 6); c. Indus bull without inscription; d-f Gulf type seals from Bahrain: d. two palm branches below a quadruped; e. two quadrupeds and pair of crescents, shooting star? F. scorpion below a pair of quadrupeds; g. vulture above a bull; h. two men drinking scene; k. fragment of cylinder seal from Mohenjo-daro with twins and another undistinguishable sign. After Fig. 10, Laurssen, 2010).

Impression drawings of inscribed seals. The numbers refer to the Table of 121 seals. (After Fig. 9, Laurssen, 2010).

Laurssen argues that these seals correspond to different areas of production and that those with inscriptions have a predominant use of the glyphs of prefixed 'twins'. He also posits that 'break-away Harappans operting in the western orbit invented the Gulf Type seals but that the type from around 2050 BCE became practically synonymous with the merchant communities in Dilmun.'[492] The predominant use of 'twins' glyph should not lead to an assumption that the language different from that of the Harappans was used on the seals invented by 'break-away Harappans.' It is possible to read rebus most of the inscriptions on such Gulf Type seals, including a reading of the 'twins' in the underlying Meluhha language of the Harappan scribes, artisans, merchants and seal-makers.

sangaḍa 'pair' (Marathi) Rebus: *jaṅgaḍ* 'entrustment articles'. *jangaḍiyo* 'military guard who accompanies treasure into the treasury' Glyph: kāḍ, to stretch oneself the whole length of one's body. (Kashmiri). Glyph: *kaṇṭa* bulbous root as of lotus, plantain; point where branches and bunches grow out of the stem of a palm (Malayalam) Rebus: kāḍ 'stone'. Ga. (Oll.) kanḍ, (S.) kanḍu (pl. kanḍkil) stone (DEDR 1298).

Two oryx in confrontation, with two figures and beneath them, holding hands; the Hili tomb. (After Fig. 8.12, Michael Rice, 1994).[493]

Possible representation of 'alliance' in late 3rd millennium BCE eastern Arabia. Ra'sal Jinz seal (with dotted circles flanking the boss of the seal on reverse). A stamp seal with two human figures holding hands, alongside a palm branch from Building VII, room 1, Ra'sal Jinz. (After Fig. 6, Serge Cleuziou, 2003; After Fig. 5, ibid.) "Two individuals holding hands beside a vegetal motif, possibly a palm branch, are engraved on a small rectangular stamp seal found inside the northern compound at RJ-2 and dated around 2300-2200 BCE (figs. 5.4 and 6.1). This theme is displayed in two other examples: a smaller stamp seal of the same period recovered in an early second millennium context at Kalba (fig. 6.2), and the bas-relief carved on the southern door of tomb 1051 at Hili (fig. 6.4), one of the most monumental graves presently known, also dated around 2300 BCE. The latter represents two individuals very close in attitude to those of the RJ-2 seal, holding hands while standing between two oryx. The context of this seal is in itself illustrative. Recovered from the same house building (building VII) were two stamp seals with three engraved characters of writing (figs. 5.2-3), a complete incense burner (fig. 5.1) and a fragment of the upper jaw of a leopard."[494]

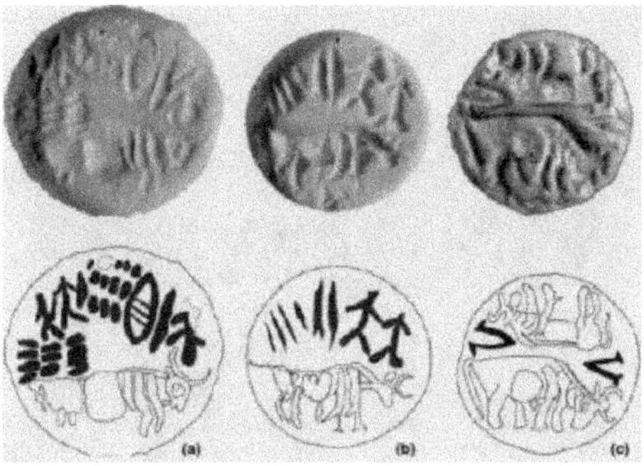

The presence of Indus texts on circular seals has been noted by a number of researchers. The pioneering effort was that of Gadd who communicated on eight circular seals, 'Seals of ancient Indian style found in Ur.'[495] A substantial number of seals without 'inscription' have been found[496] and not enough attention has been paid to the pictorial motifs or 'iconographic resemblances' of such seals which are an Indus writing continuum. Within these types of seals, some are categorised as 'Dilmun type' which show three grooves and four dots-in-circles on the reverse. The further assumption has been that the round form of the seals 'could very well have been a special trademark of some unexplored Harappan community.'[497] One guess that the round form was associated with the maritime trade.[498]

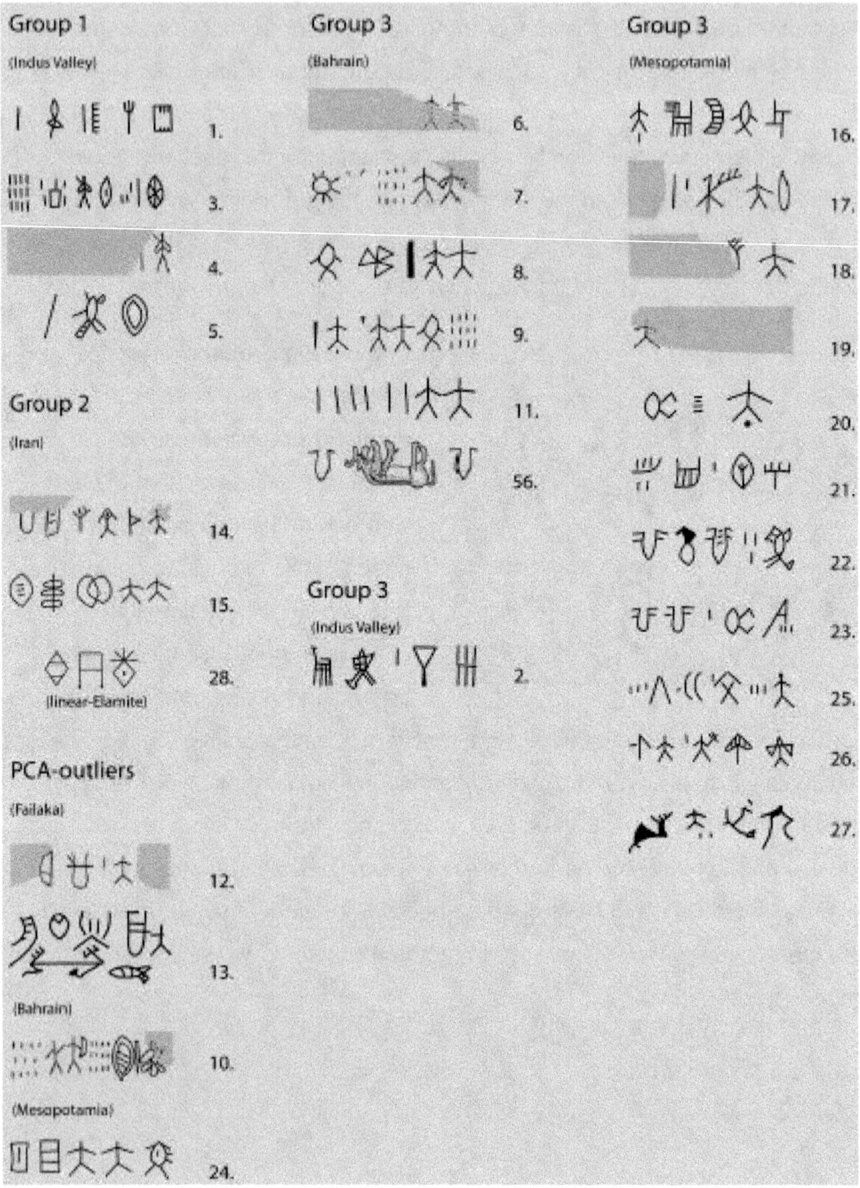
Group 1
(Indus Valley)
1.
3.
4.
5.
Group 2
(Iran)
14.
15.
28.
(linear-Elamite)
PCA-outliers
(Failaka)
12.
13.
(Bahrain)
10.
(Mesopotamia)
24.
Group 3
(Bahrain)
6.
7.
8.
9.
11.
56.
Group 3
(Indus Valley)
2.
Group 3
(Mesopotamia)
16.
17.
18.
19.
20.
21.
22.
23.
25.
26.
27.

Impressions and drawings of Gulf type steatite seals (with a white glaze and a pierced boss), with Indus text and bull motif found in Early Dilmun burial mounds. (After Fig. 1, Laurssen, 2010).

Indus inscriptions and indus-related characters on Gulf type seal impressions. Note the general abundance of 'twin' signs, especially at the beginning of the sequences. (After Fig. 11, Laurssen, 2010).Vidale suggests: "…a correlate of my hypothesis is that the 'man' and 'twins' Indus signs, in the inscriptions from Failaka and Bahrain (and Ur?), might be interpreted as patronymic logograms, to be phonetically read in one or more (still unidentified) ancient Semitic languages…"[499] Patronymic, ordered family sequences, personal or group affiliations? The answer will come from the cypher and rebus readings of Indus hieroglyphs.

The dominance of 'twin' glyphs is matched by the antithetical antelopes which

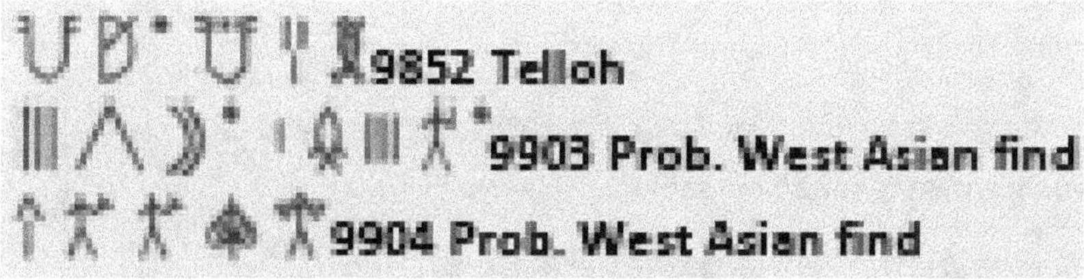

become the Gulf standard of 3rd millennium BCE.

[Pierre de talc. Louvre, AO 9036. P. Amiet, Bas-relliefs imaginaries de l'Orient ancien, Paris, 1973, p. 94, no. 274…ils proviendrait de Tello, l'ancienne Girsu, une des cites de l'Etat sumerien de Lagash. Musee National De Arts Asiatiques Guimet, 1988-1989, *Les cites oubliees de l'Indus Archeologie du Pakistan*.]

Texts related to West Asian inscriptions (either not illustrated or not linked):

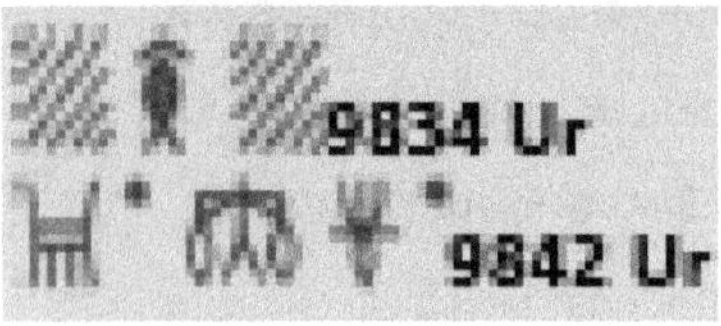

Tree in front. Fish in front of and above a one-horned bull. Cylinder seal impression (IM 8028), Ur, Mesopotamia. White shell. 1.7 cm. High, dia. 0.9 cm. [500]

"No.7...A bull, unhumped, of the so-called 'unicorn' type, raises his head towards a simplified version of a tree, and two uncertain objects, one a sort of trefoil, are shown above his back. Under his head is an unmistakable character of the Indus script, the 'fish' with cross-hatchings..." [501]

Gadd seals

What are referred to as Gadd seals are from Mesopotamia, and Gulf islands of Failaka and Bahrein (Dilmun, Magan).

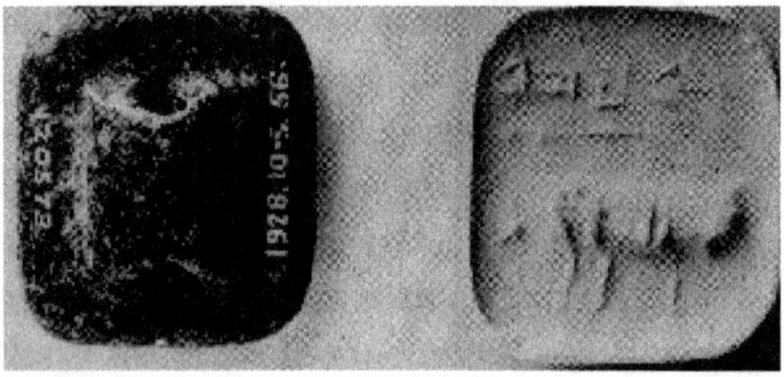

Seal impression and reverse of seal (with pierced lug handle) from Ur (U.7683; BM 120573); image of bison and cuneiform inscription; length 2.7, width 2.4, ht. 1.1 cm. cf. Gadd, PBA 18 (1932), pp. 5-6, pl. I, no.1; Mitchell 1986: 280-1 no.7 and fig. 111; Parpola, 1994, p. 131: signs may be read as (1) *sag(k)* or *ka,* (2) *ku* or *lu* or *ma*, and (3) *zi* or *ba (4)?.* SAG.KU(?).IGI.X or SAG.KU(?).P(AD)(?) The commonest value: *sag-ku-zi*

Seal; BM 122187; dia. 2.55; ht. 1.55 cm. Gadd PBA 18 (1932), pp. 6-7, pl. 1, no. 2

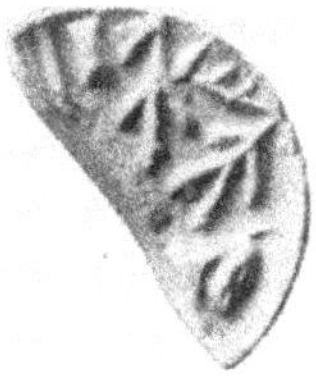

Seal; BM 122946; Dia. 2.6; ht. 1.2cm.; Gadd PBA 18 (1932), p. 7, pl. I, no.3; Legrain, *Ur Excavations*, X (1951), no. 629.

Seal; BM 118704; U. 6020; Gadd PBA 18 (1932), pp. 9-10, pl. II, no.8; two figures carry between them a vase, and one presents a goat-like animal (not an antelope) which he holds by the neck. Human figures wear early Sumerian garments of fleece.

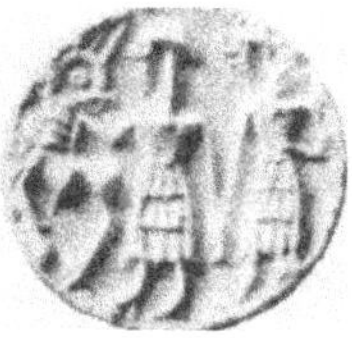

Seal; BM 122945; U. 16181; dia. 2.25, ht. 1.05 cm; Gadd PBA 18 (1932), p. 10, pl. II, no. o; each of four quadrants terminates at the edge of the seal in a vase; each quadrant is occupied by a naked figure, sitting so that, following round the circle, the head of one is placed nearest to the feet of the preceding; two figures clasp their hands upon their breasts; the other two spread out the arms, beckoning with one hand.

Seal; BM 120576; U. 9265; Gadd, PBA 18 (1932), p. 10, pl. II, no. 10; bull with long horns below an uncertain object, possibly a quadruped and rider, at right angles to the ox (counter clockwise)

Seal; UPenn; a scorpion and an elipse [an eye (?)]; U. 16397; Gadd, PBA 18 (1932), pp. 10-11, pl. II, no. 11 *bica* 'scorpion' Rebus *bica* 'stone ore'. *ḍhāḷako* = a large metal ingot (Gujarati)

Seal impression, Ur (Upenn; U.16747); dia. 2.6, ht. 0.9 cm.; Gadd, PBA 18 (1932), pp. 11-12, pl. II, no. 12; Porada 1971: pl.9, fig.5; Parpola, 1994, p. 183; water carrier with a skin (or pot?) hung on each end of the yoke across his shoulders and another one below the crook of his left arm; the vessel on the right end of his yoke is over a receptacle for the water; a star on either side of the head (denoting supernatural?). The whole object is enclosed by 'parenthesis' marks. The parenthesis is perhaps a way of splitting of the ellipse (Hunter, G.R., *JRAS*, 1932, 476). An unmistakable example of an 'hieroglyphic' seal.

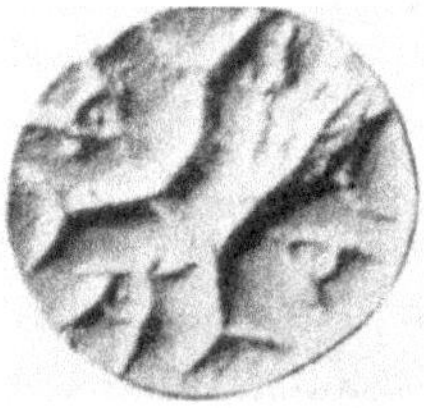

Seal; BM 122841; dia. 2.35; ht. 1 cm.; Gadd PBA 18 (1932), p. 12, pl. II, no. 13; circle with centre-spot in each of four spaces formed by four forked branches springing from the angles of a small square. Alt. four stylised bulls' heads (bucrania) in the quadrants of an elaborate quartering device which has a cross-hatched rectangle in the centre.

Seal; UPenn; cf. Philadelphia *Museum Journal*, 1929; ithyphallic bull-men; the so-called 'Enkidu' figure common upon Babylonian cylinders of the early period; all have horned head-dresses; moon-symbols upon poles seem to represent the door-posts that the pair of 'twin' genii are commonly seen supporting on either side of a god; material and shape make it the 'Indus' type while the device is Babylonian.

Seal impression; UPenn; steatite; bull below a scorpion; dia. 2.4cm.; Gadd, PBA 18 (1932), p. 13, Pl. III, no. 15; Legrain, MJ (1929), p. 306, pl. XLI, no. 119; found

at Ur in the cemetery area, in a ruined grave .9 metres from the surface, together with a pair of gold ear-rings of the double-crescent type and long beads of steatite and carnelian, two of gilt copper, and others of lapis-lazuli, carnelian, and banded sard. The first sign to the left has the form of a flower or perhaps an animal's skin with curly tail; there is a round spot upon the bull's back.

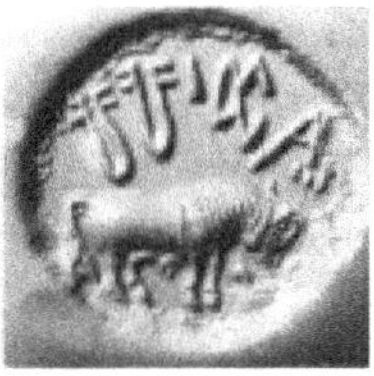

Seal impression; BM 123208; found in the filling of a tomb-shaft (Second Dynasty of Ur). Dia. 2.3; ht. 1.5 cm.; Gadd, PBA 18 (1932), pp. 13-14, pl. III, no. 16; Buchanan, *JAOS* 74 (1954), p. 149.

Seal impression, Mesopotamia (?) (BM 120228); cf. Gadd 1932: no.17; cf. Parpola, 1994, p. 132. Note the doubling of the common sign, 'jar'.

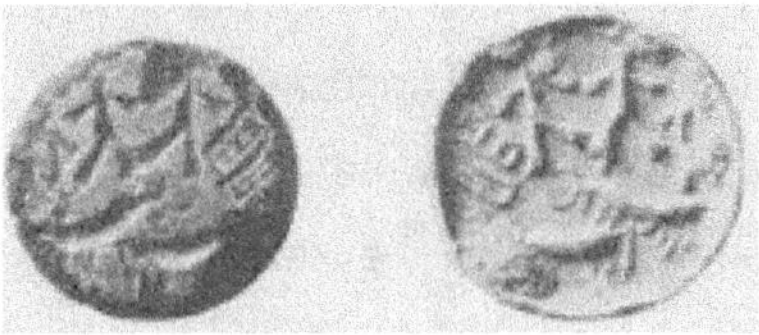

Seal and impression (BM 123059), from an antique dealer, Baghdad; script and motif of a bull mating with a cow; the tuft at the end of the tail of the cow is summarily shaped like an arrow-head; inscription is of five characters, most prominent among them the two 'men' standing side by side. To the right of these is a damaged 'fish' sign.cf. Gadd 1932: no.18; Parpola, 1994, p.219.

Failaka seal. The Yale tablet is dated to ca. the second half of the twentieth century B.C.... Trade3 on the Persian gulf was in existence well before that time-- about 2350 B.C.-- when Sargon, the first Akkadian king referred to ships from or destined for Melukhkha, Magan and Tilmun (Dilmun) at his wharves. in the Third Dynasty of Ur (around 2000), when trade apparently was centred at Magan. It is even better documented on other tablets from Ur (from about 1900 and from about 1800), belonging to various kings of Larsa. At this time the trade was centered at Tilmun... Cuneiform inscriptions naming Inzak, the god of Tilmun, were found on Failaka and, a long time ago, one on Bahrein... Failaka can be equated with Tilmun, or at least was an important part of it. (Briggs Buchanan, A dated seal impression connecting Babylonia and ancient India, Archaeology, Vol. 20, No.2, 1967, pp. 104-107).

Yale tablet. Bull's head (bucranium) between two seated figures drinking from two vessels through straws. YBC. 5447; dia. c. 2.5 cm. Possibly from Ur. Buchanan, studies Landsberger, 1965, p. 204; A seal impression was found on an inscribed tablet (called Yale tablet) dated to the tenth year of Gungunum, King of Larsa, in southern Babylonia--that is, 1923 B.C. according to the most commonly accepted ('middle') chronology of the period. The design in the impression closely matches that in a stamp seal found on the Failaka island in the Persian Gulf, west of the delta of the Shatt al Arab, which is formed by the confluence of the Tigris and Euphrates rivers.

Reduplication connotes dul 'likeness'; rebus: 'cast (metal)' to prefix the following lexemes which explain the semantics of each reduplicated glyph e.g., dul meṛed, cast iron (Mu.) dol = likeness, picture, form (Santali)

Fig. 92; Susa, stamp seal made of bitumen compound, Louvre, MDAI, 43, no. 1726; a tamer with three heavily hatched animals

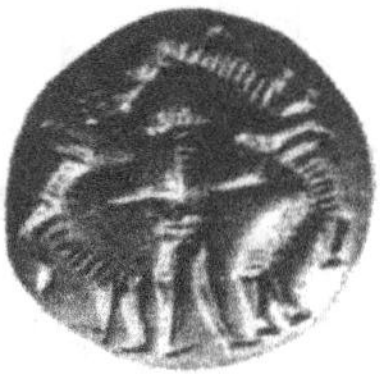

Fig. 93; Susa stamp seal made of bitumen compound, Louvre, MDAI, 43, no. 1720

Fig. 94;
Susa, stamp seal from a butimen compound,
Louvre, MDAI, 43, no. 1726

"Susa... profound affinity between the Elamite people who migrated to Anshan and Susa and the Dilmunite people... Elam proper corresponded to the plateau of Fars with its capital at Anshan. We think, however that it probably extended further north into the Bakhtiari Mountains... likely that the chlorite and serpentine vases reached Susa by sea... From the victory proclamations of the kings of Akkad we also learn that the city of Anshan had been re-established, as the capital of a revitalised political ally: Elam itself... the import by Ur and Eshnunna of inscribed objects typical of the Harappan culture provides the first reliable chronological evidence. [C.J. Gadd, Seals of ancient Indian style found at Ur, *Proceedings of the British Academy, XVIII*, 1932; Henry Frankfort, Tell Asmar, Khafaje and Khorsabad, *OIC*, 16, 1933, p. 50, fig. 22). It is certainly possible that writing developed in India before this time, but we have no real proof. Now Susa had received evidence of this same civilisation, admittedly not all dating from the Akkadian period, but apparently spanning all the closing years of the third millennium (L. Delaporte, *Musee du Louvre. Catalogues des Cylindres Orientaux...*, vol. I, 1920, pl. 25(15), S.29. P. Amiet, Glyptique susienne, *MDAI*, 43, 1972, vol. II, pl. 153, no. 1643)... B. Buchanan has published a tablet dating from the reign of Gungunum of Larsa, in the twentieth century BC, which carries the impression of such a stamp seal. (B.Buchanan, *Studies in honor of Benno Landsberger*, Chicago, 1965, p. 204, s.). The date so revealed has been whollyconfirmed by the impression of a stamp seal from the same group, fig. 85, found on a Susa tablet of the same period. (P. Amiet, Antiquites du Desert de Lut,*RA*, 68, 1974, p. 109, fig. 16. Maurice Lambert, *RA*, 70, 1976, p. 71-72). It is in fact, a receipt of the kind in use at the beginning of the Isin-Larsa period, and mentions a certain Milhi-El, son of Tem-Enzag, who, from the name of his god, must be a Dilmunite. In these circumstances we may wonder if this document had not been drawn up at Dilmun and sent to Susa, after sealing with a local stamp seal. This seal is decorated with six tightly-packed, crouching animals, characterised by their vague shapes, with legs tucked under their bodies, huge heads and necks sometimes striped obliquely. The impression of another seal of similar type, fig. 86, depicts in the centre a throned figure who seems to dominate the animals, continuing a tradition of which examples are known at the end of the Ubaid period in Assyria... Fig. 87 to 89 are Dilmun-type seals found at Susa. The boss is semi-spherical and decorated with a band across the centre and four incised circles. [Pierre Amiet, Susa and the Dilmun Culture, pp. 262-268].

Selected Sumerian texts referring to Meluhha, Dilmun, Magan

"May the land of Tukric hand over to you gold from Harali, lapis lazuli and .... May the land of Meluha load precious desirable cornelian, mec wood of Magan and the best abba wood into large ships for you. May the land of Marhasi yield you precious stones, topazes. May the land of Magan offer you strong, powerful copper, dolerite, u stone and cumin stone. May the Sea-land offer you its own ebony wood,... of a king..." Enki and Ninhursaja.[502]

gul-lum me-luh-haki: The donkey of Ancan, the bear (?) of Marhasi, the cat of Meluha, the elephant of the eastern mountains, bite off Euphrates poplars as if they were leeks. Proverbs: from Nibru[503]

gul-lum 'cat' is not unlike kol 'tiger' (Santali).

jicma2-gi4-lum me-luh-haki-a-ke4: "I will admire its green cedars. Let the lands of Meluha, Magan and Dilmun look upon me, upon Enki. Let the Dilmun boats be loaded (?) with timber. Let the Magan boats be loaded sky-high. Let the magilum boats of Meluha transport gold and silver and bring them to Nibru for Enlil, king of all the lands." Enki and the world order.[504]

The corpus comprises Sumerian texts in transliteration, English prose translations and bibliographical information for each composition. The transliterations and the translations can be searched, browsed and read online using the tools of the website.

Enki and Ninḫursaĝa: c.1.1.1
"May the land of Tukriš hand over to you gold from Ḫarali, lapis lazuli and .... May the land of Meluḫa load precious desirable cornelian, meš wood of Magan and the best abba wood into large ships for you. May the land of Marḫaši yield you precious stones, topazes. May the land ofMagan offer you strong, powerful copper, dolerite, u stone and šumin stone. May the Sea-land offer you its own ebony wood, ... of a king. May the 'Tent'-lands offer you fine multicoloured wools. May the land of Elam hand over to you choice wools, its tribute. May the manor of Urim, the royal throne dais, the city ......, load up into large ships for you sesame, august raiment, and fine cloth. May the wide sea yield you its wealth."

Enki and Ninḫursaĝa: c.1.1.1
(She said:) "For the little ones to whom I have given birth may rewards not be lacking. Ab-u shall become king of the grasses, Ninsikila shall become lord of Magan, Ningiriutud shall marry Ninazu, Ninkasi shall be what satisfies the heart, Nazi shall marry Nindara, Azimua shall marry Ninĝišzida, Ninti shall become the lady of the month, and Ensag shall become lord of Dilmun."

Enki and the world order: c.1.1.3
"I will admire its green cedars. Let the lands of Meluḫa, Magan and Dilmun look upon me, upon Enki. Let the Dilmun boats be loaded (?) with timber. Let the Magan boats be loaded sky-high. Let the magilum boats of Meluḫa transport gold and silver and bring them to Nibru for Enlil, king of all the lands."

Ninurta's exploits: a šir-sud (?) to Ninurta: c.1.6.2
"Esi (diorite), your army in battle changed sides separately (?). You spread before me like thick smoke. You did not raise your hand. You did not attack me. Since you said," It is false. The lord is alone the hero. Who can vie with Ninurta, the son of Enlil?" -- they shall extract you from the highland countries. They shall bring (?) you from the land of Magan.

You shall shape (?) Strong Copper like leather and then you shall be perfectly adapted for my heroic arm, for me, the lord. When a king who is establishing his renown for perpetuity has had its statues sculpted for all time, you shall be placed in the place of libations -- and it shall suit you well -- in my temple E-ninnu, the house full of grace."

Gilgameš and Ḫuwawa (Version A): c.1.8.1.5
"Look, Enkidu, two people together will not perish! A grappling-pole does not sink! No one can cut through a three-ply cloth! Water cannot wash someone away from a wall! Fire in a reed house cannot be extinguished! You help me, and I will help you -- what can anyone do against us then? When it sank, when it sank, when the Magan boat sank, when the magilum barge sank, then at least the life-saving grappling-pole of the boat { was rescued } { (1 ms. has instead:) was not allowed to sink }! Come on, let's get after him and get a sight of him!"

The building of Ninĝirsu's temple (Gudea, cylinders A and B): c.2.1.7
"As if at the roaring of the Anzud bird, the heavens tremble at my house, the E-ninnu founded by An, the powers of which are the greatest, surpassing all other powers, at the house whose owner looks out over a great distance. Its fierce halo reaches up to heaven, the great fearsomeness of my house settles upon all the lands. In response to its fame all lands will gather from as far as heaven's borders, even Maganand Meluḫa will come down from their mountains."

The building of Ninĝirsu's temple (Gudea, cylinders A and B): c.2.1.7
The Elamites came to him from Elam, the Susians came to him from Susa. Magan and Meluḫa loaded wood from their mountains upon their shoulders for him, and to build the house of Ninĝirsu, they gathered for Gudea at his city Ĝirsu.

Letter from Puzur-Šulgi to Ibbi-Suen about Išbi-Erra's claim on Isin: c.3.1.19
""Enlil, my lord, has ...... the shepherdship of the land. Enlil has told me to bring before Ninisina the cities, deities and troops of the region of the Tigris, Euphrates, Ab-gal and Me-Enlila watercourses, from the province of Ḫamazi { to the sea of Magan } { (1 ms. has instead:) and from the ...... of Magan }, so as to make Isin the storehouse of Enlil, to make it famous, and { to make those regions its spoils of war and to make Isin's citizens occupy their cities } { (1 ms. has instead:) to make Isin's citizens occupy the cities as spoils of war. }""

A šir-namšub to Ninurta (Ninurta G): c.4.27.07
My king, you covered the edge of the sea with rays of light. On that day from the gold (?)

of Ḫarali you are Ena-tum. From the cornelian and lapis lazuli of the land of Meluḫa you are Ena-tum. From the dušia stone of the land of Marḫaši you are Enakam. From the silver of fifteen cities you are Enakam. From the copper and tin of Magan you are Enakam. From the bronze of ...... you are Enakam (?). From the silver of Dilmun you are Ena-tum. From the im-kalaga clay of the mouth of the hills you are Enakam. From the gypsum of the shining hills you are Enakam. (10 lines missing or fragmentary)[505]

Enki and Ninḫursaĝa: c.1.1.1
Pure are the cities -- and you are the ones to whom they are allotted. Pure is Dilmun land. Pure is Sumer -- and you are the ones to whom it is allotted. Pure is Dilmun land. Pure is Dilmun land. Virginal is Dilmun land. Virginal is Dilmun land. Pristine is Dilmun land.

Enki and Ninḫursaĝa: c.1.1.1
He laid her down all alone in Dilmun, and the place where Enki had lain down with his spouse, that place was still virginal, that place was still pristine. He laid her down all alone in Dilmun, and the place where Enki had lain down with Ninsikila, that place was virginal, that place was pristine.

Enki and Ninḫursaĝa: c.1.1.1
In Dilmun the raven was not yet cawing, the partridge not cackling. The lion did not slay, the wolf was not carrying off lambs, the dog had not been taught to make kids curl up, the pig had not learned that grain was to be eaten.

Enki and Ninḫursaĝa: c.1.1.1
Ninsikila said to her father Enki: "You have given a city. You have given a city. What does your giving avail me? You have given a city, Dilmun. You have given a city. What does your giving avail me? You have given .... You have given a city. What avails me your giving?"

Enki and Ninḫursaĝa: c.1.1.1
"May the waters rise up from it into your great basins. May your city drink water aplenty from them. May Dilmun drink water aplenty from them. May your pools of salt water become pools of fresh water. May your city become an emporium on the quay for the Land. May Dilmun become an emporium on the quay for the Land."

Enki and Ninḫursaĝa: c.1.1.1
The city's dwellings are good dwellings. Dilmun's dwellings are good dwellings. Its grains are little grains, its dates are big dates, its harvests are triple ......, its wood is ...... wood.

Enki and Ninḫursaĝa: c.1.1.1
The waters rose up from it into her great basins. Her city drank water aplenty from them. Dilmun drank water aplenty from them. Her pools of salt water indeed became pools of fresh water. Her fields, glebe and furrows indeed produced grain for her. Her city indeed became an emporium on the quay for the Land. Dilmun indeed became an emporium on the quay for the Land. At that moment, on that day, and under that sun, so it indeed happened.

Enki and Ninḫursaĝa: c.1.1.1
(She said:) "For the little ones to whom I have given birth may rewards not be lacking. Ab-u shall become king of the grasses, Ninsikila shall become lord of Magan, Ningiriutud shall marry Ninazu, Ninkasi shall be what satisfies the heart, Nazi shall marry Nindara, Azimua shall marry Ninĝišzida, Ninti shall become the lady of the month, and Ensag shall become lord of Dilmun."

Enki and the world order: c.1.1.3
"I will admire its green cedars. Let the lands of Meluḫa, Magan and Dilmun look upon me, upon Enki. Let the Dilmun boats be loaded (?) with timber. Let the Magan boats be loaded sky-high. Let the magilum boats of Meluḫa transport gold and silver and bring them to Nibru for Enlil, king of all the lands."

Enki and the world order: c.1.1.3
He cleansed and purified the land of Dilmun. He placed Ninsikila in charge of it. He gave ...... for the fish spawn, ate its ...... fish, bestowed palms on the cultivated land, ate its dates...Elam and Marḫaši .... to devour ..The king endowed with strength by Enlil destroyed their houses, demolished (?) their walls. He brought their silver and lapis-lazuli, their treasure, to Enlil, king of all the lands, in Nibru.

Enlil and Sud: c.1.2.2
......, dates, figs, large pomegranates, ..., ĝipar fruits, plums (?), ḫalub nuts, almonds, acorns, Dilmun dates packed in baskets, dark-coloured date spadices, large pomegranates gathered from orchards, big clusters of grapes on high, ... trees in fruit, trees from orchards, ... grown in winter, and fruits from orchards were despatched by Enlil toward Ereš.

Inana's descent to the nether world: c.1.4.1
She abandoned the office of en, abandoned the office of lagar, and descended to the underworld. She abandoned the E-ana in Unug, and descended to the underworld. She

abandoned the E-muš-kalama in Bad-tibira, and descended to the underworld. She abandoned the Giguna in Zabalam, and descended to the underworld. She abandoned the E-šara in Adab, and descended to the underworld. She abandoned the Barag-dur-ĝara in Nibru, and descended to the underworld. She abandoned the Ḫursaĝ-kalama in Kiš, and descended to the underworld. She abandoned the E-Ulmaš in Agade, and descended to the underworld. { (1 ms. adds 8 other lines:) She abandoned the Ibgal in Umma, and descended to the underworld. She abandoned the E-Dilmuna in Urim, and descended to the underworld. She abandoned the Amaš-e-kug in Kisiga, and descended to the underworld. She abandoned the E-ešdam-kug in Ĝirsu, and descended to the underworld. She abandoned the E-šeg-meše-du in Isin, and descended to the underworld. She abandoned the Anzagar in Akšak, and descended to the underworld. She abandoned the Niĝin-ĝar-kug in Šuruppag, and descended to the underworld. She abandoned the E-šag-ḫula in Kazallu, and descended to the underworld. }

Nanna-Suen's journey to Nibru: c.1.5.1
"My Nibru, where black birch trees grow in a good place, my sanctuary Nibru, where white birch trees grow in a pure place -- my Nibru's shrine is built in a good place. The sanctuary Nibru's name is a good name. My Nibru's shrine is built in a good place. The sanctuary Nibru's name is a good name. Before Dilmun existed, palm trees grew in my city. Before Dilmun existed, palm trees grew in Nibru and the great mother Ninlil was clothed in fine linen."

The Flood story: c.1.7.4
More and more animals disembarked onto the earth. Zi-ud-sura the king prostrated himself before An and Enlil. An and Enlil treated Zi-ud-sura kindly ......, they granted him life like a god, they brought down to him eternal life. At that time, because of preserving the animals and the seed of mankind, they settled Zi-ud-sura the king in an overseas country, in the land Dilmun, where the sun rises.

Enmerkar and the lord of Aratta: c.1.8.2.3
City, majestic bull bearing vigour and great awesome splendour, Kulaba, ..., breast of the storm, where destiny is determined; Unug, great mountain, in the midst of .... There the evening meal of the great abode of An was set. In those days of yore, when the destinies were determined, the great princes allowed Unug Kulaba's E-ana to lift its head high. Plenty, and carp floods, and the rain which brings forth dappled barley were then increased in Unug Kulaba. Before the land of Dilmun yet existed, the E-ana of Unug Kulaba was well founded, and the holy ĝipar of Inana in brick-built Kulaba shone forth like

the silver in the lode. Before ...... carried ......, before ......, before ...... carried ......, before the commerce was practised; before gold, silver, copper, tin, blocks of lapis lazuli, and mountain stones were brought down together from their mountains, before ...... bathed for the festival, ..., ... time passed. (2 lines missing)

The death of Ur-Namma (Ur-Namma A): c.2.4.1.1
His (?) pleasing sacrifices were no longer accepted; they were treated as dirty (?). The Anuna gods refused his gifts. An did not stand by an "It is enough", and he could not complete his (?) days. Because of what Enlil ordered, there was no more rising up; his beloved men lost their wise one. Strangers turned into (?) .... How iniquitously Ur-Namma was abandoned, like a broken jar! His ...... with grandeur like (?) thick clouds (?). He does not ...... any more, and he does not reach out for ...." ...... Ur-Namma, alas, what is it to me?" Ur-Namma, the son of Ninsumun, was brought to Arali, the pre-eminent place of the Land, in his prime. The soldiers accompanying the king shed tears: their boat (i.e. Ur-Namma) was sunk in a land as foreign to them as Dilmun. ...... was cut. It was stripped of the oars, punting poles and rudder which it had. ......; its bolt was broken off. ...... was put aside; it stood (?) in saltpetre. His donkeys were to be found with the king; they were buried with him. His donkeys were to be found with Ur-Namma; they were buried with him. As he crossed over the ...... of the Land, the Land was deprived of its ornament. The journey to the nether world is a desolate route. Because of the king, the chariots were covered over, the roads were thrown into disorder, no one could go up and down on them. Because of Ur-Namma, the chariots were covered over, the roads were thrown into disorder, no one could go up and down on them.

A praise poem of Šulgi (Šulgi D): c.2.4.2.04
You are as strong as an ildag tree planted by the side of a watercourse. You are a sweet sight, like a fertile meš tree laden with colourful fruit. You are cherished by Ninegala, like a date palm of holy Dilmun. You have a pleasant shade, like a sappy cedar growing amid the cypresses.

A praise poem of Išme-Dagan (Išme-Dagan A + V): c.2.5.4.01
In accordance with the great destiny decided by Father Enlil, my battle-cry overspreads the remotest parts of the mountains. In the rebel cities no one approaches me or fixes their weapons against me. They bring (?) their tribute spontaneously at Enlil's command. ...... to the mountains. ...... nir-igi stone, cornelian, ... stone, { ...... their stones } { (some mss. have instead the line:) ...... time-consuming labour, ..., labour for the king }. For me the black-headed bring great timbers ...... to the Land, while Dilmun bestows

lavishly on me its linen, dates and date spadices. The Martu, who know no houses, who know no cities -- primitives who live in the hills -- bring me row upon row of woolly alum sheep. From the upland mountains, from the ...... places, cedar, zabalum, cypress and boxwood were together brought to me. Enlil, my master, who batters the foreign lands into submission, kept the people on a single track, and made them unanimous for me, who am all for Enlil, who am the beloved of E-kur.

Letter from Aradĝu to Šulgi about irrigation work: c.3.1.03
My lord, you have given me instructions about every matter, from the sea and the land of Dilmun, { from the salt waters and the borders of the land of the Martu } { (some mss. have instead:) to the salt waters and the borders of the land of the Martu }, { to } { (1 ms. has instead:) from } the { side (?) } { (1 ms. has instead:) borders (?) } of Simurrum and { the territory of ...... } { (1 ms. has instead:) the territory of Subir }:

A balbale (?) to Inana (Inana F): c.4.07.6
The heavens are mine and the earth is mine: I am heroic! In Unug the E-ana is mine, in Zabalam the Giguna is mine, in Nibru the Dur-an-ki is mine, in Urim the E-Dilmuna is mine, in Ĝirsu the Ešdam-kug is mine, in Adab the E-šara is mine, in Kiš the Ḫursaĝ-kalama is mine, in Kisiga the Amaš-kuga is mine, in Akšak the Anzagar is mine, in Umma the Ibgal is mine, in Agade the Ulmaš is mine. Which god compares with me?

A tigi to Suen (Nanna I): c.4.13.09
"In the chosen city, the shrine of my heart which I have founded in joy, like Aratta ......; in my E-mud-kura I have tended my cows." "First-born son of Enlil, where have you tended the people, Lord Ašimbabbar?" "In a place founded on a good day and given a good name, in the place chosen in my heart, my E-mud-kura, I, Ašimbabbar, have tended my cows." "First-born son of Enlil, where have you tended the people, Lord Ašimbabbar?" "In a place founded on a good day and given a good name, in the place chosen in my heart, my E-mud-kura, I, Ašimbabbar, have tended my cows." "King of the holy cattle-pen, where have you tended your cows, youthful, noble shepherd?" "In the meadow where I have built a dais for my shrine Urim and have let date palms grow as in the land of Dilmun -- there in its holy reedbeds I have tended my cows." "First-born son of Enlil, where have you tended the people, youthful, noble shepherd?" "In the meadow where I have built a dais for my shrine Urim and have let date palms grow as in the land of Dilmun -- there in its holy reedbeds I have tended my cows."

A tigi to Suen (Nanna I): c.4.13.09

(instead of lines 22-40, 1 ms. has:) "...... where have you tended your cows, youthful, noble shepherd?" "...... for my shrine Urim ...... as in the land of Dilmun -- there in the house's cattle-pen I have tended my cows." "King of the holy cattle-pen (?), where have you tended your cows, youthful, noble shepherd, Lord Ašimbabbar?" "In a place founded on a good day and given a good name, in the place chosen in my heart, E-kiš-nu-ĝal, the ...... house, I, Ašimbabbar, have tended my cows (?)."

A šir-gida to Ninisina (Ninisina A): c.4.22.1
"My house is the house of Isin, the cosmic border of heaven and earth, a fragrant cedar forest whose perfume does not diminish; its interior is a mountain established in plenteousness. Before the land of Dilmun ever existed, my house was created from a date palm. Before the land ofDilmun ever existed, Isin was created from a date palm. Its dates are like a great linen garment that hangs on a tree, heaped up into piles. The Anuna, the great gods, eat together with me. My house is a place of healing, full of opulence, the place of the formation of the Land. At night it shines to me like the moonlight; in the noonday heat it shines to me like the sunlight. My husband, Lord Pabilsaĝ, the son of Enlil, lies inside with me ......, enjoying his rest there. My watercourse is the Kir-sig watercourse, which produces plenty for eating, which spreads out over the wheat; in it the flowing water always rises high for me. Its banks make syrup and wine grow there, and make their produce rich for me."

A šir-namšub to Ninurta (Ninurta G): c.4.27.07
My king, you covered the edge of the sea with rays of light. On that day from the gold (?) of Ḫarali you are Ena-tum. From the cornelian and lapis lazuli of the land of Meluḫa you are Ena-tum. From the dušia stone of the land of Marḫaši you are Enakam. From the silver of fifteen cities you are Enakam. From the copper and tin of Magan you are Enakam. From the bronze of ...... you are Enakam (?). From the silver of Dilmun you are Ena-tum. From the im-kalaga clay of the mouth of the hills you are Enakam. From the gypsum of the shining hills you are Enakam. (10 lines missing or fragmentary)

The message of Lu-diĝira to his mother: c.5.5.1
Let me give you a third description of my mother: My mother is { rain from heaven } { (1 ms. has instead:) timely rain }, water for the finest seeds. She is a bountiful harvest of { fully-grown fine barley } { (1 ms. has instead:) ripe, exceedingly fine barley } { (1 ms. has instead:) heavenly ...... } { (1 ms. has instead:) ripe maturity (?) ...... }. She is a garden of { ...... } { (1 ms. has instead:) delights }, { full of laughter } { (1 ms. has instead:) filled with

rejoicing }. She is a well-irrigated pine tree, { an adorned juniper } { (1 ms. has instead:) adorned with pine-cones }. She is early fruit, the { products } { (1 ms. has instead:) garden's yield } of the first month. She is an irrigation ditch bringing fertilising water to the garden plots. She is a sweet Dilmun date, a prime date much sought after.

Result: 11 line(s)

c.1.1.1/Tr/Gl	kur	me-luḫ-ḫa^{ki}	^{na4}gug niĝ$_2$ al di kal-la
c.1.1.3/Tr/Gl	/kur\	[me-luḫ-ḫa^{ki}]	ma$_2$-gan^{ki} dilmun^{ki}-bi
c.1.1.3/Tr/Gl	kur	me-luḫ-ḫa^{ki}	nam-mi-ib$_2$-dib
c.2.1.5/Tr/Gl		me-luḫ-ḫa^{ki}	lu$_2$ kur gig$_2$-ga-ke$_4$
c.2.1.7/Tr/Gl	ma$_2$-gan	me-luḫ-ḫa	kur-bi-ta im-ma-ta-ed$_3$-de$_3$
c.2.1.7/Tr/Gl	ma$_2$-gan	me-luḫ-ḫa	kur-bi-ta gu$_2$ ĝiš mu-na-ab-ĝal$_2$
c.6.2.1/Tr/Gl	gul-lum	me-luḫ-ḫa^{ki}	(*šu-ra-an me-luḫ-[ḫa]*)
c.1.1.3/Tr/Gl	^{ĝiš}ma$_2$-gi$_4$-lum	me-luḫ-ḫa^{ki}-a-ke$_4$	
c.2.1.7/Tr/Gl	/urud\ nagga lagab za-gin$_3$-na kug NE gug gi-rin	me-luḫ-ḫa-da	The building of Ninĝirsu's temple (Gudea, cylinders A and B): t.2.1.7 /urud\ nagga lagab za-gin$_3$-na kug NE gug gi-rin me-luḫ-ḫa-da
c.2.1.7/Tr/Gl	gug gi-rin-e	me-luḫ-ḫa-ta	The building of Ninĝirsu's temple (Gudea, cylinders A and B): t.2.1.7 gug gi-rin-e me-luḫ-ḫa-ta

c.4.27.07/Tr/Gl ^{na_4}gug ^{na_4}za-gin$_3$ kur	me-luḫ-ḫa^{ki}-ta

ஆரம்² āram, *n.* < *āra.* Spoke of a wheel. See ஆரக்கால். ஆரஞ் சூழ்ந்த வயில்வாய் நேமியொடு (சிறுபாண். 253)(Tamil). आरा [ārā] *m* (Better आहरा *m*) A ring of grass &c; (Or आर) A spoke. (Marathi)

ஆரம்² āram Brass; பித்தளை. (அக. நி.)(Tamil) आरा [ārā] A saw.(Marathi)

Ka. (Gowda) aḍigera a pot. *Tu.* aḍḍyara earthen jar or pot. *Te.* aṭika a small earthen pot with a large mouth. *Nk.* (Ch.) aṛka earthen pot. *Go.* (Tr.) aṭkā earthen pot used for cooking; (G. Mu. Ma. S.) aṛka cooking pot; (Pat.) adka [i.e. aṛka] id.
(*Voc.* 25). *Kur.* aṛī earthen waterpot. (DEDR 75)

Ta. aṭukku (aṭukki-) to pile up one on top of another, heap up in order; *n.* pile, series, row, tier; aṭukkam pile, tier, range of mountains, mountain slope; aṭukkalseries, mountain. *Ma.* aṭukku row, pile, layer; aṭukkuka to pile up; aṭukkam a plain, field. *Ko.* aṛg- (aṛgy-) to be piled up in order; aṛk- (aṛky-) to pile up in order;aṛkm (*obl.* aṛkt-) piling up in order. *To.* oḍg- (oḍgy-) to be piled up in order; oṛk- (oṛky-) to pile. *Ka.* aḍaku, aḍuku to pack, pile as pots, heap up; aḍakil, aḍikilpiling up, a pile. *Koḍ.* aḍaŋg- (aḍaŋgi-) to be piled in order, filling space; aḍak- (aḍaki-) to heap in order, filling space, to arrange formally. *Te.* aḍuku to pile up, arrange in a set or series; *n.* a series or set of things, a compact pile of articles.(DEDR 80).

Glyphs: six (numeral) + ring of hair: आर [āra] A term in the play of इटीदांडू,--the number six. (Marathi) आर [āra] A tuft or ring of hair on the body. (Marathi) Rebus: āra 'brass'.

आर [āra] A spoke of a wheel. आरा [ārā] *m* (Better आहरा *m*) A ring of grass &c. (Or आर) A spoke. (Marathi) ará m. ' spoke of a wheel ' RV. 2. āra -- 2 MBh. v.l. [√ṛ]1. Pa. *ara* -- m., Pk. *ara* -- , *°ga* -- , *°ya* -- m.; S. *aro* m. ' spoke, cog '; P. *arn*m. ' one of the crosspieces in a cartwheel '; Or. *ara* ' felloe of a wheel '; Si. *ara* ' spoke '.2. Or. *āra* ' spoke '; Bi. *ārā* ' first pair of spokes in a cartwheel '; H. *ārā* m. ' spoke ', G. *ārɔ* m.(CDIAL 594).

आर [āra] A large serpent of the Boa-kind. (Marathi)

आरा [ārā] *m* (Better आहरा *m*) A saw. (Marathi) ā́rā f. ' shoemaker's awl ' RV. Pa. Pk. *ārā* -- f. ' awl '; Ash. *arċū́ċ* ' needle '; K. *örü* f. ' shoemaker's awl ', S. *āra* f., L. *ār* f.; P. *ār* f. ' awl, point of a goad '; N. *āro* ' awl '; A. *āl* ' sharp point, spur '; B. *ārā* ' awl ',

Or. *āra*, *āri*, Bi. *ār*, *araī*, *aruā*, (Patna) *arauā* ' spike at the end of a driving stick ', Mth. *aruā*, (SETirhut) *ār* ' cobbler's awl '; H. *ār* f. ' awl, goad ',*ārī* f. ' awl ', *araī* ' goad ', *ārā* m. ' shoemaker's awl or knife '; G. M. *ār* f. ' pointed iron spike '; M. *ārī*, *arī* ' cobbler's awl '. S.kcch. *ār* f. ' pointed iron spike '. (CDIAL 1313).

आर [āra] आर as the common termination of the words descriptive of the artisans, e. g. सोनार, सुतार, लोहार, कांसार, चाम्हार, कुंभार &c. is from the Sanskrit कार Doer or maker; thus *describing* them as doers or workers in gold, iron, brass &c. संसाराची-प्रपंचाची-रोजगाराची-आर The *goading* of worldly affairs, earthly necessities &c. *v* लाव, लाग.

Ta. āṟu six; aṟu-patu sixty; aṟu-nūṟu 600; aṟumai six; aṟuvar six persons; avv-āṟu by sixes. *Ma.* āṟu six; aṟu-patu sixty; aṟu-nnūṟu 600; aṟuvar six persons.*Ko.* a·r six; ar vat sixty; a·r nu·r 600; ar va·ṇy six pa·ṇy measures. *To.* o·ṟ six; pa·ṟ sixteen; aṟoQ sixty; o·ṟ nu·ṟ 600; aṟ xwa·w six kwa·x measures. *Ka.* āṟu six;aṟa-vattu, aṟu-vattu, ar-vattu sixty; aṟu-nūṟu, āṟu-nūṟu 600; aṟuvar, ārvaru six persons. *Koḍ.* a·rï six; a·rane sixth; aru-vadï sixty; a·r-nu·rï 600.(DEDR 2485).

<ayu?>(A) {N} ``^fish''. #1370. <yO>\\<AyO>(L) {N} ``^fish''. #3612. <kukkulEyO>,,<kukkuli-yO>(LMD) {N} ``prawn''. !Serango dialect. #32612. <sArjAjyO>,,<sArjAj>(D) {N} ``prawn''. #32622. <magur-yO>(ZL) {N} ``a kind of ^fish''. *Or.<>. #32632. <ur+Gol-Da-yO>(LL) {N} ``a kind of ^fish''. #32642.<bal.bal-yO>(DL) {N} ``smoked fish''. #15163. Vikalpa: Munda: <aDara>(L) {N} ``^scales of a fish, sharp bark of a tree''.#10171. So<aDara>(L) {N} ``^scales of a fish, sharp bark of a tree''. Indian mackerel Ta. *Ayirai, acarai, acalai* loach, sandy colour, *Cobitis thermalis*; *ayilai* a kind of fish. Ma. *Ayala* a fish, mackerel, scomber; *aila, ayila* a fish; *ayira* a kind of small fish, loach (DEDR 191) aduru native metal (Ka.); ayil iron (Ta.) ayir, ayiram any ore (Ma.); ajirda karba very hard iron (Tu.)(DEDR 192). Ta. Ayil javelin, lance, surgical knife, lancet.Ma. ayil javelin, lance; ayiri surgical knife, lancet. (DEDR 193). Aduru = gan.iyinda tegadu karagade iruva aduru = ore taken from the mine and not subjected to melting in a furnace (Ka. Siddhānti Subrahmaṇya' Śastri's new interpretation of the AmarakoŚa, Bangalore, Vicaradarpana Press, 1872, p.330); adar = fine sand (Ta.); ayir – iron dust, any ore (Ma.) Kur. Adar the waste of pounded rice, broken grains, etc. Malt. Adru broken grain (DEDR 134). Ma. Aśu thin, slender;ayir, ayiram iron dust.Ta. ayir subtlety, fineness, fine sand, candied sugar; ? atar fine sand, dust. அயிர்³ ayir, n. 1. Subtlety, fineness; நுணசம. (த_வ_.) 2. [M. ayir.] Fine sand; நுண்மணல. (மலசலப. 92.) ayiram, n. Candied sugar; ayil, n. cf. ayas. 1. Iron; 2. Surgical knife, lancet; Javelin, lance; ayilavaṉ, Skanda, as bearing a

javelin (DEDR 341).Tu. gadarů a lump (DEDR 1196) kadara— m. 'iron goad for guiding an elephant' lex. (CDIAL 2711). अयोगू: A blacksmith; Vāj.3.5. अयस् a. [इ-गतौ-असुन्] Going, moving; nimble. N. (-यः) 1 Iron (एति चलति अयस्कान्तसंनिकर्षं इति तथात्वम्; नायसोल्लिख्यते रत्नम् Śukra 4.169. अभितप्तमयो$पि मार्दवं भजते कैव कथा शरीरिषु R.8.43. -2 Steel. -3 Gold. -4 A metal in general. Ayaskāṇḍa 1 an iron-arrow. -2 excellent iron. -3 a large quantity of iron. – क_नत_(अयसक_नत_) 1 'beloved of iron', a magnet, load-stone; 2 a precious stone; °मजण_ a loadstone; ayaskāra 1 an iron-smith, blacksmith (Skt.Apte) ayas-kāntamu. [Skt.] n. The load-stone, a magnet. Ayaskāruḍu. n. A black smith, one who works in iron. ayassu. N. ayō-mayamu. [Skt.] adj. made of iron (Te.) áyas— n. 'metal, iron' RV. Pa. ayō nom. Sg. N. and m., aya— n. 'iron', Pk. Aya— n., Si. Ya. AYAŚCŪRṆA—, AYASKĀṆḌA—, *AYASKŪṬA—. Addenda: áyas—: Md. Da 'iron', dafat 'piece of iron'. ayaskāṇḍa— m.n. 'a quantity of iron, excellent iron' Pāṇ. Gaṇ. Viii.3.48 [ÁYAS—, KAA´ṆḌA—]Si.yakaḍa 'iron'.*ayaskūṭa— 'iron hammer'.

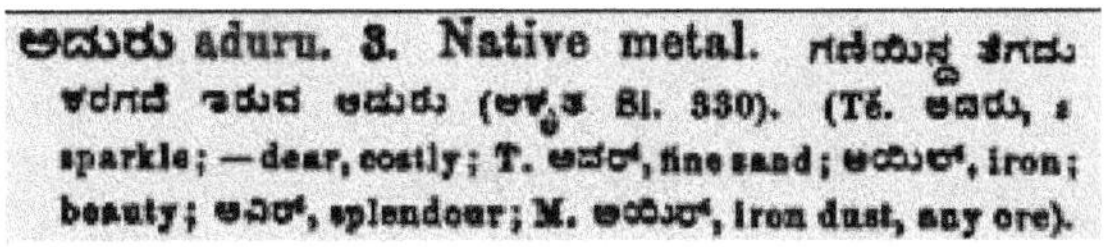
ಅದುರು aduru. 3. Native metal. ... ಅದುರು (... Bl. 330). (Tē. ..., a sparkle; —dear, costly; T. ..., fine sand; ..., iron; beauty; ..., splendour; M. ..., iron dust, any ore).

[ÁYAS—, KUU´ṬA—1] Pa. ayōkūṭa—, ayak m.; Si. Yakuḷa'sledge —hammer', yavuḷa (< ayōkūṭa) (CDIAL 590, 591, 592). Cf. Lat. Aes , aer-is for as-is ; Goth. Ais , Thema aisa; Old Germ. E7r , iron ;Goth. Eisarn ; Mod. Germ. Eisen.

Fish + corner, *aya koṇḍa*, 'metal turned, i.e. forged).

Fish + scales, *aya ās (amśu)* 'metallic stalks of stone ore'. Vikalpa: *badhoṛ* 'a species of fish with many bones' (Santali) Rebus: *baḍhoe* 'a carpenter, worker in wood'; *badhoria* 'expert in working in wood'(Santali)

Fish + splinter, *aya +* खांडा [khāṇḍā] *m* A jag, notch, or indentation (as upon the edge of a tool or weapon). Rebus: khāṇḍa 'tools, pots and pans, and metal-ware'. *Ayaskāṇḍa* is a compounde word attested in Panini.

Fish + sloping stroke, *aya ḍhāḷ* 'metal ingot'

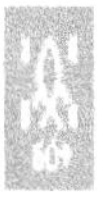
Fish + arrow or allograph, Fish + circumscribed four short strokes

ayakāṇḍa 'large quantity of metal' or *aya kaṇḍa,* 'metal fire-altar', aya. Khāṇḍa 'tools, pots and pans and metal-ware'.

ayo, hako 'fish'; *ās* = scales of fish (Santali); rebus: *aya* 'metal, iron' (G.); *ayah, ayas* = metal (Skt.) Santali lexeme, *hako* 'fish' is concordant with a proto-Indic form which

can be identified as *ayo* in many glosses, Munda, Sora glosses in particular, of the Indian linguistic area. *Beḍa hako (ayo)* 'fish' (Santali); *beḍa* 'either of the sides of a hearth' (G.) Vikalpa: badhoṛ 'a species of fish with many bones' (Santali) Rebus: *baḍhoe* 'a carpenter, worker in wood'; *badhoria* 'expert in working in wood'(Santali) Glyph: gaḍa4 m. 'young of the fish Ophiocephalus lata or Cyprinus garra', *°aka* – m. lex. B. *gaṛ, gaṛai* 'species of gilt-head fish'; Or. *Gaṛiśa, °śā* 'the fish O. lata', *gaḷa* 'a kind of fish'.(CDIAL 3970). Rebus: stone-mould to forge: Pk. *Gaḍa* – n. 'large stone'? (CDIAL 3969). Pk. *Gaḍhaï*' forms '; A. *gariba* ' to mould, form '; B. *gaṛā* ' to hammer into shape, form (CDIAL 3966).

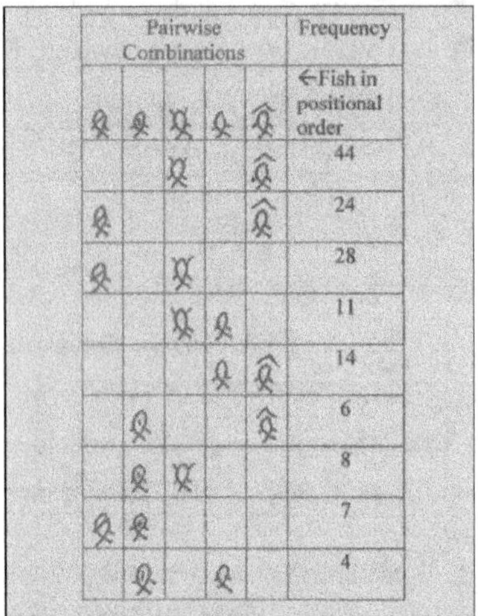

Figure 20: Positional Order of the "Fish" Signs

Fish is a frequently-used glyph on Indus script and the glyph together with ligatured glyphs has a consistent positional sequence and contextual occurrence in the inscriptions.

The glyph is frequently paired with 'circumscribed four short strokes' or with 'arrow' glyph.

Table from: The Indus Script: A Positional-statistical Approach By Michael Korvink, 2007, Gilund Press. Mahadevan notes (Para 6.5 opcit.) that 'a unique feature of the FISH signs is their tendency to form clusters, often as pairs, and rarely as triplets also. This pattern has fascinated and baffled scholars from the days of Hunter posing problems in interpretation.' One way to resolve the problem is to interpret the glyptic elements creating ligatured fish signs and read the glyptic elements rebus to define the semantics of the message of an inscription.

ayo 'fish'.

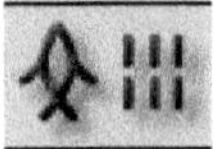

kolmo 'three' (Mu.); rebus: *kolami* 'smithy' (Te.) hence, *ayo kolmo* 'iron smithy'.

bhaṭa 'six' (G.); rebus: *bhaṭa* 'furnace' (Santali) Alternative: *āra* 'six' Rebus: *āra* 'brass'.

Four + three strokes are read (since the strokes are shown on two lines one below the other) : gaṇḍa 'four' (Santali); rebus: 'furnace, kaṇḍ fire-altar'; kolmo 'three' (Mu.) dula 'pair' (Kashmiri); rebus: dul '(fire-altar) cast metal' (Munda)

Ta. aṭi foot, footprint, *Ma.* aṭi sole of foot, footstep, measure of foot, *Ko.* aṛy foot (measure); *Ka.* aḍi foot, measure of foot, step, pace, *Tu.* aḍi bottom, base; kār aḍi footsole, footstep; *Te.* aḍugu foot, footstep, footprint, step, pace, measure of a foot, aḍi-gaṟṟa sandal, wooden shoe. *Ga.* (S.2) aḍugu footstep (< Te.). *Go.* (G.) aḍi beneath (Mu.) (DEDR 72) Rebus: *Ta.* aṭai prop. slight support; aṭaikal anvil. *Ma.* aṭa-kkallu anvil of goldsmiths. *Ko.* aṛ gal small anvil. *Ka.* aḍe, aḍa, aḍi the piece of wood on which the five artisans put the article which they happen to operate upon, a support; aḍegal, aḍagallu, aḍigallu anvil. *Tu.* aṭṭè a support, stand. *Te.* ḍā-kali, ḍā-kallu, dā-kali, dā-gali, dāyi anvil. (DEDR 76).

adhikaraṇī́ f. ' *anvil ', adhikaraṇa -- n. ' receptacle, support ' TUp. [√kr̥1] Pa. adhikaraṇī -- f. ' smith's anvil '; Pk. ahigaraṇī -- f. ' a piece of apparatus for a smith '; K. yīran, dat. yü̆rüñ f. ' anvil ', S. aharaṇi, araṇi f., L. (Jukes) ariṇ P. aihran, airaṇ, ā̃hraṇ f., WPah. bhal. arhini; roh. erṇe ' smithy ', N. āran; H. aheran, ā̃hran m. ' anvil '; -- H. Smith BSL 101, 115. S.kcch. eṇ f. ' anvil '; WPah.ktg. n/arəṇ, n/arṇi f. ' furnace, smithy '; ā́rəṇ m. prob. ← P. Him.I 4; jaun. āraṇ, airaṇ; G. eraṇi f. ' anvil ', M. aheraṇ, ahiraṇ, airaṇ, airṇī, haraṇ f. (CDIAL 252). अहेरण [ahēraṇa] f (Commonly ऐरण) An anvil. Ex. हिरा ठेविता अहेरणीं ॥ वांचे मारिता जो घनीं ॥ऐरण [airaṇa] f or णी f (H) An anvil (whether of blacksmith or of goldsmith) (Marathi)yīran यीरन्, an anvil (Kashmiri) Mth. hannā ' round block of iron pierced with a hole and placed on the perforated anvil (when iron is being pierced with holes) ' (CDIAL 13964).

aṭaikal அடைகல். (பிங்.) Anvil. *சீரிடங்காணி னெறிதற்குப் பட்ட டை* (குறள், 821). 2. [K. paṭṭaḍi.] Smithy, forge; கொல்லன் களரி.கொல்லன்பட்டடை kollaṉ-paṭṭaṭai , n. < கொல்லன் +. Anvil; அடைகல். (C. G.)அடைகுறடு aṭai-kuṟaṭu , n. < அடை[1]- +. 1. Anvil; கம்மியர் பட்டடை. (பிங்.) 2. Tongs; பற்றுக்குறடு. (W.) அடைகல்[1] aṭai-kal , n. < அடை[1]-. 1. Anvil; பட்டடை. சுட்ட வல்லிரும் படைகலைச் சுடுகலா தன் போல் (கம்பரா. பாச. 33). 2. Stone base; ஆதாரச் சிலை. ஆமையாய் மேருத் தாங்கி (சி. சி. பர. பாஞ்சரா. மறு. 11). நறுதடி naṟu-taṭi , n. prob. நறுக்கு- + தடி. Goldsmith's anvil attached to a block; அடைகல். (J.) நறுதடிக்குற்றி naṟutaṭi-k-kuṟṟi , n. < நறு தடி +. Anvil-block of goldsmith; அடைகற் கட்டை. (W.) பட்டடை[1] paṭṭaṭai , n. prob. படு[1]- + அடை[1]-. 1. [T. paṭṭika, K. paṭṭaḍe.] Anvil.

nighāti f. ' iron hammer ' lex. [Cf. nighāta -- m. ' blow ' Gaut., Pa. nighāta -- ' struck down ', °ti -- f. ' defeat ', Pk. ṇihāya -- m. ' blow '. -- √han1] N. lihi ' anvil ', B. nihāi, neh°, neyāi,

Or. nehāi, nehi, lihāi, Bi. nihāi, neh°, Mth. nehāī, nah°, lihāi, lah°; Bhoj. nahāi, nihāī f. ' anvil ', nihāu m. ' iron hammer '. nighātikūṭa 7173 *nighātikūṭa ' hammer '. [nighāti -- , kūṭa -- 1] Mth. lihāwar ' large hammer '. (CDIAL 7172, 7173)

Ta. aṭi foot, footprint, base, bottom, source, origin; Ma. aṭi sole of foot, footstep, measure of foot, Ko. aṛy foot (measure);To. oṛy foot. Ka. aḍi foot, measure of foot, step, pace,Te. aḍugu foot, footstep, footprint, step, pace, measure of a foot,aḍi-gaṟṟa sandal, wooden shoe. Ga. (S.2) aḍugu footstep (< Te.). Go. (G.) aḍi beneath; (Mu.)(DEDR 72)

Ka. (Gowda) aḍigera a pot. Tu. aḍḍyara earthen jar or pot. Te. aṭika a small earthen pot with a large mouth. Nk. (Ch.) aṛka earthen pot. Go. (Tr.) aṭkā earthen pot used for cooking; (G. Mu. Ma. S.) aṛka cooking pot; (Pat.) adka [i.e. aṛka] id. (Voc. 25). Kur. aṛī earthen waterpot. (DEDR 75).

அரணை Ta. araṇai typical lizard, Lacertidae; smooth streaked lizard, Lacerta interpunctula. Ma. araṇa green house lizard, L. interpunctula. Ka. araṇe, rāṇe, rāṇi greenish kind of lizard which is said to poison by licking, L. interpunctula. Tu. araṇe id. (DEDR 204). Rebus: eraṇi f. ' anvil ' (Gujarati)

bharāḍ = a religious service or entertainment performed by a bharāḍī; consisting of singing the praises of some idol or god with playing on the ḍaur (drum) and dancing; an order of aṭharā akhāḍe = 18 gosāyī group; bharāḍ and bhāratī are two of the 18 orders of gosāyī (Marathi) bārṇe, bāraṇe = an offering of food to a demon; a meal after fasting, a breakfast (Tulu) barada, barda, birada = a vow (Gujarati) vrata id. (Sanskrit)

baṭhi furnace for smelting ore (the same as kuṭhi) (Santali) bhaṭa = an oven, kiln, furnace; make an oven, a furnace; iṭa bhaṭa = a brick kiln; kun:kal bhaṭa a potter's kiln; cun bhaṭa = a lime kiln; cun tehen dobon bhaṭaea = we shall prepare the lime kiln today (Santali); bhaṭṭhā (H.) bhart = a mixed metal of copper and lead; bhartīyā= a barzier, worker in metal; bhaṭ, bhrāṣṭra = oven, furnace (Skt.) mẽṛhẽt baṭi = iron (Ore) furnaces. [Synonyms are: mẽt = the eye, rebus for: the dotted circle (Santali) baṭha [H. baṭṭhī (Sad.)] any kiln, except a potter's kiln, which is called coa; there are four kinds of kiln: cunabat.ha, a lime-kin, it.abat.ha, a brick-kiln, ērēbaṭha, a lac kiln, kuilabaṭha, a charcoal kiln; trs. Or intrs., to make a kiln; cuna rapamente ciminaupe baṭhakeda? How many limekilns did you make? Baṭha-sen:gel = the fire of a kiln; baṭi [H. Sad. baṭṭhi, a furnace for distilling) used alone or in the cmpds. arkibuṭi and baṭiora, all meaning a grog-shop; occurs also in ilibaṭi, a (licensed) rice-beer shop (Mundari) bhaṭi = liquor from mohwa flowers (Santali)

bhráṣṭra n. ' frying pan, gridiron ' MaitrS. [√bhrajj] Pk. bhaṭṭha -- m.n. ' gridiron '; K. büṭhü f. ' level surface by kitchen fireplace on which vessels are put when taken off fire '; S. baṭhu m. ' large pot in which grain is parched, large cooking fire ', baṭhī f. ' distilling furnace '; L. bhaṭṭh m. ' grain -- parcher's oven ', bhaṭṭhī f. ' kiln, distillery ', awāṇ. bhaṭh; P. bhaṭṭh m., °ṭhī f. ' furnace ', bhaṭṭhā m. ' kiln '; N. bhāṭi ' oven or vessel in which clothes are steamed for washing '; A. bhaṭā ' brick -- or lime -- kiln '; B. bhāṭi ' kiln '; Or. bhāṭi ' brick -- kiln, distilling pot '; Mth. bhaṭhī, bhaṭṭī ' brick -- kiln, furnace, still '; Aw.lakh. bhāṭhā ' kiln '; H. bhaṭṭhā m. ' kiln ', bhaṭ f. ' kiln, oven, fireplace '; M. bhaṭṭā m. ' pot of fire ', bhaṭṭī f. ' forge '. -- X bhástrā -- q.v. S.kcch. bhaṭṭhī keṇī ' distil (spirits) '.(CDIAL 9656). kolmo 'three' (Mu.); rebus: kolami 'smithy' (Telugu) కొలిమి [kolimi] kolimi. [Tel.] n. A pit. A fire pit or furnace. ముద్దకొలిమి a smelting forge. నీళ్లకొలిమి a reservoir. కొలిమితిత్తి a pair of bellows.(Telugu)

bēḍā f. ' boat ' lex. 2. vēḍā, vēṭī -- f. lex. 3. bhēḍa -- 3 m., bhēla -- 1, °aka -- m.n. lex.1. Pk. bēḍa -- , °aya -- m., bēḍā -- , °ḍiyā -- f. ' boat ', Gy. eur. bero, S. ḇeṛo m., °ṛī ' small do. '; L. bēṛā (Ju. ḇ --) m. ' large cargo boat ', bēṛī f. ' boat ', P. beṛā m., °ṛī f.; Ku. beṛo ' boat, raft ', N. beṛā, OAw. beḍā, H. beṛā m., G. beṛɔ m., beṛi f., M. beḍā m.2. Pk. vēḍa -- m. ' boat '.3. Pk. bhēḍaka -- , bhēlaa -- m., bhēlī -- f. ' boat '; B. bhelā ' raft ', Or. bheḷā.*bēḍḍa -- ,S.kcch. beṛī f. ' boat ', beṛo m. ' ship '; WPah.poet. beṛe f. ' boat ', J. beṛī f.3. bhēḍa -- 3: A. bhel ' raft ' (phonet. bhel) ' raft ' (CDIAL 9308).

*ḍagga -- 3 ' cattle '. 2. †*ḍhagga -- 2. [Cf. *ḍaṅgara -- 1, *daṅgara --] 1. WPah.kṭg. *ḍɔggɔ* m. 'a head of cattle', *ḍɔgge* m.pl. 'cattle', sat. (LSI ix 4, 667) *ḍōgai* ' cattle '.2. S.kcch. *ḍhago* m. ' ox ', L(Shahpur) *ḍhaggā* m. 'small weak ox', *ḍhaggī* f. ' cow ', Garh. *ḍhãgu* ' old bull '(CDIAL 5524a) *ḍaṅgara1 'cattle'. 2. *daṅgara -- . [Same as *ḍaṅ-gara* -- 2 s.v. *ḍagga -- 2 as a pejorative term for cattle]1. K. *ḍangur* m. 'bullock', L. *ḍaṅgur*, (Ju.) *ḍãgar* m. 'horned cattle'; P. *ḍaṅgar* m. 'cattle', Or. *ḍaṅgara*; Bi. *ḍãgar* 'old worn -- out beast, dead cattle', *dhūr ḍãgar* 'cattle in general'; Bhoj. *ḍāṅgar* 'cattle'; H. *ḍãgar*, *ḍãgrā* m. ' horned cattle '. 2. H. *dãgar* m. = prec.(CDIAL 5526) Rebus: N. *ḍāṅro* ' term of contempt for a blacksmith' (CDIAL 5524) Vikalpa: sal 'bos gaurus'; rebus sal 'workshop' (Santali) <sayEl>(L) {N} ``^bison, wild ^buffalo''. #59041.

Pk. dhaḍa -- n. ' trunk of body ', S. dhaṛu m., P. dhaṛ f.; Ku. dhaṛ m. ' trunk of body or tree, middle part of anything '; B. dhaṛ 'trunk of body', Or. dhaṛa ' trunk of body or tree '; Mth. dhar ' headless body '; OAw. dhara m. ' body, heart '; H. dhaṛ m. ' trunk of body ' (→ Mth. N. dhaṛ), OMarw. dhaṛa m., G. dhaṛ n.; M. dhaḍ n. ' headless body '. (CDIAL 6712).
Rebus: dhātu 'mineral' (Vedic); dhatu 'a mineral, metal' (Santali) meḍ 'body', 'dance' (Santali) meḍ 'iron' + dhatu 'mineral' (Santali)

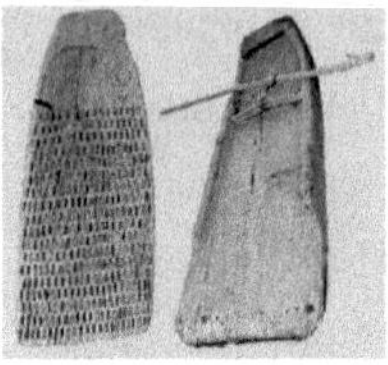

Primitive ("Orwell's") spike harrow (Archeological museum – Alanya, Turkey)

H. *dā̃tāwlī* f. ' rake, harrow '. (CDIAL 6162). Ku. *danīṛo* m. ' harrow '; N. *dā̃de* ' toothed ' sb. ' harrow '; A. *dā̃tīyā* ' having new teeth in place of the first ', *dā̃tinī* ' woman with projecting teeth '; Or. *dāntiā* ' toothed '; H. *dā̃tī* f. ' harrow '; G. *dā̃tiyɔ* m. ' semicircular comb ', *dā̃tiyɔ* m. ' harrow '. (CDIAL 6163). G. *dā̃tɔ* m. ' a kind of rake or harrow ' (CDIAL 6153).
Pk. *daṁtāla* -- m., *°lī* -- f. ' grass -- cutting instrument '; S. *ḍandārī* f. ' rake ', L. (Ju.) *ḍā̃dāl* m., *°lī* f.; Ku. *danyālo* m. ' harrow ', gng. *danyāw* (*y* from *danīṛo* < dantín --); N.*dā̃tār* ' tusked ' (← a Bi. form); A. *dā̃tāl* adj. ' tusked ', sb. ' spade '; B. *dā̃tāl* ' toothed '; G. *dā̃tāḷ* n., *°ḷī* f. ' harrow '; M. *dā̃tāḷ* ' having projecting teeth ', *dā̃tāḷ, °ḷē, dā̃tāḷ* n. ' harrow, rake '.Garh. *dā̃dāḷu* ' forked implement ', Brj. *dā̃tāl, dā̃tāro* ' toothed ', m. ' elephant '. (CDIAL 6160).

దాగలి [dāgali] or దాకలి *dāgali.* [Tel. దాయి+కలు.] n. An anvil. ఇరుకుదాగలి a carpenter's vice.
దాయి [dāyi] *dāyi.* [Tel.] n. An anvil, a work. hench, or smith's form, used as a rest or prop. దాగలి. (Telugu)

*ḍag2 ' step, pace '. 2. *ḍig -- 2. 3. *dag -- 2. 1. N. *ḍag* ' step, stride ', H. *ḍag* f., OMarw. *ḍaga* f., G. *ḍag, ḍaglũ* n.; M. *ḍag* f. ' pace ', *ḍagṇẽ* ' to step over '; -- Or. *ḍagara* ' footstep, road '; Mth. *ḍagar* ' road ', H. *ḍagar* f., *ḍagrā* m., G. *ḍagar* f. 2. P. *ḍīgh* f. ' foot, step '; N. *ḍeg, ḍek* ' pace '; Mth. *ḍeg* ' footstep '; H. *ḍig, ḍeg* f. ' pace '. 3. L. *dagg* m. ' road ', *daggaṛ rāh* m. ' wide road ' (mult. *ḍaggar rāh* < *daggaṛ*?); P. *dagaṛ* m. ' road ', H. *dagṛā* m.(CDIAL 5523).

1. Ext. -- r -- : S. ṭakuru m. ' mountain ', ṭakirī f. ' hillock ', ṭākara f. ' low hill ', ṭākirū m. ' mountaineer '; N. ṭākuro, °ri ' hill top '. 2. Or. ṭāṅgī ' hill, stony country '. -- Ext. -- r -- : Or. ṭāṅgara ' rocky hilly land '. 3. Ext. -- r -- : Or. ṭikara ' high land, sandbank ', ṭikarā, ṭīkirā ' anthill '. 4. A. ṭiṅ ' mountain peak ', ṭiṅnā ' elevated piece of land ', ṭiṅāli ' very high '. -- Ext. -- l -- in *uṭṭiṅgala -- 5. M. ṭek m.n., ṭekāḍ n., ṭekḍī, ṭẽk° f. ' hillock '. -- Ext. -- r -- : P. ṭekrā m., °rī f. ' rock, hill '; H. ṭekar, °krā m. ' heap, hillock '; G. ṭekrɔ m., °rī f. ' mountain, hillock '. 6. K. ṭẽg m. ' hillock, mound '. 7. G. ṭũk ' peak '. 8. M. ṭũg n. ' mound, lump '. -- Ext. -- r -- : Or. ṭuṅguri ' hillock '; M. ṭũgar n. ' bump, mound ' (see *uṭṭungara --); -- -- l -- : M. ṭũgaḷ, °gūḷ n. 9. K. ḍȧki f. ' hill, rising ground '. -- Ext. -- r -- : K. ḍakürü f. ' hill on a road '. 10. Ext. -- r -- : Pk. ḍaggara -- m. ' upper terrace of a house '; M. ḍagar f. ' little hill, slope '. 11. Ku. ḍāg, ḍāk ' stony land '; B. ḍāṅ ' heap ', ḍāṅgā ' hill, dry upland '; H. ḍāg f. ' mountain -- ridge '; M. ḍāg m.n., ḍāgaṇ, °gāṇ, ḍāgāṇ n. ' hill -- tract '. -- Ext. -- r -- : N. ḍaṅgur ' heap '. 12. M. ḍũg m. ' hill, pile ', °gā m. ' eminence ', °gī f. ' heap '. -- Ext. -- r -- : Pk. ḍuṁgara -- m. ' mountain '; Ku. ḍũgar, ḍũgrī; N. ḍuṅgar ' heap '; Or. ḍuṅguri ' hillock ', H. ḍũgar m., G. ḍũgar m., ḍũgrī f. 13. S. ḏũgaru m. ' hill ', H. M. ḍõgar m. 14. Pa. tuṅga -- ' high '; Pk. tuṁga -- ' high ', tuṁgīya -- m. ' mountain '; K. tŏng, tọngu m. ' peak ', P. tuṅg f.; A. tuṅg ' importance '; Si. tuṅgu ' lofty, mountain '. -- Cf. uttuṅga -- ' lofty ' MBh. 15. K. thọngu m. ' peak '. 16. H. dāg f. ' hill, precipice ', dāgī ' belonging to hill country '. 3. 12. *ḍuṅga -- : S.kcch. ḍūṅghar m. ' hillock '.(CDIAL 5423).

डोंगर [ḍ▫ṅgara] m A hill. (Marathi)

डोंगा [ḍōṅgā] m (H) A sort of boat, a canoe or doney. (Marathi)*ḍōṅga1 ' trough, dug -- out canoe, boat '. 2. *ḍaṅga -- 4. 3. *ḍiṅga -- 1. 4. *ḍēṅga -- 1. 5. *ḍōṇṭa -- 1. [Though prob. of non -- Aryan origin, it may have affected the meaning of drṓṇa -- 1] 1. Pk. ḍoṁgī -- , °galī -- f. ' small box for betel ', ḍuṁgha<-> m. ' water -- vessel made of coconut shell '; Sh. (Lor.) ḍūṅo ' small earthen vessel '; K. ḍũga m. ' a kind of covered boat '; P. ḍõgā m., °gī f., ḍõghā m., °ghī f. ' a deep boat '; Ku. ḍuṅo ' ferry boat '; N. ḍũgo, ḍuṅo ' small boat (usu. of one piece of wood) '; A. ḍoṅgā ' canoe made of plaintain -- sheath '; B. ḍoṅa, ḍuṅi ' canoe, boat '; Or. ḍuṅgi ' dug -- out canoe '; Bhoj. Aw.lakh. ḍõgī ' boat '; H. ḍõgā m. ' trough, canoe, ladle '; G. ḍũgɔ m. ' tobaccopipe '; 2. Or. ḍaṅgā ' small country boat, dug -- out canoe ', ḍaṅgi ' canoe '. 3. A. B. ḍiṅā ' boat, canoe ', Or. ḍiṅgā. 4. Bhoj. ḍẽgi ' boat '; H. ḍẽgī f. ' small boat, canoe '. 5. S. ḏũḍo m., °ḍī f. ' boat '; L. ḍõṇḍā m. ' boat ', mult. ḍūṇḍā m., (Ju.) ḏũḏī f.; N. ḍũṛ, ḍũṛh ' trough, wooden or bamboo water -- channel, gutter. '(CDIAL 5568).

ṭaṅka2 m.n. ' spade, hoe, chisel ' R. 2. ṭaṅga -- 2 m.n. ' sword, spade ' lex.1. Pa. ṭaṅka -- m. ' stone mason's chisel '; Pk. ṭaṁka -- m. ' stone -- chisel, sword '; Woṭ. ṭhõ ' axe '; Bshk. ṭhoṅ ' battleaxe ', ṭheṅ ' small axe ' (< *ṭaṅkī); Tor. (Biddulph) "tunger" m. ' axe ' (ṭ? AO viii 310), Phal. ṭhō̆ṅgi f.; K. ṭŏnguru m. ' a kind of hoe '; N. (Tarai) ṭāgi ' adze '; H. ṭākī f. ' chisel '; G. ṭāk f. ' pen nib '; M. ṭāk m. ' pen nib ', ṭākī f. ' chisel '. 2. A. ṭāṅgi ' stone chisel '; B. ṭāṅg, °gi ' spade, axe '; Or. ṭāṅgi ' battle -- axe '; Bi. ṭāgā, °gī ' adze '; Bhoj. ṭāṅī ' axe '; H. ṭāgī f. ' hatchet '.(CDIAL 5427).

Ta. iṭamāṉam double drum carried on the back of an animal; ṭamāyi kettle-drum mounted on an ox; ṭamāram, ṭamāṉam, ṭammāram, ṭammāṉam a kind of drum.*Ma.* ṭamānam, ḍhamānam kettle-drums beaten before princes. *Ka.* ḍamāra, ḍamāṇa a pair of kettle-drums. *Tu.* ḍamāra, ḍamāna a kettle-drum. *Te.* ḍamāramu, ḍamāyi id. / Cf. Skt. ḍamaru- a kind of drum (DEDR 2949) ḍamaru m. ' drum ' Rājat., *°uka* -- m. lex. 2. *ḍam- baru -- . [Onom. and perh. ← Mu. EWA i 460, PMWS 86] 1. Pk. *ḍamarua* -- m.n.; L. awāṇ. P. *ḍaurū* m. ' tabor, small drum '; Ku. *ḍaũr, ḍaũru* ' drum '; M. *ḍaur, ḍavrā* m. ' hourglass -- tabor ', *ḍaurī* m. ' itinerant musician '. 2. N. *ḍambaru, ḍamaru* ' small drum ', A. *ḍambaru,* B. *ḍamru,* Or. *ḍambaru, ḍamaru,* H. *ḍamrū* m., G. M. *ḍamru* m. Other variants: K. *ḍābürü* f. ' large drum used for proclamations '; -- Or. *ḍempha* ' shallow kettledrum '; -- N. *ḍamphu, °pho* ' small drum or tambourine '; B. *ḍamphu* drum '; -- Ku. *ḍāphṛī* ' drum ', *ḍaphulo, °uwā* ' small drum '; N. *ḍaph* ' a partic. musical instrument played during Holi '; G. *ḍaph* f.n. ' a kind of tabor '; <-> G.*ḍamkɔ* m. ' drum '.(CDIAL 5531). *ḍaṅka ' drum '. 2. *ḍakka -- 4. [Cf. *ḍakkārī* -- ' lute ' lex.] 1. P. N. B. Or. H. M. *ḍaṅkā* m. ' drum '; G. *ḍaṅkɔ* m. ' large kettledrum ', M. *ḍākā* m. 2. Pk. *ḍakka* -- m. ' a partic. musical instrument '; G. *ḍakkɔ* m. ' drum '; Si. *ḍäkkiya* ' tom -- tom '.(CDIAL 5525).

dhatu 'mineral, ore' (Santali) dhā́tu n. ' substance ' RV., m. ' element ' MBh., ' metal, mineral, ore (esp. of a red colour) ' Mn., ' ashes of the dead ' lex., ' *strand of rope ' (cf. tridhā́tu -- ' threefold ' RV., ayugdhātu -- ' having an uneven number of strands ' KātyŚr.). [√dhā] Pa. dhātu -- m. ' element, ashes of the dead, relic '; Kharl. dhatu ' relic '; Pk. dhāu -- m. ' metal, red chalk '; N. dhāu ' ore (esp. of copper) '; Or. ḍhāu ' red chalk, red ochre ' (whence ḍhāuā ' reddish '; M. dhāū, dhāv m.f. ' a partic. soft red stone ' (whence dhāvaḍ m. ' a caste of iron -- smelters ', dhāvḍī ' composed of or relating to iron '); -- Si. dā ' relic '; -- S. dhāī f. ' wisp of fibres added from time to time to a rope that is being twisted ', L. dhāī̃ f.(CDIAL 6773).

<dathom>,,<dathrom>,,<dathrom> {N} ``larger hand ^sickle for cutting grain or grass''. @5025. #6991. Mu., Bh., Ho<datrom>, H.<datri>, Sk.<datrA> `sickle'. %8011. #7931. dāta2 ' mowed ' Pāṇ.com. [√dō] Pa. dāta -- ; Or. duā ' harvested or cut (of rice) ', sb. ' harvesting of rice ', duā -- dui ' id. ' (whence duāḷi ' reaper '). dā´ti ' cuts, mows ' RV. [√dō] Pa. dāyati ' mows ', A. dāiba (pres. part. dāūtā, f. dāti), B. dāoyā; Or. dāibā ' to cut rice with a sickle, mow grass '. dā´ti -- f. ' giving ' in cmpds. RV. [√dā1] 6260 dā´tra2 n. ' knife, sickle ' RV. 2. *dātrī -- of which dāti- f. Gal. is MIA. form. [Northern word Pat. MBhāṣ. i 9, 27 which may account for NW forms in H. and Brj. <-> √dō] 1. Pa. dātta -- n. ' sickle ', Pk. datta -- n., K. drôtu m., S. ḏāṭro m., L. ḏātr m.,; P. dāttar m. ' large toothless sickle '; WPah.bhad. ḍḷāt n. ' sickle ', bhal. ḍḷāt n. ' curved knife for cutting wood ', (Joshi) dra'ṭ ' sickle '; A. dā ' large knife '; B. dā, dāo ' sickle, bill, chopper ', Or. dā, dāā, H. dā f., darāt m. (← NW), Brj. drāt; G. dātarṛũ n. ' sickle '; Si. dā̤ -- käti ' sickle ' (< nom. sg. *dātē or < *dātrī --). 2. Pk. dattiyā -- f. ' little sickle '; Paš.ar. drāet, chil. lāit ' sickle ', K. dröċü f., L. ḏātrī f., awāṇ. dātrī f., P. dātrī, ḍātrī, darātī, darāṭī, dāt(t)ī f., WPah.cur. cam. drāṭī, bhad. bhal. ḍḷāti, khaś. śeu. lāṭī, roh. dace, Garh. dāthi, datharī, Ku. dātī f., H. darātī f. (←P.), G. dātarṛ f.; -- Si. dā̤ -- see above. Ext. -- ll -- : Ku. dātulo m. ' sickle ', dataliyā ' large scythe ', gng. datul, daċhul ' sickle '; Or. dāil, °li ' small weeding sickle '. -- Pr. le/ṭēgë ' sickle ' (NTS xv 264) rather < lavitra -- . 2 [dāti -- is Eastern word: dātir lavanārthe prācyeṣu dātram udīcyeṣu Nir. 2.2.8 = Pat. 6.6.1] S.kcch. ḍātro, ḍātro, ḍāytro m. ' sickle ', WPah.kṭg. dāc m. ' large knife ', kṭg. (kc.) dacci f. ' sickle ', kṭg. dacṭi f. ' small sickle '; Brj. dātī ' sickle '. (CDIAL 6256, 6257, 6260).

A. dār ' row of teeth of fish or reptile,Pa. daṭṭhā -- f. ' large tooth, fang, tusk '; Pk. daṁṭhā -- f. ' fang 'teeth of saw or sickle ' (CDIAL 6250).

*dāṁṣṭra ' fang, tusk, beard '. [dáṁṣṭra -- n. ' tusk, fang ' RV., daṁṣṭrā -- f. Pāṇ. MBh.; daṁṣṭrikā -- f. ' tusk, beard ' lex.; dāḍhā -- f. ' tusk ' lex., dāḍhikā -- f. ' beard ' Mn., dāḍaka -- m. ' tooth ' lex. Semant. development ' fang -- tusk -- beard ' is possible (Rivet BSL 83, 143). But MIA. dāṭhā -- < daṁṣṭrā -- is phonet. difficult. On the other hand *dāṁṣṭra -- (with vṛddhi -- formation meaning ' pertaining to or collection of fangs ' (cf. A. dār below) > ' fang ', cf. Wackernagel AiGr ii 2, 130 and 132) would in MIA. become NWPk. *dāṭṭha -- (in S. P. WPah. below), central daṁṭha -- , daṭṭha -- , amg. dāṭha -- , dāḍha -- (with simplification of consonant -- group after orig. IA. long vowel), spread of which at the cost of daṭṭha -- was favoured by clash of the latter with daṭṭha -- < daṣṭa<-> and dṛṣṭá -- . Possibility of further Drav. (J. Bloch BSOS v 741) or Mu. (PMWS 63) influence cannot be excluded. -- √daṁś] Pa. daṭṭhā -- f. ' large tooth, fang, tusk '; Pk. daṁṭhā -- f. ' fang '; S. ḏāṭha f. ' molar ', P.pow. dāṭhā m.; WPah. jaun. ḍāṭho ' jaw '; -- Pk. daṁṭhi -- ' having big fangs '; S. ḏāṭhiru ' tusked '. Pa. dāṭhā -- f. (older °ṭha -- m. BSBU 146) ' large tooth, tusk ', Pk. dāḍhā -- f.; Gy. rum. hung. thar, pl. °ra f. ' back tooth ', gr. tar f. ' gums ', wel. tar f. ' jaw, gums ' (DGW iv 359 wrongly < tā´lu --); Kal.rumb. -- dōŕy*lk in dh*lndōŕy*lk ' tooth ' (see dánta --); S. ḏāṛha f. ' molar '; L. dāhaṛ f. ' molar ', (Ju.) ḏāṛh f. ' tusk, root of tooth, bite (of an animal) ', awāṇ. dā`ṛ ' long tooth '; P. dāṛh, dāhṛ f. ' molar '; Ku. dāṛ ' jaws ', gng. ' projecting tooth '; N. dāro ' tusk, fang '; A. dār ' row of teeth of fish or reptile, teeth of saw or sickle '; B. dāṛ, dāṛ(h)ā, ḍāṛ ' tooth, fang '; Or. dāṛhā ' tusk, fang, sting '; H. dāṛh, ḍāṛh f. ' molar ', dāṛhā, ḍā° m. ' large tooth, tusk '; G. dāḍh, ḍāḍh f. ' molar '; M. dāḍh f. ' fang, jaw '; Si. daḷa ' tusk, fang '. <-> Deriv. Pa. dāṭhin -- ' tusked '; Pk. dāḍhi -- ' tusked ', m. ' boar '; N. dāre ' tusked, male (of stag) '; -- S. ḏāṛhaṇu ' to bite '; Ku. dāṛaṇo ' to bite, injure '. -- X jámbha -- : S.ǰāṛha,ǰāṛī f. ' jaw '; P. jāṛh f. ' molar '; -- M. dābhāḍ n. ' jaw ' (X˙jābhāḍ < *jambhahaḍḍa --). Pa. dāṭhikā -- f. ' beard ', Pk. dāḍhiā -- f., Gy. as. (JGLS new ser. ii 259) dari, Ash. dāṛī´, Kt. däŕī´, däyī, Wg. däř, dą̄, dā, Dm. dâŕi, dâacute;ī, Tir. Paš. dāṛī´ (→ Par. dhâṛī´IIFL i 249), Shum. dā´ṛi, Woṭ. deā´ṛ, Gaw. dā´ṛī, Bshk. dɛ̀'r, Tor. dáī, Kand. däī, Mai. dhāi, Phal. dn/aṛī f. (paṇar -- dhōṛ ' greybeard '); Sh.gil. dāi, koh. gur. dáï, jij. dä´ṛī ' beard ' (all f.), pales. daī ' chin '; K. dörü f. ' beard ', kash. dāṛhi, S. ḏāṛhī f., L. dāṛhī f., (Ju.) ḏāṛhī f., khet. ḍāṛhī, P. dāṛhī f., °ṛhā m., WPah.bhal. khaś. dā`ṛi f., Ku. dāṛī, N. dāri; A. dāri, ḍāri ' beard, whiskers '; B. Or. dāṛ(h)i ' beard, chin '; Mth. dāṛh ' long beard '; Mth. Bhoj. dāṛhī ' beard '; H. dāṛhī, ḍā° f. ' beard ', ḍāṛhā m. ' hanging root of banyan tree '; G. dāḍhī f. ' beard, chin ', dāḍhũ n. (contemptuous) ' unshaven chin ', ḍhāḍhī f. ' beard ', M. dāḍhī; Si. däliya ' beard, moustache ' (rävul ' beard ' < *ḍāḍhiā -- with l -- suffix H. Smith JA 1950, 197: very doubtful). Addenda: *dāṁṣṭra -- [Burrow Shwa 6 MIA. dāṭha < *dāṣṭra<-> with full grade dāś -- ' bite ' < IE. dēk̑ -- in Gk. fut. dh/zomai, perf. de/dhgmai; dáṁṣṭra from nasalized weak grade daṁṣṭvā TāṇḍyaBr. (daṁśati Cāṇ.)] Pa. daṭṭhā -- : A. ḍâṭh (phonet. dɔth) ' elephant goad ' (or conn. daṇḍá -- , *ḍaṭṭha -- ?). Pk. daṁṭhā -- : A. dār ' teeth ' AFD 207. Pa. dāṭhā -- : S.kcch. ḍāṛ f. ' molar ', WPah.kṭg. (kc.) dáṛh, dāṛh f. (obl. -- a), J. dā'ṛ m. Pa. dāṭhikā -- : S.kcch. ḍāṛī f. ' beard ', WPah.kṭg. dáṛhi f. ' beard ', J. dāṛī f.; Md. doḷi ' jaw '. (CDIAL 6250)

ḍhol 'a drum beaten on one end by a stick and on the other by the hand' (Santali); *ḍhol* 'drum' (Nahali); *dhol* (Kurku); *ḍhol* (Hi.) *dhol* a drum (G.)(CDIAL 5608) ఢోలు [ḍōlu] [Tel.] n. A drum. *dula* 'pair' Rebus 1: *dul* 'to cast in a mould'; *dul mẽṛhẽt, dul meṛeḍ, dul; koṭe meṛeḍ* 'forged iron' (Santali) WPah.kṭg. (kc.) Rebus 2: *ḍhō`l* m. 'stone', kṭg. *ḍhòḷṭɔ* m.

'big stone or boulder', *ḍhòḷṭu* 'small id.' Him.I 87.(CDIAL 5536). <madOLO>(P) {N} ``a kind of ^musical_instrument, sounding like a ^drum''. Syn. <aRa>, <baido>, <boDokaTo>, <caG>, <DhOlO>, <Dholki>, <mou~Ni>, <nagra>. *Kh.<mandRi>(D), ~<manDri>(B), ~<mandar>(D) `drum', Mu.<mandara>, Ho<madal>, H.<ma~dArA>, ~<ma~dAlA>, Sk.<mArdAlA> `kind of drum', O.<madOLO>, Sa.<mAndAriA> `a drummer'. %21301. #21131.

dula 'pair' Rebus: dul 'cast (metal)(Santali)

Bshk. *ḍōl* ' brass pot '; K. *ḍol* m. ' bucket ', S. *ḍolu* m., P. *ḍol* m., WPah.bhal. *ḍol* n., Ku. N. B. Mth. *ḍol*, Aw. lakh. *ḍōlu*, H. *dol*, *ḍol* m., G. *ḍol* f., M. *ḍol* m. WPah.poet. *ḍōr* m. ' small pot ', kṭg. *ḍōl* m. ' bucket ', J. *ḍō̆l* m. ← H. or < **dōlla* --).(CDIAL 6583).

Rebus: eraka, er-aka any metal infusion (Ka.Tu.) eruvai 'copper' (Ta.); ere dark red (Ka.)(DEDR 446). erka = ekke (Tbh. of arka) aka (Tbh. of arka) copper (metal); crystal (Kannada) Metal: akka, aka (Tadbhava of arka) metal; akka metal (Te.) arka = copper (Skt.) erka = ekke (Tbh. of arka) aka (Tbh. of arka) copper (metal); crystal (Kannada) erako molten cast (Tulu) agasāle, agasāli, agasālavāḍu = a goldsmith (Telugu.) erakaddu = any cast thng; erake hoyi = to pour meltted metal into a mould, to cast (Ka.); cf. arika = rice beer (Santali) er-e = to pour any liquids; to pour (Ka.); ir-u (Ta.Ma.); ira- ī (Ta.); er-e = to cast, as metal; to overflow, to cover with water, to bathe (Ka.); er-e, ele = pouring; fitness for being poured (Kannada) erako molten cast (Tulu) eh-kam any weapon made of steel (Cūṭā.); eh-ku steel; eh-ku-pat.utal to melt, to soften (Cilap. 15, 210, Urai.)(Tamil) eraka, era, era = syn. erka, copper, weapons (Kannada) erakōlu = the iron axle of a carriage (Kannada.Malayalam).

Ka. eṟake, eṟaṅke, ṟakke, ṟekke wing; ṟaṭṭe, ṟeṭṭe wing, upper arm. *Koḍ.* rekke wing; raṭṭe upper arm. *Tu.* ediṅke, reṅkè wing. *Te.* eṟaka, ṟekka, rekka, neṟaka, neṟi id. *Kol.* reḍapa, (SR.) reppā id.; (P.) reṛapa id., feather. *Nk.* rekka, reppa wing. *Pa.* (S.) rekka id. *Go.* (S.) rekka wing-feather; reka (M.) feather, (Ko.) wing (*Voc.* 3045). *Koṇḍa* ṟeka wing, upper arm. *Kuwi* (Su.) rekka wing. *Ta.* ciṟai, ciṟaku, ciṟakar wing; iṟai, iṟaku, iṟakar, iṟakkai wing, feather. *Ma.* iṟaku, ciṟaku wing. *Ko.* rek wing, feather. (DEDR 2591).

ಎರಕ ēraka. (or ಎಱಕ, fr. ಎಱ್ 2?). Any metal infusion (My.; Tu.; T. ಉರುಕ್ಕು; M. ಉರುಕ್ಕ, melting; ಉರುಕ್ಕು, what is melted; fused metal; T., M. ಉರುಕ್ಕು, Tu. ಎರಗು, to melt); molten state, fusion (My.). ಎರಕದ್ದು, any cast thing (C.). — ಎರಕ ಹೊಯ್ಯು. To pour melted metal into a mould, to cast (My.). ಎರಕ ಹೊಯ್ದುದರೂ ನೆರಕ ತಪ್ಪದು (Prv.).

Rebus: eraka, e_raka = any metal infusion (Ka.Tu.); urukku (Ta.); urukka melting; urukku what is melted; fused metal (Ma.); urukku (Ta.Ma.); eragu = to melt; molten state, fusion; erakaddu = any cast (Ka.)

Ka. e_rakil, e_rake a roof, thatch. *Koḍ.* ërakï eaves. ? *Te.* e_ra, in: talliy- e_ra the uppermost well-tube which forms a parapet round a well. *Konḍa* r_ēkam roof. (DEDR 528).

Ta. erukku (erukki-) to cut, hew, strike (as a bush), beat (as a drum), kill, destroy. *Pa.* erk- to cut down bushes, etc., in clearing land. *Go.* (Ko.) erk- to cut down (grass, bushes); erkem (*pl.* erke) billhook (*Voc.* 349). *Kui* erga (ergi-) to make a clearing, clear jungle or thick grass or scrub; *n.* act of clearing a jungle. *Kuwi* (Isr.) erg- (-it-) to cut, slash. ? *Malt.* en_gde to clear away weeds, (*Gramm.*, p. 66) cut down a jungle (DEDR 824).

Ko. irg kindling (dry plants with leaves still on). *Ka.* (Hav.) ege small branch, sprout; (Bark.) eṅkli thin branch. *Tu.* eggè a branch, bough; eggelů a small branch. *Kor.* (M.) eŋkili branch. ? *Te.* rivva, rivaṭa a twig (DEDR 826).

Ta. eruvai European bamboo reed; a species of Cyperus; straight sedge tuber. *Ma.* eruva a kind of grass (DEDR 819). ērakā f. ' a kind of grass with emollient and diluent qualities ' MBh., *°kī*-- f. ' a species of plant '. Pa. *ēraka* -- n. ' Typha -- grass ', *ēragu* -- ' a kind of grass for making coverlets '; S. *eru* 'a partic. kind of plant'?(CDIAL 2516).

Ta. eruvai a kind of kite whose head is white and whose body is brown; eagle. *Ma.* eruva eagle, kite (DEDR 818).

Ka. e_ragu to bow, be bent, crouch, come down, alight, fall upon, attack, enter, join, accrue to; *n.* a bow, obeisance; e_ragisu to cause to bow, etc.; e_raka coming down, etc. *Tu.* eraguni to bow *Te.* e_rãgu, erãgu to descend, bow or make obeisance, prostrate oneself; erãguḍu bowing, salutation Ta. iṟai (-v-, -nt-) to bow before (as in salutation), worship (DEDR 516). Rebus: eraka 'copper'.

eraka, hero = a messenger; a spy (Gujarat) hēraka = spy (Skt.); ēra = to spy (Kui); er = to see (Malt.); hēru = spy (Pkt.); hēriu = spy (Kl.); hero (G.); *herũ* spying (G.); herṇẽ to spy (M.); hernā (H.); herai (Oaw.)(CDIAL 14165). heriyām = prying, peeping; heravum = to spy (Gujarat) ere = to see, behold; erye to peep, spy (Malt.); her to look at or for (Pkt.); er uk- to play 'peeping tom' (Ko.); ēra spying, scouting (Kui); hēri kiyali to see (Kuwi); ērnā (īryas) to see, look, lok for (Kur.)(DEDR 903).

Pict-108 [*Chanhu-daro Excavations*, Pl. LI, 18] erugu = to bow, to salute or make

obeisance (Te.) er-agu = obeisance (Ka.), iṛai (Ta.) er-agisu = to bow, to be bent; to make obeisance to; to crouch; to come down; to alight (Kannada) cf. arghas = respectful reception of a guest (by the offering of rice, dūrva grass, flowers or often only of water)(S'Br.14)(Sanskrit) erugu = to bow, to salute or make obeisance (Telugu)

இலை[1] ilai, *n.* [K. Tu. *ele*, M. *ila*.] 1. Leaf; மரஞ் செடிகளின் இலை. இலை வளர்குரம்பை (சீவக. 1432). 2. Petal; பூவிதழ். அகவிலை யாம்பல் (தேவா. 511, 8)

இலை[1] ilai Blade of a weapon or instrument; ஆயுதவலகு. நச்சிலை வேற்படைவீரர் (சீவக. 2209).

Sh. *jăkŭr* m. ' hair on head and body '; K. *zọ̆ku* m. ' hair of female privities '. 2. P. *jagoṭā* m. ' plaited hair worn round loins by faqirs '; N. *jagar* ' mane ', *jagaṭo* ' tangled hair ', *jagalṭo* 'matted and dishevelled hair'. (CDIAL 5075).

jāḍa 'joining, pair' < Dravidian LM333. [zata] *ḍzata*. [Tel.] n. A pair; a set. Similarity, సామ్యము. A match, an equal; a fellow. జతను వచ్చినవాండ్లు those who came with me. అవి నాకు బొత్తిగా పోయినవాటితో జతే they are as good as lost to me. adj. Equal. జతపడు *ḍzata-paḍu*. v. n. To agree, unite, suit, combine. వానికి జతపడినారు they joined him. ఆ పని జతపడలేదు the business did not succeed.(Telugu)

1. Pk. *jaḍia* -- ' set (of jewels), joined '; K. *jarun* ' to set jewels ' (← Ind.); S. *jaṛaṇu* ' to join, rivet, set ', *jaṛa* f. ' rivet, boundary between two fields '; P. *jaṛāuṇā* ' to have fastened or set

'; A. *zarāiba* ' to collect '; B. *jaṛāna* ' to set jewels, wrap round, entangle ', *jaṛ* ' heaped together '; Or. *jaṛibā* ' to unite '; OAw. *jaraï* ' sets jewels, bedecks '; H. *jaṛnā* ' to join, stick in, set ' (→ N. *jaṛnu* ' to set, be set '); OMarw. *jaṛāū* ' inlaid '; G. *jaṛvũ* ' to join, meet with, set jewels '; M. *ǰaḍṇē* ' to join, connect, inlay, be firmly established ', *ǰaṭṇē* ' to combine, confederate '.(CDIAL 5091).

jáṭā f. ' hair twisted together ' PārGr̥., ' fibrous root, root ' Bhpr. 2. *jaṭṭa -- 1. 3. *jāṭā -- . [Cf. *śaṭā* -- f. ' ascetic's matted hair ' W., *saṭā* -- f. ' braid of hair, lion's mane ' MBh. -- DED 1897 and EWA i 413 ← Drav., but eventually with PMWS 63 ← Mu. with *jatta- (**jatra* -- , **jacca* --), *jakka -- (**jagga* --), jūṭa -- (**juṇṭa* --), **jhaṇṭa* -- (**jhāṭṭha* -- , **jhiṇṭa* --), *jhuṇṭa -- (**jhōṇṭa* -- , **jhuṭṭa* -- , **jhūṭa* -- , **jhōṭṭa* --), *jhūśa -- , *jhallā -- , cū́ḍa -- 1 (*cōḍa* --3, **cōṇḍa* -- , **cōṭṭa* -- , **cunda* -- 2)] 1. Pa. *jaṭā* -- f. ' matted hair, tangled boughs '; Pk. *jaḍā*-<-> f. ' tangled or braided hair '; K. *zara* m. ' hair on scalp (esp. of infant '); S. *jaṛha* f. ' root ', L. *jaṛ*, pl. *°ṛrā* f., (Ju.) *ǰaṛh* f.; P. *jaṛ* f., *jaṛh* m. ' root ', *jaṛāu* m. ' matted hair '; WPah. rudh. *ǰaṛ* ' goat's hair '; Ku. *jaṛ* f., *°ro* m. ' root ', *°ri* f. ' small root '; N. *jari*, *°ro* ' root ', *jaruwā* ' root, bottom ', *jaire* ' hair in armpits '; A. *zar -- ban* ' medicinal herb '; B. *jaṛ* ' root ', *jaṛi -- buṭi* ' medicines '; Or. *jaṛa* ' root ', *jaṛi -- buṭi* ' herbs '; Bi. *jar* ' root, esp. sugarcane root '; Mth. *jaṛi* ' root '; OAw. *jarī* ' root of medicinal herb '; H. Marw. *jaṛ* f. ' root '; G. *jaṛ* f. ' root ', *jaṛyā* f. pl. ' root fibres '; M. *ǰaḍ* f. ' root '. 2. WPah. bhal. *ǰeṭri* ' locks of hair '; G. *jāṭ* f. ' sheep's wool '. 3. Gy. eur. *ǰar* (gr. boh. f., hung. m.) ' hair '; H. *jāṛ* f. ' root, root of teeth, gums '. jaṭilá -- ; *ujjaṭa -- , *ujjaṭati, *ujjāṭa -- , *ujjāṭayati. WPah.rudh. *ǰaṛ* ' goat's hair '; kṭg. *ǰɔṛu* m. ' lamb ', *ǰɔ̃ṛh* f. ' root ', J. *jauṛ* f. (both perh. ← P. Him.I 73), Garh. *jaṛ*, A. *jari* (phonet. *zori*) ' rope ' AFD 218.WPah.kṭg. *ǰɔ̃ṭ* f. (obl. -- *a*) ' matted twisted hair ' (lw. Him.I 73). (CDIAL 5086). jaṭilá ' having twisted hair ' Mn., m. ' ascetic ' MBh. [jaṭā --]Pa. *jaṭila* -- , *°aka* -- adj. and m., Pk. *jaḍila* -- , *°illa* -- ; Si. *duḷulu* ' ascetic with matted hair '.(CDIAL 5087).

Rhinoceros: gaṇḍá4 m. ' rhinoceros ' lex., *°aka* -- m. lex. 2. *ga- yaṇḍa -- . [Prob. of same non -- Aryan origin as khaḍgá --1: cf. *gaṇōtsāha* -- m. lex. as a Sanskritized form ← Mu. PMWS 138]1. Pa. *gaṇḍaka* -- m., Pk. *gaṁḍaya* -- m., A. *gãr*, Or. *gaṇḍā*. 2. K. *gōḍ* m., S. *geṇḍo* m. (lw. with *g* --), P. *gaĩḍā* m., *°ḍī* f., N. *gaĩṛo*, H. *gaĩṛā* m., G. *gẽḍɔ* m., *°ḍī* f., M. *gẽḍā* m. WPah.kṭg. *geṇḍɔ mirg* m. ' rhinoceros ', Md. *genḍā* ← H. (CDIAL 4000). காண்டாமிருகம் kāṇṭā-mirukam , *n.* [M. *kāṇṭāmr̥gam*.] Rhinoceros; கல்யானை. (Tamil)

Rebus 1: *kaṇḍ* 'furnace, fire-altar, consecrated fire'. Rebus 2: kaḍiyo [Hem. Des. Kaḍa-i-o = (Skt. Sthapati, a mason) a bricklayer, mason (G.)]

Buffalo: கண்டி kaṇṭi , *n.* 1. Buffalo bull; எருமைக் கடா. (தொல். பொ. 623.) kāṛā young buffalo (Go.) kaṭā, kaṭamā 'bison' (Ta.)(DEDR 1114) (glyph). Rebus 1: kāḍ 'stone'. Ga. (Oll.) kanḍ, (S.) kanḍu (pl. kanḍkil) stone (DEDR 1298). Rebus 2: *kaṇḍ* 'furnace, fire-altar, consecrated fire'. kaḍiyo [Hem. Des. kaḍa-i-o = (Skt. Sthapati, a mason) a bricklayer, mason (G.)] Pk. *gaḍa* -- n. 'large stone'? (CDIAL 3969) K. *garun*, vill. *gaḍun* ' to hammer into shape, forge, put together '. (CDIAL 3966). khār 1 खार् । लोहकारः m. (sg. abl. khāra 1 खार; the pl. dat. of this word is khāran 1 खारन्, which is to be distinguished from khāran 2, q.v., s.v.), a blacksmith, an iron worker. Or. *gaṛhibā* 'to mould, build', *gaṛhaṇa* 'building'; ghaṭ 'mould, form' (CDIAL 4407). Pk. *khaḍḍā*-- f. 'hole, mine, cave'(CDIAL 3970).

karttr̥2 m. ' spinner ' MBh. [√kr̥t2] H. *kātī* f. ' woman who spins thread '; -- Or. *kāṭiā* ' spinner ' with *ā* from verb *kātibā* < *kr̥ntati2.(CDIAL 2861).

kāgsī f. ' comb ', with metath. kāsko m., °kī f.; WPah. khaś. kāgśī, śeu. kāśkī ' a comblike fern ' (Gujarati)1. Pk. *kaṁkaya* -- m. ' comb ', *kaṁkaya* -- , *°kaï* -- m. ' name of a tree '; Gy. eur. *kangli* f.; Wg. *kuṇi -- pṟū* ' man's comb ' (for *kuṇi* -- cf. *kuṇälík* beside *kuṅälík* s.v. kr̥muka -- ; -- *pṟū* see prapavaṇa --); Bshk. *kēṅg* ' comb ', Gaw. *khēṅgī*́, Sv. *khēṅgiā*, Phal. *khyēṅgia*, *kēṅgī* f., *kāṅga* ' combing ' in *ṣiṣ k° dūm* ' I comb my hair '; Tor. *kyäṅg* ' comb ' (Dard. forms, esp. Gaw., Sv., Phal. but not Sh., prob. ← L. P. type < *kaṅgahiā -- , see 3 below); Sh. kōṅyi f. (→ Ḍ. k*lṅi f.), gil. (Lor.) kōĩ f. ' man's comb ', kōũ m. ' woman's comb ', pales. kōgōm. ' comb '; K. kanguwu m. ' man's comb ', kangañ f. ' woman's '; WPah. bhad. kā́kei ' a comb -- like fern ', bhal. kākei f. ' comb, plant with comb -- like leaves '; N. kāṅiyo, kāĩyo ' comb ', A. kākai, . kākui; Or. kaṅkāi, kaṅkuā ' comb ', kakuā ' ladder -- like bier for carrying corpse to the burning -- ghat '; Bi. kakwā ' comb ', kakahā, °hī, Mth. kakwā, Aw. lakh. kakawā, Bhoj. kakahī f.; H. kakaiyā ' shaped like a comb (of a brick) '; G. (non -- Aryan tribes of Dharampur) kākhāī f. ' comb '; M. kaṅkvā m. ' comb ', kākaī f. ' a partic. shell fish and its shell '; -- S. kaṅgu m. ' a partic. kind of small fish ' < *kaṅkuta -- ? -- Ext. with -- l -- in Ku. kāgilo, kāĩlo ' comb '.2. G. (Soraṭh) kāgaṛ m. ' a weaver's instrument '?3. L. kaṅghī f. ' comb, a fish of the perch family ', awāṇ. kaghī ' comb '; P. kaṅghā m. ' large comb ', °ghī f. ' small comb for men, large one for women ' (→ H.kaṅghā m. ' man's comb ', °gahī, °ghī f. ' woman's ', kaṅghuā m. ' rake or harrow '; Bi. kāgahī ' comb ', Or. kaṅgei, M. kaṅgvā); -- WPah.kṭg. kaṅgi f. ' comb ';

J. kāṅgṛu m. ' small comb .kaṅkatakara CDIAL 2599 *kaṅkatakara ' comb -- maker '. [káṅkata -- , kará -- 1]H. *kãgherā* m. ' caste of comb -- makers ', *°rī* f. ' a woman of this caste '.

కంచరవాడు [kañcaravāḍu] or కంచరి *kanṭsara-vaḍu.* [Tel.] n. A brazier, a coppersmith. కంచుపని చేయువాడు. కంచరది a woman of that caste. కంచరిపురుగు *kanṭsari-purugu.* n. A kind of beetle called the death watch. కంచు *kanṭsu.* n. Bell metal. కంచుకుండ a bowl or vessel or bell metal. కంచువాద్యము a cymbal made of bell metal. కంచుతీసినట్లు as bright or dazzling as the glitter of polished metal. Sunbright. ఆమె కంచుగీచినట్లు పలికె she spoke shrilly or with a voice as clear as a bell.

కంసము [kaṃsamu] *kamsamu.* [Skt.] n. Bell metal.కంచు. కంసర [kaṃsara] or కంసలల *kamsara.* [Tel.] n. Smithery; working in gold: adj. Of the goldsmith caste. కంసలది a woman of that caste. కంసలపని the business of a gold-smith. కంసాలి [kaṃsāli] or కంసాలవాడు *kamsāli.* [Tel.] n. A goldsmith or silversmith.

కంగటి [kaṅgaṭi] Same as కంకటి. (q. v.) కంగటి కాళ్లు *kangaṭi-kā!!u.* [Tel.] adj. Bowleged.

kā´ṁsya ' made of bell -- metal ' KātyŚr., n. ' bell -- metal ' Yājñ., ' cup of bell -- metal ' MBh., *°aka* -- n. ' bell -- metal '. 2. *kāṁsiya -- . [kaṁsá --1]1. Pa. *kaṁsa* -- m. (?) ' bronze ', Pk. *kaṁsa* -- , *kāsa* -- n. ' bell -- metal, drinking vessel, cymbal '; L. (Jukes) *kãjā* adj. ' of metal ', awāṇ. *kāsā* ' jar ' (← E with -- *s* -- , not *ñj*); N. *kāso* ' bronze, pewter, white metal ', *kas -- kuṭ* ' metal alloy '; A. *kãh* ' bell -- metal ', B. *kāsā*, Or. *kãsā*, Bi. *kãsā*; Bhoj. *kãs* ' bell -- metal ', *kāsā* ' base metal '; H. *kãs*, *kãsā* m. ' bell -- metal ', G. *kãsũ* n., M. *kãsẽ* n.; Ko. *kãśẽ* n. ' bronze '; Si. *kasa* ' bell -- metal '.2. L. *kãihã* m. ' bell -- metal ', P. *kãssī*, *kãsī* f., H. *kãsī* f.(CDIAL 2987).

kaṁsá1 m. ' metal cup ' AV., m.n. ' bell -- metal ' Pat. as in S., but would in Pa. Pk. and most NIA. lggs. collide with kā´ṁsya -- to which L. P. testify and under which the remaining forms for the metal are listed. 2. *kaṁsikā -- . 1. Pa. *kaṁsa* -- m. ' bronze dish '; S. *kañjho* m. ' bellmetal '; A. *kãh* ' gong '; Or. *kãsā* ' big pot of bell -- metal '; OMarw. *kāso* (= *kã* -- ?) m. ' bell -- metal tray for food, food '; G. *kãsā* m. pl. ' cymbals '; -- perh. Woṭ. *kasṓṭ* m. ' metal pot ' Buddruss Woṭ 109.2. Pk. *kaṁsiā* -- f. ' a kind of musical instrument '; A. *kãhi* ' bell -- metal dish '; G. *kãśī* f. ' bell -- metal cymbal ', *kãśiyɔ* m. ' open bellmetal pan '.(CDIAL 2576).

kaśēru 'the backbone' (Bengali. Skt.); kaśēruka id. (Skt.) Rebus: kasērā' metal worker ' (Lahnda)(CDIAL 2988, 2989) *kāṁsyakara ' worker in bell -- metal '. [See next: kā´ṁsya -- , kará – 1 L. awāṇ. *kasērā* ' metal worker ', P. *kaserā* m. ' worker in pewter ' (both ← E with -- *s* --); N. *kasero* ' maker of brass pots '; Bi. H. *kaserā* m. ' worker in pewter '. kāṁsyakāra m. ' worker in bell -- metal or brass ' Yājñ. com., *kaṁsakāra* -- m. BrahmavP. [kā´ṁsya -- , kāra -- 1]N. *kasār* ' maker of brass pots '; A. *kãhār* ' worker in bell -- metal '; B. *kãsāri* ' pewterer, brazier, coppersmith ', Or. *kãsārī*, H. *kasārī* m. ' maker of brass pots '; G.*kãsārɔ*, *kas°* m. ' coppersmith '; M. *kãsār*, *kās°* m. ' worker in white metal ', *kāsārḍā* m. ' contemptuous term for the same '.kāṁsyakuṇḍikā 2990 *kāṁsyakuṇḍikā ' bell -- metal pot '. [kā´ṁsya -- , kuṇḍa -- 1]N. *kasaũṛi* ' cooking pot '.(CDIAL 2988, 2989).

kāṁsyatāla m. ' cymbal ' Rājat. [kā´ṁsya -- , tāla -- 1] Pa. *kaṁsatāla* -- m. ' gong '; Pk. *kaṁsālā* -- , *°liyā* -- f. ' cymbal ', OB. *kaśālā*, Or. *kãsāḷa;* G. *kãsāḷũ* n. ' large bell -- metal cymbals ' with *ã* after *kãsũ* ' bell -- metal '; M. *kãsāḷ* f. ' large cymbal '; -- Si. *kastalaya* ' metal gong ' (EGS 40) is Si. cmpd. or more prob. ← Pa. kāṁsyabhāṇḍa *kāṁsyabhāṇḍa ' bell -- metal pot '. [kā´ṁsya -- , bhāṇḍa -- 1] Pa. *kaṁsabhaṇḍa* -- n. ' brass ware '; M. *kãsāḍī*, *°sãḍī* f. ' metal vessel of a partic. kind '.(CDIAL 2991, 2992).

kaṅghuā m. ' rake or harrow ' (CDIAL 2598).

kapi2 m. ' Emblica officinalis, a species of the tree Pongamia glabra, olibanum ' lex., kapikā -- f. ' Vitex negundo ' lex.Pa. kapilā -- f. ' name of two plants '; Paš. lauṛ. kayā´ ' edible pine cone ', ar. kaya ' olive '; Shum. kōu ' olive ', Gaw. kou; L. kau m. ' wild olive, Olea cuspidata '; P. kaū m. ' olive tree, Olea ferruginea '.(DEDR 2747).

kamaṇḍalu कमण्डलु *mn.* (in the वेद *f*(ऊस्). according to Pa1n2. 4-1 , 71) a gourd or vessel made of wood or earth used for water (by ascetics and religious students) , a water-jar MBh. BhP. Ya1jn5. &c (Monier-Williams lexicon, p. 252). kamaṇḍalu m.n. ' gourd or other vessel used for water ' MBh.Pa. *kamaṇḍalu* -- n. ' waterpot used by non -- Buddhist ascetics '; Pk. *kamaṁḍalu* -- m. ' drinking gourd used by ascetics '; Bi. *kãwaṇḍal* ' mendicant's wooden cup '; M. *kãvaḍaḷ* f. ' coconut used as a water vessel '; Si. *kamaňḍalā* ' ascetic's waterpot '.(CDIAL 2761). కమండలువు [kamaṇḍaluvu] *kamanḍaluvu.* [Skt.] n. A bowl or cruise carried by a Hindu ascetic. సన్న్యాసులుంచుకొనే గిన్నె వంటి మంటిపాత్రము. **కమండలి** *kamanḍali.* A hermit: "he who carries a cruise." Rebus: *Ta.* kampaṭṭam coinage, coin. *Ma.* kammaṭṭam, kammiṭṭam coinage, mint. *Ka.* kammaṭa id.; kammaṭi a coiner. (DEDR 1236).

Rebus: కమటము [kamaṭamu] *kamaṭamu.* [Telugu] n. A portable furnace for melting the precious metals. అగసాలెవాని కుంపటి.

kãwaṇḍal may be rebus *kammaṭa* 'coinage, coiner, mint'.

Allograph 1: కమఠము [kamaṭhamu] *kamaṭhamu.* [Skt.] n. A tortoise.

Allograph 2: कमटा or ठा [kamaṭā or ṭhā] *m* (कमठ S) A bow (esp. of bamboo or horn) (Marathi). Allograph 3: kamaḍha 'penance' (Pkt.)

कार [kāra] A particle affixed to a letter in naming it. Ex.अ, क, ग, become अकार, ककार, गकार. 5 An affix to Sanskrit words, signifying Maker or doer. Ex. वस्त्रकार, शस्त्रकार. 6 (For कहार) A palanquin-bearer.(Marathi)

kāra1 ' making, doing ' Prāt., m. (in cmpds.) ' action '. [√kr̥1] Pa. Pk. *kāra* -- m. ' doing, way of doing '; P. *kārā* m. ' action, business, evildoing '; Or. *kār* ' work, act; G. *kār* m. ' action, trouble '. -- X *kr̥tríma* -- : Pk. *kārima*<-> ' artificial ', G. *kārmũ* ' wonderful, strange '. *aṅkakāra -- , andhak°, alaṁkā´ra -- , ahaṁkāra -- , *ārdhikak°, karmak°, kalaṅkak°, kalahak°, kāṁsyak°, *kāccak°, kāvyak°, kumbhak°, *kulyak°, *kuśalak°, kōśak°, *krayak°, *gālikāraka -- , carmakāra -- , citrak°, *cundak°, cūrṇak°, jālak°, *ṭhaṭṭhak°, *tāpak°, tāmrak°, thūtk°, *dēhīk°, dyūtak°, *dhūnak°, *dhūrtak°, nak°, *naḍak°, namaskārá -- , *nīlakāra -- , nyakk°, pañjikāraka -- , parṇakāra -- , *piñjāk°, *pēśak°, priyak°, *balak°, balātk°, bahuk°, *burak°, bhaktak°, bhakṣak°, bhr̥ṣṭak°, maṅgalakāraka -- , maṇikārá -- , madhukāra -- , mantrak°, mālāk°, *mitrak°, mōdakak°, raṅgak°, *rasak°, *lavaṇak°, *lāvyak°, lōhak°, vaṇijyāk°, *vaṇṭak°, *vadhrik°, *vidravak°, vētrak°, śaṅkhak°, *śuṣṇak°, *satyak°, sahakāra -- 1, suvarṇakāra -- , sūtrak°, sūpak°, *hastak°. (CDIAL 3053).

kā´ri m. ' artisan, worker ' Pāṇ. 2. f. ' action, work ' Bhaṭṭ. [√kr̥1] 1. P. *kārī* m. ' worker '.2. Kt. *kår* ' work ', Wg. *k&omacrtodtod;*, Pr. *kā̃*; S. *kāri* f. ' work, occupation, use '; L. *kār* f. ' work '; P. *kārī* f. ' remedy '; Or. *kāri* ' work '. *jēmanakāri -- , *taptakāri -- , *dūtakāri -- kārín -- ' working ' Yājñ, in cmpd. ŚBr. [√kr̥1](CDIAL 3064). 3066 kārú -- , *°uka* -- m. ' artisan ' Mn. [√kr̥1] Pa. *kāru* -- , *°uka* -- m., Pk. *kāru* -- m.; A. B. *kāru* ' artist '; Or. *kāru* ' artisan, servant ', *kāruā* ' expert, deft '; G. *kāru* m. ' artisan '; Si. *karuvā* ' artist ' (ES 22 < *kāraka*--). (CDIAL 3066). कारु [kāru] *m* (S) An artificer or artisan. 2 A common term for the twelve बलुतेदार q. v. Also कारुनारु *m pl* q. v. in नारुकारु.

बलुतें [balutēm̤] *n* A share of the corn and garden-produce assigned for the subsistence of the twelve public servants of a village, for whom see below. 2 In some districts. A share of the dues of the hereditary officers of a village, such as पाटील, कुळकरणी &c.

बलुतेदार or बलुता [balutēdāra or balutā] or त्या *m* (बलुतें &c.) A public servant of a village entitled to बलुतें. There are twelve distinct from the regular Governmentofficersपाटील, कुळकरणी &c.; viz. सुतार, लोहार, महार, मांग (These four constitute पहिली or थोरली कास or वळ the first division. Of three of them each is entitled to चार पाचुंदे, twenty bundles of Holcus or the thrashed corn, and the महार to आठ पाचुंदे); कुंभार, चाम्हार, परीट, न्हावी constitute दुसरी or मधली कास or वळ, and are entitled, each, to तीन पाचुंदे; भट, मुलाणा, गुरव, कोळी form तिसरी or धाकटी कास or वळ, and have, each, दोन पाचुंदे. Likewise there are twelve अलुते or supernumerary public claimants, viz. तेली, तांबोळी, साळी, माळी, जंगम, कळवांत, डवऱ्या, ठाकर, घडशी, तराळ, सोनार, चौगुला. Of these the allowance of corn is not settled. The learner must be prepared to meet with other enumerations of the बलुतेदार (e. g. पाटील, कुळ-करणी, चौधरी, पोतदार, देशपांड्या, न्हावी, परीट, गुरव, सुतार, कुंभार, वेसकर, जोशी; also सुतार, लोहार, चाम्हार, कुंभारas constituting the first-class and claiming the largest division of बलुतें; next न्हावी, परीट, कोळी, गुरव as constituting the middle class and claiming a subdivision of बलुतें; lastly,भट, मुलाणा, सोनार, मांग; and, in the Konkaṇ̤, yet another list); and with other accounts of the assignments of corn; for this and many similar matters, originally determined diversely, have undergone the usual influence of time, place, and ignorance. Of the बलुतेदार in the Indápúr pergunnah the list and description stands thus:--First class, सुतार, लोहार, चाम्हार, महार; Second, परीट, कुंभार, न्हावी, मांग; Third, सोनार, मुलाणा, गुरव, जोशी, कोळी, रामोशी; in all fourteen, but in no one village are the whole fourteen to be found or traced. In the Panḍharpúr districts the order is:--पहिली or थोरली वळ (1st class); महार, सुतार, लोहार, चाम्हार, दुसरी or मधली वळ (2nd class); परीट, कुंभार, न्हावी, मांग, तिसरी or धाकटी वळ (3rd class); कुळकरणी, जोशी, गुरव, पोतदार; twelve बलुते and of अलुते there are eighteen. According to Grant Duff, the बलतेदार are सुतार, लोहार, चाम्हार, मांग, कुंभार, न्हावी, परीट, गुरव, जोशी, भाट, मुलाणा; and the अलुते are सोनार, जंगम, शिंपी, कोळी, तराळ or वेसकर, माळी, डवऱ्यागोसावी, घडशी, रामोशी, तेली, तांबोळी, गोंधळी. In many villages of Northern Dakhaṇ̤ the महार receives the बलुतें of the first, second, and third classes; and, consequently, besides the महार, there are but nineबलुतेदार. The following are the only अलुतेदार or नारू now to be found;--सोनार, मांग, शिंपी, भट गोंधळी, कोर- गू, कोतवाल, तराळ, but of the अलुतेदार & बलुते-दार there is much confused intermixture, the अलुतेदार of one district being the बलुतेदार of another, and vice versâ. (The word कास used above, in पहिली कास, मध्यम कास, तिसरी कासrequires explanation. It means Udder; and, as the बलुतेदार are, in the phraseology of endearment or fondling, termed बासरें (calves), their allotments or divisions are figured by successive bodies of calves drawing at the कास or under of the गांव under the figure of a गाय or cow.)

Out of 587 signs in Bryan's sign list[506], the following are at least 70 'man' glyphs with ligatures which can be identified:

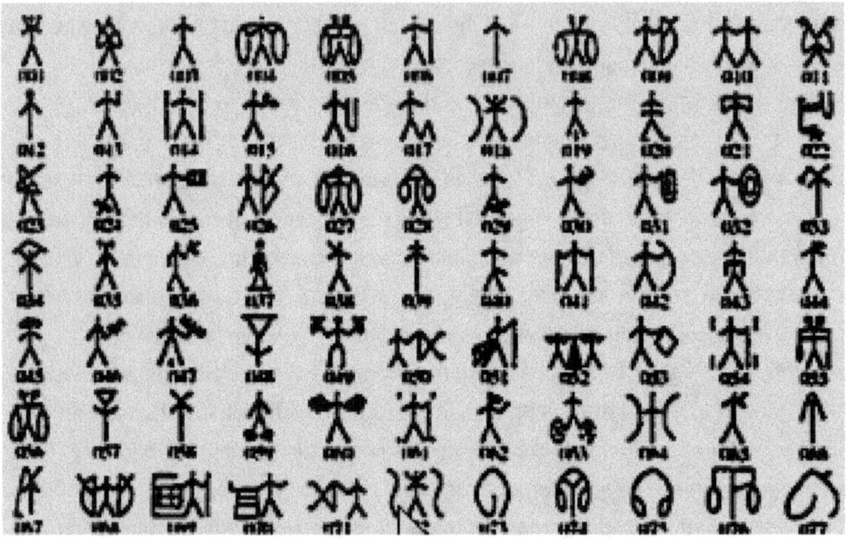

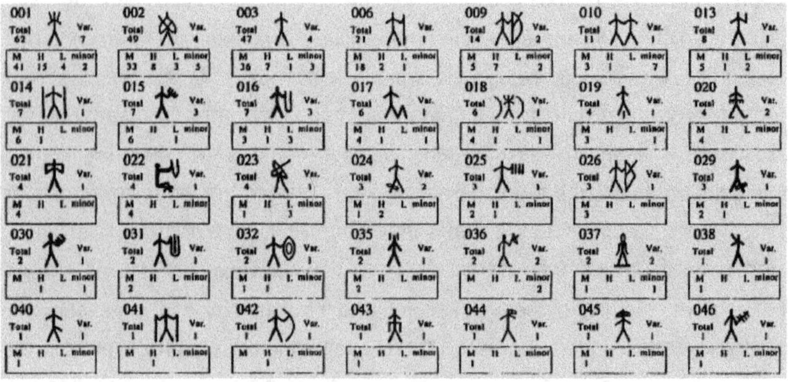

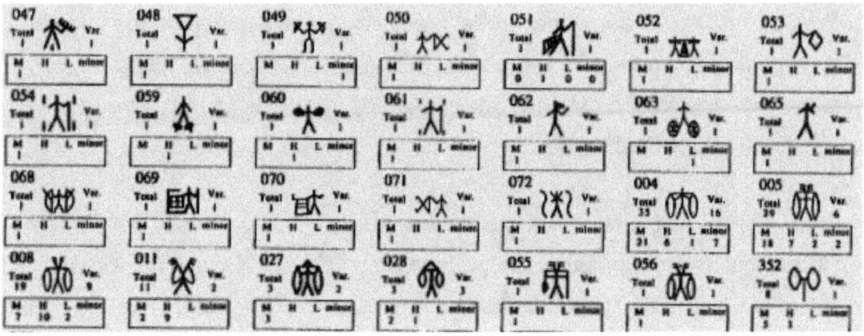

Kur. kaṇḍō a stool. *Malt.* kanḍo stool, seat. (DEDR 1179).

khaṇḍa 'tools, pots and pans and metal-ware'. kāḍ 'stone'. Ga. (Oll.) kanḍ, (S.) kanḍu (pl. kanḍkil) stone (DEDR 1298).

Ta. kaṇṭāḷam travelling sack placed on a bullock, pack-saddle. *Ka.* kaṇṭale, kaṇṭāḷa, kaṇṭāḷe, kaṇṭle double bag carried across a beast. *Te.* kaṇṭalamu, kaṇṭlamu bullock-load consisting of two bags filled with goods. / Cf. Mar. kaṇṭhāḷī a bag having opening in the middle. (DEDR 1174).

kaṇṭhá m. (*a*) ' throat, neck ' ŚBr. (*b*) ' narrowest part of a hole ' Suśr. (*c*) ' voice ' MBh., ' sound ' W. (*d*) ' *border, immediate proximity ' Pañcat.[Mayrhofer EWA i 146 accepts connexion with Drav. (T. Burrow BSOAS xi 133) but considers both IA. and Drav. forms to have originated in Muṇḍa (Kuiper PMWS 29). This is supported by the many forms with a varying degree of phonet. similarity not referable to a common IA. (*a*) Pa. *kaṇṭha* -- m. ' throat, neck '; Pk. *kaṁṭha* -- m. ' neck '; Gy. pal. *kand* ' throat ', Gaw. Sv. *khaṇṭí*; L. awāṇ. *kadhlī* ' neck -- strap '; WPah. bhal. *kaṇṭh* m. ' collar of a shirt ', *kaṇṭhi* f. ' sheep with a black neck '; Ku. gng. *kāni* ' neck ' or < skandhá -- ; Or. *kaṇṭhā* ' throat ', H. poet. *kā̃ṭhā* m.; M. *kā̃ṭhẽ* n. ' neck '; Si. *kaṭa* ' throat, mouth ' (X skandhá -- in SigGr. *kaṇḍa* ' neck '). (*b*) Wg. *káṇṭä* ' water -- channel ', Woṭ. *kaṇṭḗl* f., Gaw. *khāṇṭ*ᵉl, Bshk. *kāṇḍə.* (*c*) Kt. *kaṭī́* ' sound ', Pr. (LSI) *kuṭ*; Paš. lauṛ. *kāṇḍā* ' voice, word ', kuṛ. *kāṇ* ' shouting '; Gaw. *khaṇṭ* f. ' word '.(*d*) Pk. *kaṁṭha* -- m. ' border, edge '; L. awāṇ. *kaḍḍhā* ' bank '; P. *kaṇḍhā* m. ' bank, shore ', *°ḍhī* f. ' land bordering on a mountain '; WPah. cam. *kaṇḍhā* ' edge, border '; N. *kānlo, kā̃llo* ' boundary line of stones dividing two fields ', *kā̃ṭh* ' outskirts of a town ' ← a Mth. or H. dial.; H. *kā̃ṭhā* ' near '; OMarw. *kā̃ṭha* m. (= *kā̃°*?) ' bank of a river '; G. *kā̃ṭhɔ* m. ' bank, coast, limit, margin of a well ';

M. *kāṭh*, *kāṭh*, *°ṭhā* m. ' coast, edge, border ', *kāṭhẽ* n. ' arable land near the edge of a hill. ' -- L. P. *kaṇḍh* f. ' wall ' perh. infl. in meaning by kanthā -- 1.Addenda: kaṇṭá -- : (*a*) S.kcch. *kano* m. ' neck (of a pot) '.(*d*) S.kcch. *kaṇṭho* m. ' bank, coast '; Garh. *kāṭhu* ' throat (?), bank (?) '.(CDIAL 2680)

Gaw. *kaṭái* ' buffalo calf ', Bshk. *kaṭṓr*, Sh. (Lor.) *k*ltu* (*ṭ*?); K. *kaṭh*, dat. *°ṭas* m. ' ram, sheep in general, (contemptuous) son '; L. *kaṭṭā* m., *°ṭī* f. ' buffalo calf '; P. *kaṭṭā*m., *°ṭī* f. ' yearling buffalo ', *kaṭṭū* m. ' young buffalo bull ', *kaṭrā* m., *°ṛī* f. ' young buffalo '; WPah. khaś. rudh. marm. *kaṭru* ' buffalo calf ', bhal. *kaṭṭā* m., *°ṭī* f. ' buffalo calf ', *kaṭru* n. ' bear cub '; Ku. *kāṭo* ' young buffalo bull ', *kaṭyāro* ' young buffalo '; H. *kaṭiyā* f. ' buffalo calf ', *kaṭrā* m. ' buffalo calf ', *kaṭhṛā* m. ' young buffalo bull '; -- WPah. bhal. *sakaṭṭ* f. ' she -- bear with young ' prob. WPah. cmpd.(CDIAL 2645). 1123 *Ta.* kaṭavu, kaṭā, kaṭāy male of sheep or goat, he-buffalo; kiṭā buffalo, bull, ram; kiṭāy male of sheep; kaṭāri, kiṭāri heifer, young cow that has not calved; (PPTI) kaṭamai female of the goat. *Ma.* kaṭā, kiṭā, kiṭāvu male of cattle, young and vigorous; child, young person; kaṭacci heifer, young cow, calf; kiṭāri a cow-calf, heifer; female buffalo. *Ko.* kaṛc na·g buffalo calf between two and three years; kaṛc kurl cow calf between two and three years; ? ke·v calf of buffalo or cow, under one year (? < *kṛe·v); ? ke·n im, ke·no·ṛ im buffalo with its calf; ke·n a·v, ke·no·ṛ a·v cow with its calf. ? *To.* kaṛ pen for calves from 6 months to 1-2 years. *Ka.* kaḍasu young cow or buffalo that has not yet calved. *Koḍ.* kaḍïci id. *Tu.* gaḍasů id. *Te.* krēpu calf (? or with 1594 Ta. ciṟu). *Go.* (Ph.) kāṛā young buffalo (*Voc.* 648). *Konḍa* (BB) gṛālu calf. *Kui* (K.) grāḍu, (W.) ḍrāḍu (*pl.* ḍrāṭka) id.; (W.) gāṛo a bullock or buffalo not trained to the plough; kṛai young female buffalo or goat. *Kuwi* (Su.) ḍālu, (F. S.) dālu calf. *Kur.* kaṛā young male buffalo; kaṛī young female buffalo; kaṛrū, kaḍrū buffalo calf (male or female). *Br.* xarās bull, bullock; xaṛ ram. Cf. 1114 Ta. kaṭamā. / Cf. Turner, *CDIAL*, no. 2645*kaṭṭa- (also Skt. [*lex.*] kaṭāha- a young female buffalo whose horns are just appearing), and no. 2658 *kaḍḍa-. (DEDR 1123) *kaḍḍa ' young male animal '. Or. *kaṛā* ' castrated male buffalo ', *kaṛāi* ' young buffalo cow that has not calved ', *kaṛhi* ' lamb that has not borne '; Bi. *kāṛā* m., *°ṛī* f. ' buffalo calf ', H. *kāṛā* m.(CDIAL 2658). *kaḍḍarūpa ' young animal '. [*kaḍḍa -- , rūpá --] Bi. *kaṛrū* ' buffalo calf '.(CDIAL 2659)

gaṇḍa2 m. ' joint of plant ' lex., *gaṇḍi* -- m. ' trunk of tree from root to branches ' lex. 2. *gēṇḍa -- . 3. *gēḍḍa -- 2. 4. *gēḍa -- 1. [Cf. kāˊṇḍa -- : prob. ← Drav. DED 1619] 1. Pa. *gaṇḍa* -- m. ' stalk ', *°ḍī* -- f. ' sugarcane joint, shaft or stalk used as a bar ',

Pk. *gaṁḍa* -- m., *°ḍiyā* -- f.; Kt. *gäṇa* ' stem '; Paš. lauṛ. *gaṇḍī´* ' stem, stump of a tree, large roof beam ' (→ Par. *gaṇḍā´* ' stem ', Orm. *goṇ* ' stick ' IIFL i 253, 395), gul. *geṇḍū*, nir. *gaṇī´*, kuṛ. *gā̃ṛo*; Kal. urt. *gəṇ* ' log (in a wall) ', rumb. *goṇ* (st. *gōṇḍ* --) ' handle ', *guṇḍík* ' stick '; Kho. (Lor.) *gon*, *gonu*, (Morgenstierne) *gɔ̄`n* ' haft of axe, spade or knife ' (or < ghaná -- 2?); K. *gonḍu*, *grŏnḍu* m. ' great untrimmed log '; S.*ganu* m. ' oar, haft of a tool ', *°no* m. ' sweet stalks of millet '; P. *gannā* m. ' sugarcane ' (→ H. *gannā* m.), Bi. *gaṇḍā*, H. *gā̃ṛā* m., M. *gā̃ḍā* m. -- Deriv. Pk. *gaṁḍīrī* -- f. ' sugarcane joint '; Bhoj. *gā̃ṛērī* ' small pieces of sugarcane '; H. *gā̃ḍerī* f. ' knot of sugarcane '; G. *gā̃ḍerī* f. ' piece of peeled sugarcane '; -- Pk. *gaṁḍalī* -- ' sugarcane joint '; Kal. rumb.*gaṇḍau* (st. *°ḍāl* --) ' ancestor image '; S. *ganaru* m. ' stock of a vegetable run to seed '.2. Ku. *gino* ' block, log '; N. *gĩṛ* ' log ', *gĩṛo* ' piece of sugarcane ' (whence *gẽṛnu*, *gĩṛ°* ' to cut in pieces '); B. *gẽṛ* ' tuber '; Mth. *gẽṛī* ' piece of sugarcane chopped ready for the mill '. (CDIAL 3998).

khaḍu, khaḍī a sort of pipe-clay (Marathi) kaḍu chalk (Kannada) *gadda1 ' sediment, mud '. [Perh. < **garda* -- , cf. Pk. *geḍḍa* -- n. ' mud ' J. Bloch LM 321 < **gr̥d* -- , **gard* -- in Pers. *gil* ' dirt '. But see list s.v. karda --] B. *gād* ' dregs, lees, scum '; Or. *gāda* ' sediment, dregs '; Bi. *gād* ' low -- lying land '; Mth. *gādi* ' sediment of foul water '; H. *gād* f. ' sediment, dregs ' (→ P. *gād* m.); M.*gādā* m. ' muck, sludge '. -- Ext. with -- *l* -- : M. *gadaḷ* n. ' dirt '; -- with -- *ll* -- : H. *gadlā* ' turbid, dirty '; G. *gadlũ* ' dirty, dusty '. -- Deriv. M. *gādṇẽ* ' to become turbid '.(CDIAL 4011).

kaḍuku 'a headless trunk' (Kannada)

kaḍe, kaḍi 'a ring, a bracelet' (Kannada) kaḍī id. (Marathi) *Ta.* kaṭakam bracelet; kaṭai clasp, fastening of a neck ornament. *Ma.* kaṭakam bracelet, ring. *Ka.* kaḍaga, kaṭaka bracelet; kaḍe, kaḍeya id., ring. *Koḍ.*kaḍaga thick metal bangle. *Tu.* kaḍaga bracelet. *Te.* kaḍiyamu id.

Pa. *kaṭacchu* -- m. ' ladle, spoon ', *°uka* -- adj.; Pk. *kaḍacchu* -- f. ' ladle ', *kaḍucchu* -- m.f., *°chuya* -- , *°chaya*<-> m.; K. *kroċhu* m. ' long -- handled iron stoking shovel ',*krüċhü* f. ' cooking ladle '; S. *kaṛchu* m., *°chī* f., *kaṇchu* m., *°chī* f. ' iron ladle ', L. awāṇ. *kaṛchī*, P. *kaṛach*, *kaṛchā* m., *°chī* f., WPah. bhal. *kaṛċhī* f.; Mth. (NETirhut) *karuch*' confectioner's spoon '(CDIAL 2633). Cf. gariṭe 'spoon' (Telugu)

Ta. kāṭai rain quail, *Turnix taigoor. Ma.* kāṭa quail, *Tetras coturnix. Tu.* kāḍè id.? *Te.* kāṭigāḍu a kind of bird.(DEDR 1441).

Ta. kaṭai shop, bazaar, market. *Ma.* kaṭa market. (DEDR 1142).

kaḍe 'churning' (Kannada) kaḍecalu 'turning with a wheel or lathe' (Kannada) *Ta.* kaṭai (-v-, -nt-) to churn, turn in lathe, mash to pulp (as vegetables with the bowl of a ladle); kaṭaical polishing, enamelling, turned work in wood; kaṭaiccal turning on a lathe, that which is turned on a lathe; kaṭaiccal uḷi turner's chisel; kaṭaiyal turning in a lathe, agitating, churning. *Ma.* kaṭayuka to churn, turn on lathe, polish; kaṭa churning; kaṭaccal turning; kaṭaccil turning and polishing (wood, etc.), churning. *Ko.* kaṛv- (kaṛd-) to churn; kaṛc uḷy lathe. *To.* kaṛ- (kaṛQ-) to churn. *Ka.* kaḍe, kaḍi to churn, stir, rub together (as two pieces of wood to excite fire), turn in a lathe; kaḍe, kaḍa, kaḍaha, kaḍeta churning; kaḍayisu to cause to churn. *Koḍ.* kaḍe- (kaḍev-, kaḍand-) to grind with mortar and pestle; (Shanmugam) kaḍev grinding; kaḍace kallï mortar and pestle. *Tu.* kaḍeyuni, kaḍevuni to stir up, turn; kaḍeñcuni to knead;kaḍanda grinding; kaḍavu, kḍdcilů, karcilů a turning lathe; (B-K.) kaḍañjige kneading. *Go.* (Mu.) karrih-, (Ph.) karahtānā, (S.) karah- to churn (*Voc.* 559); (LuS.)kèrtuna id. *Koṇḍa* (BB) karas- (-t-) to stir with ladle. *Kui* kaṛsa (kaṛsi-) to knead; *n.* act of kneading. *Malt.* gaṭye to churn.(DEDR 1141).

kaḍḍe 'a bold woman' (Kannada)

Ta. kaṇṭaṉ warrior, husband; kaṇṭi buffalo bull; kaṇavaṉ husband; keṇṭaṉ robust, stout man; kiṇṭaṉ fat man, strong person. *Ma.* kaṇṭan the male, esp. of cat;kaṇavan husband; kiṇṭan big; a stout, bulky fellow; kiṇṭappan a stout and robust person. *Ko.* gaṇḍ male. *To.* koḍṇ Badaga husband. *Ka.* gaṇḍu strength, manliness, bravery; the male sex, a male, man; gaṇḍa a strong, manly male person, a husband; strength, greatness; gaṇḍasa, gaṇḍasu, gaṇḍusa, gaṇḍusu male person; gaṇḍike prowess;gaṇḍiga a valiant man; (Hav.) geṇḍã husband; geṇḍu male. *Koḍ.* kaṇḍë male (of dogs and other animals, mostly wild; not of cats). *Tu.* gaṇḍu male, valiant, stout; gaṇḍusu husband; gaṇḍůkāyi, gaṇḍůstana, gaṇḍastana manliness; garṇḍāḷů a stalwart man, giant; kaṇḍaṇi, kaṇḍaṇye husband; gaṇṭè, gaṇṭa-puccè male cat; (Bhattacharya, brahmin dial.) kaṇṭe id. *Te.* gaṇḍu bravery, strength, the male of the lower animals; gaṇḍūḍu, gaṇḍāḍu a brave, strong man; gaṇḍ-āḍu to copulate. *Nk.* gaṛek (*pl.* -er) man, male. *Malt.* geṇḍa male. / Cf. Skt. (*lex.*) gaṇḍa-, gaṇḍīra- hero. (CDIAL 1173).

Ta. kaṇ eye, aperture, orifice, star of a peacock's tail. (DEDR 1159a) Rebus 'brazier, bell-metal worker': கன்னான் kaṉṉāṉ , *n.* < கன்¹. [M. *kannān.*] Brazier, bell-metal worker, one of the divisions of the Kammāḷa caste; செம்புகொட்டி. (திவா.) *Ta.* kaṉ copper work, copper, workmanship; kaṉṉāṉ brazier. *Ma.* kannān id. (DEDR 1402). கன்¹ kaṉ , *n.* perh. கன்மம். 1. Workmanship; வேலைப்பாடு. கன்னார் மதில்சூழ் குடந்தை (திவ். திருவாய். 5, 8, 3). 2. Copper work; கன்னார் தொழில். (W.) 3. Copper; செம்பு. (ஈடு, 5, 8, 3.) 4. See கன்னத்தட்டு. (நன். 217, விருத்.) கன்² kaṉ , *n.* < கல். 1. Stone; கல். (சூடா.) 2. Firmness; உறுதிப்பாடு. (ஈடு, 5, 8, 3.)

kāṇá ' one -- eyed ' RV. Pa. Pk. *kāṇa* -- ' blind of one eye, blind '; Ash. *kā̃ṛa, °ṛī* f. ' blind ', Kt. *kā̃ŕ*, Tir. *kā´na*, Kho. *kāṇu* NTS ii 260, *kánu*BelvalkarVol 91; K. *kônu* ' one -- eyed ', S. *kāṇo*, L. P. *kāṇā̃*; WPah. rudh. śeu. *kāṇā* ' blind '; Ku. *kāṇo*, gng. ' blind of one eye ', N. *kānu;* A. *kanā* ' blind '; B. *kāṇā* ' one -- eyed, blind '; Or. *kaṇā*, f. *kāṇī* ' one -- eyed ', Mth. *kān*, *°nā*, *kanahā*, Bhoj. *kān*, f. *°ni*, *kanwā* m. ' one -- eyed man ', H. *kān*, *°nā*, G. *kāṇũ*; M. *kāṇā* ' one -- eyed, squint -- eyed '; Si. *kaṇa* ' one -- eyed, blind '. -- Pk. *kāṇa* -- ' full of holes ', G. *kāṇũ* ' full of holes ', n. ' hole ' (< ' empty eyehole '? Cf. *ā̃dhḷũ* n. ' hole ' <andhala --).S.kcch. *kāṇī* f.adj. ' one -- eyed '; WPah.kṭg. *kaṇɔ* ' blind in one eye ', J. *kāṇā*; Md. *kanu* ' blind '. (CDIAL 3019). *kāṇākṣa ' one -- eyed '. Ko. *kāṇso* ' squint -- eyed '.(CDIAL 3020).

kuṛi ' girl ', Ho *koa*, *kui*, Kūrkū *kōn*, *kōnjē*) NiDoc. *kuḍ'aǵa* ' boy ', *kuḍ'i* ' girl '; Ash. *kū´ṛə* ' child, foetus ', *istrimalī* -- *kuṛā´* ' girl '; Kt. *kŕū*, *kuŕuk* ' young of animals '; Pr. *kyúdotdot;ru* ' young of animals, child ', *kyurú* ' boy ', *kurī´* ' colt, calf '; Dm. *kúŕa* ' child ', Shum. *kuṛ*, Kal. *kūr***lk* ' young of animals '; Phal. *kuṛī* ' woman, wife '; K. *kūrü* f. ' young girl ', kash.*kōṛī*, ram. *kuṛhī*, L. *kuṛā* m. ' bridegroom ', *kuṛī* f. ' girl, virgin, bride ', awāṇ. *kuṛī* f. ' woman '; P. *kuṛī* f. ' girl, daughter ', P. bhaṭ. WPah. khaś. *kuṛi*, cur. *kuḷī*, cam. *kŏḷā* ' boy ', *kuṛī* ' girl '; -- B. *ā̃ṭ* -- *kuṛā* ' childless ' (*ā̃ṭa* ' tight ')? -- X pṓta -- 1: WPah. bhad. *kō* ' son ', *kūī* ' daughter ', bhal.*ko* m., *koi* f., pāḍ. *kuā*, *kōī*, paṅ. *koā*, *kūī.* (CDIAL 3245). Rebus: *kuṭhi* 'smelter'

kuṭhi = pubes. kola 'foetus' [Glyph of a foetus emerging from *pudendum muliebre* on a Harappa tablet.] kuṭhi = the pubes (lower down than paṇḍe) (Santali) kuṭhi = the womb, the female sexual organ; *sorrege kuṭhi menaktaea, tale tale gidrakoa* lit. her womb is near, she gets children continually (H. koṭhī, the womb) (Santali.Bodding) kōṣṭha = anyone of the large viscera

(MBh.); koṭṭha = stomach (Pali.Pkt.); kuṭṭha (Pkt.); koṭhī heart, breast (L.); koṭṭhā, koṭhā belly (P.); koṭho (G.); koṭhā (M.)(CDIAL 3545). kottha pertaining to the belly (Pkt.); kothā corpulent (Or.)(CDIAL 3510). koṭho [Skt. koṣṭha inner part] the stomach, the belly (Gujarat) kūti = pudendum muliebre (Ta.); posteriors, membrum muliebre (Ma.); ku.0y anus, region of buttocks in general (To.); kūdi = anus, posteriors, membrum muliebre (Tu.)(DEDR 188). kūṭu = hip (Tu.); kuṭa = thigh (Pe.); kuṭe id. (Mand.); kūṭi hip (Kui)(DEDR 1885). gūde prolapsus of the anus (Ka.Tu.); gūda, gudda id. (Te.)(DEDR 1891).

kuṭi, kuṭhi, kuṭa, kuṭha a tree (Kaus'.); kuḍa tree (Pkt.); kuṛā tree; kaṛek tree, oak (Pas;.)(CDIAL 3228). kuṭha, kuṭa (Ka.), kudal (Go.) kudar. (Go.) kuṭhāra, kuṭha, kuṭaka = a tree (Sanskrit) kut., kurun: = stump of a tree (Bond.a); khuṭ = id. (Or.) kuṭamu = a tree (Telugu)

Rebus: kuṭhi 'a furnace for smelting iron ore to smelt iron'; *kolheko kuṭhieda* koles smelt iron (Santali) kuṭhi, kuṭi (Or.; Sad. koṭhi) (1) the smelting furnace of the blacksmith; kuṭire bica duljad.ko talkena, they were feeding the furnace with ore; (2) the name of ēkuṭi has been given to the fire which, in lac factories, warms the water bath for softening the lac so that it can be spread into sheets; to make a smelting furnace; kuṭhi-o of a smelting furnace, to be made; the smelting furnace of the blacksmith is made of mud, cone-shaped, 2' 6" dia. At the base and 1' 6" at the top. The hole in the centre, into which the mixture of charcoal and iron ore is poured, is about 6" to 7" in dia. At the base it has two holes, a smaller one into which the nozzle of the bellow is inserted, as seen in fig. 1, and a larger one on the opposite side through which the molten iron flows out into a cavity (Mundari) kuṭhi = a factory; lil kuṭhi = an indigo factory (koṭhi - Hindi) (Santali.Bodding) kuṭhi = an earthen furnace for smelting iron; make do., smelt iron; *kolheko do kuṭhi benaokate baliko dhukana*, the Kolhes build an earthen furnace and smelt iron-ore, blowing the bellows; tehen:ko kuṭhi yet kana, they are working (or building) the furnace to-day (H. koṭhī) (Santali. Bodding) kuṭṭhita = hot, sweltering; molten (of tamba, cp. uttatta)(Pali.lex.) uttatta (ut + tapta) = heated, of metals: molten, refined; shining, splendid, pure (Pali.lex.) kuṭṭakam, kuṭṭukam = cauldron (Ma.); kuṭṭuva = big copper pot for heating water (Kod.)(DEDR 1668). gudgā to blaze; gud.va flame (Man.d); gudva, gūdūvwa, guduwa id. (Kuwi)(DEDR 1715). dāntar-kuṭha = fireplace (Sv.); kōti wooden vessel for mixing yeast (Sh.); kōlhā house with mud roof and walls, granary (P.); kuṭhī factory (A.); koṭhā brick-built house (B.); kuṭhī bank, granary (B.); koṭho jar in which indigo is stored, warehouse (G.); koṭhī lare earthen jar, factory (G.); kuṭhī granary, factory (M.)(CDIAL 3546). koṭho = a warehouse; a revenue office, in which dues are paid and collected; koṭhī a store-room; a factory (Gujarat) koḍ = the place where artisans work (Gujarati)

Rebus: kuṭhi 'a furnace for smelting iron ore to smelt iron'; *kolheko kuṭhieda* koles smelt iron (Santali) kuṭhi, kuṭi (Or.; Sad. koṭhi) (1) the smelting furnace of the blacksmith; kuṭire bica duljad.ko talkena, they were feeding the furnace with ore; (2) the name of ēkuṭi has been given to the fire which, in lac factories, warms the water bath for softening the lac so that it can be spread into sheets; to make a smelting furnace; kuṭhi-o of a smelting furnace, to be made; the smelting furnace of the blacksmith is made of mud, cone-shaped, 2' 6" dia. At the base and 1' 6" at the top. The hole in the centre, into which the mixture of charcoal and iron ore is poured, is about 6" to 7" in dia. At the base it has two holes, a smaller one into which the nozzle of the bellow is inserted, as seen in fig. 1, and a larger one on the opposite side through which the molten iron flows out into a cavity (Mundari.lex.) kuṭhi= a factory; lil kuṭhi= an indigo factory (H.kot.hi)(Santali.Bodding) kuṭhī = an earthen furnace for smelting iron; make do., smelt iron; kolheko do kut.hi benaokate baliko dhukana, the Kolhes build an earthen furnace and smelt iron-ore, blowing the bellows; tehen:ko kuṭhi yet kana, they are working (or building) the furnace to-day (H. koṭhī) (Santali. Bodding) kuṭṭhita = hot, sweltering; molten (of tamba, cp. uttatta)(Pali.lex.) uttatta (ut + tapta) = heated, of metals: molten, refined; shining, splendid, pure (Pali.lex.)

This is Sign 12 kuṭi = a woman water-carrier (Te.) kuṭi = to drink; drinking, beverage (Ta.); drinking, water drunk after meals (Ma.); kuḍt- to drink (To.); kuḍi to drink; drinking (Ka.); kuḍi to drink (Kod.); kuḍi right, right hand (Te.); kuṭī intoxicating liquor (Skt.)(DEDR 1654).

kāru కారు mosale 'wild crocodile or alligator. S. gharyālu m. ' long — snouted porpoise '; N. ghaṛiyāl ' crocodile' (Telugu)'; A. B. ghāṛiyāl ' alligator ', Or. Ghaṛiāḷa, H. ghaṛyāl, ghariār m. (CDIAL 4422) S. gharyālu m. ' long — snouted porpoise '; N. ghaṛiyāl ' crocodile' (Telugu)'; A. B. ghāṛiyāl ' alligator ', Or. Ghaṛiāḷa, H. ghaṛyāl, ghariār m. (CDIAL 4422) கரவு[2] karavu, n. < கரா. Cf. grāha. Alligator; முதலை. கரவார்தடம் (திவ். திருவாய். 8, 9, 9). கரா karā, n. prob. Grāha. 1. A species of alligator; முதலை. கராவதன் காலினைக்கதுவ (திவ். பெரியதி. 2, 3, 9). 2. Male alligator; ஆண்முதலை. (பிங்.) கராம் karām n. prob. Grāha. 1. A species of alligator ; முதலைவகை. முதலையு மிடங்கருங் கராமும் (குறிஞ்சிப். 257). 2. Male alligator; ஆண் முதலை. (திவா.)

karaḍa -- m. 'safflower', *°ḍā* -- f. ' a tree like the karañja ' (Prakrit); M. *karḍī, °ḍaī* f. ' safflower, Carthamus tinctorius and its seed '. (CDIAL 2788). *karaṭataila ' oil of safflower '. M. *karḍel* n. ' oil from the seed of safflower '.(CDIAL 2789).

kāraṇḍava m. ' a kind of duck ' MBh. [Cf. *kāraṇḍa-* m. ' id. ' R., *karēṭu* -- m. ' Numidian crane ' lex.Pa. *kāraṇḍava* -- m. ' a kind of duck '; Pk. *kāraṁḍa* -- , *°ḍaga* -- , *°ḍava* -- m. ' a partic. kind of bird '; S. *kānero* m. ' a partic. kind of water bird ' (CDIAL 3059). karaṭa1 m. ' crow ' BhP., *°aka* -- m. lex. [Cf. *karaṭu* -- , *karkaṭu* -- m. ' Numidian crane ', *karēṭu* -- , *°ēṭavya* -- , *°ēḍuka* -- m. lex., *karaṇḍa2*-- m. ' duck ' lex. Pk. *karaḍa* -- m. ' crow ', *°ḍā* -- f. ' a partic. kind of bird '; S. *karaṛa* -- *ḍhĩgu* m. ' a very large aquatic bird '; L. *karṛā* m., *°ṛī* f. ' the common teal '.(CDIAL 2787). கரண்டம் karaṇṭam , *n.* < *karaṇḍa.* 1. Water-crow, coot; நீர்க்காக்கை. கரண்டமாடு பொய் கை (திவ். திருச்சந்த. 62). 2. Jewel-box; அணி கலச்செப்பு. (பிங்.) 3. Spoon, ladle; கரண்டி. (பிங்.) 4. Water-vessel used by ascetics; கமண்டலம். (அக. நி.) karaṭa1 m. ' crow ' BhP., *°aka* -- m. lex. [Cf. *karaṭu* -- , *karkaṭu* -- m. ' Numidian crane ', *karēṭu* -- , *°ēṭavya* -- , *°ēḍuka* -- m. lex., *karaṇḍa2* -- m. ' duck ' lex: see kāraṇḍava --] Pk. *karaḍa* -- m. ' crow ', *°ḍā* -- f. ' a partic. kind of bird '; S. *karaṛa* -- *ḍhĩgu* m. ' a very large aquatic bird '; L. *karṛā* m., *°ṛī* f. ' the common teal '.(CDIAL 2787).

karadamu present to a superior (Te.) kareṭum = an annual offering and present to a godess or to an evil spirit (G.) karavṛtti (Skt.)

karaḍage, karaḍige, karaṇḍage, karḍige Tbh. Of karaṇḍaka Also, a box in which the linga is owrn.

karaḍa 'dried fodder-grass' (Kannada. Marathi)

Ta. karaṭu ankle, knot in wood. *Ma.* karaṇa knot of sugar-cane; kuraṯṯa knuckle of hand or foot. *Ka.* karaṇe, kaṇṇe clot, lump. *Te.* karuḍu lump, mass, clot.(DEDR 1266).

Ta. karaṇṭi spoon or ladle. *Ma.* karaṇṭi spoon. *Te.* garĩṭe, gaṇṭe, geṇṭe spoon, ladle. *Kol.* (SR.) gāṭe spoon; (Kamaleswaran). *Kuwi* (S.) garti (brass) spoon. (DEDR 1267).

కరమల [karamala] *karamala.* [Tel.] n. A blacksmith. కమ్మరి.

ఖరారా [kharārā] or ఖరారు *kharārā* [H.] n. An agreement. ఒడంబడిక.

కరడము or కరడు or కరుడు *karaḍamu.* [Tel.] n. A wave. అల. Parij. ii. 59. కరుళ్లు waves, billows.

खरड [kharaḍa] *f* (खरडणें) A hurriedly written or drawn piece; a scrawl; a mere tracing or rude sketch. खरडणें [kharaḍaṇēṃ] *v c* To scrape or rub off roughly: also to abrade or graze. खरडनिशी [kharaḍaniśī] *f* Scrawling, scribbling, bad writing. खरडा [kharaḍā] *m* (खरडणें) Scrapings (as from a culinary utensil). also खरडें *n* A rude sketch; a rough draught; a foul copy; a waste-book; a day-book; a note-book. खरड्या [kharaḍyā] *a* (खरडणें) That writes or shaves rudely and roughly; a mere quill-driver; a very scraper.

Pk. *karaṁḍa* -- m.n. ' bone shaped like a bamboo ', *karaṁḍuya* -- n. ' backbone '. (CDIAL 2670) కరాళము [karāḷamu] *karāḷamu.* [Skt.] n. The backbone. Pa. *piṭṭhi -- kaṇṭaka* -- m. ' bone of the spine '; Gy. eur. *kanro* m. ' penis ' (or < káṇṭaka --); Tir. *mar -- kaṇḍḗ* ' back (of the body) '; S. *kaṇḍo* m. ' back ', L. *kaṇḍ* f., *kaṇḍā* m. ' backbone ', awāṇ. *kaṇḍ, °ḍī* ' back '; P. *kaṇḍ* f. ' back, pubes '; WPah. bhal. *kaṇṭ* f. ' syphilis '; N. *kaṇḍo* ' buttock, rump, anus ', *kaṇḍeulo* ' small of the back '; B. *kā̃ṭ* ' clitoris '; Or. *kaṇṭi* ' handle of a plough '; H. *kā̃ṭā* m. ' spine ', G. *kā̃ṭɔ* m., M. *kā̃ṭā* m.; Si. *äṭa -- kaṭuva* ' bone ', *piṭa -- k°* ' backbone '. 2. Pk. *kaṁḍa* -- m. ' backbone '.(CDIAL 2670).

खरडा [kharaḍā] A leopard. खरड्या [kharaḍyā] *m* or खरड्यावाघ *m* A leopard (Marathi). Kol. keḍiak tiger. Nk. khaṛeyak panther. Go. (A.) khaṛyal tiger; (Haig) kariyāl panther Kui kṛāḍi, krānḍi tiger, leopard, hyena. Kuwi (F.) kṛani tiger; (S.) klā'ni tiger, leopard; (Su. P. Isr.) kṛa'ni (pl. -ŋa) tiger. / Cf. Pkt. (DNM) karaḍa- id. (CDIAL 1132).

करड्याची अवटी [karaḍyācī avaṭī] *f* An implement of the goldsmith. A stamp for forming the bars or raised lines called करडा. It is channeled or grooved with (or without) little cavities. करडा [karaḍā] *m* The arrangement of bars or embossed lines (plain or fretted with little knobs) raised upon a तार of gold by pressing and driving it upon the अवटी or grooved stamp. Such तार is used for the ornament बुगडी, for the hilt of a पट्टा or other sword &c. Applied also to any similar barform or line-form arrangement (pectination) whether embossed or indented; as the edging of a rupee &c. करडणें or करंडणें [karaḍaṇē or ṅkaranḍaṇēṃ] *v c* To gnaw or nibble; to wear away by biting (Marathi).

करंडा [karanḍā] *m* (करंड S) A casket (of metal, wood, ivory). 2 A covered basket of bamboo. 3 C A clump, chump, or block of wood. 4 The stock or fixed portion of the staff of the large leaf-covered summerhead or umbrella.2792 káraṇḍa1 m.n. ' basket '

BhP., °*ḍaka* -- m., °*ḍī* -- f. lex. Pa. *karaṇḍa* -- m.n., °*aka* -- m. ' wickerwork box ', Pk. *karaṁḍa* -- , °*aya* -- m. ' basket ', °*ḍī* -- , °*ḍiyā* -- f. ' small do. '; K. *kranḍa* m. ' large covered trunk ', *kronḍu*m. ' basket of withies for grain ', *krünḍü* f. ' large basket of withies '; Ku. *kaṇḍo* ' basket '; N. *kaṇḍi* ' basket -- like conveyance '; A. *karṇi* ' open clothes basket '; H.*kaṇḍī* f. ' long deep basket '; G. *karā̃ḍɔ* m. ' wicker or metal box ', *kā̃ḍiyɔ* m. ' cane or bamboo box '; M. *karā̃ḍ* m. ' bamboo basket ', °*ḍā* m. ' covered bamboo basket, metal box ', °*ḍī* f. ' small do. '; Si. *karaňḍuva* ' small box or casket '. -- Deriv. G. *kā̃ḍī* m. ' snake -- charmer who carries his snakes in a wicker basket '.

காரடம் kāraṭam, n. [T. gāraḍamu, K. gāraḍa.] See காரடவித்தை. காரடவித்தை kāraṭa-vittai, n. < காரடம் +. Juggling, legerdemain; சாலவித்தை.காரடன் kāraṭan̲, n. < id. Juggler; சால வித்தைக்காரன். காரடையாநோன்பு kāraṭaiyā-nōn̲pu, n. < காரடை + ஆம் +. A ceremonial fast observed by women when the sun passes from Aquarius to Pisces, praying for the longevity of their husbands; மாசியும் பங்குனியும் கூடும்நாளில் தம் கணவரின் தீர்க்காயுளைக் கருதிக் காரடையை உணவாகக் கொண்டு மகளிர் கைக்கொள்ளும் ஒரு விரதம்.

కర్ణము *karṇamu.* [Skt.] n. The ear. The helm of a ship చుక్కాని. కర్ణధారుడు *karṇa-dhāruḍu.* A helmsman or steers-man. ఓడనడుపువాడు. *karṇī* 'super cargo of a ship' (Marathi)

karṇadhāra m. ' helmsman ' Suśr. Pa. *kaṇṇadhāra* -- m. ' helmsman '; Pk. *kaṇṇahāra* -- m. ' helmsman, sailor '; H. *kanahār* m. ' helmsman, fisherman '.(CDIAL 2836).

kāraṇḍavamu A kind of antelope కన్నెలేడి. (Telugu)

కరటి [karaṭi] *karaṭi.* [Skt.] n. An elephant. ఏనుగు.

karaṇḍa (m. nt.) the cast skin, slough of a serpent D i.77 (=DA i.222 ahi -- kañcuka) cp. *Dial.* i.88. (Pali)

खांडा [*khāṇḍā*] *m* a jag, notch, or indentation (as upon the edge of a tool or weapon).

To. kar̲y- (kar̲c-) to make ornamental dots on metal articles, beautify (anything); kar̲y a beautified thing, beauty, ornamental dots on metal articles. *Tu.* karepuni to make a notch or incision. (DEDR 1393).

Rebus: kāḍ 'stone'. Ga. (Oll.) kanḍ, (S.) kanḍu (pl. kanḍkil) stone (DEDR 1298).

L. *kaṇḍ* f., *kaṇḍā* m. 'backbone', awāṇ. *kaṇḍ, °ḍī*' back '; P. *kaṇḍ* f. ' back, pubes '; WPah. bhal. *kaṇṭ* f. ' syphilis '; N. *kaṇḍo* ' buttock, rump, anus ', *kaṇḍeulo* ' small of the back '; B. *kā̃ṭ* ' clitoris '; Or. *kaṇṭi* ' handle of a plough '; H. *kā̃ṭā* m. ' spine ', G. *kā̃ṭɔ* m., M. *kā̃ṭā* m.; Si. *äṭa -- kaṭuva* ' bone ', *piṭa -- k°* ' backbone '. 2. Pk. *kaṁḍa* -- m. ' backbone '. 3. Pk. *karaṁḍa* -- m.n. ' bone shaped like a bamboo ', *karaṁḍuya* -- n. ' backbone '. (CDIAL 2670).

Rebus: *kaṇḍa* 'stone (ore)(Gadba)'. . Ga. (Oll.) kanḍ, (S.) kanḍu (pl. kanḍkil) stone (DEDR 1298).

kaṇḍ 'backbone' (Lahnda); rebus: *kaṇḍ* 'furnace, fire-altar' (Santali)

kharedo = a currycomb (G.) Rebus: *kharādī*' turner' (G.)

kaśēru 'the backbone' (Bengali. Skt.); kaśēruka id. (Skt.) Rebus: kasērā' metal worker ' (Lahnda)(CDIAL 2988, 2989) L. awāṇ. Kasērā ' metal worker ', P. kaserā m. ' worker in pewter ' (both ← E with — s --); N. kasero ' maker of brass pots '; Bi. H. kaserā m. ' worker in pewter '. (CDIAL 2988) கசம்¹ kacam , n. cf. ayas. (அக. நி.) 1. Iron; இரும்பு. 2. Mineral fossil; தாதுப்பொருள் (Tamil) N. kasār ' maker of brass pots '; A. kãhār ' worker in bell — metal '; B. kāsāri ' pewterer, brazier, coppersmith ', Or. Kāsārī; H. kasārī m. ' maker of brass pots '; G.kāsārɔ, kas m. ' coppersmith '; M. kāsār, kās m. ' worker in white metal ', kāsārḍā m. ' contemptuous term for the same '. (CDIAL 2989)

L. *kanērā* m. ' mat -- maker '; H. *kā̃derā* m. ' a caste of bow -- and arrow -- makers '.(CDIAL 3024).

H. *kanīrā* m. ' a caste (usu. of arrow -- makers) '.(CDIAL 3026).

Note that the flowing water issues forth from the shoulder, *khandha* (Pali):

skandhá m. ' shoulder, upper part of back ' AV., ' trunk of tree, mass (esp. of an army) ' MBh., *skándhas*<-> n. ' branching top of a tree ' RV. [Absence of any trace of initial *s* -- in Kafiri and Dardic supports possibility of IA. **kandha* -- beside *sk°* (unnecessarily assumed in ODBL 438 for NIA. *k* -- which is dissim. from *kh*<-> before *dh* as prob. in Aś. *agi -- k(h)aṁdha* --)] Pa. *khandha* -- m. ' shoulder, back, tree -- trunk ', *°aka*<-> m. ' division, chapter '; Pk. *khaṁdha* -- , *ka°* m. ' shoulder, tree trunk, wall '; Ash. *kándä* ' stem, trunk ', Kt. *kə́nē*, Wg. *kaná*; Paš.lauṛ. *xānd* ' shoulder ', ar. *kandī́*, kuṛ. *kōn* (obl. *kānda*); Shum. *kandam* ' my shoulder '; Gaw. *kandík* ' shoulder '; Bshk. *kān*(with rising tone) ' shoulder, upper part of back '; Tor. *kan* ' shoulder ', Sv. *kandike*, Phal. *kān*, *kan̄*; S. *kandhu* m. ' neck, back of neck ', *°dho* m. ' back of neck, edge ', *°dhī* f. ' bank of river ', *°dhī pāso* ' neighbourhood '; L.awāṇ. *khaddhā* ' multitude ', P. *khandhā* m. ' mass, multitude, flock of sheep or goats, herd of buffaloes ', ludh. *kannhā* m. ' shoulder ', (Ambala) *kandhā* m.; Ku. *kā̃d*, *kā̃dho*, *kāno* ' shoulder ', gng. *kāni* ' neck '; N. *kā̃dh*, *kā̃d* ' shoulder, back ' (whence *khā̃duwā*, *°dilo* ' heavy, solid ', *kā̃dheuli*, *khā̃de°* ' stick carried by coolies across shoulders to take the weight of a load '); A. *kāndh*, *kān* ' shoulder ',*kandhā*, *kanā* ' large bundle of reeds &c. carried on the shoulder ', *kā̃dhi* ' pent house, veranda, eaves '; B. *kā̃dh* ' shoulder ', *kā̃dhā* ' edge, bank '; Or. *kāndha*,*kā̃dhā* ' shoulder '; Bi. *kā̃nhe* ' on the shoulder ', (Patna) *khandh*, *°dhā* ' large area of cultivated land '; Mth. *kā̃nh*, *kanhā* ' shoulder ', Bhoj. *kā̃nh*, Aw.lakh.*kā̃dh*; H. *kā̃dh*, *°dhā* m. ' shoulder ', *kandh* m. ' tree trunk, thick branch '; G. *khā̃dhi*, *kā̃°* f. ' shoulder '; M. *khā̃d*, *°dā* m. ' shoulder, back of neck ', f. ' large bough '; Ko. *khā̃ndhu* m. ' shoulder '; Si. *kan̆da* ' shoulder, tree trunk, collection, mass ', *kan̆du* ' mountain ' (< -- *aka* --). -- With metath. K. *nakh*, dat. *°khas* m. ' shoulder '? q.v. S.kcch. *kandh* m. ' back of neck ', *kandho* m. ' shoulder '; WPah.kṭg. *kannh* m. ' shoulder ', kc. *kā̃nh*, jaun. *kā̃nn* m.; kṭg. (kc.) *khándɔ* m. ' big box along the wall of living room for grain '.(CDIAL 13627).

Glyph: sprout: కండె [kaṇḍe] *kaṇḍe* [Telugu] n. A head or ear of millet or maize. కందళము [Skt.] n. A germ or shoot, a sprout. కొత్తమొలక. కందళించు *kandaḷinṭsu*. v. n. To sprout, germinate, shoot. (Telugu)

Rebus: kaṇḍa 'fire-altar, furnace'.

కాంత [kānta] *kānta*. [Skt.] n. A fair one; a lovely woman; a lady.

కాంతము [kāntamu] *kāntamu*. [Skt.] n. A stone. రాయి, as in సూర్యకాంతము and చంద్రకాంతము. అయిస్కాంతము a lode-stone. కాంతము adj. Pleasing, charming, lovely, friendly మనోహరమైన.

కాండము [kāṇḍamu] An arrow బాణము. కాడ [kāḍa] An arrow బాణము. A. iv. 292. (Telugu) Or. *kāṇḍa*, *kāṛ* ' stalk, arrow ' (CDIAL 3013).

*kāṇḍakara ' worker with reeds or arrows '.L. *kanērā* m. ' mat -- maker '; H. *kā̃ḍerā* m. ' a caste of bow -- and arrow -- makers '. 3026 kā´ṇḍīra ' armed with arrows ' Pāṇ., m. ' archer ' lex. H. *kanīrā* m. ' a caste (usu. of arrow -- makers) '.(CDIAL 3024).

कांडेकरी [kāṇḍēkarī] A functionary at a sugar-mill. His office is to supply the mill with the कांडीं or prepared joints of cane brought to him by the कवळ्या. 2 About Kolhápúr. A carpenter.

కాడ [kāḍa] *kāḍa*. [Tel.] n. A stem, stalk, shoot, handle, shaft. తొడిమె. కాండము [kāṇḍamu] A stem or stalk ఈనె. A handle. A cluster or clump దుబ్బు (Telugu) kā´ṇḍa ' cluster, heap ' (in *tr̥ṇa -- kāṇḍa* -- Pāṇ. Kāś.). K. m. ' stalk of a reed, straw ' kāḍ 2 काँड् m. a section, part in general; a cluster, bundle, multitude (Śiv. 32). kāḍ 1 काँड् । काण्डः m. the stalk or stem of a reed, grass, or the like, straw. In the compound with dan 5 (p. 221*a,* l. 13) the word is spelt kāḍ. *kaṇḍa* -- m.n. ' joint of stalk, stalk (Pali); *kāḍ* m. ' stalk of a reed, straw ' (Kashmiri); *kāḍ* n. ' trunk, stem ' (Marathi); Or.*kāṇḍa, kāṛ* ' stalk (Oriya); *kāṛā* 'stem of muñja grass (used for thatching) (Bihari); *kānā* m. ' stalk of the reed Sara ' (Lahnda)(CDIAL 3023). कांडें [kāṇḍēṃ] The whole stem or trunk of a plant, or esp. up to the shooting of the branches. A young plant (of नाचणी, वरी &c.) fit to be transplanted. कांडें पेरें पाहून After observing the joints and points. Said in purchasing cattle &c. काड [kāḍa] *n f* Thrashed or trodden stalks of leguminous plants, pulse-straw. 2 *f* Straw (of wheat, नाचणी, उडीद, वरी and others). 3 C The chaff and bits that fall from rice-straw on beating or shaking it. 4 C Plants of rice left over from a transplantation. 5 Peeled stalks of अंबाडी or ताग.

gaṇḍa2 m. ' joint of plant ' lex., *gaṇḍi* -- m. ' trunk of tree from root to branches ' lex. 2. *gēṇḍa -- . 3. *gēḍḍa -- 2. 4. *gēḍa -- 1. [Cf. kā´ṇḍa -- : prob. ← Drav. DED 1619]1. Pa. *gaṇḍa* -- m. ' stalk ', *°ḍī* -- f. ' sugarcane joint, shaft or stalk used as a bar ', Pk. *gaṁḍa* -- m., *°ḍiyā* -- f.; Kt. *gäṇa* ' stem '; Paš. lauṛ. *gaṇḍī´* ' stem, stump of a tree, large roof beam ' (→ Par. *gaṇḍā´* ' stem ', Orm. *goṇ* ' stick ' IIFL i 253, 395), gul. *geṇḍū*, nir. *gaṇī´*, kuṛ. *gāṛo*; Kal. urt. *gəṇ* ' log (in a wall) ', rumb. *goṇ* (st. *gōṇḍ* --) ' handle ', *guṇḍík* ' stick '; Kho. (Lor.) *gon, gonu*, (Morgenstierne) *gɔ̄`n* ' haft of axe, spade or knife ' (or < ghaná -- 2?); K. *gonḍu, grŏnḍu* m. ' great untrimmed log '; S.*ganu* m. ' oar, haft of a tool ', *°no* m. ' sweet stalks of millet '; P. *gannā* m. ' sugarcane ' (→ H. *gannā* m.), Bi. *gaṇḍā*, H. *gāṛā* m., M. *gāḍā* m. -- Deriv. Pk. *gaṁḍīrī* -- f. ' sugarcane joint '; Bhoj. *gāṛērī* ' small pieces of sugarcane '; H. *gāḍerī* f. ' knot of sugarcane '; G. *gāḍerī* f. ' piece of peeled sugarcane '; -- Pk. *gaṁḍalī* -- ' sugarcane joint '; Kal. rumb.*gaṇḍau* (st. *°ḍāl* --) ' ancestor image '; S. *ganaru* m. ' stock of a vegetable run to seed '.(CDIAL 998). 2. Ku. *gino* ' block, log '; N. *gĩṛ* ' log ', *gĩṛo* ' piece of sugarcane ' (whence *gẽṛnu, gĩṛ°* ' to cut in pieces '); B. *gẽṛ* ' tuber '; Mth. *gẽṛī* ' piece of sugarcane chopped ready for the mill '. 3. Pk. *geḍḍī* -- , *giḍḍiā* -- f. ' stick '; P. *geḍī* f. ' stick used in a game ', H. *geṛī* f. (or < 4). 4. N. *gir, girrā* ' stick, esp. one used in a game ', H. *gerī* f., *geṛī* f. (or < 3), G. *geṛī* f.

Rebus: *kāṇḍa* 'tools, pots and pans, metal-ware'.

kāṭha m. ' rock ' lex. [Cf. *kānta* -- 2 m. ' stone ' lex.] (CDIAL 3018)

काँठें [kāṇṭhēṃ] *n* W (कंठ) The throat. 2 The neck.

कातारी or कांतारी [kātārī or kāntārī] m (कातणें) A turner. (Marathi)

WPah. bhal. *karoṭli* f. ' small saw '; N. *karaũti, °rāti* ' saw ', A. *karat*, B. *karāt*; Or. *karata* ' saw ', *karāta* ' goldsmith's saw '; OAw. *karavata* m. ' saw '; H. *karaut, °tā, karāt* m. ' saw ', *karautī* f. ' small do. ', B. *karātī* ' sawyer ', Or. *karatī*, H. *karātī* m., G. *karvatiyɔ* m.; -- Or. *karatibā* ' to saw ', M. *karvatṇẽ*.2. Si. *karavan* ' saw '.(CDIAL 2795).

<kapas>(K) {N} ``^cotton''. %16351. #16231. kaTA>(P) {N} ``the ^cotton ^plant''. *Sa.<kaskom>, Mu.<ka'som>, ~<ka'dsOm>, ~<kaskOm>, Ho<kaTsom>, Kh.<kapas>(D), H.<kApasA>, O.<kOpa>, Sk.<kArpasA>. %16671. #16551. (Munda etyma). kārpāsá ' made of cotton ' ĀśvŚr., *°aka* -- MBh. [kar- pā´sa --] P. *kupāhā*.(CDIAL 3072). kārpāsika ' made of cotton ' MBh. [karpā´sa --] Pa. *kappāsika* -- ' made of cotton ', n. ' cotton cloth '; Pk. *kappāsiya* -- 'made of cotton', m. ' seller of cotton ', S. *kāpāhī* m.; P. *kapāhī, kup°* ' made of cotton, light green '; A. *kapāhī* ' made of cotton ', B. *kāpāsiyā, °se*, Or. *kapāsiā*, Bhoj. *kapāsī*; H. *kapāsī* ' made of cotton, downy, light green '. (CDIAL 3073). karpaṭa n. ' patched garment, rag ' Pañcat. [← Austro- as. prefixed form of paṭa -- of which -- *pāsa* -- in karpā´sa<-> is dial. form J. Przyluski BSL xxv 70, EWA i 174]Pa. *kappaṭa* -- m. ' dirty torn rag '; Pk. *kappaḍa* -- m. ' old garment, garment, cloth '; K. *kapur* m. ' cotton cloth ', sg. or pl. ' clothes '; S. *kapaṛu* m. ' coarse cloth ', *°piṛo* m. ' garment, pl. clothes '; L. *kapṛā* m. ' cloth, pl. clothes '; P. *kappaṛ* m. ' cloth ', *kappṛā* m. ' cloth, pl. clothes, menstrual flow '; WPah. khaś. *kapṛu* n. ' cloth '; Ku. *kāpro* ' piece, bit ' (< ' rag '?); N. *chār* -- *kāpro* ' a kind of fomentation with hot ashes ', *kapar* -- *maṭṭi* ' clay and cowdung smeared on a crucible '; A. *kāpar, °por* ' cloth, garment ', B. *kāpaṛ*, Or. *kāpaṛā*; OAw. *kāpara* m. ' clothes '; H. *kapaṛ, kapṛā* m. ' cloth, clothes ' (→ N. Bi. *kapṛā*, Mth. Aw. lakh. *kapaṛā*), Marw. *kapṛo* m. ' garment '; G. *kāpaṛ* n. ' cloth ', *kāpṛũ* n. ' bodice ', *kapṛũ* n. ' any garment ' (← H.?); M. *kāpaḍ* n. ' cloth ', Ko. *kāppaḍa* n. -- Deriv. P. *kappṛī* ' requiring clothes, adult '; M. *kāpḍī* ' made of cloth '; -- B. *kāpuṛiyā, °re* ' clothseller ', Or. *kāpaṛī, kāpuṛiā*, G. *kapṛiyɔ* m.karpaṭa -- [or sanskritization of Pa. *kappaṭa* -- < *kadpaṭa* -- = *ku* -- *paṭa* --

see paṭa --]S.kcch. *kapaṛ* m. ' cloth ', *kapṛo* m. ' garment '; WPah.poet. *kapṛu* m. ' cloth ', kṭg. (kc.) *kapṛɔ* m. ' cloth, clothes '. (CDIAL 2871).

kandhi = a lump, a piece (Santali.) [The dotted circle thus connotes an ingot taken out of a kaṇḍ, furnace]. kāndavika = a baker; kandu = an iron plate or pan for baking cakes etc. (Kannada)

kaṇḍ = altar, furnace (Santali) लोहकारकन्दुः f. a blacksmith's smelting furnace (Kashmiri) payĕn-kōda पयन्-कौंद । परिपाककन्दुःf. a kiln (a potter's, a lime-kiln, and brick-kiln, or the like); a furnace (for smelting) This yajn~a kuṇḍam can be denoted rebus, by perforated beads (kandi) or on ivory (khaṇḍ):

kandi (pl. -l) beads, necklace (Pa.); kanti (pl. -l) bead, (pl.) necklace; kandit. bead (Ga.)(DEDR 1215). The three stringed beads depicted on the pictograph may perhaps be treated as a phonetic determinant of the substantive, the rimmed jar, the khaṇḍa kanka. khaṇḍa, xanro, sword or large sacrificial knife. kandil, kandi_l = a globe of glass, a lantern (Kannada)

jaṇḍ khaṇḍ = ivory (Jat.ki) khaṇḍī = ivory in rough (Jaṭkī); gaṭī = piece of elephant's tusk (S.) [This semant. may explain why the dotted circle -- i.e., kandi, 'beads' -- is often depicted on ivory objects, such as ivory combs]. See also: khaṇḍiyo [cf. khaṇḍaṇī a tribute] tributary; paying a tribute to a superior king (Gujarat) [Note glyph of a kneeling adorant]

Glyph: *khan:ghar, ghan:ghar, ghan:ghar gon:ghor* 'full of holes' (Santali)

Substantive: *kan:gar* 'portable furnace' (K.)

Go. (A.) khaṛyal tiger; (Haig) kariyāl panther Kui kṛāḍi, krānḍi tiger, leopard, hyena. Kuwi (F.) kṛani tiger; (S.) klā'ni tiger, leopard; (Su. P. Isr.) kṛa?ni (pl. -ŋa) tiger. / Cf. Pkt. (DNM) karaḍa- id. (CDIAL 1132). Rebus 2: करडा [*karaḍā*] Hard from alloy--iron, silver &c. (Marathi) *lōī* f., *lo* m.2. Pr. *ẓūwī* 'fox' (Western Pahari)(CDIAL 11140-2). Rebus 3: *loh* 'copper' (Hindi). Glyph, 'Winged': eṟaka, ṟekka, rekka, neṟaka, neṟi 'wing' (Telugu)(DEDR 2591). Rebus: eraka, eṟaka = any metal infusion (Kannada.Tulu)

క్రమ్మరు [krammaru] *krammaru.* [Tel.] v. n. To turn, return, go back. మరలు. క్రమ్మరించు or క్రమ్మరుచు *krammarintsu.* V. a. To turn, send back, recall. To revoke, annul, rescind. క్రమ్మరజేయు. క్రమ్మర *krammara.* Adv. Again. క్రమ్మరిల్లు or క్రమరబడు Same as క్రమ్మరు. krəm back'(Kho.)(CDIAL 3145) Kho. Krəm ' back ' NTS ii 262 with (?) (CDIAL 3145)[Cf. Ir. *kamaka – or *kamraka -- ' back ' in Shgh. Čůmč ' back ', Sar. Čomǰ EVSh 26] (CDIAL 2776) cf. Sang. kamak ' back ', Shgh. Čomǰ (< *kamak G.M.) ' back of an animal ', Yghn. Kama ' neck ' (CDIAL 14356). Kár, kãr 'neck' (Kashmiri) Kal. Gřä ' neck '; Kho. Goḷ ' front of neck, throat '. Gala m. ' throat, neck ' MBh. (CDIAL 4070) Rebus: karmāra 'smith, artisan' (Skt.) kamar 'smith' (Santali)

Ta. kaṇ eye, aperture, orifice, star of a peacock's tail. Ma. kaṇ, kaṇṇu eye, nipple, star in peacock's tail, bud. Ko. kaṇ eye. To. Koṇ eye, loop in string. Ka. Kaṇ eye, small hole, orifice. Koḍ. Kaṇṇï id. Te. Kanu, kannu eye, small hole, orifice, mesh of net, eye in peacock's feather. Kol. Kan (pl. kanḍl) eye, small hole in ground, cave. Ga. (Oll.) kaṇa (pl. Kaṇul) hole; (S.) kanu (pl. Kankul)eye. Go. (Tr.) kan (pl. Kank) id.; (A.) kaṛ (pl. Kaṛk) id. Konḍa kaṇ id. Pe. Kaṇga (pl. –ŋ, kaṇku) id. Manḍ. Kan (pl. –ke) id. Kui kanu (pl. Kan-ga), (K.) kanu (pl. Kaṛka) id. Kuwi (F.) kannū (pl. Kar&nangle;ka), (S.) kannu (pl. Kanka), (Su. P. Isr.) kanu (pl. Kaṇka) id. (DEDR 1159a). Pa. kanḍp- (kanḍt-) to look for, seek. Ga. (Oll.) kanḍp- (kanḍt-) to search. Ta. Kāṇ (kāṇp-, kaṇṭ-) to see, consider, investigate, appear, become visible; n. sight, beauty Te. Kanu (allomorph kān-), kāncu to see (DEDR 1443) B. kan ' eye of corn, particle ', kanā ' piece of dust, 694onta seed ', kanī ' atom, particle '; Or. kaṇa, ṇā ' particle of dust, eye of seed, atom ', kaṇi ' particle of grain '; Oaw. Kana ' drop (of dew) ' M. kaṇ m. ' grain, atom, corn ', kaṇī f. ' hard core of grain, pupil of eye, broken bit ', kaṇẽ n. ' very small particle ' (CDIAL 2661)

*khuṇṭa2 ' corner '. 2. *kuṇṭa -- 2. [Cf. *khõñca --] 1. Phal. *khun* ' corner '; H. *khū̃ṭ* m. ' corner, direction ' (→ P. *khū̃ṭ* f. ' corner, side '); G. *khū̃ṭrī* f. ' angle '. <-> X kōṇa -- : G. *khuṇ* f., *khū̆ṇɔ* m. ' corner '. 2. S. *kuṇḍa* f. ' corner '; P. *kū̃ṭ* f. ' corner, side ' (← H.).(CDIAL 3898). Rebus: kunda1 m. ' a turner's lathe ' lex. [Cf. *cunda -- 1] N. *kū̃dnu* ' to shape smoothly, smoothe, carve, hew ', *kū̃duwā* ' smoothly shaped '; A. *kund* ' lathe ', *kundiba* ' to turn and smooth in a lathe ', *kundowā* ' smoothed and rounded '; B. *kū̃d* ' lathe ', *kū̃dā, kõdā* ' to turn in a lathe '; Or. *kū̆nda* ' lathe ', *kū̃dibā, kū̃d°* ' to turn ' (→ Drav. Kur. *kū̃d* ' lathe '); Bi.*kund* ' brassfounder's lathe '; H. *kunnā* ' to shape on a lathe ', *kuniyā* m. ' turner ', *kunwā* m. (CDIAL 3295). kundakara m. ' turner ' W. [Cf. *cundakāra -

- : kunda -- 1, ka*rá* -- 1] A. *kundār*, B. *kũdār*, *°ri*, Or. *kundāru*; H. *kũderā* m. ' one who works a lathe, one who scrapes ', *°rī* f., *kũdernā* ' to scrape, plane, round on a lathe '.(CDIAL 3297). *Ta.* kuntaṉam interspace for setting gems in a jewel; fine gold (< Te.). *Ka.* kundaṇa setting a precious stone in fine gold; fine gold; kundana fine gold. *Tu.* kundaṇa pure gold. *Te.* kundanamu fine gold used in very thin foils in setting precious stones; setting precious stones with fine gold. (DEDR 1725).

Rebus: কুঁদন, কোঁদন [kuṅdana, kōṅdana] n act of turning (a thing) on a lathe; act of carving; act of bragging. কুঁদ [kuṅda] n a (turner's) lathe.কুঁদ[1] [kuṅda[1]] v to turn (a thing) on a lathe, to shape by turning on a lathe; to carve (Bengali) kunda1 m. ' a turner's lathe ' lex. N. *kũdnu* ' to shape smoothly, smoothe, carve, hew ', *kũduwā* ' smoothly shaped '; A. *kund* ' lathe ', *kundiba* ' to turn and smooth in a lathe ', *kundowā* ' smoothed and rounded '; B. *kũd* ' lathe ', *kũdā*, *kõdā* ' to turn in a lathe '; Or. *kũnda* ' lathe ', *kũdibā*, *kũd°* ' to turn ' (→ Drav. Kur. *kũd* ' lathe '); Bi. *kund* ' brassfounder's lathe '; H.*kunnā* ' to shape on a lathe ', *kuniyā* m. ' turner ', *kunwā* m. (CDIAL 3295). kundakara m. ' turner ' W. A. *kundār*, B. *kũdār*, *°ri*, Or. *kundāru*; H. *kũderā* m. ' one who works a lathe, one who scrapes ', *°rī* f., *kũdernā* 'to scrape, plane, round on a lathe'.(CDIAL 3297). **कोंद** *kōnda* 'engraver, lapidary setting or infixing gems' (Marathi) **कोंदण** [kōndaṇa] n (**कोंदणें**) Setting or infixing of gems.(Marathi) **খোদকার** [khōdakāra] n an engraver; a carver. খোদকারি n. engraving; carving; interference in other's work. **খোদাই** [khōdāi] n engraving; carving. খোদাই করা v. to engrave; to carve. খোদানো v. & n. en graving; carving. **খোদিত** [khōdita] a engraved. (Bengali) **खोदकाम** [khōdakāma] n Sculpture; carved work or work for the carver. **खोदगिरी** [khōdagirī] f Sculpture, carving, engraving: also sculptured or carved work. **खोदणावळ** [khōdaṇāvaḷa] f (**खोदणें**) The price or cost of sculpture or carving. **खोदणी** [khōdaṇī] f (Verbal of **खोदणें**) Digging, engraving &c. 2 fig. An exacting of money by importunity. V **लाव, मांड**. 3 An instrument to scoop out and cut flowers and figures from paper. 4 A goldsmith's die. **खोदणें** [khōdaṇēṃ] v c & i (H) To dig. 2 To engrave. **खोद खोदून विचारणें** or **–पुसणें** To question minutely and searchingly, to probe. **खोदाई** [khōdāī] f (H.) Price or cost of digging or of sculpture or carving. **खोदींव** [khōdīṃva] p of **खोदणें** Dug. 2 Engraved, carved, sculptured. (Marathi)

koṇḍu spine (Kashmiri)

Allograph: *kõdā* खोंड [khōṇḍa] m A young bull, a bullcalf. (Marathi)

কুঁদন, কোঁদন [kuṅdana, kōṅdana] act of rushing forward to attack or beat; act of skipping or frisking (Bengali) M. *vākudṇẽ* ' to jump about, frisk, frolic '(Marathi) kūrda m. ' jump ', *gūrda* -- m. ' jump ' Kāṭh. [√kūrd] S. *kuḍu* m. ' leap ', N. *kud*, Or. *kuda*, *°dā*, *kudā -- kudi* ' jumping about '.(CDIAL 3411). kū´rdati ' leaps, jumps ' MBh. [*gū´rdati*, *khū´rdatē* Dhātup.: prob. ← Drav. (Tam. *kuti*, Kan. *gudi* ' to spring ') T. Burrow BSOAS xii 375] S. *kuḍaṇu* ' to leap '; L. *kuḍaṇ* ' to leap, frisk, play '; P. *kuddṇā* ' to leap ', Ku. *kudṇo*, N. *kudnu*, B. *kũdā*, *kõdā*; Or. *kudibā* ' to jump, dance '; Mth. *kūdab* ' to jump ', Aw. lakh. *kūdab*, H. *kūdnā*, OMarw. *kūdaï*, G. *kudvũ*, M. *kudṇẽ*; -- ext. with -- *kk* -- : H. *kudaknā* ' to leap, caper '; G. *kudkɔ* m. ' a leap '. Addenda: kū´rdati: WPah.kṭg. (kc.) *kudṇõ* ' to jump ', Garh. *kudṇu*, Brj. *kūdno*, *kudakno*, caus. *kudlāno*; A. *kudiba* ' to romp ' (CDIAL 3412). *Ta.* kuti (-pp-, -tt-) to jump, leap, bound, frolic, leap over, escape from, splash (as water), spurt out; *n.* jump, leap; kutippu leaping. *Ma.* kuti leap, gallop;kutikka to jump, skip, boil, bubble up; kutukkuka to take a spring in order to leap. *Ka.* gudi to jump, stamp, make a noise with the feet; kuduku to trot; *n.* trotting; (Hav. S.) gudiku to jump. *Tu.* guttu a leap, jump; a stride. *Te.* kudupu to shake (*tr.*), agitate, jolt; *n.* shaking, jolting; kudulu to be shaken, jolt. (K. also) shake while walking, flutter in agony; kudilincu to shake (*tr.*); kudilika shaking, agitation, jolting. *Konḍa* gudlis- (-t-) to shake violently. *Kur.* kuddnā to move about; kudāba'ānāto make run; kudākudī in hot haste; kuduṛ-kuduṛ at a trot. (DEDR 1705).

Allographs: Go<kun>(Z),,<kunDa>(ZA),,<kunDan>(Z),<kunDa?>(Z) {N} ``^hill, ^mountain (Munda)

Re<kunda=kundi>(B) {} ``^pushing each other''.

Re<kunDu->(B) {V} ``to ^carry in one's arms''. <kunDum>(BD) {VT} ``to ^carry a child in one's arms''. #18521.
So. *konDo* `to embrace'. ~ *kUnd+b* `to grasp with the hand'.

Kh.<kunDA'b>(P), ~<kunRa'b> `back of a house, man, or animal' <ku~Ra'b>(AB),,<kunDa'b>(B) {NI} ``^back''. *@. ??VAR. #18651.

Kh.<ku~R>(D) `iron pail to draw water', ~<kunDa>(P), Mu.<kunDa> `a large earthen pitcher', Sa.<kuNDA> `bucket', H.<kUNDa>, O.<kUNDI>, B.<kU~RI>, Sk.<dUNDA> `pot'; Kh.<tim-soG>(P), Sa., Mu., Ho<seGgel>. %19292. #19142.

Ka. kunda a pillar of bricks, etc. *Tu.* kunda pillar, post. *Te.* Kunda id. *Malt.* kunda block, log. (DEDR 1723). cf. *Ta.* kuntāṇi large mortar, protective ring placed over a mortar to prevent the grain from scattering. *Ma.* kuntāṇi, kūntāṇi mortar for beating paddy.
Ka. kundaṇige, kundaṇi, kundaḷige wooden rim of a mortar so placed as to keep in the contents while beating. *Te.* kundi, kundene rim of stone or other material placed upon a mortar to prevent spilling of rice, etc. (DEDR 1726).

Ta. kuntam haystack. *Ka.* kuttaṟi a stack, rick. (DEDR 1724).

Ta. kuṭai umbrella, parasol, canopy. *Ma.* kuṭa umbrella. *Ko.* koṛ umbrella made of leaves (only in a proverb); keṛ umbrella. *To.* kwaṛ id. *Ka.* koḍe id., parasol. *Koḍ.* koḍeumbrella. *Tu.* koḍè id. *Te.* goḍugu id., parasol. *Kuwi* (F.) gūṛgū, (S.) gudugu, (Su. P.) guṛgu umbrella (< Te.). / Cf. Skt. (*lex.*) utkūṭa- umbrella, parasol.(DEDR 1663).

Pa. guḍva nilgai. *Go.* (Mu.) koḍal (māv) a kind of deer; (L.) koḍā māv, (SR.) khoḍḍa māv blue bull (*Voc.* 890); (Ko.) guṛiya māv nilgai (*Voc.* 1159). *Ga.* (S.) guri goḍbison. *Konḍa* (BB 1972) gura bison. (DEDR 1664).

Go. (Mu.) gunḍral (*pl.* gunḍrahk) a kind of quail (*Voc.* 1122). *Kur.* guṇḍrī quail.(DDR 1696).

Ka. kuṇṭe a harrow, the web-beam in a loom. *Tu.* kuṇṭè the web beam of a loom. *Te.* guṇṭaka, (*VPK*) guṇṭika, guṇṭiki, guṇṭike, guṇṭava, gūṭava a harrow. (DEDR 1689).

गुंड [guṇḍa] *a* Arch, sly, subtle. (Marathi)

गुंडा [guṇḍā] *m* A rolling or roundish stone. (Marathi)

Ma. kuṭṭa a knotty log. *Ko.* guṭḷ stake to which animal is tied, any large wooden peg. *To.* kuṭy a stump. *Ka.* (Coorg) kuṭṭu stem of a tree which remains after cutting it. *Koḍ.* kuṭṭe log. *Tu.* kuṭṭi stake, peg, stump. *Go.* (Mu.) kuṭṭa, guṭṭa, (G. Ma.) guṭṭa, (Ko.) guṭa stump of tree; (S.) kuṭṭa id., stubble; (FH.) kuta jowari stubble (*Voc.* 731). *Pe.* kuṭa stump of tree. *Kui* gūṭa, (K.) guṭa id. *Kuwi* (Su.) guṭṭu (DEDR 1676). *khuṭṭa1 ' peg, post '. 2. *khuṇṭa -- 1. [Same as *khuṭṭa -- 2? -- See also kṣōḍa -- .] 1.

Ku. *khuṭī* ' peg '; N. *khuṭnu* ' to stitch ' (der. **khuṭ* ' pin ' *khilnu* from *khil* s.v. khī´la --); Mth. *khuṭā* ' peg, post '; H. *khūṭā* m. ' peg, stump '; Marw. *khuṭī* f. ' peg '; M. *khuṭā* m. ' post '.2. Pk. *khuṁṭa* -- , *khoṁṭaya* -- m. ' peg, post '; Dm. *kuṇḍa* ' peg for fastening yoke to plough -- pole '; L. *khū̃ḍī* f. ' drum -- stick '; P. *khuṇḍ, °ḍā* m. ' peg, stump '; WPah. rudh. *khuṇḍ* ' tethering peg or post '; A. *khū̃ṭā* ' post ', *°ṭi* ' peg '; B. *khū̃ṭā, °ṭi* ' wooden post, stake, pin, wedge '; Or. *khuṇṭa, °ṭā* ' pillar, post '; Bi. (with --*ḍa* --) *khū̃ṭrā, °rī* ' posts about one foot high rising from body of cart '; H. *khū̃ṭā* m. ' stump, log ', *°ṭī* f. ' small peg ' (→ P. *khū̃ṭā* m., *°ṭī* f. ' stake, peg '); G. *khū̃ṭ* f. ' landmark ', *khū̃ṭɔ* m., *°ṭī* f. ' peg ', *°ṭũ* n. ' stump ', *°ṭiyũ* n. ' upright support in frame of wagon ', *khū̃ṭṛũ* n. ' half -- burnt piece of fuel '; M. *khū̃ṭ* m. ' stump of tree, pile in river, grume on teat ' (semant. cf. kīla -- 1 s.v. *khila -- 2), *khū̃ṭā* m. ' stake ', *°ṭī* f. ' wooden pin ', *khū̃ṭaḷṇẽ* ' to dibble '.WPah.kṭg. *khv́ndɔ* ' pole for fencing or piling grass round ' (Him.I 35 *nd* poss. wrong for *ṇḍ*); J. *khuṇḍā* m. ' peg to fasten cattle to '. (CDIAL 3893).

*khuṭṭa2 ' leg '. [Perh. same as *khuṭṭa -- 1 ' peg ', but see word -- group s.v. *kuṭṭha --]Ku. *khuṭo* ' leg, foot ', *°ṭī* ' goat's leg '; N. *khuṭo* ' leg, foot ', *khuṛkilo* ' ladder ' (< **khuṭ+kilo* ' peg ' < kīla -- 1). WPah.poet. *khvṭe* f. ' leg (of a domestic animal) '; J. *khuṭi* f.pl. ' legs '; Garh. *khuṭu* ' foot '.(CDIAL 3894).

kuṭṭa1 in cmpd. ' breaking, cutting ', *°aka* -- ' id. ', m. ' cutter, breaker, grinder '. 2. *kōṭṭa -- 2. [√kuṭṭ] 1. S. *kāṭha -- kuṭo* m. ' woodpecker '; WPah. bhal. *kuṭṭū* m. ' wooden bar serving as pivot of door, wooden peg in socket of flour mill, hip, buttock '; Ku. *kuṭo, °ṭī, °ṭlo* ' hoe ', N. *kuṭo, °ṭi*, A. *kuṭ* ' mark of punctuation '; Or. *kuṭa* ' small hammer for breaking stones ', *°ṭā* ' act of beating or pounding or husking '; M. *kuṭā -- kuṭī* f. ' fighting '.2. Pa. *koṭṭa* -- in cmpd. ' breaking '; Pk. *koṭṭaga* -- m. ' carpenter ', *koṭṭila* -- , *°illa* -- m. ' mallet '. (DEDR 3236).

Ta. kurappam currycomb. *Ma.* kurappam, kurappan id. *Ka.* korapa, gorapa id. *Te.* kurapamu, ko̱rapamu, go̱rapamu id. / ? *CDIAL*, no. 3730, (DEDR 1771). kṣurapra- ('scraper'-meanings). kṣurapra ' sharp -- edged like a razor ' BhP., m. ' sharp- edged arrow ' MBh., ' sharp -- edged knife ' Pañcat., ' a sort of hoe ' lex. Pa. *khurappa* -- m. ' arrow with a horseshoe head '; Pk. *khurappa* -- , *°ruppa* -- m. ' a kind of arrow, knife for cutting grass '; S. *khurpo* m. ' a pot -- scraper '; P. *khurpā*m., *°pī* f. ' pot -- scraper, grubber for grass '; N. *khurpo* ' sickle ', *°pi* ' weeding knife '; B. *khurpā* ' spud for grubbing up grass ' (X khanítra -- q.v.), Or. *khurapa, °pā, °pi, °rupā, °pi*;; Bi. *khurpā* ' blade of hoe ', *°pī* ' small hoe for weeding '; Mth. *khurpā, °pī* ' scraper '; H. *khurpā* m. ' weeding knife ', *°pī* f. ' small do. '; G. *kharpɔ* m. ' scraper ', *°pī* f. ' grubber ' (X *kāpvũ* in *karpī* f. ' weeding tool '); M. *khurpẽ* n. ' curved grubbing hoe ', *°pī* f. ' grub -- axe '. -- Deriv. H. *khurapnā*, *°rupnā* ' to scrape up grass '; G. *kharapvũ* ' to cut, dig, remove with a scraper '; M. *khurapṇẽ* ' to grub up '.(CDIAL 3730).

কুঁদ [kunঁda] a variety of multi-petalled jasmine (Bengali) kunda m. ' Jasminum multiflorum or pubescens ' MBh. (' olibanum or resin of Boswellia thurifera ' lex., see kunduru --), n. ' its flower '.Pa. *kunda* -- n. ' jasmine '; Pk. *kuṁda* -- m. ' a flowering tree ', n. ' a kind of flower '; B. *kũd* ' J. multiflorum ', M. *kũd* m. ' id. ', *kũdā* m. ' a partic. kind of flowering shrub '; Si. *koňda* ' jasmine '.(CDIAL 3296)

Ka. koṇḍe, goṇḍe tuft, tassel, cluster (DEDR 2081) *Kui* gunda (gundi-) to sprout, bud, shoot forth into bud or ear; *n.* a sprouting, budding. ? *Kuwi* (Isr.) kunda a very small plot of ground (e.g. for seed-bed). *Kur.* kundnā to germinate, bud, shoot out; kundrnā to be born; kundrkā birth; kundrta'ānā to generate, beget, produce. *Malt.* kunde to be born, be created. (DEDR 1729). kuṇḍa n. ' clump ' e.g. *darbha -- kuṇḍa* -- Pāṇ. [← Drav. (Tam. *koṇṭai* ' tuft of hair ', Kan. *goṇḍe* ' cluster ', &c.) T. Burrow BSOAS xii 374] Pk. *kuṁḍa* -- n. ' heap of crushed sugarcane stalks '; WPah. bhal. *kunnū* m. ' large heap of a mown crop '; N. *kunyũ* ' large heap of grain or straw ', *baṛ -- kũṛo* ' cluster of berries '. (CDIAL 3236). Mar. gōḍā cluster, tuft. *Ta.* koṇṭai tuft, dressing of hair in large coil on the head, crest of a bird, head (as of a nail), knob (as of a cane), round top. *Ma.* koṇṭa tuft of hair. *Ko.* goṇḍ knob on end of walking-stick, head of pin; koṇḍ knot of hair at back of head. *To.* kwïḍy Badaga woman's knot of hair at back of head (< Badaga koṇḍe). *Ka.* koṇḍe, goṇḍe tuft, tassel, cluster. *Koḍ.* koṇḍe tassels of sash, knob-like foot of cane-stem. *Tu.* goṇḍè topknot, tassel, cluster. *Te.* koṇḍe, (K. also) koṇḍi knot of hair on the crown of the head. Cf. 2049 Ta. koṭi. / Cf. Skt. kuṇḍa- clump (e.g. darbha-kuṇḍa), Pkt. (*DNM*) goṇḍī- = mañjarī-(DEDR 2081).

koḍa 'one' (Santali) Rebus: *koḍ* 'artisan's workshop' (Kuwi) *koḍ* = place where artisans work (Gujarati) 'Comb' glyph ligatured to a body: *kāḍ* 2 काड् । पौरुषम् m. a man's length, the stature of a man (as a measure of length) (Rām. 632, zangan kaḍun kāḍ, to stretch oneself the whole length of one's body. So K. 119). Rebus: *kāḍ* 'stone'. Ga. (Oll.) *kanḍ*, (S.) *kanḍu* (pl. kanḍkil) stone (DEDR 1298). *maypoṇḍi kanḍ* whetstone; (Ga.)(DEDR

4628). खोंड [*khōṇḍa*] *m* A young bull, a bullcalf (Marathi). *kōḍiya, kōḍe, kōda* young bull (Telugu) Rebus: *kõdā* 'to turn in a lathe', *kūdār 'turner'* (Bengali) **कोंद** *kōnda* 'engraver, lapidary setting or infixing gems' (Marathi)

कोडें [kōḍēṃ] *n* An earthen saucer-form receptacle for the oil and wicks of a lamp. 2 An enigma; a puzzling question in arithmetic; a knotty point; an obscure, perplexing stanza, passage &c. कोंडवरा [kōṇḍavarā] *a* R Deep, not shallow--a vessel &c. कोठंबी [kōṭhambī] *f* कोठमी *f* A water-jar of a wide open mouth, tapering from the bottom. कोठंबा or कोठबा [kōṭhambā or kōṭhabā] *m* See कोटंबा. कोटंबी *f* (Dim. of कोटंबा) A small wooden trough. कोटंबा [kōṭambā] *m* A square wooden vessel used by the वाघ्या or worshipers of खंडोबा in begging alms. It is worshiped on occasions. 2 A sort of wooden trough. (Marathi)

Ka. guḍḍu, guḍḍi eyeball, egg; guḍasu anything round; guḍi a circle, halo. *Tu.* kuḍu testicles of dogs, cats, etc. *Te.* g(r)uḍḍu eyeball, egg; guḍusu a circle, round; goḍḍa cylindrical stone; guḍi halo round the sun or moon. *Kol.* guḍ (*pl.* guḍl) testicle. *Nk. (Ch.)* guḍ (*pl.* -l) egg; kanta guḍḍa eyeball; ?gaḍḍa stone, pestle made of stone. *Go.* (Ko.) guḍi variety of small bead (*Voc.* 1114). *Konḍa* guḍu eyeball, egg, testicle (< Te.); gurḍu, (Sova dial.) gurzupupil, eyeball. *Kuwi* (Su.) guḍu egg (< Te.). Cf. 1695 Ta. kuṇṭu. / Cf. Skt. guṭikā-, guḍa- globe, ball, pill guḍá1 m. ' globe, ball ' MBh., *guḍikā* -- f. ' kernel ' VarBṛS., *gula* -- m. ' glans penis ', *°lī* -- f. ' pill ' lex., *°likā* -- f. ' globule ' Kād. [Cf. gōla -- 1, *gōṭṭa --] Pa. *guḷa* -- ' cluster ' in *mālā -- g°*, *guḷikā* -- f. ' little ball '; Pk. *guḍiā* -- f. ' pellet ', *gulia* -- m., *°iā* -- f. ' ball '; A. *guri* ' minute particle ', *gurā, gulī* ' sinker on fishing net or line '; B. *guṛ* ' globe, mouthful '; Or. *guṛā, guḷā* ' pill ', *goṛi* ' pebble ', *guḷī* ' round clod '; Mth. *guriā* ' bead '; H. *guriyā* f. ' glass bead ', *gulā* m. ' ball, bullet ', *gullā* m. ' small pellet '; Si. *guḷiya* ' pill, ball, lump '. (CDIAL 4181) Rebus: Ko. guṛy temple *Te.* koṭika hamlet; guḍi temple; guḍise hut, cottage, hovel. *Kol.* (SR) guḍī temple. *Pa.* guḍi temple, village resthouse. *Ga.* (Oll.) guḍi temple. *Go.*(Ko.) guḍi, (Mu.) guḍḍi, (S. Ko.) guṛi temple; guḍḍī (Ph.) temple, (Tr.) (DEDR 1655) See Turner, *CDIAL*, no. 3232, kuṭī-, no. 3493, kōṭa-, no. 3233, kuṭumba-, for most of the Skt. Forms.

குடதாடி kuṭa-tāṭi , *n.* < குடம்[1] +. Capital of a pillar; தூணின்மேல்வைக்குங் குடவடிவான உறுப்பு. (சீவக. 593, உரை.)

குடம்² kuṭam, n. cf. kūṭa. 1. Town; நகரம். (பிங்.)

kuṭa1 m.n. ' water -- pot, pitcher ' Yaśast., *kūṭa* -- 5 n. lex., *kuḍikā* -- f. lex. 2. *kuṭava -- . 3. *kōṭa -- 4. [With kuṇḍá -- 1, *kulla -- 3, kúlāla -- , *kōḍamba -- , gōla -- 2, *ghōla -- 2 ←

Drav. EWA i 221, 226 with lit. -- Cf. kuḍava --] 1. Pa. *kuṭa* -- m.n. ' pitcher '; NiDoc. *kuḍ'a* ' waterpot ', Pk. *kuḍa* -- m.; Paš. *kuṛā* ' clay pot ' (or < kuṇḍá -- 1); Kal. *kṝūṛi* ' milking pail '; H. *kuliyā* f. ' small earthen cup '; Si. *kuḷāva* ' pot, vessel for oil ' (EGS 47 wrongly < kaṭāha --), *kaḷa -- geḍiya* ' waterpot ', *kaḷaya* (or < kaláśa --).2. Pa. *kuṭava* -- ' nest ' (semant. cf. N. *gũṛ* s.v. kuṇḍá -- 1); Or. *kuṛuā* ' tall red earthen pot for cooking curry and rice offerings in the temple at Puri '.3. Pk. *kōḍaya* -- , *°ḍia* -- n. ' small earthen pot '; Dm. *kōṛī* ' milking pail '; G. *koṛiyũ* n. ' earthen cup for oil and wick '; M. *koḍẽ* n. ' earthen saucer for a lamp '. OMarw. (Vīsaḷa) loc.sg.m. *kūṛaï* ' pot '; G. *kuṛlī* f. ' small pitcher '. (CDIAL 3227).

कोठी [kōṭhī] *f* (कोष्ट S) A common term for the squares in a मिठागर or saltern-enclosure. कोट [kōṭa]A form of array of troops, the solid square. (Marathi)

कोडी [kōḍī] *f* (Probably corrupted from Score.) A score (of particular things, viz. of pieces of nankeen, or other kinds of cloth, of gold or tin foil, of panes of glass, or glass-bracelets &c.) कोड [kōḍa] *f* C (Usually कोडी q. v.) A score. (Marathi)

कोठी [kōṭhī] *f* (कोष्ट S) A granary, garner, storehouse, warehouse, treasury, factory, bank. 2 The grain and provisions (as of an army); the commissariatsupplies. कोठा [kōṭhā] *m* (कोष्ट S) A large granary, store-room, warehouse, water-reservoir &c. कोठ [kōṭha] *m* (कोट्ट S) A fort: also a castle. 2 The wall of a fort. कोट [kōṭa] *m* (कोट्ट S) A fort, fortress, castle, stronghold, tower &c. 2 The wall of a fort or town. (Marathi)

Ta. koṭṭu (koṭṭi-) to beat (as a drum, tambourine), hammer, beat (as a brazier), clap, strike with the palms, pound (as paddy); *n.* beat, stroke, drumbeat, time-measure;koṭṭāṉ, koṭṭaṉ mallet; koṭṭi time-measure; koṭṭaṇam pounding or husking paddy; koṭu (-pp-, -tt-) to thrash, abuse roundly; koṭai blows, round abuse. *Ma.* koṭṭuka to beat so as to produce a sound (as drum, metals, bells), clap hands; koṭṭu beating a drum, clapping hands, buffet,

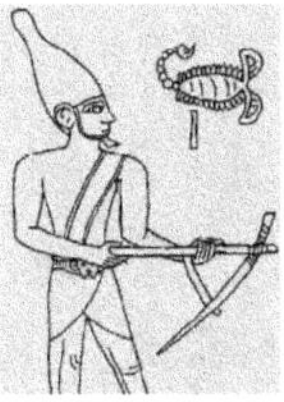

knocking of knees against each other; koṭṭi mallet; koṭṭaṇam beating the husk from paddy in a slovenly manner; koṭukka to flog. *Ko.* koṭk- (koṭky-) to strike (with small hammer), knock on (door), strike tipcat in hole in ground. *To.* kwïṭk- (kwïṭky-) to tap (on door, something with stick); kwïṭ fïḷ woodpecker. *Ka.* koḍati, koḍanti a wooden hammer; koṭṭaṇa beating the husk from paddy; koṭṭuha beating; kuḍu to beat. *Koḍ.*koṭṭ- (koṭṭi-) to tap, beat (drum). *Tu.* koḍapuni to forge, hammer; koḍapāvuni to weld, forge together; (B-K.) kuḍapu to hammer metallic objects; korpini to beat. *Te.* koṭṭu to beat, strike, knock;

strike (as a clock); *n.* a blow, stroke. *Pa.* koṭṭ- to strike with axe. *Ga.* (Oll.) koṭ- id. *Go.* koṭ- (Mu.) to cut with axe, (Ko.) strike with horn (*Voc.* 888); koṭela(A.) mallet, (Mu. Ma.) drumstick (*Voc.* 882); (SR. Tr. W. Ph.) kohkānā to crush, pound, butt, gore; kohk- (Mu.) to gore, (G.) thresh with flail; (Ma.) ko'k- to butt (*Voc.* 959); (ASu.) kohk- to grind into a paste, pound (in a mortar), beat stalks of millet, wheat, etc. on the ground so that the seeds fall down. *Pe.* koṭ- to thresh with flail. *Kuwi* (Isr.) koṭoli mallet. *Kur.* xoṭṭnā (xuṭṭyas) to break, smash, pierce, break open; xoṭrnā to be broken. *Malt.* qoṭe to break, knock, strike; qoṭre to be broken; qoṭure to knock or dash against. (DEDR 2063) Cf. 1671 Ta. kuṭṭu. / Cf. Pali koṭṭeti to beat, smash, pound; Turner, *CDIAL*, no. 3241(2). cf. Nahali koṭṭo- to pound, beat. (DEDR 2063). *Ta.* kaṉ copper work, copper, workmanship; kaṉṉāṉ brazier. *Ma.* kannān id. (DEDR 1402). கன்னான் kaṉṉāṉ. *n.* < கன்[1]. [M. *kannān.*] Brazier, bell-metal worker, one of the divisions of the Kammāḷa caste; செம்புகொட்டி. (திவா.) கொட்டன் koṭṭaṉ , *n.* < கொட்டு-. (J.) 1. Mallet (Tamil) கொட்டுக்கிடாரம் koṭṭu-k-kiṭāram , *n.* < id. +. Large boiler of beaten brass; பெரிய கொப்பரை. (W.)

Mr' hand-plough, Protodynastic Period of Egypt (from the Scorpion Macehead)

koṇḍi the sting of a scorpion (Kannada). Rebus: *kōnda* 'engraver (Marathi)

కుట్టు. v. a. To prick, bore కుట్టుతేళ్లు scorpions, villains (Telugu) *koṭṭu* [T. M. *koṭṭu.*] [Tu. *koḍapuni.*] To sting, as a scorpion, a wasp (Tamil) *Ka.* koṇḍi the sting of a scorpion. *Tu.* koṇḍi a sting. *Te.* koṇḍi the sting of a scorpion. (DEDR 2080). Rebus: *koṭhi* 'smelter' (Sad.) *kund* ' brassfounder's lathe ' (Bihari)(CDIA 3295). *kõdā* 'to turn in a lathe' (Bengali) **कोंद** *kōnda* 'engraver, lapidary setting or infixing gems' (Marathi)

கொட்டுக்கன்னார் koṭṭu-k-kaṉṉār , *n.* < கொட்டு[2] +. Braziers who work by beating plates into shape and not by casting; செம் படிக்குங் கன்னார். (W.) கொட்டுச்செம்பு koṭṭu-c-cempu , *n.* < id. +. A copper pot made by beating plates into shape; தகடடித்துச்செய்த தாமிரச்செம்பு. (W.) கொட்டுவேலை koṭṭu-vēlai , *n.* < id. +. Beaten work, dist. fr. *vārppu-vēlai*; கொட்டுக்கன்னார்வேலை. (W.) கொட்டுக்குடவை koṭṭu-k-kuṭavai , *n.* < id. +. A kettle-shaped vessel; உடுக்கைபோல் வடிவமைந்த பாத்திரம். *Tinn.*கொட்டுக்கூடை koṭṭu-k-kūṭai, *n.* < id. +. 1. Cup-shaped basket; கிண்ணவடிவான கூடை. (W.) 2. A basket-shaped metal vessel; கூடைபோன்ற வடிவுள்ள உலோகபாத்திரம். *Loc.*

கொட்டி³ koṭṭi, *n.* cf. *kōṭṭāra.* 1. Tower- gate in a temple; கோபுரவாசல். 2. Gate; வாயில். (அக. நி.)(Tamil)

koṭṭu, *n.* < கொட்டு [T. *koṭṭu.*] Granary; நெற்கூடு. (பழ. 388, உரை.)(Tamil)

Ta. koṭṭakai shed with sloping roofs, cow-stall; marriage pandal; koṭṭam cattle-shed; koṭṭil cow-stall, shed, hut; (STD) koṭambe feeding place for cattle. *Ma.* koṭṭil cowhouse, shed, workshop, house. *Ka.* koṭṭage, koṭige, koṭṭige stall or outhouse (esp. for cattle), barn, room. *Koḍ.* koṭṭï shed. *Tu.* koṭṭa hut or dwelling of Koragars; koṭyashed, stall. *Te.* koṭṭāmu stable for cattle or horses; koṭṭāyi thatched shed. *Kol.* (Kin.) koṛka, (SR.) korkā cowshed; (Pat., p. 59) konṭoḍi henhouse. *Nk.* khoṭa cowshed. *Nk. (Ch.)* koṛka id. *Go.* (Y.) koṭa, (Ko.) koṭam (*pl.* koṭak) id. (*Voc.* 880); (SR.) koṭka shed; (W. G. Mu. Ma.) koṛka, (Ph.) korka, kurka cowshed (*Voc.* 886); (Mu.) koṭorla, koṭorli shed for goats (*Voc.* 884). *Malt.* koṭa hamlet. / Influenced by Skt. goṣṭha. (DEDR 2058).

Ko. guṇḍ gal, kal guṇḍ a huge, round stone; Ka. guṇḍu anything globular, round stone for grinding, boulder, plummet, testicle of beasts, bullet; *Te.* guṇḍu bullet, rock, bead, anything spherical; rubbu-guṇḍu stone pestle or roller used in grinding things in a mortar. *Kol.* gunḍ stone; (SR.) rubgunḍ pounding stone. *Nk.* ghunḍ stone. *Ga.* (S.3) kuṇḍran round. *Go.* (S.) gunḍkula pēru bead necklace (DEDR 1695) Mar. gũḍ, gũḍā stone, esp. round stone. गुंडा [guṇḍā] *m* A rolling or roundish stone. 2 fig. A shrewd, all-knowing, capable fellow; esp. in a bad sense, as a sharper or elusive knave. 3 A ball or roll of thread, tape, twine, cord &c. 4 A large गुंड or metal vessel. 6 (Local.) A squared or onefaced stone for building. 6 A stone used by the potter in shaping his pots. (Marathi)

गोटा [gōṭā] *m* A roundish stone or pebble. 2 A marble (of stone, *lac*, wood &c.)

kol 'tiger' (Konkani) krōṣṭŕ̥ ' crying ' BhP., m. ' jackal ' RV. = *krṓṣṭu* -- m. Pāṇ. [√kruś] Pa. *koṭṭhu* -- , *°uka* -- and *kotthu* -- , *°uka* -- m. ' jackal ', Pk. *koṭṭhu* -- m.; Si. *koṭa* ' jackal ', *koṭiya* ' leopard ' GS 42; -- Pk. *kolhuya* -- , *kulha* -- m. ' jackal ' < **kōḍhu* -- ; H. *kolhā*, *°lā* m. ' jackal ', adj. ' crafty '; G. *kohlũ*, *°lũ* n. ' jackal ', M. *kolhā*, *°lā* m.(CDIAL 3615). Sa. *kul* `tiger'.Mu. *kul* ~ *kula* `tiger'.KW *kuḷ*~ *kula* @(M062)So. *k+nal* *k+D* `tiger, leopard'.Go. *kula* ~ *kul* ~ *ku:* `tiger, panther'. (Munda etyma) कोल्हा [kōlhā] *m* A jackal,

Canis aureus. Linn. कोल्हें [kōlhēṃ] *n* A jackal. Without reference to sex. (Marathi) kola 'woman' (Nahali)

Koḍ. koṭṭï katti billhook: *Ta.* koṭṭu (koṭṭi-) to sting (as a scorpion, wasp); *n.* stinging; hoe with short handle, weeding-hoe, spade; koṭukku sting of a wasp, hornet, scorpion, claws of a crab, lobster; tēṭ-koṭṭāṉ a green insect whose touch produces the same sensation as a scorpion-sting; tēṭ-kuṭicci a black bee (for tēṭ-, see 3470 Ta. tēḷ). *Ma.* koṭṭuka to sting (of scorpion);koṭukka scorpion's sting. *Ko.* koṭk- (koṭky-) (snake) strikes, bites; ? kako·ṭ hoe with sharp, broad blade (for ka-, see 1265). *Ka.* kuṭuku to sting (as a scorpion); kuḍuku to peck; kukku to peck, strike something with a stone, etc., in a pecking manner, dig up the ground slightly with a hoe; (Hav.) koḍappu to peck. *Tu.* koḍapuni, (B-K.) kuḍapu to bite (as a serpent), peck, strike with the beak; kukkuli pecking; kukkuliyuni to peck; koṭṭu, koṭrè spade; (B-K.) kuḍpoḷu a hornet. *Nk.* koṛk- to peck. *Pa.* koḍk- id.; koṭṭ- id., dig; koṭal hoe. *Ga.* (Oll.) koṭ- to dig, (fowl) to peck; koṭal hoe, spade; (S.) koṭ- to bite (as a snake). *Go.* koṭṭānā (SR. Tr.) to peck, pierce leaves and sew them for platters, (Ph.) to pierce, thrust; (A.) koṭṭ- to hoe; (M.) koṭāna to sew; (Tr.) goṭṭānā to poke or thrust with a stick or finger; kōṭstānā to have one's ears pierced (*Voc.* 888); (Sr. Tr. W. Ph.)kohkānā to prick, puncture, tattoo; (Mu. Ko.) kohk-, (Ma.) koʔk- to peck (*Voc.* 959). *Pe.* koṭ- (-t-) to dig, hoe, (snake) to bite; koḍgi hoe. *Manḍ.* kuṭ- (-t-) (snake) to bite, (hen) to peck. *Kui* (K.) koḍi hoe. *Kuwi* (Su. Mah. Isr.) koṛgi, (F.) kūrgi, (S.) korgi hoe, mattock. *Malt.* koḍkare woodpecker. (DEDR 2064).

koṭṭi mallet (Malayalam) kotti pick-axe, stone-digger, carver. (Malayalam)

Ma. koṟṟan ram, boar, tomcat; koṟṟi ewe, female cat, bandicoot; kuṟiññi, kuṟuññi she-cat. *To.* kwaṯy cat. *Ka.* kotti male or female cat. *Tu.* kuttiri a civet cat. (DEDR 2170).

Ta. koṭṭu (koṭṭi-) to pour forth, shower down, empty the contents of a basket or sack, throw into a vessel; drop (as leaves), fall off (as hair); *n.* pouring, emptying; koṭṭamflowing, pouring. *Ma.* koṭṭuka to shoot out, empty a sack. ? *Te.* koṭṭukonipōvu to be carried along by stream or air current.(DEDR 2065).

Pa. *kuṭila—* 'bent', n. 'bend'; Pk. *kuḍila—* 'crooked', *°illa—* 'humpbacked', *°illaya—* 'bent' (CDIAL 3231) Rebus: *kuṭila, katthīl* = bronze (8 parts copper and 2 parts tin) [cf. āra-kūṭa, 'brass' (Skt.)

Ta. koṭu curved, bent, crooked; koṭumai crookedness, obliquity; koṭukki hooked bar for fastening doors, clasp of an ornament; koṭuṅ-kāy cucumber; koṭuṅ-kaifolded arm; koṭu-maram bow; koṭu-vāy curved or bent edge (as of billhook); koṭu-vāḷ pruning knife, billhook, sickle, battle-axe; kuṭa curved, bent; kuṭakkam bend, curve, crookedness; kuṭakki that which is crooked; kuṭakkiyaṉ humpback; kuṭaṅku (kuṭaṅki-) to bend (*intr.*); kuṭaṅkai palm of hand; kuṭantai curve; kuṭavu (kuṭavi-) to be crooked, bent, curved; *n.* bend, curve; kuṭā bend, curve; kōṭu (kōṭi-) to bend, be crooked, go astray, be biased; *n.* crookedness, obliquity; kōṭal bending, curving; kōṭi bend, curve; kōṭṭam bend, curve, warp, partiality, crookedness (as of mind); kōṭṭu (kōṭṭi-) to bend (*tr.*); ṭoṅku crookedness. *Ma.* koṭuṅ-kai bent arm; koṭu-vāḷ hatchet, large splitting knife; kōṭuka to be crooked, twisted, awry, warp (of wood); kōṭṭuka to bend (*tr.*); kōṭṭam crookedness, distortion; kōṭṭal what is crooked, turn, way of escape. *Ko.* koṛy crick in neck from sleeping crooked or lifting heavy burden. *To.* kwïṛ magoy elbow; kwiṛ curve. *Ka.* kuḍu, kuḍa, kuḍi state of being crooked, bent, hooked, or tortuous; ḍoṅku to bend, be crooked; ḍoṅku, ḍoṅka state of being bent, curved, crooked; crookedness, a bend, a curve. *Koḍ.* koṭṭï katti billhook. *Tu.* guḍke a crooked man; ḍoṅků, ḍoṅku crookedness; crooked, curved, perverse; ḍoṅkelů crookedness; (B-K.) daṅgāvu to bend, incline. *Te.* koḍavali, (*VPK*) koḍali, koḍēli, koḍvali sickle; gōḍi-vaḍu to bend (*intr.*); gōḍi-veṭṭu id. (*tr.*); ḍoṅku curvature; ḍoṅkenaa sort of spear with a bent or curved head. *Kol.* koḍval (*pl.* koḍvasil), (Kin.) koṛva sickle; (Pat., p. 119) koṭe false. *Nk.* koṛval sickle. *Pa.* kūḍaŋgey elbow; koḍka billhook. *Ga.* (Oll.) konḍke id. *Go.* (G.) kunamkay, (Ma.) kunaŋkay, (Ko.) kunagay elbow (*Voc.* 755); (LuS.) koondakaiyoo id.; (ASu.) kōr- to bend in dancing. *Konḍa* koṛveli sickle. *Kui* konḍoṛi, konḍoni bent, winding, zigzag; kōnḍa (kōnḍi-) to curl, be curly, bent, twisted; gōṭoṛi, (P.) gōṭoni hooked, bent like a hook. *Kuwi* (P.2) ḍong- (-it-), (Isr.) ḍōṅg- (-it-) to be bent, crooked; (P.2) ḍok- (-h-), (Isr.) ḍōk- (-h-) to bend (elbow, wrist, finger); (Su. Isr.) ḍoveli, (F.) dō'velli (*pl.* dōvelka) sickle; (S.) doweli knife. *Br.* kōnḍōon all fours, bent double. Initial ḍ of some forms is < *kḍ- (*kḍoṅg-, *kḍōk-; *kḍoveli < koḍavali); ? cf. also 2983 Kol. toŋge. / Cf. Mar. ḍōgā curved, bent.(DEDR 2054).

கோலம்[1] kōlam , *n.* [T. *kōlamu*, K. *kōla*, M. *kōlam.*] Ornamental figures drawn on floor, wall or sacrificial pots with rice-flour, white stone-powder (Tamil)

koṭṭï katti billhook (Koḍagu) (DEDR 2054) <kati>(Z),,<ka?Ti>(A),,<kaTi>(A) [kati'] {N} ``^knife(A), small ^sickle(Z)''. kártati1 ' cuts ' Ep. [Later pres. formation from aor. subj., fut., &c. replacing kr̥ntáti1: with wide extension of MIA. kaṭṭ -- to distinguish from katt -- ' spin ' < *kartati2: √kr̥t1] NiDoc. ger. kartavo ' to be cut off '; Pk. kattaï, kaṭṭaï ' cuts ', Paš. kaṭ -- (→ Par. kaṭ -- IIFL i 268), K. kaṭun, ḍoḍ. kaṭṇō, S. kaṭaṇu, P. kaṭṭṇā, Ku. kāṭṇo, N. kāṭnu, A. kāṭiba, B. kāṭā, Or. kāṭibā; Bi. kāṭab ' to reap '; Mth. kāṭab ' to cut ', Aw. lakh. kāṭab, H. kāṭnā, G. kāṭvũ; M. kāṭṇẽ ' to cut ' with restricted use only, prob. ← H. -- Caus. P. kaṭāuṇā, N. kaṭāunu, B. kāṭāna, Or. kaṭāibā, H. kaṭānā, OMarw. kaṭāi. -- Intr. with a: Or. kaṭibā ' to be cut ', Mth. Aw. lakh. kaṭab, H. kaṭnā, OMarw. kaṭaï, M. kaṭṇẽ. Addenda: kártati1: WPah.kṭg. kaṭṇō ' to cut, fell ', J. kāṭṇu, kṭg. caus. kəṭauṇō; Garh. kāṭṇu ' to cut ', kaṭṇu ' to be cut '.(CDIAL 2854).

kōla ornament, decoration, form (Kannada); *kōlam* form, shape (Tamil)(DEDR 2240). Rebus: *Ta.* kol working in iron, blacksmith; kollaṉ blacksmith. *Ma.* kollan blacksmith, artificer. *Ka.* kolime, kolume, kulame, kulime, kulume, kulme fire-pit, furnace; (Bell.; U.P.U.) konimi blacksmith (Gowda) kolla id. *Koḍ.* kollë blacksmith. *Te.* kolimi furnace. *Go.* (SR.) kollusānā to mend implements; (Ph.) kolstānā, kulsānā to forge; (Tr.) kōlstānā to repair (of ploughshares); (SR.) kolmi smithy (*Voc.* 948). *Kuwi* (F.) kolhali to forge. (DEDR 2133).

Rebus: kol metal (Ta.) kol = pañcalōkam (five metals) (Tamil) kol = pañcalōkam (five metals); kol metal (Tamil) pañcalōha = a metallic alloy containing five metals: copper, brass, tin, lead and iron (Skt.); an alternative list of five metals: gold, silver, copper, tin (lead), and iron (dha_tu; Nānārtharatnākara. 82; Man:garāja's Nighaṇṭu. 498)(Ka.) *kol, kolhe*, 'the koles, an aboriginal tribe if iron smelters speaking a language akin to that of Santals' (Santali) kol = kollan-, kammāḷan- (blacksmith or smith in general)(Tamil) kollar = those who guard the treasure (Tamil) cf. golla (Telugu) khol, kholī = a metal covering; a loose covering of metal or cloth (G.) [The semant. expansions to kollāpuri or kolhāpur and also to 'kollāppaṇṭi' a type of cart have to be investigated further].

kola, kolum = a jackal (G.) kolhuyo (Dh.Des.); kulho, kolhuo (Hem.Des.); kroṣṭr̥ (Skt.) kul seren = the tiger's son, a species of lizard (Santali) kolo, koleā jackal (Konkani) Jackal: kuṛi-nari jackal (Kuṟṟā. Tala. Vēṭan-valam. 13)(Ta.); id. (Ma.)(Tamil) kul tiger; kul dander den of tiger; aṇḍkul to become tiger; huduṛ to growl as tiger; maran. d.at.kap kul a big-headed tiger (Santali.) kōlupuli = a big, huge tiger, royal or Bengal tiger; kōlu = big, great, huge (Telugu.) kula tiger; syn. of maran: kula, burukula, kamsikula, the striped royal tiger; syn. of maran: kula, laṛokula, the brown royal tiger without stripes; syn. of huṛin: kula, soncita, leopard: sinkula = the lion; kindorkula, kinduakula = the panther; tagukula (lit. the shaggy tiger), the hyena; ḍurkula, a smaller feline animal, which when attacking a man bites him in the knee, probably a tiger-cat; kula-bin: collective noun for all dangerous animals; kulabin:-o to become infested by dangerous animals; kla (Khasi.Rongao) tiger (Mundari) kroṣṭṛ = jackal (RV.); kroṣṭu = id. (Pāṇ); kroṣṭṛ = crying (BhP.); koṭṭhu, koṭṭhuka, kotthu, kotthuka = jackal (Pali); koṭṭhu (Pkt.); koṭa (Si.); koṭiya = leopard (Si.); kōlhuya, kulha = jackal (Pkt.); kolhā, kolā jackal; adj. crafty (H.); kohlū̃, kohlū jackal (G.); kolhā, kolā (M.)(CDIAL 3615). Fr. kruś = cry, call; krōśati cries out (RV)(CDIAL 3613). koṭho = a call, a messenger; koṭha invitation; koṭhaṇu = to send for (S.)(CDIAL 3614). koś to abuse, curse, blame (Gypsy); kosnā to curse (H.); kosṇā (P.); akoś to abuse (Gypsy); krośati cries out (RV)(CDIAL 3612). krośa shout (VS); kurū voice, word (Pas'); kosā curse (H.)(CDIAL 3611). kul. = the tiger, filis tigris; kul en:ga = tigress; *kul seren* 'the 'tiger's song', a species of lizard (Santali)

Ta. kural corn-ear, spike, flower-cluster, link, tie, band, stalk, sheath of millet or plantain. *Tu.* koralů, koraḷů an ear of corn.(DEDR 1775).

náva2 ' nine ' RV.Pa. nava, Pk. ṇava, Ḍ. nau, Ash. no, nū, Wg. nū, Pr. nū, Dm. nō, Tir. nāb, Paš.lauṛ. nā´wa, ar. nāu, dar. nō, Shum. nū, Niṅg. nū, Woṭ. nau, Gaw. nū, Kal.rumb. nō, Kho. nyoh (whence y? -- h from Pers.? BelvalkarVol 94), Bshk. nab, num, Tor. nom, Kand. nāũ, Mai. naũ, Sv. nōu, Phal. nau, nū, nũ, Sh.gil. náŭ, pales. nāũ, K. nav, nau, nam, pog. nāu, rām. kash. ḍoḍ. nau, S. nãvã, L. nõᵛ, khet. naũ, awāṇ. naɔ̃, P. naũ, bhaṭ. nau, WPah.bhal. paṅ. cur. nao, Ku. nau, gng. nɔ, N. nau, A. B. na, Or. na, naa, Bi. Mth. Aw.lakh. nau, H. nau, nam, OMarw. nova, G. nav, M. nav, naũ, Ko. nav, OSi. nava, Si. namaya, Md. nuva.navaka --S.kcch. nõ ' 9 ', WPah.kṭg. (kc.) nɔ̃, nɔu, J. nau, Garh. nɔ, Md. nuva.(CDIAL 6984).navaka2 ' consisting of 9 ' RVPrāt., n. ' collection of 9 ' R. [náva2] Pk. ṇavaga -- n. ' collection of 9 ', K. nomu m., H. nawwā, nammā m.; G. navvɔ m. ' the 9 in cards '.(CDIAL 6985).

``^plough'': Sa. *nahEl* `plough'. Mu. *nahEl* `plough'. KW *nahEl* @(M083) lā´ṅgala n. ' plough ' RV. [→ Ir. dial of Lar in South Persia liṅgṓr ' plough ' Morgenstierne. -- Initial n -- in all Drav. forms (DED 2368); PMWS 127 derives both IA. and Drav. words from Mu.

sources] Pa. naṅgala -- n. ' plough ', Pk. laṁgala -- , ṇa°, ṇaṁgara<-> n. (ṇaṁgala -- n.m. also ' beak '); WPah.bhad. nā̃ṅgal n. ' wooden sole of plough '; B. lāṅal, nā° ' plough ', Or. (Sambhalpur) nā̃gar, Bi.mag. lā̃gal; Mth. nā̃gano ' handle of plough '; H. nā̃gal, nāgal, °ar m. ' plough ', M. nā̃gar, °gor, nāgār, °gor m., Si. naṅgul, nagala, nagula. -- Gy. eur. nanari ' comb ' (LM 357) very doubtful. lāṅgalin -- A. lāṅgal ' plough ' (CDIAL 11006). Ta. ñāñcil, nāñcil plough. Ma. ñēṅṅōl, nēññil plough-shaft. Ko. ne·lg plough. Ka. nēgal, nēgil, nēgila id. Koḍ. ne·ŋgi id. Tu. nāyerů id. Kor. (T.) nēveri id. Te. nāgali, nāgelu, nāgēlu id. Kol. na·ŋgli, (Kin.) nāŋeli id. Nk. nāŋgar id. Nk. (Ch.) nāŋgar id. Pa. nāgil id. Ga. (Oll.) nāŋgal, (S.) nāngal id. Go. (W.) nāṅgēl, (A. SR.) nāngyal, (G. Mu. M. Ko.) nāŋgel, (Y.) nāŋgal, (Ma.) nāŋgili (pl. nāŋgisku) id. (Voc. 1956); (ASu.) nāynāl, (Koya Su.) nāṅēl, nāyṅēl id. Konḍa nāŋgel id. Pe. nāŋgel id. Manḍ. nēŋgel id. Kui nāngeli id. Kuwi (F.) nangelli ploughshare; (Isr.) nāŋgeli plough. / Cf. Skt. lāṅgala-, Pali naṅgala- plough; Mar. nāgar, H. nāgal, Beng. nāṅgal id., etc.(DEDR 2907).

lōī f., *lo* m.2. Pr. *ẕūwī* 'fox' (Western Pahari)(CDIAL 11140-2). Rebus: *loh* 'copper' (Hindi). lōpāśá m. ' fox, jackal ' RV., *lōpāśikā* -- f. lex. [Cf. *lōpāka* -- . -- *lōpi --] Wg. *liwášä*, *laúša* ' fox ', Paš.kch. *lowóć*, ar. *lṓeč* ' jackal ' (→ Shum. *lṓeč* NTS xiii 269), kuṛ. *lwāinč*; K. *lośu*, *lōh*, *lohu*, *lôhu* ' porcupine, fox '. (CDIAL 11141) *lōpi ' fox '. 2. *rōpi -- . [Cf. Av. *raopi* -- ' a sort of dog- like animal '. 1. Kho. *lōw* ' fox ', Sh.gil. *lótilde;i* f., pales. *lṓi* f., *lṓo* m., WPah.bhal. *lōī* f., *lo* m.2. Pr. *ẕūwī* ' fox '. (CDIAL 11142) lōmaṭaka m. ' fox ' Śīl. 2. *lōmaka -- or *lūmaka -- . 3. *lōmpaṭa -- 1. NiDoc. *lomaṭī* ' foxes ' Burrow KharDoc 117.2. Gaw. *Lamasík* ' fox ', Bshk. *lumáṛ*, Tor. *lamā* ' jackal ', Phal. *lūmḗi*.3. S. *lombaṛu* m. ' fox ', *lombiṛī*, *lū̃biṛī* f., L. *lū̃buṛ* m., *lū̃bṛī* f., khet. *lumbaṛ*, P. *lū̃bṛī* f., H. *lomṛī* f. (→ N. *lomṛī*); -- H.jt. *lobā*. WPah.kc. *lɔmbṛe* f. ' fox ' (→ H. *lambar* f.? -- or X lampaṭa -- Him.I 194). (CDIAL 11153).

P. *lohaṛ* m. ' lust, violence, oppression '(CDIAL 11147). Rebus: *lohār*, *lohāra* 'coppersmith, blacksmith' (Lahnda. Prakrit)

N. *lokhar* ' bag in which a barber keeps his tools '; H. *lokhar* m. ' iron tools, pots and pans '; -- X lauhabhāṇḍa -- : Ku. *lokhaṛ* ' iron tools '; H. *lokhaṇḍ* m. ' iron tools, pots and pans '; G. *lokhā̃ḍ* n. ' tools, iron, ironware '; M. *lokhā̃ḍ* n. ' iron ' (LM 400 < -- *khaṇḍa* --)(CDIAL 11171). lōhitaka ' reddish ' Āpast., n. ' calx of brass, bell- metal ' lex. [lṓhita --]K. *lŏy* f. ' white copper, bell -- metal '. (CDIAL 11166). lōhá ' red, copper -- coloured ' ŚrS., ' made of copper ' ŚBr., m.n. ' copper ' VS., ' iron ' MBh. [*rudh --] Pa. *lōha* -- m. ' metal, esp. copper or bronze '; Pk. *lōha* -- m. ' iron ', Gy. pal. *li°*, *lihi*, obl. *elhás*, as. *loa* JGLS new ser.

ii 258; Wg. (Lumsden) "*loa*" ' steel '; Kho. *loh* ' copper '; S. *lohu* m. ' iron ', L. *lohā* m., awāṇ.*lō`ā*, P. *lohā* m. (→ K.rām. ḍoḍ. *lohā*), WPah.bhad. *lõu* n., bhal. *lòtilde;* n., pāḍ. jaun. *lōh*, paṅ. *luhā*, cur. cam. *lohā*, Ku. *luwā*, N. *lohu*, *°hā*, A. *lo*, B. *lo*, *no*, Or. *lohā*, *luhā*, Mth. *loh*, Bhoj. *lohā*, Aw.lakh. *lōh*, H.*loh*, *lohā* m., G. M. *loh* n.; Si. *loho*, *lō* ' metal, ore, iron '; Md. *ratu -- lō* ' copper '.(CDIAL 11158). lōhakāra m. ' iron -- worker ', *°rī* -- f., *°raka* -- m. lex., *lauhakāra* -- m. Hit. [lōhá -- , kāra -- 1] Pa. *lōhakāra* -- m. ' coppersmith, ironsmith '; Pk. *lōhāra* -- m. ' blacksmith ', S. *luhāru* m., L. *lohār* m., *°rī* f., awāṇ. *luhār*, P. WPah.khaś. bhal. *luhār* m., Ku. *lwār*, N. B. *lohār*, Or. *lohaḷa*, Bi.Bhoj. Aw.lakh. *lohār*, H. *lohār*, *luh°* m., G. *lavār* m., M. *lohār* m.; Si. *lōvaru* ' coppersmith '. Addenda: lōhakāra -- : WPah.kṭg. (kc.) *lhwā`r* m. ' blacksmith ', *lhwàri* f. ' his wife ', Garh. *lwār* m.(CDIAL 11159). lōhahala 11161 lōhala ' made of iron ' W. [lōhá --](CDIAL 11161). Bi. *lohrā*, *°rī* ' small iron pan '(CDIAL 11160). Bi. *lohsārī* ' smithy '(CDIAL 11162). P.ludh. *lōhṭiyā* m. ' ironmonger '.(CDIAL 11163). लोहोलोखंड [lōhōlōkhaṇḍa] *n* (लोह & लोखंड) Iron tools, vessels, or articles in general.रुपेशाई लोखंड [rupēśāī lōkhaṇḍa] *n* A kind of iron. It is of inferior quality to शिक्केशाई. लोखंड [lōkhaṇḍa] *n* (लोह S) Iron. लोखंडाचे चणे खावविणें or चारणें To oppress grievously. लोखंडकाम [lōkhaṇḍakāma] *n* Iron work; that portion (of a building, machine &c.) which consists of iron. 2 The business of an ironsmith. लोखंडी [lōkhaṇḍī] *a* (लोखंड) Composed of iron; relating to iron. 2 fig. Hardy or hard--a constitution or a frame of body, one's हाड or natal bone or parental stock. 3 Close and hard;--used of kinds of wood. 4 Ardent and unyielding--a fever. 5 लोखंडी, in the sense Hard and coarse or in the sense Strong or enduring, is freely applied as a term of distinction or designation. Examples follow. लोखंडी [lōkhaṇḍī] *f* (लोखंड) An iron boiler or other vessel. लोखंडी जर [lōkhaṇḍī jara] *m* (लोखंड & जर) False brocade or lace; lace &c. made of iron.लोखंडी रस्ता [lōkhaṇḍī rastā] *m* लोखंडी सडक *f* (Iron-road.) A railroad. लोह [lōha] *n* S Iron, crude or wrought.
2 *m* Abridged from लोहभस्म. A medicinal preparation from rust of iron.लोहकार [lōhakāra] *m* (S) A smelter of iron or a worker in iron.लोहकिट्ट [lōhakiṭṭa] *n* (S) Scoriæ or rust of iron, *klinker*.लोहंगी or लोहंगी काठी [lōhaṅgī or lōhaṅgī kāṭhī] *f* (लोह & अंग) A club set round with iron clamps and rings, a sort of bludgeon.लोहार [lōhāra] *m* (H or लोहकार S) A caste or an individual of it. They are smiths or workers in iron. लोहारकाम [lōhārakāma] *n* Iron-work, work proper to the blacksmith.लोहारकी [lōhārakī] *f* (लोहार) The business of the blacksmith. लोहारडा [lōhāraḍā] *m* A contemptuous form of the word लोहार.लोहारसाळ [lōhārasāḷa] *f* A smithy.

Loha (nt.) [Cp. Vedic loha, of Idg. *(e)reudh "red"; see also rohita & lohita] metal, esp. copper, brass or bronze. It is often used as a general term & the individual application is not always sharply defined. Its comprehensiveness is evident from the classification of loha at VbhA 63, where it is said lohan ti jātilohaŋ, vijāti°, kittima°, pisāca° or natural metal, produced metal, artificial (i. e. alloys), & metal from the Pisāca district. Each is subdivided as follows: jāti°=ayo, sajjhaŋ, suvaṇṇaŋ, tipu, sīsaŋ, tambalohaŋ, vekantakalohaŋ; vijāti°=nāga -- nāsika°; kittima°=kaŋsalohaŋ, vaṭṭa°, ārakūṭaŋ; pisāca°=morakkhakaŋ, puthukaŋ, malinakaŋ, capalakaŋ, selakaŋ, āṭakaŋ, bhallakaŋ, dūsilohaŋ. The description ends "Tesu pañca jātilohāni pāḷiyaŋ visuŋ vuttān' eva (i. e. the first category are severally spoken of in the Canon). Tambalohaŋ vekantakan ti imehi pana dvīhi jātilohehi saddhiŋ sesaŋ sabbam pi idha lohan ti veditabbaŋ." -- On loha in *similes* see *J.P.T.S.* 1907, 131. Cp. A iii.16=S v.92 (five alloys of gold: ayo, loha, tipu, sīsaŋ, sajjhaŋ); J v.45 (asi°); Miln 161 (suvaṇṇam pi jātivantaŋ lohena bhijjati); PvA 44, 95 (tamba°=loha), 221 (tatta -- loha -- secanaŋ pouring out of boiling metal, one of the five ordeals in Niraya). -- kaṭāha a copper (brass) receptacle Vin ii.170. -- kāra a metal worker, coppersmith, blacksmith Miln 331. -- kumbhī an iron cauldron Vin ii.170. Also N. of a purgatory J iii.22, 43; iv.493; v.268; SnA 59, 480; Sdhp 195. -- guḷa an iron (or metal) ball A iv.131; Dh 371 (mā °ŋ gilī pamatto; cp. DhA iv.109). -- jāla a copper (i. e. wire) netting PvA 153. -- thālaka a copper bowl Nd1 226. -- thāli a bronze kettle DhA i.126. -- pāsāda"copper terrace," brazen palace, N. of a famous monastery at Anurādhapura in Ceylon Vism 97; DA i.131; Mhvs passim. -- piṇḍa an iron ball SnA 225. -- bhaṇḍa copper (brass) ware Vin ii.135. -- maya made of copper, brazen Sn 670; Pv ii.64. -- māsa a copper bean Nd1 448 (suvaṇṇa -- channa). -- māsaka a small copper coin KhA 37 (jatu -- māsaka, dāru -- māsaka+); DhsA 318. -- rūpa a bronze statue Mhvs 36, 31. -- salākā a bronze gong -- stick Vism 283. Lohatā (f.) [abstr. fr. loha] being a metal, in (suvaṇṇassa) aggalohatā the fact of gold being the best metal VvA 13. (Pali)

maṇḍū´ka m. ' frog ', *maṇḍūkī´* -- f. RV., *°kíkā* -- f. Suparṇ., *marūka* -- m. lex. 2. *maṇḍukka -- . 3. maṇḍūra -- m. lex. 4. maṇḍa -- 5 m. lex. 5. *manṭrakka -- or *maṭrakka -- . [The many aberrant forms in NIA. are due to taboo (EWA ii 561 with lit.: see also dardurá --) as well as onom. influences (as, e.g., **maṭrakka* -- ~ Gk. ba/traxos). P. Thieme's derivation (ZDMG 93, 135) as MIA. < **mr̥ṁṣṭa* -- is phonet. unacceptable. -- → Orm. *maṛyūg* ' frog ' IIFL i 401] 1. Pa. *maṇḍūka* -- m., *°kī* -- f. ' frog ', Pk. *maṁḍū`ka* -- , *°ḍūa* -- , *°ḍuga* -- m., WPah.bhiḍ. bhi*ḍõ*, pl. *°ḍū* n., bhal. *mā´ṇū* n. (+ *go* < gōdhā´ -- in*mango* f. ' large frog '), khaś. *mn*/a*ḍū*, marm. *mā̃ḍū*, Si. *maḍu -- vā*, *mäňḍi*, *mäḍi -- yā* (< *maṇḍūkī´* --). 2. Pk. *maṁḍukka* -- m., *°kiyā* -- , *°kaliyā* -- f., Ḍ. *minik* m., Ash. *muṇḍúk*, Wg. *āvmeḍák*, *āmǝ́ṛk* (*āv* -- , *ā* -- < *ā´pah* s.v. áp --), Kt. *muṇúk*,

(Kamdesh) *ṓmaṇuk*, Pr. *mā´ṇḍux, māṇḍuk, mā̃ḍək*, Paš.kuṛ. chil. *marák, °rék*, Gaw. *muṇḍā´ka, miṇ°*, Bshk. *mänā´k* (< *maṇḍ* -- or *mandr* -- AO xviii 244), Sv. *miṇḍā´ka*, Sh.*măṇū´kụ* m., K. *miñĕmŏnḍukh*, dat. *°dakas* m. (see 4), P. *mẽḍuk, °ḍak, mī̃ḍuk, °ḍak* m., WPah.rudh. *mínku*, (Joshi) *minkā* m.; Ku. *munki -- ṭaulo* ' tadpole '; OMarw. *mī̃ḍako* m. ' frog ', *mīṁḍakī* f. ' small frog ', G. *me_ḍak, meḍ°* m., *me_ḍkī, meḍ°* f.; M. *mẽḍūk -- mukh* n. ' frog -- like face '.3. Pk. *maṁḍūra* -- m.4. K. *main, mön* m., *miñ* f., *miñĕ -- mŏnḍukh* m. (orig. ' female and male frog '?).5. Wg. *āwmaṭrakōg*, Dm. *maṭrak*, Paš.lauṛ. *máṭrax*, uzb. *máṭrōk, katrṓx*, nir. kch. *maṭeṅ*, dar. *maṭḗx*, weg. *maṭék*, ar. *matrek*, Shum. *maṭərok*, Kal.rumb.*maṇḍrák*, urt. *maḍrák*, Phal. *maṭrōk* m. (CDIAL 9746).

maṇḍa6 ' some sort of framework (?) '. [In *nau -- maṇḍḗ* n. du. ' the two sets of poles rising from the thwarts or the two bamboo covers of a boat (?) ' ŚBr. (as illustrated in BPL p. 42); and in BHSk. and Pa. *bōdhi -- maṇḍa* -- n. perh. ' thatched cover ' rather than ' raised platform ' (BHS ii 402). If so, it may belong to maṇḍapá -- andmaṭha --] Ku. *mā̃ṛā* m. pl. ' shed, resthouse ' (if not < **mā̃ṛhā* < **maṇḍhaka* -- s.v. maṇḍapá --).(CDIAL 9737).

maṇḍapa m.n. ' open temporary shed, pavilion ' Hariv., *°pikā* -- f. ' small pavilion, customs house ' Kād. 1. Pa. *maṇḍapa* -- m. ' temporary shed for festive occasions '; Pk. *maṁḍava* -- m. ' temporary erection, booth covered with creepers ', *°viā* -- f. ' small do. '; Phal. *maṇḍau* m. ' wooden gallery outside a house '; K. *manḍav* m. ' a kind of house found in forest villages '; S. *manahũ* m. ' shed, thatched roof '; Ku. *mā̃ṛyā, manyā* ' resthouse '; N.*kā̃ṭhmā̃ṛau* ' the city of Kathmandu ' (*kā̃ṭh* -- < kāṣṭhá --); Or. *maṇḍuā* ' raised and shaded pavilion ', *paṭā -- maṇḍoi* ' pavilion laid over with planks below roof ', *muṇḍoi, °ḍei* raised unroofed platform '; Bi. *mā̃ṛo* ' roof of betel plantation ', *mā̃ṛuā, maṛ°, malwā* ' lean -- to thatch against a wall ', *maṛaī* ' watcher's shed on ground without platform '; Mth. *mā̃ṛab* ' roof of betel plantation ', *maṛwā* ' open erection in courtyard for festive occasions '; OAw. *mā̃ṁḍava* m. ' wedding canopy '; H. *mā̃ṛwā* m., *°wī* f., *manḍwā* m., *°wī* f. ' arbour, temporary erection, pavilion ', OMarw. *maṁḍavo, mā̃ḍhivo* m.; G. *mā̃ḍav* m. ' thatched open shed ', *mā̃ḍvɔ* m. ' booth ', *mā̃ḍvī* f. ' slightly raised platform before door of a house, customs house ', *mā̃ḍaviyɔ* m. ' member of bride's

party '; M. *mā̃ḍav* m. ' pavilion for festivals ', *mā̃ḍvī* f. ' small canopy over an idol ';
Si. *maḍu -- va* ' hut ', *maḍa* ' open hall ' SigGr ii 452.2. Ko. *māṁṭav* ' open pavilion '.3.
H. *mā̃ḍhā, mā̃ṛhā, mā̃ḍhā* m. ' temporary shed, arbour ' (cf. OMarw. *mā̃ḍhivo* in 1); --
Ku. *mā̃ṛā* m.pl. ' shed, resthouse S.kcch. *mā̃ṇḍhvo* m. ' booth, canopy '.(CDIAL 9740).

OMarw. *māṁḍaï* ' writes '; OG. *māṁḍīṁ* 3 pl. pres. pass. ' are written ', maṇḍáyati ' adorns, decorates ' Hariv., *máṇḍatē, °ti* Dhātup. Pa. *maṇḍēti* ' adorns ', Pk. *maṁḍēi, °ḍaï,* Ash. *mū̆ṇḍ* -- , *moṇ* -- intr. ' to put on clothes, dress ', *muṇḍaā́* -- tr. 'to dress'; K. *manḍun* ' to adorn ', H. *maṇḍnā,* G. *mā̃ḍvũ* ' to arrange, dispose, begin ', M. *mā̃ḍṇẽ,* Ko. *mā̃ṇḍtā*.(CDIAL 9741).

Glyph: *Ko.* meṭ- (mec-) to trample on, tread on; meṭ sole of foot, footstep, footprint: *meḍ* 'to dance' (F.)[reduplicated from me-]; me id. (M.) in Remo (Munda)(Source: D. Stampe's Munda etyma) *Ta.* meṭṭu (meṭṭi-) to spurn or push with the foot. *Ko.* meṭ- (mec-) to trample on, tread on; meṭ sole of foot, footstep, footprint. *To.* möṭ- (möṭy-) to trample on; möṭ step, tread, wooden-soled sandal. *Ka.* meṭṭu to put or place down the foot or feet, step, pace, walk, tread or trample on, put the foot on or in, put on (as a slipper or shoe); *n.* stepping, step of the foot, stop on a stringed instrument; sandal, shoe, step of a stair; meṭṭisu to cause to step; meṭṭige, meṭlastep, stair. *Koḍ.* moṭṭï footprint, foot measure, doorsteps. *Tu.* muṭṭu shoe, sandal; footstep; steps, stairs. *Te* meṭṭu step, stair, treading, slipper, stop on a lute;maṭṭu, (K. also) meṭṭu to tread, trample, crush under foot, tread or place the foot upon; *n.* treading; maṭṭincu to cause to be trodden or trampled. *Ga.* (S.3) meṭṭu step (< Te.). *Konḍa* maṭ- (-t-) to crush under foot, tread on, walk, thresh (grain, as by oxen); *caus.* maṭis-. *Kuwi* (S.) mettunga steps. *Malt.* maḍye to trample, tread. (DEDR 5057) Rebus: *meḍ* 'iron' (Mundari. Remo.)

Or. *meṇḍā* ' lump, clot '.(CDIAL 10308).
mēda m. ' a mixed caste, any one living by a degrading occupation ' Mn. [→ Bal. *mēd* ' boatman, fisher- man '. -- Cf. Tam. *metavar* ' basket -- maker ' &c. DED 4178] Pk. *mēa* -- m., *mēī* -- f. ' member of a non -- Aryan tribe '; S. *meu* m. ' fisherman ' (whence *miāṇī* f. ' a fishery '), L. *mē* m.; P. *meũ* m., f. *meuṇī* ' boatman '. -- Prob. separate from S. *muhāṇo* m. ' member of a class of Moslem boatmen ', L. *mohāṇā* m., *°ṇī* f (CDIAL 10320).

mr̥gayā́ f. ' hunting ' Mn. [*mr̥gayú* -- ' hunting ' AV. - mr̥gá --]Pa. *migavā* -- f. ' hunting ', Aś.shah. *mrugaya* f., Pk. *migayā* -- , *miaā* -- , *maaā* -- , *maïā* -- f.; Wg. *mrāī̃* ' shooting, hunting '; Kho. *mroi* ' all sorts of big game ' BelvalkarVol 93. 10272 *mr̥gahana2 ' act of hunting '. [mr̥gá -- , hana --]Kal.rumb. *mrū̃*ln ' shooting, hunting '.(CDIAL 10269).

*mr̥gadr̥ti ' deer -- skin '. [mr̥gá -- , dŕ̥ti --]Kho. *muriri* ' ibex skin '.(CDIAL 10267)

*mr̥garūpa ' animal '. [mr̥gá -- , rū́pa --]S. *mirū̃* m. ' wild animal '.(CDIAL 10270)

*mr̥gasūkara ' wild boar '. [mr̥gá -- , sūkará --]L. *mirhõ, °hū̃*, pl. *°hẽ* m. ' boar ' (*mirhõ* ' ravine deer ' for **mirū̃* (CDIAL 10271)

*mr̥gākāra ' shaped like a deer '. [mr̥gá -- , ākāra --]Sh.pales. *mayā́ro* m. ' oorial ', koh. *mā̃yā́ro* m. ' deer ', gil. (Lor.) *maiāro* ' wild animal of goat or sheep type (including markhor, ibex and oorial) '. (CDIAL 10274)

*mr̥gahanaka, *mr̥gahan(a)* -- m. ' hunter ' MBh. [mr̥gá -- , hana --]Tor. *mĩṅg* ' leopard ' (rather than < mr̥gá --); S. *muhāṇo* m. ' one of a class of fishermen and boatmen ', L. *mohāṇā* m., *°ṇī* f. (CDIAL 10273)

*mr̥gasūkara ' wild boar '. [mr̥gá -- , sūkará --]L. *mirhõ, °hū̃*, pl. *°hẽ* m. ' boar ' (*mirhõ* ' ravine deer ' for **mirū̃* < *mr̥garūpa -- ?). (CDIAL 10271)

Ka. mēke she-goat; mē the bleating of sheep or goats. *Te.* mēka, mēka goat. *Kol.* me·ke id. *Nk.* mēke id. *Pa.* mēva, (S.) mēya she-goat. *Ga.* (Oll.) mēge, (S.) mēge goat. *Go.* (M) mekā, (Ko.) mēka id. ? *Kur.* mēxnā (mīxyas) to call, call after loudly, hail. *Malt.* méqe to bleat. [*Te.* mr̤ēka (so correct) is of unknown meaning. *Br.*mēḻẖ is without etymology; see MBE 1980a.] / Cf. Skt. (*lex.*) meka- goat.(DEDR 5087). Milāca [by -- form to milakkha, viâ *milaccha> *milacca> milāca: Geiger, *P.Gr.* 622; Kern, *Toev.* s. v.] a wild man of the woods; Milakkhu [the Prk. form (A -- Māgadhī, cp. Pischel, *Prk. Gr.* 105, 233) for P. milakkha] a non -- Aryan D iii.264; milakkhuka at Vin iii.28, where Bdhgh expls by "Andha -- Damil' ādi."; Milakkha [cp. Ved. Sk. mleccha, root mlecch, onomat. after the strange sounds of a foreign tongue (Pali) B. *mech* ' a Tibeto -- Burman tribe ' ODBL 473(CDIAL 10389). Mrēcchati ~ *mlḗcchati* ' speaks indistinctly ' ŚBr. [MIA. *mr* -- < *ml* -- ? See Add. -- √mlēch] K. *briċhun*, pp. *bryuċhu* ' to weep and lament, cry as a child for something wanted or as motherless child '.(CDIAL 10384).

mḗdas n. ' fat, marrow ' RV., *mēda* -- m. ' fat ' R.Tor. (Biddulph) *mih* f. ' fat ', *mīm* f. ' brain ' (CDIAL 10323)

One word glossed in *Deśīnāmamālā* is: *meḍho* 'helper of merchant'. (See embedded text -- Deśīnāmamālā of Hemacandra).

मेढो vi. 138 वणिक्सहायः, one who helps a merchant.

Deśīnāmamālā Glossary, p. 71. *Deśīnāmamālā*[507] provides a remarkable resource for ancient lexemes of Indian linguistic area.

मेढ [mēḍha] *f* A forked stake. Used as a post. Hence a short post generally whether forked or not. मेढ [mēḍha] *f* A forked stake. Used as a post. Hence a short post generally whether forked or not.

मेंढा [mēṇḍhā] *m* (मेष S through H) A male sheep, a ram or tup. 2 A crook or curved end (of a stick, horn &c.) and *attrib.* such a stick, horn, bullock. मेढी [mēḍhī] *f* (Dim. of मेढ) A small bifurcated stake: also a small stake, with or without furcation, used as a post to support a cross piece. मेंढी [mēṇḍhī] *f* (मेंढा or H) A female sheep, a newe. மேண்டம் mēṇṭam , *n.* < *mēṇḍha.* Ram; ஆடு mēṇḍha2 m. ' ram ', *°aka* -- , *mēṇḍa* -- 4, *miṇḍha* -- 2, *°aka* -- , *mēṭha* -- 2, *mēṇḍhra* -- , *mēḍhra* -- 2, *°aka* -- m. lex. 2. *mēṇṭha-(*mēṭha* -- m. lex.). 3. *mējjha -- . [*r* -- forms (which are not attested in NIA.) are due to further sanskritization of a loan -- word prob. of Austro -- as. origin (EWA ii 682 with lit.) and perh. related to the group s.v. bhēḍra --] 1. Pa. *meṇḍa* -- m. ' ram ', *°aka* -- ' made of a ram's horn (e.g. a bow) '; Pk. *meḍḍha* -- , *meṁḍha* -- (*°ḍhī* -- f.), *°ṁḍa* -- , *miṁḍha* -- (*°dhiā* -- f.), *°aga* -- m. ' ram ', Dm. Gaw. *miṇ* Kal.rumb. *amŕn/aŕə* ' sheep ' (*a* -- ?); Bshk. *minā́l* ' ram '; Tor. *miṇḍ* ' ram ', *miṇḍā́l* ' markhor '; Chil. *mindh**l/* ' ram ' AO xviii 244 (*dh*!), Sv. *yēṛo -- miṇ*, Phal. *miṇḍ*, *miṇ* ' ram ', *miṇḍṓl* m. ' yearling lamb, gimmer '; P. *mẽḍhā* m., *°ḍhī* f., ludh. *mīḍḍhā*, *mī̃ḍhā* m.; N. *meṛho*, *meṛo* ' ram for sacrifice '; A. *mersāg* ' ram ' (-- *sāg* < *chāgya -- ?), B. *meṛā* m., *°ṛi* f., Or. *meṇḍhā*, *°ḍā* m., *°ḍhi* f., H. *meṛh*, *meṛhā*, *mẽḍhā* m., G. *mẽḍhɔ*, M. *mẽḍhā*m., Si. *mäḍayā*.2. Pk. *meṁṭhī* -- f. ' sheep '; H. *meṭhā* m. ' ram '.3. H. *mejhukā* m. ' ram '. A. also *mer* (phonet. *mer*) ' ram ' (CDIAL 10310).

मेंड [mēṇḍa] *m* (H) Edge, margin, or border of a field, esp. as raised: also a ridge or raised edge more generally.

मेंडका or क्या [mēṇḍakā or kyā] *a* (Preferably मेंढका or क्या) A shepherd. मेंढका or क्या [*mēṇḍhakā or kyā*] *a* (मेंढा) A shepherd.(Marathi) मेढंगमत, मेढजोशी, मेढदाई, मेढमत [*mēḍhaṅgamata, mēḍhajōśī, mēḍhadāī, mēḍhamata*] See मेढेमत, मेढेजोशी, मेढेदाई &c. मेढेजोशी [*mēḍhējōśī*] *m* A stake-जोशी; a जोशी who keeps account of the तिथि &c., by driving stakes into the ground: also a class, or an individual of it, of fortune-tellers, diviners, presagers, seasonannouncers, almanack-makers &c. They are Shúdras and followers of the मेढेमत q. v. 2 Jocosely. The hereditary or settled (quasi fixed as a stake) जोशी of a village. मेढेमत [*mēḍhēmata*] *n* (मेढ Polar star, मत Dogma or sect.) A persuasion or an order or a set of tenets and notions amongst the Shúdra-people. Founded upon certain astrological calculations proceeding upon the North star. Hence मेढेजोशी or डौरीजोशी.

Glyph: *Ta.* meṭṭu mound, heap of earth; mēṭu height, eminence, hillock; muṭṭu rising ground, high ground, heap. *Ma.* mēṭu rising ground, hillock; māṭu hillock, raised ground; miṭṭāl rising ground, an alluvial bank; (Tiyya) maṭṭa hill. *Ka.* mēḍu height, rising ground, hillock; miṭṭu rising or high ground, hill; miṭṭe state of being high, rising ground, hill, mass, a large number; (Hav.) muṭṭe heap (as of straw). *Tu.* miṭṭè prominent, protruding; muṭṭe heap. *Te.* meṭṭa raised or high ground, hill;
(K.) meṭṭu mound; miṭṭa high ground, hillock, mound; high, elevated, raised, projecting; (*VPK*) mēṭu, mēṭa, mēṭi stack of hay; (Inscr.) meṇṭa-cēnudry field (cf. meṭṭu-nēla, meṭṭu-vari). *Kol.* (SR.) meṭṭā hill; (Kin.) meṭṭ, (Hislop) met mountain. *Nk.* meṭṭ hill, mountain. *Ga.* (S.3, *LSB* 20.3) meṭṭa high land.*Go.* (Tr. W. Ph.) maṭṭā, (Mu.) maṭṭa mountain; (M. L.) meṭā id., hill; (A. D. Ko.) meṭṭa, (Y. Ma. M.) meṭa hill; (SR.) meṭṭā hillock (*Voc.* 2949). *Koṇḍa* meṭa id. *Kuwi* (S.) metta hill; (Isr.) meṭa sand hill.(DEDR 5058). K*a.* mede heap. *Te. (VPK*, intro. p. 128) meda id. (DEDR 5065). Or. *meṭṭā* ' hillock '(CDIAL 10308).

பணை paṇai , n. prob. பணை-. 1. Anvil; உலைக்களத்துப் பட்டடை. (குறள், 828, மணக். பக். 28.) 2. Tusk of an elephant; யானைத் தந்தம். மகரிகையு மிருபணைகளும் . . . ஒளிவிட . . . முடுகினகரிகளே (பாரத. பதினாறாம். 20).

पहार [pahāra] f पहारय f C A pointed iron-bar, used in punching rocks or the ground, a bickern, a pitcher, a crowbar.(Marathi)prahāra m. ' blow ' Mn. [√hr̥]Pa. Pk. pahāra -- m. ' blow, wound '; Kt. prōr ' wound ', Pr. pār, pārė ' wounded ' (← Ind. NTS ii 198); Dm. praā́ru, praāl ' wound ' (with dissim. of r -- r NTS xii 130), Paš.lauṛ. lahā´r, ar. plōor, weg. lahār, uz. ṣawṓr, Shum. lāar; L. pahār f. ' internal, wound '; Or. pāhāra ' blow, beating, pestle of rice -- pounding machine ' (whence pāhurāibā ' to pound with a pestle '); Bi. paharuwā ' pestle of husking machine '; Si. pahara, pāra ' blow '; Md. fāru ' wound '. -- Altern. < parighāta -- : Or. pu(h)āri ' small iron chisel '; G. pārī f. ' crowbar '; M. pahār, pahāray f. ' iron bar, crowbar '. -- Psht. parhār ' wound ' (← Ind. EVP 58) → Tir. Woṭ. parā´r m. ' wound ', Sv. Phal. parhā´r, Bshk. parā´r Buddruss Woṭ 120. Md. etifaharu ' blows '.(CDIAL 8906). Ta. pārai crowbar, small hoe for cutting grass. Ma. pāra iron crowbar, lever, bar used for digging. Ko. pa·r crowbar. To. pa·r id. Ka. pāre id., short hoe. Tu. pāreṅgi iron crowbar, lever. Te. pāra, pāṟa spade. Kol. (Kin.) gaḍḍa pāra spade (gaḍḍa clod). Nk. (Ch.) pahar crowbar. Ga. (S.3) pāra spade. Go. (A.) pāra id. (Voc. 2195). Kuwi (S.) pāra id.(DEDR 4093).

<haRisia>(P),,<aRisia>(*),,<paRisia>(*) {N} ``^axe''. *Mu., Ho<kapi>. Cf. <haDisa>, <guTia>. *H.<phArAsa>, B.<phOrsa>, Sk.<pArA$U> `axe', H.<pArAsIya> `sickle'. %12611. #12511. paraśu -- m. ' axe ' RV. 2. *pharaśu -- .1. Pa. Pk. parasu -- m. ' axe '; H. parsā ' hatchet ', parsiyā f. ' reaping hook '; Si. porova ' axe ' H. Smith JA 1950, 208 (or < 2), Md. furō.2. Pa. Pk. pharasu -- m. ' axe ', Ku.gng. phars; N. pharsā ' long -- handled battle -- axe '; B. H. pharsā m. ' axe ', G. pharśī f.; M. pharas m. ' battle -- axe ', pharśī f. ' battleaxe, large chisel '. (CDIAL 7799).

పట్టడ [paṭṭaḍa] paṭṭaḍu. [Tel.] n. A smithy, a shop. కుమ్మరి వడ్లంగి మొదలగువారు పనిచేయు చోటు.(Telugu) Glyph: S. baṭhu m. 'large pot in which grain is parched; L. bhaṭṭh m. ' grain -- parcher's oven 'M. bhaṭṭā m. ' pot of fire '(CDIAL 9656). Glyph: bhaṭa 'six' (G.) rebus: baṭa = kiln (Santali); bhaṭṭī f. ' forge '(Marathi)(CDIAL 9656). baṭa = a kind of iron (G.) bhaṭṭhī f. 'kiln, distillery', awāṇ. bhaṭh; P. bhaṭṭh m., °ṭhī f. 'furnace', bhaṭṭhā m. 'kiln'; S. bhaṭṭhī keṇī 'distil (spirits) baṭa = furnace (Santali) bhrāṣṭra = furnace (Skt.) bhaṭa 'furnace' (G.) baṭhī f. ' distilling furnace' (Sindhi) P. *bhaṭhiār, °ālā* m. 'grainparcher's shop'.(CDIAl 9658).

patākā f. ' flag ' MBh. 2. paṭākā -- f. lex. 3. *phaṭākā --. [Prob. ← a non -- Aryan word containing *p(h)aṭ* aryanized with *t* EWA ii 200]1. Pa. *patākā* -- f. ' flag '. 2. Pa. *paṭāka* -- n., Pk. *paḍāga* -- m., *paḍāyā* -- , *paḍāiā* -- f., mh. *paḍāha* -- m.; G. *paṛāi* f. ' paper kite '. 3. Kal.rumb. *phŕā* ' flag '; Or. *phaṛkā* (perh. influenced by Or. *phaṛa -- phaṛa* ' with a sudden movement ' s.v. *phaṭ --). S.kcch. *paṛāī* f. ' paper kite '.(CDIAL 7726)

Ta. pāṭi town, city, hamlet, pastoral village; pāṭam street, street of herdsmen. *Ma.* pāṭi (in *n.pr.* of villages). *Ka.* pāḍi settlement, hamlet, village. *Koḍ.* pa·ḍi hut of a Kurumba. *Te.* pāḍu village (at the end of names of places). / Cf. Skt. pāṭaka- a kind of village, half a village (from which are borrowed Ta. pāṭakam street, section of a village, Ma. pāṭakam part of a village); Turner, *CDIAL*, no. 8031, to which add Mar. pāḍā hamlet or cluster of houses of agriculturalists (also Guj., Beng., etc.)(DEDR 4064). pāṭaka m. ' quarter of a town or village '. [← Drav. T. Burrow BSOAS xii 383, but perh. same as pāṭa<-> EWA ii 245] S. *pāṛo* m. ' quarter of a town, vicinity '; H. *pāṛā* m. ' quarter of a town '. pāṭaka -- m. ' kind of village, part of village ' lex. [MIA. *pāḍa(ya)* -- ' quarter, street ' ~ Drav. Tam. *pāṭa(ka)m* id. perh. conn. pallī -- 1 ← Drav. DED 3309] Pk. *pāḍa* -- , *pāḍaya* -- m.; A. *pārā*, B. *pāṛā*, Or. *paṛā*, H. *pāṛā* m., M. *pāḍā* m. (CDIAL 8031).

Patthara [cp. late Sk. prastara. The ord. meaning of Sk. pr. is "stramentum"] 1. stone, rock S i.32. -- 2. stoneware Miln 2. (Pali) Pa. Pk. patthara -- m. ' stone ', S. patharu m., L. (Ju.) pathar m., khet. patthar, P. patthar m. (→ forms of Bi. Mth. Bhoj. H. G. below with atth or ath), WPah.jaun. pātthar; Ku. pāthar m. ' slates, stones ', gng. pāth*lr ' flat stone '; A. B. pāthar ' stone ', Or. pathara; Bi. pāthar, patthar, patthal ' hailstone '; Mth. pāthar, pathal ' stone ', Bhoj. pathal, Aw.lakh. pāthar, H. pāthar, patthar, pathar, patthal m., G. patthar, pathrɔ m.; M. pāthar f. ' flat stone '; Ko. phāttaru ' stone '; Si. patura ' chip, fragment '; -- S. pathirī f. ' stone in the bladder '; P. pathrī f. ' small stone '; Ku. patharī ' stone cup '; B. pāthri ' stone in the bladder, tartar on teeth '; Or. pathurī ' stoneware '; H. patthrī f. ' grit ', G. pathrī f. *prastarapaṭṭa -- , *prastaramr̥ttikā -- , *prastarāsa -- .Addenda: prastará -- : WPah.kṭg. pátthər m. ' stone, rock '; pəthreuṇõ ' to stone '; J. pāthar m. ' stone '; OMarw. pātharī ' precious stone '. (CDIAL 8857)

Pa. *phāla* -- m. (?) ' board, slab ', *phālaka* -- ' splitting '; Gy. eur. *phal* ' board ', wel. *phal* f. ' pailing, rail, stake '; K. *phal* f. ' strip of wood ' (or < phala --3?); S. *phāra* f. ' slice '; P. *phāl* f. ' wedge '; Ku. *phālo* ' piece of wood or metal, iron bar '; N. *phāli* ' thin strip of metal '; A. *phāli* ' strip '; B. *phālā* ' chip ', *°li* ' strip '; Or. *phāḷiā* ' chip '; Bi. *phārī* ' half a hide '; H. *phāl* m. ' lump of areca -- nut ', (poet.) *phār* m. ' piece '; G. *phāḷɔ* m. ' share '; M. *phāḷ* ' slip of wood '.(CDIAL 9073).

Rebus: phā´la ' ploughshare ' RV., ' mattock ' R. Pa. Pk. K. *phāl* m. ' ploughshare, metal blade of mattock &c. ' S.*phāru* m. ' ploughshare, steel edge of a tool '; L. *phālā* m. ' ploughshare 'Ku. *phālo*, gng. *phāw*, N. *phāli*, A. B. *phāl*, Or. *phāḷa*, (Bastar) *phāra*, Bi. *phār*, Mth. *phār*, *°rā*, *phālā*, Bhoj. *phār*, H. *phāl*, *°lā* m., *°lī* f.,*phār*, *°rā* m., M. *phāḷ* m.(CDIAL 9072). *lōhaphāla -- ' ploughshare '. [lōhá -- , phā´la --

1] WPah.ktg. *lhwā'ḷ* m. ' ploughshare ', J. *lohāl* m. ' an agricultural implement ' Him.I 197(CDIAL 11160).

pāslo = a nugget of gold or silver having the form of a die (G.) Rebus: pasra 'smithy' (Santali)

P. *pẽdā* m., *°ḍī* f. ' bottom '; N. *pĩd, pĩdh, pin* ' bottom, fundament, buttocks '; A. *penda* ' lower or inner extremity of the alimentary canal or the vagina '; Or. *pendi* ' earth bulging at bottom side of a brick when in the mould, depression at bottom of a pot, pedestal of a cup '; Bi. *pẽd(ā), °dī, penī* ' bottom of a granary ', Mth. *pẽdo*; H.*pẽdā* m. ' bottom '; M. *pẽd* n. ' tuft of grass ', *pẽdī, pẽdhī* f. ' bottom '; Si. *peňda* ' bird's tail '; Md. *fīndu* ' hips ', *fidu* ' posterior '.(CDIAL 8379). Allographs: peṇḍa female, woman (Kannada)(DEDR 4395). *Pa.* peṇḍa buttock. *Go.* (Tr. Ph.) pēnḍā female organ; pēnḍa (Mu.) id., (Ko.) buttock (*Voc.* 2362); (ASu.) pēṇḍā anus. *Kui* pinḍari rectum.(DEDR 4398). Rebus: *Pa.* penda shifting cultivation. *Go.* penda (Elwin) hillside axe cultivation, (Ma.) hill field for the cultivation of millet (DEDR 4404).
पेंढी [pēṇḍhī] *f* A bundle (of grass, कडबा &c.): also a handful of reaped corn (जोंधळा &c.) just tied, a sheaf.(Marathi)
पेंढें [pēṇḍhēṃ] पेंडकें [pēṇḍakēṃ] n Weaver's term. A cord-loop or metal ring (as attached to the गुलडा of the बैली and to certain other fixtures). पेंडें [pēṇḍēṃ] n (पेड) A necklace composed of strings of pearls. 2 A loop or ring

पेढ [pēḍha] A common name for the stones composing a handmill, a leaf.
पेढेघाट [pēḍhēghāṭa] m (पेढा & घाट) A gem (a pearl, ruby &c.) of the form of the sweetmeat called पेढा.
पुट [puṭa] *n* (S) Anything folded or doubled so as to form a cup or concavity;--as the hands, leaves &c., a valve of a shell &c. Also in comp. as अंजलिपुट, चंचुपुट, पर्णपुट, कर्णपुट. 2 A hemisphere. 3 A single application unto;--as, in preparing medicaments, of fire to bake, of sun, air &c. to dry: also a single dipping into an infusion, a single coating, plastering, smearing, overlay. Gen. in comp. as अग्निपुट, सूर्यपुट, औषधपुट, रसपुट. *v* दे. It signifies also the material so used,--the infusion, the plaster &c. 4 In comp. with नासिका or नासा or घ्राण,

as नासिकापुट &c. A nostril. 5 A crucible. Ex. जैसें पुटीं पडतां सुवर्ण ॥ तेजस्वी दिसे दैदीप्यमान ॥.(Marathi) puṭa m.n. ' cavity, small receptacle, fold '(Skt)(CDIAL 8253). పుటము [puṭamu] Burning or refining a metal, calcining a medicinal drug.(Telugu) *புடம்*[1] *puṭam, n. < puṭa.* 1. The refining or sublimating vessel or cup; புடமிடுங்கலம். (ஞானா. 15, 26.) 2. Cover; மூடி. தொகுபுடஞ் சற்றே யோங்கி (விநாயகபு. 15, 40). புடம்[2] puṭam, n. < sphuṭa. 1. (Astron.) True daily motion of a heavenly body; கிரகங் களின் உண்மையான தினசரிக்கதி. 2. (Astron.) Celestial longitude; ஒருவகை வானவளவை. *புடபாகம் puṭa-pākam, n. < puṭa-pāka.* 1. A particular method of preparing drugs in which various substances are placed in clay cups covered over with clay and heated over the fire; புடமிடுகை. புடபாகத்திற் சார்தரு முலோக மாசு தள்ளல்போல் (திருக்காளத். பு. ஞானயோ. 18). sphuṭa ' blossoming, opened ' MBh., ' clear in meaning ' R. [Perh. not conn. with √sphuṭ, but < **sphṛta* -- 2 pp. of *spharati2 ' swells '. -- √sphar2] Pa. *phuṭa* -- ' expanded, spread out over (glossed with *pharitvā*), blossoming '; Pk. *phuḍa* -- ' open, clear '; Sh.koh. *phŭṛu* m., jij. *phvṛe* ' flower ', WPah.bhad. bhiḍ.*phuṛõ* n., bhal. khaś. *phuṛu* n.; OM. *phuḍā* ' real, true ' (CDIAL 13841).

<rabca?>(D) {ADJ} ``with ^dishevelled ^hair''. Cf. <raca> `dishevelled'. #26291. <raca>(D) {ADJ} ``^dishevelled''. Syn. <kunkRu>(D). #26311. <rabca?>(D) {ADJ} ``with ^dishevelled ^hair''. #26320. Rebus, 'Glowing embers': N. *rachyān* ' dust -- hole, rubbish -- hole '; M. *rasāṇẽ* n. ' glowing embers '.(CDIAL 10554). rakṣā2 f. ' ashes ' lex. [Same as rakṣā -- 1? -- √rakṣ]Pk. *rakkhā* -- , *racchā* -- f. ' ashes ', S. *rakha* f., P. *rākh* f. (← H.?), Bi. Mth. Bhoj. *rākh*, OAw. *rākhā* f., H. *rākh*, *rākhī* f., OMarw. *rācha* f., G. M. *rākh* f.(CDIAL 10552). రాజు [rāzu] *rāḍzu.* [Tel.] v. n. To take fire, flame, begin to burn.(Telugu) రాచ (adj.) Pertaining to a stone. (Telugu) cf. *sangatarāśū* = stone cutter; *sangatarāśi* = stone-cutting (Telugu)

saman = to offer an offering, to place in front of; front, to front or face (Santali) Rebus: *samṛobica*, stones containing gold (Mundari) samanom = an obsolete name for gold (Santali)

சுக்கான்[1] cukkāṉ , *n.* < U. *sukkān.* Rudder, helm; கப்பல்திருப்புங் கருவி. சுக்கான்கிரி cukkāṉ-kiri , *n.* < U. *sukkāngīr.* Helmsman, one who steers a vessel; மாலுமி. Bi. *karuār* ' paddle '; H. *karwāl, karuār*, *karwār*, *°rā* m. ' oar, rudder, sword' (CDIAL 2796).

rīti2 f. ' yellow brass, bell metal ' Kathās., *rītika* -- n. ' calx of brass ', *°kā* -- f. ' brass ' lex. 2. rīrī -- , *rirī* -- f. ' yellow brass ' lex. [Ac. to AO xviii 248 Dard. forms < *raktikā -- 2](CDIAL 10752). 1. Dm. *rit* ' copper ', Gaw. *rīt* (→ Sv. *rīda* NoPhal 49); Bshk. *rīd* ' brass ', Tor. *žit* f. 2. Pk. *rīrī* -- f. ' brass '; Sh. *rīl* m. ' brass, bronze, copper '.

sangaḍa 'lathe' Rebus: *jangaḍa* 'entrustment articles'.Rebus 2: *samgara* 'living in the same house, guild', *sangar* 'fortified place' (Pushto). L. *sãgaṛh* m. ' line of entrenchments, stone walls for defence '.(CDIAL 12845) Hence, smith guild in a fortification, which is a characteristic architectural feature of hundreds of civilization sites.

sang 2 संग् m. a stone (Rām. 199, 143, 1412; YZ. 557). L. 65 gives a list of the most common local stones used for ornaments, and other purposes. These are (in his spelling) *bilor,* a white crystal; *sang-i-baswatri,* a yellow stone used in medicine; *sang-i-dálam,* used by goldsmiths; *sang-i-farash* (p. 64), a kind of slate; *sang-i-Nadid,* of a dark coffee colour; *sang-i-Nalchan,* a kind of soap-stone, from which cups and plates are made; *sang-i-Musá,* of a black colour; *sang-i-Ratel,* of a chocolate colour; *sang-i-Shalamar,* of a green colour; *sang-i-sumák,* coloured blue or purple, with green spots; *Takht-i-Sulimán,* coloured black, with white streaks. (Kashmiri)

sángī सह्चरः m. an associate, companion, comrade; confederate, ally, accomplice; a partner in business. (Kashmiri)

sarvalā -- , °lī -- f. ' iron club or crowbar ' lex. 2. *sambala -- (cf. śamba --). [sarvalā -- (Pk. savvala --) sanskritization of *sabbala -- ~ *sambala -- ?] 1. Pk. sabbala -- , savvala -- m., °lā -- f. ' spear '; P. sabbal f. ' crowbar (used by thieves) '; Ku. sāblo ' iron bar '; N. B. sābal ' crowbar ', Or. sābaḷa; Bi. sābar, sābrā ' round -- headed anvil ', sabrā, °rī ' tinman's small anvil (made of a bent piece of iron) ', Mth. sābal; H. sābal m.(?) ' crowbar (esp. one used by burglars), lever, small anvil '; M. sabaḷ f. ' crowbar '. 2. K. sambal f. ' crowbar ', L.poṭh. sãbbal m. ' crowbar (used by thieves for digging through a wall) '; Ku. sãplo ' iron bar ', gng. śābaw, śāpaw; M. sãbaḷ m. ' large bickern '.(CDIAL 13279). Ju(P) {N} ``^crowbar''. *Sa., Mu., Ho, H., B., O..संबळ or सबळ [sambaḷa or sabaḷa] f m A bickern that is divided at one end into two parts, a crowbar. Note. Distinction is made by some between these two words. संबळ is understood to be m, and to mean A large bickern or पहार; and सबळ to be f, and to mean Crowbar.(Marathi)

शिंगाडा [śiṅgāḍā] m (शृंगाटक or संघाटिका S through H) A form of anvil. Used for hammering nails and forming vessels &c. It is disting. from both ऐरण & संदान. (Marathi) शिंगाडी [śiṅgāḍī] A horn or a hornlike article used by shoemakers to enlarge a tight shoe. (Marathi)

शिंसळ [śiṃsaḷa] *n* R (शीस) Hair of the head hanging about disheveled and disorderly. (Marathi) salae sapae = untangled, combed out, hair hanging loose (Santali.) Rebus: *sal* workshop (Santali)

Rebus: शिंसे [śiṃsē] *n* (सीसक S through H) Lead. सीस [sīsa] & सीसक *n* S Lead. sī´sa n. ' lead ', adj. ' leaden ' VS., *sīsaka* -- m.n. Yājñ. Pa. *sīsa* -- n. ' lead ', Pk. *sīsa* -- , *°aya* -- n., S. *sīho* m., WPah.jaun. *sīsō*, Ku. *sīso*, N. *siso*, A. *xih*, B. *sisā*, Or. *sisā*, *sīsā*, H. *sīsā* m. (→ P. *sīsā* m.), G. *sīsũ* n., M.*śisē̃* n.(CDIAL 13445).

Allograph: शिंसा A honey-comb

संदान or सदान [sandāna or sadāna] n f (P) The smaller anvil of blacksmiths and forgers. On it are formed ferrules, rings, caps &c. Disting. from शिंगाडा ऐरण &c. (Marathi)P سندان sandān, s.m. (2nd) An anvil. Pl. سندانونه sandānūnah. See پلک (Pushto) saṁdhā´na n. ' joint, union ' TS., ' bell -- metal ' MW., °nī -- f. ' foundry ' lex. [√dhā]Pa. sandhāna -- n. ' union, fetter '; Pk. saṁdhāṇa -- n. ' joint'; sandhānī f. ' id., distilling, foundry ';Si. aňdun bell, gong ' (CDIAL 12909).

Ta. cuṇṭaṉ grey musk shrew; cuṇṭ-eli, (Koll.) *cuṇṭāṉ* mouse, *Mus urbanus*; cūṟaṉ grey musk shrew; mūñ-cūṟu musk-rat,*Sorex indicus. Ma.* cuṇṭ-eli mouse, musk-rat. *Ka.* suṇḍa, suṇḍ-ili, suṇḍil-ili, soṇḍ-ili, soṇḍil-ili, cuñc-ili musk-rat. *Koḍ.* Ciṇḍ-elihouse-mouse, field-mouse. *Tu.* Suṇḍ-eli musk-rat. *Te.* cuncu mouse, musk-rat; cunc-eluka, cuṇḍ-eluka mouse; cūr-eluka species of mouse *Kol* (Kin.) cinḍrag musk-rat. *Go.* (Mu. Ma.) cūci musk-rat (*Voc.* 1353); (Ma.) cuṭṭi-eli, (Mu.) cuṭi, cuṭiyal small rat (*Voc.*1344); (Ph.) coṭe mouse (*Voc* 1368). *Konḍa* (BB) susuki musk-rat. *Kur.* coṭṭō mouse. For eli, etc., see 833 Ta. Eli. Cf. 2664 Ta. cuṇṭu; the shrews seem to be differentiated from rats and mice by the length of the snout. / Cf. Skt. *śuṇḍi-mūṣikā-*, gandha-śuṇḍinī-(Burrow, *Kratylos* 15.56), cuñcu-mūṣikā-, chucchūndura-, cucundarī-; Turner, *CDIAL*, no. 5053. Cf. also Skt. Tuṭuma- mouse, rat. For similar words in Munda languages, see Pinnow, p. 95 (Santali cũnd musk-rat, etc.), and Emeneau, *JAOS* 82.109.(DEDR 2661) cunda an artist who works in ivory J vi.261 (Com: dantakāra); Miln 331. The superscript ligatures can also be read as suffixes: - *kāra* 'artisan'. *kāruvu* = mechanic, artisan, Viśvakarma, the celestial artisan (Te.); kāruvu [Skt.] n. An artist, artificer. An agent . One is a *loha-kāra* (metalsmith). The other is a *cunda-kāra* (ivory turner).

ṭaṅka3 (*a*) ' *rod, spike ', (*b*) m. ' leg ' lex. 2. ṭaṅga -- 3 m. ' leg ' lex. 1. (*a*) K. *ṭang* m. ' projecting spike which acts as a bolt at one corner of a door '; N. *ṭāṅo* ' rod, fishing rod ', *°ṅi* ' measuring rod '; H. *ṭāk* f. ' iron pin, rivet ' (→ Ku. *ṭāki* ' thin iron bar ').
(*b*) Pk. *ṭaṁka* -- m., *°kā* -- f. ' leg ', S. *ṭaṅga* f., L. P. *ṭaṅg* f., Ku. *ṭā̃g*, N. *ṭāṅ*; Or. *ṭāṅka* ' leg, thigh ', *°ku* ' thigh, buttock '. 2. B. *ṭāṅ*, *ṭeṅri* ' leg, thigh '; Mth. *ṭā̃g*, *ṭā̃gri* ' leg, foot '; Bhoj. *ṭāṅ*, *ṭaṅari* ' leg ', Aw. lakh. H. *ṭā̃g* f.; G. *ṭā̃g* f., *°gɔ* m. ' leg from hip to foot '; M. *ṭā̃g* f. ' leg '.ṭaṅka -- 4 ' peak, crag ' see Addenda: ṭaṅka -- 3. 1(*b*): S.kcch. *ṭaṅg*(*h*) f. ' leg ', WPah.kṭg. (kc.) *ṭāṅg* f. (obl. -- *a*) ' leg (from knee to foot) '.(CDIAL 5428).

*ṭaṅkati2 ' chisels '. [ṭaṅka -- 2] Pa. *ṭaṅkita -- mañca* -- ' a stone (i.e. chiselled) platform '; G. *ṭā̃kvũ* ' to chisel ', M. *ṭā̃kṇẽ*.(CDIAL 5433).

ṭaṅkaśālā -- , *ṭaṅkakaś°* f. ' mint ' lex. [ṭaṅka -- 1, śā´lā --] N. *ṭaksāl*, *°ār*,
B. *ṭā̃ksāl*, *ṭā̃k°*, *ṭek°*, Bhoj. *ṭaksār*, H. *ṭaksāl*, *°ār* f., G. *ṭā̃ksāḷ* f., M. *ṭā̃ksāl*, *ṭāk°*, *ṭā̃k°*, *ṭak°*. -- Deriv. G. *ṭaksāḷī* m. ' mint -- master ', M. *ṭā̃ksāḷyā* m. Brj. *ṭaksāḷī*, *° sārī* m. ' mint -- master '. (CDIAL 5434).

ṭaṅka2 m.n. ' spade, hoe, chisel ' R. 2. ṭaṅga -- 2 m.n. ' sword, spade ' lex.1. Pa. *ṭaṅka* -- m. ' stone mason's chisel '; Pk. *ṭaṁka* -- m. ' stone -- chisel, sword '; Woṭ. *ṭhõ* ' axe '; Bshk. *ṭhoṅ* ' battleaxe ', *ṭheṅ* ' small axe ' (< **ṭaṅkī*); Tor. (Biddulph) "*tunger*" m. ' axe ' (*ṭ*? AO viii 310), Phal. *ṭhō̆ṅgi* f.; K. *ṭŏnguru* m. ' a kind of hoe '; N. (Tarai) *ṭā̃gi* ' adze '; H. *ṭā̃kī* f. ' chisel '; G. *ṭā̃k* f. ' pen nib '; M. *ṭā̃k* m. ' pen nib ', *ṭā̃kī* f. ' chisel '.2. A. *ṭāṅgi* ' stone chisel '; B. *ṭāṅg*, *°gi* ' spade, axe '; Or. *ṭāṅgi* ' battle -- axe '; Bi. *ṭā̃gā*, *°gī* ' adze '; Bhoj. *ṭāṅī* ' axe '; H. *ṭā̃gī* f. ' hatchet '.(CDIAL 5427).

Pk. *ṭhakkura* -- m. 'Rajput, chief man of a village'; P. *ṭhākar* m. landholder, ludh. *ṭhaukar* m. ' lord '; Ku. *ṭhākur* m. ' master, title of a Rajput '; N. *ṭhākur* ' term of address from slave to master ' (f. *ṭhakurānī*), *ṭhakuri* 'a clan of Chetris' (f. *ṭhakurnī*); A. *ṭhākur* 'a Brahman', *ṭhākurānī* 'goddess'; B. *ṭhākurāni*, *ṭhākrān*, *°run* ' honored lady, goddess '; Or. *ṭhākura* ' term of address to a Brahman, god, idol ', *ṭhākurāṇī* ' goddess '; Bi. *ṭhākur* ' barber '; Maithili. *ṭhākur* ' blacksmith '; Bhoj. Aw.lakh.*ṭhākur* ' lord, master '; H. *ṭhākur* m. '

master, landlord, god, idol ', *ṭhākurāin, ṭhākurānī* f. ' mistress, goddess '; G. *ṭhākor, °kar* m. ' member of a clan of Rajputs ',*ṭhakrāṇī* f. ' his wife ', *ṭhākor* ' god, idol '; M. *ṭhākur* m. ' jungle tribe in North Konkan, family priest, god, idol '; Si. mald. "*tacourou*" ' title added to names of noblemen '; Garh. *ṭhākur* ' master '; A. *ṭhākur* also ' idol ' (CDIAL 5488).
S. *kãḍo* ' thorny ', Si. *kaṭu.* -- Deriv.: S. *kãḍero* m. ' camel -- thorn ', *°rī* f. ' a kind of thistle '(CDIAL 3022).

Ta. taṭu (-pp-, -tt-) to hinder, stop, obstruct, forbid, prohibit, resist, dam, block up, partition off, curb, check, restrain, control, ward off, avert; *n.* hindering, checking, resisting; *Ka.* taḍa impeding, check, impediment, obstacle, delay; *Koḍ.* taḍe- (taḍev-, taḍand-) to be obstructed (by person or thing); taḍï- (taḍïp-, taḍït-) to stop, obstruct, endure; taḍu lateness, delay. *Tu.* taḍavu delay, hindrance, impediment; a slowcoach or dilatory person; taḍèhindrance, obstacle, a charm for serpents; taḍepāvuni to hinder, impede, obstruct; taḍepini, taḍepuni to hold off, hinder, keep back, prevent, stop, oppose; taḍeppu stoppage, resistance, anything put up to stop a passage; taḍeyuni, taḍevuni to halt, stop, tarry, bear, endure; taḍevu a halt, stopping, tarrying, impediment, hindrance;taḍevoṇuni to bear, suffer, be patient; daḍè an obstacle, hindrance; taṭṭaṅkŭ id. *Te.* taḍayu to delay; taḍa hindrance, obstruction, prevention; taḍavu delay, loss of time; taṭāyincu to hinder, prevent (DEDR 3031). Rebus: dhatu 'mineral' (Santali)

Glyph: taṭṭai 'mechanism made of split bamboo for scaring away parrots from grain fields (Ta.); taṭṭe 'a thick bamboo or an areca-palm stem, split in two' (Ka.) (DEDR 3042)Rebus: toṭxin, toṭ.xn goldsmith (To.); taṭṭāṉ 'gold- or silver-smith' (Ta.); taṭṭaravāḍu 'gold- or silver-smith' (Te.); *ṭhaṭṭakāra 'brass-worker' (Skt.)(CDIAL 5493).

Glyph 'small ball' or 'hole': A. goṭ 'a fruit, whole piece', °ṭā 'globular, solid', guṭi 'small ball, seed, kernel'; B. goṭā 'seed, bean, whole'; Or. goṭā 'whole, undivided', goṭi 'small ball, cocoon', goṭāli 'small round piece of chalk'; Bi. goṭā 'seed'; Mth. goṭa 'numerative particle' (CDIAL 4271) Pk. *kōḍara --* , *kōla°, kōṭa°, koṭṭa°* n. ' hole, hollow '; Or. *koraṛa* ' hollow in a tree, cave, hole '; H. (X *khōla -- 2) *khoḍar* m. ' pit, hollow in a tree ', *khoṛrā* m.; Si.*kovuḷa* ' rotten tree ' (< **kōḷalla --* with H. Smith JA 1950, 197, but not < Pa. *kōḷāpa --*). (CDIAL 3496).

tāmrá ' dark red, copper -- coloured ' VS., n. ' copper ' Kauś., *tāmraka --* n. Yājñ.
Pa. *tamba --* ' red ', n. ' copper ', Pk. *taṁba --* adj. and n.; Dm. *trāmba --* ' red ' (in *trāmba -*

- *laçuk* ' raspberry ' NTS xii 192); Bshk. *lām* ' copper, piece of bad pine -- wood (< ' *red wood '?); Phal. *tāmba* ' copper ' (→ Sh.koh. *tāmbā*), K. *trām* m. (→ Sh.gil. gur. *trām* m.), S. *ṭrāmo* m., L. *trāmā*, (Ju.) *tarāmā* m., P. *tāmbā* m., WPah. bhad. *ṭḷām* n., kiũth. *cāmbā*, sod. *cambo*, jaun. *tā̃bō*, Ku. N. *tāmo* (pl. ' young bamboo shoots '), A. *tām*, B. *tā̃bā*, *tāmā*, Or. *tambā*, Bi *tā̃bā*, Mth. *tām*, *tāmā*, Bhoj.*tāmā*, H. *tām* in cmpds., *tā̃bā*, *tāmā* m., G. *trā̃bũ*, *tā̃bũ* n.;M. *tā̃bẽ* n. ' copper ', *tā̃b* f. ' rust, redness of sky '; Ko. *tāmbe* n. ' copper '; Si. *tam̆ba* adj. ' reddish ', sb. ' copper ', (SigGr) *tam*, *tama*. -- Ext. -- *ira* -- : Pk. *taṁbira* -- ' coppercoloured, red ', L. *tāmrā* ' copper -- coloured (of pigeons) '; -- with -- *ḍa* -- : S. *ṭrāmiṛo* m. ' a kind of cooking pot ', *ṭrāmiṛī* ' sunburnt, red with anger ', f. ' copper pot '; Bhoj. *tāmrā* ' copper vessel '; H. *tā̃bṛā*, *tāmṛā* ' coppercoloured, dark red ', m. ' stone resembling a ruby '; G. *tā̃baṛ* n., *trā̃bṛī*, *tā̃bṛī* f. ' copper pot '; OM. *tāṁbaḍā* ' red '. -- X trápu -- q.v.tāmrika -- ; tāmrakāra -- , tāmrakuṭṭa -- , *tāmraghaṭa -- , *tāmraghaṭaka -- , tāmracūḍa -- , *tāmradhāka -- , tāmrapaṭṭa -- , tāmrapattra -- , tāmrapātra -- , *tāmrabhāṇḍa -- , tāmravarṇa -- , tāmrākṣa -- .S.kcch. *trāmo*, *tām(b)o* m. ' copper ', *trāmbhyo* m. ' an old copper coin '; WPah.kc. *cambo* m. ' copper ', J. *cāmbā* m., kṭg. (kc.) *tambɔ* m. (← P. or H. Him.I 89), Garh.*tāmu*, *tā̃bu*. (CDIAL 5779). tāmrakāra m. ' coppersmith ' lex. Or. *tāmbarā* ' id. '.(CDIAL 5780).tāmrakuṭṭa m. ' coppersmith ' R. N. *tamauṭe*, *tamoṭe* ' id. '.Garh. *ṭamoṭu* ' coppersmith '; Ko. *tāmṭi*.(CDIAL 5781). *tāmraghaṭa ' copper pot '. Bi. *tamheṛī* ' round copper vessel '; -- *tamheṛā* ' brassfounder ' der. **tamheṛ* ' copper pot ' or < next? (CDIAL 5782).*tāmraghaṭaka ' copper -- worker '. [tāmrá -- , ghaṭa -- 2]Bi. *tamheṛā* ' brass -- founder ' or der. fr. **tamheṛ* see prec.(CDIAL 5783). tāmracūḍa ' red -- crested ' MBh., m. ' cock ' Suśr. [tāmrá -- , cū´ḍa -- 1] Pa. *tambacūḷa* -- m. ' cock ', Pk. *taṁbacūla* -- m.; -- Si. *tam̆basiluvā* ' cock ' (EGS 61) either a later cmpd. (as in Pk.) or ← Pa.(CDIAL 5784). *tāmradhāka ' copper receptacle '. [tāmrá -- , dhāká --]Bi. *tamahā* ' drinking vessel made of a red alloy '.(CDIAL 5785). tāmrapaṭṭa m. ' copper plate (for inscribing) ' Yājñ. [Cf. tāmrapattra -- . -- tāmrá -- , paṭṭa -- 1] M. *tā̃boṭī* f. ' piece of copper of shape and size of a brick '. (CDIAL 5786). tāmrapattra n. ' copper plate (for inscribing) ' lex. [Cf. tāmrapaṭṭa -- . -- tāmrá -- , páttra --] Ku.gng. *tamoti* ' copper plate '. (CDIAL 5787) tāmrapātra n. ' copper vessel ' MBh. [tāmrá -- , pā´tra --] Ku.gng. *tamoi* ' copper vessel for water '. (CDIAL 5788) *tāmrabhāṇḍa ' copper vessel '. Bhoj. *tāmaṛā*, *tāmṛā* ' copper vessel '; G. *tarbhāṇũ* n. ' copper dish used in religious ceremonies ' (< **taramhā̃ḍũ*). (CDIAL 5789). tāmravarṇa ' copper -- coloured ' TĀr. Si. *tam̆bavan* ' copper -- coloured, dark red ' (EGS 61) prob. a Si. cmpd. tāmrākṣa ' red -- eyed ' MBh. [tāmrá -- , ákṣi --]Pa. *tambakkhin* -- ; P. *tamak* f. ' anger '; Bhoj. *tamakhal* ' to be angry '; H. *tamaknā* ' to become red in the face, be angry '. (CDIAL

5790, 5791). tāmrika ' coppery ' Mn. [tāmrá --] Pk. *taṁbiya* -- n. ' an article of an ascetic's equipment (a copper vessel?) '; L. *trāmī* f. ' large open vessel for kneading bread ', poṭh. *trāmbī* f. ' brass plate for kneading on '; Ku.gng. *tāmi* ' copper plate '; A. *tāmi* ' copper vessel used in worship '; B. *tāmī, tamiyā* ' large brass vessel for cooking pulses at marriages and other ceremonies '; H.*tambiyā* m. ' copper or brass vessel '. (CDIAL 5792). *meḍak* 'small frog' (Gujarati) Rebus: *meḍ* 'iron' (Ho.)

உடு; uṭu, n. cf. huḍa. 1. Point where the arrow is pressed against the bow-string; நாணைக் கொள்ளுமிடம். (குறிஞ்சிப். 170.) 2. Arrow; அம்பு. உடுவென்னு நஞ்சந் துய்த்து (இரகு. மீட்சி. 50). 3. Feather of an arrow; அம்பினிறகு. உடுவமை பகழிவாங்க (சீவக. 2191). 4. Arrow-head; அம்புத் தலை. (பிங்.) 5. Oar, boatman's pole; ஓடம் இயக் குங் கோல். (பிங்.)

குடவன்[1] kuṭavaṉ, *n.* < குடம்[1]. cf. *huḍa-vān.* Cowherd, shepherd; இடையன். ஆம்பாற் குடவர் மகளோ (சீவக. 492). 14135 huḍa -- , *°ḍu* -- m. ' ram ' lex. 2. hunda -- 1 m. Kāśīkh. 1. Pk. *huḍa* -- m. ' ram ', WPah.bhal. *huṛ*, jaun. *hūṛ*. <-> L. *huṛeāl, huṛeār* m. ' the wild hill sheep or oorial ', P. *huṛiār* m. 2. L. *hunḍū* m. ' fighting ram ', (Shahpur) *hū̃ḍḍu* m., P. *hunḍū* m. 3. †hulu -- ' ram ' lex.: WPah.kṭg. *huḷ* m. ' ram for breeding '.

*huḍahāra ' sheep -- taker '. 2. *hunḍahāra -- . [huḍa -- , hāra -- . -- But Pk. *huḍa* -- m. ' dog ~ ram ', Or. *hunḍā* ' hyena '; and semant. cf. H.*bheṛī* ' sheep ' ~ *bheṛiyā* ' wolf ']1. Mth. *huṛār* ' wolf '. 2. N. *hũṛār* ' wolf '; Or. dial. *hunār* ' wolf, hyena '; Mth. H. *hũṛār* m. ' wolf '. (CDIAL 14137)

hunati (opt. *hunēt* Pañcar.) ' offers libation '. [From pp. **huna* -- ~ *hutá* -- (see prāhuṇa --). -- √hu] Pa. *hunitabba* -- ' to be sacrificed '; Pk. *huṇaï* ' offers oblation ', *huṇia* -- pp., *huṇaṇa* -- n.; MB. *hune* ' sacrifices ' ODBL 553, H. *hunnā.*(CDIAL 14139). ఉడుగర [uḍugara] *uḍugara.* [Tel.] n. A gift, a present, any present given to a bride or bridegroom during the celebration of their marriage, A. vi. 190. -కట్నము కానుక "గంధర్వులకుడుగరల్ దయనొసగు" N. ii. 126. లబాంధవులొసగిరపుడు కాంచన భూషలు చీరలు నరపతికింబొలతికినుడు గరలుముదము పొదలగనంతన్." Swa. v. 120. (Telugu)

Pk. *vaṭṭa* -- m.n., *°aya* -- m. ' cup '; Ash. *waṭā´k* ' cup, plate '; K. *waṭukh*, dat. *°ṭakas* m. ' cup, bowl '; S. *vaṭo* m. ' metal drinking cup '; N. *bāṭā*, ' round copper or brass vessel '; A. *bāṭi* ' cup '; B. *bāṭā* ' box for betel '; Or. *baṭā* ' metal pot for betel ', *bāṭi* ' cup, saucer '; Mth. *baṭṭā* ' large metal cup ', *bāṭī* ' small do. ', H. *baṭṛī* f.; G. M. *vāṭī* f. ' vessel '. (CDIAL

11347) Rebus: baṭa = a kind of iron (Gujarati) S. *baṭhu* m. ' large pot in which grain is parched, large cooking fire ', *baṭhī* f. ' distilling furnace '; L. *bhaṭṭh* m. ' grain -- parcher's oven ', *bhaṭṭhī* f. ' kiln, distillery ', awāṇ. *bhaṭh*; P. *bhaṭṭh* m., *°ṭhī* f. ' furnace ', *bhaṭṭhā* m. ' kiln '; N. *bhāṭi* ' oven or vessel in which clothes are steamed for washing '; A. *bhaṭā* ' brick -- or lime -- kiln '; B. *bhāṭi* ' kiln '; Or. *bhāṭi* ' brick -- kiln, distilling pot '; Mth. *bhaṭhī*, *bhaṭṭī* ' brick -- kiln, furnace, still '; Aw.lakh. *bhāṭhā* ' kiln '; H. *bhaṭṭhā* m. ' kiln ', *bhaṭ* f. ' kiln, oven, fireplace '; M. *bhaṭṭā* m. 'pot of fire', *bhaṭṭī* f. ' forge '(CDIAL 9656).

Glyph: *vartakara ' making turns (of the quail) '. [Pop. etym. for vártikā -- (*vartīra* -- m. Suśr., *°tira* -- m. lex.)? -- varta -- 1, kará -- 1] Ku. B. *baṭer* ' quail '; Or. *baṭara*, *batara* ' the grey quail '; Mth. H. *baṭer* f. ' quail '; -- → P. *baṭer*, *°rā* m., *°rī* f., L. *baṭērā* m., S. *baṭero* m.; K. *bāṭuru* m. ' a kind of quail ', *baṭēra* m. ' quail '.(CDIAL 11350). vártikā f. ' quail ' RV. 2. vārtika -- m. lex. 3. var- takā -- f. lex. (eastern form ac. to Kātyāyana: S. Lévi JA 1912, 498), *°ka* -- m. Car., *vārtāka* -- m. lex. 1. Ash. *uwŕel* ' partridge ' NTS ii 246 (connexion denied NTS v 340), Paš.snj. *waṭī́*; K. *hāra -- wüṭü* f. ' species of waterfowl ' (*hāra* -- < śā´ra --).2. Kho. *barti* ' quail, partridge ' BelvalkarVol 88.3. Pa. *vaṭṭakā* -- f., *°ka* -- in cmpds. ' quail ', Pk. *vaṭṭaya* -- m., N. *baṭṭāi* (< *vārtāka* -- ?), A. *batā -- sarāi*, B. *batui*, *baṭuyā*, Si. *vaṭuvā* ' snipe, sandpiper ' (ext. of **vaṭu* < *vartakā* --). -- With unexpl. *bh* -- : Or. *bhāṭoi*, *°ṭui* ' the grey quail Cotarnix communis ', (dial.) *bhāroi*, *°rui* (< early MIA. **vāṭāka* -- < *vārtāka* -- : cf. *vāṭī*- f. ' a kind of bird ' Car.) (CDIAL 11361) Rebus: vartaka -- 2 n. ' bell -- metal, brass ' lex. vartalōha n. ' a kind of brass (i.e. *cup metal?) ' lex. [*varta -- 2 associated with lōhá -- by pop. etym.?] Pa. *vaṭṭalōha* -- n. ' a partic. kind of metal '; L.awāṇ. *valṭōā* ' metal pitcher ', *valṭoh*, *ba°* f., *vaṭlohā*, *ba°* m.; N. *baṭlohi* ' round metal vessel '; A. *baṭlahi* ' water vessel '; B. *bāṭlahi*, *bāṭulāi* ' round brass cooking vessel '; Bi. *baṭlohī* ' small metal vessel '; H. *baṭlohī*, *°loī* f. ' brass drinking and cooking vessel ', G. *vaṭloi* f. WPah.ktg. *bəlṭóɔ* m. ' large brass vessel '.(CDIAL 11357). *pattar* merchants (Tamil); perh. Vartaka (Skt.)

Semantic clusters in *Indian Lexicon*[508] (1242 English words and Botanical species Latin)

- Economic Court: Flora and Products from Flora
- Birds
- Insects
- Fauna
- Animate phenomena: birth, body, sensory perceptions and actions
- Visual phenomen, forms and shapes

- Numeration and Mensuration
- Economic Court: Natural phenomena, Earth formations, Products of earth (excluding flora clustered in a distinct category)
- Building, infrastructure
- Work, skills, products of labour and workers (fire-worker, potter/ smith/ lapidary, weaver, farmer, soldier)
- Weapons and tools
- Language fields
- Kinship
- Social formations

Languages and dialects referenced to Meluhha glosses: CDIAL, DEDR, Munda

1. Languages and dialects (CDIAL)

Assamese
al. Alashai dialect of Pashai
amg. Ardhamāgadhī Prakrit
Ap. Apabhraṁśa
Ar. Arabic
Ār. Aryan, i.e. Indo-iranian
ar. Areti dialect of Pashai
Aram. Aramaic
Arm. Armenian
arm. Armenian dialect of Gypsy
as. Asiatic dialects of Gypsy
Aś. Aśokan, i.e. the language of the Inscriptions of Aśoka
Ash. Ashkun (Aṣkū — Kaf.)
Austro-as. Austro-asiatic
Av. Avestan (Iranian)
Aw. Awadhī
awāṇ. Awāṇkārī dialect of Lahndā
B. Bengali (Baṅglā)
Bal. Balūčī (Iranian)
bāṅg. Bāṅgarū dialect of Western Hindī
Bashg. Bashgalī (Kaf.)

bh. Bairāṭ Bhābrū Minor Rock Edict of Aśoka

bhad. Bhadrawāhī dialect of West Pahāṛī

bhal. Bhalesī dialect of West Pahāṛī

bhaṭ. Bhaṭĕāḷī sub-dialect of Ḍogrī dialect of Panjābī

bhiḍ. Bhiḍlàī sub-dialect of Bhadrawāhī dialect of West Pahāṛī

Bhoj. Bhojpurī

BHSk. Buddhist Hybrid Sanskrit

Bi. Bihārī

bir. Birir dialect of Kalasha

boh. Bohemian dialect of European Gypsy

Brah. Brāhūī (Dravidian)

Brj. Brajbhāṣā

bro. Brokpā dialect of Shina

Bshk. Bashkarīk (Dard.)

bul. Bulgarian dialect of European Gypsy

Bur. Burushaski

cam. Cameāḷī dialect of West Pahāṛī

Chil. Chilīs (Dard.)

chil. Chilasi dialect of Shina or of Pashai

cur. Curāhī dialect of West Pahāṛī

Ḍ. Ḍumāki

dar. Darrai-i Nūr dialect of Pashai

Dard. Dardic

dh. Dhauli Rock Inscription of Aśoka

Dhp. Gāndhārī or Northwest Prakrit (as recorded in the Dharmapada ed. J. Brough, Oxford 1962)

Dm. Dameli (Damε̃ḍī´ — Kaf.-Dard.)

ḍoḍ. Ḍoḍī (Sirājī of Ḍoḍā), a dialect of Kashmiri in Jammu

ḍog. Ḍogrī dialect of Panjābī

dr. Drās dialect of Shina

Drav. Dravidian

Eng. English

eng. English dialect of European Gypsy

eur. European (Gypsy)

Fr. French

G. Gujarātī

Ga. Gadba (Dravidian)

Garh. Gaṛhwālī

Gau. Gauro (Dard.)

gav. Gavīmaṭh Inscription of Aśoka

Gaw. Gawar-Bati (Dard.)

germ. German dialect of European Gypsy

ghis. Ghisāḍī dialect of wandering blacksmiths in Gujarat

gil. Gilgitī dialect of Shina

gir. Girnār Rock Inscription of Aśoka

Gk. Greek

Gmb. Gambīrī (Kaf.)

gng. Gaṅgoī dialect of Kumaunī

Goth. Gothic

gr. Greek dialect of European Gypsy

gul. Gulbahārī dialect of Pashai

gur. Gurēsī dialect of Shina

Gy. Gypsy or Romani

H. Hindī

hal. Halabī dialect of Marāṭhī

haz. Hazara Hindkī dialect of Lahndā

h.rudh. High Rudhārī sub-dialect of Khaśālī dialect of West Pahāṛī

hung. Hungarian dialect of European Gypsy

IA. Indo-aryan

IE. Indo-european

Ind. Indo-aryan of India proper excluding Kafiri and Dardic

Indo-ir. Indo-iranian or Aryan

Ir. Iranian

ish. Ishpi dialect of Pashai

Ishk. Ishkāshmī (Iranian)

isk. Iskeni dialect of Pashai

it. Italian dialect of European Gypsy

jau. Jaugaḍa Rock Inscription of Aśoka

jaun. Jaunsārī dialect of West Pahāṛī

jij. Jijelut dialect of Shina

jmag. Jaina Māgadhī Prakrit

jmh. Jaina Mahārāṣṭrī Prakrit

jt. Jāṭū sub-dialect of Bāṅgarū dialect of Western Hindī

jub. North Jubbal dialect of West Pahāṛī

K. Kashmiri (Kāśmīrī)

kach. Kāchṛī dialect of Lahndā

Kaf. Kafiri

Kal. Kalasha (Kaláṣa — Dard.)

kāl. Kālsī Rock Inscription of Aśoka

Kamd. See Kmd.

Kan. Kanarese (Kannaḍa — Dravidian)

Kand. Kandia (Dard.)

kar. Karači (Transcaucasian) dialect of Asiatic Gypsy

kash. or kiś. Kashṭawāṛī dialect of Kashmiri

Kaṭ. Kaṭārqalā (Dard.)

kāṭh. Kāṭhiyāvāḍi dialect of Gujarātī

kb. Kauśāmbī Pillar Edict of Aśoka

kc. Kocī dialect of West Pahāṛī

kcch. Kacchī dialect of Sindhī

kch. Kachur-i Sala dialect of Pashai

kgr. or kng. Kāṅgrā sub-dialect of Ḍogrī dialect of Panjābī

Kharl. MIA. forms occurring in Corpus Inscriptionum Indicarum Vol. II Pt. 1

khas. Khasa dialect of Kumaunī

khaś. Khaśālī dialect of West Pahāṛī

khet. Khetrānī dialect of Lahndā

Kho. Khowār (Dard.)

Khot. Khotanese (Iranian)

kiś. See kash.

kiũth. Kiũthalī dialect of West Pahāṛī

Kmd. or Kamd. Kāmdeshi (Kaf.), Kāmdesh dialect of Kati

kṇḍ. Kaṇḍak dialect of Pashai

kng. See kgr.

Ko. Koṅkaṇī

Koh. Kohistānī (Dard.)

koh. Kohistānī dialect of Shina

Kol. Kōlāmī (Dravidian)

kōl. Kōlā dialect of Shina

kq. Kauśāmbī (Queen's Edict) Inscription of Aśoka

Kt. Kati or Katei (Kaf.)

Ku. Kumaunī

Kur. Kurukẖ (Dravidian)

kuṛ. Kuṛaṅgali dialect of Pashai

Kurd. Kurdish (Iranian)

kurd. Kurdari dialect of Pashai

ky. Kanyawālī dialect of Maiyã

L. Lahndā

la. Lāṛī dialect of Sindhī

lagh. Laghmani dialect of Pashai

lakh. Lakhīmpurī dialect of Awadhī

Lat. Latin

lauṛ. Lauṛowānī dialect of Pashai

Lith. Lithuanian

l.rudh. Low Rudhārī sub-dialect of Khaśālī dialect of West Pahāṛī

ludh. Ludhiānī dialect of Panjābī

M. Marāṭhī

mag. Magahī dialect of Bihārī

Mai. Maiyã (Dard.)

Mal. Malayāḷam (Dravidian)

Māl. or Malw. Mālwāī

mald. See Md.

Malw. See Māl.

man. Mānsehrā Rock Inscription of Aśoka

marm. Marmatī sub-dialect of Khaśālī dialect of West Pahāṛī

Marw. Mārwāṛī

Md. or mald. Maldivian dialect of Sinhalese

mg. Māgadhī Prakrit

mh. Mahārāsṭrī Prakrit

MIA. Middle Indo-aryan

mi. Delhi Mīrat Pillar Edict of Aśoka

mid.rudh. Middle Rudhārī sub-dialect of Khaśālī dialect of West Pahāṛī

Mj. Munǰī (Iranian)

Mth. Maithilī

mth. Mathiā (Lauṛiyā-Nandangaṛh) Inscription of Aśoka

Mu. Muṇḍā

mult. Multānī dialect of Lahndā

N. Nepāli

New. Newārī

ng. Nāgārjunī Cave Inscription of Aśoka

NIA. New (modern) Indo-aryan

NiDoc. Language of `Kharoṣṭhī Inscriptions discovered by Sir Aurel Stein in Chinese Turkestan' edited by A. M. Boyer, E. J. Rapson, and E. Senart

nig. Niglīvā Inscription of Aśoka

nij. Nijelami (Neẓəlā´m) dialect of Pashai

Niṅg. Niṅgalāmī (Dard.)

nir. Nirlāmī dialect of Pashai

Nk. Naiki (Dravidian)

norw. Norwegian dialect of European Gypsy

OHG. Old High German

OPruss. Old Prussian

Or. Oṛiyā

Orm. Ōrmuṛī´ (Iranian)

OSlav. Old Slavonic

Oss. Ossetic (Iranian)

P. Panjābī (Pañjābī)

Pa. Pali

pach. See pch.

pāḍ. Pāḍarī sub-dialect of Bhadrawāhī dialect of West Pahāṛī

Pah. Pahāṛī

Pahl. Pahlavi (Iranian)

paiś. Paiśācī Prakrit

pal. Palestinian dialect of Asiatic Gypsy of the Nawar

pales. Palesī dialect of Shina

paṅ. Paṅgwāḷī dialect of West Pahāṛī

Par. Parachi (Parāčī — Iranian)

Parth. Parthian (Iranian)

Paš. Pashai (Pašaī — Dard.)
paṭ. Paṭṭanī dialect of Gujarātī
pch. or pach. Pachaghani dialect of Pashai
Pers. Persian (Iranian)
pers. Persian dialect of Asiatic Gypsy
Phal. Phalūṛa (Dard.)
Pk. Prakrit
pog. Pŏgulī dialect of Kashmiri
pol. Polish dialect of European Gypsy
poṭh. Poṭhwārī dialect of Lahndā
pow. Pōwādhī dialect of Panjābī
Pr. Prasun (Kaf.)
Prj. Parji (Dravidian)
Psht. Pashto (Iranian)
pun. Punchī dialect of Lahndā
punl. Puniali dialect of Shina
rām. Rāmbanī dialect of Kashmiri in Jammu
rdh. Radhia (Lauṛiyā Ararāj) Pillar Edict of Aśoka
Rj. Rājasthānī
roḍ. Roḍiyā dialect of Sinhalese
roh. Rohruī dialect of West Pahāṛī
rp. Rāmpurvā Rock Edict of Aśoka
ru. Rūpnāth Inscription of Aśoka
rudh. Rudhārī sub-dialect of Khaśālī dialect of West Pahāṛī
rum. Rumanian dialect of European Gypsy
rumb. Rumbūr dialect of Kalasha
rus. Russian dialect of European Gypsy
Russ. Russian
S. Sindhī
ś. Śaurasenī Prakrit
sah. Sahasrām Inscription of Aśoka
Sang. Sanglechi (Saṅlēčī — Iranian)
Sant. Santālī (Muṇḍā)
Sar. Sarīkolī (Iranian)
SEeur. South-east European dialects of Gypsy

śeu. Śeuṭī sub-dialect of Khaśālī dialect of West Pahāṛī

Sh. Shina (Ṣiṇā — Dard.)

shah. Shāhbāzgaṛhī Rock Inscription of Aśoka

sham. Shamakaṭ dialect of Pashai

she. Shewa dialect of Pashai

Shgh. Shughnī (Iranian)

Shum. Shumashti (Šumāštī — Dard.)

shut. Shutuli dialect of Pashai

Si. Sinhalese

Sik. Sikalgārī (Mixed Gypsy Language: LSI xi 167)

sir. Sirājī dialect of West Pahāṛī

sirm. Sirmaurī dialect of West Pahāṛī

Sk. Sanskrit

sn. Sārnāth Inscription of Aśoka

snj. Sanjan dialect of Pashai

sod. Sŏdōcī dialect of West Pahāṛī

Sogd. Sogdian (Iranian)

sop. Bombay-Sopārā Inscription of Aśoka

sp. Spanish dialect of European Gypsy

srk. Sirāikī dialect of Sindhī

suk. Suketī dialect of West Pahāṛī

Sv. Savi (Dard.)

Tam. Tamil (Dravidian)

Tel. Telugu (Dravidian)

Tib. Tibetan

Tir. Tirāhī (Dard.)

Toch. Tocharian

top. Delhi-Tōprā Pillar Edict of Aśoka

Tor. Tōrwālī (Dard.)

Tu. Tuḷu (Dravidian)

Turk. Turkish

urt. Urtsun dialect of Kalasha

uzb. Uzbini dialect of Pashai

vrāc. Vrācaḍa Apabhraṁśa

waz. Waziri dialect of Pashto

weg. Wegali dialect of Pashai

wel. Welsh dialect of European Gypsy

Werch. Werchikwār or Wershikwār (Yasin dialect of Burushaski)

Wg. Waigalī or Wai-alā (Kaf.)

Wkh. Wakhi (Iranian)

Woṭ. Woṭapūrī (language of Woṭapūr and Kaṭārqalā — Dard.)

WPah. West Pahāṛī

Yazgh. Yazghulami (Iranian)

Yghn. Yaghnobi (Iranian)

Yid. Yidgha (Iranian)

2. Languages and dialects (DEDR)

ba.	Baghī dialect of West Pahāṛī
barg.	Bargromatol dialect of Kāmdeshī
Bj.	Bajui (Iranian)
Brt.	Bartangi (Iranian dialect of the Shughnī Group)
cam.	Cameāḷī dialect of West Pahāṛī member of the Camba group spoken in Camba State of the Panjab
Chvar.	Chvarezmian (Iranian)
cur.	Curāhī one of Camba group of dialects of West Pahāṛī in Camba State of the Panjab
dig.	Digoric (or Western) dialect of Ossetic (Iranian)
EMIA.	Eastern Middle Indo-aryan
ga.	Gadī dialect of West Pahāṛī
Go.	Gondī

hāḍ.	Hāḍautī dialect of Mārwāṛī
Hit.	Hittite
in.sir.	Inner Sirājī dialect of West Pahāṛī
Ind.	IA. in India
J.	Tîka Râm Joshi, *A Dictionary of the Pâhari Dialects as spoken in the Punjab Himalayas.* JRASB (New Series) VII, 5, 1911 (abbrev. Joshi in CDIAL): primarily Kiũthalī dialect
kc.	Kocī dialect of West Pahāṛī. Examples in Add[2] from Hendriksen Him.I with phonetic representation of vowels (e.g. kc. *a*=J. *ā.* while kc. *ā̄*=J. *ā'* with secondary length)
kiũth.	Kiũthalī dialect of West Pahāṛī (spelling Kyoṇṭhli in Hendriksen Him.I)
kṭg.	Koṭgaṛhī dialect of West Pahāṛī (equated with Sŏdōcī dialect in LSI ix 4, 647ff.). Examples in Add[2] are from Him.I with phonetic representation of vowels; kṭg. (kc.) indicates that an analogous form, not given, is attested in Kocī
kua.	Kuarī dialect of West Pahāṛī
kul.	Kuluī dialect of West Pahāṛī
lett.	Lettish
mand.	Mandeālī dialect of West Pahāṛī
OEng.	Old English
Orosh.	Oroshori (Iranian)
Port.	Portuguese

rāmp.	Rāmpurī dialect of West Pahāṛī
Rosh.	Roshani (Iranian)
sai.	Sainjī dialect of West Pahāṛī
sat.	Satlaj dialect of West Pahāṛī
serb.	Serbian dialect of European Gypsy
surkh.	Surkhulī dialect of West Pahāṛī
Swed.	Swedish
Wj.	Wanji (Iranian)
WPah.poet.	Examples from West Pahāṛī poetry taken from Him.I, with phonetic representation of vowels
X.	Khufi dialect of Iranian Shughnī Group

3. Languages and dialects (Munda)[509]

Didey	Koraput (Orissa)	Di.	Collected by the writer in 1955
Bonda	Koraput (Orissa)	Bo.	Collected by the writer in 1951 and 1955
Gutob (i.e. Munda-speaking Gadba)	Koraput (Orissa) and Srikakulam (Andhra)	Gu.	Collected by the writer in 1951 and 1955
Parengi	Koraput (Orissa)	Pa.	As above[1]
Sora	Koraput (Orissa)	So.	*Sora-English Dictionary* by G. V. Ramamurti, 1938
Sora	Koraput (Orissa)	So. (Bhat.)	Collected by the writer in 1955
Juang	Keonjhar, Dhenkanal (Orissa)	Ju. (Ke.) Ju. (Dh.)	As above
Kharia	Ranchi (Bihar)	Kh.	Collected by the writer in 1954
Kharia	—	Kh. (R.)	*The Kharias* by S. C. Roy
Ho	Singbhum (Bihar)	—	Collected by the writer in 1954
Asur	Ranchi (Bihar)	As.	As above
Birhor	Ranchi (Bihar)	Bh.	As above
Birhor	—	Bh. (R.)	*The Birhor* by S. C. Roy
Munda	—	Mu.	*Encyclopaedia Mundarica* by Rev. John Hoffmann, S.J. in collaboration with Rev. Arthur Van Emelen S.J. 1950
Munda	—	Mu. (B.)	*Mundari-English Dictionary* by M. B. Bhaduri, 1931
Santali	—	Sa.	*A Santal Dictionary* by P. O. Bodding, 1929-1936
Koṛaku	Surguja (M.P.)	Kor.	Collected by the writer in 1959
Korwa	Jashpur-Raigarh (M.P.)	Kw.	As above
Mowasi	Chhindwara (M.P.)	Mo.	Collected by the writer in 1958
Korku	Betul, Amravati and Nimar (M.P.)	Ko.	Collected by the writer in 1955, 1956 and 1957
Korku	—	Ko. (ER.)	*A Korku Vocabulary*
Nahali	Nimar (M.P.)	Nah.	Collected by E. Ramsay in 1955[2]

Excerpt from a remarkable webpage[510] of University of Delaware

Alchemical Emblems, Glyphs and Allegories

[quote]One of the ways alchemists maintained their secrets from gold–seekers and the uninitiated was by using glyphs in lieu of words to represent various chemicals, metals, and other substances. Another common practice was to include emblems. The rich visual imagery could be "read" by those who could understand and interpret the illustrations. An adept could decipher the emblems and use them to perform the scientific and spiritual processes outlined in the image. Alchemists often used both written and visual allegories to describe various processes. The meanings of some of these emblems, glyphs, and allegories have been uncovered, and yet many others remain mysterious and unknown…

Christian Adolph Balduin

Phosphorus hermeticus, sive Magnes luminaris Christiani Adolphi Balduini.... Francofurti, Lipsiæ,: sumpt. G.H. Frommanni, 1675.

Christian Adolph Balduin (1632–1682) describes in this work his method of preparing a phosphorescent form of calcium nitrate. For this discovery he was elected Fellow of the Royal Society in 1676. Seen here is the Frankfurt edition which was printed in the same year as the Amsterdam edition, but with a different title. This fold out plate illustrates the Emerald Tablet.

Clovis Hesteau de Nuisement

Traittez dv vray sel, secret des philosophes, et de l'esprit general dv monde: contenant en son interieur les trois principes naturels, selon la doctrine de Hermes: oeuure tres vtile & necessaire à quiconque desire arriuer à la parfaitte prattique de ce pretieux elixir ou medecine uniuerselle, tant celebree des anciens, recognuë & experimentee. A Paris: Chez Ieremie Perier & Abdias Bvisard, 1621.

French poet Clovis Hesteau de Nuisement (c.1550–c.1624) was the author of several books of poems, and also wrote this alchemical treatise on salt. In this engraving, the figure is standing on a base with the inscription "Trinus et Unus" ("Three and One"), which refers to God, nature and man, being three distinct figures and one united at the same time.

Jakob Böhme

Hohe und tieffe Gründe von dem dreyfachen Leben des Menschen: nach dem Geheimnüss der dreyen Principien göttlicher Offenbahrung. Zu Amsterdam: [s.n.], gedruckt im Jahr Christi 1682.

Jakob Böhme (1575–1624) was a German mystic and theologian. His alchemical writings were influenced by the great alchemist and physician Paracelsus. Bohme was drawn to alchemy as a metaphysical science and used alchemical symbolism to describe spiritual and religious theories. Seen here is an engraving of a sphere containing alchemical symbols, with beasts below and angels in the heavens above whose energies filter down through a phoenix which is surrounded by eyes.

Medicinisch–Chymisch und Alchemistisches Oraculum: darinnen man nicht nur alle Zeichen und Abkürzungen welche so wohl in den Recepten und Büchern der Aerzte und Apothecker als auch in den Schriften der Chemisten und Alchemisten vorkommen findet. Ulm: Bey August Lebrecht Stettin, 1772.

This work is a comprehensive collection of symbols and abbreviations in alchemical medicinal works. The title page woodcut is titled "Ora et Labora" ("Prayer and Work").

Opus magni philosophia opus. [ca. 16--?].
Mss 095 Item 023

This Latin alchemical manuscript contains hand drawn illustrations by an unknown owner. Seen here is one about the Philosopher's Stone.

Fünff Curieuse Chymische Tractätlein: in welchen die allerdeutlichsten Ausdrücke derer, so jemals, als wahrhafftige Kunstbesitzer, von dem so sehr beruffenen Stein der Weisen geschrieben haben, anzutreffen sind. Leipzig: Bey Stocks Erben Schilling und Weber, 1757.

Collection of alchemical texts, some of which are not printed anywhere else. Seen here is the engraving preceding Brunnen der Weisheit ("Fountain of Wisdom").

Johannes de Monte–Snyder

Joh. de Monte–Snyders, Metamorphosis Planetarum: das ist: eine wunderbarliche Veränderung der Planeten und metallischen Gestalten in ihr erstes Wesen: mit beygefügtem Process und Entdeckung der dreyen Schlüssel, so zu Erlangung der drey Principia gehörig, und wie das universale generalislimum zu Erlangen. Frankfurt am Mayn: Verlegts Georg Heinrich Oehrling, 1700.

Little is known about German alchemist, Johannes de Monte–Snyder; however, this work contains one of the greatest alchemical allegories. Metamorphosis Planetarum ("Metamorphosis of the Planets") was immensely popular and many struggled to understand its complexities, including the renowned scientist Isaac Newton. Seen here is the engraved title page.

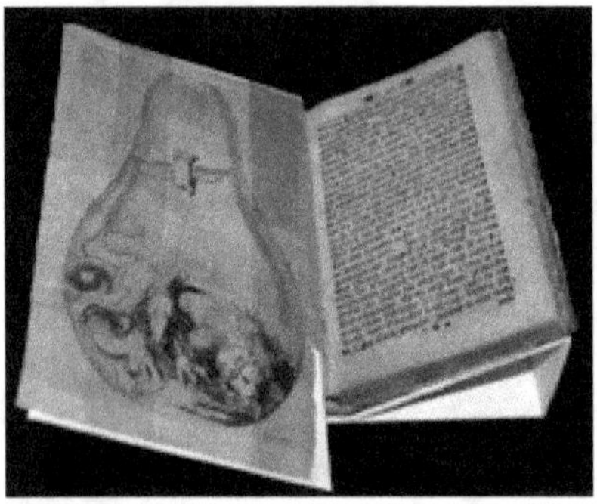

Franz Clinge

Ein richtiger Wegweiser zu der einigen Warheit in Erforschung der verborgenen Heimlichkeiten der Natuhr. Zu finden in Berlin: Bey Johann Michael Rüdiger, 1701.

Franz Clinge was a lawyer in Berlin, about whom little else is known. The engraving seen here of a lion, lobster, dragon, and a bird inside of a flask represents the process of an alchemical tincture.

Theatrvm Chemicvm: præcipvos selectorvm avctorvm tractatvs de chemiæ et lapidis philosophici antiqvitate, veritate, jure, præstantia, & operationibus, continens: in gratiam veræ chemiæ, et medicinæ chemicæ studiosorum (ut qui uberrimam inde optimorum remediorum messem facere poterunt) congestum, & in quatuor partes seu volumina digestum. Argentorati: Sumptibus Lazari Zetzneri, 1613–1622.

Theatrvm Chemicvm ("Chemical Theatre") is the earliest and most comprehensive compendium of alchemical writings. Seen here are two woodcuts. On the left is a mermaid, which often represents the mercury of the wise destroying the solid counterpart. On the right shows the sun (mercury) and the moon (sulfur) engulfed in flames, which represent the union of opposites.

Giovanni Battista Nazari

Della tramvtatione metallica sogni tre. In Brescia: Appresso Pietro Maria Marchetti, 1599.

Giovanni Battista Nazari's (c. 16th century) allegorical treatise on the transmutation of metals. This image depicts a giant donkey playing music on a flute with tiny people dancing in a circle around him.

Ouroboros

The Ouroboros symbolizes life on every level, it is both the macrocosm and the microcosm -- the serpent and the egg, the universal and the individual. The circle represents the movement of divine energy and is a pictorial representation of the dictum "my end is my beginning."

The Double Ouroborus shows two serpents which are integrated as one and symbolizes perfection and the union of opposites. The alchemical dictum associated with the double ouroboros is "Solve et Coagula" meaning "dissolve the body and coagulate the spirit." The bottom, wingless serpent must be dissolved as it represents the unenlightened body. The top, winged serpent is elusive and must be coagulated. The continual circle ends when the two are integrated and become one.

Abraham Eleazar

R. Abrahami Eleazaris Uraltes Chymisches Werk. Schwartzburgicum, P. M. & I. P. E. Erfurt, Verlegts Augustinus Crusius, 1735.

Engraving of the double ouroboros in front of a tree bare of leaves and on the left a tulip–like flower is growing. Tulips are thought to represent the attainment of spiritual awareness.

Abraham Eleazar

R. Abrahami Eleazaris Uraltes Chymisches Werk. Schwartzburgicum, P. M. & I. P. E. Leipzig, in Lankischens Buchhandlung, 1760.

Nicolas Flamel's engraving, "Crucified Serpent" appears in this volume. It represents the fixing of the volatile or the removing of poison and the making the elixir of mercury. In the left foreground a tulip–like flower is wilting and behind this a tree stump sprouts new leaves.

Caduceus

For five thousand years the Caduceus has been a symbol of healing and remains recognizable in modern medicine. Also known as the Wand of Hermes, the two snakes around the pillar represent the unity of opposites: male/female, sun/moon, soul/spirit between the heaven and earth. The crown represents divine nature and the wings represent transcendence.

Philipp Müller

*Miracula & mysteria chymico–medica: libris quinque (quorum summam pagina versa exhibet).*Amstelodami: Apud Ægidium Janssonium Valkenier, 1656.

This is one of several chemical and medical works by Philipp Müller (1585–1659), a professor of Mathematics at Leipzig University.

Johann Joachim Becher

Institutiones chimicae prodromae i.e. Ioannis Ioachimi Becheri ... Oedipus chimicus obscuriorum terminorum & principiorum chimicorum mysteria aperiens & resolvens. Opusculum, omnibus medicinae & chimiae studiosis, lectu perquàm utile & necessarium. Francofvrti, apud Hermannvm à Sande, 1664.

Alchemists took delight in their cryptic texts and often compared alchemical riddles with the riddle of Sphinx. Seen here is an engraving of Oedipus holding a caduceus approaching the Sphinx.

Johann Joachim Becher

Institutiones chimicae prodromae id est, Joannis Joachimi Becheri. Amstelodami, apud Elizeum Weyerstraten, 1664.

The frontispiece engraving for a textbook on Paracelsian medicine. Again, Oedipus meeting the Sphinx can be seen in the background of the alchemists' laboratory.

Daniel Stolcius

Hortulus hermeticus flosculis philosophorum cupro incisis conformatus, & breuissimis versiculis explicatus quo chymiatriae studiosi pro philotheca vti, fessique laboratorium ministri recreari possint. Francofurti: Impensis Lucae Jennisii, 1627.

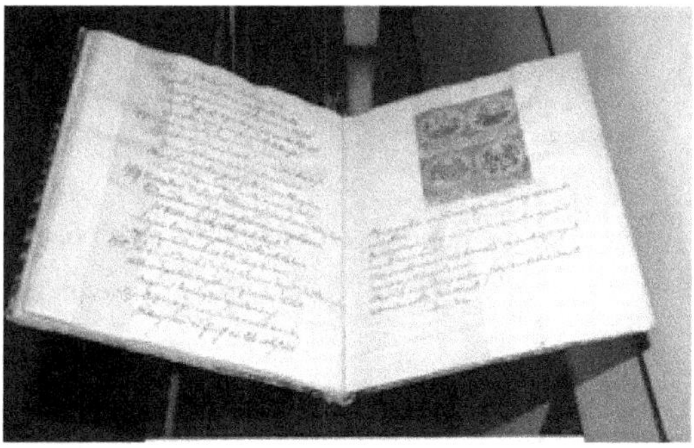

Daniel Stolcius (1600–1660) was a Bohemian physician and alchemist. He studied alchemy with Michael Maier. Seen here is his well-known emblem book displaying seals for Summa Textualis Philosophica, Codex Veritatis De Sapientia Philosophica, Oswaldus Crollius

Veteranus Philosophicae Discipulus and Johannes–Daniel Mylius, Veteranus, Philosophicae Discipulus.

Daniel Stolcius

Hortulus hermeticus flosculis philosophorum cupro incisis conformatus, et brevissimis versiculis explicates. [c. 16--?].
MSS 095 Item 026

This manuscript copy of the Stolcius's emblem book contains additional material clipped out of unidentified book. The emblems are mounted on pages with the printed material copied by an unknown hand. Open to the same seals as in the published copy on the left.

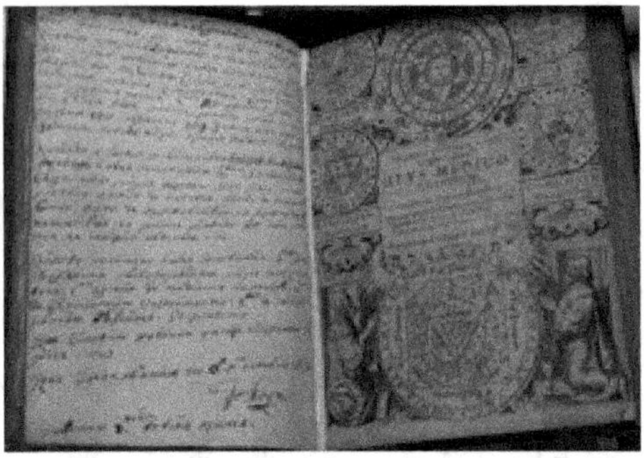

Johann Daniel Mylius

Ioannis Danielis Mylii Vetterani Hassi M.C. Opus medico–chymicum: continens tres tractatus siue Basilicas: quorum prior inscribitur Basilica medica: secundus Basilica chymica: tettius Basilica philosophica. Francofurti: Apud Lucam Iennis, 1618–1630. Volume One.

Johann Daniel Mylius (c.1583–1642) was a German philosopher, composer and alchemist, who also studied theology and medicine. He wrote many alchemical treatises, and is best known for his works on alchemical emblems. Seen here across from the beautiful title page engraving are the handwritten notes by a previous owner.

Johann Daniel Mylius

Ioannis Danielis Mylii Vetterani Hassi M.C. Opus medico–chymicum: continens tres tractatus siue Basilicas: quorum prior inscribitur Basilica medica: secundus Basilica chymica: tettius Basilica philosophica. Francofurti: Apud Lucam Iennis, 1618–1630.

Volume three of Mylius's Opus Medico–Chymicum which he wrote while still a medical student. This treatise is about Paracelsian medicine, which was highly controversial.

Johann Daniel Mylius

Ioannis Danielis Mylii T. & med. candidati vetterani hassi Philosophia reformata continens libros binos: I. Liber in septem partes diuisus est...: II. Liber continet authoritates philosophorum. Francofvrti: Apud Lucam Iennis, 1622.

This is a first edition of Mylius's best–known work, Philosophia Reformata ("Philosophy Reformed") is a beautifully illustrated book that discusses concepts of metals and the stages of alchemy.

Basil Valentine

Basil Valentine (c. 15th century) was a Benedictine monk who was incredibly knowledgeable about chemistry, medicine, philosophy, and alchemy. He reportedly became Canon of the Priory of St. Peter at Erfurt in Germany. Mysteriously there is no extant evidence to support his affiliation with the Benedictines or the Priory of St. Peter and many believe "Basil Valentine" was a pseudonym.

Regardless, he is credited with a number of important writings related to the valuable and practical experiments he performed. He discovered many chemical preparations, such as the preparation of sulphuric acid; he was the first to introduce antimony into medicine and the first to explain how to extract antimony from sulphuret.

Basilius Valentinus

Haliographia de praeparatione, vsu, ac virtutibus omnium salium, mineralium, animalium, & vegetabilium. Bononiae: [Apud Andream Salmincium], 1644.

In this work Valentine discusses the preparation of salts. Here he is the first to discuss artificial mineral baths, chiefly nitre, vitriol, alum, and salt of tartar and examine the medical benefits for treatment of skin diseases. This work is also the first to describe the process for fulminating gold.

Basilius Valentinus

Les douze clefs de philosophie de frere Basile Valentin, religieux de l'ordre Sainct Benois: traictant de la vraye medecine metalique: plus l'Azoth, ou, Le moyen de faire l'or caché des philosophes: traduction francoise. A Paris: Chez Ieremie et Christophle Perier ..., 1624.

The frontispiece engraving shows the sun and the moon, which often represent mercury and sulfur and triangle with a bird inside which represents a chemical process.

The Twelve Keys

When Basil Valentine's *The Twelve Keys* was first published in 1599 it did not contain any illustrations. A 1602 edition included woodcuts. The twelve engravings that the work is now famous for did not appear until 1618 when the alchemist Michael Maier included *The Twelve Keys* in his *Tripus Aureus* (*Golden Tripod*).

Seen here are seven of the twelve keys; each emblem is rich with alchemical symbolism and appears in many editions. The meanings of some of the symbols within each emblem are known; however, the interpretation of the keys as a whole remains an enigma to the uninitiated.

Basilius Valentinus

Les douze clefs de philosophie. A Paris: Chez Pierre Moët, 1659.

The First Key: The King and Queen represent the sun and the moon or mercury and sulfur. They stand between antimony, symbolized by the wolf and lead, symbolized by the man with the scythe, which also symbolize animality and death. The King holds up three fingers and the Queen holds three flowers suggesting that the process needs to be repeated three times. This emblem represents the chemical process of purification.

Basilius Valentinus

Les douze clefs de philosophie. A Paris: Chez Pierre Moët, 1659.

The Second Key: Mercury is standing between polar opposites, sun/moon, life/death, earth/air and the fixed/volatile. This emblem often represents the chemical process of separation.

Johann Grasshof

Dyas chymica tripartita: das ist: sechs herrliche Teutsche philosophische Tractälein, deren II. von an jtzo noch im Leben: II. von mitlern Alters: und II. von ältern philosophis beschrieben worden: nunmehr aber allen filiis doctinæ zu Nutz an Tag geben, und mit schönen Figuren gezieret. Franckfurt am Mayn: Bey Lvca Jennis zu finden, 1625.

The Seventh Key: Depicts materials of the four seasons surrounded in chaos. Inside the triangle is "water" and at the base of the triangle is "salt of the philosophers."

The Eighth Key: Depicts twelve arches representing each key or step in the process. The one hidden behind the alchemists' target is Resurrection.

The Ninth Key: Depicts a man and woman forming the shape of a cross, with four birds at their head and feet. These birds symbolize different chemical processes. For example the black crow is putrefaction and the phoenix is resurrection.

Johann Daniel Mylius

Ioannis Danielis Mylii Vetterani Hassi M.C. Opus medico-chymicum: continens tres tractatus siue Basilicas: quorum prior inscribitur Basilica medica: secundus Basilica chymica: tettius Basilica philosophica. Francofurti: Apud Lucam Iennis, 1618-1630. [Volume 4]

The Eleventh Key: Seen here the Sun and Moon, or the spirit and the soul, are united through death. This emblem sometimes represents the process of conjunction.

Johann Daniel Mylius

Ioannis Danielis Mylii Vetterani Hassi M.C. Opus medico-chymicum: continens tres tractatus siue Basilicas: quorum prior inscribitur Basilica medica: secundus Basilica chymica: tettius Basilica philosophica. Francofurti: Apud Lucam Iennis, 1618-1630. [Volume 2:]

The Twelfth Key: The alchemist achieves the creation of the Philosopher's Stone in this emblem which is represented by the golden flower and the lion eating the snake. Sometimes this emblem is used to represent the chemical process of calcification.

[unquote]

Bibliography

Algaze, Guillermo D. 2001. Initial Social Complexity in Southwestern Asia. Current Anthropology 42, no. 2: 199–233.

Allchin, Bridget, and Raymond Allchin. 1968. The Birth of Indian Civilization. Baltimore: Penguin.

———. [1988] 1996. The Rise of Civilization in India and Pakistan. New Delhi: Cambridge University Press, through Foundation Books.

Allison K. Thomason: *Luxury and Legitimation: Royal Collecting in Ancient Mesopotamia.* Aldershot 2005, S. 75ff

Anon., 1980, Ingots from wrecked ship may help to solve ancient mystery, *Inst. Archaeo-Metallurgical Studies Newsletter,* No. 1, 1-2

Art. *Industalkultur.* In: Reallexikon der Assyriologie und vorderasiatischen Archäologie. Bd. 5, S. 96ff.

Asthana, S.P. 1976. History and archaeology of India's contacts with other countires: from earliest times to 300 BC, B.R. Publications Corp., Delhi.

Bardhan, Pranab. 2000. The Nature of Institutional Impediments to Economic Development. In A Not-So-Dismal Science: A Broader View of Societies and Economies, edited by Mancur Olson and Satu Kahkonen, 245–67. Oxford: Oxford University Press.

Beck H.C. (1933) “Etched carnelian beads.” *Antiquaries Journal*, XIII, pp. 384-398.

Benson, Bruce L. 1990. The Enterprise of Law: Justice Without the State. San Francisco: Pacific Research Institute for Public Policy.

———. 2002. Justice Without Government. In The Voluntary City: Choice, Community, and Civil Society, edited by David T. Beito, Peter Gordon, and Alexander Tabarrok, 127–50. Ann Arbor: University of Michigan Press.

Benveniste, E., “Les classes sociales dans la tradition avestique,” *JA* 221, 1932, pp. 117--34.

Idem, *Les Mages dans l'ancien Iran*, Paris, 1938.

Bhan K.K., J.M. Kenoyer & M. Vidale (1994) “Harappan Technology: Theoretical and Methodological Issues.” *Man and Environment*, XIX, 2, 141-157.

Bibby, T.G., 1958. The 'ancient Indian Style' Seals from Bahrain, Antiquity 33: 243-246.

Brandenstein, W. and M. Mayrhofer, *Handbuch des Altpersischen*, Wiesbaden, 1964.

Bray, Francesca. 1986. The Rice Economies: Technology and Development in Asian Societies. Oxford: Basil Blackwell.

Bryant, Edwin, *The Quest for the Origins of Vedic Culture: The Indo-Aryan Migration Debate* (Oxford University Press, USA, 2004).

Bulliet, Richard W. [1975] 1990. The Camel and the Wheel. New York: Columbia University Press.

Byock, Jesse L. 1988. Medieval Iceland: Society, Sagas, and Power. Berkeley: University of California Press.

Calmeyer, P., “Zur Genese altiranischer Motive. Die "Statistische Landcharte des Perserreiches,"" *AMI* 15, 1982, pp. 105-87; 16, 1983, pp. 141-222.

Cameron, GC,“The Persian Satrapies and Related Matters,” *JNES* 32, 1973, pp. 47-56.

Carneiro, Robert. 1970. A Theory of the Origin of the State. Science 169: 733–38.

———. 1987. Cross-Currents in the Theory of State Formation. American Ethnologist 14, no. 4: 756–70.

———. 1988. The Circumscription Theory: Challenge and Response. American Behavioral Scientist 31, no. 4: 497–511.

Carter R. (2002a) “Prehistoric navigation and exchange in the Persian Gulf.” Paper presented at the International Congress “Early Navigation and Trade in the Indian Ocean,” Ravenna, 5 July 2002.

Carter R. H. Crawford (2002b) “The Kuwait-British Archaeological Expedition to As-Sabiyah: Report on the Third Season’s Work.” *Iraq*, LXIV, pp. 1-13.

Casanova M. (1997) *Le lapis-lazuli dans l’Orient Ancien: gisements, production, des origines au debut du second millenaire avant J.-C.* Doctorat, Universite de Paris I,Pantheon, Sorbonne (2 vols.)

Casson, Lionel. [1971] 1995. Ships and Seamanship in the Ancient World. Baltimore: Johns Hopkins University Press.

CDIAL Turner, R. L. (Ralph Lilley), Sir. *A comparative dictionary of Indo-Aryan languages.*London: Oxford University Press, 1962-1966. Includes three supplements, published 1969-1985.

Chakrabarti, D.K. 1977. India and West Asia--an alternative approach, Man and Environment 1:25-38.

Chakrabarti, D.K. 1978. Seals as evidence of Indus-West Asia Interrelations, in D. Chattopadhyaya, ed., History and Society, Essays in Honour of Prof. Niharranjan Ray, Calcutta, p. 93-116.

Chakrabarti, D.K., 1979, The problem of tin in early India--a preliminary survey, in: *Man and Environment,* Vol. 3, pp. 61-74

Chakrabarti D.K. (1982) "'Long-barrel-Cylinder' Beads and the Issue of Pre-Sargonic Contact between the Harappan Civilization and Mesopotamia." In G.L. Possehl (ed.) *Harappan Civilization: a Contemporary Perspective.* Delhi, 265-270.

Chakrabarti D.K. (1990) *The External Trade of the Indus Civilization.* New Delhi.

Claussen, Martin, OTHER AUTHORS' NAMES. 1999. Simulation of an Abrupt Change in Saharan Vegetation in the Mid-Holocene. Geophysical Research Letters 26, no. 14: 2037–40.

de Clercq, Louis. *Collection de Clercq: Catalogue Méthodique et Raisonné: Antiquités Assyriennes, Cylindres Orientauz, Cachets,Briques, Bronzes, Bas-Reliefs, Etc.* Paris: E. Leroux, 1888.

Cleuziou, S., 1978-79, Preliminary report on the second and third excavation campaigns at Hili 8, Archaeology in the United Arab Emirates, vol. 2/3, 30ff.

Cleuziou, S., and Berthoud, Th., 1982, Early tin in the Near East: a reassessment in the light of new evidence from western Afghanistan, *Expedition*, 25.

Cleuziou, S. 1992. The Oman peninsula and the Indus civilization: a reassessment, Man and Environment 17/2: 93--103.

Cleuziou S. & M. Tosi (2000) “Ra’s al-Jinz and the Prehistoric Coastal Cultures of the Ja`laan.” *The Journal of Oman Studies*, 11, pp. 19-73.

Clutton-Brock, Juliet. 1992. Horse Power: A History of the Horse and the Donkey in Human Societies. London: Natural History Publications.

Collon D. (1977) “Ivory.” In J.D. Hawkins (ed.) *Trade in the Ancient Near East*. London, pp. 219-222.

Collon D. (1990) *Near Eastern Seals*. University of California/British Museum, Berkeley.

Dikshit M.G. (1949) *Etched Beads in India*. Poona.

Corbiau, S. 1936. An Indo-Sumerian Cylinder, Iraq 3: 100-103.

Cowen, Richard. 1999. Fire and Metals. Available at: http://www-geology.ucdavis.edu/~GEL115/115CH3.html.

Cowen, Tyler, ed. 1988. The Theory of Market Failure: A Critical Examination. Fairfax, Va.: George Mason University Press.

Crabtree, Donald E., and E. L. Davis. 1968. Experimental Manufacture of Wooden Implements with Tools of Flaked Stone. Science, New Series, 159: 426–28.

Crawford, H. E. W. 1973. Mesopotamia’s Invisible Exports in the Third Millennium B.C. World Archaeology 5, no. 2: 232–41.

Daniels, Peter T. , William Bright (eds.), 1996, The *World's Writing Systems*. Oxford University Press.

Danino, Michel, “A Dravido-Harappan Connection? The issue of Methodology.,” *Indus Civilization and Tamil Language* (2009): 70 – 81.

Davies, Stephen. 2002. The Private Provision of Police during the Eighteenth and Nineteenth Centuries. In The Voluntary City: Choice, Community, and Civil Society, edited by David T. Beito, Peter Gordon, and Alexander Tabarrok, 151–81. Ann Arbor: University of Michigan Press.

DEDR, 1984, Burrow, T. and Emeneau, M.B. (eds). *A Dravidian Etymological Dictionary Revised,* 2nd edn., eds., Oxford

Deflem, Mathieu. 1999. Warfare, Political Leadership, and State Formation: The Case of the Zulu Kingdom, 1808–1879. Ethnology 38, no. 4: 371–91.

Deshpande, MM, 1979, *Sociolinguistic attitudes in India: an historical reconstruction*, Ann Arbor, MI: Karoma Publishers, 265; note 1, p. 105; note 22, p. 107

Dhavalikar, M. K. 1995. Cultural Imperialism: Indus Civilization in Western India. New Delhi: Books and Books.

During Caspers E.C.L. (1971) "Etched Carnelian Beads." *Bullettin of the Institute of Archaeology*, 10, 83-98.

During Caspers, E.C.L. 1972. Harappan trade in the Arabian Gulf in the third millennium BC, Mesopotamia 7: 167-191.

During Caspers, E.C.L. 1982. Sumerian traders and businessmen residing in the Indus Valley cities: a critical assessment of archaeological evidence, Annali 42: 337-380.

During Caspers, E.C.L. 1992. Intercultural/mercantile contacts between the Arabian Gulf and South Asia at the close of the 3rd millennium BC, Proceedings of the Seminar for Arabian Studies 22: 3--28.

Edens, Christopher. 1992. Dynamics of Trade in the Ancient Mesopotamian "World System." American Anthropologist, New Series, 94, no. 1: 118–39.

Edzard, D.O. 1976--1980. Kamm A. Philologisch, Reallexikon der Assyriologie 5: 332.

Ekelund, Robert B., OTHER AUTHORS' NAMES. 1996. Sacred Trust: The Medieval Church as an Economic Firm. Oxford: Oxford University Press.

Emeneau, MB, 1956, India as a linguistic area, Language 32, 1956, 3-16.

Emeneau, M.B., 1974, The Indian linguistic area revisited, *CCSAL*, 92-134

Falkenstein, A., Wahrsagung' in der sumerischen Ueberlieferung, *CRRA* 14: 55-56

Foster B. (1995) *From distant days... Myths, tales and poetry from ancient Mesopotamia.*Bethesda.

Frankfort, H. 1934. The Indus Civilization and the Near East, Annual Bibliography of Indian Archaeology VII: 1-12.

Franke-Vogt U. (1991) "The Glyptic Art of the Harappa Culture." In M. Jansen., M.Mulloy & G. Urban (eds.) *Forgotten cities on the Indus.* Mainz, pp. 179-187.

Franke-Vogt U. (1992) "Inscribed Objects from Mohenjo-Daro: Some Remarks on Stylistic Variability and Distribution Patterns." In C. Jarrige (ed.) *South Asian Archaeology 1989.* Madison, 103-118.

Fried, Morton H. 1967. The Evolution of Political Society: An Essay in Political Anthropology. New York: Random House.

———. 1978. The State, the Chicken, and the Egg: or, What Came First? In Origins of the State: The Anthropology of Political Evolution, edited by Ronald Cohen and Elman R. Service, 35–47. Philadelphia: Institute for the Study of Human Issues.

Friedman, David. 1979. Private Creation and Enforcement of Law—A Historical Case. Journal of Legal Studies 8, no. 2: 399–415.

Frye, RN, *The Heritage of Persia*, London, 1962.

Gadd, C.J. 1932. Seals of Ancient Indian Style found at Ur, Proc. of the British Academy, XVII: 191-210.

Gadd, C.J. and Smith, S. 1924. The new links between Indian and Babylonian Civilizations, Illus. London News, Oct. 4, p. 614-616.

Gade, Daniel W. 1992. Landscape, System, and Identity in the Post-Conquest Andes. Annals of the Association of American Geographers 82, no. 3: 460–77.

Gershevitch, I., "The Alloglottography of Old Persian," *TPS*, 1979, pp. 114-90.

Gibson, McG. 1976. The Nippur expedition, The Oriental Institute of the Univ. of Chicago Annual Report 1975/76: 26,28.

Glassner J.-J. (2002) "Dilmun et Magan: Le Peuplement, l'Organisation Politique, la Question des Amorrites et la Place de l'Ècriture. Point de Vue de l'Assyriologue." In S. Cleuziou, M. Tosi & J. Zarins (eds.) *Essays on the Late Prehistory of the Arabian Peninsula.* Roma, pp. 337-381.

Gnoli, G., *The Idea of Iran. An Essay on Its Origin*, Rome, 1989.

Good, R. 1961. The geography of the flowering plants. London: Longman.

Graber, Robert B., and Paul B. Roscoe. 1988. Introduction: Circumscription and the Evolution of Society. American Behavioral Scientist 31, no. 4: 405–15.

Hahn, Ferdinand, 1908, Grammar of the Kurukh Language, Repr. 1985, Mittal Publications

Hall, Kenneth R. 1985. Maritime Trade and State Development in Early Southeast Asia. Honolulu: University of Hawaii Press.

Hallock, Hiram. 1979. Sawmilling Roots. Available at: http://www.ls.net/~windyhill/saw-millhistory4.htm. Conference paper originally published in Electronics in the Sawmills: Proceedings of the Electronics Workshop, Sawmill and Plywood Clinic, Portland, Oregon. San Francisco: Miller Freeman.

Harris, Marvin. 1989. Our Kind. New York: Harper and Row.

Harrison, Timothy P. 1993. Economics with an Entrepreneurial Spirit: Early Bronze Trade with Late Predynastic Egypt. The Biblical Archaeologist 56, no. 2: 81–93.

Heimpel W.L., L.Gorelick & A.J.Gwinnet (1988) "Philological and archaeological evidence for the use of emery in the Bronze Age Near East." *Journal of Cuneiform Studies*, 40/2, 195-210.

Herrenschmidt, C., "Désignation de l'empire et concepts politiques de Darius I d'après ses inscriptions en vieux perse," *Stud. Ir.* 5, 1976, pp. 17-58.

Herzfeld, E., *The Persian Empire. Studies in Geography and Ethnography of the Ancient Near East*, ed. G. Walser, Wiesbaden, 1968.

Hiebert, F.T. & C.C. Lamberg-Karlovsky. 1992. Central Asia and the Indo-Iranian borderlands, Iran 30: 1--15.

Hirsch, H., 1963, Die Inschriften der Konige Von Agade, *Afo*, 20, pp. 37-38

Hock, Hans Henrich, 1991, *Principles of Historical Linguistics*, New York, Mouton de Gruyter, p. 10

Hoffmann, K., *Aufsätze zur Indoiranistik* II, Wiesbaden, 1976.

Hunter, G.R., 1932, Mohenjodaro--Indus Epigraphy *JRAS*, 476

Idem and J. Narten, *Der sasanidische Archetypus*, Wiesbaden, 1989.

Hosler, Dorothy. 1988. Ancient West Mexican Metallurgy: South and Central American Origins and West Mexican Transformations. American Anthropologist, New Series, 90, no. 4: 832–55.

Inizan M.-L. (2000) "Importation de cornalines et agates de l'Indus en Mésopotamie.Le cas de Suse et Tello." In V. Roux (ed.) *Cornaline de l'Inde. Des pratiques techniques de Cambay aux techno-systémes de l'Indus*. Paris, 473-502.

Jacobs, David K., and Dork L. Sahagian. 1993. Climate-Induced Fluctuations in Sea Level during Non-glacial Times. Nature 361: 710–12.

Jacobs, Jane. 1969. The Economy of Cities. New York: Random House.

———. 1984. Cities and the Wealth of Nations. New York: Random House.

Jayaswal, KP, 1914, 'Kleine Mitteilungen', *Zeitschrift der Deutschen Morgenlandischen Gesellschraft,*, vol. LXXII, p. 719

Joshi J.P. & A. Parpola (1987) *Corpus of Indus Seals and Inscriptions. 1. Collections in India*. Helsinki.

Junge, J., "Satrapie und Natio. Reichsverwaltung und Reichspolitik im Staate Dareios' I," *Klio* 34, 1941, pp. 1-55.

Kalyanaraman, S., 2008, Web resource on decoding Indus script (including Epigraphica Sarasvati or corpus of Indus script inscriptions) http://sites.google.com/site/kalyan97

Kalyanaraman, S. 2012. *Indian Hieroglyphs – Invention of Writing*. Herndon: Sarasvati Research Center. ISBN 978-0982897126

Kak, Subhash C., "A frequency-an alysis of the Indus script," *Cryptologia* 12, no. 3 (1988): 129.

Kak,Subhash C., "Indus and Brahmi- Further connections" *Cryptologia* 14, no. 2 (1990): 169.

Kak,Subhash C., "An Indus-Sarasvati signboard, *Cryptologia* 20, no. 3 (1996): 275.

Kaplan, Edward. 1997. Economic Change during the Early Chinese Bronze Age. Lecture given at Western Washington University. Available at: http://www.ac.wwu.edu/~Kaplan/H371/ae.05.pdf.

Keeley, Lawrence H. 1996. War before Civilization: The Myth of the Peaceful Savage. Oxford: Oxford University Press.

Kenoyer, Jonathan Mark. 1994. The Harappan State: Was It or Wasn't It? In From Sumer to Meluhha: Contributions to the Archaeology of South and West Asia in Memory of George F. Dales, Jr., edited by Jonathan Mark Kenoyer, 71–80. Madison, Wisc.: Prehistory Press.

———. 1997. Trade and Technology of the Indus Valley: New Insights from Harappa, Pakistan. World Archaeology 29, no. 2: 262–80.

———. 1998. Ancient Cities of the Indus Valley Civilization. Oxford: Oxford University Press.

Kenoyer J.M. (in print) "Indus and Mesopotamian Trade Networks: New Insights from Shell and Carnelian Artefacts." In E. Olijdam (ed.) *E. During Casper's Memorial Volume.*

Kirfel, W., 1927, *Das Purāṇa Pañcalakṣaṇa.* Bonn : K. Schroeder

Kirzner, Israel M. 1973. Competition and Entrepreneurship. Chicago: Chicago University Press.

———. 1979. Perception, Opportunity, and Profit: Studies in the Theory of Entrepreneurship. Chicago: Chicago University Press.

Kjaerum, P. 1980. Seals of Dilmun-Type from Failaka, Kuwait, PSAS 10: 45-53.

Kjaerum, P. 1983. *The Stamp and Cylinder Seals 1:1*, Failaka/Dilmun: The second millennium settlements, Jutland Arch. Soc. Publ. XVII:1, Aarhus.

Kohl, P.L. (ed.). 1981. The Bronze Age civilization of Central Asia: recent Soviet discoveries. Armonk (NY): M.E. Sharpe.

Kramer, Samuel N. *The Sumerians: Their History, Culture and Character.* Chicago, IL: University of Chicago Press, 1963.

Kuiper, FBJ, 1948, Proto-Munda words in Sanskrit, Amsterdam, Verhandeling der Koninklijke Nederlandsche Akademie Van Wetenschappen, Afd. Letterkunde, Nieuwe Reeks Deel Li, No. 3. 1948

1967, The genesis of a linguistic area, IIJ 10, 1967, 81-102

Lahiri, Nayanjot. 1992. The Archaeology of Indian Trade Routes Up to c. 200 BC: Resource Use, Resource Access, and Lines of Communication. New Delhi: Oxford University Press.

Lamberg-Karlovsky C.C. (1972) "Trade Mechanisms in Indus-Mesopotamian Interrelations."*Journal of the American Oriental Society*, 92, 2, April-June 1972, 222-229.

Lammens, Henri. 1928. Les Chrétiens à La Mecque à la veille de l'hégire: L'Arabie occidentale avant l'hégire. Beirut: Imprimerie Catholique.

Lansing, J. Stephen. 1991. Priests and Programmers: Technologies of Power in the Engineered Landscape of Bali. Princeton, N.J.: Princeton University Press.

Laufer, B. 1919. Sino-Iranica: Chinese contributions to the history of civilization in ancient Iran, with special reference to the history of cultivated plants and products. Chicago (IL): Field Museum. Publication 201.

Leemans, W.F. 1960. Foreign trade in the Old Babylonian period. Leiden: Brill.

Lenski, Gerhard, OTHER AUTHORS' NAMES. 1991. Human Societies: An Introduction to Macrosociology. New York: McGraw-Hill.

Leuze, O., *Die Satrapieneinteilung in Syrien und im Zweistromlande von 520-320*, Halle, 1935.

Lieblich, Bruno, 1918, 'Der Name Mlēccha', *ZDMG* 72, 286-7.

Mackay, E.J.H. 1925. Sumerian connections with Ancient India, JRAS: 696-701.

Mackay, E.J.H. 1931. Further Excavations at Mohenjo-daro, New Delhi.

Mackay, E.J.H. 1943. Chanhu-Daro excavations 1935--36. New Haven (CT): American Oriental Series 20.

MacKenzie, DN, *A Concise Pahlavi Dictionary*, Oxford, 1971.

Maddin, R., T.S. Wheeler and J. Muhly, 1977, Tin in the ancient Near East: old questions and new finds, *Expedition*, 19, 35-47

Mahadevan, I., 1977, *Indus Script*, Delhi, Archaeological Survey of India

Mancini, M., "Ant. pers. *dahyu-*, il segno "DH" e il problema degli ideogrammi nel cuneiforme achemenide," *Studi e Saggi Linguistici* 24, 1984, pp. 241-70.

Marshall, Sir J. 1931. Mohenjo-daro and the Indus Civilization, London. Arthur Probsthain.

Masica, CP, 1971, Defining a Linguistic area. South Asia. Chicago: The University of Chicago Press.

Masica, Colin P., 1976, *Defining a linguistic area, South Asia*, Chicago, niversity of Chicago Press

Masica, Colin, 1979, Aryan and non-Aryan elements in North Indian agriculture, in: Deshpande and Hook (eds.), *Aryan and non-Aryan in India*, Ann Arbour, Univ. of Michigan, Centre for South and Southeast Asian Studies, 55-152).

Masica, Colin P., 1991, *Indo-Aryan Languages*, Cambridge Univ. Press

Masson, V.M. and Sarianidi, V.I. 1972. Central Asia, Thames and Hudson, London.

Masson, V.M. 1981. Urban centers of early class societies, in Kohl (ed.): 135--48.

Masson, V.M. & V.I. Sarianidi. 1972. Central Asia: Turkmenia before the Achaemenids. New York (NY): Praeger.

Mate, M. S. 1985. Harappan Fortifications: A Study. In Studies in Indian Archaeology, edited by S. B. Deo and M. K. Dhavalikar, 75–84. Bombay: Popular Prakashan.

MBh., 1933-1966, *Mahabhrata* critical edition, Poona, Bhandarkar Oriental Institute

Mcintosh, Jane, *A Peaceful Realm : The Rise And Fall of the Indus Civilization* (Basic Books, 2001).

McNeill, William H. 1994. The Changing Shape of World History, History, and Theory. History and Theory 34, no. 2: 8–26.

———. [1967] 1999. A World History. New York: Oxford University Press.

———. 2000. Information and Transportation Nets in World History. In World-System History: The Social Science of Long-term Change, edited by Robert Allen Denemark, OTHER EDITORS' NAMES, 201–15. New York: Routledge

Millennio av. Cr. alla luce delle fonti letterarie e lessicali sumeriche." *Mesopotamia*, VII, 43-166.

Mises, Ludwig von. 1949. Human Action: A Treatise on Economics. New Haven, Conn.: Yale University Press.

Moe, Terry. 1980. The Organization of Interests: Incentives and the Internal Dynamics of Political Interest Groups. Chicago: University of Chicago Press.

Moorey, P.R.S., 1994, *Ancient Mesopotamian Materials and Industries,* Oxford, Clarendon Press

J.D. Muhly, 1973a, Copper and Tin, Conn.: Archon., Hamden; *Transactions of Connecticut Academy of Arts and Sciences*, vol. 43

Muhly, J.D., 1973b, Tin trade routes of the Bronze Age, *Scientific American*, 1973, 61, 404-13

Muhly, J.D., 1976, *Copper and Tin, Hamden*, Archon Books.

Muhly, J.D., 1977, New evidence for sources of and trade in bronze age tin, in: Alan D. Franklin, Jacqueline S. Olin, and Theodore A. Wertime, *The Search for Ancient Tin*, Seminar organized by Theodore A. Wertime and held at the Smithsonian Institution and the National Bureau of Standards, Washington, D.C., March 14-15, 1977

Muhly, J.D., 1985, Sources of tin and the beginnings of bronze metallurgy, *AJA* 89: 275-291

Nissen, H.J. 1982. Linking distant areas archaeologically, paper read at the 1st International Conference on Pakistan Archaeology, Peshawar.

Nissen, H.J., P. Damerow, and R.K. Englund (1993), Archaic Bookkeeping.Chicago: The University of Chicago Press.

Nock, Albert Jay. [1935] 1973. Our Enemy the State. New York: Libertarian Review Foundation.

Oates, Joan. 1993. Trade and Power in the Fifth and Fourth Millennia BC: New Evidence from Northern Mesopotamia. World Archaeology 24, no. 3: 403–22.

O'Connell, Robert L. 1995. Ride of the Second Horseman: The Birth and Death of War. New York: Oxford University Press.

Olson, Mancur. [1965] 1971. The Logic of Collective Action: Public Goods and the Theory of Groups. Cambridge, Mass.: Harvard University Press.

———. 2000. Power and Prosperity: Outgrowing Communist and Capitalist Dictatorships. New York: Basic Books.

Oppenheim, A.L. 1954. The seafaring merchants of Ur, Journal of the American Oriental Society 74: 6--17.

Oppenheim, A. Leo. *Ancient Mesopotamia: Portrait of a Dead Civilization*. Chicago, IL: University of Chicago Press, 1964.

Ozguc, T., 1962, An Assyrian trading outpost, *Scientific American*, 1962, 97 ff.

Parasher, Aloka, 1991, Mlecchas in early India. A Study in Attitudes toward Outsiders upto AD 600. New Delhi: Munshiram Manoharial Publishers Pvt. Ltd.

Parpola, Asko, S. Koskenniemi, S. Parpola and P. Aalto, 1970, *Decipherment of the Proto Dravidian Inscriptions of the Indus Valley,* no. 3, Copenhagen

Parpola A. and S. Parpola, 1975, On the relationship of the Sumerian Toponym Meluhha and Sanskrit Mleccha, *Studia Orientalia* 46

Parpola, S., Parpola, A., and Brunswig, R.H. Jr. 1977. The Meluhha village: evidence of acculturation of Harappan traders in late third millennium Mesopotamia? *Journal of the Economic and Political History of the Orient*, vol. 20, 129-165.

Parpola, A. 1984. New correspondences between Harappan and Near Eastern Glyptic Art, in B. Allchin, ed., South Asian Archaeology 1981, Univ. of Cambridge Oriental Publications 34, Cambridge.

Parpola, A. et al, 1987, *Corpus of Indus seals and inscriptions*, Vol. 1 Collections in India, Helsinki: Suomalainen Tiedeakatemia

Parpola, A. 1988. The coming of the Aryans to Iran and India and the cultural and ethnic identity of the Dasas, Studia Orientalia 64: 195--302.

Parpola,. A. et al, 1991, *Corpus of Indus seals and inscriptions*, Vol. 2 Collections in Pakistan, Helsinki: Suomalainen Tiedeakatemia.

Parpola, A., BM Pande and Peter Koskikallio,(eds.), 2010, in collaboration with Richard Meadow and J. Mark Kenoyer, Corpus of Indus Seals and inscriptions, vol. 3: New Material, Untraced Objects, and Collections Outside India and Pakistan. Pt. 1: Mohenjo-daro and Harappa. Suomalainen Tiedeakatemia, Annales Academiae Scientiarum Fennicae, Sarja, Series B, NIDE, vol. 359. Memoires of the Archaeological Survey of India, vol. 96. Helsinki, 2010.

Paton, L.B., 1908-27, Ammonites, in *Encyclopaedia of Religion & Ethics*, ed. J. Hastings, vol. I, pp. 389-393.

Pearson, G.W. & M.V. Stuivier, 1986. High-perecision calibration of the radiocarbon time scale, 500--2500 BC, Radiocarbon 28: 838--52.

Pettinato G. (1972) "Il commercio con l'estero della Mesopotamia meridionale nel 3.

Peyronel L. (2000) "Sigilli Harappani e Dilmuniti dalla Mesopotamia e dalla Susiana. Note sul Commercio nel Golfo Arabo-Persico tra III e II Mill. a.C." *Vicino Oriente*, 12, pp. 175-240.

Pezzoli-Olgiati D. (2000) "Images of cities in Ancient Religions: Some methodological considerations." Zurich. <http://www.cwru.edu/affil/GAIR/papers/2000papers/Daria.html>

Pfeiffer, Martin, 1973, Elements of Kurux historical phonology, Bill Archive

Phadtare, Netajirao R. 2000. Sharp Decrease in Summer Monsoon Strength 4000–3500 cal yr B.P. in the Central Himalaya of India Based on Pollen Evidence from Alpine Past. Quaternary Research 53, no. 1: 122–29.

Piggott, Stuart. 1950. Prehistoric India. Harmondsworth, U.K.: Penguin.

Pollock, Susan. 1996. Household Production at the Uruk Mound, Abu Salabikh, Iraq. American Journal of Archaeology 100, no. 4: 683–98.

Polunin, O. 1980. Flowers of Greece and the Balkans: a field guide. Oxford: Oxford University Press.

Porada, E., 1971, Remarks on seals found in the Gulf States. *Artibus Asiae* 33 (4): 331-7: pl.9, Figure 5

Possehl, G.L. (ed.). 1979. Ancient cities of the Indus. New Delhi: Vikas Publishing House.

Possehl G.L. (1984) "Of Men." In J.M. Kenoyer (ed.) *From Sumer to Meluhha: contributions* to the archaeology of South and West Asia in memory of George F. Dales, Jr. Wisconsin Archaeological Reports, 3, pp. 179-186.

Possehl, Gregory L. 1990. Revolution in the Urban Revolution: The Emergence of Indus Urbanization. Annual Review of Anthropology 19: 261–82.

———. 1994. Of Men. In From Sumer to Meluhha: Contributions to the Archaeology of South and West Asia in Memory of George F. Dales, Jr., edited by Jonathan Mark Kenoyer, 179–86. Madison, Wisc.: Prehistory Press.

-- *The Indus Age: The Writing System*. Philadelphia, PA: University of Pennsylvania Press.

———. 1998. Sociocultural Complexity Without the State: The Indus Civilization. In Archaic States, edited by Gary M. Feinman and Joyce Marcus, 261–91. Santa Fe: School of American Research Press.

Possehl, Gregory L., 1999, *The Indus Age: The beginnings*, Philadelhia, Univ. of Pennsylvania Press

Possehl G.L. (2002) *The Indus Civilization. A Contemporary Perspective*. Walnut Creek.

Possehl, Gregory L., 2006, Shu-ilishu's cylinder seal. In *Expedition*, Vol. 48, No. 1

Pottier, M.-H. 1984. Materiel funeraire de la Bactriane meridionale de l'Age du Bronze. Paris: Editions Recherche sur les Civilisations.

Potts, D.T. 1990. A prehistoric mound in the Emirate of Umm al-Qaiwain: excavations at Tell Abraq in 1989. Copenhagen: Munksgaard. 1991. Further excavations at Tell Abraq: the 1990 season. Copenhagen: Munksgaard. 1993. Rethinking some aspects of trade in the Arabian Gulf, World Archaeology 24: 423--40.

Potts T. (1994) *Mesopotamia and the East.* Oxford.
Potts, D., 1995, Distant Shores: Ancient Near Eastern Trade, in: Jack M. Sasson (ed.), *Civilizations of the Ancient Near East*, Vol. I, pp. 1451-1463

Potts, D.T., "A new Bactrian find from southeastern Arabia". Antiquity. FindArticles.com. 23 Sep, 2009. http://findarticles.com/p/articles/mi_hb3284/is_n256_v67/ai_n28629137/

Przyludski, J., 1929, Further notes on non-aryan loans in Indo-Aryan in: Bagchi, P. C. (ed.), Pre-Aryan and Pre-Dravidian in Sanskrit. Calcutta : University of Calcutta: 145-149

Rao S.R. (1973) *Lothal and the Indus Civilization.* Bombay.
Rao S.R. (1979) *Lothal a Harappan Port Town (1955-62).* Memoirs of the Archaeological Survey of India, 78, Volume 1. New Delhi.
Rao S.R. (1985) *Lothal a Harappan Port Town (1955-62).* Memoirs of the Archaeological Survey of India, 78, Volume 2. New Delhi.

Ratnagar, S. 1981. Encounters, the westerly trade of the Harappan Civilization, Oxford Univ. Press, Delhi

Ratnagar, Shereen. 1991. Enquiries into the Political Organization of Harappan Society. Pune, India: Ravish.

———. 2004. Trading Encounters: From the Euphrates to the Indus in the Bronze Age. New Delhi: Oxford University Press.

Ray, Himanshu Prabha. 2003. The Archaeology of Seafaring in Ancient South Asia. Cambridge, U.K.: Cambridge University Press.

Reade J. (1979) *Early Etched Beads and the Indus-Mesopotamia Trade.* London.
Reade, Julian. 2001. Assyrian King-Lists, the Royal Tombs of Ur, and Indus Origins. Journal of Near Eastern Studies 60, no. 1: 1–29.

Ridley, Matt. 1996. The Origins of Virtue. London: Penguin.

Roux V. & Matarasso P. (2000) "Les perles in cornaline harappéennes. Pratiques techniques et techno-systéme." In V. Roux (ed.) *Cornaline de l'Inde. Des pratiques techniques de Cambay aux techno-systémes de l'Indus.* Paris,417-438.
RV. *Rigveda*, 1896, tr. By Ralph TH Griffith.

Sarianidi, V. 1977. Bactrian centre of ancient art, Mesopotamia 12: 97--110. 1987. South-west Asia: migrations, the Aryans and Zoroastrians, Information Bulletin 13: 44--56.

Sax M. (1991) "The Composition of the Materials of the First Millennium BC Cylinder Seals from Western Asia." In P. Budd, B. Chapman, C. Jackson, R. Janaway & B. Ottaway (eds.) *Archaeological Sciences 1989*. Exeter.
Scheil, V., 1925, Un Nouvea Sceau Hindou Pseudo-Sumerian, *RA*, 22/3, pp. 55-56)

Schmandt-Besserat, D. (1992), Before Writing, 2 vols. Austin: The University of Texas Press.

______ (1996), How Writing Came About. Austin: The University of Texas Press.

--- 1999. The Legacy of the Middle East. Available at: http://www.humanities-interactive.org/ancient/mideast mideast_ essay.htm.

--------(2009), Tokens and Writing: The Cognitive Development. SCRIPTA, Volume 1 (September 2009): 145-154

Schwartz, M., "The Old Eastern Iranian World View According to the Avesta,"*Camb. Hist. Iran* II, 1985, pp. 640-63.

Service, Elman R. 1975. Origins of the State and Civilization: The Process of Cultural Evolution. New York: Norton.

Shaffer, J.G., 1978, *Prehistoric Baluchistan: With Excavation Report on Said Qala Tepe.* Delhi: B.R.Publishing Corp

Shaffer, Jim G. 1982. Harappan Civilization: A Reconsideration. In Harappan Civilization: A Contemporary Perspective, edited by Gregory L. Possehl, 41–50. New Delhi: Oxford-IBH.

Shaffer, J.G. 1986. The archaeology of Baluchistan: a review, Newsletter of Baluchistan Studies 3: 63--111.

Shah S.G.M. & A. Parpola (1991) *Corpus of Indus Seals and Inscriptions. 2. Collections in Pakistan*. Helsinki.
Shendge, Malati, 1977, *The civilized demons: the Harappans in Rigveda*, Abhinav Publications

Silver, Morris. 1985. Economic Structures of the Ancient Near East. Totowa, N.J.: Barnes and Noble.

Simoons F.J. (1968) *A Ceremonial Ox of India. The Mithan in Nature, Culture and History with Notes on Domestication of Common Cattle.* Madison.

Sollberger E. (1970) "The Problem of Magan and Meluhha." *Bulletin of the University of London*, 8-9, pp. 247-250.

Southworth, Franklin, C., 1993, 'Linguistics and Archaeology: prehistoric implications of some south Asian plant names' in: *South Asia archaeology studies* (81-85), ed. G. Possehl, New York, International Science; 2005, *Linguistic archaeology of the south Asian subcontinent*, London, Routledge-Curzon, Taylor and Francis Group

Southworth, F., 2005, Linguistic archaeology of South Asia, London, Routledge-Curzon.

Spycket, A. 1976--1980. Kamm B. Archaologisch, Reallexikon der Assyriologie 5: 332--5.

Stech, T. and Pigott, V.C.,1986, The Metals Trade in Southwest Asia in the Third Millennium B. C., *Iraq,* 48: 39-64.

Stein, M.A. 1937. Archaeological reconnaissances in north-western India and south-eastern Iran. London: Macmillan.

Tallon F. (1995) *Les Pierres Précieuses de l'Orient Ancien des Sumériens aux Sassanides.* Paris.

Thieme, P., *Mitra and Aryaman*, New Haven, Conn., 1957.

Thapar, B.K. 1979. Kalibangan: a Harappan metropolis beyond the Indus Valley, in Possehl (ed.): 196--202.

Thompson, Thomas J., 2006, An ancient stateless civilization: bronze age India and the state in history, *Independent Review*

Tol.Col. *Tolkaappiyam Collakaraati*, a Tamil work of grammar of ca 3rd century BCE to 10th cent. CE Full text on web address: http://www.tamil.net/projectmadurai/pub/pm0100/tolkap.pdf

Tosi, M. 1982. A possible Harappan Seaport in Eastern Arabia: Ra's Al Junayz in the Sultanate of Oman, paper read at the 1st International Conference on Pakistan Archaeology, Peshawar.

Tosi M. (1991) "The Indus Civilization beyond the Indian Subcontinent." In M. Jansen,M. Mulloy & G. Urban (eds.) *Forgotten cities on the Indus*. Mainz, 111-128.

Vats, M.S. 1940. Excavations at Harappa, Calcutta.

Vidale M. (2000) *The Archaeology of Indus Crafts. Indus craftspeople and why we study them*. IsIAO Reports and Memoirs, IV, Series Minor, Rome.

Vidale M. (2002) "Aspects of the Indian bead trade in the Bronze Age." Paper presented at the International Congress "Early navigation and Trade in the Indian Ocean," Ravenna, 5 June 2002.

Vidale M. "The Short-Horned Bull on the Indus Seals: a Symbol of the Families in the Western Trade?" Forthcoming in *South Asian Archaeology 2002*, Bonn.

Vidale M. & P. Bianchetti (1997) "Mineralogical Identification of Green Semiprecious Stones from Pakistan." In R. Allchin & B. Allchin (eds.) *South Asian Archaeology, 1995*. New Delhi, Vol. 2, 947-953.

Vidale M. & P. Bianchetti (1998-1999) "Identification of grossular (garnet) as a possible item of long-distance trade from the Indus Valley to Mesopotamia in the Third millennium BC." *Ancient Sindh*, 5, 39-43.

Walser, G., *Die Völkerschaften auf den Reliefs von Persepolis*, Berlin, 1966.

Web resource:

ancientroute.com http://www.ancientroute.com/resource/metal/tin.htm

Wikipedia http://en.wikipedia.org/wiki/Rebus

Weisgerber, G., 1980, '...und Kupfer in Oman', *Der Anschnitt*, vol. 32, 1980, 62-110

Weisgerber, G., 1981, *Makkan and Meluhha- 3rd millennium copper production in Oman and evidence of contact with the Indus valley*, Paper read in Cambridge 1981 and to appear in South Asia Archaeology 1981

Weisgerber, G., 1986, Dilmun--a trading entrepot; evidence from historical and archaeological sources, 135-142 in: Shaikha Haya Ali Al Khalifa and Michael Rice (eds.) *Bahrain through the ages: the archaeology*, London, KPI.

Wells, Bryan, "An introduction to Indus writing /–by Bryan Wells." (Ann Arbor, Mich. :UMI,, 2001), ScientificCommons.

Wheeler, REM. 1965. The Indus Civilization, Cambridge Univ. Press, Cambridge.

Wilhelm, Geiger, 1956, Jataka, XIV, 486; XVII, 524; Pali Literature and Language, tr. BK Ghosh, Calcutta.

Winkelmann S. (1999) "Ein Stempelsiegel mit alt-elamischer Strichschsrift." *Archäologischen Mitteilungen aus Iran und Turan*, 31, pp. 23-32.

Yule, P. 1981. Zu den Beziehungen zwischen Mesopotamien und dem Indusgebiet im 3. und beginnenden 2. Jahrtausend.

Zarins J. (2002) "Magan Ship Builders at the Ur-III Lagash Dockyards." Paper presented at the International Congress "Early Navigation and Trade in the Indian Ocean," Ravenna, 5 June 2002.

Zarins Y. (2003) "Magan Shipbuilders at the Ur III Lagash State Dockyards (2062-2025 BC)." In E. Olijdam & R.H. Spoor (eds.) *Intercultural Relations Between South and Southwest Asia. Studies in Commemoration of E.C.L. During Caspers (1934-1996).* Bar International Series, pp. 66-85.

Zohary, M. 1982. Plants of the Bible. London: Cambridge University Press.

Zvelebil, Kamil V., "Decipherments of the Indus Script," in The Aryan Debate *edited by Thomas R. Trautmann* (Oxford University Press, USA), 254 – 271.

A

a tergo 575

agate 76, 186, 196, 388, 425, 452, 456, 497, 556, 633

Akkadian 28, 152, 258, 262, 498, 560

alligator 41, 45, 56, 595, 686

allograph 62, 63, 93, 160, 223, 224, 233, 369, 420, 525, 527, 660

alloy 16, 19, 25, 33, 34, 36, 37, 40, 42, 43, 45, 46, 49, 53, 57, 63, 68, 69, 72, 73, 75, 79, 86, 87, 88, 94, 95, 105, 112, 115, 117, 119, 120, 123, 124, 125, 127, 128, 137, 142, 149, 158, 159, 160, 164, 168, 169, 187, 196, 197, 217, 218, 221, 223, 231, 232, 259, 333, 390, 391, 416, 435, 449, 466, 479, 480, 506, 520, 523, 524, 527, 530, 557, 558, 561, 572, 576, 581, 584, 585, 587, 598, 599, 600, 601, 675, 694, 707, 725

alloying 11, 60, 75, 137, 167, 169, 196, 198, 219, 223, 226, 308, 419, 420, 475, 479, 528, 531, 537

amśu 122, 125, 288, 348, 349, 660

ancu 53, 238, 348

angle 236, 585

antelope 28, 29, 31, 34, 35, 38, 40, 44, 45, 50, 57, 63, 96, 104, 106, 114, 123, 125, 130, 131, 144, 145, 148, 151, 152, 153, 158, 159, 162, 164, 220, 221, 223, 224, 262, 267, 275, 287, 302, 304, 344, 361, 389, 405, 418, 419, 420, 421, 422, 423, 424, 431, 470, 476, 513, 523, 524, 536, 554, 559, 569, 572, 574, 575, 576, 601, 602, 603, 604, 608, 610, 614, 619, 633, 642, 689

Anzu 211, 238, 239, 240

Arabia 171

archer 18, 127, 132, 136, 156, 157, 691

arrow 44, 45, 46, 111, 132, 200, 239, 256, 292, 369, 394, 425, 525, 526, 530, 584, 623, 644, 660, 661, 690, 691, 699

artifact 34, 49, 284, 528

artisan 42, 45, 52, 53, 56, 58, 59, 70, 71, 73, 76, 79, 80, 82, 86, 97, 99, 100, 103, 105, 106, 110, 112, 117, 118, 122, 123, 124, 128, 146, 147, 148, 154, 155, 159, 160, 163, 165, 176, 185, 234, 236, 237, 255, 264, 266, 305, 308, 424, 480, 507, 562, 563, 575, 595, 600, 626, 677, 695, 700, 723

austro-asiatic 338

awl 224, 475, 658

axe 42, 127, 131, 150, 186, 193, 232, 374, 406, 415, 424, 443, 469, 475, 493, 558, 569, 599, 682, 692, 700, 703, 705, 706, 723

ayas 40, 41, 42, 51, 82, 112, 120, 133, 170, 192, 197, 237, 348, 369, 391, 392, 405, 444, 475, 507, 523, 528, 530, 536, 575, 584, 659, 660, 690

ayo 19, 40, 41, 42, 51, 82, 109, 112, 120, 121, 122, 133, 192, 232, 237, 259, 360, 369, 392, 394, 405, 507, 520, 523, 528, 530, 536, 537, 560, 561, 575, 660, 661, 711

B

backbone 45, 46, 47, 48, 141, 676, 688, 690

Bagchi 357

Bahrain 771

bandicoot 293, 705

bangle 127, 173, 307, 410, 414, 416, 480, 682

bath 59, 685, 686

BB Lal 439

bead 154, 263, 599

beads 47, 76, 80, 105, 128, 141, 153, 154, 169, 173, 179, 195, 207, 219, 255, 256, 263, 307, 353, 354, 393, 402, 425, 456, 459, 469, 495, 500, 501, 503, 599, 628, 633, 643, 694, 752

bell-metal 50, 54, 72, 171, 219, 560, 562, 684, 703

bird41, 42, 45, 210, 211, 228, 239, 240, 258, 292, 327, 444, 454, 455, 512, 520, 539, 554, 560, 565, 568, 572, 581, 598, 600, 602, 604, 605, 608, 609, 615, 632, 649, 683, 687, 700, 727

Bisht 400

bison 108, 110, 119, 184, 259, 524, 530, 564, 570, 572, 635, 641, 664, 674, 698

blacksmith27, 34, 36, 40, 41, 43, 45, 52, 53, 56, 57, 58, 59, 66, 67, 70, 72, 75, 79, 95, 100, 104, 110, 111, 112, 113, 118, 126, 129, 148, 152, 153, 158, 159, 161, 186, 188, 191, 192, 221, 223, 224, 233, 234, 260, 263, 265, 286, 310, 369, 370, 395, 477, 478, 499, 507, 528, 530, 531, 532, 536, 558, 561, 564, 572, 575, 576, 586, 595, 598, 600, 660, 662, 664, 674, 685, 686, 687, 694, 707, 709, 710, 723

boar 115, 118, 119, 154, 263, 504, 555, 576, 590, 705, 714

boat 23, 41, 42, 43, 72, 95, 157, 194, 210, 211, 237, 240, 314, 367, 379, 428, 456, 459, 474, 495, 496, 520, 566, 604, 631, 649, 653, 664, 712

body 31, 51, 54, 57, 69, 70, 71, 79, 80, 82, 102, 109, 111, 117, 120, 121, 122, 124, 146, 150, 152, 153, 158, 159, 165, 191, 197, 258, 260, 261, 262, 283, 292, 293, 312, 350, 376, 401, 433, 446, 459, 506, 521, 531, 536, 539, 556, 572, 573, 575, 589, 604, 605, 615, 616, 626, 637, 658, 665, 671, 672, 688, 699, 700, 710, 720, 727

bos gaurus 119, 524, 664

bos indicus 161

bovine 146, 228, 229, 230, 231, 574, 614

bow 165, 672

bracelet 219, 584

branch 20

brass 31, 36, 46, 48, 51, 55, 57, 72, 75, 87, 89, 90, 97, 98, 100, 103, 104, 115, 116, 118, 121, 122, 126, 137, 142, 144, 145, 159, 165, 171, 191, 192, 198, 220, 221, 223, 224, 233, 236, 237, 257, 259, 260, 261, 265, 266, 308, 333, 402, 420, 425, 438, 463, 478,개506, 527, 531, 532, 560, 562, 564, 565, 585, 587, 589, 658, 659, 661, 670, 676, 687, 690, 703, 706, 707, 709, 721, 724, 725, 726, 727

brazier 50, 54, 90, 113, 141, 154, 263, 675, 676, 684, 690, 702

brick 685

bronze 10, 37, 39, 42, 46, 67, 72, 75, 81, 86, 87, 88, 92, 96, 100, 102, 105, 107, 116, 120, 122, 127, 138, 140, 142, 145, 146, 163, 168, 170, 173, 192, 196, 197, 198, 200, 203, 213, 217, 218, 219, 226, 237, 241, 246, 278, 284, 286, 305, 306, 308, 313, 328, 333,개335, 338, 339, 378, 415, 417, 419, 425, 427, 429, 430, 431, 433, 434, 436, 439, 440, 442, 443, 445, 446, 448, 454, 456, 457, 462, 465, 466, 467,

468, 469, 471, 473, 475, 480, 493, 495, 509, 519, 523, 528, 537, 539, 540, 542, 543, 544, 545, 546, 547, 548, 549, 550, 551, 553, 562, 563, 574, 580, 613, 649, 655, 675, 706, 709, 721, 763, 769

buffalo 70, 72, 73, 94, 96, 117, 118, 119, 187, 196, 260, 261, 497, 517, 524, 525, 526, 533, 542, 560, 564, 568, 569, 570, 596, 614, 664, 674, 681, 683

bull 40, 64, 66, 70, 73, 74, 75, 79, 80, 82, 95, 103, 104, 106, 107, 108, 117, 123, 124, 125, 128, 130, 140, 141, 146, 148, 152, 156, 157, 159, 161, 167, 168, 175, 176, 184, 188, 190, 192, 217, 221, 223, 224, 228, 256, 257, 258, 259, 260, 261, 265, 267, 286, 335, 369, 389, 401, 402, 469, 498, 499, 503, 504, 507, 508, 512, 514, 516, 517, 518, 524, 525, 526, 530, 540, 554, 555, 560, 564, 565, 566, 568, 570, 572, 573, 575, 576, 589, 590, 591, 596, 598, 599, 600, 601, 602, 608, 610, 611, 619, 620, 625, 626, 627, 636, 640, 641, 642, 643, 644, 652, 664, 674, 681, 683, 696, 698, 701

bush 148, 292, 671

C

caravan 418

carnelian 39, 78, 128, 179, 194, 196, 206, 207, 215, 238, 256, 314, 354, 381, 382, 388, 414, 425, 432, 433, 437, 449, 451, 452, 454, 456, 457, 466, 478, 479, 486, 497, 500, 503, 519, 633, 643, 752

carpenter 55, 91, 112, 115, 118, 141, 177, 286, 310, 313, 490, 499, 504, 576, 595, 660, 661, 665, 692, 699

cart 707

cast 30, 64, 65, 95, 226, 228, 232, 259, 507, 561, 585, 661, 670

casting 57, 58, 60, 76, 98, 100, 137, 141, 142, 173, 286, 306, 310, 392, 474, 546, 547, 703

chalcedony 206, 306, 401, 404, 555

Chatterjee 357

cipher 10, 76, 170, 181, 242, 291, 297, 332, 361

citadel 96, 97, 164, 229, 398, 400, 551, 552

city 28

cloth 707

comb 46, 62, 148, 556, 557, 558, 564, 665, 674, 722

community 91, 94, 104, 105, 111, 112, 130, 148, 152, 159, 215, 234, 243, 248, 252, 291, 293, 352, 369, 370, 387, 420, 502, 507, 540, 545, 585, 638

composite animal 93, 94, 102, 146, 162, 232, 353, 538, 574, 604

conch 74, 173, 307, 616

copper 11, 16, 18, 19, 20, 24, 26, 28, 29, 33, 35, 36, 37, 41, 42, 47, 50, 54, 55, 58, 60, 63, 66, 67, 72, 73, 74, 75, 76, 86, 87, 93, 94, 97, 98, 100, 103, 104, 110, 111, 112, 113, 115, 120, 121, 122, 126, 127, 128, 129, 131, 133, 135, 136, 137, 142, 143, 144, 145, 146, 147, 148, 150, 156, 157, 158, 159, 164, 165, 168, 189, 192, 196, 197, 198, 202, 203, 206, 215, 218, 219, 220, 223, 224, 226, 231, 233, 234, 235, 236, 237, 238, 240, 241, 246, 253, 255, 256, 259, 260, 262, 266, 269, 284, 297, 308, 310, 312, 313, 333, 335, 345, 361, 377, 379, 381, 382, 385, 386, 393, 405, 406, 414, 415, 416, 417, 418, 419, 421, 422, 424, 425, 426, 427, 429, 430, 432, 433, 434, 436, 437, 438, 439, 440, 441, 443, 444, 445, 448, 449, 451, 452, 454, 456, 457, 459, 463, 464, 465, 466, 467,

468, 469, 470, 471, 473, 474, 475, 478, 479, 480, 486, 495, 498, 500, 511, 516, 519, 529, 531, 532, 534, 535, 537, 547, 559, 564, 571, 572, 576, 577, 581, 584, 585, 587, 598, 599, 600, 601, 603, 609, 617, 630, 631, 632, 644, 647, 648, 649, 652, 655, 663, 670, 672, 684, 685, 694, 703, 706, 707, 709, 721, 724, 726, 770

copper tablet 157

coppersmith 129

copulation 53, 56, 152, 155, 575, 605

crab 53, 98, 120, 121, 135, 156, 157, 392, 611, 620, 705

crocodile 41, 42, 45, 53, 56, 70, 73, 112, 161, 234, 335, 469, 530, 537, 563, 575, 576, 595, 686

crown 587

currycomb 46, 68, 79, 88, 690

curve 118, 192, 612, 706

curved 16, 55, 112, 217, 228, 537, 539, 545, 546, 577, 607, 613, 619, 623, 700, 706, 715

cylinder seal 28

D

dagger 34, 72, 126, 131, 259, 260, 266, 381, 416, 421, 443, 564, 565, 574, 577

dance 67, 117, 279, 280, 293, 665, 697, 713

decipherment 352

decoded 154, 236, 263, 370, 506

deer 83, 114, 145, 158, 169, 302, 304, 359, 419, 576, 698, 714

Dholavira 97, 167

Dilmun 43, 78, 85, 100, 114, 152, 158, 164, 175, 176, 177, 179, 194, 195, 197, 199, 206, 210, 211, 238, 262, 283, 311, 312, 313, 314, 328, 374, 375, 376, 377, 378, 379, 388, 414, 426, 432, 433, 444, 445, 446, 459, 465, 467, 470, 471, 486, 504, 518, 556, 590, 591, 598, 599, 603, 617, 627, 628, 629, 630, 631, 632, 633, 635, 637, 638, 640, 641, 644, 647, 648, 649, 650, 651, 652, 653, 654, 655, 757, 760, 771

dotted circle 146, 150, 151, 153, 154, 158, 160, 256, 262, 264, 524, 529, 556, 557, 558, 634, 637, 663, 694

Dravidian 764

drill 47, 80, 500, 630

drum 68, 87, 115, 142, 181, 291, 498, 527, 550, 663, 667, 669, 671, 699, 702

duck 14, 41, 42, 562, 581, 598, 599, 600, 605, 609, 611, 615, 687

E

eagle 35, 186, 191, 213, 215, 216, 220, 221, 222, 223, 224, 225, 232, 238, 239, 240, 284, 512, 588, 591, 671

Egyptian 227, 229

electrum 169, 226, 349, 430, 614

Emeneau 248, 271, 275, 290, 309, 315, 332, 357, 722, 755, 756

epigraph 584

eraka 16, 18, 19, 26, 97, 98, 100, 111, 115, 133, 135, 136, 143, 144, 150, 158, 165, 220, 224, 232, 234, 235, 260, 529, 531, 564, 585, 598, 601, 670, 671, 672, 694

F

Fabri 357

Failaka 158, 175, 176, 194, 195, 199, 379, 500, 503, 556, 590, 591, 599, 610, 613, 614, 624, 627, 634, 640, 641, 644, 645, 760

ficus glomerata 129, 130, 571

ficus religiosa 100, 126, 129, 131, 193, 233, 255, 531, 584

fish 19, 35, 36, 38, 40, 41, 42, 50, 51, 82, 109, 112, 120, 121, 122, 133, 146, 147, 152, 187, 192, 218, 224, 232, 237, 256, 258, 259, 262, 283, 292, 330, 335, 369, 392, 393, 394, 398, 405, 432, 459, 505, 506, 507, 513, 514, 518, 523, 528, 530, 535, 536, 537, 554, 560, 561, 570, 575, 576, 584, 602, 608, 620, 621, 622, 631, 641, 644, 651, 659, 660, 661, 674

flag 17, 18, 52, 95, 237, 561, 600, 717

flow 399, 400, 409, 440, 504, 523, 536, 542, 570, 693

forge 17, 19, 24, 27, 43, 47, 55, 57, 63, 81, 86, 87, 88, 89, 90, 92, 97, 98, 105, 111, 114, 115, 117, 121, 122, 126, 130, 133, 134, 135, 136, 140, 145, 153, 154, 158, 159, 164, 185, 187, 188, 192, 216, 232, 237, 260, 262, 263, 390, 391, 392, 402, 406, 528, 531, 564, 583, 586, 599, 634, 661, 662, 664, 674, 702, 707, 717, 727

fox 33, 312, 581, 694, 709

frog 267, 582, 586, 711, 726

furnace 27, 28, 36, 42, 43, 45, 47, 52, 53, 55, 56, 57, 58, 59, 65, 66, 73, 81, 88, 90, 93, 95, 97, 98, 99, 109, 110, 111, 113, 116, 117, 118, 119, 120, 121, 122, 123, 124, 125, 127, 129, 130, 131, 132, 134, 135, 136, 140, 142, 145, 152, 153, 154, 158, 159, 160, 161, 165, 171, 188, 191, 197, 217, 218, 219, 220, 221

G

Gadd 108, 128, 141, 150, 151, 164, 171, 183, 195, 211, 256, 383, 636, 638, 641, 642, 643, 644, 646, 757

gateway 97

gloss 23, 309, 348

glosses 661

glyph 125, 153, 225, 231, 262, 263, 353, 370, 537

glyptic 506

goat 14, 16, 17, 28, 29, 31, 33, 35, 38, 44, 63, 75, 104, 116, 151, 159, 187, 190, 221, 255, 262, 327, 507, 536, 568, 570, 571, 572, 574, 575, 576, 577, 600, 603, 630, 642, 673, 681, 699, 714

goats 571

godess 587

gold 20, 36, 37, 39, 42, 56, 68, 78, 91, 94, 107, 116, 118, 128, 136, 137, 152, 164, 165, 168, 169, 179, 196, 206, 207, 211, 226, 236, 237, 238, 256, 258, 283, 312, 345, 348, 353, 354, 380, 381, 382, 388, 393, 395, 405, 414, 415, 416, 425, 427, 429, 430, 432, 434, 436, 444, 445, 453, 454, 459, 465, 467, 472, 473, 474, 477, 504, 519, 561, 585, 598, 605, 614, 632, 643, 647, 648, 649, 651, 652, 655, 659, 675, 688, 696, 702, 707, 711, 719, 720, 724

goldsmith 670

granary 685

guild 45, 47, 52, 80, 82, 91, 93, 94, 95, 98, 100, 103, 104, 105, 109, 111, 121, 129, 130, 133, 143, 148, 152, 159, 160, 163, 164, 216, 234, 236, 291, 335, 369, 370, 392, 402, 406, 420, 506, 507, 530, 536,

538, 540, 542, 545, 546, 583, 585, 621, 721

H

Haifa 100, 145, 196, 198, 209, 297, 415, 417, 418, 420, 424, 426, 430, 445, 464
hair-knot 165
hare 292, 554, 602
harrow 82, 392, 404, 529, 665, 674, 676, 698
haystack 116, 698
headdress 587
heifer 125
hieroglyph 33, 370
hieroglyphic 229, 230
hieroglyphs 153, 229, 263
hill 457, 477, 525, 572, 697, 716
hood 31, 149, 214, 222, 231, 581, 588, 600
horn 18, 40, 55, 72, 106, 124, 146, 153, 184, 255, 262, 292, 302, 359, 389, 390, 545, 546, 599, 602, 621, 677, 703, 715, 722
horns 228, 537

I

ibex 41, 126, 145, 255, 566, 714
implements 25, 27, 31, 55, 87, 188, 391, 430, 436, 443, 555, 577, 579, 580, 586, 602, 615, 707
incised 418
ingot 3, 18, 19, 20, 26, 43, 45, 47, 57, 62, 63, 67, 86, 95, 98, 115, 118, 119, 123, 124, 126, 127, 128, 135, 139, 145, 151, 153, 154, 155, 158, 159, 164, 185, 203, 219, 223, 224, 256, 262, 264, 267, 287, 297, 361, 386, 390, 417, 418, 420, 421, 449, 506, 557, 559, 572, 584, 585, 587, 600, 603, 604, 606, 610, 616, 622, 623, 627, 660, 694
inscription 157, 353, 421, 529, 531
iron 16, 17, 19, 25, 27, 28, 29, 31, 33, 36, 40, 41, 42, 43, 45, 46, 49, 50, 52, 53, 55, 56, 57, 58, 59, 63, 64, 65, 66, 67, 68, 69, 72, 73, 76, 79, 81, 82, 86, 87, 88, 89, 90, 93, 98, 103, 104, 106, 108, 109, 111, 112, 114, 115, 116, 117, 118, 119, 120, 122, 124, 125, 126, 129, 131, 132, 133, 141, 143, 145, 146, 147, 149, 150, 151, 152, 153, 154, 157, 158, 159, 160, 161, 165, 168, 169, 188, 191, 192, 197, 200, 203, 214, 217, 218, 219, 221, 222, 223, 228, 231, 233, 234, 235, 237, 255, 256, 257, 258, 260, 263, 266, 267, 278, 284, 286, 288, 291, 293, 297, 333, 335, 348, 349, 360, 361, 369, 370, 390, 391, 392, 394, 395, 405, 416, 441, 447, 459, 464, 476, 481, 484, 506, 507, 508, 509, 523, 524, 526, 527, 528, 530, 532, 534, 536, 545, 546, 557, 561, 564, 571, 575, 576, 577, 581, 582, 584, 586, 589, 595, 598, 600, 601, 626, 645, 659, 660, 661, 662, 663, 665, 669, 670, 674, 682, 685, 686, 694, 697, 707, 709, 713, 716, 718, 721, 723, 726, 727
iron ore 49, 52, 53, 59, 65, 66, 278, 370, 464, 507, 508, 685, 686

J

jackal 33, 57, 72, 233, 292, 507, 704, 707, 709
jar 26, 27, 32, 66, 85, 86, 92, 110, 120, 122, 123, 124, 125, 126, 130, 134, 139, 144, 146, 161, 170, 171, 208, 209, 236, 256, 259, 305, 392, 401, 404, 429, 468, 472, 476, 521, 524, 528, 546, 561, 567, 569,

604, 606, 611, 616, 617, 618, 619, 621, 627, 644, 653, 658, 663, 672, 673, 675, 676, 685, 694, 701

jasmine 20, 700

Jhukar 122, 123

K

Kalyanaraman 1, 251, 759

kamaḍha 18, 73, 100, 118, 129, 143, 584, 595, 677

Kashmir 167

Kenoyer 71, 94, 130, 306, 307, 346, 353, 354, 357, 500, 559, 753, 760, 765, 766

kũdār 585

Kuiper 193, 249, 270, 309, 316, 332, 349, 357, 760

kundau 585

L

ladder 103, 605, 674, 699

language 167, 170, 243, 707

languages 424

lapis lazuli 107, 207, 215, 238, 283, 312, 381, 382, 425, 430, 432, 436, 437, 449, 451, 452, 453, 455, 457, 465, 466, 467, 476, 478, 479, 499, 502, 504, 511, 520, 632, 647, 648, 649, 652, 655

lathe 13, 16, 19, 20, 30, 42, 45, 46, 47, 65, 68, 69, 71, 73, 79, 80, 82, 87, 88, 93, 95, 97, 98, 104, 106, 112, 115, 116, 118, 124, 126, 128, 129, 130, 131, 132, 134, 136, 143, 144, 167, 184, 190, 191, 192, 213, 214, 221, 236, 237, 256, 261, 267, 284, 392, 394, 402, 405, 530, 557, 565, 572, 573, 574, 581, 583, 585, 683, 695, 696, 701, 703, 721

lead 707

leafless tree 72, 147, 234, 235

Levi 357

ligature 70, 71, 74, 100, 115, 120, 157, 224, 232, 259, 392, 477, 561

ligatured 153, 154, 157, 263

lion 126, 152, 220, 221, 222, 223, 224, 225, 239, 240, 259, 260, 261, 265, 266, 312, 406, 505, 512, 518, 520, 554, 555, 560, 564, 565, 566, 567, 568, 569, 570, 587, 588, 613, 618, 632, 650, 673, 708

lizard 707

M

Mackay 94, 122, 123, 150, 155, 157, 164, 168, 207, 265, 333, 403, 500, 508, 626, 761

Magan 78, 85, 100, 114, 164, 175, 176, 177, 178, 179, 194, 197, 199, 210, 211, 237, 238, 269, 282, 283, 313, 314, 324, 327, 328, 373, 377, 378, 380, 381, 382, 383, 388, 426, 432, 433, 436, 444, 445, 446, 453, 456, 470, 471, 518, 519, 522, 598, 631, 632, 641, 644, 647, 648, 649, 651, 655, 757, 769, 771

Mahadevan 421, 423

makara 468

markhor 40, 130, 153, 255, 263, 537, 600

Marshall 258, 333, 548, 550, 561, 762

Masica 251, 309, 315, 316, 331, 332, 341, 357, 762

mason 75, 103, 105, 141, 177, 218, 219, 255, 260, 313, 526, 564, 584, 595, 674, 723

Meluhha 1, 3, 10, 23, 24, 26, 27, 28, 29, 30, 31, 32, 33, 34, 40, 42, 49, 50, 60, 62, 67,

69, 71, 74, 76, 78, 85, 86, 89, 98, 100, 114, 121, 136, 137, 139, 140, 162, 171, 172, 175, 177, 178, 179, 183, 193, 194, 195, 197, 199, 202, 204, 206, 207, 210, 211, 212, 217, 237, 245, 251, 252, 253, 269, 280, 282, 283, 284, 288, 294, 295, 299, 310, 313, 324, 325, 327, 328, 329, 332, 339, 353, 368, 372, 373, 375, 378, 379, 380, 381, 382, 383, 386, 388, 389, 402, 406, 410, 413, 414, 415, 418, 420, 432, 433, 435, 436, 437, 443, 444, 445, 451, 452, 453, 454, 455, 456, 457, 459, 464, 466, 467, 475, 476, 478, 479, 485, 486, 487, 489, 497, 502, 504, 511, 518, 519, 522, 532, 534, 540, 545, 558, 576, 577, 580, 581, 586, 598, 599, 614, 631, 632, 633, 637, 647, 658, 760, 764, 766, 769, 770

merchant 25, 27, 28, 29, 33, 41, 42, 57, 63, 66, 72, 75, 89, 91, 93, 104, 110, 111, 114, 117, 119, 123, 125, 126, 127, 131, 144, 147, 148, 151, 158, 159, 165, 172, 177, 183, 215, 223, 224, 255, 260, 266, 268, 275, 286, 287, 299, 310, 313, 332, 342, 360, 361, 394, 420, 427, 429, 431, 433, 460, 471, 472, 500, 531, 534, 538, 562, 595, 600, 614, 637, 715

Mesopotamia 28

metal 18, 20, 30, 46, 64, 65, 95, 117, 129, 143, 144, 152, 171, 221, 225, 228, 231, 259, 262, 369, 370, 561, 584, 585, 586, 660, 661, 670, 707, 770

metals 141, 170, 685, 686, 707

metalsmith 25, 26, 42, 70, 87, 112, 129, 226, 406, 431, 507, 584, 723

miner110, 111, 134, 135, 170, 392, 404, 405

mineral 17, 43, 57, 58, 64, 65, 66, 76, 81, 105, 106, 113, 116, 118, 120, 135, 144, 146, 148, 164, 198, 223, 228, 257, 338, 386, 391, 392, 416, 419, 420, 424, 425, 431, 442, 444, 457, 465, 466, 467, 468, 475, 477, 478, 481, 483, 506, 509, 528, 537, 538, 577, 586,개665, 724

mint 170

mleccha 3, 10, 28, 35, 60, 67, 71, 77, 85, 104, 111, 139, 159, 163, 164, 167, 168, 170, 176, 181, 183, 184, 193, 195, 202, 204, 217, 242, 243, 246, 251, 252, 253, 277, 278, 288, 290, 293, 294, 295, 296, 297, 299, 300, 303, 309, 314, 322, 323, 324, 336, 337, 338, 340, 341, 342, 344, 348, 349, 352, 355, 357, 358, 359, 360, 361, 362, 366, 367, 368, 369, 370, 371, 383, 385, 386, 387, 389, 405, 406, 407, 408, 409, 410, 411, 413, 414, 419, 431, 445, 538, 545, 576, 714

Mleccha 243, 764

Mohenjodaro 421

monkey 255, 266, 285, 363, 364, 432, 455, 600, 602, 616, 617, 625, 627, 634

mould 141, 670

mountain 38, 145, 214, 240, 254, 372, 425, 427, 429, 438, 440, 449, 462, 472, 473, 477, 478, 520, 556, 557, 567, 570, 571, 572, 652, 655, 658, 691, 697, 716

Muhly75, 226, 333, 418, 426, 430, 431, 434, 443, 444, 457, 464, 465, 466, 470, 474, 631, 761, 763

Munda 20, 29, 31, 33, 40, 41, 43, 51, 52, 55, 56, 59, 67, 77, 85, 88, 89, 98, 126, 128, 148, 150, 151, 153, 154, 165, 167, 190, 192, 197, 198, 200, 202, 213, 218, 224, 248, 259, 264, 267, 269, 270, 272, 273, 278, 284, 289, 290, 291, 295, 303, 308, 315, 320, 322, 331, 345, 346, 349, 351, 357, 361, 425, 476, 509, 516, 523, 524, 540, 561, 588, 659, 661, 693, 697, 704, 713, 722, 760

Mundari 59, 423, 685, 686, 708

N

Narmer 225, 226, 227, 228, 229, 230

native metal 59, 81, 82, 99, 103, 104, 133, 161, 221, 265, 360, 391, 392, 404, 529, 558, 576, 659

neck 19, 29, 54, 130, 151, 157, 184, 293, 521, 570, 605, 606, 607, 608, 611, 612, 615, 616, 617, 618, 619, 620, 621, 625, 634, 642, 682, 691, 693, 695, 706

numeral 51, 57, 89, 98, 99, 103, 121, 159, 160, 165, 191, 256, 257, 260, 261, 299, 419, 506, 531, 553, 589, 658

O

offering 165, 687, 720

ore 17, 31, 40, 41, 43, 49, 50, 51, 52, 53, 55, 56, 57, 58, 59, 64, 65, 66, 73, 97, 98, 99, 109, 115, 117, 118, 120, 121, 122, 124, 125, 126, 133, 134, 135, 137, 147, 148, 153, 154, 158, 161, 165, 168, 219, 221, 223, 236, 237, 256, 257, 263, 266, 284, 335, 360, 370, 390, 391, 392, 405, 415, 416, 418, 439, 440, 443, 456, 457, 463, 478, 480, 482, 483, 507, 508, 517, 525, 526, 537, 548, 576, 581, 583, 584, 588, 601, 659, 660, 663, 685, 686, 690, 710

organization 171

oval 43, 44, 47, 122, 123, 150, 151, 164, 169, 256, 604

overthrow 526

P

Pāṇini 369

panning 429, 472, 476, 480, 483

Parpola 423, 764

pectoral 164, 516

penance 73, 118, 143, 173, 494, 595, 677

Persian Gulf 35, 60, 100, 140, 158, 163, 199, 204, 207, 215, 267, 294, 314, 332, 377, 380, 381, 388, 425, 436, 444, 451, 466, 467, 471, 487, 558, 645, 753

pewter 46, 117, 119, 142, 149, 308, 333, 448, 524, 529, 530, 558, 675, 676, 690

phonetic 34, 228, 229

plant 148

platform 47, 69, 80, 90, 92, 94, 113, 116, 254, 304, 404, 552, 574, 575, 604, 712, 723

portable furnace 154, 263, 584

Possehl 194, 310, 333, 354, 754, 766, 768, 769, 784

pottery 171

Prakrit 16, 42, 45, 70, 72, 100, 118, 129, 156, 183, 242, 277, 281, 282, 287, 296, 297, 321, 337, 340, 342, 343, 349, 358, 362, 366, 368, 529, 531, 557, 595, 601, 687, 709

present 49, 54, 83, 167, 169, 176, 182, 204, 205, 279, 304, 309, 311, 312, 316, 317, 318, 321, 346, 425, 428, 429, 430, 440, 457, 462, 466, 472, 474, 475, 481, 485, 489, 532, 553, 687

Przyludski 357

Przyluski 269, 289, 290, 291, 332, 693

punch-marked 77, 86, 173, 241, 246, 297, 304, 306, 335, 352, 468

R

ram 28, 29, 33, 40, 41, 50, 55, 62, 63, 104, 116, 123, 125, 126, 127, 145, 148, 153, 158, 159, 162, 190, 220, 221, 225, 231,

240, 255, 260, 262, 263, 266, 267, 287, 293, 361, 420, 524, 537, 546, 570, 577, 581, 587, 600, 613, 614, 681, 684, 705, 715
rebus 28, 40, 52, 53, 64, 65, 95, 113, 121, 122, 124, 125, 145, 153, 167, 170, 221, 228, 255, 263, 291, 369, 418, 423, 424, 507, 529, 584, 586, 598, 600, 660, 661
rhinoceros 94, 96, 104, 115, 117, 119, 161, 187, 285, 442, 469, 530, 576, 595, 673
rice 670, 672
Rigveda 238, 242, 243, 318, 375, 475, 489, 490, 493, 495, 614, 767, 768
rim of jar 43, 52, 110, 111, 112, 120, 122, 123, 124, 125, 130, 134, 135, 145, 192, 236, 335, 404, 405, 528
rimless pot 81, 92, 93, 157, 161
road 125, 372, 420, 424, 425, 431, 464, 517, 665, 710

S

Sanskrit 243, 764
Santali 171, 507, 508, 670, 685, 686, 707
Sarasvati 1, 2, 24, 91, 97, 100, 141, 163, 167, 168, 172, 183, 193, 194, 223, 246, 269, 278, 289, 294, 295, 300, 304, 305, 306, 315, 322, 331, 333, 336, 338, 345, 357, 366, 375, 388, 389, 400, 407, 412, 413, 414, 415, 421, 431, 458, 465, 467, 468, 489, 495, 513, 528, 529, 554, 555, 560, 602, 630, 631, 759
Sasson 474, 767
scarf 16, 17, 63, 64, 65, 75, 76, 106, 130, 144, 228, 537, 538
scribe 43, 46, 52, 85, 86, 110, 111, 112, 120, 122, 123, 124, 125, 126, 127, 130, 134, 135, 144, 145, 153, 161, 171, 237, 259, 262, 335, 391, 392, 395, 404, 405, 518, 528, 531, 532, 538, 561
sememe 342, 492, 586
serpent 31, 240, 512, 610, 658, 689, 705
shaggy 708
shawl 305
sheep 113
ship 752
silver 16, 33, 36, 37, 42, 45, 46, 68, 69, 74, 79, 87, 88, 112, 113, 125, 169, 189, 196, 211, 226, 236, 238, 283, 353, 379, 381, 382, 388, 405, 414, 415, 425, 427, 432, 433, 444, 446, 447, 450, 453, 454, 460, 473, 474, 497, 511, 519, 528, 561, 581, 584, 598, 599, 600, 601, 632, 647, 648, 649, 651, 652, 655, 694, 707, 719, 724
slope 585
sloping 585
smelt 686
smelter 51, 52, 53, 55, 56, 57, 72, 88, 97, 98, 100, 109, 110, 111, 118, 120, 125, 129, 140, 142, 159, 165, 217, 218, 219, 237, 291, 292, 405, 424, 458, 493, 506, 565, 566, 567, 600, 684, 703, 710
smelting 153, 263, 370, 586, 686
smith 117, 120, 123, 236, 255, 266, 419, 507, 600, 626, 660, 695, 724
smithy 11, 17, 19, 27, 36, 43, 45, 47, 52, 53, 55, 63, 66, 81, 86, 87, 88, 89, 90, 92, 95, 97, 98, 101, 103, 105, 113, 115, 117, 121, 122, 126, 127, 128, 130, 133, 134, 135, 136, 145, 148, 153, 154, 155, 158, 159, 160, 164, 167, 170, 186, 187, 188, 190, 191, 192, 216, 220, 223, 224, 233, 237, 238, 254, 259, 262, 263, 264, 284, 335, 370, 389, 390, 391, 392, 395, 402, 404, 405, 406, 431, 506, 507, 526, 529, 531,

541, 545, 546, 559, 561, 575, 576, 580, 584, 586, 598, 599, 634, 661, 662, 664, 707, 710, 717, 719
Southworth 181, 193, 309, 322, 332, 336, 346, 349, 351, 355, 356, 357, 358, 769
spinner 505, 674
spokes 72, 97, 98, 115, 247, 528, 585, 658
spotted 32, 152, 262
sprachbund 11, 77, 85, 139, 140, 167, 198, 199, 200, 202, 217, 218, 241, 244, 246, 251, 290, 308, 315, 333, 335, 337, 352, 420
spy 234, 235, 672
stalk 64, 65, 156, 159, 190, 191, 348, 477, 526, 536, 538, 572, 617, 681, 691, 692, 708
standard device 157
star 263, 695
steel 145
stone 40, 165, 232, 585, 660
stool 14, 87, 116, 125, 187, 193, 217, 505, 506, 600, 601, 609, 680
stump 13, 36, 291, 540, 545, 572, 682, 685, 692, 698, 699
Sumer 10, 26, 61, 64, 77, 79, 82, 83, 85, 100, 114, 140, 168, 177, 191, 197, 199, 204, 206, 214, 225, 237, 240, 280, 283, 311, 312, 313, 325, 329, 330, 334, 377, 380, 414, 430, 465, 467, 470, 479, 487, 495, 498, 499, 504, 534, 537, 548, 562, 563, 577, 602, 630,개650, 760, 766
Sumerian 11, 23, 26, 29, 33, 35, 57, 61, 77, 78, 103, 114, 173, 177, 183, 186, 187, 190, 194, 195, 196, 203, 206, 208, 211, 221, 222, 223, 225, 226, 231, 238, 239, 240, 252, 261, 265, 266, 272, 280, 283, 309, 310, 311, 312, 313, 314, 324, 326, 329, 331, 377, 378, 380, 381, 383, 388, 414, 418, 433, 444, 446, 447, 448, 450, 453, 456, 460, 469, 470, 496, 497, 498, 499, 501, 502, 516, 522, 562, 563, 571, 579, 586, 615, 629, 631, 642, 647, 648, 755, 756, 761, 764, 768
summit 304, 477, 549, 572
Susa 13, 35, 36, 38, 39, 40, 43, 44, 53, 63, 139, 151, 176, 203, 217, 220, 221, 265, 268, 377, 386, 417, 427, 433, 450, 472, 475, 496, 501, 503, 505, 512, 513, 514, 521, 525, 535, 536, 537, 539, 540, 541, 543, 545, 546, 547, 548, 553, 562, 563, 587, 588, 593, 594, 596, 597, 603, 616, 630, 634, 645, 646, 649
svastika50, 51, 57, 146, 333, 334, 335, 468, 527, 528, 529, 531
symbols 418, 422

T

tabernae Montana 148, 151, 267
tablet 39, 43, 45, 47, 52, 53, 56, 57, 71, 76, 77, 78, 92, 110, 112, 131, 143, 144, 156, 157, 176, 231, 233, 240, 280, 379, 389, 390, 391, 414, 418, 419, 421, 422, 433, 449, 470, 486, 497, 527, 529, 530, 531, 553, 554, 570, 572, 575, 587, 590, 591, 595, 626, 631, 644, 645, 646, 684
tail 36, 41, 44, 50, 54, 73, 96, 125, 128, 129, 130, 131, 144, 145, 151, 154, 159, 187, 220, 232, 263, 419, 424, 514, 567, 580, 588, 604, 607, 612, 630, 644, 684, 695
Telugu 63, 707
temple 27, 28, 36, 52, 54, 59, 61, 65, 66, 67, 86, 95, 108, 125, 137, 179, 185, 187, 188, 194, 222, 226, 230, 237, 256, 326, 329, 330, 331, 373, 377, 378, 379, 402, 425, 434, 439, 459, 468, 497, 498, 499, 502, 508, 511, 513, 514, 516, 518, 519, 541,

542, 546, 581, 584, 586, 587, 598, 615, 625, 648, 649, 656, 701, 702, 704
Tepe Yahya 89, 156, 158, 174, 186, 211, 212, 215, 217, 220, 232, 254, 268, 416, 425, 443, 469, 476, 478, 479, 588
terracotta 58, 176, 232, 255, 303, 304, 389, 403, 456, 595
Tewari 357
throat 695
tiger 27, 33, 53, 57, 58, 62, 63, 72, 92, 96, 104, 106, 117, 118, 119, 159, 161, 213, 217, 223, 224, 225, 226, 231, 232, 234, 235, 257, 267, 284, 285, 286, 292, 507, 512, 527, 530, 554, 555, 574, 576, 602, 614, 626, 647, 688, 694, 704, 707
tin 11, 28, 36, 37, 50, 52, 55, 57, 62, 63, 64, 72, 73, 75, 76, 87, 93, 106, 116, 117, 119, 120, 122, 123, 124, 131, 133, 137, 142, 145, 148, 149, 150, 153, 159, 164, 165, 169, 192, 196, 198, 200, 207, 218, 220, 221, 226, 232, 236, 255, 260, 262, 266, 287, 297, 308, 333, 361, 391, 392, 405, 415, 416, 417, 418, 419, 420, 421, 423, 424, 425, 426, 427, 428, 429, 430, 431, 434, 436, 437, 438, 439, 440, 441, 442, 443, 444, 445, 446, 447, 448, 449, 450, 451, 452, 454, 456, 457, 464, 465, 466, 467, 470, 471, 472, 473, 474, 475, 478, 479, 480, 483, 484, 511, 519, 524, 529, 531, 536, 537, 557, 558, 565, 576, 577, 585, 587, 600, 614, 649, 652, 655, 702, 706, 707, 754, 763, 770
Tocharian 53, 122, 125, 238, 281, 288, 318, 321, 345, 348, 349
Tolkāppiyam 369
tools 170
trader 116, 119, 123, 223
tree 13, 16, 20, 25, 38, 42, 63, 92, 93, 129, 130, 147, 156, 162, 184, 193, 209, 211, 217, 218, 234, 235, 254, 266, 292, 310, 381, 383, 445, 479, 481, 493, 508, 511, 513, 514, 519, 537, 538, 539, 540, 557, 558, 567, 570, 571, 572, 574, 599, 609, 617, 618, 620,개625, 626, 627, 641, 653, 655, 659, 665, 674, 681, 685, 687, 690, 692, 698, 699, 700, 724
trough 125, 130
turner 16, 19, 20, 26, 40, 45, 46, 65, 66, 67, 68, 69, 70, 71, 72, 73, 75, 79, 80, 86, 87, 88, 93, 100, 104, 105, 106, 112, 115, 116, 117, 118, 119, 128, 129, 130, 136, 143, 144, 146, 147, 148, 170, 184, 213, 221, 234, 235, 236, 237, 261, 360, 394, 395, 402, 529, 531, 560, 562, 573, 574, 585, 595, 683, 690, 693, 695, 696, 701, 723
tusk 153, 154, 263
twig 19, 20, 293, 565, 566, 567, 633, 671

U

United Arab Emirates 754
unsmelted metal 161, 217, 234, 335, 575
Uruk 16, 53, 54, 60, 61, 62, 106, 136, 162, 166, 167, 175, 188, 189, 190, 191, 221, 225, 228, 309, 328, 373, 501, 508, 509, 513, 531, 538, 553, 555, 571, 765

V

vagina 56, 57
Vats 186, 305, 306, 401, 404, 590, 770
Vedic 64, 228, 507
vessel 213, 586

W

warehouse 95, 160, 185, 395, 685, 702

Warka 60, 61, 62, 65, 150, 267, 537, 561, 587
water-carrier 125, 219, 686
weapons 97, 98, 670
wheel 585
Wheeler 761
wing 26, 210, 220, 224, 225, 232, 513, 585, 670, 694
workshop 122, 124, 237, 291, 700, 722

Z

zebu104, 148, 152, 159, 161, 191, 211, 217, 221, 222, 265, 335, 369, 488, 558, 585, 590, 630
zinc 11, 51, 57, 72, 73, 93, 117, 137, 142, 149, 198, 219, 223, 224, 233, 236, 308, 333, 335, 425, 457, 463, 528, 529, 530, 531, 558, 585, 587

---

[1] Woods, Christopher, 2010, Visible language: inventions of writing in the ancient Near East and beyond, OIMP32, Oriental Institute Museum, Chicago http://oi.uchicago.edu/pdf/oimp32.pdf

[2] Bloch, Jules, 1920, *La formation de la Langue Marathe* Tr. The Formation Of The Marathi Language, Bloch, Jules. 2008, Formation of the Marathi Language. (Reprint, Translation from French), New Delhi, Motilal Banarsidass.

[3] http://oi.uchicago.edu/OI/IRAQ/dbfiles/objects/825.htm

[4] http://oi.uchicago.edu/pdf/oip72.pdf

[5] http://tinyurl.com/38at9b

[6] http://www.britishmuseum.org/explore/highlights/highlight_objects/me/s/stela_of_ashurnasirpal_ii.aspx Grayson, AK, *Assyrian royal inscriptions* (Wiesbaden, O. Harrassowitz, 1972); Reade, JE, *Assyrian sculpture-1* (London, The British Museum Press, 1998).

[7] Sproat, Richard,2010, Language, technology and Society, OUP, p. 89.

[8] Collection De Clercq 3rd millennium BCE. Catalogue Méthodique et Raisonné: Antiquités Assyriennes, Cylindres Orientauz, Cachets,Briques, Bronzes, Bas-Reliefs, Etc. Paris: E. Leroux, 1888.

[9] Gregory L. Possehl,Shu-ilishu's cylinder seal, Expedition, Vol. 48, Number 1, pp. 42-3. http://www.penn.museum/documents/publications/expedition/PDFs/48-1/What%20in%20the%20World.pdf

[10] Edzard, AfO 22 (1968), 15 no. 15.33. Oppenheim Anc. Mes. (Chicago 1964) 355, argues that the title eme-bal designated its bearer as one who translated from his native into a foreign language.

[11] www.museum.upenn.edu/expedition, Vol. 48, No. 1, Expedition, pp. 42-43

[12] http://www.scribd.com/doc/156872759/Total-prestation-in-marhashi-ur-relations-DT-Potts-2002-Iranica-Antiqua-Vol-XXXVII

[13] http://www.archive.org/download/mmoires01franuoft/mmoires01franuoft.pdf Jacques de Morgan, Fouilles à Suse en 1897-1898 et 1898-1899, Mission archéologique en Iran, Mémoires I, 1990

[14] http://www.iranchamber.com/history/elamite/elamite.php
[15] Source: Apkalu Angel, Fig. of Apkallu from Nimrud, ancient Mesopotamia (north-west palace, room Z, 875-860 BCE), Waw Allap, ISBN: AS-33 http://www.ashmol.ox.ac.uk/ash/amocats/anet/pdf-files/ANET-26Bronze1MesV.pdf

http://www.gorgiaspress.com/bookshop/pc-339-35-apkalu-angel.aspx
http://www.geocities.com/dominorus/oannes_2.htm

[16] Amiet Pierre, Suse 6000 ans d'histoire, Paris, Éditions de la Réunion des musées nationaux, 1988, pp. 98-99 ; fig. 57.

Benoit A. , "Les Civilisations du Proche-Orient ancien", in Manuels de l'École du Louvre ; Art et archéologie, Paris, École du Louvre, 2003, pp 358-359 ; fig. 180.

Meyers Peter, "The casting process of the statue of queen Napir-Asu in the Louvre", extrait de : Journal of Roman Archaeology, supplementary series, n 39, Portsmouth, 2000, pp.11-18. Author: Herbin Nancie

[17] Izzat Allah Nigahban, 1991, *Excavations at Haft Tepe, Iran*, The University Museum, UPenn, p. 97.

[18] 415 Seal impression HTS 128. Plate 48:III.46, ibid.
[19] http://www.iranicaonline.org/articles/elam-ii Plate V.
[20] http://www.iranicaonline.org/articles/haft-tepe
[21] Potts, DT, 2000.
[22] http://www.adias-uae.com/publications/hellyer92a.pdf
[23] Harriett EW Crawford, 1998, *Dilmun and its Gulf neighbours*, Cambridge University Press, p.16.
[24] cf. JM Kenoyer, 1998, p. 74.
[25] http://www.harappa.com/indus4/e6.html

[26] Source of table: I. Mahadevan http://www.harappa.com/arrow/indus-agricultural-terms.pdf

[27] "The deity appears to be holding a ladle (?) in his right hand. His knees are drawn up and he seems to be squatting on his haunches... The details are clearly visible in the highly enlarged photograph of the seal published in Swami Oamanda Saraswati 1975, *Ancient Seals of Haryana* (in Hindi). Rohtak.Pl. 275." Iravatham Mahadevan 1999. Murukan in the Indus script. Journal of the Institute of Asian Studies Vol. XVI, No.2, 1999, pp.21-39.
[28] Lal, BB, 1960. From Megalithic to the Harappa: Tracing back the graffiti on pottery. *Ancient India*, No.16, pp.4-24.
[29] Sorenson, John L., 2006, Out of the dust: steel in early metallurgy, *Journal of Book of Mormon Studies*, Volume 15, Issue 2, pp. 108-9, 127, Provo, Utah, Maxwell Institute.
http://maxwellinstitute.byu.edu/publications/jbms/?vol=15&num=2&id=423&print
[30] Ernst Herzfeld, Die vorgeschichtlichen Töpfereien von Samarra, Die Ausgrabungen von Samarra 5, Berlin 1930.
[31] After Ernst Herzfeld, Die Ausgrabungen von Samarra V: Die vorgeschichtischenTopfereien, Univ. of Texas Press, pl. 30. Courtesy Dietrich Reimer.
[32] Les Antiquités orientales : guide du visiteur, Paris, Éditions de la Réunion des musées nationaux, 1993, p. 188.

Bréniquet Catherine, "Du Fil à retordre : réflexions sur les idoles aux yeux et les fileuses de l'époque d'Uruk", in Collectanea Orientalia, 1996.
Caubet Annie, "L'Idole aux yeux du IVe millénaire", in La Revue du Louvre, février 1991, Paris, Éditions de la Réunion des musées nationaux, 1991, pp. 6-9.

[33]Legrain,L., 1936, Ur excavations, Vol. 3, Archaic Seal Impressions, Vol. III, Archaic Seal-impressions, Carnegie Foundation of New York. http://amar.hsclib.sunysb.edu/u?/amar,37238.

[34] Ibid.
[35] Rabe, Michael, 1996, Sexual Imagery on the "Phantasmagorical Castles" at Khajuraho, in: *International Journal of Tantric Studies*, Vol. 2 No. 2 (November 1, 1996) http://asiatica.org/ijts/vol2_no2/sexual-imagery-phantasmagorical-castles-khajuraho/

http://www.panoramio.com/photo/72198881

http://worldvisitguide.com/oeuvre/photo_ME0000135227.html

[36] cf. Photo on pg. 61 of M. Roaf's *Cultural Atlans of Mesopotamia and the Ancient Near East*).
[37] http://cdli.ox.ac.uk/wiki/doku.php?id=uruk_mod._warka

[38]

http://tc.templejc.edu/dept/Art/ASmith/ARTS1303/arts1303_2StoneAge2Sumer/Ston2Sumpage022.html
[39] *Man and Environment*, Volume XXXII, No.1, 2007.
[40] 'Snarling iron' is a technical term, a metallurgical tool. In the context of the Bronze Age, this may be called 'Snarling Bronze' used for raising vessels using the tool as an anvil.
[41] Wells, Bryan, 1998, An introduction to Indus Writing, Dept. of Archaeology, University of Calgary, Alberta, Table 3.1 by Sign Number http://www.nlc-bnc.ca/obj/s4/f2/dsk2/ftp03/MQ31309.pdf
[42] Slide 90 Harappa.com.

[43] V.M. Masson and V.I. Sarianidi, 1972, *Central Asia: Turkmenia before the Achaemenids*, New York, Praeger Publishers, p. 125, 129; pl. 46 shows the ligatured three-headed animal seal of silver.

[44] संगतराश संज्ञा पुं० [फ़ा०] पत्थर काटने या गढ़नेवाला मजदूर। पत्थरकट। २. एक औजार जो पत्थर काटने के काम में आता है। (Dasa, Syamasundara. Hindi sabdasagara. Navina samskarana. 2nd ed. Kasi : Nagari Pracarini Sabha, 1965-1975.) पत्थर या लकडी पर नकाशी करनेवाला, संगतराश, 'mason'.
[45] http://bharatkalyan97.blogspot.com/2011/08/decoding-inscription-on-indus-seal-of.html
[46] Kalyanarman, S. 1998. *Indian Lexicon – A comparative etymological dictionary of South-Asian Languages*. Manila.
https://docs.google.com/file/d/0B4BAzCi4O_l4ZXJfN0hMamowSGs/edit?usp=drive_web
[47] See decoding of Two Schoyen Indus seals. http://www.docstoc.com/docs/89158432/Decoding-inscriptions-on-two-Schoyen-Indus-seals. A significant contribution by Jeffrey I. Rose (2010) relates to the importance of Arabo-Persian Gulf. Another is by Steffen Terp Laursen (2010)

detailing the westward transmission of Indus valley sealing technology: origin and development of 'Gulf type' seal and other administrative technologies in early Dilmun, ca. 2100-2000 BCE (Published in *Arabian Archaeology and Epigraphy* 2010: vol. 21: 96–134). See Decoding in Indus Script Gulf Type Seals.

[48] Agrawal, DP, JS Kharakwal, YS Rawat, T Osada & Pankaj Goyal, 2010, Redefining the Harappan hinterland, *Antiquity*, Vol. 84, Issue 323, March 2010
http://www.antiquity.ac.uk/projgall/agrawal323/

[49] http://www.antiquity.ac.uk/projgall/agrawal323/Antiquity, D.P. Agrawal et al, Redefining the Harappan hinterland, *Anquity*, Vol. 84, Issue 323, March 2010.

[50] http://en.wikipedia.org/wiki/Kanmer

[51] LAW, R.. 2008. Letter from Pakistan: no stone unturned. *Archaeology* 61(5).
http://www.archaeology.org/0809/abstracts/letter.html

[52] http://www.schoyencollection.com/math.html#4638

[53] Schmandt-Besserat, Denise. «*Two Precursors of Writing: Plain and Complex Tokens*», in The Origins of Writing / edited by Wayne M. Senner. 1991: 27-41.
http://en.finaly.org/index.php/Two_precursors_of_writing:_plain_and_complex_tokens

[54] http://www.schoyencollection.com/math.html#9.5

[55] Denise Schmandt-Besserat, "An Ancient Token System: The Precursor to Numerals and Writing," *Archaeology* 39 (Nov.-Dec. 1986): 38; reprinted with permission from *Archaeology.*

[56] Denise Schmandt-Besserat, 2009, Tokens and writing: the cognitive development, *Scripta*, Vol. 1 (September 2009): 145-154.

[57] Kalyanarman, S. 1998. *Indian Lexicon – A comparative etymological dictionary of South-Asian Languages*. Manila.
https://docs.google.com/file/d/0B4BAzCi4O_l4ZXJfN0hMamowSGs/edit?usp=drive_web

[58] http://www.harappa.com/indus4/e6.html

[59] Kazanas, Nicholas, 2009 Economic principles in Ancient India,

[60] R P Kangle's edition, Pt I, Univ Bombay, 1965

[61] See also Ancient Hindu principles of social and economic management.

[62] http://www.hindu.com/fline/fl2712/stories/20100618271206800.htm

[63] Kalyanaraman, S., 2012, *Harosheth Hagoyim*, Herndon, Sarasvati Research Center

[64] http://tinyurl.com/d7be2qh

[65] http://www.abarim-publications.com/Meaning/Harosheth.html

[66] Wyatt, N., 1983, A press-seal, possibly of Indus type, found in Iraq. JRAS 1983: 3-6.

[67] http://bharatkalyan97.blogspot.com/2013/06/ancient-near-east-art-indus-writing.html

[68] Contenau G., Manuel d'archéologie orientale depuis les origines jusqu'à Alexandre : les découvertes archéologiques de 1930 à 1939, IV, Paris : Picard, 1947, pp. 2049-2051, fig. 1138

Parrot A., Les fouilles de Mari, première campagne (hiver 1933-1934), Extr. de : Syria, 16, 1935, paris : P. Geuthner, pp. 132-137, pl. XXVIII

Parrot A., Mission archéologique de Mari : vol. I : le temple d'Ishtar, Bibliothèque archéologique et historique, LXV, Paris : Institut français d'archéologie du Proche-Orient, 1956, pp. 136-155, pls. LVI-LVII Author: Iselin Claire

[69] Hunter, G.R., *JRAS*, 1932, 476.
[70] http://indusscriptmore.blogspot.com/2011/08/problematic-13-stroke-signs-in-indus.html.
[71] Harappa National Museum, Karachi, HM 13 710 Dimensions of right bangle: 6.13 cm dia Mohenjo-daro, DK 3457a National Museum, Karachi, NMP 51.899, HM 13.809 Mackay 1938: 535, pl. CXXXVI, 60
[72] V. Gordon Childe, 1929, *The most ancient East: the oriental prelude to European history*, London, Kegan Paul, Trench, Trubner and Co. Ltd., Fig. 72b.

[73] http://www.harappa.com/goladhoro/bagasraseals.html
[74] Biswas, Arun Kumar, 1993, The primacy of India in ancient brass and zinc metallurgy, Indian Journal of History of Science, 28(4), pp. 309-330. http://www.new1.dli.ernet.in/data1/upload/insa/INSA_1/20005b5c_309.pdf
[75] Denise Schmandt-Besserat, 2009, Tokens and writing: the cognitive development, *Scripta*, Vol. 1 (September 2009): 145-154. (Fig. 2).' (p.148, ibid.) Susa, ca. 3300 BCE.

[76] Kalyanaraman. S., 2013, *Indus writing in ancient Near East*, Herndon, Sarasvati Research Center
[77] 'Pictorial motifs' and 'signs' are two classifications used by compilers, for statistical analyses of concordances of inscriptions. Both are glyphs composed of glyptic elements. 'Pictorial motifs' generally occupy the substantial portion of the limited field on a small-sized seal or tablet and cannot be ignored while reading 'visible language' of a writing system.
[78] Revue d'Assyriologie, Vol. 22: 56.
[79] Hakemi, Ali, 1997, Comparison between the plates of Shahdad and other plates that exist in a few museums, In: Taddei, Maurizio and Giuseppe de Marco, eds., 2000, South Asian Archaeology, 1997, Vol. 1, Istituto Italiano per l'africa e l'oriente, Rome, pp. 943-959.

[80]After Pottier, M.H., 1984, *Materiel funeraire e la Bactriane meridionale de l'Age du Bronze*, Paris, Editions Recherche sur les Civilisations: plate 20.150. Ivory comb with Mountain Tulip motif and dotted circles. TA 1649 Tell Abraq. [D.T. Potts, South and Central Asian elements at Tell Abraq (Emirate of Umm al-Qaiwain, United Arab Emirates), c. 2200 BC—AD 400, in Asko Parpola and Petteri Koskikallio, *South Asian Archaeology 1993*: , pp. 615-666]

[81] After Fig. 7 Holly Pittman, 1984, *Art of the Bronze Age: Southeastern Iran, Western Central Asia, and the Indus Valley*, New York, The Metropolitan Museum of Art, pp. 29-30.
[82] The glossary of *deśi* words is a veritable lexicon of Meluhha (Mleccha) exemplified by the inscriptions of sites in Rann of Kutch using Indus writing.

[83] http://www.scribd.com/doc/158033053/Chanhudaro-Inscriptions-with-Unique-Slanted-Stroke-Glyph-S-Kalyanaraman-August-4-2013

[84] cf. Parpola, 1994, fig. 13.12.
[85] Remi Boucharlat, Archaeology and Artifacts of the Arabian Peninsula, in: Jack M. Sasson (ed.), *Civilizations of the Ancient Near East*, pp. 1335-1353. Kuwait National Museum. French

Archaeological Expedition in Kuwait. Several inscriptions at Failaka mention the Dilmunite god Enzak and his temple or Mesopotamian deities

[86] Reconstruction, courtesy: http://pubweb.cc.u-tokai.ac.jp/indus/english/image2/2_4_03_04.jpg

[87] Possehl, Gregory L., and Praveena Gullapalli, 1999. The Early Iron Age in South Asia. pp. 153–175 in: Pigott, Vincent C. (ed.), The archaeometallurgy of the Asian Old World. (MASCA Research Papers in Science and Archaeology, University Museum Monograph, volume 16.) Philadelphia: The University Museum, University of Pennsylvania.

[88] Weisgerber, Gerd, Dilmun – a trading entrepot, evidence from historical and archaeological sources, in: Al_Khaifa, Michael Rice, 1986, Bahrain through he ages, the archaeology, Routledgej, p.140.

[89] Ozguc, T., 'An Assyrian Trading Outpost', Scientific American, 1962, 97 ff. Cited after Lamberg-Karlovsky 1972. Simo Parpola/Asko Parpola/Robert H. Brunswig, 'The Meluhhan Village. Evidence of acculturation of Harappa Traders in the late Third Millennium Mesopotamia?' Journal of the Economic and Social History of the Orient, vol. 20, 1977, 129-165.

[90] Trade interactions of bronze age (After Rice, M. ed., 2000, Traces of Paradise. The archaeology of Bahrain 2500 BCE-300 CE. London: The Dilmun Committee, 15.

[91] http://www.scribd.com/doc/11114439/Ancient-Hieroglyphs

[92] Tomb MR3T.21, Mehrgarh, Period 1A, ca. 6500 BCE. After Fig. 2.10 in Kenoyer, 1998.

[93] Vallat 1978, 63-66. D. Potts, 1981, The potter's marks of Tepe Yahya, Paleorient Vol. 7/1.

[94] http://www.britishmuseum.org/explore/highlights/highlight_objects/me/c/cylinder_seal.aspx

[95] After figure in: Samuel Noah Kramer, The Indus civilization and Dilmun the Sumerian Paradise Land, Expedition, Spring, 1964, p. 47.

[96] Ibid., 137)

[97] Bibby, G., 1969, Looking for Dilmun – Origins of Arabia, New York, Knopf, p.219

[98] Paul D. LeBlanc, 2012, The Indus culture and writing system in contact, *The Ottawa Journal of Religion, La Revue des sciences des religions d'Ottawa*, Vol. 4, 2012, No. 4, 2012.

[99] Crawford, H., 2012, Meluhha. The Encyclopedia of Ancient History First Edition. Edited by Roger S. Bagnall, Kai Brodersen, Craige B. Champion, Andrew Erskine,

and Sabine R. Huebner, print pages 4424–4425.

http://onlinelibrary.wiley.com/doi/10.1002/9781444338386.wbeah24144/full

[100] Gadamer, Hans-Georg. 1976,*Philosophical Hermeneutics*, ed. and trans. by David E. Linge, Berkeley: University of California Press, xii.

[101] Natya Shastra of Bharata Muni in english THE NATYASASTRA A Treatise on Hindu Dramaturgy and Histrionics Ascribed to B H A R A T A - M r X I Vol. I. (Chapters I-XXVII) Completely translated jor the jirst tune from the original Sanskrit tuttri «u Introduction and Various Notes, Royal Asiatic Society of Bengal, Calcutta
http://archive.org/stream/NatyaShastraOfBharataMuniVolume1/NatyaShastraOfBharataMuniVolume1_djvu.txt

[102] See S. K. Chatterji, Origin and Development of the Bengali Language, Calcutta, 1926 pp. 42,178.

[103] Shafer, Robert, 1954, *Ethnography of Ancient India*, Wiesbaden, Otto Harrassowitz, p. 14; p. 33

[104] மிலேச்சிதம் milēccitam, *n.* < *mlēcchita*. (யாழ். அக.) 1. Ungrammatical speech; இலக்கண வழுவான பேச்சு. 2. Non-Sanskritic language; ஸம்ஸ்கிருதமும் அதனுட்பிரிவான பாஷைகளும் அல் லாத பிறபாஷை.(Tamil)

[105] Alain Danielou, 1994, *The complete Kama Sutra*, Park Street Press, Rochester, Vermont, pp.3-4.
[106] Wilhelm Halbfass 1990, *India and Europe: an essay in philosophical understanding*, Delhi, Motilal Banarsidass, pp. 179, 185.
[107] http://creative.sulekha.com/sanskrit-philia-and-indic-civilization_132117_blog
[108] Parpola, S., A. Parpola, and RH Brunswig, Jr., 1977, 'The Meluhha village: evidence of acculturation of Harappan traders in late third millennium Mesopotamia?', JESHO 20 (1977): 129-65.) (Parpola, A. and S., 'On the relationship of the Sumerian toponym Meluhha and Sanskrit mleccha,' Studia Orientalia 46 (1975): 205-38.
[109] http://www.metmuseum.org/explore/First_Cities/seals_meso_object_10c.R.htm
[110]

[111] cf. Southworth, F.C., 1979, Lexical evidence for early contacts between Indo-Aryan and Dravidian, in: M.M. Deshpande and P.E. Hook, eds., *Aryan and Non-Aryan in India*, Ann arbor, pp.191-233.
[112] Joshi, J.P., Madhu Bala, and Jassu Ram, 1984 "The Indus Civilization: A Reconsideration on the Basis of Distribution Maps." In *Frontiers of the Indus Civilization, Wheeler Commemoration Volume*, B.B. Lal and S.P. Gupta, editors, Indian Archaeological Society, pp. 511, 513.
[113] Chris JD Kostman, 'The Indus Valley civilization: in search of those elusive centers and peripheries', in: *JAGNES*, the Journal of the Association of Graduates in Near Eastern Studies.
[114] http://www.adventurecorps.com/archaeo/centperiph.html
[115] Possehl, Gregory. Meluhha. in: J. Reade (ed.) *The Indian Ocean in Antiquity.* London: Kegan Paul Intl. 1996a, 133–208.
[116] Landsberger, Die Welt des Orients 3. 261.
[117] Parpola, S., Parpola, A., and Brunswig, R.H. Jr. 1977. The Meluhha village: evidence of acculturation of Harappan traders in late third millennium Mesopotamia? JESHO XX: 129-165.
[118] Massimo Vidale, 2004, 'Growing in a foreign world: for a history of the 'Meluhha villages' in Mesopotamian in the 3rd millennium BC' in: A. Panaino and A. Piras (eds.), *Proceedings of the Fourth Annual Symposium of the Assyrian and Babylonian Intellectual Heritage Project*, held in Ravenna, Italy, October 13-17, 2001, Milan, Universita di Bologna and Islao, pp. 261-80. http://www.aakkl.helsinki.fi/melammu/
[119] J.D. Muhly, 1973,, *Copper and Tin*, Conn.: Archon., Hamden; *Transactions of Connecticut Academy of Arts and Sciences*, vol. 43, 221f.
[120] Thornton, C.P.; Lamberg-Karlovsky, C.C.; Liezers, M.; Young, S.M.M. (2002). "On pins and needles: tracing the evolution of copper-based alloying at Tepe Yahya, Iran, via ICP-MS analysis of Common-place items."*Journal of Archaeological Science* 29 (29): 1451–1460.
[121] Parpola, Asko; Parpola, Simo (1975). "On the relationship of the Sumerian Toponym Meluhha and Sanskrit Mleccha". *Studia Orientalia* 46: 205–238.
[122] Tewari, Rakesh, 2003, The origins of iron-working in India: new evidence from the Central Ganga Plain and the eastern Vindhyas, http://www.archaeologyonline.net/artifacts/iron-ore.html
[123] http://www.george-broderick.de/INDO-EUROPEAN.doc George Broderick, 2009, Indo-European and non-Indo-European aspects to the languages and place-names in Britain and Ireland explains non-Indo-European features of Insular Celtic in the realms of syntax, phonology, lexicon, place-names.

[124] http://alterling2.narod.ru/English/MetalAngl.doc *Valentyn Stetsyuk,* Lviv; Ukraine, 1989, About

some names of metals in Turkic and Indo-European languages

[125] George A. Lindbeck presents the nature of doctrine in his book, *The Nature of Doctrine: Religion and Theology in a Postliberal Age* (Louisville, KY: Westminster John Knox Press, 1984).

[126] E.g. Wittgenstein, *Philosophical Investigations*, §245, §247, §252-3, §257, §278, §282. For Wittgenstein's discussions on private language, see Ludwig Wittgenstein, *Philosophical Investigations*, trans. G. E. M. Anscombe (Malden, MA: Blackwell, 2005), §243-315.

http://churchandpomo.typepad.com/conversation/2007/01/lindbeck_after_.html Eric Lee, 2007, Lindbeck After Wittgenstein?

[127] Cf. Englund, Robert K. (1998). *Texts from the Late Uruk Period.* In Bauer, Josef; Englund, Robert K.; and Krebernik, Manfred (1998). *Mesopotamien: Späturuk-Zeit und Frühdynastische Zeit.* Orbis Biblicus et Orientalis 160/1; Annäherungen, 1. Freiburg, Switzerland: Academic Press Freiburg.

[128] Kalyanaraman, S., 2013, Takṣat vāk, 'incised speech' -- Evidence of Indus writing of Meluhha language in Ancient Near East http://bharatkalyan97.blogspot.in/2013/07/taksat-vak-incised-speech-evidence-of.html

[129] Parpola, S., A. Parpola and R.H. Brunswig, 1977, The Meluhha village: evidence of acculturation of Harappan traders in late third millennium Mesopotamia? *Journal of the Economic and Social History of the Orient*, Vol. 20. No. 2: 129-65.

[130] Terqa (Tell Ashara) with genetic links to Meluhha http://bharatkalyan97.blogspot.in/2013/09/terqa-tell-ashara-with-genetic-links-to.html Genetic links between India and Mesopotamia in Bronze Age Ancient Near East http://bharatkalyan97.blogspot.in/2013/09/genetic-links-between-india-and.html

[131] Source: *PLoS ONE* http://www.pasthorizonspr.com/index.php/archives/09/2013/genetic-link-shown-between-indian-subcontinent-and-mesopotamia

[132] Reade, J., 1986, Commerce of conquest: variations in the Mesopotamia-Dilmun relationship, pp. 325-334 in: Bahrain through the Ages: the Archaeology, Shaikha HA, Al-Khalifa and M. Rice, eds, KPI, London

[133] Tosi, Maurizio, 1986, Early maritime cultures of the Arabian Gulf and the Indian Ocean in: Bahrain through the ages: the Archaeology, 1986, Rouledge, pp. 94ff.

[134] Steve Glines, https://groups.google.com/forum/#!topic/sci.archaeology/9KwZXeEJ_Bs

[135] Liggett, Renata M., 1982, Ancient Terqa and its temple of Ninkarrak: the excavations of the Fifth and sixth seasons. http://128.97.6.202/tq/EL-TQ%5CLigett_1982_Ancient_Terqa_and_Its_Temple_-_NEASB_19.pdf

[136] Potts, Daniel T., 1996, *Mesopotamian civilization: the material foundations*, Cambridge University Press, p.270.

[137] http://www.iimas.org/Terqa.html

[138] http://www.silkroadgourmet.com/tag/terqa/
[139] http://www.livescience.com/39011-cinnamon-trade-found-in-israel.html
[140] Parpola, Asko, S. Koskenniemi, S. Parpola and P. Aalto, 1970, Decipherment of the Proto Dravidian Inscriptions of the Indus Valley, no. 3, Copenhagen, p. 37.
[141] Parpola et al 1970: 37.
[142] http://upload.wikimedia.org/wikipedia/commons/d/d3/Sialk1.jpg
[143] Alster, Bendt, 1972, Nirnurta and the Turtle UET 6/1 2, *Journal of Cuneiform Studies* Vol. 24, No. 4 (1972), pp. 120-125.
[144] Vallat. F.,1985, Elements de geographic elamite (resume), *PO*.11, pp.49-54.
[145] Witzel, M., 1999, Substrate languages in old Indo-Aryan (Rgvedic, Middle and Late Vedic), *Electronic Journal of Vedic Studies,* 5-1, pp. 1-67. http://www.ejvs.laurasianacademy.com/ejvs0501/0501ART.PDF
[146] http://bharatkalyan97.blogspot.com/2013/07/ancient-near-east-shahdad-bronze-age.html

[147] Benoit Agnès, "Acquisitions", in Revue du Louvre, n 3, juin 2003, p. 87. Agnès Benoit

[148] http://www.louvre.fr/en/oeuvre-notices/base-ritual-offering-carved-animals

[149] http://www.italyforiraq.esteri.it/ItalyForIraq/documenti/Iraq_Museum_GUIDE_2012.pdf

[150] This artwork is currently on display in Gallery 173 Said to be from Amathus, Cyprus. 1865–1872, found in Cyprus by General Luigi Palma di Cesnola; acquired by the Museum in 1874, purchased from General Luigi Palma di Cesnola http://www.metmuseum.org/collections/search-the-collections/30000008

[151] http://xoomer.virgilio.it/francescoraf/hesyra/palettes/narmerp.htm
[152] http://en.wikipedia.org/wiki/Narmer_Palette#cite_note-13
[153] http://www.nemo.nu/ibisportal/0egyptintro/2aegypt/index.htm
[154] Mallowan 1947; Crawford, op.cit., p. 134.
[155] Wilkinson, Toby A.H. *Early Dynastic Egypt*. p.6, Routledge, London. 1999.
[156] http://xoomer.virgilio.it/francescoraf/hesyra/palettes/narmerp.htm
[157] Brier, Bob. *Daily Life of the Ancient Egyptians*, A. Hoyt Hobbs 1999, p.202.
[158] http://en.wikipedia.org/wiki/Narmer_Palette#cite_note-13
[159] Wengrow, David, *The Archaeology of Ancient Egypt* Cambridge University Press.
[160] Janson, Horst Woldemar; Anthony F. Janson *History of Art: A Survey of the Major Visual Arts from the Dawn of History to the Present Day* Prentice Hall 1986.
[161] Breasted, , James Henry. *Ancient Records of Egypt*, Chicago 1906, part Two, §§ 143, 659, 853; part Three §§ 117, 144, 147, 285 etc.
[162] http://en.wikipedia.org/wiki/Narmer_Palette

[163] Donald P. Hansen, Erica Ehrenberg, 2002, *Leaving no stones unturned: essays on the ancient Near East and Egypt in honor of Donald P. Hansen*, Eisenbrauns, p.220.
[164] Originally published as fig. 368c in WIlliam Hayes Ward, *The Seal cylinders of Western Asia*, Washington 1910. Reprinted as fig. 3 under the heading *The Caduceus an the God Ningishzida* in A. L. Frothingham, *Babylonian Origin of Hermes the Snake-God, and of the Caduceus I*, American Journal of Archaeology, Vol. 20, No. 2 (Apr. - Jun., 1916), pp. 175-211 (p. 181). 1910 drawing of a vase of green steatite found at Telloh (Lagash), now ath the Louvre (De Sarzec, *Découvertes en Chaldée*, Paris 1883, pl. 44, fig. 2, pp. 234-236).

[165] http//www.metmuseum.org/toah/ho/02/wam/hod_41.160.192.htm

[166] Kramer, SN, 1963, *The Sumerians: their history, culture and character*, Univ. of Chicago Press, p.280.
[167] http://bharatkalyan97.blogspot.in/2013/06/tablet-of-destinies.html
[168] Legend of Anzu which stole the tablets of destiny and allegory of soma http://bharatkalyan97.blogspot.in/2013/07/legend-of-anzu-which-stole-tablets-of.html The tablets of destiny may be a reference to Indus writing corpora which were veritable stone-, mineral-, metal-ware catalogs.

http://bharatkalyan97.blogspot.in/2011/11/syena-orthography.html śyena, orthography, Sasanian iconography. Continued use of Indus Script hieroglyphs.

http://www.jtsa.edu/documents/pagedocs/janes/2009/wazana_janes31.pdf

[169] Bloch, Jules. 2008, Formation of the Marathi Language. (Reprint, Translation from French), New Delhi, Motilal Banarsidass. ISBN: 978-8120823228.
[170] David Kahn, *The Code-Breakers: The Story of Secret Writing*, New York, Macmillan, 1967, pp. 74-75.
[171171] Shendge, Malati, 1977, *The civilized demons: the Harappans in Rigveda, Rigveda*, Abhinav Publications.
[172] Tarlekar, G.H., 1975, Studies in the *Nāṭyaśāstra*, Delhi, Motilal Banarsidass, p. 38.
[173] Vidale, Massimo, 2007, "The collapse melts down", *East and West* 2007.
[174] Vidale, Massimo, 2004, "Growing in a Foreign World. For a History of the "Meluhha Villages" in Mesopotamia in the 3rd Millennium BCE." http://www.scribd.com/doc/2566221/meluhhanvillage
[175] Jain, Dhanesh, George Cardona (eds.), 2003, The Indo-Aryan languages, Routledge, pp.6-7,17-21, 26-28, 31-37.
[176] Jātaka, XIV, 486; XVII, 524; Geiger, Wilhelm, Pāli Literature and Language, tr. BK Ghosh, Calcutta, 1956; repr. New Delhi, 1978; Kern, H. Toevoegselen op't Woordenbock van Childeers, 2 pts., NR., XVI, nos. 4 and 5.
[177] Leif Jonsson // Oct 17, 2008 http://rspas.anu.edu.au/rmap/newmandala/2008/09/30/pali/#comment-568304
[178] D. Collon, *First impressions: cylinder seals* (London, The British Museum Press, 1987) http://www.britishmuseum.org/explore/highlights/highlight_objects/me/a/aragonite_cylinder_seal.aspx
[179] D.J. Wiseman, *Catalogue of the Western Asiat* (London, 1962) J. Rawson, *Animals in art* (London, The British Museum Press, 1977) http://www.britishmuseum.org/explore/highlights/highlight_objects/me/w/calcite_seal,_combat_scene.aspx

[180] http://news.nationalgeographic.com/news/2003/05/photogalleries/iraqtreasures_1/

[181] http://amar.hsclib.sunysb.edu/u?/amar,124774 DT Potts, 1998, *Ancient Magan, The secrets of Tell Abraq*, Trident Press
[182] http://www.tulane.edu/~danny/arch.html

[183] http://www.metmuseum.org/toah/hd/akka/hob_1999.325.4.htm

[184] http://www.scribd.com/doc/158033053/Chanhudaro-Inscriptions-with-Unique-Slanted-Stroke-Glyph-S-Kalyanaraman-August-4-2013

[185] http://www.thepersia.com/2012_08_01_archive.html
[186] http://www.mesopotamia.co.uk/writing/explore/seal.html
[187] http://www.honestinformation.com/articles/missing-teapot.php
[188] After Fig. 9 in: Jack M. Sasson (ed.), Civilizations of the Ancient Near East, p.2705.
[189] Sege Cleuziou, Preliminary report on the second and third excavation campaigns at Hili 8, Archaeology in the United Arab Emirates, vol. 2/3, 1978/79, 30ff.; Gerd Weisgerber, '...und Kupfer in Oman', Der Anschnitt, vol. 32, 1980, 62-110; Gerd Weisgerber, Makkan and Meluhha- 3rd millennium copper production in Oman and evidence of contact with the Indus valley, Paper read in Cambridge 1981 and to appear in South Asia Archaeology 1981; Tosi, M. 1982. A possible Harappan Seaport in Eastern Arabia: Ra's Al Junayz in the Sultanate of Oman, paper read at the 1st International Conference on Pakistan Archaeology, Peshawar. Gerd Weisgerber, Dilmun--a trading entrepot; evidence from historical and archaeological sources, 135-142 in: Shaikha Haya Ali Al Khalifa and Michael Rice (eds.) Bahrain through the ages: the archaeology, London, KPI, 1986. Simo Parpola/Asko Parpola/Robert H. Brunswig, The Meluhha village. evidence of acculturation of Harappan traders in the later third millennium Mesopotamia?, Journal of the Economic and Political History of the Orient, vol. 20, 1977, 129-165.
[190] T. Ozguc, An Assyrian trading outpost, Scientific American, 1962, 97 ff.
[191] A. Parpola and S. Parpola, 1975, On the relationship of the Sumerian Toponym Meluhha and Sanskrit Mleccha, Studia Orientalia 46.
[192] Connan, J., 1999, 'Use and Trade of Bitumen in Antiquity and Prehistory: Molecular Archaeology Reveals Secrets of Past Civilizations', Philosophical Transactions of the Royal Society London B 353: 33-50.
http://www.journals.royalsoc.ac.uk/(qoptgors11gb1p45iz5i3wup)/app/home/contribution.asp?referrer=parent&backto=issue,4,14;journal,86,116;linkingpublicationresults,1:102022,1See also: http://www.sabi-abyad.nl/tellsabiabyad/projecten/index/0/19/?sub=32&language=en which has a map pointing to origin of bitumen somewhere between Iraq and Israel.
[193] http://www.scribd.com/doc/12238039/mundalexemesinSanskrit

[194] M.B.Emeneau, India as a Linguistic Area [Lang. 32, 1956, 3-16; LICS, 196, 642-51; repr. In Collected papers: Dravidian Linguistics Ethnology and Folktales, Annamalai Nagar, Annamalai University, 1967, pp. 171-186.
[195] M.B.Emeneau, Linguistic Prehistory of India PAPS98 (1954). 282-92; Tamil Culture 5 (1956). 30-55; repr. In Collected papers: Dravidian Linguistics Ethnology and Folktales, Annamalai Nagar, Annamalai University, 1967, pp. 155-171.
[196] Kalyanarman, S. 1998. *Indian Lexicon – A comparative etymological dictionary of South-Asian Languages.* Manila.
https://docs.google.com/file/d/0B4BAzCi4O_l4ZXJfN0hMamowSGs/edit?usp=drive_web An Indian Lexicon with about 8000 semantic clusters has been compiled; this proves the *sprachbund* with evidence of glossary of words commonly used across the set of families of languages (Indo-Aryan, Indo-Iranian, Dravidian, Munda). In the book, *Indus Writing in Ancient Near East* hundreds of examples of such semantic clusters have been identified in the context of bronze-age metallurgy.

[197] Bryant, Edwin and Laurie L. Patton, 2005, The Indo-Aryan controversy: evidence and inference in Indian history, Routledge, p.197.

[198] *K. V. Sarma*, 1983, "Spread of Vedic Culture in Ancient. South India" in The *Adyar* Library *Bulletin*, *1983*, 43:1.

[199] Pischel, Richard, 1900 (German), A grammar of the Prākrit languages, (English tr. 1955) Rev. edn. 1981, Delhi, Motilal Banarsidass, p.59.
[200](Burrow, T., 1955, *The Sanskrit language*, UK, Faber & Faber Ltd., p.43, p.62.

[201] Karl H. Potter, Harold G. Coward, K. Kunjunni Raja, 1990, *Encyclopaedia of Indian philosophies: the philosophy of the Grammarians*, Delhi, Motilal Banarsidass.

[202] http://en.wikipedia.org/wiki/Gharana
[203] Harmatta, Janos, 1992: "The emergence of the Indo-Iranians: the Indo-Iranian languages", in A.H. Dani and V.M. Masson, eds., *History of Civilizations*, vol.1, UNESCO Publ., Paris 1992, p.374.
[204] Litvinsky, Boris Abramovich; Vorobyova-Desyatovskaya, M.I (1999). "Religions and religious movements". *History of civilizations of Central Asia*. Motilal Banarsidass. pp. 421–448.
[205] Elst, Koenraad, 1999, *Update on the Aryan Invasion debate*, Delhi, Aditya Prakashan http://www.bharatvani.org/books/ait/ch45.htm#37a
[206] Albright, W.F., The Mouth of the Rivers, *AJSL*, 35 (1919): 161-195).
[207] Piotr Steinkeller identified Jiroft as Marhashi. http://www.cais-soas.com/News/2008/May2008/08-05-jiroft.htm
[208] http://www.hindunet.org/hindu_history/sarasvati/lapis/lapis_lazuli.htm
[209] Carte: H. Balfet & A. Didier; Durrani, FA, 1988: pl. XVIA; Franke-Vogt, U., 2005: abb.16; Catalogue d'exposition *Les cites oubliees de l'Indus. Archeologie du Pakistan*, 1988: no. 123. Paris: Association francaise d'Action artistique; Madjidzadeh 2003: 73). (After Fig. 10 in: Didier, Aurore, 2011, L'utilisation de la couleur dans les ceramiques protohistoriques du Balochistan pakistanais et de Mundigak (Afghanistan). Identites culturelles et traditions techniques, p.126 ff. in: Annals de la Fondation Fyssen No. 26, Les Annales de la Fondation Fyssen 2011. http://www.fondationfyssen.fr/wp-content/uploads/2012/11/web150Fyssen_26.pdf

[210] Kalyanarman, S. 1998. *Indian Lexicon – A comparative etymological dictionary of South-Asian Languages.* Manila. https://docs.google.com/file/d/0B4BAzCi4O_l4ZXJfN0hMamowSGs/edit?usp=drive_web
[211] Przyluski, Non-aryan loans in Indo-Aryan, in: Bagchi, PC, *Pre-aryan and pre-dravidian,* pp.28-29 http://www.scribd.com/doc/33670494/prearyanandpredr035083mbp

[212] Emeneau, Murray. 1956. India as a Lingusitic Area. "Langauge" 32: 3-16. http://en.academic.ru/dic.nsf/enwiki/113093
[213] Berger, H. Die Burushaski-Sprache von Hunza und Nagar. Vols. I-III. Wiesbaden: Harrassowitz 1988] [Tikkanen (2005)].
[214] [G.Morgenstierne, Irano-Dardica. Wiesbaden 1973], Dravidian, Munda and Indo-Aryan language families of the Indian subcontinent. *The Munda Languages*. Edited by Gregory D. S. Anderson. London and New York: Routledge (Routledge Language Family Series), 2008.
[215] http://sites.google.com/site/kalyan97/induswriting

[216] Kalyanarman, S. 1998. *Indian Lexicon – A comparative etymological dictionary of South-Asian Languages*. Manila.
https://docs.google.com/file/d/0B4BAzCi4O_l4ZXJfN0hMamowSGs/edit?usp=drive_web
[217] Chelliah, JV, 1946, *Pattuppāṭṭu; ten Tamil idylls, translated into English verse*, South India Saiva Siddhanta Works Publishing Society, p. 91.

[218] Kirfel, W. Das *Purāṇa Pañcalakṣaṇa*.1927.Bonn : K. Schroeder.
[219]F.R. Allchin, 1959, Upon the contextual significance of certain groups of ancient signs, *Bulletin of the School of Oriental and African Studies*, London.
[220] Kalyanaraman, S., 2010, The Bronze Age Writing System of Sarasvati Hieroglyphics as Evidenced by Two "Rosetta Stones" - Decoding Indus script as repertoire of the mints/smithy/mine-workers of Meluhha. *Journal of Indo-Judaic Studies*. Number 11. pp. 47–74.
[221] http://www.iranicaonline.org/articles/dahyu-
[222] Mayrhofer, *Dictionary* II, pp. 28-29.
[223] Bailey, *Dictionary*, p. 155.
[224] Benveniste, 1932; idem, 1938, pp. 6, 13; Thieme, pp. 79ff.; Frye, p. 52; Boyce, *Zoroastrianism* I, p. 13; Schwartz, p. 649; Gnoli, pp. 15ff.
[225] cf. Leuze; Junge; Walser, pp. 27ff.; Herzfeld, pp. 228-29; Herrenschmidt, pp. 53ff.; Calmeyer, 1982, pp. 105ff.; idem, 1983, pp. 141ff.
[226] e.g., Nisāya in Media; DB 1.58; Kent, *Old Persian*, p. 118.
[227] Kent, *Old Persian*, pp. 18-19.
[228] *Frahang ī Pahlawīg* 2.3, p. 117; cf. Syr. *Mātā*.
[229] MacKenzie, p. 26.
[230] Possehl, Gregory, 2006, Shu-ilishu's cylinder seal, Expedition, Vol. 48, No. 1http://www.penn.museum/documents/publications/expedition/PDFs/48-1/What%20in%20the%20World.pdf
[231] Kalyanarman, S. 1998. *Indian Lexicon – A comparative etymological dictionary of South-Asian Languages*. Manila.
https://docs.google.com/file/d/0B4BAzCi4O_l4ZXJfN0hMamowSGs/edit?usp=drive_web
[232] https://docs.google.com/file/d/0B4BAzCi4O_l4ZXJfN0hMamowSGs/edit?usp=drive_web
[233] Steve Farmer, Richard Sproat, and Michael Witzel, 2005, The Collapse of the Indus-Script Thesis: The Myth of a Literate Harappan Civilization, *EJVS* 11-2 Dec. 13, 2005.
[234] http://huntingtonarchive.osu.edu/Makara%20Site/makara
[235] http://tinyurl.com/gonsh
[236] Kalyanaraman, S. 2012. *Indian Hieroglyphs – Invention of Writing*. Herndon: Sarasvati Research Center
[237] Schmandt-Besserat, D. 1996. *How Writing Came About.* Austin: The University of Texas Press.
[238] Schmandt-Besserat, D. (1992), *Before Writing*, 2 vols. Austin: The University of Texas Press.
[239] Ibid.
[240] Schmandt-Besserat, D. 2009. SCRIPTA, Volume 6 (September 2009): 145
[241] Kalyanaraman, S. 2012. *Indian Hieroglyphs – Invention of Writing*. Herndon: Sarasvati Research Center
[242] Nissen, H.J., Damerow, P., Englund, R.K., 1993. *Archaic Bookkeeping*, Chicago: The University of Chicago Press, pp. 64-65.
[243] Kalyanarman, S. 1998. *Indian Lexicon – A comparative etymological dictionary of South-Asian Languages*.
Manila. https://docs.google.com/file/d/0B4BAzCi4O_l4ZXJfN0hMamowSGs/edit?usp=drive_web

[244] Kalyanarman, S. 1998. *Indian Lexicon – A comparative etymological dictionary of South-Asian Languages*. Manila.
https://docs.google.com/file/d/0B4BAzCi4O_l4ZXJfN0hMamowSGs/edit?usp=drive_web

[245] See: www.sumerian.org/sumerian.pdf Sumerian Lexicon Version 3.0 by John A. Halloran

[246] Glassner, J-J. 2003. *The invention of cuneiform. Writing in Sumer*. Translated and edited by Zainab Bahrani and Marc van de Mieroop. Baltimore & London: The John Hopkins University Press.

[247] D.T.Potts, Mesopotamian Civilization: The Material Foundations, 1997, Ithaca, Cornell University Press.

[248] Samuel N. Kramer, The Indus Civilization and Dilmun: The Sumerian Paradise Land, *Expedition*, Vol. 6, No. 3, 1964, pp. 44-52.

[249] Carte: H. Balfet & A. Didier; Durrani, FA, 1988: pl. XVIA; Franke-Vogt, U., 2005: abb.16; Catalogue d'exposition *Les cites oubliees de l'Indus. Archeologie du Pakistan*, 1988: no. 123. Paris: Association francaise d'Action artistique; Madjidzadeh 2003: 73. After Fig. 10 in: Didier, Aurore, 2011, L'utilisation de la couleur dans les ceramiques protohistoriques du Balochistan pakistanais et de Mundigak (Afghanistan). Identites culturelles et traditions techniques, p.126 ff. in: Annals de la Fondation Fyssen No. 26, Les Annales de la Fondation Fyssen 2011.
http://www.fondationfyssen.fr/wp-content/uploads/2012/11/web150Fyssen_26.pdf

[250] Brugmann, K. (Tr. By Wright, J.), *Comparative Grammar of the Indo-Germanic Languages*, Vol. I (Repr. Varanasi, 1972), p. 259-321.

[251] Satya Swarup Misra, 1999, The date of the Rigveda and the Aryan Migration, Pune, Centre of Advanced Study in Sanskrit, University of Pune. SS Misra, *Fresh light on IE classification and chronology*, Varanasi, 1980

[252] http://groups.yahoo.com/group/cybalist/message/12051

[253] http://groups.yahoo.com/group/cybalist/message/12037

[254] http://home.planet.nl/~mcv/PPIE/Active_thematic.html

[255] Excerpts taken from Kazanas' article in JIES Vol. 30, Nos. 3 and 4, Fall/Winter 2002, p. 41 ff.

[256] Hans Henrich Hock, 1975, Substratum influence on (Rig-vedic) Sanskrit? In:*Studies in the Linguistic Sciences*, Urbana, Illinois, University of Illinois, Vol. 5, No. 2, Fall 1975, pp. 76-125

[257] Kazanas, N., 2002, *JIES*, Vol. 30, Nos. 3 and 4, Fall/Winter 2002.

[258] Hock, 1996: 86-7.

[259] http://www.koshur.org/Linguistic/8.html

[260] Vermaak, PS, 2008, Guabba, the Meluhhan village in Mesopotamia, in: *Journal for Semitics*, Vol. 17, No. 2 http://www.sabinet.co.za/abstracts/semit/semit_v17_n2_a12.html

[261] For the foreign tributes paid to Neo-Sumerian authorities and gun-mada-texts see Michalowski (Foreign tribute to Sumer during the Ur III Period, *ZA* 68:34-49), Steinkeller (The administrative and economic organization of the Ur III state: the core and periphery, in Gibson & Biggs 1987:19-41.) and Gelb (1973: Prisoners of war in early Mesopotamia, *Journal of Near Eastern Studies* 32:70-98.)

[262] Vermaak, PS, 2008, Guabba, the Meluhhan village in Mesopotamia, *Journal fo Semitics* 17/2, pp. 553-570.
[263] Colin Masica, 1991, Indo-Aryan Languages, Cambridge Univ. Press.

[264] Emeneau, MB, 1956, India as a linguistic area, in: Language, 32.3-16 •Kuiper, FBJ, 1967, The genesis of a linguistic area, Indo-Iranian Journal 10: 81-102 •Masica, Colin P., 1976, Defining a linguistic area, South Asia, Chicago, University of Chicago Press •Franklin Southworth, 2005, Linguistic Archaeology of South Asia, Routledge Curzon.
[265] Cited in Karl Menninger, 1969, *Number words and number symbols: a cultural history of numbers*, MIT Press, p.212. http://tinyurl.com/26ze95s
[266] Possehl, Gregory and Gullapalli, Praveena; 1999; 'The Early Iron Age in South Asia'; in Vincent C. Piggott (ed.). *The Archaeometallurgy of the Asian Old World*; University Museum Monograph, MASCA Research Papers in Science and Archaeology, Volume 16; Pgs. 153-175; The University Museum, University of Pennsylvania; Philadelphia.
[267] Sharma, Deo Prakash, ed. 2011. *Science and Metal Technology of Harappans*, New Delhi. Kaver Books.
[268] Mackay, E.J.H., Further links between ancient Sind, Sumer and elsewhere, *Antiquity*, Vol. 5, 1931, pp. 459-473.

[269] Kalyanaraman, S. 2012. *Indian Hieroglyphs – Invention of Writing.* Herndon: Sarasvati Research Center.

[270] http://www.ling.hawaii.edu/faculty/stampe/aa.html.
[271] The work is Simharaja, 1909, *Prakriti Rupavatara -- A Prakrit grammar based on the Valmikisutra*, Vol. I, Ed. by E. Hultzsch, Albermarle St., Royal Asiatic Society. Full text at: http://ia700202.us.archive.org/23/items/prakritarupavata00simhuoft/prakritarupavata00simhuoft.pdf
[272] (William Carey), Braj bhāṣā grammar (James Robert), Sindhi, Hindi, Tamil (*Tolkāppiyam*) and Gujarati which can be used as supplementary references, together with the classic *Hemacandra's Dēsīnāmamālā, Prakrit Grammar of Hemachandra* edited by P. L. Vaidya (BORI, Pune), Vararuchi's works and Richard Pischel's *Comparative Grammar of Prakrit Languages*.(Repr. Motilal Banarsidass, 1957).
[273] See also: http://www.indianetzone.com/39/prakrit_language.htm

[274] *Linguistic Survey of India* 3, pt.2, p.1.
[275] Robert Shafer, 1954, Ethnography of Ancient India, Otto Harras Sowitz, Wiesbaden, pp.14,33. http://archive.org/stream/ethnographyofanc033514mbp/ethnographyofanc033514mbp_djvu.txt
[276] Manu I.23, tr. G. Buhler 1886: 33). In Kautilya's *ArthaŚāstra mleccha* is used as a suffix to describe aṭavi or forest people. (AŚ XII.4.23; VII.10.16..
[277] Parasher, Aloka, 1991, *Mlecchas in early India*, Delhi, Munshiram Manoharlal.
[278] Cf. Bellwood, Peter, (2004), *First Farmers: The Origins of Agricultural Societies*, John Wiley & Sons., Chakrabarti et al., 2004-05, Bellwood 2005: 91-6; Shinde, V., T. Osada, MM Sharma et al. 2008. Exploration in the Ghaggar Basin and excavations at Girawad, Farmana (Rohtak District) and Mitathal (Bhiwani District), Haryana, India, pp. 77-158 in: Gepts, Paul, Thomas R. Famula, Robert L. Bettinger, Stephen B. Brush, and Ardeshir B. Damania. Biodiversity in Agriculture: Domestication, Evolution, and Sustainability. Cambridge University Press, 2012, pp.178-179.
[279] FBJ Kuiper, 1948: 9.
[280] http://ccat.sas.upenn.edu/~fsouth/LASAcontents.pdf
[281] Southworth, opcit., 2006: 58.

[282] Kannada. Siddhānti Subrahmaṇya śāstrī's new interpretation of the Amarakośa, Bangalore,Vicaradarpana Press, 1872, p. 330.
[283] de Saussure, Ferdinand. (1986). *Course in general linguistics* (3rd ed.). (R. Harris, Trans.). Chicago: Open Court Publishing Company. (Original work published 1972). p. 9-10, 15].
[284] Translation See: Narayana Iyengar, 1938, Vanmeegarum Thamizhum; http://tashindu.blogspot.com/2006_12_01_archive.html In this work, Narayana Iyengar cites that the commentator interpret mānuṣam vākyam as the language spoken in Kosala. http://www.valmikiramayan.net/sundara/sarga30/sundara_30_frame.htm

[285] Jayaswal, KP, 1914, 'Kleine Mitteilungen', Zeitschrift der Deutschen Morgenlandischen Gesellschraft,, vol. LXXII, p. 719.

[286] Dhavalikar, MK, 1997, Meluhha – the land of copper, in: *South Asian Studies* 13, 1997, p. 276.
[287] Sengupta, R., 1971, On the identity of 'mlecchas', pp. 180-187 in: *Prof. KR Nilakantha Sastri Felicitation Volume,* Prof. KAN Sastri Felicitation Committee, Madras.
[288] Paton, L.B., 1908-27, Ammonites, in *Encyclopaedia of Religion & Ethics*, ed. J. Hastings, vol. I, pp. 389-393..
[289] http://www.bharatvani.org/books/ait/ch46.htm#54a
[290] Pargiter, F.E.,1922, *Ancient Indian Historical Tradition*, p. 295.

[291] Pargiter, F.E.,1922, *Ancient Indian Historical Tradition*, pp. 56-7.

[292] Grayson, AK, 1977, 'The empire of Sargon of Akkad,' AfO 25 (1974-77): 56-64.
[293] Potts, DT, 1982,The road to Meluhha, The Journal of Nearestern Studies, Vol. 41, No. 4 (Oct., 1982), pp.279-288.
[294] Weidner, E., 1952, 'Das Reich Sargons von Akkad,' AfO 16 (1952): 6-11.)(cf. Gelb, IJ, 1970, 'Makkan and Meluhha in Early Mesopotamian Sources,' RA 64 (1970): 1-8). (Sollberger, E., 1969, 'The Problem of Magan and Meluhha,' Bull. Of the Institute of Archaeology 8-9 (1968-69): 247-50.
[295] Hans J. Nissen, The occurrence of Dilmun in the Oldest texts of Mesopotamia, pp. 335-339.
[296] Gelb 1968: 43.
[297] Captain Durand, Extracts from Report on the Islands and Antiquities of Bahrain, with notes by Major-General Sir. H.C. Rawlinson, *JRAS*, N.S. 12 (1880): 189-227, with two maps. Also suggested by Fr. Hommel, *Ethnologie und Geographie des Alten Orients*, 1904/1926, p. 24, 270.
[298] Bendt Alster, Dilmun, Bahrain, and the alleged paradise in Sumerian Myth and Literature, in: Daniel T. Potts (ed.), Dilmun: New studies in the archaeology and early history of Bahrain, Berlin, Dietrich Reimer Verlag, 1983, pp. 39-74). (See also: Daniel Potts, Dilmun: Where and When?*Dilmun: Journal of the Bahrain Historical and Archaeological Society*, 11 (1983): 15-19; Theresa Howard-Carter, The tangible evidence for the earliest Dilmun, JCS, 33 (1981): 210-223; S.N.Kramer, Quest for Paradise, *Antiquity*, 37 (1963): 112-113.
[299] T.G. Bibby, *Kuml* 1970: 345-353; cf. Michael Roaf, Weights on the Dilmun standard,*Iraq* 44 (1982): 137:141.
[300] I.J.Gelb, Makkan and Meluhha in Early Mesopotamian Sources, *RA* 64 (1970): 1-8; E. Sollberger, The Problem of Magan and Meluhha, *Bulletin of the Institute of Archaeology* 8-9 (1968-69): 247-250; John Hansman, A Periplus of Magan and Meluhha, *BOAS* 36 (1973): 554-587; E.C.L. During Caspers and A. Govindakutty, R. Thapar's Dravidian Hypothesis for the Location of Meluhha, Dilmun and Makan, *JESHO* 21 (1978): 114-145.
[301] Gelb, IJ, 1997, Makkan and Meluhha. Early Mesopotamian Sources, Revue d'Assyriologie 64 (1970): 1-7. Also in A source-book of Indian Archaeology, ed., FR Allchin and D. Chakrabarti, vol. 2:

Settlements, Technology and Trad, Delhi:
Munshiram. http://cdli.ucla.edu/cdlisearch/search/index.php?SearchMode=Text&txtID_Txt=P227514

[302] Vallat F., 1985, Elements de geographie elamite (resume). PO 11: 53.

[303] Bendt Alster, opcit., 1983, p. 41.

[304] H.W. Bailey, "Mleccha, Baloc, and Gadrosia", in: BSOAS. No. 36, London, 1973, pp. 584-87.Also see, Cf. K. Kartrunen, India in Early Greek Literature. *Studia Orientalia*, no. 65, Helsinki: Finnish Oriental Society, 1989, pp. 13-14. For evidence of Meluhha=Indus, see Leemans, Foreign Trade in the Old Babylonian Period; Sollberger, *Bull. of the Inst. of Archaeology* 1968/9 8/9:247-50; Heimple ZA 1987 77: 24-31; Leemans JESHO 1960 3:21-37; Leemans *JSEHO* 1968 11:171-226; Oppenheim *JSAOS* 1954 74:6-17; Potts *JNES* 1982 41:279-288; Landsberger, B., *ZA*, xxxv, 3, 1924, 217; Herzfeld, E., *The Persian Empire*, Wiesbaden, 1968, 63; Gelb, IJ, *RA*, lxiv, 1, 1970, 5.

[305] Gelb, I.J., 1970, Makkan and Meluhha in early Mesopotamian sources, RA LXIV, No. 1, pp.3-6.

[306]Hansman, J., ibid., p.569.

[307] For recent comments on *mleccha*, see Wackernagel, *Altindische Grammatik. Introduction generale. Nouvelle edition...par Louis Renou*, 1957, 73; M. Mayrhofer, *Kurzgefasstes etymologisches Worterbuch des Altindischen*, 699, *mleccha*." (Bailey, HW, pp.584-586).

[308] cf. Kalyanaraman, S.,2012, Indian hieroglyphs; Indus script corpora, archaeo-metallurgy and Meluhha (Mleccha), http://arxiv.org/ftp/arxiv/papers/1204/1204.3800.pdf

[309] Dhavalikar, MK, 1997, pp. 276-278.

[310] cf. K. Karttunen (1989). India in Early Greek Literature. Helsinki, Finnish Oriental Society. *Studia Orientali*a. Vol.65. 293 pages. ISBN 951-9380-10-8, pp. 11 ff et passim. Asko Parpola (1975a). Isolation and tentative interpretation of a toponym in the Harappan inscriptions. Le dechiffrement des ecritures et des langues. *Colloque du XXXIXe congres des orientalistes*, Paris Juillet 1973. Paris, Le dechiffrement des ecritures et des langues. *Colloque du XXXIXe congres des orientalistes*, Paris Juillet 1973. 121-143 and Asko Parpola (1975b). "India's Name in Early Foreign Sources." *Sri Venkateswara University Oriental Journal*, Tirupati, 18: 9-19.

[311] Parpola, Simo, Asko Parpola, and Robert H. Brunswig, Jr., 1977, "TheMeluhha Village — Evidence of Acculturation of Harappan Traders in Late Third Millenium Mesopotamia?", *Journal of the Economic and Social History of the Orient*, Volume 20, Part II.

[312] http://en.wikipedia.org/wiki/Khirasarahttp://en.wikipedia.org/wiki/Khirasara

[313] Source: http://www.persee.fr/web/revues/home/prescript/article/paleo_0153-9345_1996_num_22_2_4637#

See: http://antiquity.ac.uk/projgall/madella325/ Social and environmental transitions in arid zones: the North Gujarat Archaeological Project — NoGAP *Antiquity* Volume 084 Issue 325 September 2010

[314] See: http://chandrashekharasandprints.wordpress.com/2013/05/08/kutch-and-kathiawar-a-tryst-with-history-part-vii/ Kutch and Kathiawar: A tryst with history Seven parts.

[315] http://www.portal.gsi.gov.in/portal/page?_pageid=127,693641&_dad=portal&_schema=PORTA

[316] Malik, JN, SS Merh and V. Sridhar, 1999, Palaeo-delta complex of Vedic Saraswati and other ancient rivers of northwestern India, Vedic Sarasvati. Memoirs of Geological Society of India 42: 163-174.) (Anjana Reddy, 2008, Exploration in the Ghaggar Basin and excavations at Girwad, Farmana (Rohtak district) and Mitathal (Bhiwani district), Haryana, p.84. http://www.academia.edu/904156/Exploration_in_the_Ghaggar_Basin_and_excavations_at_Girawad_Farmana_Rohtak_District_and_Mitathal_Bhiwani_District_Haryana_India

[317] http://www.frontline.in/arts-and-culture/heritage/the-harappan-hub/article4840474.ece#test

[318] http://www.hindunet.org/saraswati/heritage1.pdf

[319] MS Vats, 1940, *Excavations at Harappa*, Vol. II, Calcutta, p.370

[320] http://www.asi.nic.in/nmma_reviews/Indian%20Archaeology%201963-64%20A%20Review.pdf

[321] tr. CH Tawney, 1880, Calcutta; rep. New Delhi, 1991, I, p. 151

[322] http://www.harappa.com/goladhoro/Shikarpur-2008-2009.pdf Excavations at Shikarpur, Gujarat 2008 - 2009

[323] ed. Ganapati Śāstri, II, p. 274.

[324] Sircar, DC, *Selected Inscriptions*, vol. I, 'Thirteenth Rock Edict Shābhāzgaṛhī, text line 7, p.37; 'Khoh Copper Plate Inscription of Saimkshobha', text line 8; *Arthaśāstra* VII.10.16; VII.4.43: *mlecchaṭavi* who were considered a threat to the state; *Arthaśāstra* IX.2.18-20 mentions *aṭavibala*, troops from forests as one of six types of troops at the disposal of a ruler.

[325] http://en.wikipedia.org/wiki/Invasion_of_India_by_Scythian_Tribes#Establishment_of_Mlechcha_Kingdoms_in_Northern_India

[326] MBh. trans. PC Roy, vol. I, p. 179.

[327] Beal, S. 1973, *The Life of Hiuen Tsiang*, New Delhi, p 57; cf. NL Dey, *Geographical Dictionary of India*, p. 113 for an identification of Lamgham (Lampakā) 20 miles north-west of Jalalabad.

[328] *Rājataranginī*, VII. 2762-64.

[329] Rapson, EJ, ed., 1922,*Cambridge History of India* , vol. I, Ancient India, Cambridge, p. 564.

[330] Law, BC, *The Buddhist Concepts of Spirits*, p 81.

[331] Dey, NL, *Geographical Dictionary*, p. 115.

[332] SK Chatterji, 1950, Kirāta-jana-kṛti --The Indo-Mongoloids: Their contributions to the and culture of India, Journal of Royal Asiatic Society of Bengal, Vol. XVI, pp.143-253.

[333] Leemans, WF, Foreign Trade in the Old Babylonian Period, 1960; 'Trade Relations on Babylonia', Journal of Economic and Social History of the Orient, vol. III, 1960, p.30 ff. 'Old Babylonian Letters and Economic History', Journal of Economic and Social History of the Orient, vol. XI, 1968, pp. 215-26; J. Hansam, 'A Periplus of Magan and Meluhha', Bulletin of the School of Oriental and African Studies, vol. 36, pt. III, 1973, pp. 554-83. Asko and Simo Parpola, 'On the Relationship of the Sumerian Toponym Meluhha and Sanskrit Mleccha', Studia Orientalia,vol. 46, 1975, pp. 205-38.

[334] Hansman, J., 'A Periplus of Magan and Meluhha', Bulletin of the School of Oriental and African Studies, vol. 36, pt. III, 1973, pp. 560.

[335] Leemans, WF, 'Old Babylonian Letters and Economic History', Journal of Economic and Social History of the Orient, vol. XI, 1968, pp. 215-26. P. Aalto, 1971, 'Marginal Notes on the Meluhha Problem,' Professor KA Nilakanta Sastri Felicitation Volume, Madras, pp. 222-23.

[336] Jain, 1984, Life in Ancient India as Described in the Jain Canon and Commentaries (6th century BC - 17th century AD, p. 150.
[337]Cowell, 1973, Jatakas Book II, p. 172 ff.
[338] Theodore A. Wertime, The search for ancient tin: the geographic and historic boundaries, in: Alan D. Franklin, Jacqueline S. Olin and Theodore A. Wertime, eds., 1977, *The Search for Ancient Tin*, Washington D.C., US Government Printing Office; See Theodore W. Wertime, In search of Ana_ku, bronze-age mystery, *Mid-East* 8, May-June 1968, pp. 10-20; J.D. Muhly, Tin trade routes of the bronze age, *American Scientist* 61, July-August 1973, pp. 403-13.
[339] R.F. Tylecote, 1976, *A History of Metallurgy*, London, The Metals Society.
[340] Tylecote, opcit., p.15.
[341] New evidence for sources of and trade in bronze age tin, in: Alan D. Franklin, Jacqueline S. Olin, and Theodore A. Wertime, *The Search for Ancient Tin*, 1977, Seminar organized by Theodore A. Wertime and held at the Smithsonian Institution and the National Bureau of Standards, Washington, D.C., March 14-15, 1977.
[342] http://www.hindunet.org/saraswati/roots.htm
[343] Anon. 1980: 1-2; Maddin et al 1977: 35-47.
[344] Muhly, James, New evidence for sources of and trade in bronze age tin, in: Alan D. Franklin, Jacqueline S. Olin, and Theodore A. Wertime, The Search for Ancient Tin, 1977, Seminar organized by Theodore A. Wertime and held at the Smithsonian Institution and the National Bureau of Standards, Washington, D.C., March 14-15, 1977, p.47.
[345] *Inst. Archaeo-Metallurgical Studies Newsletter*, No. 1, 1980, 1-2; Maddin, R., T.S. Wheeler and J. Muhly, Tin in the ancient Near East: old questions and new finds, *Expedition*, 1977, 19, 35-47.
[346] Muhly, James D.,1995, Mining and Metalwork in Ancient Western Asia, in: Jack M. Sasson, ed. 1995, *Civilizations of the Ancient Near East*, Vol. III, New York, Charles Scribner's Sons, pp. 1501-1521.
[347] Muhly, J.D., 1976, Copper and Tin, Hamden, Archon Books, p.47.
[348] P.R.S. Moorey, 1994, Ancient Mesopotamian Materials and Industries, Oxford, Clarendon Press.

[349] After Rice, M. ed., 2000, Traces of Paradise. The archaeology of Bahrain 2500 BCE-300 CE. London: The Dilmun Committee, 15.

[350] Potts, D., 1995, Distant Shores: Ancient Near Eastern Trade, in: Jack M. Sasson (ed.), *Civilizations of the Ancient Near East*, Vol. I, pp. 1451-1463.
[351] Muhly 1973: 155-535; cf. 1976: 77-136.
[352] Serge Cleuziou, Dilmun and Makkan during the third and early second millennia BC, 143-155 in: Shaikha Haya Ali Al Khalifa and Michael Rice (eds.) *Bahrain through the ages: the archaeology*, London, KPI, 1986.
[353] After Woolley 1934 and Vats 1941 and Fig. 12.28 in Possehl, G.L., 2002, The Indus civilization: a contemporary perspective, Alta Mira Press, p. 228.
[354]Vats 1940: 381; Marshall 1931: 488.
[355] Chakrabari, DK, 1979, The problem of tin in early India--a preliminary survey, in: *Man and Environment*, Vol. 3, pp. 61-74.
[356] Burney, 1977, 86; Muhly, 1973, 306-7, 449 note 542; Muhly, J.D., 1973, Tin trade routes of the Bronze Age, Scientific American, 1973, 61, 404-13.

[357] Muhly, J.D., 1976, *Copper and Tin*, Hamden, Archon Books, pp. 306-7.

[358] Pliny, *Naturalis Historia*, 34.2 and 37.44. The map and notes on Mesopotamian/Egyptian contacts are based on: D.T.Potts, 1995, Distant Shores: ancient near eastern trae with south Asia and northeast Africa, pp. 1451-1463, in: Jack M. Sasson, ed. 1995, *Civilizations of the Ancient Near East*, Vol. III, New York, Charles Scribner's Sons.

[359] Copper-bronze artefacts from Mohenjodaro exhibited at the Mohenjodaro museum. Dr. Abdul Jabbar Junejo and Mohammad Qasim Bughio, 1988, Cultural Heritage of Sind, International Arabi Conference, University of Sind, Hyderabad, Sindhi Adabi Board.

[360] Hegde, KTM, Sources of Ancient Tin in India, in: Alan D. Franklin, Jacqueline S. Olin and Theodore A. Wertime, eds., 1977, *The Search for Ancient Tin*, Washington D.C., US Government Printing Office.

[361] Tylecote, R.F., 1976, A History of Metallurgy, The Metals Society, p. 11.

[362] Penhallurick, R.D., 1986, Tin in Antiquity, London, Institute of Metals, pp. 18-32.

[363] Muhly, J.D., 1973, *Copper and Tin: the distribution of mineral resources and the nature of the metals trade in the Bronze Age*, Hamden, Connecticut, Archon Books, p. 409.

[364] Hirsch, H., 1963, Die Inschriften der Konige Von Agade, Afo, 20, pp. 37-38; Leemans, W.F., 1960, Foreign Trade in the Old Babylonian Period, p. 164; Oppenheim, A.L., 1954, The seafaring merchants of Ur, JAOS, 74, pp. 6-17.

[365] Oppenheim 1954: II, 15 n.24.

[366] Oppenheim 1954: 6-12.

[367] Raw, V. 27A, 25-7; loc.cit. Upenn University Museum, 1915, Publications of the Babylonian Section, Vol. 10' Stephen Langdon, Sumerian epic of paradise, flood and the fall of man, p.8 http://tinyurl.com/ybfhept

[368] J.D. Muhly, 1973, *Copper and Tin*, Hamden, Connecticut, Archon Books, pp.241-335.

[369] Chakrabarti, DK, 1979, The problem of tin in early India--a preliminary survey, in: Man and Environment, Vol. 3, pp. 61-74.

[370] KTM Hegde and Ericson, J.E., 1985, Ancient Indian Copper Smelting Furnaces, in: *Furnaces and Smelting Technology in Antiquity*, ed. P.T. Craddock, Occasional Paper No. 48, British Museum, London, pp. 59-67.

[371] http://www.hindunet.org/saraswati/trade1.htm

[372] http://www.harappa.com/indus4/e6.html

[373] http://www.archaeologyonline.net/artifacts/iron-ore.html

[374] Oppenheim, A. Leo, The Seafaring Merchants of Ur, *Journal of the American Oriental Society*, Vol. 74, 1954, pp. 6-17.

[375] Source: http://www.cbseacademic.in/web_material/Circulars/2012/68_KTPI/Module_8.pdf

[376] Moorey, PRS, 1994, Ancient Mesopotamian Materials and Industries, Oxford, Clarendon Press pp. 298-299).

[377] http://www.ancientroute.com/resource/metal/tin.htm

[378] Muhly, J.D., 1976, Copper and Tin, Hamden, Archon Books, pp. 306-7.

[379] http://www.turkishhan.org/trade.htm

[380] http://www.ancientroute.com/resource/metal/tin.htm

[381] Gerard Clauson and John Chadwick, 1969, Indus script deciphered?, Antiquity XLIII.
[382] Potts, 1995, p. 1457.
[383]Sheil, VE, 1925, Un nouveau scean Hindon pseudo-Sumerian, Revnue d'Assyriologie et d'Archeologie Orientale, Vol. XXII, pp. 55-56.

[384] Lamberg-Karlovsky, 1972, Trade mechanisms in Indus-Mesopotamian interrelations, Journal of American Oriental Society, Vol. 92, No. 2, pp.222-229) http://www.jstor.org/stable/600649
[385] Gelb, I.J., 1952, *A study of writing: the foundations of grammatology*, Chicago, Univerity of Chicago Press, p.218.
[386] Edwin Yamauchi, 1993, Metal sources and metallurgy in the biblical world, Oxford, OH 45056, Dept. of History, Miami University From: PSCF 45 (December 1993): 252-259. http://www.asa3.org/ASA/PSCF/1993/PSCF12-93Yamauchi.html) [See: G. Dossin, "La route de l'étain en Mesopotamie au temps de Zimri-Lim," Revue d'Assyriologie 64 (1970), 97-106. M. Heltzer, "The Metal Trade of Ugarit and the Problem of Transportation of Commercial Goods," Iraq 39 (1977), 203-11. A. Malamat, "Syro-Palestinian Destinations in a Mari Tin Inventory," Israel Exploration Journal 21 (1971), 31-38.]
[387] Adapted from: R.J.Forbes, 1954, Extracting, smelting and alloying, in: Charles Singer, E.J.Holmyard and AR Hall (eds.), 1954, A History of Technology, Oxford, Clarendon Press.
[388] Knox, Robert, 1994, A new Indus Valley Cylinder Seal, pp. 375-378 in: *South Asian Archaeology 1993, Vol. I,* Helsinki.
[389] Ibid., p. 377; cf. Lamberg- Karlovsky and Tosi 1973: pl. 137.
[390] Babu, TM, 2003, Advent of the bronze age in the Indian subcontinent in: Craddock, PT and J. Lang, Mining and Metl production through the ages, British Museum, pp.174-180.
[391] Fuller, Dorian Q., Nicole Boivin, Tom Hoogervorst & Robin Allaby, 2011, Across the Indian Ocean: the prehistoric movement of plants and animals, Antiquity 85: 544-558 http://www.antiquity.ac.uk/ant/085/0544/ant0850544.pdf

[392] Kalyanarman, S. 1998. *Indian Lexicon – A comparative etymological dictionary of South-Asian Languages.* Manila. https://docs.google.com/file/d/0B4BAzCi4O_l4ZXJfN0hMamowSGs/edit?usp=drive_web
[393] Fuller, D.Q., 2007, Non-human genetics, agricultural origins and historical linguistics, in M. Petraglia & B. Allchin, ed., *The evolution and history of human populations in south Asia: interdisciplinary studies in archaeology, biological anthropology, linguistics and genetics*: 389-439, Dordrecht: Springer).
[394] http://www.omilosmeleton.gr/pdf/en/indology/Vedic_and_Avestan.pdf
[395] Jairazbhoy, RA,1995, *Foreign Influence in Ancient Indo-Pakistan*, Karachi, Sind Book House.
[396] *The Divine Songs of Zarathushtra*, pp. 682-3, pp. 210-1.
[397] Tilak, Arctic Home in the Vedas, p. 122.
[398] Dr. Haug's trans. Vol. II, p. 207.
[399] A.A.Macdonell, Vedic Mythology, p.117
[400] Chaturvedi, P.S., 1969, Technology in Vedic Literature, Delhi, Books and Books
[401] L. Woolley , The Sumerians, pp. 46-47; cf. Ur Excavations, vol. II, pp. 390-396.
[402] See also Swami Sankarananda, Hindu States of Sumeria, Calcutta, K.L.Mukhapadhyay, 1962 for the story of Bhujyu who was the son of a king named Tugra (a worshipper of As'vina) whose boat was sunk in the mid-ocean, p. 32.

[403] Kent, Roland (1953). *Old Persian: Grammar, Texts & Lexicon.* American Oriental Series 33). American Oriental Society. p. 53*)*,http://en.wikipedia.org/wiki/Elam - cite_note-Kent_1953_53-7

[404] Jeremy Black, Andrew George & Nicholas Postgate (eds.), ed. (1999). *A Concise Dictionary of Akkadian*. Harrassowitz Verlag. p. 68.
[405] http://en.wikipedia.org/wiki/Elam
[406] McAlpin, David W., *Proto Elamo Dravidian: The Evidence and Its Implications*, American Philosophy Society (1981).
[407] Parpola S., A. Parpola & R.H. Brunswig, Jr. (1977) "The Meluhha Village. Evidence of acculturation of Harappan traders in the late Third Millennium Mesopotamia." Journal of Economic and Social History of the Orient, 20, 129-165.
[408] Hammurabi (King of Babylonia.), (University of Chicago Press, 1904).
[409] André-Salvini Béatrice, "Stèle de la musique", in Musiques au Louvre, Paris, Éditions de la Réunion des musées nationaux, 1994, pp. 10-11.

Parrot André, Tello, vingt campagnes de fouilles, 1877-1933, Paris, Albin Michel, 1948, pp. 174-176, pl. 20a.

Rutten Marguerite-Maggie, "Scènes de musique et de danse", in Revue des arts asiatiques, Paris, École française d'Extrême-Orient, 1935, p. 220, fig. 8.

Sarzec Édouard de, Découvertes en Chaldée, Paris, Leroux, 1884-1912, pp. 36 et 219-221, pl. 23.

Sillamy Jean-Claude, La Musique dans l'ancien Orient ou la théorie musicale suméro-babylonienne, Villeneuve d'Ascq, Presses universitaires du Septentrion, 1998, p. 160.Author(s): Iselin Claire (after a text by André-Salvini Béatrice)

[410] http://www.louvre.fr/en/oeuvre-notices/stele-music

[411] King, L.W., A history of Sumer and Akkad, 1910, pp. 236-7.
[412] Vidale, M., pp. 274-5.

[413] Vidale, Massimo, 2001, Growing in a foreign world. For a history of the Meluhha villages' in Mesopotamia in the 3rd millennium BCE, in: A. Panaino and A. Piras, eds., Proceedings of the fourth annual symposium of the Assyrian and Babylonian intellectual heritage project, held in Ravenna, Italy, Oct. 13-17, 2001, Milan, Universita di Bologna & Islao, 2004, pp.275-276. http://www.aakkl.helsinki.fi/melammu/pdf/vidale2004.pdf
[414] http://en.wikipedia.org/wiki/File:Relief_spinner_Louvre_Sb2834.jpg Source: http://ia600406.us.archive.org/29/items/mmoires01franuoft/mmoires01franuoft.pdf After "Kunst." Barthel Hrouda. Editor. *Der Alte Orient, Geschichte und Kultur des alten Vorderasien*. Munchen. C. Bertelsmann. Verlag GmbH. 1991, p. 360.

[415] After "Kunst." Barthel Hrouda. Editor. *Der Alte Orient, Geschichte und Kultur des alten Vorderasien*. Munchen. C. Bertelsmann. Verlag GmbH. 1991, p. 360.
[416] Hunter, G.R., 1932, Mohenjodaro--Indus Epigraphy,*JRAS*, 476.

[417] Parpola, A., New correspondences between Harappan and Near Eastern glyptic art, in: Bridget Allchin (ed.), *South Asian Archaeology, 1981*, Cambridge, Cambridge University Press, 1984.
[418] http://oi.uchicago.edu/OI/MUS/ED/TRC/MESO/writing_largewindow.html

[419] Delaporte Louis, Musée du Louvre, catalogue des cylindres, cachets et pierres gravées de style oriental, Hachette, 1920-1923, p. 106, pl. 69-8.
Amiet Pierre, La glyptique mésopotamienne archaïque, CNRS, 1980, pp. 75-77, pl. 44.

[420] A person with a vase with overflowing water; sun sign. C. 18th cent. BCE. E. Porada,1971, Remarks on seals found in the Gulf states, Artibus Asiae, 33, 31-7.

[421] Malbran-Labat Florence, Les Inscriptions de Suse : briques de l'époque paléo-élamite à l'empire néo-élamite, Paris, Éditions de la Réunion des musées nationaux, 1995, p.168-169.
Miroschedji Pierre de, "Le Dieu élamite au serpent", in : Iranica antiqua, Vol.16, 1981, Gand, Ministère de l'Éducation et de la Culture, 1989, p.13-14, pl.8.
[422] Amiet Pierre, Suse 6000 ans d'histoire, Paris, Éditions de la Réunion des musées nationaux, 1988, pp.98-99 ; fig. 57.

Miroschedji Pierre de, "Le dieu élamite au serpent", in : Iranica antiqua, vol.16, 1981, Gand, Ministère de l'Éducation et de la Culture, 1989, pp.16-17, pl. 10, fig.3.
[423] George L. Campbell, *Compendium of the World's Languages*, Routledge, London, 1991, p. 1199.
[424] R.M. Macphail, An Introduction to Santali, 1953, p.2). George L. Campbell, Compendium of the World's Languages, Routledge, London, 1991, p. 1199.
[425]
http://www.academia.edu/2360254/Temple_Sacred_Prostitution_in_Ancient_Mesopotamia_Revisited
[426] Lambert 1990, 298– 299) and probably was a patron of scribes, as was Nidaba/Nisaba (Michalowski 2002
http://www.academia.edu/2360254/Temple_Sacred_Prostitution_in_Ancient_Mesopotamia_Revisited
[427] *Records of the Past, 2nd series, Vol. II*, ed. by A. H. Sayce, [1888], at sacred-texts.com) http://www.sacred-texts.com/ane/rp/rp202/rp20221.htm http://www.sacred-texts.com/ane/rp/rp202/rp20221.htm#fr_228
[428] http://faculty.txwes.edu/csmeller/human-experience/ExpData09/01AncMed/AncMedPICs/MesPICs/Gudea/mesP_GudeaInscription.htm
[429]
http://books.google.co.in/books?id=0guVA19YUVoC&lpg=PA68&pg=PA55#v=onepage&q&f=false
Gudea and His Dynasty By Dietz Otto Edzard University of Toronto Press, 1997 (pp.34-36, p.39, p.41, p.42, p.75, p.78, p.79) The Electronic Text Corpus of Sumerian Literature
[430] http://www.worldartmuseum.cn/content/918/4070_1.shtml See also
http://bharatkalyan97.blogspot.in/2013/06/ancient-near-east-indus-writing-lokhad.html Ancient near East Gudea statue hieroglyph (Indus writing): lokhãḍ, 'copper tools, pots and pans' Rebus: lo 'overflow', kāṇḍa 'sacred water'.
[431]
http://www.britishmuseum.org/explore/highlights/article_index/g/gudea,_king_of_lagash_around.aspx

[432] Claudia E. Suter, 2000, Gudea's Temple Building: the representation of an early Mesopotamian Ruler in text and image, BRILL., II.c.i.d, pp. 62-63.

[433] After Khan 1965, pl. XVIIb; cf. Fig. 2.25 in JM Kenoyer, 1998, *Ancient cities of the Indus Valley Civilization*, Karachi, Oxford University Press.
[434] Credit Line: Gift of Nanette B. Kelekian, in memory of Charles Dikran and Beatrice Kelekian, 1999 Accession Number: 1999.325.104 http://www.metmuseum.org/Collections/search-the-collections/30006389?rpp=20&pg=1&ft=*&who=Proto-Elamite&pos=7

[435] *Reveu archéologique de* 1880, vol. xl. p. 17.

[436] Fig. 220 in: Thomas Wilson, 1894, The Swastika, The Earliest Known Symbol, and Its Migration; with Observations on the Migration of Certain Industries in Prehistoric Times, the First Report of the US National Museum for 1894, pp. 757-1011, Washington, Govt. Printing Office.

[437] G. Bongard-Levin, 1989, Archaeological Finds in Central Asia throw light on Ancient India, Jagdish Vibhakar and Usha Gard (Eds.), *Glimpses of Ancient India through Soviet Eyes*, Delhi, Sundeep Prakashan.

[438] Masson, VM, Seals of a Proto-Indian Type from Altyn-depe, pp. 149-162; V.M. Masson, Urban Centers of Early Class Society, pp. 135-148; I.N. Khlopin, The Early bronze age cemetery in Parkhai II: The first two seasons of excavations, 1977-78, pp. 3-34 in: Philip L. Kohl (ed.), 1981, The Bronze Age Civilization in Central Asia, Armonk, NY, ME Sharpe, Inc.

[439] http://tinyurl.com/yexoudu

http://www.metmuseum.org/explore/First_Cities/seals_meso_object_135.R.htm

[440] D. Collon, *Catalogue of the Western Asi-1* (London, 1982)
http://www.britishmuseum.org/explore/highlights/highlight_objects/me/g/greenstone_seal.aspx

[441] D. Collon, *Catalogue of the Western Asi-1* (London, 1982)
http://www.britishmuseum.org/explore/highlights/highlight_objects/me/g/greenstone_seal.aspx

[442] (http://www.archive.org/download/mmoires01franuoft/mmoires01franuoft.pdf Jacques de Morgan, Fouilles à Suse en 1897-1898 et 1898-1899, Mission archéologique en Iran, Mémoires I, 1990, p.160).
[443] (http://www.archive.org/download/mmoires01franuoft/mmoires01franuoft.pdf Jacques de Morgan, Fouilles à Suse en 1897-1898 et 1898-1899, Mission archéologique en Iran, Mémoires I, 1990, p.116).

http://wpcontent.answcdn.com/wikipedia/commons/thumb/5/5c/Goatfishes_Louvre_Sb19.jpg/220px-Goatfishes_Louvre_Sb19.jpg Accession Number Sb 19. Excavated by Jacques de Morgan, 1904–1905

Louvre Museum. Department of Oriental Antiquities, Richelieu, ground floor, room 11 H. 9 cm (3 ½ in.), W. 13 cm (5 in.) Accession Number Sb 2834 Excavations of Jacques de Morgan

[444] Amiet Pierre, Élam, Auvers-sur-Oise, Archée, 1966, p. 394 et pp. 467-468, fig. 298 A-B. Borne interactive du département des Antiquités orientales.

Contenau Georges, Manuel d'archéologie orientale depuis les origines jusqu'à l'époque d'Alexandre, vol. II, Histoire de l'art : IIIe et IIe millénaires avant notre ère, Paris, A. Picard, 1931, pp. 912-913, fig. 629. Herbin Nancie

[445] Source: http://www.elamit.net/elam/sit_overheads.pdf

Model of a temple, called the Sit-shamshi, made for the ceremony of the rising sun. http://www.louvre.fr/en/oeuvre-notices/sit-shamshi See the reading of the inscription at http://www.elamit.net/elam/sit_handout.pdf

[446] Gian Pietro Basello, 2003, Loan-words in Achaemenid Elamite: the spelling of old Persian Month-names, in: 5th European Conf. of Iranian Studies, October 10th 2003 http://digilander.libero.it/elam2/elam/basello_sie2003.pdf http://www.academia.edu/1706512/The_3D_Model_from_Susa_called_Sit-shamshi_An_essay_of_interpretation

The 3D Model from Susa called Sit-shamshi: An essay of interpretation by Gian Pietro Basello

[447] After Fig. 200 in Gautier 1911:145 + FW Konig, Corpus Inscriptionum Elamicarum, no. 56, Hanover 1926 + Tallon & Hurtel 1992: 140, fig. 43.

[448] http://www.louvre.fr/media/repository/ressources/sources/illustration/atlas/image_66481_v2_m56577569830704548.jpg

[449] http://bharatkalyan97.blogspot.in/2011/11/mohenjo-daro-stupa-great-bath-modeled.html
[450] http://www.mohenjodaro.net/wheelersplatform39.html
[451] http://www.mohenjodaro.net/Mohenjo-darostupa14.html

[452] Beatrice Teissier, *Ancient Near Eastern Cylinder Seals: From the Marcopoli Collection*, Berkeley, University of California Press, 1984.

[453] Poul Kjaerum, The Dilmun Seals as evidence of long distance relations in the early second millennium BC, pp. 269-277.Dilmun period shell seals from Sar El-Jisr burial mounds, Bahrain. Source: H. Khalifa and M. Ibrahim. 1982. The Seals. pp.37-39. Fig.48. In: M. Ibrahim, Excavations of the Arab Expedition at Sar El-Jisr, Bahrain. Ministry of Information, Bahrain. http://www.adias-uae.com/shellbook/shellbook.html

[454] After Fig. 2 a&b. in Potts, DT, 1993, A new Bactrian find from southeastern Arabia, Antiquity 67 (1993): 591-6. http://faculty.ksu.edu.sa/archaeology/Publications/Arabia/Bacterian%20Camel%20in%20Arabia.pdf
[455] Thapar 1979, Pl.XXVII, in: *Ancient Cities of the Indus.*
[456] After Marie-Helene Pottier, 1984, *Materiel funeraire de la Bactriane meridionale de l'age du bronze*, Recherche sur les Civilizations, Memoire 36, Paris, fig. 21; Sarianidi, V.I., 1986, Le complexe culturel de Togolok 21 en Margiane, *Arts Asiatiques 41*: fig. 6,21; Potts, 1994, fig. 53,8; Amiet, 1986, fig. 132.

[457] Potts. DT, 2000. Ancient Magan - The Secrets of Tell Abraq. Trident Press, London. p.98. http://www.adias-uae.com/shellbook/Tell-Abraq-Ficus-shell-sm1.jpg
[458] http://www.hindunet.org/hindu_history/sarasvati/lapis/lapis_lazuli.htm

[459] http://oi.uchicago.edu/OI/MUS/ED/TRC/MESO/farmers.html

[460] Amiet Pierre, Élam, Auvers-sur-Oise, Archée, 1966, p. 243, n 176.

La Cité royale de Suse, Exposition, New York, Metropolitan Museum of Art, 17 novembre 1992-7 mars 1993, Paris, Éditions de la Réunion des musées nationaux, 1994, p. 92, n 56.

[461] http://news.nationalgeographic.com/news/2003/05/photogalleries/iraqtreasures_1/

[462] http://amar.hsclib.sunysb.edu/u?/amar,124774 DT Potts, 1998, *Ancient Magan, The secrets of Tell Abraq*, Trident Press
[463] Heiser, Michael S., The myth of a 12th planet: a brief analysis of cylinder seal VA 243 http://www.michaelsheiser.com/va_243 page.htm
http://www.michaelsheiser.com/VA243seal.pdf

[464] Potts, DT, *Magan*, p. 68.
[465] D. Collon, *First Impressions – Cylinder Seals in the Ancient Near East*, (London, British Museum Press, 1987, updated 2005)
[466] Ursula Seidl, Die Babylonischen Kudurru Reliefs, p. 47 = The Babylonian Kudurru Reliefs, p. 47.
[467] Ursula Seidl, Die Babylonischen Kudurru Reliefs, p. 60 = The Babylonian Kudurru Reliefs, p. 60.

[468] Ursula Seidl, Die Babylonischen Kudurru Reliefs, p. 23 = The Babylonian Kudurru Reliefs, p. 23.

[469] Frankfort, Henri, Cylinder Seals: A Documentary Essay on the Art and Religion of the Ancient Near East (London: MacMillan and Co., 1939): Plate XXVI-seal L.
[470]Frankfort, Henri, Cylinder Seals: A Documentary Essay on the Art and Religion of the Ancient Near East (London: MacMillan and Co., 1939): Plate XXVI-seal L See the discussion in Frankfort (pp. 177-178, 236, 254) and Black, p. 168.
[471] Stolper Matthew W., The Royal City of Susa. Ancient Near Eastern Treasures in the Louvre, Exposition, New York, Metropolitan Museum of Art, 1992, n 49. Author: AB

Morgan Jacques de, Mémoires I, Leroux, 1900, p. 172, pl. XVI-3.

Scheil, Victor, Mémoires II, 1900, p. 99, pl. XXI à XXIII.Author: Pouysségur Patrick

[472] Robert H. Brunswig, Jr. et al, New Indus Type and Related Seals from the Near East, 101-115 in: Daniel T. Potts (ed.), Dilmun: New Studies in the Archaeology and Early History of Bahrain, Berlin, Dietrich Reimer Verlag, 1983; each seal is referenced by a four-digit number which is registered in the Finnish concordance.

[473] bibliography and image source: Frankfort, Henri: *Stratified Cylinder Seals from the Diyala Region*. Oriental Institute Publications 72. Chicago: University of Chicago Press, no. 642. Museum Number: IM14674 3.4 cm. high. Glazed steatite. ca. 2250 - 2200 BCE.

[507] *Deśīnāmamālā of Hemacandra* (ed. R. Pischel (1880), Bombay Sanskrit Series No. XVII; 1938, 2nd edn. by Paravastu Venkata Ramanujaswami)
[508] Kalyanarman, S. 1998. *Indian Lexicon – A comparative etymological dictionary of South-Asian Languages*. Manila.
https://docs.google.com/file/d/0B4BAzCi4O_l4ZXJfN0hMamowSGs/edit?usp=drive_web
[509] http://sealang.net/sala/archives/pdf4/bhattacharya1966munda.pdf S. Bhattacharya, Some Munda etymologies
[510] http://www.lib.udel.edu/ud/spec/exhibits/alchemy/emblems.htm

www.ingramcontent.com/pod-product-compliance
Lightning Source LLC
Chambersburg PA
CBHW051530230426
43669CB00015B/2557
9780991104819